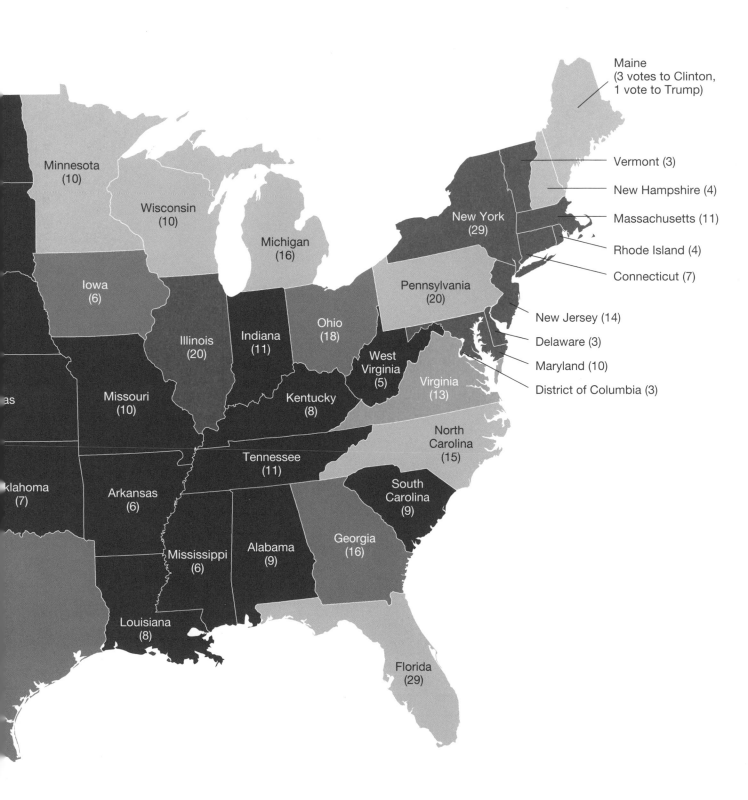

Maine
(3 votes to Clinton,
1 vote to Trump)

Vermont (3)

New Hampshire (4)

Massachusetts (11)

Rhode Island (4)

Connecticut (7)

New Jersey (14)

Delaware (3)

Maryland (10)

District of Columbia (3)

New York
(29)

Minnesota
(10)

Wisconsin
(10)

Michigan
(16)

Iowa
(6)

Pennsylvania
(20)

Illinois
(20)

Indiana
(11)

Ohio
(18)

West
Virginia
(5)

Virginia
(13)

Missouri
(10)

Kentucky
(8)

North
Carolina
(15)

klahoma
(7)

Arkansas
(6)

Tennessee
(11)

South
Carolina
(9)

Mississippi
(6)

Alabama
(9)

Georgia
(16)

Louisiana
(8)

Florida
(29)

as

ELEVENTH EDITION

We the People

AN INTRODUCTION TO AMERICAN POLITICS

ELEVENTH EDITION

We the People

AN INTRODUCTION TO AMERICAN POLITICS

Benjamin Ginsberg
THE JOHNS HOPKINS UNIVERSITY

Theodore J. Lowi
CORNELL UNIVERSITY

Margaret Weir
BROWN UNIVERSITY

Caroline J. Tolbert
UNIVERSITY OF IOWA

W. W. NORTON & COMPANY
NEW YORK   LONDON

Copyright © 2017, 2015, 2013, 2011, 2009, 2007, 2005, 2003, 2001, 1999, 1997 by W. W. Norton & Company, Inc.

Editor: Ann Shin
Associate Editor: Emily Stuart
Project Editor: Christine D'Antonio
Editorial Assistant: Shannon Jilek
Manuscript Editor: Andrew Pachuta
Managing Editor, College: Marian Johnson
Managing Editor, College Digital Media: Kim Yi
Production Manager: Ashley Horna
Media Editor: Spencer Richardson-Jones
Associate Media Editor: Michael Jaoui
Media Editorial Assistant: Ariel Eaton

Marketing Manager, Political Science: Erin Brown
Art Director: Rubina Yeh
Text Design: Lissi Sigillo
Photo Editor: Catherine Abelman
Photo Researcher: Elyse Rieder
Permissions Manager: Megan Schindel
Permissions Clearing: Elizabeth Trammell
Information Graphics: Kiss Me I'm Polish LLC, New York
Composition: Graphic World, Inc.
Manufacturing: TransContinental

Permission to use copyrighted material is included in the credits section of this book, which begins on page A91.

Library of Congress Cataloging-in-Publication Data

Ginsberg, Benjamin, author. | Lowi, Theodore J., author. | Weir, Margaret, 1952- author. | Tolbert, Caroline J., author.
We the people : an introduction to American politics / Benjamin Ginsberg, the Johns Hopkins University, Theodore J. Lowi, Cornell University, Margaret Weir, Brown University, Caroline J. Tolbert, University of Iowa.
Eleventh Edition. | New York : W.W. Norton & Company, [2017]
Tenth edition: 2015.
Includes bibliographical references and index.
LCCN 2016050517 | **ISBN 9780393283624** (hardcover)
LCSH: United States—Politics and government—Textbooks.
LCC JK276.G55 2017 | DDC 320.473—dc23 LC record available at https://lccn.loc.gov/2016050517

W. W. Norton & Company, Inc., 500 Fifth Avenue, New York, N.Y. 10110
www.wwnorton.com

W. W. Norton & Company Ltd., Castle House, 15 Carlisle Street, London W1D 3BS

1 2 3 4 5 6 7 8 9 0

To Sandy, Cindy, and Alex Ginsberg

Angele, Anna, and Jason Lowi

Nicholas Ziegler

David, Jackie, Eveline, and Ed Dowling

contents

2 ● The Founding and the Constitution 38

3 ● Federalism 74

4 ● Civil Liberties 112

5 ● Civil Rights 152

PART II   Politics

6 ● Public Opinion   198

9 ● Political Parties 326

10 ● Campaigns and Elections 368

PART III   Institutions

12 ● Congress   456

13 ● The Presidency 504

PART IV   Policy

16 ● Government and the Economy   626

17 ● Social Policy 670

18 ● Foreign Policy and Democracy 710

● Appendix

preface

This book has been and continues to be dedicated to developing a satisfactory response to the question more and more Americans are asking: Why should we be engaged with government and politics? Through the first ten editions, we sought to answer this question by making the text directly relevant to the lives of the students who would be reading it. As a result, we tried to make politics interesting by demonstrating that students' interests are at stake and that they therefore need to take a personal, even selfish, interest in the outcomes of government. At the same time, we realized that students needed guidance in how to become politically engaged. Beyond providing students with a core of political knowledge, we needed to show them how they could apply that knowledge as participants in the political process. The "Who Participates?" sections in each chapter help achieve that goal.

As events from the last several years have reminded us, "what government does" inevitably raises questions about political participation and political equality. The size and composition of the electorate, for example, affect who is elected to public office and what policy directions the government will pursue. Hence, the issue of voter ID laws became important in the 2016 election, with some arguing that these laws reduce voter fraud and others contending that they decrease participation by poor and minority voters. Other recent events have underscored how Americans from different backgrounds experience politics. Arguments about immigration became contentious during the 2016 election as the nation once again debated the question of who is entitled to be an American and have a voice in determining what the government does. And charges that the police often use excessive violence against members of minority groups have raised questions about whether the government treats all Americans equally. Reflecting all of these trends, this new Eleventh Edition shows more than any other book on the market (1) how students are connected to government, (2) why students should think critically about government and politics, and (3) how Americans from different backgrounds experience and shape politics. These themes are incorporated in the following ways:

- **Chapter introductions focus on "What Government Does and Why It Matters."** In recent decades, cynicism about "big government" has dominated the political zeitgeist. But critics of government often forget that governments do a great deal for citizens. Every year, Americans are the beneficiaries of billions of dollars of goods and services from government programs. Government "does" a lot, and what it does matters a great deal to everyone, including college students. At the start of each chapter, this theme is introduced and applied to the chapter's topic. The goal is to show students that government and politics mean something to their daily lives.

- **A twenty-first-century perspective on demographic change** moves beyond the book's strong coverage of traditional civil rights content with expanded coverage of contemporary group politics.

- **"Who Are Americans?" infographics**—including several new to the eleventh edition—ask students to think critically about how Americans from different backgrounds experience politics. These sections use bold, engaging graphics to present a statistical snapshot of the nation related to each chapter's topic. Critical-thinking questions are included in each infographic.

- *New* **"Who Participates?" infographics at the end of every chapter** show students how different groups of Americans participate in key aspects of politics and government. Each concludes with a "What You Can Do" section that provides students with specific, realistic steps they can take to act on what they've learned and get involved in politics. The InQuizitive course and Coursepack include accompanying exercises and multiple-choice questions that encourage students to engage with these features.

- **"America Side by Side" boxes** in every chapter use data figures and tables to provide a comparative perspective. By comparing political institutions and behavior across countries, students gain a better understanding of how specific features of the American system shape politics.

- **Up-to-date coverage**, with more than 20 pages and numerous graphics on the 2016 elections, including a 12-page section devoted to analysis of the 2016 elections in Chapter 10, as well as updated data, examples, and other information throughout the book.

- **"For Critical Analysis" questions** are incorporated throughout the text. "For Critical Analysis" questions in the margins of every chapter prompt students' own critical thinking about the material in the chapter, encouraging them to engage with the topic.

- **"Politics and Your Future" chapter conclusions** give students direct, personal reasons to care about politics. These sections focus on the political opportunities and challenges that students will face in their lives as a result of emerging social, political, demographic, and technological change. The conclusions reprise the important point made in the chapter introductions that *government matters* and prompt students to consider how political change will impact their futures.

- **This Eleventh Edition is accompanied by InQuizitive**, Norton's award-winning formative, adaptive online quizzing program. The InQuizitive course for *We the People* guides students through questions organized around the text's chapter learning objectives to ensure mastery of the core information and to help with assessment. More information and a demonstration are available at digital.wwnorton.com/wethepeople11.

We continue to hope that our book will itself be accepted as a form of enlightened political action. This Eleventh Edition is another chance. It is an advancement toward our goal. We promise to keep trying.

acknowledgments

W e are pleased to acknowledge the many colleagues who had an active role in criticism and preparation of the manuscript. Our thanks go to:

First Edition Reviewers

Sarah Binder, Brookings Institution
Kathleen Gille, Office of Representative David Bonior
Rodney Hero, University of Colorado at Boulder
Robert Katzmann, Brookings Institution
Kathleen Knight, University of Houston
Robin Kolodny, Temple University
Nancy Kral, Tomball College
Robert C. Lieberman, Columbia University
David A. Marcum, University of Wyoming
Laura R. Winsky Mattei, State University of New York at Buffalo
Marilyn S. Mertens, Midwestern State University
Barbara Suhay, Henry Ford Community College
Carolyn Wong, Stanford University
Julian Zelizer, State University of New York at Albany

Second Edition Reviewers

Lydia Andrade, University of North Texas
John Coleman, University of Wisconsin at Madison
Daphne Eastman, Odessa College
Otto Feinstein, Wayne State University
Elizabeth Flores, Delmar College
James Gimpel, University of Maryland at College Park
Jill Glaathar, Southwest Missouri State University
Shaun Herness, University of Florida
William Lyons, University of Tennessee at Knoxville
Andrew Polsky, Hunter College, CUNY
Grant Reeher, Syracuse University
Richard Rich, Virginia Polytechnic
Bartholomew Sparrow, University of Texas at Austin

Third Edition Reviewers

Bruce R. Drury, Lamar University
Andrew I. E. Ewoh, Prairie View A&M University
Amy Jasperson, University of Texas at San Antonio
Loch Johnson, University of Georgia
Mark Kann, University of Southern California
Robert L. Perry, University of Texas of the Permian Basin

Wayne Pryor, Brazosport College
Elizabeth A. Rexford, Wharton County Junior College
Andrea Simpson, University of Washington
Brian Smentkowski, Southeast Missouri State University
Nelson Wikstrom, Virginia Commonwealth University

Fourth Edition Reviewers

M. E. Banks, Virginia Commonwealth University
Lynn Brink, North Lake College
Mark Cichock, University of Texas at Arlington
Del Fields, St. Petersburg College
Nancy Kinney, Washtenaw Community College
William Klein, St. Petersburg College
Dana Morales, Montgomery College
Christopher Muste, Louisiana State University
Larry Norris, South Plains College
David Rankin, State University of New York at Fredonia
Paul Roesler, St. Charles Community College
J. Philip Rogers, San Antonio College
Greg Shaw, Illinois Wesleyan University
Tracy Skopek, Stephen F. Austin State University
Don Smith, University of North Texas
Terri Wright, Cal State, Fullerton

Fifth Edition Reviewers

Annie Benifield, Tomball College
Denise Dutton, Southwest Missouri State University
Rick Kurtz, Central Michigan University
Kelly McDaniel, Three Rivers Community College
Eric Plutzer, Pennsylvania State University
Daniel Smith, Northwest Missouri State University
Dara Strolovitch, University of Minnesota
Dennis Toombs, San Jacinto College–North
Stacy Ulbig, Southwest Missouri State University

Sixth Edition Reviewers

Janet Adamski, University of Mary Hardin–Baylor
Greg Andrews, St. Petersburg College

Louis Bolce, Baruch College
Darin Combs, Tulsa Community College
Sean Conroy, University of New Orleans
Paul Cooke, Cy Fair College
Vida Davoudi, Kingwood College
Robert DiClerico, West Virginia University
Corey Ditslear, University of North Texas
Kathy Dolan, University of Wisconsin, Milwaukee
Randy Glean, Midwestern State University
Nancy Kral, Tomball College
Mark Logas, Valencia Community College
Scott MacDougall, Diablo Valley College
David Mann, College of Charleston
Christopher Muste, University of Montana
Richard Pacelle, Georgia Southern University
Sarah Poggione, Florida International University
Richard Rich, Virginia Tech
Thomas Schmeling, Rhode Island College
Scott Spitzer, California State University–Fullerton
Robert Wood, University of North Dakota

Seventh Edition Reviewers

Molly Andolina, DePaul University
Nancy Bednar, Antelope Valley College
Paul Blakelock, Kingwood College
Amy Brandon, San Jacinto College
Jim Cauthen, John Jay College, CUNY
Kevin Davis, North Central Texas College
Louis DeSipio, University of California–Irvine
Brandon Franke, Blinn College
Steve Garrison, Midwestern State University
Joseph Howard, University of Central Arkansas
Aaron Knight, Houston Community College
Paul Labedz, Valencia Community College
Elise Langan, John Jay College, CUNY
Mark Logas, Valencia Community College
Eric Miller, Blinn College
Anthony O'Regan, Los Angeles Valley College
David Putz, Kingwood College
Chis Soper, Pepperdine University
Kevin Wagner, Florida Atlantic University
Laura Wood, Tarrant County College

Eighth Edition Reviewers

Brian Arbour, John Jay College, CUNY
Ellen Baik, University of Texas–Pan American
David Birch, Lone Star College–Tomball
Bill Carroll, Sam Houston State University
Ed Chervenak, University of New Orleans
Gary Church, Mountain View College
Adrian Stefan Clark, Del Mar College
Annie Cole, Los Angeles City College
Greg Combs, University of Texas at Dallas
Cassandra Cookson, Lee College
Brian Cravens, Blinn College

John Crosby, California State University–Chico
Scott Crosby, Valencia Community College
Courtenay Daum, Colorado State University, Fort Collins
Peter Doas, University of Texas–Pan American
John Domino, Sam Houston State University
Doug Dow, University of Texas–Dallas
Jeremy Duff, Midwestern State University
Heather Evans, Sam Houston State University
Hyacinth Ezeamii, Albany State University
Bob Fitrakis, Columbus State Community College
Brian Fletcher, Truckee Meadows Community College
Paul Foote, Eastern Kentucky University
Frank Garrahan, Austin Community College
Jimmy Gleason, Purdue University
Steven Greene, North Carolina State University
Jeannie Grussendorf, Georgia State University
M. Ahad Hayaud-Din, Brookhaven College
Alexander Hogan, Lone Star College–CyFair
Glen Hunt, Austin Community College
Mark Jendrysik, University of North Dakota
Krista Jenkins, Fairleigh Dickinson University
Carlos Juárez, Hawaii Pacific University
Melinda Kovas, Sam Houston State University
Boyd Lanier, Lamar University
Jeff Lazarus, Georgia State University
Jeffrey Lee, Blinn College
Alan Lehmann, Blinn College
Julie Lester, Macon State College
Steven Lichtman, Shippensburg University
Fred Lokken, Truckee Meadows Community College
Shari MacLachlan, Palm Beach Community College
Guy Martin, Winston-Salem State University
Fred Monardi, College of Southern Nevada
Vincent Moscardelli, University of Connecticut
Jason Mycoff, University of Delaware
Sugmaran Narayanan, Midwestern State University
Anthony Nownes, University of Tennessee, Knoxville
Elizabeth Oldmixon, University of North Texas
John Osterman, San Jacinto College–Central
Mark Peplowski, College of Southern Nevada
Maria Victoria Perez-Rios, John Jay College, CUNY
Sara Rinfret, University of Wisconsin, Green Bay
Andre Robinson, Pulaski Technical College
Susan Roomberg, University of Texas at San Antonio
Ryan Rynbrandt, Collin County Community College
Mario Salas, Northwest Vista College
Michael Sanchez, San Antonio College
Mary Schander, Pasadena City College
Laura Schneider, Grand Valley State University
Subash Shah, Winston-Salem State University
Mark Shomaker, Blinn College
Roy Slater, St. Petersburg College
Debra St. John, Collin College
Eric Whitaker, Western Washington University
Clay Wiegand, Cisco College
Walter Wilson, University of Texas at San Antonio

Kevan Yenerall, Clarion University
Rogerio Zapata, South Texas College

Ninth Edition Reviewers

Amy Acord, Lone Star College–CyFair
Milan Andrejevich, Ivy Tech Community College
Steve Anthony, Georgia State University
Phillip Ardoin, Appalachian State University
Gregory Arey, Cape Fear Community College
Joan Babcock, Northwest Vista College
Evelyn Ballard, Houston Community College
Robert Ballinger, South Texas College
Mary Barnes-Tilley, Blinn College
Robert Bartels, Evangel University
Nancy Bednar, Antelope Valley College
Annie Benifield, Lone Star College–Tomball
Donna Bennett, Trinity Valley Community College
Amy Brandon, El Paso Community College
Mark Brewer, The University of Maine
Gary Brown, Lone Star College–Montgomery
Joe Campbell, Johnson County Community College
Dewey Clayton, University of Louisville
Jeff Colbert, Elon University
Amanda Cook-Fesperman, Illinois Valley Community College
Kevin Corder, Western Michigan University
Kevin Davis, North Central Texas College
Paul Davis, Truckee Meadows Community College
Terri Davis, Lamar University
Jennifer De Maio, California State University, Northridge
Christopher Durso, Valencia College
Ryan Emenaker, College of the Redwoods
Leslie Feldman, Hofstra University
Glen Findley, Odessa College
Michael Gattis, Gulf Coast State College
Donna Godwin, Trinity Valley Community College
Precious Hall, Truckee Meadows Community College
Sally Hansen, Daytona State College
Tiffany Harper, Collin College
Todd Hartman, Appalachian State University
Virginia Haysley, Lone Star College–Tomball
David Head, John Tyler Community College
Rick Henderson, Texas State University–San Marcos
Richard Herrera, Arizona State University
Thaddaus Hill, Blinn College
Steven Holmes, Bakersfield College
Kevin Holton, South Texas College
Robin Jacobson, University of Puget Sound
Joseph Jozwiak, Texas A&M–Corpus Christi
Casey Klofstad, University of Miami
Samuel Lingrosso, Los Angeles Valley College
Mark Logas, Valencia College
Christopher Marshall, South Texas College
Larry McElvain, South Texas College
Elizabeth McLane, Wharton County Junior College
Eddie Meaders, University of North Texas
Rob Mellen, Mississippi State University

Jalal Nejad, Northwest Vista College
Adam Newmark, Appalachian State University
Stephen Nicholson, University of California, Merced
Cissie Owen, Lamar University
Suzanne Preston, St. Petersburg College
David Putz, Lone Star College–Kingwood
Auksuole Rubavichute, Mountain View College
Ronnee Schreiber, San Diego State University
Ronald Schurin, University of Connecticut
Jason Seitz, Georgia Perimeter College
Jennifer Seitz, Georgia Perimeter College
Shannon Sinegal, The University of New Orleans
John Sides, George Washington University
Thomas Sowers, Lamar University
Jim Startin, University of Texas at San Antonio
Robert Sterken, University of Texas at Tyler
Bobby Summers, Harper College
John Theis, Lone Star College–Kingwood
John Todd, University of North Texas
Delaina Toothman, The University of Maine
David Trussell, Cisco College
Ronald Vardy, University of Houston
Linda Veazey, Midwestern State University
John Vento, Antelope Valley Community College
Clif Wilkinson, Georgia College
John Wood, Rose State College
Michael Young, Trinity Valley Community College
Tyler Young, Collin College

Tenth Edition Reviewers

Stephen P. Amberg, University of Texas at San Antonio
Juan F. Arzola, College of the Sequoias
Thomas J. Baldino, Wilkes University
Christina Bejarano, University of Kansas
Paul T. Bellinger, Jr., University of Missouri
Melanie J. Blumberg, California University of Pennsylvania
Matthew T. Bradley, Indiana University Kokomo
Jeffrey W. Christiansen, Seminole State College
McKinzie Craig, Marietta College
Christopher Cronin, Methodist University
Jenna Duke, Lehigh Carbon Community College
Francisco Durand, University of Texas at San Antonio
Carrie Eaves, Elon University
Paul M. Flor, El Camino College Compton Center
Adam Fuller, Youngstown State University
Christi Gramling, Charleston Southern University
Sally Hansen, Daytona State College
Mary Jane Hatton, Hawaii Pacific University
David Helpap, University of Wisconsin–Green Bay
Theresa L. Hutchins, Georgia Highlands College
Cryshanna A. Jackson Leftwich, Youngstown State University
Ashlyn Kuersten, Western Michigan University
Kara Lindaman, Winona State University
Timothy Lynch, University of Wisconsin–Milwaukee
Larry McElvain, South Texas College
Corinna R. McKoy, Ventura College

Eddie L. Meaders, University of North Texas
Don D. Mirjanian, College of Southern Nevada
R. Shea Mize, Georgia Highlands College
Nicholas Morgan, Collin College
Matthew Murray, Dutchess Community College
Harold "Trey" Orndorff III, Daytona State College
Randall Parish, University of North Georgia
Michelle Pautz, University of Dayton
Michael Pickering, University of New Orleans
Donald Ranish, Antelope Valley College
Glenn W. Richardson, Jr., Kutztown University of Pennsylvania
Jason Robles, Colorado State University
Ionas Aurelian Rus, University of Cincinnati–Blue Ash
Robert Sahr, Oregon State University
Kelly B. Shaw, Iowa State University
Captain Michael Slattery, Campbell University
Michael Smith, Sam Houston State University
Maryam T. Stevenson, University of Indianapolis
Elizabeth Trentanelli, Gulf Coast State College
Ronald W. Vardy, University of Houston
Timothy Weaver, University of Louisville
Christina Wolbrecht, University of Notre Dame

Eleventh Edition Reviewers

Maria J. Albo, University of North Georgia
Andrea Aleman, University of Texas at San Antonio

Juan Arzola, College of the Sequoias
Ross K. Baker, Rutgers University
Daniel Birdsong, University of Dayton
Phil Branyon, University of North Georgia
Sheryl Edwards, University of Michigan–Dearborn
Lauren Elliott-Dorans, University of Toledo
Heather Evans, Sam Houston State University
William Feagin, Jr., Wharton County Junior College
Glen Findley, Odessa College
Heather Frederick, Slipper Rock University
Jason Ghibesi, Ocean County College
Patrick Gilbert, Lone Star–Tomball
Steven Horn, Everett Community College
Demetra Kasimis, California State University,
     Long Beach
Eric T. Kasper, University of Wisconsin–Eau Claire
Mary Linder, Grayson County College
Phil McCall, Portland State University
Carolyn Myers, Southwestern Illinois College–Belleville
Gerhard Peters, Citrus College
Michael A. Powell, Frederick Community College
Allen K. Settle, California Polytechnic State University
Laurie Sprankle, Community College of Allegheny County
Ryan Lee Teten, University of Louisiana at Lafayette
Justin Vaughn, Boise State University
John Vento, Antelope Valley College
Aaron Weinschenk, University of Wisconsin–Green Bay
Tyler Young, Collin College

We are also grateful to Melissa Michelson, of Menlo College, who contributed to the "Who Are Americans?" and "Who Participates?" infographics for this edition; Holley Hansen, of Oklahoma State University, who contributed to the "America Side by Side" boxes; and Gabrielle Ellul for research assistance.

Perhaps above all, we thank those at W. W. Norton. For its first five editions, editor Steve Dunn helped us shape the book in countless ways. Lisa McKay contributed smart ideas and a keen editorial eye to the Tenth Edition. Ann Shin carried on the Norton tradition of splendid editorial work on the Sixth through Ninth Editions and on the current Eleventh Edition. As associate editor, Emily Stuart brought intelligence and dedication to the development of this Eleventh Edition. For our InQuizitive course, Coursepack, and other instructor resources, Spencer Richardson-Jones has been an energetic and visionary editor. Ashley Horna, Michael Jaoui, Shannon Jilek, and Ariel Eaton also kept the production of the Eleventh Edition and its accompanying resources coherent and in focus. Andrew Pachuta copyedited the manuscript, and our superb project editor Christine D'Antonio devoted countless hours to keeping on top of myriad details. We thank Elyse Rieder for finding new photos and our photo editor Catherine Abelman for managing the image program. Finally, we thank Roby Harrington, the head of Norton's college department.

Benjamin Ginsberg
Theodore J. Lowi
Margaret Weir
Caroline J. Tolbert
October 2016

ELEVENTH EDITION

We the People

AN INTRODUCTION TO AMERICAN POLITICS

Most Americans share the core political values of liberty, equality, and democracy and want their government and its policies to reflect these values. However, people often disagree on the meaning of these values and what government should do to protect them.

American Political Culture

WHAT GOVERNMENT DOES AND WHY IT MATTERS Americans sometimes appear to believe that the government is an institution that does things *to* them and from which they need protection. Students may wonder why they have to fill in long, often complicated forms to apply for financial assistance. They may frown when they see the payroll tax deducted from their small paycheck. Like Americans of all ages, they may resent municipal "red-light" cameras designed to photograph traffic violators—and send them tickets.

Although most people complain about something that government does *to* them, most everyone wants the government to do a great deal *for* them. Some of the services that people expect from government are big-ticket items, such as providing national security and keeping the nation safe from terrorist attacks. We all know that government pays for and directs the military. Students attending a state university know that state and federal public dollars help support their education.

Yet many of the other services that government provides are far less visible, and often it is not even clear that government plays a role at all. For example, students grabbing a quick bite to eat between classes take it for granted that their hamburger will not contain bacteria that might make them sick. Without federal inspection of meat, however, chances of contracting food-borne illnesses would be much higher and the everyday task of eating would be much riskier. Driving to school would not be possible if not for the tens of billions of dollars spent each year on road construction and maintenance by federal, state, and municipal authorities. Like most Americans, young people expect to get reliable information about the weather for the week ahead and warnings about dangerous events such as hurricanes. The National Weather Service and the National Hurricane Center both provide reliable forecasts for such simple calculations as whether to bring an umbrella to more significant calculations made by airlines and air traffic control to get travelers safely where they need to go. These daily decisions don't seem to involve government, but in fact they do. Indeed, most Americans would not be here at all if it were not for federal immigration policies, which set the terms for entry into the United States and for obtaining citizenship.

government institutions and procedures through which a territory and its people are ruled

Government is the term generally used to describe the formal institutions through which a land and its people are ruled. As the government seeks to help and protect its citizens, it faces the challenge of doing so in ways that are true to the key American political values of liberty, equality, and democracy. Most Americans find it easy to affirm all three values in principle. In practice, however, matters are not always so clear; these values mean different things to different people, and they often seem to conflict. This is where politics comes in. **Politics** refers to conflicts and struggles over the leadership, structure, and policies of governments. As we will see in this chapter and throughout this book, much political conflict concerns policies and practices that seem to affirm one of the key American political values but may contradict another.

politics conflict over the leadership, structure, and policies of governments

chaptergoals

- Explore Americans' attitudes toward government (pp. 5–9)
- Describe the role of the citizen in politics (pp. 9–12)
- Define government and forms of government (pp. 12–16)
- Show how the social composition of the American population has changed over time (pp. 16–24)
- Analyze whether the U.S. system of government upholds American political values (pp. 24–31)

● What Americans Think about Government

Explore Americans' attitudes toward government

Since the United States was established as a nation, Americans have been reluctant to grant government too much power, and they have often been suspicious of politicians. But over the course of the nation's history, Americans have also turned to government for assistance in times of need and have strongly supported the government in periods of war. In 1933 the power of the government began to expand to meet the crises created by the stock market crash of 1929, the Great Depression, and the run on banks of 1933. Congress passed legislation that brought the government into the businesses of home mortgages, farm mortgages, credit, and relief of personal distress. More recently, when the economy threatened to fall into a deep recession in 2008 and 2009, the federal government took action to shore up the financial system, oversee the restructuring of the ailing auto companies, and inject hundreds of billions of dollars into the faltering economy. Today the national government is an enormous institution with programs and policies reaching into every corner of American life. It oversees the nation's economy, it is the nation's largest employer, it provides citizens with a host of services, it controls the world's most formidable military, and it regulates a wide range of social and commercial activities.

Much of what citizens have come to depend on and take for granted as somehow part of the natural environment is in fact created by government. Take the example of a typical college student's day, throughout which that student relies on a host of

The federal government maintains a large number of websites that provide useful information to citizens on such topics as loans for education, civil service job applications, the inflation rate, and how the weather will affect farming. These sites are just one way in which the government serves its citizens.

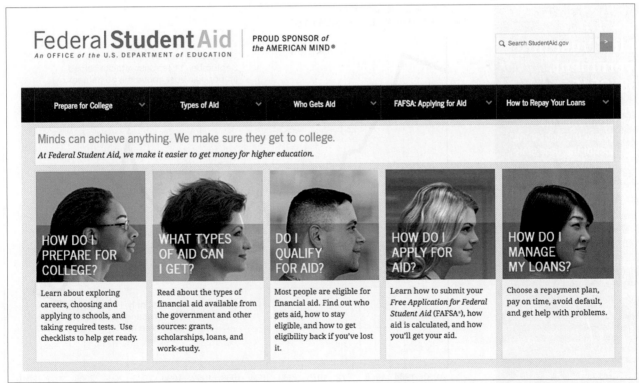

services and activities organized by national, state, and local government agencies. The extent of this dependence on government is illustrated by Table 1.1 on page 7.

Trust in Government

Ironically, even as popular dependence on the government has grown, the American public's view of government has turned more sour. Public trust in government has declined, and Americans are now more likely to feel that they can do little to influence the government's actions. The decline in public trust among Americans is striking. In the early 1960s, three-quarters of Americans said they trusted government most of the time. By 2015, only 19 percent of Americans expressed trust in government; 67 percent stated that they trusted government only some of the time[1] (see Figure 1.1). Different groups vary somewhat in their levels of trust: African Americans and Latinos express slightly more confidence in the federal government than do whites. But even among the most supportive groups, considerably more than half only trust the government some of the time.[2] These developments are important because politically engaged citizens and public confidence in government are vital for the health of a democracy.

In the aftermath of the September 11, 2001, terrorist attacks, a number of studies reported a substantial increase in popular trust in government.[3] This view, expressed during a period of national crisis, may have been indicative less of a renewed *trust* in government to do the right thing than of a fervent *hope* that it would. And, indeed, by 2004, trust in government had fallen to near its pre–September 11 level.[4]

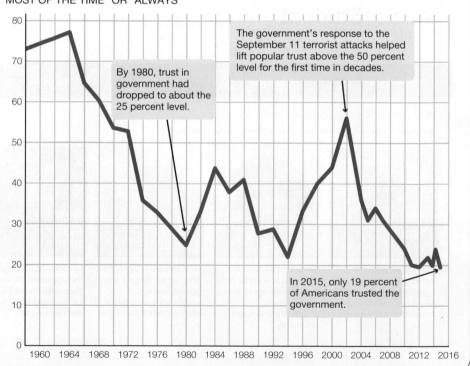

FIGURE 1.1

Public Trust in Government, 1958–2015

Participants in these polls were asked if they trusted the government to "do the right thing" always, most of the time, only some of the time, or never.

Since the 1960s, general levels of public trust in government have declined. What factors might help to account for changes in the public's trust in government? Why has confidence in government dropped again since September 11, 2001?

SOURCE: The American National Election Studies, 1958–2004; Pew Research Center, www.people-press .org/2015/11/23/beyond-distrust-how -americans-view-their-government/ (accessed 4/10/16). The Pew data after 2004 represent a "three survey moving average."

PERCENTAGE RESPONDING "MOST OF THE TIME" OR "ALWAYS"

The government's response to the September 11 terrorist attacks helped lift popular trust above the 50 percent level for the first time in decades.

By 1980, trust in government had dropped to about the 25 percent level.

In 2015, only 19 percent of Americans trusted the government.

TABLE 1.1

The Presence of Government in the Daily Life of a Student at "State University"

TIME OF DAY	SCHEDULE
7:00 A.M.	Wake up. Standard time set by the national government.
7:10 A.M.	Shower. Water courtesy of local government, either a public entity or a regulated private company. Brush your teeth with toothpaste whose cavity-fighting claims have been verified by a federal agency. Dry your hair with an electric dryer manufactured according to federal government agency guidelines.
7:30 A.M.	Have a bowl of cereal with milk for breakfast. "Nutrition Facts" on food labels are a federal requirement, pasteurization of milk required by state law, freshness dating on milk based on state and federal standards, recycling the empty cereal box and milk carton enabled by state or local laws.
8:30 A.M.	Drive or take public transportation to campus. Air bags and seat belts required by federal and state laws. Roads and bridges paid for by state and local governments, speed and traffic laws set by state and local governments, public transportation subsidized by all levels of government.
8:45 A.M.	Arrive on campus of large public university. Buildings are 70 percent financed by state taxpayers.
9:00 A.M.	First class: Chemistry 101. Tuition partially paid by a federal loan (more than half the cost of university instruction is paid for by taxpayers), chemistry lab paid for with grants from the National Science Foundation (a federal agency) and smaller grants from business corporations made possible by federal income tax deductions for charitable contributions.
Noon	Eat lunch. College cafeteria financed by state dormitory authority on land grant from federal Department of Agriculture.
12:47 P.M.	Felt an earthquake! Check the U.S. Geological Survey at www.usgs.gov to see that it was a 3.9 on the Richter scale.
2:00 P.M.	Second class: American Government 101 (your favorite class!). You may be taking this class because it is required by the state legislature or because it fulfills a university requirement.
4:00 P.M.	Third class: Computer Lab. Free computers, software, and Internet access courtesy of state subsidies plus grants and discounts from Apple and Microsoft, the costs of which are deducted from their corporate income taxes; Internet built in part by federal government. Duplication of software prohibited by federal copyright laws.
6:00 P.M.	Eat dinner: hamburger and french fries. Meat inspected for bacteria by federal agencies.
7:00 P.M.	Work at part-time job at the campus library. Minimum wage set by federal, state, or local government; books and journals in library paid for by state taxpayers.
8:15 P.M.	Go online to check the status of your application for a federal student loan (FAFSA) on the Department of Education's website at studentaid.ed.gov.
10:00 P.M.	Go home. Street lighting paid for by county and city governments, police patrols by city government.
10:15 P.M.	Watch TV. Networks regulated by federal government, cable public-access channels required by city law. Weather forecast provided to broadcasters by a federal agency.
10:45 P.M.	To complete your economics homework, visit the Bureau of Labor Statistics at www.bls.gov to look up unemployment levels since 1972.
Midnight	Put out the trash before going to bed. Trash collected by city sanitation department, financed by "user charges."

In the 2016 presidential campaign, the popularity of nonestablishment, "outsider" candidates, such as businessman and reality-TV star Donald Trump, pointed to Americans' continued frustration with and distrust of the federal government.

Several factors contributed to the decline in trust. Revelations about the faulty information that led up to the war in Iraq and ongoing concern about the war had increased Americans' distrust of government. In March 2007, 54 percent of those surveyed believed that the Bush administration had deliberately misled the American public about whether Iraq had weapons of mass destruction.

The lowest level of trust ever recorded was in October 2011, when, after a bitter congressional battle over raising the national debt limit, one poll showed that only 10 percent of Americans trusted government to do the right thing always or most of the time.[5] By 2013 intense partisan conflict further undermined trust in government. The public watched with dismay as political differences over taxing and spending led to repeated threats to shut down the federal government. When political differences over the Affordable Care Act, the social program supported by President Obama to reform the American health care system, led to a government shutdown in 2013 and yet another dramatic showdown over raising the national debt limit, public trust once again dipped to historically low levels.

Distrust of government greatly influenced the primary elections in 2015 and 2016, when a number of "outsider" candidates, critical of government, attracted wide support. This trend was especially pronounced in the Republican primaries, in which candidates known for their strong anti-government rhetoric, such as Ted Cruz, and candidates with no government experience, notably Donald Trump, unexpectedly attracted wide support. Support for such outsiders reflected deep distrust in government among Republicans, only 11 percent of whom expressed trust in goverment in 2015, compared to 26 percent of Democrats.[6] Among Democratic primary voters, strong support for Bernie Sanders, a democratic socialist, also indicated a desire to depart from business as usual in Washington. Sanders vigorously faulted the government for failing to take more forceful action against corporate misconduct and growing inequality.

Does it matter if Americans trust their government? For the most part, the answer is yes. As we have seen, most Americans rely on government for a wide range of services and laws that they simply take for granted. But long-term distrust in government can result in public refusal to pay the taxes necessary to support such widely approved public activities. Low levels of confidence may also make it difficult for government to attract talented and effective workers to public service.[7] The weakening of government as a result of prolonged levels of distrust may ultimately harm the United States' capacity to defend its national interest in the world economy and may jeopardize its national security. Likewise, a weak government can do little to assist citizens who need help in weathering periods of sharp economic or technological change.

for critical analysis

What recent events have affected Americans' trust in government? What might it take to restore Americans' trust in the federal government?

Political Efficacy

Another important trend in American views about government has been a declining sense of **political efficacy**, the belief that ordinary citizens can affect what government does, that they can make government listen to them. In 2015, 74 percent of Americans said that elected officials don't care what people like them think; in 1960, only 25 percent felt so shut out of government.[8] Accompanying this sense that ordinary people are not heard is a growing belief that government is not run for the benefit of all the people. In 2015, 76 percent of the public disagreed with the idea that the "government is really run for the benefit of all the people."[9] These views are widely shared across the age spectrum.

political efficacy the ability to influence government and politics

This widely felt loss of political efficacy is bad news for American democracy. The feeling that you can't affect government decisions can lead to a self-perpetuating cycle of apathy, declining political participation, and withdrawal from political life. Why bother to participate if you believe it makes no difference? Yet the belief that you can be effective is the first step needed to influence government. Not every effort of ordinary citizens to influence government will succeed, but without any such efforts, government decisions will be made by a smaller and smaller circle of powerful people. Such loss of broad popular influence over government actions undermines the key feature of American democracy— government by the people.

● Citizenship: Knowledge and Participation

Describe the role of the citizen in politics

The first prerequisite for achieving an increased sense of political efficacy is knowledge. Political indifference is often simply a habit that stems from a lack of knowledge about how your interests are affected by politics and from a sense that you can do nothing to affect politics. But political efficacy is a self-fulfilling prophecy: if you think you cannot be effective, chances are you will never try. Most research suggests that people active in politics have a high sense of their own efficacy. This means they believe they can make a difference—even if they do not win all the time. Most people do not want to be politically active every day of their lives, but it is essential to American political ideals that all citizens be informed and able to act.

Even though the Internet has made it easier than ever to learn about politics, the state of political knowledge in the United States today is spotty. Most Americans know little about current issues or debates. Numerous surveys indicate that the majority of Americans have significant gaps in their political knowledge. For example, in 2015 only 31 percent of those surveyed could identify all three branches of the federal government and in 2014 only 27 percent knew that it takes a two-thirds vote in the House and the Senate to override a presidential veto. On the other hand, the public is more knowledgeable about politicians and individuals who have been prominent in the national media. For example, when shown pictures of public figures in 2015, 91 percent could identify Martin Luther King, Jr., and 51 percent could identify Senator Elizabeth Warren (see Table 1.2). Rather than dwell on the widespread political ignorance of many Americans, we prefer to view this as an opportunity for the readers of this book. Those of you who make the effort to become more knowledgeable will be much better prepared to influence the political system regarding the issues and concerns that you care most about.

TABLE 1.2

What Americans Know about Government

RESPONDENTS WHO	PERCENTAGE
Could identify all three branches of government	31
Could identify the partisan balance in the House and Senate	40
Knew that it takes a two-thirds vote of the House and Senate to override a presidential veto	27
Correctly believed that the government spends more on Social Security than on foreign aid, transportation, or interest on the national debt	20
Knew that three Supreme Court justices are women	33
Could identify Senator Elizabeth Warren (from a photo)	51
Could identify Martin Luther King, Jr. (from a photo)	91

SOURCES: Pew Research Center for the People and the Press, www.people-press.org/2015/04/28/what-the -public-knows-in-pictures-words-maps-and-graphs/; www.people-press.org/2014/10/02/from-isis-to-unemployment -what-do-americans-know/; www.people-press.org/2014/06/26/section-10-political-participation-interest-and -knowledge/; and Annenberg Public Policy Center, "Is There a Constitutional Right to Own a Home or Pet? Many Americans Don't Know," September 16, 2015, www.annenbergpublicpolicycenter.org/wp-content/uploads/Civic -knowledge-survey-Sept.-2015.pdf (accessed 4/11/16).

After September 11, many commentators noted a revival in Americans' sense of citizenship, as manifested by ubiquitous flag displays and other demonstrations of patriotic sentiment. There seems to be little doubt that millions of Americans experienced a renewed sense of identification with their nation. Citizenship, however, has a broader meaning than just patriotism.

Beginning with the ancient Greeks, citizenship has meant membership in one's community. Citizenship entailed involvement in public discussion, debate, and activity designed to improve the welfare of the community. Our definition of **citizenship** derives from the Greek ideal: enlightened political engagement.[10] To be politically engaged in a meaningful way, citizens require resources, especially political knowledge and information. Democracy functions best when citizens are informed. But citizenship in the full sense, as understood first by the ancient Greeks, goes beyond an occasional visit to a voting booth. A good citizen must be politically engaged and have the knowledge needed to participate in political debate.

citizenship informed and active membership in a political community

The Necessity of Political Knowledge

Political knowledge means more than having a few opinions to offer a pollster or to guide your decisions in a voting booth. It is important to know the rules and strategies that govern political institutions and the principles on which they are based, but it is more important to know them in ways that relate to your own interests. Citizens need knowledge in order to assess their interests and to know when to act on them. Knowledgeable citizens are more attentive to and engaged in politics because they understand how and why politics is relevant to their lives.

Without political knowledge, no citizen can be aware of her interests or her stake in a political dispute. In 2015 the Supreme Court considered an important case related to the Affordable Care Act, informally known as Obamacare. At stake was the constitutionality of the federal subsidies for the health insurance of people living in states that had not established their own insurance exchanges. A negative ruling would have eliminated subsidies for millions of Americans, making insurance unaffordable for many. Even so, only 27 percent of Americans reported that they had heard some or a lot about the issue.[11] This number grew to 39 percent after the Court ruled in favor of continuing the subsidies. Less than half of Americans paid enough attention to the discussion to be able to develop an informed opinion about the issue. How many had enough of an understanding of the complex health care act to determine whether it was in their interest or not? Various public and private interest groups devote enormous time and energy to understanding alternative policy proposals and their implications so that they will know which policies to support and which to oppose. Interest groups understand something that every citizen should also understand: effective participation requires knowledge.

Citizens need political knowledge also to identify the best ways to act on their interests. If your street is rendered impassable by snow, what can you do? Is snow removal the responsibility of the federal government? Is it a state or municipal responsibility? Knowing that you have a stake in a clear road does not help much if you do not know that snow removal is a city or a county responsibility and if you cannot identify the municipal agency that deals with the problem. Americans are fond of complaining that government is not responsive to their needs, but in some cases, it is possible that citizens simply lack the information they need to present their problems to the appropriate government officials.

Citizens need political knowledge also to ascertain what they cannot or should not ask of politicians and the government. We need to balance our need for protection and service with our equally pressing need for liberty. Particularly during periods when the nation's safety is threatened, Americans may be inclined to accept increased governmental intrusion into their lives in the name of national security. Since 2001, for example, Americans have accepted unprecedented levels of governmental surveillance and the erosion of some traditional restrictions on police powers in the name of preventing terrorism. It remains to be seen whether this exchange of liberty for the promise of security was a wise choice. Political knowledge, therefore, includes knowing the limits on (as well as the possibilities for) pursuing one's own individual interests through political action. This is, perhaps, the most difficult form of political knowledge to acquire.

"Digital Citizenship"

As more and more of our social, workplace, and educational activities have migrated online, so too have opportunities for political knowledge and participation, creating a new concept of "digital citizenship." *Digital citizenship* is the ability to participate in society online, and it is increasingly important in politics. A 2015 Pew survey found that over the previous year, 65 percent of Americans had used the Internet to find data or information about government. These include visiting a local, state, or federal government website.[12] Digital citizenship benefits individuals,

When the federal government partially shut down in October 2013, millions of citizens were affected, including visitors who were turned away from the Statue of Liberty. Citizens need political knowledge to understand how such events affect their lives and what policies promote their interests.

for critical analysis

Many studies seem to show that most Americans know very little about government and politics. Can we have democratic government without knowledgeable and aware citizens?

but it also provides advantages to society as a whole. Digital citizens are more likely to be interested in politics and to discuss politics with friends, family, and coworkers than individuals who do not use online political information. They are also more likely to vote and participate in other ways in elections.

By contrast, individuals without Internet access or the skills to participate in politics and the economy online are being left further behind. Exclusion from participation online is referred to as the digital divide (which we discuss further in Chapters 7 and 8). Lower-income and less-educated Americans, racial and ethnic minorities, and the elderly are all less likely to have Internet access. For some, location is the barrier: the limits of network infrastructure mean that many rural residents have a difficult time getting Internet access. But for many, cost is the barrier to access. Internet access and digital literacy are critical for full participation in American politics in the twenty-first century. In much the same way that higher levels of education and literacy promoted democracy and economic growth in the nineteenth century, the Internet has the potential to benefit society as a whole and to facilitate political participation of individuals within society. At the same time, the rise of the Internet raises new questions about who is able to participate and whether digital politics is changing the traditional dynamics of American politics.

for critical **analysis**

Just as all Americans have the right to a public education and to be taught to read and write, should all Americans have access to the Internet and be taught skills to access and use information online?

● Government

Define government and forms of government

As we saw in the introduction to this chapter, *government* refers to the formal institutions through which a land and its people are ruled. To govern is to rule. A government may be as simple as a tribal council that meets occasionally to advise the chief or as complex as the vast establishments, with their procedures, laws, and bureaucracies, found in many large countries today. In the history of civilization, governments have not been difficult to establish. There have been thousands of them. The hard part is establishing a government that lasts. Even more difficult is developing a stable government that is compatible with liberty, equality, and democracy.

Is Government Needed?

Americans have always harbored some suspicion of government and have wondered how extensive a role it should play in their lives. Thomas Jefferson famously observed that the best government was one that "governed least." Generally speaking, a government is needed to provide those services, sometimes called "public goods," that all citizens need but are not likely to be able to provide adequately for themselves. These might include defense against foreign aggression, maintenance of public order, a stable currency, enforcement of contractual obligations and property rights, and a guarantee of some measure of social justice. These are goods that benefit everyone but that no individual or group on its own can afford to supply. Government, with its powers to tax and regulate, is typically viewed as the best way to provide public goods. However, there is often disagreement about which public goods are essential and how they should be provided. The precise extent to which government involvement in American society is needed has been debated throughout the nation's history and will continue to be a central focus of political contention.

Forms of Government

Governments vary in their structure, their size, and the way they operate. Two questions are of special importance in determining how governments differ: Who governs? And how much government control is permitted?

Some nations are governed by a single individual—a king or dictator, for example. This state of affairs is called **autocracy**. Where a small group—perhaps landowners, military officers, or the wealthy—controls most of the governing decisions, that government is said to be an **oligarchy**. If citizens are vested with the power to rule themselves, that government is a **democracy**.

Governments also vary considerably in terms of how they govern. In the United States and a small number of other nations, governments are limited as to what they are permitted to control (substantive limits) and how they go about it (procedural limits). Governments that are limited in this way are called **constitutional governments**, or liberal governments. In other nations, including many in Latin America, Asia, and Africa, the law imposes few real limits. The government, however, is nevertheless kept in check by other political and social institutions that it is unable to control and must come to terms with—such as autonomous territories, an organized religion, organized business groups, or organized labor unions. Such governments are generally called **authoritarian**. In a third group of nations, including the Soviet Union under Joseph Stalin, Nazi Germany, perhaps prewar Japan and Italy, and North Korea today, governments not only are free of legal limits but also seek to eliminate those organized social groups that might challenge or limit their authority. These governments typically attempt to dominate or control every sphere of political, economic, and social life and, as a result, are called **totalitarian** (see Figure 1.2).

Americans have the good fortune to live in a nation in which limits are placed on what governments can do and how they can do it. Many of the world's people do not live in a constitutional democracy. By one measure, just 40 percent of the global population (those living in 86 countries) enjoy sufficient levels of political and personal freedom to be classified as living in a constitutional democracy.[13] And constitutional democracies were unheard of before the modern era. Prior to the eighteenth and nineteenth centuries, governments seldom sought—and rarely

autocracy a form of government in which a single individual—a king, queen, or dictator—rules

oligarchy a form of government in which a small group—landowners, military officers, or wealthy merchants—controls most of the governing decisions

democracy a system of rule that permits citizens to play a significant part in the governmental process, usually through the election of key public officials

constitutional government a system of rule in which formal and effective limits are placed on the powers of the government

authoritarian government a system of rule in which the government recognizes no formal limits but may nevertheless be restrained by the power of other social institutions

totalitarian government a system of rule in which the government recognizes no formal limits on its power and seeks to absorb or eliminate other social institutions that might challenge it

Who governs	Type of government
One person	Autocracy
Small group (e.g., landowners, military officers, or wealthy merchants)	Oligarchy
Many people	Democracy

Limits on government	Type of government
Codified, legal substantive and procedural limits on what government can or cannot do	Constitutional
Few legal limits; some limits imposed by social groups	Authoritarian
No limits	Totalitarian

FIGURE 1.2

Forms of Government

America's Founders were influenced by the English thinker John Locke (1632–1704). Locke argued that governments need the consent of the people.

received—the support of their subjects. The available evidence strongly suggests that ordinary people often had little love for the government or for the social order. After all, they had no stake in it. They equated government with the police officer, the bailiff, and the tax collector.[14]

Beginning in the seventeenth century, in a handful of Western nations, two important changes began to take place in the character and conduct of government. First, governments began to acknowledge formal limits on their power. Second, a small number of governments began to provide ordinary citizens with a formal voice in public affairs—through the vote. Obviously, the desirability of limits on government and the expansion of popular influence were at the heart of the American Revolution in 1776. "No taxation without representation," as we shall see in Chapter 2, was fiercely asserted from the beginning of the Revolution through the Founding in 1789. But even before the Revolution, a tradition of limiting government and expanding participation in the political process had developed throughout western Europe.

Limiting Government

The key force behind the imposition of limits on government power was a new social class, the bourgeoisie, which became an important political force in the sixteenth and seventeenth centuries. *Bourgeois* is a French word for "freeman of the city," or *bourg*. Being part of the bourgeoisie later became associated with being "middle class" and with involvement in commerce or industry. In order to gain a share of control of government, joining or even displacing the kings, aristocrats, and gentry who had dominated government for centuries, the bourgeoisie sought to change existing institutions—especially parliaments—into instruments of real political participation. Parliaments had existed for centuries but were generally aristocratic institutions. The bourgeoisie embraced parliaments as means by which they could exert the weight of their superior numbers and growing economic advantage over their aristocratic rivals. At the same time, the bourgeoisie sought to place restraints on the capacity of governments to threaten these economic and political interests by placing formal or constitutional limits on governmental power.

Although motivated primarily by the need to protect and defend their own interests, the bourgeoisie advanced many of the principles that would define the central underpinnings of individual liberty for all citizens—freedom of speech, freedom of assembly, freedom of conscience, and freedom from arbitrary search and seizure. The work of political theorists such as John Locke (1632–1704) and, later, John Stuart Mill (1806–73) helped shape these evolving ideas about liberty and political rights. However, it is important to note that the bourgeoisie generally did not favor democracy as we know it. They were advocates of electoral and representative institutions, but they favored property requirements and other restrictions so as to limit participation to the middle and upper classes. Yet once these institutions of politics and the protection of the right to engage in politics were established, it was difficult to limit them to the bourgeoisie.

Access to Government: The Expansion of Participation

The expansion of participation from the bourgeoisie to ever-larger segments of society took two paths. In some nations, popular participation was expanded by

John Stuart Mill (1806–73) presented a ringing defense of individual freedom in his famous treatise On Liberty. *Mill's work influenced Americans' evolving ideas about the relationship between government and the individual.*

the Crown or the aristocracy, which ironically saw common people as potential political allies against the bourgeoisie. Thus, in nineteenth-century Prussia, for example, it was the emperor and his great minister Otto von Bismarck who expanded popular participation in order to build political support among the lower orders.

In other nations, participation expanded because competing segments of the bourgeoisie sought to gain political advantage by reaching out to and mobilizing the support of working- and lower-class groups that craved the opportunity to take part in politics—"lining up the unwashed," as one American historian put it.[15] To be sure, excluded groups often agitated for greater participation. But seldom was such agitation by itself enough to secure the right to participate. Usually, expansion of voting rights resulted from a combination of pressure from below and help from above.

The gradual expansion of voting rights by groups hoping to derive some political advantage has been typical of American history. After the Civil War, one of the chief reasons that Republicans moved to enfranchise newly freed slaves was to use the support of the former slaves to maintain Republican control over the defeated southern states. Similarly, in the early twentieth century, upper-middle-class Progressives advocated women's suffrage because they believed that women were likely to support the reforms espoused by the Progressive movement.

Influencing the Government through Participation: Politics

Expansion of participation means that more and more people have a legal right to take part in politics. *Politics* is an important term. In its broadest sense, it refers to conflicts over the character, membership, and policies of any organization to which people belong. As Harold Lasswell, a famous political scientist, once put it, politics is the struggle over "who gets what, when, how."[16] Although politics is a phenomenon that can be found in any organization, our concern in this book is narrower. Here, *politics* will be used to refer only to conflicts and struggles over the leadership, structure, and policies of governments. The goal of politics, as we define it, is to have a share or a say in the composition of the government's leadership, how the government is organized, or what its policies are going to be. Having a share is called having **power** or influence.

Politics can take many forms, including everything from blogging and posting opinion pieces online, sending emails to government officials, voting, lobbying legislators on behalf of particular programs, and participating in protest marches and even violent demonstrations. A system of government that gives citizens a regular opportunity to elect the top government officials is usually called a **representative democracy**, or **republic**. A system that permits citizens to vote directly on laws and policies is often called a **direct democracy**. At the national level, the United States is a representative democracy in which citizens select government officials but do not vote on legislation. Some states and cities, however, have provisions for direct legislation through popular initiative and ballot referendum. These procedures allow citizens to collect petitions requiring an issue to be brought directly to the voters for a decision. In 2016, 165 initiatives appeared on state ballots, dealing with matters that ranged from gun control and raising the minimum wage to legalizing marijuana. Many hot-button issues are decided by initiatives. For example, in Colorado in 2010, voters passed a referendum that called on the state to sue the federal government to enforce immigration laws. Often, broad public campaigns promote controversial referenda, attempting to persuade voters to change existing laws.

power influence over a government's leadership, organization, or policies

representative democracy (republic) a system of government in which the populace selects representatives, who play a significant role in governmental decision making

direct democracy a system of rule that permits citizens to vote directly on laws and policies

For example, in 2016 nine states considered measures that would either decriminalize marijuana or legalize it altogether. Some 82 million people would be affected by the outcome of these contests. Four states considered additional gun control regulations. Colorado voters weighed an amendment to the state constitution that would create a single-payer health system funded by a tax on employers and employees. In California, voters decided on whether to support a ban on plastic bags, the first such statewide ban.

Groups and organized interests do not vote (although their members do), but they certainly do participate in politics. Their political activities usually consist of such endeavors as providing funds for candidates, lobbying, and trying to influence public opinion. The pattern of struggles among interests is called group politics, or **pluralism**. Americans have always been ambivalent about pluralist politics. On the one hand, the right of groups to press their views and compete for influence in the government is the essence of liberty. On the other hand, Americans often fear that organized groups may sometimes exert too much influence, advancing special interests at the expense of larger public interests. (We return to this problem in Chapter 11.)

Sometimes, of course, politics does not take place through formal channels at all but instead involves direct action. Direct action politics can include either violent politics or civil disobedience, both of which attempt to shock rulers into behaving more responsibly. Direct action can also be a form of revolutionary politics, which rejects the system entirely and attempts to replace it with a new ruling group and a new set of rules. In recent years in the United States, groups ranging from animal rights activists to right-to-life advocates to the Occupy Wall Street protesters have used direct action to underline their demands. Many forms of peaceful direct political action are protected by the U.S. Constitution. The country's Founders knew that the right to protest is essential to the maintenance of political freedom, even where the ballot box is available.

pluralism the theory that all interests are and should be free to compete for influence in the government; the outcome of this competition is compromise and moderation

● Who Are Americans?

> **Show how the social composition of the American population has changed over time**

While American democracy aims to give the people a voice in government, the meaning of "we the people" has changed over time. Who are Americans? Through the course of American history, politicians, religious leaders, prominent scholars, and ordinary Americans have puzzled over and fought about the answer to this fundamental question. Since the Founding, the American population has grown from 3.9 million in 1790, the year of the first official census, to 323 million in 2016. As the American population has grown, it has become more diverse on nearly every dimension imaginable.[17] (See the "Who Are Americans?" feature on page 19.)

At the time of the Founding, when the United States consisted of 13 states arrayed along the Eastern Seaboard, 81 percent of Americans counted by the census traced their roots to Europe, mostly England and northern Europe; nearly 20 percent were of African origin, the vast majority of whom were slaves.[18] Only 1.5 percent of the black population was free. There was also an unknown number of Native Americans, the original inhabitants of the land, not counted by the census because the government did not consider them Americans. The first estimates of Native Americans and Hispanics in the mid-1800s showed that each group made up less than 1 percent of the total population.[19]

Native American societies, with their own forms of government, existed for thousands of years before the first European settlers arrived. By the time this photo of Red Cloud and other Sioux warriors was taken, around 1870, Native Americans made up about 1 percent of the American population.

Fast-forward to 1900. The country now stretched across the continent, and waves of immigrants, mainly from Europe, boosted the population to 76 million. In 1900 the United States was predominantly composed of whites of European ancestry, but this number now included many from southern and eastern as well as northern Europe; the black population stood at 12 percent. Residents who traced their origin to Latin America or Asia each accounted for less than 1 percent of the entire population.[20] The large number of new immigrants was reflected in the high proportion of foreign-born people in the United States: the foreign-born population reached its height at 14.7 percent in 1910.[21]

Immigration and Ethnic Diversity

As the European-origin population grew more diverse, anxiety about Americans' ethnic identity mounted. In 1900 the author of a *New York Times* front-page article answered his own question—"Are the Americans an Anglo-Saxon People?"—in the affirmative.[22] But the growing numbers of immigrants from southern and eastern Europe who were crowding into American cities spurred heated debates about how long Anglo-Saxons could dominate. Much as today, politicians and scholars argued about whether the country could absorb such large numbers of immigrants. Concerns ranged from whether their political and social values were compatible with American democracy to whether they would learn English to alarm about the diseases they might bring into the United States.

The distinct ethnic backgrounds and language differences of the new immigrants were not the only characteristics that worried the Anglo-Saxon natives; immigrant religious affiliations also aroused concern. The first immigrants to the United States were overwhelmingly Protestant, many of them fleeing religious persecution. The arrival of Germans and Irish in the mid-1800s began to shift that balance with increasing numbers of Catholics. Even so, in 1900, four out of five Americans were still Protestants. The large-scale immigration of the early twentieth century threatened to reduce the proportion of Protestants significantly. Many of the eastern European immigrants pouring into the country, especially those from Russia, were

Jewish; the southern Europeans, especially the Italians, were Catholic. A more religiously diverse country challenged the implicit Protestantism embedded in many aspects of American public life. For example, religious diversity introduced new conflicts into public schooling as Catholics sought public funding for parochial schools and dissident Protestant sects lobbied to eliminate Bible reading and prayer in the schools.

Anxieties about immigration sparked intense debate. Should the numbers of immigrants entering the country be limited? Should restrictions be placed on the types of immigrants to be granted entry? After World War I, Congress responded to the fears swirling around immigration with new laws that sharply limited the number who could enter the country each year. It also established a new National Origins quota system, based on the nation's population in 1890, before the wave of immigrants from eastern and southern Europe arrived.[23] Supporters of ethnic quotas hoped to turn back the clock and revert to an earlier America in which northern Europeans dominated. The new system set up a hierarchy of admissions: northern European countries received generous quotas for new immigrants, whereas eastern and southern European countries were granted very small quotas. These restrictions ratcheted down the numbers of immigrants so that by 1970 the foreign-born population in the United States reached an all-time low of 5 percent.

Immigration and Race

Official efforts to use racial and ethnic criteria to restrict the American population were not new but had been used to draw boundaries around the American community from the start. The very first census, as just mentioned, did not count Native Americans; in fact, no Native Americans became citizens until 1924. Although the Constitution infamously declared that each slave would count as three-fifths of a person for purposes of apportioning representation among the states, most people of African descent were not officially citizens until 1868, when the Fourteenth Amendment to the Constitution conferred citizenship on the freed slaves.

In the 1900s, many immigrants entered the United States through New York's Ellis Island, where they were checked for disease before being admitted. Today, individuals hoping to immigrate to the United States often apply for a visa at the U.S. consulate in their home country before traveling to the United States, where the U.S. Customs and Border Protection checks their identity and legal status.

An Increasingly Diverse Nation

Since the Founding, the American people have become increasingly diverse. This diversity and the changes in the population have frequently raised challenging questions in American politics.

Race

	1790*	1900*	2010	
= 1 million people	White 81%	White 88%	White	64%
	Black 19%	Black 12%	Black	12%
		Other 1%	Hispanic	16%
			Asian	5%
			Native American	1%
			Other	0.2%
			2 or more races	2%

TOTAL POPULATION =   3,929,214   75,994,575   308,745,538

Geography

	1790	1900	2010
	50%	28%	18%
	50%	5%	23%
		35%	22%
		32%	37%

1790: Northeast 50%   South 50%

1900: Northeast 28%   Midwest 35%   South 32%   West 5%

2010: Northeast 18%   Midwest 22%   South 37%   West 23%

Age

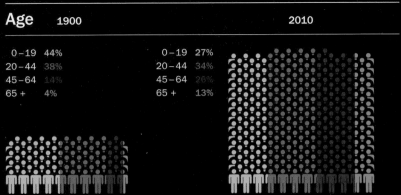

	1900		2010
0–19	44%	0–19	27%
20–44	38%	20–44	34%
45–64	14%	45–64	26%
65 +	4%	65 +	13%

for critical analysis

1. The 2010 census showed that the populations of the South and the West continued to grow more rapidly than the Northeast and Midwest. What are some of the political implications of this trend?

2. Today, Americans over age 37 outnumber Americans under 37—and older adults are more likely to participate in the political process. What do you think this means for the kinds of issues and policies taken up by the government?

* The 1790 census does not accurately reflect the population because it only counted blacks and whites. It did not include Native Americans or other groups. The 1900 census did not count Hispanic Americans.

SOURCE: U.S. Census Bureau, www.census.gov (accessed 8/16/12).

Over half a century earlier, the federal government had sought to limit the non-white population with a 1790 law stipulating that only free whites could become naturalized citizens. Not until 1870 did Congress lift the ban on the naturalization of nonwhites. In addition to the restrictions on blacks and Native Americans, restrictions applied to Asians. The Chinese Exclusion Act of 1882 outlawed the entry of Chinese laborers to the United States. These provisions were not lifted until 1943, when China became America's ally during World War II. Additional barriers enacted after World War I meant that virtually no Asians entered the country as immigrants until the 1940s. People of Hispanic origin do not fit simply into the American system of racial classification. In 1930, for example, the census counted people of Mexican origin as nonwhite but reversed this decision a decade later—after protests by the Mexican-origin population and the Mexican government. Only in 1970 did the census officially begin counting persons of Hispanic origin, noting that they could be any race.[24] As this history suggests, American citizenship has always been tied to "whiteness" even as the meaning of "white" shifted over time.

Twenty-First-Century Americans

Race and Ethnicity By 2000, immigration had profoundly transformed the nation's racial and ethnic profile once again. The primary cause was Congress's decision in 1965 to lift the tight restrictions of the 1920s, allowing for much-expanded immigration from Asia and Latin America (see Figure 1.3). One consequence of the shift has been the growth in the Hispanic, or Latino, population. Census figures for 2014 show that the total Hispanic proportion of the population is now 17.4 percent;

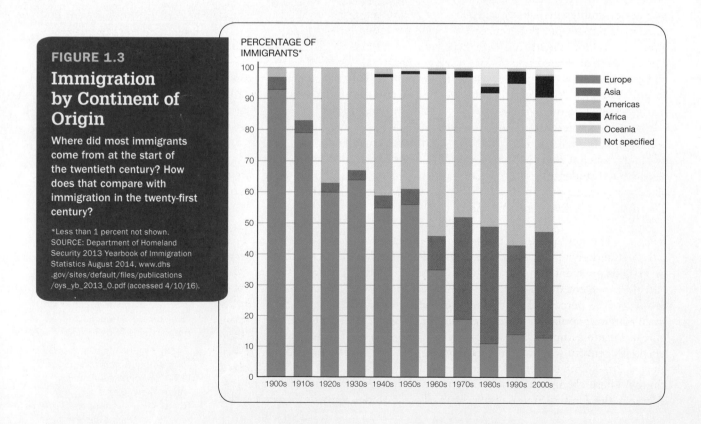

FIGURE 1.3

Immigration by Continent of Origin

Where did most immigrants come from at the start of the twentieth century? How does that compare with immigration in the twenty-first century?

*Less than 1 percent not shown.
SOURCE: Department of Homeland Security 2013 Yearbook of Immigration Statistics August 2014, www.dhs.gov/sites/default/files/publications/oys_yb_2013_0.pdf (accessed 4/10/16).

PERCENTAGE OF IMMIGRANTS*

Europe
Asia
Americas
Africa
Oceania
Not specified

1900s 1910s 1920s 1930s 1940s 1950s 1960s 1970s 1980s 1990s 2000s

the black, or African American, population is 13.2 percent of the total population. Asians make up 5.4 percent of the population. European Americans account for less than two-thirds of the population—their lowest share ever. Moreover, nearly 2.5 percent of the population now identifies itself as of "two or more races," a new category that the census added in 2000.[25] Although it is only a small percentage of the population, the multiracial category points toward a future in which the traditional labels of racial identification may be blurring, marking a major shift in the long-standing American tradition of strict racial categorization. The blurring of racial categories poses challenges to a host of policies—many of them put in place to remedy past discrimination—that rely on racial counts of the population.

Large-scale immigration means that many more residents are foreign-born. In 2014, 13.3 percent of the population was born outside the United States, a figure comparable to foreign-born rates at the turn of the previous century.[26] Over half of the foreign-born came from Latin America and the Caribbean—almost 1 in 10 from the Caribbean, nearly 4 in 10 from Central America (including Mexico), and 1 in 15 from South America.[27] Those born in Asia constituted the next-largest group, making up over one-quarter of foreign-born residents. In sharp contrast to the immigration patterns of a century earlier, fewer immigrants came from Europe. By 2014, just 11.2 percent of those born outside the United States came from Europe.[28]

These figures represent only legally authorized immigrants. One new feature of American society in recent years is the very large number of immigrants who live in the country without legal authorization. Estimates put the number of undocumented immigrants at almost 12 million, the majority of whom are from Mexico and Central America.[29] The large unauthorized population became a flashpoint for controversy as states and cities passed a variety of conflicting laws regarding illegal immigrants' access to public services. Some states have offered driver's licenses to undocumented immigrants, while others have sought to bar them from public services, such as education and emergency health care, both of which are constitutionally guaranteed to unauthorized immigrants.[30] In 1982 the Supreme Court ensured access to education when it ruled in *Plyler v. Doe* that Texas could not deny funding for undocumented students.[31] In 1986, Congress guaranteed emergency medical care to all people regardless of immigration status when it passed the Emergency Medical Treatment and Active Labor Act (EMTALA).

Religion The new patterns of immigration combined with differences in birth rates and underlying social changes to alter the religious affiliations of Americans. In 1900, 80 percent of the American adult population was Protestant; by 2014 only 46.6 percent of Americans identified themselves as Protestants.[32] Catholics made up 20.8 percent of the population, and Jews accounted for 1.9 percent. A small Muslim population had also grown, with nearly 1 percent of the population. One of the most important shifts in religious affiliation during the latter half of the twentieth century was the percentage of people who professed no organized religion: in 2014, 28.8 percent of the population was not affiliated with an organized church. These changes suggest an important shift in American religious identity; although the United States thinks of itself as a "Judeo-Christian" nation—and

Immigration remains a controversial issue in the United States. While many believe we should do more to protect our borders, others call for comprehensive immigration reform, including an easier pathway to citizenship for the country's nearly 12 million undocumented immigrants.

Global Diversity

In this chapter, we learned that the United States has become an increasingly diverse country over time. One way that the American population is diverse is in its racial and ethnic make-up. How does the racial and ethnic diversity of the United States compare to that of other countries around the world?

Racial and ethnic diversity is related not only to immigration rates but also to geography, historical legacies, and whether the government has favored certain groups over others. Many western European and Asian countries have histories of past conflict and strong state-building efforts, resulting in less diversity. For example, Japan's geographic isolation has created a racially homogeneous society, which was reinforced by the government's use of isolationism as a means to consolidate power.[a] Modern policies limiting immigration continue these historic trends. To take another example, France has historically pursued both political and cultural assimilation, using its schools as tools to socialize its citizens into a common "republican" identity. More recent waves of immigrants, however, have highlighted potential problems with this policy.[b]

As a "nation of immigrants," the United States is more diverse than many Western countries, but some former colonies are even more diverse than the United States. Many countries in sub-Saharan Africa were colonized by multiple empires, whose governments often drew borders that encompassed multiple ethnic groups in the region. State-building and nationalism are also very new to these regions, meaning that local identities remain stronger than national ones.

How might the degree of diversity shape political values in specific countries? What types of values and policies would we expect to see in countries with a high degree of diversity versus those with less diversity?

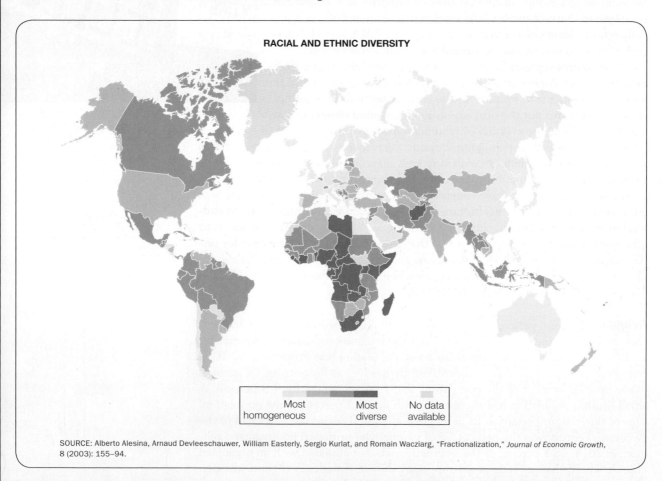

RACIAL AND ETHNIC DIVERSITY

Most homogeneous · Most diverse · No data available

SOURCE: Alberto Alesina, Arnaud Devleeschauwer, William Easterly, Sergio Kurlat, and Romain Wacziarg, "Fractionalization," *Journal of Economic Growth*, 8 (2003): 155–94.

[a]Benedict Anderson, *Imagined Communities: Reflections on the Origin and Spread of Nationalism* (London: Verso, 2006), 94–99.
[b]John R. Bowen, *Why the French Don't Like Headscarves: Islam, the State, and Public Space* (Princeton, NJ: Princeton University Press, 2007).

indeed was 95 percent Protestant, Catholic, or Jewish from 1900 to 1968—by 2014, this number had fallen to 72.5 percent of the adult population.[33]

Age As America grew and its population expanded and diversified, the country's age profile shifted with it. In 1900 only 4 percent of the population was over age 65. As life expectancy increased, the number of older Americans grew with it: by 2014, nearly 14.5 percent of the population was over 65. The percentage of children under the age of 18 also changed; in 1900 this group comprised 40.5 percent of the American population; by 2014, children 18 and under had fallen to just under one-quarter of the population.[34] Another way to think about the age of Americans is that in 1800 the median age of the population was 16 years, by 1900 it was 22.9 years, and by 2014 it was 37.7 years. Even though the median age of Americans has increased, Americans tend to be younger than citizens of many industrialized countries, mainly because of the large immigrant population in the United States. In most European countries, the median age was above 42.2 in 2014.[35] But an aging population poses challenges to the United States as well. As the elderly population grows and the working-age population shrinks, questions arise about how we will fund programs for the elderly such as Social Security.

Geography Over the nation's history, Americans have changed in other ways, moving from mostly rural settings and small towns to large urban areas. The idealization of country life in American culture traces its roots to the long period in which the majority of Americans lived in rural areas. Before 1920, less than half the population lived in urban areas; today 80.7 percent of Americans do.[36] Critics charge that the American political system—created when America was a largely rural society—underrepresents urban areas. The constitutional provision allocating each state two senators, for example, overrepresents sparsely populated rural states and underrepresents urban states, where the population is far more concentrated. In addition to becoming more urban over time, the American population has shifted regionally. During the past 50 years especially, many Americans left the Northeast and Midwest and moved to the South and Southwest. As congressional seats have been reapportioned to reflect the population shift, many problems that particularly plague the Midwest and Northeast, such as the decline in manufacturing jobs, receive less attention in national politics.

Socioeconomic Status Americans have fallen into diverse economic groups throughout American history. For much of American history most people were relatively poor working people, many of them farmers. A small wealthy elite, however, grew larger in the 1890s, in a period called "the gilded age." The top 1 percent and the top 10 percent of earners accounted for a growing share of the national income. By 1928, nearly one-quarter of the total annual income went to the top 1 percent of earners; the top 10 percent took home 46 percent of total annual income. After the New Deal in the 1930s, a large middle class took shape and the share going to those at the top dropped sharply. By 1976, the top 1 percent took home only 9 percent of the national annual income. Since then, however, economic inequality has once again widened as a tiny group of super-rich has emerged. By 2014, the top 1 percent earned 21.2 percent of annual income and the top

By 2002, Hispanics were the largest minority group in the United States. Here, Hillary Clinton poses with Janet Murguia, president and CEO of the National Council of La Raza, the largest Latino advocacy organization in the country, after addressing the group on the campaign trail in 2015.

10 percent took home 49.9 of the total national income, the highest ever recorded except for 2012.[37] At the same time, the incomes of the broad middle class have largely stagnated.[38] And 14.8 percent of the population remains below the official poverty line. As the middle class has frayed around the edges, the numbers of poor and near poor have swelled to nearly one-third of the population.[39] (See Figure 1.4.)

Population and Representation The shifting contours of the American people have regularly raised challenging questions about our politics and governing arrangements. Population growth has spurred politically charged debates about how the population should be apportioned among congressional districts. These conflicts have major implications for the representation of different regions of the country and for the balance of representation between urban and rural areas. Population growth has also transformed the close democratic relationship between congressional representatives and their constituents envisioned by the framers. For example, the framers stipulated that the number of representatives in the House of Representatives "shall not exceed one for every thirty Thousand" constituents; today the average member of Congress represents 721,641 constituents.[40] Immigration and the cultural and religious changes it entails provoked heated disputes 100 years ago and still spark passionate debate today. The different languages and customs that immigrants bring to the United States trigger fears among some that the country is changing in ways that may undermine American values and alter fundamental identities. The large number of unauthorized immigrants in the country today makes these anxieties even more acute. Yet a changing population has been one of the constants of American history. Indeed, each generation has confronted the myriad political challenges associated with answering the question anew, "Who are Americans?"

● American Political Culture

Analyze whether the U.S. system of government upholds American political values

Underlying and framing political life in the United States are agreements on basic political values but disagreements over the ends or goals of government. Most Americans affirm the values of liberty, equality, and democracy. Values shape citizens' views of the world and define their sense of what is right and wrong, just and unjust, possible and impossible. If Americans shared no values, they would have difficulty communicating, much less agreeing on a common system of government and politics. However, sharing broad values does not guarantee political consensus. We can agree on principles but disagree over their application or how they are to be balanced. Much of the debate over the role of government has been over what government should do and how far it should go to reduce the inequalities within our society and political system while still preserving essential liberties.

Even though Americans have disagreed over the meaning of such political ideals as equality, they still agree on the importance of those ideals. The values, beliefs, and attitudes that form our **political culture** and hold together the United States and its people date back to the time of the founding of the Union.

The essential documents of the American Founding—the Declaration of Independence and the Constitution—enunciated a set of political principles about the purposes of the new republic. In contrast with many other democracies, in the United States these political ideals did not just remain words on dusty documents.

political culture broadly shared values, beliefs, and attitudes about how the government should function; American political culture emphasizes the values of liberty, equality, and democracy

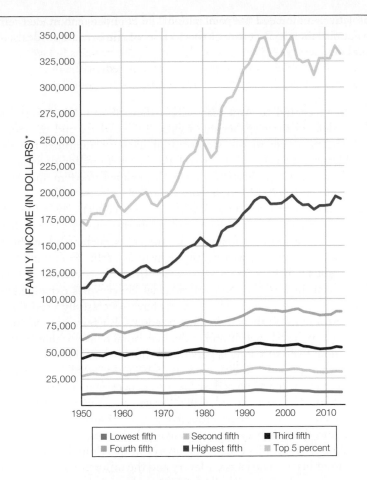

FAMILY INCOME (IN DOLLARS)*

Legend:
- ■ Lowest fifth
- ■ Fourth fifth
- ■ Second fifth
- ■ Highest fifth
- ■ Third fifth
- ■ Top 5 percent

FIGURE 1.4

Income in the United States

The top graph shows that while the income of most Americans has risen only slightly since 1950, the income of the richest Americans (the top 5 percent) has increased dramatically. The lower graph shows the portion of all income in the United States that goes to each group, with an increasing share going to the richest Americans in recent years. What are some of the ways that this shift might matter for American politics? Does the growing economic gap between the richest groups and most other Americans conflict with the political value of equality?

*Dollar values are given in constant 2014 dollars, which are adjusted for inflation so that we can compare a person's income in 1950 with a person's income today.
SOURCE: U.S. Census Bureau, Current Population Survey, www.census.gov/hhes/www/income/data/historical/inequality/index.html (accessed 2/18/16).

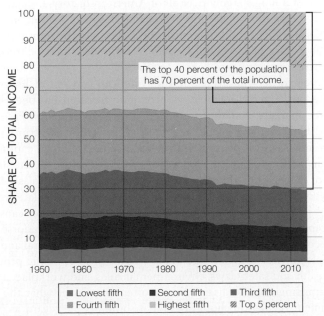

SHARE OF TOTAL INCOME

The top 40 percent of the population has 70 percent of the total income.

Legend:
- ■ Lowest fifth
- ■ Fourth fifth
- ■ Second fifth
- ■ Highest fifth
- ■ Third fifth
- ▨ Top 5 percent

Americans actively embraced the principles of the Founders and made them central to the national identity. Let us look more closely at three of these ideals: liberty, equality, and democracy.

Liberty

No ideal is more central to American values than liberty. The Declaration of Independence defined three inalienable rights: "Life, Liberty and the pursuit of Happiness." The preamble to the Constitution likewise identified the need to secure "the Blessings of Liberty" as one of the key reasons for drawing up the Constitution. For Americans, **liberty** means both personal freedom and economic freedom. Both are closely linked to the idea of **limited government**.

The Constitution's first 10 amendments, known collectively as the Bill of Rights, above all preserve individual personal liberties and rights. In fact, the word *liberty* has come to mean many of the freedoms guaranteed in the Bill of Rights: freedom of speech and writing, the right to assemble freely, and the right to practice religious beliefs without interference from the government. Over the course of American history, the scope of personal liberties has expanded as laws have become more tolerant and as individuals have successfully used the courts to challenge restrictions on their individual freedoms. Far fewer restrictions exist today on the press, political speech, and individual moral behavior than in the early years of the nation. Even so, conflicts persist over how personal liberties should be extended and when personal liberties violate community norms. For example, a number of cities have recently passed "sit-lie" ordinances, which limit the freedom of individuals to sit or lie down on sidewalks. Designed to limit the presence of the homeless and make city streets more attractive to pedestrians, the ordinances have also been denounced as infringements on individual liberties.

The central historical conflict regarding liberty in the United States was about the enslavement of blacks. The facts of slavery and the differential treatment of the races have cast a long shadow over all of American history. In fact, scholars today note that the American definition of freedom has been formed in relation to the concept of slavery. The right to control one's labor and the right to receive rewards for that labor have been central elements of our definition of freedom precisely because these freedoms were denied to slaves.[41]

In addition to personal freedom, the American concept of liberty means economic freedom. Since the Founding, economic freedom has been linked to capitalism, free markets, and the protection of private property. Free competition, unfettered movement of goods, and the right to enjoy the fruits of one's labor are all essential aspects of economic freedom and American capitalism.[42] In the first century of the Republic, support for capitalism often meant support for the doctrine of laissez-faire (literally, "leave alone" in French). **Laissez-faire capitalism** allowed very little room for the national government to regulate trade or restrict the use of private property, even in the public interest. Americans still strongly support capitalism and economic liberty, but they now also endorse some restrictions on economic freedoms to protect the public. Today, federal and state governments deploy a wide array of regulations in the name of public protection. These include health and safety laws, environmental rules, and workplace regulations.

Not surprisingly, fierce disagreements often erupt over what the proper scope of government regulation should be. What some people regard as protecting the public, others see as an infringement on their own freedom to run their businesses and use their property as they see fit. For example, many business leaders opposed

liberty freedom from governmental control

limited government a principle of constitutional government; a government whose powers are defined and limited by a constitution

laissez-faire capitalism an economic system in which the means of production and distribution are privately owned and operated for profit with minimal or no government interference

Patrick Henry's famous "Give Me Liberty or Give Me Death" speech demanded freedom at any cost and has resonated with Americans throughout the nation's history.

the Affordable Care Act, the health care reform legislation informally known as Obamacare, because it required businesses with over 50 employees to provide health coverage for their employees and establishes standards about which health services should be covered by the insurance. In addition, the law required that insurers pay for access to contraceptive care. From the perspective of the law's supporters, this provision simply ensured that women have access to basic health care. Many businesses, however, opposed the law as unwanted government intrusion. And some businesses strongly denounced the requirement to cover contraception, in particular, as a violation of their fundamental liberties to run their businesses as they see fit. In fact, in 2014 a company called Hobby Lobby successfully challenged this provision of the act when the Supreme Court ruled that family firms could be exempted on the basis of religious objections.[43]

Concerns about liberty have also arisen in relation to the government's efforts to combat terrorism and protect the nation's security. These concerns escalated in 2013 when Edward Snowden, a former National Security Agency (NSA) contractor, leaked top secret documents from the NSA to the press. The NSA is the agency charged with protecting the United States by monitoring electronic data flows—including radio, email, and cellular telephone calls—for foreign threats. The leaked documents revealed that the American government was listening in on the private communications of foreign governments, including many American allies, such as Germany and Brazil. The leaks also revealed information about domestic surveillance: the NSA had access to Americans' Facebook, Google, Apple, and Yahoo! accounts, among many other electronic data sources. It was using these "metadata" to track the connections among people, searching for suspicious ties. The revelation that the NSA had been collecting this information for three years without public knowledge set off a storm of controversy since the NSA is supposed to monitor foreign communications, not track Americans. The controversy reinforced the tech companies' commitment to privacy. In 2016, Apple refused an FBI order to unlock the iPhone used by a terrorist who killed 14 people in San Bernardino, California. The FBI dropped the case after it was able to open the phone without Apple's help. However, a new court order to Apple related to an iPhone used in a drug conspiracy case made it clear that the tension between privacy and security will continue [44]

Concerns about terrorism leave us with an extraordinary dilemma. On the one hand, we treasure liberty; but on the other hand, we recognize that the lives of thousands of Americans have already been lost and countless others are threatened by terrorism. Can we reconcile liberty and security? Liberty and order? In previous national emergencies, Americans accepted restrictions on liberty with the understanding that these would be temporary. But because the threat of terrorism has no clear end point, doubts have grown about whether special government powers that infringe on liberties should be continued.

Equality

The Declaration of Independence declares as its first "self-evident" truth that "all men are created equal." As central as it is to the American political creed, however, equality has been an even less well-defined ideal than liberty because people interpret "equality" in different ways. Few Americans have wholeheartedly embraced the ideal of full equality of results, but most Americans share the ideal of **equality of opportunity**—that is, the notion that each person should be given a fair chance to go as far as his talents will allow. Yet it is hard for Americans to reach agreement on what constitutes equality of opportunity. Must a group's *past* inequalities be

equality of opportunity a widely shared American ideal that all people should have the freedom to use whatever talents and wealth they have to reach their fullest potential

Americans struggle to define how equality of opportunity can be provided at the same time as individual liberty. One area of debate is in education. Does the fact that New Jersey spends on average $17,572 per student each year while North Carolina spends on average $8,390 per student mean that there is not an equality of opportunity for schoolchildren? (Data from www.census.gov.)

political equality the right to participate in politics equally, based on the principle of "one person, one vote"

remedied in order to ensure equal opportunity in the *present*? Should inequalities in the legal, political, and economic spheres be given the same weight? In contrast to liberty, which requires limits on the role of government, equality implies an *obligation* of the government to the people.[45]

Americans do make clear distinctions between political equality and social or economic equality. **Political equality** means that members of the American political community have the right to participate in politics on equal terms. Beginning from a very restricted definition of political community, which originally included only propertied white men, the United States has moved much closer to an ideal of political equality that can be summed up as "one person, one vote." Broad support for the ideal of political equality has helped expand the American political community and extend to all the right to participate. Although considerable conflict remains over whether the political system makes participation in it harder for some people and easier for others and whether the role of money in politics has drowned out the public voice, Americans agree that all citizens should have an equal right to participate and that government should enforce that right.

In part because Americans believe that individuals are free to work as hard as they choose, they have always been less concerned about social or economic inequality. Many Americans regard economic differences as the consequence of individual choices, virtues, or failures. Because of this, Americans tend to be less supportive than most Europeans of government action to ensure economic equality. Yet when major economic forces, such as the Great Depression of the 1930s, affect many people or when systematic barriers appear to block equality of opportunity, Americans support government action to promote equality. Even then, however, they have endorsed only a limited government role designed to help people get back on their feet or to open up opportunity.

Because equality is such an elusive concept, many conflicts have arisen over what it should mean in practice. Americans have engaged in three kinds of controversies about the public role in addressing inequality. The first is determining what constitutes equality of access to public institutions. In 1896 the Supreme Court ruled in *Plessy v. Ferguson* that "separate but equal" accommodation for blacks and whites was constitutional.[46] In 1954, in a major legal victory for the civil rights movement, the Supreme Court's decision in *Brown v. Board of Education* overturned the "separate but equal" doctrine (see Chapter 5).[47] Today, new questions have been raised about what constitutes equal access to public institutions. Some argue that the unequal financing of public schools in cities, suburbs, and rural districts is a violation of the right to equal education. To date, these claims have not been supported by the federal courts, which have rejected the notion that the unequal economic impacts of public policy outcomes are a constitutional matter.[48] Lawsuits arguing a right to "economic equal protection" stalled in 1973 when the Supreme Court ruled that a Texas school-financing law did not violate the Constitution even though the law affected rich and poor students differently.[49]

A second debate concerns the public role in ensuring equality of opportunity in private life. Although Americans generally agree that discrimination should not be tolerated, people disagree over what should be done to ensure equality of opportunity (see Table 1.3).[50] Controversies about affirmative action programs reflect these disputes. Supporters of affirmative action claim that such programs are necessary to compensate for past discrimination in order to establish true equality of opportunity today. Opponents maintain that affirmative action amounts to reverse discrimination and that a society that espouses true equality should not

TABLE 1.3

Equality and Public Opinion

Americans believe in some forms of equality more than others. How do these survey results reflect disagreement about what equality means in practice?

STATEMENT	PERCENTAGE WHO AGREE
It is very important that women have the same rights as men in our country.	91
Our society should do what is necessary to make sure that everyone has an equal opportunity to succeed.	86
Our country should have laws that protect gay, lesbian, bisexual, and transgender people against discrimination in jobs, public accommodations, and housing	69
It should be legal for gay and lesbian couples to get married.	55
The fact that some are rich and some are poor is an acceptable part of the economic system.	52
Our country needs to continue making changes to give blacks equal rights with whites (according to whites)	53
Our country needs to continue making changes to give blacks equal rights with whites (according to blacks)	86

SOURCE: Pew Research Center, www.pewresearch.org/. See endnote 50 for specific reports.

acknowledge gender or racial differences. The question of the public responsibility for private inequalities is central to gender issues. The traditional view, still held by many today, takes for granted that women should bear special responsibilities in the family. In this perspective, the challenges women face in the labor force due to family responsibilities fall outside the range of public concern. In the past 30 years especially, these traditional views have come under fire as advocates for women have argued that private inequalities *are* a topic of public concern.[51]

A third debate about equality concerns differences in income and wealth. Unlike in other countries, income inequality has not been an enduring topic of political controversy in the United States, which currently has the largest gap in income and wealth between rich and poor citizens of any developed nation. But Americans have generally tolerated great differences among rich and poor citizens, in part because of a pervasive belief that mobility is possible and that economic success is the product of individual effort.[52] This tolerance for inequality is reflected in America's tax code, which is more advantageous to wealthy taxpayers than that of almost any other Western nation. Indeed, tax changes enacted in recent years have sharply reduced the tax burdens of upper-income Americans. Debate about taxes surfaced throughout the Obama presidency and during the 2012 election. President Obama defended the need to raise the tax rate of Americans earning more than $250,000 a year to support programs that benefit the

for critical analysis

Economic inequality among Americans has been widening since at least the 1970s. Many politicians and news commentators say that inequality is threatening the middle class. Is there any evidence that the American public is worried about the growth in inequality?

The Fight for $15—a nationwide effort to increase the minimum wage to $15 an hour—first gained traction in 2013, increasing public awareness of income inequality in the United States. In November 2015, fast food workers in hundreds of cities around the country went on strike to rally for higher pay and the right to unionize.

middle class.[53] Even so, opposition among Republicans—and some Democrats—meant that tax rates increased a small amount only on those making more than $400,000 a year. The issue of inequality emerged in a new dramatic way in late 2011, when the Occupy Wall Street movement mounted protests across the country. Motivated by concerns about inequality, the movement did not develop a clear policy agenda, but concerns about inequality received new prominence. Polls showed that growing numbers of Americans believe that government should aim to reduce economic inequality. In 2015, 57 percent of Americans agreed that the government should do more to reduce the gap between rich and poor; 39 percent said government should not do more. More Americans expressed concern about the power of the rich, with 74 percent agreeing that there was too much power in the hands of large corporations.[54]

Democracy

The essence of democracy is the participation of the people in choosing their rulers and the people's ability to influence what those rulers do. In a democracy, political power ultimately comes from the people. The idea of placing power in the hands of the people is known as **popular sovereignty**. In the United States, popular sovereignty and political equality make politicians accountable to the people. Ideally, democracy envisions an engaged citizenry prepared to exercise its power over rulers. As we noted earlier, the United States is a representative democracy, meaning that the people do not rule directly but instead exercise power through elected representatives. Forms of participation in a democracy vary greatly, but voting is a key element of the representative democracy that the American Founders established.

American democracy rests on the principle of **majority rule** with **minority rights**. Majority rule means that the wishes of the majority determine what government does. The House of Representatives—a large body elected directly by the people—was designed in particular to ensure majority rule. But the Founders feared that popular majorities could turn government into a "tyranny of the majority" in which

popular sovereignty a principle of democracy in which political authority rests ultimately in the hands of the people

majority rule, minority rights the democratic principle that a government follows the preferences of the majority of voters but protects the interests of the minority

for critical analysis

In the United States, do citizens make the decisions of government, or do they merely influence them?

individual liberties would be violated. Concern for individual rights has thus been a part of American democracy from the beginning. The rights enumerated in the Bill of Rights and enforced through the courts provide an important check on the power of the majority.

Despite Americans' deep attachment to the *ideal* of democracy, many questions can be raised about our *practice* of democracy. The first is the restricted definition of the political community during much of American history. Property restrictions on the right to vote were eliminated by 1828; in 1870 the Fifteenth Amendment to the Constitution granted African Americans the vote, although later exclusionary practices denied them that right; in 1920 the Nineteenth Amendment guaranteed women the right to vote; and in 1965 the Voting Rights Act finally secured the right of African Americans to vote.

Just securing the right to vote does not end concerns about democracy, however. The organization of electoral institutions can have a significant impact on access to elections and on who can get elected. During the first two decades of the twentieth century, states and cities enacted many reforms, including strict registration requirements and scheduling of elections, that made it harder to vote. The aim was to rid politics of corruption, but the consequence was to reduce participation. Other institutional decisions affect which candidates stand the best chance of getting elected (see Chapter 10).

A further consideration about democracy concerns the relationship between economic power and political power. Money has always played an important role in elections and governing in the United States. Many argue that the pervasive influence of money in American electoral campaigns today undermines democracy. With the decline of locally based political parties that depend on party loyalists to turn out the vote and the rise of political action committees, political consultants, and expensive media campaigns, money has become the central fact of life in American politics. Money often determines who runs for office; it can exert a heavy influence on who wins; and some argue that it affects what politicians do once they are in office.[55]

Low turnout for elections and a pervasive sense of apathy and cynicism characterized American politics for much of the past half-century. The widespread interest in the 2008 election and the near-record levels of voter turnout, which, at 61.6 percent, was the highest turnout since 1980, reversed this trend.[56] Nine million voters registered and voted for the first time in 2008, including near-record numbers of voters under the age of 24.[57] Despite strong engagement in the presidential primaries and in the general election campaigns, lower turnout in the 2012 and 2016 elections suggested that public disengagement remains a challenge for American democracy.

While levels of participation in politics are relatively low for young Americans, the presidential primary campaigns of 2008 and 2016 saw the highest levels of youth turnout—to volunteer and to vote—in decades. What factors might have energized young people to become involved in these particular campaigns?

American Political Culture
and Your Future

Americans express mixed views about government. Almost everyone complains about government at one time or another, but in the past two decades, general trust in government has declined significantly. Despite mounting distrust, when asked about particular government activities or programs, a majority of Americans are more than likely to support the activities that government undertakes. These conflicting views reflect the tensions in American political culture: there is no perfect balance between liberty, equality, and democracy. In recent years, finding the right mix of government actions to achieve these different goals has become especially troublesome. Some charge that government initiatives designed to promote equality infringe on individual liberty, while others point to the need for government to take action in the face of growing inequality. Sharp political debate over competing goals alienates many citizens, who react by withdrawing from politics. Yet, in contrast to totalitarian and authoritarian forms of government, democracy rests on the principle of popular sovereignty. No true democracy can function properly without knowledgeable and engaged citizens. The "**Who Participates?**" feature on the following page shows various ways Americans were engaged with and participated in the 2012 presidential election.

The remarkable diversity of the American people represents a great strength for American democracy as well as a formidable challenge. The shifting religious, racial and ethnic, and immigration status of Americans throughout history has always provoked fears about whether American values could withstand such dramatic shifts. The changing face of America also sparks hopes for an America that embodies its fundamental values more fully. Only after a bloody civil war were slavery abolished and African Americans guaranteed citizenship and voting rights. In the early 1900s, as European immigrants flocked to American cities, fears about the stability of American democracy mounted, leading to a cutoff of immigration. The portrait of Americans shifted again after 1965, when new laws permitted more immigrants from Latin America, Asia, and Africa to enter the country. Each wave of demographic change has presented new questions about the role of government in promoting a democracy that values both liberty and equality.

Demographic changes will continue to raise thorny new questions in the coming decades. For example, as the American population grows older, programs for the elderly are expected to take up an increasing share of the federal budget. Yet to be successful, a nation must invest in its young people. And, as any college student knows, the cost of college has risen in recent years. Many students drop out as they discover that the cost of college is too high. Or they graduate and find themselves saddled with loans that will take decades to pay back. Yet, in a world of ever-sharper economic competition, higher education has become increasingly important for individuals seeking economic security. Moreover, an educated population is critical to the future prosperity of the country as a whole. Are there ways to support the elderly and the young at the same time? Is it fair to cut back assistance to the elderly, who have worked a lifetime for their benefits? If we decrease assistance to the elderly, will they stay in the labor market and make the job hunt for young people even more difficult? As these trade-offs suggest, there are no easy answers to the demographic changes that will unfold in the coming years. Undoubtedly, these questions will provoke heated political conflict as politicians and interest groups propose different strategies for supporting the young in an aging country. Informed participation of the American public, especially the participation of young people, is the only way to ensure that the steps taken to address these challenges best reflect the will of the people.

Who Participated in the 2012 Presidential Election?

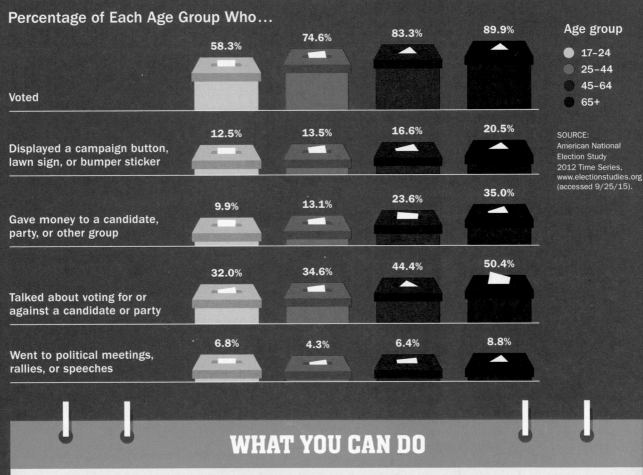

Percentage of Each Age Group Who...

Age group
- 17–24
- 25–44
- 45–64
- 65+

SOURCE:
American National
Election Study
2012 Time Series,
www.electionstudies.org
(accessed 9/25/15).

Voted
58.3% | 74.6% | 83.3% | 89.9%

Displayed a campaign button, lawn sign, or bumper sticker
12.5% | 13.5% | 16.6% | 20.5%

Gave money to a candidate, party, or other group
9.9% | 13.1% | 23.6% | 35.0%

Talked about voting for or against a candidate or party
32.0% | 34.6% | 44.4% | 50.4%

Went to political meetings, rallies, or speeches
6.8% | 4.3% | 6.4% | 8.8%

WHAT YOU CAN DO

Register to Vote

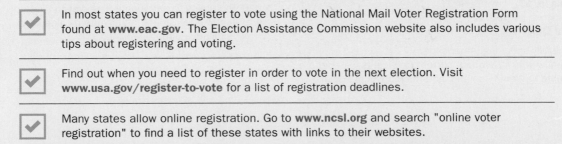

☑ In most states you can register to vote using the National Mail Voter Registration Form found at **www.eac.gov**. The Election Assistance Commission website also includes various tips about registering and voting.

☑ Find out when you need to register in order to vote in the next election. Visit **www.usa.gov/register-to-vote** for a list of registration deadlines.

☑ Many states allow online registration. Go to **www.ncsl.org** and search "online voter registration" to find a list of these states with links to their websites.

☑ If you've moved to attend college or for another reason, you can register with your new address.

studyguide

What Americans Think about Government

Explore Americans' attitudes toward government (pp. 5–9)

While Americans have always been hesitant about granting government too much power, they have frequently relied on it during times of national crisis and have become increasingly dependent on it to provide important services. Over the last few decades, Americans' trust in government and their sense of political efficacy have declined significantly. Low levels of trust and efficacy may threaten American democracy by weakening the government and reducing the public's willingness to participate in political life.

Key Terms

government (p. 4)

politics (p. 4)

political efficacy (p. 9)

Practice Quiz

1. *Political efficacy* is the belief that
   a) government is wasteful and corrupt.
   b) government operates efficiently.
   c) government has grown too large.
   d) government cannot be trusted.
   e) ordinary citizens can influence what government does.

2. Americans' trust in their government
   a) rose significantly between 1964 and 1980.
   b) increased immediately following September 11, 2001, but declined shortly thereafter.
   c) declined immediately after the September 11 attacks but has risen dramatically since 2004.
   d) reached its highest point ever in the fall of 2011.
   e) has remained the same over the last 50 years.

Citizenship: Knowledge and Participation

Describe the role of the citizen in politics (pp. 9–12)

Citizenship requires political knowledge. When citizens know about politics, they are better able to understand their interests and to identify the best way to act on those interests. Most Americans, however, do not know much about politics. While the Internet has made it easier to learn about and participate in politics, many Americans still do not go online to find information about government. Internet access and digital literacy are increasingly important for full participation in American politics.

Key Term

citizenship (p. 10)

Practice Quiz

3. Generally speaking, Americans
   a) know very little about current political issues but are able to identify some high-profile political leaders.
   b) know a great deal about current political issues but are not able to identify high-profile political leaders.
   c) know very little about current political issues and are never able to identify high-profile political leaders.
   d) know a great deal about current political issues and are able to identify high-profile political leaders.
   e) are extremely engaged with politics and trust the government to do what is right.

4. What is *digital citizenship*?
   a) a new government initiative to expand online voter registration
   b) the ability to vote online
   c) an online certification program that allows immigrants to become American citizens
   d) the ability to participate in society online
   e) a new government initiative to provide daily legislative updates online

Government

Define government and forms of government (pp. 12–16)

There are many different kinds of government. Prior to the modern era, governments accepted almost no limits on their behavior and provided citizens with few opportunities to participate in public affairs. Today, numerous countries, including the United States, are constitutional democracies. America's democracy provides citizens with the chance to elect top officials at all levels of government and even allows them to vote directly on laws in many states and localities.

Key Terms

autocracy (p. 13)

oligarchy (p. 13)

democracy (p. 13)

constitutional government (p. 13)

authoritarian government (p. 13)

totalitarian government (p. 13)

power (p. 15)

representative democracy (republic) (p. 15)

direct democracy (p. 15)

pluralism (p. 16)

Practice Quiz

5. What is the basic difference between an autocracy and an oligarchy?
   a) the extent to which average citizens have a say in government affairs
   b) the means of collecting taxes and conscripting soldiers
   c) the number of people who control governing decisions
   d) the size and political influence of the military
   e) there are no differences between autocracies and oligarchies

6. When the government is formally limited in what it can control and how it controls it, this is known as
   a) totalitarian government.
   b) authoritarian government.
   c) constitutional government.
   d) autocracy.
   e) oligarchy.

7. Although not present at the national level, a number of states and cities permit citizens to vote directly on laws and policies. What is this form of rule called?
   a) republic
   b) representative democracy
   c) direct democracy
   d) pluralism
   e) laissez-faire capitalism

8. *Pluralism* is a theory that says
   a) the means of economic production should be privately owned and operated without interference from the government.
   b) all interests in a society should be free to compete for influence over governmental decisions.
   c) government should always follow the preferences of the majority while also protecting the rights of those in the minority.
   d) American political culture should emphasize the values of liberty, equality, and democracy.
   e) one ruler should dominate all spheres of social, political, economic, and cultural life.

Who Are Americans?

Show how the social composition of the American population has changed over time (pp. 16–24)

The United States is defined, in part, by its ever-growing and changing population. During the last 200 years, America has become more racially, ethnically, geographically, and religiously diverse. Immigration has been an important reason for the country's shifting demographics, and it has frequently sparked intense debate about the nature of American identity and American democracy.

Practice Quiz

9. The percentage of foreign-born individuals living in the United States
   a) has increased significantly since reaching its low point in 1970.
   b) has decreased significantly since reaching its high point in 1970.
   c) has remained the same since 1970.
   d) has not been studied since 1970.
   e) has never been less than the percentage of native-born individuals living in the United States.

10. Which of the following statements best describes the history of income inequality in the United States?
    a) The top 1 percent has never earned more than 10 percent of the nation's annual income.
    b) The top 1 percent has never earned less than 10 percent of the nation's annual income.
    c) Income inequality has remained fairly constant since the late 1970s.
    d) Income inequality has increased considerably since the late 1970s.
    e) Income inequality has decreased considerably since the late 1970s.

American Political Culture

Analyze whether the U.S. system of government upholds American political values (pp. 24–31)

Most Americans express strong support for liberty, equality, and democracy. Agreement on these basic values does not mean, however, that political debate in the United States is without conflict. Questions about how to apply and balance the different elements of American political culture have motivated disagreements throughout the country's history.

Key Terms

political culture (p. 24)

liberty (p. 26)

limited government (p. 26)

laissez-faire capitalism (p. 26)

equality of opportunity (p. 27)

political equality (p. 28)

popular sovereignty (p. 30)

majority rule, minority rights (p. 30)

Practice Quiz

11. Which of the following is *not* related to the American conception of liberty?
    a) freedom of speech
    b) economic freedom
    c) freedom of religion
    d) freedom of assembly
    e) All of the above are related to the American conception of liberty.

12. The principle of political equality can be best summed up as
    a) "equality of results."
    b) "equality of opportunity."
    c) "one person, one vote."
    d) "equality between the sexes."
    e) "leave everyone alone."

13. Which of the following is an important principle of American democracy?
    a) popular sovereignty
    b) majority rule
    c) political equality
    d) minority rights
    e) All of the above are important principles of American democracy.

14. Which of the following is *not* part of American political culture?
    a) belief in equality of results
    b) belief in democracy
    c) belief in personal freedom
    d) belief in economic freedom
    e) belief in equality of opportunity

15. Which of the following restrictions on voting have been repealed over the last 200 years in the United States?
    a) property, gender, and race
    b) gender only
    c) race only
    d) property only
    e) race and gender only

For Further Reading

Dahl, Robert. *How Democratic Is the American Constitution?* New Haven, CT: Yale University Press, 2002.

Dalton, Russell. *The Good Citizen: How a Younger Generation Is Reshaping American Politics*, 2nd ed. Washington, DC: CQ Press, 2015.

Delli Carpini, Michael X., and Scott Keeter. *What Americans Know about Politics and Why It Matters*. New Haven, CT: Yale University Press, 1996.

Fischer, Claude S., and Michael Hout. *A Century of Difference: How America Changed in the Last One Hundred Years*. New York: Russell Sage Foundation, 2006.

Hetherington, Marc J., and Thomas J. Rudolph. *Why Washington Won't Work: Polarization, Political Trust, and the Governing Crisis*. Chicago: University of Chicago Press, 2015.

Hibbing, John R., and Elizabeth Theiss-Morse. *Stealth Democracy: Americans' Belief about How Government Should Work*. New York: Cambridge University Press, 2002.

Hochschild, Jennifer L. *Facing Up to the American Dream: Race, Class, and the Soul of the Nation*. Princeton, NJ: Princeton University Press, 1995.

Huntington, Samuel. *Who Are We? The Challenges to America's National Identity*. New York: Simon & Schuster, 2004.

Lasswell, Harold. *Politics: Who Gets What, When, How*. New York: Meridian Books, 1958.

McCarty, Nolan, Keith T. Poole, and Howard Rosenthal. *Polarized America: The Dance of Ideology and Unequal Riches*. Cambridge, MA: MIT Press, 2008.

Mettler, Suzanne. *The Submerged State: How Invisible Government Policies Undermine American Democracy.* Chicago: University of Chicago Press, 2011.

Page, Benjamin I., and Lawrence R. Jacobs. *Class War? What Americans Really Think about Economic Inequality.* Chicago: University of Chicago Press, 2009.

Putnam, Robert. *Making Democracy Work: Civic Traditions in Modern Italy.* Princeton, NJ: Princeton University Press, 1993.

Tocqueville, Alexis de. *Democracy in America.* Translated by Phillips Bradley. New York: Knopf, Vintage Books, 1945. First published 1835.

Winters, Jeffrey A. *Oligarchy.* New York: Cambridge University Press, 2011.

Recommended Websites

American Democracy Project
www.aascu.org/programs/adp
This is an effort by the American Association of State Colleges and Universities to increase political engagement among college students. See what opportunities are available for you to become politically active.

Americans for Informed Democracy
www.aidemocracy.org
A nonpartisan organization that promotes democracy and seeks to build a new generation of globally conscious leaders. Find out how you can be politically active and coordinate a town hall meeting on campus, attend a leadership retreat, or publish your opinions on democracy.

DiversityInc
http://diversityinc.com
This site is dedicated to the promotion of American diversity and education. Here you can read about the issues that directly affect American minorities.

Future of Freedom Foundation
www.fff.org
This organization promotes individual liberty, free markets, private property, and limited government. Find out how some people are trying to protect freedom in the United States.

Mobilize.org
http://mobilize.org
This all-partisan network is dedicated to educating, empowering, and energizing young people. Find out how politics affects America's youth and what they are doing about it by being engaged and active.

Pew Research Center, U.S. Politics and Policy
www.people-press.org
A nonpartisan "fact tank" that provides public opinion data about a wide range of topics related to American government and society. This site covers current issues as well as providing analyses of change over time in American politics and demographics.

The Youth Participatory Politics Research Network
http://ypp.dmlcentral.net/pages/about
A network of researchers and writers supported by the MacArthur Foundation. The network conducts studies of youth participation and contains short videos, blogs, and links to other resources about youth participation. The website provides many resources for understanding the impact of digital media on youth engagement in politics.

U.S. Census Bureau
www.census.gov
The website for the Census Bureau offers a statistical look at our country's population and economy. Check out some of the statistics to get a better idea of American diversity.

When the framers of the Constitution met in 1787, they set out to establish a political system that would protect liberty and place limits on government. They also believed a powerful government required a broad popular base. However, they debated how best to protect liberty and how to balance democracy with other concerns.

The Founding and the Constitution

WHAT GOVERNMENT DOES AND WHY IT MATTERS The framers of the U.S. Constitution knew why government mattered. In the Constitution's preamble, the framers tell us that the purposes of government are to promote justice, to maintain peace at home, to defend the nation from foreign foes, to provide for the welfare of the citizenry, and, above all, to secure the "blessings of liberty" for Americans. The remainder of the Constitution spells out a plan for achieving these objectives. This plan includes provisions for the exercise of legislative, executive, and judicial powers and a recipe for the division of powers among the federal government's branches and between the national and state governments. The framers' conception of why government matters and how it is to achieve its goals, while often a matter of interpretation and subject to revision, has been America's political blueprint for more than two centuries.

Often, Americans become impatient with aspects of the constitutional system such as the separation of powers, which often seems to be a recipe for inaction and "gridlock" when America's major institutions of government are controlled by opposing political forces. This has led to bitter fights that sometimes prevent government from delivering important services. In 2011 and again in 2013, the House and Senate could not reach agreement on a budget for the federal government or a formula for funding the public debt. For 16 days in October 2013, the federal government partially shut down; permit offices across the country no longer took in fees, contractors stopped receiving checks, research projects stalled, and some 800,000 federal employees were sent home on unpaid leave—at a cost to the economy of $2–6 billion.[1]

The framers, however, believed that a good constitution not only created a government with the capacity to act forcefully but also promoted compromise and deliberation, sometimes delaying action until tempers cooled and a variety of viewpoints could be heard. Every form of government has strengths and weaknesses. The cost of compromise and deliberation encouraged by such constitutional arrangements as the separation of powers might sometimes be gridlock, but the benefit may be a government compelled to take a variety of interests and viewpoints into account when it formulates policies.

The story of America's Founding and the Constitution is generally presented as something both inevitable and glorious: it was inevitable that the American colonies would break away from Great Britain to establish their own country, and it was glorious in that the country established the best of all possible forms of government under a new constitution. In reality, though, America's successful breakaway from Britain was by no means assured, and many of the Constitution's provisions were highly controversial.

America's long-standing values of liberty, equality, and democracy were all major themes of the Founding period and are all elements of the U.S. Constitution. However, the Constitution was a product of political bargaining and compromise, formed in very much the same way political decisions are made today. As this chapter will show, the Constitution reflects high principle as well as political self-interest and defines the relationship between American citizens and their government.

chaptergoals

- Describe the events that led to the Declaration of Independence and the Articles of Confederation (pp. 41–45)

- Analyze the reasons many Americans thought a new Constitution was needed, and assess the obstacles to a new Constitution (pp. 45–51)

- Explain how the Constitution attempted to improve America's governance, and outline the major institutions established by the Constitution (pp. 52–59)

- Present the controversies involved in the struggle for ratification (pp. 60–63)

- Trace how the Constitution has changed over time through the amendment process (pp. 63–68)

● The First Founding: Interests and Conflicts

Describe the events that led to the Declaration of Independence and the Articles of Confederation

Competing ideals and principles often reflect competing interests, and so it was in Revolutionary America. The American Revolution and the American Constitution were outgrowths and expressions of a struggle among economic and political forces within the colonies. Five sectors of society had interests that were important in colonial politics: (1) the New England merchants; (2) the southern planters; (3) the "royalists"—holders of royal lands, offices, and patents (licenses to engage in a profession or business activity); (4) shopkeepers, artisans, and laborers; and (5) small farmers. Throughout the eighteenth century, these groups were in conflict over issues of taxation, trade, and commerce. For the most part, however, the southern planters, the New England merchants, and the royal office and patent holders—groups that together made up the colonial elite—were able to maintain a political alliance that held in check the more radical forces representing shopkeepers, laborers, and small farmers. After 1760, however, by seriously threatening the interests of New England merchants and southern planters, British tax and trade policies split the colonial elite, permitting radical forces to expand their political influence, and set in motion a chain of events that culminated in the American Revolution.[2]

British Taxes and Colonial Interests

During the first half of the eighteenth century, Britain ruled its American colonies with a light hand. Evidence of British rule was hardly to be found outside the largest towns, and the enterprising colonists had found ways of evading most of the taxes nominally levied by the distant British regime. Beginning in the 1760s, however, the debts and other financial problems confronting the British government forced it to search for new revenue sources. This search rather quickly led to the Crown's North American colonies, which, on the whole, paid remarkably little in taxes to their parent country. The British government reasoned that a sizable fraction of its debt was, in fact, attributable to the expenses it had incurred in defense of the colonies during the French and Indian War, which ended in 1763, driving France from North America. The British also considered the cost of the continuing protection that British forces were giving the colonists from Indian attacks and that the British navy was providing for colonial shipping. Thus, during the 1760s, Britain sought to impose new, though relatively modest, taxes on the colonists.

Like most governments of the period, the British regime had limited ways in which to collect revenues. The income tax, which in the twentieth century became the single most important source of governmental revenues, had not yet been developed. In the mid-eighteenth century, governments relied mainly

British colonists in America shipped many goods back to England, such as furs obtained by trading with Native Americans. The British government claimed that the colonists should pay more in taxes in light of the protection their shipments received from the British navy and the expenses Britain incurred defending the colonies.

on tariffs, duties, and other taxes on commerce; and it was to such taxes, and to the Stamp Act, that the British turned during the 1760s.

The Stamp Act, and other taxes on commerce such as the Sugar Act of 1764, which taxed sugar, molasses, and other commodities, most heavily affected the two groups in colonial society whose commercial interests and activities were most extensive—the New England merchants and the southern planters. United under the famous slogan "No taxation without representation," the merchants and planters sought to organize opposition to these new taxes. In the course of the struggle against British tax measures, the planters and merchants broke with their royalist allies and turned to their former adversaries—the shopkeepers, small farmers, laborers, and artisans—for help. With the assistance of these groups, the merchants and planters organized demonstrations and a boycott of British goods that ultimately forced the Crown to rescind most of its hated new taxes.

From the perspective of the merchants and planters, this was a victorious conclusion to their struggle with the mother country. In contrast to the shopkeepers, small farmers, laborers, and artisans whom they had helped mobilize initially, merchants and planters were now anxious to end the unrest they had helped arouse; and they supported the British government's efforts to restore order. Indeed, most respectable Bostonians supported the actions of the British soldiers involved in the Boston Massacre—the 1770 killing of five colonists by British soldiers who were attempting to repel an angry mob gathered outside the Town House, the seat of the colonial government. In their subsequent trial, the soldiers were defended by John Adams, a pillar of Boston society and a future president of the United States. Adams asserted that the soldiers' actions were entirely justified, provoked by "a motley rabble of saucy boys, negroes and mulattoes, Irish teagues and outlandish Jack tars." All but two of the soldiers were acquitted.[3]

Despite the efforts of the British government and the elite members of colonial society, it proved difficult to bring an end to the political strife. The more radical forces continued to agitate for political and social change. These radicals, whose leaders included Samuel Adams, a cousin of John Adams, asserted that British power supported an unjust political and social structure within the colonies and began to advocate an end to British rule.[4]

Political Strife and the Radicalization of the Colonists

The political strife within the colonies was the background for the events of 1773–74. In 1773 the British government granted the politically powerful East India Company a monopoly on the export of tea from Britain, eliminating a lucrative form of trade for colonial merchants. To add to the injury, the East India Company sought to sell the tea directly in the colonies instead of working through the colonial merchants. Tea was an extremely important commodity during the 1770s, and these British actions posed a serious threat to the New England merchants. Together with their southern allies, the merchants once again called on their radical adversaries for support. The most dramatic result was the Boston Tea Party. In three other colonies, antitax Americans succeeded in blocking the unloading of taxed tea, which then had to be returned to Britain. The royal governor of Massachusetts, however, refused to allow three shiploads of unsold tea to leave Boston Harbor. Anti-British radicals seized this opportunity: on the night of December 16, 1773,

The British helped radicalize colonists through bad policy decisions in the years before the Revolution. For example, Britain gave the ailing East India Company a monopoly on the tea trade in the American colonies. Colonists feared that the monopoly would hurt colonial merchants' business and protested by throwing East India Company tea into Boston Harbor in 1773.

a group led by Samuel Adams, some of them hastily "disguised" as Mohawk Indians, boarded the three vessels and threw the entire cargo of 342 chests of tea into the harbor.

This event was of decisive importance in American history. The merchants had hoped to force the British government to rescind the Tea Act, but they did not support any further demands and did not seek independence from Britain. Samuel Adams and the other radicals, however, did hope to provoke the British government to take actions that would alienate its colonial supporters and pave the way for a rebellion. This was precisely the purpose of the Boston Tea Party, and it succeeded. By dumping the East India Company's tea into Boston Harbor, Adams and his followers goaded the British into enacting a number of harsh reprisals, including closing the port of Boston to commerce, changing the provincial government of Massachusetts, providing for the removal of accused persons to Britain for trial, and, most important, restricting movement to the West—further alienating the southern planters, who depended on access to new western lands. These acts of retaliation confirmed the worst criticisms of British rule and helped radicalize Americans. Radicals such as Samuel Adams had been agitating for more violent measures against the British for some time, but ultimately they needed Britain's political repression to create widespread support for independence.

Thus, the Boston Tea Party set in motion a cycle of provocation and retaliation that in 1774 resulted in the convening of the First Continental Congress—an assembly of delegates from all parts of the country—that called for a total boycott of British goods and, under the prodding of the radicals, began to consider the possibility of independence from British rule. The eventual result was the Declaration of Independence.

for critical analysis

Conflicts over taxes did not end with the American Revolution. Why is tax policy almost always controversial? What differences and similarities are there between the debates over taxes in the 1760s and today?

The Declaration of Independence

In 1776, more than a year after open warfare had commenced in Massachusetts, the Second Continental Congress appointed a committee consisting of Thomas Jefferson of Virginia, Benjamin Franklin of Pennsylvania, Roger Sherman of Connecticut, John Adams of Massachusetts, and Robert Livingston of New York to draft a statement of American independence from British rule. The Declaration of Independence, written by Jefferson and adopted by the Second Continental Congress, was an extraordinary document both philosophically and politically. In philosophic terms, the Declaration was remarkable for its assertion that certain rights—the "unalienable rights" that include life, liberty, and the pursuit of happiness—could not be abridged by governments. In the world of 1776, in which some kings still claimed to rule by divine right, this was a dramatic statement. This philosophical view was heavily influenced by the works of the philosopher John Locke, one of England's foremost liberal theorists of the seventeenth century. In his treatises on government, widely read by educated colonists, Locke asserted that all individuals were equal and possessed a natural right to defend their own lives, liberties, and possessions. Individuals created governments to help them protect these rights, and if a government failed in its duties, the citizenry had the right to alter or abolish it. In political terms, the Declaration was remarkable because, despite the differences of interest that divided the colonists along economic, regional, and philosophical lines, it focused on grievances, aspirations, and principles that might unify the various colonial groups. The Declaration was an attempt to identify and articulate a history and set of principles that might help forge national unity.[5]

The purpose of the Declaration of Independence was to explain to the world why the colonists had rebelled against the British and sought self-government. Every year, Americans celebrate the signing of the Declaration on the Fourth of July.

Articles of Confederation
America's first written constitution; served as the basis for America's national government until 1789

confederation a system of government in which states retain sovereign authority except for the powers expressly delegated to the national government

The Articles of Confederation

Having declared their independence, the colonies needed to establish a governmental structure. In November 1777 the Continental Congress adopted the **Articles of Confederation**—the United States' first written constitution. Although it was not ratified by all the states until 1781, it was the country's operative constitution for almost 12 years, until March 1789.

The first goal of the Articles was to limit the powers of the central government. The relationship between the national government and the states was called a **confederation**; as provided under Article II, "each state retains its sovereignty, freedom, and independence," much like the contemporary relationship between the United Nations and its member states. The central government was given no president or any other presiding officer. The entire national government was vested in a Congress, with execution of its few laws to be left to the individual states. And the Articles gave Congress very little power to exercise. Its members were not much more than delegates or messengers from the state legislatures: their salaries were paid out of the state treasuries; they were subject to immediate recall by state authorities; and each state, regardless of its size, had only one vote. All 13 states had to agree to any amendments to the Articles of Confederation after it was ratified.

Under the Articles of Confederation, Congress was given the power to declare war and make peace, to make treaties and alliances, to coin or borrow money, and to regulate trade with the Native Americans. It could also appoint the senior officers of the U.S. Army, but the national government had no army for those officers to command because the nation's armed forces were composed of the state militias. Moreover, the central government could not prevent one state from discriminating against other states in the competition for foreign commerce. These extreme limits on the power of the national government made the Articles of Confederation hopelessly impractical.[6]

● The Second Founding: From Compromise to Constitution

Analyze the reasons many Americans thought a new Constitution was needed, and assess the obstacles to a new Constitution

The Declaration of Independence and the Articles of Confederation were not sufficient to hold the new nation together as an independent and effective nation-state. A series of developments following the armistice with the British in 1783 highlighted the shortcomings of the Articles of Confederation.

First, many of the new country's leaders worried that the Articles of Confederation would not allow the United States to conduct its foreign affairs successfully as the federal government was unable to enforce existing treaties and there was no national military. Furthermore, competition among the states for foreign commerce allowed the European powers to play the states off one another, which created confusion on both sides of the Atlantic. At one point during the winter of 1786–87, John Adams of Massachusetts, a leader in the independence struggle, was sent to negotiate a new treaty with the British, one that would cover disputes left over from the war. The British government responded that since the United States under the Articles of Confederation was unable to enforce existing treaties, it would negotiate with each of the 13 states separately. At the same time, the United States faced a threat from Spain, which still held vast territories in North and South America. Without a national military, the nation's borders were difficult to protect against this potentially hostile foreign power.

Second, the Articles of Confederation allowed for only a weak federal government, with state governments retaining most of the powers of government. This situation became alarming to well-to-do Americans, in particular New England merchants and southern planters, when "radical" forces began to exert considerable influence in a number of state governments. The colonists' victory in the Revolutionary War had not only ended British rule but also significantly changed the balance of political power within the new states. As a result of the Revolution, one key segment of the colonial elite—the royal land, office, and patent holders—was stripped of its economic and political privileges. In fact, many of these individuals, along with tens of thousands of other colonists who considered themselves loyal British subjects, left for Canada after the British surrender. And although the prerevolutionary elite was weakened, the prerevolutionary radicals were better organized than ever and now controlled such states as Pennsylvania and Rhode Island, where they pursued economic and political policies that struck terror in the hearts of the prerevolutionary political establishment. In Rhode Island, for example, between 1783 and 1785, a legislature dominated by representatives of small farmers, artisans, and shopkeepers had instituted economic policies, including drastic currency inflation, that frightened business and property owners throughout the country. Of course, the central government under the Articles of Confederation was powerless to intervene. Similarly, the Pennsylvania government engaged in land redistribution to the chagrin of property owners.

However, the Articles of Confederation were by no means a complete failure. The Congress of the Confederation agreed upon two laws that helped to shape American history. These were the Land Ordinance of 1785 and the Northwest Ordinance of 1787. The Land Ordinance established the principles of land surveying and landownership that governed America's westward expansion. Under the Northwest Ordinance, the individual states agreed to surrender their western land claims, which opened the way for the admission of new states to the Union.

These legislative successes were not adequate to sustain the fledgling federal government, however. During the 1780s, the political and economic position of the new American states deteriorated. Europe's great powers—Britain, France, and Spain—hurt colonial commerce by adopting policies that excluded American trade. At the same time, political unrest within the 13 new states further undermined trade and investment. Something had to be done.

The Annapolis Convention

The continuation of international weakness and domestic economic turmoil led many Americans to consider whether their newly adopted form of government might not already require revision. In the fall of 1786, many state leaders accepted an invitation from the Virginia legislature for a conference of representatives of all the states, to be held in Annapolis, Maryland. Delegates from only five states actually attended, so nothing substantive could be accomplished. Still, this conference was the first step toward what is now known as the second founding. The one positive result that came out of the Annapolis Convention was a carefully worded resolution calling on the Congress to send commissioners to Philadelphia at a later time "to devise such further provisions as shall appear to them necessary to render the Constitution of the Federal Government adequate to the exigencies of the Union."[7] But the resolution did not necessarily imply any desire to do more than improve and reform the Articles of Confederation.

Shays's Rebellion

It is quite possible that the Constitutional Convention of 1787 in Philadelphia would never have taken place at all except for a single event that occurred during the winter following the Annapolis Convention: Shays's Rebellion.

Daniel Shays, a former army captain, led a mob of farmers in a rebellion against the government of Massachusetts. The purpose of the rebellion was to prevent foreclosures on their debt-ridden land by keeping the county courts of western Massachusetts from sitting until after the next election. The state militia dispersed the mob, but for several days in February 1787, Shays and his followers terrified the state government by attempting to capture the federal arsenal at Springfield, provoking an appeal to the Congress to help restore order. Within a few days, the state government regained control and captured 14 of the rebels. Later that year, a newly elected Massachusetts legislature granted some of the farmers' demands.

The effects of the incident lingered and spread. George Washington summed it up: "I am mortified beyond expression that in the moment of our acknowledged independence we should by our conduct verify the predictions of our transatlantic foe, and render ourselves ridiculous and contemptible in the eyes of all Europe."[8]

The Congress under the Confederation had been unable to act decisively in a time of crisis. This provided critics of the Articles of Confederation with precisely the evidence they needed to push the Annapolis resolution through the Congress. Thus, the states were asked to send representatives to Philadelphia to discuss constitutional revision. Seventy-four delegates were chosen. Of these, 55 would actually attend the convention, representing every state except Rhode Island, and 39 would eventually sign the newly drafted Constitution.

The Constitutional Convention

The delegates who convened in Philadelphia in May 1787 had political strife, international embarrassment, national weakness, and local rebellion fixed in their minds. Recognizing that these issues were symptoms of fundamental flaws in the Articles of Confederation, the delegates soon abandoned the plan to revise the Articles and committed themselves to a second founding—a second, and ultimately successful, attempt to create a legitimate and effective national system of government. This effort would occupy the convention for the next five months.

In the winter of 1787, Daniel Shays led a makeshift army against the federal arsenal at Springfield to protest heavy taxes levied by the Massachusetts legislature. The rebellion proved the Articles of Confederation too weak to protect the fledgling nation.

A Marriage of Interest and Principle For years, scholars have disagreed about the motives of the Founders in Philadelphia. Among the most controversial views of the framers' motives is the "economic interpretation" put forward by the historian Charles Beard and his disciples.[9] According to Beard's account, America's Founders were a collection of securities speculators and property owners whose only aim was personal enrichment. From this perspective, the Constitution's lofty principles were little more than sophisticated masks behind which the most venal interests sought to enrich themselves.

Of course, the opposite view is that the framers of the Constitution *were* concerned with philosophical and ethical principles—that, indeed, they sought to devise a system of government consistent with the dominant philosophical and moral principles of the day. But in fact these two views belong together: the Founders' interests were reinforced by their principles. The convention that drafted the American Constitution was chiefly organized by the New England merchants and southern planters. Although the delegates representing these groups did not all hope to profit personally from an increase in the value of their securities, as Beard would have it, they did hope to benefit in the broadest political and economic sense by breaking the power of their radical foes and establishing a system of government more compatible with their long-term economic and political interests. Thus, the framers sought to create a new government capable of promoting commerce and protecting property from radical state legislatures and populist forces hostile to the interests of the commercial and propertied classes.

The Great Compromise The proponents of a new government fired their opening shot on May 29, 1787, when Edmund Randolph of Virginia offered a resolution that proposed corrections and enlargements in the Articles of Confederation. The proposal, which showed the strong influence of James Madison, was not a simple motion. Rather, it provided for virtually every aspect of a new government.

The portion of Randolph's motion that became most controversial was called the **Virginia Plan**. This plan provided for a system of representation in the national legislature based on the population of each state or the proportion of each state's revenue contribution to the national government, or both. (Randolph also proposed a second chamber of the legislature, to be elected by the members of the first chamber.) Since the states varied enormously in size and wealth, the Virginia Plan was thought to be heavily biased in favor of the large states.

While the convention was debating the Virginia Plan, opposition to it began to mount as more delegates arrived in Philadelphia. William Paterson of New Jersey introduced a resolution known as the **New Jersey Plan**. Its main proponents were delegates from the less populous states, including Delaware, New Jersey, Connecticut, and New York, who asserted that the more populous states—Virginia, Pennsylvania, North Carolina, Massachusetts, and Georgia—would dominate the new government if representation were to be determined by population. The smaller states argued that each state should be equally represented in the new regime regardless of the state's population.

The issue of representation threatened to wreck the entire constitutional enterprise. Delegates conferred, factions maneuvered, and tempers flared. James Wilson

Virginia Plan a framework for the Constitution, introduced by Edmund Randolph, that called for representation in the national legislature based on the population of each state

New Jersey Plan a framework for the Constitution, introduced by William Paterson, that called for equal state representation in the national legislature regardless of population

The Constitutional Convention took place from May to September, 1787 at Independence Hall in Philadelphia, where the Declaration of Independence was signed 11 years prior. In order to keep their deliberations secret, the delegates voted to keep the hall's windows shut throughout the hot summer.

Who Benefits from the Great Compromise?

The Great Compromise attempted to balance power between large and small states in the new Congress. The figure shows the difference in representation for states in the House and Senate in the first Congress (1789–91). In the Senate each state has equal representation, which in the first Congress meant each had 1/13 of all seats. In the House the number of seats apportioned to each state is based on population; thus, the larger states have more representation.

Representation in the First Congress

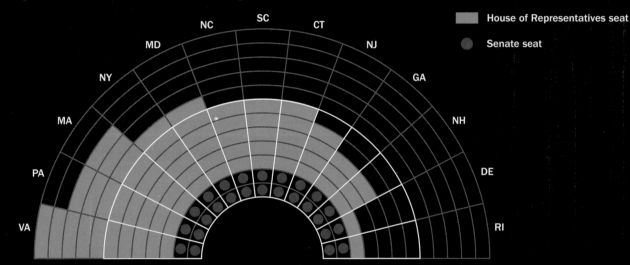

House of Representatives seat

Senate seat

State Populations, 1790*

1.	Virginia	747,610
2.	Pennsylvania	433,373
3.	North Carolina	393,751
4.	Massachusetts	378,787
5.	New York	340,120
6.	Maryland	319,728
7.	South Carolina	249,073
8.	Connecticut	237,946
9.	New Jersey	184,139
10.	New Hampshire	141,885
11.	Georgia	82,548
12.	Rhode Island	68,825
13.	Delaware	59,096

* These numbers represent the total number of persons in each state according to the 1790 census (including free white males, free white females, "all other free persons," and slaves). For the purpose of representation in the first Congress, the framers calculated the number of representatives per state in 1787 based on population estimates, which counted each slave as three-fifths of a person. This calculation is why the representation in the first Congress does not match perfectly with the total population counts reported here.

SOURCE: U.S. Census Bureau, www.census.gov (accessed 8/16/12); U.S. House of Representatives, www.history.house.gov/Institution/Apportionment/Apportionment (accessed 4/11/14).

for critical analysis

1. At the Constitutional Convention, large states supported the Virginia Plan, which would have made the whole Congress look like the House. Small states supported the New Jersey Plan, which would have made the whole Congress look like the Senate. How would each group have benefited from its favored plans?

2. What are the advantages of equal representation by states? What are the drawbacks? In your opinion, do the advantages outweigh the disadvantages?

of Pennsylvania told the small-state delegates that if they wanted to disrupt the union, they should go ahead. The separation, he said, could "never happen on better grounds." Small-state delegates were equally blunt. Gunning Bedford of Delaware declared that the small states might, if forced, look elsewhere for friends. "The large states," he said, "dare not dissolve the confederation. If they do the small ones will find some foreign ally of more honor and good faith, who will take them by the hand and do them justice." These sentiments were widely shared. The union, as Luther Martin of Maryland put it, was "on the verge of dissolution, scarcely held together by the strength of a hair."[10]

The outcome of this debate was the Connecticut Compromise, also known as the **Great Compromise**. Under the terms of this compromise, in the first chamber of Congress—the House of Representatives—the representatives would be apportioned according to the population in each state. This, of course, was what delegates from the large states had sought. But in the second branch— the Senate—each state would have equal representation regardless of its size; this provision addressed the concerns of small states. This compromise was not immediately satisfactory to all the delegates. Indeed, two of the most vocal members of the small-state faction, John Lansing and Robert Yates of New York, were so angered by the concession that their colleagues had made to the large-state forces that they stormed out of the convention. In the end, however, most of the delegates preferred compromise to the breakup of the Union, and the plan was accepted.

The Question of Slavery: The Three-Fifths Compromise

Many of the conflicts that emerged during the Constitutional Convention were reflections of the fundamental differences between the slave and the nonslave states—differences that pitted the southern planters against the New England merchants and would almost destroy the Republic in later years. Even in the midst of debate over large versus small states, James Madison observed that "the great danger" lay in the opposition of "southern and northern interests."[11] More than 90 percent of the country's slaves resided in five states—Georgia, Maryland, North Carolina, South Carolina, and Virginia—where they accounted for 30 percent of the total population. In some places, slaves outnumbered nonslaves by as many as 10 to 1. Were they to be counted in as part of a state's population even though they had no rights, thereby giving slave states increased representation in the House? If the Constitution were to embody any principle of national supremacy, some basic decisions would have to be made about the place of slavery in the general scheme. Madison hit on this point on several occasions as different aspects of the Constitution were being discussed. For example, he observed,

> It seemed now to be pretty well understood that the real difference of interests lay, not between the large and small but between the northern and southern states. The institution of slavery and its consequences formed the line of discrimination. There were five states on the South, eight on the northern side of this line. Should a proportional representation take place it was true, the northern side would still outnumber the other: but not in the same degree, at this time; and every day would tend towards an equilibrium.[12]

Whatever they thought of the institution of slavery, most delegates from the northern states opposed counting slaves in the distribution of congressional seats.

Great Compromise the agreement reached at the Constitutional Convention of 1787 that gave each state an equal number of senators regardless of its population but linked representation in the House of Representatives to population

Despite the Founders' emphasis on liberty, the new Constitution allowed slavery, counting three-fifths of all slaves in apportioning seats in the House of Representatives. In this 1792 painting, Liberty Displaying the Arts and Sciences, *the books, instruments, and classical columns at the left contrast with the kneeling slaves at the right— illustrating the divide between America's rhetoric of liberty and equality and the reality of slavery.*

James Wilson of Pennsylvania, for example, argued that if slaves were citizens, they should be treated and counted like other citizens. If, on the other hand, they were property, then why should not other forms of property be counted toward the apportionment of representatives? But southern delegates made it clear that they would never agree to the new government if the northerners refused to give in; William R. Davie of North Carolina, for example, heatedly asserted that the people of North Carolina would never enter the Union if slaves were not counted as part of the basis for representation. Without such agreement, he asserted ominously, "the business was at an end." Even southerners such as Edmund Randolph of Virginia, who conceded that slavery was immoral, insisted on including slaves in the allocation of congressional seats.

Northerners and southerners eventually reached agreement through the **Three-Fifths Compromise**. The seats in the House of Representatives would be apportioned according to a "population" in which only three-fifths of slaves would be counted. The slaves would not be allowed to vote, of course, but the number of representatives would be apportioned accordingly.

The issue of slavery was the most difficult one faced by the framers, and it nearly destroyed the Union. Although some delegates believed slavery to be morally wrong, an evil and oppressive institution that made a mockery of the ideals and values espoused in the Constitution, morality was not the issue that caused the framers to support or oppose the Three-Fifths Compromise. Indeed, northerners even agreed to permit a continuation of the odious slave trade in order to keep the South in the Union. But in due course, the disparate interests of the North and the South could no longer be reconciled, and a bloody civil war was the result.

Three-Fifths Compromise
the agreement reached at the Constitutional Convention of 1787 that stipulated that for purposes of the apportionment of congressional seats only three-fifths of slaves would be counted

● The Constitution

Explain how the Constitution attempted to improve America's governance, and outline the major institutions established by the Constitution

The political significance of the Great Compromise and the Three-Fifths Compromise was to reinforce the unity of the mercantile and planter forces that sought to create a new government. The Great Compromise reassured those in both groups who feared that a new governmental framework would reduce the importance of their own local or regional influence. The Three-Fifths Compromise temporarily defused the rivalry between the merchants and planters. Their unity secured, members of the alliance supporting the establishment of a new government moved to fashion a constitutional framework consistent with their economic and political interests.

In particular, the framers sought a new government that, first, would be strong enough to promote commerce and protect property from radical state legislatures such as Rhode Island's. This became the constitutional basis for national control over commerce and finance and for the establishment of national judicial supremacy and the effort to construct a strong presidency. (See Table 2.1 for a comparison of the Articles of Confederation to the Constitution.) Second, the framers sought to prevent what they saw as the threat posed by the "excessive democracy" of the state and national governments under the Articles of Confederation. This led to such constitutional principles as a **bicameral** legislature, **checks and balances**, staggered terms in office, and indirect election (selection of the president by an electoral college rather than directly by voters and election of senators by state legislatures). Third, the framers, lacking the power to force the states or the public at large to accept the new form of government, sought to identify principles that would help secure support. This became the basis of the constitutional provision for direct popular election of representatives and, subsequently, for the addition of the **Bill of Rights** to the Constitution. Finally, the framers wanted to be certain that the government they created did not pose an even greater threat to its citizens' liberties and property rights than did the radical state legislatures they feared and despised. To prevent the new government from abusing its power, the framers incorporated principles such as the **separation of powers** and **federalism** into the Constitution. Below, we assess the major provisions of the Constitution's seven articles to see how each relates to these objectives.

If the Declaration of Independence drew its philosophical inspiration from John Locke, the Constitution drew upon the thought of the French political philosopher Baron de La Brède et de Montesquieu (1689–1755). In Montesquieu's view, the powers of government must be divided in order to prevent any one group or institution from exercising tyrannical control over the nation. Montesquieu recommended a tripartite division, placing the executive, legislative, and judicial powers in different governmental bodies. He claimed that such a tripartite division had worked very well in the Roman Republic and in Britain. The delegates to America's Constitutional Convention referred frequently to Montesquieu's writings in devising America's new governmental structure.

The Legislative Branch

In Article I, Sections 1–7, the Constitution provides for a Congress consisting of two chambers: a House of Representatives and a Senate. Members of the House of

bicameral having a legislative assembly composed of two chambers or houses; distinguished from *unicameral*

checks and balances mechanisms through which each branch of government is able to participate in and influence the activities of the other branches; major examples include the presidential veto power over congressional legislation, the power of the Senate to approve presidential appointments, and judicial review of congressional enactments

Bill of Rights the first 10 amendments to the U.S. Constitution, ratified in 1791; they ensure certain rights and liberties to the people

separation of powers the division of governmental power among several institutions that must cooperate in decision making

federalism a system of government in which power is divided, by a constitution, between a central government and regional governments

TABLE 2.1

Comparing the Articles of Confederation and the Constitution

MAJOR PROVISIONS	ARTICLES OF CONFEDERATION	CONSTITUTION
Executive branch	None	President of the United States
Judiciary	No federal court system. Judiciary exists only at state level.	Federal judiciary headed by Supreme Court
Legislature	Unicameral legislature with equal representation for each state. Delegates to the Congress of the Confederation were appointed by the states.	Bicameral legislature consisting of Senate and House of Representatives. Each state is represented by two senators, while apportionment in the House is based on each state's population. Senators are chosen by the state legislatures (changed to direct popular election in 1913) for six-year terms and members of the House by popular election for two-year terms.
Fiscal and economic powers	The national government is dependent upon the states to collect taxes. The states are free to coin their own money and print paper money. The states are free to sign commercial treaties with foreign governments.	Congress given the power to levy taxes, coin money, and regulate international and interstate commerce. States prohibited from coining money or entering into treaties with other nations.
Military	The national government is dependent upon state militias and cannot form an army during peacetime.	The national government is authorized to maintain an army and navy.
Legal supremacy	State constitutions and state law are supreme.	National Constitution and national law are supreme.
Constitutional amendment	Must be agreed upon by all states.	Must be agreed upon by three-fourths of the states.

Representatives were given two-year terms in office and were to be elected directly by the people. Members of the Senate were to be appointed by the state legislatures (this was changed in 1913 by the Seventeenth Amendment, which instituted direct election of senators) for six-year terms. These terms were staggered so that the appointments of one-third of the senators would expire every two years. The Constitution assigned somewhat different tasks to the House and Senate. Though the approval of each body is required for the enactment of a law, the Senate alone is given the power to ratify treaties and approve presidential appointments. The House, on the other hand, is given the sole power to originate revenue bills.

The character of the legislative branch was related to the framers' major goals. The House of Representatives was designed to be directly responsible to the people in order to encourage popular consent for the new Constitution and to help enhance the power of the new government. At the same time, to guard against "excessive democracy," the power of the House of Representatives was checked by the Senate, whose members were to be appointed by the states for long terms rather than elected directly by the people. The purpose of this provision, according to Alexander Hamilton, was to avoid "an unqualified complaisance to every sudden breeze of passion, or to every transient impulse which the people may receive."[13]

Article I of the Constitution establishes the structure of Congress and lists certain specific powers of Congress. The language of the Constitution reflects the framers' desire to create government that was powerful enough to be effective but not so powerful that it would threaten individual liberty.

expressed powers specific powers granted by the Constitution to Congress (Article I, Section 8) and to the president (Article II)

elastic clause The concluding paragraph of Article I, Section 8, of the Constitution (also known as the "necessary and proper clause"), which provides Congress with the authority to make all laws "necessary and proper" to carry out its enumerated powers.

Staggered terms of service in the Senate, moreover, were intended to make that body even more resistant to popular pressure. Since only one-third of the senators would be selected at any given time, the composition of the institution would be protected from changes in popular preferences transmitted by the state legislatures. This would prevent what James Madison called "mutability in the public councils arising from a rapid succession of new members."[14] Thus, the structure of the legislative branch was designed to contribute to governmental power, to promote popular consent for the new government, and at the same time to place limits on the popular political currents that many of the framers saw as a radical threat to the economic and social order.

The issues of power and consent are important throughout the Constitution. Section 8 of Article I specifically lists the powers of Congress, which include the authority to collect taxes, borrow money, regulate commerce, declare war, and maintain an army and navy. By granting Congress these powers, the framers indicated very clearly that they intended the new government to be far more influential than its predecessor. At the same time, by defining the new government's most important powers as belonging to Congress, the framers sought to promote popular acceptance of this critical change by reassuring citizens that their views would be fully represented whenever the government exercised its new powers.

As a further guarantee to the people that the new government would pose no threat to them, the Constitution implies that any powers not listed were not granted at all. This is the doctrine of **expressed powers**: the Constitution grants only those powers specifically expressed in its text. But the framers intended to create an active and powerful government, so they also included the necessary and proper clause, sometimes known as the **elastic clause**, which declares that Congress could write laws needed to carry out its expressed powers. This clause indicates that the expressed powers could be broadly interpreted and were meant to be a source of strength to the national government, not a limitation on it. In response to the charge that they intended to give the national government too much power, the framers included language in the Tenth Amendment stipulating that powers not specifically granted by the Constitution to the federal government were reserved to the states or to the people. As we will see in Chapter 3, the resulting tension between the elastic clause and the Tenth Amendment has been at the heart of constitutional struggles between federal and state powers.

The Executive Branch

The Articles of Confederation had not provided for an executive branch, and the framers viewed this omission as a source of weakness. Accordingly, the Constitution provides for the establishment of the presidency in Article II. As Alexander Hamilton commented, the presidential article aims toward "energy in the Executive."[15] It does so in an effort to overcome the natural tendency toward stalemate that was built into the bicameral legislature and into the separation of powers among the three branches. The Constitution affords the president a measure of independence from the people and from the other branches of government—particularly the Congress.

In line with the framers' goal of increased power to the national government, the president is granted the unconditional power to accept ambassadors from other countries—this amounts to the power to "recognize" other countries—as well as the power to negotiate treaties, although their acceptance requires the approval of the Senate by a two-thirds vote. The president is also given the unconditional right to grant reprieves and pardons, except in cases of impeachment, and the powers to appoint major departmental personnel, to convene Congress in special session, and to veto congressional enactments. The veto power is formidable, but it is not absolute since Congress can override it by a two-thirds vote, reflecting the framers' concern with checks and balances.

The framers hoped to create a presidency that would make the federal government rather than the states the agency capable of timely and decisive action to deal with public issues and problems—hence the "energy" that Hamilton hoped to impart to the executive branch. At the same time, however, the framers sought to help the presidency withstand excessively democratic pressures by creating a system of indirect rather than direct election through a separate electoral college.

The Judicial Branch

In establishing the judicial branch in Article III, the Constitution reflects the framers' preoccupations with nationalizing governmental power and checking radical democratic impulses while preventing the new national government itself from interfering with liberty and property.

Under the provisions of Article III, the framers created a court that was literally a supreme court of the United States and not merely the highest court of the national government alone. The most important expression of this intention is granting the Supreme Court the power to resolve any conflicts that might emerge between federal and state laws. In particular, the Supreme Court is given the right to determine whether a power is exclusive to the national government, concurrent with the states, or exclusive to the states. In addition, the Supreme Court is assigned jurisdiction over controversies between citizens of different states. The long-term significance of this provision was that as the country developed a national economy, it came to rely increasingly on the federal judiciary, rather than on the state courts, for the resolution of disputes.

Judges are given lifetime appointments to protect them from popular politics and from interference by the other branches. This, however, does not mean that the judiciary remains totally impartial to political considerations or to the other branches, for the president is to appoint the judges and the Senate to approve the appointments. Congress also has the power to create inferior (lower) courts, change the jurisdiction of the federal courts, add or subtract federal judges, and even change the size of the Supreme Court.

No explicit mention is made in the Constitution of **judicial review**—the power of the courts to render the final decision when there is a conflict of interpretation of the Constitution or of laws between the courts and Congress, the courts and the executive branch, or the courts and the states. The Supreme Court eventually assumed the power of judicial review. Its assumption of this power, as we shall see in Chapter 15, was based not on the Constitution itself but on the politics of later decades and the membership of the Court.

judicial review the power of the courts to review and, if necessary, declare actions of the legislative and executive branches invalid or unconstitutional; the Supreme Court asserted this power in *Marbury v. Madison* (1803)

National Unity and Power

Various provisions in the Constitution addressed the framers' concern with national unity and power, including Article IV's provisions for comity (reciprocity) among states and among citizens of all states. Each state is prohibited from discriminating against the citizens of other states in favor of its own citizens. The Supreme Court is charged with deciding in each case whether a state had discriminated against goods or people from another state. The Constitution restricts the power of the states in favor of ensuring enough power to the national government to give the country a free-flowing national economy.

The framers' concern with national supremacy was also expressed in Article VI, in the **supremacy clause**, which provides that national laws and treaties "shall be the supreme Law of the Land." This means that all laws made under the "Authority of the United States" would be superior to all laws adopted by any state or any other subdivision and that the states would be expected to respect all treaties made under that authority. The supremacy clause also binds the officials of all governments—state and local as well as federal—to take an oath of office to support the national Constitution. This means that every action taken by the U.S. Congress has to be applied within each state as though the action were in fact state law.

supremacy clause Article VI of the Constitution, which states that laws passed by the national government and all treaties are the supreme law of the land and superior to all laws adopted by any state or any subdivision

Amending the Constitution

The Constitution establishes procedures for its own revision in Article V. Its provisions are so difficult that Americans have successfully availed themselves of the amending process only 17 times since 1791, when the first 10 amendments were adopted. Many other amendments have been proposed in Congress; but fewer than 40 of them have even come close to fulfilling the Constitution's requirement of a two-thirds vote in Congress, and only a fraction have gotten anywhere near adoption by three-fourths of the states. Article V also provides that the Constitution can be amended by a constitutional convention, but thus far, all the amendments to the U.S. Constitution have been approved first by Congress and then by the state legislatures. The only exception is the amendment repealing prohibition, which was approved by Congress but ratified by state conventions. No national convention has been called since the Philadelphia Convention of 1787.

Ratifying the Constitution

The rules for the ratification of the Constitution are set forth in Article VII. Nine of the 13 states would have to ratify, or agree to, the terms in order for the Constitution to be formally adopted.

Constitutional Limits on the National Government's Power

Although the framers sought to create a powerful national government, they also wanted to guard against possible misuse of that power. To that end, the framers incorporated two key principles into the Constitution—federalism and the separation of powers. A third set of limitations, in the form of the Bill of Rights, was added to the Constitution in the form of 10 amendments proposed by the first Congress and ratified by the states. Most of the framers had thought a Bill of Rights to be unnecessary but accepted the idea during the ratification debates that took place when the new constitution was submitted to the states for approval.

The Separation of Powers No principle of politics was more widely shared at the time of the 1787 Founding than the principle that power must be used to balance power. As noted earlier, the French political theorist Montesquieu believed that

Comparing Systems of Government

The U.S. Constitution is the oldest constitution still in use in the world, yet many newer democracies have chosen *not* to follow the American model when writing their own constitutions. In fact, there is tremendous variation across the world's democracies. For instance, many democracies possess a unitary system of government, with powers centralized at the national level, rather than a federal system, as in the United States.

All democracies possess some form of an executive, a legislature, and a judiciary; but the amount of power that each branch has varies. In the United States, the system of checks and balances, as described in this chapter and outlined in Figure 2.2, divides power among the branches. In the United Kingdom, power is highly concentrated in the legislature and its leader, the prime minister. Even with the recent creation of the UK Supreme Court, the judicial branch often lacks the power to overrule legislation passed by the parliament.[a]

The U.S. Constitution is also relatively short, creating a basic governmental framework but relying on experience and the courts to flesh out the original document. Over time, through usage and reinterpretation, constitutional provisions may take new shape. For example, as defined in the U.S. Constitution (and shown below), the presidency is less powerful than Congress. Over time, however, presidential power has grown as Congress has delegated significant powers, such as the war power, to the president, and as presidents have claimed additional powers. Other constitutions, such as India's, provide more specific details, leaving less to interpretation. Even so, India's prime ministers, especially when faced with a crisis, have sometimes reinterpreted the constitution in ways that have shifted power toward the central government.

Country	Written Constitution?	Year Enacted	Length (in Words)	Federal or Unitary System	Strength of Executive	Strength of Legislature	Judicial Independence
Brazil	Yes	1988	64,488	Federal	High	Medium	High
France	Yes	1958	10,180	Unitary	High	Low	Low
India	Yes	1949	146,385	Federal	Medium	Low	Medium
Israel	No	—	—	Unitary	Low	Low	Medium
South Africa	Yes	1996	43,062	Unitary	Medium	Low	High
Tunisia	Yes	2014	9,508	Unitary	High	Medium	Low
United States	Yes	1789	7,762	Federal	High*	Medium	High*
United Kingdom	No	—	—	Unitary	Low	Low	Medium

*Although the Comparative Constitutions Project classifies the formal powers of both the American presidency and the judicial branch, as originally provided for in the Constitution, as relatively *weak*, we have classified both here as strong, based on the greater powers that have developed over time.
SOURCE: Comparative Constitutions Project, "CCP Rankings," http://comparativeconstitutionsproject.org/ccp-rankings/ (accessed 7/16/15).

[a]Parliamentary sovereignty, www.parliament.uk/about/how/sovereignty/ (accessed 7/16/15).

FIGURE 2.1

The Separation of Powers

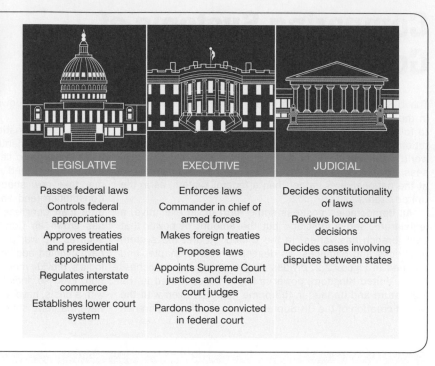

LEGISLATIVE	EXECUTIVE	JUDICIAL
Passes federal laws	Enforces laws	Decides constitutionality of laws
Controls federal appropriations	Commander in chief of armed forces	Reviews lower court decisions
Approves treaties and presidential appointments	Makes foreign treaties	Decides cases involving disputes between states
Regulates interstate commerce	Proposes laws	
Establishes lower court system	Appoints Supreme Court justices and federal court judges	
	Pardons those convicted in federal court	

for critical analysis

How does the separation of powers limit the national government's power? What are the consequences for the ability of the federal government to govern?

this balance was an indispensable defense against tyranny. His writings, especially his major work, *The Spirit of the Laws*, "were taken as political gospel" at the Philadelphia Convention.[16] Although the principle of the separation of powers is not explicitly stated in the Constitution, the entire structure of the national government was built precisely on Article I, the legislature; Article II, the executive; and Article III, the judiciary (see Figure 2.1).

However, separation of powers is nothing but mere words on parchment without a method to maintain that separation. The method became known by the popular label "checks and balances" (see Figure 2.2). Each branch is given not only its own powers but also some power over the other two branches. Among the most familiar checks and balances are the president's veto power over Congress and Congress's power over the president through its control of appointments to high executive posts and to the judiciary. Congress also has power over the president with its control of appropriations (the spending of government money) and (by the Senate) the right of approval of treaties. The judiciary has the power of judicial review over the other two branches.

Another important feature of the separation of powers is the principle of giving each of the branches a distinctly different constituency. Theorists such as Montesquieu called this a "mixed regime," with the president chosen, indirectly, by electors; the House, by popular vote; the Senate (originally), by state legislatures; and the judiciary, by presidential appointment. By these means, the occupants of each branch would tend to develop very different outlooks on how to govern, different definitions of the public interest, and different alliances with private interests.

Federalism Compared with the confederation principle of the Articles of Confederation, federalism was a step toward greater centralization of power. The delegates agreed that they needed to place more power at the national level, without

Executive over Legislative

Can veto acts of Congress

Can call Congress into a special session

Carries out, and thereby interprets, laws passed by Congress

Vice president casts tie-breaking vote in the Senate

Legislative over Judicial

Can change size of federal court system and the number of Supreme Court justices

Can propose constitutional amendments

Can reject Supreme Court nominees

Can impeach and remove federal judges

Legislative over Executive

Can override presidential veto

Can impeach and remove president

Can reject president's appointments and refuse to ratify treaties

Can conduct investigations into president's actions

Can refuse to pass laws or to provide funding that president requests

Judicial over Legislative

Can declare laws unconstitutional

Chief justice presides over Senate during hearing to impeach the president

Executive over Judicial

Nominates Supreme Court justices

Nominates federal judges

Can pardon those convicted in federal court

Can refuse to enforce Court decisions

Judicial over Executive

Can declare executive actions unconstitutional

Power to issue warrants

Chief justice presides over impeachment of president

FIGURE 2.2
Checks and Balances

completely undermining the power of the state governments. Thus, they devised a system of two sovereigns—the states and the nation—with the hope that competition between the two would be an effective limitation on the power of both.

The Bill of Rights Late in the Philadelphia Convention, a motion was made to include a list of citizens' rights in the Constitution. After a brief debate in which hardly a word was said in its favor and only one speech was made against it, the motion was almost unanimously turned down. Most delegates sincerely believed that since the federal government was already limited to its expressed powers, further protection of citizens was not needed. The delegates argued that the states should adopt bills of rights because their greater powers needed greater limitations. But almost immediately after the Constitution was ratified, a movement arose to adopt a national bill of rights. This is why the Bill of Rights, adopted in 1791, comprises the first 10 amendments to the Constitution rather than being part of the body of it. (We will have a good deal more to say about the Bill of Rights in Chapter 4.)

● The Fight for Ratification

Present the controversies involved in the struggle for ratification

The first hurdle faced by the proposed Constitution was ratification by state conventions of delegates elected by the people of each state. This struggle for ratification was carried out in 13 separate campaigns. Each involved different people, moved at a different pace, and was influenced by local and national considerations. Two sides faced off throughout the states, however, calling themselves **Federalists** and **Antifederalists** (see Table 2.2). The Federalists (who more accurately should have called themselves "Nationalists," but who took their name to appear to follow in the revolutionary tradition) supported the Constitution and preferred a strong national government. The Antifederalists opposed the Constitution and preferred a federal system of government that was decentralized; they took their name by default, in reaction to their better-organized opponents. The Federalists were united in their support of the Constitution, whereas the Antifederalists were divided over possible alternatives to the Constitution.

During the struggle over ratification of the Constitution, Americans argued about great political issues and principles. How much power should the national government be given? What safeguards would most likely prevent the abuse of power? What institutional arrangements could best ensure adequate representation for all Americans? Was tyranny of the many to be feared more than tyranny of the few?

Federalists those who favored a strong national government and supported the Constitution proposed at the American Constitutional Convention of 1787

Antifederalists those who favored strong state governments and a weak national government and who were opponents of the Constitution proposed at the American Constitutional Convention of 1787

Federalists versus Antifederalists

During the ratification struggle, thousands of essays, speeches, pamphlets, and letters were presented in support of and in opposition to the proposed Constitution. The best-known pieces supporting ratification were the 85 essays written between the fall of 1787 and the spring of 1788 under the name of "Publius," by Alexander Hamilton, James Madison, and John Jay. These *Federalist Papers*, as they are collectively known today, defended the principles of the Constitution and sought

Federalist Papers a series of essays written by Alexander Hamilton, James Madison, and John Jay supporting ratification of the Constitution

TABLE 2.2

Federalists versus Antifederalists

	FEDERALISTS	ANTIFEDERALISTS
Who were they?	Property owners, creditors, merchants	Small farmers, frontiersmen, debtors, shopkeepers, some state government officials
What did they believe?	Believed that elites were most fit to govern; feared "excessive democracy"	Believed that government should be closer to the people; feared concentration of power in hands of the elites
What system of government did they favor?	Favored strong national government; believed in "filtration" so that only elites would obtain governmental power	Favored retention of power by state governments and protection of individual rights
Who were their leaders?	Alexander Hamilton, James Madison, George Washington	Patrick Henry, George Mason, Elbridge Gerry, George Clinton

to dispel fears of a national authority. The Antifederalists published essays of their own, arguing that the new Constitution betrayed the Revolution and was a step toward monarchy. Among the best of the Antifederalist works were the essays, usually attributed to the New York State Supreme Court justice Robert Yates, that were written under the name of "Brutus" and published in the *New York Journal* at the same time the *Federalist Papers* appeared. The Antifederalist view was also ably presented in the pamphlets and letters written by a former delegate to the Continental Congress and future U.S. senator, Richard Henry Lee of Virginia, using the pen name "The Federal Farmer." These essays highlight the major differences of opinion between Federalists and Antifederalists. Federalists appealed to basic principles of government in support of their nationalist vision. Antifederalists cited equally fundamental precepts to support their vision of a looser confederacy of small republics.

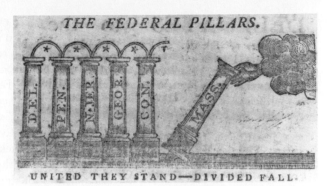

Article VII of the Constitution required 9 of the 13 states to ratify the Constitution in order for it to be adopted. In this image from January 1788, the pillars represent the first five states that ratified the Constitution, with Massachusetts as the likely sixth.

Representation One major area of contention between the two sides was the question of representation. The Antifederalists asserted that representatives must be "a true picture of the people . . . [possessing] the knowledge of their circumstances and their wants."[17] This could be achieved, argued the Antifederalists, only in small, relatively homogeneous republics such as the existing states. In their view, the size and extent of the entire nation precluded the construction of a truly representative form of government. As Brutus put it, "Is it practicable for a country so large and so numerous . . . to elect a representation that will speak their sentiments? . . . It certainly is not."[18]

Federalists, for their part, saw no reason that representatives should be precisely like those they represented. In the Federalist view, one of the great advantages of representative government over direct democracy was precisely the possibility that the people would choose as their representatives individuals possessing ability, experience, and talent superior to their own. In Madison's words, rather than serving as a mirror or reflection of society, representatives must be "[those] who possess [the] most wisdom to discern, and [the] most virtue to pursue, the common good of the society."[19]

Tyranny of the Majority A second important issue dividing Federalists and Antifederalists was the threat of **tyranny**—unjust rule by the group in power. Both opponents and defenders of the Constitution frequently affirmed their fear of tyrannical rule. Each side, however, had a different view of the most likely source of tyranny and, hence, of the way in which to forestall the threat.

From the Antifederalist perspective, the great danger was the tendency of all governments—including republican governments—to become gradually more and more "aristocratic" in character, wherein the small number of individuals in positions of authority would use their stations to gain more and more power over the general citizenry. In essence, the few would use their power to tyrannize the many. For this reason, Antifederalists were sharply critical of those features of the Constitution that divorced governmental institutions from direct responsibility to the people—institutions such as the Senate, the executive, and the federal judiciary. The last, appointed for life, presented a particular threat:

tyranny oppressive government that employs cruel and unjust use of power and authority

for critical analysis

The Antifederalists worried that the size and diversity of the United States made democratic government impossible. In what ways might a large heterogeneous population limit democracy and enhance democracy?

"I wonder if the world ever saw . . . a court of justice invested with such immense powers, and yet placed in a situation so little responsible," protested Brutus.[20]

The Federalists, too, recognized the threat of tyranny, but they believed that the danger particularly associated with republican governments was not aristocracy but majority tyranny. The Federalists were concerned that a popular majority, "united and actuated by some common impulse of passion, or of interest, adverse to the rights of other citizens," would endeavor to "trample on the rules of justice."[21] From the Federalist perspective, it was precisely those features of the Constitution that the Antifederalists attacked as potential sources of tyranny that actually offered the best hope of averting the threat of oppression. The size and extent of the nation, for instance, was for the Federalists a bulwark against tyranny because a majority would have difficulty uniting in a large and populous nation.

Governmental Power A third major difference between Federalists and Antifederalists was the issue of governmental power. Both opponents and proponents of the Constitution agreed on the principle of **limited government**. They differed, however, on the fundamentally important question of how to place limits on governmental action. Antifederalists favored limiting and enumerating the powers granted to the national government in relation both to the states and to the people at large. To them, the powers given the national government ought to be "confined to certain defined national objects."[22] Otherwise, the national government would "swallow up all the power of the state governments."[23] Antifederalists bitterly attacked the supremacy clause and the elastic clause of the Constitution as unlimited and dangerous grants of power to the national government.[24] Antifederalists also demanded that a bill of rights be added to the Constitution to place limits on the government's exercise of power over the citizenry.

Federalists favored the construction of a government with broad powers to defend the nation against foreign foes, guard against domestic strife and insurrection, promote commerce, and expand the nation's economy. Antifederalists shared some of these goals but still feared governmental power. In reply, Federalists such as Hamilton acknowledged that every power could be abused but argued that the way to prevent misuse of power was not by depriving the government of the powers needed to achieve national goals but by adopting the Constitution's internal checks and controls. As Madison put it, "the power surrendered by the people is first divided between two distinct governments (state and national), and then the portion allotted to each subdivided among distinct and separate departments. Hence, a double security arises to the rights of the people. The different governments will control each other, at the same time that each will be controlled by itself."[25] The Federalists' concern with avoiding unwarranted limits on governmental power led them to oppose a bill of rights, which they saw as nothing more than a set of unnecessary restrictions on the government.

Federalists acknowledged that abuse of power remained a possibility but felt that the risk had to be taken in order to achieve essential goals. "The very idea of power included a possibility of doing harm," said the Federalist John Rutledge during the South Carolina ratification debates. "If the gentleman would show the power that could do no harm," Rutledge continued, "he would at once discover it to be a power that could do no good."[26] This aspect of the debate between Federalists and Antifederalists, perhaps more than any other, continues

limited government a principle of constitutional government; a government whose powers are defined and limited by a constitution

Debates over how much power the national government should have continue today. Here, a man protests the presence of the FBI in Harney County, Oregon, in 2016 after an antigovernment group seized a U.S. wildlife refuge building.

to reverberate through American politics. Should the nation limit the federal government's power to tax and spend? Should Congress limit the capacity of federal agencies to issue new regulations? Should the government endeavor to create new rights for minorities, the disabled, and others? Though the details have changed, these are the same great questions that have been debated since the Founding.

Reflections on the Founding

The final product of the Constitutional Convention was an extraordinary victory for the groups that had most forcefully called for the creation of a new system of government to replace the Articles of Confederation. While Antifederalist criticisms did force the Constitution's proponents to accept the addition of a bill of rights designed to limit the powers of the national government, overall it was the Federalist vision of America that triumphed. The Constitution adopted in 1789 created the framework for a powerful national government that for more than 200 years has defended the nation's interests, promoted its commerce, and maintained national unity. In one notable instance, the national government fought and won a bloody war to prevent the nation from breaking apart. And despite this powerful national government, the system of internal checks and balances has functioned reasonably well, as the Federalists predicted, to prevent the government from tyrannizing its citizens. The national unity created under the Constitution also gradually helped America become a great world power—as many of the framers had hoped.

Of course, the groups whose interests were served by the Constitution in 1789, mainly the merchants and planters, are not the same groups that benefit from the Constitution's provisions today. Once incorporated into law, political principles often take on lives of their own and have consequences that were never anticipated by their original champions. Indeed, many of the groups that benefit from constitutional provisions today did not even exist in 1789. Who would have thought that the principle of free speech would influence the transmission of data on the Internet? Perhaps one secret of the Constitution's longevity is that it did not confer permanent advantage on any one set of economic or social forces.

Although they were defeated in 1789, the Antifederalists present us with an important picture of an America that might have been. Would Americans in the eighteenth century have been worse off if they had been governed by a confederacy of small republics linked by a national administration with severely limited powers? Were the Antifederalists correct in predicting that a government given great power in the hope that it might do good would, through "insensible progress," inevitably turn to evil purposes? Two hundred years of government under the federal Constitution are not necessarily enough to answer these questions definitively.

for critical analysis
Do you agree with Rutledge that a power that can do no harm can also do no good? How can a system of government maximize the ability of government to do good while minimizing the possibility of harm?

● The Citizen's Role and the Changing Constitution

Trace how the Constitution has changed over time through the amendment process

The Constitution has endured for more than two centuries as the framework of government. But it has not gone unchanged. Without change, the Constitution might have become merely a sacred text, stored under glass.

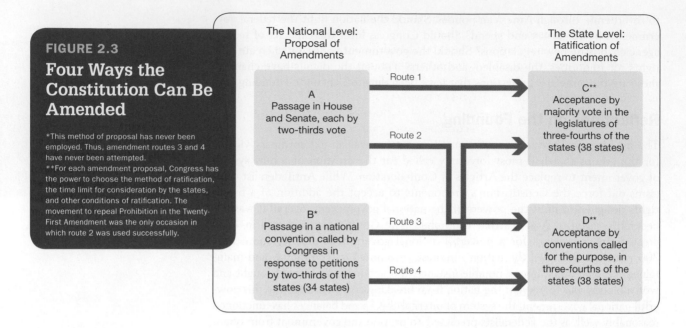

FIGURE 2.3

Four Ways the Constitution Can Be Amended

*This method of proposal has never been employed. Thus, amendment routes 3 and 4 have never been attempted.

**For each amendment proposal, Congress has the power to choose the method of ratification, the time limit for consideration by the states, and other conditions of ratification. The movement to repeal Prohibition in the Twenty-First Amendment was the only occasion in which route 2 was used successfully.

The National Level: Proposal of Amendments

A
Passage in House and Senate, each by two-thirds vote

B*
Passage in a national convention called by Congress in response to petitions by two-thirds of the states (34 states)

Route 1
Route 2
Route 3
Route 4

The State Level: Ratification of Amendments

C**
Acceptance by majority vote in the legislatures of three-fourths of the states (38 states)

D**
Acceptance by conventions called for the purpose, in three-fourths of the states (38 states)

The Constitution assigns citizens an indirect but important role in this process of change. Figure 2.3 outlines the ways in which the Constitution might be amended, all of which involve citizens through the election of members of Congress and state legislatures or, hypothetically, through the election of delegates to national and state constitutional conventions. Amending the Constitution may be difficult, but it is ultimately controlled by institutions elected by the people. Of course, the courts, whose judges are not elected by the people but appointed by the president with the consent of the Senate, also modify the Constitution and adapt it to changing circumstances. Many voters are aware that their presidential ballots may also help to shape the character of the Supreme Court and other federal courts.

Amendments: Many Are Called; Few Are Chosen

The inevitable need for change was recognized by the framers of the Constitution, and provisions for **amendment** were incorporated into Article V. Four methods of amendment are described:

amendment a change added to a bill, law, or constitution

1. Passage in House and Senate by two-thirds vote, then ratification by majority vote of the legislatures of three-fourths (now 38) of the states

2. Passage in House and Senate by two-thirds vote, then ratification by conventions called for the purpose in three-fourths of the states

3. Passage in a national convention called for by Congress in response to petitions by two-thirds of the states, ratification by majority vote of the legislatures of three-fourths of the states

4. Passage in a national convention (as in method 3), then ratification by conventions called for the purpose in three-fourths of the states

Figure 2.3 illustrates each of these possible methods. Since no amendment has ever been proposed by national convention, however, methods 3 and 4 have never been employed. And method 2 has been employed only once (the Twenty-First

Amendment, which repealed the Eighteenth Amendment, or Prohibition). Thus, method 1 has been used for all the others.

The Constitution has proved to be extremely difficult to amend. In the history of efforts to amend it, the most appropriate characterization is "many are called; few are chosen." Since 1789, more than 11,000 amendments have been formally offered in Congress. Of these, Congress officially proposed only 29, and 27 of these were eventually ratified by the states. Two of these—Prohibition and its repeal—cancel each other out, so for all practical purposes, only 25 amendments have been added to the Constitution since 1791.

Which Were Chosen? An Analysis of the 27

There is more to the amending difficulties than the politics of campaigning and voting. It would appear that only a limited number of changes can actually be made to the Constitution. Most efforts to amend the Constitution have failed because they were simply attempts to use the Constitution as an alternative to legislation for dealing directly with a specific public problem.

The 25 successful amendments, on the other hand, are concerned with the structure or composition of government (see Table 2.3). This is consistent with the dictionary, which defines *constitution* as the makeup or composition of something. And it is consistent with the concept of a constitution as "higher law" because the whole point and purpose of a higher law is to establish a framework within which government and the process of making ordinary law can take place. Even those who would have preferred more changes to the Constitution have to agree that there is great wisdom in this principle. A constitution ought to enable legislation and public policies to be enacted, but it should not determine what that legislation or those public policies ought to be.

For those whose hopes for change center on the Constitution, it must be emphasized that the amendment route to social change is, and always will be, extremely limited. Through a constitution it is possible to establish a working structure of government, and through a constitution it is possible to establish basic rights of citizens by placing limitations on the powers of that government. Of course, the Constitution cannot enforce itself. But it can and does have a real influence on everyday life because a right or an obligation set forth in the Constitution can become a cause of action in the hands of an otherwise powerless person.

Private property is an excellent example. Property is one of the most fundamental and well-established rights in the United States; but it is well established not because it is recognized in so many words in the Constitution but because legislatures and courts, working within an agreed-upon constitutional framework, have made it a crime for anyone, including the government, to trespass or to take away property without compensation. A constitution is good if it produces the cause of action that leads to good legislation, good case law, and appropriate police behavior. A constitution cannot eliminate power. But its principles can be a citizen's dependable defense against the abuse of power.

And ordinary citizens, including students, can influence America's constitution. Take the case of the Twenty-Seventh Amendment, which declares that no congressional pay increase can take effect until the next Congress is elected. This idea was proposed in 1789 along with the 10 amendments that became the Bill of Rights. This proposed amendment was ratified by several states but never achieved the three-fourths needed to be added to the Constitution. The idea was forgotten until

TABLE 2.3

Amendments to the Constitution

AMENDMENT	PURPOSE	YEAR PROPOSED	YEAR ADOPTED
I	*Limits on Congress:* Congress is not to make any law establishing a religion or abridging speech, press, assembly, or petition freedoms.	1789	1791
II, III, IV	*Limits on Executive:* The executive branch is not to infringe on the right of people to keep arms (II), is not arbitrarily to take houses for a militia (III), and is not to engage in the search or seizure of evidence without a court warrant swearing to belief in the probable existence of a crime (IV).	1789	1791
V, VI, VII, VIII	*Limits on Courts:** The courts are not to hold trials for serious offenses without provision for a grand jury (V), a petit (trial) jury (VII), a speedy trial (VI), presentation of charges (VI), confrontation of hostile witnesses (VI), immunity from testimony against oneself (V), and immunity from more than one trial for the same offense (V). Neither bail nor punishment can be excessive (VIII), and no property can be taken without just compensation (V).	1789	1791
IX, X	*Limits on National Government:* All rights not enumerated are reserved to the states or the people.	1789	1791
XI	Limited jurisdiction of federal courts over suits involving the states.	1794	1795
XII	Provided separate ballot for vice president in the electoral college.	1803	1804
XIII	Eliminated slavery and eliminated the right of states to allow property in persons.	1865	1865
XIV	(Part 1) Provided a national definition of *citizenship*.**	1866	1868
XIV	(Part 2) Applied due process of Bill of Rights to the states.	1866	1868
XV	Extended voting rights to all races.	1869	1870
XVI	Established national power to tax incomes.	1909	1913
XVII†	Provided direct election of senators.	1912	1913
XIX	Extended voting rights to women.	1919	1920
XX	Eliminated "lame-duck" session of Congress.	1932	1933
XXII	Limited presidential term.	1947	1951
XXIII	Extended voting rights to residents of the District of Columbia.	1960	1961
XXIV	Extended voting rights to all classes by abolition of poll taxes.	1962	1964
XXV	Provided presidential succession in case of disability.	1965	1967
XXVI	Extended voting rights to citizens aged 18 and over.	1971	1971††
XXVII	Limited Congress's power to raise its own salary.	1789	1992

*These amendments also impose limits on the law-enforcement powers of federal, state, and local executive branches.
**In defining *citizenship*, the Fourteenth Amendment actually provided the constitutional basis for expanding the electorate to include all races, women, and residents of the District of Columbia. Only the "18-year-olds' amendment" should have been necessary since it changed the definition of citizenship. The fact that additional amendments were required following the Fourteenth suggests that voting is not considered an inherent right of U.S. citizenship. Instead, it is viewed as a privilege.
†The Eighteenth Amendment, ratified in 1919, outlawed the sale and transportation of liquor. It was repealed by the Twenty-First Amendment, ratified in 1933.
††The Twenty-Sixth Amendment holds the record for speed of adoption. It was proposed on March 23, 1971, and adopted on July 5, 1971.

a University of Texas undergraduate, Gregory Watson, wrote his class term paper on the subject in 1982. Watson proposed a campaign to complete the ratification process. His professor awarded Watson a C grade, asserting that the proposal was unrealistic. Watson, however, was undeterred and launched a student-led campaign to complete the ratification process. In 1992, the Twenty-Seventh Amendment was added to the Constitution, more than two centuries after it was proposed.

The Supreme Court and Constitutional Change

Although the process of constitutional amendment outlined in Article V has seldom been used successfully, another form of constitutional revision is constantly at work in the United States: judicial interpretation of the Constitution and its amendments by the Supreme Court as it reviews cases. In some instances, the Court may give concrete definition to abstract constitutional principles. For example, the Constitution's Fifth Amendment asserts in general terms that individuals accused of crimes are entitled to procedural rights. The Supreme Court, in a series of decisions, established principles giving effect to those rights. Every viewer of television crime programs knows that, upon being arrested, individuals must receive Miranda warnings informing them of their right to refuse to speak and their right to counsel. These required warnings are the result of a 1966 Supreme Court decision interpreting the meaning and implications of the Fifth Amendment.

In some instances, the Supreme Court does more than interpret or flesh out constitutional provisions: it seems to modify or augment the text itself. For example, in decisions in 1965 and 1973 on birth control and abortion, respectively, the Court said that Americans were constitutionally entitled to a right of privacy. The Constitution

The Equal Rights Amendment (ERA) is an example of an amendment that almost succeeded. The proposed amendment guaranteed equality under the law for women and made gender discrimination illegal. The ERA was ratified by 35 state legislatures but failed to get the 38 necessary to equal three-fourths of the states.

The Twenty-Sixth Amendment addressed an issue of representation that came to the fore when 18-, 19-, and 20-year-olds were drafted to serve in the Vietnam War but could not vote for Congress or the president who enacted the policies that affected their lives and deaths.

does not explicitly mention the right to privacy; it is derived from the Fourteenth Amendment and several provisions in the Bill of Rights.

Of course, much of the Supreme Court's power is itself based on constitutional interpretation rather than on the text of the document. The Supreme Court claims the power of judicial review—the power to render the final decision when there is a conflict of interpretations of the Constitution or federal law among the courts, Congress, the executive branch, or the states. Nowhere does the Constitution mention this power. In a number of early cases, however, the Supreme Court asserted that the Constitution gave it the power of judicial review; and this interpretation has prevailed, enhancing the Court's power. Some commentators this as denounce constitutional amendment by the judiciary and demand that judges limit themselves to "strict construction" of the Constitution, adhering closely to the words of the document's text. Proponents of the idea of the *living Constitution*, on the other hand, assert that the Constitution is subject to change as conditions warrant; and they argue that the judiciary is the institution best qualified to adjust the Constitution's principles to new problems and times.

The Constitution
and Your Future

The Constitution's framers placed individual liberty ahead of all other political values, a concern that led many of the framers to distrust both democracy and equality. They feared that democracy could degenerate into a majority tyranny in which the populace, perhaps led by rabble-rousing demagogues, trampled on liberty. As for equality, the framers were products of their time and place; our contemporary ideas of racial and gender equality would have been foreign to them. The framers were concerned primarily with another manifestation of equality: they feared that those without property or position might be driven by what some called a "leveling spirit" to infringe on liberty in the name of greater economic or social equality. Indeed, the framers believed that this leveling spirit was most likely to produce demagoguery and majority tyranny. As a result, the basic structure of the Constitution—separated powers, internal checks and balances, and federalism—was designed to safeguard liberty, and the Bill of Rights created further safeguards for liberty. At the same time, however, many of the Constitution's other key provisions, such as indirect election of senators and the president and the appointment of judges for life, were designed to limit democracy and, hence, the threat of majority tyranny.

By championing liberty, however, the framers virtually guaranteed that democracy and even a measure of equality would sooner or later evolve in the United States. Liberty promotes the growth of political activity and the expansion of political participation, as in James Madison's famous phrase "Liberty is to faction as air is to fire."[27] Where they have liberty, more and more people, groups, and interests will almost inevitably engage in politics and gradually overcome whatever restrictions might have been placed on participation. Indeed, this is precisely what happened in the early years of the American Republic. During the Jeffersonian period, political parties formed. During the Jacksonian period, many state suffrage restrictions were removed and popular participation greatly expanded. The "**Who Participates**?" feature on the following page traces the expansion of the right to vote in the United States from the Founding to today. Over time, liberty is conducive to democracy.

Who Gained the Right to Vote through Amendments?

Adult Citizens Eligible to Vote in National Elections*

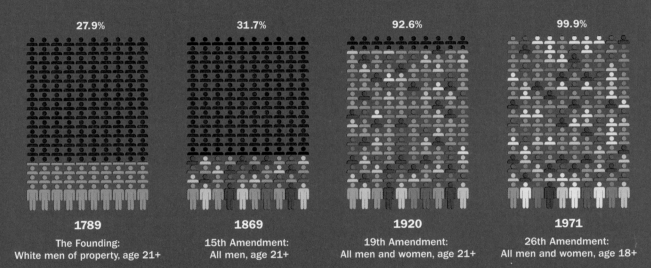

| 27.9% | 31.7% | 92.6% | 99.9% |

| **1789** | **1869** | **1920** | **1971** |
| The Founding: White men of property, age 21+ | 15th Amendment: All men, age 21+ | 19th Amendment: All men and women, age 21+ | 26th Amendment: All men and women, age 18+ |

*Percentages are of the adult (18+) population. These figures are approximate for 1789 and 1869. The voting rights of convicted felons are restricted in some states, and of noncitizens in all states.
SOURCES: U.S. Census of Population and Housing, 1790–2010, www.census.gov/prod/www/decennial.html (accessed 9/28/15); United States Elections Project, www.electproject.org/national-1789–present (accessed 9/27/15).

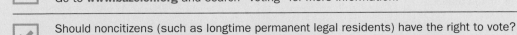

WHAT YOU CAN DO

Know Your Constitutional Rights

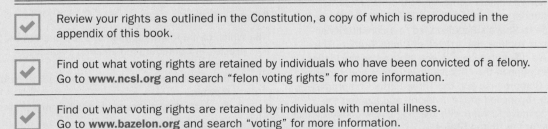

- ☑ Review your rights as outlined in the Constitution, a copy of which is reproduced in the appendix of this book.

- ☑ Find out what voting rights are retained by individuals who have been convicted of a felony. Go to **www.ncsl.org** and search "felon voting rights" for more information.

- ☑ Find out what voting rights are retained by individuals with mental illness. Go to **www.bazelon.org** and search "voting" for more information.

- ☑ Should noncitizens (such as longtime permanent legal residents) have the right to vote? Go to **www.latimes.com/citizenship** to read more and to join the conversation online.

studyguide

The First Founding: Interests and Conflicts

Describe the events that led to the Declaration of Independence and the Articles of Confederation (pp. 41–45)

Dissatisfaction with British tax policies and discontent over retaliatory acts of political repression radicalized many colonists during the 1770s to push for independence from British rule. By identifying widely shared grievances, goals, and principles, the Declaration of Independence helped forge a sense of national unity among diverse elements in colonial society. The first written constitution of the United States, the Articles of Confederation, left most governmental powers in the hands of the states and placed strong limits on the powers of the national government.

Key Terms

Articles of Confederation (p. 44)

confederation (p. 44)

Practice Quiz

1. How did the British attempt to raise revenue in the North American colonies?
   a) income taxes
   b) tariffs, duties, and other taxes on commerce
   c) expropriation and sale of Native American lands
   d) licensing fees for the mining of natural resources
   e) requests for voluntary donations

2. In their fight against British taxes, such as the Stamp Act and the Sugar Act of 1764, New England merchants and southern planters allied with which of the following groups?
   a) shopkeepers, small farmers, laborers, and artisans
   b) shopkeepers only
   c) laborers only
   d) artisans only
   e) shopkeepers and laborers only

3. The first governing document in the United States was
   a) the Declaration of Independence.
   b) the Articles of Confederation.
   c) the Constitution.
   d) the Bill of Rights.
   e) the Virginia Plan.

4. Where was the execution of laws conducted under the Articles of Confederation?
   a) the presidency
   b) the Congress
   c) the states
   d) the federal bureaucracy
   e) the federal judiciary

The Second Founding: From Compromise to Constitution

Analyze the reasons many Americans thought a new Constitution was needed, and assess the obstacles to a new Constitution (pp. 45–51)

International weakness, domestic economic problems, and the national government's inability to act decisively in response to Shays's Rebellion led to a constitutional convention to replace the Articles of Confederation. The convention's delegates were deeply divided on the issues of representation in the national government and slavery. The Great Compromise and the Three-Fifths Compromise temporarily reconciled these divisions and allowed the Founders to move forward with creating a new constitutional framework for the United States.

Key Terms

Virginia Plan (p. 48)

New Jersey Plan (p. 48)

Great Compromise (p. 50)

Three-Fifths Compromise (p. 51)

Practice Quiz

5. Which of the following was *not* a reason that the Articles of Confederation seemed inadequate?
   a) the lack of a national military
   b) the inability of the federal government to enforce treaties
   c) the persistent economic turmoil among states

d) the growing power of radical forces in state legislatures

e) the Congress of the Confederation's strict control over state governments

6. Which event led directly to the Constitutional Convention by providing evidence that the government created under the Articles of Confederation was unable to act decisively in times of national crisis?
   a) the Boston Tea Party
   b) the Boston Massacre
   c) Shays's Rebellion
   d) the Annapolis Convention
   e) the War of 1812

7. The draft constitution that was introduced at the start of the Constitutional Convention was authored by Edmund Randolph but showed the strong influence of
   a) William Patterson.
   b) Benjamin Franklin.
   c) James Madison.

d) George Clinton.
e) Thomas Jefferson.

8. Which state's proposal embodied a principle of representing states in the Congress according to their size and wealth?
   a) New Jersey
   b) Maryland
   c) Rhode Island
   d) Virginia
   e) Connecticut

9. The agreement reached at the Constitutional Convention that determined how slaves would be counted for the purposes of taxation and representation in the House of Representatives was called the
   a) Connecticut Compromise.
   b) Three-Fifths Compromise.
   c) Great Compromise.
   d) Virginia Plan.
   e) New Jersey Plan.

The Constitution

Explain how the Constitution attempted to improve America's governance, and outline the major institutions established by the Constitution (pp. 52–59)

The Founders sought to create a stronger national government than existed under the Articles of Confederation. In particular, they hoped that the new constitution would promote commerce, protect private property, and avoid the perils of "excessive democracy." The Founders' concern with national power was expressed most clearly in the supremacy clause of Article VI. The national government, however, did not have unlimited power; and there were significant constraints placed on it through the separation of powers, federalism, and the Bill of Rights.

Key Terms

bicameral (p. 52)

checks and balances (p. 52)

Bill of Rights (p. 52)

separation of powers (p. 52)

federalism (p. 52)

expressed powers (p. 54)

elastic clause (p. 54)

judicial review (p. 55)

supremacy clause (p. 56)

Practice Quiz

10. Which mechanism was instituted in the Congress to guard against "excessive democracy"?
    a) bicameralism
    b) staggered terms in office
    c) checks and balances
    d) selection of senators by state legislatures
    e) all of the above

11. Which of the following best describes the Supreme Court as understood by the Founders?
    a) the principal check on presidential power
    b) the arbiter of disputes within the Congress
    c) the body that would choose the president
    d) a figurehead commission of elders
    e) the highest court of both the national government and the states

12. The ability of the president to veto a bill passed by Congress is a good example of
    a) federalism
    b) the system of checks and balances
    c) the supremacy clause
    d) civil liberties
    e) bicameralism

The Fight for Ratification

Present the controversies involved in the struggle for ratification (pp. 60–63)

Before the Constitution could go into effect, it had to be ratified by 9 of the 13 states. In the debate over ratification, the Federalists supported the Constitution and the Antifederalists opposed it. The three major areas of disagreement between Federalists and Antifederalists were the question of representation, the threat of tyranny of the majority, and the extent of government power.

Key Terms

Federalists (p. 60)

Antifederalists (p. 60)

Federalist Papers (p. 60)

tyranny (p. 61)

limited government (p. 62)

Practice Quiz

13. Which of the following were the Antifederalists most concerned with?
    a) interstate commerce
    b) the protection of property
    c) the distinction between principles and interests
    d) abolishing slavery
    e) the potential for tyranny in the central government

The Citizen's Role and the Changing Constitution

Trace how the Constitution has changed over time through the amendment process (pp. 63–68)

The amendment process outlined in Article V of the Constitution creates significant hurdles to change that have rarely been cleared in American history. Attempts to solve specific social problems through the use of a constitutional amendment have been particularly unsuccessful at winning the support required to change the country's basic governing document. The Supreme Court, however, has provided new meaning and new substance to the Constitution on countless occasions during the last 200 years through decisions on important cases.

Key Term

amendment (p. 64)

Practice Quiz

14. Which of the following best describes the process of amending the Constitution?
    a) It is difficult and has rarely been used successfully to address specific public problems.
    b) It is difficult and has frequently been used successfully to address specific public problems.
    c) It is easy but has rarely been used successfully to address specific public problems.
    d) It is easy and has frequently been used successfully to address specific public problems.
    e) It is easy, but it has never been used for any purpose.

For Further Reading

Ackerman, Erin, and Benjamin Ginsberg. *A Guide to the United States Constitution*, 2nd ed. New York: W. W. Norton, 2011.

Amar, Akhil Reed. *America's Constitution: A Biography.* New York: Random House, 2006.

Beard, Charles. *An Economic Interpretation of the Constitution of the United States.* New York: Macmillan, 1913.

Beeman, Richard. *Plain, Honest Men: The Making of the American Constitution.* New York: Random House, 2010.

Dahl, Robert A. *How Democratic Is the American Constitution?* 2nd ed. New Haven, CT: Yale University Press, 2002.

Ellis, Joseph. *American Creation: Triumphs and Tragedies at the Founding of the Republic.* New York: Knopf, 2007.

Ellis, Joseph. *The Quartet: Orchestrating the Second American Revolution.* New York: Knopf, 2015.

Ferling, John. *The American Revolution and the War That Won It.* New York: Bloomsbury, 2015.

Hamilton, Alexander, James Madison, and John Jay. *The Federalist Papers.* Edited by Isaac Kramnick. New York: Viking, 1987.

Jensen, Merrill. *The Articles of Confederation.* Madison: University of Wisconsin Press, 1963.

Keller, Morton. *America's Three Regimes.* New York: Oxford University Press, 2009.

Lewis, Anthony. *Freedom for the Thought That We Hate: A Biography of the First Amendment.* New York: Basic Books, 2008.

Main, Jackson Turner. *The Social Structure of Revolutionary America.* Princeton, NJ: Princeton University Press, 1965.

Rossiter, Clinton. *1787: Grand Convention.* New York: Macmillan, 1966.

Stewart, David O. *Madison's Gift: Five Partnerships That Built America.* New York: Simon & Schuster, 2015.

Storing, Herbert, ed. *The Complete Anti-Federalist.* 7 vols. Chicago: University of Chicago Press, 1981.

Recommended Websites

The American Civil Liberties Union
www.aclu.org
The ACLU is committed to protecting, for all individuals, the freedoms found in the Bill of Rights. This sometimes controversial organization constantly monitors the government for violations of liberty and encourages its members to take political action.

Archiving Early America
www.earlyamerica.com
Revolutionary Americans were motivated by a variety of competing ideals, principles, and interests. Visit this website to learn more about the early colonists and the founding of our government.

Constitution Finder
http://confinder.richmond.edu
Is the American Constitution a model for the world? Explore the constitutions of many different nations and see what elements of the U.S. Constitution can be found in the governing documents of other countries.

FindLaw
http://findlaw.com/casecode/state.html
The FindLaw website provides all 50 states' constitutions. Click on your state and try to identify such constitutional principles as bicameralism, staggered terms of office, checks and balances, and separation of powers.

The National Archives
www.archives.gov
This government site provides information about and actual digital images of such founding documents as the Declaration of Independence, the U.S. Constitution, and the Bill of Rights.

The National Constitution Center
www.constitutioncenter.org
The National Constitution Center in Philadelphia maintains a website that provides in-depth instructional analysis of the U.S. Constitution. Check out the Interactive Constitution function and follow the document from its Preamble through the Twenty-Seventh Amendment.

Oyez
www.oyez.org
This website for U.S. Supreme Court media has an excellent search engine for finding information on Supreme Court cases. See how the Court has interpreted the Constitution over time.

The PBS *Liberty!* Series
www.pbs.org/ktca/liberty
The PBS *Liberty!* series on the American Revolution offers an in-depth look at the Revolutionary War and includes information on historical events such as the Constitutional Convention.

The Supreme Court of the United States
www.supremecourtus.gov
The website for the U.S. Supreme Court provides information on recent decisions. Take a moment to read some oral arguments, briefs, or opinions.

Federalism is at the center of a national debate over marijuana policy: while marijuana remains illegal under federal law, some states permit marijuana for medicinal or recreational use. Colorado legalized recreational use of marijuana in 2012, and participants in this 2015 Denver rally called for national legalization.

Federalism

WHAT GOVERNMENT DOES AND WHY IT MATTERS In 1996, voters in California approved a new law legalizing the cultivation, possession, and use of marijuana for medical purposes. As the idea spread, other states followed suit. By 2016, 26 states and the District of Columbia had approved medical marijuana. In these states, medical clinics selling marijuana have popped up in many cities. With a doctor's prescription, patients can purchase marijuana for personal use. Some states have gone even further. In 2012, voters in Washington state and Colorado approved measures to legalize the recreational use of marijuana. The laws gave adults over the age of 21 the right to buy limited amounts of marijuana. And in the 2014 and 2016 elections, ballot measures in Alaska, California, Maine, Massachusetts, Nevada, Oregon, and Washington, D.C., also legalized recreational use of marijuana.

States routinely devise their own laws on a wide variety of topics. But the marijuana laws passed over the past two decades are extraordinary because marijuana remains a controlled substance under federal law, making it illegal to grow, sell, or possess marijuana for medical or recreational purposes. States began to legalize marijuana in defiance of clear federal prohibitions.

The federal response to the states has shifted over time. As state laws began to loosen restrictions on marijuana, the federal government at first sought to assert its authority. The federal Drug Enforcement Agency staged raids on marijuana clinics and even searched individual homes to enforce the federal law prohibiting marijuana. In 2005 the Supreme Court ruled that these federal actions were constitutional. The Court affirmed the federal government's right to prohibit marijuana even as a growing number of state laws moved in the opposite direction. By 2013, however, the Justice Department, bowing to the states, announced a change of course. The department stated that it would not challenge state laws so long as the states maintained a close watch over their marijuana markets. Instead the federal government would focus its enforcement efforts on specific issues, including trafficking by gangs, sales to minors, and selling across state lines. Washington's governor, Jay Inslee, issued a joint statement with the state's attorney general noting that the decision "reflects a balanced approach by the federal government that respects the states' interests in implementing these laws and recognizes the federal government's role in fighting illegal drugs and criminal activity."[1]

The debates about marijuana policy engage some of the oldest questions in American government: What is the responsibility of the federal government, and what is the responsibility of the states? When should there be uniformity across the states, and when is it better to let states adopt their own laws based on the needs and desires of their population, which may result in a diverse set of laws across the country? Which approach serves the common good?

The United States is a federal system, in which the national government shares power with lower levels of government. Throughout American history, lawmakers, politicians, and citizens have wrestled with questions about how responsibilities should be allocated across the different levels of government. Some responsibilities, such as international relations, clearly lie with the federal government. Others, such as divorce laws, are controlled by state governments. In fact, most of the rules and regulations that Americans face in their daily lives are set by state and local governments. However, many government responsibilities are shared in American federalism and require cooperation among local, state, and federal governments. The debate about "who should do what" remains one of the most important discussions in American politics.

chaptergoals

- Describe what the Constitution says about the powers of the national government and of the states (pp. 77–82)

- Consider how the relationship between the federal and state governments has changed over time (pp. 82–89)

- Trace developments in the federal framework leading to a stronger national government (pp. 89–95)

- Analyze the developments in the federal framework since the 1970s (pp. 96–105)

Federalism in the Constitution

Describe what the Constitution says about the powers of the national government and of the states

The Constitution has had its most fundamental influence on American life through **federalism**. *Federalism* can be defined as the division of powers and functions between the national government and the state governments. Governments can organize power in a variety of ways. One of the most important distinctions is between unitary and federal governments. In a **unitary system**, the central government makes the important decisions and lower levels of government have little independent power. In such systems, lower levels of government primarily implement decisions made by the central government. In France, for example, the central government was once so involved in the smallest details of local activity that the minister of education boasted that by looking at his watch he could tell what all French schoolchildren were learning at that moment because the central government set the school curriculum. In a federal system, by contrast, the central government shares power or functions with lower levels of government, such as regions or states. Nations with diverse ethnic or language groupings, such as Switzerland and Canada, are most likely to have federal arrangements. In federal systems, lower levels of government often have significant independent power to set policy in some areas, such as education and social programs, and to impose taxes. Yet the specific ways in which power is shared vary greatly: no two federal systems are exactly the same.

The United States was the first nation to adopt federalism as its governing framework. With federalism, the framers sought to limit the national government by creating a second layer of state governments. By granting a few "expressed powers" to the national government and reserving all the rest to the states, the original Constitution recognized two sovereigns: state governments and the federal government. Table 3.1 indicates which level of government has responsibility for some of the actions that affect our everyday lives.

The Powers of the National Government

As we saw in Chapter 2, the **expressed powers** granted to the national government are found in Article I, Section 8, of the Constitution. These 17 powers include the power to collect taxes, coin money, declare war, and regulate commerce. Article I, Section 8, also contains another important source of power for the national government: the **implied powers** that enable Congress "to make all Laws which shall be necessary and proper for carrying into Execution the foregoing Powers." Not until several decades after the Founding did the Supreme Court allow Congress to exercise the power granted in this **necessary and proper clause**, but as we shall see later in this chapter, this doctrine allowed the national government to expand considerably the scope of its authority, although the process was a slow one. In addition to these expressed and implied powers, the Constitution affirmed the power of the national government in the supremacy clause (Article VI), which made all national laws and treaties "the supreme Law of the Land."

The Powers of State Government

One way in which the framers sought to preserve a strong role for the states was through the Tenth Amendment to the Constitution. The Tenth Amendment states

federalism a system of government in which power is divided, by a constitution, between a central government and regional governments

unitary system a centralized government system in which lower levels of government have little power independent of the national government

expressed powers specific powers granted by the Constitution to Congress (Article I, Section 8) and to the president (Article II)

implied powers powers derived from the necessary and proper clause of Article I, Section 8, of the Constitution; such powers are not specifically expressed but are implied through the expansive interpretation of delegated powers

necessary and proper clause Article I, Section 8, of the Constitution, which provides Congress with the authority to make all laws "necessary and proper" to carry out its expressed powers

TABLE 3.1

The Presence of Federal, State, and Local Government in the Daily Life of a Student at "State University"

TIME	SCHEDULE	LEVEL OF GOVERNMENT
7:00 A.M.	Wake up. Standard time set by the national government.	Federal and state
7:10 A.M.	Shower. Water courtesy of local government, either a public entity or a regulated private company.	Local
7:18 A.M.	Brush your teeth with toothpaste whose cavity-fighting claims have been verified by a federal agency.	Federal
7:30 A.M.	Have a bowl of cereal with milk for breakfast. "Nutrition Facts" on food labels are a federal requirement, pasteurization of milk required by state law, freshness dating on milk based on state and federal standards.	Federal and state
7:57 A.M.	Recycle the empty cereal box and milk carton.	State or local
8:30 A.M.	Drive or take public transportation to campus. Air bags and seat belts required by federal and state laws. Roads and bridges paid for by state and local governments, speed and traffic laws set by state and local governments, public transportation subsidized by all levels of government.	Federal, state, and local
8:45 A.M.	Arrive on campus of large public university. Buildings are 70 percent financed by state taxpayers.	State
9:00 A.M.	First class: Chemistry 101. Tuition partially paid by a federal loan (more than half the cost of university instruction is paid for by taxpayers), chemistry lab paid for with grants from the National Science Foundation (a federal agency) and smaller grants from business corporations made possible by federal income tax deductions for charitable contributions.	Federal
2:00 P.M.	Second class: American Government 101 (your favorite class!). You may be taking this class because it is required by the state legislature or because it fulfills a university requirement.	State
4:00 P.M.	Third class: Computer Lab. Free computers, software, and Internet access courtesy of state subsidies plus grants and discounts from IBM and Microsoft, the costs of which are deducted from their corporate income taxes; Internet built in part by federal government. Duplication of software prohibited by federal copyright laws.	Federal and state
6:00 P.M.	Eat dinner: hamburger and french fries. Meat inspected for bacteria by federal agencies.	Federal
7:00 P.M.	Work at part-time job at the campus library. Minimum wage set by federal government; some states and cities set a higher minimum. Books and journals in library paid for by state taxpayers.	Federal, state, local
8:15 P.M.	Go online to check the status of your application for a federal student loan (FAFSA) on the Department of Education's website at studentaid.ed.gov.	Federal
10:00 P.M.	Go home. Street lighting paid for by county and city governments, police patrols by city government.	Local
10:15 P.M.	Watch Netflix. Broadband Internet service regulated by federal government. Check app for tomorrow's weather. Weather forecast provided by a federal agency.	Federal
10:45 P.M.	To complete your economics homework, visit the Bureau of Labor Statistics at www.bls.gov to look up unemployment levels since 1972.	Federal
Midnight	Put out the trash before going to bed. Trash collected by city sanitation department, financed by "user charges."	Local

that the powers the Constitution does not delegate to the national government or prohibit to the states are "reserved to the States respectively, or to the people." The Antifederalists, who feared that a strong central government would encroach on individual liberty, repeatedly pressed for such an amendment as a way of limiting national power. Federalists agreed to the amendment because they did not think it would do much harm, given the powers of the Constitution already granted to the national government. The Tenth Amendment is also called the "**reserved powers** amendment" because it aims to reserve powers to the states.

reserved powers powers, derived from the Tenth Amendment to the Constitution, that are not specifically delegated to the national government or denied to the states

The most fundamental power that the states retain is that of coercion—the power to develop and enforce criminal codes, to administer health and safety rules, and to regulate the family via marriage and divorce laws. These issues touch closely on state and local values, which the Founders saw as appropriately differing from state to state (see Figure 3.1). States also have the power to regulate individuals' livelihoods; if you're a doctor or a lawyer or a plumber or a barber, you must be licensed by the state. Even more fundamentally, the states have the power to define private property—private property exists because state laws against trespass define who is and is not entitled to use a piece of property. If you own a car, your owner-ship isn't worth much unless the state is willing to enforce your right to possession by making it a crime for anyone else to drive your car without your consent. These are fundamental matters, and the powers of the states regarding these domestic issues are much greater than the powers of the national government.

A state's authority to regulate these fundamental matters is commonly referred to as the **police power** of the state and encompasses the state's power to regulate the health, safety, welfare, and morals of its citizens. Policing is what states do—they coerce you in the name of the community in order to maintain public order. And this was exactly the type of power that the Founders intended the states, not the federal government, to exercise.

police power power reserved to the state government to regulate the health, safety, and morals of its citizens

In some areas, the states share **concurrent powers** with the national government, whereby they retain and share some power to regulate commerce and affect the currency—for example, by being able to charter banks, grant or deny corporate charters, grant or deny licenses to engage in a business or practice a trade, regulate the quality of products or the conditions of labor, and levy taxes. Wherever there is a direct conflict of laws between the federal and the state levels, the issue will most likely be resolved in favor of national supremacy.

concurrent powers authority possessed by *both* state and national governments, such as the power to levy taxes

States' Obligations to One Another

The Constitution also creates obligations among the states. These obligations, spelled out in Article IV, were intended to promote national unity. By requiring the states to recognize actions and decisions taken in other states as legal and proper, the framers aimed to make the states less like independent countries and more like components of a single nation.

Article IV, Section 1, calls for "Full Faith and Credit" among states, meaning that each state is normally expected to honor the "Public Acts, Records, and Judicial Proceedings" that take place in any other state. So, for example, if a person has a re-straining order placed on a stalker or batterer in one state, other states are required to enforce that order as if they had issued it.

Notwithstanding, some courts have found exceptions to the **full faith and credit clause**: if a law is against the "strong public policy" of a state, that state may not be obligated to recognize it—even if it has been sanctioned by other states.[2] A look

full faith and credit clause provision from Article IV, Section 1, of the Constitution requiring that the states normally honor the public acts and judicial decisions that take place in another state

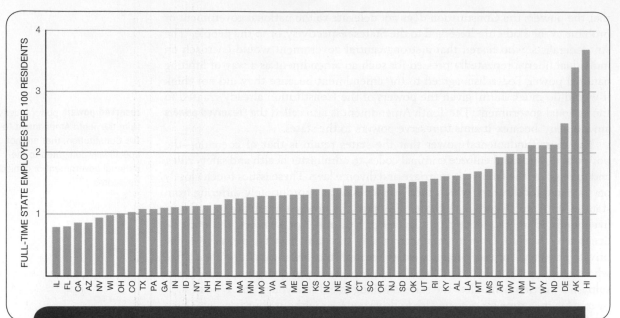

FIGURE 3.1

The Size of State Governments

The Founders believed that local needs and values varied from state to state and thus left many powers and responsibilities to state governments rather than the national government. State governments vary substantially in their relative size (how many state employees per 100 residents). How might these differences reflect differing needs and values?

SOURCES: U.S. Census Bureau, 2014 Annual Survey of Public Employment and Payroll, www.census.gov/govs/apes/index.html (accessed 4/12/16); U.S. Census Bureau, "Table 1. Annual Estimates of the Resident Population for the United States, Regions, States, and Puerto Rico: April 1, 2010 to July 1, 2014 (NST-EST2014-01)," www.census.gov/popest/data/state/totals/2014/ (accessed 4/12/16).

at the history of interracial marriage, for example, offers some perspective on how much leeway states have to recognize marriages performed in other states. In 1952, 30 states prohibited interracial marriage. Many of the states that prohibited interracial marriage also refused to recognize such marriages performed in other states.[3] For example, in the 1967 *Loving v. Virginia* case, which successfully challenged the ban on interracial marriage, the Lovings (a black woman and a white man) were married in the District of Columbia. However, when they returned to their home state of Virginia, which prohibited interracial marriage, the state refused to recognize them as a married couple.[4]

Until recently, same-sex marriage was in a similar position to interracial marriage half a century ago. Thirty-five states had passed "Defense of Marriage Acts" or had adopted constitutional amendments that defined marriage as a union between one man and one woman. Anxious to show its disapproval of gay marriage, Congress passed the Defense of Marriage Act in 1996, which declared that states would not have to recognize a same-sex marriage from another state. The act also said that the federal government would not recognize same-sex marriage—even if it were legal under state law—and that same-sex marriage partners would not be eligible for the federal benefits, such as Medicare and Social Security, normally available to spouses.[5] In 2013, however, the Supreme Court in *United States v. Windsor* struck down the Defense of Marriage Act in part, requiring that same-sex married couples receive equal treatment on issues relating to taxes, inheritance, and other federal laws.[6] After *Windsor*, many state courts struck down the state bans on same-sex marriage.

On the second anniversary of the *Windsor* ruling, the Supreme Court, in a historic and long-awaited decision, ruled in June 2015 that the Fourteenth Amendment guaranteed a fundamental right to same-sex marriage. The case, *Obergefell v. Hodges*, combined four lawsuits by same-sex couples challenging their home states' refusals to grant same-sex marriage licenses or recognize same-sex marriages performed out of state.[7] While 37 states recognized same-sex marriage on the eve of the *Obergefell* announcement, the Court's 5–4 decision immediately required that number to jump to 50: all states must offer marriage licenses to two people of the same sex and recognize same-sex marriages licensed out of state. In one stroke, same-sex marriage turned from a state-level policy choice to a nationally recognized right. In the aftermath of the *Obergefell* decision, several of the 13 states that were mandated to lift their bans on same-sex marriage protested the ruling. Ken Paxton, the attorney general of Texas, for example, called the decision "unlawful" and pledged to provide legal assistance to local officials who refused to carry out the new law.[8] However, such resistance ebbed as it became clear that the courts would enforce the constitutional right to same-sex marriage.

Article IV, Section 2, known as the "comity clause," also seeks to promote national unity. It provides that citizens enjoying the **privileges and immunities** of one state should be entitled to similar treatment in other states. What this has come to mean is that a state cannot discriminate against someone from another state or give special privileges to its own residents. For example, in the 1970s, when Alaska passed a law that gave residents preference over nonresidents in obtaining work on the state's oil and gas pipelines, the Supreme Court ruled the law illegal because it discriminated against citizens of other states.[9] The comity clause also regulates criminal justice among the states by requiring states to return fugitives to the states from which they have fled. Thus, in 1952, when an inmate escaped from an Alabama prison and sought to avoid being returned to Alabama on the grounds that he was being subjected to "cruel and unusual punishment" there, the Supreme Court ruled that he must be returned according to Article IV, Section 2.[10] This example highlights the difference between the obligations among states and those among different countries. For example, in 2013, Russia refused to extradite Edward Snowden, a government contractor who leaked important intelligence documents about U.S. government spying. Although the Justice Department stated that it would not seek the death penalty for Snowden, Russia declined to hand Snowden over to American authorities. The Constitution clearly forbids states from doing something similarly.

States' relationships with one another are also governed by the interstate compact clause (Article I, Section 10), which states that "No State shall, without the Consent of Congress . . . enter into any Agreement or Compact with another State." The Court has interpreted the clause to mean that states may enter into agreements with one another, subject to congressional approval. Compacts are a way for two or more states to reach a legally binding agreement about how to solve a problem that crosses state lines. In the early years of the republic, states turned to compacts primarily to settle border disputes. Today compacts are used for a wide range of issues but are especially important in regulating the distribution

Previously a state-level policy, same-sex marriage was declared a fundamental right nationwide by the Supreme Court in 2015. The decision prompted a brief backlash when clerks in some states refused to issue marriage licenses to same-sex couples.

privileges and immunities clause provision, from Article IV, Section 2, of the Constitution, that a state cannot discriminate against someone from another state or give its own residents special privileges

TABLE 3.2

90,107 Governments in the United States

TYPE	NUMBER
National	1
State	50
County	3,031
Municipal	19,519
Townships	16,360
School districts	12,880
Other special districts	38,266

SOURCE: U.S. Census Bureau, www2.census.gov/govs/cog/g12_org.pdf (accessed 11/2/13).

of river water, addressing environmental concerns, and operating transportation systems that cross state lines.[11] One unusual use of the interstate compact is the effort to enact the National Popular Vote compact. Initiated after George W. Bush won the presidency without winning the popular vote, the compact aims to make the popular vote, not the electoral college results, the criterion for victory. In signing the compact, a state agrees to award all its electoral college votes to the winner of the national popular vote. The measure has thus far failed to win sufficient support: by 2015, with 10 states and the District of Columbia supporting the compact, the movement had obtained only 61 percent of the 270 electoral votes needed for it to be effective.[12]

Local Government and the Constitution

Local government occupies a peculiar but very important place in the American system (see Table 3.2). In fact, the status of American local government is probably unique in world experience. First, it must be pointed out that local government has no status in the U.S. Constitution. *State* legislatures created local governments, and *state* constitutions and laws permit local governments to take on some of the responsibilities of the state governments. Local governments have always been subject to ultimate control by the states. This imbalance of power means that state governments could legally dissolve local governments or force multiple local governments to consolidate into one large locality. Most states amended their own constitutions to give their larger cities **home rule**—a guarantee of noninterference in various areas of local affairs. But local governments enjoy no such recognition and have no protected standing at all in the federal Constitution.[13]

Local governments became administratively important in the early years of the Republic because the states possessed little administrative capability. They relied on local governments—cities and counties—to implement state laws. Local government was an alternative to a statewide bureaucracy.

home rule power delegated by the state to a local unit of government to manage its own affairs

● The Changing Relationship between the Federal Government and the States

Consider how the relationship between the federal and state governments has changed over time

At the time of the Founding, the states far surpassed the federal government in their power to influence the lives of ordinary Americans. In the system of shared powers between the states and the federal government, the states were most active in economic and social regulation, while the federal government took a much more hands-off approach. Even so, the federal government gradually expanded its powers in the wake of important Supreme Court decisions. However, it was not until the New Deal in the 1930s that the federal government gained vast new powers.

Restraining National Power with Dual Federalism

As we have noted, the Constitution created two layers of government: the national government and the state governments. The consequences of this **dual federalism** are fundamental to the American system of government in theory and in practice; they have meant that states have done most of the fundamental governing. For evidence, look at Table 3.3, which lists the major types of public policies by which Americans were governed for the first century and a half under the Constitution. We call it the "traditional system" because it prevailed for much of American history and because it closely approximates the intentions of the framers of the Constitution.

Under the traditional system, the national government was quite small compared with both the state governments and the governments of other Western nations. Not only was it smaller than most governments of that time, but in fact it was also very narrowly specialized in the functions it performed. The national government built or sponsored the construction of roads, canals, and bridges (internal improvements). It provided cash subsidies to shippers and shipbuilders and distributed free or low-priced public land to encourage western settlement and business ventures. It placed relatively heavy taxes on imported goods (tariffs),

dual federalism the system of government that prevailed in the United States from 1789 to 1937 in which most fundamental governmental powers were shared between the federal and state governments

---

TABLE 3.3

The Federal System: Specialization of Governmental Functions in the Traditional System, 1789–1937

NATIONAL GOVERNMENT POLICIES (DOMESTIC)	STATE GOVERNMENT POLICIES	LOCAL GOVERNMENT POLICIES
Internal improvements	Property laws (including slavery)	Adaptation of state laws to local conditions
Subsidies	Estate and inheritance laws	Public works
Tariffs	Commerce laws	Contracts for public works
Public land disposal	Banking and credit laws	Licensing of public accommodation
Patents	Corporate laws	Zoning and other land-use regulation
Currency	Insurance laws	Basic public services
	Family laws	
	Morality laws	
	Public health laws	
	Education laws	
	General penal laws	
	Eminent domain laws	
	Construction codes	
	Land-use laws	
	Water and mineral laws	
	Criminal procedure laws	
	Electoral and political party laws	
	Local government laws	
	Civil service laws	
	Occupations and professions laws	

not only to raise revenues but also to protect "infant industries" from competition from the more advanced European enterprises. It protected patents and provided for a common currency, which encouraged and facilitated enterprises and expanded markets.

What do these functions of the national government reveal? First, virtually all the functions were aimed at assisting commerce. It is quite appropriate to refer to the traditional American system as a "commercial republic." Second, virtually none of the national government's policies directly coerced citizens. The emphasis of governmental programs was on assistance, promotion, and encouragement—the allocation of land or capital to meet the needs of economic development.

Meanwhile, state legislatures were also actively involved in economic regulation during the nineteenth century. In the United States, then and now, private property exists only in state laws and state court decisions regarding property, trespass, and real estate. American capitalism took its form from state property and trespass laws and from state laws and court decisions regarding contracts, markets, credit, banking, incorporation, and insurance. Laws concerning slavery were a subdivision of property law in states where slavery existed, though Article I, Section 2 of the Constitution (known as the fugitive slave clause) ensured that slavery would be protected even in free states. This clause obliged free states to return runaway slaves to the state from which they escaped. The practice of important professions, such as law and medicine, was (and is) illegal except as provided for by state law. To educate or not to educate a child has been a decision governed more by state laws than by parents. It is important to note also that until recent decades, virtually all criminal laws—regarding everything from trespass to murder—have been state laws. Since 1970, there has been a considerable growth in the number of federal criminal laws adopted by Congress, many of which overlap existing state laws.[14] Roughly 40 percent of the federal criminal statutes passed since the Civil War were enacted between 1970 and 1998.[15]

All this (and more, as shown in the middle column of Table 3.3) demonstrates that most of the fundamental governing in the United States was done by the

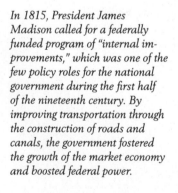

In 1815, President James Madison called for a federally funded program of "internal improvements," which was one of the few policy roles for the national government during the first half of the nineteenth century. By improving transportation through the construction of roads and canals, the government fostered the growth of the market economy and boosted federal power.

states. The contrast between national and state policies, as shown by Table 3.3, demonstrates the difference in the power vested in each. The list of items in the middle column could actually have been made longer. Moreover, each item on the list is a category of law that fills many volumes of statutes and court decisions.

By allowing state governments to do most of the fundamental governing, the Constitution saved the national government from many policy decisions that might have proven too divisive for a large and very young country. There is little doubt that if the Constitution had provided for a unitary rather than a federal system, the war over slavery would have come in 1789 or not long thereafter rather than in 1861; and if it had come that early, the South might very well have seceded and established a separate, slaveholding nation. In helping the national government remain small and aloof from the most divisive issues of the day, federalism contributed significantly to the political stability of the nation, even as the social, economic, and political systems of many of the states and regions of the country were undergoing tremendous, profound, and sometimes violent change.[16] The most fundamental impact of federalism on the way the United States is governed comes not from any particular provision of the Constitution but from the framework itself, which has determined which level of government does what and, through that, the political development of the country. As we shall see, some important aspects of federalism have changed, but the federal framework has survived two centuries and a devastating civil war.

Federalism and the Slow Growth of the National Government's Power

As the nation grew, disputes arose about the powers of the federal government versus the powers of the states. In the first several decades after the Founding, the Supreme Court decided several critical cases that expanded federal powers and facilitated trade across the states. These decisions removed barriers to trade in the new nation and laid the groundwork for a national economy. However, by the end of the nineteenth century, as reformers began to enact laws regulating businesses through such measures as child labor restrictions, the Court took a much more restrictive view of federal power. Not until well into the New Deal in 1937 did the federal government gain the expansive powers it exercises today.

The Supreme Court's early decisions to expand federal power rested on its pro-national interpretation of Article I, Section 8 of the Constitution. That article enumerates the powers of Congress, including the power to tax, raise an army, declare war, establish post offices, and "regulate commerce with foreign nations, and among the several States and with the Indian tribes." This **commerce clause** would later form the basis for expansive federal government control over the economy, but its scope initially remained unclear.

The Court's early decisions began to define national power by favoring federal control over the economy when there was a conflict between the states and the federal government. The first and most important such case was *McCulloch v. Maryland* (1819), which involved the question of whether Congress had the power to charter a national bank—an explicit grant of power nowhere to be found in Article I, Section 8.[17] Chief Justice John Marshall answered that this power could be "implied" from other powers that were expressly delegated to Congress, such as the "powers to lay and collect taxes; to borrow money; to regulate commerce; and to declare and conduct a war." Marshall's decision rested on "the necessary and

commerce clause Article I, Section 8, of the Constitution, which delegates to Congress the power "to regulate commerce with foreign nations, and among the several States and with the Indian tribes"; this clause was interpreted by the Supreme Court in favor of national power over the economy

In 1916, the national government passed the Keating-Owen Child Labor Act, which excluded from interstate commerce all goods manufactured by children under age 14. The act was ruled unconstitutional by the Supreme Court, and the regulation of child labor remained in the hands of state governments until the 1930s.

proper clause" of Article I, Section 8, which gave Congress the power to enact laws "necessary and proper" for executing its substantive powers.

By allowing Congress to use the necessary and proper clause to interpret its delegated powers expansively, the Supreme Court created the potential for an unprecedented increase in national government power. Marshall also concluded that whenever a state law conflicted with a federal law (as in *McCulloch*), the state law would be deemed invalid since the Constitution states that "the Laws of the United States . . . shall be the supreme Law of the Land." Both parts of this great case are pro-national, yet Congress did not immediately seek to expand the policies of the national government.

Another major case, *Gibbons v. Ogden* (1824), reinforced this nationalistic interpretation of the Constitution. The important but relatively narrow issue was whether the state of New York could grant a monopoly to Robert Fulton's steamboat company to operate an exclusive service between New York and New Jersey. Chief Justice Marshall argued that New York state did not have the power to grant this particular monopoly, so Marshall had to define what Article I, Section 8 meant by "commerce among the several states." He insisted that the definition was "comprehensive," extending to "every species of commercial intercourse." However, this comprehensiveness was limited "to that commerce which concerns more states than one." *Gibbons* is important because it established the supremacy of the national government in all matters affecting what later came to be called "interstate commerce."[18] But the precise meaning of interstate commerce would remain uncertain during several decades of constitutional discourse. Backed by the implied-powers decision in *McCulloch* and by the broad definition of "interstate commerce" in *Gibbons*, Article I, Section 8 was a source of power for the national government as long as Congress sought to facilitate commerce through subsidies, services, and land grants.

Later in the nineteenth century, though, any effort of the national government to *regulate* commerce in such areas as fraud, the production of substandard goods, the use of child labor, or the existence of dangerous working conditions or long hours was declared unconstitutional by the Supreme Court as a violation of the concept of interstate commerce. Such legislation meant that the federal government was entering the factory and the workplace—local areas—and was attempting to regulate goods that had not yet passed into interstate commerce. To enter these local workplaces was to exercise police power—a power reserved to the states. No one questioned the power of the national government to regulate businesses that intrinsically involved interstate commerce, such as railroads, gas pipelines, and waterway transportation. But well into the twentieth century the Supreme Court used the concept of interstate commerce as a barrier against most efforts by Congress to regulate local conditions.

This aspect of federalism prevailed during an epoch of tremendous economic development, the period between the Civil War and the 1930s. It gave the American economy a freedom from federal government control that closely approximated the ideal of free enterprise. The economy was never entirely free, of course; in fact, entrepreneurs themselves did not want complete freedom from government. They needed law and order. They needed a stable currency. They needed courts and police to enforce contracts and prevent trespass. They needed roads, canals, and railroads. But federalism, as interpreted by the Supreme Court for 70 years after the Civil War, made it possible for business to have its cake and eat it, too: entrepreneurs enjoyed the benefits of national policies facilitating commerce and were protected by the courts from policies regulating commerce by protecting the rights of consumers and workers.[19]

All this changed after 1937, when the Supreme Court issued a series of decisions that laid the groundwork for a much stronger federal government. Most significant was the Court's dramatic expansion of the commerce clause. By throwing out the old distinction between interstate and intrastate commerce, the Court converted the commerce clause from a source of limitations to a source of power for the national government. The Court upheld acts of Congress protecting the rights of employees to organize and engage in collective bargaining, regulating the amount of farmland in cultivation, extending low-interest credit to small businesses and farmers, and restricting the activities of corporations dealing in the stock market.[20] The Court also upheld many other laws that contributed to the construction of the "welfare state." With these rulings, the Court decisively signaled that the era of dual federalism was over. In the future, Congress would have very broad powers to regulate activity in the states.

The Changing Role of the States

As we have seen, the Constitution's commerce clause contained the seeds of a very expansive national government. However, for much of the nineteenth century, federal power remained limited. The Tenth Amendment was used to bolster arguments in favor of **states' rights**, which in their extreme version claimed that the states did not have to submit to national laws whenever they believed the national government had exceeded its authority. Prior to the Civil War, sharp differences between the North and the South over tariffs and slavery gave rise to arguments supporting nullification. Most fully articulated by John C. Calhoun, vice

states' rights the principle that the states should oppose the increasing authority of the national government; this principle was most popular in the period before the Civil War

John C. Calhoun, one of the most prominent advocates of states' rights, argued that states should have the right to veto any federal law they found to be unconstitutional.

president under Andrew Jackson and later a senator from South Carolina, the doctrine of nullification proposed that states were not bound by federal laws that they considered unconstitutional. Such arguments were voiced less often after the Civil War, but the Supreme Court continued to use the Tenth Amendment to strike down laws that it thought exceeded national power, including the Civil Rights Act passed in 1875.

In the early twentieth century, however, reformers began to press for national regulations to limit the power of large corporations and to preserve the health and welfare of citizens. The Supreme Court approved some of these laws, but it struck down others, including a law combating child labor. The Court stated that the law violated the Tenth Amendment because only states should have the power to regulate conditions of employment. By the late 1930s, however, the Supreme Court had approved such an expansion of federal power that the Tenth Amendment appeared irrelevant. The desire to promote equal working conditions across the country had elevated the federal government over the states. In fact, in 1941, Justice Harlan Fiske Stone declared that the Tenth Amendment was simply a "truism," that it had no real meaning.[21]

Yet the idea that some powers should be reserved to the states did not go away. One reason is that groups with substantive policy interests often support states' rights as a means for achieving their policy goals. For example, in the 1950s, southern opponents of the civil rights movement revived the idea of states' rights to support racial segregation. In 1956, 96 southern members of Congress issued a "Southern manifesto" in which they declared that southern states were not constitutionally bound by Supreme Court decisions outlawing racial segregation. They believed that states' rights should override individual rights to liberty and formal equality. With the eventual triumph of the civil rights movement, the slogan of "states' rights" became tarnished by its association with racial inequality.

The 1990s saw a revival of interest in the Tenth Amendment and important Supreme Court decisions limiting federal power. Much of the interest in the Tenth Amendment stemmed from conservatives who believed that a strong federal government encroached on individual liberties. They believed such freedoms were better protected by returning more power to the states through the process of devolution. In 1996, Bob Dole, the Republican presidential candidate, carried a copy of the Tenth Amendment in his pocket as he campaigned, pulling it out to read aloud at rallies.[22] The Supreme Court's 1995 ruling in *United States v. Lopez* fueled further interest in the Tenth Amendment.[23] In that case, the Court, stating that Congress had exceeded its authority under the commerce clause, struck down a federal law that barred handguns near schools. This was the first time since the New Deal that the Court had limited congressional powers in this way. In 1997 the Court again relied on the Tenth Amendment to limit federal power in *Printz v. United States.*[24] The decision declared unconstitutional a provision of the Brady Handgun Violence Prevention Act that required state and local law-enforcement officials to conduct background checks on handgun purchasers. The Court declared that this provision violated state sovereignty guaranteed by the Tenth Amendment because it required state and local officials to administer a federal regulatory program.

for critical analysis

How have Supreme Court decisions affected the balance of power between the federal government and the states? Has the Supreme Court favored the federal government or the states?

In 1995, the Supreme Court ruled that the Gun-Free School Zones Act was an unconstitutional application of the commerce clause, leaving this area of regulation to the states. In striking down a federal law, the Supreme Court ruled that regulating guns near schools is a state prerogative.

Thus, the expansion of the power of the national government has not left the states powerless. State governments continue to make important laws. No better demonstration of the continuing influence of the federal framework can be offered than that in the middle column of Table 3.2, which is still a fairly accurate characterization of state government today. In each of these domains, however, states must now share power with the federal government.

● Who Does What? Public Spending and the Expanding Federal Framework

Trace developments in the federal framework leading to a stronger national government

Questions about how to divide responsibilities between the states and the national government first arose more than 200 years ago, when the framers wrote the Constitution to create a stronger union. But they did not solve the issue of who should do what. There is no "right" answer to that question; each generation of Americans has provided its own answer. In recent decades, many Americans have grown distrustful of the federal government and have supported giving more responsibility to the states.[25] Even so, they still want the federal government to set standards, promote equality, and provide security.

In political debates about the division of responsibility, some people argue for a strong federal role to set national standards, whereas others say the states should do more. These two goals are not necessarily at odds. The key is to find the right balance. In this section we will look at how the balance has shifted, and then we will consider current efforts to reshape the relationship between the national government and the states.

The New Deal

The door to increased federal action opened when states proved unable to cope with the demands brought on by the Great Depression of the 1930s. Before this national economic catastrophe, states and localities took responsibility for addressing the needs of the poor, usually through private charity. But the extent of the need created by the depression quickly exhausted local and state capacities. By 1932, 25 percent of the workforce was unemployed. The jobless lost their homes and settled into camps all over the country, called "Hoovervilles," after President Herbert Hoover. Elected in 1928, the year before the depression hit, Hoover steadfastly maintained that the federal government could do little to alleviate the misery caused by the depression. It was a matter for state and local governments, he said.

Yet demands mounted for the federal government to take action. In Congress, some Democrats proposed that

The New Deal expanded the scope of the federal government. One of the largest and most effective New Deal programs, the Works Progress Administration (WPA) employed millions of Americans in projects such as constructing highways, bridges, and public parks.

the federal government finance public works to aid the economy and put people back to work. Other members of Congress introduced legislation to provide federal grants to the states to assist them in their relief efforts. Most of these measures failed to win congressional approval or were vetoed by President Hoover.

When Franklin Delano Roosevelt took office in 1933, he energetically threw the federal government into the business of fighting the depression through a number of proposals known collectively as the New Deal. He proposed a variety of temporary measures to provide federal relief and work programs. Most of the programs he proposed were to be financed by the federal government but administered by the states. In addition to these temporary measures, Roosevelt presided over the creation of several important federal programs designed to provide future economic security for Americans. The New Deal signaled the rise of a more active national government.

Federal Grants

grants-in-aid programs through which Congress provides money to state and local governments on the condition that the funds be employed for purposes defined by the federal government

For the most part, the new national programs that the Roosevelt administration developed did not directly take power away from the states. Instead, the national government typically redirected states by offering them **grants-in-aid**, whereby Congress appropriates money to state and local governments on the condition that the money be spent for a particular purpose defined by Congress (see Figure 3.2). Franklin Roosevelt's New Deal expanded the range of grants-in-aid into social programs, providing grants to the states for financial assistance to poor children. Congress added more grants after World War II, creating new programs to help states fund activities such as providing school lunches and building highways. Sometimes the national government required state or local governments to match the national contribution dollar for dollar, but in some programs, such as the development of the interstate highway system, the congressional grants provided 90 percent of the cost of the program.

categorical grants congressional grants given to states and localities on the condition that expenditures be limited to a problem or group specified by law

These types of federal grants-in-aid are also called **categorical grants** because the national government determines the purposes, or categories, for which the money can be used. For the most part, the categorical grants created before the 1960s simply helped the states perform their traditional functions.[26] During the 1960s, however, the national role expanded and the number of categorical grants increased dramatically. For example, during the 89th Congress (1965–66) alone, the number of categorical grant-in-aid programs grew from 221 to 379.[27] The *value* of categorical grants also has risen dramatically, increasing from $2.3 billion in 1950 to an estimated $667 billion in 2016. The grants authorized during the 1960s announced national purposes much more strongly than did earlier grants. One of the most important—and expensive—was the federal Medicaid program, which provides states with grants to pay for medical care for the poor, the disabled, and many nursing home residents.

project grants grant programs in which state and local governments submit proposals to federal agencies and for which funding is provided on a competitive basis

formula grants grants-in-aid in which a formula is used to determine the amount of federal funds a state or local government will receive

Many of the categorical grants enacted during the 1960s were **project grants**, which require state and local governments to submit proposals to federal agencies. In contrast to the older **formula grants**, which used a formula (composed of such elements as need and state and local capacities) to distribute funds, the project grants made funding available on a competitive basis. Federal agencies would give grants to the proposals they judged to be the best. In this way, the national government acquired substantial control over which state and local governments got money, how much they got, and how they spent it.

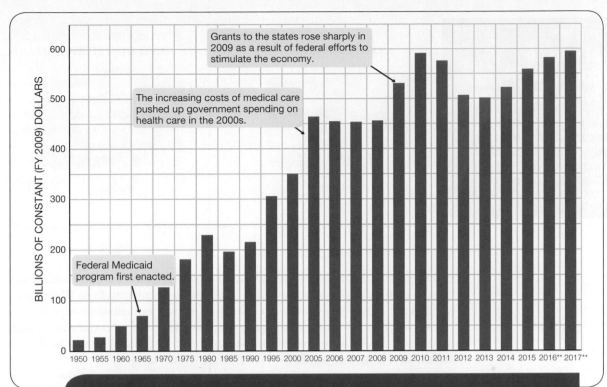

FIGURE 3.2

Historical Trend of Federal Grants-in-Aid,* 1950–2017

Spending on federal grants-in-aid to the states and local governments has grown dramatically since 1990. These increases reflect the growing public expectations about what government should do. What has been the most important cause of the steady increase in these grants?

*Excludes outlays for national defense, international affairs, and net interest.

**Estimate.

SOURCES: Office of Management and Budget, U.S. Budget for Fiscal Year 2017, "Historical Tables: Table 12.2, Total Outlays for Grants to State and Local Governments, by Function and Fund Group: 1940-2021," www.whitehouse.gov/omb/budget/Historicals (accessed 4/12/16); Office of Management and Budget, U.S. Budget for Fiscal Year 2017, "Historical Tables: Table 10.1, Gross Domestic Product and Deflators Used in the Historical Tables: 1940–2021," www.whitehouse.gov/omb/budget/Historicals (accessed 4/12/16).

Cooperative Federalism

The growth of categorical grants created a new kind of federalism. If the traditional system of two sovereigns performing highly different functions could be called dual federalism, historians of federalism suggest that the system since the New Deal could be called **cooperative federalism**. The political scientist Morton Grodzins characterized this as a move from "layer cake federalism" to "marble cake federalism,"[28] in which intergovernmental cooperation and sharing have blurred a once-clear distinguishing line, making it difficult to say where the national government ends and the state and local governments begin (see Figure 3.3). Figure 3.4 demonstrates the financial basis of the "marble-cake" idea.

For a while in the 1960s, however, it appeared as if the state governments would become increasingly irrelevant to American federalism. Many of the new federal

cooperative federalism a type of federalism existing since the New Deal era in which grants-in-aid have been used strategically to encourage states and localities (without commanding them) to pursue nationally defined goals; also known as *intergovernmental cooperation*

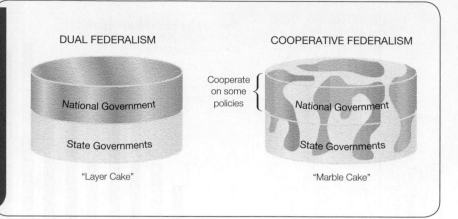

FIGURE 3.3

Dual versus Cooperative Federalism

In layer-cake federalism, the responsibilities of the national government and state governments are clearly separated. In marble-cake federalism, national policies, state policies, and local policies overlap in many areas.

DUAL FEDERALISM

National Government

State Governments

"Layer Cake"

Cooperate on some policies

COOPERATIVE FEDERALISM

National Government

State Governments

"Marble Cake"

grants bypassed the states and instead sent money directly to local governments and even to local nonprofit organizations. The theme heard repeatedly in Washington was that the states simply could not be trusted to carry out national purposes.[29]

One of the reasons that Washington distrusted the states was the way African American citizens were treated in the South. The southern states' forthright defense of segregation, justified on the grounds of states' rights, helped tarnish the image of the states as the civil rights movement gained momentum. The national officials who planned the War on Poverty during the 1960s pointed to the racially exclusionary practices of the southern states as a reason for bypassing state governments. The political scientist James Sundquist described how this thinking affected the War on Poverty: "In the drafting of the Economic Opportunity Act, an 'Alabama syndrome' developed. Any suggestion within the poverty task force that the states be given a role in the administration of the act was met with the question, 'Do you want to give that kind of power to [then–Alabama governor] George Wallace?'"[30]

Yet even though many national policies of the 1960s bypassed the states, other new programs, such as Medicaid—the health program for the poor—relied on state governments for their implementation. In addition, as the national government expanded existing programs run by the states, states had to take on more responsibilities. These new responsibilities meant that the states were playing a very important role in the federal system.

Regulated Federalism and National Standards

The question of who decides what each level of government should do goes to the very heart of what it means to be an American citizen. How different should things be when one crosses a state line? In what policy areas is it acceptable for states to differ? In what areas should states be similar? How much inequality among the states is acceptable? Supreme Court decisions about the fundamental rights of American citizens provide the most important answers to these questions. Over time, the Court has pushed for greater uniformity across the states. In addition to legal decisions, the national government uses two other tools to create similarities across the states: grants-in-aid and regulations.

Grants-in-aid, as we have seen, are incentives: Congress gives money to state and local governments if they agree to spend it for the purposes Congress specifies.

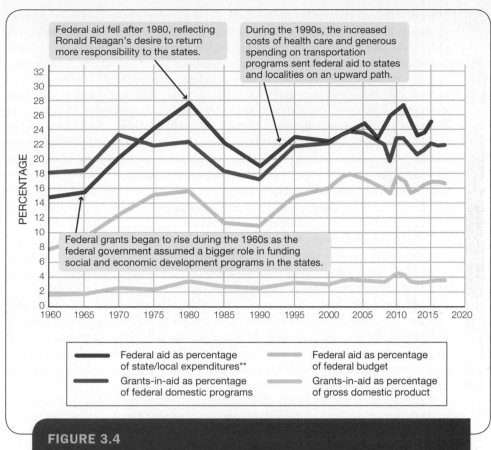

Federal aid fell after 1980, reflecting Ronald Reagan's desire to return more responsibility to the states.

During the 1990s, the increased costs of health care and generous spending on transportation programs sent federal aid to states and localities on an upward path.

Federal grants began to rise during the 1960s as the federal government assumed a bigger role in funding social and economic development programs in the states.

Legend:
- Federal aid as percentage of state/local expenditures**
- Grants-in-aid as percentage of federal domestic programs
- Federal aid as percentage of federal budget
- Grants-in-aid as percentage of gross domestic product

FIGURE 3.4

The Rise, Decline, and Recovery of Federal Aid, 1960–2017*

The level of federal aid has varied over the past several decades as program costs and politics have affected the role the national government plays in funding state and local services. The data in this figure show the rise, decline, and recovery of federal aid. What factors contributed to each of these trends?

*Excludes national defense, international affairs, net interest, and undistributed offsetting receipts. Data for 2016 and 2017 are estimated.
**Estimates for state and local expenditures in 2016 and 2017 are not available.
SOURCES: Office of Management and Budget, U.S. Budget for Fiscal Year 2017, "Analytical Perspectives: Table 15.1: Trends in Federal Grants to State and Local Governments," www.whitehouse.gov/sites/default/files/omb/budget/fy2017/assets/ap_15_state_and_local.pdf (accessed 4/13/16); Government Publishing Office, Budget of the United States Government, www.gpo.gov/fdsys/browse/collectionGPO.action?collectionCode=BUDGET (accessed 4/13/16).

But as Congress began to enact legislation in new areas, such as environmental policy, it also imposed additional regulations on states and localities. Some political scientists call this a move toward **regulated federalism**.[31] The national government began to set standards of conduct or to require the states to set standards that met national guidelines. The effect of these national standards is that state and local policies in the areas of environmental protection, social services, and education are more uniform from coast to coast than are other nationally funded policies.

regulated federalism a form of federalism in which Congress imposes legislation on states and localities, requiring them to meet national standards

Some national standards require the federal government to take over areas of regulation formerly overseen by state or local governments. Such **preemption** occurs when state and local actions are found to be inconsistent with federal requirements. In some cases, federal laws and regulations are more stringent than state laws. For example, as federal regulations proliferated after the 1970s, Washington increasingly preempted state and local action in many different policy areas. These preemptions required the states to abide by tougher federal rules in policies as diverse as air and water pollution, occupational health and safety, and access for the disabled. The regulated industries often oppose such laws because they increase the cost of doing business. After 1994, when Republicans retook control of Congress, the federal government used its preemption power in business's favor, limiting the ability of states to tax and regulate industry. For example, the Internet Tax Freedom Act, first enacted by Congress in 1998 and subsequently renewed, prohibits states and localities from taxing Internet access services.

Congress is not the only federal body that can preempt the states; federal regulatory agencies can also issue rules that override state law. One controversial case involved a 2006 Food and Drug Administration drug-labeling rule preempting state laws that allow individuals to sue drug companies in state courts. Opponents—many of them trial lawyers—charged that such rules amounted to "stealth preemption" that "will deprive consumers of their right to hold negligent corporations accountable for injuries caused by defective products."[32] Supporters claimed that the rules were a proper use of federal authority. Although the Republicans came to power promising to grant more responsibility to the states, they ended up reducing state control in many areas by preemption.

State and local governments often contest federal preemptions. For example, in 2001, Attorney General John Ashcroft declared that Oregon's law permitting doctor-assisted suicide was illegal under federal drug regulations. The state, a physician, a pharmacist, and several terminally ill state residents challenged Ashcroft's rule; and in January 2006 the Supreme Court ruled in a 6–3 vote that the attorney general did not have the authority to outlaw the Oregon law.[33] Individuals have also challenged federal preemption. In 2009 the Supreme Court ruled against a drug manufacturer and in favor of a woman whose arm had to be amputated after she was improperly injected with a drug designed to counter nausea.[34] Although the drug company knew that such complications could arise, it argued that it was not responsible for the amputation because federal regulations did not require it to warn against this danger in labeling the drug. The Court, however, found the company liable for the damage. In its decision, the Court made it clear that federal regulations could not preempt state consumer protections and that states had the power to adopt stricter protections than those of the federal government.

In 2009, after only a few months in office, President Obama reversed the George W. Bush administration's use of federal regulations to limit state laws. Under the new policy, federal regulations should preempt state laws only in extraordinary cases. The president directed agency leaders to review the regulations that had been put in place over the past 10 years and consider amending them if they interfered with the "legitimate prerogatives of the states."[35] But as we will see, the Obama administration did use its power of preemption to challenge state immigration laws, charging that states were making laws in a domain reserved for federal authority.

The growth of national standards has created some new problems and has raised questions about how far federal standardization should go. One problem that emerged in the 1980s was the increase in **unfunded mandates**—the product of a Democratic Congress that wanted to achieve liberal social objectives and

Republican presidents who opposed increased social spending. Between 1983 and 1991, Congress mandated standards in many policy areas, including social services and environmental regulations, without providing additional funds to help the states meet those standards. Altogether, Congress enacted 27 laws that imposed new regulations or required states to expand existing programs.[36] For example, the 1973 Rehabilitation Act prohibited discrimination against the disabled in programs that were partly funded by the federal government. The new law required state and local governments to make public transit accessible to disabled people with wheelchair lifts in buses, elevators in train stations, and special transportation systems where needed. These requirements were estimated to cost state and local governments $6.8 billion over 30 years.[37] But Congress did not supply additional funding to help states meet these new requirements; the states had to shoulder the increased financial burden themselves.

States and localities quickly began to protest the cost of unfunded mandates. Although it is very hard to determine the exact cost of federal regulations, the Congressional Budget Office estimated that between 1983 and 1990 new federal regulations cost states and localities between $8.9 and $12.7 billion.[38] States complained that mandates took up so much of their budgets that they were not able to set their own priorities. These burdens became part of a rallying cry to reduce the power of the federal government—a cry that took center stage when a Republican Congress was elected in 1994. One of the first measures the new Congress passed was an act to limit the cost of unfunded mandates, the Unfunded Mandates Reform Act (UMRA). Under this law, the Congressional Budget Office must assess the cost of any mandate that it believes would exceed the threshold established in UMRA ($76 million in 2014 adjusted for inflation). Bills that would impose sizable costs on the private sector must also be assessed. The goal is to ensure that Congress knows how much it is expecting of state and local governments and the private sector. Congress must identify funding sources for bills that exceed the threshold established in UMRA. Of all public laws enacted since 1996, fewer than 5 percent have included private-sector mandates with costs estimated to exceed the threshold, while fewer than 1 percent have contained intergovernmental mandates (mandates on state or local governments) with such costs.[39]

New national problems inevitably raise the question "Who pays?" Recently, concern about unfunded mandates has arisen around health care reform. The major health care reform enacted during Obama's first two years as president, the Affordable Care Act of 2010, called for a major expansion of Medicaid. But because Medicaid is partly funded by the states, any major increase in the number of Medicaid recipients could impose a significant fiscal burden on the states. Although the law provided additional federal aid to support the new requirements, the Medicaid provisions became a target for state challenges to the health care law. One of the central claims in the 26 states' lawsuits charged that the federal government did not have the power to withhold Medicaid funds from states that did not implement the new expansions.[40] The Supreme Court ultimately ruled that states could decline to expand Medicaid coverage without losing their existing Medicaid funds. After the Court's decision, 25 states, all led by Republican governors, announced that they would not implement the expanded coverage. Some began to reconsider this decision. By 2016, 32 states had decided to expand Medicaid, 2 states were debating the question, and 17 had decided to not expand Medicaid. It is clear that the Court's decision injected a whole new set of issues into the question "Who pays?"

The federal government frequently passes laws that impose mandates on the states, such as the 1990 Americans with Disabilities Act, which protects against discrimination based on disability. States were required to pay for changes to meet federal standards for accessibility in public transportation and public facilities.

for critical analysis

Should states be required to implement unfunded mandates? How much of the funding should the federal government provide for policies or standards that it sets?

● New Federalism and State Control

Analyze the developments in the federal framework since the 1970s

In 1970 the mayor of Oakland, California, told Congress that his city had 22 separate employment and training programs but that few poor residents were being trained for jobs that were available in the local labor market.[41] National programs had proliferated as Congress enacted many small grants, but little effort was made to coordinate or adapt programs to local needs. Today many governors argue for more state and local control over such national grant programs. They complain that national grants do not allow for enough local flexibility and instead take a "one-size-fits-all" approach.[42] These criticisms point to a fundamental challenge in American federalism: how to get the best results for the money spent. Do some divisions of responsibility between states and the federal government work better than others? Since the 1970s, as states became more capable of administering large-scale programs, the idea of **devolution**—transferring responsibility for policy from the federal government to the states and localities—has become popular.

devolution a policy to remove a program from one level of government by delegating it or passing it down to a lower level of government, such as from the national government to the state and local governments

Proponents of more state authority have looked to **block grants** as a way of reducing federal control. Block grants are federal grants that allow the states considerable leeway in spending federal money. President Nixon led the first push for block grants in the early 1970s, as part of his **New Federalism**. Nixon's approach consolidated programs in the areas of job training, community development, and social services into three large block grants. These grants imposed some conditions on states and localities as to how the money should be spent but not the narrow regulations contained in the categorical grants. In addition, Congress provided an important new form of federal assistance to state and local governments, called **general revenue sharing**. Revenue sharing provided money to local governments and counties with no strings attached; localities could spend the money as they wished. In enacting revenue sharing, Washington acknowledged both the critical role that state and local governments play in implementing national priorities and their need for increased funding and enhanced flexibility in order to carry out that role (see Figure 3.5). Reagan's version of New Federalism also looked to block grants. Like Nixon, Reagan wanted to reduce the national government's control and return power to the states. But unlike Nixon, whose block grants increased federal spending, Reagan's block grants cut federal funding by 12 percent. His view was that the states could spend their own funds to make up the difference, if they chose to do so. Revenue sharing was also eliminated during the Reagan administration, leaving localities to fend for themselves. In all, Congress created 12 new block grants between 1981 and 1990.[43]

block grants federal grants-in-aid that allow states considerable discretion in how the funds are spent

New Federalism attempts by presidents Nixon and Reagan to return power to the states through block grants

general revenue sharing the process by which one unit of government yields a portion of its tax income to another unit of government, according to an established formula; revenue sharing typically involves the national government providing money to state governments

The Republican Congress elected in 1994 took this strategy even further, making substantial cuts in federal programs as well as supporting block grants. Their biggest success was the 1996 welfare reform law, which delegated to states important new responsibilities. Most of the other major proposed block grants or spending reductions, however, failed to pass Congress or were vetoed by President Clinton. The Republican congressional leadership had found that it was much easier to promise a "devolution revolution" than to deliver on that promise.[44]

Neither block grants nor reduced federal funding have proven to be magic solutions to the problems of federalism. For one thing, there is always a trade-off between accountability—that is, whether the states are using funds for the purposes intended—and flexibility. If the objective is to have accountable and efficient

Government Spending in Federal and Unitary Systems

A key difference between unitary and federal systems of government is in the amount of power that is reserved for state and local governments. In federal systems, subnational units are given considerable taxation and spending power, whereas in unitary systems, the federal (or central) government carries out most of these tasks.

The graph here shows the percentage of total government expenditures by the central government and by the state and/or local governments. The central governments of France, the United Kingdom, and New Zealand, all unitary countries, spend a larger percentage than federal countries such as Mexico and the United States.

South Korea is a unitary country where local governments operate under a great deal of autonomy, carrying out many of the country's administrative functions. Local government spending in South Korea is thus higher than in many unitary countries, and, as a result, its spending behavior falls somewhere in the middle of the federal–unitary divide. This example shows that while the distinction between federalism and unitary systems is important, it is not the only factor in determining who holds power in a country.

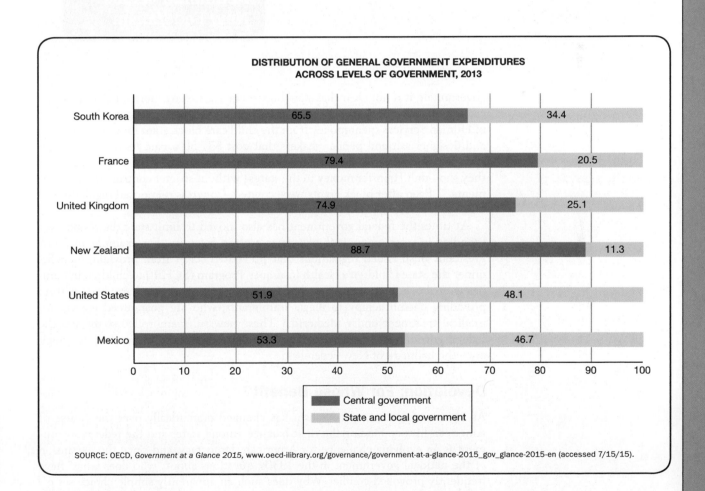

DISTRIBUTION OF GENERAL GOVERNMENT EXPENDITURES ACROSS LEVELS OF GOVERNMENT, 2013

Country	Central government	State and local government
South Korea	65.5	34.4
France	79.4	20.5
United Kingdom	74.9	25.1
New Zealand	88.7	11.3
United States	51.9	48.1
Mexico	53.3	46.7

SOURCE: OECD, *Government at a Glance 2015*, www.oecd-ilibrary.org/governance/government-at-a-glance-2015_gov_glance-2015-en (accessed 7/15/15).

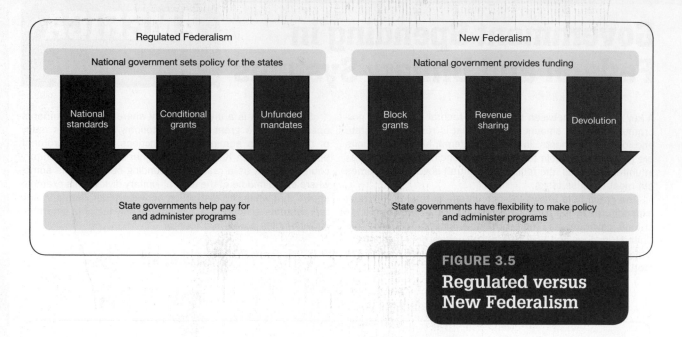

FIGURE 3.5
Regulated versus New Federalism

government, it is not clear that state bureaucracies are any more efficient or more capable than national agencies. In Mississippi, for example, the state Department of Human Services spent money from the child care block grant for office furniture and designer salt and pepper shakers that cost $37.50 a pair. As one Mississippi state legislator said, "I've seen too many years of good ol' boy politics to know they shouldn't [transfer money to the states] without stricter controls and requirements."[45] Even after block grants were created, Congress reimposed regulations in order to increase the states' accountability.

At times the federal government has also moved to limit state discretion over spending in cases where it thinks states are too generous. For example, in 2007, President Bush issued regulations that prevented states from providing benefits under the State Children's Health Insurance Program (SCHIP) to children in families well above the poverty line. The Bush administration also barred states from providing chemotherapy to illegal immigrants, who are guaranteed emergency medical treatment under Medicaid.[46] These new rules embroiled states and the federal government in sharp conflicts over state discretion in spending decisions, once the hallmark of New Federalism.

Devolution: For Whose Benefit?

As Figure 3.6 indicates, federalism has changed dramatically over the course of American history. Finding the right balance among states and the federal government is an evolving challenge for American democracy, and since the expansion of the national government in the 1930s, questions about "who does what" have frequently provoked conflict. Why does such an apparently simple choice set off such highly charged political debate? One reason is that many decisions about federal-versus-state responsibility have implications for who benefits from government action.

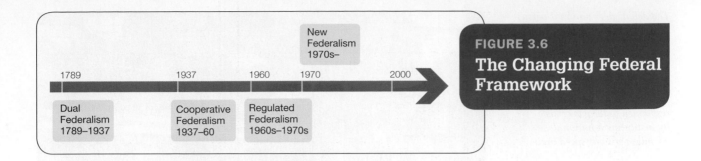

FIGURE 3.6
The Changing Federal Framework

Let's consider the benefits of federal control versus devolution in the realm of **redistributive programs**—programs designed primarily for the benefit of the poor. Many political scientists and economists maintain that states and localities should not be in charge of redistributive programs. They argue that since states and local governments have to compete with one another, they do not have the incentive to spend their money on the needy people in their areas. Instead, they want to keep taxes low and spend money on things that promote economic development.[47] In this situation, states might engage in a "race to the bottom": if one state cuts assistance to the poor, neighboring states will institute similar or deeper cuts both to reduce expenditures and to discourage poorer people from moving to their states. As one New York legislator put it, "The concern we have is that unless we make our welfare system and our tax and regulatory system competitive with the states around us, we will have too many disincentives for business to move here. Welfare is a big part of that."[48]

In 1996, when Congress enacted major welfare reform, it followed a different logic. By changing welfare from a combined federal–state program into a block grant to the states, Congress gave the states more responsibility for programs that serve the poor. Supporters of the change hoped to reduce welfare spending and argued that states could act as "laboratories of democracy" by experimenting with many different approaches in order to find those that best met the needs of their citizens.[49] As states altered their welfare programs in the wake of the new law, they did indeed design diverse approaches. For example, Minnesota adopted an incentive-based approach that offers extra assistance to families that take low-wage jobs, while six other states imposed very strict time limits on receiving benefits, allowing welfare recipients less than the five-year limit in the federal legislation. After the passage of the law, welfare rolls declined dramatically. On average, they declined by more than half from their peak in 1994; in 12 states the decline was 70 percent or higher. Politicians have cited these statistics to claim that the poor have benefited from greater state control of welfare, yet most studies have found that the majority of those leaving welfare remain in poverty.

In some decisions about federalism, local concerns are overridden in the name of the national interest. The question of speed limits, traditionally a state and local responsibility, provides an example. In 1973, at the height of the oil shortage, Congress passed legislation to withhold federal highway funds from states that did not adopt a maximum speed limit of 55 miles per hour in order to reduce fuel consumption. Although Congress had not formally taken over the authority to set speed limits, the power of its purse was so important that every state adopted the new speed limit. As the crisis faded, concern about energy conservation diminished.

> **redistributive programs** economic policies designed to control the economy through taxing and spending, with the goal of benefiting the poor

The debate over national-versus-state control of speed limits arose in 1973, when gas prices skyrocketed and supplies became scarce. Drivers nationwide were forced to wait in long lines at gas stations. The federal government responded to the gas crisis by instituting a national 55-mile-per-hour speed limit.

The national speed limit lost much of its support, even though it was found to have reduced the number of traffic deaths. In 1995, Congress repealed the penalties for higher speed limits, and states once again became free to set their own speed limits. Many states with large rural areas raised their maximum to 75 miles per hour; Montana initially set unlimited speeds in its rural areas during daylight hours. Research indicates that the number of highway deaths has indeed risen in the states that increased the limits.[50]

Because the division of responsibility in the federal system has important implications for who benefits, few conflicts over state-versus-national control will ever be settled once and for all. New evidence about the costs and benefits of different arrangements provides fuel for ongoing debates about what are properly the states' responsibilities and what the federal government should do. Likewise, changes in the political control of the national government usually provoke a rethinking of responsibilities as new leaders seek to alter federal arrangements for the benefit of the groups they represent.

Federalism since 2000

Since the year 2000, the political polarization between Republicans and Democrats that has characterized national politics and divided states has been played out through the federal system as well. This does not mean that all decisions about federalism have divided along political lines. But many of the most controversial issues in American politics—including the appropriate size of public social spending, the rights and benefits of immigrants (legal as well as undocumented), government response to global climate change, and questions about whether and how government should regulate business and moral behavior—have been fought through the federal system. Politicians of all stripes have regularly turned to the federal government to override policies they don't like that were made at the state level. The reverse is also true: when the federal government proves unable or unwilling to act, activists and politicians instead try to achieve their goals in states and localities. Sometimes, states seek to go their own way regardless of federal law. It is often then up to the courts to decide which level of government should have the final say. In many cases, the federal government has succeeded in advancing its policy agenda through the states. However, the era since 2000 has been marked by a considerable amount of back-and-forth between the states and the federal government as debates over federalism have become politically prominent.

Although conservatives proclaim their preference for a small federal government and their support for more state autonomy, in fact they often expand the federal government and limit state autonomy. During the presidency of George W. Bush, the growth of government; the activist, free-spending Republican Congress; and a series of Supreme Court rulings supporting federal power over the states made it clear that conservatives do not always support small government, nor do they always favor returning power to the states. Once in power, many conservatives discovered not only that they needed a strong federal government to respond to public demands but also that they could use federal power to advance conservative policy goals.

For President Bush, the importance of a strong federal government dawned with force after the terrorist attacks in 2001. Aware that the American public was looking to Washington for protection, Bush worked with Congress to pass the USA PATRIOT Act, which greatly increased the surveillance powers of the federal government. A year later he created the enormous new federal Department of Homeland Security. Democrats supported the president in both initiatives.

President Bush, with the support of Democrats, also expanded federal control and increased spending in policy areas far removed from concerns about security. The 2001 No Child Left Behind Act introduced unprecedented federal intervention in public education, traditionally a state and local responsibility. New, detailed federal testing requirements and provisions stipulating how states should treat failing schools were major expansions of federal authority in education. When a number of states threatened to defy some of the new federal requirements, Bush's Department of Education relaxed its tough stance and became more flexible in enforcing the act. The Obama administration increased flexibility even more by granting waivers to 43 states. The waivers released the states from the federal mandates around school accountability and performance, replacing them with state measures. But in other ways Obama increased federal authority over schools. In 2009, the administration introduced a new competitive grant program called "Race to the Top." States were required to apply for the funds; states that had adopted the administration's favored reforms were best positioned to win. In 2015 mounting dissatisfaction with federal influence over education led Congress to enact a new education law called Every Student Succeeds, which gave more power to the states to evaluate schools.

In the Supreme Court, too, many decisions began to support a stronger federal role over the states. This was surprising to many observers because in the 1990s it had appeared that the Rehnquist Court was embarked on a "federalism revolution" designed to return more power to the states. Instead, in several key decisions, the Court reaffirmed the power of the federal government. Decisions to uphold the federal Family and Medical Leave Act and the Americans with Disabilities Act

for critical analysis

The role of the national government has changed significantly from the Founding era to the present. Do you think the framers of the Constitution would be pleased with the current balance of power between the national government and the state governments?

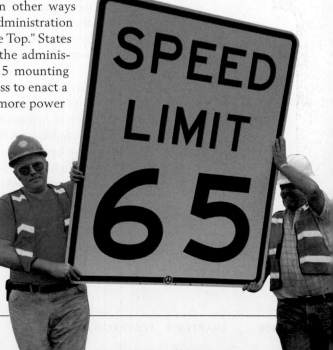

In 1995, Congress removed its speed limit restrictions and allowed states to raise the limit above 55 miles per hour without losing federal highway funds. As a result, speed limits went up on many highways.

asserted federal authority against state claims of immunity from the acts. In one important 2005 case, the Court upheld the right of Congress to ban medical marijuana, even though 11 states had legalized its use. Overturning a lower-court ruling that said Congress did not have authority to regulate marijuana when it had been grown for noncommercial purposes in a single state, the Supreme Court ruled that the federal government did have the power to regulate use of all marijuana under the commerce clause.[51] Even so, as we have seen, by 2016, 26 states and the District of Columbia had legalized medical marijuana. Amid this legal confusion, a medical marijuana industry began to flourish. In 2012, Colorado and Washington went further by legalizing recreational marijuana even though it is a prohibited substance by federal law. Alaska, Oregon, and the District of Columbia joined them in 2014, and in 2016, California, Maine, Massachusetts, and Nevada followed suit. Although the federal government has not endorsed these laws, it has made prosecution of marijuana in these states a low priority.

The move to a stronger federal role has not been uniform, however; in some cases the Supreme Court has granted more authority to the states. One closely watched federalism case in 2006 was the challenge to Oregon's "right to die" law, discussed earlier, which allows doctors to prescribe lethal doses of medicine for terminally ill patients who request it. Challengers claimed the law was illegal because Congress has the right to outlaw such use of drugs under the Controlled Substances Act, which regulates prescription drugs. In a 6–3 decision, the Court ruled in Oregon's favor.[52] Despite the ruling, only Washington state, Vermont, Montana, California, and Colorado followed in Oregon's footsteps to make physician-assisted suicide legal.[53]

On some issues, the majority of the states have pressed the federal government to act, but it has not responded. One issue on which most states would like the federal government to establish uniform law is Internet sales. Current law requires Internet retailers to collect sales tax on online purchases only when the business has a physical presence in the buyer's state. This has become a major issue for states, most of which rely on sales taxes for a significant part of their revenue. One study estimated that states would lose $23 billion in 2012 from Internet sales on which no taxes were collected.[54] In 2013, the Senate—with support from both Democrats and Republicans—passed the Marketplace Fairness Act, which would require online retailers to collect state sales taxes. However, in the House, some Republicans opposed the measure as a tax increase. By 2016, with the issue still unresolved in Congress, officials in 13 states had begun to impose taxes on out-of-state Internet sales. Frustrated by congressional inaction, the states aimed to push Congress to act or to throw the matter into the courts, where they hoped for a decision that would support them.[55]

The tug-of-war between the federal and state governments for policy control is particularly evident in the field of immigration. Faced with federal inaction on immigration reform, states and localities have forged their own policies. Some states, such as Arizona and Georgia, have adopted policies more restrictive than those of the federal government, while other states, such as California and Connecticut, have enacted laws to limit cooperation with federal immigration authorities. In the first half of 2013, state legislatures enacted 377 laws and resolutions related to immigration, exceeding the number passed in all of 2012.[56] Many state and local laws that govern immigration are not controversial, but others raise critical questions about what is the federal government's role and what are the responsibilities of state and local governments. In April 2010, Arizona enacted an extremely controversial immigration measure requiring immigrants to carry identity documents

Who Benefits from Federal Spending?

Federal Grants to State and Local Governments, 2014

Health	Income security	Education	Transportation	Other
$320 billion	$101 billion	$60 billion	$62 billion	$33 billion

Although Americans often think they pay a lot in federal taxes, they receive much in return in the form of federal money for state and local programs. Federal outlays for grants to state and local governments have grown from $51.5 billion in 1950 to $539 billion in 2014 (in constant dollars).

Fiscal Transfers between the States and the Federal Government, 2013

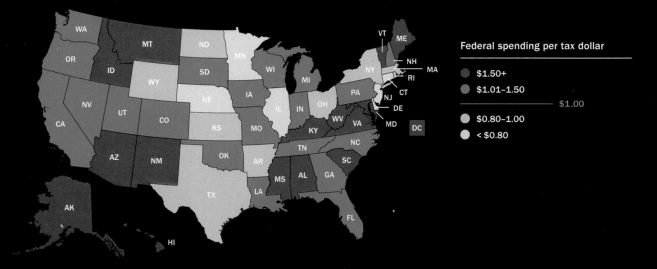

Federal spending per tax dollar

- $1.50+
- $1.01–1.50
- $1.00
- $0.80–1.00
- < $0.80

Every U.S. state contributes to the federal government through the federal taxes paid by the state's citizens, and every state receives money from federal spending. Federal spending is a broad category that includes the federal grants described above as well as spending on military bases and federal procurement. Not every state receives the same amount from the federal government, however. The map above shows how much federal spending each state received for each dollar paid in federal taxes in 2013.

SOURCES: "Federal Grants to State and Local Governments: A Historical Perspective on Contemporary Issues," Congressional Research Service, March 5, 2015, www.fas.org/sgp/crs/misc/R40638.pdf (accessed 2/18/16); Internal Revenue Service, *2013 Internal Revenue Service Data Book*, www.irs.gov/pub/irs-soi/13databk.pdf (accessed 3/10/16); Pew Charitable Trusts, "Federal Spending in the States," December 2, 2014, www.pewtrusts.org/en/research-and-analysis/issue-briefs/2014/12/federal-spending-in-the-states (accessed 3/10/16).

for critical analysis

1. What are some of the benefits of federal grants to state and local governments?

2. What is the rationale behind transfers from one state to another? Is it fair that some states pay more in federal taxes than they receive? What might explain why some states are net recipients and some net contributors?

and requiring police to ask about immigration status when they stop drivers they suspect of being illegal immigrants. The federal Department of Justice joined several other groups in challenging the law. In the words of then–attorney general Eric Holder, "It is clearly unconstitutional for a state to set its own immigration policy."[57] In 2012 the Supreme Court overturned three of four provisions in Arizona's law. But it ruled in favor of the most divisive provision, which allows state police to check the immigration status of anyone stopped or arrested.[58]

Immigration policy once again became embroiled in federal–state conflict after 2014. Frustrated by congressional inaction on immigration, President Obama issued an executive order that would provide temporary legal status to those who had been brought to the United States as children and would extend legal status to the parents of U.S. citizens and legal residents. Approximately 5 million undocumented immigrants could receive work permits under the new program. However, led by Texas, 26 states challenged the executive order in court, charging that it exceeded executive authority and would impose unreasonable costs on states, which would bear additional costs, such as issuing driver's licenses. The program was never implemented because the Supreme Court, in the wake of the death of Justice Antonin Scalia, deadlocked in a 4–4 decision, leaving in place lower-court decisions that sided with the states.[59]

President Obama also announced the termination of the controversial Secure Communities program in 2014. Initially launched in 2008, Secure Communities required state and local authorities to check the fingerprints of people being booked into jail against a Homeland Security database. The policy led to a record number of deportations in 2009 and 2010, leading several states and localities to pull out of the agreement with the federal government on the grounds that the

The federal government brought Arizona to court over law SB1070, which imposed strict requirements on immigrants. The Supreme Court found that three provisions of the law were preempted by federal law, meaning Arizona did not have the authority to make the regulation. However, the controversial "show me your papers" provision of the law was upheld.

law was detaining too many undocumented immigrants who had never committed a crime. The administration softened its deportation policy in 2011, but sustained opposition as well as federal court decisions that challenged the constitutionality of elements of the policy ultimately led the government to end the program in late 2014. In its place, the Obama administration launched the Priority Enforcement Program in July 2015, which adopts a more limited deportation policy than the one formerly mandated by Secure Communities.[60]

In some ways, the Obama White House allowed the states more leeway for action than they had experienced under the Bush administration. This was particularly true in the domains of social policy and the environment when states sought to enact laws more stringent than those of the federal government. In the memo reversing the Bush policy of preemption, the White House noted, "Throughout our history, State and local governments have frequently protected health, safety, and the environment more aggressively than has the national Government."[61] Its new policy aimed to keep the federal government from infringing on these more aggressive state actions.

The most significant Obama law to affect the states was the 2010 health care overhaul. As we have seen, one controversial part of that legislation required states to expand their Medicaid programs to cover more low-income residents. The Court's ruling that the federal government could not impose all-or-nothing conditions on the states—implement the expansion or lose all Medicaid funding—represented a sharp departure from the past. The ruling has far-reaching potential to change the federal government's power to impose conditions on the states when it supplies the funds. The other controversial provision of the Affordable Care Act was the "individual mandate," the requirement that individuals without health care insurance be required to purchase such insurance. The 26 states suing the federal government charged that Congress had no power to force individuals to purchase a product and that it had exceeded its power under the commerce clause. In defending the law, the federal government argued the opposite: that the complex interactions of the health care market made the individual mandate constitutional under the commerce clause.[62] Everyone is part of the health care economy. Even if a person does not have health insurance, federal law requires that hospitals provide treatment in an emergency, costs which are borne by all of the people who do pay for health insurance. The Court rejected this argument on the grounds that the federal government cannot regulate economic inactivity, that is, the failure to purchase health insurance. Instead, it found that the Affordable Care Act could be justified by Congress's power to tax. The law required individuals who do not receive insurance from their employers or their parents and are not eligible for Medicaid to purchase insurance or pay a penalty. The Court reasoned that the penalty could be considered a tax and, in that sense, passed constitutional muster. The complex and surprising decision marked a new era in American federalism. The Court placed limits on two of the key powers that have expanded the reach of the federal government since the New Deal—the power to regulate commerce and the power to spend for the general welfare. The decision will surely invite challenges to federal power in diverse areas, possibly including education programs, the drinking age, and environmental regulations.

The Affordable Care Act law survived another challenge in 2015 when the Supreme Court ruled that federal subsidies to help pay for insurance should be available to residents in states that offered insurance through the federal exchange as well as in states that had formed their own state insurance marketplaces. The outcome of *King v. Burwell* ensured that subsidies would be available in all states.[63]

Federalism
and Your Future

It is often argued that liberals prefer a strong federal government because they value equality more than liberty. Conservatives are said to prefer granting more power to states and localities because they care most about liberty. Although this greatly oversimplifies liberal and conservative views, such arguments underscore the reality that ideas about federalism are linked to different views about the purposes of government. For what ends should government powers be used? What happens when widely shared national values conflict in practice? The connections between federalism and our fundamental national values have made federalism a focus of political contention throughout our nation's history.

In recent years, sharp differences in Americans' views on many economic and social issues have been reflected in the federal system. Until 2015, when the Supreme Court ruled that state-level bans on same-sex marriage were unconstitutional, 37 states allowed same-sex marriage and 13 did not. Today, nearly half of the 50 states have legalized medical marijuana, while four have gone further and legalized recreational marijuana. More states are likely to change their laws on marijuana, but differences across the states are likely to persist for many years. Half of the states welcomed the expansion of Medicaid, the program that provides medical assistance to the poor. The other half, concerned about costs and the growing role of government in the economy, has declined to implement the expansion. Some states actively welcome immigrants and seek to opt out of restrictive federal laws; other states go beyond the federal government in enacting restrictive immigration laws. Yet while states have the authority to devise their own laws on a variety of important issues, Americans' participation in state and local politics remains low (see the "**Who Participates?**" feature on the facing page).

For young people, differences across the states provoke important questions about the future. Our history of federalism means that we are comfortable with the idea that states should have the freedom to enact laws that best serve their residents, within the bounds set by Congress and the courts. We expect states to act as "laboratories of democracy" that try out new policies. But the great variation across the states today poses questions that will have to be answered in the coming decades. Is the federal government endangering people by allowing states to legalize marijuana? Is it fair that a transgender person in California can legally change the sex on her birth certificate, but a transgender person in Tennessee would be denied the same? Each generation confronts a different set of questions about how much variation across the states is appropriate. Are some of the issues on which the states differ fundamental rights that should be uniform across the country? Is it important to preserve state choice on most matters? As today's youth help to answer these questions in the coming decades, they will be remaking American federalism.

American federalism remains a work in progress. As public problems shift and as local, state, and federal governments change, questions about the relationship between American values and federalism naturally emerge. The different views that people bring to this discussion suggest that federalism will remain a central issue in American democracy.

Who Participates in State and Local Politics?

Turnout in 2014 Election, by State
Percentage of Voting-Eligible Population*

● 25–34%　◐ 35–44%　● 45–54%　● 55–64%

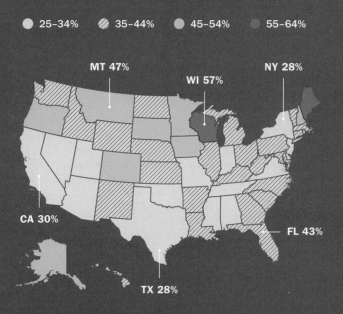

MT 47%

WI 57%

NY 28%

CA 30%

FL 43%

TX 28%

Turnout in Most Recent Municipal Election
Percentage of Voting-Age Population in Selected Cities*

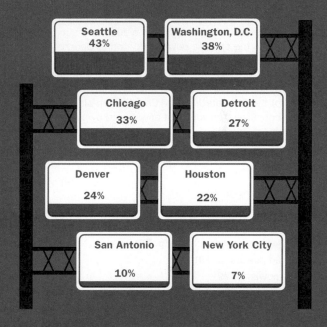

Seattle 43%	Washington, D.C. 38%
Chicago 33%	Detroit 27%
Denver 24%	Houston 22%
San Antonio 10%	New York City 7%

*The voting-eligible population excludes noncitizens and people who are institutionalized or not allowed to vote in some states because they are ex-felons. The voting-age population includes everyone over 18.
SOURCES: 2014 November General Election Turnout Rates, United States Election Project, www.electproject.org/2014g (accessed 9/27/15); Voting Age Population by Citizenship and Race (CVAP), U.S. Census American Community Survey, www.census.gov/rdo/data/voting_age_population_by_citizenship_and_race_cvap.html (accessed 9/27/15).

WHAT YOU CAN DO

Get Involved in State and Local Politics

 Attend a board of supervisors, city council, planning commission, or other local government meeting. Agendas and minutes will usually be available on county and city websites.

☑ Visit the state capitol. If you make an appointment, you might be able to meet with your local representative. Committee meetings and hearings are generally open to the public, as are meetings of the legislature.

 Attend a session of your local or state judiciary. Cases on the docket are available online, as are rules for attendance and behavior when the court is in session.

studyguide

Federalism in the Constitution

> **Describe what the Constitution says about the powers of the national government and of the states (pp. 77–82)**

While the Founders wanted a national government that was stronger than it had been under the Articles of Confederation, they also wanted to preserve the autonomy of the states. The necessary and proper clause, the supremacy clause, and the specific powers granted to Congress in Article I demonstrate the nation-centered focus of the Constitution. The Tenth Amendment, which grants all undelegated powers to the states, shows the state-centered focus of the Constitution. The Constitution also includes some concurrent powers that are shared by both the federal government and state governments.

Key Terms

federalism (p. 77)

unitary system (p. 77)

expressed powers (p. 77)

implied powers (p. 77)

necessary and proper clause (p. 77)

reserved powers (p. 79)

police power (p. 79)

concurrent powers (p. 79)

full faith and credit clause (p. 79)

privileges and immunities clause (p. 81)

home rule (p. 82)

Practice Quiz

1. Which term describes the division of powers between the national government and the state governments?
   a) home rule
   b) separation of powers
   c) federalism
   d) checks and balances
   e) unitary system

2. Which amendment to the Constitution stated that the powers not delegated to the national government or prohibited to the states were "reserved to the states"?
   a) First Amendment
   b) Fifth Amendment
   c) Tenth Amendment
   d) Fourteenth Amendment
   e) Twenty-Sixth Amendment

3. A state government's authority to regulate the health, safety, and morals of its citizens is frequently referred to as
   a) the reserved power.
   b) the police power.
   c) the expressed power.
   d) the concurrent power.
   e) the implied power.

4. Which constitutional clause requires that states normally honor the public acts and judicial decisions of other states?
   a) privileges and immunities clause
   b) necessary and proper clause
   c) interstate commerce clause
   d) preemption clause
   e) full faith and credit clause

5. Many states have amended their constitutions to guarantee that large cities will have the authority to manage local affairs without interference from state government. This power is called
   a) home rule.
   b) devolution.
   c) preemption.
   d) states' rights.
   e) New Federalism.

The Changing Relationship between the Federal Government and the States

The relative importance of states and the federal government has changed significantly over time. During the first 100 years of American history, the national government was small and focused on assisting commerce. Beginning in the 1930s, the Supreme Court dramatically expanded the power of the federal government through its expansive interpretation of the commerce clause. The growing power of the national government has not, however, left the states powerless, and state governments continue to make important laws.

Key Terms

dual federalism (p. 83)

commerce clause (p. 85)

states' rights (p. 87)

Practice Quiz

6. The relationship between the states and the national government from 1789 to 1937 is known as
   a) unitary government.
   b) New Federalism.
   c) dual federalism.
   d) cooperative federalism.
   e) regulated federalism.

7. In which case did the Supreme Court create the potential for increased national power by ruling that Congress could use the necessary and proper clause to interpret its delegated powers broadly?
   a) *United States v. Lopez*
   b) *Printz v. United States*
   c) *Loving v. Virginia*
   d) *McCulloch v. Maryland*
   e) *Gibbons v. Ogden*

8. In 1937 the Supreme Court laid the groundwork for a stronger federal government by issuing a number of decisions that
   a) dramatically narrowed the definition of the commerce clause.
   b) dramatically expanded the definition of the commerce clause.
   c) struck down the supremacy clause.
   d) struck down the privileges and immunities clause.
   e) struck down the full faith and credit clause.

Who Does What? Public Spending and the Expanding Federal Framework

The Great Depression effectively ended the traditional system of dual federalism in which the states and the federal government performed very different functions. Political debates continue about the division of responsibility between states and the national government in search of the right balance. The New Deal, federal grants, and cooperative and regulated federalism are all part of the shift in power and responsibility.

Key Terms

grants-in-aid (p. 90)

categorical grants (p. 90)

project grants (p. 90)

formula grants (p. 90)

cooperative federalism (p. 91)

regulated federalism (p. 93)

preemption (p. 94)

unfunded mandates (p. 94)

Practice Quiz

9. Which of the following tools has the federal government used in the past to create similarities across states?
   a) states' rights.
   b) general revenue sharing.
   c) grants-in-aid.
   d) eminent domain.
   e) home rule.

10. The principle that allows the federal government to take over areas of regulation formerly overseen by states or local governments is called
    a) project grants.
    b) preemption.
    c) devolution.
    d) categorical grants.
    e) formula grants.

11. When state and local governments must conform to costly federal regulations or conditions in order to receive grants but do not receive reimbursements for their expenditures it is called
    a) a reciprocal grant.
    b) an unfunded mandate.
    c) general revenue sharing.
    d) a concurrent grant.
    e) a counterfunded mandate.

New Federalism and State Control

Analyze the developments in the federal framework since the 1970s (pp. 96–105)

Today, American federalism includes elements of cooperative, coercive, and "new" federalism. Most of the important public policy issues in recent years, including controversies about government spending, immigration, climate change, health care, and economic regulation, are debated and addressed through the United States' unique system of federalism.

Key Terms

devolution (p. 96)

block grants (p. 96)

New Federalism (p. 96)

general revenue sharing (p. 96)

redistributive programs (p. 99)

Practice Quiz

12. The process of returning more of the responsibilities of governing from the national level to the state level is known as
    a) devolution.
    b) dual federalism.
    c) incorporation.
    d) home rule.
    e) preemption.

13. To what does the term *New Federalism* refer?
    a) the era of federalism initiated by President Roosevelt during the late 1930s
    b) the national government's regulation of state action through grants-in-aid
    c) the type of federalism that uses categorical grants to influence state action
    d) efforts to return more policy-making discretion to the states through the use of block grants
    e) the recent emergence of local governments as important political actors

14. A notable example of the process of giving the states more responsibility for administering government programs is
    a) campaign finance reform.
    b) prison reform.
    c) Social Security.
    d) welfare reform.
    e) trade reform.

For Further Reading

Bowman, Ann O'M., and Richard C. Kearney. *The Resurgence of the States*. Englewood Cliffs, NJ: Prentice-Hall, 1986.

Derthick, Martha. *Keeping the Compound Republic: Essays on American Federalism*. Washington, DC: Brookings Institution Press, 2001.

Elazar, Daniel. *American Federalism: A View from the States*. 3rd ed. New York: Harper & Row, 1984.

Feiock, Richard C., and John T. Scholz. *Self-Organizing Federalism: Collaborative Mechanisms to Mitigate Institutional Collective Action Dilemmas*. New York: Cambridge University Press, 2009.

Gerston, Larry N. *American Federalism: A Concise Introduction*. Armonk, NY: M. E. Sharpe, 2007.

Grodzins, Morton. *The American System*. Chicago: Rand McNally, 1974.

Johnson, Kimberly S. *Governing the American State: Congress and the New Federalism, 1877–1929*. Princeton, NJ: Princeton University Press, 2007.

Kettl, Donald. *The Regulation of American Federalism.* Baltimore: Johns Hopkins University Press, 1987.

Mettler, Suzanne. *Dividing Citizens: Gender and Federalism in New Deal Public Policy.* Ithaca, NY: Cornell University Press, 1998.

Pierceson, Jason. *Same-Sex Marriage in the United States: The Road to the Supreme Court.* Lanham, MD: Rowman and Littlefield, 2013.

Robertson, David Brian. *Federalism and the Making of America.* New York: Routledge, 2011.

Van Horn, Carl E. *The State of the States.* 4th ed. Washington, DC: CQ Press, 2005.

Recommended Websites

Constitution Finder
http://confinder.richmond.edu

Governments can organize power in either a unitary or a federal system. Examine the constitutions of different countries throughout the world, and try to identify how those governments organize power.

Council of State Governments
www.csg.org

This organization provides information on a variety of state–federal policy areas. See what current issues concerning federalism are of prime importance to the state governments on this site.

Governing.com
www.governing.com

See what state–federal issues are important to your local government officials on the website for *Governing* magazine.

National Conference of State Legislatures
www.ncsl.org

National Governors Association
www.nga.org

These are two of the largest organizations dedicated to representing state and local government interests at the federal level.

Oyez: U.S. Supreme Court Media
www.oyez.org

Read here about one of the most important U.S. Supreme Court decisions regarding the division of federal and state power in the case of *McCulloch v. Maryland*.

Pew Charitable Trusts Stateline
www.pewtrusts.org/en/research-and-analysis/blogs/stateline/about

This nonprofit site provides news coverage in the states, focusing on four issues: fiscal and economic issues, health care, demographics, and the business of government. It also offers a weekly newsletter that includes the highlights of its reporting.

Supreme Court of the United States Blog
www.scotusblog.com

Supreme Court of the United States blog provides independent scholarly analysis of court rulings. The site provides timely discussion of pending and recent court decisions including *Obergefell v. Hodges*, the decision that made same-sex marriage legal in all states.

U.S. Census Bureau
www.census.gov

The Census Bureau maintains one of the largest collections of data about social and economic conditions of the nation's 50 states.

World Federalist Movement
www.wfm.org

This international organization is dedicated to the division of power and authority among all local, state, and international governmental agencies. Generally, it promotes federalism and constitutional democracy throughout the world.

The Bill of Rights protects Americans from government surveillance and searches without reasonable cause. Some people worry that increased government surveillance in the fight against terrorism represents a turn away from protecting civil liberties.

Civil Liberties

WHAT GOVERNMENT DOES AND WHY IT MATTERS Today in the United States, we often take for granted the liberties contained in the Bill of Rights. In fact, few people in recorded history, including many American citizens before the 1960s, have enjoyed such protections. For more than 170 years after its ratification by the states in 1791, the Bill of Rights meant little to most Americans. As we shall see in this chapter, guaranteeing the liberties articulated in the Bill of Rights to all Americans required a long struggle. As recently as the early 1960s, criminal suspects in state cases did not have to be informed of their rights, some states required daily Bible readings and prayers in their public schools, and some communities regularly censored books that they deemed to be obscene.

Often, the government presents restraints on liberty, particularly in such realms as speech, assembly, and privacy, as necessary to protect the nation's security. Today, for example, many Americans seem to accept the necessity of full-body scans at airports, though many question whether extensive electronic surveillance of email and phone conversations is necessary to protect the nation against attack. The framers of the Constitution had qualms about such invasions of privacy. To the framers, political freedom required that citizens be protected from government surveillance and searches into citizens' private affairs. Indeed, this concern for privacy lies at the heart of the Constitution's Fourth Amendment, which prohibits "unreasonable searches and seizures."

The framers were concerned that government agents were inclined to search private homes for evidence of political dissidence, a British practice that the framers wanted to put a stop to in the new United States. But what if the dissidents are terrorists bent on violence? What are the limits of the Fourth Amendment? This was the question underlying the 2016 FBI/Apple controversy in which the Apple Corporation refused FBI demands to unlock the iPhone that belonged to Syed Farook. In 2015, Farook, along with his wife Tashfeen Malik, had carried out a mass shooting in San Bernardino, California, leaving 14 dead. Civil libertarians applauded the company's position, arguing that the demand that Apple develop a software to unlock iPhones undermined customers' privacy and led to a slippery slope by giving the government back-door access to any phones it pleased. Other Americans, however, were aghast at Apple's refusal. They expressed concern for the nation's security and believed that the FBI should have access to data that could aid a terrorist investigation. Eventually the case became moot when the FBI "hacked" the phone on its own, but this new kind of privacy issue remains.

Thomas Jefferson said that a bill of rights "is what people are entitled to against every government on earth." Note the wording: *against government.* Civil liberties are *protections from* improper government action. Some of these restraints are substantive liberties, which put limits on *what* the government shall and shall not have power to do, such as establishing a religion or seizing private property without just compensation. Other restraints are procedural liberties, which deal with *how* the government is supposed to act. Civil liberties require a delicate balance between governmental power and governmental restraint. The government must be kept in check, with strict limits on its powers; yet, at the same time, the government must be given enough power to defend liberty and its benefits. According to the Constitution's Preamble, after all, one of the chief purposes of government is "to secure the blessings of liberty." This chapter will explore how this balance is struck. We will see how the Supreme Court, an inherently undemocratic institution, is especially important in establishing the balance. In a sense, civil liberties can be thought of as limits on democracy, providing an important check on the power of the majority. They are the "minority rights" in the principle of "majority rule with minority rights."

chaptergoals

- Explain the origins and evolution of the civil liberties in the Bill of Rights as they apply to the federal government and the states (pp. 115–20)
- Describe how the First Amendment protects freedom of religion (pp. 120–23)
- Describe how the First Amendment protects free speech and freedom of the press (pp. 123–31)
- Explore whether the Second Amendment means people have a right to own guns (pp. 131–32)
- Explain the major rights that people have if they are accused of a crime (pp. 133–40)
- Assess whether people have a right to privacy under the Constitution (pp. 140–45)

A Brief History of the Bill of Rights

Explain the origins and evolution of the civil liberties in the Bill of Rights as they apply to the federal government and the states

When the first Congress under the newly ratified Constitution met in late April of 1789, the most important item of business was the consideration of a proposal to add a bill of rights to the Constitution. Such a proposal had been turned down with little debate in the waning days of the Philadelphia Constitutional Convention in 1787, not because the delegates were against rights but because, as the Federalists, led by Alexander Hamilton, later argued, it was "not only unnecessary in the proposed Constitution but would even be dangerous."[1] First, according to Hamilton, a bill of rights would be irrelevant to a national government that was given only delegated powers in the first place. To put restraints on "powers which are not granted" could provide a pretext for governments to claim more powers than were in fact granted: "For why declare that things shall not be done which there is no power to do?"[2] Second, the Constitution was to Hamilton and the Federalists a bill of rights in itself, containing provisions that amounted to a bill of rights without requiring additional amendments (see Table 4.1). For example, Article I, Section 9 included the right of **habeas corpus**, which prohibits the government from depriving a person of liberty without an open trial before a judge. Many of the framers, moreover, saw the very structure of the Constitution, including checks and balances, as protective of citizens' liberties.

habeas corpus a court order demanding that an individual in custody be brought into court and shown the cause for detention

Despite the power of Hamilton's arguments, when the Constitution was submitted to the states for ratification, Antifederalists, most of whom had not been delegates in Philadelphia, picked up on the argument of Thomas Jefferson (who also had not been a delegate) that the omission of a bill of rights was a major imperfection of the new Constitution. The Federalists conceded that to gain ratification they would have to make an "unwritten but unequivocal pledge" to add a bill of rights that would include a confirmation (in what would become the Tenth Amendment) of the understanding that all powers not expressly delegated to the national government or explicitly prohibited to the states were reserved to the states.[3]

TABLE 4.1

Rights in the Original Constitution (Not in the Bill of Rights)

CLAUSE	RIGHT ESTABLISHED
Article I, Section 9	Guarantee of habeas corpus
Article I, Section 9	Prohibition of bills of attainder
Article I, Section 9	Prohibition of ex post facto laws
Article I, Section 9	Prohibition against acceptance of titles of nobility, etc., from any foreign state
Article III	Guarantee of trial by jury in state where crime was committed
Article III	Treason defined and limited to the life of the person convicted, not to the person's heirs

bill of attainder a law that declares a person guilty of a crime without a trial

ex post facto laws laws that declare an action to be illegal after it has been committed

TABLE 4.2

The Bill of Rights

Amendment I: Limits on Congress	Congress cannot make any law establishing a religion or abridging freedoms of religious exercise, speech, assembly, or petition.
Amendments II, III, IV: Limits on the executive	The executive branch cannot infringe on the right of the people to keep arms (II), cannot arbitrarily take houses for militia (III), and cannot search for or seize evidence without a court warrant swearing to the probable existence of a crime (IV).
Amendments V, VI, VII, VIII: Limits on the judiciary	The courts cannot hold trials for serious offenses without provision for a grand jury (V), a trial jury (VII), a speedy trial (VI), presentation of charges and confrontation by the accused of hostile witnesses (VI), and immunity from testimony against oneself and immunity from trial more than once for the same offense (V). Furthermore, neither bail nor punishment can be excessive (VIII), and no property can be taken without "just compensation" (V).
Amendments IX, X: Limits on the national government	Any rights not enumerated are reserved to the state or the people (X), and the enumeration of certain rights in the Constitution should not be interpreted to mean that those are the only rights the people have (IX).

Bill of Rights the first 10 amendments to the U.S. Constitution, ratified in 1791; they ensure certain rights and liberties to the people

civil liberties areas of personal freedom constitutionally protected from government interference

"After much discussion and manipulation . . . at the delicate prompting of Washington and under the masterful prodding of Madison," the House of Representatives approved 17 amendments; of these, the Senate accepted 12. Ten of the amendments were ratified by the necessary three-fourths of the states on December 15, 1791; from the start, these 10 were called the **Bill of Rights** (see Table 4.2).[4] The protections against improper government action contained in the Constitution and the Bill of Rights represent important **civil liberties**.

Nationalizing the Bill of Rights

The First Amendment provides that "Congress shall make no law. . . ." But this is the only amendment in the Bill of Rights that addresses itself exclusively to the national government. For example, the Second Amendment provides that "the right of the people to keep and bear Arms, shall not be infringed." And the Fifth Amendment says, among other things, that "no person shall . . . be twice put in jeopardy of life or limb" for the same crime. Since the First Amendment is the only part of the Bill of Rights that is explicit in its intention to put limits on Congress and therefore on the national government, a fundamental question inevitably arises: Do the remaining provisions of the Bill of Rights put limits only on the national government, or do they limit the state governments as well?

The Supreme Court first answered this question in 1833 by ruling that the Bill of Rights limited only the national government and not the state governments.[5] But in 1868, when the Fourteenth Amendment was added to the Constitution, the question arose once again. The Fourteenth Amendment reads as if it were meant to impose the Bill of Rights on the states:

> No State shall make or enforce any law which shall abridge the privileges or immunities of citizens of the United States; nor shall any State deprive any person of life, liberty, or property, without due process of law; nor deny to any person within its jurisdiction the equal protection of the laws.

This language sounds like an effort to extend the Bill of Rights in its entirety to all citizens, wherever they might reside.[6] Yet this was not the Supreme Court's interpretation of the amendment for nearly 100 years. Within five years of ratification of the Fourteenth Amendment, the Court was making decisions as though the amendment had never been adopted.[7]

The only change in civil liberties during the first 50-odd years following the adoption of the Fourteenth Amendment came in 1897, when the Supreme Court held that the due process clause of the Fourteenth Amendment did in fact prohibit states from taking property for a public use without just compensation.[8] However, the Supreme Court had selectively "incorporated" into the Fourteenth Amendment only the property protection provision of the Fifth Amendment and no other clause of the Fifth or any other amendment of the Bill of Rights. In other words, although according to the Fifth Amendment "due process" applied to the taking of life and liberty as well as property, only property was incorporated into the Fourteenth Amendment as a limitation on state power.

No further expansion of civil liberties via the Fourteenth Amendment occurred until 1925, when the Supreme Court held that freedom of speech is "among the fundamental personal rights and 'liberties' protected by the due process clause of the Fourteenth Amendment from impairment by the states."[9] In 1931 the Court added freedom of the press to that short list of freedoms protected by the Bill of Rights from state action; in 1939 it added freedom of assembly.[10]

But that was as far as the Court was willing to go. In the 1937 case of *Palko v. Connecticut*, the Court gave its blessing to the preservation of a legal framework in which the states had the power to determine their own laws on a number of fundamental issues. In that case, a Connecticut court had found Frank Palko guilty of second-degree murder and sentenced him to life in prison. Unhappy with the verdict, the state of Connecticut appealed the conviction to its highest court, won the appeal, got a new trial, and then succeeded in getting Palko convicted of first-degree murder. Palko appealed to the Supreme Court on what seemed an open-and-shut case of double jeopardy, which is prohibited by the Fifth Amendment. Yet, although the majority of the Court agreed that this could indeed be considered a case of double jeopardy, they decided that double jeopardy was *not* one of the provisions of the Bill of Rights incorporated into the Fourteenth Amendment as a restriction on the powers of the states. It took more than 30 years for the Court to nationalize the constitutional protection against double jeopardy. Because Frank Palko lived in the state of Connecticut rather than in a state whose constitution included a guarantee against double jeopardy, he was eventually executed for the crime.

The *Palko* case established the principle of **selective incorporation**, by which the provisions of the Bill of Rights were to be considered one by one and selectively applied as limits on the states through the Fourteenth Amendment. In order to make clear that "selective incorporation" should be narrowly interpreted, Justice Benjamin Cardozo, writing for an 8–1 majority, asserted that although many rights have value and importance, some rights do not represent a "principle of justice so rooted in the traditions and conscience of our people as to be ranked as fundamental."[11] *Palko* left states with most of the powers they had possessed even before the adoption of the Fourteenth Amendment, such as the power to engage in searches and seizures without a warrant, to deprive accused persons of trial by jury, and to

---

Philadelphia, Pennsylvania   *December 15, 1791*

Congress Adds a Bill of Rights to the Federal Constitution

10 AMENDMENTS TO GUARANTEE INDIVIDUAL RIGHTS

Madison leads the fight for passage

The promise of a bill of rights was instrumental to securing ratification of the Constitution. The first 10 amendment approved by Congress and ratified by three-fourths of the states were known from the start as the Bill of Rights.

selective incorporation the process by which different protections in the Bill of Rights were incorporated into the Fourteenth Amendment, thus guaranteeing citizens protection from state as well as national governments

prosecute accused persons more than once for the same crime.[12] Few states chose to use these kinds of powers, but some did.

So, until 1961 (see Table 4.3), only the First Amendment and one clause of the Fifth Amendment had been clearly incorporated into the Fourteenth Amendment as binding on the states as well as on the national government.[13] After that, one by one, almost all the provisions of the Bill of Rights were incorporated into the Fourteenth Amendment and applied to the states. Table 4.3 shows the progress of this revolution in the interpretation of the Constitution. Before we leave the topic, it is worth mentioning that one element of the Fourteenth Amendment is being called into question today. This is the idea that all persons "born or naturalized" in the United States are citizens. Some politicians and public figures, most notably Donald Trump, have argued that the children of illegal immigrants should not be considered U.S. citizens and might be subject to deportation. Though we are a nation of immigrants, struggles over who may lawfully engage in the opportunities provided by American democracy can become bitter.

TABLE 4.3

Incorporation of the Bill of Rights into the Fourteenth Amendment

These cases are significant because they represent the first instance that the Supreme Court acknowledged that the selected provision or amendment was binding on the states. In some cases this meant the Supreme Court overturned the state or local law under contention. In other cases the Court held that the law did not violate the Constitution, so the law was upheld.

SELECTED PROVISIONS AND AMENDMENTS	INCORPORATED	KEY CASE
Eminent domain (V)	1897	*Chicago, Burlington, and Quincy R.R. v. Chicago* The city of Chicago was required to compensate a railroad company for seizing its property for the purpose of widening a city road.
Freedom of speech (I)	1925	*Gitlow v. New York* Upheld Gitlow's conviction for "criminal anarchy" for publishing a left-wing manifesto. The Court held the First Amendment allowed the states to suppress speech directly advocating the overthrow of the government.
Freedom of press (I)	1931	*Near v. Minnesota* Overturned Minnesota's permanent injunction against those who created a "public nuisance" by publishing, selling, or distributing a "malicious, scandalous and defamatory newspaper, magazine or other periodical" as an infringement on freedom of the press.
Free exercise of religion (I)	1934	*Hamilton v. Regents of the University of California* Students filed suit to protest mandatory military training at the University of California on religious grounds. The Court upheld the right of California to mandate that its students receive military training as permissible under the First Amendment's free exercise of religion clause.
Freedom of assembly (I) and freedom to petition the government for redress of grievances (I)	1937	*DeJonge v. Oregon* DeJonge's conviction for addressing a meeting of the Communist Party was overturned as an infringement on freedom of assembly.

SELECTED PROVISIONS AND AMENDMENTS	INCORPORATED	KEY CASE
Free exercise of religion (I)	1940	*Cantwell v. Connecticut* State governments may not prohibit the dissemination or expression of religious views.
Nonestablishment of state religion (I)	1947	*Everson v. Board of Education* Applying the establishment clause, the Court found that using taxpayer money to bus students to private religious schools did not constitute establishing a religion because busing was a "separate" function from the school's religious purpose.
Freedom from warrantless search and seizure (IV) ("exclusionary rule")	1961	*Mapp v. Ohio* The Court overturned the conviction of Dollree Mapp for possession of obscene materials because the evidence was obtained in violation of the Fourth Amendment's requirement of a warrant for conducting a search.
Freedom from cruel and unusual punishment (VIII)	1962	*Robinson v. California* The Court overturned a California law imposing a 90-day jail sentence on persons found guilty of "addiction to the use of narcotics" as cruel and unusual punishment for what amounted to illness.
Right to counsel in any criminal trial (VI)	1963	*Gideon v. Wainwright* Gideon requested a lawyer at his trial for a felony crime but was denied under Florida law. The Supreme Court held the right to counsel in the Sixth Amendment applied to the states, so Gideon got a new trial with counsel.
Right against self-incrimination and forced confessions (V)	1964	*Malloy v. Hogan* Malloy was imprisoned for contempt after refusing to answer questions about gambling activities on grounds it might implicate him. The Supreme Court held the Fifth Amendment secures defendants against self-incrimination so Malloy could not be forced to testify.
Right to remain silent (V)	1964	*Escobedo v. Illinois* Police denied repeated requests by Escobedo to see his lawyer during interrogation; Escobedo eventually incriminated himself in a murder. The Court held Escobedo's Sixth Amendment rights to counsel and to the right to remain silent were violated.
Right to counsel and to remain silent (V)	1966	*Miranda v. Arizona* Miranda was questioned by police and signed a statement of confession without being informed of his right to counsel and protection from self-incrimination. The Court held defendants in police custody must be informed of their rights.
Right against double jeopardy (V)	1969	*Benton v. Maryland* Benton was tried twice for the same crime of larceny. The Supreme Court held "double jeopardy" as impermissible under the Fifth Amendment.
Right to bear arms (II)	2010	*McDonald v. Chicago* The Supreme Court struck down a Chicago firearms ordinance making it extremely difficult to own a gun within city limits as violating the Second Amendment.

The best way to examine the Bill of Rights today is the simplest way: to take the major provisions one at a time. Some of these provisions are settled areas of law; others are not. The Court can reinterpret any one of them at any time.

● The First Amendment and Freedom of Religion

| Describe how the First Amendment protects freedom of religion | Congress shall make no law respecting an establishment of religion, or prohibiting the free exercise thereof; or abridging the freedom of speech, or of the press; or the right of the people peaceably to assemble, and to petition the Government for a redress of grievances. |

The Bill of Rights begins by guaranteeing freedom of religion, and the First Amendment provides for that freedom in two distinct clauses: "Congress shall make no law [1] respecting an establishment of religion, or [2] prohibiting the free exercise thereof." The first clause is called the "establishment clause," and the second is called the "free exercise clause."

Separation between Church and State

establishment clause the First Amendment clause that says that "Congress shall make no law respecting an establishment of religion"; this law means that a "wall of separation" exists between church and state

The **establishment clause** and the idea of "no law" regarding the establishment of religion could be interpreted in several possible ways. One interpretation, which probably reflects the views of many of the First Amendment's authors, is that the government is prohibited from establishing an official church. Official state churches, such as the Church of England, were common in the eighteenth century and were viewed by many Americans as inconsistent with a republican form of government. Indeed, many American colonists had fled Europe to escape persecution for having rejected state-sponsored churches. A second possible interpretation is the view that the government may not take sides among competing religions but is not prohibited from providing assistance to religious institutions or ideas as long as it shows no favoritism. The United States accommodates religious beliefs in a variety of ways, from the reference to God on U.S. currency to the prayer that begins every session of Congress. These forms of religious establishment have never been struck down by the courts. The third view regarding religious establishment, the most commonly held today, is the idea of a "wall of separation" between church and state—Jefferson's formulation—that cannot be breached by the government. For two centuries, Jefferson's words have had a powerful impact on our understanding of the proper relationship between church and state in America.

Despite the seeming absoluteness of the phrase "wall of separation," there is ample room to disagree on how high the wall is. One area of contestation over the appropriate boundary between church and state is in public education. For example, the Court has been consistently strict in cases of school prayer, striking down such practices as Bible reading,[14] nondenominational prayer,[15] a moment of silence for meditation, and pregame prayer at public sporting events.[16] In each of these cases, the Court reasoned that school-sponsored religious observations, even of an apparently nondenominational character, are highly suggestive of school sponsorship and therefore violate the prohibition against establishment of religion.

For decades, the Court has faced cases involving government financial support for religious schools. In 1971, the Court attempted to specify some criteria to guide its decisions and those of lower courts, indicating the circumstances under which state financial assistance to religious schools was constitutionally permissible. The case was *Lemon v. Kurtzman*; in its decision, the Supreme Court established three criteria to guide future cases. Collectively, these came to be called the **Lemon test**. The Court held that government aid to religious schools would be accepted as constitutional if (1) it had a secular purpose, (2) its effect was neither to advance nor to inhibit religion, and (3) it did not entangle government and religious institutions in each other's affairs.[17]

Although these restrictions make the *Lemon* test hard to pass, imaginative authorities are finding ways to do so, and the Supreme Court has demonstrated a willingness to let them. For example, in 1995 the Court narrowly ruled that a student religious group at the University of Virginia could not be denied student activities funds merely because it was a religious group espousing a particular viewpoint about a deity. The Court called the denial "viewpoint discrimination" that violated the free speech rights of the group.[18]

In 2004 the question of whether the phrase "under God" in the Pledge of Allegiance violated the establishment clause was brought before the Court. Written without any religious references in 1892, the pledge had long been used in schools. But in 1954, in the midst of the Cold War, Congress voted to change the pledge in response to the "godless Communism" of the Soviet Union.

Ever since the change was made, there has been a steady murmuring of discontent from those who object to an officially sanctioned profession of belief in a deity as a violation of the establishment clause of the First Amendment. In 2003, Michael A. Newdow, the atheist father of a kindergarten student, brought suit against the local California school district, arguing that the reference to God turned the daily recitation of the pledge into a religious exercise. The case was appealed to the Supreme Court, which ruled that Newdow lacked a sufficient personal

Lemon test a rule articulated in *Lemon v. Kurtzman* that government action toward religion is permissible if it is secular in purpose, neither promotes nor inhibits the practice of religion, and does not lead to "excessive entanglement" with religion

The First Amendment affects everyday life in a multitude of ways. Because of the amendment's ban on state-sanctioned religion, the Supreme Court ruled in 2000 that student-initiated public prayer in school is illegal. Pregame prayer at public schools violates the establishment cause of the First Amendment.

free exercise clause the First Amendment clause that protects a citizen's right to believe and practice whatever religion he or she chooses

stake in the case to bring the complaint. This inconclusive decision by the Supreme Court left "under God" in the pledge while keeping the issue alive for possible resolution in a future case.

Another realm of contestation over the meaning of the establishment clause is in public displays of religious symbols, such as city-sponsored nativity scenes in commercial or municipal areas. This realm remains contested, in part because the Supreme Court's rulings on such cases have been inconclusive, as demonstrated by two 2005 cases involving displays of the Ten Commandments. In *Van Orden v. Perry*, the Court decided that a display of the Ten Commandments outside the Texas state capitol did not violate the Constitution.[19] However, in *McCreary County v. American Civil Liberties Union of Kentucky*, the Court determined that a display of the Ten Commandments inside two Kentucky courthouses was unconstitutional.[20] Justice Stephen Breyer, the deciding vote in the two cases, said that the display in *Van Orden* had a secular purpose, whereas the displays in *McCreary* had a purely religious purpose. The key difference between the two cases is that the Texas display had been exhibited in a large park for 40 years with other monuments related to the development of American law, whereas the Kentucky display was erected much more recently and initially by itself, suggesting to some justices that its posting had a religious purpose. But most observers saw little difference between the two cases. Clearly, the issue of government-sponsored displays of religious symbols has not been settled.

Free Exercise of Religion

The **free exercise clause** protects the right to believe and to practice whatever religion one chooses; it also protects the right to be a nonbeliever. The precedent-setting case involving free exercise is *West Virginia State Board of Education v. Barnette* (1943), which involved the children of a family of Jehovah's Witnesses who refused to salute and pledge allegiance to the American flag on the grounds that their religious faith did not permit it. Three years earlier, the Court had upheld such a requirement and had permitted schools to expel students for refusing to salute the flag. But the entry of the United States into a war to defend democracy, coupled with the ugly treatment to which the Jehovah's Witnesses' children had been subjected, induced the Court to reverse itself and to endorse the free exercise of religion even when it may be offensive to the beliefs of the majority.[21]

Although the Supreme Court has been fairly consistent and strict in protecting the free exercise of religious belief, it has taken pains to distinguish between religious beliefs and *actions* based on those beliefs. The 1940 case of *Cantwell v. Connecticut* established the "time, place and manner" rule. The case arose from the efforts of two Jehovah's Witnesses to engage in door-todoor fund-raising. Americans are free to adhere to any religious beliefs, but the time, place, and manner of their exercise are subject to regulation in the public interest.[22]

In recent years, the principle of free exercise has been bolstered by statutes prohibiting religious discrimination by public and private entities in a variety of realms including hiring, land use, and the treatment of prison inmates. Two recent cases illustrating this point are *Holt v. Hobbs*[23] and *Equal Employment Opportunity Commission v. Abercrombie & Fitch Stores, Inc.*[24] The *Holt* case involved a Muslim prisoner in an Arkansas jail. The prisoner, Gregory Holt, asserted that his religious beliefs required him to grow a beard. Thus, according to Holt, an Arkansas prison policy prohibiting beards was a violation of his ability to exercise his religion. The Court held that the prison policy was a violation of the free exercise clause and violated a federal statute designed to protect the ability of prisoners to worship as they pleased. In the second case, the Equal Employment Opportunity Commission brought suit against Abercrombie & Fitch for refusing to hire a Muslim woman who wore a head scarf in violation of the company's dress code. The Court held that the store's actions amounted to religious discrimination in hiring, a violation of Title VII of the U.S. Code.

Does it violate the free exercise clause if a private business does not allow its employees to wear religious headscarves to work? In 2015 the Court ruled in favor of Samantha Elauf, declaring that Abercrombie and Fitch could not make an applicant's religious practice a factor in employment decisions.

● The First Amendment and Freedom of Speech and of the Press

> Describe how the First Amendment protects free speech and freedom of the press

Congress shall make no law . . . abridging the freedom of speech, or of the press.

Freedom of speech and freedom of the press have a special place in American political thought. To begin with, democracy depends on the ability of individuals to talk to one another and to disseminate information. It is difficult to conceive how democratic politics could function without free and open debate. Such debate, moreover, is seen as an essential mechanism for determining the quality or validity of competing ideas. As Justice Oliver Wendell Holmes said in 1919, "The best test of truth is the power of the thought to get itself accepted in the competition of the market. . . . That at any rate is the theory of our Constitution."[25] What is sometimes called the "marketplace of ideas" receives a good deal of protection from the courts. In 1938 the Supreme Court held that any legislation that attempts to restrict speech "is to be subjected to a more exacting judicial scrutiny . . . than are most other types of legislation."[26] This higher standard of judicial review came to be called "strict scrutiny."

The doctrine of strict scrutiny places a heavy burden of proof on the government if it seeks to regulate or restrict speech. Americans are assumed to have the right to speak and to broadcast their ideas unless some compelling reason can be identified to stop them. But strict scrutiny does not mean that speech can never be regulated. Over the past 200 years, the courts have scrutinized many different forms of speech and constructed different principles and guidelines for each. According to the courts, although virtually all speech is protected by the Constitution, some forms of speech are entitled to a greater degree of protection than others.

Political Speech

Political speech was the activity of greatest concern to the framers of the Constitution, even though some found it the most difficult form of speech to tolerate. Within seven years of the ratification of the Bill of Rights in 1791, Congress adopted the infamous Alien and Sedition Acts (long since repealed), which, among other things, made it a crime to say or publish anything that might tend to defame or bring into disrepute the government of the United States.

The first modern free speech case arose immediately after World War I. It involved persons who had been convicted under the federal Espionage Act of 1917 for opposing U.S. involvement in the war. The Supreme Court upheld the Espionage Act and refused to protect the speech rights of the defendants on the grounds that their activities—appeals to draftees to resist the draft—constituted a **"clear and present danger"** to national security.[27] This is the first and most famous, though since discarded, "test" for when government intervention or censorship can be permitted.

It was only after the 1920s that real progress toward a genuinely effective First Amendment was made. Since then, political speech has been consistently protected by the courts even when it has been deemed "insulting" or "outrageous." In the 1969 case *Brandenburg v. Ohio*, the court ruled that as long as speech falls short of actually inciting action, it cannot be prohibited, even if it is hostile to or subversive of the government and its policies. This decision came in the case of a Ku Klux Klan leader, Charles Brandenburg, who had been arrested and convicted of advocating "revengent" action against the president, Congress, and the Supreme Court, among others, if they continued "to suppress the white, Caucasian race." Although Brandenburg was not carrying a weapon, some of the members of his audience were. Nevertheless, the Supreme Court reversed the state courts and freed Brandenburg while also declaring Ohio's Criminal Syndicalism Act unconstitutional because it punished persons who "advocate, or teach the duty, necessity, or propriety [of violence] as a means of accomplishing industrial or political reform" or who publish materials or "voluntarily assemble . . . to teach or advocate the doctrines of criminal syndicalism." The Supreme Court argued that the statute did not distinguish "mere advocacy" from "incitement to imminent lawless action."[28] It would be difficult to go much further in protecting freedom of speech.

Another area of political speech that has recently received much attention is the First Amendment status of monetary contributions to political campaigns. Campaign finance reform laws of the early 1970s, arising out of the Watergate scandal, sought to put severe limits on campaign spending. In the 1976 case *Buckley v. Valeo*, a number of important provisions were declared unconstitutional on the basis of a new principle that spending money by or on behalf of candidates is a form of speech protected by the First Amendment.[29] (For more details, see Chapter 10.)

The issue came up again in 2003 with passage of a new and still more severe campaign finance law, the Bipartisan Campaign Reform Act (BCRA). In *McConnell v. Federal Election Commission*, the 5–4 majority seriously reduced the area of speech protected by the *Buckley v. Valeo* decision by holding that Congress was well within its power to put limits on campaign spending. The Court argued that "the selling of access . . . has given rise to the appearance of undue influence [that justifies] regulations impinging on First Amendment rights . . . in order to curb corruption or the appearance of corruption."[30] In the *McConnell* case, the Court also upheld BCRA's limitations on "issue advertising." The act prohibited political advocacy groups from running ads that mentioned a candidate within 30 days of a primary election and 60 days of a general election. This ban was justified with the argument that wealthy special interests could affect election outcomes with last-minute ad campaigns. However, in its 2007 decision in the case of *Federal Election Commission v. Wisconsin Right to Life*, the Court reversed itself, declaring

---

"clear and present danger" test used to determine whether speech is protected or unprotected, based on its capacity to present a "clear and present danger" to society

that such ads were protected speech and could not be prohibited so long as they focused mainly on issues and were not simply appeals to vote for or against a specific candidate.[31]

Even more recently, in the 2010 case of *Citizens United v. Federal Election Commission*, the Supreme Court declared that the First Amendment prohibited BCRA's ban on corporate funding of independent political broadcasts aimed at electing or defeating particular candidates.[32] In its 5–4 decision, the Supreme Court ruled that the Constitution prohibits the government from regulating political speech and that therefore the government could not ban this type of political spending by corporations. In 2014 the Court again expanded its protection of campaign expenditures under the First Amendment by overturning aggregate limits restricting how much money a donor may contribute.[33] As a result of this decision several wealthy donors contributed more than $10 million to presidential candidates in 2016. The Court's decisions in both cases have been controversial. Republicans hailed the decisions as a victory for free speech, while Democrats denounced the decisions. President Obama called *Citizens United* "a major victory for big oil, Wall Street banks, health insurance companies, and the other powerful interests that marshal their power every day in Washington to drown out the voices of everyday Americans."[34]

Fighting Words and Hate Speech

Freedom of speech does have limits, however. Speech can also lose its protected position when it moves toward the sphere of action. "Expressive speech," for example, is protected until it moves from the symbolic realm to the realm of actual conduct—to direct incitement of damaging conduct with the use of so-called **fighting words**. In 1942 a man called a police officer a "goddamned racketeer" and "a damn Fascist" and was arrested and convicted of violating a state law forbidding the use of offensive language in public. When his case reached the Supreme Court, the arrest was upheld on the grounds that the First Amendment provides no protection for such offensive language because such words "are no essential part of any exposition of ideas."[35] This decision was reaffirmed in the important 1951 case of *Dennis v. United States* when the Supreme Court held that there is no substantial public interest in permitting certain kinds of utterances: the lewd and obscene, the profane, the libelous, and the insulting or "fighting" words—those which by their very utterance inflict injury or tend to incite an immediate breach of the peace.[36] Since that time, however, the Supreme Court has reversed almost every conviction based on arguments that the speaker had used "fighting words."

In recent years, the increased activism of minority and women's groups has prompted a movement against words that might be construed as offensive to members of a particular group. Scores of universities have attempted to develop speech codes to suppress utterances deemed to be racial or ethnic slurs. Similar developments have taken place in large corporations, both public and private, with many successful complaints and lawsuits alleging that the words of employers or their supervisors created a "hostile or abusive working environment." The Supreme Court has held that a "hostile working environment" results from "sexual harassment," including "unwelcome sexual advances, requests for sexual favors, and other *verbal* or physical conduct of a sexual nature [emphasis added]."[37] A fundamental free speech issue is involved in these regulations of hostile speech.

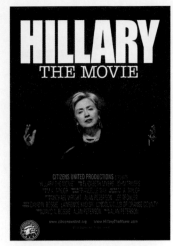

During the 2008 presidential primaries, the conservative organization Citizens United released a documentary criticizing Hillary Clinton. A lower court found that ads for the film violated the BCRA's ban on corporate funding of ads for or against a particular candidate. In 2010 the Court declared the BCRA ban unconstitutional under the First Amendment.

fighting words speech that directly incites damaging conduct

for critical analysis

Is there speech that should be banned because it does not contribute to the exchange of ideas? How do we determine what speech should be protected because it contributes to this exchange and what speech does not?

Many jurisdictions have drafted ordinances banning hate speech—forms of expression designed to assert hatred toward one or another group, be they African Americans, Jews, Muslims, or others. Such ordinances seldom pass constitutional muster. The leading Supreme Court case in this realm is the 1992 decision in *R.A.V. v. City of St. Paul*.[38] Here, a white teenager was arrested for burning a cross on the lawn of a black family in violation of a municipal ordinance that banned cross burning. The Court ruled that such an ordinance must be *content neutral*—that is, it must not prohibit actions directed at some groups but not others. The statute in question prohibited only cross burning, which is typically directed at African Americans. Since a statute banning all forms of hateful expression would be deemed overly broad, the *R.A.V.* standard suggests that virtually all hate speech is constitutionally protected.

Student Speech

One category of conditionally protected speech is the speech of high school students in public schools. In 1986 the Supreme Court backed away from a broad protection of student free speech rights by upholding the punishment of a high school student for making a sexually suggestive speech. The Court opinion held that such speech interfered with the school's goal of teaching students the limits of socially acceptable behavior.[39] Two years later the Supreme Court took another conservative step by restricting students' speech and press rights even further, defining them as part of the educational process and not to be treated with the same standard as adult speech in a regular public forum.[40] A later case involving high school students is the 2007 case of *Morse v. Frederick*.[41] This case dealt with the policies of Juneau-Douglas High School in Juneau, Alaska. In 2002 the Olympic torch relay had passed through Juneau on its way to Salt Lake City for the opening of the Winter Olympics. As the torch passed Juneau-Douglas High, a senior, Joseph Frederick, unfurled a banner reading "BONG HITS 4 JESUS." The school's principal promptly suspended Frederick, who then brought suit for reinstatement, alleging that his free speech rights had been violated. Like most of America's public schools, Juneau-Douglas High prohibits assemblies or expressions on school grounds that advocate illegal drug use, saying that some federal aid is contingent on this policy. Civil libertarians, of course, see such policies as restricting students' right to free speech. Speaking for the Court's majority, Chief Justice Roberts said that the First Amendment did not require schools to permit students to advocate illegal drug use.

The Supreme Court has ruled that high school students' speech can be restricted. In a 2007 case involving a student who displayed the banner below, the Court found that the school principal had not violated the student's right to free speech by suspending him.

Commercial Speech

Commercial speech, such as newspaper or television advertisements, does not have full First Amendment protection because it cannot be considered political speech. Initially considered to be entirely outside the protection of the First Amendment, commercial speech today is subject to limited regulation. For example, the prohibition of false and misleading advertising by the Federal Trade Commission is an old and well-established power of the federal government. The Supreme Court has upheld city ordinances prohibiting the posting of all commercial signs on public property (as long as the ban is total so that there is no hint of selective censorship).[42]

However, the gains far outweigh the losses in the effort to expand the protection of commercial speech under the First Amendment. "In part, this reflects the growing appreciation that commercial speech is part of the free flow of information necessary for informed choice and democratic participation."[43] For example, in 1975 the Supreme Court struck down a state statute making it a misdemeanor to sell or circulate newspapers encouraging abortions; the Court ruled that the statute infringed on constitutionally protected speech and on the right of the reader to make informed choices.[44] On a similar basis, the Court reversed its own earlier decisions upholding laws that prohibited lawyers, dentists, and other professionals from advertising their services. For the Court, medical service advertising was a matter of health that could be advanced by the free flow of information.[45] And in a 2001 case, the Court ruled that a Massachusetts ban on all cigarette advertising violated the First Amendment right of the tobacco industry to advertise its products to adult consumers.[46] These instances of commercial speech, significant in themselves, are all the more significant because they indicate the breadth and depth of the freedom existing today to direct appeals to a large public, not only to sell goods and services but also to mobilize people for political purposes.

Symbolic Speech, Speech Plus, and the Rights of Assembly and Petition

The First Amendment treats the freedoms of religion and political speech as equal to the freedoms of assembly and petition—speech associated with action. For this reason, the long record of Supreme Court cases largely protects an individual's right to symbolic speech, assembly, and petition. Freedom of speech and freedom of assembly are closely related by the "public forum doctrine." In the 1939 case of *Hague v. Committee for Industrial Organization*, the Court declared that the government may not prohibit speech-related activities such as demonstrations or leafleting in public areas traditionally used for that purpose, though, of course, the government may impose rules designed to protect the public safety so long as these rules do not discriminate against particular viewpoints.[47]

Generally, the Supreme Court has sought to protect actions that are designed to send a political message. One example is the burning of the American flag as a protest. In 1984, at a political rally held during the Republican National Convention in Dallas, Texas, a political protester burned an American flag, thereby violating a Texas statute that prohibited desecration of a venerated object. In a 5–4 decision, the Supreme Court declared the Texas law unconstitutional on the grounds that flag burning was expressive conduct protected by the First Amendment.[48] Since 1995 the House of Representatives has seven times passed a resolution for a constitutional amendment to ban this form of expressive conduct, but each time the Senate has failed to go along.[49]

In the 2011 case of *Snyder v. Phelps*, the Court sought to protect another form of symbolic speech. Members of the Westboro Baptist Church had frequently demonstrated at military funerals, claiming that the deaths of the soldiers were a sign that God disapproved of the acceptance of homosexuality in the United States. The father of a soldier killed in Iraq brought suit against the church and its pastor, claiming that the demonstrators had caused him and his family severe emotional distress. The Supreme Court ruled, however, that the First Amendment protected free speech in a public place against such suits.[50]

Should the First Amendment's protection of free speech apply even when that speech is seen as offensive? In 2011 the Supreme Court ruled 8–1 that members of the Westboro Baptist Church had a right to picket soldiers' funerals to demonstrate what they take as a sign of God's disapproval of homosexuality.

"speech plus" speech accompanied by conduct such as sit-ins, picketing, and demonstrations; protection of this form of speech under the First Amendment is conditional, and restrictions imposed by state or local authorities are acceptable if properly balanced by considerations of public order

prior restraint an effort by a governmental agency to block the publication of material it deems libelous or harmful in some other way; censorship; in the United States, the courts forbid prior restraint except under the most extraordinary circumstances

Closer to the original intent of the assembly and petition clause is the category of **"speech plus"**—following speech with physical activity such as picketing, distributing leaflets, and other forms of peaceful demonstration or assembly. Such assemblies are consistently protected by courts under the First Amendment; state and local laws regulating such activities are closely scrutinized and frequently overturned. But the same assembly on private property is quite another matter and can in many circumstances be regulated. For example, the directors of a shopping center can lawfully prohibit an assembly protesting a war or supporting a ban on abortion. Assemblies in public areas can also be restricted under some circumstances, especially when the assembly or demonstration jeopardizes the health, safety, or rights of others. This condition was the basis of the Supreme Court's decision to uphold a lower-court order that restricted the access that abortion protesters had to the entrances of abortion clinics.[51]

Freedom of the Press

For all practical purposes, freedom of speech implies and includes freedom of the press. With the exception of the broadcast media, which are subject to federal regulation, the press is protected under the doctrine against **prior restraint**. Beginning with the landmark 1931 case of *Near v. Minnesota*, the U.S. Supreme Court has held that, except under the most extraordinary circumstances, the First Amendment of the Constitution prohibits government agencies from seeking to prevent newspapers or magazines from publishing whatever they wish.[52] Indeed, in the case of the 1971 *New York Times Co. v. United States* (the so-called Pentagon Papers case), the Supreme Court ruled that the government could not block publication of secret Defense Department documents furnished to the *New York Times* by an opponent of the Vietnam War who had obtained the documents illegally.[53] In a 1990 case, however, the Supreme Court upheld a lower court order restraining Cable News Network (CNN) from broadcasting tapes of conversations between the former Panamanian dictator Manuel Noriega and his lawyer, supposedly recorded by the U.S. government. By a vote of 7 to 2, the Court held that CNN could be restrained from broadcasting the tapes until the trial court in the Noriega case had listened to the tapes and decided whether their broadcast would violate Noriega's right to a fair trial.[54]

Another press freedom issue that the courts have often been asked to decide is the question of whether journalists can be compelled to reveal their sources of information. Journalists assert that if they cannot ensure their sources' confidentiality, the flow of information will be reduced and press freedom effectively curtailed. Government agencies, however, aver that names of news sources may be relevant to criminal or even national security investigations. More than 30 states have "shield laws," which, to varying degrees, protect journalistic sources. There is, however, no federal shield law and no special constitutional protection for journalists. The Supreme Court has held that the press has no constitutional right to withhold information in court.[55] In 2005 a *New York Times* reporter, Judith Miller, was jailed for contempt of court for refusing to tell a federal grand jury the name of a confidential source in a case involving the leaked identity of the CIA analyst Valerie Plame. Plame's husband, Joseph Wilson, had been critical of the Bush administration's Iraq policies.

In addition to prosecuting journalists for refusing to reveal their sources, the government may seek to prosecute individuals who leak information to the press. During the Obama presidency, seven individuals were charged or prosecuted for disclosing classified information. These cases included Pfc. Bradley Manning, an army intelligence analyst sent to prison for providing classified documents to WikiLeaks, which published many of the documents, and Edward Snowden, an employee of the National Security Agency (NSA) who fled the country to escape arrest after revealing the details of NSA domestic spying operations. Another whistle-blower, Thomas Drake, was prosecuted after revealing the details of financial improprieties at the NSA to a *Baltimore Sun* reporter. Many journalists have been sharply critical of the Obama administration for its unprecedented efforts to halt whistle-blowing.[56]

Should reporters be obligated to reveal sources if the information will aid a government investigation? In 2005, New York Times reporter Judith Miller served almost three months' jail time for refusing to reveal a confidential source.

Libel and Slander Some speech is not protected at all. If a written statement is made in "reckless disregard of the truth" and is considered damaging to the victim because it is "malicious, scandalous, and defamatory," it can be punished as **libel**. If such a statement is made orally, it can be punished as **slander**.

Most libel suits today involve freedom of the press, and the realm of free press is enormous. Historically, newspapers were subject to the law of libel, which provided that newspapers that printed false and malicious stories could be compelled to pay damages to those they defamed. In recent years, however, American courts have greatly narrowed the meaning of libel and made it extremely difficult, particularly for politicians or other public figures, to win a libel case against a newspaper. In the important 1964 case of *New York Times Co. v. Sullivan*, the Court held that to be deemed libelous, a story about a public official not only had to be untrue but also had to result from "actual malice" or "reckless disregard" for the truth.[57] In other words, the newspaper had to print false and malicious material deliberately. In practice, it is nearly impossible to prove that a paper *deliberately* printed maliciously false information, and it is thus especially difficult for a politician or other public figure to win a libel case. Essentially, the print media have been able to publish anything they want about a public figure.

However, the Court has opened up the possibility for public officials to file libel suits against the press. The Court has held since the 1970s that the press was immune to libel suits only when the printed material was "a matter of public concern."[58] In other words, a newspaper would have to show that the public official was engaged in activities that were indeed *public*. This principle has made the press more vulnerable to libel suits, but it still leaves an enormous realm of freedom for the press.

With the emergence of the Internet as an important communications medium, the courts have had to decide how traditional libel law applies to Internet content. In 1995 the New York courts held that an online bulletin board could be held responsible for the libelous content of material posted by a third party. To protect Internet service providers, Congress subsequently enacted legislation absolving them of responsibility for third-party posts. The federal courts have generally upheld this law and declared that service providers are immune from suits regarding the content of material posted by others.[59]

libel a written statement made in "reckless disregard of the truth" that is considered damaging to a victim because it is "malicious, scandalous, and defamatory"

slander an oral statement made in "reckless disregard of the truth" that is considered damaging to the victim because it is "malicious, scandalous, and defamatory"

Obscenity and Pornography If libel and slander cases can be difficult because of the problem of determining the truth of statements and whether those statements are malicious and damaging, cases involving pornography and obscenity can be even trickier. Not until 1957 did the Supreme Court confront this problem, and it did so with a definition of obscenity that may have caused more confusion than it cleared up. In writing the Court's opinion, Justice William Brennan defined obscenity as speech or writing that appeals to the "prurient interest"—that is, whose purpose is to excite lust, as this appears "to the average person, applying contemporary community standards." Even so, Brennan added, the work should be judged obscene only when it is "utterly without redeeming social importance."[60] In 1964, Justice Potter Stewart confessed that, although he found pornography impossible to define, "I know it when I see it."[61]

The vague and impractical standards that had been developed meant ultimately that almost nothing could be banned on the grounds that it was pornographic and obscene. An effort was made to strengthen the restrictions in 1973, when the Supreme Court expressed its willingness to define pornography as a work that (1) as a whole, is deemed prurient by the "average person" according to "community standards"; (2) depicts sexual conduct "in a patently offensive way"; and (3) lacks "serious literary, artistic, political, or scientific value." This definition meant that pornography would be determined by local rather than national standards. Thus, a local bookseller might be prosecuted for selling a volume that was a best-seller nationally but that was deemed pornographic locally.[62] This new definition of standards did not help much either, and not long after 1973, the Court began again to review all such community antipornography laws, reversing most of them.

In recent years, the battle against obscene speech has targeted "cyberporn"—pornography on the Internet. Opponents of this form of expression argue that it should be banned because of the easy access children have to the Internet. The first major effort to regulate the content of the Internet occurred in 1996, when Congress passed the Telecommunications Act. Attached to it was an amendment, called the Communications Decency Act (CDA), designed to regulate the online transmission of obscene material. The constitutionality of the CDA was immediately challenged in court by a coalition of interests led by the American Civil Liberties Union. In the 1997 case of *Reno v. American Civil Liberties Union*, the Supreme Court struck down the CDA, ruling that it suppressed speech that "adults have a constitutional right to receive" and that governments may not limit the adult population to messages that are fit for children. Supreme Court justice John Paul Stevens described the Internet as the "town crier" of the modern age and said that the Internet was entitled to the greatest degree of First Amendment protection possible.[63] In 2003, Congress enacted the PROTECT Act, which outlawed efforts to sell child pornography via the Internet. The Supreme Court upheld this act in the 2008 case of *United States v. Williams*, in which the majority said that criminalizing efforts to purvey child pornography did not violate free speech guarantees.[64]

In 2000 the Supreme Court extended the highest degree of First Amendment protection to cable (not broadcast) television. In *United States v. Playboy Entertainment Group*, the Court struck down a portion of the 1996 Telecommunications Act that required cable TV companies to limit the broadcast of sexually explicit programming to late-night hours. In its decision, the Court noted that the law already provided parents with the means to restrict access to sexually explicit cable channels through various blocking devices. Moreover, such programming could come into the home only if parents decided to purchase such channels in the first place.[65]

Closely related to the issue of obscenity is the matter of violent broadcast content. Can a state or the federal government prohibit broadcasts or publications deemed to be excessively violent? Here, too, the Court has generally upheld freedom of speech. For example, in the 2011 case of *Brown v. Entertainment Merchants Association*, the Court struck down a California law banning the sale of violent video games to children, saying that the law violated the First Amendment.[66]

● The Second Amendment and the Right to Bear Arms

Explore whether the Second Amendment means people have a right to own guns

A well regulated Militia, being necessary to the security of a free State, the right of the people to keep and bear Arms, shall not be infringed.

The point and purpose of the Second Amendment is the provision for militias; they were to be the backing of the government for the maintenance of local public order. "Militia" was understood at the time of the Founding to be a military or police resource for state governments, and militias were specifically distinguished from armies and troops, which came within the sole constitutional jurisdiction of Congress. Many individuals, though, have argued that the Second Amendment also establishes an individual right to bear arms.

The judicial record of Second Amendment cases is far sparser than that of First Amendment cases, and for almost 60 years the Court made no Second Amendment decisions. In the absence of a ruling that would apply to the entire country, localities across the country have very different gun ownership standards, the result of a patchwork of state and local laws. For instance, in Wyoming, there is no ban on owning any type of gun, there is no waiting period to purchase a firearm, and individuals are not required to obtain a permit for carrying a concealed weapon. In California, in contrast, the possession of assault weapons is banned, there is a 10-day waiting period to purchase a firearm, and a permit is required to carry a concealed weapon. Figure 4.1 shows the percentage of adults in each state who own guns.

A string of recent mass shootings in the United States, including the shooting of nine people during a prayer service at a church in Charleston, South Carolina, have prompted calls for legislation to limit the availability of guns.

The Court's silence on the application of the Second Amendment ended in 2008, when the Supreme Court made the first of two rulings in favor of expansive rights of gun ownership by individuals. In the case *District of Columbia v. Heller*, at issue was a strict Washington, D.C., law that banned handguns. In a 5–4 decision, the Court ruled that the Second Amendment provides a constitutional right to keep a loaded handgun at home for self-defense, a view that had long been subject to debate. In the majority opinion, Justice Antonin Scalia stated that the decision was not intended to cast doubt on all laws limiting firearm possession, such as the prohibition on gun ownership by felons or the mentally ill.[67] In his dissenting opinion, Justice Stevens asserted that the Second Amendment only protects the rights of individuals to bear arms as part of a militia force, not in an individual capacity.

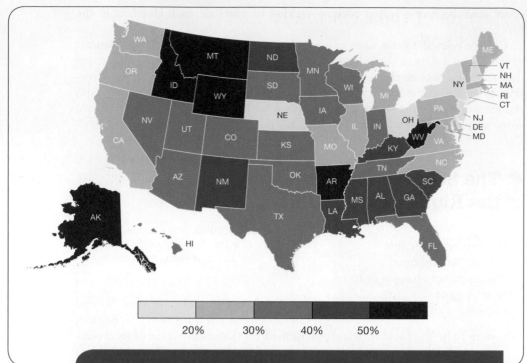

20%   30%   40%   50%

FIGURE 4.1

Gun Ownership by State

Although state gun laws must conform to the Second Amendment as interpreted by the U.S. Supreme Court, laws concerning gun sales and ownership vary widely from state to state. It is much more difficult to buy a gun in, say, New York or California than in Texas or Kentucky. This map shows the percentage of the adult population in each state owning a gun in 2013.

SOURCE: Bindu Kalesan, Marcos D. Villarreal, Katherine M. Keyes, and Sandro Galea, "Gun Ownership and Social Gun Culture," June 29, 2015, http://injuryprevention.bmj.com/content/early/2015/06/09/injuryprev-2015-041586.full.pdf?keytype=ref&ijkey=doj6vxOlaFZMsQ2 (accessed 6/13/16).

The District of Columbia is an entity of the federal government, and the Court did not indicate that its ruling applied to state firearms laws. However, in the 2010 case of *McDonald v. Chicago*, the Supreme Court applied the Second Amendment to the states, making this decision the first new incorporation decision by the Court in 40 years. The case concerned a Chicago ordinance that made it extremely difficult to own a gun within city limits, and the Court's ruling had the effect of overturning the law.[68]

Despite these rulings, the debate over gun control continues to loom large in American politics today. A recent series of tragic shootings (including the killing of 20 elementary school students in Newtown, Connecticut; 9 parishioners at a Charleston, South Carolina, church; and 50 people at a nightclub in Orlando, Florida) has kept the issue of gun laws firmly on the national agenda. In 2016, President Obama issued several executive orders designed to expand background checks for gun purchasers and licensure requirements for firearms dealers but these did not end the debate.

Rights of the Criminally Accused

Explain the major rights that people have if they are accused of a crime

Except for the First Amendment, most of the battle to apply the Bill of Rights to the states has been fought over the various protections granted to individuals who are accused of a crime, who are suspects in the commission of a crime, or who are brought before the court as a witness to a crime (Table 4.4). The Fourth, Fifth, Sixth, and Eighth amendments, taken together, are the essence of the **due process of law**, even though these precise words for this fundamental concept do not appear until the end of the Fifth Amendment. In the next sections, we will look at specific cases that illuminate the dynamics of this important constitutional issue. The procedural safeguards that we will discuss may seem remote to most law-abiding citizens, but they help define the limits of government action against the personal liberty of every citizen. Many Americans believe that "legal technicalities" are responsible for setting many actual criminals free. In some cases, this is true. In fact, setting defendants free is the very purpose of the requirements that constitute due process, and few convictions are actually lost because of excluded evidence. One of America's traditional and most strongly held juridical values is that "it is far worse to convict an innocent man than to let a guilty man go free."[69] In civil suits, verdicts rest on "the preponderance of the evidence"; but in criminal cases, guilt has to be proven "beyond a reasonable doubt"—a far higher standard. The provisions for due process in the Bill of Rights were added in order to improve the probability that the standard of "reasonable doubt" would be respected.

TABLE 4.4

The Rights of the Accused from Arrest to Trial

No improper searches and seizures (Fourth Amendment)

No arrest without probable cause (Fourth Amendment)

Right to remain silent (Fifth Amendment)

No self-incrimination during arrest or trial (Fifth Amendment)

Right to be informed of charges (Sixth Amendment)

Right to counsel (Sixth Amendment)

No excessive bail (Eighth Amendment)

Right to grand jury (Fifth Amendment)

Right to open trial before a judge (Article I, Section 9)

Right to speedy and public trial before an impartial jury (Sixth Amendment)

Evidence obtained by illegal search not admissible during trial (Fourth Amendment)

Right to confront witnesses (Sixth Amendment)

No double jeopardy (Fifth Amendment)

No cruel and unusual punishment (Eighth Amendment)

due process of law the right of every individual against arbitrary action by national or state governments

The Fourth Amendment and Searches and Seizures

> The right of the people to be secure in their persons, houses, papers, and effects, against unreasonable searches and seizures, shall not be violated, and no Warrants shall issue, but upon probable cause, supported by Oath or affirmation, and particularly describing the place to be searched, and the persons or things to be seized.

The purpose of the Fourth Amendment is to guarantee the security of citizens against unreasonable (i.e., improper) searches and seizures. In 1990 the Supreme Court summarized its understanding of the Fourth Amendment brilliantly and succinctly: "A search compromises the individual interest in privacy; a seizure deprives the individual of dominion over his or her person or property."[70] But how are we to define what is reasonable and what is unreasonable?

The 1961 case of *Mapp v. Ohio* illustrates one of the most important of the principles that have grown out of the Fourth Amendment—the **exclusionary rule**, which prohibits evidence obtained during an illegal search from being introduced

exclusionary rule the ability of courts to exclude evidence obtained in violation of the Fourth Amendment

Under what circumstances can the police search an individual's car? The Fourth Amendment protects against "unreasonable searches and seizures," but the Supreme Court has had to interpret what is unreasonable.

in a trial. Acting on a tip that Dollree (Dolly) Mapp was harboring a suspect in a bombing incident, several policemen forcibly entered Mapp's house, claiming they had a warrant to look for the bombing suspect. The police did not find the bombing suspect but, in an old trunk in the basement, did find some materials they declared to be obscene. Although no warrant was ever produced, the evidence that had been seized was admitted by a court, and Mapp was charged and convicted of illegal possession of obscene materials.

The question before the Court was whether any evidence produced under the circumstances of the search of her home was admissible. The Court's opinion affirmed the exclusionary rule: under the Fourth Amendment (applied to the states through the Fourteenth Amendment), "all evidence obtained by searches and seizures in violation of the Constitution . . . is inadmissible."[71] This means that even people who are clearly guilty of the crime of which they are accused must not be convicted if the only evidence for their conviction was obtained illegally. This idea was expressed by Supreme Court justice Benjamin Cardozo nearly a century ago, when he wrote that "the criminal is to go free because the constable has blundered."

The exclusionary rule is the most dramatic restraint imposed by the courts on police behavior because it rules out precisely the evidence that produces a conviction; it frees those people who are *known* to have committed the crime of which they have been accused. Thus, in recent years the Court has softened the application of the exclusionary rule, and federal courts have relied on its discretionary use, whereby they make a judgment as to the "nature and quality of the intrusion."[72] In 2006, in the case of *United States v. Grubbs*, the Supreme Court ruled that the police could conduct searches using such "anticipatory warrants"—warrants issued when the police know that incriminating material is not yet present but have reason to believe that it will eventually arrive at a particular premises.[73] The warrants are held until the police are ready to conduct their search. In some instances, such as during an arrest, the authorities can conduct searches without obtaining any warrants at all.

The Fourth Amendment is also at issue in the controversy over mandatory drug testing. Such tests are most widely applied to public employees. In 1989 the Supreme Court upheld the U.S. Customs Service's drug-testing program for its employees[74] and drug and alcohol tests for railroad workers if they were involved in serious accidents.[75] Since then, more than 40 federal agencies have initiated mandatory employee drug tests, giving rise to public appeals against the general practice of "suspicionless testing" of employees, in violation of the Fourth Amendment. A 1995 case, in which the Court upheld a public school district's policy requiring all students participating in interscholastic sports to submit to random drug tests, surely contributed to the efforts of federal, state, and local agencies to initiate random and suspicionless drug and alcohol testing.[76]

The most recent cases suggest, however, that the Court is beginning to consider limits on the war against drugs. In a decisive 8–1 decision in 1997, the Court applied the Fourth Amendment as a shield against "state action that diminishes personal privacy" in cases that do not involve high-risk or safety-sensitive tasks.[77] And in 2013, the Court held that the use of a drug-sniffing dog on the front porch of a home constituted a search that violates the Fourth Amendment in the absence of consent of a warrant. The majority opinion, written by Justice Antonin Scalia, rested on traditional property notions.[78]

Changes in technology have also had an impact on Fourth Amendment jurisprudence. In the 2012 case of *United States v. Jones*, the Court held that prosecutors violated Jones's rights when they attached a Global Positioning System (GPS) device to his Jeep and monitored his movements for 28 days.[79] On the other hand, in *Maryland v. King*, the Court upheld DNA testing of arrestees without the need for individualized suspicion. Writing for the majority, Justice Anthony Kennedy characterized DNA testing as an administrative tool for identifying the arrestee and thus legally indistinguishable from photographing and fingerprinting.[80] In the 2014 case of *Riley v. California*, the Court held that the police were constitutionally prohibited from seizing and searching the digital contents of a cell phone during an arrest. As new technologies develop, the Court will continue to face the question of what constitutes a reasonable search.[81] In 2016, the FBI sought to compel the Apple Corporation to unlock the cell phone used by Syed Farook, an alleged terrorist who, along with his wife Tashfeen Malik, had killed 14 people in San Bernardino, California. Apple asserted that creating a new software to enable the FBI to unlock the phone would allow the agency to invade the privacy of millions of iPhone users. The case became moot when the FBI was able to unlock the phone without Apple's help.

Fourth Amendment issues have also been raised by aggressive police tactics, particularly the tactic known as "stop and frisk." This is a tactic in which the police confront an individual whom they believe to be acting "suspiciously," question the individual, and conduct a search for weapons. The practice was reviewed by the Supreme Court in the 1968 case of *Terry v. Ohio*, and the Court then held that if an officer had "probable cause" to believe the individual was armed, such a search was permitted.[82] In recent years, some police departments, most notably the New York City police, have made stop and frisk a routine practice, searching thousands and thousands of individuals whom they deemed to look suspicious. The police aver that this aggressive tactic has reduced crime rates. In August 2013 a federal judge, Shira Scheindlin, noted that most police stops occurred in minority communities and

The policing tactic of "stop and frisk" is intended to protect communities from violent crime. But opponents view it as invasion of privacy and unreasonable search without sufficient cause. Furthermore, opponents charge that such tactics damage the relationship between the police and the community.

amounted to a form of racial profiling. The judge's order ending the practice, however, was stayed by a federal appeals court that removed Judge Scheindlin from the case and accused her of improper bias. In 2014, the City of New York dropped its appeal and agreed to engage in a process of mediation with community groups to curtail the practice. After his election in 2014, Mayor Bill de Blasio announced an end to aggressive stop-and-frisk tactics. Critics charged that the mayor's orders were responsible for a subsequent increase in New York crime rates.

Finally, the Fourth Amendment places limits on government surveillance of individuals, an ongoing and controversial issue in the United States today. For example, a federal judge in Washington, D.C., recently ruled that an NSA program that collected millions of records of telephone calls was impermissible under the Fourth Amendment.[83]

The Fifth Amendment

No person shall be held to answer for a capital, or otherwise infamous crime, unless on a presentment or indictment of a Grand Jury, except in cases arising in the land or naval forces, or in the Militia, when in actual service in time of War or public danger; nor shall any person be subject for the same offence to be twice put in jeopardy of life or limb; nor shall be compelled in any criminal case to be a witness against himself, nor be deprived of life, liberty, or property, without due process of law; nor shall private property be taken for public use, without just compensation.

grand jury jury that determines whether sufficient evidence is available to justify a trial; grand juries do not rule on the accused's guilt or innocence

Grand Juries The first clause of the Fifth Amendment, the right to a **grand jury** to determine whether a trial is warranted, is considered "the oldest institution known to the Constitution."[84] A grand jury is a body of citizens that must agree that the prosecutor has sufficient evidence to bring criminal charges against a suspect. Grand juries play an important role in federal criminal cases. However, the provision for a grand jury is the one important civil liberties provision of the Bill of Rights that was not incorporated into the Fourteenth Amendment to apply to state criminal prosecutions. Thus, some states operate without grand juries. In such states, the prosecuting attorney simply files a "bill of information" affirming that there is sufficient evidence available to justify a trial. If the accused person is to be held in custody, the prosecutor must take the available information before a judge to determine that the evidence shows probable cause.

double jeopardy the Fifth Amendment right providing that a person cannot be tried twice for the same crime

Double Jeopardy "Nor shall any person be subject for the same offence to be twice put in jeopardy of life or limb" is the constitutional protection from **double jeopardy**, or being tried more than once for the same crime. The protection from double jeopardy was at the heart of the *Palko* case in 1937, which, as we saw earlier in this chapter, also established the principle of selective incorporation of the Bill of Rights. In the *Palko* case, the Supreme Court ruled that the Fifth Amendment's prohibition of double jeopardy did not apply to the states. However, in the 1969 case of *Benton v. Maryland*, the Court expressly overruled *Palko* and declared that the double jeopardy clause did, in fact, apply to the states.[85] In this case, the state of Maryland sought to try a defendant, John Benton, for larceny even though he had previously been acquitted by a jury. Maryland's constitution did not prohibit such a proceeding, and at the second trial Benton was convicted. The Supreme Court, however, ruled that the second trial violated Benton's rights under the U.S. Constitution. Double jeopardy now joined those rights "incorporated" via the Fourteenth Amendment.

Self-Incrimination Perhaps the most significant liberty found in the Fifth Amendment, and the one most familiar to the many Americans who watch television crime shows, is the guarantee that no citizen "shall be compelled in any criminal case to be a witness against himself." The most famous case concerning self-incrimination is one of such importance that Chief Justice Earl Warren assessed its results as going "to the very root of our concepts of American criminal jurisprudence."[86] Twenty-three-year-old Ernesto Miranda was sentenced to between 20 and 30 years in prison for the kidnapping and rape of an 18-year-old woman. The woman had identified him in a police lineup, and after two hours of questioning, Miranda confessed, subsequently signing a statement that his confession had been made voluntarily, without threats or promises of immunity. These confessions were admitted into evidence and served as the basis for Miranda's conviction. After his conviction, Miranda argued that his confession had not been truly voluntary and that he had not been informed of his right to remain silent or his right to consult an attorney. The Supreme Court agreed and overturned the conviction. Following one of the most intensely and widely criticized decisions ever handed down by the Supreme Court, Ernesto Miranda's case produced the rules the police must follow before questioning an arrested criminal suspect. The reading of a person's "Miranda rights" became a standard scene in every police station and on virtually every dramatization of police action on television and in the movies. *Miranda* advanced the civil liberties of accused persons not only by expanding the scope of the Fifth Amendment clause covering coerced confessions and self-incrimination but also by confirming the right to counsel (discussed later). The Supreme Court under Burger and Rehnquist considerably softened the *Miranda* restrictions, but the **Miranda rule** still stands as a protection against egregious police abuses of arrested persons.

Eminent Domain The other fundamental clause of the Fifth Amendment is the "takings clause," which extends to each citizen a protection against the "taking" of private property "without just compensation." Although this part of the Fifth

Miranda rule the requirement, articulated by the Supreme Court in *Miranda v. Arizona*, that persons under arrest must be informed prior to police interrogation of their rights to remain silent and to have the benefit of legal counsel

The case of Ernesto Miranda resulted in the creation of Miranda rights, which must be read to those arrested to make them aware of their constitutional rights.

DEFENDANT	LOCATION
SPECIFIC WARNING REGARDING INTERROGATIONS	

1. You have the right to remain silent.

2. Anything you say can and will be used against you in a court of law.

3. You have the right to talk to a lawyer and have him present with you while you are being questioned.

4. If you cannot afford to hire a lawyer one will be appointed to represent you before any questioning, if you wish one.

SIGNATURE OF DEFENDANT	DATE
WITNESS	TIME

☐ REFUSED SIGNATURE   SAN FRANCISCO POLICE DEPARTMENT   PR.9.1.4

Amendment is not specifically concerned with protecting persons accused of crimes, it is nevertheless a fundamentally important instance where the government and the citizen are adversaries. The power of any government to take private property for public use—a power essential to the very concept of sovereignty—is called **eminent domain**. The Fifth Amendment puts limits on that inherent power through procedures that require a showing of a public purpose and the provision of fair payment for the taking of someone's property. This provision is now universally observed in all U.S. principalities, but it has not always been meticulously observed.

eminent domain the right of government to take private property for public use

The first modern case confronting the issue of public use involved a mom-and-pop grocery store in a run-down neighborhood of the District of Columbia. In carrying out a vast urban redevelopment program, the city government took the property as one of a large number of privately owned lots to be cleared for new housing and business construction. The owner of the grocery store took the government to court on the grounds that it was an unconstitutional use of eminent domain to take property from one private owner and eventually to turn that property back, in altered form, to another private owner. In 1945 the store owner lost the case. The Supreme Court's argument was a curious but very important one: the "public interest" can mean virtually anything a legislature says it means. In other words, since the overall slum clearance and redevelopment project was in the public interest, according to the legislature, the eventual transfers of property were justified.[87] This principle was reaffirmed in the 2005 case of *Kelo v. City of New London*, where the Court held that the city could seize land from one private owner and transfer it to another as part of a redevelopment plan.[88]

The Sixth Amendment and the Right to Counsel

In all criminal prosecutions, the accused shall enjoy the right to a speedy and public trial, by an impartial jury of the State and district wherein the crime shall have been committed, which district shall have been previously ascertained by law, and to be informed of the nature and cause of the accusation; to be confronted with the witnesses against him; to have compulsory process for obtaining witnesses in his favor, and to have the Assistance of Counsel for his defence.

Some provisions of the Sixth Amendment, such as the right to a speedy trial and the right to confront witnesses before an impartial jury, are not very controversial in nature. The "right to counsel" provision, like the exclusionary rule of the Fourth Amendment and the self-incrimination clause of the Fifth Amendment, is notable for sometimes freeing defendants who seem to be guilty as charged.

Gideon v. Wainwright (1963) is the perfect case study because it involved a disreputable person who seemed patently guilty of the crime of which he was convicted. In and out of jails for most of his 51 years, Clarence Earl Gideon received a five-year sentence for breaking and entering a poolroom in Panama City, Florida. While serving time in jail, Gideon became a fairly well-qualified "jailhouse lawyer," made his own appeal on a handwritten petition, and eventually won the landmark ruling on the right to counsel in all felony cases.[89]

The right to counsel has been expanded during the past few decades, even as the courts have become more conservative. For example, although at first the right to counsel was met by judges assigning lawyers from the community as a formal public obligation, now most states and cities have created an office of public defender; these state-employed professional defense lawyers typically provide poor defendants with much better legal representation. In addition, defendants have the right to appeal a conviction on the grounds that the counsel provided by the state was deficient. For example, in 2003 the Supreme Court overturned the death sentence of a Maryland death-row inmate, holding that the defense lawyer had failed to inform the jury fully of the defendant's history of "horrendous childhood abuse."[90] Moreover, the right to counsel extends beyond serious crimes to any trial, with or without a jury, that holds the possibility of imprisonment.[91]

The Eighth Amendment and Cruel and Unusual Punishment

> Excessive bail shall not be required, nor excessive fines imposed, nor cruel and unusual punishment inflicted.

Virtually all the debate over Eighth Amendment issues focuses on the last clause of the amendment: one of the greatest challenges in interpreting this provision consistently is that what is considered "cruel and unusual" varies from culture to culture and from generation to generation.

In 1972 the Supreme Court overturned several state death penalty laws, not because they were cruel and unusual but because they were being applied unevenly—that is, blacks were much more likely than whites to be sentenced to death, the poor more likely than the rich, and men more likely than women.[92] Very soon after that decision, a majority of states revised their capital punishment provisions to meet the Court's standards, and the Court reaffirmed that the death penalty could be used if certain standards were met.[93] Since 1976, the Court has consistently upheld state laws providing for capital punishment, although the Court also continues to review death penalty appeals each year.

Between 1976 and October 2016, states executed 1,439 people. Most of those executions occurred in southern states, with Texas leading the way at 538. As of 2016, 31 states had statutes providing for capital punishment for specified offenses, a policy supported by a majority of Americans, according to polls. On the other hand, 19 states bar the death penalty, and since the end of the 1990s, both the number of death sentences and the number of executions have declined annually.[94]

Despite the seeming popularity of the death penalty, the debate has become, if anything, more intense. Many death penalty supporters assert its deterrent effects on other would-be criminals. Although studies of capital crimes usually fail to demonstrate any direct deterrent effect, this failure may be due to the lengthy delays—typically years and even decades—between convictions and executions. A system that eliminates undue delays might enhance deterrence. And deterring even one murder or other heinous crime, proponents argue, is ample justification for such laws.

Death penalty opponents are quick to counter that the death penalty has not been proved to deter crime, either in the United States or abroad. In fact, America is the only Western nation that still executes criminals. If the government is to serve as an example of proper behavior, say foes of capital punishment, it has no business sanctioning killing when incarceration will similarly protect society. Furthermore, execution is time-consuming and expensive—more expensive than life imprisonment—precisely because the government must make every effort to ensure that it is not executing an innocent person. Curtailing legal appeals would make the possibility of a mistake too great. And although most Americans do

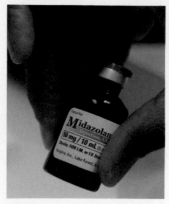

Opponents argue that the death penalty constitutes cruel and unusual punishment. In recent years the use of lethal injection drugs including Midazolam has come under scrutiny after some troubling executions where the process was drawn-out and painful. In 2015 the Supreme Court upheld the use of lethal injection.

support the death penalty, people also support life imprisonment without the possibility of parole as an alternative. Race also intrudes in death penalty cases: people of color are disproportionately more likely than whites charged with identical crimes to be given the ultimate punishment.

The Supreme Court has long struggled to establish principles to govern executions under the Eighth Amendment. In recent years, the Court has issued a number of death penalty opinions, declaring that death was too harsh a penalty for the crime of rape of a child,[95] prohibiting the execution of a defendant with an IQ under 70 and of a youthful defendant, and invalidating a death sentence for a black defendant after the prosecutor improperly excluded African Americans from the jury.[96] In 2015 the Court upheld lethal injection as a mode of execution despite arguments that this form of execution was likely to cause considerable pain.[97]

The question of cruel and unusual punishment goes beyond the death penalty. Federal courts have on occasion held that overcrowding and other dangerous conditions within prisons, such as inadequate food, medical care, and sanitation, may constitute cruel and unusual punishment. Also, prison officials employing threats and beatings against inmates may be guilty of violating this Eighth Amendment right.[98] The Court has also been concerned with punishments meted out to the mentally disabled and to juveniles. In a recent case, the Court held that life imprisonment without parole for a juvenile, even one convicted of murder, constituted cruel and unusual punishment.[99] The "Who Are Americans?" feature takes a look at the U.S. prison population.

● The Right to Privacy

right to privacy the right to be left alone, which has been interpreted by the Supreme Court to entail individual access to birth control and abortions

> **Assess whether people have a right to privacy under the Constitution**

A **right to privacy** was not granted in the Bill of Rights, but a clause in the Fourth Amendment provides for "the right of the people to be secure in their persons, houses, papers, and effects, against unreasonable searches and seizures." In a 1928 case, Justice Louis Brandeis argued in a dissent that the Fourth Amendment should be extended to a more general principle of "privacy in the home."[100] Another step in this direction was taken when several Jehovah's Witnesses directed their children not to salute the flag or say the Pledge of Allegiance in school because the first of the Ten Commandments prohibits the worship of "graven images." They lost their case in 1940, but the Supreme Court, reversing itself in 1943, held that the 1940 case had been "wrongly decided" and recognized "a right to be left alone" as part of the free speech clause of the First Amendment.[101] Another small step was taken in 1958, when the Supreme Court recognized "privacy in one's association" in its decision that the state of Alabama could not use the membership list of the National Association for the Advancement of Colored People (NAACP) in state investigations.[102]

Birth Control

The sphere of privacy was formally recognized in 1965, when the Court ruled that a Connecticut statute forbidding the use of contraceptives violated the right of marital privacy. Estelle Griswold, the executive director of the Planned Parenthood

Who Is in Prison?

Despite the many freedoms protected by the Bill of Rights, the United States imprisons more of its people than any other country. Although African Americans make up only about 13 percent of the total U.S. population, they make up 35.7 percent of the prison population. Incarceration rates by state range from a low of 189 per 100,000 residents in Maine to a high of 1,072 per 100,000 residents in Louisiana.*

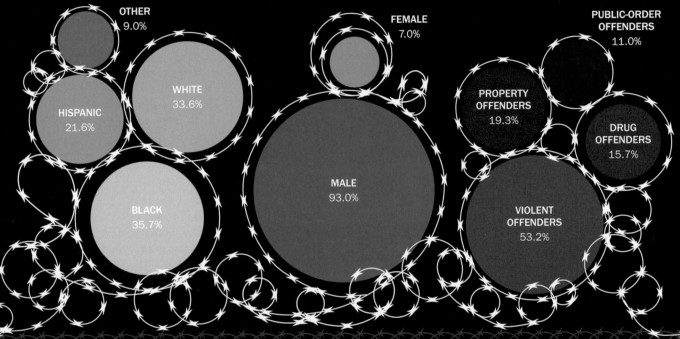

- OTHER 9.0%
- HISPANIC 21.6%
- WHITE 33.6%
- BLACK 35.7%
- FEMALE 7.0%
- MALE 93.0%
- PUBLIC-ORDER OFFENDERS 11.0%
- PROPERTY OFFENDERS 19.3%
- DRUG OFFENDERS 15.7%
- VIOLENT OFFENDERS 53.2%

*Violent offenses include murder, manslaughter, rape/sexual assault, robbery, and aggravated or simple assault. Property offenses include burglary, motor vehicle theft, and fraud. Drug offenses include trafficking and possession. Public order offenses include weapons, drunk driving, and indecency.

Incarceration Rates by State

Number of incarcerated individuals per 100,000 residents

- >300
- 300–399
- 400–499
- 500–599
- 600+

SOURCE: U.S. Department of Justice, "Prisoners in 2014," September 2015, www.bjs.gov/index.cfm?ty=pbdetail&iid=5387 (accessed 2/18/16).

for critical analysis

1. Due process guarantees the same legal protections to anyone accused of a crime. However, studies have shown that African Americans and Hispanics are more likely to be jailed—and jailed for longer—than whites convicted of similar crimes. Is this a violation of civil liberties?

2. Some people have argued that prison terms for relatively minor drug offenses violate the Eighth Amendment's ban on cruel and unusual punishment. What do you think?

League of Connecticut, was arrested by the state of Connecticut for providing information, instruction, and medical advice about contraception to married couples. She and her associates were found guilty as accessories to the crime and fined $100 each. The Supreme Court reversed the lower-court decisions and declared the Connecticut law unconstitutional because it violated "a right of privacy older than the Bill of Rights—older than our political parties, older than our school system."[103] Justice William O. Douglas, author of the majority decision in the *Griswold* case, argued that this right of privacy is also grounded in the Constitution because it fits into a "zone of privacy" created by a combination of the Third, Fourth, and Fifth amendments. A concurring opinion, written by Justice Arthur Goldberg, attempted to strengthen Douglas's argument by adding that "the concept of liberty . . . embraces the right of marital privacy though that right is not mentioned explicitly in the Constitution [and] is supported by numerous decisions of this Court . . . and *by the language and history of the Ninth Amendment* [emphasis added]."[104] The Ninth Amendment provides that "the enumeration in the Constitution, of certain rights, shall not be construed to deny or disparage others retained by the people." According Justice Goldberg, this language means, in effect, that just because the Constitution does not specifically mention a particular right to privacy does not mean that the people do not retain that right. The language of the Ninth Amendment, when taken with the evidence provided by the First, Third, Fourth, and Fifth amendments, was sufficient for the Court to find that the Bill of Rights implies a constitutional right to privacy.

Abortion

The right to privacy was confirmed and extended in 1973 in an important Supreme Court decision: *Roe v. Wade*. This decision established a woman's right to seek an abortion and prohibited states from making abortion a criminal act prior to the point at which the fetus becomes viable, which in 1973 was the twenty-seventh week.[105] The Burger Court's decision in *Roe* took a revolutionary step toward establishing the right to privacy. It is important to emphasize that the preference for privacy rights and for their extension to include the rights of women to control

for critical analysis

Read the Third, Fourth, Fifth, and Ninth amendments in the appendix at the end of this book. In your opinion, do American citizens have a constitutional right to privacy?

One of the most important cases related to the right to privacy was Roe v. Wade, which established a woman's right to seek an abortion. However, the decision has remained highly controversial, with opponents arguing that the Constitution does not guarantee this right.

their own bodies was not something the Supreme Court invented in a vacuum. Most states did not regulate abortions in any fashion until the 1840s, at which time only six of the 26 existing states had any regulations governing abortion. In addition, many states had begun to ease their abortion restrictions well before the 1973 *Roe* decision, although in recent years a number of states have reinstated some restrictions on abortion including lowering the viability standard: 20 weeks (Texas), 12 weeks (Arkansas), and 6 weeks (North Dakota).

By extending the umbrella of privacy, this sweeping ruling dramatically changed abortion practices in America. In addition, it galvanized and nationalized the abortion debate. Groups opposed to abortion, such as the National Right to Life Committee, organized to fight the liberal new standard, while abortion rights groups have sought to maintain that protection. While the Supreme Court has continued to affirm a woman's right to seek an abortion, the Court has since qualified that right as the legal standard shifted against abortion rights supporters. In *Webster v. Reproductive Health Services* (1989), the Court narrowly upheld (by a 5–4 majority) the constitutionality of restrictions on the use of public medical facilities for abortion.[106] And in the 1992 case of *Planned Parenthood of Southeastern Pennsylvania v. Casey*, another 5–4 majority of the Court upheld *Roe* but narrowed its scope, refusing to invalidate a Pennsylvania law that significantly limits freedom of choice. The Court's decision defined the right to an abortion as a "limited or qualified" right subject to regulation by the states as long as the regulation does not constitute an "undue burden."[107] In the 2006 case of *Ayotte v. Planned Parenthood of Northern New England*, the Court held that a law requiring parental notification before a minor could obtain an abortion was not an undue burden.[108] And in the 2007 *Gonzales v. Carhart* decision, the Court effectively upheld the federal partial-birth abortion ban, which outlaws a particular type of abortion procedure.[109]

Sexual Orientation

In the last three decades, the right to be left alone began to include the privacy rights of gay people. One morning in Atlanta, Georgia, in the mid-1980s, a police officer came to the home of Michael Hardwick to serve a warrant for Hardwick's arrest for failure to appear in court to answer charges of drinking in public. One of Hardwick's unknowing housemates invited the officer to look in Hardwick's room, where he found Hardwick and another man engaging in "consensual sexual behavior" and then proceeded to arrest him under Georgia's laws against heterosexual and homosexual sodomy. Hardwick filed a lawsuit against the state, challenging the constitutionality of the Georgia law, and won his case in the federal court of appeals. The state of Georgia, in an unusual move, appealed the court's decision to the Supreme Court. In 1986 the majority of the Court reversed the lower-court decision, holding against Hardwick on the grounds that "the federal Constitution confers [no] fundamental right upon homosexuals to engage in sodomy" and that therefore there was no basis to invalidate "the laws of the many states that still make such conduct illegal and have done so for a very long time."[110]

Seventeen years later, and to almost everyone's surprise, in *Lawrence v. Texas* (2003) the Court overturned *Bowers v. Hardwick* with a dramatic pronouncement that gays are "entitled to respect for their private lives"[111] as a matter of constitutional due process. Drawing from the tradition of negative liberty, the Court maintained, "In our tradition the State is not omnipresent in the home. And there are other spheres of our lives and existence outside the home, where the State should not be a dominant presence." Explicitly encompassing lesbians and gay men

Civil Liberties around the World

Elections are only a small part of what makes a democracy a democracy. *Liberal democracies*—a term political scientists use to refer to countries they consider fully democratic—also have extensive civil rights and civil liberties.

Freedom House, an independent watchdog organization focusing on freedom and democracy around the world, collects data on political rights and civil liberties from each country. They measure freedom of expression and belief, respect for the "rule of law,"[a] the right to organize and form associations, and personal autonomy and individual rights to rank countries as free, partly free, and not free (shown below).

All countries vary in how they prioritize specific liberties. The United States is generally comparable to other democracies when it comes to the freedom of expression and belief and the right to organize and form associations, but the United States places exceptionally high emphasis on personal autonomy and individual rights. In comparison, Latvia is ranked slightly higher on the right to organize and form associations, but concerns regarding the treatment of women and minorities mean their individual rights score is lower.

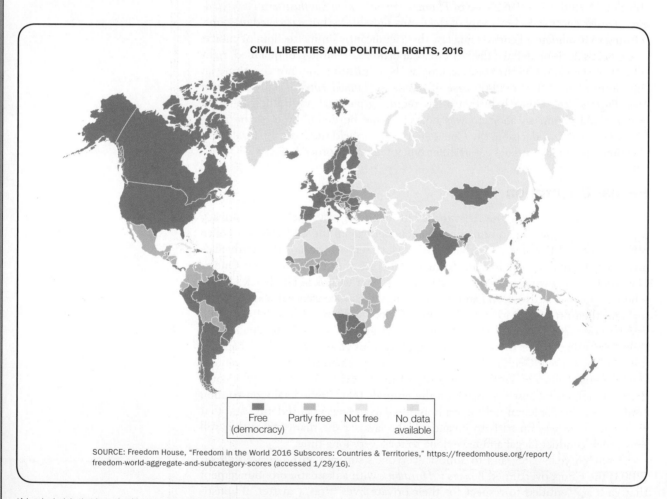

CIVIL LIBERTIES AND POLITICAL RIGHTS, 2016

Free (democracy)   Partly free   Not free   No data available

SOURCE: Freedom House, "Freedom in the World 2016 Subscores: Countries & Territories," https://freedomhouse.org/report/freedom-world-aggregate-and-subcategory-scores (accessed 1/29/16).

[a]A legal principle that laws should govern a country—including its leaders—rather than having decisions made arbitrarily by individuals in the government.

within the umbrella of privacy, the Court concluded that the "petitioners are entitled to respect for their private lives. The State cannot demean their existence or control their destiny by making their private sexual conduct a crime."[112] This decision added substance to the "right of privacy."[113] In 2015 the Court took another important step in the protection of gay rights by declaring that state bans on same-sex marriage were unconstitutional.[114] The Court said that the refusal to issue marriage licenses to same-sex couples constituted a violation of the Fourteenth Amendment's equal protection and due process clauses. See Chapter 5 for more on same-sex marriage.

The Right to Die

Another area ripe for litigation and public discourse is the so-called right to die. A number of highly publicized physician-assisted suicides in the 1990s focused attention on whether people have a right to choose their own death and to receive assistance in carrying it out. Can this become part of the privacy right? Or is it a new substantive right? The Supreme Court has not definitively answered this question. However, the Court refused to intervene in the well-publicized case of Terri Schiavo, a woman who suffered irreversible brain damage and was kept alive in a vegetative state via a feeding tube for 15 years. During this period, Schiavo's husband wanted to withdraw life support, citing his wife's wishes, while her parents wanted support continued indefinitely. The case was heard multiple times in the Florida state courts and the federal courts. In 2005, Schiavo's husband finally prevailed, and she was removed from life support and subsequently died. In the 2006 case of *Gonzales v. Oregon*, the Supreme Court did intervene to uphold a law allowing doctors to use drugs to facilitate the deaths of terminally ill patients who requested such assistance.[115] Thus, although the Court has not ruled definitively on the right-to-die question, it does not seem hostile to the idea.

Civil Liberties
and Your Future

One of the major civil liberties questions facing Americans today and into the future is the matter of government surveillance. Government eavesdropping on communications, travel, and personal conduct has become a fact of American life. Revelations in the summer of 2013 of extensive electronic surveillance by the NSA of Americans' phone and Internet communications caused considerable consternation in Congress and in the news media. Such surveillance, however, is not a new phenomenon in the United States. As early as 1920, the Cipher Bureau, remembered today as the "Black Chamber," an office jointly funded by the army and the State Department, secretly inspected telegrams in the Western Union system.

Today, the Black Chamber seems a quaint relic of a long-forgotten past as Americans find themselves subject to more or less constant government surveillance via electronic interception of telephone calls and examination of email communications and social media postings, to say nothing of ubiquitous security cameras now tied to crowd-scanning software, traffic monitoring, airport searches, and so forth. And while the Black Chamber sifted through transcripted telegrams by hand,

National Intelligence Director James Clapper and other defense officials testified before Congress following revelations in 2013 of extensive government surveillance programs. Electronic monitoring allows the government to gather vast quantities of data from private communications.

peering at their contents, today the work is done by sophisticated computer software that allows the government to process and analyze enormous quantities of data, looking for possible indications of illicit activity among seemingly disparate bits of information.

Many Americans believe that they are the beneficiaries rather than the potential victims of government surveillance. Those who have nothing to hide, goes the saying, have nothing to fear. However, as law professor Daniel Solove shows, surveillance can entrap even the most innocent individuals in a web of suspicions and allegations from which they may find it extremely difficult to extricate themselves.[116]

The issue of government surveillance is tied to a larger question of political power. Popular government requires that citizens possess a good deal of knowledge about the actions of the state. Knowledge is necessary to permit citizens to evaluate rulers' claims and to hold rulers accountable for their conduct. In essence, citizens must undertake their own surveillance of the government and its officials as a precondition for exerting influence over them.

At the same time, citizens' ability to exercise power also requires that they have considerable protection from the state's scrutiny. To begin with, those intent on expressing anything but support for the groups in power need privacy to plan, organize, and mobilize lest their plans be anticipated and disrupted. Terrorists are not the only ones who need privacy. Even in the mundane realm of partisan politics, the efforts of the party out of power can certainly be compromised if its rivals in government become privy to its plans. Known political dissidents, moreover, often face some risk of official reprisal. Accordingly, some citizens may refrain from acting upon their political beliefs for fear that they will draw attention to themselves and become targets for tax audits and other government efforts to find evidence of criminality, fraud, or other misconduct that can be used against them.

Thus, popular government requires a combination of government transparency and citizen privacy. To exercise influence over it, citizens must know what the government is doing. At the same time, citizens seeking to exercise influence over the government need protection from retaliation and intimidation. Question about privacy will continue to grow as surveillance technologies become more sophisticated and we, as citizens, will be challenged to adapt eighteenth-century constitutional protections to twenty-first-century issues. How have new technologies affected the government's ability to monitor its citizens? What are your expectations of privacy in your email conversations, your plane tickets, your reading habits?

These issues, along with questions about the right to bear arms, the use of the death penalty, and religious freedom (see the "**Who Participates?**" feature on the facing page) are unlikely to go away any time soon and will continue to challenge Americans in the years to come.

Religious Affiliation and Freedom of Religion

Percentage of American Adults in Each Religious Tradition

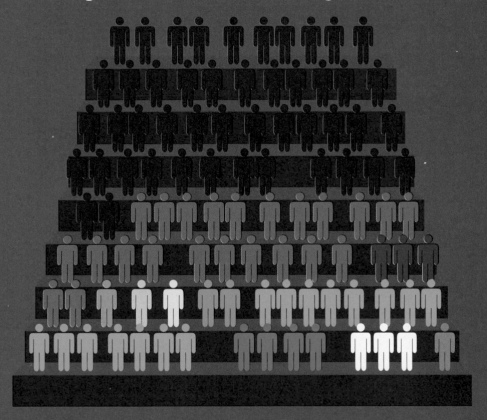

Under the First Amendment, Americans enjoy the freedom to practice (or not practice) the religion of their choice. Most Americans identify with and participate in some form of religion.

- Protestant **46.5%**
- Catholic **20.8%**
- Other Christian **3.3%**
- Jewish **1.9%**
- Muslim **0.9%**
- Buddhist **0.7%**
- Hindu **0.7%**
- Other faiths **1.7%**
- Nothing in particular **15.8%**
- Agnostic **4%**
- Atheist **3.1%**
- Don't know **0.6%**

SOURCE: Pew Research Center, "America's Changing Religious Landscape," www.pewforum.org/2015/05/12/americas-changing-religious-landscape (accessed 9/20/15).

WHAT YOU CAN DO

Know Your First Amendment Rights

 Learn more about freedom of religion from a variety of legal scholars at **www.constitutioncenter.org**.

 Share your opinion about the First Amendment and religion on campus with your school newspaper. Find information about students' religious rights at **www.thefire.org**.

 Learn more about your other First Amendment rights, such as free speech on the Internet, at **www.eff.org**.

studyguide

A Brief History of the Bill of Rights

> Explain the origins and evolution of the civil liberties in the Bill of Rights as they apply to federal government and the states (pp. 115–20)

Although some of the framers believed that a bill of rights was unnecessary and potentially dangerous, the Federalists made a pledge to add one in order to secure support for the Constitution during the ratification process. Over the course of the first 100 years of American history, the Bill of Rights was interpreted to limit only the actions of the federal government. One by one, most of the important provisions of the first 10 amendments have been incorporated into the Fourteenth Amendment and applied to the states.

Key Terms

habeas corpus (p. 115)

bill of attainder (p. 115)

ex post facto laws (p. 115)

Bill of Rights (p. 116)

civil liberties (p. 116)

selective incorporation (p. 117)

Practice Quiz

1. From 1789 until the end of the nineteenth century, the Bill of Rights put limits on
   a) the national government only.
   b) the state government only.
   c) both the national and state governments.
   d) neither the national nor the state government.
   e) political parties and interest groups.

2. Which of the following rights was *not* included in the original Constitution?
   a) prohibition of bills of attainder
   b) prohibition of ex post facto laws
   c) guarantee of habeas corpus
   d) guarantee of trial by jury in the state where the crime was committed
   e) None. They were all included in the original Constitution.

3. The process by which some of the liberties in the Bill of Rights were applied to the states is known as
   a) preemption.
   b) selective incorporation.
   c) judicial activism.
   d) civil liberties.
   e) establishment.

4. Which of the following provisions of the Bill of Rights was incorporated in 2010?
   a) the right to counsel in any criminal trial
   b) the right against self-incrimination
   c) freedom from unnecessary searches and seizures
   d) freedom to petition the government for redress of grievance
   e) the right to bear arms

The First Amendment and Freedom of Religion

> Describe how the First Amendment protects freedom of religion (pp. 120–23)

Two parts of the First Amendment touch on religious freedom: the establishment clause and the free exercise clause. The courts have been somewhat inconsistent in determining how solid the establishment clause's "wall of separation" between church and state actually is in practice. While the courts have been more consistent in protecting the free exercise of religious beliefs, they have taken pains to distinguish between religious beliefs and actions based on those beliefs.

Key Terms

establishment clause (p. 120)

Lemon test (p. 121)

free exercise clause (p. 122)

Practice Quiz

5. The Supreme Court's ruling in *Lemon v. Kurtzman*, which led to the *Lemon* test, concerned the issue of
   a) school desegregation.
   b) aid to religious schools.
   c) cruel and unusual punishment.
   d) obscenity.
   e) prayer in school.

The First Amendment and Freedom of Speech and of the Press

Describe how the First Amendment protects free speech and freedom of the press (pp. 123–31)

Given the importance of freedom of speech and of the press to the functioning of democratic government, Americans are assumed to have the right to speak and broadcast their ideas unless there is some compelling reason to stop them. According to the courts, although virtually all speech is protected by the Constitution, some forms of speech are entitled to a greater degree of protection than others. Libel, slander, and speech that incites lawless action are examples of speech that can be limited by the government.

Key Terms

"clear and present danger" test (p. 124)

fighting words (p. 125)

"speech plus" (p. 128)

prior restraint (p. 128)

libel (p. 129)

slander (p. 129)

Practice Quiz

6. Which of the following protections is *not* contained in the First Amendment?
   a) the establishment clause
   b) the free exercise clause
   c) freedom of the press
   d) the right to peaceably assemble
   e) the right to privacy

7. The judicial doctrine that places a heavy burden of proof on the government when it seeks to regulate or restrict speech is called
   a) judicial restraint.
   b) judicial activism.
   c) habeas corpus.
   d) prior restraint.
   e) strict scrutiny.

8. Which of the following describes a written statement made in "reckless disregard of the truth" that is considered damaging to a victim because it is "malicious, scandalous, and defamatory"?
   a) slander
   b) libel
   c) speech plus
   d) fighting words
   e) expressive speech

The Second Amendment and the Right to Bear Arms

Explore whether the Second Amendment means people have a right to own guns (pp. 131–32)

The Second Amendment granted Americans the right "to keep and bear Arms" in order to provide for state militias. Prior to 2010, the Second Amendment was not incorporated. In *McDonald v. Chicago*, the Supreme Court asserted that the right to bear arms applies to both state governments and the federal government.

Practice Quiz

9. In *McDonald v. Chicago*, the Supreme Court ruled that
   a) states can require citizens to own firearms.
   b) federal grants can be used to support the formation of state militias.
   c) felons can be prevented from purchasing assault rifles.
   d) the Second Amendment applies to states as well as the federal government.
   e) the Second Amendment applies only to the federal government and not to states.

Rights of the Criminally Accused

Explain the major rights that people have if they are accused of a crime (pp. 133–40)

The essence of the Constitution's due process of the law is found in the Fourth, Fifth, Sixth, and Eighth amendments. The Fourth Amendment protects individuals from unreasonable searches and seizures. The Fifth Amendment provides individuals with the right to a grand jury, protection from double jeopardy, and a guarantee against self-incrimination. The Sixth Amendment provides the right to legal counsel, the right to a speedy trial, and the right to confront witnesses before an impartial jury. The Eighth Amendment protects individuals against "cruel and unusual" punishment.

Key Terms

due process of law (p. 133)

exclusionary rule (p. 133)

grand jury (p. 136)

double jeopardy (p. 136)

Miranda rule (p. 137)

eminent domain (p. 138)

Practice Quiz

10. The Fourth, Fifth, Sixth, and Eighth amendments, taken together, define
    a) freedom of religion.
    b) due process of law.
    c) free speech.
    d) the right to bear arms.
    e) civil rights of minorities.

11. In *Mapp v. Ohio*, the Supreme Court ruled that
    a) evidence obtained from an illegal search could not be introduced in a trial.
    b) the government must provide legal counsel for defendants who are too poor to provide it for themselves.
    c) persons under arrest must be informed prior to police interrogation of their rights to remain silent and to have the benefits of legal counsel.
    d) the government has the right to take private property for public use if just compensation is provided.
    e) a person cannot be tried twice for the same crime.

12. Which famous case deals with the Sixth Amendment's guarantee of the right to counsel?
    a) *Roe v. Wade*
    b) *Mapp v. Ohio*
    c) *Gideon v. Wainwright*
    d) *Terry v. Ohio*
    e) *Miranda v. Arizona*

The Right to Privacy

Assess whether people have a right to privacy under the Constitution (pp. 140–45)

A right to privacy is never explicitly mentioned in the Constitution. In fact, it was not until 1965 that the Supreme Court interpreted the Third, Fourth, Fifth, and Ninth amendments to create a constitutional "zone of privacy." The right to privacy has since been used to strike down laws limiting access to birth control, outlawing abortion, and criminalizing gay and lesbian sexual activity.

Key Term

right to privacy (p. 140)

Practice Quiz

13. In which case was a right to privacy related to the use of birth control first formally recognized by the Court?
    a) *Griswold v. Connecticut*
    b) *Roe v. Wade*
    c) *Lemon v. Kurtzman*
    d) *Planned Parenthood v. Casey*
    e) *Baker v. Carr*

14. In which case did the Supreme Court rule that state governments no longer had the authority to make private sexual behavior a crime?
    a) *Texas v. Johnson*
    b) *Webster v. Reproductive Health Services*
    c) *Gonzales v. Oregon*
    d) *Lawrence v. Texas*
    e) *Bowers v. Hardwick*

For Further Reading

Amar, Akhil Reed. *The Law of the Land: A Grand Tour of Our Constitutional Republic*. New York: Basic Books, 2015.

Brandon, Mark. *The Constitution in Wartime*. Durham, NC: Duke University Press, 2005.

Cash, Arthur. *John Wilkes: The Scandalous Father of Civil Liberties*. New Haven, CT: Yale University Press, 2007.

Cook, Byrne. *Reporting the War: Freedom of the Press from the American Revolution to the War on Terror*. New York: Palgrave Macmillan, 2007.

Domino, John. *Civil Rights and Liberties in the 21st Century*. 3rd ed. New York: Longman, 2015.

Dworkin, Ronald. *Justice in Robes*. Cambridge, MA: Belknap Press, 2006.

Friendly, Fred W. *Minnesota Rag: The Dramatic Story of the Landmark Supreme Court Case That Gave New Meaning to Freedom of the Press*. New York: Vintage, 1982.

Lewis, Anthony. *Freedom for the Thought That We Hate: A Biography of the First Amendment*. New York: Basic Books, 2010.

Lewis, Anthony. *Gideon's Trumpet*. New York: Random House, 1964.

O'Brien, David M. *Constitutional Law and Politics: Civil Rights and Civil Liberties*. 8th ed. Vol. 2. New York: W. W. Norton, 2011.

Richards, Neil. *Intellectual Privacy: Rethinking Civil Liberties in the Digital Age*. New York: Oxford University Press, 2015.

Smith, Steven D. *The Rise and Decline of American Religious Freedom*. Cambridge, MA: Harvard University Press, 2014.

Solove, Daniel. *Nothing to Hide: The False Tradeoff between Privacy and Security*. New Haven, CT: Yale University Press, 2011.

Sundby, Scott. *A Life and Death Decision: A Jury Weighs the Death Penalty*. New York: Palgrave Macmillan, 2007.

Waldron, Jeremy. *The Harm in Hate Speech*. Cambridge, MA: Harvard University Press, 2012.

Recommended Websites

The American Civil Liberties Union (ACLU)
www.aclu.org

The ACLU is committed to protecting for all individuals the freedoms found in the Bill of Rights. This sometimes controversial organization constantly monitors the government for violations of liberty and encourages its members to take political action.

Electronic Privacy Information Center
http://epic.org/privacy

For an extensive list of privacy issues, go to the web page for the Electronic Privacy Information Center. Here you will find civil liberties concerns as they relate to all forms of information technology, including the Internet.

The Free Expression Network
www.freeexpression.org

The Free Expression Network is an organization "dedicated to preserving the right to free expression." On its website you can find links to important First Amendment issues and organizations.

Freedom Forum
www.freedomforum.org

Freedom of speech and freedom of the press are considered critical in any democracy; however, only some kinds of speech are fully protected against restrictions. Freedom Forum is a nonpartisan agency that investigates and analyzes such First Amendment restrictions.

National Abortion and Reproductive Rights Action League
www.naral.org

National Right to Life Committee
www.NRLC.org

The National Abortion and Reproductive Rights Action League and the National Right to Life Committee are two of the nation's largest interest groups weighing in on the abortion issue. See what these opposing groups have to say about privacy rights.

Religious Freedom
http://guides.lib.virginia.edu/content.php?pid=147534&sid=1255449

The establishment clause of the U.S. Constitution has been interpreted to mean a "wall of separation" between government and religion. On the Religious Freedom Page you can find information on a variety of issues pertaining to religious freedom in the United States and around the world.

U.S. Supreme Court Media
www.oyez.org

This website for U.S. Supreme Court media has a great search engine for finding information on cases affecting civil liberties, such as *Lemon v. Kurtzman*, *Miranda v. Arizona*, *Mapp v. Ohio*, and *New York Times v. Sullivan*, to name a few.

Though the black civil rights movement of the 1960s addressed civil and political rights, many people worry that African Americans still face structural racism in the United States. The Black Lives Matter movement gained momentum in response to a number of incidents of excessive police force against African Americans.

Civil Rights

WHAT GOVERNMENT DOES AND WHY IT MATTERS In this chapter, we will turn from a discussion of civil liberties to an examination of civil rights. Rights and liberties are related but are not one and the same. Civil liberties are limitations on the power of the government. The concept of civil liberties defines certain spheres of activity, such as speech or worship, in which the government's authority to interfere with individuals is limited. Civil rights, on the other hand, are the rules governing who may participate in the political process and regulating the ways in which the government may or may not treat its citizens. As we shall see, among the most important rights guaranteed by the American Constitution are "equal protection" under the law and "due process" of law, concepts that will be at the heart of this chapter. Civil liberties and civil rights are both aspects of political freedom and, while specific rights may conflict with particular liberties, in a broad sense rights and liberties reinforce each other. The Constitution's Bill of Rights includes liberties such as freedom of speech and rights such as trial by jury.

As in the case of civil liberties, Americans agree with the basic principle of civil rights but quarrel frequently over their application. The question of who has the constitutional right to do what underlies some of the major controversies of American history. Fifty years ago, the African American struggle for equal rights took center stage. Many goals of the civil rights movement that once aroused bitter controversy are now widely accepted as part of the American commitment to equal rights. But even today the question of what is meant by "equal rights" is hardly settled. To what extent can states mandate racial preferences in college admissions? Do transgender individuals have the right to use a public restroom based upon their gender identification rather than their physical characteristics? What rights do undocumented immigrants possess?

The Black Lives Matter movement has gained momentum in recent years in response to highly publicized incidents of excessive police force against African Americans. Supporters of the movement have charged that the police are inclined to use particularly harsh tactics against minorities in general and African Americans in particular. Some critics have replied by asserting that *all* lives matter or that the police officers are simply doing their job, but the Black Lives Matter protesters maintain that police brutality against African Americans is a reflection of continued institutional racism. The Black Lives Matter movement has fueled the fire of the ongoing debate about how serious a problem racism is in the United States today.

Ideas about civil rights do not change easily; advocates who have challenged barriers to civil rights often struggled against strong resistance. This chapter will show how inequalities between races and genders were tolerated and even enforced by law during much of our country's history. Although the United States was founded on the ideals of liberty, equality, and democracy, its history of civil rights reveals a gap between these principles and actual practice. This history also demonstrates how the struggle to attain those ideals has helped narrow this gap. The election of Barack Obama as the nation's first black president was a testament to the successes of those struggles but did not by itself alter persistent social and economic differences across racial lines.

chaptergoals

- Trace the legal developments and social movements that expanded civil rights (pp. 155–74)

- Describe how different groups have fought for and won protection of their civil rights (pp. 174–89)

- Contrast arguments for and against affirmative action (pp. 189–91)

The Struggle for Civil Rights

Trace the legal developments and social movements that expanded civil rights

In the United States the history of slavery and legalized racial **discrimination** against African Americans coexists uneasily with a strong tradition of individual liberty. Indeed, for much of our history Americans have struggled to reconcile such exclusionary racial practices with our notions of individual rights. With the adoption of the Fourteenth Amendment in 1868 **civil rights** became part of the Constitution, guaranteed to each citizen through "equal protection of the laws." This **equal protection clause** launched a century of political movements and legal efforts to press for racial equality.

For African Americans, the central fact of political life for most of American history has been a denial of full citizenship rights. By accepting the institution of slavery, the Founders embraced a system fundamentally at odds with the "Blessings of Liberty" promised in the Constitution. Their decision set the stage for two centuries of African American struggles to achieve full citizenship.

For women, electoral politics was a decidedly masculine world. Until 1920, not only were women barred from voting in national politics but electoral politics was closely tied to such male social institutions as lodges, bars, and clubs. Yet the exclusion of women from this political world did not prevent them from engaging in public life. Instead, women carved out a "separate sphere" for their public activities. Emphasizing female stewardship of the moral realm, women became important voices in social reform well before they won the right to vote.[1] Prior to the Civil War, women played leading roles in the abolitionist movement.

discrimination the use of any unreasonable and unjust criterion of exclusion

civil rights obligation imposed on government to take positive action to protect citizens from any illegal action of government agencies and of other private citizens

equal protection clause provision of the Fourteenth Amendment guaranteeing citizens "the equal protection of the laws." This clause has been the basis for the civil rights of African Americans, women, and other groups

African American men won the right to vote after the Civil War, and many former slaves began registering and voting in state elections as early as 1867. This political influence soon evaporated in the face of Jim Crow laws and the end of Reconstruction.

Slavery and the Abolitionist Movement

No issue in the nation's history so deeply divided Americans as that of slavery. The importation and subjugation of Africans kidnapped from their native lands was a practice virtually as old as the country itself: the first slaves brought to what became the United States arrived in 1619, a year before the Plymouth colony was established in Massachusetts. White southerners built their agricultural economy (especially cotton production) on a large slave labor force. By 1840 nearly half of the populations of Alabama and Louisiana consisted of black slaves. Even so, only about one-quarter of southern white families owned slaves.

Slavery was so much a part of southern culture that efforts to restrict or abolish the institution were met with fierce resistance. Despite the manifest cruelties of the slave system, southerners referred to it merely as their "peculiar institution." This quaint label meant little to slavery's opponents, however; and an abolitionist movement grew and spread among northerners in the 1830s (although abolitionist sentiment could be traced back to the prerevolutionary era). The abolitionist movement spread primarily through local organizations in the North. Soon two political parties emerged, the staunchly antislavery Liberty Party and the more moderate Free Soil Party, which sought primarily to restrict slavery from spreading into new western territories. Some opponents of slavery took matters into their own hands, aiding in the escape of runaway slaves along the Underground Railroad. In the South, a similar, if contrary, fervor prompted mobs to break into post offices in order to seize and destroy antislavery literature.

In 1857, the Supreme Court inflamed this tense atmosphere with its infamous decision in *Dred Scott v. Sanford*. Dred Scott was a slave who had been taken by his owner to the free state of Illinois and the territory of Wisconsin, where slavery was forbidden. Scott sued for his freedom, arguing that his residence in a free territory meant he was a free man. The Court, however, disagreed, holding that slaves—indeed, all blacks—were not citizens of the United States. Scott had no due process rights because, as a slave, he was his master's permanent property, regardless of his master's having taken him to a free state or territory.[2] This decision split the country deeply over the issue of slavery; the emotional power of the slavery issue was such that it precipitated the nation's bloodiest conflict, the Civil War. From the ashes of the Civil War came the Thirteenth, Fourteenth, and Fifteenth amendments, which would redefine civil rights from that time on.

The Link to the Women's Rights Movement

The quiet upstate New York town of Seneca Falls played host to what would later come to be known as the starting point of the modern women's movement. Convened in July 1848 and organized by the activists Elizabeth Cady Stanton and Lucretia Mott, the Seneca Falls Convention drew 300 delegates to formulate plans for advancing the political and social rights of women.

The centerpiece of the convention was its Declaration of Sentiments and Resolutions. Patterned after the Declaration of Independence, the Seneca Falls document declared, "We hold these truths to be self-evident: that all men and women are created equal" and "The history of mankind is a history of repeated injuries and usurpations on the part of man toward woman, having in direct object the establishment of an absolute tyranny over her." The most controversial provision of the declaration, nearly rejected as too radical, was the call for the right to vote for women. Although most of the delegates were women, about 40 men participated,

including the renowned abolitionist Frederick Douglass. The link to the antislavery movement was not new. Stanton and Mott had attended the World Anti-Slavery Convention in London in 1840 but had been denied delegate seats because of their sex. This rebuke helped precipitate the 1848 convention in Seneca Falls.

The convention and its participants were subjected to widespread ridicule, but similar conventions were organized in other states; and in the same year as the Seneca Falls Convention, New York State passed the Married Women's Property Act in order to restore the right of married women to own property.

The Civil War Amendments to the Constitution

The hopes of African Americans for achieving full citizenship rights initially seemed fulfilled when three constitutional amendments were adopted after the Civil War: the **Thirteenth Amendment** abolished slavery, the **Fourteenth Amendment** guaranteed equal protection under the law, and the **Fifteenth Amendment** guaranteed voting rights for blacks. Protected by the presence of federal troops, African American men were able to exercise their political rights immediately after the war. Between 1869 and 1877, blacks were elected to many political offices: two black senators were elected from Mississippi, and a total of 14 African Americans were elected to the House of Representatives. African Americans also held many state-level political offices. As voters and public officials, black citizens found a home in the Republican Party, which had secured the ratification of the three constitutional amendments guaranteeing black rights. After the war, the Republican Party continued to reach out to black voters as a means to build party strength in the South.[3]

This political equality was short-lived, however. The national government withdrew its troops from the South and turned its back on African Americans in 1877, when Reconstruction ended. In the Compromise of 1877, southern Democrats agreed to allow the Republican candidate, Rutherford B. Hayes, to become president after a disputed election. In exchange, northern Republicans dropped their support for the civil liberties and political participation of African Americans. After

Thirteenth Amendment one of three Civil War amendments; it abolished slavery

Fourteenth Amendment one of three Civil War amendments; it guaranteed equal protection and due process

Fifteenth Amendment one of three Civil War amendments; it guaranteed voting rights for African American men

Jim Crow laws laws enacted by southern states following Reconstruction that discriminated against African Americans

that, southern states erected a "Jim Crow" system of social, political, and economic inequality that made a mockery of the promises in the Constitution. The first **Jim Crow laws** were adopted in the 1870s, in each southern state, to criminalize intermarriage of the races and to segregate trains and depots. These were promptly followed by laws segregating all public accommodations, and within 10 years all southern states had adopted laws segregating the schools.

Immediately after the Civil War, when male ex-slaves won the franchise, some women pressed for the right to vote at the national level; but politicians in both parties rejected women's suffrage as disruptive and unrealistic. Women also started to press for the vote at the state level in 1867, when a referendum to give women the vote in Kansas failed. Frustration with the general failure to win reforms accelerated suffrage activism. In 1872, Susan B. Anthony and several other women were arrested in Rochester, New York, for illegally registering and voting in that year's national election. (The men who allowed the women to register and vote were also indicted; Anthony paid their expenses and eventually won presidential pardons for them.) At Anthony's trial, Judge Ward Hunt ordered the jury to find her guilty without deliberation. Yet Anthony was allowed to address the court, saying, "Your denial of my citizen's right to vote is the denial of my right of consent as one of the governed, the denial of my right of representation as one of the taxed, the denial of my right to a trial of my peers as an offender against the law."[4] Hunt assessed Anthony a fine of $100 but did not sentence her to jail. She refused to pay the fine.

Civil Rights and the Supreme Court: "Separate but Equal"

Resistance to equality for African Americans in the South led Congress to adopt the Civil Rights Act of 1875, which attempted to protect blacks from discrimination by proprietors of hotels, theaters, and other public accommodations. But the Court declared the legislation unconstitutional on the grounds that the act sought to protect blacks against discrimination by *private* businesses, whereas the Fourteenth Amendment, according to the Court's interpretation, was intended to protect individuals from discrimination only against actions by *public* officials of state and local governments.

The 1896 Supreme Court case of Plessy v. Ferguson *upheld legal segregation and created the "separate but equal" rule, which fostered national segregation. Overt discrimination in public accommodations was common.*

In the infamous case of *Plessy v. Ferguson* (1896), the Court went still further by upholding a Louisiana statute that *required* segregation of the races on trolleys and other public carriers (and, by implication, in all public facilities, including schools). Homer Plessy, a man defined as "one-eighth black," had violated a Louisiana law that provided for "equal but separate accommodations" on trains and levied a $25 fine on any white passenger who sat in a car reserved for blacks or on any black passenger who sat in a car reserved for whites. The Supreme Court held that the Fourteenth Amendment's equal protection clause was not violated by racial distinction as long as the facilities were equal, thus establishing the **"separate but equal" rule** that prevailed through the mid-twentieth century. People generally pretended that segregated accommodations were equal as long as some accommodation for blacks existed. The Court said that although "the object of the [Fourteenth] Amendment was undoubtedly to enforce the absolute equality of the two races before the law . . . it could not have intended to abolish distinctions based on color, or to enforce social, as distinguished from political, equality, or a commingling of the two races upon terms unsatisfactory to either."[5] What the Court was saying in effect was that the use of race as a criterion of exclusion in public matters was reasonable.

Organizing for Equality

The creation of a Jim Crow system in the southern states and the lack of a legal basis for "equal protection of the laws" prompted the beginning of a long process in which African Americans built organizations and devised strategies for asserting their constitutional rights.

The National Association for the Advancement of Colored People One such strategy sought to win political rights through political pressure and litigation. This approach was championed by the National Association for the Advancement of Colored People (NAACP), established in 1909 by a group of black and white reformers that included W. E. B. Du Bois, one of the twentieth century's most influential and creative thinkers on racial issues. Because the northern black vote was so small in the early 1900s, the NAACP relied primarily on the courts to press for black political rights. After the 1920s it built a strong membership base, with some strength in the South, which would be critical when the civil rights movement gained momentum in the 1950s.

Women's Organizations and the Right to Suffrage The 1886 unveiling in New York Harbor of the Statue of Liberty, depicting liberty as a woman, prompted women's rights advocates to call it "the greatest hypocrisy of the nineteenth century," in that "not one single woman throughout the length and breadth of the Land is as yet in possession of political Liberty."[6]

The climactic movement toward women's suffrage had been formally launched in 1878 with the introduction of a proposed constitutional amendment in Congress. Parallel efforts were made in the states. Many states granted women the right to vote before the national government did; western states with less entrenched political systems opened politics to women earliest. When Wyoming became a state in 1890, it was the first state to grant full suffrage to women. Colorado, Utah, and Idaho all followed suit in the next several years. Suffrage organizations grew—the National American Woman Suffrage Association (NAWSA), formed in 1890, claimed 2 million members by 1917 and staged mass meetings, parades, petitions, and protests.

"separate but equal" rule doctrine that public accommodations could be segregated by race but still be considered equal

for critical analysis
What were the consequences of the "separate but equal" policy for southern society and for blacks' civil rights?

Women have had the right to vote in the United States for less than 100 years. The women who fought for this basic political right were often ridiculed as man-haters, as depicted in this cartoon. However, the suffragettes believed both men and women should enjoy the same political rights.

NAWSA organized state-by-state efforts to win the right for women to vote. Members of a more militant group, the National Woman's Party, staged pickets and got arrested in front of the White House to protest President Wilson's opposition to a constitutional amendment granting women this right. When the Nineteenth Amendment was ratified in 1920, women were finally guaranteed the right to vote.

Litigating for Equality after World War II

The shame of discrimination against black military personnel during World War II, plus revelations of Nazi racial atrocities, moved President Harry S. Truman finally to bring the problem of racial discrimination to the White House and national attention, with the appointment in 1946 of the President's Commission on Civil Rights. In 1948 the commission submitted its report, *To Secure These Rights*, which laid bare the extent of the problem and its consequences and revealed the success of experiments with racial integration in the armed forces during World War II, to demonstrate to southern society that it had nothing to fear. But the commission recognized that the national government had no clear constitutional authority to pass and implement civil rights legislation. It proposed tying such legislation to the commerce power described in Article I of the Constitution, which allows Congress to regulate interstate commerce, although it was clear that discrimination was not itself related to the flow of interstate commerce.[7] The committee even suggested using the treaty power as a source of constitutional authority for civil rights legislation.[8]

The Supreme Court had begun to change its position on racial discrimination before World War II by being stricter about the criterion of equal facilities in the "separate but equal" rule. In 1938, for example, the Court rejected Missouri's policy of paying the tuition of qualified blacks to out-of-state law schools rather than admitting them to the University of Missouri Law School.[9]

After the war, modest progress resumed. In 1950 the Court rejected Texas's claim that its new "law school for Negroes" afforded education equal to that of the all-white University of Texas Law School, anticipating its future civil rights rulings by opening the question of whether *any* segregated facilities could be truly

equal.[10] But in ordering the admission of blacks to all-white state law schools, the Supreme Court did not directly confront the "separate but equal" rule. The same had been true in 1944, when the Supreme Court struck down the southern practice of "white primaries," which legally excluded blacks from participation in the nominating process. Here the Court simply recognized that primaries could no longer be regarded as the private affairs of the parties but were an integral aspect of the electoral process, making parties "an agency of the State." Therefore, any practice of discrimination against blacks was "state action within the meaning of the Fifteenth Amendment."[11] The most important pre-1954 decision was probably *Shelley v. Kraemer*, in which the Court ruled against the widespread practice of "restrictive covenants" whereby the seller of a home added a clause to the sales contract requiring the buyer to agree never to sell the home to any non-Caucasian, non-Christian, and so on. The Court ruled that such covenants could not be judicially enforced since the Fourteenth Amendment prohibits any organ of the state, including the courts, from denying equal protection of its laws.[12]

Although none of those pre-1954 cases confronted "separate but equal" and the principle of racial discrimination as such, they were extremely significant to black leaders in the 1940s and gave them encouragement to believe that at last they had an opportunity and enough legal precedent to change the constitutional framework itself. Much of this legal work was done by the Legal Defense and Educational Fund of the NAACP, which until the late 1940s had concentrated on winning small victories within the existing framework. In 1948, the Legal Defense Fund upgraded its approach by simultaneously filing suits in different federal districts and through each level of schooling, with complaints ranging from unequal provision of kindergarten for blacks to unequal sports and science facilities in all-black high schools. After nearly two years of these mostly successful equalization suits, the lawyers decided the time was ripe to confront the "separate but equal" rule head-on, but they felt they needed some heavier artillery to lead the attack. Their choice was the African American lawyer Thurgood Marshall, who had been fighting, and often winning, equalization suits since the early 1930s. Marshall was pessimistic about the readiness of the Supreme Court for a full confrontation with segregation itself and the constitutional principle sustaining it. But the unwillingness of Congress after the 1948 election to consider fair-employment legislation seems to have convinced Marshall that the courts were the only hope.

The NAACP was formed in 1909 to promote the political rights of blacks. In the decades following, the NAACP expanded its membership significantly and played an important role in the civil rights movement of the 1950s and '60s.

During the next four years there emerged a clear indication that the Supreme Court was willing to take more civil rights cases on appeal. Yet this was no guarantee that the Court would reverse *on principle* the "separate but equal" precedent of *Plessy v. Ferguson*. All through 1951 and 1952, as cases were winding slowly through the lower-court litigation maze, intense discussions and disagreements arose among NAACP lawyers as to whether a full-scale assault on *Plessy* was good strategy or whether it might not be better to continue with specific cases alleging unequal treatment and demanding relief with a Court-imposed policy of equalization.[13]

In the fall of 1952, the Court had on its docket cases from Delaware, Kansas, South Carolina, Virginia, and the District of Columbia challenging the constitutionality of school segregation. Of these, the case filed in Kansas became the one chosen by the NAACP. This case was further along in the process of adjudication in its district court, and it had the advantage of being located in a state outside the Deep South, a fact which would minimize any local opposition to a favorable decision.[14]

Oliver Brown, the father of three girls, lived "across the tracks" in a low-income, racially mixed Topeka neighborhood. Every school day, Linda Brown took the school bus to the Monroe Elementary School, for black children, about a mile away. In September 1950, Oliver Brown took Linda to the all-white Sumner School, which was closer to home, to enter her into the third grade, in defiance of state law and local segregation rules. When they were refused, Brown took his case to the NAACP, and soon thereafter, the case **Brown v. Board of Education** was born. In mid-1953 the Court announced that the several cases on their way up would be reargued within a set of questions having to do with the intent of the Fourteenth Amendment. Almost exactly a year later, the Court responded to those questions in one of the most important decisions in its history.

In deciding the *Brown* case, the Court, to the surprise of many, basically rejected as inconclusive all the learned arguments about the intent and the history of the Fourteenth Amendment and committed itself instead to considering only the consequences of segregation:

> Does segregation of children in public schools solely on the basis of race, even though the physical facilities and other "tangible" factors may be equal, deprive the children of the minority group of equal educational opportunities? We believe that it does. . . . We conclude that in the field of public education the doctrine of "separate but equal" has no place. Separate educational facilities are inherently unequal.[15]

The *Brown* decision altered the constitutional framework in two fundamental respects. First, after *Brown*, the states no longer had the power to use race as a criterion of discrimination in law. Second, the national government from then on had the power (and eventually the obligation) to intervene with strict regulatory policies against the discriminatory actions of state or local governments, school boards, employers, and many others in the private sector.

Civil Rights after *Brown v. Board of Education*

Brown v. Board of Education withdrew all constitutional authority to use race as a criterion of exclusion, and it signaled more clearly the Court's determination to use the **strict scrutiny** test in cases related to racial discrimination. This meant that the burden of proof would fall on the government to show that the law in question *was* constitutional—not on the challengers to show the law's *un*constitutionality.[16]

Brown v. Board of Education the 1954 Supreme Court decision that struck down the "separate but equal" doctrine as fundamentally unequal; this case eliminated state power to use race as a criterion of discrimination in law and provided the national government with the power to intervene by exercising strict regulatory policies against discriminatory actions

strict scrutiny a test used by the Supreme Court in racial discrimination cases and other cases involving civil liberties and civil rights that places the burden of proof on the government rather than on the challengers to show that the law in question is constitutional

"Massive resistance" among white southerners attempted to block the desegregation efforts of the national government. For example, at Little Rock Central High School in 1957, an angry mob of white students prevented black students from entering the school.

Although the use of strict scrutiny would give an advantage to those attacking racial discrimination, the historic decision in *Brown v. Board of Education* was merely a small opening move. First, most states refused to cooperate until sued, and many ingenious schemes were employed to delay obedience (such as paying the tuition for white students to attend newly created "private" academies). Second, even as southern school boards began to cooperate by eliminating their legally enforced (**de jure**) school segregation, extensive actual (**de facto**) school segregation remained, in the North as well as in the South, as a consequence of racially segregated housing that could not be addressed by the 1954–55 *Brown* principles. Third, discrimination in employment, public accommodations, juries, voting, and other areas of social and economic activity was not directly touched by *Brown*.

School Desegregation, Phase One Although the District of Columbia and some of the school districts in the border states began to respond almost immediately to court-ordered desegregation, the states of the Deep South responded with a carefully planned delaying tactic commonly called "massive resistance." Southern politicians stood shoulder to shoulder to declare that the Supreme Court's decisions and orders were without effect. The legislatures in these states enacted statutes ordering school districts to maintain segregated schools and state superintendents to terminate state funding wherever there was racial mixing in the classroom. Some southern states violated their own long traditions of local school autonomy by centralizing public school authority under the governor or the state board of education, and they gave themselves the power to close the schools and to provide alternative private schooling wherever local school boards might be inclined to obey the Supreme Court.

Most of these plans of "massive resistance" were tested in the federal courts and struck down as unconstitutional.[17] But southern resistance was not confined to legislation. Perhaps the most serious incident occurred in Arkansas in 1957, when Governor Orval Faubus mobilized the Arkansas National Guard to intercede against enforcement of a federal court order to integrate Little Rock Central High School. President Eisenhower was compelled to deploy U.S. troops and place the city under

de jure literally, "by law"; refers to legally enforced practices, such as school segregation in the South before the 1960s

de facto literally, "by fact"; refers to practices that occur even when there is no legal enforcement, such as school segregation in much of the United States today

for critical analysis

Describe the changes in American society between the *Plessy v. Ferguson* and the *Brown v. Board of Education* decisions. How have changes in civil rights policy since the *Brown* case impacted society?

martial law. This action by the federal government underlined that a right was at issue. The Supreme Court considered the Little Rock confrontation so historically important that the opinion it rendered in that case was not only agreed to unanimously but, unprecedentedly, signed personally by every one of the justices.[18]

The end of massive resistance, however, became simply the beginning of still another southern strategy. "Pupil placement" laws authorized school districts to place each pupil in a school according to a variety of academic, personal, and psychological considerations, never mentioning race at all. This put the burden of transferring to an all-white school on the nonwhite children and their parents, making it almost impossible for a single court order to cover a whole district, let alone a whole state, thereby delaying desegregation awhile longer.[19]

Social Protest after *Brown* Ten years after *Brown*, fewer than 1 percent of black school-age children in the Deep South were attending schools with whites.[20] A decade of frustration made it fairly obvious to all observers that adjudication alone would not succeed. The goal of "equal protection" required positive, or affirmative, action by Congress and by administrative agencies. And given massive southern resistance and a generally negative national public opinion toward racial integration, progress would not be made through courts, Congress, or federal agencies without intense, well-organized support. Figure 5.1 shows the increase in the number of civil rights demonstrations for voting rights and public accommodations during the years following *Brown*.

The number of organized demonstrations began to mount slowly but surely after *Brown v. Board of Education*. Only a year after *Brown*, black citizens in Montgomery, Alabama, challenged the city's segregated bus system with a yearlong boycott.

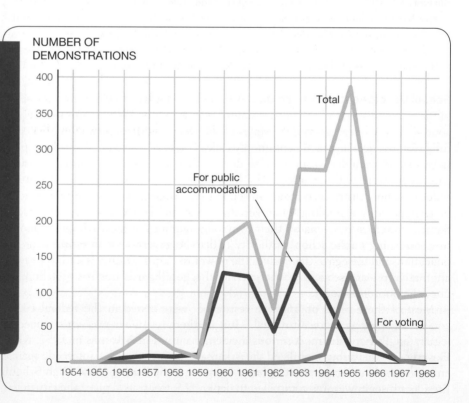

FIGURE 5.1

Peaceful Civil Rights Demonstrations, 1954–68

Peaceful demonstrations were an important part of the civil rights movement. Why did the number of demonstrations grow after 1955? Why do you think the focus shifted from public accommodations to voting rights after 1964?

NOTE: The data are drawn from a search of the *New York Times* index for all references to civil rights demonstrations.
SOURCE: Jonathan D. Casper, *The Politics of Civil Liberties* (New York: Harper and Row, 1972), 90.

The boycott began with the arrest of Rosa Parks, who refused to give up her seat for a white man. A seamstress who worked with civil rights groups, Parks eventually became a civil rights icon, as did one of the ministers leading the boycott, Martin Luther King, Jr. After a year of private carpools and walking, Montgomery's bus system desegregated, but only after the Supreme Court ruled the system unconstitutional.

By the 1960s the many organizations that made up the civil rights movement had accumulated experience and built networks capable of launching large-scale direct action campaigns against southern segregationists. The Southern Christian Leadership Conference, the Student Nonviolent Coordinating Committee, and many other organizations had built a movement that stretched across the South, using the media to attract nationwide attention and support. The image of protesters being beaten, attacked by police dogs, and set upon with fire hoses did much to win broad sympathy for the cause of black civil rights and to discredit state and local governments in the South. In the massive March on Washington in 1963, the Reverend Martin Luther King, Jr., staked out the movement's moral claims in his famous "I Have a Dream" speech. Steadily, the movement created intense pressure for a reluctant federal government to take more assertive steps to defend black civil rights.

Protests against discriminatory practices toward African Americans did not end in the 1960s. In recent years, a variety of local protests coalesced under the banner Black Lives Matter to focus attention on allegations of police misconduct directed at African Americans. The movement took off in Ferguson, Missouri, after the shooting of an unarmed black man by a white police officer and spread across the nation as the media carried reports, photos, and videos of police violence against blacks in Chicago, South Carolina, Baltimore, New York, and many other cities. African Americans had long asserted that they were often victims of racial profiling and more likely than whites to be harassed, physically harmed, or arrested by the police. Police departments had often replied that blacks were more likely than whites to be engaged in criminal activity. Reports and film footage of killings, however, proved difficult for the police to justify and seemed likely to lead to new rules governing police behavior.

The 1955–56 Montgomery bus boycott began with the arrest of Rosa Parks, who refused to give up her seat for a white man. The boycott lasted a year and drew national attention to the cause of civil rights.

The Civil Rights Acts

It is important to observe here the mutual dependence of the courts and legislatures: the legislatures need constitutional authority to act, and the courts need legislative and administrative assistance to implement court orders and focus political support. Consequently, even as the U.S. Congress finally moved into the field of school desegregation (and other areas of "equal protection"), the courts continued to exercise their powers, not only by placing court orders against recalcitrant school districts but also by extending and reinterpreting aspects of the equal protection clause to support legislative and administrative actions (see Table 5.1).

Three civil rights acts were passed during the first decade after the 1954 Supreme Court decision in *Brown v. Board of Education*. But these acts were of only marginal importance. The first one, in 1957, created the U.S. Commission on Civil Rights, to study abuses. The second, in 1960, established that the Fourteenth Amendment to the Constitution, adopted almost a century earlier, could no longer be disregarded,

TABLE 5.1

Cause and Effect in the Civil Rights Movement

Political action and government action worked in tandem to produce dramatic changes in American civil rights policies.

JUDICIAL AND LEGAL ACTION	POLITICAL ACTION
1954 *Brown v. Board of Education*	**1955** Montgomery, Alabama, bus boycott
1956 Federal courts order school integration; of special note is one ordering Autherine Lucy admitted to the University of Alabama, with Governor Wallace officially protesting	
1957 Civil Rights Act creating Civil Rights Commission; President Eisenhower sends 101st Airborne Division paratroops to Little Rock, Arkansas, to enforce integration of Central High School	**1957** Southern Christian Leadership Conference formed, with Martin Luther King, Jr., as president
1960 First substantive Civil Rights Act, primarily voting rights	**1960** Student Nonviolent Coordinating Committee formed to organize protests, sit-ins, freedom rides
1961 Interstate Commerce Commission orders desegregation on all buses and trains and in terminals	
1961 President Kennedy (JFK) favors executive action over civil rights legislation	
1963 JFK shifts, supports strong civil rights law; JFK's assassination; President Johnson asserts strong support for civil rights	**1963** Nonviolent demonstrations in Birmingham, Alabama, lead to King's arrest and his "Letter from Birmingham Jail"
	1963 March on Washington
1964 Congress passes historic Civil Rights Act covering voting, employment, public accommodations, education	
1965 Voting Rights Act	**1965** King announces drive to register 3 million blacks in the South
1966 War on Poverty in full swing	**Late 1960s** Movement diverges: part toward litigation, part toward community action programs, part toward war protest, part toward more militant "Black Power" actions

particularly with regard to voting. The third, the Equal Pay Act of 1963, was more important; but it was concerned with women, did not touch the question of racial discrimination, and, like the 1960 legislation, had no enforcement mechanisms.

By far the most important piece of legislation passed by Congress concerning equal opportunity was the Civil Rights Act of 1964. It not only put some teeth in the voting rights provisions of the 1957 and 1960 acts but also went far beyond voting to attack discrimination in public accommodations, segregation in the schools, and, at long last, the discriminatory conduct of employers in hiring, promoting, and laying off their employees. Discrimination against women was also included, extending the important 1963 provisions. The 1964 act seemed bold at the time, but it was enacted fully 10 years after the Supreme Court had declared racial discrimination "inherently unequal" and long after blacks had demonstrated that discrimination was no longer acceptable.

Public Accommodations After the passage of the 1964 Civil Rights Act, public accommodations quickly removed some of the most blatant forms of racial discrimination. Signs defining "colored" and "white" restrooms, water fountains, waiting rooms, and seating arrangements were removed; and a host of other practices that relegated black people to separate and inferior arrangements were ended. In addition, the federal government filed more than 400 antidiscrimination suits in federal courts against hotels, restaurants, taverns, gas stations, and other "public accommodations."

Many aspects of legalized racial segregation—such as separate Bibles to swear in black and white witnesses in the courtroom—seem like ancient history today. But the issue of racial discrimination in public settings is by no means over. In 1993, six African American Secret Service agents filed charges after a Denny's restaurant in Annapolis, Maryland, failed to serve them. Similar charges citing discriminatory service at Denny's restaurants surfaced across the country. Faced with evidence of a pattern of systematic discrimination and numerous lawsuits, Denny's paid $45 million in damages to plaintiffs in Maryland and California in what is said to be the largest settlement ever in a public accommodations case.[21] In addition to the settlement, the chain vowed to expand employment and management opportunities for minorities in its restaurants. Other forms of racial discrimination in public accommodations are harder to challenge, however. For example, there is considerable evidence that taxicabs often refuse to pick up black passengers.[22] Such practices may be common, but they are difficult to prove and remedy through the law.

School Desegregation, Phase Two The 1964 Civil Rights Act also declared discrimination by private employers and state governments (school boards, etc.) illegal and then went further to provide for administrative agencies to help the courts implement these laws. Title IV of the act, for example, authorized the executive branch, through the Justice Department, to implement federal court orders to desegregate schools and to do so without having to wait for individual parents to bring complaints. Title VI of the act vastly strengthened the role of the executive branch and the credibility of court orders by providing that federal grants-in-aid to state and local governments for education must be withheld from any school system practicing racial segregation. Title VI became the most effective weapon for desegregating schools outside the South because the situation in northern communities was subtler and more difficult to address. In the South, the problem was segregation by law coupled with overt resistance to the national government's efforts to change the situation. In contrast, outside the South, segregated facilities were the outcome of hundreds of thousands of housing choices made by individuals and families. Once racial residential patterns emerged, racial homogeneity, property values, and neighborhood schools and churches were defended by real estate agents, neighborhood organizations, and the like. Thus, in order to eliminate discrimination nationwide, the 1964 Civil Rights Act gave (1) the president, through the Justice Department's Office for Civil Rights, the power to withhold federal education grants[23] and (2) the attorney general of the United States the power to initiate suits (rather than having to await complaints) wherever there was a "pattern or practice" of discrimination.[24]

In the decade following the 1964 Civil Rights Act, the Justice Department brought legal action against more than 500 school districts. During the same period, administrative agencies filed lawsuits against 600 school districts, threatening to suspend federal aid to education unless real desegregation steps were taken.

The 1964 Civil Rights Act made desegregation a legal requirement. The policy of busing from black neighborhoods to white schools bitterly divided the black and white communities in Boston. In 1976 a protester waved an American Flag threateningly at an innocent black bystander—a lawyer on his way to his office— as another white man sought to help him get out of the way.

for critical analysis

Brown v. Board of Education led to the end of de jure segregation. However, de facto segregation remains in many areas, including housing and schooling. Should there be legal or social efforts to address de facto segregation?

Busing One step taken toward desegregation was busing children from poor urban school districts to wealthier suburban ones. In 1971 the Supreme Court held that state-imposed desegregation could be brought about by busing children across school districts.[25] But the decision went beyond that, adding that under certain limited circumstances even racial quotas could be used as the "starting point in shaping a remedy to correct past constitutional violations" and that pairing or grouping schools and reorganizing school attendance zones would also be acceptable.

Three years later, however, this principle was severely restricted when the Supreme Court determined that only cities found guilty of deliberate and de jure racial segregation would have to desegregate their schools,[26] effectively exempting most northern states and cities from busing because school segregation in northern cities is generally the de facto result of segregated housing and thousands of acts of private discrimination against blacks and other minorities.

Boston provides a good illustration of the agonizing problem of making further progress in civil rights in the schools under the constitutional framework established by these decisions. Boston school authorities were found guilty of deliberately building school facilities and drawing school district bound aries "to increase racial segregation." After vain efforts by Boston school authorities to draw up an acceptable plan to remedy the segregation, in 1974 federal judge W. Arthur Garrity ordered an elaborate desegregation plan of his own, involving busing between the all-black neighborhood of Roxbury and the nearby white, working-class community of South Boston. The city's schools were so segregated and uncooperative that even the conservative administration of President Richard Nixon had already initiated a punitive cutoff of funds. But even many liberals criticized Judge Garrity's plan as being badly conceived for involving two neighboring communities with a history of tension and mutual resentment. The plan did work well at the elementary school level but proved explosive at the high school level, generating a continuing crisis for the city of Boston and for the whole nation.[27]

The prospects for further school integration diminished with a 1991 Supreme Court decision holding that lower federal courts could end supervision of local school boards if they could show "good faith" compliance with court orders to desegregate and that "vestiges of past discrimination" had been eliminated "to the extent practicable."[28] It is not necessarily easy for a school board to prove that the new standard has been met, but this was the first time since *Brown* and the 1964 Civil Rights Act that the Court had opened the door at all to retreat.

In 2007 the Court's ruling in *Parents Involved in Community Schools v. Seattle School District No. 1* limited school integration measures still further.[29] By making race one factor in assigning students to schools, the cities of Seattle, Washington, and Louisville, Kentucky, had hoped to achieve greater racial balance across the public schools. The Court ruled that these plans were unconstitutional because they discriminated against white students on the basis of race. Many observers described the decision as the end of the *Brown* era because it eliminated one of the few public strategies left to promote racial integration. Others argued that Justice Anthony Kennedy's concurring opinion, which recognized the harm of racial isolation, may provide the basis for new efforts to promote integration in the future.[30]

Outlawing Discrimination in Employment   Despite the agonizingly slow progress of school desegregation, some progress was made in other areas of civil rights during the 1960s and '70s. Voting rights were established and fairly quickly began to revolutionize southern politics. Service on juries was no longer denied to minorities. But progress in the right to participate in politics and government dramatized the relative lack of progress in the economic domain, where battles over civil rights were increasingly being fought.

The federal courts and the Justice Department entered this area through Title VII of the Civil Rights Act of 1964, which outlawed job discrimination by all private and public employers, including governmental agencies (such as fire and police departments) that employed more than 15 workers. Title VII makes it unlawful to discriminate in employment on the basis of color, religion, sex, or national origin, as well as race.

Title VII delegated some of the powers to enforce fair-employment practices to the Justice Department's Civil Rights Division and others to a new agency created in the 1964 act, the Equal Employment Opportunity Commission (EEOC). By executive order, these agencies had the power of the national government to revoke public contracts for goods and services and to refuse to engage in contracts with any private company that could not guarantee that its rules for hiring, promotion, and firing were nondiscriminatory. And in 1972, President Nixon and a Democratic Congress cooperated to strengthen the EEOC by giving it authority to initiate suits rather than wait for grievances.

But one problem with Title VII was that the complaining party had to show that deliberate discrimination was the cause of the failure to get a job or a training opportunity. Rarely, of course, does an employer explicitly admit discrimination on the basis of race, sex, or any other illegal reason. Recognizing this, the courts have allowed aggrieved parties (the plaintiffs) to make their case if they can show that an employer's hiring practices had the *effect* of exclusion. A leading case in 1971 involved a "class action" by several black employees in North Carolina attempting to show with statistical evidence that blacks had been relegated to only one department in the Duke Power Company, which involved the least desirable manual-labor jobs, and that they had been kept out of contention for better jobs because the employer had added attainment of a high school education and the passing of specially prepared aptitude tests as qualifications for higher jobs. The Supreme Court held that although the statistical evidence did not prove intentional discrimination and although the requirements were race-neutral in appearance, their effects were sufficient to shift the burden of justification to the employer to show that the requirements were a "business necessity" that bore "a demonstrable relationship to successful performance."[31] The ruling in this case was subsequently applied to other hiring, promotion, and training programs.[32]

Voting Rights Although 1964 was the *most* important year for civil rights legislation, it was not the only important year. In 1965, Congress significantly strengthened legislation protecting voting rights by barring literacy and other tests as a condition for voting in six southern states,[33] by setting criminal penalties for interference with efforts to vote, and by providing for the replacement of local registrars with federally appointed registrars in counties designated by the attorney general as significantly resistant to registering eligible blacks to vote. The right to vote was further strengthened with ratification in 1964 of the Twenty-Fourth Amendment, which abolished the poll tax, and in 1975 with legislation permanently outlawing literacy tests in all 50 states and mandating bilingual ballots or oral assistance for Spanish speakers; Chinese, Japanese, and Korean speakers; and Native Americans and Alaska natives.

In the long run, the laws extending and protecting voting rights could prove to be the most effective of all the great civil rights legislation because the progress in black political participation produced by these acts has altered the shape of American politics. In 1965, in the seven states of the Old Confederacy covered by the Voting Rights Act, 29.3 percent of the eligible black residents were registered to vote, compared with 73.4 percent of the white residents (see Table 5.2). Mississippi was the extreme case, with 6.7 percent black and 69.9 percent white

TABLE 5.2

Registration by Race and State in Southern States Covered by the Voting Rights Act (VRA)

The VRA had a direct impact on the rate of black voter registration in the southern states, as measured by the gap between white and black voters in each state. Further insights can be gained by examining changes in white registration rates before and after passage of the VRA and by comparing the gaps between white and black registration. Why do you think registration rates for whites increased significantly in some states and dropped in others? What impact could the increase in black registration have had on public policy?

	BEFORE THE ACT*			AFTER THE ACT* 1971–72		
	WHITE %	BLACK %	GAP** %	WHITE %	BLACK %	GAP %
Alabama	69.2	19.3	49.9	80.7	57.1	23.6
Georgia	62.6	27.4	35.2	70.6	67.8	2.8
Louisiana	80.5	31.6	48.9	80.0	59.1	20.9
Mississippi	69.9	6.7	63.2	71.6	62.2	9.4
North Carolina	96.8	46.8	50.0	62.2	46.3	15.9
South Carolina	75.7	37.3	38.4	51.2	48.0	3.2
Virginia	61.1	38.3	22.8	61.2	54.0	7.2
TOTAL	73.4	29.3	44.1	67.8	56.6	11.2

*Available registration data as of March 1965 and 1971–72.
**The gap is the percentage-point difference between white and black registration rates.

SOURCE: U.S. Commission on Civil Rights, *Political Participation* (1968), Appendix VII: Voter Education Project, attachment to press release, October 3, 1972.

One of the most contentious areas of voting rights today is voter ID laws. Proponents say ID requirements prevent fraud, while opponents argue the rules purposely keep the poor and minorities, who are less likely to have picture IDs, from the polls.

registration. By 1972 the gap between black and white registration in the seven states was only 11.2 points, and in Mississippi the gap had been reduced to 9.4 points. At one time, white leaders in Mississippi had attempted to dilute the influence of this growing black vote by **gerrymandering** districts to ensure that no blacks would be elected to Congress. But the black voters changed Mississippi before Mississippi could change them. In 1988, 11 percent of all elected officials in Mississippi were black—still well below the percentage of blacks in the state's voting-age population, which was 32 percent in 1990, but progress nonetheless.[34]

Several provisions of the 1965 act were scheduled to expire in 2007. However, in 2006, responding to charges that black voters still faced discrimination at the polls, Congress renewed the act for another 25 years. Pressure for renewal of the act had been intense since the disputed 2000 presidential election. The U.S. Commission on Civil Rights conducted hearings on the election in Florida, at which black voters testified about being turned away from the polls and wrongly purged from the voting rolls and about the unreliable voting technology in their neighborhoods. On the basis of this testimony and after an analysis of the vote, the commission charged that there had been extensive racial discrimination.[35] Most recently, Texas has come under fire for gerrymandering congressional districts that discriminate against Latino voters. Due to population growth, most of it among Latinos, Texas gained four new congressional seats after the 2010 census. The heavily Republican state legislature drew a map designed to ensure that three of the new seats would go to Republican candidates. However, a coalition of minority groups and the Justice Department contested the map in court, charging that it failed to create a sufficient number of majority-minority districts. After extensive legal wrangling, the new redistricting plan included three majority-minority districts.[36]

The 1965 Voting Rights Act had also required some state and local governments to obtain federal preclearance before making any changes to their voting laws or practices. The designation of which jurisdictions needed preclearance was based upon a formula that calculated each jurisdiction's history of past voting discrimination. In the 2013 case *Shelby County v. Holder*, the Supreme Court overturned the formula, saying it was based on data more than 40 years old.[37] The Obama administration was critical of the decision, but there seemed little possibility that Congress would take action to devise a new preclearance formula.

A new area of controversy in the realm of voting rights concerns is so-called voter ID laws. Some 34 states have enacted legislation requiring voters to show

gerrymandering the apportionment of voters in districts in such a way as to give unfair advantage to one racial or ethnic group or political party

positive identification at the polls. As of 2016, seven of these states required prospective voters to show an official photo ID before they would be allowed to cast ballots. Republicans generally support such laws, arguing that they deter voter fraud. Democrats generally oppose such laws, countering that they are particularly burdensome to poor and minority voters, who they say are less likely than others to possess such IDs. Several studies of this question have been conducted but have produced inconclusive results. Cases have been brought in several states challenging the laws on equal protection grounds. The laws have been upheld by some courts and struck down by others. In 2008 the Supreme Court upheld the constitutionality of Indiana's voter ID law, affirming the states' "valid interest" in improving election procedures and deterring fraud.[38] On the other hand, in 2013 the Supreme Court struck down an Arizona law requiring that individuals produce proof of U.S. citizenship in order to register to vote. In 2016 voter ID laws were struck down or modified by courts in Kansas, North Carolina, North Dakota, Texas, and Wisconsin, indicating increased judicial suspicion of these statutes. Given the political controversy over voter ID laws, it seems likely that the Court will be asked to rule yet again on the question.

Housing The Civil Rights Act of 1964 did not address housing, but in 1968 Congress passed another civil rights act specifically to outlaw housing discrimination. Called the Fair Housing Act, the law prohibited discrimination in the sale or rental of most housing—eventually covering nearly all the nation's housing. Housing was among the most controversial of discrimination issues because of deeply entrenched patterns of residential segregation across the United States. Such segregation was not simply a product of individual choice. Local housing authorities deliberately segregated public housing, and federal guidelines had sanctioned discrimination in Federal Housing Administration mortgage lending, effectively preventing blacks from joining the exodus to the suburbs in the 1950s and '60s. Nonetheless, Congress had been reluctant to tackle housing discrimination, fearing

The mortgage crisis that led to foreclosures on many homes in 2008 and 2009 hit minority communities especially hard. Civil rights organizations argued that some lenders discriminated against African Americans and Latino home buyers, making it harder for them to get a fair deal on a mortgage.

the tremendous controversy it could arouse. But just as the housing legislation was being considered in April 1968, the civil rights leader Martin Luther King, Jr., was assassinated; this tragedy brought the measure unexpected support in Congress.

Although it pronounced sweeping goals, the Fair Housing Act had little effect on housing segregation because its enforcement mechanisms were so weak. Individuals who believed they had been discriminated against had to file suit themselves. The burden was on the individual to prove that housing discrimination had occurred, even though such discrimination is often subtle and difficult to document. Although local fair housing groups emerged to assist individuals in their court claims, the procedures for proving discrimination constituted a formidable barrier to effective change. These procedures were not altered until 1988, when Congress passed the Fair Housing Amendments Act. This new law put more teeth in the enforcement procedures and allowed the Department of Housing and Urban Development (HUD) to initiate legal action in cases of discrimination.[39]

Other attempts to challenge residential segregation had similarly mixed success. HUD tried briefly in the early 1970s to create racially "open communities" by withholding federal funds to suburbs that refused to accept subsidized housing. Confronted with charges of "forced integration" and bitter local protests, however, the administration quickly backed down. Efforts to prohibit discrimination in lending have been somewhat more promising. Several laws passed in the 1970s required banks to report information about their mortgage lending patterns, making it more difficult for them to engage in **redlining**, the practice of refusing to lend to entire neighborhoods. The 1977 Community Reinvestment Act required banks to lend in neighborhoods in which they do business. Through vigorous use of this act, many neighborhood organizations have reached agreements with banks that, as a result, have significantly increased investment in some poor neighborhoods.

Even so, racial discrimination in home mortgage lending remains a significant issue. In 2007 the issue of predatory lending—offering loans well above market rates, often with complex provisions that borrowers do not understand—attracted nationwide attention as the number of home foreclosures skyrocketed. In 2009, civil rights organizations, several states, and some cities filed charges against banks and other lenders claiming they had illegally discriminated against African American and Latino home buyers. Minority home buyers, the suits charged, had been offered subprime mortgage products with higher interest rates, in contrast to whites with similar income levels, who were offered loans at lower interest rates. By 2012 some of these lawsuits had resulted in the largest financial settlements ever issued for lending discrimination. In announcing one settlement, the Justice Department vowed to "vigorously pursue those who would take advantage of certain Americans because of their race, national origin, gender or disability," noting that such discrimination "betrays the promise of equal opportunity that is enshrined in our Constitution and our legal framework."[40]

Marriage The Civil Rights Act of 1964 was also silent on the question of interracial marriage, which 16 states continued to outlaw in 1967. In that year, the Supreme Court ruled in *Loving v. Virginia* that such state laws were unconstitutional. The case concerned a Virginia couple, a white man and a black woman, who married in Washington, D.C.,

redlining a practice in which banks refuse to make loans to people living in certain geographic locations

The Supreme Court ruled in 1967 that state laws banning interracial marriage were unconstitutional. The case Loving v. Virginia *was invoked numerous times in the Court's decision almost 50 years later declaring marriage a fundamental right for same-sex couples.*

where such unions were legal. When they moved back to Virginia, which outlawed interracial marriage, authorities charged the couple with violating Virginia law. The Lovings moved back to Washington, D.C., and challenged the Virginia law. Nine years later the Supreme Court struck down state laws banning marriage on the basis of racial classifications. In so doing, the Court declared marriage "one of the 'basic civil rights of man,' fundamental to our very existence and survival."[41]

● Extending Civil Rights

> Describe how different groups have fought for and won protection of their civil rights

Even before equal employment laws began to have a positive effect on the economic situation of blacks, something equally dramatic began happening: the extension of civil rights to other groups. The right not to be discriminated against was being successfully claimed by the other groups listed in Title VII of the 1964 Civil Rights Act, those defined by sex, religion, or national origin, and eventually by still other groups defined by age or sexual orientation. This extension of civil rights has become the new frontier of the civil rights struggle.

Once racial discrimination began to be seen as an important civil rights issue, other groups rose to demand recognition and active protection of their civil rights. Under Title VII, any group or individual can try, and in fact is encouraged to try, to convert goals and grievances into questions of rights and of the deprivation of those rights. A plaintiff must establish only that his or her membership in a group is an unreasonable basis for discrimination. In the United States today, a large number of individuals and groups have and are claiming illegal discrimination.

Levels of Scrutiny under the Equal Protection Clause

Before we examine the civil rights movements of the past 60 years, it is useful to take a moment to describe how the courts have analyzed laws in cases where an individual or group has claimed discrimination. As has already been made clear, the courts have been a very important actor in the contest for rights protections. Recall that civil rights are the rules governing who may participate in the political process and regulating the ways in which the government may or may not treat its citizens. The equal protection clause of the Fourteenth Amendment does not require that everyone be treated equally. State and federal laws often create classifications allowing some, but not other, individuals to engage in activities or receive benefits. States, for example, allow only those with certain qualifications to engage in various occupations (such as medical professions) and set a minimum age for driving automobiles, voting, and consuming alcohol. Courts generally recognize the need for such systems of classification. Some systems of classification, on the other hand, such as those based on race, gender, or religion, raise serious constitutional questions. When dealing with challenges to state-imposed systems of classification, the courts employ a three-tiered approach, placing a greater burden of proof on the government to defend some types of classificatory schemes than others. The three tiers are often called "levels of scrutiny."

First Level The first and lowest level of scrutiny is applied by the courts to most state and federal regulatory schemes, such as motor vehicle and occupational licensing as well as laws setting a minimum age for the purchase of alcohol and cigarettes. Here, the courts will generally apply the "rational basis test." Under this level of scrutiny, the burden of proof is on the plaintiff to show that there is no rational basis whatsoever for the government's rules. Such a showing is extremely difficult, and few plaintiffs succeed. For example, in the case of *FCC v. Beach Communications*, a cable television provider challenged a Federal Communications Commission ruling dertermining which cable operators did and did not require local government franchises to operate their systems. The Supreme Court said that whether the FCC's decision was correct or not, it had a rational basis and did not infringe upon fundamental constitutional rights.[42]

Second Level The next level of judicial review of state action under the equal protection clause is **intermediate scrutiny** (or exacting scrutiny). Here, there is a greater burden on the government to show that its classification scheme not only is rational but also serves an important interest. Courts generally apply intermediate scrutiny to laws that afford differential treatment to men and women or that discriminate against the inheritance and property rights of illegitimate children. In recent years, federal courts have generally applied intermediate scrutiny in cases involving gender orientation. For example, in the 2013 case of *Windsor v. United States* the Second Circuit Courts of Appeals employed *intermediate scrutiny* in holding that the federal Defense of Marriage Act, which applied the terms *marriage* and *spouse* only to heterosexual unions, served no legitimate state interest.[43] The U.S. Supreme Court affirmed the decision but did not indicate which level of scrutiny it had applied.

intermediate scrutiny a test used by the Supreme Court in gender discrimination cases that places the burden of proof partially on the government and partially on the challengers to show that the law in question is unconstitutional

Third Level The highest level of scrutiny employed by the courts, "strict scrutiny," places the burden of proof on the government to show that discrimination serves a "compelling interest," that the law is "narrowly tailored to achieve that goal," and that the government has used the "least restrictive means" for achieving its compelling interest. Strict scrutiny generally applies to laws that discriminate on the basis of race, religion, or national origin. These are termed *suspect classifications*. Strict scrutiny also applies to laws that hinder the exercise of fundamental rights, such as access to the courts or the right to vote. When a federal court employs strict scrutiny, the government is seldom able to meet its burden of proof. All race-based classifications are automatically subject to strict scrutiny.[44] In 2013, the Supreme Court also applied strict scrutiny to a case involving a claim of reverse discrimination. In the case of *Fisher v. University of Texas*, a white plaintiff charged that she had been rejected in favor of less qualified minority applicants.[45] The Supreme Court remanded the case for reconsideration by a lower federal court, which was instructed to apply strict scrutiny to the school's admissions process. The court of appeals still rejected Fisher's claim, and in 2016 the Supreme Court upheld the university's procedures.[46]

Women and Gender Discrimination

Title VII provided a valuable tool for the growing women's movement in the 1960s and '70s. In fact, in many ways the law fostered the growth of the women's movement. The first major campaign of the National Organization for Women (NOW) involved picketing the EEOC for its refusal to ban sex-segregated employment advertisements. NOW also sued the *New York Times* for continuing to

Political equality did not end discrimination against women in the workplace or in society at large. African Americans' struggle for civil rights in the 1950s and '60s spurred a parallel equal rights movement for women in the 1960s and '70s.

publish such ads after the passage of Title VII. Another organization, the Women's Equity Action League (WEAL), pursued legal action on a wide range of gender-discrimination issues, filing lawsuits against law schools and medical schools for discriminatory admission policies, for example.

Building on these victories and the growth of the women's movement, feminist activists sought an "Equal Rights Amendment" (ERA) to the Constitution. The proposed amendment was short: its substantive passage stated that "equality of rights under the law shall not be denied or abridged by the United States or by any State on account of sex." The amendment's supporters believed that such a sweeping guarantee of equal rights was a necessary tool for ending all discrimination against women and for making gender roles more equal. Opponents charged that the amendment would be socially disruptive and would introduce changes (such as unisex restrooms) that most Americans did not want. The amendment easily passed Congress in 1972 and won quick approval in many state legislatures, but it fell three states short of the 38 needed to ratify it by the 1982 deadline.[47]

Despite the failure of the ERA, efforts to stop gender discrimination expanded dramatically as an area of civil rights law. In the 1970s the conservative Burger Court (under Chief Justice Warren Burger) helped establish gender discrimination as a major and highly visible civil rights issue. Although the Supreme Court refused to treat gender discrimination as the equivalent of racial discrimination,[48] it did make it easier for plaintiffs to file and win suits on the basis of gender discrimination by applying an "intermediate" level of review to these cases, as described earlier.[49]

In recent years, laws and court decisions designed to deal with discrimination against women have been used by groups representing transgender individuals to press for equal rights, especially in the realm of employment. For example, Title VII of the 1964 Civil Rights Act makes it unlawful to discriminate in employment on the basis of color, religion, sex, national origin, or race. The act is enforced by the EEOC. Pressed by groups representing transgender workers, in July 2015 President Obama issued an executive order prohibiting federal contractors from discriminating against workers based on their sexual orientation or gender identity. Two months later, the EEOC filed its first-ever lawsuits to protect transgender workers under Title VII of the Civil Rights Act. In late December, then–attorney general Eric Holder announced that, going forward, the Justice Department would consider discrimination against transgender people as covered by the Civil Rights Act's prohibition of sex discrimination.[50] Nonetheless, attempts have been made to pass legislation requiring transgender individuals to use public bathrooms that correspond to the gender designated on their birth certificates. In 2016, North

Carolina enacted such a law, leading to boycotts and protests, with several corporations announcing plans to reduce their operations in the state. When the Department of Justice warned North Carolina that the law violated the Civil Rights Act, the state sued the federal government in order to defend its new law.

Equality in Education Title IX of the 1972 Education Act forbade gender discrimination in education, but it initially sparked little litigation because of its weak enforcement provisions. In 1992, the Supreme Court ruled in *Franklin v. Gwinnett County Public Schools* that monetary damages could be awarded for gender discrimination, opening the door for more legal action in the area of education.[51] The greatest impact has been in the areas of sexual harassment (the subject of the *Franklin* case) and in equal treatment of women's athletic programs. The potential for monetary damages has made universities and public schools take the problem of sexual harassment more seriously. And in the two years after the *Franklin* case, complaints to the Education Department's Office for Civil Rights about unequal treatment of women's athletic programs nearly tripled. In several high-profile legal cases, some prominent universities were ordered to create more women's sports programs, prompting many other colleges and universities to follow suit in order to avoid potential litigation.[52] In 1997 the Supreme Court refused to hear a petition by Brown University challenging a lower-court order that the university establish strict sex equity in its athletic programs. The Court's decision meant that in colleges and universities across the country, varsity athletic positions for men and women must reflect the schools' overall enrollment numbers.[53] By 2012, 40 years after Title IX was first enacted, it was clear that the ruling had a major impact on college athletic programs. But advocates for gender equality note that many differences between male and female students continue to exist. They point to gender barriers in important fields such as science, technology, engineering, and math, which female students are much less likely to enter.[54]

In 1996 the Supreme Court made another important decision about gender and education by putting an end to all-male schools supported by public funds. It ruled that the Virginia Military Institute's (VMI) policy of not admitting women was unconstitutional.[55] Along with the Citadel, an all-male military college in South Carolina, VMI had never admitted women in its 157-year history. VMI argued that the unique educational experience it offered (including intense physical training and the harsh treatment of freshmen) would be destroyed if women were admitted. The Court, however, ruled that the male-only policy denied "substantial equality" to women. Two days after the ruling, the Citadel announced that it would accept women. Even without formal barriers to entry, the experience of the new female cadets at these schools was not easy. The first female cadet at the Citadel, Shannon Faulkner, won admission in 1995 under a federal court order but quit after four days. Of the four women admitted to the Citadel after the Supreme Court decision, two quit within months. They charged harassment from male students, including attempts to set the female cadets on fire.[56]

Sexual Harassment Courts began to find sexual harassment to be a form of sex discrimination during the late 1970s. Most such law has been developed by courts through interpretation of Title VII of the 1964 Civil Rights Act. In 1986 the

The integration of women in the U.S. military has been a slow process. Only in 2013 did then–Secretary of Defense Leon Panetta announce that the military would lift its official ban on women serving in combat. This decision in part reflected the reality that female service members frequently found themselves in combat in Iraq and Afghanistan.

for critical analysis

Has Title IX created equality in men's and women's college athletic programs? Should there be public efforts to encourage more female students to enter well-paid fields such as science and technology, or is that mainly a matter of individual choice?

Supreme Court recognized two forms of sexual harassment. One type is "quid pro quo" harassment, which involves an explicit or strongly implied threat that submission is a condition of continued employment. The second is harassment that creates offensive or intimidating employment conditions amounting to a "hostile environment."[57] Employers and many employees have complained that "hostile environment" sexual harassment is too ambiguous. When can an employee bring charges? When is the employer liable? In 1986 the Court said that sexual harassment may be legally actionable even if the employee did not suffer tangible economic or job-related losses in relation to it and in 1993 added that tangible psychological costs did not have to be a result either to warrant legal action.[58] In two 1998 cases, the Court further strengthened the law when it said that whether or not sexual harassment results in economic harm to the employee, an employer is liable for the harassment if it was committed by someone with authority over the employee—by a supervisor, for example. But the Court also said that an employer may defend itself by showing that it had a sexual harassment prevention and grievance policy in effect.[59]

Sexual harassment remains an issue today. Recently, a number of cases of sexual harassment of female members of the U.S. military have come to light. These cases have led to several courts-martial of both officers and noncommissioned officers. Some observers argue that the problem is systemic, however, and have urged the military to enact reforms that would hopefully have the effect of stemming the abuse of women in the military.

Equality in Employment Women have also pressed for civil rights in employment. In particular, women have fought against pay discrimination, which occurs when a male employee is paid more than a female employee of equal qualifications in the same job. In the 1960s, pay discrimination was common. After the Equal Pay Act of 1963 made such discrimination illegal, women's pay slowly moved toward the level of men's pay. In 2007 this movement received a setback when the Supreme Court ruled against a claim of pay discrimination. The case, *Ledbetter v. Goodyear Tire and Rubber Co.*, involved a female supervisor named Lily Ledbetter, who learned late in her career that she was being paid up to 40 percent less than male supervisors, including those with less seniority. Ledbetter filed a grievance with the EEOC, charging sex discrimination.[60] The Supreme Court denied her claim, ruling that, according to the law, workers must file their grievance 180 days after the discrimination occurs. Many observers found the ruling unfair because workers often do not know about pay differentials until well after the initial decision to discriminate has been made. Justice Ruth Bader Ginsburg, the only female member of the Court at the time, marked her disagreement by reading her dissent aloud, a rare occurrence. In January 2009 the Lily Ledbetter Fair Pay Act became the first bill that President Obama signed into law. The new law gave workers expanded rights to sue in cases, such as Ledbetter's, when an employee learns of discriminatory treatment well after it has started.

The fight against gender discrimination as an important part of the civil rights struggle has coincided with the rise of women's politics as a discrete movement in American politics. As with the struggle for racial equality, the relationship between changes in government policies and political action suggests that, to a great degree, changes in government policies produce political action. The inclusion of gender as a protected class in the 1964 Civil Rights Act prompted women to take steps to press for their rights where they were denied in education and employment. The "Who Are Americans?" feature on considers the progress on women's rights.

Have Women Achieved Equal Rights?

Title VII of the 1964 Civil Rights Act prohibits gender discrimination, and the Supreme Court has consistently upheld the principle that women should have the same rights as men. Since 1960, the United States has made great strides toward gender equality in some areas but, as the data show, still has a long way to go in other areas.

Education

■ Percentage of college students who are women

1960	39%
1970	39%
1980	42%
1990	45%
2000	48%
2010	56%

Politics

■ Percentage of members of Congress who are women   ■ Percentage of state legislators who are women

1960	4%
1970	2%
1980	11% / 2%
1990	17% / 6%
2000	23% / 13%
2010	25% / 17%

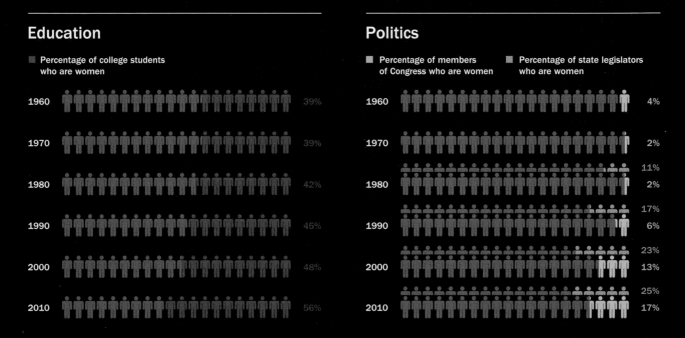

Median Weekly Earnings by Race and Gender

Based on the median weekly earnings for full-time workers (which excludes self-employed and full-time workers who work only part of the year), in 2014 women earned 82.5 percent as much as men. In 1979 women earned 62.3 percent as much as men.

White		African American		Latino		Asian American	
Men	Women	Men	Women	Men	Women	Men	Women
$897	$734	$680	$611	$616	$548	$1,080	$841

SOURCES: Bureau of Labor Statistics, "Labor Force Statistics from the Current Population Survey," www.bls.gov/cps/tables.htm; U.S. Bureau of Labor Statistics, "Highlights of Women's Earnings in 2014," November 2015, www.bls.gov/cps/earnings.htm/ (accessed 2/27/16).

for critical analysis

1. How much do each of these factors—education, political office, and income— say about gender equality in the United States?

2. While most Americans support the principle of equal opportunity for all groups, there is disagreement over how much the government should do to ensure equal outcomes. Discuss the difference between equal opportunity and equal outcomes in the context of women's rights.

Latinos

The labels *Latino* and *Hispanic* encompass a wide range of groups with diverse national origins, distinctive cultural identities, and particular experiences. As a result, civil rights issues for them have varied considerably by group and by place. For example, the early political experiences of Mexican Americans were shaped by race and by region. In 1848, under the Treaty of Guadalupe Hidalgo, Mexico ceded to the United States territory that now comprises Arizona, California, New Mexico, and parts of Colorado, Nevada, and Utah, as well as extending the Texas border to the Rio Grande. Although the treaty guaranteed full civil rights to the residents of these territories, Mexican Americans in fact experienced ongoing discrimination, which they sought to remedy through the courts. In 1898 the courts reconfirmed Mexican Americans' formal political rights, including the right to vote. In many places, however, and especially in Texas, Mexican Americans were segregated and prevented from voting through such means as the white primary and the poll tax.[61] Texas established separate schools for Mexicans, a practice also common in southern California. In the housing markets, Mexicans were often banned by restrictive covenants from buying or renting houses in many neighborhoods.

The earliest Mexican American independent political organizations included the League of United Latin American Citizens (LULAC), founded in 1929, and the GI Forum, created in 1948. Both groups worked to stem discrimination against Mexican Americans. LULAC pursued a legal strategy like the NAACP's to eliminate the segregation of Mexican American students. One of its earliest victories came in 1930, when it successfully challenged a Texas school district's decision to establish separate schools for Anglos and Mexicans.[62] LULAC also litigated the 1946–47 *Mendez v. Westminster* case, which overturned school segregation in Orange County, California.[63] This case was an important precursor to *Brown v. Board of Education*, and many of the same actors were involved. For example, Thurgood Marshall of the NAACP, the lead attorney on *Brown* (and later a Supreme Court justice), filed a brief supporting desegregation in the *Mendez* case. Moreover, Earl Warren, the California governor who signed the legislation outlawing school segregation there after the *Mendez* decision, served as chief justice when the Supreme Court ruled on *Brown* seven years later. By the late 1950s the first Mexican American was elected to Congress, and four others followed in the 1960s.

In the 1960s a new kind of Mexican American political movement was born. A central inspiration for political mobilization emerged from the United Farm Workers union and its charismatic leader, César Chávez. In an era of unprecedented economic prosperity, California's farmworkers, mainly Mexican migrants, remained poorly paid and lacked basic rights for fair treatment on the job. Employing novel tactics such as the national grape boycott, the union drew Americans' attention to the plight of farmworkers and the injustices that confronted Mexican migrants and Mexican Americans in the fields. Chávez, whose hunger strikes and inspirational speeches kept the movement in the public eye, came to symbolize the quest for Mexican American civil rights more broadly.[64] The fields were not the only focus of conflict. In the late 1960s, Mexican American students, inspired by the black civil rights movement, launched boycotts of high school classes in East Los Angeles, Denver, and San Antonio, demanding bilingual education, an end to discrimination, and more cultural recognition. They were soon joined by students in colleges and universities across California.

Since that time, Latino political strategy has developed along two tracks. One is a traditional ethnic group path of voter registration and voting along ethnic lines. The other is a legal strategy using the various civil rights laws designed to ensure fair access to the political system. The Mexican American Legal Defense

César Chávez, a leader of the United Farm Workers, advocated for the rights of Mexican Americans. During the 1960s, Chávez and his supporters used hunger strikes and other protests to draw attention to the discriminatory treatment of Mexican Americans.

and Education Fund (MALDEF), founded in 1968, has played a key role in designing and pursuing the latter strategy.

Immigrants and Civil Rights Since the 1960s, rights for Latinos have been intertwined with immigrant rights. For much of American history, legal immigrants were treated much the same as citizens. But growing immigration—including an estimated 300,000 unauthorized immigrants per year—and mounting economic insecurity have undermined this sense of equality. Groups of voters across the country now strongly support drawing a sharper line between immigrants and citizens. The Supreme Court has ruled that unauthorized immigrants are eligible for education and emergency medical care but can be denied other social benefits. The movement to deny benefits to noncitizens gathered steam in California, which experienced sharp economic distress in the early 1990s and has the highest levels of immigration of any state. In 1994, an ultimately unsuccessful movement in California sought to deny unauthorized immigrants all services except emergency medical care in an attempt to discourage unauthorized immigration and to pressure those already in the country to leave.

Questions about the rights of unauthorized immigrants became especially contentious in 2007. That year, Congress considered a complex compromise bill—running some 761 pages long—that attempted to accomplish three goals: increase border security to reduce illegal immigration, provide unauthorized immigrants who had been in the country for at least five years with a pathway to legal citizenship, and ensure employers an adequate supply of temporary immigrant workers through a guest worker program. The compromise failed in the face of opposition from conservatives, who disliked the provision for creating a path to legal citizenship, and from liberals, who opposed the proposed guest worker program.

Unauthorized immigration has continued to be a hot-button political issue. One priority for advocacy groups has been the issue of undocumented immigrants who came to the United States as young children, were raised in the United States, and have no real ties to the nation in which they were born. One proposed piece of legislation to benefit such individuals is the Development, Relief, and Education Act for Alien Minors, known as the DREAM Act. This proposal would provide a route to permanent residency for such individuals via military service or

In 2010 young adults demonstrated their support for the DREAM Act by staging a sit-in protest on the floor of Senator John McCain's headquarters in Tucson, Arizona. The DREAM Act would provide a path to permanent residency via military service or college attendance for individuals who were brought to the U.S. illegally as children by their parents.

college attendance. The DREAM Act was introduced in Congress in 2001 but has been defeated every year on the grounds that it would encourage illegal immigration. Absent legislation, the Department of Homeland Security has instituted its own policy, Deferred Action for Childhood Arrivals (DACA), instructing immigration officials to take no action to deport law-abiding individuals who entered the United States illegally as children. In 2014, President Obama issued executive orders granting quasi-legal status and work permits to some 5 million individuals who entered the U.S. illegally as children or who have children who are American citizens. The president's orders were challenged in the federal courts, and in 2016 a 4–4 tie in the Supreme Court left in place a lower-court decision disallowing the president's plan.[65]

Efforts to curb illegal immigration have led to civil rights violations of legal immigrants. Latino organizations opposed the Immigration Reform and Control Act of 1986 because it imposed sanctions on employers who hire undocumented workers. Such sanctions, they feared, would lead employers to discriminate against Latinos. These suspicions were confirmed in a 1990 report by the General Accounting Office that found employer sanctions had created a "widespread pattern of discrimination" against Latinos and others who appear foreign.[66]

Another ongoing issue is federal cooperation with local and state law-enforcement agencies to enforce federal immigration laws. Programs initiated by the Department of Homeland Security in the final years of the George W. Bush administration led to immigrant "sweeps," which rounded up Latinos, many of whom were legal immigrants or even American citizens. A broad coalition of civil rights organizations opposed the program for engaging in racial profiling and violating civil rights, and the congressional Hispanic Caucus called on the next president to end it. Yet, the Obama administration's Secure Communities program, which initially sought to focus on major drug offenders, violent criminals, and those already in prison, came under fire for illegally detaining citizens and legal immigrants. Secure Communities requires state and local police to run the fingerprints of individuals they have arrested against the Department of Homeland Security's immigration database. If the individual is not a U.S. citizen and is not in the database, Immigration and Customs Enforcement is notified.[67] The Secure Communities Program was terminated in 2014 in favor of an effort to refocus law enforcement attention on serious criminals.

Finally, as we saw in Chapter 3, a number of states, including Arizona, Utah, South Carolina, Indiana, Georgia, and Alabama, passed very strict immigration laws within the past few years. Civil rights groups have contested the laws in court, and the federal Justice Department has instituted its own legal challenges. Arizona's 2010 law provided the inspiration for these far-reaching state measures. Arizona's law required immigrants to carry identity documents with them at all times, made it a crime for an undocumented immigrant to apply for a job, gave the police greater powers to stop anyone they suspected of being an unauthorized immigrant, and required them to check the immigration status of a person they detain if they suspect that person is an unauthorized immigrant. The Justice Department challenged the law on the grounds that the federal government was responsible for making immigration law, not the states. The Supreme Court's 2012 decision was a partial victory for the federal government. The court struck down three parts of the Arizona law on the grounds that they preempted federal responsibility. These included the provision that immigrants carry identity papers, that undocumented immigrants cannot apply for jobs, and that police can stop persons they suspect of being undocumented immigrants. The Court let stand the provision that required local police to check the immigration status of an individual detained for other reasons if they had grounds to suspect that the person was in the country illegally. Opponents of the police checks vowed to challenge that part of the law on the grounds that it led to illegal racial profiling.[68]

Immigration became an even more divisive topic during the 2016 presidential election. During the campaign for the GOP nomination, Donald Trump asserted that he would build a wall along the U.S. border with Mexico, institute a temporary ban on Muslims seeking to travel to the United States, and end the administration's program to accept several thousand Syrian refugees every year. Trump was denounced by Democrats and some Republicans, but his views seemed to express the opinions of many Americans and vaulted him to a leadership position in the party as the Republican nominee in the 2016 presidential race.

for critical analysis

Why are immigration and the rights of immigrants so controversial?

Asian Americans

Like the term *Latino*, the label *Asian American* encompasses a wide range of people from very different national backgrounds who came to the United States at different moments in history. As a consequence, Asian Americans have had very diverse experiences.

The early Asian experience in the United States was shaped by a series of naturalization laws dating back to 1790, the first of which declared that only white aliens were eligible for citizenship. Chinese immigrants began arriving in California in the 1850s, drawn by the boom of the gold rush, but they were immediately met with virulent antagonism. In 1870, Congress declared Chinese immigrants ineligible for citizenship; in 1882 the first Chinese Exclusion Act suspended the entry of Chinese laborers.

At the time of the Exclusion Act, the Chinese community was composed predominantly of single male laborers, with few women and children. The few Chinese children in San Francisco were initially denied entry to the public schools; only after parents of American-born Chinese children pressed legal action were the children allowed to attend public school. Even then, however, they were segregated into a separate Chinese school. American-born Chinese children could not be denied citizenship, however; this right was confirmed by the Supreme Court in 1898, when it ruled in *United States v. Wong Kim Ark* that anyone born in the United States was entitled to full citizenship.[69] Still, new Chinese immigrants were barred from the United States until 1943, after China had become a key wartime ally and Congress repealed the Chinese Exclusion Act and permitted Chinese residents to become citizens.

Asian immigrants faced discrimination through much of American history. During World War II, Americans of Japanese descent were forced from their homes and confined in internment camps. At the time, the Supreme Court supported this denial of civil rights as a necessary security measure.

The earliest Japanese immigrants, who came to California in the 1880s, at the height of the anti-Chinese movement, faced similar discrimination. Like Chinese immigrants, Japanese immigrants were ineligible to become citizens because of their race. During the first part of the twentieth century, California and several other western states enacted laws that denied Japanese immigrants the right to own property. The denial of basic civil rights to Japanese Americans culminated in the decision to forcibly remove Americans of Japanese descent as well as Japanese noncitizen residents from their homes and confine them in internment camps during World War II. After the Japanese government launched its attack on Pearl Harbor, America's Japanese residents and citizens were suspected of disloyalty. Some 120,000 individuals of Japanese descent or heritage, including 90,000 American citizens, were forcibly relocated from their homes to 10 internment camps located in California, Idaho, Utah, Arizona, Wyoming, Colorado, and Arkansas. Conditions in the camps were poor and characterized by overcrowding, food rationing, and primitive sanitary facilities. Despite a vigorous legal challenge, the Supreme Court ruled that the internment was constitutional on the grounds of military necessity.[70] In 1944, President Roosevelt rescinded the order that began the internment process and closed the camps. Many of the internees, however, had suffered property losses and health problems during the period of internment and would never recover from its effects. Not until the Civil Liberties Act of 1988 did the federal government formally acknowledge this denial of civil rights as a "grave injustice" that had been "motivated largely by racial prejudice, wartime hysteria, and a failure of political leadership."[71]

Asian immigration increased rapidly after the 1965 Immigration Act, which lifted discriminatory quotas. In spite of this and other developments, limited English proficiency barred many new Asian American (in addition to Latino) immigrants from full participation in American life. Two developments in the 1970s, however, established rights for language minorities. In 1974 the Supreme Court ruled in *Lau v. Nichols*, a suit filed on behalf of Chinese students in San Francisco, that school districts have to provide education for students whose English is limited.[72] It did not mandate bilingual education, but it established a duty to provide instruction that the students could understand. As we saw earlier, the 1970 amendments to the Voting Rights Act permanently outlawed literacy tests in all 50 states and mandated bilingual ballots or oral assistance for those who speak Chinese, Japanese, Korean, Spanish, or Native American or Alaskan languages.

Native Americans

The political status of Native Americans was left unclear in the Constitution. But by the early 1800s the courts had defined each of the Indian tribes as a nation. As members of Indian nations, Native Americans were thus declared noncitizens of the United States. The political status of Native Americans changed in 1924, when congressional legislation granted citizenship to all persons born in the United States. A variety of changes in federal policy toward Native Americans during the 1930s paved the way for a later resurgence of their political power. Most important was the federal decision to encourage Native Americans on reservations to establish local self-government.[73] Since the 1920s and '30s, Native American tribes have sued the federal government for illegal land seizures; both monetary reparations and land have been awarded as damages but only in small amounts. Native American tribes have been more successful at winning federal recognition of their sovereignty.

The Native American political movement gathered force in the 1960s as Native Americans began to use protest, litigation, and assertion of tribal rights to improve their situation. The federal government responded to the rise in Native American activism with the Indian Self-Determination and Education Assistance Act, which began to give Native Americans more control over their own land.[74]

As a language minority, Native Americans also benefited from the 1975 amendments to the Voting Rights Act and the *Lau* decision, which established the right of Native Americans to be taught in their own languages. This marked quite a change from the boarding schools run by the Bureau of Indian Affairs, where members of Native American tribes were forbidden to speak their own languages until reforms began in the 1930s. In addition to these language-related issues, Native Americans have sought to expand their rights on the basis of their sovereign status. Most significant in economic terms was a 1987 Supreme Court decision that freed Native American tribes from most state regulations prohibiting gambling. The establishment of casino gambling on Native American lands has brought a substantial flow of new income to desperately poor reservations.

Disabled Americans

The concept of rights for the disabled began to emerge in the 1970s as the civil rights model spread to other groups. The seed was planted in a little-noticed provision of the 1973 Rehabilitation Act, which outlawed discrimination against individuals on the basis of disabilities. As in many other cases, the law itself helped give rise to the movement demanding rights for the disabled.[75] Inspired by the NAACP's use of a legal defense fund, the disability movement founded the Disability Rights Education and Defense Fund to press its legal claims. The movement achieved its greatest success with the passage of the Americans with Disabilities Act (ADA) of 1990, which guarantees equal employment rights and access to public businesses for the disabled and prohibits discrimination in employment, housing, and health care. Claims of discrimination in violation of this act are considered by the EEOC. The impact of the law has been far-reaching as businesses and public facilities have installed ramps, elevators, and other devices to meet the act's requirements.[76]

Gay Men and Lesbians

In less than 50 years, the lesbian, gay, bisexual, transgender, and queer (LGBTQ) movement has become one of the largest civil rights movements in contemporary America. For much of the country's history, any sexual orientation other than heterosexuality was considered "deviant" and many states criminalized sexual acts considered to be "unnatural." Gay people were often afraid to reveal their sexual orientation for fear of reprisals, including being fired from their jobs; and the police in many cities raided bars and other establishments where it was believed that gay people gathered. While no formal restrictions existed on their political participation, gay people faced the possibility of ostracization, discrimination, and even prosecution.[77]

The contemporary gay rights movement began in earnest in the 1960s. In 1962, Illinois became the first state to repeal its sodomy laws. The movement drew national attention in 1969, when patrons at the Stonewall Inn, a popular gay bar in Greenwich Village, New York, rioted when police attempted to raid the establishment. The first gay pride parade was held in New York City the following year to commemorate the anniversary of the Stonewall riots, and gay pride parades now take place in dozens of cities across the country.

Gay rights drew national attention again in 1993, when President Bill Clinton confronted the question of whether gays should be allowed to serve in the military. As a candidate, Clinton had said he favored lifting the ban on gay people in the military. The issue set off a huge controversy in the first months of Clinton's presidency. After nearly a year of deliberation, the administration enunciated a compromise: its "Don't Ask, Don't Tell" policy allowed gay men and lesbians to serve in the military as long as they did not openly proclaim their sexual orientation or engage in homosexual activity. The administration maintained that the ruling would protect gay men and lesbians against witch-hunt investigations, but many gay rights advocates expressed disappointment, charging the president with reneging on his campaign promise. After nearly 20 years of challenges, President Obama signed an executive order repealing "Don't Ask, Don't Tell"; and beginning in September 2011, gay men and lesbians could serve openly in the military.

But until 1996 there was no Supreme Court ruling or national legislation explicitly protecting gay men and lesbians from discrimination. In the first gay rights case it decided, *Bowers v. Hardwick*, the Court ruled against a right to privacy that would protect consensual homosexual activity.[78] After the *Bowers* decision, the gay rights movement sought suitable legal cases to test the constitutionality of discrimination against gay men and lesbians, much as the black civil rights movement had done in the late 1940s and '50s. Test cases stemmed from local ordinances restricting gay rights (including the right to marry), allowing job discrimination, and affecting family law issues such as adoption and parental rights. In 1996 the Supreme Court, in *Romer v. Evans*, explicitly extended fundamental civil rights protections to gay men and lesbians by declaring unconstitutional a 1992 amendment to the Colorado state constitution that prohibited local governments from passing ordinances to protect gay rights.[79] In its decision, the Court highlighted the connection between gay rights and civil rights.

Finally, in *Lawrence v. Texas* (2003), the Court overturned *Bowers* and struck down a Texas statute criminalizing certain intimate sexual conduct between consenting partners of the same sex.[80] This significant victory for gay men and lesbians extends the right to privacy to sexual minorities.

However, this decision did not undo the various exclusions that deprive gay men and lesbians of full civil rights, including the right to marry. In 1993, Hawaii's supreme court declared the state's ban on same-sex marriage discriminatory, raising the possibility that such marriages could become legal. In Washington, D.C., the Republican congressional majority responded with the Defense of Marriage Act, which defined marriage as the union of a man and a woman for purposes of federal law and benefits, such as Social Security.

Edith Windsor (left) won her case in 2013 when the Supreme Court struck down the portion of the Defense of Marriage Act denying federal benefits to married same-sex couples. Two year later, the Court legalized same-sex marriage nationwide. The Obama administration showed its support by illuminating the White House in rainbow light (right).

In 2015 the Supreme Court clarified the law concerning same-sex marriage. In the case of *Obergefell v. Hodges*, the Court ruled that the Constitution's equal protection clause and the Fourteenth Amendment's due process clause guarantee same-sex couples the right to marry in all states and require states to recognize same-sex marriages performed in other jurisdictions.[81] Some local officials briefly refused to issue marriage licenses to same-sex couples, but opposition soon melted away. Though deemed controversial, the Court's decision actually reflected a shift in public opinion on same-sex unions, with a majority of Americans now favoring the right of same-sex couples to wed.

Gay rights advocates won a significant victory of a different kind in national politics in 2009 when new legislation extended the definition of hate crimes to include crimes against gay and transgender people. Such legislation had been sought since the 1998 murder of Matthew Shepard, a Wyoming college student who was brutally slain because of his sexual orientation. The new law allowed for tougher penalties when a crime is designated a hate crime. In another win in 2013, the Senate approved a law that bans discrimination in the workplace based on sexual orientation and gender identity (discussed above), with a vote of 64 to 32 in which 10 Republicans joined 54 Democrats. The House did not take up the bill, however, so it has not yet become law. Like other minorities fighting for civil rights, the LGBTQ community is organized politically to support such measures. The Human Rights Campaign is the primary national political action committee (PAC) focused on gay rights; it provides campaign financing and volunteers to work for political candidates endorsed by the group. The movement has also formed legal rights organizations, including the Lambda Legal Defense and Education Fund.

Do the Poor Have Civil Rights?

One category often omitted from discussions of rights is the poor. Yet, America's poor have also struggled for recognition as a group with rights that should be protected. From the colonial period until the early nineteenth century, state income and property restrictions excluded the poor from voting and officeholding. In modern times, advocates have argued that the poor have a right (a claim upon government action) to education, health care, and other social benefits. Such rights are guaranteed in many European constitutions. And, in the United States, various social policies discussed in Chapter 17 appear to recognize such rights.

forcriticalanalysis

Political conflicts over gay rights have been carried out in the courts, in state legislatures, in Congress, and in elections. What are some of the decisions that have been reached in each of these different decision-making arenas? Where should decisions about gay rights be made?

Same-Sex Marriage around the World

When the U.S. Supreme Court legalized same-sex marriage in 2015, the United States joined the roughly 20 countries in the world that allow gay marriage. As the map shows, most of these countries are in Western Europe and the Americas, and we see in the time line that most have only legalized same-sex marriage in the past several years.

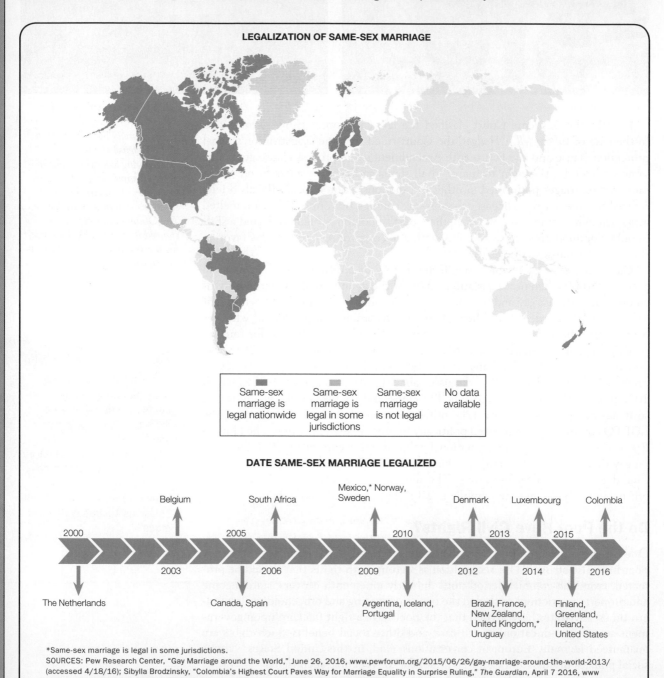

LEGALIZATION OF SAME-SEX MARRIAGE

Same-sex marriage is legal nationwide

Same-sex marriage is legal in some jurisdictions

Same-sex marriage is not legal

No data available

DATE SAME-SEX MARRIAGE LEGALIZED

Belgium	2003 — The Netherlands
South Africa (2005)	2006 — Canada, Spain
Mexico,* Norway, Sweden	2009 — Argentina, Iceland, Portugal
Denmark (2012)	2012 — Brazil, France, New Zealand, United Kingdom,* Uruguay
Luxembourg (2014)	2014
Colombia (2016)	2016 — Finland, Greenland, Ireland, United States

Timeline markers: 2000, 2005, 2010, 2013, 2015

*Same-sex marriage is legal in some jurisdictions.

SOURCES: Pew Research Center, "Gay Marriage around the World," June 26, 2016, www.pewforum.org/2015/06/26/gay-marriage-around-the-world-2013/ (accessed 4/18/16); Sibylla Brodzinsky, "Colombia's Highest Court Paves Way for Marriage Equality in Surprise Ruling," *The Guardian*, April 7 2016, www .theguardian.com/world/2016/apr/07/colombia-court-gay-marriage-ruling (accessed 4/18/16).

One area in which there is currently a disparity is in access to high-speed Internet. A 2014 Census department survey found that among those who earn less than $10,000 per year, only 46 percent have high-speed Internet access at home. This compares with 92 percent of those making at least $75,000 a year.[82] As more and more economic and political activity moves online, including job listings and applications for government services, this disparity has the potential to reinforce inequalities.

● Affirmative Action

> **Contrast arguments for and against affirmative action**

Over the past half-century or so, the relatively narrow goal of equalizing opportunity by eliminating discriminatory barriers evolved into the broader goal of **affirmative action**, compensatory action to overcome the consequences of past discrimination and encourage greater diversity. Affirmative action policies take race or some other status into account in order to provide greater opportunities to groups that have previously been at a disadvantage due to discrimination.

affirmative action government policies or programs that seek to redress past injustices against specified groups by making special efforts to provide members of those groups with access to educational and employment opportunities

In 1965, President Lyndon Johnson issued executive orders promoting minority employment in the federal civil service and in companies doing business with the government. But affirmative action did not become a prominent goal of the national government until the 1970s.

Affirmative action also took the form of efforts by the agencies in the Department of Health, Education, and Welfare to shift their focus from "desegregation" to "integration."[83] Federal agencies, sometimes with court orders and sometimes without them, required school districts to present plans for busing children across district lines, for closing certain schools, and for redistributing faculties as well as students or face the loss of grants-in-aid from the federal government. These efforts dramatically increased the number of black children attending integrated classes.

Affirmative action was also initiated in the area of employment opportunity. The EEOC has often required plans whereby employers must attempt to increase the number of their minority employees with the same threat of contract revocation. These programs did not require the use of formal quotas.

The Supreme Court and the Burden of Proof

Efforts by the executive, legislative, and judicial branches to shape the meaning of affirmative action today tend to center on one key issue: What is the appropriate level of review in affirmative action cases—that is, on whom should the burden of proof be placed: the plaintiff, to show that discrimination has not occurred, or the defendant, to show that discrimination has occurred? Affirmative action was first addressed formally by the Supreme Court in the case of Allan Bakke (see Table 5.3). Bakke, a white male, brought suit against the University of California at Davis Medical School on the grounds that, in denying him admission, the school had discriminated against him on the basis of his race. (That year, the school had reserved 16 of 100 available slots for minority applicants.) Bakke argued that his grades and test scores ranked him well above many students who were accepted and that he had been rejected because he was white, whereas those others accepted were black or Latino. In 1978, Bakke won his case before the Supreme Court and was admitted to the medical school, but the Court stopped short of declaring affirmative action unconstitutional. The Court

TABLE 5.3

Supreme Court Rulings on Affirmative Action

CASE	COURT RULING
Regents of the University of California v. Bakke, 438 U.S. 265 (1978)	Affirmative action upheld, but quotas and separate admission for minorities rejected; burden of proof on defendant
Wards Cove Packing Co., Inc. v. Atonio, 490 U.S. 642 (1989)	All affirmative action programs put in doubt: burden of proof shifted from defendant to plaintiff (victim), then burden of proof shifted back to employers (defendants)
St. Mary's Honor Center v. Hicks, 509 U.S. 502 (1993)	Required victim to prove discrimination was intentional
Adarand Constructors v. Peña, 515 U.S. 200 (1995)	All race-conscious policies must survive "strict scrutiny," with burden of proof on government to show the program serves "compelling interest" to redress past discrimination
Hopwood v. Texas, 78 F.3d 932 (5th Cir., 1996)	Race can *never* be used as a factor in admission, even to promote diversity (Supreme Court refusal to review limited application to the Fifth Circuit—Texas, Louisiana, Mississippi)
Gratz v. Bollinger, 539 U.S. 244 (2003)	Rejection of a "mechanical" point system favoring minority applicants to University of Michigan as tantamount to a quota; *Bakke* reaffirmed
Grutter v. Bollinger, 539 U.S. 306 (2003)	Upheld race-conscious admission to Michigan Law School, passing strict scrutiny with diversity as a "compelling" state interest, as long as admission was "highly individualized" and not "mechanical," as in *Gratz*
Fisher v. University of Texas, 570 U.S. __ (2013)	Held that strict scrutiny should be applied to college admissions policies that used race as a factor even if the intent was to favor black applicants

rejected the procedures at the University of California because its medical school had used both a quota *and* a separate admissions system for minorities. The Court accepted the argument that achieving "a diverse student body" was a "compelling public purpose" but found that the method of a rigid quota of student slots assigned on the basis of race was incompatible with the Fourteenth Amendment's equal protection clause. Thus, the Court permitted universities (and presumably other schools, training programs, and hiring authorities) to continue to consider minority status but limited the use of quotas to situations (1) in which previous discrimination had been shown and (2) where quotas served more as a guideline for social diversity than as a mathematically defined ratio.[84]

For nearly a decade after *Bakke*, the Court was tentative and permissive about efforts by universities, corporations, and governments to experiment with affirmative action programs.[85]

But in 1995, another Supreme Court ruling further weakened affirmative action. This decision stated that race-based policies, such as preferences given by the government to minority contractors, must survive strict scrutiny, placing the burden on the government to show that such affirmative action programs serve a compelling government interest and address identifiable past discrimination.[86]

This betwixt-and-between status of affirmative action was how things stood in 2003, when the Supreme Court took two cases against the University of Michigan. The first suit alleged that by automatically awarding 20 points (out of 150) to African American, Latino, and Native American applicants, the university discriminated unconstitutionally against white students of otherwise equal or superior academic qualifications. The Supreme Court agreed, arguing that something tantamount to a quota was involved because undergraduate admissions lacked the necessary "individualized consideration" and had employed instead a "mechanical one," based too much on the favorable minority points.[87]

The second case, *Grutter v. Bollinger*, broke new ground. Barbara Grutter sued the law school on the grounds that it had discriminated in a race-conscious way against white applicants with equal or superior grades and law boards. A 5–4 decision for the first time aligned the majority of the Supreme Court with Justice Powell's lone plurality opinion in *Bakke*. Powell had argued that (1) diversity in education is a compelling state interest and (2) race could be constitutionally considered as a plus factor in admissions decisions. In *Grutter*, the Court reiterated Powell's holding and, applying strict scrutiny to the law school's policy, found that the law school's admissions process was tailored to the school's compelling state interest in diversity because it gave a "highly individualized, holistic review of each applicant's file" in which race counted but was not used in a "mechanical" way.[88] The Court's ruling that racial categories can be deployed to serve a compelling state interest put affirmative action on stronger ground. The Court reaffirmed its decision in *Grutter* in 2013 when it decided *Fisher v. University of Texas*, in which a white student challenged the use of race as one factor among many in the admissions decision. In a 7–1 decision, the Court sent the case back to the district court with instructions to apply "strict scrutiny" to the school's policy, as articulated in *Grutter*.[89] As noted above, the Court eventually accepted the university's plan.

Affirmative action remains controversial. In 2008, Abigail Fisher brought suit against the University of Texas for making race one factor in its admissions decisions. In 2016 the Supreme Court upheld the university's procedures.

Civil Rights
and Your Future

The election of Barack Obama as the nation's first black president fueled discussions about whether America's racial problems had been solved. Polls taken just before Obama's inauguration revealed a sharp upturn in positive views about progress toward racial equality, but the euphoria about racial equality did not last for long. After Obama's election, the proportion of those believing that racism against blacks was widespread dropped somewhat. Even so, in a July 2015 Pew survey, 73 percent of blacks and 44 percent of all whites continued to view racism against blacks as a widespread problem.[90]

The debate about civil rights and affirmative action is ongoing because Americans hold fundamentally different views about whether and how the government should recognize racial distinctions. At the risk of gross oversimplification, we can divide those with differing views into two groups and label them *liberals* and *conservatives*.[91] Conservatives argue, first, that rights in the American tradition are *individual* rights and that affirmative action violates this concept by concerning itself with "group rights," an idea said to be alien to the American tradition. Second, conservatives argue that the Constitution is "color-blind" and that any discrimination, even if it is called positive or benign, must inevitably rely on quotas and thus ultimately violate the equal protection clause.

Liberals agree that rights ultimately come down to individuals but argue that since the essence of discrimination is the unreasonable and unjust exclusion of *an entire group* from something valuable the society has to offer, discrimination itself has to be attacked on a group basis. Despite progress toward racial equality, liberals argue that race still matters. They can also cite Supreme Court history because the first definitive interpretation of the Fourteenth Amendment by the Court, in 1873, stated that

> the existence of laws in the state where the newly emancipated Negroes resided, which discriminated with gross injustice and hardship against them *as a class*, was the evil to be remedied by this clause [emphasis added].[92]

As to the conservative argument concerning quotas, the liberal response is that the Supreme Court has already accepted ratios (a form of quota) that are admitted as evidence to prove a "pattern or practice of discrimination" sufficient to reverse the burden of proof—to obligate the employer to show that there was *not* an intent to discriminate. Further, benign quotas have often been used by Americans both to compensate for some bad action in the past and to provide some desired distribution of social characteristics—that is, diversity. For example, a long-respected policy in the United States is the "veterans' preference" by which the government automatically gives extra consideration in hiring to persons who have served in the country's armed forces. And the goal of social diversity has long justified "positive discrimination," especially in higher education. For example, many private colleges and universities regularly reserve admissions places for the children of loyal alumni and of their own faculty, even when, in a pure competition based solely on test scores and high school records, many of those same students would not have been admitted. These practices underscore the liberal argument that affirmative or compensatory action for minorities is not alien to American experience. Because our nation has a history of slavery and legalized racial discrimination and because discrimination continues to exist (although it has declined), the issue of racial justice, more than any other, highlights the difficulty of reconciling our values to our practice.

The civil rights revolution, a revolution that began with African Americans, has broadened to include women and Latinos and to address such matters as sexual orientation and immigration status. The **"Who Participates?"** feature on the following page shows a time line of groups that have fought for their rights throughout American history. As our nation becomes more and more diverse, equal protection of the laws will become more and more important. If we are to succeed and prosper as a nation, we must be inclusive. The tumultuous history of civil rights in America demonstrates that exclusion is a recipe for national calamity. It also demonstrates that struggles for civil rights often take a long time, beginning with political action by a small group of committed individuals and often ending with legislation and legal decisions from the highest court in the country. What civil rights battles now appear on the country's horizon? What can and should be done to remedy past wrongs that have current consequences, such as when past discrimination results in an economic underclass for a racial or ethnic minority? And, most fundamentally, how does a country based on the democratic principle of majority rule ensure that the civil rights of minorities are protected?

The election of Barack Obama as the country's first black president in 2008 raised questions about whether the United States' racial problems had been solved and whether policies such as affirmative action were still needed. Does the election of an African American as president mean we are closer to achieving racial equality?

Who Has Fought for Their Rights?

Time Line of Major Civil Rights Movements

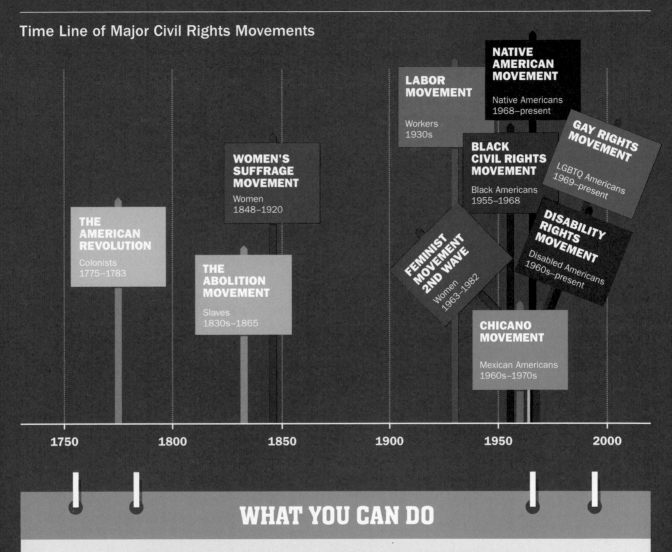

NATIVE AMERICAN MOVEMENT
Native Americans
1968–present

LABOR MOVEMENT
Workers
1930s

GAY RIGHTS MOVEMENT
LGBTQ Americans
1969–present

WOMEN'S SUFFRAGE MOVEMENT
Women
1848–1920

BLACK CIVIL RIGHTS MOVEMENT
Black Americans
1955–1968

DISABILITY RIGHTS MOVEMENT
Disabled Americans
1960s–present

THE AMERICAN REVOLUTION
Colonists
1775–1783

FEMINIST MOVEMENT 2ND WAVE
Women
1963–1982

THE ABOLITION MOVEMENT
Slaves
1830s–1865

CHICANO MOVEMENT
Mexican Americans
1960s–1970s

1750   1800   1850   1900   1950   2000

WHAT YOU CAN DO

Advocate Your Position on Civil Rights

☑ To learn more about your civil rights, explore the Civil Rights page of the U.S. Department of Health and Human Services at **www.hhs.gov/ocr**.

☑ Do you think the government should do more to protect civil rights in your community? Speak out about civil rights on social media. Post to your Facebook page or Tumblr, launch a hashtag campaign on Twitter, or start an online petition at **www.change.org**.

☑ Make a phone call to voice your opinion on civil rights. Call the White House (**202-456-1111**) or your members of Congress (**202-224-3121**). You can also contact the White House online (**www.whitehouse.gov/contact**) or email your members of Congress (**www.congress.gov/members**).

studyguide

The Struggle for Civil Rights

> Trace the legal developments and social movements that expanded civil rights (pp. 155–74)

Discrimination against individuals on the basis of their race and gender was tolerated and even enforced by government policy through much of American history. With the adoption of the Fourteenth Amendment in 1868, civil rights became a part of the Constitution. The political struggles of African Americans and women have narrowed the gap between Americans' belief in equality and the reality of life in the United States, but they have not eliminated it.

Key Terms

discrimination (p. 155)

civil rights (p. 155)

equal protection clause (p. 155)

Thirteenth Amendment (p. 157)

Fourteenth Amendment (p. 157)

Fifteenth Amendment (p. 157)

Jim Crow laws (p. 158)

"separate but equal" rule (p. 159)

Brown v. Board of Education (p. 162)

strict scrutiny (p. 162)

de jure (p. 163)

de facto (p. 163)

gerrymandering (p. 171)

redlining (p. 173)

Practice Quiz

1. When did civil rights become part of the Constitution?
   a) in 1789 at the Founding
   b) with the adoption of the Fourteenth Amendment in 1868
   c) in 2008 when Barack Obama was elected president
   d) with the adoption of the Nineteenth Amendment in 1920
   e) in the 1954 *Brown v. Board of Education* decision

2. Which of the following could be described as a Jim Crow law?
   a) a law forcing blacks and whites to ride on separate trains
   b) a law criminalizing interracial marriage
   c) a law requiring blacks and whites to attend different schools
   d) a law segregating all public accommodations, such as hotels, restaurants, and theaters
   e) All of the above are examples of Jim Crow laws.

3. Which civil rights case established the "separate but equal" rule?
   a) *Plessy v. Ferguson*
   b) *Grutter v. Bollinger*
   c) *Brown v. Board of Education*
   d) *Regents of the University of California v. Bakke*
   e) *Adarand Constructors v. Peña*

4. Which of the following organizations established a legal defense fund to challenge segregation?
   a) the Association of American Trial Lawyers
   b) the National Association of Evangelicals
   c) the National Association for the Advancement of Colored People
   d) the Student Nonviolent Coordinating Committee
   e) the Southern Christian Leadership Council

5. *Massive resistance* refers to efforts by southern states during the late 1950s and early 1960s to
   a) build public housing for poor blacks.
   b) defy federal mandates to desegregate public schools.
   c) give women the right to have an abortion.
   d) bus black students to white schools.
   e) stage large-scale protests against Jim Crow laws.

6. Which of the following made discrimination by private employers and state governments illegal?
   a) the Fourteenth Amendment
   b) the Fifteenth Amendment
   c) *Brown v. Board of Education*
   d) the 1964 Civil Rights Act
   e) *Regents of the University of California v. Bakke*

7. The Voting Rights Act of 1965 significantly extended and protected voting rights by doing which of the following?
   a) barring literacy tests as a condition for voting in six southern states
   b) requiring all voters to register two weeks before any federal election
   c) eliminating all federal-level registration requirements
   d) allowing voters to sue election officials for monetary damages in civil court
   e) requiring that all voters show a valid government-issued photo ID

Extending Civil Rights

In the 1970s the civil rights model created by African Americans began to spread beyond racial and ethnic groups to include groups defined by sex, religion, national origin, age, and sexual orientation. For many of these groups, government polices played an important role in giving rise to movements that demanded equal treatment.

Key Term

intermediate scrutiny (p. 175)

Practice Quiz

8. The judicial test that places the burden of proof on government to show that a race-based policy serves a compelling government interest and is narrowly tailored to address identifiable past discrimination is called
   a) strict scrutiny.
   b) intermediate scrutiny.
   c) limited scrutiny.
   d) de facto segregation.
   e) de jure segregation.

9. Which of the following declared that "equality of rights under the law shall not be denied or abridged by the United States or by any State on account of sex"?
   a) the Lily Ledbetter Fair Pay Act
   b) Title IV of the 1964 Civil Rights Act
   c) the DREAM Act
   d) the Equal Rights Amendment
   e) *Obergefell v. Hodges*

10. The Supreme Court's decision in *Mendez v. Westminster* was significant because it
    a) served as a precursor for *Brown v. Board of Education* by ruling that the segregation of Anglos and Mexican Americans into separate schools was unconstitutional.

    b) determined that anyone born in the United States was entitled to full citizenship.
    c) allowed school districts to achieve racial integration through busing.
    d) held that public accommodations could be segregated by race but still be equal.
    e) eliminated state power to use race as a criterion for discrimination in law.

11. In *United States v. Wong Kim Ark,* the Supreme Court ruled that
    a) school districts must provide bilingual education for students whose English is limited.
    b) the internment of Japanese Americans during World War II was constitutional on the grounds of military necessity.
    c) the 1882 Chinese Exclusion Act was an unconstitutional form of racial discrimination.
    d) anyone born in the United States was entitled to full citizenship.
    e) Chinese immigrants were ineligible for citizenship in the United States.

12. Which of the following cases extended fundamental civil rights protections to gay men and lesbians?
    a) *Bowers v. Hardwick*
    b) *Lau v. Nichols*
    c) *Romer v. Evans*
    d) *Regents of the University of California v. Bakke*
    e) There has never been a Supreme Court ruling extending fundamental civil rights protections to gay men and lesbians.

Affirmative Action

Affirmative action policies take race or some other status into account in order to provide greater educational and employment opportunities to groups that have been discriminated against. The Supreme Court has ruled that the government must show evidence that affirmative action programs serve a compelling government interest and are narrowly tailored to address identifiable past discrimination in order to be ruled constitutional. In recent years, challenges to affirmative action have also emerged at the state and local levels.

Key Term

affirmative action (p. 189)

Practice Quiz

13. In which case did the Supreme Court find that rigid quotas are incompatible with the equal protection clause of the Fourteenth Amendment?
    a) *Regents of the University of California v. Bakke*
    b) *Korematsu v. United States*
    c) *Brown v. Board of Education*
    d) *United States v. Nixon*
    e) *Immigration and Naturalization Service v. Chadha*

14. The Supreme Court's decision in *Grutter v. Bollinger* was significant because
    a) it stated that race can never be used as a factor in university admissions.
    b) it stated that diversity is a compelling state interest and that university admissions that take racial categories into account are constitutional as long as they are highly individualized.
    c) it outlawed quotas and separate university admission standards for members of minority groups.
    d) it rejected mechanical point systems that favor minority applicants in university admissions.
    e) it declared that affirmative action policies would no longer be subject to strict scrutiny from the courts.

For Further Reading

Ackerman, Bruce. *We the People.* Vol. 3, *The Civil Rights Revolution.* Cambridge, MA: Harvard University Press, 2014.

Chen, Anthony S. *The Fifth Freedom: Jobs, Politics, and Civil Rights in the United States, 1941–1972.* Princeton, NJ: Princeton University Press, 2009.

Davis, Lennard J. *Enabling Acts: The Hidden Story of How the Americans with Disabilities Act Gave the Largest US Minority Its Rights.* Boston: Beacon Press, 2015.

Garrow, David J. *Bearing the Cross: Martin Luther King, Jr., and the Southern Christian Leadership Conference: A Personal Portrait.* New York: Morrow, 1986.

Greenberg, Jack. *Crusaders in the Courts: How a Dedicated Band of Lawyers Fought for the Civil Rights Revolution.* New York: Basic Books, 1994.

Katznelson, Ira. *When Affirmative Action Was White: The Untold Story of Racial Inequality in Twentieth-Century America.* New York: W. W. Norton, 2006.

Lee, Sonia Song-Ha. *Building a Latino Civil Rights Movement.* Chapel Hill: University of North Carolina Press, 2014.

McClain, Paula D., and Joseph Stewart Jr. *"Can We All Get Along?" Racial Minorities in American Politics.* 6th ed. Boulder, CO: Westview Press, 2013.

Mink, Gwendolyn. *Hostile Environment: The Political Betrayal of Sexually Harassed Women.* Ithaca, NY: Cornell University Press, 2000.

Nichols, Walter J. *The DREAMers: How the Undocumented Youth Movement Transformed the Immigrant Rights Debate.* Stanford, CA: Stanford University Press, 2013.

Rosenberg, Gerald N. *The Hollow Hope: Can Courts Bring about Social Change?* Chicago: University of Chicago Press, 2008.

Russell, Nancy. *Freedom Is Not Enough: The Opening of the American Workplace.* Cambridge, MA: Harvard University Press, 2006.

Sainsbury, Diane. *Welfare States and Immigrant Rights: The Politics of Inclusion and Exclusion.* New York: Oxford University Press, 2012.

Taylor, Jami Kathleen, and Donald P. Halder-Markel, eds. *Transgender Rights and Politics.* Ann Arbor: University of Michigan Press, 2015.

Valelly, Richard. *The Voting Rights Act.* Washington, DC: CQ Press, 2005.

Recommended Websites

ADA Home Page
www.ada.gov
The Americans with Disabilities Act (ADA), enacted in 1990, guarantees equal employment rights and access to public businesses for the physically disabled. The U.S. Department of Justice maintains this website, which offers general information on ADA standards, changes in regulation, and policy enforcement.

Equal Employment Opportunity Commission
www.eeoc.gov
This website provides information on the federal agency and current employment laws. At this site you can even find out how someone might file a harassment or discrimination charge against an employer.

Equality Now
www.equalitynow.org

This is an organization dedicated to ending gender discrimination around the world. Read about how this group is fighting for the rights of women in Africa or campaigning against female genital mutilation and sex trafficking.

Federal Bureau of Investigation
www.fbi.gov/hq/cid/civilrights/hate.htm

Civil rights violations fall under the jurisdiction of the Federal Bureau of Investigation (FBI). Find out what steps the FBI is taking to combat the problem of hate crimes, and view some comprehensive statistical data.

Feminist Majority Foundation
www.feminist.org

National Organization for Women
www.now.org

These leading women's rights groups continue to fight for gender equality and equal rights.

The Martin Luther King, Jr., Research and Education Institute
http://mlk-kpp01.stanford.edu

Dr. Martin Luther King, Jr., was a key leader in the fight for civil rights and desegregation. At this website you can find Dr. King's important speeches and papers, as well as other information about social injustice.

Gay and Lesbian Alliance against Defamation
www.glaad.org

Human Rights Campaign
www.hrc.org

These two prominent interest groups are dedicated to equal rights for lesbians and gay men and ending gender discrimination.

League of United Latin American Citizens
www.lulac.org

The League of United Latin American Citizens has worked to stem discrimination against Mexican Americans since World War II and is now the largest and oldest Latino organization in the United States. See what this group is doing to guarantee racial equality based on the Fourteenth Amendment's equal protection clause.

Mexican American Legal Defense and Education Fund
www.maldef.org

The Mexican American Legal Defense and Education Fund (MALDEF) is the leading nonprofit Latino litigation, advocacy, and educational outreach institution in the United States. At this site, you will learn about litigation and other activities that MALDEF has initiated related to the rights of Latinos and of immigrants more generally.

NAACP
www.naacp.org

The NAACP is one of the oldest and largest civil rights organizations that is dedicated to equal rights and putting an end to racial discrimination. This group was particularly influential in the landmark case *Brown v. Board of Education*, which led to the desegregation of public schools.

U.S. Commission on Civil Rights
www.usccr.gov

The U.S. Commission on Civil Rights was created by Congress in the late 1950s and continues to investigate complaints of discrimination in American society.

U.S. Supreme Court Media
www.oyez.org

This website has a good search engine for finding information on such landmark civil rights cases as *Plessy v. Ferguson*, *Brown v. Board of Education*, *Lawrence v. Texas*, and *United States v. Wong Kim Ark*, to name only a few.

What accounts for changing public opinion? Before 2011, most Americans did not think income inequality was a problem, whereas today the issue is at the forefront of the political agenda. The recent movement to increase the minimum wage to $15 an hour has continued the national discussion on wealth distribution in the United States.

Public Opinion

WHAT GOVERNMENT DOES AND WHY IT MATTERS The "consent of the governed"—demanded in the Declaration of Independence—is critical for the functioning of a democracy. We expect government to pay attention to the people, and research has shown that public opinion does indeed have a significant impact on public policy. There are debates among scholars, however, about whether the public is sufficiently informed about politics, as well as whether elected officials represent the interests of all Americans or only some Americans.

Consider public opinion on certain economic policies. A primary goal of democracy is to promote economic opportunity. In the abstract, most Americans believe that a combination of equal opportunity and hard work is the best path to financial success; in a 2009 study, more than three-fourths of the public agreed that it is possible for someone who is poor to become rich through hard work.[1] But do all Americans have an equal chance to succeed? Has public opinion on this issue changed over time?

Today in the United States, income inequality—the gap between the affluent and the rest of the population—is the highest it has been since 1928 and continues to increase. In 2015 the average household income in the United States was $56,516. The top 20 percent of earners, however, had a household income of at least $117,003, and the top 5 percent earned at least $214,463.[2] In recent years, the incomes of the richest Americans have grown rapidly, while most Americans' wages have remained about the same (after adjusting for inflation).[3] Between 1993 and 2013, the income of the top 1 percent of Americans grew 62.4 percent, while the income of the other 99 percent grew 7.3 percent.[4]

Are Americans aware of this growing economic inequality? Public opinion polls have shown that while most Americans acknowledge the large gap between the rich and the poor in the United States, only 47 percent thought the gap between the rich and the poor was a serious problem in 2013.[5] In 2015 public opinion on inequality of wealth began to shift, with 67 percent of Americans believing the gap between the rich and the poor was getting larger, a major increase from two years prior. Six in 10 Americans now say that it is mainly just a few people at the top who have a chance to get ahead.[6]

Partisanship continues to have a significant effect on opinion. In 2015, 89 percent of Democrats agreed with the statement that wealth should be more evenly distributed, but only 44 percent of Republicans agreed. Still, concern about inequality is growing on both sides and challenges long-held beliefs about economic opportunity. Today, large majorities of Americans favor proposals aimed at strengthening workers' rights, including paid sick leave and paid family leave, and raising taxes on the wealthy. A recent movement to increase the minimum wage to $15 an hour sparked rallies in many cities around the country, as organized labor and anti-poverty groups worked to draw attention to income inequality.

What caused this shift in public opinion on economic inequality? Will policy makers in government respond to these changing opinions and, if so, how? As we will see in this chapter, an informed public is crucial in order for citizens to have their voices heard, and what people think about politics matters.

chaptergoals

- Define public opinion, and identify broad types of values and beliefs Americans have about politics (pp. 201–8)

- Explain the major factors that shape specific individual opinions (pp. 208–19)

- Explore when and why public opinion changes and what role political knowledge plays (pp. 219–26)

- Describe the major forces that shape public opinion (pp. 226–29)

- Analyze how public opinion shapes government policy and influences elected officials (pp. 229–31)

- Describe basic survey methods and other techniques researchers use to measure public opinion (pp. 231–41)

Defining Public Opinion

Define public opinion, and identify broad types of values and beliefs Americans have about politics

The term **public opinion** refers to the attitudes that people have about issues, events, elected officials, and, of course, politics and policy. It is useful to distinguish between values and beliefs, on the one hand, and attitudes and opinions, on the other. **Values (or beliefs)** constitute a person's basic orientation to politics and include guiding principles. Values are not limited to the political arena, but they underlie deep-rooted goals, aspirations, and ideals that shape an individual's perceptions of society, political issues, and events. Liberty, democracy, and equality of opportunity, for example, are basic political values held by most Americans.

Another useful term for understanding public opinion is *ideology*. **Political ideology** refers to a set of beliefs and values that, as a whole, form a general philosophy about government. For example, many Americans believe that governmental solutions to problems are inherently inferior to solutions offered by the private sector. Such a philosophy about government may predispose individuals to form negative views of specific government programs, even before they know much about the policy.

An **attitude (or opinion)** is a specific view about a particular issue, person, or event. An individual may have an attitude toward American policy in Iraq or an opinion about economic inequality in America. The attitude or opinion may have emerged from a broad belief about military intervention or about the role of government in the economy, but the opinion itself is very specific. Some attitudes may be short-lived and can change based on changing circumstances or new information; others may change over a few years.

To determine the public's opinion on an issue, one must study the individual opinions of thousands or millions of people aggregated together; it is a way to gauge what Americans think about politics and policy. When we think of public opinion, we often think in terms of differences of opinion. The media are fond of reporting political differences between Democrats and Republicans, blacks and whites, men and women, the young and the old, and so on. Certainly, Americans differ on many issues, and often these differences are associated with partisanship, economic status, or social characteristics. For example, opinion polls show that roughly half of Americans sympathized with the Tea Party movement and half with the Occupy Wall Street movement. Those who supported Occupy Wall Street have very different beliefs regarding the cause of the poor economy (that banks and elected officials are held captive by corporate interests) from those of people supporting the Tea Party (that government regulation is strangling the private sector, preventing an economic rebound). While both Occupy Wall Street and the Tea Party are populist economic movements, they have different underlying opinions, attitudes, and ideologies about the economy and government.

Factors such as race and ethnicity, gender, income, education, age, religion, and region—which not only affect individuals' interests but also shape their experiences and upbringing—do influence Americans' beliefs and opinions. For example, individuals whose incomes differ substantially have varying views on many important economic and social programs, including government health care. In general,

public opinion citizens' attitudes about political issues, leaders, institutions, and events

values (or beliefs) basic principles that shape a person's opinions about political issues and events

political ideology a cohesive set of beliefs that forms a general philosophy about the role of government

attitude (or opinion) a specific preference on a particular issue

the poor, who are the chief beneficiaries of these programs, support them more strongly than do those who are wealthier and pay more of the taxes that fund the programs. Blacks and whites have different views on issues that touch on civil rights, criminal justice, and race relations, reflecting differences of interest and experience. Political attitudes are also strongly influenced by partisanship (Republicans versus Democrats), ideology (conservatives versus liberals), and core values.

Traditionally, there was an assumption that political attitudes were wholly rooted in rational factors, such as economic self-interest. Now political scientists have a renewed understanding that opinions about issues and politics have emotional underpinnings as well.[7] Emotional responses to candidates, events, or policies run the gamut from strongly positive to strongly negative. These emotions are usually measured by survey questions asking if a candidate (or another individual, event, or issue) makes the respondent feel angry, fearful, anxious, or enthusiastic. Contrary to the idea that public opinion is purely rational, feelings are complicated and often irrational; once individuals become emotionally attached to particular beliefs, they tend to hold on to them even in the face of contradictory information. Using emotions as a guide, individuals form opinions quickly in response to current events. An important study called this "affective [meaning emotional] intelligence."[8]

Research has shown that individuals usually monitor political news by responding to familiar political figures or issues in a habitual and unthinking manner. However, when we encounter a new political actor, event, or issue, we tend to form a new evaluation. Anxiety triggered by a change in the political environment, such as a foreign enemy or an opposing party's candidate, can then trigger increased interest and attention and even prompt a change of opinion. These findings suggest that even individuals with strong opinions might abandon their political habits if they have feelings of anxiety.

Take, for example, public opinion about foreign policy and global terrorism. When President Obama entered the White House in 2008, Americans had tired of the Iraq War (begun in 2003), and large majorities wanted the United States

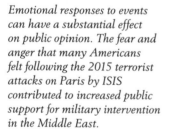

Emotional responses to events can have a substantial effect on public opinion. The fear and anger that many Americans felt following the 2015 terrorist attacks on Paris by ISIS contributed to increased public support for military intervention in the Middle East.

to withdraw troops from the region. But in 2015, most Americans again favored military intervention in Iraq and Syria. Why? Emotions may be part of the answer.

Viral news spread rapidly beginning in 2014 when an extremist militia group in Iraq and Syria calling itself the Islamic State of Iraq and Syria (ISIS), used the Internet to distribute gruesome videos of beheadings of foreign journalists, soldiers, and Christians. ISIS gained momentum quickly, taking over large swaths of Iraq and Syria, including key cities, trade routes, and oil fields. With a $2 billion dollar budget in 2015 from oil revenue and criminal activity, the organization's goal is to create a worldwide Sunni Islamic empire (or caliphate) across countries in the Middle East.[9] The group used a sophisticated online propaganda campaign to convince thousands of foreigners to join the fight. Media coverage of the mass executions fueled emotions of fear, and by 2015 more than twice as many approved as disapproved (63 percent and 30 percent, respectively) of the military campaign against ISIS.[10]

Emotions can lead individuals to reconsider their views regarding not only policy issues but also political candidates. For example, negative political campaign ads aim to make individuals feel uneasy about a particular candidate, thereby convincing viewers to change their minds about whom to vote for.

Political Values

Despite their differences, most Americans share a common set of values, including a belief in the principles, if not always the actual practice, of liberty, equality, and democracy. The United States was founded on the principle of individual **liberty**, or freedom. Americans have always voiced strong support for the idea of liberty and typically support the notion that governmental interference with individuals' lives and property should be kept to a minimum. Liberty is, after all, tied inextricably to the birth of our nation—Puritans fled to America to escape persecution in England for their religious beliefs—and it remains as important in contemporary politics as it was during the Founding era. Americans have stronger views about the importance of liberty and freedom of expression than do citizens in other democratic countries. One example is the growing concern with civil liberties related to privacy and security of personal information online. A 2015 Pew survey found that 54 percent of Americans oppose the government collecting cell phone and Internet data on its citizens as part of its antiterrorism efforts.[11] More broadly, three in four Americans don't see a need to sacrifice liberty (privacy and freedom) to be safe from terrorism.[12] Support for freedom of speech, a free Internet, and a free press is higher in the United States than in most other countries in the world: 71 percent of Americans believe it is very important that "people can say what they want without state or government censorship," compared to a global average of 56 percent.[13] These data underscore the fact that government surveillance is of increasing concern to most Americans and that the value of liberty matters.

Similarly, **equality of opportunity** has always been an important theme in American society. Most Americans believe that all individuals should be allowed to seek personal and economic success. Moreover, most people generally believe that such success should be the result of individual effort and ability, rather than family connections or other forms of special privilege. Quality public education is one of the most important mechanisms for obtaining equality of opportunity in that it allows individuals, regardless of personal or family wealth, a chance to get ahead. Today, Internet access is emerging as an important form of equality of opportunity by

liberty freedom from governmental control

equality of opportunity a widely shared American ideal that all people should have the freedom to use whatever talents and wealth they have to reach their fullest potential providing access to job opportunities, news, politics, commerce, and other benefits of digital citizenship.[14] The minimum wage is another issue related to inequality. A 2014 survey found that 73 percent of people favored an increase in the federal minimum wage to $10.10 an hour, a proposal that failed to move ahead in Congress in 2014.[15] Economic opportunity, defined as access to a good job and a decent standard of living, is a core value in American politics. Growing inequality of wealth, as discussed above, challenges this core value of equality.

Most Americans also believe in democracy and the rule of law. They believe that every citizen should have the opportunity to take part in the nation's governmental and policy-making processes and to have some say in determining how they are governed, including the right to vote in elections.[16] (See Chapter 8 for a discussion of rules affecting voting in elections.) Figure 6.1 shows there is consensus among Americans on fundamental values: for instance, 86 percent believe society should do what it takes to ensure equality of opportunity, and 95 percent believe people should be able to make statements that criticize the government and its policies.

Obviously, the political values that Americans espouse have not always been put into practice. For 200 years, Americans embraced the principles of equality of opportunity and individual liberty while denying them in practice to generations of African Americans. Ultimately, proponents of slavery and, later, of segregation were defeated in the arena of public opinion because their practices differed so sharply from the fundamental principles accepted by most Americans.

Yet even when there is broad agreement over principles, practical *interpretations* of principles can differ. For example, in contemporary politics Americans' fundamental commitment to equality of opportunity has led to divisions over affirmative action programs, with both proponents and opponents citing their belief in equality of opportunity as the justification for their position. Proponents of these programs see them as necessary to ensure equality of opportunity, whereas opponents believe that affirmative action is a form of preferential

for critical analysis

The news often focuses on issues on which public opinion is sharply divided, but in fact there are many issues on which Americans largely agree. What other issues do you think have strong consensus among Americans?

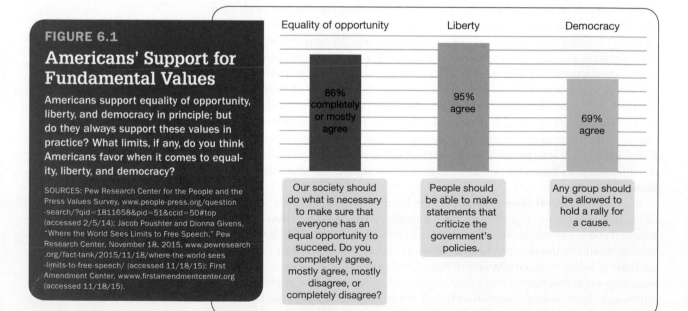

FIGURE 6.1

Americans' Support for Fundamental Values

Americans support equality of opportunity, liberty, and democracy in principle; but do they always support these values in practice? What limits, if any, do you think Americans favor when it comes to equality, liberty, and democracy?

SOURCES: Pew Research Center for the People and the Press Values Survey, www.people-press.org/question-search/?qid=1811658&pid=51&ccid=50#top (accessed 2/5/14); Jacob Poushter and Dionna Givens, "Where the World Sees Limits to Free Speech," Pew Research Center, November 18, 2015, www.pewresearch.org/fact-tank/2015/11/18/where-the-world-sees-limits-to-free-speech/ (accessed 11/18/15); First Amendment Center, www.firstamendmentcenter.org (accessed 11/18/15).

Equality of opportunity — 86% completely or mostly agree — Our society should do what is necessary to make sure that everyone has an equal opportunity to succeed. Do you completely agree, mostly agree, mostly disagree, or completely disagree?

Liberty — 95% agree — People should be able to make statements that criticize the government's policies.

Democracy — 69% agree — Any group should be allowed to hold a rally for a cause.

treatment that violates basic American values (see Chapter 5).[17] We form our individual preferences and interpretation of values through interaction with family members, friends, teachers, and others in our social groups and networks in a process called "socialization."

Political Ideology

Americans share many fundamental political values, but the application of these values to specific policies varies. The set of underlying ideas and beliefs through which we come to understand and interpret politics is called a *political ideology*. Ideologies take many different forms. Some people may view politics primarily in religious terms. During the course of European political history, for example, Protestantism and Catholicism were often political ideologies as much as they were religious creeds. The conflict in Iraq today is among two religious political ideologies, the Sunnis and the Shiites. Each set of beliefs includes not only elements of religious practice but also distinct ideas about secular authority and political action.

In the United States the definitions of the two most common political ideologies—liberalism and conservatism—have changed over time. To some extent, contemporary liberalism and conservatism can be seen as differences in emphasis with regard to the fundamental American political values of liberty and equality. For liberals, equality is the most important of the core values. Liberals encourage government action in such areas as the economy and progressive taxation, worker's rights, college admissions, and business practices to enhance race, class, and gender equality of opportunity. For conservatives, on the other hand, liberty is the core value. Conservatives oppose many efforts of the government, however well intentioned, to interfere in private life and free markets.

Liberalism In classical political theory, a liberal was someone who favored individual initiative and was suspicious of the motives of government and of its ability to manage economic and social affairs—a definition akin to that of today's libertarian. The proponents of a larger and more active government called themselves progressives. In the early twentieth century, many liberals and progressives coalesced around the doctrine of "social liberalism," which held that government action might be needed to preserve individual liberty. Today's liberals are social liberals rather than classical liberals.

In contemporary politics being a **liberal** has come to mean supporting political and social reform, government intervention in the economy, the expansion of federal social services and health care, more vigorous efforts on behalf of the poor and minorities, and greater concern for protecting the environment. For example, Senator Elizabeth Warren (D-Mass.) is a leading liberal politician. Warren is an active consumer protection advocate whose work led to the establishment of the U.S. Consumer Financial Protection Bureau, which protects individuals from bankruptcy. Liberals generally support abortion rights and rights for gays and lesbians and are concerned with protecting the rights of people accused of crimes. In international affairs, liberals often support foreign aid to poor nations, arms control, and international organizations that promote peace such as the United Nations and the European Union. Many liberals are opposed to military wars, but under President Obama some liberals tolerated military interventions in other countries.

Although liberalism and conservatism are the most common political ideologies in the United States today, other ideologies, such as libertarianism, offer different perspectives on the role of government, policy issues, and society.

liberal today this term refers to those who generally support social and political reform, governmental intervention in the economy, more economic equality, expansion of federal social services, and greater concern for consumers and the environment

Profile of a Liberal: Senator Elizabeth Warren

- Supports stricter environmental protections

- Favors expanded health coverage for all Americans

- Advocates increased funding for education

- Supports same-sex marriage

- Supports abortion rights and birth control

- Supports an increase in the minimum wage

- Supports more equitable tax policy that benefits middle-class Americans and imposes higher taxes on corporations

conservative today this term refers to those who generally support the social and economic status quo and are suspicious of efforts to introduce new political formulas and economic arrangements; conservatives believe that a large and powerful government poses a threat to citizens' freedom

Conservatism By contrast, **conservatives** believe strongly that a large government poses a threat to the freedom of individual citizens and to free markets and democracy. Ironically, today's conservatives support the views of classical liberalism. Today, conservatives generally oppose the expansion of governmental activity, asserting that solutions to many social and economic problems can and should be developed in the private sector or local communities. Many conservatives are opposed to increasing taxes, preferring to cut government spending instead. Conservatives oppose efforts to impose government regulation on business, maintaining that regulation frequently leads to economic inefficiency, is costly, and can lower the entire nation's standard of living by making U.S. manufactured products more expensive and less competitive. Wisconsin governor Scott Walker is a leading conservative politician who made national headlines when he developed a budget plan that limited collective bargaining (that is, union) powers for most public employees. In terms of social policy, many conservatives support traditional family values and generally oppose abortion and same-sex marriage. They often oppose environmental protections that interfere with private business. In international affairs, conservatism has come to mean support for military intervention and the maintenance of American military power. There is a split among conservatives in terms of immigration, with pro-business conservatives often accepting immigration and social conservatives strongly opposing immigration to the United States.

libertarian someone who emphasizes freedom and believes in voluntary association with small government

Libertarianism Other political ideologies also influence American politics. **Libertarians**, for example, argue that government interferes with freedom of expression, free markets, and society and thus should be limited to as few spheres of activity as possible (public education being a notable exception for many libertarians). In 2016, Republican presidential candidate Rand Paul, also a libertarian, gained widespread support based on his opposition to foreign wars and his commitment to civil liberties and smaller government.

socialist someone who generally believes in social ownership, strong government, free markets, and reducing economic inequality

Socialism While libertarians believe in less government intervention in economic and social realms, **socialists** argue that more government is necessary to promote

Profile of a Conservative: Governor Scott Walker

- Wants to trim the size of the federal government

- Wants to reduce government regulation of business

- Supports capital punishment for certain crimes

- Opposes restrictions on the right to bear arms

- Supports using traditional energy sources and opposes climate change action that reduces manufacturing jobs

- Opposes many affirmative action programs

- Favors tax cuts

justice and to reduce economic and social inequality. To take an example, 2016 Democratic presidential candidate Bernie Sanders called himself a "democratic socialist." Like the Social Democratic parties in Europe, Sanders supports free markets and private enterprise but wants government to ensure more equality of opportunity for citizens such as free public college. He also supports government policies to protect workers' rights and unions. Socialists are more to the ideological left than the mainstream Democratic Party.

Americans' Ideologies Today Although many Americans subscribe to libertarianism, socialism, or other ideologies in part, most describe themselves as either liberals, conservatives, or moderates. Figure 6.2 shows that the percentage of Americans who consider themselves moderates, liberals, or conservatives has remained relatively constant for the past 15 years. Gallup surveys indicate that as of 2015 37 percent of Americans considered themselves conservatives, 35 percent moderates, and 24 percent liberals.[18] These numbers have remained virtually unchanged since the 1990s. But among young people aged 18–33, trends are different: just 15 percent identify as conservative, while 41 percent identify as liberals and 44 percent as moderates (and independent from the political parties).[19]

Within each ideological group, individual beliefs often vary. Many conservatives support at least some government social programs. Republican president George W. Bush called himself a "compassionate conservative," to indicate that he favored programs that assist the poor and needy. In contrast, staunch conservatives hold much more critical views of government's role in the economy and society. Many joined the rising Tea Party movement in 2009 to protest President Obama's efforts to expand the role of the federal government, especially in health care.

And while President Obama supported health care reform and other social programs, he was criticized by those on the left for extending the tax policies of his Republican predecessor, George W. Bush, which benefited the affluent; for expanding U.S. military involvement overseas; and for historic deportations of illegal

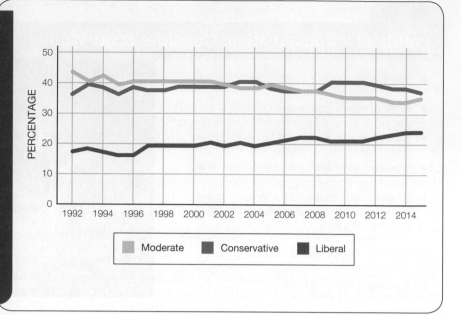

Americans' Ideology

More Americans identify themselves as "conservatives" than "liberals." During the period shown in this figure, however, Americans have had two Democratic presidents and have several times elected Democratic majorities to a house of Congress. What might account for this apparent discrepancy? What role do moderates play in the electorate? How stable is Americans' ideology over time?

SOURCE: Lydia Saad, "Conservatives Hang On to Ideology Lead by a Thread," Gallup, January 11, 2016, www.gallup.com/poll /188129/conservatives-hang-ideology-lead -thread.aspx (accessed 10/3/16).

immigrants. In short, some of Obama's domestic, economic, and foreign policies are associated with conservatives and some with liberals. The real political world is far too complex to be seen simply in terms of a struggle between liberals and conservatives. Political candidates who claim to be moderates in a large number of policy areas, tend to overlap with the ideologies of the majority of Americans and, thus, often win elections.

● How We Form Political Opinions

Explain the major factors that shape specific individual opinions

As noted above, broad ideologies do not necessarily determine every political opinion a person holds. Though conservatives generally support small government, most also support some federal programs, such as the military, and national security, and wish to see them—and hence the government—expanded. Some conservatives are not opposed to immigration and accept same-sex marriage. Though most liberals do not favor American military intervention abroad, many do favor military intervention for what they deem to be humanitarian purposes or to prevent terrorist attacks. How are political opinions formed?

Political Socialization

People's attitudes about political issues and elected officials tend to be shaped by their underlying political beliefs and values. For example, an individual who has negative feelings about government regulation of the economy would probably be predisposed to oppose the development of new social and health care programs. Similarly, someone who distrusts the military tends to be suspicious of a call for the use of U.S. troops. The processes through which these underlying political beliefs and values are formed are collectively called **political socialization**.

Probably no nation, and certainly no democracy, could survive if its citizens did not share some fundamental beliefs. In contemporary America, some elements of the socialization process tend to produce differences in outlook, whereas others, such as public education, promote similarities. The **agents of socialization** that foster differences in political opinions include the family and social networks, education, membership in social groups, religion, party affiliation, self-interest, and political environment.

Of course, no list of the agents of socialization can fully explain an individual's basic political beliefs. In addition to the factors that are important for everyone, experiences and influences that are unique to each individual play a role in shaping political orientation. An early encounter with an important mentor (for example, a teacher, coach, or religious leader), can have a lasting impact on an individual's views. A major political event, such as the terrorist attacks of September 11, 2001, can leave an indelible mark on a person's political consciousness. And some deep-seated personality characteristic, such as paranoia or openness to new experiences, may strongly influence the formation of political beliefs. One recent experiment found that people who have physiological reactions to sudden noises and threatening visual images were more likely to favor defense spending, capital punishment, patriotism, and military force. That is, people who tend to be more fearful appear to support policies that protect the existing social structure from both external and internal threats.[20]

Some new research has found that political beliefs may have a genetic basis and thus be "hard-wired." While it is common knowledge that genes predispose individuals to be tall or short, blond or brunet, brown- or blue-eyed, recent studies have suggested that our genes shape our political beliefs and opinions. Using data from a large sample of twins, scholars found that genes may contribute, in combination with environmental factors, to our ideology.[21] Individual backgrounds, experiences, and social factors also explain people's political attitudes. Below we look at some of the most important agents of socialization that affect individuals' beliefs.

The Family and Social Networks Most people acquire their initial orientation to politics from their families. As might be expected, differences in family background tend to produce divergent political perspectives. Although relatively few parents spend significant time directly teaching their children about politics, political conversations occur in many households, and children tend to absorb the political views of parents and other caregivers, often without realizing it. Studies find, for example, that party preferences are initially acquired at home, even in households that don't explicitly talk about politics. Children raised in households in which the primary caregivers are Democrats tend to become Democrats, whereas children raised in homes where their caregivers are Republicans tend to favor the Republican Party.[22] Of course, not all children absorb their parents' political views. Two of the late Republican president Ronald Reagan's three children, for instance, rejected their parents' conservative values and became active on behalf of Democratic candidates.

Nevertheless, family, friends, coworkers, and neighbors are an important source of political orientation for nearly everyone. Political scientist Betsy Sinclair argues that

political socialization the induction of individuals into the political culture; learning the underlying beliefs and values on which the political system is based

agents of socialization social institutions, including families and schools, that help to shape individuals' basic political beliefs and values

Children are socialized into political environments in ways large and small, from attending political rallies with their parents to hearing offhand comments at the dinner table. What political opinions did you learn from your parents?

individuals are "social citizens" whose political opinions and behavior are significantly shaped by peer influence, including friends and family.[23] Sinclair shows that social networks can and do have the power to change an individual's opinion. When members of a social network express a particular political opinion or belief, Sinclair finds, others notice and conform, particularly if their conformity is likely to be highly visible. The conclusion is that basic political acts are surprisingly subject to social pressures.

Online social networks such as Facebook and Twitter may increase the role of peers in shaping public opinion. For example, after the June 2015 Supreme Court decision to legalize same-sex marriage nationwide, Facebook launched a "Celebrate Pride" tool that enabled users to give their profile pictures a rainbow-tinted background to show support for gay rights, signalling to friends and family their opinion on this issue. Similarly, the widely shared Facebook meme of an equal sign against a red background in 2013 communicated support for gay rights at the same time that the U.S. Supreme Court was deciding two controversial court cases affecting gay and lesbian marriage rights. This social media discussion was associated with upticks in public support for gay marriage nationally. In 2015 a record high 55 percent of Americans believed marriages between same-sex couples should be recognized by law, an increase of almost 20 percent from 2005 when only 36 percent of Americans felt this way.[24]

Education After family, formal education can be an important source of differences in political perspectives. Governments use public education to try to teach all children a common set of civic values; it is mainly in school that Americans acquire their basic beliefs in liberty, equality, and democracy. In history classes, students are taught that the Founders fought for the principle of liberty. In the course of studying such topics as the Constitution, the Civil War, and the civil rights movement, students are taught the importance of equality. Research finds formal education to be a strong predictor of tolerance for racial minorities.[25]

At the same time, differences in formal education are strongly associated with differences in political opinions. In particular, those who attend college are often exposed to modes of thought that will distinguish them from their friends and neighbors who do not pursue college diplomas. Education is one of the most important factors in predicting who engages in behaviors that increase political knowledge, such as regularly following the news, voting, and participating in politics.[26]

Social Groups and Public Opinion

The social groups to which individuals belong comprise another important source of political values. Social groups include those that individuals haven't chosen (national, religious, gender, and racial groups, for example) and those they join willingly (political parties, labor unions, the military, and environmental, educational, and occupational groups). Membership in a particular group can give individuals experiences and perspectives that shape their view of political and social life.

Race Race plays an important role in shaping political attitudes and opinions, among both minorities and whites. The experiences of blacks, whites, and Asian Americans, for example, can differ significantly. Blacks are a minority and have been victims of persecution and discrimination throughout American history, while many Asians are relatively recent immigrants to the United States. Blacks and whites also have different occupational opportunities, often live in separate communities, and frequently attend separate schools. Such differences tend to produce distinctive political views. Many black Americans perceive other blacks as members of a group with a common identity and a shared political interest in overcoming persistent racial and economic inequality. Political scientists refer to this phenomenon as "linked fate": African Americans see their fate as linked to other members of the black community.[27] This linked fate acts as a sort of filter through which black Americans evaluate information and determine their own opinions and policy preferences.

That black and white Americans have different views is reflected in public perception of fair treatment across racial groups in the United States. Figure 6.3 shows that 70 percent of African Americans believe that slavery and discrimination have made it difficult for blacks to work their way out of the lower class compared to just 30 percent of white non-Hispanics. In a striking difference, 81 percent of blacks support affirmative action policies compared to just 27 percent of whites.

Differences in public opinion among blacks and whites are also found in views of the role of race in the criminal justice system. In 2009, 80 percent of African Americans said blacks and other minorities do not get equal treatment under the law; the number of whites giving this response was just 40 percent.[28] In the past few years, however, widely publicized incidents of excessive use of police force against African Americans around the country have begun to cause a shift in public opinion on this issue. The activist movement Black Lives Matter took off in 2014 after the killing of Michael Brown, an unarmed, 18-year-old African American, by a white police officer in Ferguson, Missouri. Protests erupted across the nation when the officer, Daren Wilson, was not indicted. One month after that verdict, a white police officer in New York was not indicted despite video evidence that he had used a chokehold and other means of force on Eric Garner, an African American man, heard repeatedly asserting that he could not breathe. The Black Lives Matter movement has quickly gained momentum in response to the growing number of these incidents. By 2015, 90 percent of African Americans agreed that blacks and whites are not treated equally by police, and 54 percent of whites felt the same way (see Figure 6.3), showing that while there is still a racial divide on this issue,

Let's Celebrate Pride

Here's your new profile picture.
Go to News Feed

From all of us at Facebook, happy Pride!

Social networks influence our opinions on many issues. We learn and absorb the opinions of friends and family from their words as well as their actions, such as displaying memes or using hashtags associated with a particular movement.

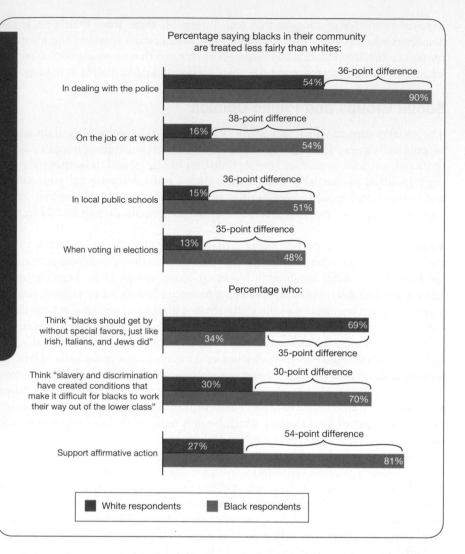

Percentage saying blacks in their community are treated less fairly than whites:

In dealing with the police — 54% / 90% — 36-point difference

On the job or at work — 16% / 54% — 38-point difference

In local public schools — 15% / 51% — 36-point difference

When voting in elections — 13% / 48% — 35-point difference

Percentage who:

Think "blacks should get by without special favors, just like Irish, Italians, and Jews did" — 69% / 34% — 35-point difference

Think "slavery and discrimination have created conditions that make it difficult for blacks to work their way out of the lower class" — 30% / 70% — 30-point difference

Support affirmative action — 27% / 81% — 54-point difference

White respondents ■   Black respondents ■

opinions on it have changed significantly over the past few years.[29] Strikingly, half of all Americans now agree that racism is a big problem, compared to only 26 percent in 2009.[30]

Race can also shape opinions about political candidates. In 2008 Barack Obama made history as the first African American elected president of the United States of America. Political scientists Michael Tesler and David O. Sears looked at the importance of racial attitudes, in predicting evaluations of the 2008 presidential candidates compared with evaluations of previous presidential candidates over many decades. They found that racial attitudes in 2008 were a more important predictor of support for or opposition to the presidential candidates than any time in the last four decades; specifically, whites with a high level of racial resentment were less likely to vote for Obama regardless of partisanship or ideology. Attitudes about President Obama illustrated that race remains a salient cue in shaping the public opinion of both whites and minorities.[31]

Ethnicity Ethnicity also affects policy attitudes. Latinos are the fastest-growing minority population in the United States. While most Latinos are white in race, their shared Hispanic ethnicity contributes to a group consciousness that shapes opinions. Today, Latinos made up 17.4 percent of the total population and 9 percent of the electorate.[32] The U.S. Latino population is diverse, comprising individuals of Central American, South American, and Caribbean descent, and thus their backgrounds and circumstances can be quite different. Moreover, there are significant generational differences among Latinos, especially among generations born outside and within the United States. However, in spite of the differences, the Latino population has a growing sense of "linked fate."

Unsurprisingly, immigration is one of the most important policy issues among Latinos, with significant majorities of Latinos concerned about restrictive immigration policies. The number of first-generation immigrants—or foreign-born citizens—living in the United States quadrupled from almost 10 million in 1970 to about 41 million in 2013. Most immigrants legally reside in the United States.[33] Sharp differences in opinion are found between Latinos and white non-Hispanics over immigration. In 2014, 42 percent of white non-Hispanics said they would grant legal status to immigrants working in the United States, while 64 percent of Latinos believed legal status should be given to all immigrants.[34]

With respect to ideology, Latinos typically are supportive of government policy to improve the lives of citizens and to reduce prevailing inequality, which includes favoring public funding for education, health, and welfare; Latinos generally see an active government as a good thing and favor liberal economic policies. While Latinos tend to be fairly religious, Latino Decision surveys find they do not allow their religious beliefs to dictate their political decisions—they are thus less likely to vote for conservative politicians because of social issues.[35] This helps explains why a majority of Latinos supported Democratic candidate Hillary Clinton for president.

Gender Men and women have important differences of opinion as well. Reflecting differences in social roles and occupational patterns, women tend to oppose military intervention more than men do, are more likely than men to favor gun control, and are more supportive of government social programs (see Figure 6.4). Perhaps because of these differences on issues, women are more likely than men to vote for Democratic candidates. In the 2016 presidential election, there was an especially large gap between men's and women's opinions of the candidates, Democrat Hillary Clinton and Republican Donald Trump. This tendency of men's and women's opinions to differ is known as the **gender gap**.

Political knowledge may play a role in explaining differences in opinion. For example, research suggests that women are more politically knowledgeable about welfare, education, and health policies than men are, but women are less politically knowledgeable regarding other issues. If, however, there is a female Congress member, women in that congressional district are as likely as men to be able to name their senator. Higher female representation in government is associated with greater political efficacy among woman and an increased ability to name their representatives.[36]

Religion Religion is a more important predictor of opinion on a wide range of issues than previously recognized. Religious individuals are usually defined in surveys as frequent church attenders and those who indicate that religion and prayer are important in their lives. One of the fastest-growing groups in America are those without religious affiliation, rising from 5–6 percent of the population in the 1990s

gender gap a distinctive pattern of voting behavior reflecting the differences in views between women and men

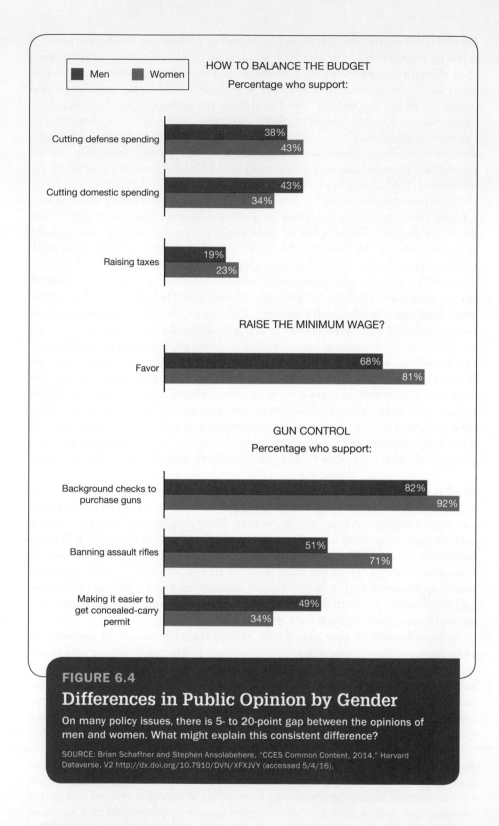

FIGURE 6.4

Differences in Public Opinion by Gender

On many policy issues, there is 5- to 20-point gap between the opinions of men and women. What might explain this consistent difference?

SOURCE: Brian Schaffner and Stephen Ansolabehere, "CCES Common Content, 2014," Harvard Dataverse, V2 http://dx.doi.org/10.7910/DVN/XFXJVY (accessed 5/4/16).

Women are more likely to support gun control than men. The movement One Million Moms for Gun Control formed following the mass shooting of 20 first graders and six adults in Newtown, Connecticut, in 2012. Today the group has hundreds of thousands of members—both women and men—across all 50 states.

to 23 percent today.[37] Among religious groups, white evangelical Protestants and Catholics tend to have more conservative views on moral issues than mainline Protestants and individuals of other denominations. Among the religious groups with more conservative views, evangelical Protestants tend to be even more conservative than Catholics. A 2014 study found that only 31.5 percent of evangelical Protestants believe abortion rights for women should always be permitted, compared to 56 percent of Catholics and 75 percent of those without religious affiliation. Similarly sharp differences in opinion are also found across religious groups in terms of attitudes about same-sex marriage: only 35 percent of evangelical Protestants support same-sex marriage compared to 60 percent of Catholics and 76 percent of the nonreligious.[38] Religion also helps us understand opinions on gambling, teaching evolution in the public schools, immigration, partisanship, ideology, and other issues. White evangelicals and weekly churchgoers are much more likely to hold conservative views and be Republican, while black Protestants, Hispanic Catholics, Jews, and the religiously unaffiliated are more likely to hold liberal views and favor the Democratic Party.

Party Affiliation Political party membership is one of the most important factors affecting political orientation. We can think of partisanship as red- or blue-tinted glasses that color opinion on a vast array of issues. Self-identified partisans (individuals affiliating with the Republican or Democratic Party) tend to rely on party leaders and the media for cues on the appropriate positions to take on major political issues.[39]

In recent years, party polarization has become a defining feature of Congress and many state legislatures. As a result, the leadership of the Republican Party has become increasingly conservative, whereas that of the Democratic Party has become more liberal, a shift reflected in public opinion. Geographic sorting— where liberals choose to live in neighborhoods, cities, counties, and states that are more liberal, while conservatives move to areas with populations with more conservative views—also contributes to mass polarization. Large cities, such as New York City, Chicago, and Los Angeles, have predominantly Democratic populations, while Republicans are more numerous in rural and suburban areas.

According to recent studies, differences between Democratic and Republican partisans on a variety of political and policy questions are greater today than during any other period for which data are available. Across a wide range of issues, Democrats and Republicans strongly disagree. For example, 76 percent of Democrats strongly favor government policies to protect the environment compared to just 30 percent of Republicans, and 72 percent of Republicans oppose granting legal citizenship for immigrants with jobs in the United States, but only 34 percent of Democrats do.[40] Figure 6.5 offers a more detailed look at Americans' attitudes toward immigration, broken down by party affiliation and by education. Wide differences in public opinion exist based on partisanship involving immigration, energy, income inequality, infrastructure, job creation, climate change, national defense, budget deficit, taxes, terrorism, trade, and much more. Democrats and Republicans also have different policy priorities.

Despite the fact that the rift between the "red" (Republican-leaning) and "blue" (Democrat-leaning) states seems deeper than ever, political scientist Morris Fiorina

FIGURE 6.5

Attitudes on Immigration

Americans remain widely divided on the issue of immigration. There is stark disagreement across party lines, with Republicans far more likely than Democrats to oppose citizenship for working immigrants. A less striking, but still significant, difference can be found when it comes to level of education. Are people with more formal education more or less likely to support citizenship for immigrants with jobs? What do you think explains this trend?

*Highest level attained.
SOURCE: Brian Schaffner and Stephen Ansolabehere, "CCES Common Content, 2014," Harvard Dataverse, V2 http://dx.doi .org/10.7910/DVN/XFXJVY (accessed 5/4/16).

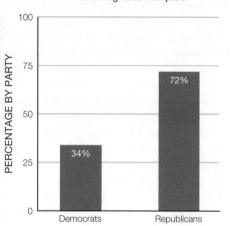

Americans who oppose citizenship for immigrants with jobs:

PERCENTAGE BY PARTY

Democrats: 34%
Republicans: 72%

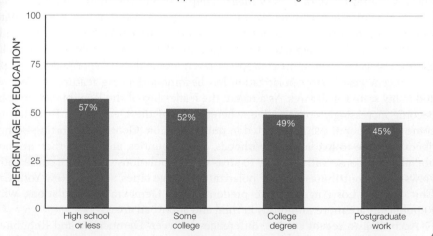

Americans who oppose citizenship for immigrants with jobs:

PERCENTAGE BY EDUCATION*

High school or less: 57%
Some college: 52%
College degree: 49%
Postgraduate work: 45%

and colleagues argue that most Americans hold moderate opinions.[41] While political elites and members of Congress may be highly polarized, there is general agreement among most Americans even on those issues thought to be most divisive. Thus, evidence of partisan polarization in public opinion is mixed: some see deep divisions, while others see evidence of popular consensus.

Economic Class and Group Self-Interest Another way that membership in groups can affect political beliefs is through what might be called rational political interest. On many economic issues, for example, the interests of the rich and the poor differ significantly. Inevitably, these differences in interests will produce differences in political outlook. The framers of the Constitution thought that the inherent gulf between the rich and the poor would always be the most important source of conflict in political life. More recently, Occupy Wall Street protesters decried the chasm between the 99 percent of income earners and the top 1 percent, while the movement to raise the minimum wage to $15 an hour—"Fight for $15"—has quickly gained momentum since 2013. Such struggles over the minimum wage, unemployment benefits, job creation, taxing the wealthy, health care and welfare policy, Social Security, and other issues are fueled by differences in interest between wealthier and poorer Americans. For example, protecting the environment is often seen as a trade-off with job creation and the economy. One-third of individuals earning less than $30,000 a year strongly favor environmental regulations compared to 42 percent of Americans earning $150,000 or more.[42]

However, some researchers have found that people don't necessarily translate broad concerns about inequality or their own economic self-interest into specific policy preferences.[43] For instance, two-thirds of Americans favored the 2001 and 2003 federal tax cuts supported by President George W. Bush, even though the tax reduction disproportionately benefited the very wealthy and therefore increased inequality. The poor, middle class, and affluent alike favored the tax cuts. Political scientist Larry Bartels concluded that the public did not seem able to translate a concern for economic self-interest into policy preferences that would benefit average citizens because they lacked necessary information about the effects of the tax cuts.[44]

Differences in interest also exist among the generations. Senior citizens and younger Americans have different views on such diverse issues as the war on drugs, Social Security, and criminal justice. The young, for example, are much more accepting of legalization of marijuana than are older citizens. The young are also more likely to favor same-sex marriage than are older age cohorts, and they are more concerned about the high cost of a college education and privacy and security online (government surveillance). Older citizens are more concerned with protecting social security benefits than are the young. Some of these differences are rooted in where individuals learn about politics and media consumption; the young are significantly more likely to get their news online and are less likely to watch television news (see Chapter 7).

Nevertheless, group membership can never fully explain a given individual's political views. An individual's unique personality and life experiences may produce political views very different from those of the group to which one might nominally belong. Some African Americans are conservative Republicans, and the occasional wealthy businessperson is also very liberal. Group membership is conducive to particular outlooks, but it is not determinative.

forcritical analysis

Political scientists have observed "geographic sorting" in the United States, where liberals live in areas with other liberals and conservatives live in areas with other conservatives. Is the area where you live strongly liberal, conservative, or evenly mixed? What are the political consequences of geographic sorting?

Political Environment A final set of factors that shape political attitudes and values are the conditions under which individuals are recruited into and become involved in political life. Although political beliefs are influenced by family background and group membership, the content and character of these views is, to a large extent, determined by political circumstances. For example, the baby-boom generation that came of age in the 1960s was exposed to the Vietnam War and the resulting widespread antiwar protests on college campuses and in urban areas throughout the nation. As a result, this generation has generally opposed foreign wars. Young people today who were born around the time of the September 11, 2001, terrorist attacks on the Twin Towers in New York City, or came of age during that time, may be less opposed to foreign wars.

Similarly, the views held by members of a particular group can shift drastically over time as political circumstances change. For example, white southerners were staunch members of the Democratic Party from the Civil War through the 1960s. As Democrats, they became key supporters of liberal New Deal and post–New Deal social programs that greatly expanded the size and power of the national government and provided social welfare programs. The 1960s mark the beginning of the South's move from the Democratic to the Republican camp—mainly because of white southerners opposed to the Democratic Party's integrationist racial policies. Since the 1960s a majority of southern whites have shifted to the Republican Party. Now southern whites provide a solid base of support for efforts to scale back social programs and sharply reduce the size and power of the national government—hence the popularity of the Tea Party movement.[45] It was not a change in the character of white southerners but a change in the political environment in which they found themselves that induced this major shift in partisanship in the South.

Another example of public opinion change can be seen in the evolving political environment in the West. California's Republican governor in the 1970s, Ronald Reagan, went on in the 1980s to become one of the most admired Republican presidents, ushering in major tax reform and deregulating many government policies. But since the 1990s, California, once a Republican stronghold, has become solidly Democratic. Some argue that the shift began with a series of Republican-endorsed ballot measures targeting racial and ethnic minorities—including immigration, affirmative action, and bilingual education—which triggered a backlash especially among Latinos, who had previously participated in politics in very low numbers. In the 1990s, the number of Latino voters who favored more liberal public policy increased dramatically. With Latinos and blacks combined making up more than 50 percent of California's population, this demographic environmental change moved California to a solid Democratic state.[46] In this case, immigration and demographic change, two environmental factors, caused public opinion in the nation's largest state to change over time. Some analysts predict that even Texas, a solidly Republican state, may turn "blue" in future presidential elections, given that Latinos make up 45 percent of the state's population and tend to vote for Democratic candidates.

The terrorist attacks of September 11, 2001 certainly influenced public opinion in the months immediately following the attacks and likely also had a long-term effect on many Americans' basic political beliefs.

In sum, public opinion and orientations are shaped by the political circumstances in which individuals and groups find themselves, and those outlooks can change as circumstances change.

Political Knowledge and Changes in Public Opinion

Explore when and why public opinion changes and what role political knowledge plays

The section above described what factors shape individuals' opinions, including political socialization, group identity, and political environment. These factors are relatively constant: one's level of education, for example, is generally set by early adulthood. However, these are not the only influences on individuals' opinions. Individuals encounter new information from political leaders and the media throughout their lives. What role does political knowledge and information play in forming opinions? What causes people's opinions to change over time?

Stability of Public Opinion One of the most important studies of how public opinion is formed is by political scientist John Zaller.[47] Zaller argues that individuals learn about politics by converting information from the news, elected officials, and other sources into opinions. His model of opinion formation works in three stages. In the "receive" stage, an individual receives information from a number of different sources. In the "accept" stage, the individual assesses this information through the lens of her own political views and accepts only those messages that are in line with previously held beliefs, meaning that some political information will be rejected. Finally, in the "sample" stage, the individual selects some of the accepted information—often the information that is most recent—and forms an opinion from it. So, according to this theory, if you receive information from various sources about a proposed tax cut, you will then assess the different messages based on your own previously held beliefs about tax cuts. If you believe tax cuts are generally good, you will likely reject information that suggests this particular cut is bad and accept only the messages suggesting that it is good.

The decision to accept or reject information is based on political knowledge. When asked about his opinion on a topic, the individual selects the most relevant or most recently acquired and accepted information from his "bucket" of information (the third stage above). Citizens with more political knowledge can differentiate between information that fits or does not fit with their beliefs—and then correctly accept or reject it. For less-informed individuals, the media and political leaders may play a larger role in influencing public opinion. This reliance on politicians and the media, Zaller concludes, means that the public's opinions are often unstable and unreliable because these sources provide competing, changing information. As a result, public opinion is often a reflection of whatever recent message (or media story) an individual has stored in her short-term memory. As we will see later in the chapter, this effect is called priming.

The public is constantly exposed to competing messages from political elites. Following the death of Supreme Court Justice Antonin Scalia in 2016, Republican members of Congress, led by Senate Majority Leader Mitch McConnell (left), urged President Obama to leave the task of appointing Scalia's replacement to the next president. At the same time, Democrats such as Senator Diane Feinstein (right) called on Republicans to do their duty and allow a vote on Obama's nominee.

Another way of understanding how individuals form political opinions is the online-processing model, advanced by the political scientist Milton Lodge and colleagues.[48] According to Lodge and his colleagues, an individual keeps a running tally of information and uses that tally to form an opinion on a policy issue or to decide which candidate to vote for. However, by the time an individual actually votes or voices an opinion on a specific issue, she may have forgotten some of the older information included in her decision-making process. This effect leads to the misconception that voters are uninformed, when in fact their opinion is informed but they have not retained all of the facts used to form that opinion. This model also implies a large role for political elites and the media but does not necessarily suggest that opinion is unstable.

If public opinion is easily manipulated, the democratic process, which relies on citizens to play a significant part in the government, would be at risk. But other research has shown that individuals are quite stable in their policy attitudes.[49]

To take a closer look at whether and how public opinion changes, see Figure 6.6. The Pew Research Center tracks public opinion over time with annual surveys asking identical questions. Some opinions are relatively stable: support for abortion, for example, has remained virtually unchanged over the past decade, with 55 percent saying abortion should be legal in all or most cases and 40 percent saying illegal in all or most cases, on average. Opinions about the economy and personal finances, however, experienced a gradual change triggered by the financial crisis in 2008. In 2004, 48 percent of Americans described their personal finances as poor or fair and half described their finances as good or excellent. By 2015, 56 percent of Americans described their personal finances as poor or fair. Opinion on same-sex marriage has changed dramatically over the past two decades. In 1996, 65 percent of Americans opposed marriage for gays and lesbians. As of 2015, only 39 percent opposed same-sex marriage and 55 percent favored marriage rights. Notice that when public opinion has shifted, the shift has occurred fairly steadily in one direction; it doesn't simply jump around.[50]

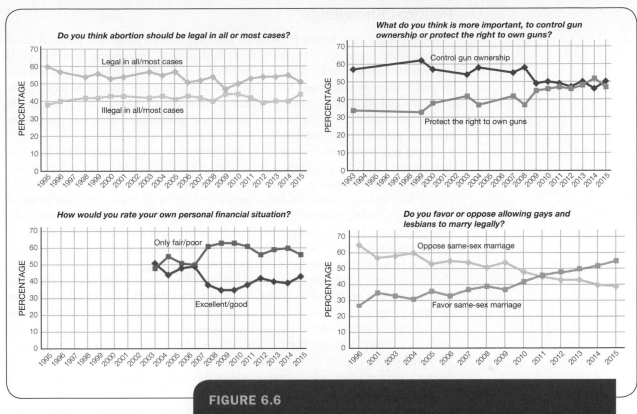

FIGURE 6.6

Stability in Public Opinion

Public opinion on some issues has stayed stable in the last two decades, while opinion on other issues has shifted. What might explain why opinion on personal finance and same-sex marriage has changed, while opinion on abortion has stayed relatively constant?

SOURCES: Pew Research Center, www.pewresearch.org/data-trend/domestic-issues/abortion/; www.people-press.org/2015/08/13/continued-bipartisan-support-for-expanded-background-checks-on-gun-sales/8-12-2015-3-57-45-pm/; http://www.pewresearch.org/data-trend/national-conditions/personal-finances/; www.pewforum.org/2015/07/29/graphics-slideshow-changing-attitudes-on-gay-marriage/ (all accessed 12/23/15).

The shift in public opinion on same-sex marriage has occurred partly in response to government policy. Political scientists call this "policy feedback." In 2009, Iowa was just the third U.S. state to allow same-sex marriages when the state Supreme Court issued a unanimous and at the time unpopular decision in the case *Varnum v. Brien*.[51] Changes in opinion immediately before and after the court decision were large. A survey of Iowans conducted immediately before and after the court legalized same-sex marriage showed that certain groups—Democrats, educated, young, nonreligious, non-evangelical, and people who have gay/lesbian family or friends— were the most likely to change their opinion in favor of same-sex marriage.[52] In 2015, the U.S. Supreme Court ruled in favor of legalizing same-sex marriage in all 50 states. Favorable public opinion may have helped pave the way for national policy change.[53]

Political Knowledge

What best explains whether citizens are generally consistent in their political views or inconsistent and open to the influence of others? In general, knowledgeable citizens are better able to evaluate new information and determine if it is relevant to and consistent with their beliefs and opinions; they are also more likely to be partisans and to have an ideology (such as liberal or conservative).[54] As a result, better-informed individuals can recognize their political interests and act consistently to further those interests.[55]

Using public-opinion surveys, political scientist Adam Berinsky found that certain segments of the population may lack sufficient knowledge of public policy to give informed opinions. When asked about preferences toward social welfare policy, for instance, disadvantaged groups are more likely than any other group to abstain from giving answers (that is, are more likely to say they don't know). This tendency not only leads to a potential underreporting of support for social welfare policy among the poor but also limits the political voice of those who are most likely to benefit from goverment policy in this area.[56]

This variation raises the question of how much political knowledge is necessary for one to act as an effective citizen. In an important study of political knowledge political scientists Michael X. Delli Carpini and Scott Keeter found that the average American exhibits little formal knowledge of political institutions, processes, leaders, or policy debates; many Americans could not name their member of Congress and did not know that U.S. senators serve six-year terms.[57] Delli Carpini and Keeter also found that political knowledge is not evenly distributed throughout the population. Those with higher education, income, and occupational status and who are members of social or political organizations are more likely to know about and be active in politics. As a result, individuals with more income and education also have a disproportionate share of knowledge and influence and thus are better able to get what they want from government.

But some groups have high information on specific issues. Latinos, for example, have higher levels of political knowledge on immigration than average Americans. Republican presidential candidate Mitt Romney won only 30 percent of the Latino vote in 2012, in part due to his position on immigration and his harsh rhetoric against immigrants. Latino Decisions surveys show three-quarters of Latinos wanted the federal government not to deport young people who would be eligible for the DREAM Act (Development, Relief, and Education for Alien Minors).[58] President Obama issued an executive order implementing parts of the DREAM Act in 2012. Obama's and Romney's different policies shaped Latinos' opinions of the candidates and their voting behavior in the 2012 elections. In 2016, Republican candidate Donald Trump made immigration a central issue with even harsher language against illegal immigration than Romney's in 2012. In response, Latinos strongly opposed Trump and favored his Democratic opponent, Hillary Clinton.

Shortcuts and Cues Because being informed politically requires a substantial investment of time and energy, most Americans seek to acquire political information and to make political decisions "on the cheap" by making use of shortcuts for political evaluation and decision making rather than engaging in a lengthy process of information-gathering. As noted above, researchers have found that individuals rely on cues from trusted party elites, interest groups, and the media to aid in

People often rely on cues from party elites in forming political opinions. During the 2016 presidential campaign, some people took their cue on whom to support from former vice presidential candidate Sarah Palin when she endorsed Republican Donald Trump.

attitude formation.[59] Other "inexpensive" ways to become informed involve taking cues from trusted friends, social networks and social media, relatives, colleagues, and perhaps religious leaders. Political scientists Richard Lau and David Redlawsk contend that using informational shortcuts, average citizens can form political opinions that are, in most instances, consistent with their underlying preferences. They call this "voting correctly."[60] Even individuals with low levels of political knowledge are able to make relatively informed political choices by relying on these voter cues. It is generally accepted by scholars that people rely on shortcuts in forming public opinion on politics and public policy.[61] From this perspective, lower levels of political knowledge about politics, or instability of opinions, may not be a serious problem.

The public's reliance on elite cues has taken on new significance in today's era of party polarization. As elected officials have become increasingly polarized, has this change affected the way that citizens arrive at their opinions? Political scientists James Druckman and colleagues have found stark evidence that polarized political environments change how citizens make decisions and form opinions. Notably, polarization between the parties means that party endorsements (of an issue or candidate) have a larger impact on public opinion formation than they used to. At the same time, polarization decreases the impact of other information on public opinion—that is, party polarization may actually reduce levels of political knowledge. Thus, elite polarization may have negative implications for public opinion formation.[62]

Skim and Scan Another factor affecting political knowledge is the *form* in which people consume information. The transformation of political information in the digital era has had a profound effect on the way the news is reported and how citizens learn about politics. A 2012 survey found that one in three social networking site users say those sites are important for their political information, and more than three in four Americans read the news online or seek political information online.[63] Recent research also indicates a trend in journalism toward shorter articles and

In the digital era, many Americans obtain news by skimming and scanning headlines from online publications rather than by reading in-depth articles.

flashier headlines. Americans today are likely to read the news by scanning and skimming multiple headlines online, in bits and bytes, rather than by reading long news articles.[64] There is a debate about whether the shift to digital media creates a more informed public, given the broader diversity of information sources and more personalized communication of the news via social media, or a public that is less informed because of a tendency to favor scanning and skimming over in-depth reading. However, as we've seen in this chapter, some research indicates that most individuals use simple cues and shortcuts to process political information. If this is correct, scanning and skimming headlines might provide a reasonable way to be informed about politics without extensive time or effort.

Costs to Democracy Political knowledge is necessary for effective citizenship. Those who lack political information cannot effectively defend their own political interests and can easily become losers in political struggles and government policy. The presence of large numbers of politically ignorant individuals means that political power can more easily be manipulated by political elites, the media, and wealthy special interests that seek to shape public opinion. If knowledge is power, then a lack of knowledge can contribute to growing political and economic inequality. When individuals are unaware of their interests or how to pursue them, it is virtually certain that political outcomes will not favor them. The answer is to get informed and stay informed.

One of the most important areas of government policy is taxation. As discussed in the introduction to this chapter, the United States has one of the largest gaps between the rich and the poor of any nation in the world. But rather than raise taxes, over the past several decades the United States has substantially reduced the rate of taxation levied on its wealthiest citizens. Most recently, tax cuts signed into law by George W. Bush in 2001, and extended by President Obama, provided a substantial tax break mainly for the top 1 percent of the nation's wage earners. Political scientist Larry Bartels has shown that, surprisingly, most Americans favored the tax cuts, including millions of middle- and lower-middle-class citizens who did not stand to benefit from the tax policy. Additionally, 40 percent of Americans had no opinion at all regarding the Bush tax cuts. The explanation for this odd state of affairs appears to be a lack of political knowledge. Millions of individuals who were unlikely to derive benefit from President Bush's tax policy thought they would. Since most Americans think they pay too much in taxes, they favored the policy, even if the wealthy benefited much more than the middle class. (See the "Who Are Americans?" feature for public opinion on income inequality.)

Bartels has employed the cartoon character Homer Simpson to explain how people don't realize what is in their economic interest: Homer wants a tax cut, and even if he gets only $1 and Mr. Burns, his boss, takes home $10,000, Homer still wants his dollar in savings.[65] But Homer is misguided in wanting his dollar in tax savings: the overall lost tax revenues, collected mainly from the wealthy, would have funded programs that benefit middle-class taxpayers like Homer. Upper-bracket taxpayers, who are more informed and knowledgeable, are more likely to see to it that their

Who Thinks Economic Inequality Is a Problem?

Percentage who said the government should do more to reduce the gap between the rich and the poor in the United States

An individual's party identification, gender, and income may influence his or her opinions on specific issues. As this study showed, there are significant differences of opinion about the government's role in reducing the income gap between men and women and across income groups, but the most pronounced differences were between Democrats and Republicans.

By Income

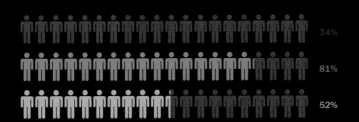

<$50,000	65%
$50,000–$99,999	53%
>$100,000	45%

By Party

Republicans	34%
Democrats	81%
Independents	52%

By Gender

Men	50%
Women	63%

for critical analysis

1. Do the findings in this study show that opinions are shaped by economic self-interest? Why or why not?

2. Which of these groups is most likely to support government action to address inequality? Are the other groups not concerned about inequality? Use the data to explain your answers.

SOURCE: The New York Times/CBS News Poll, "Americans' Views on Income Inequality and Workers' Rights," *New York Times*, June 3, 2015, www.nytimes.com/interactive/2015/06/03/business/income-inequality-workers-rights-international-trade-poll.html (accessed 3/15/16).

economic self-interest aligns with government policy—and vice versa. This example illustrates that basic political knowledge matters in American politics.

● The Media, Government, and Public Opinion

Describe the major forces that shape public opinion

When individuals attempt to form opinions about particular political issues, events, and personalities, they seldom do so in isolation. Typically, they are confronted with—sometimes bombarded by—the efforts of a host of individuals and groups seeking to persuade them to adopt a particular point of view. In the approach to the 2016 presidential election, someone trying to decide what to think about Hillary Clinton or Donald Trump could hardly avoid an avalanche of opinions expressed through the media, in meetings, or in conversations with friends. The **marketplace of ideas** is the interplay of opinions and views that takes place as competing forces attempt to persuade as many people as possible to accept a particular position on a particular issue. Given this constant exposure to the ideas of others, it is virtually impossible for most individuals to resist some modification of their own beliefs. Three forces that play important roles in shaping opinions in the marketplace are the government, private groups, and the news media.[66]

marketplace of ideas the public forum in which beliefs and ideas are exchanged and compete

Political Leaders

All governments try to influence, manipulate, or manage their citizens' beliefs. But the extent to which public opinion is actually affected by governmental public relations can be limited. Often, governmental claims are disputed by the media, by interest groups, and increasingly by the opposing political party.

This hasn't stopped modern presidents from focusing a great deal of attention on shaping public opinion to boost support for their policy agendas. Franklin Delano Roosevelt promoted his policy agenda directly to the American people through his famous "fireside chat" radio broadcasts. A hallmark of the Clinton administration was the establishment of a political "war room" similar to the one that operated in his campaign headquarters, where representatives from all departments met daily to discuss and coordinate the president's public-relations efforts.[67] The George W. Bush administration developed an extensive public-relations program to bolster popular support for the president's policies, including the war against terrorism.[68] Bush was especially effective in building support for the Iraq War and antiterrorism policies via theatric State of the Union addresses. Using the runway of an aircraft carrier as his stage, a confident Commander in Chief Bush, dressed in military fatigues, proclaimed the end of the Iraq War in 2003. His statement was premature by nearly a decade, but it effectively maintained public support for the war effort.

Like its predecessors, the Obama administration sought to shape public opinion in the United States and abroad, relying upon the power of the president's oratorical skills to build support for his administration's initiatives in domestic and foreign policy. But Obama's White House was unique in using digital media and social media to promote the president's policy agenda. Facebook posts promoted his policies and served to personalize the president. Obama was especially adept at using Twitter, with 70 million followers on that network. He used multiple Twitter accounts including his official account for the U.S. president (@POTUS), as well as the White House's Twitter account (@WhiteHouse). Obama's use of Twitter to shape public opinion in favor of his policies allowed him to communicate directly with the people without having to be interviewed by the media.

One realm in which presidential messages seem to routinely impact public opinion is foreign policy. Because most Americans have relatively low levels of knowledge about foreign policy, political elites have more influence in shaping opinion on such matters.[69] As will be described in more detail in Chapter 18, the president plays a key role in deciding and implementing U.S. foreign policy, particularly in moments of crisis. One prominent example is the decision to invade Iraq, which was strongly endorsed by President George W. Bush. In 2002, Congress passed the Joint Resolution to Authorize the Use of United States Armed Forces Against Iraq. Public opinion in favor of invading Iraq remained above 50 percent between June and November of 2002, according to Gallup polls. By the time the invasion occurred, in March 2003, after months of presidential messages, public support had reached over 70 percent.[70]

Interest Groups

The ideas that become prominent in political life are developed and spread not only by government officials but also by important economic and political groups searching for issues that will advance their causes. One notable example is the abortion issue, which has inflamed American politics over the past 30 years. The

To promote their ideas and influence public opinion, left-leaning public interest groups, such as the National Organization for Women, do extensive lobbying work but also rely on grassroots campaigns—organizing marches, rallies, and acts of civil disobedience—to push for social change.

notion of a fetal "right to life," whose proponents seek to outlaw abortion and over-turn the Supreme Court's 1973 *Roe v. Wade* decision, was developed by conservative politicians who saw the issue of abortion as a means of uniting Catholic and Protestant conservatives and linking both groups to the Republican Party.[71] To advance their cause, leaders of the right-to-life movement sponsored well-publicized Senate hearings at which testimony, photographs, films (such as *The Silent Scream*), and other exhibits were presented to illustrate the movement's claim that abortion amounted to the murder of millions of unborn human beings. Finally, Catholic and Evangelical Protestant religious leaders were organized to denounce abortion from their church pulpits and, increasingly, from their electronic pulpits on the Christian Broadcasting Network and the various other television forums available for religious programming. Religious leaders have also organized demonstrations, pickets, and disruptions at abortion clinics throughout the nation.[72]

Ideas are marketed most effectively by groups with access to financial resources, public or private institutional support, and well-coordinated media campaigns that attract interest and support. The promotion of conservative ideas in recent years has been greatly facilitated by the millions of dollars that conservative corporations and business organizations such as "Super PACs" (see Chapter 10), the U.S. Chamber of Commerce, and the Public Affairs Council spend each year on public information. In much the same way, liberal organizations vie for public attention armed with ample financial assets, access to the media, and well-honed skills in strategic communication and grass-roots mobilization. In recent decades, various left-leaning public interest groups, relying heavily on voluntary contributions of time, effort, and money from their members, have organized in parallel with the rise of such institutions on the right. Through groups such as New Democrat Coalition, MoveOn.org, Common Cause, the National Organization for Women, EMILY's List, and the World Wildlife Federation, liberal intellectuals and professionals have been able to apply their organizational skills and educational resources to developing and promoting their ideas.[73]

The Mass Media

The media are among the most powerful forces operating in the marketplace of ideas. As we shall see in Chapter 7, the mass media are not simply neutral messengers for ideas developed by others. Instead, the media are opinion makers in their own right and have an enormous impact on popular attitudes. For example, since the publication of the Pentagon Papers by the *New York Times* and the exposure of the Watergate scandal led by the *Washington Post* in the 1970s, the national news media have relentlessly investigated personal and official wrongdoing on the part of politicians and public officials. Today, *Follow the Money*'s new website, www.darkmoney.org, plays a similar role in exposing money in politics and potential government corruption. Media revelation of corruption in government has contributed to the cynicism and distrust of government that prevail in much of the general public.

At the same time, the ways in which media coverage interprets or "frames" specific events can have a major impact on popular responses and opinions about these events (see Chapter 7).[74] Given the critical importance of media framing to the way the public perceives the news, the Bush administration went to great lengths to persuade broadcasters to follow its lead in their coverage of both terrorism and America's response to terrorism in the months following the September 11, 2001, attacks. The media acquiesced, presenting the administration's military

for critical **analysis**

Does it matter what news sources an individual reads? How can the news influence public attitudes on issues of public policy?

campaigns in Afghanistan and Iraq, as well as its domestic antiterrorist efforts, in a positive light. Even supposedly liberal newspapers such as the *New York Times* published articles supportive of the military invasion of Iraq in March 2003, when President Bush ordered the invasion.

● Public Opinion and Government Policy

> **Analyze how public opinion shapes government policy and influences elected officials**

In 1960 the authors of a book titled *The American Voter* argued that few Americans think about politics ideologically or consistently, so one would naturally expect public opinion to vary, as discussed earlier.[75] In fact, one of the reasons elected officials sometimes do not follow public opinion is that it tends to be unpredictable. Given generally low levels of political knowledge among voters and the changing nature of public opinion, it's little wonder that politicians are sometimes unwilling to act solely on the basis of public opinion. John Zaller's explanation of how Americans form specific opinions calls into question whether government leaders should consult public opinion when they make policy decisions—but consulting public opinion is their democratic duty. So how responsive is government policy to public opinion?

Government Responsiveness to Public Opinion

Studies generally find that elected officials are influenced by the preferences of the public. For example, political scientists Benjamin Page and Robert Shapiro explored the relationship between broad changes in opinion toward various political issues and the policy outcomes that most closely correspond to the issues.[76] The results showed that shifts in public opinion on particular issues do in fact tend to lead to changes in public policy. This is especially true when there are wide swings in opinion regarding particularly high-profile issues that are relatively simple, such as legalization of same-sex marriage. Other researchers have found similar

To what extent do political leaders listen to the opinions of their constituents? To what extent should they listen? Is Calvin's father right that leaders should do what they believe is right, not what the public wants?

evidence that government policy generally does track public opinion. Political scientists Gerald Wright, Robert Erikson, and John McIver have found, unsurprisingly, that states where conservative opinions predominate tend to adopt more conservative laws and states with more liberal public opinion adopt more liberal policies.[77] Another example is in health care. A July 2009 Pew survey found that 65 percent of Americans favored a law "requiring all Americans to have health insurance, and government aid for those unable to afford it."[78] The federal government adopted the Affordable Health Care Act for America in 2010, which required health insurance for all citizens.

However, there is reason to question whether prevailing public opinion causes politicians to make policies that reflect the general will or whether government policy in fact causes changes in public opinion. The relationship between government policy and opinion may be dynamic, wherein policy responds to opinion but opinion also shifts based on new government policies.[79] Recent studies have found policy to have an effect on opinion in various areas, such as the environment, health care, welfare reform, the death penalty, and smoking bans. For example, researchers found that in states that adopted smoking bans, public opinion then shifted to become more critical of cigarette smoking than in states without such bans.[80] Scholars have suggested a number of possible mechanisms to explain this process. New policy may expose the public to new ideas, causing opinion to change, or experience with a successful or unsuccessful policy gives the public new information. A policy might act as a "signal" of a moral or ethical view (such as a smoking ban acting as a "signal" that smoking should be stigmatized).

Of course, sometimes public opinion and policy do not align. At times, officials act on their own preferences if they believe it will benefit government or society, and lawmakers typically do use their own judgment when making policy choices.[81] When elected officials pursue policies not aligned with public opinion, it is often because they view particular groups of the electorate as more important than others. Inevitably, loyal voting blocs or interest groups that regularly contribute to a candidate may have their interests more closely represented than the general public.[82]

Although the American political system is open to everyone, some voices are more likely to be listened to than others. During the 2016 presidential election, Hillary Clinton was criticized for having close ties with Wall Street. Over the years Goldman Sachs (whose CEO Lloyd Blankfein appears here with Clinton) has contributed over $800,000 to Clinton's campaigns.

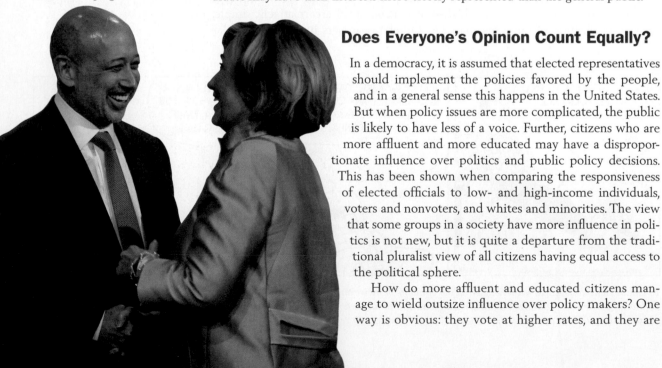

Does Everyone's Opinion Count Equally?

In a democracy, it is assumed that elected representatives should implement the policies favored by the people, and in a general sense this happens in the United States. But when policy issues are more complicated, the public is likely to have less of a voice. Further, citizens who are more affluent and more educated may have a disproportionate influence over politics and public policy decisions. This has been shown when comparing the responsiveness of elected officials to low- and high-income individuals, voters and nonvoters, and whites and minorities. The view that some groups in a society have more influence in politics is not new, but it is quite a departure from the traditional pluralist view of all citizens having equal access to the political sphere.

How do more affluent and educated citizens manage to wield outsize influence over policy makers? One way is obvious: they vote at higher rates, and they are more likely to contribute money to political campaigns. As we will discuss in Chapter 8, voters and individuals making political contributions tend to be more affluent and educated than nonvoters. Indeed, there is new evidence supporting the common, but generally untested, assumption that voters are better represented than nonvoters. In a comparative study of the roll-call votes of U.S. senators, political scientists John Griffin and Brian Newman demonstrated that elected officials are indeed responsive to the policy preferences of voters but not to those of nonvoters.[83]

In regard to income group, research has found that U.S. senators from both the Republican and Democratic parties are less likely to respond to the opinions of low-income constituents than to those of constituents with higher incomes.[84] Senate votes on such varied issues as the minimum wage, civil rights, and abortion are more likely to reflect the opinions of the rich. The influence of affluent Americans may explain government policies such as tax cuts for the very wealthy, failure to increase the minimum wage, and the elimination of the inheritance tax which contribute to growing income inequality.[85]

As an alternative to analyzing legislative votes, political scientist Martin Gilens has used survey results to confirm that those with higher incomes are more likely to have their policy preferences represented by actual policies.[86] He considered public opinion surveys on a wide variety of policy issues conducted over 20 years and compared the responses of upper- and lower-income groups with related federal policy outcomes. Gilens found a relationship between what the public wants and what the government actually does, albeit with a strong bias toward the status quo. But when Americans with different income levels differ in their policy preferences, policies strongly reflect the preferences of the most affluent and show little or no relationship to the preferences of poor or middle-income Americans. Political scientist Robert Dahl may be right when he argues that every American citizen has an equal right to voice opinions in the political arena, but his critics are also right to point out that some voices receive a very attentive listening, while others are hardly heard at all.[87]

● Measuring Public Opinion

Describe basic survey methods and other techniques researchers use to measure public opinion

A century ago American political leaders gauged public opinion by the presence of crowds at meetings and their applause. This direct exposure to the people's views did not necessarily produce accurate knowledge of public opinion. It did, however, give political leaders confidence in their public support—and therefore confidence in their ability to govern by consent.

Abraham Lincoln and Stephen Douglas debated each other seven times during the summer and autumn of 1858, two years before they became presidential nominees. Their debates took place before audiences in parched cornfields and courthouse squares. A century later, the presidential debates, although seen by millions, often take place in television studios, and audiences are instructed not to applaud or make noise. The 2016 presidential candidates, however, often engaged in large rallies and campaign events attended by thousands

Public Opinion on Climate Change

When it comes to public opinion on climate change, different security or economic interests may influence global attitudes. Some people are opposed to increasing environmental regulations out of fear that they will impose costs on businesses and slow economic growth. People who live in regions particularly susceptible to the effects of climate change and flooding, such as countries with low-lying coastal areas, tend to express greater concern for the environment. Public opinion surveys also show higher levels of concern in developing countries that are less equipped to deal with the consequences of climate change.

In Latin America and Africa, for example, most of the population considers climate change to be the *most* significant international issue, while other countries rank this concern much lower. What do you think are possible explanations for these global differences?

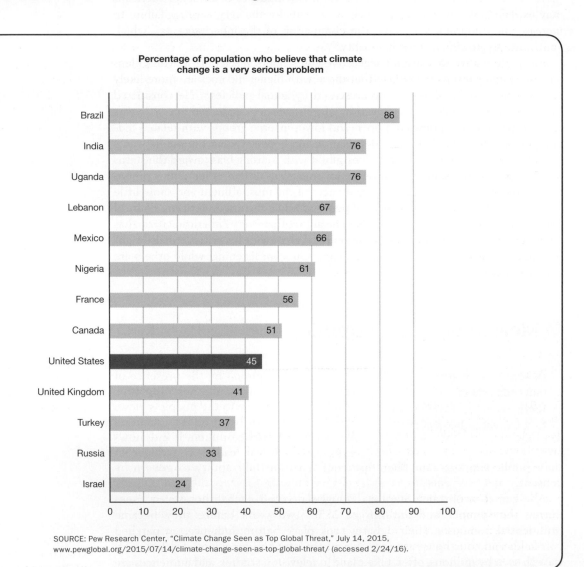

Percentage of population who believe that climate change is a very serious problem

Country	Percentage
Brazil	86
India	76
Uganda	76
Lebanon	67
Mexico	66
Nigeria	61
France	56
Canada	51
United States	45
United Kingdom	41
Turkey	37
Russia	33
Israel	24

SOURCE: Pew Research Center, "Climate Change Seen as Top Global Threat," July 14, 2015, www.pewglobal.org/2015/07/14/climate-change-seen-as-top-global-threat/ (accessed 2/24/16).

of people, which allowed them to gauge the public's response directly.[88] Retail politics is where candidates meet citizens face-to-face to discuss politics.[89]

As Chapter 7 on the media illustrates, the media convey information to millions of people, but the media are not yet as efficient at getting information back to leaders—although the rise of social media, such as Facebook and Twitter, has created improved feedback for elected officials. Today, public officials make extensive use of **public-opinion polls** to help them decide whether to run for office, what policies to support, how to vote on important legislation, and what types of appeals to make in their campaigns. All recent presidents and other major political figures have worked closely with polls and pollsters.

public-opinion polls scientific instruments for measuring public opinion

Measuring Public Opinion from Surveys

It is not feasible to interview the more than 300 million Americans residing in the United States on their opinions of who should be the next president or what should be done about important policy issues such as how to improve the economy and create jobs. Instead, pollsters take a **sample** of the population and use it to make inferences (e.g., predictions and educated guesses) about the preferences of the population as a whole. For a political survey to be an accurate representation of the population, it must meet certain requirements, including an appropriate sampling method (i.e., randomization), a sufficient sample size, and the avoidance of selection bias.[90] While some are skeptical of sampling, random sample surveys, which are used extensively in business and marketing as well as politics, ensure that the samples are accurate and reliable predictions of the underlying population.

sample a small group selected by researchers to represent the most important characteristics of an entire population

Websites such as RealClearPolitics.com list the results of every political survey released each day; during elections, this can be as many as 20 different surveys daily. Every week, the opinions of Americans regarding candidates and public policies are measured, as well as opinions on a vast array of products (toothpaste), entertainment (movie star romances), and even college political science textbooks!

Representative Samples One way to obtain a representative sample is what statisticians call a **simple random sample (or probability sample)**. To take such a sample, one would need a complete list of all the people in the United States, and individuals would be *randomly* selected from that list. Imagine that everyone's name were entered into a lottery, with names then drawn blindly from an enormous box. If everyone had an equal chance of selection, we would have a truly random sample. Since we don't have a complete list of all Americans, pollsters use census data, lists of households (for in-person or telephone surveys), and telephone numbers (cell phones and landlines) to create lists, drawing samples from regions and then neighborhoods within regions. Rolls of registered voters are often used in political surveys designed to predict the outcome of an election. If respondents are chosen randomly and everyone has an equal chance of being selected, then their results can be used to predict behavior for the overall population. If randomization is not used or some people are excluded from the chance to be selected, then the sample will be biased and cannot be used to generalize to the population accurately.

simple random sample (or probability sample) a method used by pollsters to select a representative sample in which every individual in the population has an equal probability of being selected as a respondent

Another method of drawing samples of the national population is a technique called **random digit dialing** of landline and cell phone numbers (but not business phones or inoperative home telephones). A computer random number generator is used to produce a list of 10-digit telephone numbers. Given that 95 percent

random digit dialing a polling method in which respondents are selected at random from a list of 10-digit telephone numbers, with every effort made to avoid bias in the construction of the sample

of Americans have telephones (cell phones or landlines), this technique usually results in a random national sample because almost every citizen has a chance of being selected for the survey. Telephone surveys are fairly accurate, cost-effective, and flexible in the type of questions that can be asked; but many people refuse to answer political surveys, and response rates—the percent of those called who actually answer the survey—have been falling steadily, averaging less than 15 percent.[91]

Sample Size A sample must be large enough to provide an accurate representation of the population. Surprisingly, though, the size of the population being measured doesn't matter, only the size of the *sample*. A survey of 1,000 people is almost as effective for measuring the opinions of all Texans (26 million residents) as the opinions of all Americans (over 314 million residents).

Flipping a coin shows how this works. After tossing a coin 10 times, the number of heads and tails may not be close to 5 and 5. After 100 tosses of the coin, though, the percentage of heads should be close to 50 percent and after 1,000 tosses, very close to 50 percent. In fact, after 1,000 tosses, there is a 95 percent chance that the number of heads will be somewhere between 46.9 percent and 53.1 percent. This 3.1 percent variation from 50 percent is called the **sampling error (or margin of error)**: the chance that the sample used does not accurately represent the population from which it is drawn. In this case, 3.1 percent is the amount of uncertainty we can expect with a typical 1,000-person survey. If we conduct a national survey and find candidate A leads candidate B by 5 percent in the upcoming election and the uncertainty in the survey is 3 percent, it means candidate A leads candidate B by anywhere between 2 (5 − 3) and 8 (5 + 3) percentage points (see Figure 6.7). Normally, samples of 1,000 people are considered sufficient for accurately measuring public opinion through the use of surveys.

Larger sample sizes can yield more accurate predictions of the opinions of a population, but there is a trade-off in terms of cost since it is also more expensive to poll more people. Why is a sample size of only 1,000 generally accepted as adequately representative of much larger populations? Consider the "diminishing returns" of sampling more and more people. The sample error from a sample of 500 people is 4.4 percent. With 1,000 respondents, it drops to 3.1 percent and with 1,500 to 2.5 percent. That is, the smaller and smaller gains in accuracy have to be weighed

sampling error (or margin of error) polling error that arises based on the small size of the sample

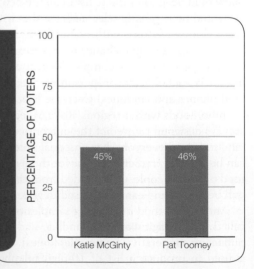

FIGURE 6.7

Sample Size and Margin of Error

In September 2016 preelection polling showed Pennsylvania senatorial candidate Pat Toomey ahead of his rival Katie McGinty by 1 percentage point. With a margin of error of plus or minus 3.5 percentage points, however, this poll effectively showed a tie between the two candidates. Would a larger sample size eliminate the margin of error?

NOTE: A sample of 778 likely voters were interviewed by telephone. Margin of error: +/− 3.5%.
SOURCE: Quinnipiac University Poll. "Republicans Lead in Florida, North Carolina, Ohio Senate Races; Pennsylvania Is Close, Quinnipiac University Swing State Poll Finds," September 9, 2016, www.qu.edu/images/polling/ps /ps09092016_prbt47q.pdf (accessed 10/17/16).

against the steadily increasing costs of polling more people. The consensus among statisticians and pollsters is that the optimal trade-off point is 1,000—hence 1,000 is the "gold standard." But today many surveys conducted online include thousands and thousands of respondents, making their predictions even more accurate.

When an election poll of 1,000 people indicates that 51 percent of voters surveyed favor the Republican candidate and 49 percent support the Democratic candidate, the outcome is considered too close to call because the difference, 2 percent, is within the margin of error of 3.1 percent. That is, a figure of 51 percent really means that between 48 percent and 54 percent of voters in the population *probably* favor the Republican, while a figure of 49 percent indicates that between 46 percent and 52 percent of all voters *probably* support the Democrat. Thus, in this example, a 52-to-48 percent Democratic victory would still be consistent with polls predicting a 51-to-49 percent Republican triumph.

Survey Design and Question Wording Even with a good sample design, surveys may fail to reflect the true distribution of opinion within a target population. One frequent source of measurement error is the wording of survey questions. The words used in a question can have an enormous impact on the answers it elicits. The reliability of survey results can also be adversely affected by poor question format, the ordering of questions, poor vocabulary, ambiguity of questions, or questions with built-in biases.

Often, minor differences in the wording of a question can convey vastly different meanings to respondents and thus produce quite different response patterns (see Box 6.3). For example, for many years the University of Chicago's National Opinion Research Center has asked respondents whether they think the federal government is spending too much, too little, or about the right amount of money on "assistance for the poor." Answering the question posed this way, about two-thirds of all respondents seem to believe that the government is spending too little. However, the same survey also asks whether the government spends too much, too little, or about the right amount for welfare. When the word *welfare* is substituted for "assistance for the poor," about half of all respondents indicate that too much is being spent.[92]

Internet Surveys Today, pollsters are increasingly turning to the use of online surveys, often using similar techniques to those of telephone surveys. Internet surveys can be more efficient, less costly, and more accurate than standard phone surveys; and they include larger samples of young people and yield more accurate results within age cohorts. But many surveys you will find online do not use probability sampling (random sampling) and thus are not representative of the American population. Instead, they reflect those willing to take a quiz online.

Knowledge Networks (KN) and YouGov are leaders in Internet polling using random sampling methods in which respondents complete surveys online instead of being interviewed on the phone. KN has a large population of respondents (hundreds of thousands of individuals) identified using probability sampling, so the sample is representative of the American population in terms of age, education, income, gender, race, political interest, region, religion, partisanship, and other attributes. Individuals without Internet access are given free subscriptions and, if necessary, a computer or WebTV; those with Internet access are given free subscriptions to complete the surveys. If a client commissions a survey, KN randomly draws a sample of, say, 1,000 respondents from its population of online

BOX 6.3

It Depends on How You Ask

THE SITUATION

The public's desire for tax cuts can be hard to measure. In 2000, pollsters asked what should be done with the nation's budget surplus and got different results depending on the specifics of the question.

THE QUESTION

President [Bill] Clinton has proposed setting aside approximately two-thirds of an expected budget surplus to fix the Social Security system. What do you think the leaders in Washington should do with the remainder of the surplus?

VARIATION 1

Should the money be used for a tax cut, or should it be used to fund new government programs?

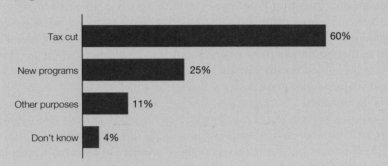

VARIATION 2

Should the money be used for a tax cut, or should it be spent on programs for education, the environment, health care, crime fighting, and military defense?

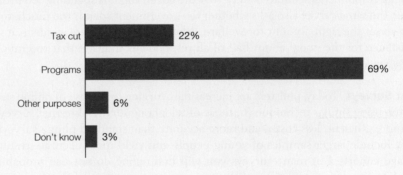

SOURCE: Pew Research Center, reported in the *New York Times*, January 30, 2000, WK 3.

respondents. Because respondents have agreed to complete a number of surveys in exchange for free Internet access, they are more likely to complete the surveys.

Other polling companies use different methods for conducting Internet surveys, often by using statistical weights to make the surveys generally representative of the American population.[93] Internet surveys such as the Cooperative Congressional Election Study can have very large samples, up to 50,000 people. In the future, Internet surveys may be more representative of the American population than traditional telephone surveys and may replace telephone surveys entirely, especially given falling response rates and the growing number of households without land-line phones but using cell phones exclusively.

Critics of Internet surveys contend that the samples may still be biased by not including enough respondents from groups that are more likely to be offline, especially non–English speakers, Latinos, the elderly, and the poor. Online surveys may include more respondents who are interested in politics than the normal population. Proponents contend that minorities and the poor are increasingly online, even via mobile access, and that the samples are representative of the American population. Because online surveys from sites such as YouGov have proved to be more accurate in forecasting elections than many telephone surveys relying on cell phones and landlines, online surveys are likely here to stay.[94]

Face-to-Face Surveys With more than 60 years' experience studying American politics, the American National Election Studies (ANES) is the premier broad general survey. The ANES traditionally has conducted surveys using face-to-face interviews, but because interviewing respondents in person is very costly, the ANES uses a multistage, stratified probability sample of 2,000-plus respondents from regions of the country (what they call "primary sampling units"). While this method approximates a simple random sample of the entire population, it does not guarantee random samples within states; all respondents from Iowa may be from Des Moines, for example. This can cause problems for generalizing the results for individual states. Even the ANES has begun experimenting with adding Internet surveys to its traditional face-to-face surveys. However, in-person surveys remain one of the most valuable and accurate ways to conduct interviews, and thus, the ANES is an important source of survey data in political science.

Though pollsters are increasingly turning to online surveys, face-to-face interviews remain an important method for data collection as they are often more accurate, have higher response rates, and enable the interviewer to better observe the attitude and behavior of respondents.

Framing Experiments within Surveys

Surveys are increasingly drawing on experimental techniques in which one group of respondents is given a treatment, or unique question wording, and responses are compared with a control group of respondents that does not receive the treatment. For example, the widespread tendency to base survey responses on the way questions are worded or "framed" provides a way to measure public opinion—through what are called "framing experiments." Because of the media's power to shape public opinion, framing experiments are an important tool for measuring how the media and government shape political attitudes.

Researchers often use framing experiments (in surveys or laboratory experiments) to understand how subtle changes in the structure of political information can result in the expression of different political opinions. In one experiment, individuals in one group were exposed to a frame arguing that affirmative action is necessary to correct past discrimination, while those in a second group received a competing frame arguing that affirmative action gives African Americans special treatment. Not surprisingly, those in the first group showed greater support for affirmative action than did those in the second group for the same policies. By using a treatment and control group design, framing experiments provide more leverage in assessing cause and effect in measuring changes in public opinion.

The researchers Dennis Chong and Jamie Druckman have extended how we measure framing effects on public opinion by testing the effect of competing frames to create more realistic models of real-world political debate, where citizens are exposed to multiple perspectives on candidates and political issues.[95] Such competing frames can be expected to have different effects in shaping public opinion on a policy. In the marketplace of ideas, it matters whether, say, the wealthiest Americans are characterized as the 1 percent or alternatively as "business leaders" and "job creators." Framing experiments help researchers understand how public opinion changes in the face of new information. Framing by the media, political groups, or candidates matters because individuals often form opinions based on the latest information and arguments they are exposed to—what is "on the top of their heads"—and as a result, public-opinion polls often merely measure whatever recent elite cues (or media stories) individual respondents happen to have stored in their short-term memory.[96] Thus, framing experiments are an important way to understand how public opinion moves in response to political elites and the mass media.

When Polls Are Wrong

The history of polling over the past century contains many instances of getting it wrong and learning valuable lessons in the process. As a result, polling techniques have grown more and more sophisticated, and pollsters have a more and more nuanced understanding of how public opinion is formed and how it is revealed. Polls are best understood as best guesses of a political outcome but not a prediction of fact.

Social Desirability Effects Political scientists have found that survey results can be inaccurate when the surveys include questions about sensitive issues for which individuals do not wish to share their true preferences. For example, respondents tend to overreport voting in elections and the frequency of their church attendance because these activities are deemed socially appropriate. Political scientist Adam Berinsky calls this the **social desirability effect**, whereby respondents report what they expect the interviewer wishes to hear or whatever they think is socially acceptable, rather than what they actually believe or know to be true.[97] On other topics, such as questions about income or alcohol and drug use, respondents may feel self-conscious and choose not to answer.

Questions that ask directly about race or gender are particularly problematic. Social desirability makes it difficult to learn voters' true opinions about touchy subjects such as racial attitudes because respondents hide their preferences from the interviewer for fear of social retribution (against what might be deemed "politically incorrect" opinions). Berinsky, for example, found respondents in surveys didn't want to admit that they opposed school integration and would not vote for the black candidate and, therefore, abstained from answering the question. Measuring public opinion can be a challenge; measuring opinions incorrectly can bias the findings. However, surveys using experiments can be designed to tap respondents' latent or hidden feelings about sensitive issues without directly asking them to express overt opinions.

Selection Bias The importance of accurate sampling was brought home early in the history of political polling. A 1936 *Literary Digest* poll predicted that the Republican candidate, Alf Landon, would defeat the Democratic incumbent, Franklin Roosevelt, in that year's presidential election. The actual election, of course, ended in a Roosevelt landslide. The main problem with the survey was what is called **selection bias** in drawing the sample. The pollsters had relied on telephone directories and automobile registration rosters to produce the survey sample. During the Great Depression, though, only wealthier Americans owned telephones and automobiles. Thus, the millions of working-class Americans who constituted Roosevelt's base of support were excluded from the sample.

social desirability effect
the effect that results when respondents in a survey report what they expect the interviewer wishes to hear rather than what they believe

selection bias (surveys) polling error that arises when the sample is not representative of the population being studied, which creates errors in overrepresenting or underrepresenting some opinions

Selection bias was also at play in preelection polls in the 2012 presidential election, when Gallup significantly overestimated Latino support for the Republican candidate, suggesting a close race between the Republican candidate, Mitt Romney, and the Democratic candidate, Barack Obama. The Gallup numbers were incorrect because of selection bias (that is, they had too few Latinos in their sample and therefore their predictions were inaccurate). Estimates based on aggregating information from many different statewide public opinion polls were more accurate.[98] In the 2016 presidential election, although most polls predicted the direction of the popular vote correctly in Hillary Clinton's favor, they failed to predict the size of the vote margin and the election outcome (see Figure 6.8). Not since the 1936 presidential election have the polls been so wrong. Clinton won the popular vote, but she lost to Donald Trump in the electoral college. Reasons for the polling inaccuracies included the use of "likely voter models," which left out some groups

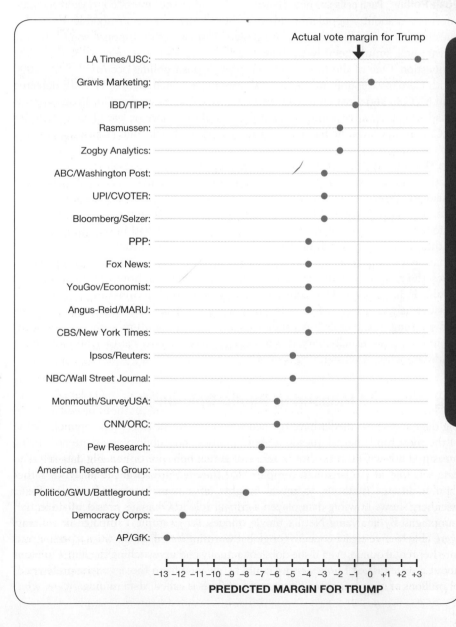

Actual vote margin for Trump

PREDICTED MARGIN FOR TRUMP

FIGURE 6.8

Accuracy of Final Preelection Polls, 2016

A large number of news organizations conducted polls to predict the outcome of the 2016 election. For how many of these polls was the actual result within their margin of error, assuming a sample size of 1,000 and a margin of error of plus or minus 3.1 percent? What might explain why some respected organizations, like Pew and Politico, were so far off the mark?

SOURCES: All poll data, except LATimes/USC, from HuffPost Pollster, www.elections.huffingtonpost.com/pollster (accessed 11/10/16). Poll results are from the most recent polls prior to election day in the database. USC/LATimes data from www.cesrusc.org/election/ (accessed 11/11/16). Popular vote margin data from "CNN 2016 Election Results," www.cnn.com/election/results (accessed 11/11/16).

that ended up voting at higher-than-usual rates, such as rural and blue-collar voters who supported Trump in large numbers; social desirability bias in which respondents didn't want to admit their support for Trump; and "nonresponse bias," where Trump supporters were less likely to respond to surveys. The LA Times/USC survey accurately predicted a Trump win, relying on a different methodology than the others.

In recent years, the issue of selection bias has been complicated by the fact that growing numbers of individuals refuse to answer pollsters' questions, or they use such devices as answering machines and caller ID to screen unwanted callers. If pollsters could be certain that those who responded to their surveys simply reflected the views of those who refused to respond, there would be no problem. Some studies, however, suggest that the views of respondents and nonrespondents can differ, especially along social class lines. This can lead to incorrect inferences of public opinion.

push poll a polling technique in which the questions are designed to shape the respondent's opinion

Push Polling **Push polls** are not scientific polls and are not intended to yield accurate information about a population. Instead, they involve asking a respondent a loaded question about a political candidate designed to elicit the response sought by the pollster and, simultaneously, to shape the respondent's perception of the candidate in question. One of the most notorious uses of push polling occurred in the 2000 South Carolina Republican presidential primary, in which George W. Bush defeated John McCain and went on to win the presidency. Callers working for Bush supporters asked conservative white voters if they would be more or less likely to vote for McCain if they knew he had fathered an illegitimate black child (a false statement).

bandwagon effect a shift in electoral support to the candidate whom public opinion polls report as the front-runner

The Bandwagon Effect Public-opinion polls can influence political realities and elections. In fact, sometimes polling can even create its own reality. The so-called **bandwagon effect** occurs when polling results convince people to support a candidate marked as the probable victor. This is especially true in the presidential nomination process, where there may be multiple candidates within one party vying to be the party's nominee. Todd Donovan and his coauthors found that the change in national media coverage received by a candidate before and after the Iowa caucuses, the first nominating event, was a major predictor of how well the candidate would do in the New Hampshire primary (the second nominating event) and in presidential primaries nationwide, controlling for other factors including money and standing in the polls.[99] A candidate who has "momentum"—that is, one leading in the polls—usually finds it considerably easier to raise campaign funds than a candidate whose poll standing is poor.

for critical analysis

Is it important that public-opinion polls be accurate? How might polls fail to be accurate? What are the consequences if polls are systematically inaccurate?

Big Data and Measuring Public Opinion

Big data and social media have opened new ways to measure mass opinion. Some of the most fundamental questions about politics and public opinion are now being measured not with surveys but in terms of actual behavior online. Big data refers to data sets that are so large and complex that they require advanced analytics, rather than traditional methods, to reveal insights on a massive scale. Journalist Sasha Issenberg shows how big data played a critical role in Obama's presidential election campaigns. By analyzing Netflix movie queues, for example, campaign consultants were able to investigate concern for global warming based on the titles a person puts into her rental queue, even if she does not actually end up watching the film. Opinions about a wide range of policy issues could be gleaned from the aggregate preferences of millions of movie viewers. This type of analysis is called "data mining."[100]

Though public opinion is important, it is not always easy to interpret, and polls often fail to predict accurately how Americans will vote. In 1948, election-night polls showed Thomas Dewey defeating Harry S. Truman for the presidency. The Chicago Daily Tribune *trusted the polls and incorrectly printed a banner headline proclaiming Dewey the winner, which a triumphant Truman displayed when he won the election by a margin of approximately 4 percent.*

Twitter, the preferred medium of candidates and political elites, introduces another way to measure public opinion and agenda setting using text analysis. A new study analyzed the number of Twitter followers for the 2016 presidential candidates and tracked changes over time, as well as tracking mentions of any of the candidates based on millions of tweets. A candidate's lead in positive Twitter coverage may be more important to winning the White House than a lead in traditional public-opinion polls. Coding large amounts of Twitter data can also be valuable for measuring phenomena that are difficult or impossible to measure with standard telephone surveys, such as the use of racial slurs.

Beyond Twitter, big data are playing a role in forecasting and predictive analytics. As noted above, blogger Nate Silver became an overnight sensation in 2008 by aggregating thousands of public-opinion polls conducted in each of the 50 states to predict the winner of the presidential election state by state more accurately than any single polling house—a feat he repeated in 2012 though he was often incorrect in predicting the winner in the tumultuous 2016 primaries.[101]

The Democratic Party and the Republican Party now use a database of 240 million Americans including a wide range of data from voting history and party registration, social media, consumer purchasing patterns, and so on. Using big data and data mining, researchers can predict factors that make a person more likely to vote in the first place and whether he will cast a vote for the Republican or Democratic candidate. Data mining has been used for years in business, marketing, and economics but is growing in importance in campaigns, elections, and policy. The study of politics has been on the forefront of this big data revolution with sophisticated analyses of massive amounts of data including text scraping and text analysis of social media. These are just a few examples of how very large sample data—millions and millions of data points—are changing how we measure public opinion in the digital age.

Public Opinion, Democracy, **and Your Future**

This chapter has focused on the role of public opinion in American politics. A major purpose of democratic government, with its participatory procedures and representative institutions, is to ensure that political leaders will heed the public will. And, indeed, a good deal of evidence suggests that they do. There are many instances in which public policy and public opinion do not coincide, but often the government's actions are consistent with citizens' preferences, at least in the most general sense.[102]

Some political scientists argue, however, that government policy is much less responsive to public opinion on the issues that really count and that when the interests of elites are at stake, government officials are much more likely to represent the opinions of the affluent than the poor.[103] People in lower income groups, however, are less likely to actively seek out ways to express their political opinions than are wealthier people (see the "**Who Participates?**" feature on the facing page).

New technology may be able to help. The migration of politics online has greatly expanded the amount of information available and the ease of becoming informed. And as we will see in Chapter 7, online media are more diverse than traditional media. Given this new media environment, we might expect public opinion to be more accurate, even about the nuances of public policy. Digital citizenship offers the promise of a more informed electorate, with citizens having multiple venues in which to translate their opinions into political action and demand improved representation from political leaders. At the same time, the Internet raises new concerns about the accuracy and consistency of public opinion.

As Chapter 7 will show, Americans may become trapped in a "filter bubble" in which they are exposed only to news consistent with their political preferences. There are Internet vandals, or "bomb throwers," who defame other people and their opinions in ways that may negatively color public opinion. Misinformation—rumor masked as legitimate news—may be more common, especially in blogs. Some research finds that the gap between the haves and the have-nots in terms of political knowledge actually increases with the availability of more information. The implications are significant, given the explosion of political coverage online. The research suggests that with more information, public opinion may actually be less consistent.[104]

The Internet may be reshaping what is public opinion. The effects of new media—vast and still unfolding—include the wide dissemination of public-opinion polls and the rise of Internet polling. Do new media make public opinion more or less important? Do they make elected officials more or less responsive to the citizens? Time will tell.

Who Expresses Their Political Opinions?

By income group

⊘ < $20,000   ● $20,000–$39,999   ● $40,000–$74,999   ● $75,000+

Attended a town or city council meeting

13%   16%   21%   27%

Signed a petition

25%   30%   38%   43%

Attended a protest march

5%   6%   7%   7%

Tried to contact a member of Congress

13%   15%   22%   31%

SOURCE: American National Election Study 2012 Time Series, www.electionstudies.org (accessed 9/25/15).

WHAT YOU CAN DO

Be an Informed Consumer of Opinion Polls

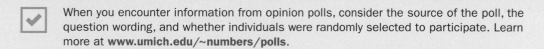

☑ When you encounter information from opinion polls, consider the source of the poll, the question wording, and whether individuals were randomly selected to participate. Learn more at **www.umich.edu/~numbers/polls**.

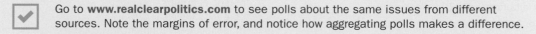

☑ Go to **www.realclearpolitics.com** to see polls about the same issues from different sources. Note the margins of error, and notice how aggregating polls makes a difference.

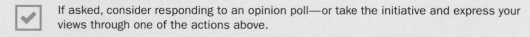

☑ If asked, consider responding to an opinion poll—or take the initiative and express your views through one of the actions above.

study guide

Defining Public Opinion

> **Define public opinion, and identify broad types of values and beliefs Americans have about politics (pp. 201–8)**

Public opinion refers to the attitudes that people have about issues, events, elected officials, and public policy. Despite differences in opinion on many issues, most Americans share a common set of values, including a belief in the principles of liberty, equality, and democracy. Contemporary liberalism and conservatism have different emphases with regard to the values of liberty and equality.

Key Terms

public opinion (p. 201)

values (or beliefs) (p. 201)

political ideology (p. 201)

attitude (or opinion) (p. 201)

liberty (p. 203)

equality of opportunity (p. 203)

liberal (p. 205)

conservative (p. 206)

libertarian (p. 206)

socialist (p. 206)

Practice Quiz

1. The term *public opinion* is used to describe
   a) the speeches and writings made by a president during his or her term in office.
   b) the analysis of events broadcast by news reporters during the evening news.
   c) the beliefs and attitudes that people have about issues, events, elected officials, and policies.
   d) decisions of the Supreme Court.
   e) any political statement that is made by a citizen outside of his or her home.

2. Today, the term _____ refers to an ideology that supports social and political reform, greater economic equality, and expansion of government social services.
   a) libertarianism
   b) liberalism
   c) conservatism
   d) democracy
   e) moderate

3. Libertarianism refers to
   a) a political ideology that emphasizes social ownership and strong government.
   b) a political ideology that emphasizes freedom and voluntary association with small government.
   c) a political ideology that argues for the need to place strict limitations on voting rights and civil liberties.
   d) a political ideology that argues a single ruler should have total control over every aspect of people's lives.
   e) a political ideology that argues governments are inherently repressive and should be abolished entirely.

How We Form Political Opinions

> **Explain the major factors that shape specific individual opinions (pp. 208–19)**

A number of factors, including the family, education, membership in social groups, self-interest, and the political environment, help form people's underlying political beliefs and values.

Key Terms

political socialization (p. 209)

agents of socialization (p. 209)

gender gap (p. 213)

Practice Quiz

4. The process by which Americans learn political beliefs and values is called
   a) brainwashing.
   b) propaganda.
   c) indoctrination.
   d) political socialization.
   e) political development.

5. Which of the following is an agent of socialization?
   a) the family
   b) social groups
   c) education
   d) political environment
   e) All of the above are agents of socialization.

Political Knowledge and Changes in Public Opinion

As people encounter new information, it may (or may not) influence their opinions. Many people acquire political information and make political decisions by relying on cues from party elites, interest groups, trusted acquaintances, and the mass media. However, inadequate knowledge can prevent individuals from effectively defending their political interests.

Practice Quiz

6. Which of the following statements about political knowledge is not accurate?
   a) In general, citizens with high levels of political knowledge are more likely to be partisans (Democrats or Republicans).
   b) In general, citizens with high levels of political knowledge are more likely to have an ideology (liberal or conservative).
   c) In general, citizens with high levels of political knowledge are better able to evaluate new information and determine if it is consistent with their beliefs and opinions.
   d) In general, citizens with high levels of political knowledge are less likely to belong to political organizations and to be active in politics.
   e) In general, citizens with high levels of political knowledge are better able to recognize their political interests and to act to further those interests.

7. Recent research in political science indicates that partisan polarization has
   a) prevented party endorsements of an issue or candidate from ever playing a role in the formation of public opinion.
   b) led party endorsements of an issue or candidate to have a smaller impact on the formation of public opinion than they used to.
   c) led party endorsements of an issue or candidate to have a larger impact on the formation of public opinion than they used to.
   d) led to an exponential increase in the amount of political knowledge most Americans possess.
   e) had no effect on public opinion or on how people form their political attitudes.

The Media, Government, and Public Opinion

When individuals form opinions about specific issues, events, and politicians, they do not do so in isolation. They are bombarded by the efforts of many individuals and groups seeking to persuade them. Government officials and interest groups rely on messaging and a variety of media to get their messages across to citizens. The news media also serve as a powerful force in creating opinion and influencing popular attitudes.

Key Term

marketplace of ideas (p. 226)

Practice Quiz

8. Which of the following are the most important external influences on how political opinions are formed in the marketplace of ideas?
   a) the government, private groups, and the news media
   b) the unemployment rate, the Dow Jones industrial average, and the NASDAQ composite
   c) random digit dialing surveys, push polls, and framing experiments
   d) the Constitution, the Declaration of Independence, and the *Federalist Papers*
   e) the legislative branch, the executive branch, and the judicial branch

Public Opinion and Government Policy

Analyze how public opinion shapes government policy and influences elected officials (pp. 229–31)

Although there are many instances where government policy differs from the desires of the public, research has shown that there is generally a strong connection between what government does and what people want. Research has also shown, however, that more affluent and more educated citizens have a disproportionate influence over policy decisions.

Practice Quiz

9. Which statement best describes the relationship between public opinion and government policy?
   a) Public opinion almost never influences government policy.
   b) Government policy almost never influences public opinion.
   c) The relationship between government policy and public opinion is dynamic, wherein government policy responds to public opinion but public opinion also shifts based on new government policies.
   d) Public opinion always influences government policy because lawmakers are legally bound to enact the majority's preferences.
   e) Government policy never influences public opinion because most Americans pay very little attention to politics.

Measuring Public Opinion

Describe basic survey methods and other techniques researchers use to measure public opinion (pp. 231–41)

Surveys can provide a very accurate description of public opinion on an issue if they employ an appropriate sampling method, include a sufficient sample size, and avoid selection bias. In addition to the characteristics of the sample, the reliability of surveys is determined by the ordering and wording of the questions pollsters choose to ask.

Key Terms

public-opinion polls (p. 233)

sample (p. 233)

simple random sample (or probability sample) (p. 233)

random digit dialing (p. 233)

sampling error (or margin of error) (p. 234)

social desirability effect (p. 238)

selection bias (p. 238)

push poll (p. 240)

bandwagon effect (p. 240)

Practice Quiz

10. Which of the following is the term used in public-opinion polling to denote the small group representing the opinions of the whole population?
    a) control group
    b) sample
    c) micropopulation
    d) respondents
    e) median voters

11. A *push poll* is a poll in which
    a) the questions are designed to shape the respondent's opinion rather than measure the respondent's opinion.
    b) the questions are designed to measure the respondent's opinion rather than shape the respondent's opinion.
    c) the questions are designed to reduce measurement error.
    d) the sample is chosen to include only undecided or independent voters.
    e) the sample is not representative of the population it is drawn from.

12. A familiar polling problem is the *bandwagon effect*, which occurs when
    a) the same results are used over and over again.
    b) polling results influence people to support the candidate marked as the probable victor in a campaign.
    c) polling results influence people to support the candidate who is trailing in a campaign.
    d) background noise makes it difficult for a pollster and a respondent to communicate with each other.
    e) a large number of people refuse to answer a pollster's questions.

For Further Reading

Asher, Herbert. *Polling and the Public: What Every Citizen Should Know*. 8th ed. Washington, DC: CQ Press, 2011.

Barreto, Matt, and Gary M. Segura. *Latino America: How America's Most Dynamic Population Is Poised to Transform the Politics of the Nation*. New York: Public Affairs, 2014.

Bartels, Larry. *Unequal Democracy*. Princeton, NJ: Princeton University Press, 2008.

Berinsky, Adam. *Silent Voices: Public Opinion and Political Participation in America*. Princeton, NJ: Princeton University Press, 2005.

Clawson, Rosalee, and Zoe Oxley. *Public Opinion: Democratic Ideals and Democratic Practice*. Washington, DC: CQ Press, 2008.

Delli Carpini, Michael, and Scott Keeter. *What Americans Know about Politics and Why It Matters*. New Haven, CT: Yale University Press, 1997.

Erikson, Robert, Michael MacKuen, and James Simson. *The Macro Polity*. New York: Cambridge University Press, 2002.

Gallup, George. *The Pulse of Democracy*. New York: Simon and Schuster, 1940.

Gilens, Martin. *Affluence and Influence: Economic Inequality and Political Power in America*. Princeton, NJ: Princeton University Press, 2012.

Ginsberg, Benjamin. *The Captive Public: How Mass Opinion Promotes State Power*. New York: Basic Books, 1986.

Griffin, John, and Brian Newman. *Minority Report: Evaluating Political Equality in America*. New York: Cambridge University Press, 2008.

Hutchings, Vincent. *Public Opinion and Democratic Accountability: How Citizens Learn about Politics*. Princeton, NJ: Princeton University Press, 2005.

Lau, Richard, and David Redlawsk. *How Voters Decide: Information Processing in an Election Campaign*. New York: Cambridge University Press, 2006.

Lee, Taeku. *Mobilizing Public Opinion*. Chicago: University of Chicago Press, 2002.

Lippmann, Walter. *Public Opinion*. 1922. http://xroads .virginia.edu/~Hyper2/CDFinal/Lippman/cover.html.

Lodge, Milton, and Charles S. Taber. *The Rationalizing Voter*. New York: Cambridge University Press, 2013.

Marcus, George E., W. Russell Neuman, and Michael MacKuen. *Affective Intelligence and Political Judgment*. Chicago: University of Chicago Press, 2000.

Norrander, Barbara, and Clyde Wilcox. *Understanding Public Opinion*. Washington, DC: CQ Press, 2009.

Tesler, Michael, and David O. Sears. *Obama's Race: The 2008 Election and the Dream of a Post-Racial America*. Chicago: University of Chicago Press, 2010.

Wlezien, Christopher, and Stuart Soroka. *Degrees of Democracy: Politics, Public Opinion, and Policy*. New York: Cambridge University Press, 2010.

Zaller, John. *The Nature and Origins of Mass Opinion*. New York: Cambridge University Press, 1992.

Recommended Websites

American Association for Public Opinion Research
www.aapor.org
This website is one of the premier academic sites for public opinion data on a host of political and social topics.

FiveThirtyEight
www.fivethirtyeight.com/politics
FiveThirtyEight, named for the number of electors in the Electoral College, was founded as a polling aggregator site by political analyst Nate Silver. The blog now covers a broad range of topics, but it is still widely known for Silver's election forecasts.

Gallup
www.gallup.com
The Gallup Organization has been involved in the scientific study of public opinion for more than 70 years and is highly regarded. This website contains public-opinion data archives, video archives, and international polls.

Latino Decisions
www.latinodecisions.com
A leader in Latino opinion research, Latino Decisions presents data and analysis on Latino American political opinions, attitudes, and engagement.

Pew Religion and Public Life
www.pewforum.org
Pew Religion and Public Life conducts public opinion polling, demographic research, and content analyses of attitudes about religion and politics. Pew Research Center is an independent, nonpartisan think tank that also explores attitudes toward numerous other political issues.

Real Clear Politics
www.realclearpolitics.com
This website aggregates top news stories, analyses, editorials, videos, and polls with the goal of providing users with ideological diversity. The "Polls" section averages polling data for presidential and congressional races and has often been an effective predictor of election outcomes.

Political candidates who receive positive news coverage gain momentum, which helps them attract campaign contributions and endorsements and eventually win votes. The influence of the media on political campaigns is just one example of its important role in American democracy.

The Media

WHAT GOVERNMENT DOES AND WHY IT MATTERS The Constitution's First Amendment guarantees freedom of the press, and most Americans believe that a free press is an essential condition for both liberty and democratic politics. Today, the media play a central role in American politics, not only in setting the agenda of topics that Americans think about and discuss but also in swaying public opinion on political issues and politicians.

The digital revolution has rapidly changed the media industry, journalism, and how citizens get their news, fundamentally altering the media's role in politics. Just 20 years ago the majority of Americans got their political news by reading a daily newspaper, listening to the radio, or watching the local and national evening news from one of the three major networks (ABC, CBS, and NBC). Today, more Americans read the news online than read a print newspaper, and those reading digital news are more likely to vote and participate in politics in other ways.[1] In 2015, 1 in 10 Americans found political news on Twitter, 4 in 10 on Facebook, and 3 in 4 on social media of some sort—platforms that did not exist before 2000. Traditional media such as newspapers and television must also compete with digital-only media that tailor news to their readers and viewers.[2]

Political communication and news have entered a new era in which there is interplay between older and new media forms. Often, traditional media offer detailed coverage of news that is first broken online via social media. Ordinary citizens navigate the terrain of hybrid media—a blend of traditional and digital media—daily as they seek political information. In this new landscape, political news is generated by a wider range of individuals and groups than ever before, including professional journalists, parties and election campaigns, activists, researchers, politicians, celebrities, and the government. Sometimes citizens make headline news as their video cameras and tweets record political protests, police shootings, or scandals as they unfold on the ground.

The political implications of this media system are significant. Politics is increasingly defined by the individuals and groups who are best able to blend older and newer media—using, for example, both television and digital media to promote their message.[3] Sometimes politicians bypass traditional media altogether, going directly to their supporters using social media.

Digital media such as Twitter have caused the public's demand for round-the-clock, real-time news to skyrocket. The 2016 presidential candidates used Twitter extensively in their political campaigns. Notably, Donald Trump frequently tweeted provocative attacks on his rivals and even members of his own party. The number of articles written about the 2016 candidates also increased dramatically compared to previous elections. Trump in particular received an extraordinary level of media attention. Was the media capitalizing on Trump's novel campaign style, including his Twitter rants, for profits and traffic? Or was the media simply fulfilling their watchdog role by informing the public?

The sharing of information, whether via traditional or digital media, is an essential component of American democracy. Discussing the right of press freedom, Thomas Jefferson wrote, "The basis of our government being the opinion of the people, the very first object should be to keep that right; and were it left to me to decide whether we should have a government without newspapers or newspapers without a government, I should not hesitate a moment to prefer the latter."[4]

chaptergoals

- Describe trends in the role of print and broadcast media in providing political information (pp. 251–58)

- Explain how the Internet has transformed the news media (pp. 258–67)

- Analyze the ways the media can influence public opinion and politics (pp. 267–74)

- Explain how politicians and others try to shape the news (pp. 274–77)

- Trace the evolution of rules that govern broadcast media (pp. 277–80)

Traditional Media

Describe trends in the role of print and broadcast media in providing political information

The American news **media** are among the world's freest and most diverse. Americans have thousands of available options in political reporting. The wide variety of local and national newspapers, newsmagazines, broadcast media, and digital sources regularly present information that is at odds with the government's claims; and editorial opinions that are sharply critical of high-ranking officials. The freedom to speak one's mind is one of the most cherished of American political values. Without the news media's investigations, citizens would be forced to rely entirely on information provided by politicians and the government and would be deprived of information necessary to evaluate issues carefully and form reasoned opinions.

Americans get their news from (1) print media, including newspapers and magazines; (2) **broadcast media** (radio and television); and, increasingly, (3) digital media. While television remains the public's top source for news, digital media are now second most important. Among those under 50 years of age, digital media are where the majority get their news. This pattern is found across racial and ethnic groups. Within the category of digital media, social media have become a primary source of news for many Americans, and today reading news on mobile devices and cell phones has become more common than reading from desktop computers or reading print newspapers.

This picture is very different from that in the early 2000s, when most Americans said that after television, newspapers were their main source for news and less than 20 percent used the Internet as a primary source (see Figure 7.1).[5] The rise of the Internet has led to a profound shift in the media and politics over the past two decades. In 1998, the first year the U.S. Census began asking about Internet use at home, just 25 percent of Americans had Internet access.[6] Today, over 80 percent of Americans use the Internet. Among Internet users three in four read the news online.[7]

Each of these three sources—print, broadcast, and digital—has distinctive characteristics. We discuss trends in print and broadcast media in this section, and in the next section we will take a close look at the vast world of digital media and how it is changing the media industry and the way Americans get political news.

Print Media

Newspapers are the oldest medium for the dissemination of the news. Though no longer the primary news source for most Americans, print newspapers remain important because they are influential among the political elite, who rely on the detailed coverage provided by professional journalists to inform their views about public matters. The print media may have a smaller audience than their newer cousins in broadcasting and digital media, but they have an especially influential audience because they help set the political agenda for the nation. As discussed below, some of the top digital news sources are online versions of print newspapers.

The emergence of newspapers (and later radio and television networks) as mass-production businesses driven primarily for profit had major implications for the role of the media in politics in the late nineteenth and early twentieth

media print and digital forms of communication, including television, newspapers, radio, and the Internet, intended to convey information to large audiences

broadcast media television, radio, or other media that transmit audio and/or video content to the public

The circulation and newsstand sales of traditional newspapers and news magazines have fallen in the last decade. However, because the remaining audience includes political elites and politically engaged citizens, they remain important forums in the marketplace of ideas.

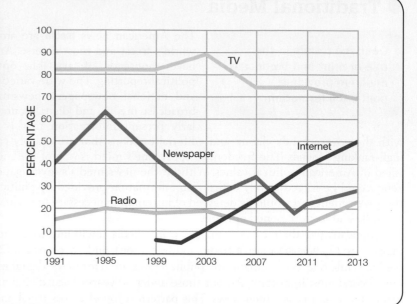

FIGURE 7.1

Americans' Main Sources for News

The media landscape for news has seen remarkable shifts in a short period of time. Twenty years ago, more than 80 percent of Americans watched news on television and more than half read news in a newspaper. Today, fewer Americans watch news on TV and just over one-quarter read the newspaper. What media source has gained rather than lost its audience?

SOURCE: Pew Research Center, "Amid Criticism, Support for Media's 'Watchdog' Role Stands Out." August 8, 2013, www.people-press.org/2013/08/08/amid-criticism-support-for-medias-watchdog-role-stands-out (accessed 4/27/14).

centuries. For example, the development of standardized reporting and writing practices that emphasized "objectivity" in political news coverage was due in large part to this shift in the structure of media organizations. The owners of large newspaper companies, concentrated in urban areas, determined that the best way to make a profit was to appeal to as broad an audience as possible, which meant not alienating potential readers who held liberal or conservative political views. This, in turn, required methods to train and "discipline" reporters to produce a standardized, seemingly neutral news product. Specialized journalism schools and major journalism prizes were founded largely with money from media moguls (Joseph Pulitzer, William Randolph Hearst) who owned the first large news corporations, rewarding standardized news reporting. In contrast, some digital news, as discussed in the next section, is much less likely to be value-neutral like journalism from legacy media outlets.

These journalistic practices were successful in attracting audiences, and for a long time, most cities and towns in the country had their own newspaper. However, the long reign of newspapers as leading political news sources appears to be waning, and for most traditional newspapers, recent decades have been ruinous. Competition from broadcast media and, more recently, free content online, combined with simultaneous declines in advertising revenue and circulation levels, have undermined the traditional business model of newspapers, bringing financial disaster to traditional print media.[8] In 2015 there were roughly 36,000 working journalists, down from a high of 60,000 a decade before, a 40 percent decline.[9] Estimates indicate daily newspaper print circulation has declined by over 30 percent over the past 20 years.[10] Advertising revenue at print newspapers is half of what is was in 2005 (see Figure 7.2).[11]

For most newspapers today, non-ad revenue comes mainly from digital subscriptions rather than print circulation. The *New York Times*, for example, reported an average weekday print circulation of fewer than 650,000 copies in

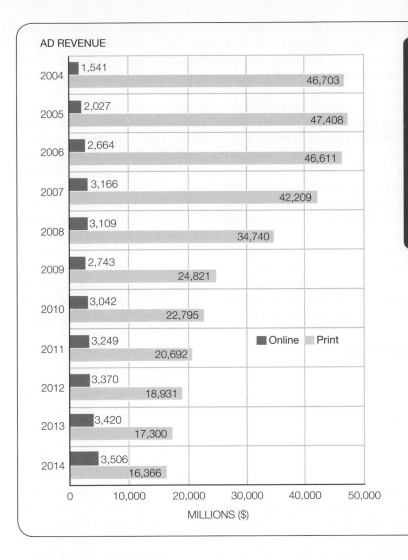

AD REVENUE

Year	Online	Print
2004	1,541	46,703
2005	2,027	47,408
2006	2,664	46,611
2007	3,166	42,209
2008	3,109	34,740
2009	2,743	24,821
2010	3,042	22,795
2011	3,249	20,692
2012	3,370	18,931
2013	3,420	17,300
2014	3,506	16,366

MILLIONS ($)

FIGURE 7.2

Advertising Revenue

Media is a business, not a branch of government, so media rely on subscription and advertising money to fund their services. As print newspapers' readership declined, their advertising revenue fell sharply. Some of this money shifted to online advertising, including ads for mobile devices.

SOURCE: Newspaper Association of America (2003–2013), Pew Research analysis of BIA/Kelsey data (2014), www .journalism.org/media-indicators/newspaper-print-and -online-ad-revenue/ (accessed 2/3/16).

September 2014, but by 2015 the *Times* had 1.4 million paid subscribers.[12] Many of the newspapers with the highest digital traffic are also those with the greatest circulation.

People continue to turn to traditional news organizations, but increasingly to their digital versions, as most print newspapers now have a significant online presence. Faced with shrinking revenues from print, news organizations such as the *Washington Post*, the *New York Times*, and the *Economist* were among the first to charge customers for reading the news online. Paid digital news is increasing revenue and improving content. This metered model allows a certain number of free visits before requiring users to pay and appears to be a viable business model for the digital press.

Text-based, print newspapers face the greatest competition from digital-only news outlets, such as Politico, the Drudge Report, the Huffington Post, and a host of others discussed below. Pew reports that there are so many new media platforms and so much experimentation in digital media that it is difficult to measure—but the pace of technological change in the news media shows no signs of slowing down.[13]

As a result of financial losses, newspapers have had to make dramatic cutbacks. Employment in print newsrooms continues to fall each year. These cutbacks have affected papers both big and small. For example the *Chicago Tribune*, the *Minneapolis Star Tribune*, and the *Philadelphia Inquirer* have sought bankruptcy protection; and many others have gone out of business altogether.

The effects of a decade of newsroom cutbacks are evident in the political sphere. During the 2012 presidential election, one report showed that campaign reporters were acting primarily as megaphones, rather than as investigators, of the claims made by the candidates. These findings indicate a decline in investigative reporting by journalists to interpret the claims made by the candidates resulting in the media playing less of a watchdog role than in previous years. Readers, too, noticed this shift: Pew found that nearly one-third of U.S. adults had stopped turning to a news outlet because it no longer provided them with the quality of news they were used to receiving.[14] The media were widely criticized during the 2016 presidential campaign for a lack of scrutiny and uneven coverage of candidates, but at the same time, some coverage was investigative. Investigative articles in the *Washington Post*, for example, revealed the history around candidate Donald Trump's casino bankruptcies as well as his ties to mafia-controlled organizations, while others focused on the defunct and fraudulent Trump University.[15]

Broadcast Media

Television news reaches more Americans than any other single news source. It is estimated that over 95 percent of Americans have a television, and tens of millions of people watch national and local news programs every day. Television news, however, generally covers relatively few topics and provides little depth of coverage. It serves the important function of alerting viewers to issues and events—headline news—via brief quotes and short characterizations of the day's events, often little more than a few seconds in length. Furthermore, broadcast media do very little of their own reporting, instead relying on leading newspapers such as the *New York Times* or, increasingly, digital media to set their news agenda. For example, sensational charges that President Bill Clinton had had an affair with a White House intern were reported first by the Drudge Report, a popular news website, and then picked up by the *Washington Post* and *Newsweek* before being trumpeted around the world by the broadcast media. Print and digital media, as written text, also provide more detailed and complete information than radio or television media, offering a better context for analysis.

Because they are aware of the character of television news coverage, politicians and others often seek to manipulate the news by providing the media with sound bites that will dominate news coverage for at least a few days. Sound bites can work for or against politicians. During the 2016 Republican primary races, calls for deporting illegal immigrants were a frequent sound bite topic from candidates such as Donald Trump and Ted Cruz. When another candidate, Marco Rubio, repeated the same statement criticizing Barack Obama four times during one debate, the media quickly latched onto the sound bite, mocking him as "Robot-Rubio."

Twenty-four-hour cable news stations such as Microsoft National Broadcasting Company (MSNBC) and Fox News offer more detail and commentary than the half-hour evening news shows found on the three broadcast news stations—ABC, NBC, and CBS. But even these channels offer more headlines and sound bites than news analysis, especially during their prime-time broadcasts.

Politicians generally consider local broadcast news a friendlier venue than the national news. National reporters are often inclined to criticize and question, whereas local and state reporters are more likely to accept the pronouncements of national leaders at face value. During the 2016 presidential campaign, Republican Donald Trump took a new strategy in responding to tough questioning by national reporters. After the first televised Republican presidential primary debate in 2015, the national media widely reported that Trump stumbled badly in responding to some tough questions about prior sexist remarks. In retaliation, Trump went on a Twitter rampage against one of the debate's moderators, Fox News host Megyn Kelly, in the early morning hours after the event. His angry public response resulted in more national media attention than the televised presidential debate itself. Strategically playing new media against old, Trump turned to social media to promote his message when traditional media threw him a hard ball. The result was a rise in his polling numbers.

As more Americans turn online for news and entertainment, cable television has experienced modest declines. The Pew Research Center found that cable news experienced an 8 percent decline in viewership across the three channels—Fox News, MSNBC, and CNN—in 2014. Local TV continues to be a major source of news, especially for older Americans, though its importance as a news source is decreasing among the younger generation in favor of social media such as Facebook (see Figure 7.3). Generally, however, Americans' reliance on television does not appear to be going away. From 2014 to 2015, network television experienced audience growth of 5 percent in evening news and 2 percent in morning news, with an average evening viewership of roughly 24 million across all networks.[16]

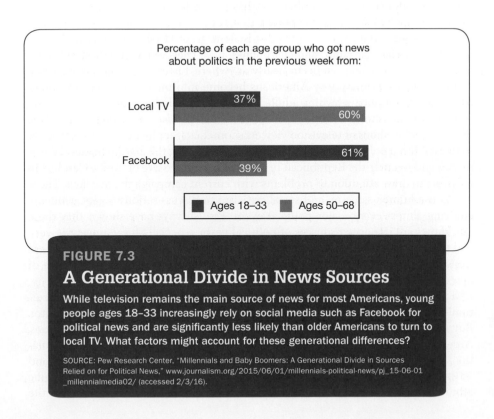

Percentage of each age group who got news about politics in the previous week from:

Local TV: 37% (Ages 18–33), 60% (Ages 50–68)

Facebook: 61% (Ages 18–33), 39% (Ages 50–68)

Ages 18–33 ■ Ages 50–68

FIGURE 7.3

A Generational Divide in News Sources

While television remains the main source of news for most Americans, young people ages 18–33 increasingly rely on social media such as Facebook for political news and are significantly less likely than older Americans to turn to local TV. What factors might account for these generational differences?

SOURCE: Pew Research Center, "Millennials and Baby Boomers: A Generational Divide in Sources Relied on for Political News," www.journalism.org/2015/06/01/millennials-political-news/pj_15-06-01 _millennialmedia02/ (accessed 2/3/16).

As the Hispanic population continues to grow, Latino-oriented news outlets are increasingly influential. Jorge Ramos is a popular news anchor on the Spanish-language network Univision, which in recent years has beat out major networks ABC, CBS, Fox, and NBC for the number one primetime spot.

Radio is another broadcast news source that has evolved in response to the rise of new media. In the 1990s talk radio became an important source of commentary as well as entertainment. Conservative radio hosts, such as Rush Limbaugh and Sean Hannity, have huge audiences and have helped to mobilize support for conservative political causes and candidates. In the political center or center left, National Public Radio (NPR) is a coveted source for in-depth political reporting. In recent years radio news listening has experienced significant growth; in 1990 there were 400 radio stations, a number that has grown to over 2,000 today. In 2015 more than half of Americans reported that they had listened to online radio in the past month; NPR's podcast downloads alone grew 41 percent. Mobile devices, including wireless car radios and cell phones, have triggered a growth in radio use as online radio listening can occur nearly anywhere. Listening to radio news while commuting is a primary way Americans become informed about politics; today, one in three cell phone–owning adults listens to online radio in the car.[17]

Comedy talk shows with political content, such as *The Daily Show* or *The Late Show*, attract millions of television viewers. Comedian Stephen Colbert went so far as to establish a political action committee (PAC) during the 2012 presidential primaries and to enter the Republican primary in his home state of South Carolina in an effort to draw attention to problems with current campaign finance laws. These shows use humor, sarcasm, and social criticism to discuss serious topics, generally covering almost every major political event. Pew surveys have shown that these talk shows are important sources of political news, especially for younger viewers, and that followers of comedic talk shows are well informed about politics.[18] These shows combine political news and entertainment and are an important source of news for young people.

The broadcast media are also diversifying as America becomes more multicultural. In 2014 the *New York Times* had its first African American executive editor. But racial minorities remain underrepresented at major U.S. news organizations. Although blacks and Latinos make up over one-third of the adult U.S. population, they account for only 22 percent of the local television news workforce and 13 percent of the local print media workforce.[19] News outlets aimed at specific ethnic groups, however, have become common in many areas. For example, the

Latino-oriented television channels Telemundo, Univision, and MSN Latino attract large audiences and may focus on topics or perspectives of particular interest to their audience, which are sometimes significantly different from those of mainstream media. Pew's "State of the Media" found that some of these outlets have faced financial hardship as more Latinos transition to English rather than Spanish only.[20]

Mass Media Ownership

One noteworthy feature of the traditional media in the United States is the concentration of its ownership. A small number of giant corporations control a wide swath of media holdings, including television networks, movie studios, record companies, cable channels and local cable providers, book publishers, magazines, and newspapers. **Media monopolies**, such as Disney, have prompted questions about whether enough competition exists among traditional media to produce a truly diverse set of views on political matters.[21] As major newspapers, television stations, and radio networks fall into fewer hands, the risk increases that politicians and citizens who express less popular or minority viewpoints will have difficulty finding a public forum. Ultimately, media are private corporations whose business is to sell audiences to advertisers, not to supply news or protect democracy.

Despite the appearance of substantial numbers overall, the number of traditional news-gathering sources operating nationally is actually quite small—several wire services, four broadcast networks, a few elite print newspapers, and a smattering of other sources, such as a few large local papers and several small, independent radio networks. More than three-fourths of the daily print newspapers in the United States are owned by large media conglomerates such as the Hearst, McClatchy, and Gannett corporations. Much of the national news that is published by local newspapers is provided by one wire service, the Associated Press. More than 500 of the nation's television stations are affiliated with one of just four networks and carry that network's evening news programs.

The trend in concentration of traditional media ownership occurred in large part due to the relaxation of government regulations in the 1980s and '90s. The enactment of the 1996 Telecommunications Act opened the way for additional consolidation in the media industry, and a wave of mergers and consolidations has further reduced the field of independent media across the country. For example, the Australian press baron Rupert Murdoch owns the Fox network plus a host of radio, television, and newspaper properties around the world, known collectively as News Corporation, the world's second-largest media conglomerate, which owned 800 media companies in more than 50 countries before its 2013 split into the new News Corporation and 21st Century Fox. Murdoch remains chair of both. But as more digital-only news sources come online, these trends toward concentration in media ownership may reverse.

One negative consequence of media concentration combined with party polarization may be a growing distrust of mainstream media. The political scientist Jonathan Ladd argues that 50 years ago the political parties were less polarized and were less likely to attack one another in the press.[22] During this period, newspaper editors also had less incentive to attack their competitors. Ladd cites a 1956 study that found 66 percent of Americans thought newspapers were fair. Party polarization increased with the Nixon presidency, and over the past 50 years, political candidates, especially Republican candidates, have made prominent attacks on the mainstream media. Ladd argues that as competition increased in party politics

media monopoly the ownership and control of the media by a few large corporations

for critical analysis

In recent years, a number of major media corporations have acquired numerous newspapers, television stations, and radio properties. Is media concentration a serious problem? Why or why not?

Though the media generally attempt to remain unbiased, a number of media figures and outlets are distinctly left- or right-leaning, such as Rachel Maddow of MSNBC and Megyn Kelly of Fox News. Consumers are increasingly turning to partisan media, reflecting a tendency to self-select information that already conforms with their beliefs, making it more difficult to evaluate information objectively.

and journalism, the public's distrust of the mass media grew, leading the public to reject the mainstream press's reporting and turn to alternative partisan media sources—those expressly favored by Republicans or Democrats. As recent as 2011, Pew reports that just 16 percent of Americans say the press deals fairly with all sides of the issues.[23] Recently, political fact-checking websites such as Politifact have grown in importance and popularity.

In an age of digital media, it is more important than ever for citizens to find and evaluate information (see the "What You Can Do" section at the end of the chapter). Across print and broadcast news media, journalists provide the content, whereas both journalists and amateurs create the content of the news in digital media.

● New Media and Online News

Explain how the Internet has transformed the news media

The twenty-first century has already experienced a profound transformation of the media. The impact of the Internet in mass communication parallels that of the printing press in nineteenth-century America, which saw the rise of the **penny press** and widespread literacy.[24] Today, even as the print newspaper business has consolidated, readership of online news has soared. Digital media have become the medium of choice for all age groups below 50 years to consume entertainment, news, and information about politics. In 2000, just 35 percent of adult Internet users said they looked for news or information about politics or the upcoming campaigns online.[25] As of 2015, that number rose to 6 in 10 Americans.[26] Besides digital-only newspapers, other forums include news websites, blogs, YouTube, podcasts, and social media. (See the "Who Are Americans?" feature on p. 269 for more information on where Americans get their news.)

News aggregators, such as Google News, Reddit, and RealClear Politics, cover thousands of news stories each day, as well as the latest public-opinion polls and their own synthesis of the headline news. Mirroring the digital revolution, digital

penny press cheap, tabloid-style newspaper produced in the nineteenth century, when mass production of inexpensive newspapers first became possible due to the steam-powered printing press; a penny press newspaper cost one cent compared with other papers, which cost more than five cents

news aggregator an application or feed that collects web content such as news headlines, blogs, podcasts, online videos, and more in one location for easy viewing

advertising has grown as a percentage of total media advertising across all platforms. The main benefactors of digital advertising continue to be social media and technology companies, such as Google and Facebook.

The Internet is particularly convenient for obtaining news, and formats for doing so are becoming more diverse and interactive. For example, it is increasingly common to watch online campaign ads, and one in three Internet users report having done so in the last election cycle. Streaming live videos is a growing substitute for television for some viewers. Presidential addresses are now regularly streamed live, and millions of people tune in to hear the president in this format.[27]

Rather than merely providing a forum to connect with friends and family, social media are increasingly places for learning about politics and now a primary source for news—a dramatic change from just a few years ago. A 2016 Pew survey found that 66 percent of Facebook users and 59 percent of Twitter users read the news from these platforms.[28] When we look at the American adult population as a whole, a majority—62 percent—gets news on social media. The trend in using social media for political information continues to grow at a rapid rate across all demographic groups. Social media are discussed in more detail below.

The rise of digital media has changed the way that people get information and share it, affecting everything from political activism, campaign organization, and voter mobilization to public opinion. Online media are more diverse and have created a more participatory press, one in which citizens and nonprofit organizations now play a prominent role. Readers can now post comments online, upload videos, and participate in a community, providing feedback on almost all online news articles. Digital media, by representing a wider range of political views than traditional media, have created more information and a more vibrant media environment.

The term *digital citizenship* refers to the ability to participate in culture and politics online. In much the same way that education and literacy promoted democracy and economic growth in the nineteenth century, today's Internet has the potential to benefit society as a whole by facilitating political participation and social inclusion through greater access to political information and news.[29] The Internet helps provide the information and skills needed for democratic engagement and economic opportunity.[30]

However, regular and effective use of the Internet requires high-speed access and literacy to evaluate and use information online.[31] Individuals without the access or skills to use the Internet may be increasingly uninformed and excluded from the world of politics online. As of 2014, 8 in 10 Americans were **digital citizens**, individuals with home Internet access, and more than 8 in 10 Americans used the Internet at some location (for example, at school, a library, or a friend's house). There are important differences in Internet access rates across race and ethnicity; in 2015, 75 percent of white non-Hispanic Americans and 75 percent of Asian Americans had high-speed Internet access at home compared to 64 percent of African Americans and 61 percent of Hispanic Americans. Among Hispanic Americans who speak only Spanish, 43 percent had home access compared to 72 percent of those who speak at least some English.[32] Access to the Internet is also shaped by income and education. While only half of the working poor (those earning less than $20,000 a year) had home broadband, 85 percent of those earning more than $100,000 a year did. Sixty-three percent of high school graduates have home broadband compared with almost 90 percent of college graduates.[33] These

The rise of digital media has made it easier for Americans to get political news, but one in five Americans still lacks home Internet access. People without high-speed Internet access at home often get free access in public libraries, but access is restricted to certain times.

digital citizen a daily Internet user with broadband (high-speed) home Internet access and the technology and literacy skills to go online for employment, news, politics, entertainment, commerce, and other activities

digital divide the gap in access to the Internet among demographic groups based on education, income, age, geographic location, and race/ethnicity

data suggest that there are significant inequalities in access to digital media, what is called the **digital divide**.[34]

Today, mobile Internet on smartphones is ever more important for news and participation in society. Similar inequalities based on demographic factors such as income and education are also found for mobile Internet access. High monthly subscription rates and data usage caps make mobile access a poor substitute for a broadband connection at home. Affordability is a major barrier to access, with the poor more likely to cite cost as a reason why they are offline. Because digital media are essential to participation in society, some argue that government has a responsibility to provide affordable access.

In this section we look at the major types of online news available to citizens today. While many traditional news sources, such as newspapers, now publish online, other digital-only outlets tend to be smaller and more specialized and have lower personnel and overhead costs than mainstream publishers. According to Pew Research Center, the major online political news websites in 2015 included a few major newspapers, such as the *New York Times*; radio programs, such as those on NPR; economic sources, such as Business Insider; and news sources whose audiences tend to lean to the ideological left or right.[35]

Today, streaming videos on YouTube, Netflix, and Amazon are fundamentally altering broadcast news, as dedicated channels provide political analysis, commentary, full-length features, and comedy. Similarly, podcasts are restructuring radio news by allowing listeners to tune into the news at any time online. Digital news sources include digital journalism, social media, citizen journalism and blogs, and nonprofit journalism.

Digital Journalism

niche journalism news reporting devoted to a targeted portion (subset) of a journalism market sector or for a portion of readers/viewers based on content or ideological presentation

In the gap opened by the decline of traditional print media, the last decade has seen the rise of **niche journalism** and digital-only publications. Bloomberg News, one of the most successful specialty online sources, has hundreds of thousands of readers paying a large annual fee for detailed business-related news. In politics, the Huffington Post, Vice, Buzzfeed, Gawker, the Drudge Report, and others are the niche leaders with detailed political reporting. FiveThirtyEight specializes in data journalism providing election forecasts but also broad coverage including sports, science, and lifestyle. Niche journalism feeds citizens' interest in politics across the full range of the political spectrum.

More and more news sources are digital-only, including the *Christian Science Monitor*, one of the five leading national newspapers. Hybrid media helps explains why yesterday's reporters from traditional media are today's entrepreneurs of digital news media. For example, digital-only Vox Media launched in 2014 under the leadership of former *Washington Post* journalist Ezra Klein and now ranks 35th in the top 50 news sites with 14 million unique visitors.[36] Similarly, Politico, another established leader in digital news, was founded in 2007 by two former *Washington Post* reporters. The oversight of professional journalists helps ensure that the quality of these online news outlets is high. A significant trend in media today is the sharp increase in the number of professionally trained journalists working for digital news platforms.[37]

The rise of digital news and niche journalism has fundamentally changed how Americans consume news and what they read. News consumers have shifted from a few general-purpose sources, such as the evening television news and a local newspaper, to a large number of niche publications and specialized sources: business news from one source; weather from another; sports, politics, and commentary from others. The radio has long been a primary medium for information about local traffic, but Google Maps on smartphones provides up-to-the-minute traffic information and routing with the touch of a screen. Sports fans once depended on local evening news for information about their favorite teams but now find it online at EPSN.com and Deadspin.

Social Media

The rise of **social media**, such as Twitter and Facebook, is the single most important trend in news and political communication. Worldwide, Facebook had over 1.7 billion users in 2016, with 190 million users in the United States. More than 70 percent of Americans use social media.[38] As of 2016, roughly 67 percent use Facebook and 16 percent use Twitter, both of which have high rates of exposure to political news.[39]

Because they are more personalized and interactive than anonymous news organizations, social media allow Americans to learn about politics and political news from each other. Growing use of social media for news is evident across demographic groups, including those under and over 35 years of age, women and men, and groups defined by race, education, and income. (Figure 7.4 shows the percentage of adults who use each social networking site as well as the percentage who

social media web- and mobile-based technologies that are used to turn communication into interactive dialogue among organizations, communities, and individuals; social media technologies take on many different forms including text, blogs, podcasts, photographs, streaming video, Facebook, and Twitter

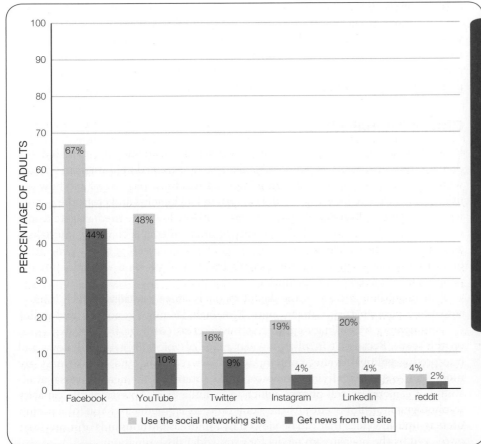

FIGURE 7.4

Social Media as a News Source

Many Americans who use social media use those sites as a way to obtain political news. This graph shows the percentage of American adults who use each social media site compared with the percentage who report getting news from that site. What are the advantages of getting news on social media, and what are some potential drawbacks?

SOURCE: Jeffrey Gottfriend and Elisa Shearer, "News Use across Social Media Platforms 2016," Pew Research Center, May 26, 2016, www.journalism.org/2016/05/26/news-use-across-social-media-platforms-2016/ (accessed 6/17/16).

get news from that site.) As previously shown in Figure 7.3, social media tend to be a secondary source for news after television for many Americans but a primary source for the young, with 61 percent of those 18–33 years old reporting that they got political news from Facebook in a given week in 2015. The high rate of exposure to political news online is notable since young Americans overall are less engaged in politics—just 35 percent of 18–33 year-old say they talk about politics at least a few times a week. As the Internet becomes an increasingly important source for political news, young people may become more engaged in politics.[40]

Facebook provides a more interactive forum for learning about politics than does Twitter. A 2015 Pew survey found that Facebook users are more likely to post and respond to news about government and politics, while Twitter users are more likely to follow news organizations. Twitter's strength is providing news coverage as it happens, focusing on live events. Twitter users are more than twice as likely to say they use the site for breaking news compared to Facebook. More than two-thirds of users of both sites say they posted about news at least at some point. Compared to passively watching television or reading the news, this is a high rate of engagement with political news.[41]

Both Facebook and Twitter have contributed to political mobilization and information sharing by creating virtual social networks where groups of like-minded individuals can quickly and easily share information. Social networking is a key feature of the dissemination of news through social media platforms; a majority of social media users follow links to full news stories after learning about a story from friends and family.

Finally, social media also provide a platform for citizens to be directly engaged with political candidates and elected officials, who have been quick to adopt Facebook and Twitter as means of communicating with their supporters and providing them a continual feed of new information. Obama was the first American president to use social media extensively for governing.

Citizen Journalism

Related to social media is the concept of citizen journalism and blogs. The old media system was dominated by professional journalists, trained in journalism schools, who served as gatekeepers in determining what was front-page news and how political events were to be interpreted. This system had benefits and costs: the quality was high, but the diversity of opinions was relatively low. The media's gatekeeper role continues, but the incredible diversity of online media is changing journalism and the very nature of "news coverage." Digital news is creating a new generation of whistle-blowers, enhancing the media's traditional role as a watchdog for the people against government corruption.

citizen journalism news reported and distributed by citizens, rather than professional journalists and for-profit news organizations

A distinguishing feature of the digital media is **citizen journalism**, which is interactive and participatory. Citizen journalism includes news reporting and political commentary by ordinary citizens and even crisis coverage from eyewitnesses on the scene. Because it involves a wider range of voices in gathering news and interpreting political events, contemporary news reporting and commentary are more democratic. Magnifying the power of the Internet is the near-universal availability of cameras on cell phones, which gives millions of Americans the capacity to photograph or film events. At the same time, social media and YouTube permit users to upload videos that can be viewed by hundreds of thousands of subscribers or relayed by the mainstream media for even wider dissemination.

During the 2011 Occupy Wall Street protests, many ordinary citizens recorded videos—both of the protests themselves and of police responses to them— that were widely shared on the Internet and sometimes made headline news.

Citizen journalism is enhanced by the ease of starting a blog. There are millions of blogs, covering virtually every topic imaginable, and a large share of these include political news and commentary on local, national, and world events. Many blogs are citizen-run and more interactive and representative of the diversity of American views than traditional news, which generally reflects the priorities of political elites. A number of blogs, such as the *Daily Kos* and the *Monkey Cage*, have thousands of loyal readers who regularly critique stories presented by the print and broadcast media. These online discussion forums create a community for readers, further interpreting the news.

Citizen journalism supplements the work of professional journalists in many important ways. The diversity of online media has created new opinion leaders and new voices and has even, at times, improved information. In recent years, for example, bloggers have uncovered major factual errors in media reports and forced the networks and newspapers to issue corrections. Furthermore, because bloggers and social media posts do not have strict editorial boards, they can post a story within minutes. This ability to scoop the mainstream media means bloggers can frame stories about political candidates before they break in the mainstream media.[42] By sharply lowering the technological and financial barriers that previously prevented all but a few individuals from reaching mass audiences, blogs increase the ability of ordinary people to engage in effective political action. (In Chapter 8, we will take a closer look at the Internet's effects on political participation.)

To be sure, the freewheeling nature of blogging and social media often means that there is less traditional quality control employed by professional journalists and institutional old media. Because they do not face the burden of fact-checking required for the mainstream media or some digital-only news outlets, even well-meaning bloggers can post false information. This could be one reason why misinformation about some political issues is higher among blog readers than those reading online news from the mainstream press.[43]

Nonprofit Journalism

As traditional news organizations have cut budgets and especially investigative journalism, political information is increasingly emanating from universities, think tanks, nonprofit organizations, and private foundations. For example, the *Washington*

Post, one of the nation's premier newspapers known for the investigative journalism that broke the Watergate scandal, is now run as a nonprofit and owned by the chief executive officer of the technology giant Amazon.com, Jeffrey Bezos. Think tanks such as the Brookings Institution, the Cato Institute, the Hoover Institution, the Heritage Foundation, and the Center for American Progress provide news and analysis on current events to influence public debate. Universities have expanded their public outreach, encouraging faculty to explain their findings for a general audience; as a result, university faculty are increasingly cited in the mainstream media, and many are bloggers themselves. Community-based nonprofit newspapers are supported by local foundations seeking to fill the void in local news as local papers close their doors. The Kaiser Family Foundation was early in creating *Kaiser Health News*. The Bill and Melinda Gates Foundation, established by Microsoft founder Bill Gates, provides extensive funding to National Public Radio.

Benefits of Online News

As digital news media become mainstream, it is worthwhile to reexamine why Americans appear to prefer online news. The reasons include (1) the convenience of getting news online, (2) the up-to-the-minute currency of the information available online, (3) the depth of the information available online, (4) the diversity of viewpoints, and (5) the low cost.[44] At the same time, changes to the media arising from the rapid proliferation of the Internet have raised some concerns, as we will see in the following sections.

Convenience Information online is convenient and always available for those with access to the Internet at home or, increasingly, through mobile devices such as smartphones. Pew surveys show that nearly half of those who use online news and political information cite its convenience, with much more depth than that found when tuning in to the national evening news on television.[45] Because political knowledge is central to the formation of political attitudes, the convenience of online news may lead to a more informed and engaged citizenry. Use of digital media is associated with more interest in politics, greater knowledge of politics, and a greater likelihood of discussing politics with friends and family, as well as voting.[46]

Currency One of the fundamental changes ushered in by an era of online news is the speed with which local, national, and international events are covered, as well as the scope of coverage. Major news stories regularly break first online. Social media have accelerated even further the speed with which news travels around the globe. For example, news of Osama bin Laden's death in May 2011 spread rapidly through messaging and social media even before it could be verified by traditional media.

Depth Online news provides more information than the 60-second sound bites found in television and radio news. By blending more detailed treatment of topics with the visual and emotive appeal of streaming videos, the Internet shares qualities both of print media (promoting knowledge) and of the visual aspects of television (promoting interest and engagement).[47] The multimedia capacity of the Internet notwithstanding, most websites still rely heavily upon written text, and most political "web surfing" consists mainly of reading, which facilitates greater recall of information and, in turn, encourages the acquisition of political knowledge.[48]

The Internet has facilitated both diversity and specialization in news media. Websites such as FactCheck.org exist solely for the purpose of evaluating statements made by U.S. politicians. The site corrects misinformation every day, such as incorrect claims about the Syrian refugee crisis.

Diversity Online sources are much more diverse than those found in the traditional media, and this diversity may lead to an increase in political knowledge and interest.[49] While major players online certainly do include mainstream outlets,[50] the Internet remains populated by a wide range of information sources. By making foreign media such as the British Broadcasting Company (BBC) and Al Jazeera television easily available, the Internet has reduced the importance of physical proximity and created more global news. Such a vast array of voices, of course, means that online sources also can provide misinformation or outright lies—just as can happen in mainstream media, campaign events, and even presidential debates. To verify media reports found in both traditional and online media, there are new websites, such as FactCheck.org and PolitiFact.com, devoted exclusively to checking the veracity of political claims.

Concerns about Online News

While online news holds significant promise for improving access to the political information citizens need, the shift toward online media has also given rise to several major concerns. These potential disadvantages include a decline in investigative journalism, uneven quality in news content, and negative effects on knowledge and tolerance.

Loss of Investigative Power In a democracy, the press is expected to be a watchdog for the people and to inform citizens about government abuses of power. Stated another way, democracies depend on news organizations to inform the people about current events and help citizens hold their leaders accountable for their actions. The greatest challenge for journalism organizations is to generate enough revenue to finance traditional investigative journalism.[51] This activity requires more time and resources than other aspects of the news, and it may be the most important. When readers paid subscription fees to read the news, circulation was high and advertising provided sufficient revenue to allow newspapers and broadcasters to cover both basic news (weather, sports, business) and political events. Revenue from publishing basic news subsidized political analysis and

Without traditional media's commitment to fact-checking, digital media sometimes spread innacurate information and rumors. In 2008, the false claim that President Obama was not a natural-born U.S. citizen spread rapidly online and remained a top story even after Obama released his official long-form birth certificate.

investigative journalism. By breaking apart mainstream news organizations, digital news may actually reduce the media's ability to engage in the kind of sustained, in-depth reporting that is critical to the media's watchdog role and thus to the health of American democracy. In the 2016 presidential election, the media were criticized for focusing coverage on some candidates, most notably Donald Trump, much more than others and for a lack of more critical reporting.

More Variation in the Quality of News As already noted, the growing diversity of digital news has led to substantial variation in the quality of available information. Multiple perspectives create a stronger marketplace of ideas, but the freewheeling nature of the Internet also means that hate speech, unsubstantiated rumors, and factual errors can overwhelm thoughtful, original, and civic-oriented voices. And while viral media may elevate the watchdog function of the media, the misinformation and unsubstantiated rumors that are part of viral media can substitute for objective truth as claims are widely repeated. This is especially so in anonymous online forums. Political scientist Dianne Bystrom has noted that "the online universe of political commentary operates outside traditional media editorial boundaries and is sometimes incisive but often offensive and unsubstantiated."[52]

Political candidates and political leaders are particularly susceptible to attack when negative stories go viral and spread quickly without the traditional media filters of fact-checking and respect for the privacy of public figures. False rumors that President Obama and 2016 Republican presidential candidate Ted Cruz were not natural-born citizens and therefore not eligible to be president under Article II of the U.S. Constitution spread rapidly online and spilled into mainstream news. In Obama's case, the "birther movement" conspiracy theories alleged that he was born in Kenya, not Hawaii, and that his birth certificate was a forgery. Extensive media coverage allowed what many viewed as an attack against a sitting president to become headline news, something that may not have occurred in a pre-Internet era. Belief in these theories has persisted, despite Obama's preelection release of his official long-form birth certificate from Hawaii in 2008, the posting of a copy of his birth certificate online, and confirmation by the Hawaii Department of Health based on the original documents.

Potential Effects on Knowledge and Tolerance Perhaps the greatest concern about politics in the digital age goes to the heart of modern democracy: Does the Internet ultimately help or hinder progress toward the ideal of a well-informed citizenry that can govern itself effectively? The very diversity of online news may actually *lower* tolerance for social, religious, and political diversity. Digital media often do not abide by traditional media's principle of objective journalism, in which both sides of an argument are reported. Instead, the specialization of information online and on cable television means that liberals and conservatives alike can self-select media that are consistent with their underlying assumptions and avoid exposure to information that might challenge their preconceived beliefs.[53] The natural tendency to select news that conforms with our own beliefs is exacerbated by the way search engines cater to our individual preferences—what one scholar has called the "filter bubble," or "self-selection bias," which screens out exposure to information that might challenge or broaden our worldview.[54]

The benefits and possibilities created by digital media for the American political process may well outweigh these concerns about accuracy, reliability, ethical practices, and depth of reporting. If the new media are to create a more informed democratic process, citizens must have "information literacy" or the ability to find and evaluate information.[55] Greater access to information online makes education and critical thinking among citizens more important than ever before.

Social Media as Propaganda Another concern about the Internet as a source of political information is that its accessibility has enabled violent groups to spread political propaganda more effectively. Social media have been a primary means to distribute the political propaganda of the extremist militia group the Islamic State of Iraq and Syria (ISIS), creating headline news worldwide. The group's sophisticated media campaign, including the use of Twitter, YouTube, and other forums, distributes a multitude of social media messages daily and has helped mobilize thousands of people to fight on behalf of the group's cause. In the most significant terrorist attack on U.S. soil since September 11, 2001, Omar Mateen, an American citizen of Afghan descent, carried out a mass shooting at a gay nightclub in Orlando, Florida, in 2016. Mateen killed 49 people and wounded dozens more. He took to social media immediately following the killings to pledge his loyalty to ISIS. Just six months earlier, a husband and wife team carried out a terrorist attack in San Bernardino, California, leaving 14 Americans dead. According to the FBI, the couple was inspired, if not directed, by extremists via social media.

ISIS has also used social media to distribute gruesome videos of public executions, beheadings, and burnings of foreign journalists, soldiers, and other ordinary individuals. These videos, in combination with mass media coverage of ISIS's actions in the Middle East, fueled fear and calls for government action in countries around the world.[56]

● Media Influence

Analyze the ways the media can influence public opinion and politics

The content and character of news and public affairs programming—what the media choose to present and how they present it—can have far-reaching political consequences. The media can shape and modify, if not fully form, the public's perception of events, issues, and institutions. Media coverage can rally support for, or intensify opposition to, national policies on matters as weighty as health care, the economy, or international wars. Media disclosures can greatly enhance or fatally damage the careers of public figures, as discussed earlier. At the same time, the media are influenced by the individuals or groups who are subjects of the news. The president in particular has the power to set the news agenda through speeches and actions. All politicians, for that matter, seek to shape or manipulate their media images by cultivating good relations with reporters and through news leaks and staged news events.

In recent American political history, the media have played a central role in many major events. For example, the media were a critically important factor in the civil rights movement of the 1950s and '60s. Television images showing peaceful civil rights marchers attacked by club-swinging police helped to generate sympathy among northern whites for the civil rights struggle and greatly increased the pressure on Congress to bring an end to segregation.[57] The media were also instrumental in compelling the Nixon administration to negotiate an end to American involvement in the Vietnam War. Beginning in 1967 the media, reacting in part to a shift in elite opinion, portrayed the war as misguided and unwinnable and, as a result, helped turn popular sentiment against continued American involvement.[58]

The media were also central actors in the Watergate affair, the cluster of scandals that ultimately forced President Richard Nixon, the landslide victor in the 1972 presidential election, to resign from office in disgrace just two years later. A relentless series of investigations launched by the *Washington Post*, the *New York Times*, and the television networks led to disclosures of the various abuses of which Nixon was guilty, ultimately forcing him to choose between resignation and almost certain impeachment.

Harsh media coverage of Iraqi leader Saddam Hussein, combined with White House claims that Iraq was harboring weapons of mass destruction (WMDs), led 70 percent of Americans to approve of the U.S. decision to invade Iraq in 2003. (It was later determined that, in fact, Iraq did not have any WMDs.) The Pew Research Center reported that individuals getting the news from mainstream American media were more supportive of the Iraq invasion, while those relying on foreign news coverage or online news were more likely to oppose the invasion.

Conservatives have long charged that the liberal biases of reporters and journalists result in distorted news coverage.[59] Though many professional journalists do lean Democratic, they generally defend their professionalism, insisting that

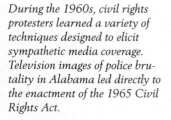

During the 1960s, civil rights protesters learned a variety of techniques designed to elicit sympathetic media coverage. Television images of police brutality in Alabama led directly to the enactment of the 1965 Civil Rights Act.

Where Do Americans Get Their News?

Percentage of each age group who got news about politics and government in the previous week from...

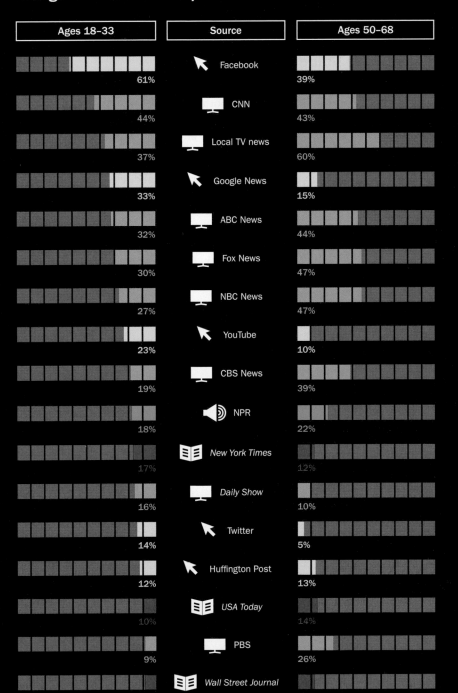

Ages 18–33	Source	Ages 50–68
61%	Facebook	39%
44%	CNN	43%
37%	Local TV news	60%
33%	Google News	15%
32%	ABC News	44%
30%	Fox News	47%
27%	NBC News	47%
23%	YouTube	10%
19%	CBS News	39%
18%	NPR	22%
17%	New York Times	12%
16%	Daily Show	10%
14%	Twitter	5%
12%	Huffington Post	13%
10%	USA Today	14%
9%	PBS	26%
9%	Wall Street Journal	12%

In a democracy like the United States, people need information to understand current issues and the government's actions. But not all Americans get their news from the same place. Outlets for news vary by medium (print, TV, radio, and Internet) as well as source (e.g., *The Daily Show*, Fox News).

SOURCE: Pew Research Center, "Political Media Habits across Millennials, Gen Xers and Baby Boomers," June 1, 2015, www.journalism.org/interactives/generational-media-habits/ (accessed 3/8/16).

for critical analysis

1. Are there differences between how younger adults and older adults get their news? Which age group is more likely to get news from television versus the Internet?

2. What might be some consequences of such differences?

their personal political leanings do not affect the way they perform their jobs.[60] Moreover, journalists represent liberals, conservatives, and moderates. Those who decry "the liberal media" seldom acknowledge the partisan or ideological leanings of media owners. Rupert Murdoch, the chief executive officer of News Corporation and 21st Century Fox, is a politically active conservative. Philip Anschutz, owner of the *Examiner* newspapers in San Francisco, Washington, and other cities, has been a major financial contributor to the Republican Party and its candidates. Many news sources are distinctly left- or right-leaning, and, as discussed above, people have a tendency to select news that conforms with their own ideology. Table 7.1 shows where different ideological groups get political news. The diversity of online news, however, may mean that debates about liberal or conservative bias in the mainstream media are becoming less important.

How the Media Influence Politics

Traditional and digital media influence American politics in a number of important ways.[61] The power of all media collectively, both traditional and online, lies in their ability to shape what issues Americans think about (agenda setting) and what opinions Americans hold about those issues (framing and priming).

Agenda Setting and Selection Bias The first source of media power is **agenda setting**; that is, the media help to set the agenda for political discussion. Agenda setting involves identifying the issues that politicians will pay attention to: some things are deemed important, while others are not. Groups and forces that wish to bring their ideas before the public in order to generate support for policy proposals or political candidacies must secure media coverage. If the media are persuaded that an idea is newsworthy, then they may declare it an "issue" that must be confronted

for critical analysis

To what extent, do you think, are the media biased? As more news sources have become available, has this led to more or less bias in the media?

agenda setting the power of the media to bring public attention to particular issues and problems

TABLE 7.1

Media and Viewers' Ideology

Percentage of each ideological group who got news about politics in the previous week from each source

SOURCE	CONSISTENTLY LIBERAL	MOSTLY LIBERAL	MIXED	MOSTLY CONSERVATIVE	CONSISTENTLY CONSERVATIVE
CNN	52	48	49	32	20
Fox News	10	24	39	61	84
ABC News	33	38	42	32	26
NBC News	37	44	40	29	21
CBS News	30	32	32	24	22
MSNBC	38	32	25	23	13
NPR	53	23	12	10	8

SOURCE: Pew Research Center, "Where News Audiences Fit on the Political Spectrum," www.journalism.org/interactives/media-polarization/table/consume/ (accessed 3/7/16).

or a "problem" to be solved, thus clearing the first hurdle in the policy-making process. If, on the other hand, an idea lacks or loses media appeal, its chance of resulting in new programs or policies is diminished.

After September 11, 2001, President George W. Bush had little difficulty convincing the media that terrorism and his administration's efforts to forestall further terrorist attacks merited a dominant place on the national agenda. Not surprisingly, the American-led military campaigns in Afghanistan and Iraq dominated the news throughout 2002 and 2003. Some stories have such overwhelming significance that the main concern of political leaders is not whether a story will receive attention—wars and natural disasters always receive attention—but whether the leaders themselves will figure prominently and positively in media accounts. Yet many important issues are not on the media's agenda, such as alternative energy sources to fossil fuels (oil and gas). Likewise, these issues are often absent from major policy discussions.

Media attention plays a central role in whether or not officials act on a policy issue, but how policy issues make the news in the first place has remained a puzzle. Political scientist Amber Boydstun has shown that there are two different patterns of media attention that determine which issues are brought before the public: media storms and general coverage.[62] The media have two modes: an "alarm mode" for breaking stories and a "patrol mode" for covering them in greater depth. The incentive to reach a wider audience (and generate ad revenue) often initiates "alarm mode" around a story, after which news outlets go into watchdog "patrol mode" to monitor policy implications until the next big media storm hits. This pattern results in skewed coverage of political issues, with a few issues receiving the majority of media attention while others receive none at all.

Today, digital and social media are increasingly defining what becomes headline news as it is often social media, especially Twitter, that sets off "alarm mode" by breaking news and causing it to go viral. A 2014 study found that the top media sources linked to in tweets are not traditional media, with the exception of the *New York Times*, but rather alternative and niche media, YouTube, and other

Through agenda setting, the media have the power to influence which issues the public pays attention to. Although drinking water contamination in Flint, Michigan, began in April 2014, it didn't gain national media attention until almost a year later. Mass media coverage eventually led to governmental action when Governor Rick Snyder declared a state of emergency almost two years later in January 2016.

social media. In this way, social media more broadly, and Twitter especially, play an important role in setting the overall news media agenda.[63]

Political candidates need the media's agenda-setting role to win elections. Candidates who receive positive news coverage gain momentum, pick up political endorsements, attract campaign contributions, and win support from voters.[64] In the 2008 presidential campaign, Barack Obama exceeded the media's expectations with his early win in the Iowa caucuses, in which he upset the front-runner, Hillary Clinton, in the Democratic primaries for president. Obama's unexpected victory earned him increased press attention and eventually led the first African American president to the White House.[65] In 2016, Donald Trump exceeded media expectations by coming in second in Iowa and wining New Hampshire. But candidates who disappoint media expectations, such as 2016 Republican candidate Jeb Bush, see their political endorsements, campaign contributions, and polling numbers dwindle. The influence of the media on political candidates is just one example of the media's vitally important role in American democracy.

Often, the media serve as conduits for agenda-setting efforts by competing groups and forces. Occasionally, however, journalists themselves are instrumental in setting the agenda of political discussion. The Watergate scandal that destroyed Nixon's presidency was in some measure initiated and driven by the *Washington Post* and the national television networks.

Because the media are businesses and seek to attract the largest possible audiences, they naturally tend to cover stories with dramatic or entertainment value, giving less attention to important stories that they deem less compelling. News coverage often focuses on crimes and scandals, especially those involving prominent individuals. **Selection bias** means that the news media may provide less information about important political issues that the public depends upon. For example, there was a media frenzy in January 1998 when reports surfaced that Democratic president Clinton might have had an affair with a White House intern. In 2016, Donald Trump's sensationalist statements during the course of his campaign dominated headline news for months. Partisanship and ideology notwithstanding, the age-old journalistic instinct for sensational stories often trumps both the media's responsibility to inform the public about what really matters and the public's responsibility to demand that from the media.

selection bias (news) the tendency to focus news coverage on only one aspect of an event or issue, avoiding coverage of other aspects

What the mainstream media decide to report on and what they ignore has important implications. For example, the Bush tax cuts of 2001 and 2003, extended under Obama in 2008, had widespread effects, dramatically increasing the federal budget deficit and widening the income gap between the super-rich and most other Americans. But the media provided little coverage of these measures, the result being that 40 percent of Americans had no opinion on whether they favored the massive tax cuts in 2001.[66]

Access to the print and broadcast media is such an important political resource that political forces that lack media access, such as the Black Lives Matter or Occupy Wall Street protestors, have only a very limited opportunity to influence the political process. The skewed coverage of traditional media, however, may be balanced out by the diversity of media sources available online, especially the growing influence of social media.

framing the power of the media to influence how events and issues are interpreted

Framing The language and context in which the media present the news, known as **framing**, can determine how the American people interpret political events. Robert Entman defines *framing* as the social construction of social phenomena by the mass media, political or social movements, political leaders, or other political actors and organizations. Frames shape how individuals perceive meaning from words or phrases, photographs, or video.[67] Knowing this, politicians take care to choose language that presents their ideas in the most favorable light possible. Public opinion on politics naturally changes with facts, but few citizens read legislation, so when forming opinions about policy and politics, the public relies on media coverage. This means that arguments made by elected officials and other political actors, or frames, are critical in how the public interprets events and policy.

For example, Obama's health care initiative was framed differently by Democrats and Republicans. The Obama administration labeled the initiative the Patient Protection and Affordable Care Act, thus framing the proposal as a matter of compassionate responsibility and good economic sense. As the bill was debated in Congress, early press coverage framed it as "health care reform." Sensing that Americans generally approve of the idea of "reform," Republican opponents of the legislation chose different language: the law's provisions for limiting excessive medical testing were labeled as "health care rationing," for example, and proposals to create committees to advise patients about end-of-life care were called "death panels." Other opponents called it "Obamacare." The Democrats framed the initiative as achieving the positive goal of reform, while the Republicans framed it as achieving the negative outcome of rationing.

Priming A third important way the media can shape political events is known as **priming**. Priming involves "calling attention to some matters while ignoring others" when evaluating political officials.[68] As a result, the public will be *primed* to use certain criteria when evaluating a politician or an issue and ignore other criteria. For example, the media's intensive focus on terrorism and security in the wake of the September 11, 2001, terrorist attacks primed the public to evaluate President Bush's performance in office based on his ability to defend the nation from terrorism and not on, say, his ability to manage the economy at the time. In 2008, however, the serious economic recession took the media spotlight. As a result the economy—far more than national security—became one of the most important lenses through which the public evaluated the 2008 presidential candidates.

In the case of political candidates, the media's focus on which candidate "has momentum" and "is winning the horse race" can prime the public to evaluate the candidates based on their likelihood to win the election rather than on their positions on policy issues. For example, as noted earlier, the media declared that Donald Trump had momentum after his unexpected victories and polling numbers exceeded expectations early in the primary season, and he went on to clinch the Republican nomination. News media are not alone in agenda setting, framing, and priming; elected officials, interest groups, and other political players compete over all three in hopes of influencing public opinion.

Media and Public Knowledge

In general, individuals who frequently consume political news are more likely to be interested in politics, to have political knowledge, and to vote in elections. There are several reasons why exposure to political information increases participation in politics. Exposure to political news increases political knowledge, which in turn increases turnout because people know whom to vote for and are more likely to perceive differences between candidates. Learning from exposure to political

priming process of preparing the public to bring specific criteria to mind when evaluating a politician or issue

for critical analysis

How do the media distort political reality? How do politicians use the media for their own purposes? What are the consequences for American democracy when the electorate is informed through such a filter? How might the quality of political information in America be improved?

information on cable television news and online news also increases people's interest in electoral campaigns, which in turn affects voter turnout.[69]

The media in all their varying forms—traditional and digital—lead to a more informed public, but also to growing gaps between the informed and uninformed.[70] A puzzle remains, however. Despite the dramatic rise in political information and the diversity of the media, average levels of political knowledge in the population have remained constant for the last few decades.[71] One widely discussed reason has been proposed by Cass Sunstein. He argues that individuals "customize" the political information they receive through their choice of news outlets to follow.[72] This customization leads to a polarized news environment in which media users are unlikely to encounter information that challenges their partisan viewpoints, which is related to selective exposure and the filter bubble, discussed above.

● News Coverage

> **Explain how politicians and others try to shape the news**

News coverage, or the content of the news, comes from numerous sources. Governments, politicians, corporations, interest groups, nonprofit organizations, and others issue press releases to draw attention to an issue and tell their side of the story. Journalists also gain information through investigative journalism and media leaks.

Press Releases

Each year, thousands of press releases are seamlessly incorporated into daily news reports. These press releases are written by advocates or publicists and distributed to the media in the hope that journalists will publish them, under the journalists' own bylines, with little or no revision. The originator of the press release, or news release, was a well-known New York public-relations consultant named Ivy Lee. In 1906 a train operated by one of Lee's clients, the Pennsylvania Railroad, was involved in a serious wreck. Lee quickly wrote a story about the accident that presented the railroad in a favorable light, and he distributed the account to reporters. Many papers published Lee's slanted story as their own objective account of the events, and the railroad's reputation for quality and safety remained untarnished.

Consistent with Lee's example, today's press release presents facts and perspectives that serve an advocate's interests but is written in a way that mimics the factual news style of the paper, periodical, or television news program to which it has been sent. A well-designed press release can be nearly impossible to distinguish from an actual news story. Newspapers, of course, understand that in publishing press releases they are allowing themselves to be used, but they have a strong financial incentive to publish material that, in effect, allows them to fill their pages at little cost. The White House regularly issues press releases—for example, in preparation for a State of the Union address or major legislation supported by the president. Polling companies, such as Gallup, use press releases to share the results of election surveys.

Media Leaks

The media may also report information that is leaked by government officials. A leak is the disclosure of confidential information to the news media. Leaks may

emanate from a variety of sources, including "whistle-blowers," lower-level officials who hope to publicize what they view as their bosses' or the government's improper activities. In 1971, for example, Daniel Ellsberg, a minor Defense Department staffer, sought to discredit official justifications for America's military involvement in Vietnam by leaking top-secret documents to the press. The Pentagon Papers—the Defense Department's own secret history of the war—were published by the *New York Times* and the *Washington Post* after the U.S. Supreme Court ruled that the government could not block their release.[73] The Pentagon's credibility was severely damaged, hastening the erosion of public support for the war.

Leaks of classified information have sparked significant debate over what the government should classify as "secret" and what deserves to be public knowledge. After Edward Snowden leaked thousands of classified documents, he fled the United States to escape arrest and prosecution. His actions have been both defended and denounced.

Most leaks, though, originate not with low-level whistle-blowers but rather with senior government officials, prominent politicians, and political activists. Journalists are likely to regard high-level sources of confidential information as valuable assets whose favor must be retained. For example, during the George W. Bush administration, Lewis "Scooter" Libby, Vice President Dick Cheney's chief of staff, was apparently such a valuable source of leaks to so many journalists that his name was seldom even mentioned in the newspapers, despite his prominence in Washington and his importance as a decision maker.[74]

Digital technology has taken the cat-and-mouse game of leaks to a new level. WikiLeaks, an independent nonprofit organization dedicated to publishing classified information, posts leaked documents to its website and uses an anonymous drop-box system so that leakers cannot be identified. In recent years, WikiLeaks has released thousands of secret government documents involving instances of government corruption, war crimes in Afghanistan and Iraq, torture at U.S. military detention camps, maps of U.S. military drone attacks on civilians around the world, and numerous embarrassing private communiqués sent by U.S. diplomats abroad.

In 2013, Edward Snowden, a former employee of the Central Intelligence Agency (CIA) and contractor for the National Security Agency (NSA), disclosed thousands of classified digital documents to journalists and international media in what has been called the most significant leak in U.S. history. The leaks revealed widespread global surveillance programs by the U.S. government working with telecommunication companies. The world learned the NSA was searching millions of emails and tapping cell phones, even of foreign political leaders. For revealing the mass surveillance programs, Snowden has been called a hero, a whistle-blower, a dissident, and a traitor. The leaks garnered intense media attention and sparked heated public debate over government surveillance and privacy of information for individuals.

Critics of WikiLeaks and Snowden argue that governments must have some secrets and that the release of some government documents may jeopardize American soldiers and their local allies by revealing their identities, as well as national security. The whistle-blower behind the Pentagon Papers, Daniel Ellsberg, defended WikiLeaks in 2010, arguing that it has played a vital role in informing the public of government wrongdoings in terms of foreign policy and infringement of privacy and security in a digital age.

Adversarial Journalism

The political power of the news media vis-à-vis the government has greatly increased in recent years through the growing prominence of *adversarial journalism*,

This famous photograph of the aftermath of a napalm attack was one of many media images that shaped the American public's views on the Vietnam War. Media accounts critical of the war helped to turn public opinion against it and hastened the withdrawal of American troops.

a form of reporting in which the media adopt a skeptical or even hostile posture toward the government and public officials.

During the nineteenth century, American newspapers were subordinate to the political parties. Newspapers depended on official patronage (legal notices and party subsidies) for their financial survival and were controlled by party leaders. At the turn of the twentieth century, with the development of commercial advertising, newspapers became financially independent, making possible the emergence of a formally nonpartisan press.

Presidents were the first national officials to make use of the opportunities presented by this development. By communicating directly to the electorate through newspapers and magazines, Theodore Roosevelt and Woodrow Wilson established political constituencies for themselves, independent of party organizations, and thereby strengthened their own power relative to that of Congress. President Franklin Delano Roosevelt used the radio, most notably in his famous fireside chats, to reach out to voters throughout the nation and to make himself the center of American political life. Subsequent presidents have all sought to use the media to enhance their popularity and power.

During the 1950s and early 1960s a few members of Congress also made successful use of the media, especially television, to mobilize national support for their causes; but through the mid-1960s the executive branch continued to generate the bulk of news coverage, and the media became a cornerstone of presidential power.

The Vietnam War shattered this amicable relationship between the press and the presidency. During the early stages of U.S. involvement, American officials in Vietnam who disapproved of the way the war was being conducted leaked to reporters information critical of administrative policy. Publication of this material infuriated the White House, which pressured publishers to block its release. However, the national broadcast media and especially the two leading national newspapers, the *Washington Post* and the *New York Times*, discovered an audience for critical coverage and investigative reporting among segments of the public skeptical of administration policy. As the Vietnam War dragged on, adverse media coverage fanned antiwar sentiment. In turn, these shifts in popular and congressional sentiment emboldened journalists and publishers to continue to present news reports critical of the war. Gradually, a generation of journalists developed a commitment to adversarial journalism, and a constituency emerged that would rally to the defense of the media whenever it came under attack from the White House.

To take a more recent example, during her campaign for the presidency in 2016, Hillary Clinton became embroiled in controversy regarding her use of a private email address during her tenure as secretary of state, despite protocol that official government email should be used for security reasons. In response, the Justice Department demanded that Clinton turn over her entire private email server. Through investigative journalism, McClatchy News Service reported that two of the four classified emails on her server were top secret, the highest security classification. Clinton had previously denied sending or receiving any classified material via her email account.[75] An investigation by the FBI recommended no criminal charges against Clinton for her handling of classified information using email while she was secretary of state. To warrant a criminal charge there had to be evidence that Clinton "intentionally transmitted or willfully mishandled classified information." The investigation found neither.[76]

Aggressive use of the techniques of investigation, publicity, and exposure has allowed the national media to enhance their autonomy and carve out a prominent place for themselves in American government and politics. Without investigative journalism, would we have known of the illegal break-in to the Democratic Party headquarters in the Watergate building by Nixon's "Committee to Re-elect the President" and the White House's subsequent cover-up of the scandal? Would we have known the extent of government surveillance of American citizens? Without aggressive media coverage, important questions about the conduct of American foreign and domestic policy, police violence, drone attacks, and civil liberty violations may not ever be raised. It is easy to criticize the media for their aggressive tactics, but our democracy may not function effectively without the critical role of the press. Independent media are needed as the watchdogs of American politics. Digital technology has provided a new means by which the media are a watchdog of government wrongdoing. One advantage of digital media is that they are less likely to be co-opted by the government, taking the adversarial role of the press to new heights.

● Regulation of the Media

Trace the evolution of rules that govern broadcast media

In many countries, such as China, the government exercises strict control over traditional media content. In others, the government owns the broadcast media (for example, the BBC in Britain) but does not tell the media what to say.

In the United States, the print and online media are essentially free from government interference. The broadcast media, on the other hand, are subject to federal regulation. American radio and television are regulated by the Federal Communications Commission (FCC), an independent agency established in 1934. Radio and TV stations must have FCC licenses, which must be renewed every five years. Through regulations prohibiting obscenity, indecency, and profanity, the FCC has

After Janet Jackson's "wardrobe malfunction" during a live performance at the Super Bowl in 2004 led to indecent exposure, the FCC increased fines for indecency and profanity violations. In turn, many networks increased their broadcast delays for live performances.

sought to prohibit radio and television stations from airing explicit sexual and excretory references between 6 A.M. and 10 P.M., the hours when the audience is most likely to include children. Generally speaking, FCC regulation applies only to the over-the-air broadcast media. It does not apply to cable television, the Internet, or satellite radio.

In 1996, Congress passed the Telecommunications Act, a broad effort to end most regulations. The legislation loosened restrictions on media ownership and allowed telephone companies, cable television providers, and broadcasters to compete with one another to provide telecommunication services. Following the passage of this act, mergers between telephone and cable companies and different entertainment media produced a greater concentration of media ownership than had been possible since regulation of the industry began in 1934.

Though the act loosened many regulations, it did include an attempt to regulate the content of material transmitted over the Internet. This law, known as the Communications Decency Act, made it illegal to make "indecent" sexual material on the Internet accessible to those under age 18. The act was immediately denounced by civil libertarians, and in 1997 the Supreme Court ruled that the Communications Decency Act was an unconstitutional infringement of the right to freedom of speech guaranteed by the First Amendment (see Chapter 4).

Although the government's ability to regulate the content of the Internet is limited, the FCC has used its licensing power to impose several regulations that can affect the political content of radio and TV broadcasts. The first of these is the **equal time rule**, under which broadcasters must provide to candidates for the same political office equal opportunities to communicate their messages to the public. Under the terms of the Telecommunications Act, during the 45 days before an election, broadcasters are required to make time available to candidates at the lowest rate charged for that time slot.

The second regulation affecting the content of broadcasts is the **right of rebuttal**, which requires that individuals be given the opportunity to respond to personal attacks. In the 1969 case of *Red Lion Broadcasting Company v. FCC*, for example, the U.S. Supreme Court upheld the FCC's determination that a radio station was required to provide a liberal author with an opportunity to respond to a conservative commentator's attack that the station had aired.[77] For many years, a third important federal regulation was the *fairness doctrine*. Under this rule, broadcasters that aired programs on controversial issues were required to provide time for opposing views. In 1985, however, the FCC stopped enforcing the fairness doctrine on the grounds that there were so many radio and television stations—to say nothing of newspapers and newsmagazines—that in all likelihood many different viewpoints were already being presented without each station being required to try to present all sides of every argument. Critics of this FCC decision charge that in many media markets the number of competing viewpoints is actually quite small.

The rise of online media challenges our thinking about regulation of the media as it is more difficult—some say impossible—to regulate political content online. In 2011 the United Nations declared that access to the Internet is a human right.[78] While this declaration came in response to threats by authoritarian governments

equal time rule the requirement that broadcasters provide candidates for the same political office equal opportunities to communicate their messages to the public

right of rebuttal a Federal Communications Commission regulation giving individuals the right to have the opportunity to respond to personal attacks made on a radio or television broadcast

Press Freedom around the world

The First Amendment to the U.S. Constitution guarantees that the media are essentially free from government interference. A free press is a necessary component of a functioning democracy, as critical media help hold leaders accountable for their actions. However, many countries limit freedom of the press in at least some ways. For example, in some democratic countries, such as Hungary, rules limiting hate speech or protecting privacy rights can inhibit critical journalism. Some non-democratic governments, such as in China or Cuba, exercise strict control over the media.

When we think about attacks on the freedom of the press, it's often government arrests and the killing of journalists that make the headlines, but threats to media freedom can be more subtle. In Russia, for example, journalists who criticize government officials may find themselves targets of expensive libel or slander lawsuits. In an ideal world, should all media be free from interference? Is there ever a reason to place limits on press freedom?

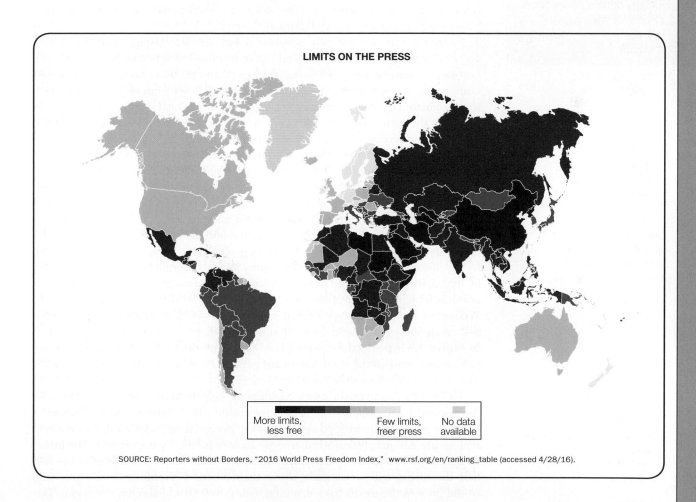

LIMITS ON THE PRESS

More limits, less free · Few limits, freer press · No data available

SOURCE: Reporters without Borders, "2016 World Press Freedom Index," www.rsf.org/en/ranking_table (accessed 4/28/16).

against Internet access, it demonstrates the significance of information technology in modern life.[79]

The Media, Democracy, *and Your Future*

forcriticalanalysis

In wartime, can media criticism of government action aid the nation's enemies? Should there be limits on media criticism of the government during times of war? Or does criticism actually enhance the nation's strength?

The freedom of the press is essential to democratic government. Ordinary citizens depend on the media to investigate wrongdoing, publicize and explain governmental policy, evaluate politicians, and bring to light matters that might otherwise be known to only a handful of governmental insiders. In short, without free and active media, democratic government would be virtually impossible. Citizens would have few means through which to know or assess the government's actions—other than the claims or pronouncements of the government itself. Moreover, without active (indeed, aggressive) media, citizens would be hard-pressed to make informed choices among competing candidates at the polls.

Today's media are not only adversarial but also increasingly partisan. Blogs, digital journalism, social media, and other Internet outlets can be unabashedly partisan. To some extent, increasing ideological and partisan stridency is an inevitable result of the expansion and proliferation of news sources. When the news was dominated by three networks and a handful of national papers, each sought to appeal to the entire national audience. This required a moderate and balanced tone so that consumers would not be offended and transfer their attention to a rival network or newspaper. Today, there are so many news sources that few can aim for a broad-based national audience. Instead, many target a partisan or ideological niche and aim to develop a strong relationship with consumers in that audience segment by catering to their biases and predispositions.

The rise of citizen journalism, social media, and digital media has fundamentally changed how political information is gathered and distributed. News today is participatory and involves citizens as well as professional journalists. Wikipedia, the free online encyclopedia founded by Jimmy Wales, has millions of pages compiled by legions of volunteers and provides relatively unbiased content on virtually every political topic imaginable. Social media (Facebook, Twitter, and countless others), Wikipedia, and all Wiki-type sites involve people working collaboratively to write and create information and transmit knowledge. Social media also enable citizens to express their political opinions. (The "**Who Participates?**" feature on the facing page shows some of the ways Americans participate in politics via social media.) Is such a system the future of the news media?

The media can make or break reputations, help to launch or destroy political careers, and build support for or rally opposition to programs and institutions.[80] Wherever there is so much power, at least the potential exists for its abuse or overly zealous use. All things considered, free media are so critically important to the maintenance of a democratic society that Americans must be prepared to take the risk that the media will occasionally abuse their power. Governmental controls that would prevent the media from misusing their power would also limit freedom. The ultimate beneficiaries of free and active media are the American people.

Who Participates via Social Media?

Percentage of Adults Who Have...

Age group
- 18–29
- 30–49
- 50–64
- 65+

Posted pictures or videos related to political or social issues in the last 12 months

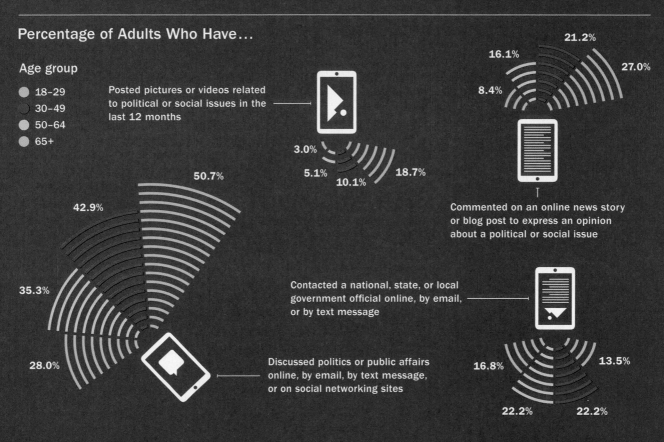

21.2%
16.1%
27.0%
8.4%

3.0%
5.1%
10.1%
18.7%

Commented on an online news story or blog post to express an opinion about a political or social issue

50.7%
42.9%
35.3%
28.0%

Contacted a national, state, or local government official online, by email, or by text message

Discussed politics or public affairs online, by email, by text message, or on social networking sites

16.8%
13.5%
22.2%
22.2%

SOURCE: Pew Research Center, "Civic Engagement in the Digital Age." www.pewinternet.org/2013/04/25/civic-engagement-in-the-digital-age/ (accessed: 10/5/15).

WHAT YOU CAN DO

Be an Informed Consumer of Media

☑ Gather information from a variety of news sources rather than relying on just one. You can set up a news aggregator with a variety of free downloadable apps, including Flipboard (**www.flipboard.com**) and Feedly (**www.feedly.com**).

☑ Check media watchdog organizations such as the Columbia Journalism Review (**www.cjr.org**), Fairness & Accuracy in Reporting (**www.fair.org**), and Accuracy in Media (**www.aim.org**) for reports of media bias and censorship.

☑ For information on the factual accuracy of what is said by political players, go to **www.factcheck.org**. For investigative journalism in the public interest, go to **www.propublica.org**. For reporting on the accuracy of news rumors, go to **www.snopes.com**.

studyguide

Traditional Media

Describe trends in the role of print and broadcast media in providing political information (pp. 251–58)

Americans have traditionally gotten their political information from broadcast media (radio and television) and print media (newspapers and magazines). Television reaches the largest audience but provides little depth of coverage. Radio news provides important sources of commentary as well as entertainment. Newspapers, by contrast, are read for their in-depth coverage and are important in setting the agenda of the broadcast media.

Key Terms

media (p. 251)

broadcast media (p. 251)

media monopoly (p. 257)

Practice Quiz

1. _____ play an important role in American politics because they are influential among the political elite.
   a) Academic journals
   b) Newspapers
   c) Facebook posts
   d) Political cartoons
   e) YouTube videos

2. The vast majority of daily print newspapers are owned by
   a) large media conglomerates.
   b) the national government.
   c) small local companies.
   d) private individuals.
   e) the employees who run them.

New Media and Online News

Explain how the Internet has transformed the news media (pp. 258–67)

Online political information includes online-only newspapers, news aggregation websites, niche journalism, social media, citizen journalism, blogs, and nonprofit journalism. The convenience, currency, depth, and diversity of online news have led many Americans to prefer it to more traditional sources. Changes arising from the emergence of the Internet have also raised concerns that online news may produce a decline in investigative journalism, a decrease in the quality of news content, and a reduction in political knowledge and tolerance.

Key Terms

penny press (p. 258)

news aggregator (p. 258)

digital citizen (p. 259)

digital divide (p. 260)

niche journalism (p. 260)

social media (p. 261)

citizen journalism (p. 262)

Practice Quiz

3. Digital citizenship requires
   a) an online subscription to one or more online newspapers.
   b) high-speed Internet access and the skills to use and evaluate online information.
   c) a social media account.
   d) maintaining a political blog.
   e) registering one's computer with the government.

4. News reporting devoted to a targeted portion of readers based on content or ideological presentation is called
   a) nonprofit journalism.
   b) for-profit journalism.
   c) niche journalism.
   d) citizen journalism.
   e) adversarial journalism.

5. Which of the following is *not* a reason that many Americans appear to prefer online news?
   a) the convenience of getting news online
   b) the up-to-the-minute currency of the information available online
   c) the depth of the information available online
   d) the diversity of online viewpoints
   e) the accuracy and objectivity compared to traditional media outlets

Media Influence

The content and character of news programming can have far-reaching political consequences. In recent American political history, the media have played a central role in numerous major events, such as the civil rights movement of the 1950s and '60s, the Vietnam War, and the Watergate affair. The power of the media lies in their ability to shape what issues Americans think about (agenda setting) and what opinions Americans hold about those issues (framing and priming).

Key Terms

agenda setting (p. 270)

selection bias (news) (p. 272)

framing (p. 272)

priming (p. 273)

Practice Quiz

6. The media's powers to determine what becomes a part of political discussion and to shape how political events are interpreted are known as
   a) media consolidation and selection bias.
   b) issue definition and protest power.
   c) agenda setting and framing.
   d) the illusion of saliency and the bandwagon effect.
   e) the equal time rule and the right of rebuttal.

7. Which of the following best describes the media's role in the Watergate affair?
   a) They played a central role in reporting on President Nixon's resignation but did little to reveal his abuses of power while he was president.
   b) They played a central role in President Nixon's decision to resign from the presidency by revealing his abuses of power to the public.
   c) They played a central role in disproving claims that President Nixon had abused his power while in office.
   d) They played almost no role in the Watergate affair because they were legally prohibited from discussing ongoing police investigations.
   e) They played almost no role in the Watergate affair because they refused to investigate claims that President Nixon had abused his power.

News Coverage

Press releases, leaks, and the tradition of adversarial journalism are important in determining the content of news coverage. Leaks, which are confidential pieces of information disclosed to members of the media, have driven press coverage on issues ranging from foreign policy to government corruption. Also incorporated into daily news coverage are thousands of press releases authored by advocates of influential political interests. Adversarial journalism, a form of reporting in which the media adopt a skeptical or even hostile posture toward public officials, has increased the political power of the press in recent years.

Practice Quiz

8. Which of the following best describes the media's use of press releases?
   a) Press releases are never incorporated into daily news reports because it is illegal under federal law.
   b) Press releases are never incorporated into daily news reports because reporters view the information they contain as biased and politically motivated.
   c) Thousands of press releases are incorporated into daily news reports every year because press releases allow news organizations to fill their pages at little cost.
   d) Press releases are rarely incorporated into daily news reports because reporters view the information as biased and politically motivated.
   e) Every press release written by a political party, interest group, candidate, or government official is incorporated into daily news reports because reporters view the information as newsworthy.

9. Most leaks originate with
   a) low-level government whistle-blowers.
   b) senior government officials, prominent politicians, and political activists.
   c) members of the public who witness misbehavior.
   d) ambassadors from foreign countries.
   e) members of the media.

10. *Adversarial journalism* refers to
   a) the recent shift in American society away from general-purpose sources of information and toward narrowly focused niche sources.
   b) an era in American history when political parties provided all of the financing for newspapers.
   c) a form of reporting in which the media adopt a skeptical or even hostile posture toward the opinions and behaviors of their audience.
   d) a form of reporting in which the media adopt an accepting and friendly posture toward the government and public officials.
   e) a form of reporting in which the media adopt a skeptical or even hostile posture toward the government and public officials.

11. Which event shattered the amicable relationship between the press and the presidency?
   a) September 11, 2001
   b) the Vietnam War
   c) Watergate
   d) World War II
   e) the Monica Lewinsky affair

Regulation of the Media

Trace the evolution of rules that govern broadcast media (pp. 277–80)

Although American print and online media are free from government interference, broadcast media are subject to significant federal regulation. Radio and television stations in the United States are licensed by the Federal Communications Commission (FCC). The FCC has used its licensing power to impose several regulations, such as the equal time rule, the right of rebuttal, and the fairness doctrine, that affect the political content of radio and television broadcasts.

Key Terms

equal time rule (p. 278)

right of rebuttal (p. 278)

Practice Quiz

12. In general, FCC regulations apply only to
   a) cable television.
   b) Internet websites.
   c) over-the-air broadcast media.
   d) satellite radio.
   e) newspapers and magazines.

13. The now defunct requirement that broadcasters provide time for opposing views when they air programs on controversial issues was called
   a) the equal time rule.
   b) the free speech doctrine.
   c) the fairness doctrine.
   d) the right of rebuttal.
   e) the response rule.

For Further Reading

Boydstun, Amber E. *Making the News: Politics, the Media, and Agenda Setting*. Chicago: University of Chicago Press, 2013.

Carr, Nicholas. *The Shallows: What the Internet Is Doing to Our Brains*. New York: W. W. Norton, 2011.

Chadwick, Andrew. *The Hybrid Media System: Politics and Power*. New York: Oxford University Press, 2013.

Fenton, Tom. *Bad News: The Decline of Reporting, the Business of News, and the Danger to Us All*. New York: Harper Collins, 2005.

Hamilton, James T. *All the News That's Fit to Sell*. Princeton, NJ: Princeton University Press, 2004.

Iyengar, Shanto. *Media Politics: A Citizen's Guide*. New York: W. W. Norton, 2015.

Iyengar, Shanto, and Donald Kinder. *News That Matters: Television and American Public Opinion*. Chicago: University of Chicago Press, 2010.Jamieson, Kathleen, and Paul Waldman. *The Press Effect*. New York: Oxford University Press, 2004.

Jenkins, Henry. *Convergence Culture: Where Old and New Media Collide*. New York: New York University Press, 2008.

Jenkins, Henry, Sam Ford, and Joshua Green. *Spreadable Media: Creating Value and Meaning in a Networked Culture*. New York: New York University Press, 2013.

Mossberger, Karen, Caroline Tolbert, and Ramona McNeal. *Digital Citizenship: The Internet, Society, and Participation*. Cambridge, MA: MIT Press, 2008.

Pariser, Eli. *The Filter Bubble: What the Internet Is Hiding from You*. New York: Penguin, 2011.

Shirky, Clay. *Here Comes Everybody: The Power of Organizing without Organizations*. New York: Penguin, 2009.

West, Darrell. *The Next Wave: Using Digital Technology to Further Social and Political Innovation*. Washington, DC: Brookings Institution Press, 2011.

Recommended Websites

Accuracy in Media
www.aim.org

This nonprofit watchdog group attempts to ensure accuracy in media reporting by identifying botched or slanted stories and then "setting the record straight."

G. R. Boynton's New Media and Politics
ir.uiowa.edu/polisci_nmp/

This website contains a collection of research on new media trends such as microblogging, streaming video, and Twitter, with a focus on how these developments have shaped the way people share political information.

Journalism.org
www.journalism.org

This nonprofit, nonpolitical site, sponsored by the Project for Excellence in Journalism, examines the overall performance of the press as providers of information. Its aim is to help both consumers and producers of the news.

National Telecommunication and Information Administration
www.ntia.doc.gov

The National Telecommunication and Information Administration advises the president on telecommunications policies for the technological advancement of the nation. The "Broadband" section of the website includes "Digital Nation Reports" on Internet usage in the United States.

Pew Internet, Science, and Tech
www.pewinternet.org

Pew Internet, Science, and Tech conducts public opinion polling, demographic research, and content analyses of trends around Internet, Science, and Technology. Pew Research Center is an independent, nonpartisan think tank that also explores attitudes toward numerous other political issues.

Shorenstein Center on Media, Politics, and Public Policy
www.shorensteincenter.org

This research center based out of Harvard University explores the intersection of the press, politics, and public policy. The "News and Events" section includes a weekly roundup of "Must-Reads" on the media and politics.

For much of the country's history, large groups of Americans were denied the right to vote. Most restrictions on voting have been eliminated for Americans age 18 and older, but turnout remains relatively low, especially among young voters. Will changes in voting laws increase participation?

POLLING PLACE
投票站 CASILLA ELECTORAL
投票所 LUGAR NG BOTOHAN
투표소 PHÒNG PHIẾU

Political Participation and Voting

8

WHAT GOVERNMENT DOES AND WHY IT MATTERS Who votes affects who is elected and what issues politicians put at the top of their agenda. Voters tend to be more affluent, educated, and older than nonvoters. Elected officials adopt policies consistent with the preferences of voters, rather than nonvoters. Thus who votes matters. The United States has relatively low voter participation, setting it apart from other democracies in the developed world. Even in the high-turnout presidential election of 2008, only 62 percent of Americans voted;[1] in 2016, the turnout rate was 59 percent.[2] In most democratic countries, residents are automatically registered to vote in elections at adult age. In the United States, citizens must actively register to vote and, in most states, must do so in advance of the election—sometimes 30 days beforehand.

The registration requirement accounts in large part for low voting rates among Americans. One of the most common reasons that people in the United States give for not voting is that they are not registered; on average more than 5 percent of Americans indicate that registration problems prevented them from voting, adding up to millions of people. Young people especially are less likely to register to vote than are older Americans.[3] In an effort to boost voter turnout, a number of states have begun to offer same-day registration, which means that people can both register and vote when they go to the polls on Election Day. As of 2016, 13 states plus Washington, D.C., had same-day registration laws. Of the 10 states with the highest average voting rates, 7 offer same-day registration.[4]

Five states—California, Oregon, Connecticut, Vermont, and West Virginia—have recently gone even further and have adopted laws that will automatically register their residents to vote in elections.

These new laws place more responsibility for increasing voter turnout on the government rather than on citizens, requiring information sharing between two government agencies collecting similar information, the Department of Motor Vehicles and the secretary of state's office. Though all five states have adopted these laws, automatic voter registration was only in effect in Oregon for the 2016 election. Though turnout in Oregon did not increase in 2016 from 2012, some scholars believe automatic voter registration is more likely to have an impact on turnout in state in local elections, rather than in presidential elections when voters are better informed and don't need a reminder to vote.[5]

Although this kind of election reform may seem wholly positive at first, it triggers controversial debate and deep partisan conflict. Opponents contend that these laws make the states' voter rolls more vulnerable to fraud. Supporters say the new system may be more secure than traditional paper registration because rather than simply attesting to their eligibility with a signature, individuals have to submit proof of citizenship to the Department of Motor Vehicles. Automatic voter registration is generally favored by Democrats, who want expanded access to the ballot box; Republicans, on the other hand, often don't want to add new voters who may be more likely to support the Democratic Party. It is important to note, however, that lawmakers are not always correct about which party will benefit from increased voter registration.

Voting is just one form of political participation, and voter-registration requirements are just one factor that affects who participates in American politics. As we will see in this chapter, who participates and how they participate matter a great deal—in elections and in influencing government policy.

chapter goals

- Describe the major forms of traditional and digital participation in politics (pp. 289–99)
- Describe the patterns of participation among major demographic groups (pp. 299–310)
- Explain the factors in the political environment that influence whether individuals vote or not (pp. 310–13)
- Explain the effect of electoral laws on voting (pp. 314–19)

● Forms of Political Participation

Describe the major forms of traditional and digital participation in politics

We can think of political participation as falling into two major categories. Traditional participation in politics includes not only voting but also attending campaign events, rallies, and fund-raisers, volunteering on behalf of candidates and political organizations, canvassing, displaying campaign signs, contacting elected officials, contributing money to candidates and parties, or even challenging a law in court. Protests, demonstrations, and strikes, too, are age-old forms of participatory politics.

In addition to traditional participation, there is a growing world of digital politics, which includes not only the exchange of information but also fund-raising and voter mobilization. Most experts now agree that digital politics is just a new way of engaging in traditional politics. As digital politics becomes more common, it continues to change participation in important ways that may increase engagement in politics overall.

Traditional Political Participation

Traditional political participation refers to a wide range of activities designed to influence government, politics, and policy. For most citizens today, voting is the most common form of participation in politics. Yet ordinary people took part in politics long before the advent of the election or any other formal mechanism of popular involvement in political life. If there is any natural or spontaneous form of popular political participation, it is not the election but the riot. In fact, for much of American history, fewer Americans exercised their right to vote than participated in urban riots and rural uprisings as voting for a long time was limited to white, male, landowning citizens.

The vast majority of Americans reject rioting or violence for political ends, but peaceful **protest** is protected by the First Amendment and generally recognized as a legitimate and important form of political activity. During the height of the civil rights movement in the 1960s, hundreds of thousands of Americans took part in peaceful protests to demand social and political rights for African Americans. Peaceful marches and demonstrations have been employed by a host of groups, including opponents of the war in Iraq and the 2011 Occupy Wall Street protests against unemployment, undue corporate influence on government, and growing income inequality.

Growing concern over police discrimination and excessive use of police force against African Americans has led to both peaceful protests and civil unrest. The Black Lives Matter campaign took off after the killing of Michael Brown, an 18-year-old unarmed black man, by a white police officer in Ferguson, Missouri, in 2014. The incident sparked protests in Ferguson that began peacefully but soon became unruly. Mass media attention and an ongoing investigation—in which the police officer was not indicted—put the incident on the forefront of the American political scene, triggering protests in 170 American cities. Since then, a number of similar incidents of police force resulting in the deaths of African Americans have kept the issue in the spotlight. In July 2016 the widely publicized deaths of two black men at the hands of police within one day of each other again spurred nationwide protests. While most of the protests were peaceful, a sniper killed five police officers at a protest in Dallas, Texas. The events indicated that nearly two years after the death of Michael Brown, tensions around race relations in the United States

traditional political participation activities designed to influence government, including voting and face-to-face activities such as volunteering for a campaign or working on behalf of a candidate or political organization

protest participation that involves assembling crowds to confront a government or other official organization

One advantage of protest is visibility: through media attention, protesters can raise awareness, attract like-minded individuals, and put pressure on politicians, all of which are goals of Black Lives Matter protests.

remain very high, and protests and civil unrest in response to the issue are unlikely to go away any time soon.

People participate in public protests to attract media attention, raise public awareness, and send a message to politicians about the policies they enact. The Black Lives Matter campaign has prompted discussion and political action around police reform, including revamped training programs and calls to equip police officers with body cameras. Opinion polls suggest that both white and black Americans increasingly feel that racism is a problem in American society.[6] The Occupy Wall Street movement and protests were similarly successful in raising awareness of income inequality. For example, a Pew survey found that in 2014 two-thirds of Americans (66 percent) believed there were "very strong" or "strong" conflicts between the rich and the poor—an increase of 19 percentage points since 2009.[7] As noted in Chapter 6, a larger number of Americans have concerns with rising economic inequality.

Elections, of course, are the hallmark of political participation in a democracy. In addition to voting (discussed below), citizens can give money to candidates or political organizations, volunteer in campaigns, contact political officials, sign petitions, attend public meetings, join organizations, display campaign signs and pins, write letters to the editor, and attend rallies. They can also lobby their representatives in Congress; they can even sue the government or run for elected office. Such activities can communicate much more detailed information to public officials than voting can. Voters may support a candidate for many reasons; their votes do not indicate which specific policies they support or how strongly they feel about particular issues. By volunteering for a political campaign, writing or emailing their member of Congress, or contributing money to a political organization, people can convey their specific opinions, making these other political activities often more satisfying than voting.[8] However, these other forms of political action generally require more time, effort, and/or money than voting. As a result, as Figure 8.1 shows, the percentage of the population that participates in ways other than voting is relatively low.

Participation through Voting For most Americans, voting is the single most important political act. Voting is the most common way that individuals interact with politics. The right to vote gives ordinary Americans an equal voice in politics as each vote has the same value. Voting is especially important because it selects the officials who make the laws that the American people must follow.

The right to vote, or **suffrage**, is a legal right. During the colonial and early national periods of American history, suffrage was generally restricted to white males over the age of 21. Many states further limited voting to those who owned property or paid more than a specified amount of annual tax. Until the early 1900s, state legislatures elected U.S. senators, and there were no direct elections for members of the Electoral College (who in turn elect the president). As a result, elections for the U.S. House as well as state and local offices were the primary venue for citizen participation in government.

suffrage the right to vote; also called *franchise*

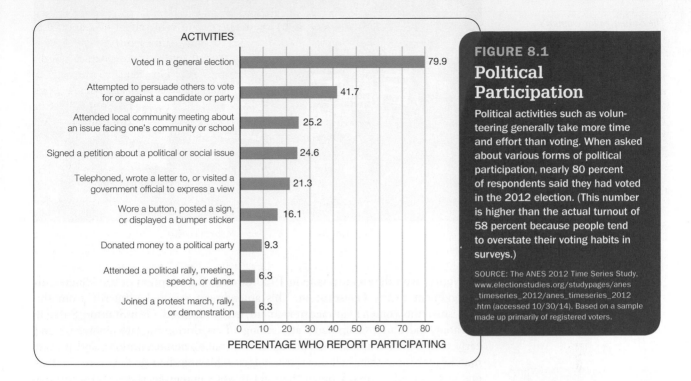

ACTIVITIES

Activity	Percentage
Voted in a general election	79.9
Attempted to persuade others to vote for or against a candidate or party	41.7
Attended local community meeting about an issue facing one's community or school	25.2
Signed a petition about a political or social issue	24.6
Telephoned, wrote a letter to, or visited a government official to express a view	21.3
Wore a button, posted a sign, or displayed a bumper sticker	16.1
Donated money to a political party	9.3
Attended a political rally, meeting, speech, or dinner	6.3
Joined a protest march, rally, or demonstration	6.3

PERCENTAGE WHO REPORT PARTICIPATING

FIGURE 8.1

Political Participation

Political activities such as volunteering generally take more time and effort than voting. When asked about various forms of political participation, nearly 80 percent of respondents said they had voted in the 2012 election. (This number is higher than the actual turnout of 58 percent because people tend to overstate their voting habits in surveys.)

SOURCE: The ANES 2012 Time Series Study, www.electionstudies.org/studypages/anes_timeseries_2012/anes_timeseries_2012.htm (accessed 10/30/14). Based on a sample made up primarily of registered voters.

During the nineteenth and early twentieth centuries, states often acted to restrict suffrage, initially through poll taxes (fees to vote) and literacy tests (reading tests) designed to curtail immigrant voting in northern cities. These laws were later imported to the southern states to prevent African Americans and uneducated whites from voting during the Jim Crow era, the period after the Civil War and before the 1960s (see Chapter 5). Voter eligibility requirements often varied greatly from state to state. Some states openly prevented the right to vote on the basis of race; others did not. Some states required property ownership for voting; others had no such restrictions.[9]

Over the past two centuries of American history, a dominant trend has been federal statutes, court decisions, and constitutional amendments designed to override state voting laws and expand suffrage to nonlandowners, African Americans, Asian Americans, women, young adults, and others.[10] In the South, voting rights for black men were established by the Fifteenth Amendment in 1870, which prohibited denying the right to vote on the basis of race. Despite the Fifteenth Amendment, the voting rights of African American men were effectively rescinded during the 1880s by the states of the former Confederacy with voting laws such as poll taxes and literacy tests, as discussed above. A goal of the civil rights movement in the 1950s and '60s led by Martin Luther King, Jr., was voting rights for African Americans. This goal was partially achieved with the enactment of the 1965 Voting Rights Act, which authorized the federal government to register voters in states that discriminated against minority citizens. The result was the re-enfranchisement of southern blacks for the first time since the 1860s.

The campaign for women's suffrage gathered strength in the United States in the mid-eighteenth century. Activists fought for decades—with tactics ranging from protests to pickets to hunger strikes—before the Nineteenth Amendment to the Constitution granted all adult women the right to vote in 1920.

turnout the percentage of eligible individuals who actually vote

Women won the right to vote in 1920 through the adoption of the Nineteenth Amendment to the Constitution. This amendment resulted primarily from the activism of the women's suffrage movement, led by Elizabeth Cady Stanton, Susan B. Anthony, and Carrie Chapman Catt, among others, during the late nineteenth and early twentieth centuries. The suffragists held rallies, demonstrations, and protest marches for more than half a century before achieving their goal. Before the federal government granted women the right to vote, numerous states and territories adopted women's suffrage, paving the way for women to earn the right to vote nationally. The cause of women's suffrage was ultimately advanced by World War I, when President Woodrow Wilson and members of Congress argued that women would be more likely to support the war effort if they were granted the right to vote.

The most recent expansion of the right to vote in the United States, the Twenty-Sixth Amendment, lowered the voting age from 21 to 18. Ratified during the Vietnam War, in 1971, it was intended to channel the disruptive protest activities of students involved in the anti–Vietnam War movement into peaceful participation at the ballot box.

Current Trends in Voter Turnout Today, voting rights are granted to all American citizens aged 18 and above, although some states revoke this right from those who have committed a felony or are mentally incompetent. Although eligibility to vote is now almost universal for citizens aged 18 and above, America's overall rate of voting participation, or **turnout**, is moderately low. Since the 1960s about 60 percent of eligible Americans vote in presidential elections, and turnout for midterm elections (elections that fall between presidential elections) is typically around one-third of the eligible population. Turnout in state and local races, especially those that do not coincide with national contests or primaries, is typically much lower.[11] This means that many Americans choose not to participate in elections that impact local, state, and national issues, including education and public works.

Participation in U.S. presidential elections has declined over the past four decades from a high of 64 percent in 1960. In 1996 participation reached a modern low when only 52 percent of eligible voters went to the polls. Since then, however, overall trends have improved in presidential elections due to major efforts to get out the vote. Turnout reached a modern high point of 62 percent in 2008 when presidential candidate Barack Obama mobilized many new voters. In 2016 turnout

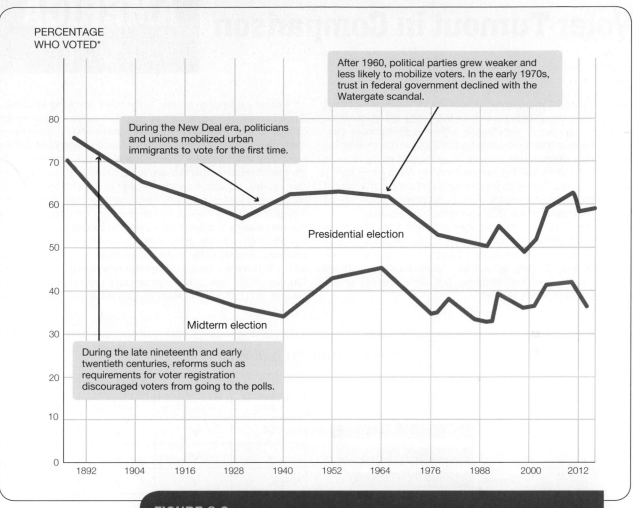

PERCENTAGE
WHO VOTED*

During the New Deal era, politicians and unions mobilized urban immigrants to vote for the first time.

After 1960, political parties grew weaker and less likely to mobilize voters. In the early 1970s, trust in federal government declined with the Watergate scandal.

Presidential election

Midterm election

During the late nineteenth and early twentieth centuries, reforms such as requirements for voter registration discouraged voters from going to the polls.

FIGURE 8.2

Voter Turnout in Presidential and Midterm Elections, 1892–2016

Since the 1890s, participation in elections has declined substantially. One pattern is consistent across time: more Americans tend to vote in presidential election years than in years when only congressional and local elections are held. What are some of the reasons that participation rose and fell during the last century?

*Percentage of voting-eligible population
SOURCES: Erik Austin and Jerome Clubb, *Political Facts of the United States since 1789* (New York: Columbia University Press, 1986); United States Election Project, www.electproject.org (accessed 11/14/16).

was 59 percent of eligible voters.[12] Midterm elections with only congressional elections at the national level tend to have much lower voter turnout; in 2014, 36 percent voted, down from almost 42 percent in 2010 (see Figure 8.2). Despite these overall trends, there are significant differences in voter turnout rates across the states. We'll learn more about why voter turnout rates vary so much across the states later in this chapter.

Voter Turnout in Comparison

Over the past 20 years, voter turnout in U.S. national elections has hovered around 45 percent of the voting-age population. While the number is significantly higher in presidential elections than in midterm elections (in the 2014 midterm election, for example, turnout was roughly 33 percent),[a] voting rates in the United States still lag behind those in many other democratic countries. Australia, for instance, had almost 80 percent of their voting-age population (roughly 93 percent of registered voters) participate in the 2013 parliamentary election.

So why does voter turnout vary so much from country to country? Part of the explanation rests in how we calculate who is eligible to vote. In the United States, noncitizens and ex-felons are denied voting rights. If we exclude those populations when calculating voter percentages, U.S. turnout would be several percentage points higher.[b]

Another explanation relates to the rules governing elections. Some countries have rules that make it easier or harder for citizens to vote, while others penalize those who do not vote. In many democracies, citizens are automatically registered to vote when they reach a certain age; in contrast, U.S. citizens generally have to register themselves, reregister if they move, and, in many states, register a certain number of days before the election. Many countries hold their elections on a Sunday, send their ballots through the mail, or declare their election day a national holiday, meaning that fewer voters have to choose between going to work or going to the polls. Voting is also compulsory in many countries. Australia, for instance, charges a $20 fine (about $17 U.S. dollars) unless a citizen can provide a good excuse for why she did not vote.[c] These factors help explain why turnout is lower in the United States than in many other countries.

TURNOUT IN NATIONAL ELECTIONS*

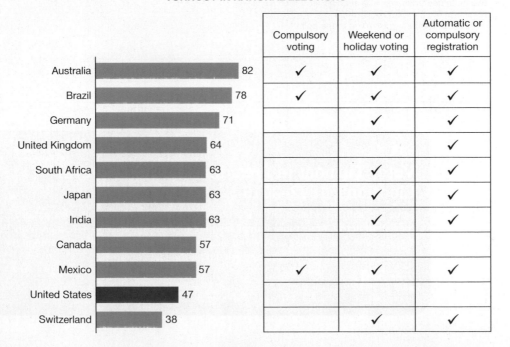

Country	Turnout	Compulsory voting	Weekend or holiday voting	Automatic or compulsory registration
Australia	82	✓	✓	✓
Brazil	78	✓	✓	✓
Germany	71		✓	✓
United Kingdom	64			✓
South Africa	63		✓	✓
Japan	63		✓	✓
India	63		✓	✓
Canada	57			
Mexico	57	✓	✓	✓
United States	47			
Switzerland	38		✓	✓

*Average 1990–2016.
SOURCES: International Institute for Democracy and Electoral Assistance (IDEA) Voter turnout database, www.idea.int/vt/viewdata. cfm and the ACE Electoral Knowledge Network, www.aceproject.org/epic-en/CDMap?question=VR008&f= (accessed 3/27/16).

[a]International Institute for Democracy and Electoral Assistance (IDEA), Voter Turnout Database, www.idea.int/vt/viewdata.cfm (accessed 3/27/16).
[b]Michael P. McDonald, "National General Election VEP Turnout Rates, 1789–Present," United States Election Project, June 11, 2014, www.electproject.org/national -1789-present (accessed 6/24/16).
[c]Juliet Lapidos, "Doing Democracy Right," Slate, October 17, 2008, www.slate.com/articles/news_and_politics/how_they_do_it/2008/10/doing_democracy_right.html (accessed 6/24/16).

Digital Political Participation

Digital political participation is rapidly changing the way Americans experience politics. The Internet gives citizens greater access to political information about candidates and campaigns and, at least potentially, a greater role in politics than ever before. Digital politics builds on traditional forms of participation, but social media, email, text messaging, and online news make many of these activities easier and give citizens greater potential for community building. The Internet offers an active, two-way form of communication with feedback, rather than the more passive, one-way communication involved in reading printed newspapers, watching television, or listening to the radio. It allows for person-to-person communication as well as broadcast capability especially through social media, video, and visual images where information can be widely shared.

Digital participation includes discussing issues or mobilizing supporters through social media (such as Facebook, Twitter, and Snapchat), emailing and text messaging, reading blogs and online news stories, viewing online videos and campaign ads, commenting and sharing opinions on the Internet, contributing money to candidates, campaigning on social networking sites, working on behalf of candidates, and organizing face-to-face neighborhood meetings online. Digital participation is the most common way average Americans participate in politics outside of voting.

Recent survey data illustrate how widespread digital politics has become. Today, a majority of American adults—62 percent in 2016—get news about politics and government on social media.[13] One in three social media users have encouraged others to vote, and roughly the same percentage have shared their own thoughts or comments on politics or government using social media.[14] About the same percentages of Democrats, Republicans, and independents use social media for politics.[15]

Twitter in particular has become a key networking tool for politics and a preferred platform of candidates and political organizations. Twitter users represented just 17 percent of the American adult population in 2015, but Twitter news consumers are younger, more mobile, and more educated than average Americans.[16] Twitter's forte is sharing breaking news about politics. While older and more affluent individuals are more likely to vote, it is young people and individuals making less than $75,000 a year who are more likely to post political news on Twitter and other social media. Social media may help level the democratic playing field, allowing the young, people with lower incomes, and racial and ethnic minorities to play a larger role in news and politics.[17]

With each successive election, political news continues to reach a greater number of Americans as the Internet creates new platforms for communication and political mobilization. The 2008 presidential election ushered in the modern era of digital politics. Democratic candidates and their left-leaning political organizations in particular built comprehensive Internet strategies that did more than just duplicate offline efforts to mobilize supporters, and citizens made unprecedented use of digital media to learn about candidates and to participate in campaigns.[18] While only 4 percent of likely voters went online for election information in 1996, a full 61 percent reported looking at information online or discussing politics online in 2012.[19]

In 2016 every serious presidential candidate had a Facebook page and Twitter account, with millions of fans who received daily updates from the candidates and campaigns. These fans, in turn, signaled to their "friends" which candidates they

digital political participation
activities designed to influence politics using the Internet, including visiting a candidate's website, organizing events online, and signing an online petition

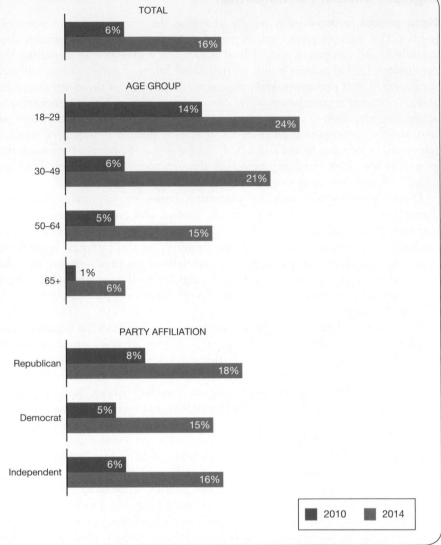

SOURCE: Monica Anderson, "More Americans Are Using Social Media to Connect with Politicians," May 19, 2015, www.pewresearch.org/fact-tank/2015/05/19/more-americans-are-using-social-media-to-connect-with-politicians/ (accessed 3/8/16).

FIGURE 8.3

Registered Voters Who Follow Political Figures on Social Media

While younger Americans are more likely to follow political figures on social media than are older Americans, there is little difference across party lines. The total number of registered voters who follow political figures on social media rose drastically from 2010 to 2014. What might have accounted for such a change? Would you expect a similar increase from 2014 to today?

supported for elected office, making politics a seamless part of everyday discussion. The number of registered voters who follow candidates or other political figures on social media rose to 16 percent in 2014, more than double the number from four years prior (see Figure 8.3), and rose even higher in 2016. Those who follow political figures on social media not only receive frequent updates directly from the candidates but also report feeling more directly connected to the candidates.[20]

With each election cycle the population turning to digital politics expands, much like the rapid diffusion of literacy with the invention of the printing press centuries ago.[21] Those who benefit most from online politics are likely to be those who are most active online, including the young and more educated.[22] Mobile technology is especially important for the organization necessary in campaigns, elections, and other forms of political participation. A Pew survey found that 27 percent of registered voters used their cell phone for news related to elections or political events in 2012.[23] Candidates and political campaigns continue to turn to digital politics to reach their audience. If these trends are sustained, they may result in greater overall levels of political interest and activity.

Does Online Participation Lead to Offline Participation?

An important question is whether online political participation influences offline participation, especially voting. Political participation requires that people have an interest in the outcome of the election. They must have the knowledge or capacity to understand how to participate, and they must be mobilized.[24] Digital politics encourages information-gathering and interaction among users and elected officials by combining the content of traditional media with interpersonal communication. It is this combination of information and interactivity that gives the Internet the potential to promote interest in politics and increase participation.

Digital politics also goes hand in hand with other types of traditional campaign engagement. A growing body of research finds that online activities such as reading digital news, commenting on blogs, and using email or social media for politics increases the likelihood of voting. Digital politics is associated with contributing to political campaigns, volunteering on behalf of candidates, and even contacting elected officials. Online participation is also linked with discussing politics with friends or family, developing an interest in politics in general, and being politically knowledgeable.[25]

Like the traditional "I Voted" stickers, political messages shared on social media may remind and encourage others to participate too. In recent elections, Facebook users could click an "I Voted" button to announce that they had cast a ballot.

Researchers who study this subject have suggested a number of possible reasons that digital politics may foster participation. First, information and political news are easier to obtain online and available 24 hours a day for those who have Internet access. Online news is often breaking news than can spread rapidly, and it is generally free.

Second, digital politics may engage individuals who otherwise would not be involved in politics. The Internet creates a form of "accidental mobilization" for those who are greeted by political news when they open their email, check social media, or conduct online searches—sometimes politics finds the individual, rather than the other way around.[26] For example, candidates regularly place political ads on social media sites and in Google searches, prompting the individuals exposed to these ads, who may be online for entirely separate reasons, to learn about politics.

Third, digital media have unique characteristics that enhance participation. Streaming video online combines the qualities of print media that promote knowledge with the visual aspects of television that generate interest, engagement, and emotion.[27] News online covers events and issues with the same immediacy as television but with the in-depth treatment that is typical of newspapers. Emotional responses to political candidates or issues learned from online media or social media have been shown to trigger interest in politics and engagement.[28]

Fourth, online politics makes it easier for people to participate in politics because it requires less effort. By its very nature, digital politics occurs in ways that are less location-dependent than traditional politics: *community* takes on a very different meaning in an online social network compared with a voter's actual neighborhood precinct or a local political party office. The Internet facilitates participation that is potentially broad but with looser connections among participants than in more traditional networks of coworkers or neighbors.[29] A large but more loosely knit online community may promote extensive organizing efforts and improve political knowledge, interest, and participation, but it also encourages forms of participation that can be low in intensity and sporadic, possibly attracting individuals with only moderate political interest. The political scientist Bruce Bimber has shown that some interest groups are responding to this new political climate of sporadic participation by focusing more outreach on the web and by making it possible for individuals to support a specific issue or campaign without making a commitment to membership in the organization as a whole.[30] In this way, online politics widens the pool of political participation. On the downside, some argue that digital politics fosters what has been termed "slacktivism"—or point-and-click activism involving minimal personal effort or sustained engagement with political issues or a campaign.

Finally, the Internet enables new forms of political expression through blogs, videos, social media, and websites. The expressive capacity of technology can lead to increased citizen involvement in politics.[31] For many citizens, becoming a fan or follower of a candidate online is a first step toward active participation in politics.

For all these reasons, digital media may foster a new kind of community building that has the potential to reverse the trends in declining political participation since the 1960s. Some analysts have cited reduced trust in government, unresponsive elected officials, and a diminishing stock of what Robert Putnam, author of *Bowling Alone*, calls social capital—community networks that motivate political participation—to explain low voter turnout in the United States.[32] By making political information, discussion, communication, and mobilization easier, the Internet, and especially social media, may help Americans grow a new kind of digital social capital, one based on shared political experiences online.[33]

Expressive Politics Political scientist Russell Dalton has argued that participation in politics is becoming more expressive than ever before, largely aided by social media. Today, voting and volunteering are not enough. Individuals turn to social media to express their opinions on issues or candidates. This trend was exemplified by the response to the Supreme Court ruling on same-sex marriage. In 2015 the Supreme Court declared marriage a fundamental constitutional right for opposite-sex and same-sex couples alike. The Court decision made same-sex marriage legal in all 50 states; previously, 37 of the 50 states had recognized same-sex marriages.

In the wake of the decision, digital politics created a media firestorm as responses to the decision took over the Internet. The immediacy with which the news spread was remarkable. Traditional media and social media converged to celebrate or denounce the news that marriage for same-sex couples was the new law of the land. Google news listed thousands of stories, but social media, especially Twitter, generated the most energy and participation by average citizens. Social media enabled citizens to share their opinions in uniquely expressive ways, including through hashtags and displaying rainbow images. While multiple hashtags were used, including #SCOTUSMarriage and #GayMarriage, the most popular was #LoveWins. This hashtag was used almost 5.5 million times in 24 hours, even by celebrities and President Obama to recognize the Court's decision. Overall there were 10 million tweets about the Supreme Court decision in less than 12 hours.[34]

Facebook networks were also ablaze with activity. Millions of people used Facebook's tool to add a rainbow-colored background

News about the Supreme Court's 2015 decision to legalize same-sex marriage spread rapidly, in part through viral activity on social media. Sites such as Twitter provided users with a highly visible platform to show support.

#LoveWins

to their profile pictures or shared news stories and memes using rainbow images to show their support for marriage rights. The rainbow-colored backdrop draped over profile pictures was a particularly expressive means of sharing a political opinion. Corporate America even joined in to express support for the Court decision, renaming products and displaying rainbow images. Increased participation in digital politics, especially through social media, may force elected officials to better represent the people.[35]

Are There Drawbacks to Digital Participation? As the above examples illustrate, traditional political participation and digital politics are not mutually exclusive. Many people are equally comfortable in both worlds, using the Internet to facilitate organizing face-to-face neighborhood meetings or seek out information about a local campaign event or where to vote.

As we described in Chapter 1, digital citizens are daily Internet users who have regular access to high-speed broadband and the skills to use that technology, including language skills.[36] A barrier to digital participation is the digital divide—defined as the gap between those with and those without home Internet or mobile access. Today, over 20 percent of Americans don't have home broadband.[37] Those on the wrong side of the divide tend to be poorer, less educated, African American or Latino, and older. The digital divide creates new inequalities as the world of politics moves online.[38] These groups are more likely to cite affordability as a reason for lacking Internet access at home compared with other groups. Inequality in access to information online and the skills to use digital information is an important public policy issue, separating the digital "haves" from the "have-nots."

Despite these limitations, perhaps the most transformative aspect of digital media is how they affect not the participation of ordinary citizens but rather that of candidates and parties. Political candidates find campaigning online particularly attractive because it is cost-efficient and can reach a wide audience of prospective voters. Running for office can be enormously expensive, but new media may level the playing field by reducing candidate reliance on money from corporations, special interests, and wealthy donors. Despite recent Supreme Court rulings against legislative attempts to limit the influence of money in politics,[39] digital politics holds the promise of reinvigorating a more grassroots and participatory democracy.[40] In 2016 presidential candidate Bernie Sanders largely rejected Super PAC funding for his campaign and relied heavily on digital media. Grassroots funding in turn may allow political leaders to better represent the people, rather than special interests.

● Who Participates?

Describe the patterns of participation among major demographic groups

The factors that predict whether an individual will vote in elections are also related to the other, nonvoting forms of political participation discussed above, including working on behalf of a candidate or party. Because the affluent have more resources, they are significantly more likely to donate money to candidates and political organizations. But voting remains the primary focus of the study of political behavior. In the end, the candidate with the majority of the votes cast in an election wins political office—so patterns in voting behavior matter.

Even though polls on the West Coast hadn't closed, Obama achieved the 270 electoral votes he needed to win the 2012 election by evening on the East Coast. With the outcome already determined, Americans living in Pacific time zones who hadn't yet voted had little incentive to do so.

A common starting point for understanding who votes and who does not is to consider that individuals face a number of costs and benefits related to their decision to become involved in politics, just as in any other activity in life. According to such an analysis, an individual is likely to participate only if the benefits of voting in an election outweigh the costs.[41] One benefit associated with voting, for instance, may be the favorable policies that might result from having one's preferred candidate or party in office, which the potential voter weighs against the slim likelihood of her vote actually influencing the outcome of the election. Another benefit of voting is the sense of pride gained from fulfilling one's civic duty or efficacy from helping a candidate from one's preferred party win office. The costs related to voting can include the time and resources needed to become informed and to cast a ballot, which may help explain why the poor and the less educated are less likely to vote and participate in politics in other ways.

To understand who votes, it helps to understand why some Americans don't vote. The U.S. Census indicates the top reason for not voting in the 2012 presidential election was being "too busy or conflicting schedules," cited by almost one in five nonvoters. Minorities were more likely to cite conflicting schedules, which can include holding multiple jobs or balancing work and family. Sixteen percent of nonvoters said they were "not interested in politics," followed by 14 percent who had an illness or disability which prevented them from voting. Even personal health can be a predictor of voting, with the healthier more likely to participate in politics.[42] Thirteen percent of nonvoters said they "didn't like the candidates running for office or the campaign issues."[43]

Another factor affecting voting is people's political environments. State residence, for example, matters for participation in politics. For example, if headline news stories declare an early winner based on exit polls in a presidential election, there is little incentive for individuals to vote at that point. This occurs every four years when voters on the West Coast, located in a time zone three hours behind that of the East Coast, learn that the presidential race is effectively over. Turnout in California and other western states naturally plummets. The political environment can also positively affect voter turnout. For instance, citizens living in presidential battleground states (states with roughly equal numbers of Democrats and Republicans in the population) are exposed to a torrent of campaigns ads, candidate visits, and grassroots mobilization efforts. These individuals are more knowledgeable about presidential elections, are more interested in the campaign, and have a higher probability of voting than residents of states that are "safe" for either the Republican Party, such as Texas, or the Democratic Party, such as New York or California.

The factors that help us explain voting in elections can be grouped into three general categories: (1) a person's social and demographic background and attitudes about politics; (2) the political environment in which elections take place, such as campaigns that seek to mobilize voters and whether an election is contested among two political candidates; and (3) the state electoral laws that shape the electoral process. We examine each in turn.

Socioeconomic Status

One of the most important and consistent findings from surveys about participation is that Americans with higher levels of education, more income, and higher-level occupations—collectively, what social scientists call higher **socioeconomic status**—participate much more in politics than do those with less education and less income.[44] Education is the single most important factor in predicting not only whether an individual will vote but also most kinds of participation. Unsurprisingly, income is an important factor when it comes to making contributions, as well as voting. People who are more affluent have the money, time, and capacity to participate effectively in the political system. Among the age group with the highest overall turnout (people aged 45–64), for example, the 2012 Census found that 86 percent of individuals earning over $100,000 a year voted compared to 53 percent of those earning less than $20,000 per year.[45] These characteristics are also related to attitudes toward politics. Higher levels of political interest and psychological involvement in politics, such as political efficacy, are associated with individuals higher on the socioeconomic scale.[46]

Figure 8.4 shows the differences in voter turnout linked to ethnic group, education level, employment status, and age. Just 50 percent of those with only a high school diploma voted in the recent presidential election compared with 70 percent of college graduates.[47]

Education is one of the most important predictors of voting, and it also leads to other forms of participation. A 2014 Pew survey found that one in two registered voters with a college education or more encouraged other people to vote or support an issue compared to 34 percent of those with a high school degree or less. Eighteen percent of college graduates contributed money to candidates in 2014 compared to 7 percent of those with only a high school degree.[48]

Age and Participation

Older people have much higher rates of participation than do young people, in part because homeownership and property taxes, more common among older individuals, lead to a greater awareness of the importance of government. In the 2008 presidential elections, youth turnout was at its highest level in decades, with 44 percent of those aged 18 to 24 voting—still significantly lower, however, than the estimated 70 percent of older (65 and over) voters who turned out.[49] In 2016 youth turnout remained lower than the average across all age groups. Moreover, in midterm elections, youth turnout has historically been extremely low. In 2014, for example, only 20 percent of people ages 18 to 29 turned out to vote, the lowest in 40 years.[50] The primary reason young people don't vote is that they lack an interest in politics or have not been mobilized to participate. Studies have found that if young people do vote, they tend to maintain this habit throughout their lifetime.[51]

Another reason younger people vote less is that political campaigns rarely target young voters. A study of political advertising found that 64 percent of campaign television advertising was directed at people over 50. Only 14.2 percent of advertising was aimed at 18- to 34-year-olds.[52] Political campaigns strategically target older voters because they are more likely to turn out to vote. The most important organization representing the elderly is the AARP (formerly the American Association of Retired People), which has a membership of 40 million. AARP's ability to mobilize many thousands of individuals to weigh in on policy proposals has made the organization one of the most powerful in Washington. Young people have no comparable organization.

Since the early 1990s, several campaigns have sought to increase the participation of young voters. Rock the Vote enlists musicians and actors to urge young people to vote. It has spawned other initiatives aimed at young voters, including

socioeconomic status status in society based on level of education, income, and occupational prestige

for critical analysis

As voter turnout has declined since its peak in the late 1800s, inequality in political participation has become more severe. Why are upper-income Americans more likely to be voters than lower-income Americans?

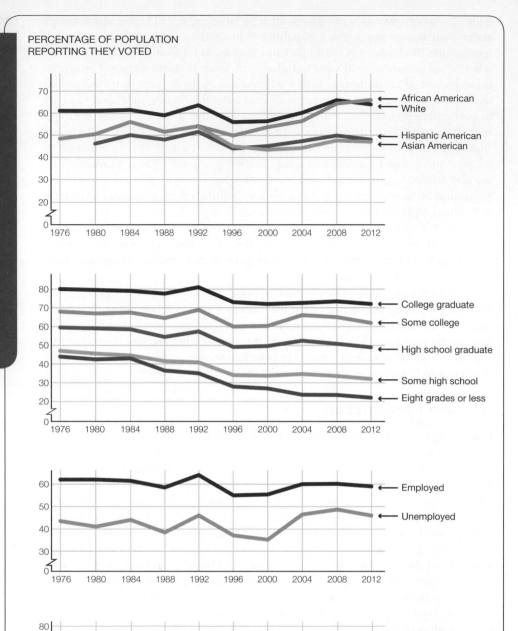

FIGURE 8.4

The Percentage of Americans Who Voted, 1976–2012

Voting rates vary substantially by race and ethnicity, education, employment status, and age. Which groups have the highest rates of voter turnout? Among which groups has participation increased the most since 1992?

SOURCES: U.S. Census Bureau, "Reported Voting and Registration by Race, Hispanic Origin, Sex, and Age Groups: November 1964 to 2012"; "Reported Voting and Registration by Region, Educational Attainment, and Labor Force: November 1964 to 2012," www.census.gov (accessed 4/24/14).

PERCENTAGE OF POPULATION
REPORTING THEY VOTED

In the 2016 presidential primaries, Democratic candidate Bernie Sanders energized young people and swept the youth vote, despite trailing Hillary Clinton overall. Still, 18- to 24-year-olds turned out at lower rates than all other age groups.

Rap the Vote and Rock the Vote a lo Latino. The Obama campaign made young voters central to its electoral strategy in 2008 and 2012, winning a significantly higher percent of the youth vote (66 percent in 2008 and 60 percent in 2012) than his opponents.[53] The Obama campaign posted videos on YouTube and used social media to reach out to young people rather than focusing primarily on television ads (which target older voters). It also worked to increase participation of young voters through major voter-registration drives on college campuses. In 2016, Democratic presidential candidate Bernie Sanders was also effective in inspiring youth participation in politics. Although Sanders failed to secure his party's nomination, election polls consistently showed 85 percent of people aged 18 to 29 preferred him to his opponent, Hillary Clinton. Sanders called for a political revolution and focused on ending a corrupt campaign finance system, combating economic inequality, and providing free college tuition. Young people were drawn to the candidate's reputation of honesty and authenticity.

Relatively low voter turnout by the young has implications for the policies addressed by government at the local, state, and federal levels. For example, young people share older Americans' concerns about the economy and national security, but they tend to be more concerned about economic inequality, have more positive views about the role of government, and express support for stronger environmental laws, funding for public education and colleges, and more tolerance for personal freedoms than older people do. A recent survey of 13- to 25-year-olds showed the consequences of coming of age in an era of hyper-partisanship and scandal; most saw the political system as ineffective and broken, and 9 out of 10 would not consider running for office.[54] At the same time young people have a strong interest in community service, and nearly 20 percent are involved in community service projects, with numbers higher among those with college experience.[55] The distinctive attitudes of today's young people suggest that higher levels of political participation by this group could change government policy and politics.

African Americans

As we saw in Chapter 5, during much of the twentieth century in the South, the widespread use of the poll tax, literacy tests, and other measures such as the white

for critical analysis

When the Twenty-Sixth Amendment changed the voting age from 21 to 18 in 1971, observers expected that the youth vote would add a significant new voice to American politics. Why has the youth vote turned out to be less important than was hoped? What changes would engage more young people in the political system?

primary deprived African Americans (and many poor whites) of the right to vote. This system of legal segregation meant that black Americans in the South had few avenues for participating in politics. Through a combination of protest, legal action, and political pressure, the civil rights movement compelled a reluctant federal government to enforce black civil and political rights.

The victories of the civil rights movement made blacks full citizens and stimulated a tremendous growth in the number of African American elected officials as blacks exercised their newfound political rights. The movement drew on an organizational base and network of communication rooted in black churches, the National Association for the Advancement of Colored People (NAACP), and black colleges. By voting as a cohesive bloc, African American voters began to wield considerable political power. When such legal barriers as the poll tax and literacy tests were removed in the 1960s, black political participation shot up, with rates of turnout approaching those of southern whites as early as 1968.[56] Today, state laws requiring government voter identification have created a new impediment for black voters in some states.

The increase in the number of black elected officials, in turn, had positive effects on the level of participation. One study found that African Americans in cities run by a black mayor were more likely to vote, participate in campaigns, and contact public officials.[57] African Americans are also more likely to vote when residing in states with increased representation in the state legislature, as measured by the percentage of black lawmakers.[58] African Americans represented by a black member of Congress are more likely to vote in elections and to have a sense of efficacy—the belief that the government is responsive to them—and higher levels of political knowledge.[59]

With Barack Obama running in 2008 as the first black major-party candidate for president, African American interest in the election surged. Exit polls indicated that 95 percent of African Americans who voted cast ballots for Obama. The 2008 and 2012 elections also witnessed a significant increase in minority participation. The black–white gap went from 7 percent in 2004 to 1 percent in 2008 as many African Americans voted for the first time (see Figure 8.4).[60] In 2012, blacks were more likely to vote than whites.[61] In 2016, however, black voter turnout was lower than in 2008 and 2012.

Yet despite these successes, racial segregation remains a fact of life in the United States, and new problems have emerged. Most troubling is the persistence of black urban poverty, now coupled with social and economic isolation.[62] These conditions, often called *concentrated poverty*, raise new questions about African American political participation. As the previous section on socioeconomic status described, participation (for blacks as well as whites) is highly correlated with more income, more education, and higher-level occupations. The persistence of poverty among African Americans in urban areas is thus a troubling issue in that participation may remain low in this group, with the result that their interests will not be represented as effectively in politics.

On the other hand, African Americans who feel a shared sense of collective identity, a concept called *linked fate*, are more likely to vote and participate politically. Political scientist Michael Dawson argues that black linked fate is a major predictor of political behavior. Dawson uses the construct of *linked fate* to measure the degree to which African Americans believe that their own self-interests are linked to the interests of the race.[63] That is, the experiences of African Americans with race and racial discrimination in the United States, including a history of slavery, unify their personal interests in seeking a candidate and policies that benefit their racial group. Black civic, community, religious, and political organizations are also important in increasing political participation for this group.

Latinos

For many years, analysts called the Latino vote "the sleeping giant" because Latinos, while accounting for a large portion of the population, as a group had relatively low levels of political participation. For instance, 48 percent of Latinos voted in the 2012 presidential election compared to 62 percent of non-Hispanic whites and 57 percent of blacks.[64] Political scientists Matt Barreto and Gary Segura have helped explain why voting rates are lower for Latinos compared to whites and African Americans. As a group, more Latinos are recent immigrants to this country and thus have fewer opportunities, such as access to a quality education, than do other ethnic and racial groups; therefore, they are more likely to lack resources for participation in politics such as money, time, and language skills.[65]

Today, politicians, political parties, and scholars view Latinos, the largest and fastest-growing minority in the United States, as a political group of critical importance. Latinos make up 17 percent of the population and represent 1 in 10 voters. In large states such as California and Texas, Latinos are approaching 50 percent of the population.[66] Although Latino registration and turnout are lower than those of whites and African Americans, these numbers have been steadily increasing. In 2016 approximately 27.3 million Latinos were eligible to vote, amounting to 11 percent of the electorate.[67] Rapid population growth, increased registration and voting, and uncertain party attachment all magnify the importance of the Latino vote.

While Latinos have tended to favor the Democrats in national elections, many Republicans believe that the tendency of Latino voters to be more socially conservative on issues such as family, abortion, and religion provides the GOP with an opportunity to attract support from this growing constituency. However, staunch Republican opposition to immigration has caused Latinos to generally prefer Democratic candidates. Furthermore, while Latinos tend to be religious, national surveys of

In the 2016 presidential election, Republican candidate Donald Trump's harsh proposals on immigration and his claims that immigrants were disproportionately criminals offended many Latinos. Democratic candidate Hillary Clinton won a majority of Latino votes.

for critical analysis

How significant a factor was the Latino vote in the 2016 election? Why does the percentage of eligible Latinos who vote still lag behind that of other groups?

Latinos find that they often do not allow their religious beliefs to dictate their political decisions and therefore may be less likely to vote for conservative politicians because of their positions on social issues related to religious values, such as abortion.[68] Latinos also favor an easier path to citizenship for noncitizen immigrants and more liberal economic policies, stances more in line with the Democratic Party. In 2016, Latinos strongly favored Democratic candidate Hillary Clinton over Republican candidate Donald Trump. Trump made ending illegal immigration a major theme of his campaign, proposing to build a wall between the United States and Mexico.

One study found that traditional explanations of vote choice based on economic evaluations and other predictors fail to take into account factors important to Latino voters, including perceptions of shared ethnic identity. Latinos in the United States have been especially concerned with changes in U.S. immigration policy, and responses to immigration policy might act to create a more cohesive Latino collective identity, similar to the linked fate for African Americans discussed above. Using national surveys of Latinos, political scientists Loren Collingwood, Matt Barreto, and Sergio García-Ríos evaluated Barack Obama's and Mitt Romney's cross-racial mobilization of Latino voters during the 2012 presidential election. They found that the candidates' policy stances vis-à-vis immigration and their ability to convey care and concern for the Latino community were important factors that shaped Latino vote choice.[69]

Similar to African Americans, Latinos are also more likely to vote when residing in states with increased representation in the state legislature, as measured by the percentage of Latino lawmakers, or in a district with a Latino member of Congress.[70] This phenomenon is commonly referred to as *descriptive representation*—when individuals are represented in government by officials of their same race, ethnicity, or gender. In this context, minority groups may have a greater ability to affect policy outcomes, thus incorporating minority populations and their concerns and interests into the political system. Descriptive representation may also confer symbolic benefits, such as reducing levels of political alienation among racial and ethnic minorities.[71] As the Latino population continues to grow, this group will continue to shape who wins and who loses in U.S. elections.

Asian Americans

Asian Americans are a smaller group than whites, Latinos, or African Americans, comprising 5.6 percent of the population in 2014. Today, over 17 million people of Asian descent call the United States home. The largest ethnic groups are Chinese, followed by Filipino, Indian, Vietnamese, Korean, and Japanese. In particular states, such as California, home to 33 percent of the nation's Asian American population, the group has become an important political presence. In terms of socioeconomic status, Asian Americans have education and income levels closer to those of whites than of Latinos or African Americans; but they are less likely to vote or participate in politics than whites or African Americans.[72] Asian Americans have voter turnout rates similar to Latinos.

No one national group dominates among the Asian American population, and this diversity has impeded the development of group-based political power. Asian Americans often have different political concerns, stemming from their different national backgrounds and experiences in the United States. Historically, these groups have united most effectively around common issues of ethnic discrimination or anti-Asian violence, federal immigration policies, and discriminatory mortgage loan practices.

Turnout rates among Asian Americans have been generally lower than those of other groups, though they have been gradually increasing: in 2012, 47.3 percent of

Asian Americans turned out to vote, their third-highest percentage turnout since the census began tracking their participation in 1990.[73] In terms of political orientation, Asian Americans are a diverse group; but they have been moving, along with other minority groups, toward the Democratic Party in recent elections. Although a majority of Asian Americans voted Republican in the early 1990s, in the 2000s they have been voting increasingly Democratic; and 65 percent of Asian Americans voted for Hillary Clinton in 2016.[74] The U.S. electorate in 2016 was the country's most racially and ethnically diverse ever; one in three eligible voters on Election Day was Hispanic, black, Asian or another racial or ethnic minority.

Gender and Participation

Today, women register and vote at rates similar to or higher than those of men. The ongoing significance of gender issues in American politics is best exemplified by the **gender gap**—a distinctive pattern of male and female voting decisions—in electoral politics. Women tend to vote in higher numbers for Democratic candidates, whereas Republicans win more male votes. In 1980 men voted heavily for the Republican candidate, Ronald Reagan; women divided their votes between Reagan and the incumbent Democratic president, Jimmy Carter. Since that election, gender differences have emerged in congressional and state elections as well. The gender gap runs around 10 points in presidential elections.

Behind these voting patterns are differing assessments of key policy issues. Women are more likely than men to oppose military activities, especially war, and to support social spending for health care, public education, and welfare, as well as gun control. In 2014, 71 percent of women supported banning assault rifles compared to just 50 percent of men.[75] Over the past 30 years Democratic candidates have received much higher support from women than from men. The 2016 presidential election saw the first female major party candidate, Democrat Hillary Clinton, and the largest gender gap in history: surveys showed that 54 percent of women supported Clinton compared to 41 percent among men, a 13-point advantage.[76] These differences, of course, do not mean that all women vote more liberally than all men.

One key development in gender politics in recent decades is the growing number of women in elective office (see Figure 8.5), an increasingly significant form of descriptive representation. Journalists dubbed 1992 the "Year of the Woman" because so many women were elected to Congress: women doubled their numbers in the House and tripled them in the Senate. Following the 2016 elections, 21 women served in the Senate, including Catherine Cortez Masto (D-Nev.), the first Latina elected to the Senate. In 2016, 84 women were elected to the House of Representatives, or 19.3 percent of the body. Women have been elected to the House of Representatives from 44 of the 50 states.

Recent research has shown that one key to increasing the number of women in political office is to encourage more women to run for political office. Although women are just as likely as men to win an election, women are less likely to run for office, even if they are equally qualified. Because women are less likely than men to hold office, they also are less likely to benefit from the advantage of incumbency.[77] Organizations supporting female candidates have worked to encourage more women to run for office and have supported them financially. In addition to the bipartisan National Women's Political Caucus, the Women's Campaign Fund and EMILY's List provide prochoice Democratic women with early campaign financing, which is critical to establishing electoral momentum.

gender gap a distinctive pattern of voting behavior reflecting the differences in views between women and men

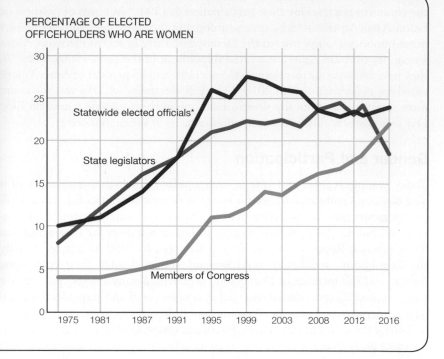

FIGURE 8.5

Increase in Number of Women in Elective Office, 1975–2016

The number of women holding elected office has always been larger in state offices than in Congress. When did the percentage of women elected to office begin to rise more rapidly?

*Governors, attorneys general, etc.
SOURCES: Cynthia Costello, Shari Miles, and Anne J. Stone, eds., *The American Woman, 2001-2002* (New York: W. W. Norton, 2002), 328; and Center for American Women and Politics, www.cawp.rutgers.edu (accessed 11/11/16).

PERCENTAGE OF ELECTED
OFFICEHOLDERS WHO ARE WOMEN

Statewide elected officials*

State legislators

Members of Congress

Why does the gender gap matter? Although women in public office by no means take uniform positions on policy issues, surveys show that, on the whole, female legislators are more supportive of women's rights and education and health care spending and are more attentive to children's and family issues.[78]

Religious Identity

Religious identity plays an important role in American life. For many citizens, religious groups provide an organizational infrastructure for political participation, especially around issues of special group concern. Black churches, for example, were instrumental in the civil rights movement, and black religious leaders continue to play important roles in national and local politics. Jews have also been active as a group in politics but less through religious bodies than through a variety of social action agencies, including the American Jewish Congress, the American Jewish Committee, and the Anti-Defamation League.

For most of American history, religious language, symbols, and values have been woven deeply into the fabric of public life. Until the mid-twentieth century, public school students generally began the day with prayers or Bible readings, and city halls displayed crèches during the Christmas season. But over the past half-century a variety of court decisions greatly reduced this kind of overt religious influence on public life. In 1962 the Supreme Court ruled in *Engel v. Vitale* that prayer in public schools was unconstitutional—that government should not be in the business of sponsoring official prayers.[79] These decisions helped to spawn a countermovement of religious activists seeking to roll back these decisions and restore the prominent role of religion in civic life. The mobilization of religious organizations that seek to infuse moral views into the public sphere has been one of the most significant political developments of the past few decades. Some of the most divisive conflicts in politics today, such as those over abortion, birth control, and same-sex relationships, hinge on differences over religious beliefs. These divisions have become so salient that they now constitute what is called a "culture war," with repercussions throughout the political system and many policy areas.

One of the most significant drivers of this new politics was the mobilization of white evangelical Protestants into a cohesive political force. The Moral Majority, the first broad-based political organization of evangelical Christians, was founded in 1979 and quickly rose to prominence in the 1980 election when it aligned with the Republican Party, eventually backing Ronald Reagan for president. Over the next few years, evangelicals strengthened their movement by registering voters and mobilizing them. Their success was evident in the 1984 election, when 8 in 10 evangelical Christian voters cast their ballots for Reagan. The 1988 election was a turning point in the political development of the Christian right. The televangelist Pat Robertson ran for president, and although his candidacy was unsuccessful, his effort laid the groundwork for future political strength. Robertson's supporters gained control of some state Republican parties and won positions of power in others. President George W. Bush was closely aligned with religious conservatives, and the religious right played an important role in mobilizing voters to support him in the 2000 and 2004 elections. Bush's faith-based initiatives, for example, sought to funnel government assistance to religious groups engaged in charitable work.[80] In 2016, Republican presidential candidates Ted Cruz and Ben Carson received strong support from evangelical Christians, most of whom came around to supporting Trump in the general election.

Religious adherents can also be mobilized to participate in politics to protect their group. In his examination of the 2004 presidential election results, political scientist David Campbell found that voting preferences among white evangelical Christians are determined, to a large extent, by their community context. The

Religious identity remains a significant factor in voting patterns. For Republicans in particular, evangelical Christian groups tend to form a very cohesive and sought-after voting bloc. In the 2016 presidential primaries, evangelicals overwhelmingly supported Republican candidate Ted Cruz.

higher the number of secularists in their communities, the more likely evangelical Christians are to hold conservative views and vote Republican.[81]

But individual-level factors are not the only explanations for voter turnout or other forms of political participation. Our incomplete understanding of participation is evident when we compare voting across countries. If more political resources lead to a greater likelihood of voting, why does the United States, one of the most prosperous countries in the world, have only moderate voting rates? And Americans have become more educated over the past century, with more people finishing high school and attending college; given the well-documented links between educational attainment and voting, why has participation declined during this period?[82] These puzzles mean that we need to look beyond the socioeconomic characteristics of individuals and to the larger political environment in which participation occurs.

● Political Environment and Participation

Explain the factors in the political environment that influence whether individuals vote or not

Political environments matter a great deal in understanding individual political behavior. Whether or not people feel engaged or are recruited to participate in politics depends on their social setting—what their parents are like, what state they live in, what associations they belong to. As discussed above, in the United States churches are one example of an important social institution that often fosters political participation. Through their church activities people learn the civic skills that prepare them to participate in the political world.

Mobilization

A critical aspect of political environments is whether people are mobilized—by parties, candidates, campaigns, interest groups, and social movements. A recent comprehensive study of the decline in political participation in the United States found that half of the drop-off could be accounted for by reduced **mobilization** efforts.[83] People become much more likely to participate when someone—especially someone they know—asks them to get involved.

mobilization the process by which large numbers of people are organized for a political activity

A series of experiments conducted by the political scientists Donald Green and Alan Gerber demonstrate the importance of personal contact for mobilizing voters. Evaluating the results of several get-out-the-vote drives, the researchers showed that face-to-face interaction with a canvasser greatly increased the chances that the person contacted would go to the polls. They estimated that personal contact boosted voter turnout by almost 10 percent. The impact of direct mail was much smaller, increasing turnout by just 0.5 percent.[84] Robocalls from a phone bank had no measurable effect on voter turnout. Green and Gerber also evaluated the impact of mobilization on young voters by studying a series of get-out-the-vote campaigns conducted near college campuses. They found that phone contacts that were chattier and more informal than standard phone-bank messages increased turnout by an estimated 5 percent, while face-to-face contacts increasing turnout by 8.5 percent.[85] Social networks also matter. In a large study involving 61 million users on Facebook, political scientists said that turnout in the 2010 midterm election increased by 340,000 additional people (who otherwise would not have voted). Importantly, users' closest friends on the network had the most influence in getting them to vote. Thus, online and offline networks both played a role in mobilizing voters.[86]

In previous decades, political parties and social movements relied on personal contact to mobilize voters. As we will see in Chapter 9, during the nineteenth century, American political party machines employed hundreds of thousands of workers to bring voters to the polls. The result was a very high turnout rate, typically more than 90 percent of eligible voters.[87] But political party machines began to decline in strength at the beginning of the twentieth century. By the late twentieth century, political parties had become essentially fund-raising and advertising organizations rather than mobilizers of people. Without party workers to encourage them to go to the polls, and even bring them there if necessary, many eligible voters will not participate.

Nevertheless, competitive presidential elections since 2000 have once again motivated both parties to build strong grassroots organizations to reach voters and turn them out on Election Day. In the 2004 elections, Republicans were more successful in their organizational efforts than Democrats, building an organization with more than 1.4 million volunteers who were trained to make calls, go door to door to register voters, write letters in favor of President Bush, post blogs online, and phone local radio call-in shows. During the 2008 campaign, it was the Democrats who built a more extensive organization to contact and turn out voters. Barack Obama's campaign made mobilization a centerpiece of its strategy from the start, organizing a base of volunteers to go door to door seeking support for their candidate. Many of Obama's crucial primary victories relied on direct voter mobilization. The campaign then created a nationwide organization, opening more than 700 field offices, where paid staff coordinated the work of tens of thousands of volunteers. Obama campaigned in all 50 states, rather than focusing on battleground states as his predecessors had done. The expansion of the electorate through mobilization, including the use of the Internet, became a central pillar of the Obama strategy.

By mobilizing support in places where Democrats had not seriously contended in the past, the Obama campaign expanded the electoral map. For the first time in decades, turnout rates were comparable to those in 1960. The marriage of technology, money, early voting, and field organization that the Obama campaign assembled for the 2008 campaign was repeated in 2012 and will surely be imitated in future elections. In 2016 political campaigns shifted to social media as a primary way to mobilize voters and directly provide their supporters with election updates. Three in 10 Americans received digital messages about news and the elections, with far more Americans turning to the candidates' social media posts rather than to their websites or emails.[88]

In the past, social movements, such as the labor movement in the 1930s and the civil rights movement in the 1960s, played an important role in mobilizing people into politics. Since then, interest groups and political parties have generally reduced their efforts at direct mobilization, although some have revived direct mobilization in recent years. The Tea Party movement in particular has engaged in widespread grassroots mobilization, as have organizations on the left such as MoveOn.org.[89]

for critical analysis

Why do efforts toward direct mobilization seem to be more successful than television advertising in promoting voter turnout? How is the Internet becoming an important tool for increasing political participation?

People are more likely to turn out to vote if someone asks them face-to-face. Direct mail and impersonal phone calls are less likely to have an effect on turnout.

Electoral Competition

To be motivated to vote, individuals must be interested in the election and knowledgeable about the candidates. An important factor, often overlooked in analyzing political participation, is whether elections are competitive; that is, whether there are at least two parties (and their candidates) actively contesting a position in government.[90] Competitive elections, and the campaign spending and mobilization efforts that go along with them, have been identified as playing a key role in turnout in the United States and cross-nationally.[91] Conversely, limited exposure to competitive elections may be one reason for the lower levels of turnout recorded since the 1960s. In many congressional, statewide, and local races, a candidate (often the incumbent) runs unopposed or is expected to win by such a large margin that the challenger's chances are virtually nil. When congressional districts are drawn to favor one political party over another—what is termed *gerrymandering*—election outcomes are thus often highly lopsided in favor of one candidate over another. Relatively uncompetitive elections are a primary reason why most members of Congress win by landslides.

One political scientist, Todd Donovan, uses a baseball analogy to explain the importance of competitive elections in mobilizing people to participate in politics: "People watch a game to see their team win, or because of interest in an important game. Perfect scoring is meaningless if only one team takes the field, and attendance will suffer if two teams are playing that no one can cheer for."[92] When candidates and political parties spend more effort and money to compete for an elected office, more information becomes available to voters in the form of media ads, news coverage, door-to-door campaigns, online campaigns, and more. Electoral competition reduces the cost to individuals of becoming informed, leading to higher turnout. Conversely, if elections are uncompetitive or uncontested, they generate little political information. Without active campaigns, individuals have few opportunities to be interested in an election and may not vote.[93]

Individual states vary dramatically in the competitiveness of congressional elections, gubernatorial elections, ballot measures, and how they experience presidential elections. Some U.S. House districts are so uncompetitive that a single candidate often runs in an uncontested election; in some states, up to one-third of congressional races are uncontested in some election years.[94] With only one name appearing on the election ballot, there is little incentive for a rational citizen to vote as voting will not affect the outcome. Every two years only two dozen U.S. House races are very competitive, which is defined as the winning candidate beating the losing candidate by 5 percentage points or less. Many studies have shown that more electoral competition and increased campaign spending on the part of candidates lead to higher voter turnout, while uncontested elections lead to lower political participation.[95]

An important source of variation in electoral competition is the United States' unique structure for presidential elections. No other country uses an electoral college to mediate between a national or direct vote for presidential candidates and the actual winner. To win, a U.S. presidential candidate must receive a majority of the votes in the electoral college. Each state is given a set number of votes in the electoral college based on the size of its congressional delegation. (The electoral college is covered in more detail in Chapter 10.) Some citizens reside in competitive battleground states, such as Ohio, Florida, and Pennsylvania. These states are defined by high levels of competition between the parties, with half the voters affiliating with the Republicans and half with the Democrats. Most Americans, however, live in nonbattleground states (also called "safe" states) such as California, New York, and Texas, where one of the major parties is generally assured of victory in presidential elections. Every four years, residents of battleground states get smothered with attention from candidates and media, while citizens in states with few electoral votes or where one political party has a solid majority barely get noticed. Hence, presidential elections are often decided by a relatively small number of voters in the United States' dozen or so battleground states. One study found that voter turnout is higher in battleground states than in nonbattleground states and less skewed in terms of lower participation by the poor and young.[96] Since the number of battleground states has been decreasing, fewer Americans are exposed to high-intensity presidential campaigns, which may be another reason for lower levels of turnout since the 1960s.

Even the structure for nominating presidential candidates has implications for participation in government. Selecting presidential candidates involves a sequence of statewide primary elections and caucuses. The early phase of this process is dominated by a handful of small-population states. The privileged position of Iowa and New Hampshire, sites of the nation's first caucus and first primary election, respectively, can boost political participation in those states. Similarly, studies have shown that citizens residing in "Super Tuesday" states (the states that hold primaries or caucuses on a single day about six weeks after the New Hampshire primary) are more likely to vote in presidential primaries and be interested in the election.[97] Among residents of late-voting states, by contrast, turnout in primaries is often very low. Frequently, the nomination contest is over almost before it starts as one candidate secures a significant lead in early primaries, leaving many citizens with no role in selecting their party's nominee. Turnout in these later states naturally plummets.

Ballot Measures

Beyond candidate races, ballot measures (initiatives and referenda) have been found to increase voter turnout.[98] Elections that include controversial initiatives on the state ballot—in which citizens vote directly on policy questions such as affirmative action, the minimum wage, immigration, legalization of marijuana, or taxation—have also been found to increase voter turnout, political interest, and contributions to interest groups.[99] In many states, ballot-measure campaigns are important for mobilizing voters and can have spillover effects on candidate races.[100] When citizens are asked to vote directly on controversial policy issues, public awareness of politics and policy debates increases. Initiatives often involve high campaign spending by proponents and opponents of the proposed laws, which generates mass media coverage. The *Los Angeles Times* estimated that $452 million was spent in California alone on controversial ballot measures including legalizing the recreational use of marijuana, repealing the death penalty, and banning plastic bags.[101] Additionally, simply being asked to vote on issues—salient or otherwise—can increase participation. This has been called the "educative effects" of direct democracy as voters are forced to make a yes-or-no binary choice on the policy issue.[102]

The most robust finding of the educative effects of ballot measures is the positive impact of direct democracy on voter turnout. Scholars have found that statewide initiatives on the ballot increases turnout in elections, especially in lower-profile, midterm elections but also in U.S. presidential elections and in cross-national contexts.

Voters often turn out in higher numbers when there are controversial initiatives on the ballot. In 2016 groups for and against Proposition 62 in California, which would repeal the death penalty, spent millions of dollars on media and mobilization campaigns.

State Electoral Laws and Participation

Explain the effect of electoral laws on voting

As stipulated by the Constitution, the states retain control of voter registration and voting itself. This decentralized system continues to create wide variation in the laws governing elections and voting, and thus participation in politics.[103] Voter turnout in presidential elections in the last decade ranges from a high of over 70 percent of eligible voters in Minnesota to 45 percent in Mississippi, a 25-point difference. State electoral laws can create barriers to voting that can reduce participation and help explain the differences in turnout across states.

Registration Requirements

An important factor reducing voter turnout is our nation's unique state-by-state patchwork of registration rules. In most other democracies in the world, citizens are automatically registered to vote, making voter turnout rates higher; but the United States requires a two-step process: registering to vote and then voting. In every American state but North Dakota, individuals who are eligible to vote must register with the state election board before they are actually allowed to vote, although a growing number of states allow same-day registration, as discussed in the introduction to this chapter. Registration requirements were introduced by Progressive reformers at the turn of the nineteenth century who wanted to limit political corruption and discourage immigrant and working-class voters from going to the polls so that political parties would be more responsive to middle-class voters and professionals. In some states, these registration requirements reduced voter turnout by as much as 50 percent.

Registration requirements particularly reduce voting by the young, those with lower levels of education, and the less affluent because registration requires a greater degree of political involvement to become informed (a cost) than does the act of voting itself. Once individuals become interested in the election and learn about the candidates, it may be too late for them to register, especially if they live in states that require registration up to a month before the election. And because young people tend to change residences more often than older people, registration requirements place a greater burden on them. As a result, voter-registration requirements not only diminish the size of the electorate but also tend to create an electorate that is, on average, better educated, more affluent, and composed of fewer young people and minorities than the citizenry as a whole (see Figure 8.6). Advocates of voting reform hope that more states adopt automatic registration laws, which may help expand the electorate.

Voter Identification Requirements A barrier to voting is the requirement that voters provide proof of identity. As of the 2016 election, 32 states require all voters to show some form of ID before voting at the polls. Seven of these states have strict laws requiring a photo ID (Georgia, Indiana, Kansas, Mississippi, Tennessee, Virginia, and Wisconsin), while another nine request photo IDs but may count the vote with a nonphoto ID under certain circumstances.[104] Photo identification is a partisan issue: Republicans argue that such laws protect against voter fraud and ensure that the vote is fair, regardless of party; opponents, mainly Democrats, counter that there have been almost no significant instances of voter fraud in the modern era and that these laws suppress the vote of segments of the

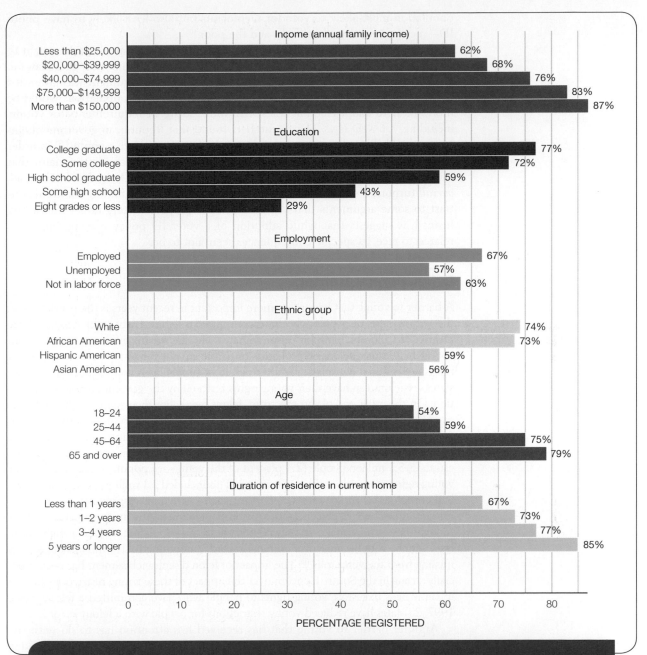

FIGURE 8.6

Voter-Registration Rates by Social Group, 2012

Some political analysts argue that registration requirements depress turnout. The percentage of the population that is registered to vote varies according to education level, employment status, race and ethnicity, and age. Are people with a lower income more or less likely to register to vote? Are less educated people more or less likely to register? Would the rates of participation among these groups change if registration requirements were altered?

SOURCES: U.S. Census Bureau, "Voting and Registration in the Election of 2012," www.census.gov/hhes/www/socdemo/voting/publications/p20/2012/tables.html (accessed 5/24/14).

population most likely to vote for Democrats but also least likely to have photo ID—racial minorities, the elderly, and the poor.[105]

A study by political scientists Rene Rocha and Tetsuya Matsubayashi sought to understand what factors drive states to adopt voter ID laws and how these laws in turn affect voter turnout of whites and minorities. Their argument was grounded in a hypothesis that posits that states with higher minority populations would be more likely to adopt election rules with more stringent requirements for voting, including voter ID laws. The researchers found that Republican governments increase the likelihood that a new law requiring citizens to have a photo ID in order to vote will be passed.[106] But their data offer little evidence for the claim that minority and Latino turnout is uniquely affected by voter ID regulations. Instead, *overall* turnout is reduced with more stringent ID laws. This finding stands in contrast to some arguments that voter ID laws disproportionately target minorities. Instead, it suggests that while adoption of a voter ID policy may be indirectly related to race, its specific consequences seem not to be.

Other Formal Barriers

A barrier to voting that has grown more important in recent years is the restriction on the voting rights of people who have committed a felony. Forty-eight states and the District of Columbia prohibit prison inmates who are serving a felony sentence from voting. In 29 states, felons on probation or parole are not permitted to vote, but voting rights are restored automatically after parole or probation is complete. In nine other states, ex-felons can have their voting rights restored by the governor's or a court's action. On the other end of the spectrum, felons never lose their right to vote in Maine and Vermont. Generally, felons who have already served their sentences still face numerous restrictions on voting. With the sharp rise in incarceration rates over the past three decades, these restrictions have had a significant impact on voting rights. By one estimate, 5.3 million people (2.4 percent of the voting-age population) have lost their voting rights as a result of these restrictions. This included 2.1 million ex-offenders who had completed their sentences.[107] Further, such restrictions disproportionately affect minorities because 59 percent of the prison population is African American or Latino, though these groups make up only 30 percent of the population.[108] One in eight black men cannot vote because of a criminal record, amounting to 1.5 million black men missing from the voter rolls.[109] The impact of felon disenfranchisement has been especially strong in the South. Concern over the impact of these voting restrictions has led to campaigns to restore voting rights to people who have committed a felony. Since 1997, 23 states have reduced voting restrictions for people with a felony record.[110]

Another barrier to voting that has received less attention has to do with the fact that in the United States elections are held on Tuesdays—regular working days when most Americans face significant commute times in addition to hours worked. In most European countries, by contrast, elections are held on Sundays or holidays. Holding elections on working days may make it difficult for some people to vote due to the demands of work and family. This problem has been addressed somewhat by expanding the use of absentee ballots, early voting, and voting by mail. Some reformers have called for an Election Day holiday, as is commonly used in Europe. This would underscore the importance of voting in America, making democratic participation a priority. The sometimes odd rules of American elections reflect long-standing traditions extending back centuries when the country was an agrarian society and work schedules were more flexible.

for critical analysis

Why is voter turnout so low in the United States? What are the consequences of low voter turnout?

Which States Make Voting Easier?

Convenience Voting, 2016

States have increasingly passed laws to make voting easier, such as early voting, which allows voters to cast a ballot before Election Day; "no-excuse" absentee voting, which permits voters to request an absentee ballot without providing justification; all-mail voting, whereby voters fill in their ballot at home and mail it, eliminating polling places altogether; and same-day and automatic voter registration. At the same time, many states have passed voter identification requirements, which make voting harder for some people. The maps show these laws by state as of the 2016 election.

- ■ Early voting
- ■ Early voting and no-excuse absentee voting
- ■ All-mail voting
- ■ No convenience voting
- ○ Same-day registration
- □ Automatic registration*

Voter ID Requirements, 2016

*Four additional states have adopted automatic registration to take effect after 2016.

SOURCES: National Conference of State Legislatures, "Absentee and Early Voting," January 5, 2016, www.ncsl.org/research /elections-and-campaigns/absentee-and-early -voting.aspx (accessed 9/22/16) and Ballot Pedia, "Voter identification laws by state," ballotpedia.org/Voter_identification_laws_by _state#tab=Map (accessed 9/22/16).

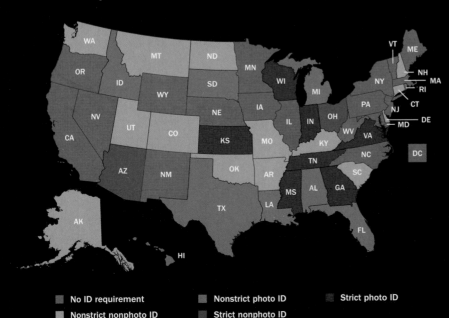

- ■ No ID requirement
- ■ Nonstrict nonphoto ID
- ■ Nonstrict photo ID
- ■ Strict nonphoto ID
- ▨ Strict photo ID

for critical analysis

1. Find your state on the map. Do you think your state's voting laws affected turnout in the 2016 election?

2. In which regions of the country do we find the most states with convenience voting? Why might this be the case?

Voting and Registration Reforms

Election reform efforts over the past century have focused on making voter registration and voting more accessible and convenient. **Same-day registration** (SDR) combines the two-step process of voting—registering to vote and casting a ballot on Election Day—into one, enabling citizens to both register to vote and actually cast a ballot on the same day. Eleven states plus the District of Columbia have SDR laws; three other states have adopted but not yet implemented the law.[111] Concern over SDR focuses on fraud and noncitizens voting. As might be expected, in states that allow registration on the day of the election, not only is voter turnout higher than the national average but younger and less educated voters are more likely to participate.[112] Still, the real effect of state election reforms may be in altering *who* turns out to vote, rather than *how many* turn out. On average, SDR increases overall turnout by 5 percent.[113]

As discussed in this chapter's introduction, five states have further simplified voting by adopting automatic voter registration, adding hundreds of thousands of new voters to the rolls. The new law, the first of its kind in the states, combines the processes of obtaining a government ID such as a driver's license and registering to vote as the same requirements are needed for each. In Oregon, for example, the Department of Transportation shares with the secretary of state an individual's proof of residency, age, and citizenship. These data are used to register Oregon citizens who haven't yet signed up to vote. Citizens then receive postcards notifying them that they have been automatically registered.

In 1998, Oregon was also the first state to create a system for voting exclusively by mail, thus eliminating polling places altogether. Individual voters fill in their ballot at home and place it in the mail or in drop boxes throughout the state. Washington State and Colorado followed suit a few years later, and the majority of Californians and other western state citizens now cast votes using **permanent absentee ballots**, which are mailed.[114] In Colorado, a state that promotes absentee voting, 77 percent of the vote was cast via absentee ballot in 2012.[115] Twenty-seven states and the District of Columbia allow "no excuse" absentee voting, which

same-day registration the option in some states to register on the day of the election, at the polling place, rather than in advance of the election

permanent absentee ballots the option in some states to have a ballot sent automatically to your home for each election, rather than having to request an absentee ballot each time

Convenience voting, such as early voting and voting by mail, removes the need to stand in a potentially long line to cast a vote and may result in increased voter turnout.

means any voter can request an absentee ballot without providing a justification. (See inside the back cover of your textbook to find voter-registration requirements in your state.) The western states tend to have higher voter turnout than other parts of the country besides the Midwest, making it difficult to disentangle whether mail voting or regional political culture drives higher turnout.

Another reform that has been adopted by many states is **early voting**, which allows registered voters to cast a ballot at their regular polling place up to 40 days before the election. As of 2016, 34 states allow early voting in which any qualified voter may cast a ballot in person during a designated period prior to Election Day.[116] Three of these states go so far as to mail a ballot to all registered voters. Some studies find that the effects of early voting laws on turnout and the demographic composition of who votes are not yet clear.[117] One study from Oregon found that voting by mail tends to advantage upper-class and older citizens, who are more likely to vote anyway.[118] But others contend that early voting does increase turnout among groups that are traditionally less likely to vote, including minorities. The outcome of the 2012 presidential race, for example, was ultimately determined by Florida, where 53 percent of total votes were cast early, in large part because Obama's campaign took advantage of early voting laws, employing a sophisticated voter-registration database to call, message, and email supporters until they confirmed that a ballot had been cast.[119] For a campaign, a vote cast early is like securing another dollar in the bank. Even though the Republican-controlled Florida state legislature had recently reduced the number of days allowed for early voting from 14 prior to the election to 8, including eliminating some weekend polling hours when many African Americans voted after church, Obama still won Florida. Comparing who voted early in 2008 (before the law change) to 2012 (after the law change), one study found that restricting early voting in Florida disproportionately hurt Democrats and African American turnout, implying that early voting can advantage these demographic and partisan groups.[120] This example also illustrates that Republicans tend to prefer laws that reduce voter turnout, while Democrats prefer more lenient laws.

Overall, SDR has been found to have the greatest effect in boosting voting rates and making participation by different demographic groups more equal. These laws reduce the information and effort needed to participate in politics. An individual need not become aware of the registration process in order to register to vote; he merely needs to know the date of the election and the location of the polling place, where registering to vote and voting can happen at the same time. Having the ability to vote at the last minute helps many people who otherwise may not vote, particularly young adults and individuals with a high school–level education or less.[121]

early voting the option in some states to cast a vote at a polling place or by mail before the election

Political Participation
and Your Future

The American political community has expanded over the course of history, with new groups winning and asserting political rights. This expansion has brought American politics more closely into line with the fundamental values of liberty, equality, and democracy. But for much of the twentieth century, the electoral system in the United States failed to mobilize an active citizenry, giving rise to an uneven pattern of political participation that gives some people more of a voice in politics than others. Since 2000 a series of highly competitive presidential elections has spurred political campaigns to pay more attention to drawing greater numbers of voters into the political process; even so, many Americans still do not participate in politics. The "**Who Participates?**" feature on the following page shows who turned out to vote in the 2012 presidential election. Turnout followed similar patterns in 2016.

Naturally enough, one of the most important factors in sustaining participation is a sense of political efficacy, the feeling that average citizens can help shape what government actually does. One important study found that elected officials respond more to the preferences of voters than nonvoters, confirming long-held assumptions that affluent, more educated, and older citizens have more voice in politics and public policy.[122] A study by the political scientist Larry Bartels showed that senators (both Republicans and Democrats) are much less responsive to the policy preferences of low-income citizens—who are also less likely to be active voters.[123] If the voices of only the more affluent are heard during election time, the issues that concern lower-income Americans may not find a place at the top of the political agenda.

What would it take to increase political engagement among citizens of all backgrounds? Several recent developments promise to give a greater number of people more of a voice in American government. Over the past few decades, innovative states have led the way by reforming and modernizing America's patchwork election system, with reforms ranging from automatic and same-day voter registration to early and mail voting. Hawaii registers all high school students to vote, while permanent voter registration, akin to voting systems used in European countries, is an increasingly popular reform at the state level. Some states, such as Iowa and California, use nonpartisan boards to draw legislative districts, which tend to boost competition in congressional and state legislative races. Increased competition, in turn, often results in a more informed and energized electorate, thus increasing turnout. Drawing on the American states as laboratories of democracy allows policy makers to test what works and what does not. Reforms found to be successful at the state level may be adopted at the national level.

If more Americans voted, the policies adopted by their governments would be more representative of the majority preferences in this country. What other innovations might the states implement to encourage or enable more people to vote? How useful might it be to end registration requirements, particularly for young voters, who are the most mobile? Already, military personnel deployed overseas are allowed to vote by email in some states. Would you support vote-by-email?

The explosive growth in digital communication as a means of organizing political participation has been especially apparent during recent elections. New technologies have supplied political leaders and candidates with new avenues for reaching out to citizens and have given citizens novel (and even enjoyable) ways to learn about and engage with politics. As we have learned, individuals who learn about politics online are more likely to vote and participate in politics in myriad other ways. Astonishingly diverse online news sources have given rise to new opinion leaders and new voices. Whatever promise digital politics holds for increasing political participation, it also raises the same fundamental questions that have arisen with every major new development in America's political history: How can citizens turn participation in politics into meaningful representation in government? And how, in turn, can representation result in public policies that reflect the needs of the greatest number of American citizens?

For much of American history, formal barriers restricted the right to vote and created a pattern of unequal participation in politics. Today, most of those barriers have been eliminated, but voter turnout remains relatively low, especially among young voters. In 2008 these voters cast their ballots at a polling station in a fraternity house near the UCLA campus.

Who Voted in 2012?

Age

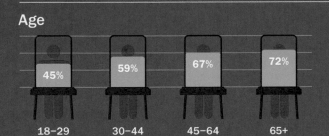

45%	59%	67%	72%
18–29	30–44	45–64	65+

Income

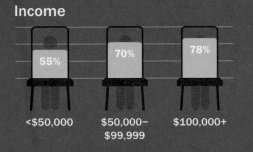

55%	70%	78%
<$50,000	$50,000–$99,999	$100,000+

Race

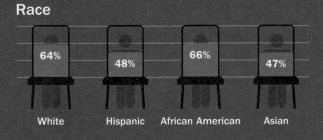

64%	48%	66%	47%
White	Hispanic	African American	Asian

Sex

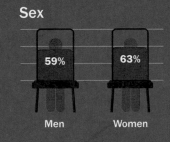

59%	63%
Men	Women

Education*

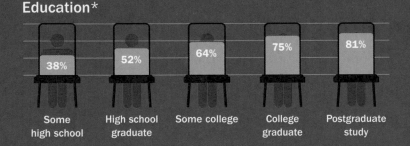

38%	52%	64%	75%	81%
Some high school	High school graduate	Some college	College graduate	Postgraduate study

*Highest level attained

SOURCE: U.S. Census Bureau, Current Population Survey, November 2012, www.census.gov/hhes/www/socdemo/voting/publications/p20/2012/tables.html?cssp=SERP (accessed 12/5/15).

WHAT YOU CAN DO

Vote

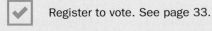

- ☑ Register to vote. See page 33.

- ☑ Find out what's on the ballot in upcoming elections in your state and district by entering your address at **www.vote411.org** (a website from the League of Women Voters).

- ☑ Cast your vote on Election Day. Consider encouraging others to vote too. Research shows that people are more likely to turn out to vote if a friend or family member asks them to.

studyguide

Forms of Political Participation

Political participation refers to a wide range of activities designed to influence government, politics, and policy. These activities fall into two major categories: traditional political participation, which includes voting, engaging in protest, volunteering, and contributing to a candidate; and digital political participation, which refers to a newer set of activities carried out through the Internet, such as posting comments on a social media site or visiting a political party's website. Voting is the most common form of political participation, but voter turnout is relatively low today in the United States.

Key Terms

traditional political participation (p. 289)

protest (p. 289)

suffrage (p. 290)

turnout (p. 292)

digital political participation (p. 295)

Practice Quiz

1. Which of the following is not a form of traditional political participation?
   a) volunteering for a campaign
   b) attending an abortion rights rally
   c) contributing money to the Democratic Party
   d) voting in an election
   e) signing an online petition

2. Which group won voting rights most recently?
   a) 18- to 20-year-olds
   b) Asian Americans
   c) white property owners
   d) women
   e) African Americans

3. The *digital divide* means
   a) some citizens watch television news and some do not.t
   b) newspapers rarely publish the same stories on their websites that they do in their print editions.
   c) few politicians maintain websites once they are elected to office.
   d) not all citizens have equal access to the Internet.
   e) people who learn about politics online are less informed than those who learn about it through traditional media.

Who Participates?

Race, gender, age, and religious affiliation are associated with different levels and types of political participation. Generally speaking, whites, older people, and women vote most frequently. In recent elections, African Americans, Latinos, women, and young people have been more likely to support Democratic candidates than whites, males, and older people.

Key Terms

socioeconomic status (p. 305)

gender gap (p. 307)

Practice Quiz

4. Which of the following statements about young people's political attitudes is most accurate?
   a. Younger people are less supportive of strong environmental laws than older people.
   b. Younger people are less likely to oppose military intervention overseas than older people.
   c. Younger people are more concerned about privacy than older people.
   d. Younger people are significantly less concerned with the economy and national security than older people.
   e. Younger people are more supportive of funding for public education and colleges than older people.

5. African Americans
   a) almost never participate in politics.
   b) consistently support the Republican Party in elections.
   c) vote at much higher rates than whites.
   d) have never voted as a cohesive bloc.
   e) are more likely to participate when they feel a shared sense of collective identity.

6. Which of the following statements about Latinos is *not* accurate?
   a) Latinos have tended to favor Democratic candidates in recent national elections.
   b) In some large states, such as California and Texas, Latinos are approaching 50 percent of the population.
   c) Latinos have tended to favor Republican candidates in recent national elections.

   d) Latinos make up approximately 17 percent of the population.
   e) Latino registration and turnout rates have been lower than those of whites and African Americans in recent elections.

7. One reason that there are fewer women than men in elected office is that
   a) there is a limit set by the Constitution on the number of women who can serve in the House of Representatives.
   b) fewer women are eligible to run for office under the rules created by state and local governments.
   c) women are less likely to vote in elections than men.
   d) women are less likely to run for office than men.
   e) women are less likely to win elections than men.

Political Environment and Participation

Explain the factors in the political environment that influence whether individuals vote or not (pp. 310–13)

Three general factors in the political environment influence whether individuals vote or not: (1) People who are mobilized by political parties, candidates, campaigns, interest groups, and social movements are more likely to participate than those who are not. (2) In competitive elections, there are more opportunities for individuals to become interested in and informed about the race as each side campaigns intensely to get its message out to the public. (3) People may also make the effort to turn out if state ballot measures address issues that are important to them.

Key Term

mobilization (p. 310)

Practice Quiz

8. Which of the following techniques is considered most effective in mobilizing voters?
   a) mass mailings
   b) robocalls
   c) phone calls made by volunteers
   d) face-to-face contact
   e) television advertisements

9. On average, how many U.S. House races can be classified as "very competitive" in each election?
   a) 0
   b) 24
   c) 100
   d) 217
   e) 435

State Electoral Laws and Participation

Explain the effect of electoral laws on voting (pp. 314–19)

As stated in the Constitution, states retain control of voter registration and voting. In practice, there is wide variation in the laws governing elections and voting from state to state. Voter-registration requirements and other barriers, such as ID requirements, may reduce participation. States have experimented with reforms, such as same-day registration, automatic registration, and early voting, to make it easier to vote.

Key Terms

same-day registration (p. 318)
permanent absentee ballots (p. 318)
early voting (p. 319)

Practice Quiz

10. Voter-registration requirements and processes are determined and controlled by
a) local governments.
b) the federal government.
c) the U.S. Constitution.
d) the states.
e) an independent organization.

11. Which of the following factors is *not* currently an obstacle to voting in the United States?
a) registration requirements
b) that elections occur on Tuesdays
c) the restriction of voting rights for people who have committed a felony
d) literacy tests
e) voter identification laws

12. In states that allow registration on the day of the election,
a) overall voter turnout rates are lower than in other states.
b) no significant difference in overall voter turnout has been measured.
c) younger and less educated voters turn out in larger percentages.
d) widespread voter fraud has called a number of election outcomes into question.
e) younger and less educated voters turn out in lower numbers.

For Further Reading

Barreto, Matt, and Gary Segura. *Latino America: How America's Most Dynamic Population Is Poised to Transform the Politics of the Nation*. New York: PublicAffairs, 2014.

Bowler, Shaun, and Todd Donovan. *The Limits of Electoral Reform*. Oxford: Oxford University Press, 2013.

Cain, Bruce E., Todd Donovan, and Caroline J. Tolbert, eds. *Democracy in the States: Experiments in Election Reform*. Washington, DC: Brookings Institution Press, 2008.

Crenson, Matthew A., and Benjamin Ginsberg. *Downsizing Democracy: How America Sidelined Its Citizens and Privatized Its Public*. Baltimore: Johns Hopkins University Press, 2004.

Dalton, Russell J. *The Good Citizen: How a Younger Generation Is Reshaping American Politics*. Washington, DC: CQ Press, 2008.

Donovan, Todd, and Shawn Bowler. *Reforming the Republic: Democratic Institutions for the New America*. Upper Saddle River, NJ: Pearson/Prentice Hall, 2004.

Green, Donald P., and Alan S. Gerber. *Get Out the Vote! How to Increase Voter Turnout*. Washington, DC: Brookings Institution Press, 2004.

Griffin, John D., and Brian Newman. *Minority Report: Evaluating Political Equality in America*. Chicago: University of Chicago Press, 2008.

Hanmer, Michael J. *Discount Voting: Voter Registration Reforms and Their Effects*. New York: Cambridge University Press, 2009.

Karpf, David. *The MoveOn Effect: The Unexpected Transformation of American Political Advocacy*. New York: Oxford University Press, 2012.

Lewis-Beck, Michael S., William G. Jacoby, Helmut Norpoth, and Herbert F. Weisberg. *The American Voter Revisited*. Ann Arbor: University of Michigan Press, 2008.

Manza, Jeff, and Christopher Uggen. *Locked Out: Felon Disenfranchisement and American Democracy*. New York: Oxford University Press, 2006.

McDonald, Michael P., and John Samples, eds. *The Marketplace of Democracy: Electoral Competition and American Politics*. Washington, DC: Brookings Institution Press, 2006.

Mossberger, Karen, Caroline Tolbert, and Ramona McNeal. *Digital Citizenship: The Internet, Society and Participation*. Cambridge, MA: MIT Press, 2008.

Nicholson, Steven P. *Voting the Agenda: Candidates Elections and Ballot Propositions*. Princeton, NJ: Princeton University Press, 2005.

Piven, Frances Fox, and Richard Cloward. *Why Americans Don't Vote*. New York: Pantheon, 1988.

Putnam, Robert. *Bowling Alone:* The Collapse and Revival of American Community. New York: Simon & Schuster, 2000.

Rosenstone, Steven J., and John Mark Hansen. *Mobilization, Participation, and Democracy in America*. New York: Macmillan, 1993.

Schattschneider, E. E. *The Semisovereign People: A Realist's View of Democracy in America*. Boston: Wadsworth-Cengage Learning, 1975.

Sinclair, Betsy. *The Social Citizen: Peer Networks and Political Behavior*. Chicago: University of Chicago Press, 2010.

Smith, Daniel, and Caroline Tolbert. *Educated by Initiative: The Effects of Direct Democracy on Citizens and Political Organizations in the American States*. Ann Arbor: University of Michigan Press, 2004.

Springer, Melanie. *American Electoral Institutions and Voter Turnout, 1920–2000*. Chicago: University of Chicago Press, 2014.

Verba, Sidney, Kay Lehman Schlozman, and Henry Brady. *Voice and Equality: Civic Voluntarism in American Politics*. Cambridge, MA: Harvard University Press, 1995.

Recommended Websites

League of Women Voters
www.lwv.org
> Established in 1920 as part of the women's suffrage movement, the League of Women Voters encourages informed and active participation in government.

Open Secrets
www.opensecrets.org/elections/
> Campaign contributions are a form of political participation that is both necessary and controversial. This website uses data from the Federal Election Commission to publish the names of those who give elected officials campaign money and those who may be receiving preferential treatment.

Project Vote
www.projectvote.org
> Since 1982, Project Vote has worked to increase the participation of low-income, minority, youth, and other marginalized and underrepresented voters. The organization sponsors voter registration drives and get-out-the-vote programs and monitors election laws across the states. As a community organizer, Barack Obama worked for Project Vote, registering voters in Chicago.

Project Vote Smart
www.votesmart.org
> This nonpartisan site is dedicated to providing citizens with information on political candidates and elected officials. Here you can easily view candidates' biographical information, positions on issues, and voting records so that you can make an informed choice on Election Day.

United States Election Project
www.electproject.org
> Click on "Voter turnout data" for the best and most reliable source for voter turnout rates nationally and by state in presidential and midterm elections from 1980–2016.

U.S. Census Bureau: Voting and Registration
www.census.gov/population/www/socdemo/voting.html
> The U.S. Census Bureau collects statistics on voting and registration by various demographic and socioeconomic characteristics. See if you can find differences in voter turnout by race, age, gender, or socioeconomic status.

In the 2016 presidential election, Bernie Sanders challenged the Democratic Party establishment. While Americans express frustration over partisan conflict, political parties play an important role in organizing American politics and government.

Political Parties

WHAT GOVERNMENT DOES AND WHY IT MATTERS In the United States, political parties help the government respond to the needs and desires of its citizens. Political parties organize the mass public, who, as individuals, might lack the resources and knowledge to compete with wealthy elites, businesses, and interest groups for a voice in politics. Strong parties and competition between party candidates can make it more likely that elected officials will represent the views and wishes of the American people. Moreover, democracy is promoted when parties mobilize large numbers of individuals to participate in the political arena and to vote. Compared with interest groups, which generally seek narrow policy objectives, political parties are capable of mobilizing much more of the electorate to win control of government.

However, in 2016 the major American political parties faced an unprecedented populist uprising during the presidential nomination process, when massive numbers of voters preferred "outsider" candidates. Self-described democratic socialist Bernie Sanders (running for the Democratic nomination) and television celebrity and businessman Donald Trump (running for the Republican nomination) positioned themselves as outsiders who would better represent ordinary Americans than the "establishment" candidates would. Sanders's campaign message directed outrage at Wall Street and the wealthiest 1 percent, who have prospered while the wages of average Americans have stalled. His proposals included free college tuition at state schools, single-payer health insurance, increasing the minimum wage to $15 an hour, imposing a tax on financial transactions on Wall Street, and raising taxes on the wealthiest Americans. Republican candidate Donald Trump dominated national media headlines for months with his highly controversial statements and proposals, which included building a wall at the Mexican border to stop illegal immigration and enacting a temporary ban on Muslims entering the United States.

Trump and Sanders represented a radical departure for the American political system, which has generally turned to insiders when choosing political leaders. Both initially received few endorsements from party elites and appealed to working-class white voters, independents, and young voters. Both also challenged the status quo by refusing contributions from big business and outside funding by Super PACs. Sanders's campaign received a record-breaking $206 million in individual contributions, of which $129 million was small contributions.[1] As a representative of big business who had donated hundreds of thousands to political candidates, Trump positioned himself as one who could not be bought off as a candidate. He stated, "My whole life I've been greedy, greedy, greedy. I've grabbed all the money I could get. I'm so greedy. But now I want to be greedy for the United States."[2] He claimed he would redirect his competitive capitalist charisma toward the public good. Trump's and Sanders's surprising victories—both won many key state primaries and caucuses and Trump went on to secure the Republican nomination—posed a challenge to the two major political parties.

As we will see in this chapter, a revolt against the political parties by rank-and-file members occurs very rarely in American history. Parties play an important role in American democracy, but the widespread support for populist, outsider candidates in 2016 indicated that large segments of the American public were frustrated with the status quo and no longer felt that the major-party "establishment" represented their interests.

chaptergoals

- Define political parties and their functions in politics (pp. 329–34)
- Explain the roles that parties play in elections (pp. 334–36)
- Describe how the major American parties are structured at the national, state, and local levels (pp. 336–40)
- Explain how parties organize legislative business and influence policy (pp. 340–42)
- Identify the reasons for and sources of party identification (pp. 342–50)
- Describe how the party system in the United States has changed over time and its main features today (pp. 350–62)

What Are Political Parties?

Define political parties and their functions in politics

Political parties, like interest groups, are organizations that seek influence over government. They can generally be distinguished from interest groups on the basis of their orientation. A party seeks to control the government by nominating candidates and electing its members to office. As we will see in Chapter 11, interest groups do not control the operation of government and its personnel but rather try to influence government policies, often through lobbying elected officials and contributing to campaigns.

political parties organized groups that attempt to influence the government by electing their members to important government offices

Although the Founders did not envision the rise of political parties and George Washington, a military general, was elected the nation's first president without association with a political party, parties quickly became a core feature of the American political system. Parties and **partisanship** organize the political world and simplify complex policy debates for citizens and elected officials alike. They are the interface through which most policy debates in American politics, and media coverage of politics, are framed. Parties also play central roles in mobilizing citizens to vote, informing the public of government policy, and ensuring that the public voice is heard in policy debates.

partisanship identification with or support of a particular party or cause

The relationship between parties and government is complex. Political parties have been the chief points of contact between government, on the one side, and individual citizens and interest groups, on the other. Through organized political parties, citizens and groups can influence government policies. As political scientist Walter Dean Burnham wrote, political parties "generate . . . collective power on behalf of the many [who are] individually powerless against the relatively few who are individually or organizationally powerful."[3] It may be difficult for ordinary citizens to have any real influence on government acting as individuals, but they can have an impact on what government does when they act collectively. Political parties also seek to organize and influence important groups in society to win elections and gain political power. All political parties have this dual character: they are instruments through which citizens and government attempt to influence each other.

In a landmark book written over a half-century ago, political scientist E. E. Schattschneider advocated for a political system run by party politics instead of interest groups.[4] To be an equal democracy where rich and poor, educated and noneducated, young and old, and white and minority are represented, there must be competitive and responsible political parties that provide real choices to the electorate so that the public can participate in the government's decision-making process. Parties, he believed, are able to mobilize more people than interest groups because they can expand the "scope of conflict" or the policy debate to include most or all of the electorate. While interest groups benefit from focusing on specific policy issues, political parties must expand political conflict to the public arena and focus on a range of policy issues from the economy to foreign policy in order to win elections.

It is not enough, however, to simply have political parties: parties must be "competitive" and "responsible." When political parties compete with one another to win elections, Schattschneider contended, they have incentives to continually expand public debates to include nonvoting members of the electorate in order to gain a majority of voters and win the election. This strategy has been evident in the extremely competitive presidential elections since 2000, with widespread voter-mobilization campaigns on the part of the Democratic and Republican parties. Voter turnout in 2008 was at the highest level since 1960, largely because of the get-out-the-vote campaign drives organized by the political parties.

Political parties must also act "responsibly" by continually informing the people of current political issues that are in their best interests. And once in power, political parties must enact policies that represent their members' interests, rather than responding to the demands of interest groups. In this idealized view, competitive and responsible parties can help increase voter turnout, creating more equal representation for those in lower socioeconomic classes.

However, some political scientists argue that Schattschneider's vision is far from reality. Today, we have strong political parties, but party candidates are often subsidized by big businesses and the wealthy. Political scientist Larry Bartels has found that on economic issues both the Democratic and Republican parties are more responsive to the preferences of the upper and middle classes and ignore the policy wishes of the lower class. Bartels calls this "unequal democracy."[5] Stagnating wages for the middle class and rising income inequality help explain why many voters have grown increasingly frustrated by the Democratic and Republican parties; as noted in the introduction, in the 2016 presidential election, many supported populist candidates, such as Donald Trump on the right and Bernie Sanders on the left, who sought to reform the political system.

Another criticism of parties stems from the idea that they are in fact controlled more by interest groups and campaign contributions than by politicians and the public are thus less likely to respond to voter preferences and may even take advantage of the public's lack of attention to politics to promote their own agenda.[6] Part of the appeal of Trump and Sanders in 2016 was that they challenged Wall Street's influence (through financial contributions) over the political parties and focused on a strategy of collecting smaller-sum donations from their supporters rather than relying mainly on Super PACs or major donors.

Studies have shown that both Democratic and Republican members of Congress respond more to the interests of affluent and middle-class Americans, while neither party represents the policy preferences of the poor.

Some observers believe that the problem in the United States today is that the two parties and political elites in Congress are too polarized along liberal and conservative lines, whereas the majority of Americans hold moderate opinions and values; thus, Congress and the parties do a poor job of representing the citizens.[7] Others argue that the rules governing our election system need to be updated— what is called "election reform"—so that there are more than two major political parties to better represent citizens' views.[8] Both of these topics are covered in more detail near the end of this chapter.

As long as political parties have existed, they have been criticized for introducing selfish, "partisan" concerns into public debates and national policy. Yet political parties are extremely important to the functioning of a democracy. As we will see, parties can increase participation in politics, provide a central cue for citizens to cast informed votes, and organize the business of legislatures and governing.

How Do Political Parties Form?

Historically, parties form in one of two ways. The first, which could be called *internal mobilization*, occurs when political conflicts prompt officials and competing factions within government to mobilize popular support. This is precisely what happened during the early years of the American Republic. Competition in Congress between northeastern merchants and southern farmers led first the southerners and then the northeasterners to attempt to organize their supporters. The result was the foundation of America's first national parties: the Jeffersonians or Antifederalists, whose primary base was in the South, and the Federalists, whose strength was greatest in the New England states.

The second way that parties form is called *external mobilization*, which takes place when a group of politicians outside of government organizes popular support to win governmental power. For example, during the 1850s, a group of state politicians who opposed slavery, especially the expansion of slavery in the United States' territorial possessions, built what became the Republican Party by constructing party organizations and mobilizing popular support in the Northeast and West.

America's two major parties now, of course, are the Democrats and the Republicans. Both trace their roots back over 150 years to the nineteenth century, and both have evolved over time. Since they were formed, the two major parties have undergone significant shifts in their policy positions and their membership. These changes have been prompted both by issues and events (economic change, the civil rights movement, immigration, etc.) and by demographic and social developments in the United States. As noted above, a lack of trust in and frustration with the federal government mobilized many to support "outsider" candidates in the 2016 presidential campaign. The success of outsider candidates possibly signaled that a change, or even a realignment, of the political parties is under way.

Growing differences in demographic profiles of Republicans and Democrats suggest more changes for the party system as the parties compete with each other to win support among voters and interest groups. One of the most recent changes is the rapid growth of the Latino population and Latinos' increased participation in presidential elections. Latinos have strongly favored the Democratic Party since 2008. Younger voters and other racial and ethnic minorities also increasingly affiliate with the Democratic Party, while white voters, the religious, and older people are more likely to vote Republican.

The United States' Two-Party System

Over the past 200 years, Americans' conception of political parties has changed considerably. In the early years of the Republic, parties were seen as threats to the social order and were referred to as "factions." In the *Federalist Papers*, both Alexander Hamilton and James Madison condemned factions that pursued narrow self-interest over the broader well-being of the nation as a whole.[9] In his 1796 Farewell Address, President George Washington warned his countrymen to shun partisan politics. Nonetheless, a **two-party system** emerged early in the history of the new Republic. Beginning with the Federalists and the Jeffersonian Republicans in the late 1780s, two major parties have dominated national politics, although which particular two parties has changed with the times and issues. (The development of the party system in U.S. history will be discussed later in the chapter.)

Most other countries in the world use a proportional representation system, in which seats in government are allocated to political parties based on their share of the total vote cast in the election. In contrast, the United States uses geographic single-member districts combined with winner-take-all elections. It doesn't matter, for example, if the contest for a U.S. House seat is won with 40 percent or 80 percent of the total vote; the candidate with the largest number of votes (a plurality) in that district wins the seat in Congress. That is why the system is "winner take all": unlike in proportional systems, runners-up do not gain seats in government. The U.S. system is also called "first past the post" because the candidate with the most votes wins the election, even if she did not win a majority of the popular vote. In the United States, proportional voting rules are uncommon, especially above the local level, and are absent at the national level.

The winner-take-all system has helped create our two party–dominant system, and third parties have generally not won seats in Congress, state legislatures, or the presidency. Election rules largely determine how many political parties there are in a country. Under U.S. election rules, voters have an incentive not to vote for small- or third-party candidates for fear of "wasting" their vote when only one party (usually one of the two largest parties) can win the election. Concern about wasting one's vote on third parties is called the spoiler effect or strategic voting. (Third parties are discussed in more detail later in this chapter). What is important to remember is that U.S. election rules create our two-party system. Proportional representation systems used in many other countries tend to result in multiple parties in government. If the rules were to change, the number of political parties would likely change as well.

What Political Parties Do

Without political parties, democracy as we know it would be difficult to achieve. In the United States, citizens take for granted that leaders will run for public office, that there will be competition among candidates, that they will have the opportunity to learn about candidates and issues from campaigns, and that once

two-party system a political system in which only two parties have a realistic opportunity to compete effectively for control

for critical analysis

What rules governing the American electoral process promote a two-party system? How might different rules impact the party system?

Two-Party Systems and Multi-Party Systems

The American political system is dominated by two political parties, the Republican Party and the Democratic Party, but many other countries have more than two parties. The number varies depending on the electoral rules in place. Countries such as the United States, which use a first-past-the-post system (in which the candidate with the most votes wins the seat), tend to have two major parties that dominate the system. In contrast, the Netherlands uses a proportional representation system (in which seats are apportioned based on the share of votes a party receives) that has led to a total of eleven parties in the legislature, with three to four major parties.

In proportional representation systems like the Netherlands, voters select parties to represent them nationally rather than candidates to represent their region, and parties receive roughly the same percentage of votes in parliament as they received in the election. Thus, the legislature tends to more accurately resemble how the national electorate voted. The party representation in the 2013 Dutch parliament is almost identical to the 2012 national vote, whereas in the United States, the largest parties tend to be overrepresented while smaller parties lose out.

UNITED STATES, 2014 HOUSE OF REPRESENTATIVES ELECTION

Percentage of Votes in the Election

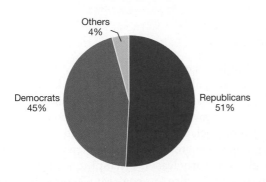

NETHERLANDS, 2012 LOWER HOUSE (TWEDE CAMER) ELECTION

Percentage of Votes in the Election

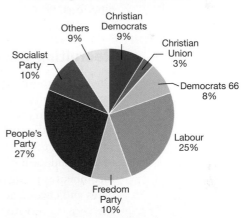

Percentage of Seats in the Legislature

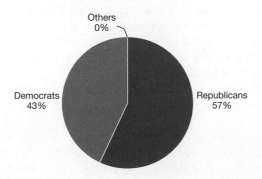

Percentage of Seats in the Legislature

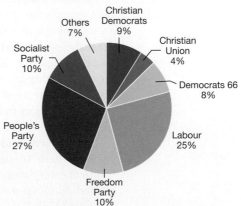

SOURCES: The U.S. Federal Election Commission, www.fec.gov/pubrec/fe2014/federalelections2014.pdf and the NSD European Election Database, www.nsd.uib.no/european_election_database/country/netherlands/parliamentary_elections.html (accessed 4/20/10).

in office, political leaders will work together to make policy and govern. Each of these tasks is complex, however, and would be all the more so if political parties did not exist. Parties mobilize citizens in the electorate to vote, offer choices to voters in elections, and provide officeholders with organization for running government. As political scientist John Aldrich argues in *Why Parties*, parties solve three fundamental problems of democracy: how to regulate the number of people seeking public office, how to mobilize voters, and how to achieve and maintain the majorities needed to accomplish legislative goals once in office.[10] In the sections that follow, we describe several democratic functions that parties serve. The next sections consider parties in the electorate, parties as organization, and parties in government.

● Parties, Voter Mobilization, and Elections

Explain the roles that parties play in elections

Parties have always been central to the electoral process, and in recent years they have taken on a renewed role in recruiting candidates, coordinating campaigns, mobilizing voters, and raising money.[11] Parties succeed when they win elections; thus, we begin with parties and elections.

Recruiting Candidates

One of the most important but least noticed party activities is the recruitment of candidates for local, state, and national office. As Schattschneider argued, "responsible parties" recruit candidates who are loyal to the party's philosophy and policy agenda with the goal of controlling government and adopting policies that are consistent with the party's platform. Each election year, candidates run for thousands of state and local offices as well as congressional seats. When they do not have an incumbent running for re-election, party leaders attempt to identify strong candidates and encourage them to run for office in open-seat elections. In recent years, the very conservative Tea Party wing of the Republican Party has been especially successful at recruiting candidates to run in Republican primary elections.

An ideal candidate will have a strong leadership record and the capacity to raise enough money to mount a serious campaign, especially if he must challenge an incumbent or will face a well-funded opponent from the other party in the general election. Party leaders are usually not willing to provide financial backing to candidates who are unable to raise substantial funds on their own. For a U.S. House seat, this can mean several hundred thousand dollars; for a Senate seat, a serious candidate must be able to raise several million dollars. Presidential candidates raise hundreds of millions of dollars, an amount that continues to rise with every election cycle.

Often, party leaders have difficulty finding competitive candidates and persuading them to run. Candidate recruitment is problematic in an era when political candidates must assume that their personal lives will be intensely scrutinized on social media, in the press, and in negative campaign ads run by their opponents.[12]

Party Nominations and Primaries

Nomination is the process by which a party selects a single candidate to run for each elective office. Parties want only one candidate on the general-election ballot so that members of the same party do not take votes from one another, allowing the other party's candidate to win. So parties undertake an internal process of nomination to settle on one candidate who will be on the ballot in the general election. The party nomination process varies from state to state and office to office, but it usually involves a **primary election** or **caucus** among multiple candidates from the same party. Voters in the primary election select just one candidate to go on to the general election.

Scholars have found that although the nomination process appears democratic in that average citizens have a say, party elites play an outsized role in selecting the candidates who will compete to be the next president of the United States.[13] Political parties determine which candidates can credibly compete in primary elections—that is, they narrow the field of which candidates have a chance to win in the primaries. Without money and endorsements from one of the two major parties, most candidates cannot get out of the primary. Candidates' reliance on party money results in rigid partisan voting blocs within government.[14] In 2016, however, the Republican Party insiders had less control over the process; reality-TV star Donald Trump secured the nomination despite the fact that many members of the party emphatically spoke out against him.

General Election and Mobilizing Voters

The general-election period begins immediately after the nominations conclude. Throughout American history, this is a time of heightened partisanship and fanfare, when popular support for the parties is high. All the paraphernalia of party committees—from signs, bumper stickers, and buttons to social

nomination the process by which political parties select their candidates for election to public office

primary elections elections held to select a party's candidate for the general election

caucus (political) a normally closed political party business meeting of citizens or lawmakers to select candidates, elect officers, plan strategy, or make decisions regarding legislative matters

With no incumbent running for Maryland's 8th Congressional District seat, Democratic candidates debated one another in the primaries. Jamie Raskin defeated seven other Democratic candidates to secure the party's nomination in the general election.

Research by political scientists and campaign organizations has shown that face-to-face, in-person contacts are much more effective than mailings, robocalls, or TV advertising in mobilizing voters.

media slogans and YouTube ads—are on display, and committee members are activated into local party workforces. The first step involves voter registration. Party workers collaborate with nonprofit organizations, local community groups, and other organizations to turn out the vote. Even so, the parties and candidate campaigns still mail notices, call voters, organize voter-registration drives on college campuses, and knock on doors to ensure that citizens are registered. Confirming that citizens are registered to vote or helping them register, however, is only the first step.

Convincing voters to actually show up to cast a ballot on Election Day is one of the hardest tasks that the parties face as it involves getting individuals to go to the polls, stand in line, and vote for the party's candidates on the ballot. If they are voting by mail—absentee ballots or mail voting is how one in three Americans now vote—they have to request the ballot, fill it out, and return it (see Chapter 8). Voter mobilization, once an art, has now become a science. Campaigns now organize wide-scale voter-mobilization drives involving field offices with hundreds of thousands of volunteers and party workers contacting millions of voters. In recent years, the two major parties have developed an extensive database of over 240 million potential adult voters, combining census and consumer behavior data, which allows the parties to more accurately seek out votes, contributions, and campaign volunteers. Using these vast computerized databases, data mining, social media, and other new techniques such as micro-targeting, modern political campaigns can predict who you will vote for; and they are extremely effective at turning out the voters who are most likely to vote for their candidates. *Micro-targeting* means tailoring campaign messages to individuals in small, homogeneous groups (e.g., suburban housewives) and emphasizing specific, often heated issues, rather than a one-size-fits-all campaign message. This technique enables political parties to identify small groups based on specific characteristics, including geography, and to target candidates' strategies and messages to these groups.

Big data and targeted messages have revolutionized how parties and candidates conduct voter-mobilization drives. It doesn't matter, after all, which party has more support if that party's voters stay home on Election Day. In 2008 the Obama campaign learned that face-to-face and in-person contacts are much more effective than mailings or robocalls at getting out the vote.[15] The lessons of 2008 were improved on in 2016 as both parties built more accurate databases to use when developing their messages and turning out the vote.

● Parties as Organizations

party organization the formal structure of a political party, including its leadership, election committees, active members, and paid staff

> **Describe how the major American parties are structured at the national, state, and local levels**

In the United States **party organizations** exist at virtually every level of government (see Figure 9.1). These organizations are usually committees made up of a number of active party members. State law and party rules prescribe how such committees are constituted. Usually, committee members are elected at local party business meetings, called caucuses, or as part of the regular primary election. The best-known examples of these committees are at the

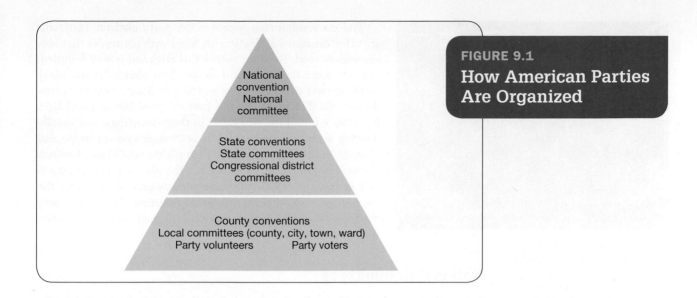

FIGURE 9.1
How American Parties Are Organized

National
convention
National
committee

State conventions
State committees
Congressional district
committees

County conventions
Local committees (county, city, town, ward)
Party volunteers   Party voters

national level: the Democratic National Committee and the Republican National Committee.

National Convention

At the national level, the party's most important institution is the **national convention**. The convention, held every four years, is attended by delegates from each of the 50 states. As a group, they nominate the party's presidential and vice-presidential candidates, draft the party's campaign platform for the presidential race, and approve changes in the rules and regulations governing party procedures. Before World War II, presidential nominations occupied most of the time at the national convention, requiring days of negotiation and compromise. In recent years, however, presidential candidates have been chosen by winning enough delegates in state primary elections and caucuses to win the official nomination on the first ballot. Today, the actual convention often serves as a media event to promote the party's candidates, not a forum to decide which presidential candidate will represent the party.

The convention's other two tasks, determining the party's rules and its platform, are also important. Party rules can determine the influence of competing groups within the party and can also increase or decrease the party's chances for electoral success. In 1972, for example, the Democratic National Convention adopted a new set of rules favored by the party's liberal wing. State delegations to the Democratic Convention were required to include women and members of minority groups in rough proportion to those groups' representation among the party's membership in that state. The change also called for the use of the proportional voting rules (i.e. quotas), which have improved representation of rank-and-file party members. In the case of the Democratic Party, proportional representation increased the likelihood of women and minority delegates being elected, while in the Republican Party, which used proportional representation voting for the first time in 2012, it worked to increase representation of social conservatives and Tea Party affiliates.

national convention convened by the Republican National Committee or the Democratic National Committee to nominate official candidates for president and vice president in the upcoming election, establish party rules, and adopt the party's platform

platform a party document, written at a national convention, that contains party philosophy, principles, and positions on issues

Today, the parties use their national conventions to provide more entertainment than substantive policy in order to attract media attention and promote their candidate. Here, crowds react to a performance by the Foo Fighters at the Democratic National Convention in 2012.

soft money money contributed directly to political parties and other organizations for political activities, such as voter mobilization drives, that is not regulated by federal campaign spending laws

The convention also approves the party **platform**. Platforms are often dismissed as documents filled with platitudes that voters seldom read. To some extent this criticism is well founded: not one voter in a thousand so much as glances at the party platform, and even the news media pay little attention to the documents. Furthermore, the parties' presidential candidates make little use of the platforms in their campaigns and usually develop their own themes, such as Obama's use of "hope and change" in 2008 and Donald Trump's slogan "Make America Great Again" in 2016. Nonetheless, the platform is understood as a contract in which the various party groups attending the convention state their terms for supporting the ticket. Party platforms should be seen more as internal party documents than as public pledges.

National Committees

Between conventions, each national political party is technically headed by its national committee. For the Democrats and Republicans, these are called the Democratic National Committee and the Republican National Committee, respectively. Much of what these national committees do is raise money for party candidates—a big job, given that elections are more expensive in the United States than in any other country in the world. The national committees also try to minimize disputes within the party and work to enhance the party's media image. The work of each national committee is overseen by its chairperson.

The Democratic National Committee and the Republican National Committee each used to raise tens of millions of dollars of so-called **soft money** every election cycle, which could be used to support party candidates throughout the nation. The 2002 Bipartisan Campaign Reform Act, sometimes known as the McCain-Feingold bill, outlawed this practice. To circumvent the Bipartisan Campaign Reform Act and raise the large amounts of money needed for political campaigns, however, each party and most candidates establish Super PACs as sources of outside money. These Super PACs, made up of 527 committees, promote and publicize political issues, including airing negative campaign ads. As nonprofit political advocacy groups, Super PACs can claim tax-exempt status under Section 527 of the Internal Revenue Code. As mentioned above, the 2016 presidential campaign of Bernie Sanders was unique in rejecting Super PACs.

527 committees can raise and spend unlimited amounts of money as long as their activities are not coordinated with those of the formal party organizations or the candidates and if the aim is to inform the public and increase voter turnout. Although some 527 committees are actually independent, many are directed by former Republican and Democratic party officials and run shadow campaigns on behalf of the parties.[16] Beginning with the 2008 elections, nonprofit organizations that formed specifically to support particular candidates became an additional source of soft money.

Another important trend is the rise of 501(c)(4)s, politically active nonprofits whose funding is called dark money because, unlike 527s, donors and amounts contributed do not have to be made public. Under federal law, these nonprofits can spend unlimited amounts on political campaigns, as long as doing so is not their primary purpose. Additionally, while these organizations may engage in political activities, those activities cannot take up more than 50 percent of their time. (Campaign funds are discussed in more detail in Chapter 10.)

Congressional Campaign Committees

Each party also forms House and Senate campaign committees, whose efforts may or may not be coordinated with the activities of the national committees. Within the party that controls the White House, the national committee and the congressional campaign committees are often rivals since both groups are seeking donations from the same people but for different candidates: the national committee seeks funds for the presidential race, while the congressional campaign committees approach the same contributors for support for the congressional contests. In recent years, both parties have attempted to coordinate the fund-raising activities of all of their committees. Congressional committees direct funds to the handful of very competitive House and Senate races each election, which are increasingly important.

State and Local Party Organizations

Each of the two major parties has a central committee in each state. The parties traditionally also have county committees and, in some instances, state Senate district committees, judicial district committees, and, in the case of larger cities, citywide party committees and local assembly district "ward" committees.

During the nineteenth and early twentieth centuries, many cities, counties, and occasionally even a few states had such well-organized parties that they were called **party machines**, whose leaders were called "bosses." The famous old machines of New York, Chicago, and Boston relied on "precinct captains" and a fairly tight group of party members around them. Precinct captains were usually members of long standing in neighborhood party clubhouses, which were important social centers and places for distributing favors (or bribes) to constituents.[17] Traditional party machines depended heavily on **patronage**, their power to control government jobs. With thousands of jobs to dispense, party bosses were able to recruit armies of political workers to turn out the vote. Voting for the party could mean the guarantee of a government job, such as a police officer, firefighter, or garbage collector. The party machines also helped immigrants process paperwork for citizenship and even distributed free turkeys on Thanksgiving, all in exchange for support of the party on Election Day.

Some of the major reform movements in American history, such as the Progressive movement, were motivated by the excessive powers and abuses of these party machines and their bosses. Progressive reformers changed the rules of politics to reduce the power of political parties and give voters more voice in deciding who was elected to public office. A few of the many reforms advocated by the Progressives to weaken the party machines included the direct election of U.S. senators; the secret ballot and long ballot, where the names of candidates running for both parties were listed; primary elections; and voter registration.

Few, if any, political machines are left today. With civil service reform and the merit system party leaders no longer control many government jobs. Nevertheless, state and local party organizations are very active in recruiting candidates and conducting voter-registration drives. In addition, under current federal law, state and local party organizations can spend unlimited amounts of money on "party-building"

party machines strong party organizations in late nineteenth- and early twentieth-century American cities; these machines were led by often corrupt "bosses" who controlled party nominations and patronage

patronage the resources available to higher officials, usually opportunities to make partisan appointments to offices and to confer grants, licenses, or special favors to supporters

Political parties used to be ruled by powerful local "bosses," who handed out jobs and favors in exchange for loyalty on Election Day. The cartoon shows New York boss Richard Croker controlling the Democratic Party organization (the donkey) with his pit bulls.

activities such as voter-registration and get-out-the-vote drives (though in some states such practices are limited by state law). As a result, for many years the national party organizations, which had enormous fund-raising abilities but were restricted by law in how much they could spend on candidates, transferred millions of dollars to the state and local organizations. The state and local parties, in turn, spent this soft money to promote national, state, and local political activities. Through the transfer of party campaign money, local organizations became linked financially to the national parties and American political parties became more integrated. At the same time, the state and local party organizations came to control large financial resources and play important roles in elections despite the collapse of the old party machines.[18]

● Parties in Government

> **Explain how parties organize legislative business and influence policy**

When the dust of the campaign has settled, does it matter which party has won? It does. Especially when the parties are sharply divided ideologically, as they have been in recent years, the party that controls government can make significant changes by moving policy in new directions.

Parties and Policy

One of the most familiar complaints about American politics is that the two major parties try to be all things to all people and are therefore indistinguishable from each other. But since the 1980s, fundamental differences emerged between the positions of Democratic and Republican party leaders on a number of key issues. For example, the national leadership of the Republican Party supports strict immigration laws, maintaining high levels of military spending, cuts in social programs, tax relief for upper-income voters, tax incentives for businesses, and a social agenda backed by members of conservative religious denominations, including opposition to abortion and same-sex marriage. The national Democratic leadership, on the other hand, supports expanded funding for social services and national health care, public spending for infrastructure such as highways and bridges, cuts in military spending, increased regulation of business to address climate change, raising taxes on the wealthy and corporations, and a variety of consumer protection programs. In the current era of party polarization, the Republican and Democratic parties in Congress are less likely to compromise and are often faced with stalemates. For example, partisan gridlock in 2013 over raising the debt ceiling resulted in government shutdown as the government ran out of money to pay federal employees until a new budget deal was reached.

The parties have different philosophies and seek to appeal to different core constituencies. The Democratic Party at the national level seeks to unite organized labor, the poor and working class, members of racial minorities, the young, and liberal upper-middle-class professionals. The Republicans, by contrast, appeal to business, upper-middle- and upper-class groups in the private sector, white working-class voters, military families, religious and social conservatives, and libertarian-leaning conservatives who want less government interference in all aspects of society and the economy. Rural and suburban areas provide more votes for the Republicans, while urban areas are dominated by Democrats.

Party leaders often seek to develop issues they hope will add new groups to their party's constituent base. During the 1980s, for example, under the leadership of Ronald Reagan, the Republicans devised a series of social issues, including support for school prayer, opposition to abortion, and opposition to affirmative action, designed to cultivate the support of white southerners. This effort was successful at increasing Republican strength in the once solidly Democratic South. In the 1990s, under the leadership of Bill Clinton, who called himself a "new Democrat," the Democratic Party sought to develop new social programs designed to solidify the party's base among working-class voters and somewhat more conservative economic programs aimed at attracting the votes of the middle- and upper-middle-class.

As these examples suggest, party leaders can play the role of **policy entrepreneurs**, developing ideas and programs that will expand their party's base of support while eroding that of the opposition. Like their counterparts in the business world, party leaders seek to identify and develop programs and policies that will appeal to the public. The public, of course, has the ultimate voice. With its votes it decides whether or not to "buy" new policy offerings.

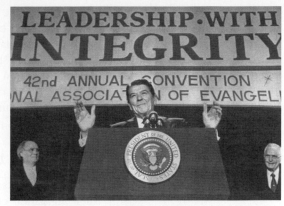

Beginning in the 1980s the Republican Party, led by Ronald Reagan, sought to expand its base by focusing on social issues that mattered to conservative religious voters. In 1984, President Reagan spoke to the National Association of Evangelicals about outlawing abortion and instituting prayer in public schools.

policy entrepreneur an individual who identifies a problem as a political issue and brings a policy proposal into the political agenda

Parties in Congress

Congress depends more on the party system than is generally recognized as the parties form the basic organization for running Congress. The speakership of the House is essentially a party office. All the members of the House take part in the election of the Speaker. But the actual selection is made by the **majority party**—the party that holds a majority of seats in the House. (The other party is known as the **minority party**.) When the majority party caucus presents a nominee for Speaker to the entire House, its choice is invariably ratified in a straight vote along party lines. The committee system of both houses of Congress is also a product of the two-party system. For example, each party is assigned a quota of members for each committee, depending on the percentage of total seats held by the party. As we shall see in Chapter 12, the assignment of individual members to committees is a party decision. Each party has a "committee on committees" to make such decisions. Granting a member of Congress permission to transfer to another committee is also a party decision, as is advancement up the committee ladder toward serving as committee chair. Since the late nineteenth century, most advancements have been automatic—based on the length of continual service on the committee. This seniority system has existed only because of the support of the two parties, however, and either party can depart from it by a simple vote.

The importance of parties in Congress first became especially evident in the months after the Republicans won control of Congress in 1994 and were able to maintain nearly unanimous support among party members. Democrats were rarely

majority party the party that holds the majority of legislative seats in either the House or the Senate

minority party the party that holds the minority of legislative seats in either the House or the Senate

for critical analysis
How do parties attract the popular support they need to win elections?

able to match the Republicans' strong party discipline. After 2006, however, when Democrats won back the Congress, they showed considerably more party discipline than they had in past decades. During Obama's tenure, Republican members of Congress also showed remarkable party discipline in their united party-line voting in opposition to the president's initiatives, ranging from economic stimulus to major health care reform. The Republicans won unified control of Congress in 2014 and retained it in 2016. We revisit the role of parties in Congress today when we discuss party polarization later in this chapter.

Parties and the President's Policy Agenda

Strong presidents with broad popular support often depend on party ties to get their legislation enacted in Congress. Yet there has been a trade-off in using the party machinery to support the president's legislative agenda and using it to support the party in congressional elections. Political scientist Daniel Galvin argues that since the Eisenhower presidency, Republicans have paid much more attention to party building than have Democrats.[19] Given their party's minority status in the electorate for much of the past 50 years, Republican presidents have sought to enhance the party's capabilities to turn out their base and win elections. Democratic presidents have put much less energy into building the party apparatus, focusing instead on their legislative agenda and their own re-election. It was only after their 2004 presidential election defeat that Democrats began to pour their energies into building a stronger party. Under the chair of Howard Dean, the Democratic National Committee invested heavily in new technology and in creating party-mobilizing capabilities in states across the country, not just the traditionally "blue" states that have reliably voted Democratic.

The Obama campaign was able to use the party as a springboard for its own mobilizing organization, Obama for America. With detailed information about Democratic Party activists, Obama for America's database became, in turn, an important political resource for the mobilizing capacities of the Democratic Party and for legislative candidates. After Obama took office, the organization was renamed Organizing for America, which mobilized grassroots support for Obama's legislative agenda. Organizing for America, separate from the Democratic National Committee, provides training for volunteers to learn how to become organizers; and it has established offices in nearly every state.

● Party Identification

party identification an individual voter's psychological ties to one party or another

Identify the reasons for and sources of party identification

One reason why parties are so important is that individual voters tend to develop **party identification** with one of the major political parties. Party identification has been compared with wearing blue- or red-tinted glasses: they color voters' understanding of politics in general and are the most important cue in how to vote in elections. That is, most Republicans vote for Republican Party candidates, and most Democrats vote for Democratic Party candidates. Slightly less than one-third of Americans are Republicans, while Democrats and Independents each make up slightly more than one-third of the population. However, most independents lean toward one of the major parties, and political scientists often consider independents who lean as identifying with that party. The number of people identifying as Democrats has outnumbered Republican identifiers for a long time (see Figure 9.2).

Although it is an emotional tie, party identification also has a rational component. Voters generally form attachments to the party that reflects their views and interests. Once those attachments are formed, usually in youth, they are likely to persist and even be handed down to children, unless some very strong factors convince individuals that their party is no longer serving their interests. In some sense, party identification is similar to brand loyalty in the marketplace: consumers choose a brand of automobile for its appearance or mechanical characteristics and stick with it out of loyalty, habit, and unwillingness to reexamine their choices. But they may eventually change if the old brand no longer serves their interests.

On any general-election ballot, there are a number of candidates about whom the average voter has little information. Without knowledge of local or judicial races, most voters fall back on their partisanship, voting for Republican candidates or Democratic candidates for these positions. Some states allow a straight-ticket voting option, where individuals may check one box to cast a ballot for all the Republican or Democratic party candidates up and down the ballot, from local to national offices.

Party identification gives citizens a stake in election outcomes that goes beyond the particular race at hand. This is why strong party identifiers are more likely to go to the polls, to be contacted by political campaigns, and to support the party with which they identify. **Party activists** are drawn from the ranks of the strong identifiers. Activists are those who not only vote but also contribute their time and effort to party affairs, organization, and elections. No party could

party activists partisans who contribute time, energy, and effort to support their party and its candidates

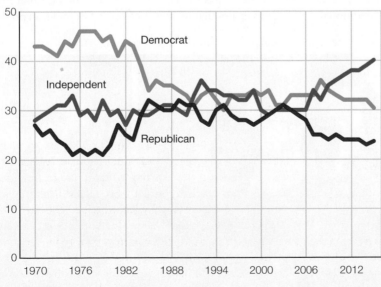

PERCENTAGE IDENTIFYING
THEMSELVES AS . . .

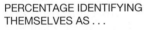

SOURCE: Pew Research Center, "Party Identification," www.pewresearch.org /data-trend/political-attitudes/party -identification/ (accessed 10/18/16).

FIGURE 9.2

Trends in Party Identification, 1939–2015

Over time, the Democrats have lost strength as more Americans identified themselves as Republicans and independents. Since 2004, however, the number of Democrats has held steady and the number of Republicans has declined, while the number of Americans identifying as independent of either party has increased to an all-time high. Why do you think this is?

succeed without the thousands of volunteers who undertake the tasks needed to keep the organization going. Many party activists devote their time to politics because they have strong beliefs on particular policy issues. Across a range of issues, the views of Democratic activists are more liberal than those of Democratic voters, whereas the views of Republican activists are more conservative than those of Republican voters.

Who Are Republicans and Democrats?

The Democratic and Republican parties are currently the only truly national parties in the United States. They are the only political organizations that draw support from most regions of the country and from Americans of every racial, economic, religious, and ethnic group. The two parties do not draw equal support from members of every social stratum, however. In the United States today, several group characteristics are associated with party identification. These include race and ethnicity, gender, religion, class, ideology, region, and age.

Race and Ethnicity The United States' growing racial and ethnic diversity is reflected in changing partisanship and growing divisions among the Republican and Democratic parties. Since the 1930s and Franklin Delano Roosevelt's New Deal, African Americans have been overwhelmingly Democratic in their party identification. More than 90 percent of African Americans describe themselves as Democrats and support Democratic candidates in national, state, and local elections. In 2016, 92 percent of African Americans voted for Democrat Hillary Clinton for president.[20]

Latino voters are less monolithic, by contrast. Cuban Americans, for example, have generally leaned Republican in their party affiliations, whereas Mexican Americans have favored the Democrats. As a group, however, Latinos increasingly support the Democratic Party. A strong shift toward the Democratic Party occurred in 2008, when the exit polls showed that 67 percent of Latinos supported Obama. This trend has continued, with 65 percent voting for Hillary Clinton in 2016. Latino party affiliation is particularly important because it has the potential to alter the electoral map and change traditionally "red" states (states that reliably vote for the Republican presidential

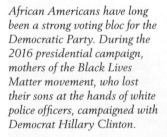

African Americans have long been a strong voting bloc for the Democratic Party. During the 2016 presidential campaign, mothers of the Black Lives Matter movement, who lost their sons at the hands of white police officers, campaigned with Democrat Hillary Clinton.

candidate) to "blue" states (states that reliably vote for the Democratic presidential candidate). In 2016 early voting among Latinos in Florida increased by 100 percent from 2012, though Democrats still lost the state.[21] Asian Americans have been divided in past elections but have also begun leaning Democratic; in 2016, 65 percent of Asian Americans voted for Hillary Clinton, and 29 percent voted for Donald Trump, according to exit polls. Presidential voting often defines party identification.

The affiliation of African Americans and Latinos with the Democratic Party can be traced to the party's historical policy positions. The Democrats were the party of the civil rights movement, desegregation, and affirmative action policies that solidified African American support. Similarly, Democrats tend to be more supportive than Republicans of policies that favor an easier path to citizenship for immigrants. Support for immigration is often key for Latino and Asian voters. The Republican Party's opposition to immigration negatively affects many Latinos, Asian Americans, and their extended families. These affiliations are particulary important in states like California, where 28 percent of the population are legal immigrants. The majority of immigrants in California are of Asian and Latino decent.

Gender Women are somewhat more likely to support Democrats than Republicans, and men are somewhat more likely to support Republicans. This reflects the fact that women and the Democratic Party tend to prioritize health, education, and social services, while men and the Republican Party tend to prioritize fiscal and economic issues and national security. This difference is known as the **gender gap**. The gender gap has hovered at 10 percent since 1992. For example, George W. Bush's first election, in 2000, had a sizable gender gap: he received 53 percent support among men and 43 percent among women. The gender gap was even larger in 2016 with the first female presidential candidate. 54 percent of women supported Democrat Hillary Clinton, compared to 41 percent of men.[22] Her opponent, Donald Trump, fared particularly poorly among women in part due to past comments about women that many deemed offensive and sexist.

gender gap a distinctive pattern of voting behavior reflecting the differences in views between women and men

Religion Just as racial and ethnic diversity continues to grow, so does religious diversity in the United States. Jews are among the Democratic Party's most loyal constituent groups and have been since the New Deal. Nearly 90 percent of all Jewish Americans describe themselves as Democrats. Catholics were also once a strongly pro-Democratic group but have been shifting toward the Republican Party since the 1970s, when Republicans began focusing on abortion and other social issues important to Catholics. White Protestants are more likely to identify with the Republican Party. Evangelical Protestants (or born-again Christians), in particular, have been drawn to the Republicans' conservative stands on social issues, such as marriage and abortion. The importance of religious conservatives to the Republican Party became more evident after 2000, when George W. Bush awarded federal grants and contracts to religious groups. By using so-called faith-based groups as federal contractors, Bush sought to ensure that these groups would have a continuing stake in Republican success. Religious conservatives, particularly white born-again Christians, overwhelmingly supported Bush in 2004, accounting for one-third of his votes. In 2012 and 2016, white evangelical Protestants continued to vote overwhelmingly Republican.[23] A growing segment of the population, roughly 25 percent, are unaffiliated with a religion and tend to vote Democratic.[24]

Class Rising income inequality is an important trend in American politics that has recently led to economic populism. The patterns of class voting that emerged from the New Deal of the 1930s were simple: upper-income Americans were considerably more likely to be Republican whereas lower-income Americans were far more likely to identify with the Democrats. This divide is reflected in the differences between the two parties on economic issues. In general, Republicans support cutting taxes, decreased regulation of business, and lower social spending—positions that reflect the interests of the wealthy. The Democrats, however, favor increasing social spending and in some cases raising taxes on the wealthy—a position consistent with the interests of less affluent Americans. But beginning in the 1970s, many white working-class voters turned to the Republican Party. When class is measured by education, white workers without a college degree have favored Republicans in recent elections. While both the Democratic and Republican parties appeal to working-class voters, working-class whites with low levels of education tend to vote Republican, while working-class minorities tend to vote Democratic.[25] This trend accelerated in 2016, contributing to Republicans' electoral success.

Ideology Ideology and party identification are very closely linked. Most individuals who describe themselves as conservatives identify with the Republican Party, whereas most who call themselves liberals support the Democrats. This division has increased in recent years as the two parties have taken very different positions on social and economic issues. Before the 1970s, when party differences were more blurred, it was not uncommon to find Democratic conservatives and Republican liberals. Both of these species are rare today.

There are now deeper divisions within both the Democratic and Republican parties than in previous decades. The Pew Research Center's political typology finds that 36 percent of Americans are "ideological" and identify strongly with one of the two major parties. That group includes social conservatives, who are especially concerned about social issues such as immigration, abortion, and same-sex marriage; business conservatives, who care most about reducing government regulation and taxes; and people who identify as solidly liberal and vote Democratic. The Republican Party includes both groups of conservatives, but at times the interests of these two groups conflict. In the 2016 Republican presidential primaries, for example, Ted Cruz represented the social conservatives, while Jeb Bush represented business conservatives.

For most Americans, however, party and ideological identification are not so clear-cut: 54 percent of Americans are less partisan and less predictable as to which candidates they will support. These voters are only sporadically interested in politics, such as during an election cycle. Finally, the remaining 10 percent of Americans are completely on the sidelines of politics—this group tends to be young and diverse.[26] This varied political typography of our nation suggests that the categories of liberal and conservative may not capture the full picture.

Region After the 2000 election, red and blue maps appeared showing the regional distribution of the vote. Democrats, represented as "blue America," tend to be clustered on the coasts, the upper Midwest, and across the northern states. Republicans, represented as "red America," tend to be concentrated in the Mountain West and the South.

The explanations for these regional variations are complex. Between the Civil War and the 1960s, the solid South was a Democratic bastion. Today, the South is solidly Republican. Southern Republicanism has come about because conservative white southerners associate the Democratic Party with liberal positions and policies that benefit urban and minority voters. Republican strength in the South is also related to the weakness of organized labor in this region and a dependence on military programs supported by the Republicans. Democratic strength in the Northeast and Midwest is a function of the continuing influence of organized labor in the large cities of these regions and of the regions' large populations of minority voters, who benefit from Democratic social programs. The coastal West, especially California and the Pacific Northwest, shifted toward the Democrats in the 1990s, in part because of the growing importance of the Latino vote, concerns with the environment, and a growing population of the religiously unaffiliated (see Figure 9.3).[27]

Age Age is another factor associated with partisanship. Today young people are much more likely to be Democratic, while the oldest voters, called the "silent generation," affiliate with the Republican Party. Why does age matter for partisanship? Individuals from the same age cohort are likely to have experienced a similar set of events during the period when their party loyalties were formed. Thus, older Americans who came of political age during the Cold War, Vietnam, and civil rights era. Voters whose initial perceptions of politics were shaped during this period generally responded favorably to the role played by the Democrats, who were antiwar and pro–civil rights, than to the actions of the Republicans. Young people who came of age during the Bush presidency also have a strong identification with the Democratic Party; in 2008, there was a particularly striking shift among young voters toward the Democratic Party. In recent years, however, there has been a striking uptick in the percentage of young people who identify as independent from either political party, which may be a reflection of increasing frustration with government (see Figure 9.4).

for critical analysis

What are the major components of each party's political coalition? What factors tie these groups to their respective parties?

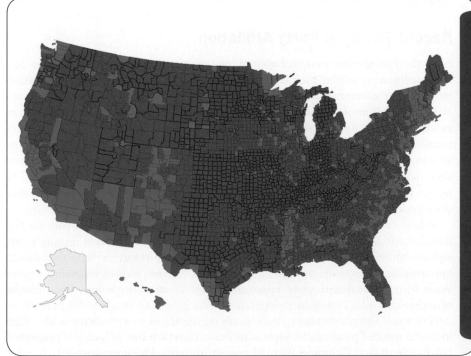

FIGURE 9.3

Presidential Vote by County, 2016

In 2016 the Republicans dominated in most counties in the center of the country. Although the map shows more "red" counties than "blue," covering a greater geographic area, Hillary Clinton and the Democrats won many of the most populous counties and several of the states with the most votes in the electoral college (see Chapter 10).

NOTE: County-level data for Alaska were not available.
SOURCE: "Presidential Election Results: Donald Trump Wins," *New York Times*, www.nytimes.com/elections/results/president (accessed 11/17/16).

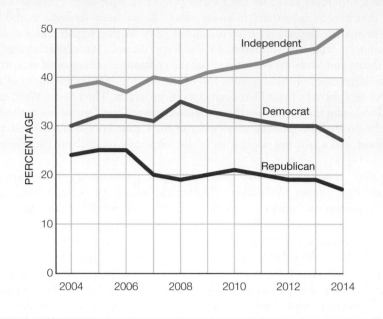

FIGURE 9.4

Party Identification of Young Americans

Young Americans ages 18-33 are more likely to be Democratic than Republican, but even more identify as independent. The years since 2008 have seen a sharp uptick in the percentage of young Americans who do not identify with either major party. What might account for these trends?

SOURCE: Pew Research Center, "Millennials Increasingly Identify as Political Independents," March 5, 2014, http://www.pewsocialtrends .org/2014/03/07/millennials-in-adulthood /sdt-next-america-03-07-2014-1-01/ (accessed 3/10/16).

Despite widely identifying as independent, in a general election young people are much more likely to vote for the Democratic candidate. In 2016, 55 percent of people ages 18–29 voted for Hillary Clinton.[28] As a group, young people have distinct policy preferences that overlap with those of the Democratic Party, including strong support for same-sex relationships, legalization of marijuana, environmental protection, and more economic equality.

Recent Trends in Party Affiliation

After the 1960s, many analysts began to express concern that American parties had become too weak to play their vital role in converting popular political participation into effective government. These scholars noted such trends as a decline in partisan attachment within the electorate, the growth in the numbers of voters identifying as independent, and a rise in so-called split-ticket voting. This overall trend, sometimes termed **dealignment**, was seen as a product of growing social diversity and educational attainment, which made voters less reliant on parties to guide their political decision making. The growth of the mass media, particularly television, also seemed to reduce the role of parties in elections as television tends to focus on the personality of individual candidates rather than the "institution" of the party.

dealignment a movement away from the major political parties; a decline in partisan attachment

While independents often lean toward one of the two parties and vote for the Republicans or Democrats in national elections, independents have unique views and are more supportive of third parties and election reform efforts that create opportunities for groups outside of government to have a voice in government.[29] With congressional and party approval ratings at an all-time low, the number of individuals identifying as independents has grown to roughly 40 percent of Americans.[30] The percentage of individuals registering as independents is very high in western states particularly, such as in Arizona, which has 37 percent registered independents, and Colorado, with 34 percent registered independents.[31]

Who Identifies with Which Party?

Party identification varies by income, race, and gender. For example, as these statistics from 2015 show, Americans with higher incomes are more supportive of the Republican Party than are Americans with lower incomes. Women are significantly more likely than men to identify with the Democratic Party, whereas more men identify as independents.

Republican Party

Democratic Party

Independent

Category	Group		Republican	Democratic	Independent
Gender	Men		24%	45%	26%
	Women		23%	35%	37%
Age	18–33		18%	48%	28%
	34–49		22%	40%	32%
	50–68		25%	35%	34%
	69–86		33%	29%	33%
Race	White		30%	40%	25%
	Black		5%	26%	64%
	Hispanic		13%	44%	34%
	Asian		11%	46%	37%
Education	Postgraduate		20%	38%	38%
	College graduate		26%	39%	31%
	Some college		25%	40%	30%
	High school diploma or less		22%	40%	31%
Income	< $30,000		17%	42%	35%
	$30,000–74,999		24%	40%	32%
	$75,000+		30%	38%	29%

NOTE: Percentages do not add to 100 because the category "Other/don't know" is omitted.

SOURCE: Pew Research Center, "A Deep Dive into Party Affiliation," April 7, 2015, www.people-press.org/2015/04/07/a-deep-dive-into-party-affiliation/ (accessed 2/27/16).

for critical analysis

1. How do younger Americans differ from older Americans in their party identification? What is the best predictor of party identification?

2. Do you think of yourself as a Democrat, Republican, or independent? Are other Americans of your gender, age, race, and income level likely to share your references?

Today, party loyalties in America continue to be in a state of flux. On the one hand, the percentage of voters who declare no party loyalty remains at an all-time high.[32] On the other hand, party identification among a large number of the most active voters has grown stronger.[33] The "Who Are Americans?" feature indicates the relationship between party identification and a number of social criteria. Race and ethnicity, age, education, religion, region, and income seem to have the greatest influence on Americans' party affiliations.

● Party Systems

> **Describe how the party system in the United States has changed over time and its main features today**

Historians often refer to the set of parties that are important at any given time as a nation's party system. The United States has usually had a two-party system, meaning that only two parties have a serious chance to win national elections. But the nation has not always had the same two parties, and as we shall see, minor parties often put forward candidates.

The term *party system*, however, refers to more than just the number of parties competing for power. It also includes the organization of the parties, the dominant form of campaigning, the main divisions between the parties, the balance of power between and within party coalitions, the parties' social and institutional bases, and the issues and policies around which party competition is organized. Seen from this broader perspective, the character of a nation's party system can change even if the number of parties remains the same and even when the same two parties seem to be competing for power. Today's American party system is very different from the country's party system of 100 years ago, but the Democrats and Republicans continue to be the major competing forces.

The nation's party system has profound consequences for the nation's political agenda and government policies such as the distribution of wealth and economic inequality. The contemporary American political parties mainly compete for the support of different groups of middle- and upper-class Americans. As a result, issues that concern the middle and upper classes, such as the environment, health care, retirement benefits, and taxation, are very much on the political agenda, whereas issues that concern working-class and poorer Americans, such as welfare and criminal justice, receive short shrift from both parties.[34] Over the course of American history, changes in political forces and alignments have produced six distinctive party systems.

The First Party System: Federalists and Jeffersonian Republicans

The first party system emerged in the 1790s and pitted the Federalists, who favored a strong national government, against the Jeffersonian Republicans, or Antifederalists, who favored a weak national government with the states retaining power. The Federalists were the establishment party at the time, and the Antifederalists were the outsiders. The Federalists represented mainly New England merchants and supported a program of protective tariffs to encourage manufacturing, forgiving states' Revolutionary War debts, the creation of a national bank, and commercial ties with Britain. The Jeffersonians, led by southern agricultural interests, opposed these policies and instead favored free trade, the promotion of agricultural over commercial interests, and friendship with France. The Federalists sought, unsuccessfully, to use the force of law against the Jeffersonians by enacting the Alien and Sedition Acts to outlaw criticism of the government. These acts, however, proved virtually impossible to enforce, and the Jeffersonians gradually expanded their base from the South into the Middle Atlantic states. In the election of 1800, Thomas Jefferson defeated the incumbent Federalist president, John Adams, and led his party to power. Over the following years, the Federalists gradually weakened. The party disappeared after the pro-British sympathies of some Federalist leaders during the War of 1812 led to charges of treason against the party.

From the collapse of the Federalists until the 1830s, America had only one political party, the Jeffersonian Republicans, who gradually came to be known as the Democrats. This period of one-party politics was defined by an absence of party competition. Throughout this period, however, there was intense conflict within the Democratic Party, particularly between the supporters and opponents of General Andrew Jackson, America's great military hero of the War of 1812. Jackson was the first populist president with a wide base of mass support; he sought to give rank-and-file members more say in party politics. Jackson's opponents united to deny him the presidency in 1824, but Jackson won elections in 1828 and 1832. Jackson's support was in the South and West, and he generally espoused a program of free trade and policies that appealed to those regions.

In the 1830s the Whig Party emerged as the Democrats' main rival. This drawing depicts a Whig rally and parade during the 1840 election.

The Second Party System: Democrats and Whigs

During the 1830s, groups opposing Jackson united to form a new political force, the Whig Party, giving rise to the second American party system. Both the Democrats and the Whigs built party organizations throughout the nation and sought to enlarge their bases of support by expanding the right to vote. They increased the number of eligible voters—still only white males—through the elimination of the requirement of property ownership in order to be able to vote. Support for the new Whig Party was stronger in the Northeast than in the South and West and among merchants than among small farmers. Hence, in some measure, the Whigs were the successors of the Federalists. Yet conflict between the two parties revolved more around personalities than policies. The Whigs were a diverse group united more by opposition to the Democrats than by agreement on programs. In 1840 the Whigs won their first presidential election under the leadership of General William Henry Harrison. The Whig campaign carefully avoided issues—since the party could agree on almost none—and emphasized the personal qualities and heroism of the candidate. They also invested heavily in campaign rallies and entertainment to win the hearts, if not exactly the minds, of the voters.

During the late 1840s and early 1850s, conflicts over slavery produced sharp divisions within both the Whig and the Democratic parties, despite the efforts of party leaders to develop compromises. By 1856 the Whig Party had all but disintegrated under the strain, and many Whig politicians and voters, along with antislavery Democrats, joined the new Republican Party, which pledged to ban slavery from the western territories. In 1860 the Republicans nominated Abraham Lincoln for the presidency. Lincoln's victory in a four-way candidate race for president strengthened southern calls for secession from the Union and, soon thereafter, for all-out civil war.

The Civil War and Post–Civil War Party System: Republicans and Democrats

During the course of the war, President Lincoln depended heavily on Republican governors and state legislatures to raise troops, provide funding, and maintain popular support for a long and bloody military conflict. The secession of the South had stripped the Democratic Party of many of its leaders and supporters, but the Democrats remained politically competitive throughout the war and nearly won the 1864 presidential election because of war weariness on the part of the northern public. With the defeat of the Confederacy in 1865, some congressional Republicans sought to convert the South into a Republican bastion through a program of Reconstruction that would grant the right to vote to newly freed slaves, thus creating a large pro-Republican voting bloc. This Reconstruction program collapsed in the 1870s as a result of disagreement within the Republican Party in Congress and violent resistance by southern whites via the Ku Klux Klan. With the end of Reconstruction, the former Confederate states regained full control of their internal affairs and party politics. Throughout the South, African Americans were deprived of political rights, including the right to vote, despite post–Civil War constitutional guarantees to the contrary. From the end of the Civil War to the 1890s, the Republican Party remained the party of the North, with strong business and middle-class support, while the Democrats were the party of the South, with support also from working-class and immigrant groups.

Following the Civil War, the Republican Party remained dominant in the North. This poster supporting Republican Benjamin Harrison in the 1888 election promises protective tariffs and other policies that appealed to the industrial states in the North.

The System of 1896: Republicans and Democrats

During the 1890s, profound and rapid social and economic changes led to the emergence of a variety of protest parties, including the Populist Party, which won the support of hundreds of thousands of voters in the South and West. The Populists appealed mainly to small farmers but also attracted western mining interests and urban workers. In the 1892 presidential election, the Populist Party carried four states and elected governors in eight. In 1896 the Populist Party effectively merged with the Democrats, who nominated William Jennings Bryan, a Democratic senator with pronounced Populist sympathies, for the presidency. The Republicans nominated the conservative senator William McKinley. In the ensuing campaign, northern and midwestern businesses made an all-out effort to defeat what they saw as a radical threat from the Populist–Democratic alliance. When the dust settled, the Republicans had won a resounding victory. The GOP ("Grand Old Party"), or Republican Party, had carried the more heavily populated northern and midwestern states and confined the Democrats to their smaller bases of support in the South and far West. For the next 36 years, the Republicans were the nation's majority party, carrying seven of nine presidential elections and controlling both houses of Congress in 15 of 18 contests. The Republican Party of this era was very much the party of American business, advocating low taxes, high tariffs on imports, and a minimum of government regulation. Southern Democrats, moreover, were too concerned with maintaining the region's autonomy on issues of race to challenge the Republicans on other fronts.

The New Deal Party System: Reversal of Fortune

Soon after the Republican presidential candidate Herbert Hoover won the 1928 presidential election, the nation's economy collapsed. The Great Depression, which produced unprecedented economic hardship, stemmed from a variety of causes; but from the perspective of millions of Americans, the Republican Party did not do enough to promote economic recovery. In 1932, Americans elected Franklin Delano Roosevelt and a solidly Democratic Congress. Roosevelt developed a program for economic recovery that he dubbed the "New Deal." Under the auspices of the New Deal, the size and reach of America's national government increased substantially. The federal government took responsibility for economic management and social welfare to an extent that was unprecedented in American history. Roosevelt designed many of his programs specifically to expand the political base of the Democratic Party. He rebuilt and revitalized the party around a nucleus of unionized workers, upper-middle-class intellectuals and professionals, southern farmers, Jews, Catholics, and African Americans—the so-called New Deal coalition that made the Democrats the nation's majority party for the next 36 years. Groping for a response to the New Deal, Republicans often wound up supporting popular New Deal programs such as Social Security in what was sometimes derided as "me too" Republicanism. Even the relatively conservative administration of Dwight D. Eisenhower in the 1950s left the principal New Deal programs intact.

The New Deal coalition was severely strained during the 1960s by conflicts over civil rights and the Vietnam War. The struggle over civil rights initially divided northern Democrats, who supported the civil rights cause, from white southern Democrats, who defended the system of racial segregation. Subsequently, as the civil rights movement launched a northern campaign aimed at securing access to jobs and education and an end to racial discrimination in such realms as housing, northern Democrats also split, often along income lines. The struggle over the Vietnam War further divided the Democrats, with upper-income liberal Democrats strongly opposing the Johnson administration's decision to greatly expand the numbers of U.S. troops fighting in Southeast Asia. These schisms within the Democratic Party provided an opportunity for the GOP, which returned to power in 1968 under the leadership of Richard Nixon.

The Contemporary American Party System

The Republican Party widened its appeal in the second half of the twentieth century. In 1964, for example, the Republican presidential candidate Barry Goldwater argued in favor of substantially reduced levels of taxation and spending, less government regulation of the economy, and the elimination of many federal social

Richard Nixon's "southern strategy" helped broaden the Republican Party's base in the late 1960s and the 1970s by appealing to white southerners. Here, Nixon meets supporters in Georgia in 1973.

programs. Though Goldwater was defeated by Lyndon Johnson, the ideas he espoused continued to be major themes for the Republican Party. It took Richard Nixon's "southern strategy" to give the GOP the votes it needed to end Democratic dominance of national politics. Nixon appealed to disaffected white southerners, and he sparked the shift that gave the party a strong position in all the states of the former Confederacy. The movement of white southerners to the Republican Party was in part because of opposition to desegregation of the South and to the civil rights movement supported by Democratic leaders, including President Kennedy. During the 1980s, under the leadership of President Ronald Reagan, Republicans added two additional important groups to their coalition. The first were religious conservatives, who were offended by Democratic support for abortion and gay rights and by alleged Democratic disdain for traditional cultural and religious values. The second were working-class whites, who were drawn to Reagan's tough approach to foreign policy and positions against affirmative action. Many Republicans consider Reagan's tenure in office as a "golden era" that saw deregulation of many industries, reduced government intervention in the economy, and particularly strong economic growth.

While Republicans built a political base around economic and social conservatives and white southerners, the Democratic Party maintained its support among a majority of unionized workers and upper-middle-class professionals. Democrats also appealed strongly to racial and ethnic minorities. The 1965 Voting Rights Act had greatly increased black voter participation in the South and helped the Democratic Party retain some House and Senate seats in southern states. And whereas the Republicans appealed to social conservatives, the Democrats appealed strongly to Americans concerned with inequality, abortion rights, gay rights, women's rights, environmentalism, and other progressive social causes.

Despite the success of Republican presidential candidates in attracting votes from groups previously associated with the Democratic Party, Republicans generally did not do as well at the state and local levels until the 1990s, when conservative religious groups made a concerted effort to expand their influence within the Republican Party. This effort led to conflict between these members of the "religious right" and more traditional fiscal Republicans, whose major concerns were economic matters such as taxes and federal regulation of business. The two factions of the party came together when the Republicans won control of both houses of Congress in 1994 (the first time in almost half a century). In 2000, George W. Bush united the party's centrist and right wings behind a program of tax cuts, education reform, military strength, and family values.

However, Republicans fared poorly in the 2008 elections, campaigning during the worst financial crisis since the 1930s. Democrats won control of Congress as well as the presidency that year. Though Barack Obama was reelected for a second term in 2012, Republicans gained control of the House in 2010 and both the House and the Senate in 2014. In 2016 they retained both chambers and captured the presidency in a tight race, signaling that sharp partisan differences and intense party conflict would continue to characterize American politics.

This history of the party system has focused on parties at the national level. However, as discussed earlier, parties operate at the local and state levels as well, serving the same functions as at the federal level. While support for political parties at the local and state levels tends to follow national-level patterns, there are important differences. For example, the ideology of Republican candidates in

Massachusetts, which has one of the most liberal populations in the country, is typically more liberal than that of national-level Republican candidates. The reverse is true for conservative states, such as many southern states.

Electoral Alignments and Realignments

Transitions in the party systems over time are sometimes called **electoral realignments**. During these periods, the coalitions that support the parties and the balance of power between the parties change and are redefined. In historical terms, realignments occur when new issues, combined with economic or political crises, mobilize new voters and persuade large numbers of them to reexamine their traditional partisan loyalties and permanently shift their support from one party to another. Figure 9.5 charts the sequence of party systems and realignments in American history.

Although scholars dispute the timing of realignments, there is some agreement that five have occurred since the Founding. The first took place around 1790–1800, when the Jeffersonian Republicans defeated the Federalists and became the dominant force in American politics. The second realignment occurred in 1828, when the Jacksonian Democrats seized control of the White House and the Congress. In the third period of realignment, centered on the 1860 election, the newly founded Republican Party, led by Abraham Lincoln, won power, in the process destroying the Whig Party, which had been one of the nation's two major parties since the 1830s. Many northern voters who had supported the Whigs or the Democrats on the basis of their economic policies shifted their support to the Republicans as slavery replaced tariffs and economic concerns as the central issue on the nation's agenda. Many southern Whigs shifted their support to the Democrats. The new regional alignment of forces that emerged was solidified by the trauma of the Civil War and persisted almost to the turn of the century.

In the 1890s, this alignment was at least partially supplanted by a party realignment based on economic and demographic factors, bringing about the fourth electoral realignment. In the election of 1896, the Republican candidate, William McKinley, emphasizing business, industry, and urban interests, defeated the Democrat, William Jennings Bryan, who spoke for populist economic interests, farmers, and miners. Republican dominance lasted until the fifth realignment, during the period 1932–36, when the Democrats, led by Franklin Delano Roosevelt, took control of the White House and Congress during the economic crisis of the Great Depression. Despite sporadic interruptions, the Democrats maintained control of both through the 1960s. Since that time, American party politics has been characterized by **divided government**, wherein the presidency is controlled by one party while the other party controls one or both houses of Congress

Major partisan realignments are rare in America, occurring on average about once every 50 years. There are frequent false alarms, when pundits describe elections as realignments and they turn out not to be. But periods of real electoral realignment in American politics have had very important policy consequences. Realignments occur when new issues or societal problems, coupled with economic or political crises, weaken the established political elite and allow new groups of politicians to create coalitions capable of capturing the reins of governmental power. The construction of new governing coalitions during these realigning periods has effected major changes in American governmental institutions and policies. Each period of realignment, such as expanding suffrage to African American men and later to all women, was a turning point in American politics. The choices made by the national electorate during these periods helped shape the course of American

electoral realignment the point in history when a new party supplants the ruling party, becoming in turn the dominant political force; in the United States, this has tended to occur roughly every 30 years

divided government the condition in American government wherein the presidency is controlled by one party while the opposing party controls one or both houses of Congress

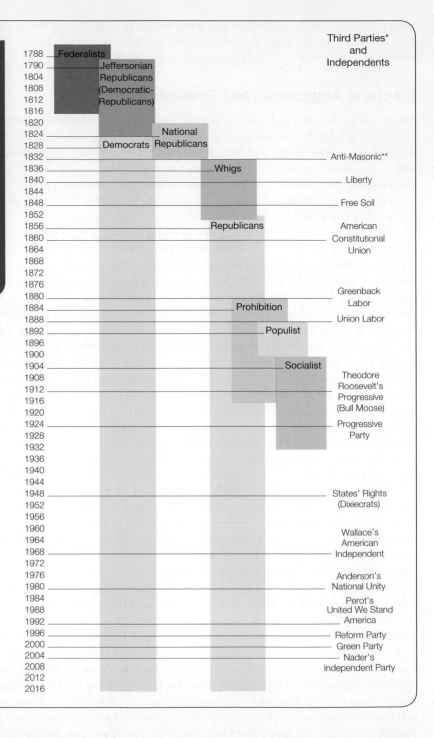

FIGURE 9.5

How the Party System Evolved

During the nineteenth century, the Democrats and Republicans emerged as the two dominant parties in American politics. As the American party system evolved, many third parties emerged; but few of them remained in existence for very long.

*Or, in some cases, fourth parties; most of these parties lasted through only one term.
**The Anti-Masonics had the distinction of being not only the first third party but also the first party to hold a national nominating convention and the first to announce a party platform.

Third Parties* and Independents

1788	Federalists
1790	Jeffersonian Republicans (Democratic-Republicans)
1804	
1808	
1812	
1816	
1820	
1824	National Republicans
1828	Democrats
1832	Anti-Masonic**
1836	Whigs
1840	Liberty
1844	
1848	Free Soil
1852	
1856	Republicans / American
1860	Constitutional Union
1864	
1868	
1872	
1876	
1880	Greenback Labor
1884	Prohibition
1888	Union Labor
1892	Populist
1896	
1900	
1904	Socialist
1908	Theodore Roosevelt's Progressive (Bull Moose)
1912	
1916	
1920	
1924	Progressive Party
1928	
1932	
1936	
1940	
1944	
1948	States' Rights (Dixiecrats)
1952	
1956	
1960	Wallace's American Independent
1964	
1968	
1972	
1976	Anderson's National Unity
1980	
1984	Perot's United We Stand America
1988	
1992	
1996	Reform Party
2000	Green Party
2004	Nader's Independent Party
2008	
2012	
2016	

political history for the following generation.[35] In the 2016 presidential election, significant factions of the Republican Party were in disagreement over Donald Trump's candidacy, leading some observers to question whether the election was the beginning of a new party realignment. Many high-profile Republican politicians refused to support Trump, and some withdrew their support during the course of the campaign.

Party Polarization

A distinguishing feature of the contemporary party system is **party polarization**. The vast and growing gap between Democrats and Republicans has become a defining feature of American politics today, with more Democrats holding liberal positions and more Republicans holding conservative views (see Figure 9.6). In Congress, polarization is measured by party unity in roll-call votes. Over 90 percent of the time, members of Congress vote in agreement with the majority of their party.[36] With this kind of party-line voting, legislation is often enacted by the slimmest of vote margins in Congress if at all. The 114th Congress was one of least productive in history, with just 2 percent of bills voted into law.[37]

The extent of party polarization in Congress was exemplified by the conflict over replacing the vacant seat on the U.S. Supreme Court after the unexpected death of conservative justice Antonin Scalia in February 2016. Under the Constitution, it is the president's job to appoint federal judges and the Senate's to confirm the nominees. Following Scalia's death, the Republican-controlled Senate called on Obama to leave the task of appointing Scalia's replacement to the next president and refused to hold confirmation hearings for a nominee. At the same time, Senate Democrats accused the Republicans of not doing their job and urged them to hold confirmation hearings. The stalemate between the political parties over the judicial replacement on the Supreme Court was unprecedented in American history.

Though most Republican lawmakers in Congress are strong conservatives and Democrats strong liberals, the majority of Amricans hold moderate views, suggesting

party polarization the division between the two major parties on most policy issues, with members of each party unified around their party's positions with little crossover

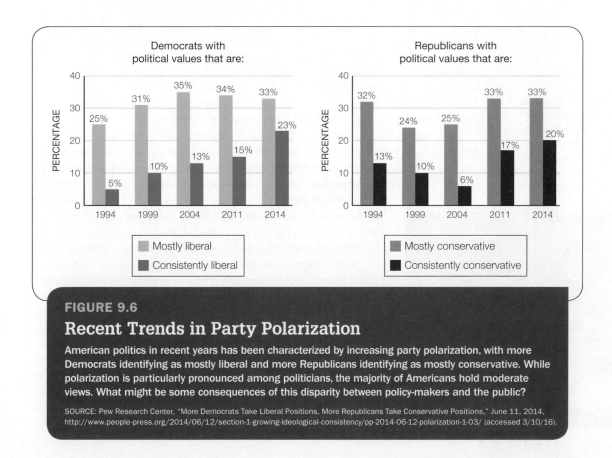

FIGURE 9.6
Recent Trends in Party Polarization

American politics in recent years has been characterized by increasing party polarization, with more Democrats identifying as mostly liberal and more Republicans identifying as mostly conservative. While polarization is particularly pronounced among politicians, the majority of Americans hold moderate views. What might be some consequences of this disparity between policy-makers and the public?

SOURCE: Pew Research Center, "More Democrats Take Liberal Positions, More Republicans Take Conservative Positions," June 11, 2014, http://www.people-press.org/2014/06/12/section-1-growing-ideological-consistency/pp-2014-06-12-polarization-1-03/ (accessed 3/10/16).

that party polarization has created a Congress that does not match the aggregate ideology of the American public. Some political scientists argue that this phenomenon is in part the result of how congressional representatives are elected. Every 10 years, congressional district geographic boundaries are redrawn so that each district has roughly the same population. These districts are increasingly drawn to be "safe" for one political party or another so that the district has a clear majority of either Republicans or Democrats. This process is known as gerrymandering. Most lawmakers are elected from safe districts, where a majority of voters identify with their party, which means they have little chance of losing in the next election. The average winning margin of victory in the House is over 40 percentage points. That means incumbents, on average, win 70 percent of the popular vote compared with challengers' 30 percent.[38] Uncompetitive elections in Congress and safe seats are associated with growing party polarization. Without facing competition from the other party during general elections, Congress members are increasingly strong liberals or strong conservatives. This phenomenon is also a result of the fact that lawmakers face the greatest threats during their own party's primary elections, which can have the effect of moving candidates more to the ideological extremes of their party in order to win in the primary.

Other political scientists argue that party polarization has occurred not because of how congressional districts are drawn but because individuals segregate themselves by choosing to live in liberal or conservative geographic areas. This is known as self-sorting. No matter what the cause, lawmakers elected from solidly safe districts have less incentive to compromise; thus, homogeneous Democratic and homogeneous Republican districts add to the polarization of the political parties.

A specific event that contributed to party polarization was the rise of the Tea Party movement in 2010. The Tea Party is an extremely conservative faction of the Republican Party. After the election of Barack Obama in 2008, a number of high-profile Tea Party candidates went on to win office in the 2010 midterm elections, defeating several incumbents and candidates endorsed by the Republican Party. In total, the Tea Party succeeded in electing about 32 percent of its candidates in 2010—a strong showing for a newly organized group—and its electoral influence was felt again in the 2014 and 2016 congressional elections.

As Congress has become more ideologically extreme, members have given more power to their party leaders, who have changed the rules in Congress so that the majority can control the legislative process more easily, further intensifying party polarization. The ability to debate legislation on the floor of the House has been restricted, and individual members exercise less personal choice in deciding how to vote. In the Senate, which has unlimited debate over legislation, the situation still isn't much better. The filibuster, the use of which was once relegated to a handful of major national issues in a given Congress, has become a routine weapon of obstruction, applied even to widely supported bills or presidential nominations.

But even strong party leaders are not immune to the pressure from their most ideologically extreme members. In 2015, House Speaker John Boehner resigned in the middle of his term. The historic event occurred because of deep divisions within the Republican Party, especially the opposition of 40 of the most conservative House members—Tea Party activists—who wanted him to take a harder line against Obama and the Democrats. Boehner's resignation illustrated a height in party polarization in Congress and divisions within the parties.

The Tea Party emerged after the election of Barack Obama in 2008. During the 2010 midterm elections, Tea Party activists around the country rallied to "reclaim the Capitol" and succeeded in electing a number of their candidates to office, which further increased party polarization in Congress.

Should we believe the media pundits who tell us that Americans are deeply divided between the red states and the blue states? Is the American population really polarized on hot-button moral, economic, and cultural issues? As noted above, many political scientists believe that in fact most Americans are moderates in terms of their opinions on major issues and that polarization among the parties in Congress does not match the ideology of the American public.[39] However, this issue continues to be debated.

for critical analysis

What are the principal issues dividing the two major parties today? What are the chief areas of agreement between the two parties?

Third Parties

Although the United States has a two party–dominant system, it has always had more than two parties. Typically, **third parties** in the United States have represented social and economic interests that for one or another reason were not given voice by the two major parties.[40] Such parties have had a good deal of influence on ideas and elections in the United States. The Populists, a party centered in the rural areas of the West and Midwest, and the Progressives, spokespersons for the urban middle class in the late nineteenth and early twentieth centuries, are the most important examples in the past 100 years. More recently, H. Ross Perot, who ran in 1992 as an independent and in 1996 as the Reform Party's nominee, won the votes of almost one in five Americans.

Because third parties almost always lose at the national level, such parties exist mainly as a protest movement against the two parties or to promote specific issues. Third parties often are sources of new ideas and party realignment, and they can profoundly affect American elections, taking votes from one of the major parties and enabling the other to win. In the extremely close 2000 presidential election, for example, third-party candidate Ralph Nader won just 3 percent of the popular vote, but that split the Democratic vote enough to swing the election in favor of Republican George W. Bush. Leaders in both major political parties fear third-party challenges in presidential elections.

Table 9.1 lists the top candidates in the presidential election of 2016, including the top third-party and independent candidates who ran. Third-party candidates fared better in 2016 than in the last three presidential elections, leading some observers to suggest that third parties were one reason Clinton lost key battleground states and thus the election.

third parties parties that organize to compete against the two major American political parties

In the United States, third parties are unlikely to win at the national level but may take votes from one of the two major parties. In the 2000 presidential election, Green Party candidate Ralph Nader split the Democratic vote, which helped Republican George W. Bush. Four years later, many Democrats, such as the protesters shown here, urged Nader not to run.

TABLE 9.1

Parties and Candidates in 2016

CANDIDATE	PARTY	VOTE TOTAL*	PERCENTAGE OF VOTES
Hillary Clinton	Democratic	65,147,421	48%
Donald Trump	Republican	62,634,907	46%
Gary Johnson	Libertarian	4,454,855	3%
Jill Stein	Green	1,426,922	1%
Other candidates		1,047,140	0.8%

*Preliminary counts as of December 1, 2016.
SOURCE: U.S. Election Atlas, "2016 Presidential General Election Results," www.uselectionatlas.org/RESULTS
/national.php?year=2016&minper=0&f=0&off=0&elect=0 (accessed 12/1/16).

Third Parties at the State and Local Levels Third-party and independent candidacies also arise at the state and local levels. The Libertarian and Green parties in particular run candidates in many state and local elections. In 2012 independent candidates won Senate races in Maine and Vermont. Because the policy agendas of the two major parties are necessarily so broad, many reformers believe third parties would improve representation for average Americans in government.

Obstacles Facing Third Parties Americans usually assume that only candidates nominated by one of the two major parties have any chance of winning an election. As noted above, voters who would prefer a third-party candidate may feel compelled to vote for the major-party candidate whom they regard as the "lesser of two evils," to avoid wasting their votes in a futile gesture. This is called *strategic voting*.

Under federal election law, only parties that receive more than 5 percent of the national presidential vote are entitled to federal funds. The Reform Party qualified by winning 8.2 percent in 1996, but since then third parties have not won federal matching money. As discussed earlier, third-party prospects are also hampered by America's single-member district system for allocating seats. In many other nations, several individuals can be elected to represent each legislative district—a system of multiple-member districts, which are more favorable to minor-party candidates. Some American states do have multiple-member districts for state legislature, but the vast majority do not. The plurality, or winner-take-all, system of voting discussed earlier in this chapter also discourages many minor parties in the United States.[41] In the proportional system used in other countries, parties can earn seats in government with 15–20 percent of the popular vote.

The Influence of Third Parties Although the Republican Party was the only American third party to make itself permanent (by replacing the Whigs), other third parties have enjoyed an influence far beyond their electoral size. This is because large parts of their programs were adopted by one or both of the major parties, which sought to appeal to the voters mobilized by the new party and thus expand their own electoral strength. The Democratic Party, for example, became a great deal more liberal when it adopted most of the Progressive Party reforms in the early twentieth century. Many socialists felt that President Franklin Roosevelt's New Deal had adopted most of their party's program, including unemployment compensation and laws guaranteeing workers the right to organize into unions. This kind of influence explains the short lives of third parties. Their causes are usually eliminated when the major parties absorb their programs and draw their supporters into the mainstream.

Election Reform and Third Parties In part because third parties have become increasingly common in American politics, despite election rules favoring a two-party system, one-third of all winning presidential candidates since the Civil War have been elected with a plurality (simply more votes than any other candidate) but not a majority (more than 50 percent of all votes) of the national popular vote.[42] If the party that wins the presidency in one out of three elections is not favored by a majority of voters, that calls into question the legitimacy of our election system. Some scholars suggest that the failure to secure majorities may continue in the future with the rise of independent candidates and dissatisfaction with the two major political parties.[43]

Some proponents of election reform argue that two major parties are not sufficient to represent the varied interests of America's 320 million people and that more political parties would improve representation. Forms of proportional representation, multiple-member districts, or instant runoff voting would increase the probability of third-party representation in American politics. State ballot access laws are another major impediment for third parties. Third parties often fail to meet criteria to get on the ballot, such as registration fees or petition requirements in which a certain number of voters must sign a petition in order for the third-party or independent candidate to gain ballot access. Those who favor a stronger role for third parties argue that states should make it easier to get on the ballot. Supporters of the current system, on the other hand, contend that America's two-party system creates stability in governing and prevents the need for a coalition government, where multiple small parties work together to form a majority to govern.

Ranked Choice Voting An example of an election reform that may reduce party polarization and increase opportunities for third parties is ranked choice voting. Ranked choice voting (or preference voting) is a ballot form used in countries around the world, notably Australia, that is growing in popularity in numerous American cities. Rather than casting a single vote for one's most preferred choice, a voter ranks candidates from the most preferred to the least preferred (usually the top three) on the ballot. If a candidate wins a majority of first-place votes (50 percent plus one), the candidate is declared the winner and second- or third-place votes are not counted. But if the top candidate does not receive a majority of the votes cast, the candidate with the fewest first-choice votes is eliminated, and those voters' ballots are redistributed to their second-choice candidates. The ballots are recounted; if the leading candidate has a majority of votes cast, a winner is declared. The process is repeated until a majority winner is declared. This system eliminates the "spoiler" effect that occurs when votes for a third-party or minor candidate are discarded.

Research suggests that ranked choice voting leads to more civility in political campaigns, fewer negative campaigns, and cooperation among candidates who seek to be a voter's second choice if they cannot be a first choice. It is also associated with more grassroots mobilization of voters. Ranked choice voting is a form of instant runoff voting in that it guarantees that the winner of an election has support from a majority of those voting in the election, rather than a plurality. Though ranked choice voting is used in many countries around the world, in the United States only the state of Maine uses it, as well as a handful of local districts, including San Francisco and Oakland, California; Cambridge, Massachusetts; and

Minneapolis, Minnesota. Successful local experiments in election reform may open the doors to use of this process at the state or even national level.

Political Parties
and Your Future

Political parties are bulwarks of liberty and freedom. As noted earlier, in the first years of the Republic, it was not the Constitution or the courts that preserved free speech in the face of Federalist efforts to silence the government's critics; it was the vigorous opposition of the Jeffersonian Republicans. To this day, the presence of an opposition party is a fundamentally important check on attempts by those in power to skirt the law and infringe on citizens' liberties. Competition among the political parties is also a key factor in stimulating voter turnout. Competition gives citizens an incentive to vote and politicians an incentive to get them to vote.[44] Voter mobilization remains one of political parties' most important tasks, as voter turnout in the United States remains relatively low, especially in primaries and caucuses (see the "**Who Participates?**" feature on the facing page). As early as the 1790s, political parties used diverse techniques to mobilize voters, many of which remain familiar today: "mass meetings, barbecues, stump-speaking, festivals of many kinds, processions and parades, runners and riders, door-to-door canvassing, the distribution of tickets and ballots . . . free transportation to the polls, outright bribery and corruption of other kinds."[45]

Parties in the United States are considered to be ground-up organizations, meaning that they get their power from the members of the mass public who support them at the local level. However, until fairly recently, political party bosses controlled the party platform, the party message, and often, through early money to candidates, who held elected office and who won the nomination for president.

While this elite-driven process still occurs today, the process of party formation and many aspects of party politics have been turned upside down with the digital revolution. Four resources that political parties use to contest and win elections (time, money, expertise, and organization) have all been altered by the Internet. Digital media are decentralizing party power as citizens can volunteer and give money to the party without ever being contacted by a party official. Online fundraising allows millions of donors to give small contributions to parties, and social media allow the party to spread its message far and wide online. These changes are beneficial for parties because more people are involved, but at the same time, there are more divergent opinions that must be recognized and appeased. No longer can party leaders craft their own message and relay it to the field; they must also listen to what their supporters want.

The question remains, however, what influence these new groups and parties will have on politics given current U.S. election rules. Will the ability of the mass public to make their desires known to party leaders mean that party leaders pay more attention to these preferences? Is the two-party system the optimal system for American politics, or would electoral reforms encourage more parties to form and, hence, more choice for voters?

Parties help to crystallize a world of possible government actions into a set of distinct choices. In so doing, they make it easier for ordinary citizens to understand politics, evaluate candidates, and make their own choices.

Who Votes in Primaries and Caucuses?

Turnout in 2008 Primaries
Percentage of voting-eligible population

Turnout in 2008 Caucuses
Percentage of voting-eligible population

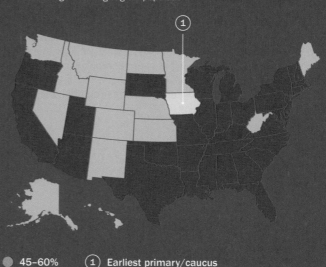

● 1–14%   ● 15–29%   ● 30–44%   ● 45–60%   ① Earliest primary/caucus

SOURCE: Michael P. McDonald, "2008 Presidential Nomination Contest Turnout Rates," United States Election Project, October 10, 2008, www.electproject.org/2008p (accessed 12/22/15).

NOTES: Idaho, Nebraska, New Mexico: Primary data are for Republican primaries. Caucus data are for Democratic caucuses.

Montana: Caucus data are for credentialed Republicans (only party leaders are allowed to vote). Both parties participated in the primary.

South Carolina: Data are for Democratic primary only. No data available for Republican primary.

Washington: The Democratic primary was a straw vote only; Democratic delegates were selected at the caucus. Republicans selected delegates by a combination of primary and caucus.

West Virginia: Primary data are for Democratic primary. Caucus data are for Republican caucus.

WHAT YOU CAN DO

Get Involved with Your Preferred Party

 Participate in the next primary or caucus in your state. When you register to vote (see p. 33), you may be asked to indicate your party affiliation.

 If you're unsure which party best represents your views, visit **www.politicalcompass.org/tests/** to take a test to find out.

 Volunteer to help your preferred party with a political campaign neighborhood by making phone calls, knocking on doors, distributing literature, and otherwise working to get out the vote. You can sign up with the Republican Party at **www.gop.com/get-involved** and with the Democratic Party at **www.democrats.org/volunteer**, and with other parties through their websites.

studyguide

What Are Political Parties?

Define political parties and their functions in politics (pp. 329–34)

A political party is an organization that seeks influence over government by electing its members to office. Although some people are critical of political parties, they are extremely important to the functioning of a democracy because they increase participation in politics, provide a central cue for citizens to cast informed votes, and organize the business of Congress and governing.

Key Terms

political parties (p. 329)

partisanship (p. 329)

two-party system (p. 332)

Practice Quiz

1. A political party is different from an interest group in that a political party
   a) seeks to control the government by nominating candidates and electing its members to office.
   b) is constitutionally exempt from taxation.
   c) is entirely nonprofit.
   d) has a much larger membership.
   e) has a much smaller membership.

2. The congressional election system in the United State is called "first past the post" because
   a) candidates must win both a primary election and a general election before taking office.
   b) seats in the House of Representatives and Senate are allocated to political parties based on their share of the total vote cast in the election.
   c) the candidate with the most votes wins even if she did not win a majority of the popular vote.
   d) a candidate can win an election only if he wins a majority of the popular vote.
   e) more Americans now vote by mail than at their local polling places.

Parties, Voter Mobilization, and Elections

Explain the roles that parties play in elections (pp. 334–36)

Because parties succeed when they win elections, parties have a large role in recruiting candidates, coordinating campaigns, mobilizing voters, and raising money.

Key Term

nomination (p. 335)

primary election (p. 335)

caucus (political) (p. 335)

3. The practice of tailoring campaign messages to individuals in small, homogeneous groups is referred to as
   a) indexing.
   b) micro-targeting.
   c) winnowing.
   d) external mobilization.
   e) internal mobilization.

Parties as Organizations

Describe how the major American parties are structured at the national, state, and local levels (pp. 336–40)

Party organizations exist at virtually every level of government in the United States, and they play an important role in structuring electoral competition. At the national level, for example, party organizations assemble conventions every four years that nominate the party's presidential and vice-presidential candidates, draft the party's campaign platform for the presidential race, and approve changes in the rules governing party procedures. Similarly, at the state and local levels, party organizations are active in recruiting candidates to run for office and in conducting voter registration and get-out-the-vote drives.

Key Terms

party organization (p. 336)

national convention (p. 337)

platform (p. 337)

soft money (p. 338)

party machines (p. 339)

patronage (p. 339)

Practice Quiz

4. Which of the following is *not* determined at a party's national convention?
   a) the party's candidate for president
   b) the party's candidate for vice president
   c) the party's campaign platform for the presidential race
   d) the congressional committees party representatives will be assigned to
   e) the rules and regulations governing party procedures

5. The 2002 Bipartisan Campaign Reform Act outlawed
   a) patronage.
   b) primaries.
   c) hard money.
   d) soft money.
   e) dark money.

6. The strength of traditional party machines depended most heavily on
   a) patronage.
   b) primaries.
   c) hard money.
   d) soft money.
   e) dark money.

Parties in Government

Explain how parties organize legislative business and influence policy (pp. 340–42)

Political parties exert a great deal of influence over public policy, the structure of Congress, and the behavior of presidents. The sharp ideological divisions between Democrats and Republicans in recent years mean that election outcomes matter greatly for the kinds of laws that government enacts. Many of the most important organizational features of Congress, such as the role of the House Speaker, the committee system, and seniority, also depend on the party system. In order to overcome their minority status in the electorate, Republican presidents have spent significantly more time mobilizing voters than Democratic presidents.

Key Terms

policy entrepreneur (p. 341)

majority party (p. 341)

minority party (p. 341)

Practice Quiz

7. By identifying problems and proposing policies that will expand their party's base of support, party leaders can act as
   a) party bosses.
   b) convention delegates.
   c) patrons.
   d) policy entrepreneurs.
   e) party activists.

8. Which of the following features of the House of Representatives is determined by a vote of the whole membership rather than by decisions within each party?
   a) the assignments of individual members to particular committees.
   b) advancement up the committee ladder.
   c) the ability of individual members to transfer from one committee to another.
   d) the use of the seniority system for determining committee chairs.
   e) selection of the Speaker of the House.

Party Identification

Identify the reasons for and sources of party identification (pp. 342–50)

Party identification refers to the psychological and emotional attachments people have to one of the political parties. In contemporary American politics, a wide variety of group characteristics, including race, ethnicity, gender, religion, class, ideology, region, and age, are associated with an individual's party identification. Party loyalties in the United States are currently in a state of flux, and roughly one-third of Americans identify themselves as independents rather than as Democrats or Republicans.

Key Terms

party identification (p. 342)

party activists (p. 343)

gender gap (p. 345)

dealignment (p. 348)

Practice Quiz

9. The decline in partisan attachment in the electorate is referred to as
   a) polarization.
   b) independentification.
   c) unalignment.
   d) realignment.
   e) dealignment.

Party Systems

Describe how the party system in the United States has changed over time and its main features today (pp. 350–62)

A nation's party system refers to the organization of the parties within the country, the dominant form of campaigning, the main divisions between the parties, the balance of power between and within party coalitions, the parties' social and institutional bases, and the issues and policies around which party competition is organized. Over the course of American history, changes in political forces and alignments have produced six distinctive party systems. Although third parties have occasionally influenced election outcomes and placed new ideas on the political agenda, numerous factors limit their long-term success and they have rarely been able to win elections at the national level.

Key Terms

electoral realignment (p. 355)

divided government (p. 355)

party polarization (p. 357)

third parties (p. 359)

Practice Quiz

10. Which party pledged to ban slavery from the western territories in 1850?
    a) American Independent
    b) Prohibition
    c) Republican
    d) Democratic
    e) Whig

11. The so-called New Deal coalition was severely strained
    a) during the 1860s by conflicts over slavery and Southern secession.
    b) during the 1890s by conflicts over the gold standard.
    c) during the 1930s by conflicts over the Great Depression and America's involvement in World War II.
    d) during the 1960s by conflicts over civil rights and the Vietnam War.
    e) during the 1990s by conflicts over abortion and affirmative action.

12. The periodic episodes in American history in which an "old" dominant political party is replaced by a "new" dominant political party are called
    a) constitutional revolutions.
    b) divided governments.
    c) unified governments.
    d) dealignments.
    e) electoral realignments.

13. Third parties have influenced national politics mainly by
    a) electing their candidates to the presidency.
    b) electing their candidates to Congress.
    c) supporting the major parties' platforms.
    d) promoting specific issues and ideas.
    e) preventing realignments.

For Further Reading

Aldrich, John H. *Why Parties? A Second Look*. Chicago: University of Chicago Press, 2011.

Bartels, Larry. *Presidential Primaries and the Dynamics of Public Choice*. Princeton, NJ: Princeton University Press, 1988.

Burnham, Walter Dean. *Critical Elections and the Mainsprings of American Politics*. New York: W. W. Norton, 1970.

Cohen, Marty, David Karol, Hans Noel, and John Zaller. *The Party Decides: Presidential Nominations before and after Reform*. Chicago: University of Chicago Press, 2008.

Donovan, Todd, and Shaun Bowler. *Reforming the Republic: Democratic Institutions for the New America*. Englewood Cliffs, NJ: Prentice Hall, 2003.

Green, Donald, Bradley Palmquist, and Eric Schickler. *Partisan Hearts and Minds: Political Parties and the Social Identities of Voters*. New Haven, CT: Yale University Press, 2002.

Maisel, L. Sandy. *Political Parties and Elections: A Very Short Introduction*. New York: Oxford University Press, 2007.

McCarty, Nolan, Keith Poole, and Howard Rosenthal. *Polarized America: The Dance of Ideology and Unequal Riches*. Cambridge, MA: MIT Press, 2006.

Polsby, Nelson W. *The Consequences of Party Reform*. New York: Oxford University Press, 1983.

Redlawsk, David, Caroline Tolbert, and Todd Donovan. *Why Iowa? How Caucuses and Sequential Elections Improve the Presidential Nominating Process*. Chicago: University of Chicago Press, 2011.

Schattschneider, E. E. *The Semisovereign People: A Realist's View of Democracy in America*. New York: Holt, Rinehart and Winston, 1960.

Shefter, Martin. *Political Parties and the State: The American Historical Experience*. Princeton, NJ: Princeton University Press, 1994.

Recommended Websites

D.C.'s Political Report
www.dcpoliticalreport.com/Disclaimer.htm

Here you can find almost every organization that identifies itself as a political party, including such obscure groups as the American Beer Drinker's Party and the Scorched Earth Party.

Democratic Party
www.democrats.org

Republican Party
www.GOP.com, www.rnc.org

These are the official websites for the Democrats and Republicans. Compare the platforms of the two main U.S. parties and see whether there's "not a dime's worth of difference" between them.

Green Party
www.gp.org

Libertarian Party
www.lp.org

The Green Party and Libertarian Party are two of the largest and most successful third parties in recent years. Find out what these parties are trying to accomplish.

National Annenberg Election Survey
http://annenbergpublicpolicycenter.org

Individual voters tend to develop psychological ties to one party or another. The National Annenberg Election Survey uses survey data to track party identification by state every two years. Find out if your state has more Democratic or Republican identifiers.

Pew Research Center, Political Polarization
www.pewresearch.org/packages/political-polarization

This Pew Research Center series presents interactive graphics illustrating dramatic shifts in party polarization over time as it explores the current political landscape and the implications of party polarization for the American public.

In the 2016 general election, Donald Trump and Hillary Clinton competed for the presidency. Elections determine who is in government and thus influence what issues and policies will be taken up by the government.

Campaigns and Elections

10

WHAT GOVERNMENT DOES AND WHY IT MATTERS Elections are the core of any democracy. In a democratic system like the United States, citizens self-govern by choosing among candidates and electing leaders to represent them in government. The rules for elections affect who runs, how they run, who votes, and who wins.

The presidential election of 2016 saw the nation's first female major-party candidate: Democrat Hillary Clinton. After a successful career as a lawyer, Clinton came to national prominence as first lady in 1993 and through electoral politics built her path to the presidential nomination. As first lady, Clinton was directly involved in policy making, notably leading the president's commission to create a national health care system. After leaving the White House, she established New York residency and drew on the networks she shared with her husband to win a Senate seat in 2000.

Clinton was easily re-elected to the Senate in 2006, and soon after announced her candidacy in the 2008 presidential election. With strong name recognition and considerable campaign funds, she quickly became the front-runner for the Democratic nomination. Her challenger was a relatively unknown candidate, a one-term senator from Illinois named Barack Obama. Obama, however, proved to be a master campaigner, orator, and grassroots community organizer. Clinton suffered a startling loss to Obama in the Iowa caucuses at the start of the primary season, foreshadowing her eventual loss in the Democratic presidential primary. As president, Obama named Clinton as his secretary of state. In her four years in this role, Clinton negotiated treaties, alliances, and trade as the nation's leader in foreign policy. With Obama's second term ending in 2016, Clinton seemed poised for another run for the Democratic nomination for president.

Clinton announced her candidacy in April 2015. In the 2016 presidential primaries, she again faced a tough challenge from a Democratic rival, Vermont senator Bernie Sanders. Sanders succeeded in mobilizing younger voters by focusing on both parties' failures to address economic inequality and political corruption. The race was a close one and extended well into the spring as Sanders won several key state primaries and caucuses—but eventually Clinton secured the party's nomination.

On the Republican side, reality-TV star and real estate tycoon Donald Trump became the frontrunner in a pool of more than a dozen Republican candidates. Trump was known for his tough talk, anti-immigration and pro-business views, no-nonsense solutions, and provocative comments, often delivered via Twitter. Trump went on to win the Republican nomination, presenting Clinton with a new and different kind of opponent. Clinton and Trump ran against one another in one of the most unusual presidential elections in American history. The nation's choice between an experienced, inside-the-beltway politician or a populist "outsider" candidate rested with the voters.

In this chapter, we will learn about how elections work in the United States and how electoral rules and other considerations influence campaign strategy. We will see how election laws, the candidates' campaigns, and voters' choices determined the outcome of the 2016 presidential and congressional elections, and thus determined who represents the American people in government.

chaptergoals

- Describe the major rules and procedures of elections in the United States (pp. 371–82)
- Explain how campaigns are typically conducted (pp. 383–91)
- Describe how candidates raise the money they need to run (pp. 391–96)
- Identify the major factors that influence voters' decisions (pp. 396–400)
- Analyze the strategies, issues, and outcomes of the 2016 elections (pp. 400–12)

● Elections in America

Describe the major rules and procedures of elections in the United States

Elections are a remarkable feature of democratic government: every few years, the citizens are provided the means with which to change the government and select new leaders. In the United States, tens of thousands of political offices at the local, state, and national levels are subject to popular election. Although most Americans do not often vote directly on specific policies and laws, they exert tremendous influence over political outcomes through the regular selection of their leaders. By allowing citizens to hold their elected representatives accountable for their actions, elections are at the heart of democracy.

In the United States, elections are highly routinized events that occur on fixed dates and are subject to specific rules. National presidential elections take place every four years, on the first Tuesday after the first Monday in November. Congressional elections are held every two years, also on the first Tuesday after the first Monday in November. Congressional elections that do not coincide with a presidential election are often called **midterm elections**. Localities and states can choose when to hold their elections. Most Americans have the opportunity to vote in several elections each year. Voting in elections is the most common form of participation in American politics.

midterm elections congressional elections that do not coincide with a presidential election; also called *off-year elections*

Elections are the most important way that Americans participate in politics. Some of the rules for American elections have been in place since the Founding, while others have evolved over time. This painting shows Election Day in Philadelphia in 1815.

In the American federal system, the responsibility for running elections is decentralized, resting largely with state and local governments. Elections are administered by state, county, and city election boards that are responsible for establishing and staffing polling places, processing mail-in ballots, and verifying the eligibility of voters. State laws influence who may vote, how they vote, and where they vote. For example, states must choose whether to require photo identification to vote and whether or not to allow their residents to cast a ballot by mail, to vote early at an official polling place, and to register to vote and vote on the same day.

Election season begins with **primary elections**, which are held to select each party's candidates for the general election. Primary elections are used in races for office at the national, state, and often local levels. A primary election is like a preliminary match in a sporting event. It is used to select the best candidate to represent the political party in the general election. Thus, primary elections are races where Democrats compete against Democrats and Republicans against Republicans (except in states that have "top two primaries," in which candidates from all parties run against one another and the top two face each other in the general election; California and Washington State use this method). The winners of primary elections face one another as their parties' nominees in the **general election**, the decisive electoral contest. The winner of the general election is elected to office for a specified term.

The United States is one of the few nations in the world to hold primary elections. In most countries, nominations are controlled completely by party officials, as they once were in the United States. Primary elections were introduced at the turn of the twentieth century by reformers who hoped to weaken the power of party leaders; the introduction of primary elections for the first time enabled voters, rather than party elites, to pick the candidates to compete in the general election. In states with **closed primaries,** only registered members of a political party may vote in a primary election to select that party's candidates. States with **open primaries** allow all registered voters, including independents, to choose which party's primary they will participate in.

What It Takes to Win

On the surface, the basic idea of how an election works may seem simple: voters select their preferred candidate on the ballot, votes are counted, and the candidate with the most votes wins the election. But there are actually many possible variations in how people vote and how the votes are counted. In some countries, a candidate must receive an absolute majority (50 percent plus 1) of all the votes cast in the relevant district in order to win the election. This type of electoral system is called a **majority system**. Majority systems usually include a provision for a **runoff election** between the two top candidates because if the initial race draws several candidates, there is little chance that any one will receive a majority.

In many electoral systems, candidates for office need not win an absolute majority of the votes cast to win an election. Instead, victory is awarded to the candidate who receives the most votes, regardless of the actual percentage this represents. A candidate receiving 50 percent, 30 percent, or even 20 percent of the popular vote can win if no other candidate receives more votes. This type of electoral system is called a **plurality system** and is used in most elections in the United States. The winning candidate needs to win a plurality (the most but not necessarily a majority) of the votes cast in the election. In the 2016 Republican primaries, for example, Donald Trump was frequently referred to by the media as the winner, but in most states he only won around 35 percent of the vote because there were three or more candidates in the race.

primary elections elections held to select a party's candidate for the general election

general election a regularly scheduled election involving most districts in the nation or state, in which voters select officeholders; in the United States, general elections for national office and most state and local offices are held on the first Tuesday after the first Monday in November in even-numbered years (every four years for presidential elections)

closed primary a primary election in which voters can participate in the nomination of candidates but only of the party in which they are enrolled for a period of time prior to primary day

open primary a primary election in which the voter can wait until the day of the primary to choose which party to enroll in to select candidates for the general election

majority system a type of electoral system in which, to win a seat in the parliament or other representative body, a candidate must receive a majority of all the votes cast in the relevant district

runoff election a "second-round" election in which voters choose between the top two candidates from the first round

plurality system a type of electoral system in which, to win a seat in the parliament or other representative body, a candidate need only receive the most votes in the election, not necessarily a majority of the votes cast

Most European nations and other advanced democracies employ a third type of electoral system, called **proportional representation**. Under proportional rules, competing political parties are awarded legislative seats in rough proportion to the percentage of popular votes that each party wins. A party that wins 30 percent of the popular vote will receive roughly 30 percent of the seats in the parliament or other representative body. Proportional representation benefits smaller groups and third parties, such as the Green Party or the Libertarian Party, because it usually allows a party to win legislative seats with fewer votes than would be required under a majority or plurality system. A party that wins 10 percent of the national vote might win 10 percent of the parliamentary seats. In the United States, by contrast, a party that wins 10 percent of the vote would probably win no seats in Congress. Because they give small parties little chance of success, plurality and majority systems tend to reduce the number of political parties that can hold power. This is one of the reasons that the United States has only two significant political parties (see Chapter 9 for more on the two-party system in the United States).

proportional representation a multiple-member district system that allows each political party representation in proportion to its percentage of the total vote

The Ballot

Before the 1890s, voters cast ballots according to political parties. Each party printed its own ballots, listed only its own candidates for each office, and employed party workers to distribute the ballots at the polls. Because voters had to choose which party's ballot to use, it was very difficult for a voter to cast anything other than a **straight-ticket vote**, selecting candidates from the same political party for all offices on the ballot. The advent of a new, neutral ballot at the turn of the twentieth century brought a significant change to electoral procedure. The new ballot—called the Australian ballot or long-form ballot—was prepared and administered by the government rather than the political parties. Each ballot was identical and included the names of all candidates running for public office. This ballot reform made it possible for voters to make their choices on the merits of the individual candidates, rather than the overall party.

straight-ticket voting selecting candidates from the same political party for all offices on the ballot

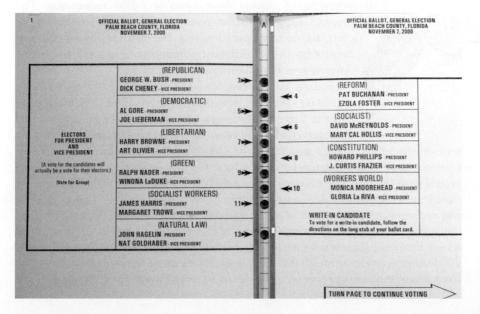

Some of the devices that have been used to record votes in the United States are notably prone to errors that can affect election results. For example, in 2000 in Florida's Palm Beach County, some voters were confused by the "butterfly ballot," which made it difficult to match candidates and votes. Use of the butterfly ballot was discontinued after 2000.

Because all candidates for the same office now appeared on the same ballot, voters were no longer forced to choose straight-ticket voting. This practice gave rise to the phenomenon of split-ticket voting, where voters may, for example, vote for a Democrat for Senate and a Republican for governor. If a voter supports candidates from more than one party in the same election, he is said to be casting a split-ticket vote.

The actual ballots used by voters vary from county to county. In the United States, it is the states, not the federal government, that run elections. Most states administer elections at the county level. Some counties employ paper ballots, while most now use electronic or computerized systems. The controversial presidential election of 2000 led to a closer look at different ballot forms and voting systems in use in the country. In 2000, the margin of victory for Republican George W. Bush over Democrat Al Gore in Florida was so small that the state ordered a recount. Careful examination of the results revealed that the punch card voting machines and butterfly ballot used in Florida had led to many voting and counting errors. The controversy made its way to the Supreme Court, which effectively reversed Florida's recount order, awarding the presidency to Bush. In the wake of the controversial election, Congress adopted the Help Americans Vote Act (HAVA) in 2003, requiring the states to introduce computerized voting systems. Critics of HAVA feared that such systems might be vulnerable to unauthorized use or hacking. However, computerized voting machines have generally worked well and have significantly updated America's election system. HAVA also required the states to use computerized voter-registration databases that have reduced problems with voter registration.

redistricting the process of redrawing election districts and redistributing legislative representatives; this happens every 10 years, to reflect shifts in population or in response to legal challenges in existing districts

The drawing of electoral districts is always a matter of controversy, with opponents accusing one another of "gerrymandering"— drawing district boundaries in such a way as to serve a particular group's interests. The original gerrymander was a districting plan attributed to the Massachusetts governor Elbridge Gerry (1744–1814) that had the shape of a salamander.

Legislative Elections and Electoral Districts

The boundaries for some elected offices are straightforward: all eligible U.S. citizens 18 years or older may vote for president; all eligible residents of each such as Texas, may vote for that state's governor and senators. Other political offices, such as members of the House of Representatives and many state legislatures, are elected from geographic legislative districts whose boundaries are drawn by the states. The boundaries for congressional and state legislative districts are redrawn every 10 years to reflect population changes, as determined by the U.S. Census. This redrawing of district boundaries is called **redistricting**. The geographic shape of district boundaries is influenced by several factors, including population size, the partisanship of the residents who live in different communities, as well as existing government boundaries such as counties.

Federal court decisions have played a major role in how legislative districts are drawn. In a 1962 landmark case *Baker v. Carr*, the Supreme Court ruled that federal courts can intervene on the issue of drawing legislative districts. In a series of decisions in 1963 and 1964, the Court held that legislative districts for Congress and state legislatures must include roughly equal populations so as to accord with the principle of "one person, one vote."[1] Prior to these decisions, many state legislative districts were simply county boundaries, with each county electing one representative, regardless of the population of the county. Drawing districts with roughly equal populations shifted power from rural areas to urban centers, where the population was higher. Today, average U.S. House districts have roughly 700,000 people (up from 30,000 people in 1800). State legislative districts vary from a few thousand people in some states to nearly a million (931,000) in the

California Senate. During the 1980s the Supreme Court also declared that legislative districts should, insofar as possible, be contiguous, compact, and consistent with existing political subdivisions.[2]

Despite these legal requirements, state lawmakers who are responsible for drawing the district boundaries for Congress and state legislatures regularly seek to influence electoral outcomes to favor one political party over another (or incumbents over challengers). This strategy of drawing legislative districts to favor a political party is called **gerrymandering**; gerrymandering is named for a nineteenth-century Massachusetts governor, Elbridge Gerry, who was alleged to have designed an odd-shaped district in the shape of a salamander to promote his party's interests. The principle behind gerrymandering is simple: different populations of voters in districts can produce different electoral results. For example, by dispersing the members of a particular party across two or more districts, state legislators can dilute that group's voting power and prevent it from electing a representative in any district. Alternatively, by concentrating the members of a party in as few districts as possible, state lawmakers can try to ensure that their opponents will elect as few representatives as possible. The widespread practice of gerrymandering has created many "safe" districts in Congress, and state legislatures where incumbents rarely face a serious challenger. This contributes to the frequency with which members of Congress are re-elected in landslide elections. In 2014, 96 percent of incumbents were reelected.[3] When candidates do not face serious challengers in elections there is concern that public officials will not represent the interests of the people but will instead make laws that benefit special interests.

The federal government has often supported congressional districts made up primarily of minority group members, a practice intended to increase the number of African Americans and Latinos elected to public office in accordance with the 1965 Voting Rights Act. Beginning with the 1993 case of *Shaw v. Reno*, however, the Supreme Court has generally opposed efforts to force the creation of **majority-minority districts**.[4] The Court has asserted that districting based exclusively on race/ethnicity is unlawful. However, most majority-minority districts in the United States occur naturally in states and geographic areas with large minority populations. Most African Americans in Congress, for example, are elected from majority black districts.

gerrymandering the apportionment of voters in districts in such a way as to give unfair advantage to one racial or ethnic group or political party

for critical analysis

How do district boundaries affect elections for the U.S. House and state legislatures? Should districts be drawn based on partisan considerations or other criteria?

majority-minority district an electoral district, such as a congressional district, in which the majority of the constituents belong to racial or ethnic minorities

Presidential Elections

While many of the rules applying to presidential and congressional elections are the same, presidential elections have special rules. The president is technically elected by the electoral college, not by popular vote of the citizens. Moreover, presidential candidates from the two major parties are officially nominated at the parties' national conventions, following a series of state-by-state primary elections and caucuses to select delegates to the conventions. While primary elections are also used to select candidates in Congressional and other types of elections, the national convention delegate system for nominating candidates is unique to presidential elections.

Nominating Presidential Candidates: Primaries and Caucuses How do we pick presidential candidates in the United States? Before the presidential election every four years, the parties must select candidates to represent them in the general election. The process starts with primary elections and caucuses (essentially a party business meeting) that are held by the major political parties to choose a candidate who will face the nominee from the other major party during the general election. Most states hold primary elections, but about one-third use caucuses instead. Citizens attending local caucuses typically elect delegates to statewide conventions, at which delegates to the national party conventions are chosen.

The Iowa caucus is especially famous, as the first state to select presidential candidates in the calendar year. The New Hampshire primary is the second election in the presidential nomination process. Both the Iowa caucus and New Hampshire primary are characterized by **grassroots politics**, where presidential candidates spend a great deal of time in the state to meet with voters face to face. Like the general elections, early primaries and caucuses tend to be highly contested, with high levels of mass media coverage and intensive voter mobilization drives.

The primaries and caucuses traditionally begin in January of a presidential election year and end six months later, in June (see Table 10.1). Iowa and New Hampshire each play a disproportionate role in picking presidential candidates because they are the first states to cast votes in the primaries and caucuses. These early voting states are important because they can help candidates gain momentum by securing national media attention, money in the form of campaign contributions, and increased standing in public-opinion polls. This momentum is so important to presidential hopefuls that former president George H. W. Bush called it the "Big Mo" in describing the boost from winning Iowa. Candidates spend months courting voter support in these two states. A candidate who performs better than expected in Iowa and New Hampshire will usually be able to win public support and media coverage for subsequent races. A candidate who fares poorly in these two states may be written off as a loser and drop out of the race. In 2016, Democrat Hillary Clinton and Republican Ted Cruz gained momentum by winning the Iowa caucuses, while their party rivals Bernie Sanders and Donald Trump did the same by winning the New Hampshire primary. Today, the presidential nomination has become "front-loaded," with states vying to increase their political influence by holding their nominating processes earlier in the calendar year in order to receive more attention from candidates and the media.

One study found that the change in mass media coverage that candidates receive before and after the Iowa caucuses predicts how well they will do in the

grassroots politics political campaigns that operate at the local level, often using face-to-face communication to generate interest and momentum by citizens

Campaigning for early primaries and caucuses typically involves grassroots politics, with candidates attempting to connect directly with citizens. Here, 2016 presidential candidate Ted Cruz speaks to potential voters at a local diner in Keene, New Hampshire.

TABLE 10.1

The 2016 Primaries and Caucuses Calendar

STATE	2016 PRESIDENTIAL PRIMARY DATE	STATE	2016 PRESIDENTIAL PRIMARY DATE
Alabama	March 1	Montana	June 7
Alaska	March 1 (R)/March 26 (D) both caucuses	Nebraska	March 5 (D) caucus/May 10 primary (R)
Arizona	March 22	Nevada	Feb. 20 (D)/Feb. 23 (R) both caucuses
Arkansas	March 1	New Hampshire	Feb. 9
California	June 7		
Colorado	March 1 caucuses (both parties)	New Jersey	June 7
Connecticut	April 26	New Mexico	June 7
Delaware	April 26	New York	April 19
Florida	March 15	North Carolina	March 15
Georgia	March 1	North Dakota	March 1 (R)/June 7 (D) both caucuses
Hawaii	March 8 (R)/March 26 (D) both caucuses	Ohio	March 15
Idaho	March 8 (R) primary/March 22 (D) caucus	Oklahoma	March 1
Illinois	March 15	Oregon	May 17
Indiana	May 3	Pennsylvania	April 26
Iowa	Feb. 1 caucuses (both parties)	Rhode Island	April 26
Kansas	March 5 caucuses (both parties)	South Carolina	Feb. 20 (R)/Feb. 27 (D) both primaries
Kentucky	March 5 (R) caucus/May 17 primary (D)	South Dakota	June 7
Louisiana	March 5	Tennessee	March 1
Maine	March 5 (R)/March 6 (D) both caucuses	Texas	March 1
		Utah	March 22 caucuses (both parties)
Maryland	April 26	Vermont	March 1
Massachusetts	March 1	Virginia	March 1
Michigan	March 8	Washington	Feb. 20 (R)/March 26 (D) both caucuses
Minnesota	March 1 caucuses (both parties)	West Virginia	May 10
Mississippi	March 8	Wisconsin	April 5
Missouri	March 15	Wyoming	March 1 (R)/April 9 (D) both caucuses

SOURCE: National Conference of State Legislatures, http://www.ncsl.org/research/elections-and-campaigns/2016-state-primary-dates.aspx#Pres (accessed 3/27/16).

New Hampshire primary and in presidential primaries nationwide measured by vote share.[5] This finding suggests that it is not winning the Iowa caucuses that matters but doing better than expected by the national media. For example, if Barack Obama had not won Iowa in 2008, unexpectedly beating presumed Democratic front-runner Hillary Clinton, most commentators believe he would not have gone on to capture the Democratic nomination. Similarly, Republican candidate Donald Trump fared much better than expected by political elites and the mass media by placing second in the Iowa caucuses and first in the New Hampshire primary. If Trump hadn't done well in these states, he likely would not have gone on to win the Republican nomination. In an era of viral digital media—most significantly Twitter—media coverage of early nominating events is even greater than before and may further increase the importance of states holding early primaries and caucuses.[6]

The result of the presidential primary or caucus determines how each state's **delegates** will vote at their party's national convention. In states such as Michigan and Iowa, party caucuses choose many of the delegates who will actually attend the national convention. In most of the remaining states, primary elections determine how a state's delegation will vote on the first ballot.

As noted in Chapter 9, the Democratic Party requires that state presidential primaries allocate delegates on the basis of proportional representation; Democratic candidates win delegates in rough proportion to their percentage of the primary vote. The Republican Party does not require proportional representation, but many states now use the system. A few states use the winner-take-all system, by which the candidate with the most votes wins all the party's delegates in that state. When the primaries and caucuses are concluded, it is usually clear which candidates have won their parties' nominations.

Nominating Presidential Candidates: Party Conventions For more than 50 years after America's Founding, presidential nominations were controlled by each party's congressional caucus—all the party's members in the House and the Senate. Critics referred to this process as the "King Caucus" and charged that it did not fairly represent the views of party members throughout the nation. Thus, the King Caucus process was replaced by the system of national conventions. As it developed over the next century, the convention became the decisive institution in the presidential nominating processes of the two major parties. Composed of delegates from each state, the convention was a deliberative body in which party elites argued, negotiated, and eventually chose a single candidate to support. The size of a state's delegation depended on the state's population, and each delegate was allowed one vote for the purpose of nominating the party's presidential and vice-presidential candidates.

Between the 1830s and World War II, national convention delegates were generally selected by a state's party leaders. Usually, the delegates were public officials, political activists, and party notables from all regions of the state, representing most major party factions. Typically, many votes were held before the nomination could be decided. Often deadlocks developed among the most powerful party factions, and state leaders would be forced to compromise, sometimes choosing a little-known candidate. Among the more famous "dark horse" nominees were James Polk in 1844 and Warren Harding in 1920. Although he was virtually unknown, Polk won the Democratic nomination when it became clear that none of the more established candidates could win. Similarly, Harding, another political unknown, won the Republican nomination after the major candidates had fought one another to a standstill.

for critical analysis

Is it fair that two relatively small states (in terms of population) such as Iowa and New Hampshire should have such outsize influence in picking presidents?

delegate a representative who votes according to the preferences of his or her constituency

Over time, reformers viewed the convention as a symbol of rule by party elites. Around the turn of the twentieth century, many states adopted direct primary elections to choose presidential candidates, enabling average citizens to have a voice in picking their president. As we saw earlier in this chapter, today the nomination is determined in a series of primary elections and local party caucuses held in all 50 states during the months prior to the party's national convention. These primaries and caucuses determine how each state's convention delegates will vote. Candidates usually arrive at the convention knowing who has enough delegate support in hand to assure a victory in the first round of balloting. If one candidate does not win a majority of delegates, a second ballot is issued, and delegates can choose to vote for a different candidate.

Both parties also allow superdelegates to play a role in nominations. Superdelegates are party elites who are not bound to the voting results in their state primaries and can vote as they wish. At the 2016 Democratic National Convention, most superdelegates backed Hillary Clinton, giving her a significant advantage over her opponent Bernie Sanders.

Even though the party convention no longer controls presidential nominations, it still has a number of important tasks. The convention makes the rules concerning delegate selection and future presidential primary elections. In 1972, for example, the Democratic Party adopted rules requiring convention delegates to be broadly representative of the party's membership in terms of race and gender. The Democratic Party refused to seat several state delegations that were deemed not to meet this standard. Another important task for the convention is the drafting of a **party platform**, a statement of principles and pledges around which the delegates can unite.

The convention is also an opportunity for the party to showcase its candidate in anticipation of the upcoming general election. Most importantly, the presidential and vice-presidential nominees deliver acceptance speeches. These speeches are opportunities for the nominees to begin their formal general-election campaigns and make a positive impression on the media. In her speech at the 2016 Democratic National Convention, Hillary Clinton repeated three times the theme of her general election campaign, "stronger together," insisting that the phrase was "not just a slogan for our campaign," but "a guiding principle for the country we've always been and the future we're going to build."

The Electoral College After they are officially nominated at the party convention, presidential candidates compete in the general election. As noted earlier, the presidential election differs from other elections in an important way: the voters do *not* directly elect the president. In the early history of popular voting, nations often made use of indirect elections. In these elections, voters would choose the members of an intermediate body. These members would, in turn, select public officials. The assumption underlying such a process was that ordinary citizens were not qualified to choose their leaders and could not be trusted to do so. The last vestige of this procedure in the United States is the **electoral college**, the group of electors who formally select the president and vice president of the United States.

When Americans go to the polls on Election Day, they are technically not voting directly for presidential candidates, even though they mark ballots as such; they are instead choosing among slates of electors selected by each party in the state and pledged, if elected, to support that party's presidential candidate. Electors are

Although the party's nominees for the president and vice president are officially announced at the party conventions, they are actually selected much earlier through caucuses and primary elections. In 2016, Hillary Clinton and Tim Kaine formally accepted the Democratic nomination at the national convention.

party platform a party document, written at a national convention, that contains party philosophy, principles, and policy positions

electoral college the presidential electors from each state who meet after the general election to cast ballots for president and vice president

allocated to each state based on the size of the state's congressional delegation (senators and House members). Larger-population states thus have more votes in the electoral college. North Dakota, for example, has 3 votes in the electoral college (based on its 2 senators plus 1 representative), while California has 55 (2 senators plus 53 representatives).

The president of the United States is the winner of the electoral college—the candidate who wins at least 270 of the college's 538 votes—not necessarily the candidate with the most votes from the people. This is in part because the electoral college and most elections in the United States are governed by plurality, winner-take-all rules. With only two exceptions, each state awards *all* of its electors to the candidate who receives the most votes in the state.[7] Thus, in 2016, Trump received all 29 of Florida's electoral votes, though he won only 49 percent of the votes in the state.

Only four times in the nation's history has the winner of the electoral college not won the popular vote (the most votes from the people). Since electoral votes are won on a state-by-state basis, it is mathematically possible for a candidate who receives the most popular votes nationwide to fail to carry states whose electoral votes would add up to a majority. Thus, in 1876, Rutherford B. Hayes was the winner in the electoral college despite receiving fewer popular votes than his rival, Samuel Tilden. In 1888, Grover Cleveland received more popular votes than Benjamin Harrison but fewer electoral votes. The third instance was the election of 2000, discussed above, when the lengthy legal battle over recounting votes in Florida ultimately ended with the Supreme Court's decision in *Bush v. Gore* that handed George W. Bush the presidency.[8] Bush had won a majority in the electoral college, but Democratic candidate Al Gore won 500,000 more votes from the people nationwide. In the most recent presidential election Donald Trump won the majority in the electoral college but Hillary Clinton won about 2.5 million more votes (based on preliminary tallies).

Calls for eliminating the electoral college and using a national popular vote for president are widespread, and public-opinion polls continue to show that most Americans prefer a direct election for the president.[9] Replacing the electoral college with another system would require a constitutional amendment that most agree would be extremely difficult to pass. However, reform is still possible since the Constitution allows states to choose the method of selecting presidential electors. One example of a recent attempt to reform the electoral college is the National Popular Vote plan, which has been introduced and adopted in a number of state legislatures.[10] Under the proposed rule change, a state's electoral college votes would go to the candidate who won the national popular vote, not the candidate with a plurality of votes in that specific state. States would enter a compact with other states making the same change, which would go into effect when a number of states representing a majority in the electoral college (270 electoral votes) approved it. The reform would effectively bypass the electoral college without the need for an amendment to the U.S. Constitution. As of 2014, 10 states plus Washington, D.C., representing 165 electoral votes, had enacted the bill into law. Under a national popular vote, competition would no longer be confined to a few large battleground states, but would likely focus more on urban areas.[11]

Another limitation of the electoral college system is that some presidents do not have widespread support. Few democracies in the world elect a president who does not win a majority of the popular vote. Since the Civil War, roughly one-third of American presidents have been elected with only a plurality (less than 50 percent) rather than a majority vote.[12] Notably, Abraham Lincoln won just 40 percent of the

Replacing the electoral college with the popular election of the president would have a significant impact on how campaigns are waged. Presidential candidates would have a greater incentive to campaign in large population centers, like San Francisco and Houston. Opponents worry that less populated rural areas would be ignored.

popular vote in a four-way tie, and Bill Clinton was elected with just 43 percent of the popular vote in 1992.[13] This often happens when a third-party candidate receives a significant percentage of votes. If the third-party candidate is more closely aligned ideologically with the losing major-party candidate, then a majority of voters may not support the winning presidential candidate.

Direct-Democracy Elections

Beyond presidential and congressional elections, 24 states also provide for the initiative process. **Ballot initiatives** allow citizens to circulate petitions to place policy change or proposed laws directly on the ballot for a popular vote. If a ballot initiative receives majority support, it becomes law. Controversial issues, such as proposals to raise the minimum wage, legalize marijuana, and reform the election process, frequently appear on the ballots of states with the initiative process. In recent years, voters in several states have voted to raise taxes on the wealthy, prohibit social services for illegal immigrants, end affirmative action, provide universal health care, create nonpartisan redistricting, protect open space and the environment, and prevent offshore drilling. At the turn of the twentieth century, ballot initiatives were used to grant women the right to vote, prevent child labor, limit the workday to eight hours, adopt progressive taxes, and allow voters to elect U.S. senators directly (rather than having them chosen by state legislatures). All 50 states have the legislative **referendum**, in which the state legislature refers certain laws to the voters for a popular vote. Referendum votes are required for changes to state constitutions.

The initiative and the referendum, both referred to as *ballot measures,* are examples of direct democracy. They allow voters to govern directly and make laws without intervention by government officials or the political parties. Ballot measure campaigns often involve high spending by proponents and opponents, and mass media campaigns that can rival those of congressional and presidential candidates

ballot initiative a proposed law or policy change that is placed on the ballot by citizens or interest groups for a popular vote

referendum the practice of referring a proposed law passed by a legislature to the vote of the electorate for approval or rejection within a state. The validity of ballot measure results, however, is subject to judicial action. If a court finds that an initiative violates the state or national constitution, it can overturn the result. This happened in 2012 when the federal courts overturned California's Proposition 8, which banned same-sex marriage.[14]

Ballot initiatives not only change policy but also appear to affect political behavior. One study found that states with initiatives on the ballot have higher voter turnout over time. Citizens living in direct-democracy states report more interest in politics and are more likely to discuss politics. Why is this so? If electoral rules offer citizens more opportunities to participate in policy decisions, those rules may have an "educative" effect on the people.[15] Representative democracy allows citizens to vote on who gets to make political decisions; ballot propositions go further, offering voters the possibility of directly making public policy. When they have more opportunities to act politically, citizens may learn to participate more and come to believe their participation has meaning.

Elections with policy choices on the ballot provide information to voters in the form of political campaigns and attention in the mass media. Ballot measures concerning controversial policy issues generate their own campaigns, with television, newspaper, and digital media; hire professional campaign consultants; and rely on volunteers for mobilization drives that contact potential voters.[16] Hundreds of initiatives and referenda appear on state election ballots every two years. In 2016 ballot measures included a plastic bag ban in California, background checks for gun purchases in Nevada, and numerous statewide initiatives to raise the minimum wage. An initiative in Maine created a new system of voting called "ranked choice voting," in which voters choose three candidates to rank in order of preference, rather than choosing only one. The new voting system applies to gubernatorial, congressional, and state legislative elections. Ballot initiatives are increasingly common: more initiatives and referenda have appeared on state ballots over the last 30 years than at any other time in American history, outside of the Progressive era at the turn of the twentieth century. In 2016, 163 ballot measures were certified for the ballot in 35 states.[17]

In addition, ballot measures can have spillover effects, shaping both the national agenda and evaluations of and voting for gubernatorial and congressional candidates.[18] Ballot measures banning same-sex marriage placed on the ballot of 13 states may have primed voting for the Republican presidential candidate in the 2004 election, George W. Bush. In 2006 coordinated ballot measures raising the minimum wage in multiple states may have influenced voters to focus on the economy, priming voters to cast ballots for Democrats in Congress and for Democratic governors. Placing issues on the ballot as part of an effort to influence candidate elections is an important strategy for political campaigns attempting to shape the political agenda.

recall a procedure to allow voters to remove state officials from office before their terms expire by circulating petitions to call a vote

Eighteen states also have legal provisions for **recall** elections, which allow voters to remove governors and other state officials from office prior to the expiration of their terms. In California, for example, if 12 percent of those who voted in the last general election sign petitions demanding a special recall election, one must be scheduled by the state board of elections. In 2003, many California voters blamed Governor Gray Davis for the state's $38 billion budget deficit; Davis became only the second governor in American history to be recalled by his state's electorate; the actor Arnold Schwarzenegger was elected in his place. In 2012, Wisconsin governor Scott Walker won a highly visible recall election, keeping his position. Federal officials, such as the president and members of Congress, are not subject to recall.

● Election Campaigns

Explain how campaigns are typically conducted

A **campaign** is an effort by political candidates (and their supporters) to win the backing of donors, political activists, and voters in their quest for elected office. Campaigns precede every primary and general election. Because of the complexity of the campaign process and the amount of money that candidates must raise, presidential campaigns often begin almost two years before the November election and congressional campaigns, 12 months in advance of the election. The campaign for any office consists of a number of steps. Candidates often organize an exploratory committee consisting of supporters who will help them raise funds and bring their names to the attention of the media, potential donors, and voters. Money is an important component of U.S. elections since public funding is limited. **Incumbents**, who already hold elected office, have an advantage over the candidates challenging them. Incumbents usually are already well known and have little difficulty attracting supporters and campaign contributors—unless, of course, they have been subject to damaging publicity while in office.

campaign an effort by political candidates and their supporters to win the backing of donors, political activists, and voters in their quest for political office

incumbent a candidate running for re-election to a position that he or she already holds

Advisers

A formal organization and advisers are critical for campaign success (see Figure 10.1). For a local campaign, candidates generally need hundreds of volunteers and some paid professionals. State-level campaigns call for thousands of volunteers, and presidential campaigns require tens of thousands of volunteers nationwide. Virtually all serious contenders for national and statewide office retain the services of professional campaign consultants. Most candidates need a professional campaign manager, media consultants, pollsters, financial advisers, a press spokesperson, and staff directors to coordinate the activities of volunteer and paid workers. Consultants offer candidates the expertise necessary to craft appealing campaign messages, conduct accurate opinion polls, produce television and digital

Candidates for national office rely on campaign advisers to guide their campaigns and direct volunteers. Here, Hillary Clinton collaborates with Huma Abedin, her longtime aid and her campaign's vice chairwoman; Brian Fallon, her national press secretary; and Nick Merrill, her traveling press secretary.

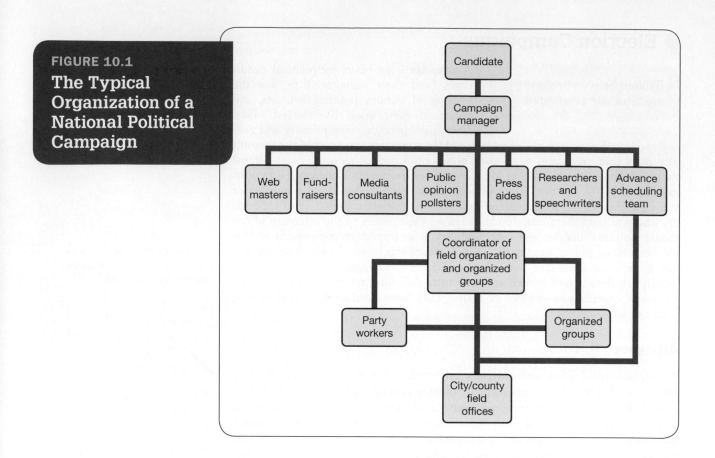

FIGURE 10.1

The Typical Organization of a National Political Campaign

Candidate

Campaign manager

Web masters

Fund-raisers

Media consultants

Public opinion pollsters

Press aides

Researchers and speechwriters

Advance scheduling team

Coordinator of field organization and organized groups

Party workers

Organized groups

City/county field offices

ads, organize direct-mail campaigns, open field offices, and leverage valuable information about their constituents from massive digital voter files or from surveys. Professional political consultants have taken the place of the old-time party bosses who once controlled political campaigns, and naturally they prefer to work for candidates who seem to have a reasonable chance of winning. Most consultants who direct campaigns specialize in politics, although some are drawn from the ranks of corporate advertising and strategic communication, public relations, and informatics and computing. They may work with commercial clients in addition to politicians.

Fundraising

Modern national political campaigns are fueled by enormous amounts of money, with more money necessary for highly competitive elections and federal offices. Candidates generally begin raising funds long before they face an election, and many politicians spend more time soliciting donations than engaging in any other campaign activity. Members of Congress spend a significant portion of their time fundraising; the Democratic leadership recommends that 40 to 50 percent of their time be spent on fundraising.[19] Serious fundraising efforts involve appealing to both small and large donors. To have a reasonable chance of winning a seat in the House of Representatives, a candidate may need to raise more than $1 million; in 2014, candidates in the most competitive House races spent $10 million or more. In the 2014 Senate races, candidates in the most competitive elections spent

$85–115 million. Presidential candidates in particular must raise huge amounts of money. In 2012 fundraising by the presidential campaigns shattered previous records. The Obama campaign, the Democratic Party, and the Priorities USA Action Super political action committee (PAC) raised $934 million, while Mitt Romney's campaign, the Republican Party, and the Restore Our Future Super PAC raised $881 million. All told, $4 billion was spent in the 2012 presidential elections. These figures are unprecedented.[20]

Once in office, members of Congress find it much easier to raise campaign funds and are thus able to outspend their challengers (see Figure 10.2).[21] Incumbents

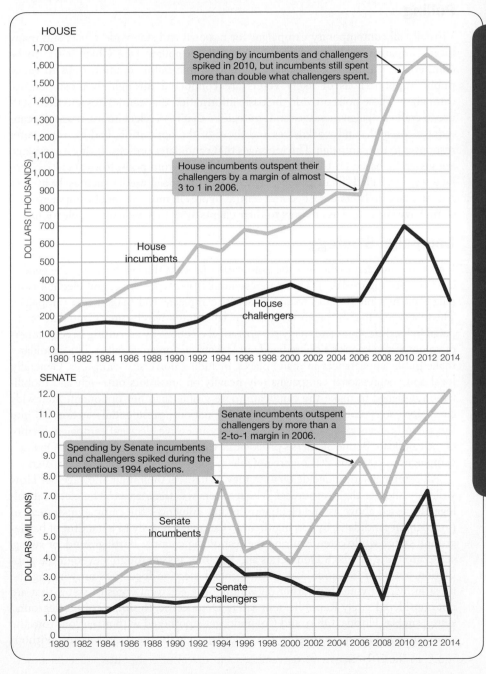

FIGURE 10.2

Average House and Senate Campaign Expenditures, 1980–2014

The average amount spent by House and Senate incumbents to secure re-election has risen sharply in recent years, whereas spending by challengers has remained more stable. What would you expect to see as a consequence of this trend? Is legislation needed to level the playing field?

SOURCES: Norman J. Orstein, Thomas E. Mann, and Michael J. Malbin, eds., *Vital Statistics on Congress, 2001–2002* (Washington, DC: American Enterprise Institute, 2002), 87, 93; Norman J. Orstein, Thomas E. Mann, Michael J. Malbin, Andrew Rugg, and Raffaela Wakeman, "Vital Statistics on Congress Data on the U.S. Congress—A Joint Effort from Brookings and the American Enterprise Institute," July 2013, www.brookings.edu/vitalstats (accessed 6/20/14); and OpenSecrets.org, "Incumbent Advantage," www.opensecrets.org/overview/incumbs.php (accessed 3/23/16).

can out-raise their opponent by significant amounts because most of the interest group contributions and PAC money donations go to incumbents. These groups seek a voice in government from their investment in campaign contributions; thus, these organizations—businesses, labor unions, public interest groups, and others—want to invest in the candidate most likely to win, and incumbents win a large percentage of the time. Members of the majority party in the House and Senate are particularly attractive to donors who want access to those in power.[22] In the "Money and Politics" section later in this chapter, we will discuss further the critical role that money plays in the electoral process.

Polling

Virtually all contemporary campaigns for national and statewide office, and many local campaigns, make extensive use of opinion polling (see Chapter 6). To be competitive, a candidate must use random sample public-opinion polls to gauge public support. Polls of likely voters are conducted throughout most political campaigns. These polls provide the basic information that candidates and their staff use to craft campaign messages and strategies—that is, to select issues, assess the candidates' strengths and weaknesses and those of the opposition, and measure voter responses to the campaign. The messages that candidates present during a campaign are generally based on the voter feedback they get from polls, from small face-to-face sessions called "focus groups," as well as from social media such as Twitter. In recent years, pollsters have become central figures in most national campaigns, and some have continued as advisers to their clients after they've won the election.

Campaign Strategy

For those candidates who win the nomination process, the last hurdle is the general election (see Figure 10.3). There are essentially two types of general election campaigns in the United States today, grassroots campaigns and mass media campaigns. The first type is the organizationally driven, labor-intensive election. Candidates campaign in local elections and many congressional elections by recruiting large numbers of volunteers to knock on doors, hand out leaflets, and organize rallies. The candidates make public appearances in many places, including university campuses. Generally, local and congressional campaigns rely heavily on grassroots outreach and mobilization designed to make the candidate more visible than her opponent. Statewide campaigns, some congressional races, and the national presidential election fall into the second category: the media-driven, money-intensive electoral campaign. Democratic candidate Bernie Sanders's presidential campaign in 2016 and Barack Obama's campaigns in 2008 and 2012 were notable in combining both types of campaigns.

All campaigns must decide on a strategy: What will their main message be? How will they allocate their resources? Which voters will they target? The electoral college, discussed above, is one election rule that influences the campaign strategy of presidential candidates by forcing them to campaign heavily in a handful of battleground states, while often ignoring the rest of the country. Battleground, or swing, states are those in which Democrats and Republicans are roughly even in the population. Presidential candidates in the general election focus not on winning the most individual votes but rather on winning the electoral votes of states that are not considered safely Republican or safely Democratic. Residents of battleground states, such as Florida, Ohio, and Colorado, get smothered with attention from the candidates and media as presidential candidates vie for that state's votes. Without

FIGURE 10.3

Electing the President: Steps in the Process

Formation of an Exploratory Committee
Formed 18 to 24 months before the election, this committee begins fundraising and bringing the candidate's name to the attention of the media and influential groups.

Fundraising
Presidential candidates must develop fundraising strategies, hire expert fundraisers, and quickly build a substantial "war chest" early on to show they are serious contenders.

Campaigning
Months before the primaries, candidates begin meetings with local leaders, public appearances, ad campaigns, and other strategies.

Primaries and Caucuses
Candidates need to do well in early contests such as Iowa and New Hampshire in order to build momentum and win their party's nomination. Party debates give candidates an opportunity to impress large television audiences.

The Convention
The Democratic and Republican parties hold national conventions in September prior to the November general election. The parties nominees for president and vice president are "officially" announced.

The General Election Campaign
In the months leading up to the November election, candidates focus on battleground or swing states as they aim to win at leat 270 votes in the electoral college. They run television ads and use new media to reach voters. They must continue to raise money throughout this process.

The Debates
In October, the major party candidates engage in several televised debates along with one vice presidential debate.

The General Election
On the Tuesday following the first Monday in November, voters in each state cast ballots. In most states, the candidate who wins the most votes in the state wins all of the state's votes in the electoral college.

The Electoral College
The electors meet in their state capitals in December, and their votes are officially counted in January.

The Inauguration
The president is officially inaugurated on January 20.

electoral competition in safe states, the needs and concerns of the residents may well be ignored.

Contemporary political campaigns also rely on a number of communication tools to reach the voters they want to target for support, including social media, massive computerized debates, and micro-targeting. Digital communication strategy is especially important in mobilizing citizens to vote.

The Media Extensive use of the broadcast media, television in particular, is the hallmark of the modern political campaign. Airing television ads is the primary cost faced by presidential and congressional candidates. Two media techniques that became important in the 1990s are the talk show interview and the town hall meeting. The **town hall meeting** format allows candidates the opportunity to interact with ordinary citizens, thus showing the candidates' concern with the views and needs of the voters. Both talk show appearances and town hall meetings (when televised) allow candidates to deliver their messages to millions of Americans without the input of journalists or commentators who might criticize or question the candidates' assertions.

Candidates spend millions of dollars for *paid media* time in the form of television and radio ads, as discussed in the previous section. Many of these ads consist of 15-, 30-, or 60-second spots (advertisements) that deliver a candidate's message to a target audience before uninterested or hostile viewers can tune it out. Notable examples include George H. W. Bush's 1988 "Willie Horton" ad, which implied that Bush's opponent, Michael Dukakis, coddled criminals, and Lyndon Johnson's 1964 "daisy" ad, which suggested that Johnson's opponent, Barry Goldwater, would lead the United States into nuclear war. Television ads are used to establish candidate name recognition, create a favorable image of the candidate and a negative image of the opponent, link the candidate with desirable groups in the community, and communicate the candidate's stands on selected issues.

Often in the later stages of a campaign, candidates and the political advocacy groups that support them will "go negative," airing ads that criticize their opponents' policy positions, qualifications, or character. Though voters consistently say they reject so-called negative campaigning, arguing that such ads undermine elections and even democratic government itself, political scientist John Geer found that negative campaign ads actually benefit voters more than positive ads do.[23] Negative ads are more likely to address important policy differences and provide supporting evidence, while positive ads tend to focus on candidates' personal characteristics. And even when negative ads are misleading or patently false, they are effective in that voters remember more from negative ads than from positive ads, possibly because negative ads are designed to elicit emotional responses, such as fear, anxiety, or anger.

In addition to ads sponsored by the candidates, a growing percentage of campaign ads are sponsored by the political parties and by political advocacy groups seeking to influence the outcome of the election. The 2010 *Citizens United* decision (discussed below) allowed corporations and unions to spend unlimited amounts of their own money to advocate for political candidates. Corporations, unions, and interest groups can form Super PACs and run unlimited campaign ads for or against candidates, as long as the organizations are "independent" of the candidate's campaign. The effect of unlimited spending on television advertising remains unclear.

town hall meeting an informal public meeting in which candidates meet with ordinary citizens; allows candidates to deliver messages without the presence of journalists or commentators

Attack ads can be effective in inspiring fear and instilling doubt about an opposing candidate. Lyndon Johnson's "Daisy" ad 1964 juxtaposed a young girl counting flower petals with a countdown to a nuclear explosion, suggesting that Johnson's opponent, Barry Goldwater, would lead the country to nuclear war.

Candidates also benefit from free media, where the cost of airtime is borne by the media themselves when the media cover the candidates' statements and activities as news. In the 2016 presidential primaries, Republican candidate Donald Trump benefited more than any other candidate from free media coverage. For example, all three major cable news channels—CNN, Fox, and MSNBC—aired 45 uninterrupted minutes of Trump's speech after he won the Mississippi primary, amounting to what would otherwise have cost millions of dollars in airtime, while providing no coverage of Hillary Clinton, the Democratic winner of the primary.[24] Critics claimed that the networks' tendency to focus on Trump, rather than provide balanced political coverage of all candidates, occurred because he drew the biggest audience.

Digital media are often free as well and have become a major weapon in modern political campaigns as more Americans turn to the Internet and social media for news. Today, every presidential campaign and most campaigns for Congress and major state offices develop a social media strategy for fundraising, generating interest in the candidate, mobilizing supporters, and getting out the vote. (See Chapters 7 and 8 for a fuller discussion of political candidates' digital strategy.) One reason digital media are so effective at organizing presidential campaigns is cost: the Internet allows the organization of volunteers at a fraction of the cost of traditional campaigns and offers more opportunities for free advertising, such as on YouTube. Online political videos may be more effective than television ads because viewers make a conscious choice to watch them, instead of having their television program interrupted by an unwanted ad. According to reports released by the Pew Research Center soon after the 2012 election, fully 55 percent of registered voters watched political videos online, including news reports about the election, debates, humorous and parody videos, and political ads.[25]

Debates Public debates were a critical part of the democratic process of ancient Greece, where they were both a vital form of public entertainment and the principal means of what today would be called "voter education." Many successful American politicians, such as Abraham Lincoln and Barack Obama, came to prominence largely because of their skill as debaters. Today, both presidential and vice-presidential candidates hold debates, as do candidates for statewide and even local offices. Debates give voters the opportunity to see how the candidates fare in direct, face-to-face exchanges outside the "campaign bubble" of stage-managed public appearances and carefully scripted speeches. Candidates who can think on their feet may be seen as demonstrating the kind of on-the-spot decision making that is more like actual governing than anything else they do in a campaign.

Televised presidential debates began with the famous 1960 Kennedy–Nixon clash. Kennedy's strong performance in the debate and the perception of many voters that the youthfully vigorous Kennedy "looked presidential" were major factors in bringing about his victory over the much better-known Richard Nixon. Indeed, candidates can make or break their campaigns with the strength of their debate performances, including high-profile gaffes during the debates and even unconscious gestures and the nuances of their facial expressions. Because debates force candidates to react spontaneously, many voters believe that they provide the most important and revealing moments of a campaign. Presidential debates usually involve civilized disagreement about substantive policy issues. The Republican primary debates in 2016, however, uncharacteristically included fierce arguments, harsh character attacks, and personal insults, many of which stemmed from the bombastic style of Donald Trump and his opponents' occasional attempts to match it.

Voters who watch debates can be swayed by personal characteristics such as the appearance, voice, and gestures of the candidates. In the first televised national debate in 1960, John F. Kennedy was largely thought to be the winner over Richard Nixon, in part because his youthful aspect "looked presidential."

When Trump faced off against Democrat Hillary Clinton in the general election, the antagonistic tone continued, and their first televised debate broke viewership records as the most watched in U.S. history.[26]

Micro-Targeting The media and debates allow candidates to communicate their policy goals and promises to voters. While this method is efficient for campaigns, it is also blunt; different voters care about different issues, after all. As we saw in Chapter 9, the idea behind micro-targeting is to send different campaign ads or messages to different demographic groups of voters and potential voters. Suburban "soccer moms," for instance, would be targeted with ads different from those targeting rural "cowboy dads."

Republican president George W. Bush is credited with successfully using micro-targeting in the 2000 and 2004 presidential elections. His campaign focused on wedge issues—issues where a voter's preferences diverge from those of his political party. By targeting such voters with messages focusing on Bush's position on the wedge issue, the campaign hoped to convince these voters to cast a ballot for Bush rather than his opponent.[27]

Micro-targeting became more sophisticated during the 2008 presidential campaign as Democrats built an extensive organization to contact and turn out voters. The Obama campaign made use of an unprecedented volume of ongoing survey work, conducting thousands of short- and long-form interviews each week to gauge voters' preferences. Statistical algorithms looked for patterns in these opinions and the many other data points the campaign had assembled for every voter (a total of 160 million people) based on voter-registration records, consumer data warehouses, and past campaign contacts. The campaign used this mountain of information to generate different, carefully targeted messages for different demographic, regional, and ideological groups to persuade them to turn out and vote for Obama.[28] It was the first time big data (see Chapter 6) had been used to win a presidential election. Because of micro-targeting, millions of Americans heard from other Americans about issues that mattered the most to them.

Once campaigns have identified specific groups of voters, they reach out via face-to-face contacts, phone calls, mailings, and social media to their target audiences. Personal contact is thought to be extremely effective at mobilizing voters to turn out but requires field offices and volunteers. Staffs of paid or volunteer telephone callers, using computer-assisted dialing systems and prepared scripts, also place calls to deliver their candidate's message. The targeted groups are generally those identified by polls as either uncommitted or weakly committed, but even strong supporters of the candidate are contacted and simply encouraged to vote. Since 2008, the presidential campaigns of both parties have also placed hundreds of thousands of automated "robocalls" urging voters to support their candidates.

Direct mail is another vehicle for communicating with voters. After obtaining the appropriate mailing lists, candidates usually send pamphlets, letters, and brochures describing themselves and their views to voters believed to be sympathetic. Often, the letters sent to voters are personalized: the recipient is addressed by name in the text, and the letter appears actually to have been signed by the candidate. Of course, these "personal" letters and even the signatures are generated by a computer. In addition to its use as a political advertising medium, direct mail has become an important source of campaign funds. Computerized mailing lists permit campaign strategists to pinpoint individuals whose interests, background, and activities suggest that they may be potential donors to the campaign.

Contemporary presidential campaigns gather large amounts of data on potential voters in order to effectively tailor campaign messages to specific demographics. Armed with this data, volunteers for both the Trump and Clinton campaigns made thousands and thousands of phone calls to urge individuals to support their candidate on Election Day in 2016.

"People power" remains important in modern political campaigns. Research suggests that direct mail and robocalls are less effective than in-person and phone contacts.[29] Candidates continue to use the political services of tens of thousands of volunteers, especially for grassroots get-out-the-vote drives. Still, even the recruitment of campaign volunteers has become a job for electronic technology. Employing a technique called "instant organization," paid staff use phone banks to contact not only potential voters but also potential campaign workers in areas targeted by a computer. Volunteer workers are recruited from among those called.

for critical analysis

Do American political campaigns help voters make a decision? Or do they produce more confusion than enlightenment?

Money and Politics

Describe how candidates raise the money they need to run

Today, campaign activities depend increasingly on surveys, computers, and electronic communication. Although the Internet has made it less expensive to coordinate and communicate with supporters, other aspects of the modern campaign require a great deal of money. A 60-second spot on prime-time network television costs hundreds of thousands of dollars each time it is aired. Polling expenses in a statewide race can easily reach or exceed the six-figure mark. Campaign consultants can charge substantial fees. Even a direct-mail campaign requires at least $1 million in "front-end cash" to pay for mailing lists, printing, envelopes, and postage.[30]

In the nineteenth century, labor-intensive campaigns allowed parties whose chief support came from groups nearer the bottom of the socioeconomic scale to use their numerical superiority as a partial counterweight to the institutional and economic resources more readily available to the opposition. As many as 2.5 million individuals worked on political campaigns during the 1880s.[31] The money-intensive campaign of the modern era, by contrast, has given a major boost to the political fortunes of candidates whose supporters are able to furnish the large sums now needed to compete effectively.[32]

Candidates with the most campaign dollars often win. In 2008 and 2012, Barack Obama outfundraised his Republican opponents. In 2016, however, though Hillary Clinton spent more than her opponent, Donald Trump, she did not win. Nonetheless, the 2016 election shattered previous records. Combined spending by candidates, parties, and interest groups on the congressional and presidential races was $6.9 billion in 2016 compared with $6.2 billion in 2012 and $5.3 billion in 2008. Of the $6.9 billion, $4.3 billion was spent on congressional races and $2.6 billion on the presidential race.[33]

The Courts and Campaign Spending

The United States is rare among democracies in allowing candidates to raise unlimited sums of money to spend on their campaigns. In most democratic countries, publically financed campaigns are the norm; in such a system, candidates or parties are provided with a set amount of money to spend by the government. In the United States, candidates may raise ever-increasing amounts of money from private individuals, corporations, and interest groups. Reformers have long been concerned about the potential for corruption that exists when candidates are actively soliciting private interests for funding. In an attempt to limit the influence of private money, the federal government has adopted a number of laws to limit and regulate contributions to political campaigns. But three Supreme Court decisions adopted over a 40-year period have dismantled most of these restrictions on money in politics.

The first, *Buckley v. Valeo* (1976), was a landmark Supreme Court case that struck down several provisions of the Federal Election Campaign Act of 1974, including limits on candidate spending, independent expenditures, and use of personal funds. (Independent expenditures are sums of money spent to influence a campaign, but the donating organization is not allowed to coordinate with a candidate's official campaign.) The decision introduced the idea that money (in this case, campaign contributions) counts as "speech" under the First Amendment and that candidates could spend unlimited amounts of their own money on their own campaign. However, the Court left intact the provision of the law that sets limits on individuals' campaign contributions.[34]

In 2010 the U.S. Supreme Court ruled in *Citizens United v. Federal Election Commission* that the government could not restrict independent expenditures by corporations or unions to political campaigns.[35] The Court said restrictions on independent expenditures violated the First Amendment. With this decision, the United States entered a new era of campaign finance in which corporations and unions can spend unlimited sums. Following the *Citizens United* decision, *SpeechNow v. FEC* allowed wealthy individuals and organizations to form committees, called Super PACs, which can raise unlimited amounts of money to run advertising for and against candidates so long as their efforts are not coordinated with those of the candidates.[36] This resulted in a significant increase in campaign spending in the 2010 midterm election and unprecedented spending in the 2012 and 2016 presidential elections. Obama, the Democratic National Committee, and its affiliated Super PACs spent $1.11 billion in 2012, while Romney, the Republican National Committee, and its affiliated Super PACs spent $928 million, or almost $1 billion, swamping previous general election totals.

In 2014, Shaun McCutcheon successfully challenged the federal limit on the amount of money any one individual can donate to political campaigns and candidates. However, many people worry that recent Supreme Court decisions overturning campaign spending limits reinforce the influence of the very affluent in American politics at the expense of everyone else.

In 2014 the Supreme Court removed additional limits on individuals' campaign contributions, again with the argument that such limits violated First Amendment freedoms, in its decision in *McCutcheon et al. v. Federal Election Commission*.[37] The case challenged the two-year cap on the amount of money an individual could give to federal candidates, PACs, and political party committees. The Court decision held that there was no evidence that making campaign contributions to large numbers of candidates led to the donor controlling the actions of elected officials. Thus, the Court held, such restrictions were not justified. The Court let stand the limit on the amount of money that an individual can give to any one candidate in a two-year election cycle (currently set at $2,700).

As the Court struggles to balance free speech with preventing political corruption, the sum of these three court decisions tips the scale in favor of speech. Opponents raise concerns that unlimited spending by wealthy donors, corporations, and other organizations could worsen existing corruption in American politics. This concern is bolstered by a number of new studies finding that members of Congress make decisions that represent the interests of wealthy campaign donors, not average voters.[38]

Sources of Campaign Funds

Although restrictions remain on how money is raised and spent on elections, there is today a great deal of latitude on where money comes from and what it is used for. Campaigns have at least six potential sources of funds.

Individual Donors Politicians spend a great deal of time asking people for money. Money is solicited via direct mail, through the Internet, over the phone, and in numerous face-to-face meetings. Under federal law, individuals may donate as much as $2,700 per candidate per election, $5,000 per federal PAC per calendar year, $33,400 per national party committee per calendar year, and $10,000 to state and local committees per calendar year. (There is no limit to the number of candidates or

for critical analysis

What purpose do limits on monetary contributions to political campaigns serve? Should there be limits? How do monetary contributions affect the outcomes of elections?

Campaign Laws in Comparison

Electoral campaigns are more expensive in the United States than in any other country, with only India even approaching the same amount of spending (roughly $5 billion in 2014).[a] Both the United States and India are large federal countries, so spending is high partly because these countries have multiple levels of government to elect. India's population, however, is approximately four times the U.S. population, so the United States still spends significantly more per voter, as shown in the table below. Critics have argued that the amount of money in these campaigns creates an unfair advantage for certain candidates, increases the importance (and political influence) of large campaign donors, and potentially undermines the quality of democracy.

Some countries have rules that limit campaign contributions or campaign spending. The United States has extensive rules regarding campaign contributions (at least for candidates, as Super PACs have few limits), but the United States has few spending limits. The United Kingdom, in contrast, does not limit contributions but has strict rules on campaign spending. Some countries also allow qualified parties and/or candidates free or subsidized access to media, which reduces the need to raise huge sums.

However, a considerable amount of campaign spending is determined by the nature of the election. Norway bans political advertising on television and the radio (which is where most U.S. campaign money goes), and the election itself only runs two weeks. Even though Norway sets no restrictions on campaign spending or fundraising, most campaign money—roughly 74 percent—comes from public funds.[b]

	United States	India	United Kingdom	Norway
Campaign spending in a recent election (in U.S. dollars)	$7.1 billion (2012)	Roughly $5 billion (2014)	$69 million (2015)	Roughly $6.5 million (2013)
Length of national election	Unlimited	2+ weeks[*]	One month	2 weeks
Are public funds available?	Only for presidential candidates (federal funds)	No	Yes	Yes
Is media access free or subsidized?	No	Yes (for parties, not candidates)	Yes (for parties, not candidates)	No
Bans on television advertising?	No	No	No	Yes
Approximate spending per voter (in U.S. dollars)	$29.47	$6.35	$1.35	$1.76

[*]While the Electoral Commission of India lists the official campaign as only 2 weeks (http://eci.nic.in/eci_main1/the_function.aspx#campaign) with all campaigning required to end the day before the election, polling took 5 weeks in 2014, as different regions of the country were scheduled to go to the polls on different days.
SOURCE: Campaign laws from The International Institute for Democracy and Electoral Assistance Political Finance Database, www.idea.int/political-finance/ (accessed 4/30/16); The U.S. Federal Election Commission, www.fec.gov/press/press2013/20130419_2012-24m-Summary.shtml (accessed 4/20/16); "General Election 2015 explained," *The Independent*, April 17, 2015, www.independent.co.uk/news/uk/politics/generalelection/general-election-2015-explained-who-finances-the-parties-who-gets-the-most-and-how-much-does-the-10186008.html (accessed 4/30/16); and "International campaign finance," CNN World, reporting of the 2013 election campaign contributions from Statistics Norway, www.ssb.no/en/valg/statistikker/valgkamp (accessed 4/30/16).

[a]Sruthi Gottipati and Rajesh Kumar Singh, "India Set to Challenge U.S. for Election-Spending Record" Reuters, March 9, 2014, www.reuters.com/article/2014/03/09/us-india-election-spending-idUSBREA280AR20140309#XxEPYA752ikcQRB5.97 (accessed 4/30/16).
[b]Nick Thompson, "International Campaign Finance: How Do Countries Compare?" CNN, March 5, 2012, *World*, www.cnn.com/2012/01/24/world/global-campaign-finance/ (accessed 4/30/16).

PACs that an individual can give to, however—a result of the Supreme Court's decision in *McCutcheon*.[39]) Democrat Bernie Sanders' 2016 presidential campaign raised an unprecedented $1.1 million in individual contributions, $850 million of which was made up of small contributions.[40] The "Who Participates?" feature at the end of this chapter looks at the characteristics of donors to political campaigns.

Political Action Committees **Political action committees (PACs)** are organizations established by corporations, labor unions, or interest or advocacy groups to channel the contributions of their members and employees into political campaigns. Under the terms of the 1971 Federal Election Campaign Act, which governs campaign finance in the United States, PACs are permitted to make larger contributions to any given candidate than individuals are allowed to make. Moreover, allied or related PACs often coordinate their campaign contributions, greatly increasing the amount of money a candidate actually receives from the same interest group. More than 4,600 PACs are registered with the Federal Election Commission, which oversees campaign finance practices in the United States. Nearly two-thirds of all PACs represent corporations, trade associations, and other business and professional groups. Many congressional and party leaders have established PACs, known as "leadership PACs," to provide funding for their political allies.

Independent Spending: 527, 501(c)(4), and Super PAC Committees Committees known as **527s** and **501(c)(4)s** are independent groups that are currently not covered by the campaign spending restrictions imposed in 2002 by the Bipartisan Campaign Reform Act. These groups, named for the sections of the tax code under which they are organized, can raise and spend unlimited amounts on political advocacy as long as their efforts are not coordinated with those of any candidate's campaign. A 527 is a group established specifically for the purpose of political advocacy and is required to report to the IRS. A 501(c)(4) is a nonprofit group that also engages in advocacy but may not spend more than half its revenue for political purposes. Unlike a 527, a 501(c)(4) is not required to disclose where it gets its funds or exactly what it does with them—as a result, its funding has earned the name "dark money" and has raised growing concern that the lack of transparency in campaign funding threatens fair elections. Indeed, it has become a common practice for wealthy and corporate donors to route campaign contributions through 501(c)(4)s to avoid the legal limits on contributions through other channels.

Independent expenditures, or outside spending via 527s and 501(c)(4)s, played an unprecedented role in the 2012 and 2016 presidential races as outside groups ran extensive television ads. Super PACs on both sides relied on very large contributions. A growing concern is that elections in the United States can be bought with big money from corporations and wealthy donors, who will then hold significant influence when that candidate is elected. Political corruption and undue influence from Wall Street were recurring themes among the 2016 presidential candidates. But 2016 was characterized by lopsided campaign spending: Clinton raised and spent double that of the Trump campaign. As of October 2016, Clinton had raised nearly $500 million, with an additional $189 million from outside money (Super PACs) compared to just $247 million raised by Trump, with another $59 million from outside money.

Political Parties Before 2002 most campaign dollars took the form of "soft money," unregulated contributions to the national parties nominally to assist in

political action committee (PAC) a private group that raises and distributes funds for use in election campaigns

527 committees nonprofit independent groups that receive and disburse funds to influence the nomination, election, or defeat of candidates as long as their activities are not coordinated with the candidate campaigns; named after Section 527 of the Internal Revenue Code, which defines and grants tax-exempt status to nonprofit advocacy groups

501(c)(4) committees politically active nonprofits; under federal law, these nonprofits can spend unlimited amounts on political campaigns and not disclose their donors as long as their activities are not coordinated with the candidate campaigns and political activities are not their primary purpose

party building or voter registration efforts rather than for particular campaigns. Federal campaign finance legislation crafted by senators John McCain and Russell Feingold and enacted in 2002 sought to ban soft money by prohibiting the national parties from receiving contributions from corporations, unions, or individuals and preventing them from directing such funds to their affiliated state parties. However, it did not reduce the overall importance of money in politics, and political parties continue to play a major role in financing political campaigns. Under federal rules, a national political party committee may make unlimited "independent expenditures" advocating support for its own presidential candidate or advocating the defeat of the opposing party's candidate as long as these expenditures are not coordinated with the candidate's own campaign.

Public Funding The Federal Election Campaign Act also provides for public funding of presidential campaigns, as discussed above. As they seek a major-party presidential nomination, candidates become eligible for public funds by raising at least $5,000 in individual contributions of $250 or less in each of 20 states. Candidates who reach this threshold may apply for federal funds to match, on a dollar-for-dollar basis, all individual contributions of $250 or less that they receive. Currently, candidates who accept matching funds may spend no more than $48.07 million, including the matching funds, in their presidential primary campaigns. The funds are drawn from the Presidential Election Campaign Fund. Major-party presidential candidates receive a lump sum (about $96 million in 2016) during the summer prior to the general election. They must meet all their general expenses from this money. Third-party candidates are eligible for public funding only if they received at least 5 percent of the vote in the previous presidential race. This stipulation effectively blocks preelection funding for third-party or independent candidates, although a third party that wins more than 5 percent of the vote can receive public funding after the election.

Under current law, no candidate is required to accept public funding for either the nominating races or the general presidential election. Candidates who do not accept public funding are not affected by any expenditure limits. In 2008, John McCain accepted public funding for the general election campaign, receiving $84 million, but Barack Obama declined, choosing to rely on his own fundraising prowess. Obama was ultimately able to outspend McCain by a wide margin. Candidates who accept public funding may not engage in fundraising for their own campaigns. Neither major-party candidate accepted public financing in 2012 or 2016. As a result, many observers believed that the 2008 race was the last time that a major-party candidate would forgo personal fundraising in favor of public funding.

The Candidates Themselves On the basis of the Supreme Court's 1976 decision in *Buckley v. Valeo*, the right of individuals to spend their *own* money to campaign for office is a constitutionally protected matter of free speech and is not subject to limitation.[41] Thus, extremely wealthy candidates often contribute millions of dollars to their own campaigns; Donald Trump, for example, spent millions of his own money on his 2016 campaign, as did Ross Perot in 1992 and 1996. The only exception to the *Buckley* rule concerns presidential candidates who accept federal funding for their general-election campaigns. Such individuals are limited to $50,000 in personal spending.

● How Voters Decide

Identify the major factors that influence voters' decisions

Even if well-funded groups and powerful individuals influence the electoral process, it is the millions of individual decisions on Election Day that ultimately determine electoral outcomes. Sooner or later the choices of voters weigh more heavily than the schemes of campaign advisers or the leverage of interest groups.

Three factors influence voters' decisions at the polls: partisan loyalty, issues and policy preferences, and candidate characteristics.

Partisan Loyalty

Most voters feel a certain sense of identification or kinship with the Democratic Party or the Republican Party. This sense of identification is often handed down from parents to children and reinforced by social and cultural ties (see Chapter 9). Partisan identification predisposes voters to favor their party's candidates and oppose those of the other party (see Figure 10.4). At the level of the presidential contest, issues and candidate personalities may become very important. But partisanship is more likely to assert itself in the less visible races, where issues and the candidates are not as well known. State legislative races, for example, are often decided by voters' partisanship.

Once formed, voters' partisan loyalties seldom change. Individuals tend to keep their party affiliations unless some crisis causes them to reexamine the bases of their loyalties and to conclude that they have not given their support to the appropriate party. During these relatively infrequent periods of electoral change, millions of voters can change their party ties. For example, at the beginning of the

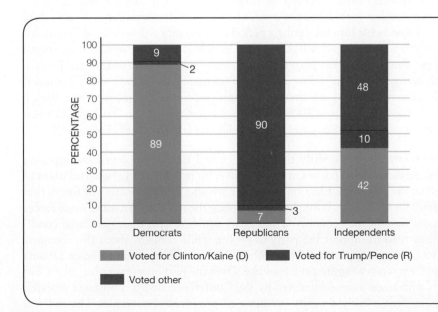

FIGURE 10.4

The Effect of Party Identification on the Vote, 2016

In 2016 around 90 percent of Democrats and Republicans supported their party's presidential candidate. Should candidates devote their resources to converting voters who identify with the opposition or to winning more support among independents? What factors might make it difficult for candidates to simultaneously pursue both courses of action?

New Deal era, between 1932 and 1936, millions of former Republicans transferred their allegiance to Franklin Roosevelt and the Democrats.

Issues and Policy Preferences

Policy preferences are a second factor influencing voters' choices at the polls. Voters may cast their ballots for the candidate whose position on economic issues they believe to be closest to their own or the candidate who has what they believe to be the best record on foreign policy or immigration. Though candidates for the presidency or Congress are often held accountable for the economy, other policy issues vary in importance depending on the election. In the 2016 election, for example, Donald Trump made curbing immigration a key issue in his campaign for the presidency. If candidates articulate and publicize very different positions on important policy issues, voters are more likely to be able to identify and act on whatever policy preferences they may have.

The ability of voters to make choices on the basis of policy preferences is diminished, however, if competing candidates do not differ substantially or do not focus their campaigns on policy matters. Often, candidates deliberately take the safe course and emphasize positions that will not offend any voters, trumpeting, for example, their opposition to corruption, crime, and inflation. Such a strategy, though perfectly rational, makes it extremely difficult for voters to make their issue or policy preferences the basis for their choices at the polls.

Voters' issue choices usually involve a mix of their judgments about the past behavior of competing parties and candidates and their hopes and fears about candidates' future behavior. Political scientists call choices that focus on future behavior **prospective voting**, whereas those based on past performance are called **retrospective voting**. Retrospective economic voting, in which voters evaluate candidates on the strength of the economy, has been found to be more important that prospective voting. To some extent, whether prospective or retrospective evaluation is more important in a particular election depends on the strategies of competing candidates. Candidates always endeavor to define the issues of an election in terms that will serve their interests. Incumbents running during a period of prosperity will seek to take credit for the economy's strength and will define the election as revolving around their record of success. This strategy encourages voters to make retrospective judgments. By contrast, an insurgent running during a period of economic uncertainty will tell voters it is time for a change and ask them to make prospective judgments. Thus, Barack Obama focused on change in 2008 and the need to stay course in 2012 and, through well-crafted media campaigns, was able to define voters' agenda of choices.

The Economy As we identify the strategies and tactics employed by opposing political candidates and parties, we should keep in mind that the best-laid plans of politicians often go awry. Election outcomes are affected by a variety of forces that candidates for office cannot fully control. Among the most important of these forces is the condition of the economy. If voters are satisfied with their economic conditions, they tend to support the party in power, while concern about the economy tends to favor the opposition. Thus, the 2008 financial crisis gave Barack Obama and the Democrats a significant advantage. Over the past quarter-century, the Consumer Confidence Index, calculated by the Conference Board, a business research group, has been a fairly accurate predictor of presidential outcomes. The index is based on surveys asking voters how optimistic they are about the future of the economy. It would appear that a generally rosy view, indicated by a score over 100,

prospective voting voting based on the imagined future performance of a candidate or political party

retrospective voting voting based on the past performance of a candidate or political party

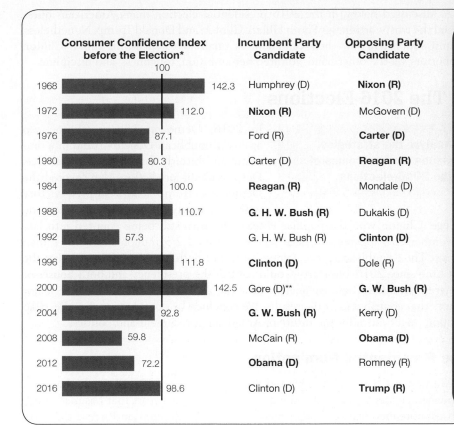

Consumer Confidence Index before the Election*

Year	Index	Incumbent Party Candidate	Opposing Party Candidate
1968	142.3	Humphrey (D)	**Nixon (R)**
1972	112.0	**Nixon (R)**	McGovern (D)
1976	87.1	Ford (R)	**Carter (D)**
1980	80.3	Carter (D)	**Reagan (R)**
1984	100.0	**Reagan (R)**	Mondale (D)
1988	110.7	**G. H. W. Bush (R)**	Dukakis (D)
1992	57.3	G. H. W. Bush (R)	**Clinton (D)**
1996	111.8	**Clinton (D)**	Dole (R)
2000	142.5	Gore (D)**	**G. W. Bush (R)**
2004	92.8	**G. W. Bush (R)**	Kerry (D)
2008	59.8	McCain (R)	**Obama (D)**
2012	72.2	**Obama (D)**	Romney (R)
2016	98.6	Clinton (D)	**Trump (R)**

FIGURE 10.5

Consumer Confidence and Presidential Elections

Since 1968 the Consumer Confidence Index has been a fairly reliable predictor of incumbents' political fortunes. Was the result of the 2016 election consistent with this trend? What issues other than the economy influenced the 2016 election?

*Survey was bimonthly prior to 1977 so figures for 1968, 1972, and 1976 are for October and they are for September from 1983 on.
**Gore won the popular vote, but Bush was elected by the electoral college.
NOTE: A score above 100 means most people are optimistic about the economy. A score below 100 means most people are pessimistic about the economy. The candidate who won the election appears in bold.
SOURCE: The Conference Board, www.conference-board.org/data/consumerdata.cfm (accessed 10/25/16).

bodes well for the party in power. An index score under 100, indicating that voters are pessimistic about the economy's trend, suggests that incumbents should worry about their own job prospects (see Figure 10.5). In 2016 personal economic conditions were an important factor in explaining voter decisions in the election.

Candidate Characteristics

Candidates' personal attributes always influence voters' decisions. The more important candidate characteristics that affect voters' choices are race, ethnicity, religion, gender, geography, and social background. In general, voters may be proud to see someone of their gender or of their ethnic, religious, or geographic background in a position of leadership. They may presume that such candidates are likely to have views and perspectives close to their own. This is why, for many years, politicians sought to "balance the ticket," making certain that their party's ticket included members of as many important groups as possible.

Just as candidates' personal characteristics may attract some voters, they may repel others. Some voters are prejudiced against candidates from certain ethnic, racial, or religious groups. And for many years, voters were reluctant to support the candidacies of women, although this appears to be changing. Indeed, the fact that the 2008 Democratic candidate was a black man and the 2016 Democratic candidate a woman indicates the increasing diversity of candidates for public office.

Voters also pay attention to candidates' personality characteristics, such as "decisiveness," "honesty," and "vigor." In recent years, integrity has become a key election issue.

for critical analysis

What factors influence voters' choices? What factors matter most to you when you decide how to cast your ballot?

As discussed below, in the 2016 presidential election many Americans questioned the trustworthiness of both Hillary Clinton and Donald Trump. Nonetheless, Trump supporters saw their candidate as unafraid to speak his mind. Clinton supporters, on the other hand, admired her ambition, toughness, and discipline.

● The 2016 Elections

> **Analyze the strategies, issues, and outcomes of the 2016 elections**

In 2016, Democrat Hillary Clinton ran against Republican Donald Trump in a dramatic and bitterly fought presidential race. Despite media predictions that favored the Democrats, Trump won a surprise victory with a majority of votes in the electoral college. Clinton won the popular vote; with votes still being counted into late November, she appeared to have received around 2.5 million more votes than Trump. The Republicans also retained control of both houses of Congress. For the first time since 2010, one party would control the presidency and both houses of Congress. In this section, we analyze how the 2016 race unfolded and the major factors that contributed to the results. We conclude by considering what the 2016 election might mean for the future of American government and politics.

The Presidential Nomination

As we saw in Chapter 9, the United States' two major political parties have experienced an ideological realignment during the past 50 years that has made both parties more ideologically homogeneous. Today, the Republican Party is the party of conservatives, while the Democratic Party is more progressive and liberal. But within each party there are growing differences. The Democratic camp includes different varieties of liberal opinion ranging from traditional social welfare liberalism, which traces its roots to the New Deal, to left-liberal progressivism, which envisions an expanded role for the federal government. The Republican camp, too, includes many shades of conservative opinion, from business conservatives who support reducing government regulation and taxes to social conservatives who oppose abortion and same-sex marriage. In 2016 each party's nomination was sharply contested by candidates representing different factions within the two parties and by "outsider" populist candidates.

The Democratic Primaries On the Democratic side, Hillary Clinton faced a serious challenge from Vermont senator Bernie Sanders, a left-liberal progressive and self-described Democratic Socialist. Though Clinton's experience, control of the party machinery, support in minority communities, and fund-raising prowess seemed to make her nomination a foregone conclusion, Sanders mounted an aggressive candidacy that gained momentum in large part through mobilizing young voters. Sanders's populist platform called for a political revolution to counter political corruption, corporate influence, and inequality. To many young people who came of age in the twenty-first century, Clinton seemed associated with the "old" politics of corruption, compromise, and special interests. While Clinton focused on traditional social programs, health care, foreign policy, and trade, Sanders appeared to promise bold new ideas, including reducing income inequality, creating free college tuition, and aggressively combating climate change. Both candidates favored raising taxes on the wealthy and addressing racial inequality in the justice system.

Though outmatched in money and organization, Sanders proved a tough competitor. He was widely seen as more trustworthy and "authentic" than Clinton, especially by young Americans. The Democratic caucuses and primaries saw very high voter turnout, just short of the historical record set in 2008. Young voters under 30 overwhelmingly supported Sanders, who won more of their votes than Clinton and Trump combined.[42] In the 2016 Iowa caucuses, the nation's first nominating event, Clinton beat Sanders by less than 1 percentage point. This early win, albeit by a slim margin, helped propel Clinton to victory for her party; but the primary was close enough to extend well into the spring. Clinton did not secure enough delegates to ensure the nomination until just six weeks before the Democratic National Convention in July. Ultimately, Sanders won 43 percent of the Democratic primary vote and carried 23 states compared to Clinton's 34.

The close competition between Sanders and Clinton highlighted divisions within the party and led to claims that the rules to select the Democratic nominee were not fair. Clinton's support among superdelegates helped secure her win over Sanders, even though throughout the primaries both candidates were in almost a dead heat in terms of the popular vote. As we saw in Chapter 9, superdelegates are party elites who are not bound to the voting results in their state primaries. To many Sanders supporters these rules seemed undemocratic, even while some studies found that Clinton would likely have won the nomination even without the superdelegates.[43] Furthermore, leaked emails from members of the Democratic National Committee revealed that party leaders, including chair Debbie Wasserman Schultz, favored Clinton over Sanders. This revelation fueled further claims that the system was undemocratic and that party insiders were actively undermining the Sanders campaign. Although Sanders eventually endorsed Clinton at the Democratic National Convention, many Democrats also worried that the bitter primary fight weakened her candidacy in the general election.

In the summer of 2016, emails from the Democratic National Committee were leaked, revealing that party leaders who purported to be neutral favored Hillary Clinton over Bernie Sanders. At the national convention, Sanders supporters protested what they felt was a corrupt system.

The Republican Primaries On the Republican side, the conflict over the 2016 presidential nomination laid bare even deeper divisions within the party. Seventeen candidates competed in the Republican primaries, from "establishment" candidates such as Jeb Bush and Marco Rubio to libertarian Rand Paul and social conservatives such as Ted Cruz. Real estate mogul and reality-TV star Donald Trump was an "outsider" populist candidate, claiming to represent the interests of the people. Trump was the first major-party presidential candidate since 1940 who had neither elected political experience nor military experience. His platform included harsher immigration laws, bringing jobs back to America, cleaning up corruption in politics, and increasing military strength. Trump's ideology more closely mirrored that of European nationalistic candidates than traditional mainstream conservatives in the United States and contributed to the divides within the Republican Party.

As the Republican race got under way, Donald Trump was not taken seriously as a presidential candidate by most pundits and party leaders. During the Republican primaries, however, Trump campaigned cleverly, making use of social media, especially Twitter, and the propensity of the broadcast media to focus on sound bites and sensationalism. At the first televised Republican presidential primary debate in August 2015, Trump sought to drive the agenda by insulting his rivals and making bold and even outlandish political claims that served to make his opponents'

for critical analysis

Turnout in the 2016 primaries (around 28 percent) was higher than average but still represented only a small fraction of eligible voters. If more people voted in primaries, would that affect which candidates are chosen? How?

carefully developed talking points seem pale and boring. Throughout the course of his campaign, Trump continued to command headlines with controversial and incendiary comments, including his assertions that he would build a wall along the U.S.–Mexican border and place a temporary ban on Muslim immigration to the United States. As Trump's provocative statements dominated the news media for much of the primary season, other Republican candidates faded into the background.

The 2016 Republican primaries were historic both in terms of competition within a crowded field of candidates and in terms of voter turnout. Trump was the plurality winner with roughly 40 percent of the popular vote in the primaries. Trump won more votes (over 13 million) in the presidential primaries than any Republican candidate in history, but he also received more votes *against* him than any candidate in history, with 16 million votes cast for other Republican candidates. Within the Republican Party Trump gained the votes from far-right conservatives, including nationalists, isolationists, and those suspicious of free trade, as well as from many working-class white men. Social conservatives were concerned about what they saw as Trump's personal moral deficiencies as a man who had been married three times and who often spoke in vulgar terms, but most were willing to overlook these, especially when he named one of their own, Mike Pence, as his running mate. Business conservatives, including the Bush family and the 2012 Republican presidential nominee Mitt Romney, were strongly opposed to Trump. Business conservatives speak for Wall Street and those elements of the American business community that benefit from free trade and open access to world markets. They viewed Trump's opposition to free trade and his nationalism as serious threats to the world order that they had forged and from which they continued to profit. Many of these party elites endorsed Trump reluctantly once he secured the nomination, while others refused to support him at all, vowing instead to focus on electing Republicans to Congress. But to many Americans, Trump seemed authentic—a candidate with a bold vision he was not afraid to assert. As the nominee, he seemed to represent a large percentage of Americans who have felt disenfranchised and left behind in recent years as the status quo is changing.

The General Election

With their parties' nominations in hand, Clinton and Trump faced one another in the general election. Clinton seemed to possess several critical advantages, especially the Democrats' apparent edge in the electoral college. Based on voting patterns in recent elections, states with a total of roughly 217 electoral votes were considered either safely Democratic or favorable to the Democrats. States with another 32 electoral votes leaned toward the Democrats, potentially putting the Democratic candidate within 21 of the 270 votes needed to win. The Republicans, by contrast, could generally only count on around 191 electoral votes from reliably "red" states. Moreover, Democratic candidates usually get support from the most dynamic and rapidly growing segments of the electorate—namely, minority voters and immigrants—along with women and young people. The GOP, on the other hand, relies primarily on the votes of white Americans, especially men, who represent a declining fraction of the electorate. As recently as 1976, 89 percent of the electorate was white, while in

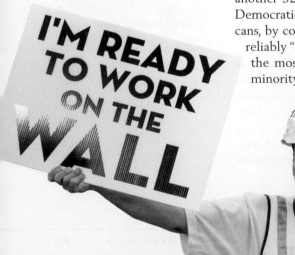

Donald Trump's provocative campaign rhetoric, including a promise to build a wall at the U.S.–Mexican border, helped energize supporters and generate media coverage.

2016 only about 69 percent was white.[44] Clinton also entered the race with an enormous fund-raising edge over Trump (see below). This ultimately allowed the former secretary of state to spend more than twice as much as her rival.

The Trump campaign was confident that it would be able to overcome the Democrats' advantages. Trump believed that his appeal to blue-collar white voters would make him competitive in Democratic strongholds in Midwestern states. He also calculated that he would increase Republican support among white voters sufficiently to offset the Democratic edge among nonwhite voters. Moreover, Trump hoped that his provocative style would continue to encourage extensive free media coverage, offsetting Clinton's fund-raising advantage and ability to spend on paid campaign ads.

As the general-election race kicked off, several trends emerged. First, Clinton and Trump were the two most disliked presidential nominees in modern American history. Both candidates had far lower favorability ratings than past presidential candidates, and as scandals raged on throughout the general-election campaign, many Americans reported that the election left them feeling "disgusted."[45]

Second, gender played a significant, though ultimately not decisive, role in 2016. Not only did this election see the first female presidential candidate for a major party, but gender issues were also headline news throughout much of the election. Donald Trump made comments about women that many people deemed offensive. Similar past comments of his were unearthed, including a recording from 2005 (discussed below) where Trump was heard talking about women in a lewd manner, bragging about actions that many felt, if true, amounted to sexual assault. The Trump campaign countered that Clinton's husband had also treated women inappropriately and that Clinton herself had been involved in aggressive efforts to discredit those women's claims. Nonetheless, by November, exit polls showed a gender gap of 13 percentage points, with 54 percent of women supporting Clinton compared with 41 percent of men.

Third, the media played an outsized role in 2016. Many observers, including President Obama, criticized the media for focusing excessively on Trump, with the goal of making headlines and viral news. In the general election, Trump received more than double the free media attention than Clinton did.[46] He excelled on the campaign trail, tweeting his daily campaign messages and effectively writing his own headline news. At the same time, some people, including Trump himself, believed that the news media's political bias favored Clinton. Some Trump voters saw themselves as voting against the "liberal media."

And fourth, money mattered—and it didn't. Most modern presidential elections have seen major-party candidates with similar campaign spending and organization. In 2012, the major-party candidates and their Super PACs both raised and spent roughly $1 billion each. But 2016 was characterized by lopsided campaign spending: Clinton raised and spent double the amount of the Trump campaign. According to opensecrets.org, as of October 2016 Clinton had raised nearly $500 million, with an additional $189 million from outside money (Super PACs) compared to just $247 million raised by Trump's campaign and $59 million from Super PACs. The Clinton campaign also had superior organization, with more field offices than the Trump campaign in almost every state. However, Trump's enormous free media coverage (estimated to be worth $1 billion) helped offset Clinton's campaign advantages as he didn't need to spend as much on television ads.

Finally, both campaigns calculated that the opposing candidate was quite vulnerable to personal attacks, so both campaigns as well as operatives associated with the Democratic and Republican parties invested months in opposition research, hoping to uncover information that would prove damaging to their rivals.

Personal Attacks, Scandal, and Campaign Strategy From the earliest years of the Republic, personal attacks have been an important weapon in the arsenals of competing political forces. The Jeffersonian press, for example, made much of Alexander Hamilton's illegitimate birth, while the papers allied with Hamilton raised many questions about Thomas Jefferson's parentage, religious beliefs, and alleged sexual improprieties. Modern-day politics is an extension of these practices, and the 2016 campaign seemed to many observers to represent a new phase in aggressive mudslinging.

Leading up to the presidential election, Republicans opened fire in 2015 by launching a congressional investigation of Hillary Clinton's role in the deaths of U.S. embassy officials in Benghazi, Libya, and another investigation of Clinton's use of a private email server to handle official State Department correspondence during her tenure as secretary of state. Democrats charged that the primary purpose of these investigations was to damage Clinton's reputation as it was presumed that she would be the 2016 Democratic presidential nominee. While neither investigation led to formal charges against Clinton, both served to convince many Americans that the former secretary of state was dishonest and untrustworthy. During the course of the race, WikiLeaks made available a large quantity of hacked Clinton emails, which painted an unflattering portrait of Clinton and her inner circle. The leaks seemed to show a candidate who said different things in public and private, who had used her position as secretary of state to obtain favorable treatment for donors to her foundation, and who seemed disconnected from ordinary Americans. Democrats disputed the content of the leaks and suggested that WikiLeaks had been given its information by the Russian government, which had launched hacks as part of an effort to influence the American election.

For their part, Democratic opposition researchers had begun to develop a dossier on Trump as soon as he emerged as a potential GOP candidate. Democrats latched onto his many controversial remarks—such as his comments about women and statements blaming illegal immigrants for drugs, rape, and other crime—labeling them as offensive and Trump as xenophobic, racist, and sexist. On October 7, 2016, with one month before the November election, the *Washington Post* released a video from 2005 that showed Trump making lewd comments about women and boasting about how his celebrity status gave him license to touch women inappropriately—comments that many people felt condoned sexual assault. The release of the tape was followed by allegations from more than a dozen women who reported having experienced unwanted sexual advances by Trump or who accused the candidate of sexual assault. Most of these accounts concerned events that had taken place some years prior, and Trump contested their veracity. However, an increasingly unflattering image of Trump emerged. The video, which Trump could not dispute, created explosive negative media coverage and a sharp drop in his polling numbers.

Another issue was Trump's failure to release his tax returns, unprecedented among major-party presidential candidates during the last four decades. In the second general-election debate, Trump acknowledged that he had not paid federal income taxes for decades, implying that he had taken advantage of legal loopholes. Investigative journalism revealed a 1995 tax return showing that Trump claimed $916 million in losses, which enabled him to avoid paying federal income taxes.[47]

Widely publicized reports also exposed Trump's long history of questionable business dealings, including his multiple casino bankruptcies, his refusal to pay contractors for work they had done, his employment of undocumented workers, and an ongoing fraud investigation of Trump University.

Following these revelations, by mid-October most polls showed Clinton with a strong lead over Trump. Other remarks that Trump had made during the debates, including the statement that he would imprison Clinton if he won and his refusal to state that he would accept a losing result on Election Day, set off intense criticism from the Democrats. Eleven days before the election, however, the scandal and personal attacks turned back on Clinton. FBI director James Comey sent a letter to Congress saying his agency was investigating 650,000 newly discovered emails that could be pertinent to their earlier investigation of Clinton's use of a private email server during her time as secretary of state. The letter effectively reopened the investigation of Clinton's mishandling of email communications and the possibility of a national security breach, and the Trump campaign capitalized on the announcement as further proof of Clinton's alleged corruption. The FBI in turn faced a torrent of criticism, including from the Department of Justice, Senate Democratic leader Harry Reid, and President Obama. Critics said the agency's actions may have been unlawful for interfering in a presidential election so close to Election Day. Two days before the election, Comey announced that the emails in fact did not support new charges; and as Americans went to the polls, most analysts gave Clinton a 70 to 80 percent chance of winning. Based on Clinton's apparently comfortable lead, the Democrats also hoped to take the Senate back from the Republicans by winning at least five additional seats in 2016.

Understanding the 2016 Results

In the end, the 2016 presidential election was a historic upset in which the national media and the polling forecasts got it wrong. On election night, the forecasts swung wildly, from the earlier predictions of a safe Clinton victory to reports indicating a Trump victory by wide margins. Many Americans who had been following the opinion polls and media analyses before the election were stunned by Trump's surprise win and by the Republicans' success in retaining control of both houses of Congress.

Trump swept every southern state and nearly all of the Midwest. He won most of the 15 battleground states that were considered competitive in the 2016 election. First winning Florida by just 1 percentage point, then Ohio by a solid margin, he went on to "flip" several more states that Barack Obama had carried in 2012. Trump's unexpected success in the northern industrial states of Michigan, Wisconsin, and Pennsylvania—all of which had gone to Obama in 2012—ultimately tipped the balance, leading to his victory in the electoral college (see Figure 10.6 and the "Who Are Americans?" feature on the facing page). For only the fourth time in U.S. history the candidate who won the electoral college did not win the popular vote. Trump prevailed in the electoral college with 306 votes to Clinton's 232 votes, but Hillary Clinton won the popular vote by around 2 percent, or approximately 2.5 million votes (based on preliminary tallies).

Voter Turnout Approximately 59 percent of eligible voters participated in the 2016 general election.[48] In 2016, 136 million ballots were cast (from a total of 231 million eligible voters), numbers close to the modern record of 62 percent turnout and more than 134 million ballots cast in the presidential election between Barack Obama and John McCain in 2008. The 2016 election saw high rates of early voting and a high number of first-time voters, many of whom were mobilized by Donald Trump's campaign. Youth turnout in 2016 was around 50 percent, an increase from 2012 but still lower than the average of 56 percent across all age groups. The surge that had been predicted in Latino and female

for critical analysis

In 2016, more Americans chose Hillary Clinton for president, but Donald Trump won the electoral college and thus the presidency. Should the electoral college system be replaced?

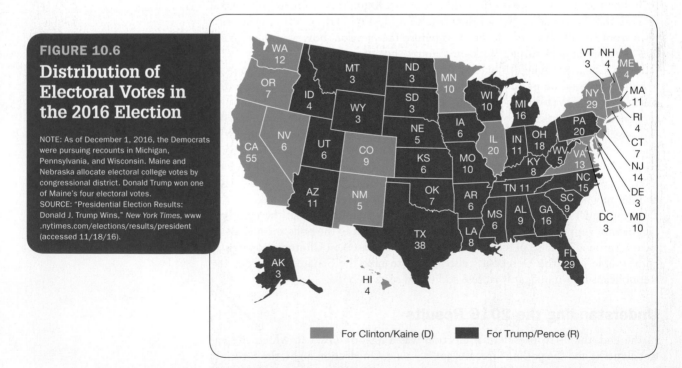

FIGURE 10.6

Distribution of Electoral Votes in the 2016 Election

NOTE: As of December 1, 2016, the Democrats were pursuing recounts in Michigan, Pennsylvania, and Wisconsin. Maine and Nebraska allocate electoral college votes by congressional district. Donald Trump won one of Maine's four electoral votes.
SOURCE: "Presidential Election Results: Donald J. Trump Wins," *New York Times*, www.nytimes.com/elections/results/president (accessed 11/18/16).

For Clinton/Kaine (D)   For Trump/Pence (R)

Who Supported Trump in 2016?

Donald Trump won enough votes in the electoral college to defeat Hillary Clinton in the 2016 presidential election, though he lost the popular vote. The map in Figure 10.6, to the left, shows who won each state; there, red clearly dominates. If we adjust the map to show each state in proportion to its population (below), red states still dominate, but there is more blue on the map, reflecting the fairly tight race.

Election Results by State's Population

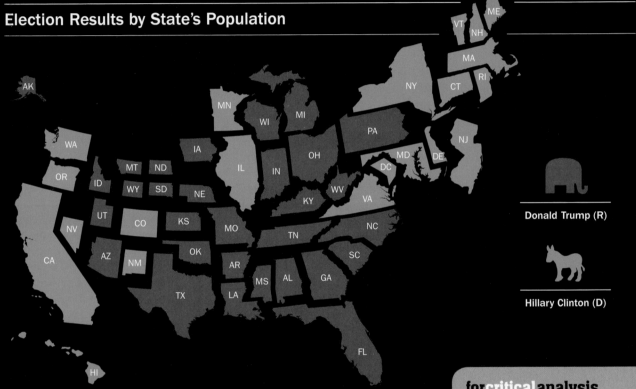

Donald Trump (R)

Hillary Clinton (D)

Votes in Electoral College

55 California	10 Maryland	06 Utah
38 Texas	10 Minnesota	05 New Mexico
29 Florida	10 Wisconsin	05 Nebraska
29 New York	10 Missouri	05 West Virginia
20 Illinois	09 Colorado	04 Hawaii
20 Pennsylvania	09 Alabama	03 / 01 Maine
18 Ohio	09 South Carolina	04 New Hampshire
16 Michigan	08 Louisiana	04 Rhode Island
16 Georgia	08 Kentucky	04 Idaho
15 North Carolina	07 Connecticut	03 Delaware
14 New Jersey	07 Oregon	03 District Of Columbia
13 Virginia	07 Oklahoma	03 Vermont
12 Washington	06 Iowa	03 Alaska
11 Massachusetts	06 Nevada	03 Montana
11 Indiana	06 Arkansas	03 North Dakota
11 Arizona	06 Kansas	03 South Dakota
11 Tennessee	06 Mississippi	03 Wyoming

for critical analysis

1. Clinton won three of the five states with the largest populations: California, New York, and Illinois. How are these states different from states with smaller populations? What do these differences tell us about the political differences between more densely populated areas (urban areas) and those with lower populations (rural areas)?

2. What do you think causes the differences between urban and rural America? Do you think these differences will continue long into the future?

voter turnout did not occur.[49] Turnout across many demographic groups remained similar to 2012, but as we will see below, a shift among working-class white voters away from the Democratic Party and changes in younger voters' preferences gave Trump the advantage.

Voters' Choices Trump's popularity among working-class white Americans was crucial to his winning coalition. This demographic group had the most negative views of the economy and was generally opposed to the trade policies favored by the Democrats and mainstream conservatives. Many voters looked to Trump to bring back factory jobs that had moved overseas and saw Clinton as representing Wall Street, government, and—as one Trump ad put it—"more of the same." According to exit polls, Trump won 67 percent of the votes among whites without a college degree compared to just 28 percent for Clinton—a 14 percentage point gain for Trump compared with the Republican vote from this group in 2012. This support enabled Trump to build a winning coalition that also included traditional Republican partisans. He won 90 percent of the votes among registered Republicans, 81 percent of the vote among ideological conservatives, and 81 percent among white born-again or evangelical Christians. The exit polls revealed that Trump also earned more of the votes among men, white voters in general, and voters over age 45. He did better among blacks and Hispanics than had been expected. Among respondents who felt the country was "seriously off track," Trump won almost 70 percent of their votes.[50]

Among those who felt the country was generally going in the right direction, Hillary Clinton won 90 percent support. Clinton also received a majority of votes from women, African Americans, Latinos, Asian Americans, and college-educated voters, although blacks and Latinos voted at slightly lower rates for Clinton than they had for Obama four years earlier. She won 71 percent of the votes of nonwhite college graduates and 75 percent of nonwhite individuals without a college degree. Young voters favored Clinton (55 percent compared to only 37 percent for Trump). Four years earlier the youth vote had helped elect Barack Obama, but some young voters who supported Bernie Sanders in the Democratic primary in 2016 remained opposed to Clinton. High youth support for third-party candidates (10 percent, up from 3 percent in 2012) meant lower support for the Democratic candidate. In the swing states of Michigan, Pennsylvania, and Wisconsin, votes for third-party candidates may have cost Clinton those very close races. In the weeks following, Clinton supporters called for recounts in these states.

While less media coverage was devoted to policy issues in 2016 than in previous elections, the issues mattered. Clinton won more votes from individuals who felt foreign policy or the economy was the most important issue. Trump won more votes from those who felt immigration or terrorism was most important. Among voters saying their preferred candidate could bring needed change, 83 percent favored Trump. Among voters who said their preferred candidate had the right experience, 90 percent favored Clinton. In the end, a desire for change edged out the importance of experience.

Why Were the Media Predictions So Wrong? Most of the media consistently underestimated the strength of Trump's support and national movement throughout the campaign. The polls and the election forecasts based on those polls turned out to be inaccurate, and the media did not take full account of the anger that a large portion of the electorate felt over economic insecurity and threats to their jobs.

Two groups that were crucial to Trump's success were men and white working-class voters. White working-class voters in particular were unhappy with the economy and turned to Trump to bring factory jobs back to the United States. Here, Trump supporters celebrate his victory on election night.

In 2008 many national opinion polls underestimated support for Barack Obama. After the election, analysts concluded that the samples used in those opinion polls didn't include enough Latinos, a group that has a higher proportion of people who are difficult to reach by phone, and who supported the Democrats by a significant margin. In 2016 many polls didn't include enough non-college-educated white voters, independents, or people who had not previously voted in elections. These individuals can be hard reach, as they may lack expensive landline phones and may be often unavailable via cell phones—but they turned out to be crucial to Trump's victory. (See Chapter 6 for additional discussion of polling errors in 2016.) Without an accurate picture of these citizens' opinions, most media outlets missed the boat and portrayed Clinton and the Democrats in the lead, right up until the actual vote counts started coming in. Because the election was considered "safe" for Clinton, such forecasts may have demobilized Democrats, reducing voter turnout as well as voter mobilization efforts and campaign fundraising.

Congressional Races and Ballot Measures Because Clinton and Trump were so disliked, a record number of people opted out of voting for president at all and only voted on lower-level races.[51] However, most voters appeared to vote straight-ticket, from the president down to lower-ballot races, which helped the Republican Party to retain its control of Congress, with 51 of the 100 seats in the Senate and a majority (239) of the 435 seats in the House. Despite earlier concerns that some of Trump's controversial statements would hurt other candidates from his party, most competitive Senate races went to the Republicans, especially in states that Trump carried. The

Democrats' hopes of winning control of the Senate were dashed as they only won two of the five additional seats they would have needed for a majority.

The 2016 election also featured some high-profile ballot-measure contests, including Maine's referendum vote to become the first state to use ranked choice voting (see earlier section) for all state and federal elections.[52] California voters adopted Proposition 64, legalizing recreational marijuana in the nation's most populous state. Similar ballot measures for recreational marijuana were also adopted in Maine, Massachusetts, and Nevada. Minimum-wage measures were popular at the ballot box. Voters in Arizona, Colorado, Ohio, and Washington approved measures to raise wages. With few federal restrictions on guns, voters adopted ballot measures to restrict access to guns in Nevada, California, and Washington state. Colorado voters rejected a ballot measure that would have established a single-payer health insurance system known as ColoradoCare.[53]

Ramifications of the 2016 Election

As the long and bitterly fought 2016 election drew to a close, President-elect Trump, President Obama, Hillary Clinton, and a host of commentators and pundits declared that it was time to bring the nation back together. It seemed more likely, however, that competing political forces would lick their wounds and move their battles from the electoral arena to the nation's capital. The election also raised questions about several key political institutions and public trust in those institutions.

Trump's Agenda During the course of his campaign, Trump had outlined an ambitious agenda of domestic and foreign policies. With the House and Senate in Republican hands, Democrats would be hard-pressed to block Trump's efforts. Democratic congressional leaders, nevertheless, prepared to wage pitched and possibly prolonged battles over several major issues.

One of the first issues facing Trump concerned the appointment of a new Supreme Court justice to replace the late Antonin Scalia. After Scalia's death in early 2016, President Obama designated Merrick Garland, a moderate Democrat, as his replacement. Senate Republicans refused to move on the Garland nomination, which would have given the Court a 5–4 Democratic majority; and the seat remained open through the end of Obama's term. Trump promised that he would designate a conservative jurist, but Democrats vowed to battle any such nominee who, if confirmed, would restore the 5–4 conservative majority of the Scalia years. Some analysts predicted that this battle could produce a Democratic Senate filibuster (see Chapter 12) and a Republican effort to change Senate rules to bring an end to this long-standing tactic—an outcome that would have a major impact on both the Senate and the Court.

A second battle would be fought over the Affordable Care Act (colloquially known as Obamacare). During the campaign, Trump frequently asserted that the repeal or modification of Obamacare would be among his first priorities. For the most part, House and Senate Republicans agreed that Obamacare should be repealed, and many supported the idea of replacing it with health savings accounts. However, Democrats prepared to mount a fierce battle to defend health care.

Many of the other policies Trump proposed on the campaign trail also seemed likely to result in fierce conflicts in Congress. Trump famously declared that he would build a wall along the U.S. border with Mexico, prevent illegal immigrants from entering the country, and increase deportations of noncitizens who committed crimes in the United States. Much of the U.S.–Mexican border is already strongly fenced and heavily patrolled, but Democrats view the Hispanic community as an important constituency and will resist harsher immigration laws. Trump also promised to revisit America's trade and international environmental agreements to obtain terms more favorable to American firms and workers. Democrats argued that under the pretext of helping American workers Trump and the Republicans would undermine the health and safety rules that protect American workers, while offering unproductive but politically powerful American firms protection from foreign competition. Trump's foreign policies regarding China and Russia also faced opposition. Thus, it appeared that the conclusion of the election marked the end of just one battle in a longer struggle over the nation's future.

Questions about Parties and Future Elections The events of 2016 also raised major questions about the future of America's political parties and the viability of America's electoral processes. Donald Trump's candidacy upended the Republican Party. Most observers thought his unprecedented rejection by party elders would doom the Trump ticket. Trump, however, mobilized millions of blue-collar voters from traditionally Democratic constituencies to win the election. The question for Republicans was whether established GOP leaders would be able to reconcile themselves to the new GOP and work with Trump to permanently tie his followers to the Republican coalition. Republicans also needed to confront the fact that their party's base of support was overwhelmingly white and male in an increasingly diverse society.

For the Democrats, Hillary Clinton's defeat prompted leaders of the party's left-liberal wing to assert that the Democratic Party needed to embrace a more progressive platform of environmentalism, reduced military spending, and multiculturalism to recapture the White House. More moderate Democrats answered that Clinton was defeated because of her particular shortcomings, not her policy platform, and that a shift to the political left would wreck, rather than strengthen, the party.

Republicans and Democrats both were left to grapple with questions about the structure of America's electoral system. Should the parties reconsider their nominating rules? The GOP's open and fluid rules allowed the nomination to be captured by an outsider; the Democrats' more closed rules gave the nomination to a candidate with more support among party elites than voters. Moreover, was it finally time to reconsider the electoral college which produced a Trump victory even though Clinton won more popular votes?

Trust in Government after the 2016 Election As we saw in Chapter 1, the public's trust in government has been relatively low in recent decades, and the 2016 election may have not only reflected this trend but also contributed to it. Some observers worried that Trump's repeated claims of election fraud and rigged elections would cast doubt the ability of the government to hold free and fair elections. While Trump had raised eyebrows before the election by saying he might not accept the validity of the results, anti-Trump protesters after the election refuted the legitimacy of the outcome, chanting, "Not my president," and pointing to the fact that Clinton had won more popular votes. Trump's intense criticism of the national media throughout the campaign also challenged the important role of the media in informing the public. After the election, some Democrats added to this criticism by blaming the media for Clinton's defeat.

for critical analysis

In what ways did the 2016 election reflect Americans' decreased trust in government? In what ways did it contribute to that distrust?

Moreover, the high reliance on social media for news in 2016 may have affected the election. A study after the election showed that fake news stories, which are often circulated via Facebook and other social media, were more likely to go viral than authentic news stories.[54] The blurring of fact and fiction on social media made it difficult for the public to know what information to trust when it came to politics and government.

The 2016 election is now history, but the ways in which these trends and developments will shape the American political system in the future are yet to be seen.

Campaigns, Elections,
and Your Future

As politicians ponder the questions discussed above, individual Americans must think about what the 2016 election might mean for them. Will Republican economic policies create more jobs or leave Americans with less secure economic futures? What will Republican plans to eliminate Obamacare mean for Americans' access to medical services? Will Republican national security policies make us more or less safe? How will America's diverse communities be affected by potential GOP efforts to crack down on illegal immigration? Should we be more critical consumers of opinion polls and the political information circulated on social media?

Another question about elections concerns campaign finance and whose interests will be represented in government. Donald Trump was a unique candidate who was able to generate unprecedented free media coverage, but his campaign still raised and spent hundreds of millions of dollars, much of it collected as small donations from individuals. In a nation as large and diverse as the United States, to be sure, campaign contributors represent many different groups and, often, clashing interests. The fact remains, however, that those with more money will be able to give more and that, once in office, elected officials can be expected to represent the interests of those who supported them. The "**Who Participates?**" feature on page 413 shows who donated to the 2012 presidential campaign.

Two trends in campaign finance may play a role in how elections are funded in the future and, thus, who is elected to office and what policies are enacted. On the one hand, recent decisions by the Supreme Court have overturned federal laws that sought to set some limits on who could give and how much they could give. The laws existed in hopes of limiting the influence of affluent interests over the electoral process and government. But the Court has held that giving money is (in some circumstances) a form of political speech that is essential to the country's democratic process. Will moneyed interests continue to play a large role in the election process? What new laws may be needed to make the rules of the game fair? Will campaign spending increase to the point that the citizens of tomorrow enact reform for public financing or free media for all qualified candidates?

Who Donates to Political Campaigns?

Percentage of Adults Who Donated, 2012*

*To a political campaign, candidate, or organization

Income

11.2% | <$20k **15.4%** | $20–$40k **25.2%** | $40–$80k **38.9%** | $80k+

Age

13.5% | 18–25 **16.8%** | 26–44 **28%** | 45–64 **34%** | 65+

Education**

**Highest level attained

12.2% | High school or less **26.2%** | Some college **33.6%** | College diploma **44.2%** | Postgraduate degree

Sources of Funds in the 2012 Campaign

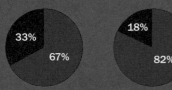

Obama — 33% / 67%
Romney — 18% / 82%

● Small individual contributions
● Large individual contributions ($200 or more)

SOURCES: Cooperative Congressional Election Study (CCES) 2012, www.projects.iq.harvard.edu/cces/home (accessed 12/15/15) and 2012 Presidential Race Fundraising, Open Secrets, www.opensecrets.org/pres12/ (accessed 12/22/15).

WHAT YOU CAN DO

Your Views on Money in Politics

 Track campaign contributions at the federal level at **www.opensecrets.org** and at the state level a **www.followthemoney.org**.

☑ If you're concerned about the role of money in politics, voice your opinion on social media platforms such as Facebook and Twitter.

☑ You can also contact groups working to raise awareness of the role of money in politics, such as Common Cause (**www.commoncause.org**), Move to Amend (**www.movetoamend.org**), or Democracy Is for People (**www.democracyisforpeople.org**).

studyguide

Elections in America

American elections are subject to many specific rules. The responsibility for administering elections rests mainly with states and counties, and most elections in the United States today use the Australian ballot and operate under a plurality, rather than a majority or proportional representation, system. Unlike members of the House of Representatives, who are elected through a direct vote from districts that are redrawn every 10 years, presidents are elected indirectly by the electoral college.

Key Terms

midterm elections (p. 371)

primary elections (p. 372)

general election (p. 372)

closed primary (p. 372)

open primary (p. 372)

majority system (p. 372)

runoff election (p. 372)

plurality system (p. 372)

proportional representation (p. 373)

straight-ticket voting (p. 373)

redistricting (p. 374)

gerrymandering (p. 375)

majority-minority district (p. 375)

grassroots politics (p. 376)

delegate (p. 378)

party platform (p. 379)

electoral college (p. 379)

ballot initiative (p. 381)

referendum (p. 381)

recall (p. 382)

Practice Quiz

1. A closed primary is a primary election in which
   a) one's vote is made public.
   b) only registered members of the party may vote.
   c) voters choose which party's primary they will participate in on the day of the primary.
   d) only two candidates are allowed to run.
   e) voting is conducted by mail.

2. To win under the plurality system used in most American elections a candidate must receive
   a) more than 50 percent of the popular vote.
   b) more than 50 percent in the runoff election.
   c) more than two-thirds of the popular vote.
   d) more than 75 percent of the popular vote.
   e) more votes than his or her opponents, regardless of the percentage.

3. When a voter casts a ballot for a party's presidential candidate and then "automatically" votes for the rest of that party's candidates, it is referred to as
   a) primary voting.
   b) one-way voting.
   c) proportional representation.
   d) straight-ticket voting.
   e) split-ticket voting.

4. If a state has 10 members in the U.S. House of Representatives, how many votes in the electoral college does that state have?
   a) 2
   b) 10
   c) 12
   d) 20
   e) The number of votes cannot be determined from this information.

Election Campaigns

Explain how campaigns are typically conducted (pp. 383–91)

In order to successfully run for national or statewide office, candidates must create formal campaign organizations that employ a campaign manager, a media consultant, a pollster, a financial adviser, a press spokesperson, and a staff director. Campaigns must decide on a message and a strategy for communicating that message to the voters they want to target.

Key Terms

campaign (p. 383)

incumbent (p. 383)

town hall meeting (p. 388)

Practice Quiz

5. An incumbent is a candidate who
   a) does not currently hold office.
   b) has the support of both major parties.
   c) already holds the office he or she is running for.
   d) has won his or her party's primary election.
   e) has been nominated at the party convention.

6. In nearly every election since 1980, the average amount of money spent by House incumbents to secure reelection has
   a) been about the same as the average amount of money spent by challengers.
   b) been less than the average amount of money spent by challengers.
   c) been greater than the average amount of money spent by challengers.
   d) been $0 due to federal laws that provide campaign funds for incumbents.
   e) been $1 million due to federal laws that provide campaign funds for incumbents.

Money and Politics

Describe how candidates raise the money they need to run (pp. 391–96)

Modern political campaigns in the United States are enormously expensive, and candidates with the most money often win. Supreme Court cases since the mid-1970s have removed many restrictions on campaign finance. Candidates finance their campaigns with money from individual donors, political action committees, political parties, and the candidates' own bank accounts. Election spending by Super PACs and non-profit groups must be independent of candidates' campaigns. The Federal Elections Campaign Act also provides for public funding of presidential campaigns.

Key Terms

political action committee (PAC) (p. 395)

527 committees (p. 395)

501(c)(4) committees (p. 395)

Practice Quiz

7. In *Buckley v. Valeo*, the Supreme Court ruled that
   a) PAC donations to campaigns are constitutionally protected.
   b) candidates cannot spend any of their own money to run for office.
   c) the right of individuals to spend their own money to campaign is constitutionally protected.
   d) there is no limit to the number of candidates to whom an individual can contribute.
   e) the Bipartisan Campaign Reform Act is unconstitutional.

8. The main difference between a 527 committee and a 501(c)(4) committee is that
   a) a 527 is not legally required to disclose where it gets its money while a 501(c)(4) is legally required to do so.
   b) a 501(c)(4) is not legally required to disclose where it gets its money while a 527 is legally required to do so.
   c) a 527 can only contribute to one campaign while a 501(c)(4) can contribute to many.
   d) a 501(c)(4) can only contribute to one campaign while a 527 can contribute to many.
   e) a 527 can legally coordinate its spending with a candidate's campaign while a 501(c)(4) cannot.

9. In the 2016 presidential election, public funding
   a) was accepted by both major-party candidates.
   b) was accepted by Hillary Clinton only.
   c) was accepted by Donald Trump only.
   d) was declined by both major-party candidates.
   e) was not available.

How Voters Decide

Identify the major factors that influence voters' decisions (pp. 396–400)

Three factors influence the decisions that voters make at the polls: partisan loyalty, issues and policy preferences, and candidate characteristics. Partisan attachments do not change frequently and are an important influence on which candidates a voter chooses to support. Voters may also consider the past and future behavior of competing parties and candidates. A candidate's race, ethnicity, religion, gender, and social background are also weighed by voters on Election Day.

Key Terms

prospective voting (p. 398)

retrospective voting (p. 398)

Practice Quiz

10. When a voter decides which candidate to vote for based on past performance, the voter is engaged in
    a) prospective voting.
    b) retrospective voting.
    c) introspective voting.
    d) straight-ticket voting.
    e) split-ticket voting.

11. The Consumer Confidence Index
    a) measures how business leaders rate the federal government's regulation of the economy during election years.
    b) was a federal government program designed to increase economic growth during the Reagan administration.
    c) has been an inaccurate predictor of presidential outcomes.
    d) has been a fairly accurate predictor of presidential outcomes.
    e) is based on government reports of objective economic indicators.

The 2016 Elections

Analyze the strategies, issues, and outcomes of the 2016 elections (pp. 400–12)

In 2016 voters elected Republican Donald Trump to the presidency even though the vast majority of pre-election polling showed Democrat Hillary Clinton in the lead. Republicans retained control of both the House of Representatives and the Senate. Throughout the 2016 campaigns both parties argued that they had a better plan for addressing the many challenges facing the nation.

Practice Quiz

12. In the 2016 general election, voters who said they felt the country and the economy were headed in the wrong direction were most likely to vote for
    a) Hillary Clinton
    b) Donald Trump
    c) Jill Stein
    d) Gary Johnson
    e) Jeb Bush

13. In 2016, Trump and the Republicans received a majority of votes from
    a) whites and Asian Americans
    b) whites, Latinos, and women
    c) whites and men
    d) African Americans and more affluent voters
    e) Latinos and young voters

14. Which of the following states flipped from Democratic to Republican in the 2016 election?
    a) Florida, Ohio, and Pennsylvania
    b) California, New York, and Massachusetts
    c) Texas, Alabama, and Kentucky
    d) West Virginia, Missouri, and Kansas
    e) Oregon, Washington, and Delaware

For Further Reading

Abramson, Paul, John Aldrich, and David Rohde. *Change and Continuity in the 2008 Elections*. Washington, DC: CQ Press, 2009.

Ackerman, Bruce, and Ian Avres. *Voting with Dollars*. New Haven, CT: Yale University Press, 2004.

Browning, Graeme. *Electronic Democracy*. New York: Cyberage, 2002.

Ginsberg, Benjamin, and Martin Shefter. *Politics by Other Means: Institutional Conflict and the Declining Significance of Elections in America*. New York: W. W. Norton, 1999.

Heilemann, John, and Mark Halperin. *Game Change: Obama and the Clintons, McCain and Palin, and the Race of a Lifetime*. New York: Harper, 2010.

Maass, Matthias. *The World Views of the 2008 U.S. Presidential Election*. New York: Palgrave, 2009.

Nelson, Michael, ed. *The Elections of 2008*. Washington, DC: CQ Press, 2009.

Polsby, Nelson, Aaron Wildavsky, and David Hopkins. *Presidential Elections*. 12th ed. New York: Rowman and Littlefield, 2007.

Raymond, Allen, and Ian Spiegelman. *How to Rig an Election*. New York: Simon & Schuster, 2008.

Schier, Steven. *You Call This an Election?* Washington, DC: Georgetown University Press, 2003.

Wayne, Stephen. *Is This Any Way to Run a Democratic Election?* 3rd ed. Washington, DC: CQ Press, 2007.

Recommended Websites

Dark Money
www.opensecrets.org/dark-money/
Dark money refers politically active organizations whose do not need to be disclosed. Learn more about how dark money spending works, and its growing influence on election campaigns.

ElectionMail.com
www.electionmail.com
Are you thinking about running for office? Whether you aspire to be student government president or president of the United States, here you can find links to affordable political printing, including political brochures, campaign literature, and campaign signs.

FairVote
www.fairvote.org
FairVote is dedicated to open access to voting, equal representation, and a voice for all Americans. Read about some of their electoral reform proposals such as runoff elections, proportional representation, and alternatives to the electoral college.

Federal Election Commission
www.fec.gov
The Federal Election Commission (FEC) is an independent government agency that was created in 1975 to administer and enforce the Federal Election Campaign Act. At the official FEC website you can read about the rules and regulations that govern the financing of federal elections and other topics of interest.

JibJab.com
www.jibjab.com
This website became famous for its political video clips during the 2004 presidential campaign. For a good laugh check out some of the political jokes or rummage through the video archives to find one of the original Bush or Kerry clips.

National Archives and Records Administration
www.archives.gov/federal-register/electoral-college/index.html
The National Archives and Records Administration's U.S. Electoral College page is a great resource on presidential elections. Find answers to frequently asked questions about our electoral system, read about how electors vote, or try predicting who will win the next presidential election with the electoral college calculator.

OpenSecrets.org
www.opensecrets.org
Campaign funds come from a variety of sources, including individual donors, political action committees, self-contributions, independent spending, parties, and public funding. At this site you can research funding for all federal officials, including your own members of Congress.

Pew Research Center, Election 2016
www.pewresearch.org/topics/2016-election/
Pew Research Center's resource for the 2016 presidential election includes survey data, facts, figures, and public opinion.

Project Vote Smart
www.votesmart.org
Project Vote Smart is a nonpartisan site dedicated to providing citizens with information on political candidates and elected officials. Here you can easily view a candidate's biographical information, position on issues, and voting record so that you can make an informed choice on Election Day.

Voter Information Services
www.vis.org
Voter Information Services is a nonpartisan, nonprofit organization dedicated to helping interested citizens learn about their elected members of Congress. Here you can obtain a Congressional Report Card for your members of Congress and find out where they stand on the issues.

The use of "fracking" to recover gas has brought environmental groups into conflict with the energy industry. Both sides have tried to influence government regulations related to fracking.

Groups and Interests

WHAT GOVERNMENT DOES AND WHY IT MATTERS For the past several years, environmental groups and the nation's energy industry have been locked in a struggle over the issue of "hydraulic fracking." This is a method for recovering natural gas trapped in shale formations deep beneath the earth's surface. The energy industry, which stands to make enormous profits from extracting the gas, asserts that fracking is the key to achieving American energy independence. Environmental groups, on the other hand, argue that fracking produces greenhouse gas emissions, undermines air quality, increases the risk of earthquakes and tremors, and contaminates drinking water, while discouraging investment in cleaner, renewable forms of energy.

Despite these environmental concerns, large sections of the United States, including land in New York, Pennsylvania, and Ohio, are being fracked for their natural gas. Environmental groups appear to be losing the battle. Why? First, fracking produces revenues and jobs. The second reason, though, is political. The energy industry, organized in groups such as the Natural Gas Alliance, the Independent Petroleum Association of America, and the American Gas Association, has deployed an army of nearly 800 lobbyists, including former members of Congress and other former high-ranking government officials, to promote their cause on Capitol Hill and in the state capitals. The industry has also spent tens of millions of dollars on advertising and campaign contributions—filling the coffers of Democrats and Republicans alike.

The case of fracking exemplifies the power of interest groups in action. Tens of thousands of organized groups have formed in the United States, ranging from civic associations to huge nationwide organizations such as the National Rifle Association (NRA), whose chief cause is opposition to restrictions on gun ownership, and Common Cause, a public interest group that advocates for such issues as limits on campaign spending. Despite the array of interest groups in American politics, however, not all interests are represented equally, and the results of competition among various interests are not always consistent with the common good. In this chapter we will examine the nature and consequences of interest group politics in the United States.

chaptergoals

- Describe the major types of interest groups and whom they represent (pp. 421–28)

- Describe how interest groups and social groups organize (pp. 428–34)

- Analyze why the number of interest and advocacy groups has grown in recent decades (pp. 434–36)

- Explain how interest groups try to influence government and policy (pp. 436–49)

Defining Interest Groups

Describe the major types of interest groups and whom they represent

Alexis de Tocqueville, a famous nineteenth-century French writer, once wrote that America was "a nation of joiners."[1] This defining characteristic of American political life has not changed since Tocqueville made his observation. Americans are much more likely to join political and social organizations than people in other countries, and America has more organized interest groups than other nations. Many believe this unique trend has a positive impact on democracy. But others worry that the power wielded by these groups can dominate Congress and the political process at the expense of average citizens and the public welfare.

The framers of the U.S. Constitution also feared the power that could be wielded by organized interests. Yet they believed that interest groups thrived because of liberty—the freedom that all Americans have to organize and to express their views. If the government were given the power to regulate or in any way to forbid efforts by organized interests to interpose themselves in the political process, it would in effect have the power to suppress liberty. The solution to this dilemma was presented by James Madison in the *Federalist Papers* no. 10:

> Take in a greater variety of parties and interests [and] you make it less probable that a majority of the whole will have a common motive to invade the rights of other citizens. . . . [Hence the advantage] enjoyed by a large over a small republic.[2]

According to Madison, a good government encourages multitudes of interests so that no single interest, which he called a "faction," can ever consistently dominate the others. Expanding the arena of contestation from local to state government and from state to the federal government should make it more likely that there are overlapping and cross-cutting interests (or factions) where a majority cannot systematically tyrannize a minority. The basic assumption is that all the competing interests will regulate one another, producing balance.[3]

Today, this Madisonian principle is called **pluralism**. Pluralism is a theory of democracy based on the balancing of interests in society via groups that compete for policy outcomes from government. While an interest group may lose on one issue, it may win on the next; and overall the vast majority of society will be represented in government. According to pluralist theory, all interests are and should be free to compete for influence. Moreover, according to the theory of pluralism, the outcome of this competition is compromise and moderation since no group is likely to be able to achieve any of its goals without accommodating itself to some of the views of its many competitors.[4]

Pluralism is the dominant view in political science, but critics point out that not all interests are equally represented in the competition for political influence. Some interests speak with loud voices, while others can barely make themselves heard. Pluralism does not guarantee political equality. Indeed, important research indicates that through group politics economic elites have considerably more influence than mass-based forces in the American political process.[5]

An **interest group** is an organized group of people that makes policy-related appeals to government. This definition includes membership organizations (citizen groups) as well as businesses, corporations, universities, unions, and other institutions

pluralism the theory that all interests are and should be free to compete for influence in the government; the outcome of this competition is compromise and moderation

interest group individuals who organize to influence the government's programs and policies

Although public school teachers are a minority of the total population, they are an influential interest group in many states because they are highly informed and act as a group in support of issues related to their profession, including teachers' salaries.

that restrict membership to particular occupational groups or other categories of persons. Individuals form groups to increase the chance that their views will be heard and their interests treated favorably by the government. Interest groups are sometimes referred to as "lobbies," "special interests," or "pressure groups." They are also sometimes confused with political action committees (PACs), which are groups that raise and distribute money for use in election campaigns (see Chapter 10). Many interest groups create PACs in their name to be the money-giving arm of the interest group. For example, the NRA PAC donates money to political candidates and officeholders on behalf of the NRA, which represents the interests of gun owners. One final distinction is that interest groups are also different from political parties: interest groups tend to focus on the *policies* of government; parties tend to concern themselves with the *personnel* of government in that parties organize to win elected office and interest groups do not.

The number of interest groups in the United States is enormous, and millions of Americans are members of one or more groups, at least to the extent of paying dues, attending an occasional meeting, or being on an email list. By representing the interests of such large numbers of people and encouraging political participation, organized groups can and do enhance American democracy. Organized groups educate and mobilize their members for elections and grassroots lobbying efforts. Groups lobby members of Congress and the executive, engage in litigation, and generally represent their members' interests in the political arena. Interest groups also monitor government programs to make certain that these programs do not adversely affect their members. In all these ways, organized interests can be said to promote democratic politics.

Because not all interests are represented equally, interest group politics works to the advantage of some and the disadvantage of others. Furthermore, not all organized interests are successful. Organized interest groups in the United States are predominantly economic groups; groups working on behalf of businesses and industry far outweigh citizen groups in terms of their number of registered lobbyists in Washington, D.C., and in state capitals and of their financial resources to influence government and elections. The ability of economic groups to mobilize resources often results in legislative victories. Examples of such groups include the oil and gas industries, telecommunication firms, pharmaceutical companies, and trial lawyers.

But even large groups that are well represented in Washington are sometimes defeated in political struggle. On January 18, 2012, the Recording Industry Association of America received a political blow when antipiracy legislation it promoted in Congress—known as the Stop Online Piracy Act (SOPA) and the Protect Intellectual Property Act (PIPA)—was defeated by a massive online protest. Thousands of websites blacked out their content to protest the proposed legislation that threatened free speech and Internet freedom. Wikipedia reports more than 162 million people viewed its protest banner, and Google collected over 7 million signatures to boycott companies supporting the legislation.

Common Types of Interest Groups

Economic and Corporate Groups Interest groups come in as many shapes and sizes as the interests they represent. The most obvious are groups with a direct economic interest in governmental policy. Businesses and corporations make up over 31 percent of those with lobbying offices in Washington, with trade associations comprising another 23 percent and labor unions just 2 percent of groups registered to lobby.[6] Trade associations are generally supported by groups of producers or manufacturers in a particular economic sector, such as the National Association of Manufacturers, the American Fuel and Petrochemical Manufacturers, the Recording Industry Association of America, and the American Farm Bureau Federation. Trade associations care about broad industrywide issues that are important to them, and they lobby and make financial contributions to gain access to elected officials. In addition to these broadly representative groups, specific companies, such as Dow Chemical, DuPont, AT&T, Apple, Google, Microsoft, Comcast, Exxon, and General Motors, may be active in Washington on certain issues that are of particular concern to them. Combined, over 6 in 10 groups lobbying in Washington represent businesses, corporations, or trade associations.

Which industry spends the most money on lobbying activities? Table 11.1 lists the top spenders from 1998 to 2015. At the top of the list is the pharmaceutical industry, which has spent more than $3 billion lobbying lawmakers in an effort to maintain high drug prices and patent protection for their products.

Labor Groups Labor organizations are also active in lobbying government. The AFL-CIO, the United Mine Workers, and the Teamsters all lobby on behalf of organized labor. Other groups have arisen to further the interests of public employees. However, according to one study, labor unions represent just 2 percent of the total number of interest groups registered to lobby in Washington.[7] The America Side by Side on page 426 compares union membership in the United States with other advanced democracies.

Despite being out-lobbied, labor unions continue to exercise influence in Washington. Union members vote, and organized labor can have a significant impact upon elections. Few members of Congress can ignore labor's power at the polls.

Professional Associations Professional lobbies such as the American Bar Association and the American Medical Association have been particularly successful at furthering their members'

Wealthy corporate interest groups usually find it easier to gain attention from elected officials than do other types of groups. Here, Maine governor Paul LePage speaks at a news conference to discuss a report from the Pharmaceutical Research and Manufacturers of America (PhRMA), an interest group representing biopharmaceutical companies and researchers.

TABLE 11.1

Top Spending on Lobbying by Industry, 1998–2015

INDUSTRY	TOTAL
Pharmaceuticals and health products	$3,201,700,687
Insurance	$2,234,406,387
Electric utilities	$2,040,767,304
Electronics manufacturing and equipment	$1,853,401,085
Business associations	$1,843,001,912
Oil and gas	$1,750,292,836
Miscellaneous manufacturing and distributing	$1,442,454,755
Education	$1,419,742,157
Hospitals and nursing homes	$1,332,659,332
Telecom Services	$1,291,773,209
Securities and investment	$1,287,763,285
Civil servants and public officials	$1,235,683,915
Real estate	$1,234,327,542
Health professionals	$1,221,281,450
Air transport	$1,145,018,349
Miscellaneous issues	$947,365,535
Automotive	$905,452,098
Defense aerospace	$902,703,485
Health services and HMOs	$880,256,913
Television, movies, and music	$867,514,016

SOURCE: Center For Responsive Politics, "Top Spenders," www.opensecrets.org/lobby/top.php?showyear=a&indextype=i (accessed 12/11/15).

interests in state and federal legislatures. Professional associations comprise 13 percent of the total number of groups lobbying in Washington. Financial institutions, represented by organizations such as the American Bankers Association and the National Savings and Loan League, although often less visible than other lobbies, also play an important role in shaping legislative policy.

Citizen Groups (or Public Interest Groups) Recent years have witnessed the growth of a powerful "public interest" lobby, purporting to represent the general good rather than its own economic interests. **Citizen groups** have been most visible in the consumer protection and environmental policy areas, although public interest groups cover a broad range of issues. Citizen groups comprise only 20 percent of the groups with lobbying offices in Washington. However, a survey of 315 lobbyists and government officials about 98 randomly selected policy issues found that citizen groups were more likely to be mentioned as being influential in the debate than any other type of group.[8]

citizen groups groups that claim they serve the general good rather than only their own particular interests

The Natural Resources Defense Council, the Sierra Club, the National Civic League, and Common Cause are all examples of public interest groups. Claims to represent *only* the public interest should be viewed with caution, however: it is not uncommon to find decidedly private interests seeking to hide behind the term *public interest*. For example, the benign-sounding Partnership to Protect Consumer Credit is a coalition of credit card companies fighting for less federal regulation of credit abuses, and Project Protect is a coalition of logging interests promoting increased timber cutting.[9]

Ideological Groups Closely related to and overlapping with public interest groups are ideological groups, organized in support of a particular political or philosophical perspective. The National Right to Life and the Christian Coalition, for example, promote conservative values and social goals, such as opposing same-sex marriage. The National Taxpayers Union campaigns to reduce the size of the federal government. Liberal-leaning groups, including EMILY's List and MoveOn.org, support causes such as women's representation and increasing the minimum wage.

Public-Sector Groups The perceived need for representation on Capitol Hill has generated a public-sector lobby in the past several years, including the National League of Cities, the National Conference of State Legislatures, the National Governor's Association, and the "research" lobby. The latter group comprises think tanks and universities that have an interest in obtaining government funds for research and support, and it includes such diverse institutions as Harvard University, the Brookings Institution, and the American Enterprise Institute. Indeed, universities have expanded their lobbying efforts even as they have reduced faculty positions and course offerings.[10] These groups represent 11 percent of the total number of groups lobbying in Washington.

What Interests Are Not Represented?

It is difficult to categorize unrepresented interests precisely because they are not organized and are not able to represent to government their identity and their demands. The political scientist David Truman referred to these interests as "potential interest groups."[11] He is undoubtedly correct that at any time, as long as there is freedom, it is possible that any interest shared by a lot of people can develop through "voluntary association" into a genuine interest group that can demand, usually successfully. But the fact remains that many widely shared interests are not represented by organized groups. Two such "potential" groups are the homeless and the poor. Both groups have shared interests in policy outcomes, such as job programs and affordable housing. But the groups lack organization through which to push for government policy to address these concerns.[12]

Unequal Representation and the Upper-Class Bias of Group Membership
Despite the benefits of interest groups in terms of mobilizing and educating the

Labor Union Membership in Global Decline

Labor union membership in the United States is lower than in most other advanced democracies. This difference is due, in part, to each country's economic history, as strong agricultural economies tend to have less unionization than industrial economies. Another reason is that class consciousness was historically much higher in Europe. European school systems funnel their students early into class-based categories, having distinct paths for vocational training and higher learning. Social interactions also reinforce class divisions, as accents, titles, and lifestyles are strong cues of class belonging.[a]

Many of Europe's socialist parties, such as the United Kingdom's Labour Party, were originally formed by union leaders and often maintain strong union ties. Europe's working class, therefore, has much higher economic, political, and social incentives to belong to a labor union than does the American working class.

Despite these differences, there has been one common pattern across advanced democracies in recent years: a decline in union membership. Part of this change is due to the significant economic restructuring of modern economies. In today's advanced economies, most of the labor force tends to be employed in the service sector or in hi-tech industries rather than in manufacturing. While some unions have formed to represent these groups, unions have been less successful in recruiting members or organizing politically than those representing manufacturing workers.

Given that labor unions have historically been a major force for mobilizing the working class and transmitting their policy interests to politicians, their decline raises an important representation question: In the absence of labor unions, who will represent the working class in policy debates?

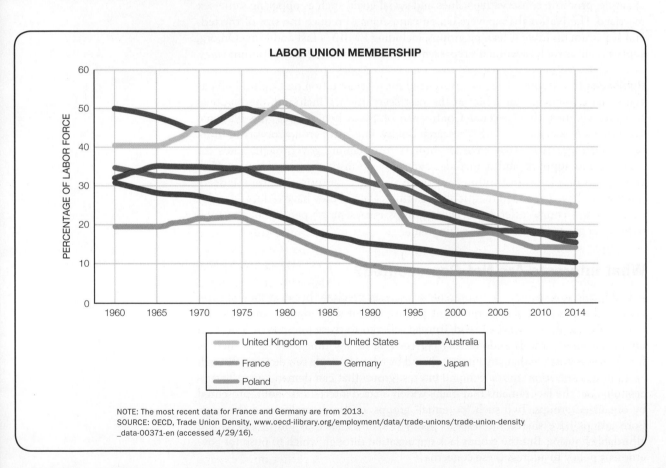

LABOR UNION MEMBERSHIP

Legend: United Kingdom, United States, Australia, France, Germany, Japan, Poland

NOTE: The most recent data for France and Germany are from 2013.
SOURCE: OECD, Trade Union Density, www.oecd-ilibrary.org/employment/data/trade-unions/trade-union-density_data-00371-en (accessed 4/29/16).

[a] Markus M. L. Crepaz, and Jürg Steiner, *European Democracies*, 6th ed. (New York: Pearson, 2013).

In a demonstration of the upper-class bias of interest group politics, Congress worked swiftly to relieve flight delays caused by budget cuts in 2013, prioritizing the issue over concerns about funding for public health and education affecting lower-income Americans.

public and the arguments in favor of pluralism, there are concerns about the influence of special interests in the United States. One long-standing critic is E. E. Schattschneider, who argued in a famous quote, "The flaw in the pluralist heaven is that the heavenly chorus sings with a strong upper-class accent."[13] Critics contend that pressure politics, or interest group politics, is heavily skewed in favor of corporate, business, and upper-class groups, leaving those with lower socioeconomic status less able to participate in and influence politics.

This is because people with higher incomes, more education, and management or professional occupations are much more likely to become members of groups than are those who occupy the lower rungs on the socioeconomic ladder.[14] Well-educated, upper-income business and professional people are more likely to have the time, money, and skills needed to play a role in a group or association. Moreover, for business and professional people, group membership may provide personal contacts and access to information that can help advance their careers. At the same time, of course, corporate entities—businesses and the like—usually have ample resources to form or participate in groups that seek to advance their interests.

The result is that interest group politics in the United States tends to have a pronounced upper-class bias. Certainly, many interest groups and political associations have a working- or lower-class membership—labor organizations or welfare rights organizations, for example—but the vast majority of interest groups and their members are drawn from the middle and upper-middle classes. Even when interest groups take opposing positions on issues and policies, the conflicting positions they espouse usually reflect divisions among upper-income strata rather than conflicts between the upper and lower classes. Thus, when the political system is run by interest groups, democracy will be unequal.

Schattschneider believed that in order to have equal representation in government America needs strong competitive, responsible political parties willing and able to mobilize the lower classes and nonvoters. That is, citizens from the bottom rungs of the socioeconomic ladder must be organized on the massive scale associated with political parties. Competitive political parties provide alternative choices so that the public can participate in the government's decision-making process. While interest groups benefit from a limited scope, political parties must expand political conflict to the public arena to win elections. When political parties compete with one another to win elections, they have incentives to continually expand

Not all groups organize to promote their common interests. Those who are well-educated and well-off financially are more likely to have the time, money, and skills needed to organize and mobilize an interest group. One result is that the needs of such groups as the homeless are often not heard in political debate.

political discussion to nonvoting members of the electorate to gain a majority of voters. Finally, political parties must also act "responsibly" by informing the public of salient political issues in the public interest, not narrow economic interests.

By representing broad public interests, competitive parties could bring more equal representation to democracy. Thus, the relative importance of political parties and interest groups in American politics has far-ranging implications for the distribution of political power in the United States and for how well the interests of America's lower and middle classes are represented. (It should be noted that some public interest groups, such as membership groups and netroots groups, discussed below, seek to educate and inform the public and bring in new members.)

● How Groups Organize

> **Describe how interest groups and social groups organize**

Although interest groups are many and varied, most share certain key organizational components. These include leadership, money, an agency or office, and members.

Leadership and decision-making structure are critical for group organization. For some groups, this structure is very simple. For others, it can be quite elaborate and involve hundreds of local chapters that are melded into a national apparatus. Interest group leadership is, in some respects, analogous to business leadership. Political entrepreneurs initially organize interest groups with a strong commitment to a particular set of goals. Such entrepreneurs see the formation of a group as a means both for achieving those goals and for enhancing their own influence in the political process. And just as is true in the business world, successful groups often become bureaucratized; a paid professional staff replaces the initial entrepreneurial leadership. In the 1960s, for example, Ralph Nader led a ragtag band of consumer advocates (Nader's Raiders) in a crusade for product safety that resulted in the enactment of numerous laws and regulations, such as the requirement that all new cars be equipped with seat belts. Today, Nader remains active in the consumer movement, and his loosely organized band of raiders has been transformed into a well-organized and well-financed phalanx of interlocking groups led by professional staff.

New **netroots** or online advocacy groups often have a streamlined staff structure with little bureaucracy. However, entrepreneurship may be even more important in the world of organizing online. As computer scientist Clay Shirky explains in *Here Comes Everybody*, the Internet has given rise to a proliferation of online organizations without formal organizing structures.[15] Examples include Wikipedia, whose content is provided by volunteers from around the world. But the real impact of the digital media revolution is not politics without groups but the advent of new forms of organization. Leadership remains a priority for online organizations; entrepreneurship and leadership are important for all interest groups but especially so for those with little staff and formal organization as the leader holds the organization together.

The second key organizational component of interest groups is a financial structure capable of sustaining the organization and funding the group's activities. Because the cost of maintaining online organizations is lower than for traditional groups, more and varied types of netroots will be able to form and succeed. Most interest groups rely on membership dues or voluntary contributions from sympathizers. Many also sell some ancillary services to members, such as insurance and vacation tours. In addition, many groups establish an agency that actually carries out the group's tasks, which may be a research organization, a public relations office, or a lobbying office in Washington or a state capital.

Finally, almost all interest groups must attract and keep members, whether membership is defined formally or informally. Groups must persuade individuals to invest the money, time, energy, or effort required to take part in the group's activities. Members play a larger role in some groups than in others. In **membership associations**, group members actually serve on committees and engage in projects. In the case of labor unions, members pay significant dues and attend rallies or march in picket lines; in the case of political or ideological groups, members may participate in demonstrations and protests. In another set of groups, **staff organizations**, a professional staff conducts most of the group's activities; members are called on only to make contributions. Among the well-known public interest groups, some, such as the National Organization for Women (NOW), are membership groups; others, such as Defenders of Wildlife and the Children's Defense Fund, are staff organizations. Finally, for netroots organizations, which do not have formal membership, membership means simply receiving email, signing online petitions, or making financial contributions.

The "Free-Rider" Problem Whether they need individuals to volunteer or merely to write checks, both types of groups need to recruit and retain members. Yet many groups find this task difficult, even when it comes to recruiting members who agree strongly with the group's goals. Why? As the economist Mancur Olson explains, the benefits of a group's success are often broadly available and cannot be denied to nonmembers.[16] Such benefits are called **collective goods**. This term is usually associated with certain government benefits, but it can also be applied to beneficial outcomes of interest group activity.

Olson offers this example: suppose a number of private property owners live near a mosquito-infested swamp. Each owner wants this swamp cleared. But if one or a few of the owners were to clear the swamp alone, their actions would benefit all the other owners as well, without any effort on the part of those other owners. Each of the inactive owners would be a **free rider** on the efforts of the ones who

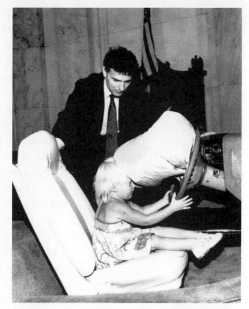

The consumer activist Ralph Nader successfully established a network of consumer advocacy groups that has endured for 50 years. One of his earliest campaigns was to support mandatory airbags in cars.

netroots grassroots online activist organizations that have redefined membership and fund-raising practices and streamlined staff structure

membership association an organized group in which members play a substantial role, sitting on committees and engaging in group projects

staff organization a type of membership group in which a professional staff conducts most of the group's activities

collective goods benefits sought by groups that are broadly available and cannot be denied to nonmembers

free riders those who enjoy the benefits of collective goods but did not participate in acquiring or providing them

cleared the swamp. Thus, there is a disincentive for any of the owners to undertake the job alone. Since the number of concerned owners is small in this particular case, they might eventually be able to organize themselves to share the costs as well as to enjoy the benefits of clearing the swamp.

But suppose the number of interested people is increased. Suppose the common concern is not the neighborhood swamp but polluted air or groundwater involving thousands or even millions of residents. National defense is the most obvious collective good whose benefits are shared by all residents, regardless of the taxes they pay or the support they provide. As the number of involved persons increases or as the size of the group increases, the free-rider phenomenon becomes more of a problem. The group would no doubt be more influential if all concerned individuals were active members—if there were no free riders. This collective action problem is one of the major reasons why many groups do not form.

Why Join Groups? Individuals do not have much incentive to become active members and supporters of a group that is already working more or less on their behalf. To overcome this free-rider problem, groups offer members "selective benefits" available only to group members. These benefits can be informational, material, solidary, or purposive. Of course, groups sometimes offer combinations of benefits. A community association, for example, can offer its members a sense of belonging (solidary benefit), involvement in community decision making (purposive benefit), and reduced rates on homeowners' insurance (material benefit) or a community swimming pool (material benefit). Table 11.2 gives some examples of the range of benefits in each of these categories.

Informational benefits are the most widespread and important category of selective benefits offered to group members. Information is provided through online communication such as email, conferences, training programs, and newsletters and other periodicals sent automatically to those who have paid membership dues. **Material benefits** include anything that can be measured monetarily, such as gifts, discount purchasing, shared advertising, and, perhaps most valuable of all, health and retirement insurance. **Solidary benefits** include the friendship and networking opportunities that membership provides. Extremely important to many of the newer citizen groups and netroots is "consciousness-raising," including the satisfaction of working toward a common goal with like-minded individuals. One example of this can be seen in the claims of many women's organizations that active participation conveys to each member an enhanced sense of her own value and a stronger ability to advance individual as well as collective rights. Members of associations based on ethnicity, race, or religion also derive solidary benefits from interacting with individuals they perceive as sharing their own backgrounds, values, and perspectives.

A fourth type of benefit involves the appeal of the purpose of an interest group. An example of these **purposive benefits** is businesses joining trade associations to further their economic interests. Similarly, individuals join consumer, environmental, or other civic groups to pursue goals important to them. Many of the most successful interest groups of the past 20 years have been citizen groups or public interest groups organized largely around shared ideological goals, including government reform, election and campaign reform, civil rights, economic equality, "family values," and even opposition to government itself.

informational benefits special newsletters, periodicals, training programs, conferences, and other information provided to members of groups to entice others to join

material benefits special goods, services, or money provided to members of groups to entice others to join

solidary benefits selective benefits of group membership that emphasize friendship, networking, and consciousness-raising

purposive benefits selective benefits of group membership that emphasize the purpose and accomplishments of the group

TABLE 11.2

Selective Benefits of Interest Group Membership

CATEGORY	BENEFITS
Informational benefits	Conferences
	Professional contacts
	Publications
	Coordination among organizations
	Research
	Legal help
	Professional codes
	Collective bargaining
Material benefits	Travel packages
	Insurance
	Discounts on consumer goods
Solidary benefits	Friendship
	Networking opportunities
Purposive benefits	Advocacy
	Representation before government
	Participation in public affairs

SOURCE: Adapted from Jack Walker, Jr., *Mobilizing Interest Groups in America: Patrons, Professions, and Social Movements* (Ann Arbor: University of Michigan Press, 1991), 86.

The Internet and Interest Groups

How interest groups foster participation in politics and sustained collective action by citizens is changing because of the Internet. Political scientist and former vice president of the Sierra Club David Karpf has argued that digital media and social media have created a new kind of interest group politics in America that has revolutionized political advocacy. New netroots political associations, such as the liberal-leaning MoveOn.org and conservative-leaning Americans for Prosperity, have arisen in the past decade to play an increasingly important role in citizen participation in politics. These grassroots online activist organizations have redefined membership and fund-raising practices via innovative methods for communicating with their members, measuring the opinions of their members, and moving their members into action—in terms of both influencing public opinion and working on behalf of the organization.[17]

Traditional interest groups are expensive to organize (which is one reason why group membership has an upper-class bias), and they rely on professional advocates and direct mail. They are also slow to change. By contrast, netroots associations are relatively inexpensive to organize and quick to adapt to an ever-changing world of politics. Rather than requiring an annual membership fee to join, like traditional interest groups, membership in netroots is free and defined by receiving emails/communication from the group or working on behalf of the group. Use of targeted fund-raising drives over local, state, or federal government legislation, over a salient event, or over an election is how the organization raises funds to maintain itself, rather than through annual dues. While most traditional interest groups are focused on a single issue—for instance, the Sierra Club seeks protection of the environment while AARP (formerly the American Association of Retired Persons) lobbies on behalf of older Americans—netroots associations are often issue generalists that have a wide umbrella of issues for which they lobby.

Netroots groups are less expensive to organize because they have a streamlined staff structure with fewer staff who often work from virtual offices. In contrast, traditional interest groups must maintain offices in Washington, D.C., and other regional locations. The modified staff structure of netroots groups engages in different work routines that prioritize communication with members through email, Twitter, and other digital platforms rather than mailing expensive glossy newsletters or engaging in direct lobbying of members of Congress. Netroots associations employ grassroots strategies to pressure elected officials, including using online media to organize rallies, fund-raising events, letter-writing campaigns, boycotts, and protests. Membership and fund-raising practices that were pioneered by MoveOn.org have spread across the political advocacy system to more traditional interest groups. Netroots groups may improve representation for citizens, counteracting the disproportionate influence of business and corporate interests in Washington.

Netroots organizations may also differ from traditional groups in the types of benefits they offer members, as the cases of MoveOn and AARP illustrate.

MoveOn and the Benefits of Membership Rather than offering members material selective incentives to join the group, online activist groups like MoveOn offer informational selective benefits to members via daily or weekly news updates and solidary benefits of volunteering or donating money on behalf of the organization. Unlike mainstream media, netroots are decidedly partisan in the information they

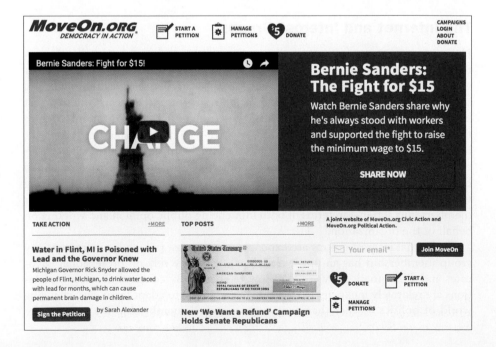

MoveOn.org pioneered a new model of interest group membership and operations. Founded in 1998 and claiming 2 million members, MoveOn seeks to leverage technology to lower the barriers to political participation. This model has since been replicated by other interest groups

provide members. In addition, netroots associations offer their members purposive benefits—the knowledge that one is contributing to a dearly held cause. Purposive benefits may be the most important of all in maintaining the new online citizen advocacy groups.

AARP and the Benefits of Membership One group that has been extremely successful in recruiting members and mobilizing them for political action is AARP. The organization was founded as the American Association of Retired Persons in 1958 as a result of the efforts of a retired California high school principal, Ethel Percy Andrus, to find affordable health insurance for herself and the thousands of members of the National Retired Teachers Association. For the insurer, it provided an expanded market; for Andrus, it was a way to serve the ever-growing elderly population, whose problems and needs were expanding along with their numbers and their life expectancy. Today, AARP is a large and powerful organization with 38 million members and an annual income of $900 million. In addition, the organization receives $90 million in federal grants. Its national headquarters in Washington, D.C., staffed by nearly 3,000 full-time employees, is so large that it has its own zip code. Its monthly periodical, *AARP: The Magazine*, has a circulation larger than that of America's leading newsmagazines.

How did this large organization overcome the free-rider problem and recruit 38 million older people as members? First, no other organization has ever more successfully provided the selective benefits necessary to overcome the free-rider problem. It helps that AARP began as an organization to provide affordable health insurance for aging members rather than as an organization to influence public policy. But that fact only strengthens the argument that members need short-term individual benefits if they are to invest effort in a longer-term and less concrete set of benefits. As AARP evolved into a political interest group, its leadership added more selective benefits for individual members. It provided guidance against consumer fraud, offered low-interest credit cards, evaluated and endorsed products that were deemed valuable to members, and provided auto insurance and a discounted mail-order pharmacy.

AARP is one of the largest interest groups in the country. One way that AARP attracts members is through selective benefits, such as hotel discounts, credit and identity theft prevention, free health tests, and all types of affordable insurance coverage.

The resources of AARP are so extensive that its leadership has been able to mobilize itself on issues of importance to the group. One of its most successful methods of mobilization for political action is the "telephone tree," with which AARP leaders can quickly mobilize thousands of members for and against proposals that affect Social Security, Medicare, and other questions of security for the aging. A "telephone tree" in each state enables the state AARP chair to phone all of the AARP district directors, who then can phone the presidents of the dozens of local chapters, who can call their local officers and individual members. Within 24 hours, thousands of individual AARP members can be contacting local, state, and national officials to express their opposition to proposed legislation. It is no wonder that AARP is respected and feared throughout Washington. Other organizations have borrowed strategy from AARP, creating digital versions of the telephone tree using social media and email to allow members to contact their elective representatives over important policy issues.

● The Growth of Interest and Advocacy Groups

Analyze why the number of interest and advocacy groups has grown in recent decades

Interest groups and concerns about them are not new phenomena. As long as there is government, as long as government makes policies that add value or impose costs, and as long as there is liberty to organize, interest groups will abound. If government expands, so will interest groups. There was, for example, a spurt of growth in the national government during the 1880s and '90s, arising largely from the first government efforts at economic intervention to fight large monopolies and to regulate some aspects of interstate commerce. In response, a parallel spurt of growth occurred in national interest groups, including the imposing National Association of Manufacturers and numerous other trade associations. Many groups organized around specific agricultural commodities as well. This period also marked the beginning of the expansion of trade unions as interest groups. Later, in the 1930s, interest groups with headquarters and representation in Washington began to grow significantly, concurrent with that decade's historic and sustained expansion within the national government (see Chapter 3).

Over the past half-century there has been an even greater increase both in the number of interest groups seeking to play a role in the American political process and in their ability to influence that process. Interest and advocacy groups have become much more numerous, more active, and more influential in American politics, with lobby groups and Super PACs playing major roles in Congress and in electoral politics. This explosion of interest group activity has two basic origins: first, the expansion of the role of government during this period and, second, the coming-of-age of a new and dynamic set of political forces in the United States—forces that have relied heavily on "public interest" groups to advance their causes.

The Expansion of Government

Modern governments' extensive economic and social programs have powerful politicizing effects, often sparking the organization of new groups and interests. The activities of organized groups are usually viewed in terms of their effects on governmental action. But interest group activity is often as much a consequence as an antecedent of governmental programs. Even when national policies begin as responses to the appeals of pressure groups, government involvement in any area can be a powerful stimulus for political organization and action by those whose interests are affected.

For example, during the 1970s, expanded federal regulation of the automobile, oil, gas, education, and health care industries impelled each of these interests to increase substantially its efforts to influence the government's behavior. These efforts, in turn, spurred the organization of other groups to augment or counter the activities of the first.[18] Similarly, federal social programs have sparked political organization. For example, federal programs and court decisions in such areas as abortion and school prayer were one factor leading to the rise of fundamentalist religious groups. Thus, the expansion of government in recent decades has also stimulated increased group activity and organization.

Like the federal government, the states too have expanded their scope of government and have likewise witnessed a growth in the number and diversity of interest groups. But interest group activity isn't uniform across the states, and scholars have measured this activity in a variety of sophisticated ways. One study used the number of trade associations to stand in for the number of interest groups for the years 1990–2005. The researcher found that large-population, affluent states with higher per capita income and higher government expenditures have more trade associations than other states. These large-population, affluent states legislate on more policy areas and, thus, activate the business community to lobby to protect their economic interests. Economists call this "rent seeking."[19]

Growth of Public Interest Groups in the 1960s and '70s

The second factor accounting for the explosion of interest group activity was the emergence of a new set of forces in American politics that can collectively be called the "New Politics movement," which began in the 1960s and '70s. For this cohort of upper-middle-class professionals and intellectuals, the civil rights and antiwar movements were formative political experiences. They formed groups to crusade against racial discrimination and the Vietnam War, and this experience taught them the political efficacy of organized group activity to affect politics. In more recent years, these citizens have focused attention on issues such as environmental protection, women's rights, rights for gay men and lesbians, and nuclear disarmament.

Members of this movement founded or strengthened public interest groups such as Common Cause, the Sierra Club, the Environmental Defense Fund, and NOW. Such groups were able to influence the media, Congress, and even the judiciary and enjoyed a remarkable degree of success during the late 1960s and early '70s in securing the enactment of environmental, consumer, and occupational health and safety legislation. Technology aided in the rise and success of these public interest groups. In the 1970s and '80s, computerized direct-mail campaigns allowed public interest groups to reach hundreds of thousands of potential sympathizers and contributors. Today, the Internet and digital platforms such as social media, Twitter, email, and blogs serve the same function even more efficiently, giving rise to a new generation of activist online

Public interest groups often advocate for interests that are not addressed by traditional lobbies. For example, in addition to many other activities, the Public Interest Research Group (PIRG) publishes an annual toy safety report to help protect consumers and to encourage policy makers to address problems in this area.

groups. Email allows relatively small groups to identify their adherents and mobilize them throughout the nation.

Some have called social media the "weapon of the weak" because they allow small groups with limited resources to send their message across the nation and even around the world.[20] However, social media can be used by the strong as well as the weak, and major corporate interests have also become adept at using Twitter, Instagram, and Facebook. Technology is not a certain answer to inequality. Liberal and conservative groups alike have been better able to organize and affect government policy in the past decade with the help of the Internet and social media.

● Interest Group Strategies

> **Explain how interest groups try to influence government and policy**

Interest groups work to improve the likelihood that their policy interests will be heard and treated favorably by all branches and levels of the government. The quest for political influence or power takes many forms. Insider strategies include access to key decision makers, lobbying, and litigating cases in courts. Outsider strategies include going public and using electoral politics. These strategies do not exhaust all the possibilities, but they paint a broad picture of ways that groups use their resources in the fierce competition for power (see Figure 11.1).

Many groups employ a mix of insider and outsider strategies. For example, environmental groups such as the Sierra Club lobby members of Congress and key congressional staff members, participate in bureaucratic rule making by offering comments and suggestions to agencies on new environmental rules, and bring lawsuits under various environmental acts such as the Endangered Species Act, which authorizes groups and citizens to come to court if they believe the act is being violated. At the same time, the Sierra Club attempts to influence public opinion through media campaigns and to influence electoral politics by supporting candidates who it believes share its environmental views and by opposing candidates it views as foes of environmentalism. While most groups win sometimes and lose sometimes when advocating for their policy goals, in general groups that are well organized and have resources, including citizen groups, are more effective.

Direct Lobbying

lobbying a strategy by which organized interests seek to influence the passage of legislation by exerting direct pressure on government officials

Lobbying is an attempt by a group to influence the policy process through persuasion of government officials. Most Americans tend to believe that interest groups exert their influence through direct contact with members of Congress, but lobbying encompasses a broad range of activities that groups engage in with all sorts of government officials and the public as a whole.

The 1946 Federal Regulation of Lobbying Act defines a lobbyist as "any person who shall engage himself for pay or any consideration for the purpose of attempting to influence the passage or defeat of any legislation of the Congress of the United States." The 1995 Lobbying Disclosure Act requires all organizations employing lobbyists to register with Congress and to disclose whom they represent, whom they lobby, what they are looking for, and how much they are paid. Approximately 12,000 lobbyists are currently registered.[21]

Lobbying involves a great deal of activity on the part of someone speaking for an interest, and lobbyists attempt to influence the policy process in a variety of

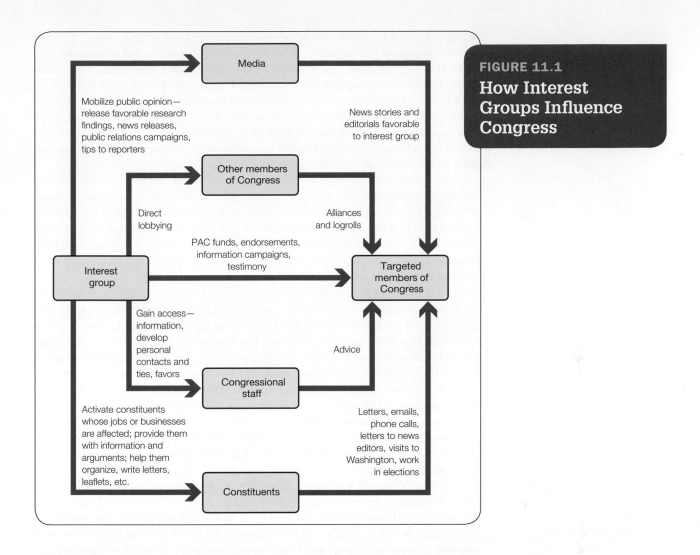

FIGURE 11.1

How Interest Groups Influence Congress

Media

Mobilize public opinion—release favorable research findings, news releases, public relations campaigns, tips to reporters

News stories and editorials favorable to interest group

Other members of Congress

Direct lobbying

Alliances and logrolls

Interest group

PAC funds, endorsements, information campaigns, testimony

Targeted members of Congress

Gain access—information, develop personal contacts and ties, favors

Advice

Congressional staff

Activate constituents whose jobs or businesses are affected; provide them with information and arguments; help them organize, write letters, leaflets, etc.

Letters, emails, phone calls, letters to news editors, visits to Washington, work in elections

Constituents

ways.[22] Lobbyists first and foremost provide information to lawmakers about their interests and the legislation at hand. They communicate this information to lawmakers, administrators, and committee staff members with facts about pertinent issues. They often testify on behalf of their clients at congressional committee and agency hearings. Lobbyists talk to reporters, place ads in newspapers, and organize letter-writing, phone call, and email campaigns. They also play an important role in fund-raising, helping to direct clients' contributions to certain members of Congress and presidential candidates.

Lobbying Congress Traditionally, the term *lobbyist* referred mainly to individuals who sought to influence the passage of legislation in Congress. The First Amendment to the Constitution provides for the right to "petition the Government for a redress of grievances." But as early as the 1870s, *lobbying* became the common term for petitioning. And since petitioning cannot take place on the floor of the House or Senate, petitioners must confront members of Congress in the lobbies of the legislative chamber—hence the term *lobbying*.

Sophisticated lobbyists win influence by providing information about policies to busy members of Congress. Although interest groups do not necessarily buy votes, they do buy time, expertise, and influence. Studies have found that those interest groups providing the most money to representatives are more likely to be consulted by that representative and asked to provide information and expertise in discussing a bill pertaining to that group's area of interest. This, in essence, gives interest groups a voice in shaping how legislation is written; and while it cannot ensure votes for laws preferred by the group, by participating in the policy process, organized interests are influencing policy.

The influence of lobbyists, in many instances, is based on personal relationships and the behind-the-scenes services they are able to perform for lawmakers. Many of Washington's top lobbyists have close ties to important members of Congress or were themselves important political figures, thus virtually guaranteeing that their clients will have direct access to congressional leaders. Some important lobbyists have more than a business relationship to lawmakers: quite a few, in fact, are married to prominent political figures.

Through their lobbyists, interest groups also have substantial influence in setting the legislative agenda. They help to craft specific language in legislation and build coalitions and comprehensive campaigns around particular policy issues.[23] These coalitions do not rise from the grassroots but instead are put together by Washington lobbyists who launch comprehensive campaigns that combine simulated grassroots activity with information and campaign funding for members of Congress.

What happens to interests that do not engage in extensive lobbying? They often find themselves "Microsofted," that is, marginalized in the political process. In 1998 the software giant was facing antitrust action from the Justice Department and had few friends in Congress. One member of the House, Representative Billy Tauzin (R-La.), told Microsoft's chair, Bill Gates, that without an extensive investment in lobbying, the corporation would continue to be "demonized." Gates responded by quadrupling Microsoft's lobbying expenditures and hiring lobbyists with strong ties to Congress. The result was congressional pressure on the Justice Department that led to a settlement of the Microsoft suit on terms favorable to the company.[24]

Similarly, in 1999, members of Congress advised Wal-Mart that its efforts to win approval to operate savings and loans in its stores were doomed to failure if the retailer did not greatly increase its lobbying efforts. "They don't give money. They don't have congressional representation—so nobody here cares about them," said one influential member. Like Microsoft, Wal-Mart learned its lesson, hired more lobbyists, and got what it wanted.[25] By 2005, Wal-Mart had become a seasoned political player, creating a "war room" in its Arkansas headquarters. Staffed by a phalanx of veteran political operatives from both parties, the war room is the nerve center of the giant retailer's lobbying and public-relations efforts.[26] Today, Wal-Mart spends more than $5 million a year on its lobbying efforts.[27]

Lobbying the President So many individuals and groups clamor for the president's time and attention that only the most skilled and best-connected members of the lobbying community can hope to influence presidential decisions. Typically, a president's key political advisers and fund-raisers will include individuals with ties to the lobbying industry who can help their friends gain access to the White House.

Many Americans feel that lobbyists have too much influence over politicians. A number of prominent politicians are even married to lobbyists. Hadassah Lieberman, wife of former senator and vice-presidential candidate Joe Lieberman, was for many years a lobbyist for the pharmaceutical industry.

Interest groups may also try to influence the president's decisions. In 2009, President Obama met with business leaders to discuss how a new health care policy would affect their employees' health insurance plans.

During the 2008 presidential campaign, Barack Obama said, "Lobbyists won't find a job in my White House." Soon after his election, however, Obama appointed David Axelrod as his senior adviser. Before joining the Obama campaign and administration, Axelrod was a partner in ASK Public Strategies, a consulting group that had helped the giant Illinois utility Commonwealth Edison obtain a major rate hike. In the end, Obama did not break the pattern of having advisers with ties to the lobbying industry, at least 30 other senior Obama administration officials had a lobbying background.[28] The lobbying industry is so much a part of Washington that it probably would have been impossible for the president to keep his campaign pledge.

Lobbying the Executive Branch Even when an interest group is successful at getting its bill passed by Congress and signed by the president, the prospect of full and faithful implementation of that law is not guaranteed. Often a group and its allies do not pack up and go home as soon as the president turns the new law they lobbied for over to the appropriate agency. In some respects, interest group access to the executive branch is promoted by federal law. The Administrative Procedure Act, first enacted in 1946 and frequently amended in subsequent years, requires most federal agencies to provide notice and an opportunity for comment before implementing proposed new rules and regulations. This "notice and comment rule making" is designed to allow interests an opportunity to make their views known and to participate in the implementation of federal legislation that affects them. In 1990, Congress enacted the Negotiated Rulemaking Act to encourage administrative agencies to engage in direct and open negotiations with affected interests when developing new regulations. These two pieces of legislation—which have been strongly enforced by the federal courts—have played an important role in opening the bureaucratic process to interest group influence. Today, few federal agencies would consider attempting to implement a new rule without consulting affected interests, known in Washington as "stakeholders."[29]

Iron Triangles The creation of government policy is the product of the so-called **iron triangle**, which has one angle in an executive branch program, another angle in a Senate or House legislative committee or subcommittee, and a third angle in some highly stable and well-organized interest group. For the most part, access to decision makers does not require bribes or other forms of illegal activity. In many areas, interest groups, government agencies, and congressional committees routinely work together for mutual benefit. The interest group provides campaign contributions for members of Congress, and it lobbies for larger budgets for the agency. The agency, in turn, provides government contracts for the interest group and constituency services for friendly members of Congress. The congressional committee or subcommittee, meanwhile, supports the agency's budgetary requests and the programs the interest group favors. The angles in the triangular relationship are mutually supporting and can last over a long period of time, especially if a committee member has considerable seniority in Congress. An interest cannot feel comfortable about its access to Congress until it has one or more of its "own" people with 10 or more years of continuous service on the relevant committee or subcommittee. Figure 11.2 illustrates an important iron triangle in recent American political history: that of the defense industry.

iron triangle the stable, cooperative relationship that often develops among a congressional committee, an administrative agency, and one or more supportive interest groups; not all of these relationships are triangular, but the iron triangle is the most typical

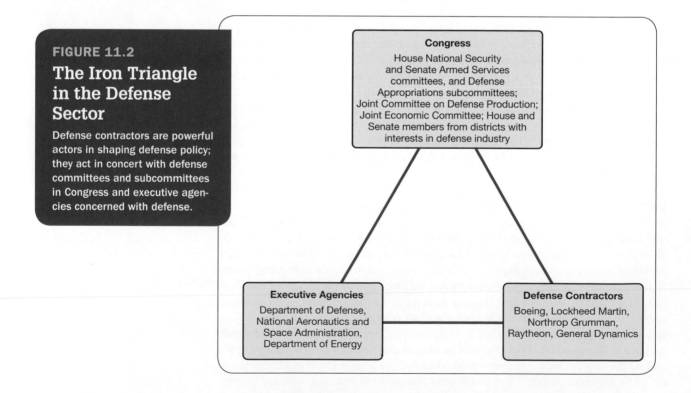

FIGURE 11.2

The Iron Triangle in the Defense Sector

Defense contractors are powerful actors in shaping defense policy; they act in concert with defense committees and subcommittees in Congress and executive agencies concerned with defense.

Congress
House National Security and Senate Armed Services committees, and Defense Appropriations subcommittees; Joint Committee on Defense Production; Joint Economic Committee; House and Senate members from districts with interests in defense industry

Executive Agencies
Department of Defense, National Aeronautics and Space Administration, Department of Energy

Defense Contractors
Boeing, Lockheed Martin, Northrop Grumman, Raytheon, General Dynamics

A number of important policy domains, such as the environment and welfare, are controlled not by highly structured and unified iron triangles but by broader **issue networks**. These networks consist of like-minded politicians, consultants, public officials, political activists, and interest groups that care about the issue in question. Activists and interest groups recognized as being involved in the issue (the stakeholders) are customarily invited to testify before congressional committees or give their views to government agencies considering action in their domain. Issue networks and iron triangles may be overlapping and may coexist.

issue network a loose network of elected leaders, public officials, activists, and interest groups drawn together by a specific policy issue

Regulating Lobbying

Sometimes the actions of lobbyists are outside of the law. In 2005 a prominent Washington lobbyist, Jack Abramoff, was indicted on numerous charges of fraud and violations of federal lobbying laws. During the investigation of his activities, it was revealed that Abramoff, along with his associate Michael Scanlon, had collected tens of millions of dollars from several American Indian tribes that operated lucrative gambling casinos. (Indian gambling is currently a $30 billion industry in the United States.) What Abramoff provided in exchange was access to key Republican members of Congress, who helped his clients shut down rival casino operators. Abramoff was closely associated with several House members, including the former House majority leader Tom DeLay. Millions of tribal dollars found their way into the campaign war chests of Abramoff's friends in Congress. Thus, through a well-connected lobbyist, money had effectively purchased access and influence. Abramoff and several of his associates subsequently pleaded guilty to federal bribery and fraud charges, and Abramoff was sentenced to more than five years in prison.

Because lobbyists are so influential in Washington, D.C., Congress has tried to limit their role by adopting stricter guidelines. However, the effectiveness of the new rules is unclear. For example, businesses may no longer deduct lobbying costs as a business expense. Trade associations must report to members the proportion of their dues that goes toward lobbying, and that proportion of the dues may not be reported as a business expense. The most important new regulation was the 1995 Lobbying Disclosure Act, which expanded the definition of the organization and individuals that must register to lobby.

In 1996, Congress passed legislation limiting the size of gifts to its own members: no gift could be worth more than $50, and no member could receive more than $100 from a single source. It also banned the practice of honoraria for giving speeches, which special interests had used to supplement congressional salaries. In 2007 congressional Democrats secured the enactment of a new package of ethics rules designed to fulfill their 2006 campaign promise to bring an end to lobbying abuses. The new rules prohibited lobbyists from paying for most meals, trips, parties, and gifts for members of Congress. Lobbyists were also required to disclose the amounts and sources of small campaign contributions they collected from clients and "bundled" into large contributions. And interest groups were required to disclose the funds they used to rally voters to support or oppose legislative proposals. According to the *Washington Post*, however, within a few weeks, lobbyists had learned how to circumvent many of the new rules, and lobbying firms were as busy as ever.[30]

Using the Courts

Interest groups sometimes turn to litigation when they lack access or when they feel they have insufficient influence to change a policy. Interest groups can use the courts to affect public policy in at least three ways: (1) by bringing suit directly on behalf of the group itself, (2) by financing suits brought by individuals, or (3) by filing a companion brief as an *amicus curiae* (literally "friend of the court") to an existing court case (see Chapter 15 for a discussion of amicus briefs).

Among the best-known illustrations of using the courts for political influence is found in the history of the National Association for the Advancement of Colored People (NAACP). The most important of these court cases was *Brown v. Board of Education of Topeka, Kansas*, in which the U.S. Supreme Court held that legal segregation of the schools was unconstitutional.[31] Later, extensive litigation accompanied the women's rights movement in the 1960s and the movement for rights for gays and lesbians in the 1990s. In 2015, the case of *Obergefell v. Hodges* illustrated the success of this litigation strategy as the Supreme Court declared that the Fourteenth Amendment prohibited states from refusing to issue marriage licenses to same-sex couples.[32]

The 1973 Supreme Court case of *Roe v. Wade*, which took away a state's power to ban abortions, sparked a controversy that brought conservatives to the fore on a national level.[33] Since 1973, conservative groups have made extensive use of the courts to whittle away at the scope of the privacy doctrine initially defined by the Supreme Court in *Roe v. Wade*. They obtained rulings, for example, that prohibit the use of federal funds to pay for voluntary abortions. And in 1989, right-to-life groups were able to use the case of *Webster v. Reproductive Health Services* to restore the right of states to place restrictions on abortion, thus undermining the *Roe v. Wade* decision (see Chapter 4).[34] The *Webster* case brought more than 300 interest groups on both sides of the abortion issue to the Supreme Court's door. On the other side of the political spectrum, the American Civil Liberties Union (ACLU) regularly uses litigation to challenge state and federal laws that restrict the rights of individuals and groups. This includes recent successful challenges to laws ending affirmative action in the states.

Litigation involving large businesses is voluminous in such areas as taxation, antitrust, interstate transportation, patents, and product quality and standardization. Often a business is brought to litigation against its will by virtue of initiatives taken against it by other businesses or by government agencies. But many individual businesses bring suit themselves to influence government policy, and business groups also frequently use the courts because of the number of government programs applied to them. Major corporations and their trade associations pay tremendous amounts of money each year in fees to the most prestigious Washington law firms. Much of this money is used to keep the best and most experienced lawyers prepared to represent the corporations in court or before administrative agencies when necessary.

Mobilizing Public Opinion

Going public is a strategy that attempts to mobilize the widest and most favorable climate of opinion and a favored strategy of citizen groups and netroots or online activist groups. Many groups consider it imperative to

When the Food and Drug Administration (FDA) required cigarette packages to carry new warning labels such as the one below, a coalition of tobacco companies sued the government, claiming the labels violated First Amendment rights. The companies won their suit. In response, anticigarette groups such as the Campaign for Tobacco-Free kids are urging the FDA to develop new warnings.

maintain this climate at all times. As early as the 1930s, political analysts were distinguishing between the "old lobby" of direct group representation before Congress and the "new lobby" of public-relations professionals addressing the public at large as a way to ultimately reach Congress.[35]

One of the best-known ways of going public is the use of **institutional advertising**. A casual scanning of major mass-circulation magazines, newspapers, and television ads will provide numerous examples of expensive and well-designed ads by the major oil and gas companies, automobile and steel companies, other large corporations, and trade associations. The ads show how much these organizations are doing for the country, for the protection of the environment, or for the defense of the American way of life. The purpose of the ads is to create and maintain a positive association between an organization and the community at large in the hope of drawing on these favorable feelings as needed for specific political campaigns later on.

Citizen groups and online netroots organizations rely heavily on mobilizing the public opinion of their members via social media, Twitter campaigns, and targeted email messages. On any given day a new viral media story may become headline news, and in most cases an interest group is behind the story. Such groups span the ideological spectrum from liberal to conservative and can wield significant pressure on elected officials to act.

Protests and Demonstrations Many groups resort to going public because they lack the resources, the contacts, or the experience to use other political strategies. The sponsorship of boycotts, sit-ins, mass rallies, and marches by Martin Luther King, Jr.'s, Southern Christian Leadership Conference and related organizations during the 1950s and '60s is one of the most significant and successful cases of going public to create a more favorable climate of opinion by calling attention to abuses. The success of these events inspired similar efforts by women's groups. Organizations such as NOW used public strategies in their drive for legislation and in their efforts to gain ratification of the Equal Rights Amendment. The 2010 Republican takeover of the House of Representatives began with the spontaneous self-organization of the Tea Party movement in 2009 as an angry response to the Obama administration's health care initiatives. In 2011 the Occupy Wall Street movement sparked demonstrations across America and around the world, giving voice to those who are outraged by economic inequality. In 2014 the Black Lives Matter movement took off after the shooting of a black teenager by police in Ferguson, Missouri, spreading across the nation. Police shootings of young black men in Baltimore, New York, Chicago, and many others cities led to major demonstrations protesting institutionalized racism, and calling in particular for the elimination of racial inequality in the criminal justice system. In 2015, students on a number of college campuses launched protests demanding that colleges create environments that recognized the value of racial and gender diversity.

Grassroots Mobilization Another form of going public is **grassroots mobilization**, in which a lobby group mobilizes its members and their families throughout the country to write or email their elected representatives in support of the group's position. Among the most effective users of the grassroots effort in contemporary American politics is the religious right. Networks of evangelical churches have the capacity to generate hundreds of thousands of letters, phone calls, and emails to Congress and the White House. Similarly, the NRA maintains a powerful grassroots lobbying effort, spending more on mobilization of its members than on

institutional advertising
advertising designed to create a positive image of an organization

grassroots mobilization a lobbying campaign in which a group mobilizes its membership to contact government officials in support of the group's position

Seeking to reform the criminal justice system and call attention to continued racism in the United States, the movement Black Lives Matter formed in 2012 and earned national attention following a series of high-profile shootings of African Americans by white police officers.

professional lobbyists. The NRA's 3.5 million dues-paying members can be mobilized to flood congressional offices with letters and phone calls, and few members of Congress are eager to pick a fight with the group.[36]

Grassroots campaigns have been so effective in recent years that a number of Washington consulting firms have begun to specialize in this area. In 2007, for example, a grassroots firm called Grassfire.org led the drive to kill the immigration reform bill supported by President George W. Bush and a number of congressional Democrats that would have legalized the status of many illegal immigrants. Grassfire.org used the Internet and talk radio programs to generate a campaign that yielded 700,000 signatures on petitions opposing the bill. The petitions, along with tens of thousands of phone calls, letters, and emails generated by Grassfire and several other groups, led to the bill's defeat in the U.S. Senate.[37]

A notorious online grassroots organization is Anonymous, a loosely associated network of activists and hackers that specializes in online protests. Some consider the group to be outside of the law, while others consider its members to be freedom fighters. The group became known for a series of well-publicized hacks and distributed denial-of-service attacks on government, religious organizations (specifically, the Church of Scientology), and corporate websites. Anonymous prioritizes Internet freedom and has mounted protests against anti–digital piracy campaigns by the motion picture and recording industry trade association and by government; recently, the organization has been active in promoting the rights of gays and lesbians. Anonymous, like other online organizations that do not engage in cyber attacks, prioritizes mobilizing public opinion over insider strategies, such as lobbying, and has been especially effective in mounting citizen protests.

Sometimes, what initially appears to be an upswelling of grassroots mobilization is not in fact a genuine grassroots campaign but instead represents "Astroturf lobbying" (a play on the name of the artificial grass used on many sports fields). Such campaigns, often using email, have increased in frequency in recent years as members of Congress have grown more and more skeptical of Washington lobbyists and far more attentive to demonstrations of support for a particular issue by their actual constituents.

Using Electoral Politics

In addition to attempting to influence members of Congress and other government officials, interest groups seek to use the electoral process to elect the right legislators in the first place and to ensure that those who are elected will owe them a debt of gratitude for their support. If we view matters in perspective, groups invest more resources in lobbying than in electoral politics. Nevertheless, financial support and campaign activism can be important tools for organized interests.

Political Action Committees By far the most common electoral strategy employed by interest groups is that of giving financial support to political parties or specific candidates running for office. But such support can easily cross the threshold into outright bribery. Therefore, Congress has occasionally attempted to regulate this strategy. For example, the Federal Election Campaign Act of 1971 (amended in 1974) requires that each candidate or campaign committee itemize the full name and address, occupation, and principal business of each person who contributes more than $100. These provisions have been effective up to a point, resulting in numerous indictments, resignations, and criminal convictions in the aftermath of the 1972 Watergate scandal.

The Watergate scandal was triggered by the illegal entry of a group of clandestine agents employed by the president's re-election committee into the office of the Democratic National Committee in the Watergate apartment and hotel complex. An investigation quickly revealed numerous violations of campaign finance laws, involving millions of dollars in unregistered cash from corporate executives to President Nixon's re-election committee. Reaction to Watergate produced further legislation on campaign finance in 1974 and 1976, but the effect was to restrict individuals rather than interest group campaign activity. In the 2015–16 election cycle, individuals could contribute no more than $2,700 to any candidate for federal office in any primary or general election. A **political action committee (PAC)**, however, can contribute $5,000, provided it contributes to at least five different federal candidates each year. (Campaign finance regulations are discussed in more detail in Chapter 10.) Beyond this, the laws permit corporations, unions, and other interest groups to form PACs and to pay the costs of soliciting funds from private citizens for the PACs. In other words, PACs operate in the electoral arena by representing interest groups. The option to form a PAC was made available by law in the early 1970s. Before then it was difficult, if not downright illegal, for corporations, including unions, to get directly involved in elections by supporting parties and candidates.

political action committee (PAC) a private group that raises and distributes funds for use in election campaigns

The United Brotherhood of Carpenters and Joiners was one of the top contributors in the 2016 and 2012 election cycles. In the 2012 election cycle, it donated $11.9 million to various Super PACs. (Data from Open Secrets, www.opensecrets.org /orgs/list.php?cycle=2012.)

The flurry of reform legislation in the 1970s attempted to reduce the influence that special interests have over elections, but the effect has been almost the exact opposite. Electoral spending by interest groups has been increasing steadily. The number of PACs has also increased significantly—from 480 in 1972 to more than 5,000 in 2014. Opportunities for legally influencing campaigns are now widespread. In the 2016 presidential election, independent expenditures totaled about $1.3 billion of which $594 million came from Super PACs. Hillary Clinton outspent Donald Trump, raising about $500 million compared to his $250 million, though she still lost the race. These numbers do not include all outside spending since certain kinds of ads are not required to be reported to the government.[38]

Given the enormous costs of television commercials, polls, computers, and other elements of contemporary political technology, most politicians are eager to receive PAC contributions and at least willing to give a friendly hearing to the needs and interests of contributors. Most politicians probably will not simply sell their services to the interests that fund their campaigns, but there is some evidence that interest groups' campaign contributions do influence the overall pattern of political behavior in Congress and in the state legislatures. (See the "Who Are Americans?" feature for one depiction of who is represented by PACs.)

Concern about PACs grew through the 1980s and '90s, creating a constant drumbeat for reform of federal election laws. Proposals to abolish PACs were introduced in Congress on many occasions, with perhaps the most celebrated being the McCain-Feingold bill, which became the Bipartisan Campaign Reform Act of 2002. When originally proposed in 1996, McCain-Feingold was aimed at reducing or eliminating PACs. But in a stunning about-face, when campaign finance reform was adopted in 2002, it did not restrict PACs in any significant way. Rather, it eliminated unrestricted "soft money" donations to the national political parties.

One consequence of this reform, as seen in Chapter 10, was the creation of a host of new organizations, which includes 527 committees, organizations created to promote particular ideas or candidates, and **Super PACs**, formally called "independent expenditure-only committees," which were created for the purpose of promoting whatever candidacies their organizers wish. Super PACs may raise unlimited sums of money from corporations, unions, and individuals but are not permitted to contribute to or coordinate directly with parties or candidates. This change has had the effect of strengthening interest groups and weakening parties. As long as a group's campaign expenditures are not coordinated with those of a candidate's campaign, the group is free to spend as much money as it wishes. Such expenditures are viewed as "issue advocacy" and are protected by the First Amendment. The Supreme Court's landmark decision *Citizens United v. Federal Election Commission* (2010) dramatically increased the flow of money from interest groups, 527s, and Super PACs into politics and electoral campaigns. *Citizens United* removed restrictions on corporate and union political spending, freeing business to back whatever politicians it chose.[39] Individuals and organizations can give an unlimited amount to Super PACs. In the 2014 congressional elections, Super PACs spent $339 million. In 2016, Super PACs spent more than $1.1 billion on House and Senate races.[40]

Campaign Activism Financial support is not the only way that organized groups seek influence through electoral politics. Sometimes activism can be even

Super PAC an independent political action committee that may raise unlimited sums of money from corporations, unions, and individuals but is not permitted to contribute to or coordinate directly with parties or candidates

Who Is Represented by PACs?

In the presidential election cycles of 2000, 2004, 2008, and 2012, political action committees (PACs) spent a grand total of $1.4 billion to elect and defeat political candidates. PACs representing labor groups spent the most, followed closely by the financial sector. For many sectors, the amount donated to Democratic candidates and Republican candidates was fairly even.

PAC Contributions to Federal Candidates, 2000–12

■ Democratic candidates   ■ Republican candidates

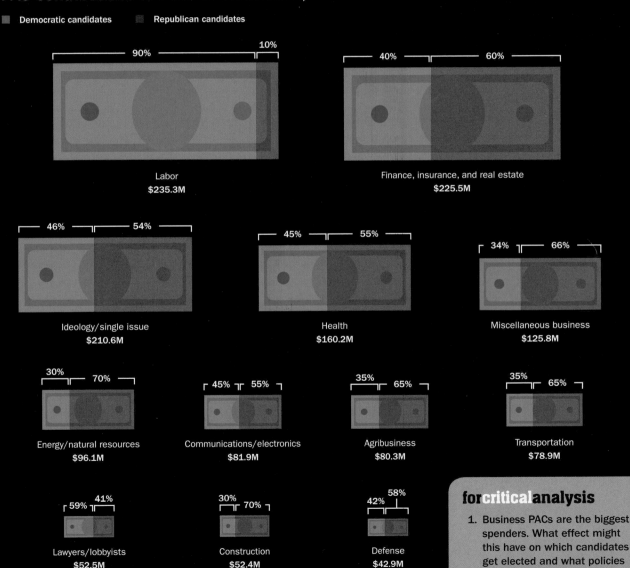

90%   10%

Labor
$235.3M

40%   60%

Finance, insurance, and real estate
$225.5M

46%   54%

Ideology/single issue
$210.6M

45%   55%

Health
$160.2M

34%   66%

Miscellaneous business
$125.8M

30%   70%

Energy/natural resources
$96.1M

45%   55%

Communications/electronics
$81.9M

35%   65%

Agribusiness
$80.3M

35%   65%

Transportation
$78.9M

59%   41%

Lawyers/lobbyists
$52.5M

30%   70%

Construction
$52.4M

42%   58%

Defense
$42.9M

for critical analysis

1. Business PACs are the biggest spenders. What effect might this have on which candidates get elected and what policies they pass?

2. Which party benefits the most from PAC donations? Why do you think this is?

SOURCES: Open Secrets, www.opensecrets.org/pacs/ (accessed 4/12/14)

The amount of money spent by organized interests on elections has increased dramatically in the last decade. This cartoon raises the concern that influence in government is for sale and only the extremely wealthy can buy it.

more important than campaign contributions. Campaign activism on the part of conservative groups played a very important role in bringing about the Republican capture of both houses of Congress in 1994. For example, Christian Coalition activists played a role in many races, including those in which Republican candidates were not strongly identified with the religious right. One postelection study suggested that more than 60 percent of the more than 600 candidates supported by the Christian right were successful in state, local, and congressional races in 1994, especially in the South.[41] In many congressional districts, Christian Coalition efforts were augmented by grassroots campaigns launched by the NRA, which had been outraged by Democratic support for gun control legislation. Both groups are well organized at the local level and were able to mobilize their members across the country to participate in congressional races. In the 2012 presidential elections, prochoice groups mobilized their supporters to turn out and vote for Democratic candidate Obama via telephone get-out-the-vote drives. Similarly, in 2016, fearing a Republican victory, prochoice groups worked vigorously on behalf of Democratic nominee Hillary Clinton.

Ballot Initiatives Another political tactic that interest groups sometimes use is sponsorship of ballot initiatives at the state level. The initiative, a device adopted by half the states around 1900, allows proposed laws to be placed on the general election ballot and submitted directly to the state's voters, bypassing the state legislature and the governor. The initiative was originally promoted by late nineteenth-century Populists and Progressives as a mechanism that would allow the people to govern directly—an antidote to interest group influence in the legislative process.

Some studies have suggested that, ironically, many initiative campaigns today are actually sponsored by interest groups seeking to circumvent legislative opposition to their goals. In recent years, for example, initiative campaigns have been sponsored by the insurance industry, the automobile industry, trial lawyers' associations, and tobacco companies.[42] The success of business groups promoting antitax initiatives and conservative activists seeking, albeit without success, to ban same-sex marriage has led liberal activists to develop their own issue campaigns. In 1998, liberal activists established the Ballot Initiative Strategy Center to provide national coordination for these efforts, which led to successes such as the 2010 Oregon campaign for Propositions 66 and 67, which increased taxes for corporations and high-income wage earners. In 2014, corporate groups had some success with initiatives. For example, a Georgia initiative gave the private operators of student dormitories and parking garages at the University of Georgia system a substantial tax break. At the same time, grassroots groups used the initiative process to decriminalize marijuana use in several states.

While businesses may sponsor ballot initiatives, such measures are much more likely to be rejected by voters on Election Day than initiatives sponsored by citizen groups. In an important study, political scientist Elisabeth Gerber finds that citizens groups and unions are the most effective at sponsoring ballot measures, whereas businesses, trade associations, and professional associations are more effective at lobbying state legislatures. The implication is that mechanisms of direct democracy, like the initiative process, favor citizen interests while lobbying favors economic interests.[43]

Interest Groups
and Your Future

We would like to think that government policies are products of legislators representing the public interest. The truth of the matter is that few programs and policies ever reach the public agenda without the vigorous efforts of important national interest groups. In the realm of economic policy, social policy, and international trade policy, the activity of interest groups is of critical importance.

James Madison wrote that "liberty is to faction as air is to fire."[44] By this he meant that the organization and proliferation of interests are inevitable in a free society. As long as competition among different interests was free, open, and vigorous—that is, as long as pluralism thrived—there would be some balance of power among them, and no one interest would be able to dominate the political or governmental process.

Indeed, there is considerable competition among organized groups in the United States. Prochoice and antiabortion forces, for example, continue to be locked in a bitter struggle. Nevertheless, interest group politics is not as balanced as Madisonian theory and pluralism might suggest. Although the weak and poor do occasionally become organized to assert their interests, interest group politics is generally a form of political competition best suited to the wealthy and powerful.

Moreover, although groups sometimes organize to promote broad public concerns, they more often represent relatively narrow, selfish interests. Small groups seeking narrow interests can be organized much more easily than large and diffuse collectives. The members of relatively small groups—say, bankers or hunting enthusiasts—are usually able to recognize their shared interests and the need to pursue them in the political arena. Members of large and diffuse groups—say, consumers or the unemployed—often find it difficult to recognize their shared interests or the need to engage in collective action to achieve them.[45]

As this chapter has shown, major changes to political or social institutions can have a significant impact on the number and identity of interest groups. One of the major social trends of our time is demographic change. Notably, the baby boomers, a large generation of Americans born in the period after World War II (1946–64), are now reaching retirement and old age. Elderly Americans are highly organized and are represented by interest groups, such as AARP, that lobby government for benefits, including health care subsidies, to keep the cost of their medical care low. Because resources are limited, however, benefits to elderly Americans may come at the expense of social goals that may be more important to other generations. Today's college students are part of the millennial generation, born 1980–2001, who are more numerous than baby boomers. Young people are most affected by the cost of a college education and the job opportunities that exist when they graduate, rather than health care, since the young tend to be relatively healthy but need education and experience. Yet it is difficult to organize college students and the millennial generation on a national or statewide scale to lobby government to spend more on higher education or job opportunities. Why are young people's interests poorly represented and elderly people better represented? Could new organizational opportunities from netroots help young people organize?

Interest groups sometimes seem to have a greater impact than voters on the government's policies and programs, especially through lobbying and financial contributions to political candidates. (The "**Who Participates?**" feature on the facing page shows how much major grounds spend on lobbying activities). Yet, before we decide that we should do away with interest groups, we should think carefully: If there were no organized interests, would the government pay more attention to ordinary voters? Would young people be better or worse off if there were no interest groups in the United States? Or would the government simply pay less attention to everyone? In his work *Democracy in America*, Alexis de Tocqueville argued that the proliferation of groups promoted democracy by encouraging governmental responsiveness. Does group politics foster democracy or impede democracy? It does both.

How Much Do Major Groups Spend?

Lobbying Expenditures, 2011–15 (By selected major groups)

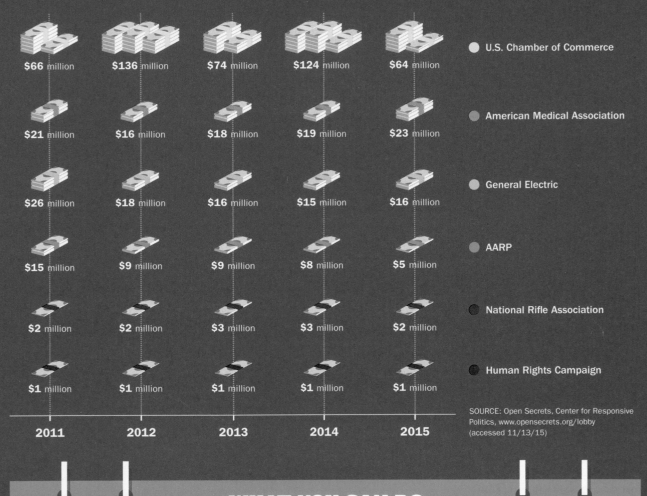

	2011	2012	2013	2014	2015	
U.S. Chamber of Commerce	$66 million	$136 million	$74 million	$124 million	$64 million	
American Medical Association	$21 million	$16 million	$18 million	$19 million	$23 million	
General Electric	$26 million	$18 million	$16 million	$15 million	$16 million	
AARP	$15 million	$9 million	$9 million	$8 million	$5 million	
National Rifle Association	$2 million	$2 million	$3 million	$3 million	$2 million	
Human Rights Campaign	$1 million	$1 million	$1 million	$1 million	$1 million	

SOURCE: Open Secrets, Center for Responsive Politics, www.opensecrets.org/lobby (accessed 11/13/15)

WHAT YOU CAN DO

Get Involved with Interest Groups and Lobbying

☑ Find an interest group that appeals to you at **votesmart.org/interest-groups**, then follow that group on Facebook or Twitter.

☑ Find out which groups give the most money to your representatives in Congress by clicking "Congress" at **www.opensecrets.org/politicians**. You can look up your representatives by zip code.

☑ Contact your Center for Campus Life to find out if groups you're interested in have chapters on your campus. Many groups will gladly help students start campus chapters.

studyguide

Defining Interest Groups

An interest group is an organized group of people that makes policy-related appeals to government. Common types of interest groups include economic and corporate groups, labor groups, and citizen (or public interest) groups. Well-educated, upper-income, professional people are more likely to have the time, money, and skills to participate in interest groups.

Key Terms

pluralism (p. 421)

interest group (p. 421)

citizen groups (p. 425)

Practice Quiz

1. The theory that competition among organized interests will produce balance and compromise, with all the interests regulating one another, is
   a) pluralism.
   b) elite power politics.
   c) democracy.
   d) socialism.
   e) libertarianism.

2. Groups that claim to serve the general good, rather than their own particular interests, are referred to as
   a) membership associations.
   b) citizen groups.
   c) professional associations.
   d) ideological groups.
   e) public-sector groups.

How Groups Organize

Describe how interest groups and social groups organize (pp. 428–34)

Almost all interest groups share a similar set of organizational components, including leadership, money, an office, and members. In order to overcome the free-rider problem, interest groups attempt to provide their potential members with informational, material, solidary, and purposive benefits. New online advocacy groups known as *netroots organizations* have established new approaches to organization and membership.

Key Terms

netroots (p. 429)

membership association (p. 429)

staff organization (p. 429)

collective goods (p. 429)

free riders (p. 429)

informational benefits (p. 430)

material benefits (p. 430)

solidary benefits (p. 430)

purposive benefits (p. 430)

Practice Quiz

3. To overcome the free-rider problem, groups
   a) lobby Congress.
   b) litigate.
   c) provide selective benefits.
   d) provide collective goods.
   e) go public.

4. Friendship and networking are examples of
   a) purposive benefits.
   b) informational benefits.
   c) solidary benefits.
   d) material benefits.
   e) member dues.

5. Discount purchasing and health insurance are examples of
   a) purposive benefits.
   b) informational benefits.
   c) solidary benefits.
   d) material benefits.
   e) member dues.

The Growth of Interest and Advocacy Groups

In recent decades there has been a significant growth in the number of interest groups seeking to influence the American political process. One reason for this change has been the dramatic expansion of the role of American government over the last four decades. Another reason for this change has been the emergence of a new set of political forces in the United States called the "New Politics" movement.

Practice Quiz

6. Which of the following is an important reason for the enormous increase in the number of groups seeking to influence the American political system?
   a) the decrease in the size and activity of government during the last few decades
   b) the increase in the size and activity of government during the last few decades
   c) the increase in the amount of soft money in election campaigns in recent decades
   d) the increase in legal protection provided to interest groups as a result of the Supreme Court's evolving interpretation of the First Amendment
   e) the increase in the number of people identifying themselves as independent in recent decades

7. Which types of interest groups are most often associated with the New Politics movement?
   a) political action committees
   b) professional associations
   c) public-sector groups
   d) labor groups
   e) public interest groups

Interest Group Strategies

Interest groups take action to improve the probability that their policy interests will be treated favorably by all branches and all levels of government. These actions often take many different forms. Insider strategies include direct lobbying, cultivating access to decision makers, and using the court system. Outsider strategies include mobilizing public opinion and using electoral politics.

Key Terms

lobbying (p. 436)

iron triangle (p. 440)

issue network (p. 441)

institutional advertising (p. 443)

grassroots mobilization (p. 443)

political action committee (PAC) (p. 445)

Super PAC (p. 446)

Practice Quiz

8. Which of the following best describes the federal government's laws regarding lobbying?
   a) Federal law allows lobbying but only on issues related to taxation.
   b) Federal law allows lobbying but only if the lobbyists receive no monetary compensation for their lobbying.
   c) Federal law strictly prohibits any form of lobbying.
   d) Federal law requires all organizations employing lobbyists to register with Congress and to disclose whom they represent, whom they lobby, what they are looking for, and how much they are paid.
   e) There are no laws regulating lobbying because the federal government has never passed any legislation on the legality of the activity.

9. A loose network of elected leaders, public officials, activists, and interest groups drawn together by a public policy issue is referred to as
   a) an issue network.
   b) a public interest group.
   c) a political action committee.
   d) pluralism.
   e) an iron triangle.

10. Which of the following is a way that interest groups use the courts to influence public policy?
    a) supplying judges with solidary benefits
    b) joining an issue network
    c) creating an iron triangle
    d) forming a political action committee
    e) filing *amicus curiae* briefs

11. Which of the following are examples of the "going public" strategy?
    a) free riding, pluralism, and issue networking
    b) donating money to political parties, endorsing candidates, and sponsoring ballot initiatives
    c) institutional advertising, grassroots advertising, and protests and demonstrations
    d) providing informational benefits, providing solidary benefits, and providing material benefits
    e) filing an amicus brief, bringing a lawsuit, and financing those who are filing a lawsuit

12. Which of the following is *not* an activity in which interest groups frequently engage?
    a) starting their own political party
    b) litigation
    c) sponsoring ballot initiatives at the state level
    d) lobbying
    e) contributing to campaigns

13. Following the *Citizens United* decision in 2010, electoral spending by interest groups and Super PACs
    a) declined dramatically.
    b) declined slightly.
    c) remained roughly the same.
    d) increased slightly.
    e) increased dramatically.

For Further Reading

Alexander, Robert, ed. *The Classics of Interest Group Behavior*. New York: Wadsworth, 2005.

Baumgartner, Frank, Jeffrey M. Berry, Beth L. Leech, David C. Kimball, and Marie Hojnacki. *Lobbying and Policy Change: Who Wins, Who Loses, and Why*. Chicago: University of Chicago Press, 2009.

Berry, Jeffrey. *Interest Group Society*. 5th ed. New York: Longman, 2008.

Cigler, Allan J., and Burdett A. Loomis, eds. *Interest Group Politics*. 9th ed. Washington, DC: CQ Press, 2015.

Drutman, Lee. *The Business of America Is Lobbying: How Corporations Became Politicized and Politics Became More Corporate*. New York: Oxford University Press, 2015.

Goldstein, Kenneth. *Interest Groups, Lobbying, and Participation in America*. New York: Cambridge University Press, 2008.

Herrnson, Paul, and Christopher Deering. *Interest Groups Unleashed*. Washington, DC: CQ Press, 2012.

Holyoke, Thomas. *Interest Groups and Lobbying: Pursuing Political Interests in America*. Boulder, CO: Westview, 2014.

Kaiser, Robert. *So Damn Much Money: The Triumph of Lobbying and the Corrosion of American Government*. New York: Vintage, 2010.

Karpf, David. *The MoveOn Effect: The Unexpected Transformation of American Political Advocacy*. New York: Oxford University Press, 2012.

Lessig, Lawrence. *Republic, Lost: How Money Corrupts Congress—and a Plan to Stop It*. New York: Twelve/Hachette Book Group, 2011.

Lowi, Theodore J. *The End of Liberalism: The Second Republic of the United States*. 2nd ed. New York: W. W. Norton, 1979.

Moe, Terry M. *The Organization of Interests: Incentives and the Internal Dynamics of Political Interest Groups*. Chicago: University of Chicago Press, 1980.

Nownes, Anthony. *Total Lobbying: What Lobbyists Want and How They Try to Get It*. New York: Cambridge University Press, 2006.

Olson, Mancur, Jr. *The Logic of Collective Action: Public Goods and the Theory of Groups*. Cambridge, MA: Harvard University Press, 1965.

Shirky, Clay. *Here Comes Everybody: The Power of Organizing without Organizations*. New York: Penguin Press, 2008.

Strolovitch, Dara. *Affirmative Advocacy: Race, Class, and Gender in Interest Group Politics*. Chicago: University of Chicago Press, 2007.

Recommended Websites

AARP
www.aarp.org
AARP (formerly the American Association of Retired Persons) is one of the largest and most significant interest groups in the United States. Read about the history of this organization, its group benefits, and how it is affecting political issues and elections.

AFL-CIO Legislative Alerts
www.aflcio.org/Legislation-and-Politics/Legislative-Alerts
Created in 1955, the AFL-CIO represents more than 10 million working men and women. See how this influential labor group is active and involved in political issues.

American Civil Liberties Union
www.aclu.org

American Conservative Union
www.conservative.org
The American Civil Liberties Union and the American Conservative Union are two of the nation's largest and most influential ideological interest groups. See what these opposing groups have to say about our government and current political issues.

American Israel Public Affairs Committee
www.aipac.org
Due to globalization, interest groups cannot limit their activities to one country. Decisions made in Washington,

D.C., can affect countries around the world. The American Israel Public Affairs Committee works with Republicans and Democrats to maintain a strong relationship between the United States and Israel.

MoveOn
www.moveon.org

This progressive interest group is dedicated to bringing ordinary citizens back into the political process and electing liberal members of government. See how this group uses electoral politics, via political action committees and campaign activism, to achieve its agenda.

National Rifle Association
www.nra.org

Coalition to Stop Gun Violence
www.csgv.org

Brady Campaign to Prevent Gun Violence
www.bradycampaign.org

Lobbying is an attempt by a group to influence the policy process by persuading government officials. These three groups employ a variety of lobbying techniques on the issue of gun control.

U.S. Public Interest Research Group
www.uspirg.org

This public interest group stands up for ordinary citizens. Its special emphasis is on consumer rights and the environment. U.S. Public Interest Research Group (U.S. PIRG) mobilizes public opinion via institutional advertising, social movements, and grassroots efforts. U.S. PIRG chapters can be found in most states and at many colleges and universities.

World Wildlife Fund
www.wwf.org

The World Wildlife Fund is dedicated to protecting nature. It provides information to policy makers about conservation and advocates for policies to help preserve the natural environment.

In addition to its lawmaking powers, Congress plays a critical role in American democracy as a representative institution. The members of Congress—100 senators and 435 representatives—represent the voices of the people across America. Yet some observers worry that Congress does not represent all voices equally.

Congress

WHAT GOVERNMENT DOES AND WHY IT MATTERS In October 2015, Congress confronted two big deadlines. It had to approve a budget by the end of the month to avoid a government shutdown. It also had to raise the debt limit to keep the government from defaulting on its debt. Failure to act on either would have serious consequences, as members of Congress knew well. Partisan stalemate on the budget had caused a government shutdown in 2013 that laid off workers, shuttered government facilities, and ultimately cost the economy billions of dollars.[1] Failure to raise the debt ceiling in 2015 threatened even more dire financial consequences by risking the credit rating of the American government in international markets. With the clock ticking down, Congress showed no signs of reaching a decision. Yet, just when it seemed that agreement would not be possible, congressional leaders and the president, meeting in secret over a long weekend, managed to strike a deal. With a two-year budget framework in place and a suspension of the debt ceiling until 2017, the federal government was back in business.

But on other important issues, the 114th Congress was unable to reach agreement. Judicial appointments proved particularly divisive. Supreme Court Justice Antonin Scalia's sudden death in February 2016 had left the nation's highest court with only eight members. Although President Obama nominated a highly experienced replacement, the Senate refused to hold confirmation hearings until after Obama left office. Left with only eight members for most of 2016, the Court's deliberations ended in ties on several important decisions. Even more significant was the mounting number of vacancies in the district courts as Congress failed to approve appointees. By fall 2016, 12 percent of district court judgeships remained unfilled, a significantly higher rate than in earlier decades. Without enough judges, lower courts proved unable to manage growing caseloads, leaving cases undecided for prolonged periods.[2] Once Republican Donald Trump was elected to the presidency, however, Senate leaders signaled their willingness to swiftly consider the new president's nominee to the Supreme Court.

Congress has vast authority over many aspects of American life. In addition to federal judicial appointments, laws related to federal spending, taxing, regulation, and federal judicial appointments all pass through Congress. While the debates over these laws may seem hard to follow because they are often complex and technical or because heated, partisan struggles distract from the substance of the issue, it is important for the American people to learn about what Congress is doing. As the example of the near government shutdown indicates, actions taken—or not taken—in Congress affect the everyday experiences we take for granted. With its power to spend and tax, Congress also affects the choices that people face and the opportunities they can expect in life. With so much information about Congress available on the Internet, it is not hard to get beyond the heated rhetoric and simplistic headlines and ask your own questions about a proposed law. How will it affect my life and the lives of people I care about? What is the impact on my country? Making laws is a complex and often messy process. Even so, it is vital for citizens to monitor what Congress does because the laws it passes are so central to their lives.

chaptergoals

- Describe who serves in Congress and how they represent their constituents (pp. 459–72)

- Explain how party leadership, the committee system, the staff system, and caucuses help structure congressional business (pp. 472–80)

- Outline the steps in the process of passing a law (pp. 480–85)

- Analyze the factors that influence which laws Congress passes (pp. 485–94)

- Describe Congress's influence over other branches of government (pp. 495–97)

Congress: Representing the American People

Describe who serves in Congress and how they represent their constituents

Congress is the most important representative institution in American government. Each member's primary responsibility in theory is to the district, to his or her **constituency**, not to the congressional leadership, a party, or even Congress itself. Yet the task of representation is not a simple one. Views about what constitutes fair and effective representation differ, and constituents may have very different expectations of their representatives. Members of Congress must consider these diverse views and expectations as they represent their districts.

constituency the residents in the area from which an official is elected

House and Senate: Differences in Representation

The framers of the Constitution provided for a **bicameral** legislature—that is, a legislative body consisting of two chambers. As we saw in Chapter 2, the framers intended each of these chambers, the House of Representatives and the Senate, to serve a different constituency. Members of the Senate, appointed by state legislatures for six-year terms, were to represent society's elite. Today, members of both the House and the Senate are elected directly by the people. The 435 members of the House are elected from districts apportioned according to population; the 100 members of the Senate are elected in a statewide vote, with two senators from each state. Senators continue to have much longer terms in office and usually represent much larger and more diverse constituencies than do their counterparts in the House (see Table 12.1).

bicameral having a legislative assembly composed of two chambers or houses, distinguished from *unicameral*

The House and Senate play different roles in the legislative process. In essence, the Senate is the more deliberative of the two bodies—the forum in which any and all ideas that senators raise can receive a thorough public airing. The House is the more centralized and organized of the two bodies—better equipped to play a routine role in the governmental process. In part, this difference stems from the different rules governing the two bodies. These rules give House leaders more

TABLE 12.1
Differences between the House and the Senate

	HOUSE	SENATE
Minimum age of member	25 years	30 years
U.S. citizenship	At least 7 years	At least 9 years
Length of term	2 years	6 years
Number representing each state	1–53 per state (depends on population)	2 per state
Constituency	Local	Local and statewide

For its first 128 years, Congress was a decidedly masculine world. In 1917, Jeanette Rankin (R-Mont.; pictured back row, far right) became the first woman to serve in the House or Senate. As of 2016, a total of 297 women had served as U.S. representatives or senators, while 11,804 men have served.

delegate a representative who votes according to the preferences of his or her constituency

trustee a representative who votes based on what he or she thinks is best for his or her constituency

control over the legislative process and allow House members to specialize in certain legislative areas. The rules of the much smaller Senate give its leadership relatively little power and discourage specialization.

Both formal and informal factors contribute to differences between the two chambers of Congress. Differences in the length of terms and requirements for holding office, specified by the Constitution, generate differences in how members of each body develop their constituencies and exercise their powers of office. For the House, the small size and relative homogeneity of their constituencies and the frequency with which they must seek re-election—every two years—make members more attuned to the legislative needs of local interest groups. The result is that members of the House most effectively and frequently serve as the agents of well-organized local interests with specific legislative agendas—for instance, used-car dealers seeking relief from regulation, labor unions seeking more favorable legislation, or farmers looking for higher subsidies. Because House members seek re-election every two years, they are interested in doing what their constituents want right *now*.

Senators, on the other hand, serve larger and more heterogeneous constituencies. As a result, they are somewhat better able than members of the House to act as the agents for groups and interests organized on a statewide or national basis. Moreover, with longer terms in office (six years), senators have more time to consider "new ideas" or to bring together new coalitions of interests rather than simply serving existing ones.

Trustee versus Delegate Representation

For the Founders, Congress was the national institution that best embodied the ideals of representative democracy. But what is the role of a representative? A member of Congress can interpret her job as representative in two different ways: as a **delegate**, acting on the express preferences of her constituents, or as a **trustee**, more loosely tied to constituents and empowered to make the decisions she thinks best. The delegate role appears to be the more democratic because it forces representatives to heed the desires of their constituents. But this requires the representative to be in constant touch with constituents; it also requires constituents to follow each policy issue very closely. The problem with this form of representation is that most people do not follow every issue so carefully; instead, they focus only on the issue or issues of particular interest to them. Many people are too busy to get the information necessary to make informed judgments even on issues they care about. Thus, adhering to the delegate form of representation runs the risk that the voices of only a few active and informed constituents get heard. Although it seems more democratic at first glance, the delegate form of representation may actually open Congress up to even more influence by special interests.

When congressional members act as trustees, on the other hand, they may not pay sufficient attention to the wishes of their constituents. In this scenario, the only way the public can exercise influence is by voting every two years for representatives and every six years for senators. In fact, most members of Congress take this electoral check very seriously. They try to anticipate the wishes of their constituents even when they don't know exactly what those wishes are because they know that unpopular decisions can be used against them in the coming election.

Sociological versus Agency Representation

We have become so accustomed to the idea of representative government that we tend to forget what a peculiar concept representation really is. A representative claims to act or speak for some other person or group. But how can one person be trusted to speak for another? How do we know that those who call themselves our representatives are actually speaking on our behalf, rather than simply pursuing their own interests?

There are two circumstances under which one person reasonably might be trusted to speak for another. The first occurs if the two individuals are so similar in background, character, interests, and perspectives that anything said by one would very likely reflect the views of the other as well. This principle is at the heart of what is sometimes called **sociological representation**—the sort of representation that takes place when representatives have the same racial, gender, ethnic, religious, or educational backgrounds as their constituents. The assumption is that sociological similarity helps to promote good representation; thus, the composition of a properly constituted representative assembly should mirror the composition of society.

The second circumstance under which one person might be trusted to speak for another occurs if the two are formally bound together so that the representative is in some way accountable to those he is supposed to represent. If representatives can somehow be punished for failing to speak properly for their constituents, then we know they have an incentive to provide good representation even if their own personal backgrounds, views, and interests differ from the backgrounds of those they represent. This principle is called **agency representation**—the sort of representation that takes place when constituents have the power to hire and fire their representatives.

Both sociological and agency representation play a role in the relationship between members of Congress and their constituencies, but in many ways, members of Congress do not reflect the American population (see the "Who Are Americans?" feature on p. 463).

The Social Composition of the U.S. Congress The extent to which the U.S. Congress is representative of the American people in a sociological sense can be seen by examining social characteristics of the House and Senate today. For example, the religious affiliations of members of both the House and Senate are overwhelmingly Protestant—the distribution is very close to the proportion in the population at large. Catholics are the second-largest category of religious affiliation and Jews a much smaller, third category.[3] Religious affiliations directly affect congressional debate on a limited range of issues where different moral views are at stake, such as abortion.

African Americans, women, Latinos, and Asian Americans have increased their congressional representation in the past two decades (see Figure 12.1), but the representation of minorities in Congress is still not comparable to their proportions in the general population. After the 2016 elections, Congress was 9 percent African American, 9 percent Latino, and 2 percent Asian American. By contrast, the American population was far more diverse, with 13.3 percent African Americans, 17.6 percent Latinos, and 5.6 percent Asian Americans.[4] As the United States has

sociological representation a type of representation in which representatives have the same racial, gender, ethnic, religious, or educational backgrounds as their constituents; it is based on the principle that if two individuals are similar in background, character, interests, and perspectives, then one can correctly represent the other's views

agency representation a type of representation in which a representative is held accountable to a constituency if he or she fails to represent that constituency properly; this is incentive for the representative to provide good representation when his or her personal backgrounds, views, and interests differ from those of his or her constituency

for critical analysis

Why is sociological representation important? If congressional representatives have racial, religious, or educational backgrounds similar to those of their constituents, are they better representatives? Why or why not?

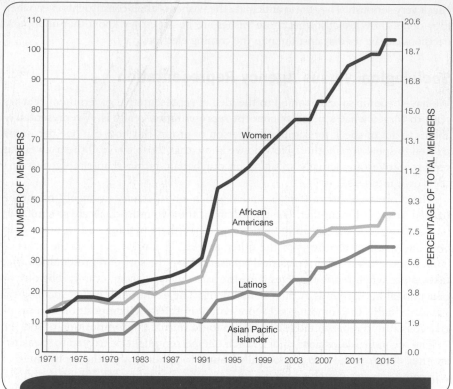

FIGURE 12.1

Women, African Americans, and Latinos in the U.S. Congress, 1971–2016

Congress has become much more socially diverse since the 1970s. After a gradual increase from 1971 to 1990, the number of female and African American members grew quickly during the first half of the 1990s. How closely does the number of female, African American, and Latino representatives reflect their proportion of the total U.S. population?

SOURCES: Harold W. Stanley and Richard G. Niemi, eds., *Vital Statistics on American Politics 2003–2004* (Washington, DC: CQ Press, 2003), 207, Table 5–2; Jennifer E. Manning, *Membership of the 113th Congress: A Profile*, Congressional Research Service 7-5700, January 13, 2014, www.fas.org/sgp/crs/misc/R42964.pdf (accessed 2/24/14); Jennifer E. Manning, *Membership of the 114th Congress: A Profile*, Congressional Research Service, 7-5700 September 17, 2015, www.fas.org/sgp/crs/misc/R43869.pdf (accessed 9/28/15); R. Eric Petersen, *Representatives and Senators: Trends in Member Characteristics since 1945*, Congressional Research Service 7-5700, February 17, 2012, www.fas.org/sgp/crs/misc/R42365.pdf (accessed 9/28/15).

become a more diverse nation, Congress has lagged behind in sociological representation. Similarly, the number of women in Congress continues to trail far behind their proportion of the population. In 2006, Nancy Pelosi (D-Calif.) became the first female Speaker of the House. Following the 2016 elections, the 115th Congress (2016–18) included 82 women in the House of Representatives and 21 women in the Senate, an all-time high. Since many important contemporary issues cut along racial and gender lines, pressure for reform in the representative process is likely to continue until all groups are fully represented.

Who Are the Members of Congress?

Gender

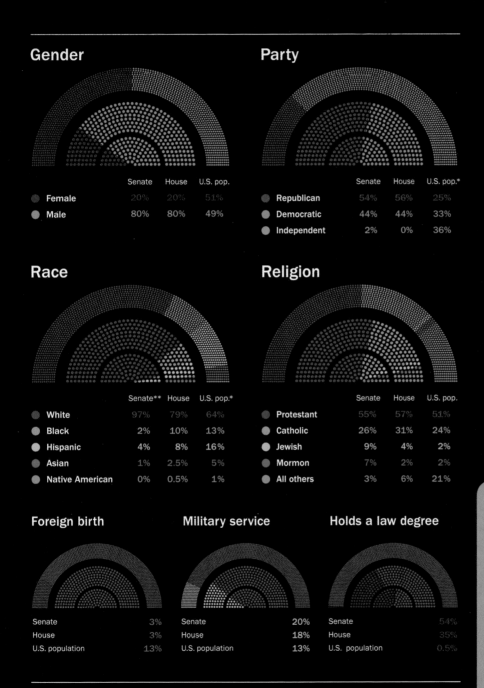

	Senate	House	U.S. pop.
● Female	20%	20%	51%
● Male	80%	80%	49%

Party

	Senate	House	U.S. pop.*
● Republican	54%	56%	25%
● Democratic	44%	44%	33%
● Independent	2%	0%	36%

Key

U.S. population

Senate

House of Representatives

Although the number of women, African Americans, and Latinos in Congress has increased in recent decades, Congress is still much less diverse than the American population. Members of Congress are predominantly male, white, Protestant, and a large percentage hold a law degree. These data compare the 114th Congress, which took office in 2015, with the U.S. population as a whole.

Race

	Senate**	House	U.S. pop.*
● White	97%	79%	64%
● Black	2%	10%	13%
● Hispanic	4%	8%	16%
● Asian	1%	2.5%	5%
● Native American	0%	0.5%	1%

Religion

	Senate	House	U.S. pop.
● Protestant	55%	57%	51%
● Catholic	26%	31%	24%
● Jewish	9%	4%	2%
● Mormon	7%	2%	2%
● All others	3%	6%	21%

Foreign birth

Senate	3%
House	3%
U.S. population	13%

Military service

Senate	20%
House	18%
U.S. population	13%

Holds a law degree

Senate	54%
House	35%
U.S. population	0.5%

Average age

Senate 61   House 57   U.S. population 37

*Percentages do not sum to 100 because some Americans identify with other categories.
**Percentages sum to more than 100 because several senators identify as more than one race.
SOURCES: Jennifer E. Manning, "Membership of the 114th Congress: A Profile," Congressional Research Service, www.fas.org/sgp/crs/misc/R43869.pdf (accessed 3/6/16); U.S. Census Bureau, www.census.gov/population/age/data/2012comp.html (accessed 3/19/14).

for critical analysis

1. Does it matter if the backgrounds of members of Congress reflect the population as a whole? Can members still represent their constituents effectively if they do not come from similar backgrounds?

2. Visit www.house.gov and www.senate.gov to identify your representatives in Congress and visit their web pages. How similar are their backgrounds to yours? How closely do their policy positions, as expressed on their web pages, match your own?

To more effectively promote a legislative agenda addressing issues that disproportionately affect racial and ethnic minority groups, members of Congress from those groups have formed caucuses. Here, members of the Congressional Black Caucus announce their endorsement of 2016 Democratic presidential candidate Hillary Clinton.

The occupational backgrounds of members of Congress have always been a matter of interest because many issues split along economic lines that are relevant to occupations and industries. The legal profession is the dominant career of most members of Congress prior to their election, and public service or politics is also a significant background. In addition, many members of Congress have important ties to business and industry.[5] Moreover, members of Congress are much more highly educated than most Americans. More than 9 in 10 members hold university degrees, and more than one-third of them have law degrees.[6] This is not a portrait of the U.S. population; Congress is not a sociological microcosm of American society.

Can Congress still legislate fairly or take account of a diversity of views and interests if it is not a sociologically representative assembly? There is reason to believe it can. Representatives, as we shall see shortly, can serve as the agents of their constituents even if they do not precisely mirror their sociological attributes. Yet sociological representation is a matter of some importance. At the least, the social composition of a representative assembly is important for symbolic purposes: to demonstrate to groups in the population that the government takes them seriously. If Congress is not representative symbolically, then its own authority, and indeed that of the entire government, is reduced.[7]

Representatives as Agents A good deal of evidence indicates that whether or not members of Congress share their constituents' sociological characteristics, they *do* work very hard to speak for their constituents' views and to serve their constituents' interests. The idea of representative as agent is similar to the relationship of lawyer and client. True, the relationship between the House member and an average of 710,767 "clients" in the district, or the senator and millions of "clients" in the state, is very different from that of the lawyer and client. But the criteria of performance are comparable. One expects at the very least that each representative will constantly seek to discover the interests of the constituency and take those interests into account as she governs. Whether members of Congress always represent the interests of their constituents is another matter, as we will see later in this chapter.[8]

There is constant communication between constituents and congressional offices, and the volume of email from constituents and advocacy groups has grown so large so quickly that congressional offices have struggled to find effective ways to respond in a timely manner.[9] At the same time, members of Congress have found new ways to communicate with constituents. They have created websites describing their achievements, established a presence on social networking sites, and issued e-newsletters that alert constituents to current issues. Many also have set up blogs and Twitter accounts to establish a more informal style of communication with constituents.

The seriousness with which members of the House attempt to behave as representatives can be seen in the amount of time they spend on behalf of their constituents. One way to measure the amount of time members of Congress devote to constituency service (called "casework") is to look at the percentage of personal House and Senate staff (personal staff being non-committee member staff) assigned to district and state offices. In 1972, 22.5 percent of House members' personal staff were located in district offices; by 2010 the number had grown to 48.9 percent. For the Senate, the staff in state offices grew from 12.5 percent in 1972 to 41 percent in 2005.[10] The service that these offices provide is not merely a matter of handling correspondence. It includes talking to constituents; providing them with minor services; presenting special bills for them; attempting to influence decisions by regulatory commissions on their behalf; helping them apply for federal benefits, such as Social Security and Small Business Administration loans; and assisting them with immigration cases. For example, during his fight for re-election in 2014, Senate Minority Leader Mitch McConnell (R-Ky.) ran a campaign ad featuring Noelle Hunter, a Kentucky resident whose ex-husband abducted their daughter and took her to Africa. According to Hunter, McConnell "took up my cause personally" and worked with the State Department to bring her daughter back home. Senator Pat Roberts (R-Kans.) struck a similar tone when touting his success in helping Kate Forristall, a Kansan whose daughter was taken hostage while teaching English in Ethiopia. Roberts says in the ad, "We got the call. Top priority. We went to work."[11]

In many districts, there are two or three issues that are top priorities for constituents and, therefore, for the representatives. For example, representatives from districts that grow wheat, cotton, or tobacco will likely give legislation on these subjects great attention. In oil-rich states such as Oklahoma and Texas, senators and members of the House are likely to be leading advocates of oil interests. For one thing, representatives are probably fearful of voting against their district interests; for another, the districts are unlikely to have elected representatives who would *want* to vote against them. On the other hand, on many issues, constituents do not have very strong views, and representatives are free to act as they think best. Foreign policy issues often fall into this category.

The influence of constituencies is so pervasive that both parties generally agree that nothing should be done to endanger the re-election chances of any member. Party leaders obey this rule fairly consistently by not asking any member to vote in a way that might conflict with a district interest.

The Electoral Connection

The sociological composition of Congress and the activities of representatives once they are in office are very much influenced by electoral considerations. Three factors related to the U.S. electoral system affect who gets elected and what they do once in office. The first factor concerns who decides to run for office and which candidates have an edge over others. The second issue is that of incumbency advantage. Finally, the way congressional district lines are drawn can greatly affect the outcome of an election. Let us examine more closely the impact that these considerations have on representation.

Who Runs for Congress Voters' choices are restricted from the start by who decides to run for office. In the past, decisions about who would run for a particular elected office were made by local party officials. A person who had a record of service to the party, who was owed a favor, or whose "turn" had come up might be nominated by party leaders. Today, few party organizations have the power to slate candidates in this way. Instead, parties try to ensure that well-qualified candidates run for Congress. During the 1990s, the Republican Party developed "farm teams" of local officials who were groomed to run for Congress. Their success led Democrats to attempt a similar strategy. Even so, the decision to run for Congress is a personal one, and one of the most important factors determining who runs for office is an individual candidate's ambition.[12] A potential candidate may also assess whether he can attract enough money to mount a credible campaign. The ability to raise money depends on connections with other politicians, interest groups, and national party organizations.

Features distinctive to each congressional district also affect the field of candidates. For example, the way the congressional district overlaps with state legislative boundaries may affect a candidate's decision to run. A state-level legislator who is considering running for the U.S. Congress is more likely to assess her prospects favorably if her state district coincides with the congressional district (because the voters will already know her).

incumbency holding the political office for which one is running

Incumbency **Incumbency** plays a very important role in the American electoral system and in the kind of representation citizens get in Washington. Once in office, members of Congress gain access to an array of tools they can use to stack the deck in favor of their re-election. Their success in winning re-election is evident in the high rates of re-election for congressional incumbents: as high as 98 percent for House members and 90 percent for members of the Senate in recent years (see Figure 12.2). It is also evident in what is called "sophomore surge"—the tendency for candidates to win a higher percentage of the vote when seeking subsequent terms in office. In 2016 approximately 97 percent of incumbents in the House and 93 percent in the Senate were re-elected.[13] Furthermore, incumbents often win by large margins: in 2014 only 49 of the 435 House races were decided by a margin of less than 10 percent. The average margin of victory was 22.6 percent in the Senate and 35.8 in the House.[14]

Incumbency can help a candidate by scaring off potential challengers. In many races, potential candidates may decide not to run because they fear that the incumbent simply has too much money or is too well liked or too well known or that a district's partisan leanings are too unfavorable. The efforts of incumbents to raise funds to ward off potential challengers start early. A Connecticut Democrat, Joe Courtney, won his seat in 2006 by a very small margin, with only 91 more votes than his opponent. He began fund-raising for the 2008 election even before he was sworn in for his first term. In addition, the Democratic Congressional Campaign Committee placed him on its "Frontline" team, a group of the 29 most vulnerable Democrats. The Democratic leadership took special efforts to raise the profile of

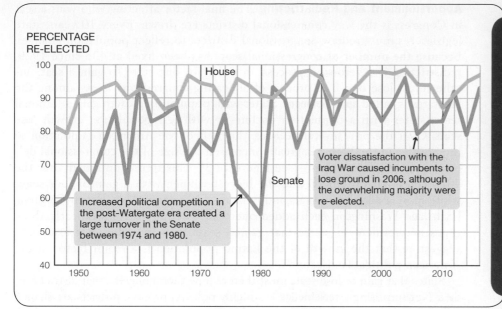

PERCENTAGE
RE-ELECTED

House

Senate

Increased political competition in the post-Watergate era created a large turnover in the Senate between 1974 and 1980.

Voter dissatisfaction with the Iraq War caused incumbents to lose ground in 2006, although the overwhelming majority were re-elected.

FIGURE 12.2

The Power of Incumbency

Members of Congress who run for re-election have a very good chance of winning. Has the incumbency advantage generally been greater in the House or in the Senate? What are the consequences of the incumbency advantage for who serves in Congress?

SOURCES: Norman J. Ornstein et al., eds., *Vital Statistics on Congress, 1999–2000* (Washington, DC: AEI Press, 2000), 57–8; and authors' update.

these members of Congress. For example, Courtney and others on the Frontline team received high-profile speaking assignments on the floor of Congress and were appointed to key congressional committees. In 2008, Courtney won his seat by a comfortable margin, and he was easily re-elected in the four following elections as well.[15]

The advantage of incumbency thus tends to preserve the status quo in Congress. This fact has implications for the social composition of Congress. For example, incumbency advantage makes it harder for women to increase their numbers in Congress because most incumbents are men. Women who run for open seats—that is, seats for which there are no incumbents—are just as likely to win as male candidates.[16] Supporters of **term limits** argue that such limits are the only way to get new faces into Congress. They believe that incumbency advantage and the tendency of many legislators to view politics as a career mean that very little turnover will occur in Congress unless limits are imposed on the number of terms a legislator may serve.

Yet the percentage of incumbents who are returned to Congress after each election also depends on how many members decide to run again. Because each year some members decide to retire, turnover in Congress is greater than the re-election rates of incumbents suggest. On average, 10 percent of the House and Senate decide to retire each election.

The precarious economy and the backlash against the party in power made 2008 and 2010 difficult election years for some incumbents, particularly Democrats, given that their party controlled the presidency and both houses of Congress in a year when economic woes contributed to strong anti-incumbent sentiment.[17] Incumbents have fared better in recent elections. In 2016, Trump's surprise victory in the presidential race benefited Republican incumbents, who appeared to be in danger of losing their seats. As Wisconsin and Pennsylvania threw their support to Trump, Senate incumbents in those states won re-election as well.

term limits legally prescribed limits on the number of terms an elected official can serve

Apportionment and Redistricting The final factor affecting who wins a seat in Congress is the way congressional districts are drawn. Every 10 years, state legislatures must redraw congressional districts to reflect population changes. Because the number of congressional seats has been fixed at 435 since 1929, redistricting is a zero-sum process: in order for one state to gain a seat, another must lose one. The process of allocating congressional seats among the 50 states is called **apportionment**. States with population growth gain additional seats; states with a population decline or with less population growth lose seats. Over the past several decades, the shift of the American population to the South and the West has greatly increased the size of the congressional delegations from those regions (see Figure 12.3). This trend continued after the 2010 census. Texas emerged as the biggest winner, with a gain of four seats, while Florida added two seats and Arizona, Georgia, Nevada, South Carolina, Utah, and Washington each added one seat.[18] Latino voters are nearly three times as prevalent in states that gained seats than in states that lost seats, suggesting that the growth of the Latino population is a major factor in the American political landscape.[19]

States that gain or lose seats must then redraw their congressional district borders. Not surprisingly, **redistricting** is a highly political process: districts are shaped to create an advantage for the party with a majority in the state legislature, which controls the redistricting process in most states. In this complex process, those charged with drawing districts use sophisticated computer technologies to come up with the most favorable district boundaries. Redistricting can create open seats and may pit incumbents of the same party against one another, ensuring that one of them will lose. Redistricting can also give an advantage to one party by clustering voters with some ideological or sociological characteristics in a single district or by

apportionment the process, occurring after every decennial census, that allocates congressional seats among the 50 states

redistricting the process of redrawing election districts and redistributing legislative representatives; this happens every 10 years to reflect shifts in population or in response to legal challenges to existing districts

FIGURE 12.3

Results of Congressional Reapportionment, 2010

States in the South and the West were the big winners in the reapportionment of House seats following the 2010 census. The old manufacturing states in the Midwest and Mid-Atlantic regions were the biggest losers. Which states have the greatest number of House seats?

SOURCES: U.S. Census Bureau, 2010 Apportionment of the U.S. House of Representatives Map, www.census.gov /library/visualizations/2010/dec/2010 -map.html (accessed 8/15/16).

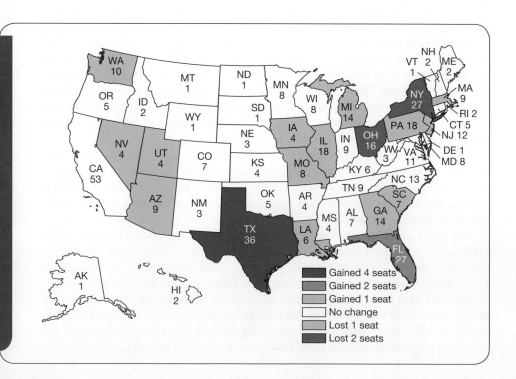

Redrawing legislative districts is a difficult task because it has implications for who will be elected. Here, the attorney for Arizona's Independent Redistricting Commission discusses a possible layout with a city council member from Casa Grande. Arizona gained one congressional seat following the 2010 census.

separating those voters into two or more districts. The manipulation of electoral districts to serve the interests of a particular group is known as **gerrymandering** (see Chapter 10).

Some analysts claim that Republicans have benefited from partisan gerrymandering since the 2010 redistricting cycle because they controlled the majority of state legislatures at the time. To support this argument, they point to the 2012 congressional election, in which the Republican Party maintained its majority in the House despite winning 1.4 million fewer votes than Democratic House candidates.[20] But others question whether districting that favors Republicans is a product of deliberate gerrymandering. They argue that these districts may reflect the natural clustering of Democrats in urban areas, not deliberate bias.[21] Even so, concern about partisan gerrymandering has led some states to take redistricting power away from state legislatures and give it to independent commissions. In the 2010 redistricting cycle, six states—California, Arizona, Idaho, New Jersey, Washington, and Montana—required district lines to be drawn by commissions.[22] In 2015, a challenge to the use of commissions failed when the Supreme Court upheld the legality of relying on commissions to draw congressional district lines. [23]

As we saw in Chapter 10, since the passage of the 1982 amendments to the Voting Rights Act of 1965, race has become a major, and controversial, consideration in drawing voting districts. These amendments, which encouraged the creation of districts in which members of racial minorities have decisive majorities, have greatly increased the number of minority representatives in Congress. After the 1990 redistricting cycle, the number of predominantly minority districts doubled, rising from 26 to 52. Among the most fervent supporters of the new minority districts were white Republicans, who used the opportunity to create more districts dominated by white Republican voters. These developments raise thorny questions about representation. Some analysts argue that the system may grant minorities greater sociological representation but has made it

gerrymandering the apportionment of voters in districts in such a way as to give unfair advantage to one racial or ethnic group or political party

for critical analysis

How does redistricting alter the balance of power in Congress? Why do political parties care so much about the redistricting process?

more difficult for minorities to win substantive policy goals, while others dispute this argument.[24]

In the case of *Miller v. Johnson* (1995), the Supreme Court limited racial redistricting by ruling that race could not be the predominant factor in creating electoral districts.[25] The distinction between race being the "predominant" factor and its being one factor among many is hazy. As a result, concerns about redistricting and representation have not disappeared.[26] Questions about minority representation emerged in 2011 in Texas, which gained four new seats as a result of reapportionment. The Republican legislature drew a map that advantaged Republicans in three of those districts. But the plan drew a legal challenge on the grounds that it underrepresented Hispanic voters, who accounted for most of the state's population growth. Although federal judges drew a map more favorable to minorities (and Democrats), the Supreme Court ruled that the state did not have to use the map drawn by judges. The state ultimately agreed to a map that added two Latino-dominated districts. However, federal courts ruled that this map also weakened Latino and African American political power by creating too few minority districts.

The future of race in redistricting became more uncertain after the 2013 Supreme Court decision in *Shelby County v. Holder*. That decision invalidated a section of the Voting Rights Act requiring that the Justice Department approve the redistricting plans of jurisdictions with a history of racial discrimination.[27] Many Democrats expressed disappointment with the decision, fearing that the previously covered states, several of which are controlled by Republican majorities, might try to redraw district lines to partisan ends and further bias districts toward Republicans.[28] In 2015, Alabama's black legislators challenged that state's redistricting under the Voting Rights Act. They charged that the Republican legislature had diluted the vote of African Americans by packing black voters into districts that already had strong minority representation, thus enhancing the chances of white Republican candidates in the remaining districts. The legislature claimed, on the contrary, that it was acting in accordance with the Voting Rights Act by concentrating black voters. Although the Supreme Court did not declare the districting unconstitutional, it ruled that the lower court had erred in approving the districts.[29] The ruling signaled that state legislatures would not be able to use the Voting Rights Act to justify packing minority voters into districts. Because the drawing of district boundaries affects incumbents as well as the field of candidates who decide to run for office, it continues to be a key battleground on which political parties fight about the meaning of representation.

Direct Patronage

As agents of their constituents, members of Congress have numerous opportunities to provide direct benefits, or **patronage**, for their districts. The most important such opportunity for direct patronage is in so-called **pork-barrel** legislation, which specifies a project to be funded within a particular district. Many observers of Congress argue that pork-barrel bills are the only ones that some members are serious about moving toward actual passage because they are seen as so important to members' re-election bids.

A common form of pork-barreling is the "earmark," by which members of Congress insert into bills language that provides special benefits for their own constituents. When the Democrats took over Congress in 2007, they vowed to limit the use of earmarks, which had grown from 1,439 per year in 1995 to 15,268 in

patronage the resources available to higher officials, usually opportunities to make partisan appointments to offices and to confer grants, licenses, or special favors to supporters

pork barrel (or pork) appropriations made by legislative bodies for local projects that are often not needed but that are created so that local representatives can win re-election in their home districts

2006. More troubling, earmarks were connected to congressional scandals. For example, the Republican House member Randy "Duke" Cunningham (R-Calif.) was sent to jail in 2005 for accepting bribes by companies hoping to receive earmarks in return.[30] The House passed a new rule requiring that those representatives supporting each earmark identify themselves and guarantee that they have no personal financial stake in the requested project. A new ethics law applied similar provisions to the Senate. The new requirements appear to have had some impact: the 2007 military bill, for example, passed with only half the dollar amount of earmarks as the military bill passed in 2006 contained. But in the midst of the sharp economic downturn in 2009, Congress passed an economic stimulus bill that contained more than 8,000 earmarks. In many cases, Republicans and some Democrats who voted against the bill were later happy to take credit from their constituents for the earmarks they had placed in it. In his 2010 State of the Union address, President Obama called for Congress to publish a list of all earmark requests on a single website. Congress not only failed to enact such legislation but in 2010 set a new record by passing 11,320 earmarks worth $32 billion. Still, in 2011 the House and the Senate agreed to a two-year moratorium on earmarks in spending bills and renewed the ban for the 113th and 114th Congresses.[31] Some analysts claim that the lack of earmarks contributes to congressional gridlock. They argue that earmarks provide congressional leaders with incentives to promote compromise among members. Supporters of this position contend that earmarks are not inherently an abuse of power and note that they often support legitimate district projects, such as transportation and parks.[32]

Highway bills are a favorite vehicle for congressional pork-barrel spending. A 2005 highway bill was full of such items, containing more than 6,000 projects earmarked for specific congressional districts. These measures often have little to do with transportation needs, instead serving as evidence for constituents that congressional members can bring federal dollars back home. Perhaps the most extravagant item in the 2005 bill—and the one least needed for transportation—was a bridge in Alaska designed to connect a barely populated island to the town of Ketchikan, population just under 8,000. At a cost that could soar to $2 billion, the bridge would have replaced an existing five-minute ferry ride. Alaska's representative, Don Young (R), proudly claimed credit. After Hurricane Katrina, "the bridge to nowhere" became a symbol of wasteful congressional spending. Sensitive to this criticism, Congress removed the earmarks for the bridge from the final legislation.

There are a few other types of direct patronage (see Figure 12.4). One important form of constituency service is intervention with federal administrative agencies on behalf of constituents. Members of the House and Senate and their staff spend a great deal of time on the telephone and in administrative offices seeking to secure favorable treatment for constituents and supporters. For example, members of Congress can assist senior citizens who are having Social Security or Medicare benefit eligibility problems. Most members of Congress have a "constituent services" section on their websites, providing information about what they can and cannot do to assist their constituents. For example, House Speaker Paul Ryan's (R-Wisc.) website puts it this way: "one of the most important jobs I have is to provide assistance to my constituents. Providing help with a problem involving a federal agency or helping obtain an American flag flown over the U.S. Capitol are only a few examples of the number of services that I provide to those I represent."[33]

for critical analysis

Would Congress work more effectively if it brought back earmarks? Why are earmarks so difficult to eliminate?

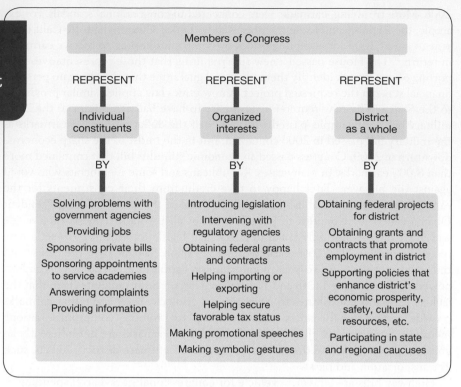

FIGURE 12.4

How Members of Congress Represent Their Districts

Members of Congress

REPRESENT — Individual constituents — BY

- Solving problems with government agencies
- Providing jobs
- Sponsoring private bills
- Sponsoring appointments to service academies
- Answering complaints
- Providing information

REPRESENT — Organized interests — BY

- Introducing legislation
- Intervening with regulatory agencies
- Obtaining federal grants and contracts
- Helping importing or exporting
- Helping secure favorable tax status
- Making promotional speeches
- Making symbolic gestures

REPRESENT — District as a whole — BY

- Obtaining federal projects for district
- Obtaining grants and contracts that promote employment in district
- Supporting policies that enhance district's economic prosperity, safety, cultural resources, etc.
- Participating in state and regional caucuses

private bill a proposal in Congress to provide a specific person with some kind of relief, such as a special exemption from immigration quotas

A different form of patronage is the **private bill**. Unlike a public bill, which is supposed to deal with general rules and categories of behavior, people, and institutions, a private bill proposes to grant some kind of relief, special privilege, or exemption to the person named in the bill. As many as 75 percent of all private bills introduced (and one-third of those that pass) are concerned with obtaining citizenship for foreign nationals who do not have resident status in the United States. Other private bills address a diverse set of issues involving a claim against the federal government, such as problems with veterans' benefits or taxation. Private legislation is a congressional privilege that can be abused, but it is impossible to imagine members of Congress completely giving up one of the easiest, cheapest, and most effective forms of patronage available to them. It can be defended as an indispensable part of the process by which members of Congress seek to fulfill their role as representatives. And obviously they like the privilege because it helps them win re-election.

● The Organization of Congress

> **Explain how party leadership, the committee system, the staff system, and caucuses help structure congressional business**

The U.S. Congress is not only a representative assembly but also a legislative body. To exercise its power to make laws, Congress must first bring about something close to an organizational miracle. The building blocks of congressional organization include the political parties, the committee system, congressional staff, the caucuses, and the parliamentary rules of the House and Senate. Each of these factors plays a key role in the organization of Congress and in the process through which Congress formulates and enacts laws.

Party Leadership in the House

Every two years, at the beginning of a new Congress, the members of each party gather to elect their House leaders. House Republicans call their gathering the **conference**. House Democrats call theirs the **caucus**. The elected leader of the majority party is later proposed to the whole House and is automatically elected to the position of **Speaker of the House**, with voting along straight party lines. The House majority conference or caucus then also elects a **majority leader**. The minority party goes through the same process and selects a **minority leader**. Each party also elects a **whip** to line up party members on important votes and to relay voting information to the leaders.

Next in order of importance for each party after the Speaker and majority or minority leader is what Democrats call the Steering and Policy Committee—Republicans have a separate steering committee and a separate policy committee—whose tasks are to assign new legislators to committees and to deal with the requests of incumbent members for transfers from one committee to another. At one time, party leaders strictly controlled committee assignments, using them to enforce party discipline. Today, in principle, representatives receive the assignments they want. But often several individuals seek assignments to the most important committees, which gives the leadership an opportunity to cement alliances when it resolves conflicting requests.

Generally, representatives seek assignments that will allow them to influence decisions of special importance to their districts. Representatives from farm districts, for example, may request seats on the Agriculture Committee.[34] Seats on powerful committees such as Ways and Means, which is responsible for tax legislation, and Appropriations are especially popular.

Party Leadership in the Senate

Within the Senate, the majority party usually designates a member with the greatest seniority to serve as president pro tempore, a position of primarily ceremonial leadership. Real power is in the hands of the majority leader and minority leader, each elected by party conference. Together they control the Senate's calendar, or agenda for legislation. Each party also elects a policy committee, which advises the leadership on legislative priorities. The structure of majority party leadership in the House and the Senate is shown in Figures 12.5 and 12.6.

The Committee System

The committee system is central to the operation of Congress. At each stage of the legislative process, Congress relies on committees and subcommittees to do the hard work of sorting through alternatives and writing legislation. There are several different kinds of congressional committees: standing committees, select committees, joint committees, and conference committees.

Standing Committees The most important arenas of congressional policy making are **standing committees**. These committees remain in existence from one session

conference a gathering of House Republicans every two years to elect their House leaders; Democrats call their gathering the "caucus"

caucus (political) a normally closed political party business meeting of citizens or lawmakers to select candidates, elect officers, plan strategy, or make decisions regarding legislative matters

Speaker of the House the chief presiding officer of the House of Representatives; the Speaker is the most important party and House leader and can influence the legislative agenda, the fate of individual pieces of legislation, and members' positions within the House

majority leader the elected leader of the majority party in the House of Representatives or in the Senate; in the House, the majority leader is subordinate in the party hierarchy to the Speaker of the House

minority leader the elected leader of the minority party in the House or Senate

whip a party member in the House or Senate responsible for coordinating the party's legislative strategy, building support for key issues, and counting votes

standing committee a permanent committee with the power to propose and write legislation that covers a particular subject, such as finance or agriculture

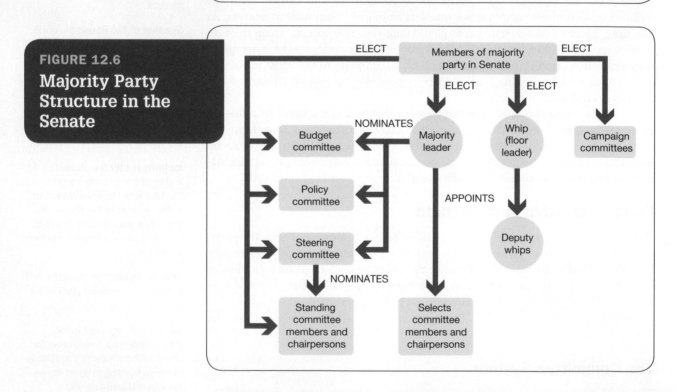

FIGURE 12.5

Majority Party Structure in the House of Representatives

*Includes Speaker, majority leader, chief and deputy whips, caucus chair, chairs of five major committees, members elected by regional caucuses, members elected by recently elected representatives, and at-large members appointed by the Speaker.

ELECT — Members of majority party in House — ELECT

ELECT ELECT ELECT ELECT

Rules committee — NOMINATES — Speaker

Budget committee

Majority leader

Whip

Committee members and chairpersons — NOMINATES — Policy committee*

APPOINTS

Campaign committee

FIGURE 12.6

Majority Party Structure in the Senate

ELECT — Members of majority party in Senate — ELECT

ELECT ELECT

Budget committee — NOMINATES — Majority leader

Whip (floor leader)

Campaign committees

Policy committee

Steering committee

APPOINTS

Deputy whips

Standing committee members and chairpersons — NOMINATES

Selects committee members and chairpersons

of Congress to the next; they have the power to propose and write legislation. The jurisdiction of each standing committee covers a particular subject matter, which in most cases parallels a major department or agency in the executive branch (see Table 12.2). Among the most important standing committees are those in charge of finances. The House Ways and Means Committee and the Senate Finance Committee are powerful because of their jurisdiction over taxes, trade, and expensive entitlement programs such as Social Security and Medicare. The Senate and

TABLE 12.2

Permanent Committees of Congress

HOUSE COMMITTEES

Agriculture	Financial Services	Oversight and Government Reform
Appropriations	Foreign Affairs	Rules
Armed Services	Homeland Security	Science, Space, and Technology
Budget	House Administration	Small Business
Education and the Workforce	Intelligence	Transportation and Infrastructure
Energy and Commerce	Judiciary	Veterans' Affairs
Ethics	Natural Resources	Ways and Means

SENATE COMMITTEES

Agriculture, Nutrition, and Forestry	Energy and Natural Resources	Intelligence
Appropriations	Environment and Public Works	Judiciary
Armed Services	Finance	Rules and Administration
Banking, Housing, and Urban Affairs	Foreign Relations	Small Business and Entrepreneurship
Budget	Health, Education, Labor, and Pensions	Veterans' Affairs
Commerce, Science, and Transportation	Homeland Security and Governmental Affairs	

House Appropriations committees also play important ongoing roles because they decide how much funding various programs will actually receive; they also determine exactly how the money will be spent. A seat on an appropriations committee allows a member the opportunity to direct funds to a favored program—perhaps one in his home district.

Except for the House Rules Committee, all standing committees receive proposals for legislation and process them into official bills. The House Rules Committee decides the order in which bills come up for a vote on the House floor and determines the specific rules that govern the length of debate and opportunity for amendments. The Senate, which has less formal organization and fewer rules, does not have a rules committee.

Select Committees **Select committees** are usually not permanent and usually do not have the power to present legislation to the full Congress. (The House and Senate Select Intelligence committees are permanent, however, and do have the power to report legislation, which means they can send legislation to the full House or Senate for consideration.) These committees hold hearings and serve as focal points for the issues they are charged with considering. Congressional leaders form select committees when they want to take up issues that fall outside

select committees (usually) temporary legislative committees set up to highlight or investigate a particular issue or address an issue not within the jurisdiction of existing committees

Committees hold hearings to gather information for legislation. The Committee on Homeland Security was set up as a select committee in the wake of 9/11 and is now a permanent committee. In February 2014, the committee listened to testimony from U.S. Homeland Security Secretary Jeh Johnson on challenges and priorities facing his department.

the jurisdictions of existing committees, to highlight an issue, or to investigate a particular problem. For example, the Senate set up the Senate Watergate Committee in 1973 to investigate the Watergate break-in and cover-up. More recently, the House Select Committee on Benghazi was established to investigate the 2012 attack on the U.S. Embassy in Benghazi, Libya. In 2015 the committee held hearings to investigate Hillary Clinton's use of private email services during her tenure as secretary of state.

Select committees set up to highlight ongoing issues have included the House Select Committee on Hunger, established in 1984, and the House Select Committee on Energy Independence and Global Warming, created in 2007 but abolished in 2011, when Republicans assumed control of the House. In 2003 an important select committee, the House Select Committee on Homeland Security, was created to oversee the new Department of Homeland Security. Unlike most select committees, this one had the ability to present legislation. Initially the committee had only temporary status. It was made a regular permanent committee in 2005.

Joint Committees **Joint committees** involve members from both the Senate and the House. There are four such committees: economic, taxation, library, and printing. These joint committees are permanent, but they do not have the power to present legislation. The Joint Economic Committee and the Joint Taxation Committee have often played important roles in collecting information and holding hearings on economic and financial issues. In 2011, Congress created the Joint Select Committee on Deficit Reduction and, in an unusual move, gave the committee the power to write and report legislation. Informally known as "the super-committee," the committee was charged with coming up with $1.2 trillion in debt reduction. Formed after a contentious debate about raising the debt limit (usually a routine matter), the super-committee proved unable to come to an agreement and disbanded less than four months after it was created.

Conference Committees Finally, **conference committees** are temporary committees whose members are appointed by the Speaker of the House and the presiding

joint committees legislative committees formed of members of both the House and Senate

conference committees joint committees created to work out a compromise on House and Senate versions of a piece of legislation

officer of the Senate. These committees are charged with reaching a compromise on legislation once it has been passed by the House and the Senate. Conference committees play an extremely important role in determining the laws that are actually passed because they must reconcile any differences in the legislation passed by the House and Senate.

When control of Congress is divided between two parties, each is guaranteed significant representation in conference committees. When a single party controls both houses, the majority party is not obligated to offer such representation to the minority party. In 2003, Democrats complained that Republicans took this power to the extreme by excluding them and adding new provisions to legislation at the conference committee stage. Democrats even prevented several conference committees from convening to protest their near exclusion from conference committees on major energy, health care, and transportation laws. After they returned to power in 2007, the Democrats also largely bypassed the conference committees; when their early efforts to reach compromises in committee were derailed by partisan differences, the Democrats began making closed-door agreements between top leaders in the House and the Senate. Although the process facilitated compromises across the two chambers, it meant that important changes to bills were made in private, without the transparency that would have been part of the conference committee process. After 2010, Congress continued to avoid conference committees. Instead, the Republican House and Democratic Senate exchanged amendments as they sought to reach agreement on the final version of a bill, a practice known informally as "ping pong."[35]

Politics and the Organization of Committees Within each committee, hierarchy has usually been based on **seniority**, determined by years of continuous service on that particular committee. In general, each committee is chaired by the most senior member of the majority party. But the principle of seniority is not absolute. When the Republicans took over the House in 1995, they violated the principle of seniority in the selection of key committee chairs. House Speaker Newt Gingrich defended the new practice, saying, "You've got to carry the moral responsibility of fielding the team that can win or you cheat the whole conference."[36] Since then, Republicans have continued to depart from the seniority principle, often choosing committee chairs on the basis of loyalty or fund-raising abilities rather than seniority. In 2007, Democrats returned to the seniority principle for choosing committee chairs but altered traditional practices in other ways by offering freshmen Democrats choice committee assignments to increase their chances of re-election.[37]

Over the years, Congress has reformed its organizational structure and operating procedures. Most changes have been made to improve efficiency, but some reforms have also been a response to political considerations. In the 1970s, for example, Congress increased the number of subcommittees and gave greater autonomy to subcommittee chairs. (Subcommittees are responsible for considering a specific subset of issues under a committee's jurisdiction.) By enhancing subcommittee power and allowing more members to chair subcommittees and appoint subcommittee staff, the reforms undercut the power of committee chairs. Yet the reforms of the 1970s created new problems for Congress: power became more fragmented, making it harder to reach agreement on legislation. The Republican leadership of the 104th Congress (1995–97), seeking to reverse this fragmentation of congressional power and concentrate more authority in the party leadership, reduced the number of subcommittees and limited the time committee chairs

seniority the ranking given to an individual on the basis of length of continuous service on a committee in Congress

could serve to three terms. They made good on this in 2001, when they replaced 13 committee chairs.

As a consequence of these changes, committees no longer have the central role they once held in policy making. Furthermore, sharp partisan divisions have made it difficult for committees to deliberate and bring bipartisan expertise to bear on policy making as in the past. With committees less able to engage in effective decision making, they typically do not deliberate for very long or call witnesses, and it has become more common in recent years for party-driven legislation to go directly to the floor, bypassing committees altogether.[38] Nonetheless, committees continue to play a role in the legislative process, especially on issues that are not sharply partisan.[39]

The Staff System: Staffers and Agencies

The congressional institution second in importance only to the committee system is the staff system. Every member of Congress employs many staff members whose tasks include handling constituent requests and, to a large extent, dealing with legislative details and the activities of administrative agencies. Staffers often bear the primary responsibility for formulating and drafting proposals, organizing hearings, dealing with administrative agencies, and negotiating with lobbyists. Indeed, legislators typically deal with one another through staff, rather than through direct personal contact. Staffers even develop policy ideas, draft legislation, and, in some instances, have a good deal of influence over the legislative process. Representatives and senators together employ roughly 11,500 staffers in their Washington and home offices. In addition, Congress employs more than 2,000 committee staffers.[40] These individuals make up the permanent staff that stays attached to every House and Senate committee regardless of turnover in Congress and that is responsible for organizing and administering the committee's work, including doing research, scheduling, organizing hearings, and drafting legislation. Committee staffers can play key roles in the legislative process.

One example of the importance that members of Congress attach to committee staffers was the conflict over hiring a new staff director for the House Ethics Committee in 2005. The Committee on Ethics has the power to investigate members for unethical practices and can issue reprimands or censures when it finds that members have violated House rules. In 2010, with allegations of ethics violations swirling around several prominent House members, including long-serving representative Maxine Waters (D-Calif.) and the successful censuring of Charles Rangel (D-N.Y.), then the powerful chair of the Ways and Means Committee, the Committee on Ethics was at the center of congressional conflict. But following a series of tumultuous shakeups in which the staff director resigned and two deputy attorneys were effectively fired over allegations of mishandling the Waters investigation, the committee was at a standstill for more than four months as Republicans and Democrats struggled to agree on an acceptable staff director replacement.[41]

Not only does Congress employ personal and committee staff, but it has also established **staff agencies** designed to provide the legislative branch with resources and expertise independent

staff agencies legislative support agencies responsible for policy analysis

Members of Congress rely heavily on their personal staffs and on committee staffs, who often play an important role in the legislative process.

Legislatures in Comparison

While in most democracies, the executive takes the lead role in initiating and directing the legislative process (with the parliament limited to amending or vetoing legislation), the U.S. Constitution gives this power to Congress. Reflecting this greater power, the budget of the U.S. Congress is the highest in the world, as is the number of staff members working for it.

The membership of the U.S. Congress also *looks* different than that of most other legislative bodies; its members tend to be older, and there are fewer women, than the global democracy average. While countries like Finland are nearing gender equality in their representation, women make up less than one-fifth of the U.S. Congress. Many countries have set compulsory or voluntary gender quotas for their list of candidates running for election, or have reserved a percentage of seats for women in their parliament. The United States has no such quotas. However, it is unclear whether quotas lead to more women in parliament, or whether the societies that value women's representation (and therefore already elect more women) choose to create gender quotas.

Another difference is that the U.S. Congress has more "professional politicians"—representatives who have only had political careers—than other legislatures. Professionalization has been on the rise in parliaments around the world, which has sparked a debate about whether increasing numbers of professional politicians is good or bad for democracy. While some analysts have argued that professional politicians are more "out of touch" with life outside of politics, others point out that professional politicians are more knowledgeable and effective at navigating the political system, and thus better able to represent their constituents' interests.

	United States (114th Congress)	Democracy Average*	Finland
Structure of Legislature			
Bicameral or unicameral?	Bicameral	Unicameral more common	Unicameral
Number of representatives	535	214	200
Citizens per representative	588,100	70,100	26,600
Budget (in U.S. dollars)	$5.1 billion	$264.8 million	$145.3 million
Cost per inhabitant	$16.27	$22.30	$27.29
Average number of staff per member	29.7	3.3	2.36
Membership Demographics			
"Professional politicians"	62%	13.3%	18%
Average age	57 (House) 61 (Senate)	54	52
Women	19.4% (House) 20% (Senate)	21.8% (Lower House) 26.7% (Upper House)	41.5%

*Of the 129 parliaments who provided voluntary data to *2012 Global Parliamentary Report,* only 86 were rated as "free" that year according to Freedom House. These 86 were selected to represent the democracy average.

SOURCES: Jennifer E. Manning, "Membership of the 114th Congress: A Profile," October 13, 2015, www.senate.gov/CRSReports/crs-publish.cfm?pid=%260BL*RLC2%0A (accessed 11/30/15); IPU and UNDP, *Global Parliamentary Report,* 2012; www.ipu.org/gpr-e/downloads/index.htm (accessed 4/29/16); and IPU Parline Database, "Women in National Parliaments," 2015, www.ipu.org/wmn-e/classif.htm (accessed 4/30/16).

of the executive branch. These agencies enhance Congress's capacity to oversee administrative agencies and to evaluate presidential programs and proposals. They include the Congressional Research Service, which performs research for legislators who wish to know the facts and competing arguments relevant to policy proposals or other legislative business; the Government Accountability Office, through which Congress can investigate the financial and administrative affairs of any government agency or program; and the Congressional Budget Office, which assesses the economic implications and likely costs of proposed federal programs.

Informal Organization: The Caucuses

caucuses (congressional)
associations of members of Congress based on party, interest, or social group, such as gender or race

In addition to the official organization of Congress, an unofficial organizational structure also exists: the caucuses. **Caucuses** are groups of senators or representatives who share certain opinions, interests, or social characteristics. A large number of caucuses are composed of legislators representing particular economic or policy interests, such as the Travel and Tourism Caucus, the Steel Caucus, and Concerned Senators for the Arts. Legislators who share common backgrounds have organized caucuses such as the Congressional Black Caucus, the Congressional Caucus for Women's Issues, and the Congressional Hispanic Caucus. All these caucuses seek to advance the interests of the groups they represent by promoting legislation, encouraging Congress to hold hearings, and pressing administrative agencies for favorable treatment. In recent years, some caucuses have evolved into powerful lobbying organizations, well funded by interest groups. For example, the Sportsmen's Caucus receives funds from a nonprofit foundation that itself benefits from donations from the National Rifle Association, sports equipment manufacturers, and firearms manufacturers. In 2010 conservative Republicans in the House and Senate formed the Tea Party Caucus to advance antispending policies.

● Rules of Lawmaking: How a Bill Becomes a Law

> **Outline the steps in the process of passing a law**

The institutional structure of Congress is a key factor in shaping the legislative process. A second and equally important set of factors is the rules of congressional procedure. These rules govern everything from the introduction of a **bill** through its submission to the president for signing (see Figure 12.7). Not only do these regulations influence the fate of every bill, but they also help determine the distribution of power in the Congress.

bill a proposed law that has been sponsored by a member of Congress and submitted to the clerk of the House or Senate

Committee Deliberation

The first step in getting a law passed is drafting legislation. Members of Congress, the White House, and federal agencies all take roles in developing and drafting initial legislation. Bills can originate in the House or the Senate, but only the House can introduce "money bills," those that spend or raise revenues. The framers inserted this provision in the Constitution because they believed that the chamber closest to the people should exercise greater authority over taxing and spending.

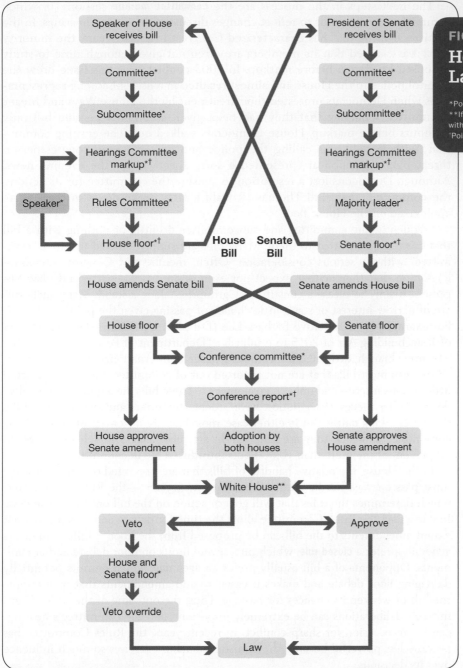

FIGURE 12.7

How a Bill Becomes a Law

*Points at which a bill can be amended.
**If the president neither signs nor vetoes a bill within 10 days, it automatically becomes law.
†Points at which a bill can die.

Speaker of House receives bill → **Committee*** → **Subcommittee*** → **Hearings Committee markup*†** → **Rules Committee*** → **House floor*†**

Speaker*

President of Senate receives bill → **Committee*** → **Subcommittee*** → **Hearings Committee markup*†** → **Majority leader*** → **Senate floor*†**

House Bill   **Senate Bill**

House amends Senate bill   **Senate amends House bill**

House floor   **Senate floor**

Conference committee*

Conference report*†

House approves Senate amendment   **Adoption by both houses**   **Senate approves House amendment**

White House**

Veto   **Approve**

House and Senate floor*

Veto override

Law

The bill is then officially submitted by a senator or representative to the clerk of the House or Senate and referred to the appropriate committee for deliberation. During the course of its deliberations, the committee typically refers the bill to one of its subcommittees, which may hold hearings, listen to expert testimony, and amend the proposed legislation before referring it to the full committee for consideration. The full committee may then accept the recommendation of the subcommittee or hold its own hearings and prepare its own amendments.

committee markup the session in which a congressional committee rewrites legislation to incorporate changes discussed during hearings on a bill

The next steps in the process are the **committee markup** sessions, in which committees rewrite bills to reflect changes discussed during the hearings. In the partisan fighting that has characterized Congress in recent years, the minority party has charged that its members are often not given enough time to study proposed legislation before markup. In 2003 conflict over this issue drew the Capitol police to the House and almost resulted in a fistfight among representatives when Democrats protested their treatment by the House Ways and Means Committee. Charging that they had been given a complex pension bill only 10 hours before markup, House Democrats walked out. The ensuing commotion, with Republicans calling the police and a Democratic congressperson threatening a Republican, presented a sorry spectacle for the evening news. Although Democrats lost a resolution to censure the committee for its actions, the committee chair, Bill Thomas (R-Calif.), later broke down in tears as he apologized on the House floor.

Frequently, the committee and subcommittee do little or nothing with a bill that has been submitted to them. Many bills are simply allowed to "die in committee" without serious consideration. Often, members of Congress introduce legislation that they neither expect nor even desire to see enacted into law but present mainly to please a constituency group by taking a stand. Many such bills are of narrow interest or stand little chance of passing given the political climate. For example, Representative Barbara Lee (D-Calif.) introduced the Department of Peacebuilding Act of 2015 to establish a "Department of Peacebuilding" in the executive branch, dedicated to promoting peace in international affairs.

As with most bills that are not reported out of committee, Lee's bill attracted little serious interest and only 26 cosponsors.[42] These bills die a quick and painless death. Other pieces of legislation have ardent supporters and die in committee only after a long battle. But in either case, most bills are never reported out of the committees to which they are assigned. In a typical congressional session, 80 to 90 percent of the more than 10,000 bills introduced die in committee.[43]

In the House, the relative handful of bills that are presented out of committee must pass one last hurdle within the committee system—the Rules Committee, which determines the rules that will govern action on the bill on the House floor. In particular, the Rules Committee allots the time for debate and decides to what extent amendments to the bill can be proposed from the floor. A bill's supporters generally prefer a **closed rule**, which puts severe limits on floor debate and amendments. Opponents of a bill usually prefer an **open rule**, which permits potentially damaging floor debate and makes it easier to add amendments that may cripple the bill or weaken its chances for passage. Thus, the outcome of the Rules Committee's deliberations can be extremely important, and the committee's hearings can be an occasion for sharp conflict. In recent years, the Rules Committee has become less powerful because the House leadership exercises so much influence over its decisions.

closed rule a provision by the House Rules Committee limiting or prohibiting the introduction of amendments during debate

open rule a provision by the House Rules Committee that permits floor debate and the addition of new amendments to a bill

Debate

The next step in getting a law passed is debate on the floor of the House and Senate. Party control of the agenda is reinforced by the rule giving the Speaker of the House and the president of the Senate the power of recognition during debate on a bill. Usually the chair knows the purpose for which a member intends to speak well in advance of the occasion. Spontaneous efforts to gain recognition are often foiled. For example, the Speaker may ask, "For what purpose does the member rise?" before deciding whether to grant recognition.

In the House, virtually all the time allotted by the Rules Committee for debate on a given bill is controlled by the bill's sponsor and by its leading opponent. In almost every case, these two people are the committee chair and the ranking minority member of the committee that processed the bill—or those they designate. These two participants are, by rule and tradition, granted the power to allocate most of the debate time in small amounts to members who are seeking to speak for or against the measure. Preference in the allocation of time goes to the members of the committee whose jurisdiction covers the bill.

Filibuster In the Senate, the leadership has much less control over floor debate. Indeed, the Senate is unique among the world's legislative bodies for its commitment to unlimited debate. Once given the floor, a senator may speak as long as she wishes. On a number of memorable occasions, senators have used this opportunity to prevent action on legislation that they opposed. Through this tactic, called the **filibuster**, small minorities or even one individual in the Senate can force the majority to give in. Filibusters can be ended by a Senate vote to cut off debate, called **cloture**. From 1917 to 1975, it took two-thirds of the Senate or 67 votes to end a filibuster. In 1975 the Senate changed the rules to three-fifths of the Senate or 60 votes needed for cloture. The threat of a filibuster ensures that, in crafting legislation and proposing judicial appointments, the majority takes into account the viewpoint of the political minority.

For much of American history, senators only rarely used the filibuster, though during the 1950s and '60s, opponents of civil rights legislation often used filibusters to block its passage. In the last 20 years, the filibuster has become so common that observers routinely note that it takes 60 votes to get anything passed in the Senate. While the 109th Congress (2005–06) held only 54 cloture votes (the vote to end a filibuster), the 113th Congress (2013–14) broke the record with 218 cloture votes.[44]

In 2013 the Democratic Senate leader Harry Reid (Nev.) mobilized his party to alter the filibuster rules for the first time in many decades. Frustrated by the repeated failure of the Senate to vote on many of the president's nominees to fill positions in the executive branch. As well as judgeships to important federal courts, Reid invoked what senators had come to call "the nuclear option," a change to the filibuster rules. Under the new rules, nominees for positions in the executive branch and the federal courts—except the Supreme Court—cannot be filibustered. This means that they can be approved by a simple majority vote. Not surprisingly, the two parties had different views on the decision. Reid defended it as necessary, due to what he called "unbelievable, unprecedented obstruction." Republicans denounced the new rule, stating, in the words of Pat Roberts (R-Kans.), "We have weakened this body permanently."[45] After they assumed leadership of the Senate in 2015, Republicans retained Reid's filibuster rules for some executive branch nominees but have retained the filibuster for legislation despite calls from some Republicans to eliminate the filibuster altogether.[46]

Amendments and Holds The filibuster is not the only technique used to block Senate debate. Under Senate rules, members have virtually unlimited ability to propose amendments to a pending bill. Each amendment must be voted on before the bill can come to a final vote. The introduction of new amendments can be stopped

Once a senator is granted the floor, Senate rules permit him to speak for as long as he wishes. Although "talking filibusters" are rare today, in May 2015 Senator Rand Paul (R-Ky.) spoke continuously for 10½ hours, challenging the legality of government surveillance in his opposition to renew the Patriot Act.

filibuster a tactic used by members of the Senate to prevent action on legislation they oppose by continuously holding the floor and speaking until the majority backs down; once given the floor, senators have unlimited time to speak, and it requires a vote of three-fifths of the Senate to end a filibuster

cloture a rule or process in a legislative body aimed at ending debate on a given bill; in the U.S. Senate, 60 senators (three-fifths) must agree in order to impose a time limit and end debate

only by unanimous consent. This, in effect, can permit a determined minority to filibuster by amendment, indefinitely delaying the passage of a bill. Senators can also place "holds," or stalling devices, on bills to delay debate. Senators place holds on bills when they fear that openly opposing them will be unpopular. Because holds are kept secret, the senators placing the holds do not have to take public responsibility for their actions. There have been several efforts to eliminate holds. In 2007 reformers succeeded in passing the Honest Leadership and Open Government Act. Although the new law did not eliminate holds, it contained provisions requiring senators who imposed a hold to identify themselves in the *Congressional Record* after six days and state the reasons for the hold.[47] Even with this provision, senators continued to impose holds on legislation and especially on presidential appointees. Senator Lindsey Graham (R-S.C.) aroused the ire of the White House in 2013 for threatening to use holds on all of President Obama's nominees unless the administration made survivors of the 2012 terrorist attack on the U.S. mission in Benghazi, Libya, available to Congress for questioning.[48]

Voting Once a bill is debated on the floor of the House and the Senate, the leaders schedule it for a vote on the floor of each chamber. Leaders do not bring legislation to the floor unless they are fairly certain it is going to pass. On rare occasions, the last moments of the floor vote can be very dramatic as each party's leadership puts its whip organization into action to make sure that wavering members vote with the party. In 2015, the House of Representatives failed to pass a spending bill to fund the Department of Homeland Security hours before the agency was to run out of money and begin to shut down. Despite having a majority in the chamber and an early vote that suggested that the bill would pass easily, House Republican Party leaders failed to prevent the most conservative members of the party from suddenly abandoning the bill over objections that it left out provisions to block President Obama's executive actions on immigration. As midnight approached, the House agreed on a one-week extension to keep the department open.[49] Leaders later secured sufficient support to enact longer-term funding for Homeland Security.

Conference Committee: Reconciling House and Senate Versions of Legislation

Getting a bill out of committee and through both houses of Congress is no guarantee that the bill will be enacted into law; it must be considered by a conference committee. Frequently, bills that begin with similar provisions in both chambers emerge with little resemblance to each other. Alternatively, a bill may be passed by one chamber but undergo substantial revision in the other chamber. In such cases, a conference committee composed of the senior members of the committees or subcommittees that initiated the bill may be required to iron out differences between the two now dissimilar pieces of legislation. Sometimes members or leaders will let objectionable provisions pass on the floor, knowing that they will get the chance to make changes in conference. Usually, conference committees meet behind closed doors. Agreement requires a majority of each of the two delegations. Legislation that emerges successfully from a conference committee is more often a compromise than a clear victory for one side. In recent years, as we have seen, polarization in Congress has led to much less reliance on conference committees. Instead, leaders exchange amendments in the hope of reaching agreement.

When a bill comes out of conference, it faces one more hurdle. Before it can be sent to the president for signing, the House–Senate conference committee's version of the bill must be approved on the floor of each chamber. Usually such approval is given quickly. Occasionally, however, a bill's opponents use this round of approval as one last opportunity to defeat a piece of legislation.

Presidential Action

The final step in passing a law is presidential approval. Once adopted by the House and Senate, a bill goes to the president, who may choose to sign the bill into law or veto it. If the president does not sign the bill or veto it within 10 days and Congress is in session, the bill automatically becomes law. The **veto** is the president's constitutional power to reject a piece of legislation. To veto a bill, the president returns it unsigned within 10 days to the house of Congress in which it originated. If Congress adjourns during the 10-day period and the president has taken no action, the bill is also considered to be vetoed. This latter method is known as the **pocket veto**. The possibility of a presidential veto affects how willing members of Congress are to push for different pieces of legislation at different times. If they think a proposal is likely to be vetoed, they might shelve it until a later time.

A presidential veto may be overridden by a two-thirds vote in both the House and Senate. A veto override says much about the support that a president can expect from Congress, and it can deliver a stinging blow to the executive branch. Presidents will often back down from a veto threat if they believe that Congress will override the veto.

veto the president's constitutional power to turn down acts of Congress; a presidential veto may be overridden by a two-thirds vote of each house of Congress

pocket veto a presidential veto that is automatically triggered if the president does not act on a given piece of legislation passed during the final 10 days of a legislative session

● How Congress Decides

> **Analyze the factors that influence which laws Congress passes**

What determines the kinds of legislation that Congress ultimately produces? According to the simplest theories of representation, members of Congress respond to the views of their constituents. In fact, the process of creating a legislative agenda, drawing up a list of possible measures, and deciding among them is a very complex one, in which a variety of influences from inside and outside government play important roles. External influences include a legislator's constituency and various interest groups. Influences from inside government include party leadership, congressional colleagues, and the president. Let us examine each of these influences individually and then consider how they interact to produce congressional policy decisions.

Constituency

Because members of Congress, for the most part, want to be re-elected, we would expect the views of their constituents to be a primary influence on the decisions that they make. Yet constituency influence is not so straightforward. In fact, most constituents pay little attention to politics and often do not even know what policies their representatives support. Nonetheless, members of Congress spend a lot of time worrying about what their constituents think because they realize that the choices they make may be scrutinized in a future election and used as

Representatives spend a lot of time meeting with constituents in their districts to explain how they have helped their district and learn what issues their constituents care about. Such meetings are often informal events at local restaurants or fairs.

ammunition by an opposing candidate. Because of this possibility, members of Congress do try to anticipate their constituents' policy views, especially if they think that voters will take them into account during elections.[50] In this way, constituents may affect congressional policy choices even when there is little direct evidence of their influence. In October 1998, for example, 31 House Democrats broke party ranks and voted in favor of an impeachment inquiry against President Clinton because they believed a "no" vote could cost them re-election that November. In 2015, despite a 40-minute visit by President Obama to Capitol Hill, where he urged Democrats to "vote your values," House Democrats defeated the Trade Adjustment Assistance bill—and, along with it, the ability of the Obama administration to fast-track negotiations on the Transpacific Partnership Trade Pact—citing the legislation's adverse impact on American workers.[51]

Interest Groups

Interest groups are another important external influence on congressional policies. Members of Congress pay close attention to interest groups for a number of reasons: interest groups can mobilize constituents, serve as watchdogs on congressional action, and supply candidates with money.

When members of Congress are making voting decisions, those interest groups that have some connection to constituents in particular districts are most likely to be influential, and those groups with the ability to mobilize followers in many congressional districts may be especially influential. In recent years, Washington-based interest groups with little grassroots strength have recognized the importance of locally generated activity. Accordingly, they have sought to simulate grassroots pressure with so-called Astroturf lobbying (see Chapter 11). Such campaigns encourage constituents to sign form letters, postcards, or emails, which are then sent to congressional representatives. Lobbying campaigns set up toll-free telephone numbers for a system in which simply reporting your name and address to the listening computer will generate a letter to your congressional representative. One Senate office estimated that such organized campaigns to demonstrate "grassroots" support account for two-thirds of the mail the office received. As such campaigns increase, however, they become less influential because members of Congress are aware of how rare real constituent interest actually is.[52]

Many interest groups also use legislative "scorecards" that rate how members of Congress vote on issues of importance to that group. A high or low rating by an important interest group may provide a potent weapon in the next election. Interest groups can increase their influence over a particular piece of legislation by signaling their intention to include it in their scoring. Among the most influential groups that use scorecards, often posting them on their websites for members and the public to see, are the National Federation of Independent Business, the American Federation of Labor–Congress of Industrial Organizations (AFL-CIO), National Right to Life, the League of Conservation Voters, and the National Rifle Association.

Interest groups also have substantial influence in setting the legislative agenda and in helping to craft specific language in legislation. Today, sophisticated lobbyists win influence by providing information about policies, as well as campaign contributions, to busy members of Congress. The $1.1 trillion end-of-year spending bill passed at the end of 2014 included an amendment exempting many financial transactions from federal regulation under the Dodd-Frank Act. The amendment language was taken from a bill originally written by Citigroup lobbyists, with 70 of 85 lines of the bill directly copying Citigroup's language.[53] In recent years, interest groups have also begun to build broader coalitions and comprehensive campaigns around particular policy issues. These coalitions do not rise from the grass roots but instead are put together by Washington lobbyists, who launch comprehensive lobbying campaigns that combine simulated grassroots activity with information and campaign funding for members of Congress.

Close financial ties between members of Congress and interest group lobbyists often raise eyebrows because they suggest that interest groups get special treatment in exchange for political donations. Concerns about the influence of lobbyists in Congress mounted in the early 2000s when Republicans launched the K Street Project, named after the street in Washington where many high-powered lobbyists have offices. The K Street Project placed former Republican staffers in key lobbying positions and ensured a large and steady flow of corporate cash into Republican coffers. Congressional relationships to lobbyists came under close scrutiny when the lobbyist Jack Abramoff, a self-proclaimed big supporter of the K Street Project, pleaded guilty in early 2006 to charges of conspiracy, mail fraud, and tax evasion.

Concern over such corruption led Congress to enact new ethics legislation in 2007. The new law sets new restrictions on the gifts lobbyists can bestow on lawmakers and limits privately funded travel. The law also prohibits members of Congress from lobbying for two years after they retire and requires lawmakers to identify the earmarks they insert in legislation. Further, it aims to shine light on the practice of "bundling," whereby lobbyists assemble money from a number of clients to make a single political donation. Now lobbyists are required to disclose the names of the individual contributors to these political donations. Although the new law provides additional transparency, revealing more about the relationship between lobbyists and members of Congress, it is widely viewed as lacking sufficient authority to go after those who are suspected of ethics violations.[54] Moreover, the large sums of cash raised by "Super PACs" (political action committees)—discussed in Chapter 10—have introduced a whole new set of questions about the role of special interests in politics, especially because donors to Super PACs can remain anonymous. Although they cannot openly coordinate with candidates, Super PACs can endorse candidates by name and are often run by people close to the candidates they support. Interest group allies of both parties mobilized to influence outcomes in the 2014 midterms. That year Super PACs made donations totaling $33 million to congressional candidates. In 2016 Super PACs poured unprecedented sums of money into the race for president, but they also targeted key congressional contests in an effort to affect the balance of power between the parties in Congress.

Party

In both the House and Senate, party leaders have a good deal of influence over the behavior of their party members. This influence, sometimes called "party discipline," was once so powerful that it dominated the lawmaking process. In the late 1800s, party leaders could often command the allegiance of more than 90 percent of their members. A vote in which half or more of the members of one party take one position while at least half of the members of the other party

for critical analysis

How does congressional ethics legislation address concerns about corruption? Why is it important that lawmakers identify the earmarks they add to legislation?

party unity vote a roll-call vote in the House or Senate in which at least 50 percent of the members of one party take a particular position and are opposed by at least 50 percent of the members of the other party

roll-call vote a vote in which each legislator's yes or no vote is recorded as the clerk calls the names of the members alphabetically

take the opposing position is called a **party unity vote**. At the beginning of the twentieth century, nearly half of all **roll-call votes** in the House of Representatives were party votes. For much of the twentieth century, the number of party votes declined as bipartisan legislation became more common. The 1990s witnessed a return to strong party discipline as partisan polarization drew sharper lines between Democrats and Republicans, and congressional party leaders aggressively used their powers to promote party discipline. In 2005 party discipline was close to its all-time high.

Typically, party unity is greater in the House than in the Senate. House rules grant greater procedural control of business to the majority party leaders, which gives them more influence over House members. In the Senate, however, the leadership has few sanctions over its members. The former Senate minority leader Tom Daschle once observed that a Senate leader seeking to influence other senators has as incentives "a bushel full of carrots and a few twigs."[55]

Though it has not reached nineteenth-century levels, party unity has been on the rise in recent years because the divisions between the parties have deepened on many high-profile issues such as abortion, health care, and financial reform (see Figure 12.8). Party unity scores rise when congressional leaders try to put a partisan

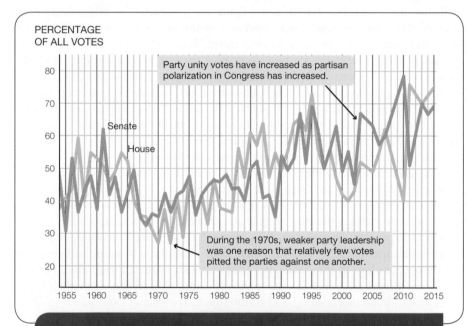

PERCENTAGE OF ALL VOTES

Party unity votes have increased as partisan polarization in Congress has increased.

Senate

House

During the 1970s, weaker party leadership was one reason that relatively few votes pitted the parties against one another.

FIGURE 12.8

Party Unity Votes by Chamber

Party unity votes are roll-call votes in which a majority of one party lines up against a majority of the other party. Party unity votes increase when the parties are polarized and when the party leadership can enforce discipline. Why did the percentage of party unity votes decline in the 1970s? Why has it risen in recent years?

SOURCES: CQ Roll Call's Vote Studies, http://media.cq.com/votestudies (accessed 6/9/14); Eliza Newlin Carney, "Standing Together against Any Action," *CQ Weekly* (March 16, 2015); and "2015 Vote Studies: Party Unity Remained Strong," *CQ Weekly* (February 8, 2016).

stamp on legislation. For example, in 1995, then-Speaker Newt Gingrich sought to enact a Republican "Contract with America" that few Democrats supported. The result was more party unity in the House than in any year since 1954. Since then, the polarization of political parties has resulted in very high party unity scores. In 2015, House Democrats voted with the majority 92 percent of the time, matching the all-time high previously reached in 2007 and 2008. That year Senate Democrats voted with their caucus 91 percent of the time, three points below the record set in 2013. Republicans were also very united. In 2015, House Republicans voted with their party 92 percent of the time, matching the record high set in 2013; Senate Republicans voted with their party 89 percent of the time, the highest level seen since 2010.[56]

To some extent, party unity is based on ideology and background. Republican members of the House are more likely than Democrats to have been elected by rural or suburban districts. Democrats are likely to be more liberal on economic and social questions than their Republican colleagues in both houses. These differences certainly help to explain roll-call divisions between the two parties. Ideology and background, however, are only part of the explanation for party unity. The other part has to do with party organization and leadership. Among the resources that party leaders have at their disposal to reward loyal members who vote with the party are (1) leadership PACs, (2) committee assignments, (3) access to the floor, (4) the whip system, (5) logrolling, and (6) the presidency.

Leadership PACs Leaders have increased their influence over members in recent years with aggressive use of leadership PACs. Leadership PACs are organizations that members of Congress use to raise funds that they then distribute to other members of their party running for election. Republican congressional leaders pioneered the aggressive use of leadership PACs to win their congressional majority in 1995, and the practice has spread widely since that time. The former House majority leader Tom DeLay was especially aggressive in raising funds, creating several important PACs, including Americans for a Republican Majority (ARMPAC), Retain Our Majority Program (ROMP), and the Republican Majority Issues Committee. In recent years, Democrats have also formed well-funded leadership PACs. Money from leadership PACs can be directed to the most vulnerable candidates or to candidates who are having trouble raising money. For example, Kirsten Gillibrand, the junior Democratic senator from New York, has used her leadership PAC to promote Democratic women candidates running for Congress. In 2016 the PAC, which she named Off the Sidelines, supplied funds to 61 candidates running for seats in the House and 10 for the Senate, all of them women.[57]

Committee Assignments Party leaders can create debts among members by helping them get favorable committee assignments. These assignments are made early in the congressional careers of most members and cannot be taken from them if they later balk at party discipline. Nevertheless, if the leadership goes out of its way to get the right assignment for a member, this effort is likely to create a bond of obligation that can be called on without any other payments or favors. This is one reason the Republican leadership gave freshmen favorable assignments when the Republicans took over Congress in 1995. When Nancy Pelosi assumed the position of Speaker in 2007, she sought to spread power more widely by limiting the number of committees that any one member could chair. She also gave freshmen representatives access to key committees that would raise their political stature.[58] By offering attractive committee assignments to members in competitive races, especially to new members, she sought to boost her party's chances in the next elections. And she engendered loyalty to the party among its new members.

Access to the Floor The most important everyday resource available to the parties is control over access to the floor. With thousands of bills awaiting passage and most members clamoring for access in order to influence a bill or publicize themselves, floor time is precious. In the Senate, the leadership allows ranking committee members to influence the allocation of floor time (who will speak for how long); in the House, the Speaker, as head of the majority party (in consultation with the minority leader), allocates large blocks of floor time. Thus, floor time is allocated in both houses of Congress by the majority and minority leaders. More important, the Speaker of the House and the majority leader in the Senate possess the power of recognition. This seemingly insubstantial authority is, in fact, quite formidable and can be used to stymie a piece of legislation completely or frustrate a member's attempts to speak on a particular issue. Because the power is significant, members of Congress usually attempt to stay on good terms with the Speaker and the majority leader to ensure they will continue to be recognized.

As House Speaker, Nancy Pelosi was particularly generous in offering freshmen Democrats and other especially vulnerable Democrats an opportunity to speak on the floor. When Republicans assumed control of the House in 2010, they likewise ensured that the voices of freshmen Republicans were heard on the House floor.[59]

When John Boehner became Speaker of the House in 2010, he was overwhelmingly backed by House Republicans. By 2015, the most conservative factions of the party, frustrated that Boehner hadn't been more effective against the Obama administration, pressured him to resign.

The Whip System Some influence accrues to party leaders through the whip system, which is primarily a communications network for conveying the leaders' wishes and plans to the members. Between 12 and 20 assistant and regional whips are selected to operate at the direction of the majority or minority leader and the whip. They poll all the members to learn their intentions on specific bills, enabling the leaders to know if they have enough support to allow a vote as well as whether the vote is so close that they will need to put pressure on undecided members. In those instances, the Speaker or a lieutenant will go to a few party members who have indicated they will switch if their vote is essential—an expedient that the leaders try to limit to a few times per session.

The whip system helps maintain party unity in both houses of Congress, but it is particularly critical in the House of Representatives because of the large number of legislators whose positions and votes must be accounted for. The majority and minority whips and their assistants must be adept at inducing compromise among legislators who hold widely differing viewpoints. The whips' personal styles and their perception of their function significantly affect the development of legislative coalitions and the compromises that emerge. As Republican House whip from 1995 to 2002, Tom DeLay established a reputation as an effective vote counter and a tough leader, earning the nickname "The Hammer." DeLay also expanded the reach of the whip, building alliances with Republicans outside Congress, particularly those in ideological and business-oriented groups. Since 2010, when Republicans retook control of the House, the whip operation has been faced with significant challenges from conservative members. In 2015, a group of conservative Republicans, organized into the House Freedom Caucus, regularly disputed the positions of the party leadership. Frustrated with the lack of discipline, House majority whip Steve Scalise (R-La.) expelled several members from his whip team for failing to support party positions.[60] Indeed, conflict with these same rebellious Republicans prompted Speaker John Boehner to make the stunning announcement in September 2015 of his retirement from the speakership and from the House.

Logrolling An agreement between two or more members of Congress who have nothing in common except the need for support is called **logrolling**. The agreement states, in effect, "You support me on bill X, and I'll support you on another bill of your choice." Since party leaders are the center of the communications networks in the two chambers, they can help members create large logrolling coalitions. Hundreds of logrolling deals are made each year, and although there are no official record-keeping books, it would be a poor party leader whose whips did not know who owed what to whom. In some instances, logrolling produces strange alliances. A most unlikely alliance emerged in Congress in October 1991, an alliance that one commentator dubbed "the corn for porn plot."[61] The alliance joined Senate supporters of the National Endowment for the Arts (NEA) with senators seeking limits on the cost of grazing rights on federal lands. The NEA, which provides federal funding to the arts, had been under fire from the conservative senator Jesse Helms (R-N.C.) for funding some controversial artists whose work Helms believed to be indecent. In an effort to block federal support for such works, Helms attached a provision to the NEA's funding that would have prohibited the agency from awarding grants to any work that in a "patently offensive way" depicted "sexual or excretory activities or organs." Supporters of the NEA condemned such restrictions as a violation of free speech and pointed out that many famous works of art could not have been funded under such restrictions. When it appeared that the amendment would pass, NEA supporters offered western senators a deal. In exchange for voting down the Helms amendment, they would eliminate a planned hike in grazing fees. Republican senators from 16 western states switched their votes and defeated the Helms amendment. Although Helms called his defeat the product of "back-room deals and parliamentary flimflam," his amendment was simply the victim of the time-honored congressional practice of logrolling.[62]

logrolling a legislative practice whereby agreements are made between legislators in voting for or against a bill; vote trading

The Presidency Of all the influences that maintain the clarity of party lines in Congress, the influence of the presidency is probably the most important. Indeed, the office is a touchstone of party discipline in Congress. Since the late 1940s, under President Harry Truman, presidents each year have identified a number of bills that they want to be considered part of their administration's program. By the mid-1950s, both parties in Congress began to look to the president for these proposals, which became the most significant part of Congress's agenda. The president's support is a criterion for party loyalty, and party leaders are able to use it to rally some members. Party polarization limited Obama's agenda-setting powers for the majority of his presidency, which saw a Republican-controlled House for his last six years and a Republican-controlled Senate for his last two. Instead, his proposals became targets for congressional opponents.

When Congress Can't Decide

We've considered the major factors that influence congressional decisions, but what happens if Congress as a whole can't decide and fails to act? Recent congresses have been notable for their inability to pass laws. The 113th Congress (2013–14) and the 112th Congress (2012–13) were the two least productive Congresses in modern history.[63]

Indeed, many high-profile bills ended in failure throughout 2012 and 2013. In 2013, House Republicans refused to pass a bill funding government operations or extending the debt ceiling unless the spending bill included language delaying implementation of the Affordable Care Act (ACA).[64] As a consequence, the federal government shut down for the first time in almost two decades. Despite then–House Speaker John Boehner's warnings to the Republican conference that the Republican Party would be blamed for the shutdown and his attempts to negotiate with Senate Democrats and the White House to reopen the government, House Republicans stood firm on their insistence to tie any deal to delaying the ACA.[65] Eventually, with public ire rising over the continued shutdown, the House voted to pass a Senate bill—which contained virtually no concessions to the Republican Party—to reopen the government and extend the debt limit for four months, just hours before the United States was set to cross the debt-ceiling deadline.[66] Democrats and Republicans succeeded in averting a second showdown over the debt ceiling when both sides agreed on a budget deal in late 2013.

In 2015, bitter political disagreements among House Republicans prompted the resignation of House Speaker John Boehner. A small group of conservative Republicans announced their intention to block any budget bill that included funding for Planned Parenthood, an organization that provides a variety of health services to women, including abortion. Yet, it was apparent that the Senate would not approve a bill that failed to fund Planned Parenthood and that President Obama would veto such a bill. Even so, House conservatives refused to back down. Without congressional approval on a short-term budget, the federal government once again faced the prospect of a shutdown. Weary of tangling with members of his own party, Boehner stunned the political world by announcing his resignation as House Speaker. Blasting House conservatives and the outside groups associated with them as "false prophets," Boehner expressed his frustration, stating that "We got groups here in town, members of the House and Senate here in town, who whip people into a frenzy believing they can accomplish things they know—they know!—are never going to happen."[67] His decision allowed conservatives to claim a victory and led them to approve the short-term spending bill to keep the government open. But the divisions that led to Boehner's resignation promised to create more challenges to congressional efforts to enact legislation.

These legislative stand-offs tarnished Congress's reputation with the public. In November 2013, Congress received the lowest levels of approval ever recorded in a public-opinion poll. Just 9 percent of those questioned approved of the job Congress was doing, while 86 percent disapproved. That reputation had improved little by 2015, when 14 percent of Americans stated that they approved of the job that Congress was doing.[68] The public's disapproval of Congress crossed party lines, with both Democrats and Republicans expressing dissatisfaction with Congress. Despite their majority status

After the resignation of Speaker of the House John Boehner in 2015, Republicans recruited Paul Ryan to take over the role. Initially reluctant, Ryan decided to run after receiving support from different factions of Republicans, who hoped that he would be a unifying figure for a divided party.

in both houses of Congress, a majority of Republicans polled expressed disapproval of Congress for failing to challenge President Obama more strongly.[69]

The partisan divisions that prevented Congress from making decisions were especially acute because the unusually large class of freshmen Republicans, many associated with the Tea Party movement, and later organized as the Freedom Caucus, believed they had been sent to Congress to put an end to business as usual. Dedicated to reducing government spending, they used their power to hold up routine decisions, such as extension of the debt limit, as a way to extract concessions on government spending. As we have seen, many of the usual procedures through which Congress enacted laws in the past—congressional committees to consider legislation, conference committees to reconcile House and Senate versions of legislation, a whip system to support leaders in the House of Representatives, logrolling, and presidential agenda setting—no longer function when Congress is so divided. Moreover, former Speaker Boehner's decision to let the House "work its will" allowed Republican conservatives considerable freedom to obstruct legislation they opposed. The inability to legislate was reinforced by Boehner's decision to follow the Hastert rule, named after former speaker Dennis Hastert (R-Ill.). According to the informal rule, the Speaker would not allow any bill to reach the floor unless it had the support of a majority of Republican members of the House. This meant that bills that could have won a majority in the House with bipartisan support from Democrats and Republicans never reached the floor for a vote.

When Paul Ryan (R-Wisc.) became Speaker in October 2015, many were hopeful that congressional stalemate would be a thing of the past. Ryan enjoyed support from all wings of the Republican Party. Although the new Speaker avoided the open confrontation with the Freedom Caucus, he, too, faced governing challenges, as conservative members of his own party defeated key legislation.[70]

Congressional Polarization Congress's inability to decide reflects the deep ideological differences that separate the two parties. Efforts to measure the ideological distance between the two parties show that since the mid-1970s Republicans and Democrats have been diverging sharply and are now more polarized than at any time in the last century. Democrats have become more liberal and Republicans have become more conservative on issues related to the economy and the role of government.[71] But as Figure 12.9 shows, the Republican Party has experienced the greatest ideological shift, becoming sharply more conservative. Moreover, because congressional districts are increasingly homogeneous in their ideology—in part due to gerrymandering but mainly because of natural clustering of the population— most members of Congress are in safe seats. Their constituents will not punish them for failing to compromise. Moreover, active mobilization by organizations on the right, such as the Club for Growth, means that Republican members of Congress who support compromises might be punished. These outside organizations have financed alternative candidates to challenge members who vote against the organizations' positions. Despite rebukes by Republican congressional leadership, groups such as the Club for Growth actively worked to recruit and support candidates in the 2016 election.[72]

Partisan polarization also affected the effort to fill the Supreme Court seat left vacant by Justice Antonin Scalia's death, as we saw in the introduction to this chapter. When President Obama nominated Merrick Garland, a well-respected moderate judge, many Republicans, who had called on Obama to let the next president fill the vacancy, vowed never to meet with the nominee. The Senate Judiciary committee declined to schedule hearings, but once Donald Trump was

for critical analysis

Why has it become so difficult for members of Congress to compromise? How is American democracy harmed when Congress is unable to agree on major pieces of legislation?

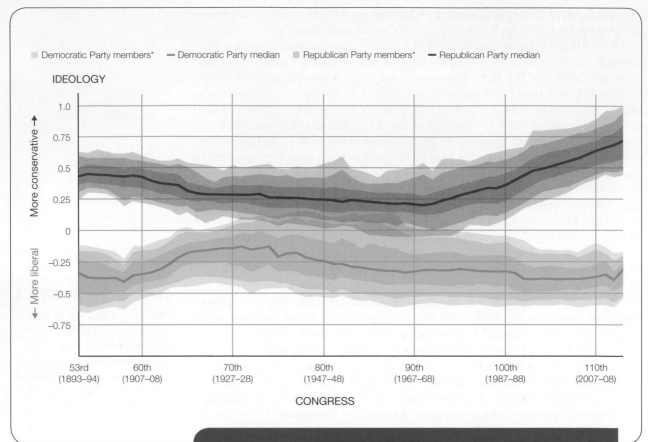

IDEOLOGY

Democratic Party members*   — Democratic Party median   Republican Party members*   — Republican Party median

More conservative →

1.0
0.75
0.5
0.25
0

← More liberal

−0.25
−0.5
−0.75

53rd
(1893–94)

60th
(1907–08)

70th
(1927–28)

80th
(1947–48)

90th
(1967–68)

100th
(1987–88)

110th
(2007–08)

CONGRESS

FIGURE 12.9

Polarization in Congress

In recent decades Democrats and Republicans in Congress are increasingly polarized as Democrats have become more liberal and Republicans more conservative. One way of measuring polarization is to estimate the ideology of members of Congress based on their roll-call votes and then graph the ideologies of each party's members. As the graph shows, polarization was lower in the 1940s and 1950s, with some Democrats and some Republicans even overlapping in their ideologies.

*The lightest shade represents the range of ideologies of party members in the 5th–95th percentiles. The next lightest shade represents the 10th–90th percentiles. The darkest shade represents the 25th–75th percentiles.
SOURCE: Voteview, http://voteview.com/dwnl.htm (accessed 6/17/16).

for critical analysis

How does polarization contribute to congressional gridlock? How has the use of congressional procedures made it more difficult to enact legislation in recent years?

elected, the Senate expressed its willingness to hold hearings on the new president's nominee.

However, congressional polarization is here to stay so long as voters elect representatives with sharply different views about what government should and shouldn't do. Until there is more agreement about the role of government and the best way to manage the budgetary challenges that face the country, congressional stand-offs on major legislation will remain a regular feature of American politics.

Beyond Legislation: Other Congressional Powers

Describe Congress's influence over other branches of government

In addition to the power to make the law, Congress has at its disposal an array of other instruments through which to influence the process of government. The Constitution gives the Senate the power to approve treaties and appointments. And Congress has a number of other powers through which it can share with the other branches the capacity to administer the laws.

Oversight

Oversight, as applied to Congress, refers to the effort to oversee or to supervise how the executive branch carries out legislation. Oversight is carried out by committees or subcommittees of the Senate or the House, which conduct hearings and investigations to analyze and evaluate bureaucratic agencies and the effectiveness of their programs. Their purpose may be to locate inefficiencies or abuses of power, to explore the relationship between what an agency does and what a law intends, or to change or abolish a program. Most programs and agencies are subject to some oversight every year during the course of hearings on **appropriations**, the funding of agencies and government programs.

Committees or subcommittees have the power to subpoena witnesses, administer oaths, cross-examine, compel testimony, and bring criminal charges for contempt (refusing to cooperate) and perjury (lying under oath). Hearings and investigations are similar in many ways, but they differ on one fundamental point. A hearing is usually held on a specific bill, and the questions asked are usually intended to build a record with regard to that bill. In an investigation, the committee or subcommittee does not begin with a particular bill but examines a broad area or problem and then concludes its investigation with one or more proposed bills.

In recent years, congressional oversight power has increasingly been used as a tool of partisan politics. The Republican Congress aggressively investigated President Clinton but failed to scrutinize seriously the actions of the George W. Bush administration during Bush's first six years in office. The investigation into the abuse of prisoners in Iraq's Abu Ghraib prison, for example, entailed only 12 hours of sworn testimony.

When the Democrats took control of Congress in 2007, congressional oversight increased dramatically. To highlight the importance of oversight, Democrats renamed the House Government Reform Committee, calling it the Committee on Oversight and Government Reform, and added four new subcommittees dedicated to oversight. They also hired more than 200 new investigative staffers.[73] Armed with these resources, Congress stepped up the number of oversight hearings: during its first six months in power, the Democratic Congress held 942 oversight hearings compared with 579 for the same period when Republicans controlled Congress in 2005.[74] Congressional leaders are quite aware of oversight hearings as political tools. Since 2010, the Republican House has used the oversight power to highlight the politically weak points in President Obama's record, holding extensive hearings on the Affordable Care Act and on the militant attack of the American consulate in Benghazi, Libya, that resulted in American deaths.[75] First convened in 2014, the Select Committee on Benghazi became enmeshed in partisan contention after Hillary Clinton, secretary of

oversight the effort by Congress, through hearings, investigations, and other techniques, to exercise control over the activities of executive agencies

appropriations the amounts of money approved by Congress in statutes (bills) that each unit or agency of government can spend

state during the attacks, announced that she would run for president. In 2015, as revelations emerged that Clinton had used a private email during her tenure as secretary of state, the committee began to investigate whether appropriate procedures had been followed and whether national security was compromised.[76] When the F.B.I. undertook an investigation into the matter in 2016, F.B.I. Director James Comey recommended no criminal charges against Clinton but also questioned her judgment and called her actions "extremely careless." The next day, Attorney General Loretta Lynch accepted the F.B.I.'s findings, affirming that the Justice Department would not seek criminal charges.

Advice and Consent: Special Senate Powers

The Constitution has given the Senate another special power, one that is not based on lawmaking. The president has the power to make treaties and to appoint top executive officers, ambassadors, and federal judges—but only "with the Advice and Consent of the Senate" (Article II, Section 2). For treaties, two-thirds of those present must concur; for appointments, a simple majority is required.

The power to approve or reject presidential requests includes the power to set conditions. In fact, the Senate only occasionally exercises its power to reject treaties and appointments, and despite recent debate surrounding judicial nominees, only a handful of judicial nominees have been rejected by the Senate during the past century, whereas hundreds have been approved. However, the recent increase in use of the filibuster to block judicial nominees led the Democratic Senate to bar the filibuster in deliberations about judicial and executive branch appointments.

Most presidents make every effort to take potential Senate opposition into account in treaty negotiations with foreign powers. Instead of treaties, presidents frequently resort to **executive agreements** that do not need Senate approval. The Supreme Court has held that such agreements are equivalent to treaties.[77] In the past, presidents sometimes concluded secret agreements without informing Congress of the agreements' contents or even their existence. For example, American involvement in the Vietnam War grew in part out of a series of secret arrangements made between American presidents and the South Vietnamese during the 1950s and '60s. Congress did not even learn of the existence of these agreements until 1969. In 1972, Congress passed the Case Act, which requires that the president inform Congress of any executive agreement within 60 days of its having been reached. This provides Congress with the opportunity to cancel agreements it opposes. In addition, Congress can limit the president's ability to conduct foreign policy through executive agreement by refusing to appropriate the funds needed to implement an agreement. In this way, for example, Congress can modify or even cancel executive agreements to provide American economic or military assistance to foreign governments.

Impeachment

The Constitution also grants Congress the power of impeachment over the president, vice president, and other executive officials. **Impeachment** means to charge a government official (president or otherwise) with "Treason, Bribery, or other high Crimes and

executive agreement an agreement, made between the president and another country, that has the force of a treaty but does not require the Senate's "advice and consent"

impeachment the formal charge by the House of Representatives that a government official has committed "Treason, Bribery, or other high Crimes and Misdemeanors"

The Senate possesses the power to impeach federal officials. In American history, 16 federal officials have been impeached, including two presidents. In 1998 the House impeached President Bill Clinton for lying under oath about his affair with White House intern Monica Lewinsky.

Misdemeanors" and bring him before Congress to determine guilt. Impeachment is thus like a criminal indictment in which the House of Representatives acts like a grand jury, voting (by simple majority) on whether the accused ought to be impeached. If a majority of the House votes to impeach, the impeachment trial moves to the Senate, which acts like a trial jury by voting whether to convict and forcibly remove the person from office (which requires a two-thirds majority of the Senate). The impeachment power is a considerable one; its very existence in the hands of Congress is a highly effective safeguard against the executive tyranny so greatly feared by the framers of the Constitution. The House has initiated impeachment proceedings more than 60 times in U.S. history. Fewer than 20 officials were ultimately impeached, and only eight—all federal judges—were convicted by the Senate and removed from office.[78]

Controversy over Congress's impeachment power has arisen over the grounds for impeachment, especially the meaning of "high Crimes and Misdemeanors." A strict reading of the Constitution suggests that the only impeachable offense is an actual crime. But a more common working definition is that "an impeachable offense is whatever the majority of the House of Representatives considers it to be at a given moment in history."[79] In other words, impeachment, especially impeachment of a president, is a political decision.

The political nature of impeachment was very clear in the two instances of presidential impeachment that have occurred in American history. In the first, in 1867, President Andrew Johnson, a southern Democrat who had battled a congressional Republican majority over Reconstruction, was impeached by the House but saved from conviction by one vote in the Senate. In 1998 the House impeached President Bill Clinton on two counts, for lying under oath and obstructing justice during the investigation into his sexual affair with the White House intern Monica Lewinsky. The vote was highly partisan, with only five Democrats voting for impeachment on each charge. In the Senate, where a two-thirds majority was needed to convict the president, only 45 senators voted to convict on the first count of lying and 50 voted to convict on the second charge of obstructing justice. As in the House, the vote for impeachment was highly partisan, with all Democrats and only five Republicans supporting the president's ultimate acquittal.

for critical analysis

Under what circumstances should Congress exercise its power of impeachment? Why has impeachment been used so rarely in U.S. history?

Congress
and Your Future

Much of this chapter has described the major institutional components of Congress and has shown how they work as Congress makes policy. But what do these institutional features mean for how Congress represents the American public? Does the organization of Congress promote the equal representation of all Americans? Or are there institutional features of Congress that allow some interests more access and influence than others?

As we noted at the beginning of this chapter, Congress instituted a number of reforms in the 1970s to make itself more accessible and to distribute power more widely within the institution. These reforms sought to respond to public views that Congress had become a stodgy institution ruled by a powerful elite that made decisions in private. We have seen that these reforms increased the number of subcommittees, prohibited most secret hearings, and increased the staff support for Congress. These reforms spread power more evenly throughout the institution and opened new avenues for the public to contact and influence Congress.

But the opening of Congress ultimately did not benefit the broad American public as reformers had envisioned. In fact, the congressional reforms enacted during the 1970s actually made Congress less effective and, ironically, more permeable to special interests. Open committee meetings made it possible for sophisticated interest groups to monitor and influence every aspect of developing legislation. The unanticipated, negative consequences of these reforms highlighted the trade-off between representation and effectiveness in Congress.[80] Efforts to improve representation by opening Congress up made it difficult for Congress to be effective.

When Congress is ineffective, American democracy suffers. As we have seen in this chapter, prolonged stalemates in Congress have led to a reduction in America's credit rating and a costly government shutdown. Moreover, Americans have lost confidence in Congress as it has lurched from crisis to crisis. Is it time for some major changes to make Congress work better? Disillusionment with congressional gridlock has led some to say that the United States should become a parliamentary system, where the winning party can enact the legislation it promised in its party platform. Such a system is more accountable to voters and less prone to stalemate. But Americans would have to jettison the presidency and become a unicameral body to operate as a true parliamentary system, like that of Britain.

Short of such major institutional transformations, are there changes that would make Congress work better? One measure that might lead to more bipartisan agreement—the appointment of citizen commissions to draw district lines—has been adopted in some states. If this practice became more widespread, it is possible that it would lead to election of more moderate candidates, making it easier to compromise in Congress. Changes in the way Congress conducts its business could also promote more bipartisan decision making. For example, former House Speaker John Boehner decided that he would only bring legislation to the floor if a majority of Republicans supported it. Boehner's successor, Paul Ryan, also vowed to follow the same practice. The "Hastert rule," as this practice is called, after former speaker Dennis Hastert, is not a formal rule of Congress, rather it is a norm that Boehner decided to implement. It is a practice that could easily be abandoned, allowing bipartisan majorities to enact legislation. Another significant change—eliminating the filibuster in the Senate—would heighten partisan differences but ease gridlock. As we have seen, the Senate voted to eliminate the filibuster for executive branch appointments and judicial candidates (except for the Supreme Court) in 2013. Abandoning the filibuster altogether would allow legislation to move more smoothly through the Senate. Will any of these changes—or other measures—be adopted? Each carries risks to political parties and to politicians. Yet, gridlock also carries political risks, as the public grows frustrated with congressional inaction on important policy areas. What areas of public policy might suffer if Congress continues its inability to decide? How politicians weigh these different choices will shape how—and whether—Congress fills its central position in American democracy.

Gridlock and bitter disagreements in Congress turn some Americans off to politics. However, as the core representative institution of government, Congress is supposed to represent all Americans. As the "**Who Participates?**" feature on the facing page shows, the electorate that turns out to vote for Congress is on average older, whiter, and more affluent than the average American.

Who Elects Congress?

2014 Voters as Compared with U.S. Population

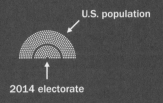

U.S. population

2014 electorate

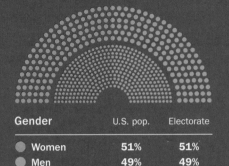

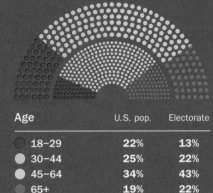

Gender	U.S. pop.	Electorate
Women	51%	51%
Men	49%	49%

Age	U.S. pop.	Electorate
18–29	22%	13%
30–44	25%	22%
45–64	34%	43%
65+	19%	22%

SOURCES: CNN House Exit Polls, www.cnn.com/election/2014/results/race/house#exit-polls (accessed 9/29/15); Wage Statistics for 2014, www.ssa.gov/cgi-bin/netcomp.cgi?year=2014 (accessed 10/22/15); U.S. Census Bureau 2014 American Community Survey, www.census.gov/programs-surveys/acs/data.html (accessed 10/22/15).

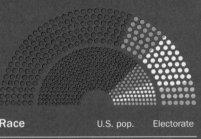

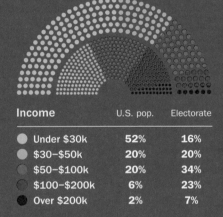

Race	U.S. pop.	Electorate
White	62%	75%
Black	13%	12%
Latino	17%	8%
Asian	5%	3%
Other	3%	3%

Income	U.S. pop.	Electorate
Under $30k	52%	16%
$30–$50k	20%	20%
$50–$100k	20%	34%
$100–$200k	6%	23%
Over $200k	2%	7%

WHAT YOU CAN DO

Know Your Members of Congress

 Vote in the next congressional election. If you haven't registered, see page 33 instructions on how to do so.

 Discover what bills are currently under consideration in Congress by visiting **www.congress.gov**.

 Contact your member of Congress to state your opinion. Go to **www.house.gov** and enter your ZIP code to find your representative. Go to **www.senate.gov** and find your state in the drop-down menu to find your two U.S. senators.

studyguide

Congress: Representing the American People

A member of Congress's primary responsibility is to his or her district and to his or her constituency. The House and Senate operate according to different sets of rules and play different roles in the legislative process. Although members of Congress often do not share their constituents' sociological characteristics, they do work hard to speak for their constituents' views and to serve their constituents' interests. Generally speaking, there are three factors related to the U.S. electoral system that affect who gets elected and what they do once in office: who decides to run for Congress, the incumbency advantage, and the way congressional districts are drawn.

Key Terms

constituency (p. 459)

bicameral (p. 459)

delegate (p. 460)

trustee (p. 460)

sociological representation (p. 461)

agency representation (p. 461)

incumbency (p. 466)

term limits (p. 467)

apportionment (p. 468)

redistricting (p. 468)

gerrymandering (p. 469)

patronage (p. 470)

pork-barrel (or pork) (p. 470)

private bill (p. 472)

Practice Quiz

1. Which of the following is a way in which the House and the Senate are different?
   a) The House is a more deliberative legislative body than the Senate.
   b) The House is more centralized and organized than the Senate.
   c) Senators serve smaller and more homogeneous constituencies than members of the House.
   d) Senators are often more attuned to the legislative needs of local interest groups than members of the House.
   e) There are no important differences between the House and the Senate.

2. What type of representation is described when constituents have the power to hire and fire their representative?
   a) agency representation
   b) sociological representation
   c) philosophical representation
   d) ideological representation
   e) economic representation

3. Which of the following statements best describes the social composition of the U.S. Congress?
   a) The majority of representatives do not have university degrees.
   b) Men and women are equally represented in Congress.
   c) Most members of Congress do not affiliate with any specific religion.
   d) The legal profession is the dominant career of most members of Congress prior to their election.
   e) The number of African American, Latino, and Asian American representatives has decreased over the last 20 years.

4. The Supreme Court has ruled that
   a) congressional districts cannot be drawn in a way to favor the incumbent candidate.
   b) race can be the predominant factor in drawing congressional districts.
   c) race cannot be the predominant factor in drawing congressional districts.
   d) states cannot use unelected, nonpartisan committees to draw congressional districts.
   e) the use of computer technologies to draw congressional districts is unconstitutional.

5. An "earmark" is
   a) a rule in the House of Representatives that limits who can be heard during legislative debates.
   b) a congressional district drawn to advantage candidates from a certain racial or ethnic group.
   c) a law that grants some special privilege or exemption to a single individual.
   d) language inserted into a bill by a member of Congress that provides special benefits for the member of Congress's constituents.
   e) a weekly, informal meeting between members of Congress and their constituents.

The Organization of Congress

Congress is not only a representative body but also a lawmaking institution. The political parties, the committee system, congressional staff, the caucuses, and the parliamentary rules of the House and Senate play key roles in the process by which Congress formulates and enacts law. The committee system is particularly important because Congress relies on committees and subcommittees to do the difficult work of sorting through alternatives and writing bills.

Key Terms

conference (p. 473)

caucus (political) (p. 473)

Speaker of the House (p. 473)

majority leader (p. 473)

minority leader (p. 473)

whip (p. 473)

standing committee (p. 473)

select committees (p. 475)

joint committees (p. 476)

conference committees (p. 476)

seniority (p. 477)

staff agencies (p. 478)

caucuses (congressional) (p. 480)

Practice Quiz

6. Which of the following types of committees include members of both the House and the Senate?
   a) standing committee
   b) select committee
   c) conference committee
   d) rules committee
   e) No committees include both House members and senators.

7. A series of reforms instituted by Congress in the 1970s, including an increase in the number of subcommittees and greater autonomy for subcommittee chairs, had the effect of
   a) reducing the power of committee chairs.
   b) increasing the power of committee chairs.
   c) eliminating the incumbency advantage in congressional elections.
   d) ending the filibuster.
   e) expanding the number of joint committees in Congress.

Rules of Lawmaking: How a Bill Becomes a Law

The rules of congressional procedure influence the fate of every bill and determine the distribution of power in Congress. Debate over bills is much less restricted in the Senate than in the House, and the filibuster gives tremendous power to individual senators. The president's veto power also exerts an important influence on Congress's lawmaking because the possibility of a presidential veto affects how willing members of Congress are to push for different pieces of legislation.

Key Terms

bill (p. 480)

committee markup (p. 482)

closed rule (p. 482)

open rule (p. 482)

filibuster (p. 483)

cloture (p. 483)

veto (p. 485)

pocket veto (p. 485)

Practice Quiz

8. The difference between a closed rule and an open rule in the House is
   a) a closed rule puts severe limits on floor debate and amendments, whereas an open rule permits floor debate and makes amendments easier.
   b) an open rule puts severe limits on floor debate and amendments, whereas a closed rule permits floor debate and makes amendments easier.
   c) a closed rule allows journalists and members of the public to listen to debates about a bill, whereas an open rule prevents journalists and members of the public from listening to debates about the bill.
   d) an open rule allows journalists and members of the public to listen to debates about a bill, whereas a closed rule prevents journalists and members of the public from listening to debates about the bill.
   e) a closed rule prevents the federal judiciary from declaring a bill unconstitutional once passed, whereas an open rule allows the federal judiciary to declare a bill unconstitutional.

9. Which of the following is not a technique that can be used to block debate about or action on a bill in the Senate?
   a) filibuster
   b) caucus
   c) the introduction of new amendments
   d) cloture
   e) placing holds on bills

How Congress Decides

Analyze the factors that influence which laws Congress passes (pp. 485–94)

A variety of influences from inside and outside government play a role in congressional decision making. External influences include the policy preferences of the legislator's constituency and the lobbying of various interest groups. Party leaders within Congress use many methods, including leadership PACs, logrolling, and the president's support, to influence how representatives behave.

Key Terms

party unity vote (p. 488)

roll-call vote (p. 488)

logrolling (p. 491)

Practice Quiz

10. Members of Congress take their constituents' views into account because
    a) the Supreme Court can invalidate laws passed without majority support in the public.
    b) interest groups are forbidden from lobbying during legislative votes.
    c) most constituents pay close attention to what's going on in Congress at all times.
    d) they worry that their voting record will be scrutinized at election time.
    e) they can be impeached if they go against their constituents' policy preferences.

11. Which of the following is not a resource that party leaders in Congress use to create party discipline?
    a) leadership PACs
    b) committee assignments
    c) access to the floor
    d) the whip system
    e) party unity votes

12. An agreement between members of Congress to trade support for each other's bills is known as
    a) oversight.
    b) filibuster.
    c) logrolling.
    d) patronage.
    e) cloture.

Beyond Legislation: Other Congressional Powers

Describe Congress's influence over other branches of government (pp. 495–97)

Congress has many other powers than simply lawmaking. Using hearings, investigations, and other techniques, Congress exercises control over the agencies of the executive branch. Under the Constitution, the president can only make treaties and appoint top executive officers, ambassadors, and federal judges "with the Advice and Consent of the Senate." The Constitution also grants Congress the power of impeachment over the president, vice president, and other executive officials.

Key Terms

oversight (p. 495)

appropriations (p. 495)

executive agreement (p. 496)

impeachment (p. 496)

Practice Quiz

13. When Congress conducts an investigation to explore the relationship between what a law intended and what an executive agency has done, it is engaged in
    a) oversight.
    b) advice and consent.
    c) appropriations.
    d) executive agreement.
    e) direct patronage.

14. Which of the following statements about impeachment is not true?
    a) The president is the only official who can be impeached by Congress.
    b) Impeachment means to charge a government official with "Treason, Bribery, or other high Crimes and Misdemeanors."
    c) The House of Representatives decides by simple majority vote whether the accused ought to be impeached.
    d) The Senate decides whether to convict and remove the person from office.
    e) There have only been two instances of impeachment in American history.

For Further Reading

Adler, E. Scott, and John D. Wilkerson. *Congress and the Politics of Problem Solving*. New York: Cambridge University Press. 2013.

Binder, Sarah. *Minority Rights, Majority Rule: Partisanship and the Development of Congress*. Cambridge, MA: Cambridge University Press, 1997.

Dodd, Lawrence C., and Bruce I. Oppenheimer, eds. *Congress Reconsidered*. 10th ed. Washington, DC: CQ Press, 2012.

Dodson, Debra L. *The Impact of Women in Congress*. New York: Oxford University Press, 2006.

Fenno, Richard F. *Homestyle: House Members in Their Districts*. Boston: Little, Brown, 1978.

Fiorina, Morris. *Congress: Keystone of the Washington Establishment*. 2nd ed. New Haven, CT: Yale University Press, 1989.

Fowler, Linda, and Robert McClure. *Political Ambition: Who Decides to Run for Congress?* New Haven, CT: Yale University Press, 1989.

Koger, Gregory. *Filibustering: A Political History of Obstruction in the House and Senate*. Chicago: University of Chicago Press, 2010.

Lee, Frances E. *Beyond Ideology: Politics, Principles, and Partisanship in the U.S. Senate*. Chicago: University of Chicago Press, 2009.

Mann, Thomas E., and Norman J. Ornstein. *It's Even Worse Than It Looks: How the American Constitutional System Collided with the New Politics of Extremism*. New York: Basic Books, 2012.

Mayhew, David R. *Congress: The Electoral Connection*. New Haven, CT: Yale University Press, 1974.

Palmer, Barbara, and Denise Simon. *Breaking the Political Glass Ceiling: Women and Congressional Elections*. 2nd ed. New York: Routledge, 2008.

Schickler, Eric, and Frances E. Lee. *The Oxford Handbook of the American Congress*. New York: Oxford University Press, 2011.

Tate, Katherine. *Concordance: Black Lawmaking in the U.S. Congress from Carter to Obama*. Ann Arbor: University of Michigan Press, 2014.

Wawro, Gregory J., and Eric Schickler. *Filibuster: Obstruction and Lawmaking in the U.S. Senate*. Princeton, NJ: Princeton University Press, 2006.

Recommended Websites

Cook Political Report
www.cookpolitical.com
The Cook Political Report, by Charlie Cook, is a nonpartisan analysis of electoral politics. Check out current House and Senate races for an in-depth analysis of past elections and previews of future congressional elections.

Library of Congress: Thomas
http://thomas.loc.gov/home/thomas.php
The Library of Congress's Thomas website is a superb place to find information about the U.S. Congress. Roll-call votes, current legislation, the full text of the *Congressional Record* and of committee reports are just a few of the archives you will find.

National Committee for an Effective Congress
www.ourcampaigns.com
Congressional redistricting is the process of redrawing House districts every 10 years to account for shifts in population. For information about redistricting in your state, log on to the Redistricting Resource Center, provided by the National Committee for an Effective Congress.

Roll Call
www.rollcall.com
Roll Call, the newspaper of Capitol Hill, provides daily coverage on the members, legislation, and events taking place in and around the U.S. legislature.

The Sunlight Foundation and Taxpayers for Common Sense Open Congress
www.opencongress.org
Informative and very user-friendly means to explore legislation passed and proposed, compare legislators, and keep up with recent action on bills.

U.S. House of Representatives
www.house.gov

U.S. Senate
www.senate.gov
These are the official websites for the U.S. House of Representatives and the U.S. Senate. Here you can find information on your members of Congress, key congressional leaders, bills currently under consideration, and legislative committees.

When Donald Trump succeeded Barack Obama as president in 2017, he inherited numerous challenges, but also a presidency more powerful than the institution imagined by the Founders.

The Presidency

WHAT GOVERNMENT DOES AND WHY IT MATTERS By 2016, President Barack Obama could look back over his two terms in office and reasonably claim that he had achieved a number of the goals he had set for himself. Under the president's leadership, the nation's health care system had been significantly redesigned so that, beginning in 2014, health insurance was offered to 32 million previously uninsured Americans. With the president's signature in 2010, the Dodd-Frank Wall Street Reform and Consumer Protection Act imposed a major set of new regulations on the financial services sector, whose practices had been blamed for the "Great Recession" of 2008. The president brought most American troops home from Iraq and Afghanistan. Terrorist mastermind Osama bin Laden was killed by U.S. special operations troops. And, in pitched battles with congressional Republicans, the president forced Congress to end the 2013 government shutdown, agree to an increase in the national debt limit, accept several of his most controversial judicial and executive branch nominees, and in 2015 enact a controversial nuclear weapons agreement with Iran. In 2014, Obama issued executive orders providing undocumented immigrants with a path toward permanent residence and citizenship; later, the executive branch issued controversial guidelines to the states requiring them to recognize the rights of transgender individuals.

The president's actions reflect the considerable power of the contemporary presidency. But President Obama also suffered a number of significant setbacks and raised new questions about the propriety of the president's use of power. His efforts to persuade Congress to enact immigration reforms were blunted, as were his attempts to induce Congress to enact gun control legislation. Some of the president's actions, such as the Iran agreement—ending economic sanctions against Iran in exchange for an Iranian promise to slow the development of nuclear weapons—remained highly controversial and were seen by critics as exemplifying presidential overreach and failure to fully consult Congress in matters of foreign policy. Moreover, with the departure of American forces, Iraq descended into chaos and sectarian violence, and new terrorist groups such as the Islamic State of Iraq and Syria (ISIS) arose in the vacuum left by the quick departure of American forces. Indeed, some of the early successes of ISIS were achieved using weapons left behind by American forces when they were recalled from the region. Even the president's health care triumph was tempered by the errors, mismanagement, and confusion surrounding the rollout of the program in 2014. And, of course, the nation continued to confront major problems including budget deficits, unemployment, failing schools, and challenges abroad, which would need to be addressed by the new president and new Congress elected in 2016.

In this chapter, we examine the foundations of the American presidency and assess the origins and character of presidential power in the twenty-first century. National emergencies are one source of presidential power, but presidents are also empowered by democratic political processes and, increasingly, by their ability to control and expand the institutional resources of the office. But, as we will see, presidential power is not without limit, nor should it be. America's Constitution emphasizes checks and balances, not unlimited power. The framers thought a powerful and energetic president would make America's government more effective but knew that presidential power needed to be subject to constraints to prevent it from becoming a threat to citizens' liberties.

chaptergoals

- Explain the role of the president in the American political system and how it has evolved (pp. 507–9)

- Understand the expressed, delegated, and inherent powers of the presidency (pp. 509–21)

- Identify the institutional resources presidents have to help them exercise their powers (pp. 521–26)

- Explain how modern presidents have become even more powerful (pp. 526–36)

● Establishing the Presidency

Explain the role of the president in the American political system and how it has evolved

The presidency was established by Article II of the Constitution, which begins by asserting, "The executive power shall be vested in a President of the United States of America." Article II describes the manner in which the president is to be chosen and defines the basic powers of the presidency. By vesting the executive power in a single president, the framers were emphatically rejecting proposals for various forms of collective leadership. Some delegates to the Constitutional Convention had argued in favor of a multiheaded executive or an "executive council" in order to avoid undue concentration of power in the hands of one individual. Most of the framers, however, wanted to provide for "energy" in the executive and thought that a unitary executive would be more energetic than some form of collective leadership. They believed that a powerful executive would help protect the nation's interests vis-à-vis other nations and promote the federal government's interests relative to the states.

The presidential selection process defined by Article II resulted from a struggle between those delegates who preferred that the president be elected directly by the people and those who wanted the president to be selected by, and thus be responsible to, Congress. Direct popular election would create a more independent and more powerful presidency. With the adoption of a scheme of indirect election through an electoral college, with electors to be selected by the state legislatures (and elections failing to produce an electoral college majority to be resolved in the House of Representatives), the framers hoped to achieve a "republican" solution: a strong president responsible to state and national legislators rather than directly to the electorate.

The framers' idea that electors would be chosen by the state legislatures gave way during the nineteenth century to various systems of popular selection of the electors. This made the presidency a more democratic institution and the president more directly responsible to the American people than to the states. Today, in 48

The election of the American president does not formally conclude on Election Day in November. In December, electors from each state cast their votes for president. The state electoral votes are then counted in January in the House of Representatives, which announces the victor.

of the 50 states, the candidate who wins the state's popular vote wins all the electoral college votes for that state. The presidential candidate with a majority of votes in the electoral college—not necessarily the candidate with the most votes from the people—becomes president. The number of electors preassigned to each state is equal to its number of senators plus representatives; small states are thus overrepresented in the electoral college. As a result, the electoral college system can sometimes distort the outcomes of presidential races, although it does not undermine the principle of popular selection of the nation's leaders.

The presidency was strengthened somewhat in the 1830s with the introduction of the national convention system of nominating presidential candidates. Until then, presidential candidates had been nominated by their party's congressional delegates through a caucus system, derisively called "King Caucus" because any candidate for president was beholden to the party's leaders in Congress both for the party's nomination and for their support in the presidential election. The national nominating convention arose outside Congress in order to provide some representation for a party's voters who lived in districts where they were in the minority. The political party in each state made its own provisions for selecting delegates to attend the presidential nominating convention, and in virtually all states, the selection was dominated by the party leaders. The convention system quickly became the most popular method of nominating candidates for all elective offices and remained so until well into the twentieth century, when it succumbed to the criticism that it was undemocratic and dominated by a few leaders in a "smoke-filled room." But during the nineteenth century, the convention system was seen as a victory for democracy against the congressional elite. Furthermore, the national convention gave the presidency a base of power independent of Congress.

This additional independence did not immediately transform the presidency into the office familiar to us today, but the national convention did begin to open the presidency to larger social forces and newly organized interests in society. In other words, it gave the presidency a broader popular base that would eventually demand and support increased presidential power. Improvements in the telegraph, the telephone, and other forms of mass communication enabled individuals to share their complaints and allowed national leaders (especially presidents and presidential candidates) to reach out directly to the people. Eventually, though more slowly, the presidential selection process began to be further democratized with the adoption of primary elections through which millions of ordinary citizens were given an opportunity to take part in the presidential nominating process by popular selection of convention delegates.

But despite political and social conditions favoring the enhancement of the presidency, the development of presidential government as we know it today did not mature until the middle of the twentieth century. For a long period, even as the national government began to grow, Congress was careful to keep a tight rein on the president's power. The real turning point in the history of American national government came during the administration of Franklin Delano Roosevelt (FDR). Roosevelt greatly enlarged the bureaucracies of the executive branch, created the Executive Office of the President, and expanded presidential responsibility for the nation's budget. He also led by example in the use of executive orders in place of

New and improving forms of mass communication have enabled modern presidents to connect with the people in a variety of ways, but interacting with citizens face-to-face remains an extremely effective way to develop a broad popular base.

legislation and executive agreements in place of treaties, reducing the congressional role in domestic and foreign policy; subsequent presidents have continued both practices. Since FDR and his "New Deal" of the 1930s, every president has been strong whether or not he was committed to the goal of strengthening the presidency.

● The Constitutional Powers of the Presidency

Understand the expressed, delegated, and inherent powers of the presidency

Whereas Section 1 of Article II of the Constitution explains how the president is to be chosen, Sections 2 and 3 outline the powers and duties of the president. These two sections identify two sources of presidential authority. Some presidential powers, called the **expressed powers** of the office, are specifically established by the language of the Constitution. For example, the president is authorized to make treaties, grant pardons, and nominate judges and other public officials. These specifically defined powers cannot be revoked by Congress or any other agency without an amendment to the Constitution. Other expressed powers include the authority to receive ambassadors and the command of the military forces of the United States.

expressed powers specific powers granted by the Constitution to Congress (Article I, Section 8) and to the president (Article II)

The list of expressed presidential powers is brief, but these expressed powers have become the foundation of a second set of presidential powers, the so-called **implied powers** of the office. An implied power is one that can be considered necessary to allow the president to exercise his expressed power. For example, the Constitution expressly gives the president the power to appoint "all other officers of the United States . . . which shall be established by law." Article II does not, however, expressly grant the president the power to remove such officials from office. From the earliest years of the Republic, though, presidents claimed that the removal power was implied by the appointment power. In 1926 the U.S. Supreme Court affirmed this idea in the case of *Myers v. United States*.[1]

implied powers powers derived from the necessary and proper clause of Article I, Section 8, of the Constitution; such powers are not specifically expressed but are implied through the expansive interpretation of delegated powers

In addition to the president's expressed and implied powers, Article II declares that the president "shall take Care that the Laws be faithfully executed." Since the laws are enacted by Congress, this language implies that Congress is to delegate to the president the power to implement or execute its will. Powers given to the president by Congress are called **delegated powers**. In principle, Congress delegates to the president only the power to identify or develop the means through which to carry out its decisions. So, for example, if Congress determines that air quality should be improved, it might delegate to a bureaucratic agency in the executive branch the power to identify the best means of bringing about such an improvement as well as the power to implement the actual cleanup process. By delegating power to the executive branch, Congress substantially enhances the importance of the presidency. In most cases, Congress delegates power to bureaucratic agencies in the executive branch rather than to the president, but as we shall see, contemporary presidents have found ways to capture a good deal of this delegated power for themselves.

delegated powers constitutional powers that are assigned to one governmental agency but that are exercised by another agency with the express permission of the first

Expressed Powers

The president's expressed powers, as defined by Sections 2 and 3 of Article II, fall into several categories:

1. *Military.* Article II, Section 2, provides for the power as "Commander in Chief of the Army and Navy of the United States, and of the Militia of the several States, when called in to the actual Service of the United States."
2. *Judicial.* Article II, Section 2, also provides the power to "grant Reprieves and Pardons for Offences against the United States, except in Cases of Impeachment."
3. *Diplomatic.* Article II, Section 2, further provides the power "by and with the Advice and Consent of the Senate to make Treaties." Article II, Section 3, provides the power to "receive Ambassadors and other public Ministers."
4. *Executive.* Article II, Section 3, also authorizes the president to see to it that all the laws are faithfully executed; Section 2 gives the chief executive power to appoint, remove, and supervise all executive officers and to appoint all federal judges.
5. *Legislative.* Article I, Section 7, and Article II, Section 3, give the president the power to participate authoritatively in the legislative process.

Military Power The president's military powers are among the most important exercised by the chief executive. The position of **commander in chief** makes the president the highest military authority in the United States, with control of the entire defense establishment. The president is also head of the nation's intelligence network, which includes not only the Central Intelligence Agency (CIA) but also the National Security Council (NSC), the National Security Agency (NSA), the Federal Bureau of Investigation (FBI), and a host of less well-known but very powerful international and domestic security agencies.

commander in chief the role of the president as commander of the national military and the state National Guard units (when called into service)

Military Sources of Domestic Power The president's military powers extend into the domestic sphere. Article IV, Section 4, provides that the "United States shall [protect] every State . . . against Invasion . . . and . . . domestic Violence." Congress has made this an explicit presidential power through statutes directing the president as commander in chief to discharge these obligations.[2] The Constitution restrains the president's use of domestic force by providing that a state legislature (or governor when the legislature is not in session) must request federal troops before the president can send them into the state to provide public order. Yet this proviso is not absolute. First, presidents are not obligated to deploy national troops merely because the state legislature or governor makes such a request. More important, the president may deploy troops in a state or city without a specific request from the state legislature or governor if the president considers it necessary to maintain an essential national service during an emergency, enforce a federal judicial order, or protect federally guaranteed civil rights.[3]

One historic example of the unilateral use of presidential emergency power, even when the states don't request it, is the decision by President Dwight D. Eisenhower in 1957 to send troops into Little Rock, Arkansas, against the wishes of the state of Arkansas, to enforce court orders to integrate Little Rock's Central High School. The governor of Arkansas, Orval Faubus, had posted the Arkansas National Guard at the entrance to Central High School to prevent the court-ordered admission of nine black students. After an effort to negotiate with Governor Faubus failed,

President Eisenhower reluctantly sent 1,000 paratroopers to Little Rock; they stood watch while the black students took their places in the all-white classrooms.

In most instances of domestic disorder, whether from human or from natural causes, presidents tend to exercise unilateral power by declaring a "state of emergency," thereby making available federal grants, insurance, and direct assistance. In 2005, President George W. Bush declared a state of emergency to allow the Federal Emergency Management Agency (FEMA) to coordinate the government's response to Hurricane Katrina, an immense storm that devastated the city of New Orleans, resulting in approximately 1,830 deaths. Chaos reigned in the days immediately following the storm, including looting and violence. Bush sent some 22,000 federal troops to bolster local efforts to restore order and offer aid.

Judicial Power The presidential power to grant reprieves, pardons, and amnesty involves power over all individuals who may be a threat to the security of the United States. Presidents may use this power on behalf of a particular individual, as did Gerald Ford when he pardoned Richard Nixon in 1974 "for all offenses against the United States which he . . . has committed or may have committed." Or they may use it on a large scale, as did President Andrew Johnson in 1868, when he gave full amnesty to all southerners who had participated in the "Late Rebellion," and President Jimmy Carter in 1977, when he declared an amnesty for all the draft evaders of the Vietnam War.

Diplomatic Power The president is America's "head of state," its chief representative in dealings with other nations, having the power to make treaties for the United States (with the advice and consent of the Senate) as well as the power to "recognize" other countries. Diplomatic recognition means that the United States acknowledges a government's legitimacy and territorial claims. In 2015, President Obama restored American diplomatic ties with Cuba, which had been severed by

As the head of state, the president is America's chief representative in dealings with other countries. Here, President Obama meets with Cuban president Raúl Castro in 2016, after restoring diplomatic relations with Cuba more than 50 years after Dwight D. Eisenhower had severed ties with the country.

executive agreement an agreement, made between the president and another country, that has the force of a treaty but does not require the Senate's "advice and consent"

executive privilege the claim that confidential communications between a president and close advisers should not be revealed without the consent of the president

President Eisenhower in 1961 after the United States' relations with the Castro regime deteriorated.

In recent years, presidents have expanded the practice of using executive agreements instead of treaties to establish relations with other countries.[4] An **executive agreement** is exactly like a treaty because it is a contract between two countries, but it does not require Senate approval. There are actually two types of executive agreements. One is the *executive–congressional agreement*. For this type of agreement, the president will submit the proposed arrangement to Congress for a simple majority vote in both houses, usually easier for presidents to win than the two-thirds approval of the Senate that is required for a treaty. The United States' 2015 accord with Iran is a recent example of an executive–congressional agreement. The other type of executive agreement is the *sole executive agreement*, which is simply an understanding between the president and a foreign state and is not submitted to Congress for approval. In the past, sole executive agreements were used to flesh out commitments already made in treaties or to arrange for matters well below the level of policy. Since the 1930s, however, presidents have entered into sole executive agreements on important issues when they were uncertain about their prospects for securing congressional approval. For example, the General Agreement on Tariffs and Trade (GATT), one of the cornerstones of U.S. international economic policy in the post–World War II era, was based on an executive agreement. The courts have held that executive agreements have the force of law, as though they were formal treaties.

Executive Power The Constitution focuses executive power and legal responsibility on the president. The most important basis of the president's power as chief executive is found in Article II, Section 3, of the Constitution, which stipulates that the president must see that all the laws are faithfully executed, and Section 2, which provides that the president will appoint and supervise all executive officers and appoint all federal judges (with Senate approval; after some early controversy, presidents' sole power to remove executive branch officials was accepted). The power to appoint the principal executive officers and to require each of them to report to the president on subjects relating to the duties of their departments makes the president the true chief executive officer (CEO) of the nation. The president is subject to some limitations because the appointment of all such officers, including ambassadors, ministers, and federal judges, is subject to a majority approval by the Senate. But these appointments are at the discretion of the president, and the loyalty and the responsibility of each appointee are presumed to be directed toward the president.

Another component of the president's power as chief executive is **executive privilege**, the claim that confidential communications between a president and close advisers should not be revealed without presidential consent. Presidents have made this claim ever since George Washington refused a request from the House of Representatives to deliver documents concerning negotiations of an important treaty. Washington refused (successfully) on the grounds that, first, the House was not constitutionally part of the treaty-making process and, second, diplomatic negotiations required secrecy.

Although many presidents have claimed executive privilege, the concept was not tested in the courts until the 1971 "Watergate" affair when President

Richard Nixon refused congressional demands that he turn over secret White House tapes that congressional investigators suspected would establish his complicity in illegal activities. In *United States v. Nixon* (1974), the Supreme Court ordered Nixon to turn over the tapes.[5] The president complied with the order and was forced to resign from office. The *United States v. Nixon* case is often seen as a blow to presidential power, but in actuality, the Court's ruling recognized for the first time the legal validity of executive privilege, though holding that it did not apply in this particular instance. Subsequent presidents have cited *United States v. Nixon* in support of their claims of executive privilege. The Obama administration invoked executive privilege once, in response to congressional demands for records from Attorney General Eric Holder relating to Operation Fast and Furious, an arms-trafficking sting operation that went awry, with federal agents losing track of hundreds of guns they sold to suspected gun smugglers.

The Supreme Court's decision in United States v. Nixon *is often seen as a blow to presidential power because Nixon was required to turn over secret tapes related to the Watergate scandal, despite his claims of executive privilege. Here, Nixon points to transcripts of the tapes that he is turning over to House impeachment investigators.*

Legislative Power The president plays a role not only in the administration of government but also in the legislative process. Two constitutional provisions are the primary sources of the president's power in the legislative arena. The first of these is the portion of Article II, Section 3, providing that the president "shall from time to time give to the Congress Information of the State of the Union, and recommend to their Consideration such Measures as he shall judge necessary and expedient." Delivering a "State of the Union" address may at first appear to be little more than the president's obligation to make recommendations for Congress's consideration. But as political and social conditions began to favor an increasingly prominent presidential role, each president, especially since FDR, began to rely on this provision in order to become the primary initiator of proposals for legislative action in Congress and the most important single participant in legislative decision making, as well as the principal source for public awareness of national issues.[6]

The second of the president's legislative powers is the veto power assigned by Article I, Section 7.[7] The **veto** is the president's constitutional power to reject acts of Congress (see Figure 13.1), making the president the most important single legislative leader.[8] No bill vetoed by the president can become law unless both the House and Senate override the veto by a two-thirds vote. In the case of a **pocket veto**, Congress does not have the option of overriding the veto but must reintroduce the bill in the next session. Usually, if a president is presented with a bill and does not sign it within 10 days, it automatically becomes law. But this is true only while Congress is in session. If a president chooses not to sign a bill presented within the last 10 days of a legislative session and Congress is out of session when the 10-day limit expires, instead of becoming law, the bill is vetoed.

Use of the veto varies according to the political situation each president confronts. During his last two years in office, when Democrats had control of both houses of Congress, Republican president George W. Bush vetoed 10 bills, including legislation designed to prohibit the use of harsh interrogation tactics, saying it "would take away one of the most valuable tools in the war on terror."[9] Similarly, 10 of President Obama's 12 vetoes occurred during his last two years in office, when Republicans held the majority in both Houses. Among Obama's most significant vetoes was his 2015 decision to veto a bill authorizing construction of the Keystone XL oil pipeline that would have carried oil from Canada to U.S. refineries. The

veto the president's constitutional power to turn down acts of Congress; a presidential veto may be overridden by a two-thirds vote of each house of Congress

pocket veto a presidential veto that is automatically triggered if the president does not act on a given piece of legislation passed during the final 10 days of a legislative session

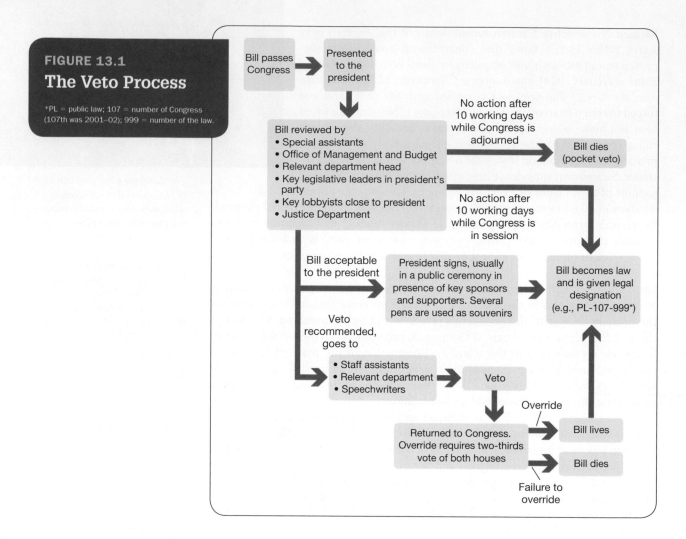

FIGURE 13.1

The Veto Process

*PL = public law; 107 = number of Congress (107th was 2001–02); 999 = number of the law.

Bill passes Congress → Presented to the president

Bill reviewed by
- Special assistants
- Office of Management and Budget
- Relevant department head
- Key legislative leaders in president's party
- Key lobbyists close to president
- Justice Department

No action after 10 working days while Congress is adjourned → Bill dies (pocket veto)

No action after 10 working days while Congress is in session

Bill acceptable to the president → President signs, usually in a public ceremony in presence of key sponsors and supporters. Several pens are used as souvenirs → Bill becomes law and is given legal designation (e.g., PL-107-999*)

Veto recommended, goes to
- Staff assistants
- Relevant department
- Speechwriters → Veto

Returned to Congress. Override requires two-thirds vote of both houses

Override → Bill lives

Failure to override → Bill dies

bill had been opposed by environmentalists and other interests. An attempt to override the president's veto failed to obtain the necessary two-thirds majority of both houses of Congress. Since the time of George Washington, presidents have used their veto power over 3,000 times, and on only 111 occasions has Congress overridden them. As shown in Figure 13.2, the number of presidential vetoes is higher when Congress is controlled by the opposite party.

Though not explicitly, the Constitution provides the president with the power of **legislative initiative**—the implied power to bring a legislative agenda before Congress. The framers of the Constitution clearly saw legislative initiative as one of the keys to executive power. *Initiative* implies the ability to formulate proposals for important policies, and the president, as an individual with a great deal of staff assistance, is able to initiate decisive action more frequently than Congress, with its large assemblies that have to deliberate and debate before taking action. With some important exceptions, Congress depends on the president to set the agenda of public policy. For example, Congress has come to expect the president to propose the government's budget. And quite clearly, initiative confers the power of being able to set the terms of discourse in the making of public policy.

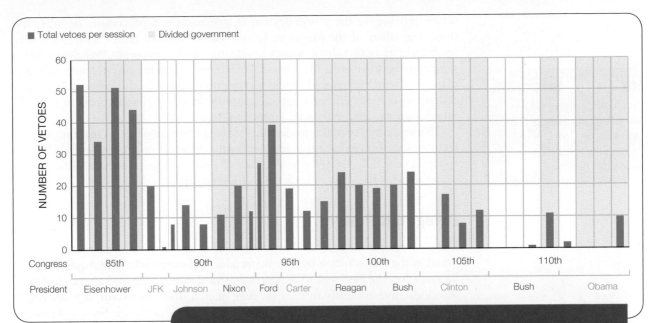

FIGURE 13.2

The Presidential Use of the Veto

One of the president's checks over the legislative branch is the use of the veto. The use of the veto has varied considerably over the course of American history. The bars in the graph show the number of vetoes each president made per session of Congress. What is the overall trend for vetoes? Why might this be? What is the relationship between the number of vetoes and whether Congress is controlled by the same party as the president (unified government) or the opposite party (divided government)?

NOTE: Congress changed party control mid-sessions in 1953–54 and 2001. The first president Bush shown here is George H. W. Bush (101st and 102nd Congresses); the second is George W. Bush (107th–110th Congresses).
SOURCE: The American Presidency Project, www.presidency.ucsb.edu/data/vetoes.php (accessed 5/16/16).

For example, during the weeks immediately following September 11, George W. Bush took many presidential initiatives to Congress, and each was given almost unanimous support. President Obama made health care his chief domestic priority and engaged in sharp battles with congressional Republicans to bring about the enactment of the Affordable Care Act, informally known as "Obamacare."

The president's initiative does not end with congressional policy making and the making of laws in the ordinary sense of the term. The president has still another legislative role (in all but name) within the executive branch. This is designated as the power to issue **executive orders**, sometimes in the form of presidential memoranda to the executive branch. President Obama preferred to issue memoranda to avoid being accused of issuing too many executive orders, though there is actually little difference between the two. The executive order or memorandum is first and foremost simply a normal tool of management, a power that virtually any CEO has to make "company policy"—rule-setting procedures, etiquette, chains of command, functional responsibilities, and so on. But evolving out of this normal management practice is a recognized presidential power to promulgate rules that have the effect and the formal status of legislation. Most presidential executive

executive order a rule or regulation issued by the president that has the effect and formal status of legislation

for critical analysis

Although Congress passes laws, the president has influence too. What is the president's role in the legislative process?

orders provide for the reorganization of structures and procedures or otherwise direct the affairs of the executive branch—to be applied either across the board to all agencies or to a single agency or department. For example, President Obama signed an executive order in January 2016 aimed at reducing gun violence, including plans to extend background checks and improve mental health services. Executive orders can also establish new agencies, as with President Nixon's order in 1970–71 establishing the Environmental Protection Agency (EPA).

This legislative or policy leadership role of the presidency is an institutionalized feature of the office that exists independently of the occupant of the office. That is to say, anyone duly elected president would possess these powers regardless of his or her individual energy or leadership characteristics.[10]

Delegated Powers

Many of the powers exercised by the president and the executive branch are not found in the Constitution but are the products of congressional statutes and resolutions. Over the past century, Congress has voluntarily delegated a great deal of its own legislative authority to the executive branch. To some extent, this delegation of power has been an almost inescapable consequence of the expansion of government activity in the United States since the New Deal. Given the vast range of the federal government's responsibilities, Congress cannot execute and administer all the programs it creates and the laws it enacts. Inevitably, Congress must turn to the hundreds of departments and agencies in the executive branch or, when necessary, create new agencies to implement its goals. Thus, for example, in 2002, when Congress sought to protect America from terrorist attacks, it established the Department of Homeland Security, with broad powers in the realms of law enforcement, public health, and immigration.

As they implement congressional legislation, federal agencies collectively develop thousands of rules and regulations and issue thousands of orders and findings every year. Agencies interpret Congress's intent, promulgate rules aimed at implementing that intent, and issue orders to individuals, firms, and organizations to impel them to conform to the law. When it establishes an agency, Congress sometimes grants it only limited discretionary authority, providing very specific guidelines and standards that must be followed by the administrators charged with the program's implementation. Take the Internal Revenue Service (IRS), for example. Most Americans view the IRS as a powerful agency whose dictates can have an immediate and sometimes unpleasant impact on their lives. In fact, congressional tax legislation is very specific and detailed, leaving little to the discretion of IRS administrators.[11] The agency certainly develops numerous rules and procedures to enhance tax collection. It is Congress, however, that establishes the structure of the tax liabilities, tax exemptions, and tax deductions that determine each taxpayer's burdens and responsibilities.

In most instances, though, congressional legislation is not very detailed. Often, Congress defines a broad goal or objective and delegates enormous discretionary power to administrators to determine how that goal is to be achieved. Agency administrators have enormous discretionary power to draft rules and regulations that have the effect of law. Indeed, the courts treat these administrative rules like congressional statutes. For all intents and purposes, when Congress creates an agency such as the Department of Homeland Security, giving it a broad mandate to achieve some desirable outcome, it transfers its own legislative power to the executive branch.

Executive Branches in Comparison

All democracies have an executive branch, but the specific form it takes varies. In presidential systems, such as the United States, the position of the *head of state* (the symbolic leader of a country) and the *head of government* (the leader in charge of the day-to-day running of the government) is combined into one position—the president. In parliamentary systems, these roles are often held by different people, with the head of government being the more powerful position. For example, in Germany, the head of government is the prime minister (called the chancellor), while the head of state is the president, who plays a largely ceremonial role similar to the United Kingdom's queen.

Most democracies use parliamentary executive systems, though presidential systems are common in the Americas, in part due to the historical influence of the United States. Political scientists have long debated which system is "best," contrasting parliamentary and presidential systems on their effectiveness, stability, and representativeness. In presidential systems, for example, the separation of powers may protect against the "tyranny of the majority," in which a majority pursues its interests without regard to those of minority groups (see Chapter 2), but it can also lead to deadlock, policy inefficiencies, and polarization.

A small but growing group of countries uses a hybrid "semi-presidential" system. France, for instance, divides the executive between a powerful head of state (the president) and the head of government (the prime minister) who have different but (theoretically) equal powers. While this arrangement is intended to combine the best of both systems, conflict can emerge in semi-presidential systems between the prime minister and president over differences in legislation or constitutional authority. In most semi-presidential systems, the president holds the majority of the power, including the power to appoint and dismiss the prime minister. Occasionally, presidents in these systems can use their power advantage to undermine the legislature and threaten democracy.

	Presidential	Parliamentary
Examples	United States, Mexico, Brazil, Chile, Ghana, South Korea	United Kingdom, India, Germany, Japan, Canada, Austria, Norway
Executive title	President	Prime Minister, Chancellor, etc.
Is the executive the . . .		
Head of state?	Yes	No
Head of government?	Yes	Yes
Executive elected by . . .	voters*	parliament
Term in office	Fixed by law	Subject to support of the parliament
Separation of powers	Yes	No; the Prime Minister is a member of the parliament
Executive role in legislating	Veto power	Initiates most bills

*In the United States, the president is elected by the Electoral College, not by the voters directly. Other presidential systems have the voters directly elect the president.

The influence of the president and the executive branch is widespread as the executive is responsible for the implementation of many laws that Congress passes. For example, after Congress passed the Affordable Care Act, it was up to the executive branch to orchestrate the health insurance enrollment process for millions of Americans.

During the nineteenth and early twentieth centuries, Congress typically wrote laws that provided fairly clear principles and standards to guide executive implementation. For example, the 1922 Fordney-McCumber Tariff Act empowered the president to increase or decrease duties on certain manufactured goods in order to reduce the difference in costs between domestically produced products and those manufactured abroad. The act authorized the president to make the final determination, but his discretionary authority was quite constrained. The statute listed the criteria the president was to consider, fixed the permissible range of tariff changes, and outlined the procedures to be used to calculate the cost differences between foreign and domestic goods. When an importer challenged a particular executive decision as an abuse of delegated power, the Supreme Court had no difficulty finding that the president was merely acting in accordance with Congress's directives.[12]

At least since the New Deal, however, Congress has tended to give executive agencies broad mandates and to draft legislation that offers few clear standards or guidelines for implementation by the executive. For example, the 1933 National Industrial Recovery Act gave the president the authority to set rules to bring about fair competition in key sectors of the economy without ever defining what the term meant or how it was to be achieved.[13] This pattern of broad delegation became typical in the ensuing decades. The 1972 Consumer Product Safety Act, for example, authorizes the Consumer Product Safety Commission to reduce unreasonable risk of injury from household products but offers no suggestions to guide the commission's determination of what constitutes reasonable and unreasonable risks or how these are to be reduced.[14] This means the executive branch, under the president's direction, has wide discretion to make rules that impact American citizens and businesses. A recent example of the executive branch's role is the 2011 Affordable Care Act. After the law passed, several members of Congress admitted that they did not fully understand how the act would work and were depending upon the Department of Health and Human Services, the agency with primary administrative responsibility for the act, to explain it to them. The case of the Affordable Care Act is fairly typical. As administrative scholar Jerry L. Nashaw has observed, "Most public law is legislative in origin but administrative in content."[15]

This shift from the nineteenth-century pattern of relatively well-defined congressional guidelines for administrators to the more contemporary pattern of broad delegations of congressional power to the executive branch is, to be sure, partially a consequence of the great scope and complexity of the tasks that America's contemporary government has undertaken. During much of the nineteenth century, the federal government had relatively few domestic responsibilities, and Congress could pay close attention to details. Today, the operation of an enormous executive establishment and literally thousands of programs under varied and changing circumstances requires that administrators be allowed some considerable measure of discretion to carry out their jobs. Nevertheless, the end result is to shift power from Congress to the executive branch.

Inherent Powers

Presidents have claimed a fourth source of power beyond expressed, implied, and delegated powers. These are powers not specified in the Constitution or the law but "powers over and beyond those expressly granted in the Constitution or reasonably to be implied from express grants."[16] Referred to as the

Who Are America's Presidents?

American presidents have all been men. Until the election of Barack Obama in 2008, they had all been white. As the data show, a majority of presidents have come from the eastern United States, with Virginia producing the most American presidents, especially in the nation's first decades.

Gender

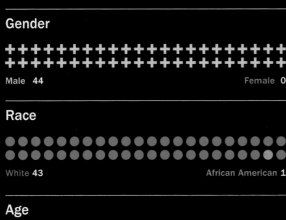

Male **44**　　　　　　　　　　　　　　　　　　　　Female **0**

Race

White **43**　　　　　　　　　　　　　　　African American **1**

Party*

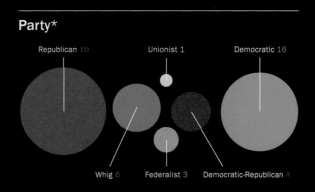

Republican 19　　　　Unionist 1　　　　Democratic 16

Whig 6　　　Federalist 3　　　Democratic-Republican 4

Age

Number of presidents

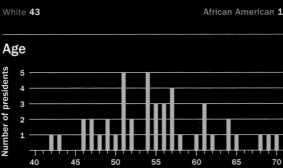

Age of president when first elected

Top Occupations**

Number of presidents

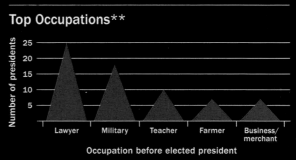

Lawyer　Military　Teacher　Farmer　Business/merchant

Occupation before elected president

Region†

Presidents

- ○ 0
- ● 1
- ● 2
- ● 4
- ● 5
- ● 7
- ● 8

NOTE: Grover Cleveland served as America's 22nd and 24th presidents. He is counted only once in the demographic data here, thus the total number of people who have served as U.S. president is 43.

*Some presidents switched parties during their political careers, thus the numbers sum to more than 43.

**This chart reflects the top nonpolitical careers of U.S. presidents. (All presidents except George Washington and Donald Trump had previous political and/or public service experience.) Presidents may have had more than one occupation, and some occupations do not appear on this list, thus the numbers do not sum to 43.

†Andrew Jackson was born in the Waxhaw area, on the North Carolina–South Carolina border.

SOURCES: Roper Center, www.ropercenter.uconn.edu/elections/common/pop_vote.html; David Leip, http://uselectionatlas.org/RESULTS/; the American Presidency Project, www.presidency.ucsb.edu/showelection.php?year=1840; Miller Center, University of Virginia, http://millercenter.org/president (accessed 3/17/14).

for critical analysis

1. Why do you think all presidents have been men and all but one have been white? Do you think this is likely to change in coming years?

2. Why do you think so many presidents have come from the South and the East? What electoral or historical factors may have produced this trend?

inherent powers powers claimed by a president that are not expressed in the Constitution but are inferred from it

inherent powers of the presidency, they are most often asserted by presidents in times of war or national emergency. Yet, not all powerful presidents claimed inherent powers.

For example, after the fall of Fort Sumter and the outbreak of the Civil War, President Abraham Lincoln issued a series of executive orders for which he had no clear legal authority. Without even calling Congress into session, Lincoln combined the state militias into a 90-day national volunteer force, called for 40,000 new volunteers, enlarged the regular army and navy, diverted $2 million in unspent appropriations to military needs, instituted censorship of the U.S. mail, ordered a blockade of southern ports, suspended the writ of habeas corpus in the border states, and ordered the arrest by military police of individuals whom he deemed to be guilty of engaging in or even merely contemplating treasonous actions.[17] Lincoln asserted that these extraordinary measures were necessary to confront this crisis. Later, when Congress convened, Lincoln reported his actions to it and Congress enacted legislation retroactively codifying the president's actions. Lincoln's example of act first and ask later was cited by later presidents including George W. Bush in the wake of the September 11 terror attacks.[18]

War and Inherent Presidential Power The Constitution gives Congress the power to declare war. Presidents, however, have gone a long way toward capturing this power for themselves. Congress has not declared war since June 1942,[19] but since then American military forces have engaged in numerous campaigns throughout the world under the orders of the president. When North Korean forces invaded South Korea in June 1950, Congress was actually prepared to declare war; but President Harry S. Truman asserted that the president and not Congress could decide when and where to deploy America's military might. Truman dispatched American forces to Korea without a congressional declaration, and in the face of the emergency, Congress felt it had to acquiesce and approved money to finance the conflict. This became the pattern for future congressional–executive relations in the military realm: the wars in Vietnam, Bosnia, Afghanistan, and Iraq, as well as a host of lesser conflicts, were all fought without declarations of war. Approximately 102,000 U.S. troops have died in these military engagements, with half of that total occurring during the Vietnam War.

War Powers Resolution a resolution of Congress that the president can send troops into action abroad only by authorization of Congress or if American troops are already under attack or serious threat

In 1973, Congress responded to presidential unilateralism by passing the **War Powers Resolution** over President Richard M. Nixon's veto. This resolution reasserted the principle of congressional war power, required the president to inform Congress of any planned military campaign, and stipulated that forces must be withdrawn within 60 days if there is no specific congressional authorization for their continued deployment. Presidents, however, have generally ignored the War Powers Resolution, claiming inherent executive power to defend the nation. Thus, President George W. Bush responded to the September 11, 2001, attacks by Islamist terrorists by organizing a major military campaign to overthrow the Taliban regime in Afghanistan, which had sheltered the terrorists. In 2003, Bush ordered the invasion of Iraq, which he accused of posing a threat to the United States. U.S. forces overthrew the government of the Iraqi dictator, Saddam Hussein, and occupied the country. In both instances, Congress passed resolutions approving the president's actions, but the president was careful to assert that he did not need congressional authorization. The War Powers Resolution was barely mentioned on Capitol Hill and was ignored by the White House. President Obama, for his part, made frequent use of special operations forces and unmanned aerial vehicles (or drones) to conduct military operations, and Congress was not consulted. Thus, in 2015, members of Congress, along with other Americans, learned of drone strikes against ISIS leaders only as these were being reported by the media.

Military emergencies have typically also led to expansion of the domestic powers of the executive branch. This was true during the First and Second World Wars and has been true in the wake of the "war on terror" as well. Within a month of the September 11, 2001, attacks, the White House had drafted and Congress had enacted the USA PATRIOT Act, expanding the power of government agencies to engage in domestic surveillance activities, including electronic surveillance, and restricting judicial review of such efforts. The act also gave the attorney general greater authority to detain and deport aliens suspected of having terrorist affiliations. The act expired in 2015, but important sections were reinstated by Congress. Also following September 11, Congress created the Department of Homeland Security, combining offices from 22 federal agencies into one huge new Cabinet department that would be responsible for protecting the nation from attack and responding to natural disasters. As an executive agency, the Department of Homeland Security is overseen by the president.

Many, if not most, of President Obama's international initiatives were based on the idea of inherent powers. These included sending troops to deal with the Ebola crisis in West Africa as well as strikes by special operations troops, the bombing campaign in Libya in 2014, and the above-mentioned drone strikes.

for critical analysis

Presidents have expressed, delegated, and inherent sources of power. Which of the three do you think most accounts for the powers of the presidency?

The Presidency as an Institution

Identify the institutional resources presidents have to help them exercise their powers

The framers of the Constitution, as we saw, created a unitary executive because they thought this would make the presidency a more energetic institution. Nevertheless, since the ratification of the Constitution, the president has been joined by thousands of officials and staffers who work for, assist, or advise the chief executive (see Figure 13.3). Collectively, these individuals could be said to make up the institutional presidency and to give the president a capacity for action that no single individual, however energetic, could duplicate. The first component of the institutional presidency is the president's Cabinet.

The Cabinet

In the American system of government, the **Cabinet** is the traditional but informal designation for the heads of all the major federal government departments. The Cabinet has no constitutional status. Unlike in Great Britain and many other parliamentary countries, where the cabinet *is* the government, the American Cabinet is not a collective body. It meets but makes no decisions as a group. Each appointment must be approved by the Senate, but Cabinet members are not responsible to the Senate or to Congress at large.

Since cabinet appointees generally have not shared political careers with the president or with one another and since they may meet literally for the first time only after their selection, this motley collection of appointees is unlikely to form an effective governing group. Although President Bill Clinton's insistence on a Cabinet

Cabinet the secretaries, or chief administrators, of the major departments of the federal government; Cabinet secretaries are appointed by the president with the consent of the Senate

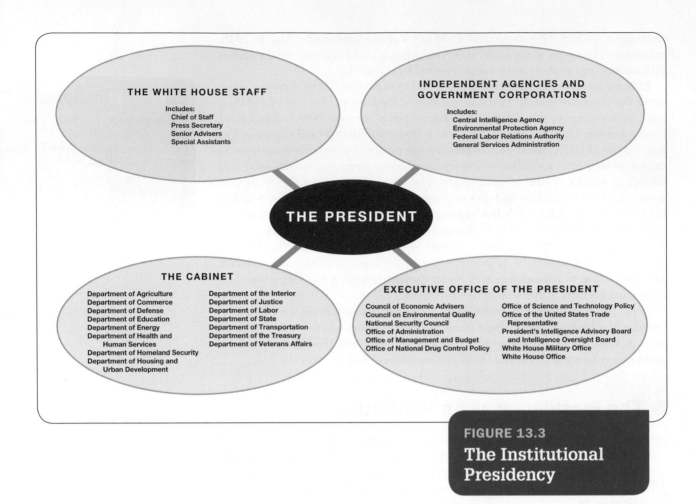

FIGURE 13.3

The Institutional Presidency

THE WHITE HOUSE STAFF

Includes:
Chief of Staff
Press Secretary
Senior Advisers
Special Assistants

INDEPENDENT AGENCIES AND
GOVERNMENT CORPORATIONS

Includes:
Central Intelligence Agency
Environmental Protection Agency
Federal Labor Relations Authority
General Services Administration

THE PRESIDENT

THE CABINET

Department of Agriculture
Department of Commerce
Department of Defense
Department of Education
Department of Energy
Department of Health and
　Human Services
Department of Homeland Security
Department of Housing and
　Urban Development

Department of the Interior
Department of Justice
Department of Labor
Department of State
Department of Transportation
Department of the Treasury
Department of Veterans Affairs

EXECUTIVE OFFICE OF THE PRESIDENT

Council of Economic Advisers
Council on Environmental Quality
National Security Council
Office of Administration
Office of Management and Budget
Office of National Drug Control Policy

Office of Science and Technology Policy
Office of the United States Trade
　Representative
President's Intelligence Advisory Board
　and Intelligence Oversight Board
White House Military Office
White House Office

diverse enough "to look like America" could be considered an act of political wisdom, it virtually guaranteed that few of his appointees had ever spent much time working together or even knew the policy positions or beliefs of the other appointees.[20]

Some presidents have relied more heavily on an "inner Cabinet." This includes the **National Security Council (NSC)**. The NSC, established by law in 1947, is composed of the president, the vice president, the secretary of state, the secretary of defense, and other officials invited by the president. It has its own staff of foreign policy specialists run by the special assistant to the president for national security affairs. For these highest appointments, presidents often turn to people from outside Washington, usually longtime associates. The inner Cabinet also can include the ranking officials of the White House staff.

The White House Staff

The **White House staff** is composed mainly of analysts and advisers.[21] Although many of the top White House staff members are given the title "special assistant" for a particular task or sector, the judgments and advice they are supposed to provide are a good deal broader and more generally political than those coming from the

National Security Council (NSC)
a presidential foreign policy
advisory council composed of the
president, the vice president, the
secretary of state, the secretary
of defense, and other officials
invited by the president

White House staff analysts and
advisers to the president, each
of whom is often given the title
"special assistant"

Executive Office of the President or from the Cabinet departments. The members of the White House staff also tend to be more closely associated with the president than are other presidentially appointed officials.

From an informal group of fewer than a dozen people (popularly called the **Kitchen Cabinet**) and no more than four dozen at its height during the Roosevelt presidency in 1937, the White House staff has grown substantially.[22] Richard Nixon employed 550 people in 1972. Jimmy Carter, who found so many of the trappings of presidential power distasteful and who publicly vowed to keep his staff small and decentralized, built an even larger and more centralized staff. In Obama's second term, the White House staff numbered approximately 450. In the spirit of transparency, the White House lists their names, positions, and salaries on the White House website.[23]

Kitchen Cabinet an informal group of advisers to whom the president turns for counsel and guidance; members of the official Cabinet may or may not also be members of the Kitchen Cabinet

The Executive Office of the President

Created in 1939, the **Executive Office of the President (EOP)** is a major part of what is often called the "institutional presidency"—the permanent agencies that perform defined management tasks for the president. Somewhere between 1,500 and 2,000 highly specialized people work for EOP agencies.[24] The importance of each agency in the EOP varies according to the personal orientation of each president. The most important and the largest EOP agency is the Office of Management and Budget (OMB). Its roles in preparing the national budget, designing the president's program, reporting on agency activities, and overseeing regulatory proposals connect the OMB to every conceivable presidential responsibility. The status and power of the OMB have grown in importance with each successive president, and the director of the OMB is now one of the most powerful officials in Washington. At one time the process of budgeting was a "bottom-up" procedure, with expenditure and program requests passing from the lowest bureaus through the departments to "clearance" in the OMB and thence to Congress, where each agency could be called in to explain what its "original request" was before the OMB revised it. Now the budgeting process is "top-down": the OMB sets the terms of discourse for agencies as well as for Congress.

Executive Office of the President (EOP) the permanent agencies that perform defined management tasks for the president; created in 1939, the EOP includes the OMB, the CEA, the NSC, and other agencies

The staff of the Council of Economic Advisers (CEA) constantly analyzes the economy and economic trends in order to help the president anticipate events, rather than waiting and reacting to them. The Council on Environmental Quality was designed to do for environmental issues what the CEA does for economic issues. The NSC—the "inner Cabinet" mentioned earlier—is composed of designated Cabinet officials who meet regularly with the president to give advice on the large national security picture. The staff of the NSC assimilates and analyzes data from all intelligence-gathering agencies (CIA, etc.). Other EOP agencies perform more specialized tasks.

The Vice Presidency

The vice presidency is a constitutional anomaly, even though the office was created along with the presidency by the Constitution. The vice president exists for two purposes only: to succeed the president in case of death, resignation, or incapacity and to preside over the Senate, casting a tie-breaking vote when necessary.[25]

The main value of the vice president as a political resource for the president is electoral. Traditionally, presidential candidates choose running mates who can win the support of at least one state (preferably a large one) that may not otherwise support the ticket. It is very doubtful that John Kennedy would have won in 1960 without his vice-presidential candidate, Lyndon Johnson, and the contribution Johnson made to winning in Texas. Another traditional guideline holds that the vice-presidential nominee should provide some regional balance and, wherever possible, ideological or ethnic balance as well. In 2016, Donald Trump chose Governor Mike Pence of Indiana as his running mate for a number of reasons. First, Indiana is a state Trump had to carry to win the election. Second, Pence, a former host of conservative radio and television talk shows, was well known among conservatives. Third, Pence served in Congress for 12 years. He worked to reassure skeptical party leaders that Trump was a qualified candidate. Fourth and most important, Pence is a devout Christian who is very well regarded by social conservatives.

As the institutional presidency has grown in size and complexity, most presidents of the past 25 years have sought to use their vice presidents as a management resource after the election. President George W. Bush granted unprecedented power and responsibility to his vice president, Dick Cheney, who helped shape the "war on terror." In the Obama White House, Vice President Biden was said to be regarded as the "skeptic-in-chief."[26] Biden's role was to question and criticize policy recommendations made to the president—until, of course, the president made a decision, at which point the vice president fell loyally into step.

The vice president is also important because, in the event of the death or incapacity of the president, he or she will succeed to the nation's highest office. During the course of American history, eight vice presidents have had to replace presidents who died in office. One vice president, Gerald Ford, found himself at the head

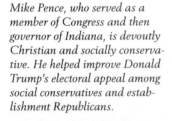

Mike Pence, who served as a member of Congress and then governor of Indiana, is devoutly Christian and socially conservative. He helped improve Donald Trump's electoral appeal among social conservatives and establishment Republicans.

of the nation when President Richard Nixon was forced to resign as a result of the Watergate scandal. During the 2004 vice-presidential debates, Dick Cheney sought to distinguish himself from the Democratic vice-presidential nominee, John Edwards, by averring that he, unlike the less experienced Edwards, had been chosen for his ability to serve as president if that became necessary.

Until the ratification of the Twenty-Fifth Amendment in 1965, the succession of the vice president to the presidency was a tradition, launched by John Tyler when he assumed the presidency after William Henry Harrison's death, rather than a constitutional or statutory requirement. The Twenty-Fifth Amendment codified this tradition by providing that the vice president would assume the presidency in the event of the chief executive's death or incapacity and setting forth the procedures that would be followed. In the event that both the president and vice president are killed, the Presidential Succession Act of 1947 establishes an order of succession, beginning with the Speaker of the House and continuing with the president pro tempore of the Senate and the Cabinet secretaries. This piece of legislation, adopted during the Cold War and prompted by fear of a nuclear attack, has taken on new importance in an age of global terrorism.

The First Spouse

The president serves as both chief executive and chief of state—the equivalent of Great Britain's prime minister and monarch rolled into one, simultaneously leading the government and representing the nation at official ceremonies and functions.

Because they are generally associated exclusively with the head-of-state aspect of America's presidency, presidential spouses are usually not subject to the same sort of media scrutiny or partisan attack as that aimed at the president. Traditionally, most first ladies have limited their activities to the ceremonial portion of the presidency: greeting foreign dignitaries, visiting other countries, and attending important national ceremonies.

Some first spouses, however, have had considerable influence over policy. Franklin Roosevelt's wife, Eleanor, was widely popular but also widely criticized for her active role in many elements of her husband's presidency. During the 1992

First Lady Melania Trump is an immigrant from Slovenia and a former model. During the 2016 presidential campaign, Mrs. Trump campaigned for her husband, speaking at the Republican National Convention and occasionally at rallies.

campaign, Bill Clinton often implied that his wife would be active in the administration; he joked that voters would get "two for the price of one." And indeed, after the election, Hillary Clinton took a leading role in many policy areas, most notably heading the administration's health care reform effort. She also became the first first lady to seek public office on her own, winning a seat in the U.S. Senate in 2000 and then running for president in 2008 and 2016, having served in between as President Obama's secretary of state. Melania Trump is the first foreign-born first lady in almost 200 years. With no political or public affairs experience, Mrs. Trump said that she would be a traditional first lady. Given the current expectation that the first spouse should assume some public responsibility, however, Mrs. Trump seems likely to take on some visible role in the Trump administration, such as becoming a visible advocate for an important social cause.

At one time, historians and journalists liked to debate the question of strong versus weak presidents. Some presidents, such as Abraham Lincoln and FDR, were called "strong" for their leadership and their ability to guide the nation's political agenda. Others, such as James Buchanan and Calvin Coolidge, were seen as "weak" for failing to develop significant legislative programs and seeming to observe, rather than shape, political events. Today, the strong-versus-weak categorization has become moot. Every president is strong, not so much as a function of personal charisma or political savvy but as a reflection of the increasing power of the presidency. Let us see how this came about.

● The Contemporary Bases of Presidential Power

> **Explain how modern presidents have become even more powerful**

During the nineteenth century, Congress was America's dominant institution of government, and members of Congress sometimes treated the president with disdain. Today, however, no one would assert that the presidency is unimportant. Presidents seek to dominate the policy-making process and claim the power to lead the nation in time of war. The expansion of presidential power over the course of the past century has come about not by accident but as the result of an ongoing effort by successive presidents to enlarge the powers of the office.

Generally, presidents can expand their power in two primary ways: through popular mobilization and through the administration. First, presidents may use popular appeals to create a mass base of support that will allow them to dominate their political foes, a tactic called "going public."[27] Second, presidents may seek to bolster their control of established executive agencies or to create new administrative institutions and procedures that will reduce their dependence on Congress and give them a more independent governing and policy-making capability. Perhaps the most obvious example of this is the use of executive orders to achieve policy goals in lieu of seeking to persuade Congress to enact legislation.

Presidents do have a third, less reliable tool: their political party. Each president has relied on his own party to implement his legislative agenda. For example, in 2015, President Obama relied on congressional Democrats to prevent rejection of his Iran treaty in the face of virtually unanimous Republican opposition. However, the president does not control his party; party members have considerable autonomy. Moreover, in America's system of separated powers, the president's party may be in the minority in Congress and unable to do much for the chief executive's programs. Obama's legislative agenda floundered after the Republican Party took control of both houses of Congress in the 2014 elections. Consequently, although the party is valuable to chief executives, it has not been a fully reliable presidential tool. As a result, contemporary presidents are more likely to use the two other methods, popular mobilization and executive administration, to achieve their political goals.

Going Public

In the nineteenth century, it was considered inappropriate for presidents to engage in personal campaigning on their own behalf or in support of programs and policies. When Andrew Johnson broke this unwritten rule and made a series of speeches vehemently seeking public support for his Reconstruction program, even some of his supporters were shocked at what they saw as his lack of decorum and dignity. The president's opponents cited his "inflammatory" speeches in one of the articles of impeachment drafted by the Congress.[28]

In the twentieth century, though, popular mobilization became a favored weapon in the political arsenals of most presidents. The first to make systematic use of appeals to the public were Theodore Roosevelt and Woodrow Wilson, but the president who used public appeals most effectively was Franklin Delano Roosevelt. FDR was "firmly persuaded of the need to form a direct link between the executive office and the public."[29] He developed a number of tactics for forging such a link. He often embarked on speaking trips around the nation to promote his programs. On one such tour, he told a crowd, "I regain strength just by meeting the American people."[30] In addition, FDR made effective use of a new electronic medium, the radio, to reach millions of Americans. In his famous "fireside chats," the president's voice could be heard in every living room in the country, discussing programs and policies and generally assuring Americans that Franklin Delano Roosevelt was aware of their difficulties and working diligently toward solutions.

Roosevelt was also an innovator in the realm of what now might be called press relations. When he entered the White House, FDR faced a mainly hostile press, typically controlled by conservative members of the business establishment.[31] To circumvent the editors and publishers who were generally unsympathetic to his goals, the president worked to cultivate the reporters who covered the White House. FDR made himself available for biweekly press conferences, where he offered candid answers to reporters' questions and made certain to make important policy announcements that would provide the reporters with significant stories for their papers.[32] FDR was the first president to designate a press secretary, Stephen Early, who was charged with organizing the press conferences and making certain that reporters observed the informal rules distinguishing those presidential comments that could be attributed directly to the president from those that were off the record.

Every president since FDR has sought to craft a public-relations strategy that would emphasize the incumbent's strengths and maximize his popular appeal. For John F. Kennedy, handsome and quick-witted, the televised press conference was an excellent

President Franklin Delano Roosevelt's direct appeals to the American people allowed him to "reach over the heads" of congressional opponents and force them to follow his lead because their constituents demanded it.

public-relations vehicle. Both Bill Clinton and Barack Obama made extensive use of televised town meetings—carefully staged events that gave the president an opportunity to appear to consult with rank-and-file citizens about his goals and policies without having to face the sorts of pointed questions preferred by reporters.

Bill Clinton introduced an innovation that continued to be used by Bush and Obama. This was to make the White House Communications Office an important institution within the EOP. The Communications Office became responsible not only for responding to reporters' queries but also for developing and implementing a coordinated communications strategy—promoting the president's policy goals, developing responses to adverse news stories, and making certain that a favorable image of the president would, insofar as possible, dominate the news.

Going Public Online President Obama was the first chief executive to make full use of another new communication medium—the Internet. Drawing on the interactive tools of the web, Obama's 2008 and 2012 campaigns changed the way politicians organize supporters, advertise to voters, defend against attacks, and communicate with their constituents.[33] In the 2016 presidential campaign, candidates Donald Trump and Hillary Clinton made particular use of Twitter to communicate with millions of voters, bypassing traditional media. The campaigns, and the candidates themselves, often tweeted many times a day.

The Internet has changed not only the way modern presidents campaign but also how they govern. The Whitehouse.gov website keeps the president's constituents abreast of his policy agenda with a weekly streaming video address by the president, press briefings, speeches and remarks, a daily blog, photos of the president, the White House schedule, and other information. Virtually everything the president does is recorded online. YouTube aired Obama's press conferences and public appearances on a daily basis. Every presidential address is now streamed live online. Obama also created a Website that allowed citizens to submit petitions to the White House. Any petition receiving 100,000 signatures was slated for review by the administration and a response issued. For example, in 2015 the president issued extensive comments on the death of Michael Brown, a black man shot by a white police officer in Ferguson, Missouri, in response to citizen petitions demanding a federal investigation of the incident.

Circumventing television and other traditional media, the Internet allows the president to broadcast his policy ideas directly to the citizens. In March 2012, Obama broke new media ground again, appearing on Bill Simmons's "B.S. Report" (a regular series of podcasts on ESPN's website) in the first ever podcast with a sitting U.S. president. Obama's Facebook page personalizes the president's connection with his constituents and the causes they care about. In summer 2016, Obama claimed 76 million Twitter followers. Websites, podcasts, Facebook, and other new media forums facilitate direct communication between the president and the people, creating a virtual network of constituents. Like FDR in the 1930s and '40s and Kennedy in the 1960s, Obama may have changed how presidents govern for some time to come.

The Limits of Going Public Some presidents have been able to make effective use of popular appeals to overcome congressional opposition. Popular support, though, has not been a firm foundation for presidential power: the public is notoriously fickle. President George W. Bush maintained an approval rating of over 70 percent for more than a year following the September 11 terrorist attacks. By

for critical analysis

What are the advantages and disadvantages of presidents governing via digital media? How do these pros and cons compare with "going public" in the age of television?

the end of 2005, however, Bush's approval rating had dropped to 39 percent as a result of the growing unpopularity of the Iraq War, the administration's inept handling of hurricane relief, and a number of White House scandals, including the conviction of Vice President Cheney's chief of staff on charges of lying to a federal grand jury. Between the time President Obama took office in January 2009 and May 2016, his public approval ranged from a high of 76 percent in January 2009 to a low of 36 percent in the fall of 2014.[34] Such declines in popular approval during a president's term in office are nearly inevitable and follow a predictable pattern.[35] Both before and after they are elected, presidents generate popular support by promising to undertake important programs that will contribute directly to the well-being of large numbers of Americans. Almost without exception, presidential performance falls short of promises and popular expectations, leading to a decline in public support and the ensuing weakening of presidential influence.[36] It is a rare American president, such as Bill Clinton, who exits the White House more popular than when he went in.

The Administrative Strategy

Contemporary presidents have increased the administrative capabilities of their office in three ways. First, they have enhanced the reach and power of the EOP. Second, they have sought to increase White House control over the federal bureaucracy. Third, they have expanded the role of executive orders and other instruments of direct presidential governance. Taken together, these three components of what might be called the White House "administrative strategy" have given presidents a capacity to achieve their programmatic and policy goals even when they are unable to secure congressional approval. Indeed, some recent presidents have been able to accomplish a great deal with remarkably little congressional, partisan, or even public support.

The Growth of the EOP The EOP has grown from six administrative assistants in 1939 to several hundred employees working directly for the president in the White House office, along with some 2,500 individuals staffing the several divisions of the Executive Office. The creation and growth of the White House staff give the president an enormously enhanced capacity to gather information, plan programs and strategies, communicate with constituencies, and exercise supervision over the executive branch. The staff multiplies the president's eyes, ears, and arms, becoming a critical instrument of presidential power.[37]

In particular, the OMB serves as a potential instrument of presidential control over federal spending and hence a mechanism through which the White House has greatly expanded its power. The OMB has the capacity to analyze and approve all legislative proposals, not only budgetary requests, emanating from all federal agencies before being submitted to Congress. This procedure, now a matter of routine, greatly enhances the president's control over the entire executive branch. All legislation originating in the White House as well as all executive orders also go through the OMB.[38] Thus, through one White House agency, the president has the means to exert major influence over the flow of money and the shape and content of national legislation.

Regulatory Review A second tactic that presidents have used to increase their power and reach is the process of regulatory review, through which presidents have sought to seize control of rule making by the agencies of the executive branch (see also Chapter 14). Whenever Congress enacts a statute, its actual implementation requires the promulgation of hundreds of rules by the agency charged with administering the law and effecting the will of Congress. Some congressional statutes are quite detailed and leave agencies with relatively little discretion. Typically, however, Congress enacts a relatively broad statement of legislative intent and then delegates to the appropriate administrative agency the power to fill in many important details.[39] In other words, Congress typically says to an administrative agency, "Here is the problem: deal with it."[40] The discretion that Congress delegates to administrative agencies has provided recent presidents with an important avenue for expanding their own power.

For example, during the course of his presidency, Bill Clinton issued 107 directives to administrators ordering them to propose specific rules and regulations. George W. Bush vigorously continued the Clinton-era practice of issuing presidential directives to agencies, spurring them to issue new rules and regulations. Obama's first regulatory director, Cass Sunstein, not only issued a number of major regulatory directives to federal agencies but also launched a "look back" program. Under this program, the administration sought to eliminate several hundred existing federal rules it deemed obsolete.[41] While eliminating some rules, Obama ordered federal agencies to adopt many others. In 2015, Obama sought new regulations governing power plant emissions, overtime pay for workers, the educational practices of career colleges, and a host of other matters.

Governing by Decree: Executive Orders and Memoranda A third mechanism through which contemporary presidents have sought to enhance their power to govern unilaterally is through the use of executive orders and other forms of presidential decrees, including executive agreements, national security findings and directives, proclamations, reorganization plans, and memoranda signing statements.[42] Executive orders have a long history in the United States and have been the vehicles for a number of important government policies, including the purchase of Louisiana, the annexation of Texas, the emancipation of the slaves, the internment of Japanese Americans, the desegregation of the military, the initiation of affirmative action, and the creation of important federal agencies, among them the EPA and the Food and Drug Administration (see Figure 13.4).[43]

Although wars and national emergencies produce the highest volume of executive orders, such presidential actions also occur frequently in peacetime. In the realm of foreign policy, unilateral presidential actions in the form of executive agreements have virtually replaced treaties as the nation's chief foreign policy instruments.[44] Presidential decrees, however, are often used for purely domestic purposes. In November 2014, President Obama issued executive orders that would protect some 4 million undocumented immigrants from the threat of deportation. These orders provoked an outcry from congressional Republicans, and in 2016, the eight-member Supreme Court (in the wake of Justice Antonin Scalia's death) divided 4–4 on the case, leaving intact a lower court ruling blocking the order within its own jurisdiction, but not invalidating the order itself.[45]

Presidents may not use executive orders to issue whatever commands they please. The use of such decrees is bound by law. If a president issues an executive order, proclamation, directive, or the like, in principle it is done pursuant to the powers granted by the Constitution or delegated by Congress, usually through a statute. When presidents issue such orders, they generally state the constitutional or statutory basis for their actions. For example, when President Truman ordered the desegregation of the armed services, he did so pursuant to his constitutional powers as commander in chief. Where an executive order has no statutory or constitutional basis, the courts have held it to be void. The most important such case is *Youngstown Co. v. Sawyer* (1952).[46] Here, the Supreme Court ruled that President Truman's seizure of the nation's steel mills during the Korean War had no statutory or constitutional basis and was thus invalid.

A number of court decisions, though, have established broad boundaries that leave considerable room for presidential action. For example, the courts have held that Congress might approve presidential action after the fact or, in effect, ratify presidential action through "acquiescence" by not objecting for long periods of time or by continuing to provide funding for programs established by executive orders. Further, the courts have indicated that some areas, most notably the realm of military policy, are presidential in character, allowing presidents wide latitude to make policy by executive decree. Thus, within the very broad limits established by the courts, presidential orders can be important policy tools.

During his time in office, President Obama issued a number of executive orders, memoranda, and other decrees, many of which rescinded Bush-era orders. Thus, Obama ordered the closing of the Guantánamo prison and ordered an end to what were deemed unlawful methods of interrogation of terror suspects. In June 2012, Obama issued an order designed to halt the deportation of undocumented immigrants who had come to the United States as children. These individuals would become eligible for work permits. Immigrant rights groups hailed the order, while

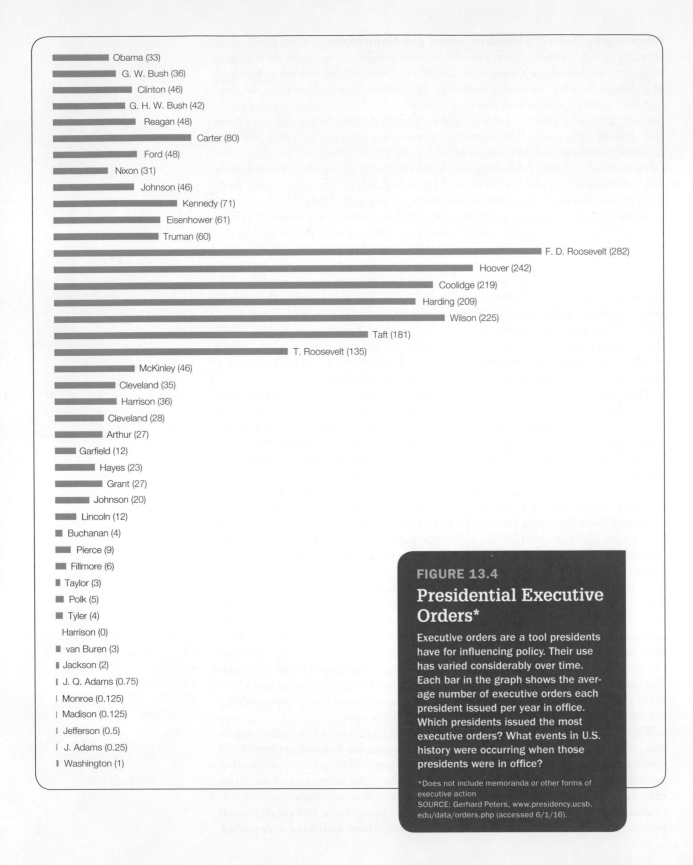

FIGURE 13.4

Presidential Executive Orders*

Executive orders are a tool presidents have for influencing policy. Their use has varied considerably over time. Each bar in the graph shows the average number of executive orders each president issued per year in office. Which presidents issued the most executive orders? What events in U.S. history were occurring when those presidents were in office?

*Does not include memoranda or other forms of executive action
SOURCE: Gerhard Peters, www.presidency.ucsb.edu/data/orders.php (accessed 6/1/16).

In 2014, President Obama issued an executive order that would shield millions of immigrants from deportation. In 2016 the validity of Obama's order was called into question when the Supreme Court split 4–4 over a lower-court decision against the president.

Republicans criticized the president for circumventing Congress. During the first seven years of his presidency Obama issued 242 executive orders and 219 presidential memoranda. Some of his orders were mundane, such as the order to close federal offices for the day on December 24, and others significant, such as his order blocking the deportation of millions of undocumented immigrants.

Signing Statements To negate congressional actions to which they objected, recent presidents have made frequent and calculated use of presidential **signing statements** when signing bills into law.[47] The signing statement is an announcement made by the president, at the time of signing a congressional enactment into law, that offers the president's interpretation of the law and usually innocuous remarks predicting the many benefits the new law will bring to the nation. Occasionally, presidents have used signing statements to point to sections of the law they have deemed improper or even unconstitutional and to instruct executive branch agencies how to execute the law.[48] In 2013, for example, President Obama signed a bill containing a provision requiring the president to notify Congress before transferring any prisoner from Guantánamo Bay. In his signing statement Obama declared that the provision was unconstitutional and ignored the legislation.

Presidents have made signing statements throughout American history, though many were not recorded and did not become part of the official legislative record.

signing statements
announcements made by the president when signing bills into law, often presenting the president's interpretation of the law

Ronald Reagan's attorney general, Edwin Meese, is generally credited with transforming the signing statement into a routine tool of presidential direct action.[49] Meese believed that carefully crafted signing statements would provide a basis for action by executive agencies and, perhaps even more important, would become part of the history and context of a piece of legislation if and when judicial interpretation became necessary. Indeed, to make certain of this, Meese reached an agreement with the West Publishing Company to include them in its authoritative texts of federal legislation.[50]

With the way thus paved, Reagan—and every president since—proceeded to use detailed and artfully designed signing statements, prepared by the Department of Justice, to reinterpret congressional enactments. George W. Bush issued 161 signing statements. Within these 161 statements, however, Bush inserted nearly 1,200 specific signing statement provisions—more than twice as many provisions as all past presidents combined—using them to rewrite the law on numerous occasions. As a candidate, Obama criticized Bush's prolific use of signing statements but did not entirely abandon the practice as president. As of November 2016, Obama had issued 38 signing statements containing more than 100 specific provisions.[51] In 2016, for example, Obama again resisted congressional efforts to prevent the closing of the Guantánamo Bay detention facility. Congress had included language in the 2016 appropriations bill that would extend the operation of the facility, but in his signing statement the president declared that this language violated the separation of powers and would be ignored.

for critical analysis

In recent years, presidents have expanded their power through increased use of executive orders, executive agreements, and other unilateral instruments. Is the United States becoming a "presidential republic"? Is this a development to be feared or welcomed?

Presidential Nonenforcement of Laws A final instrument of direct presidential governance is nonenforcement of statutes. Congress may make the law, but presidents implement and enforce it. If the president decides that a particular law is not to his liking and refuses to enforce it, Congress may find that its intent is stymied. President Obama, for example, suspended enforcement of portions of the Affordable Care Act when the rollout of "Obamacare" produced public confusion. Since the president is the nation's chief law enforcer, refusal to enforce a law can become a unilateral negation of its effects.

The Advantages of the Administrative Strategy Through the course of American history, party leadership and popular appeals have played important roles in presidential efforts to overcome political opposition, and both continue to be instruments of presidential power. Reagan's tax cuts and Clinton's budget victories were achieved with strong partisan support. George W. Bush, lacking the oratorical skills of Reagan or Roosevelt, nevertheless made effective use of sophisticated communications strategies to promote his agenda. Yet, as we have seen, in the modern era parties have waned in institutional strength, and the effects of popular appeals have often proven evanescent. The limitations of the alternatives have increasingly impelled presidents to try to expand the administrative capabilities of the office and their own capacity for unilateral action as means of achieving their policy goals. And in recent decades, the expansion of the Executive Office, the development of regulatory review, and the use of executive orders and signing statements have given presidents a substantial capacity to achieve significant policy results despite congressional opposition to their legislative agendas.

In principle, perhaps, Congress could respond more vigorously to unilateral policy making by the president than it has. Certainly, a Congress willing to impeach a president should have the mettle to overturn the chief executive's administrative directives. But the president has significant advantages in such struggles with Congress. In battles over presidential directives and orders, Congress is on the defensive, reacting to presidential initiatives. The framers of the Constitution saw "energy," or the ability to take the initiative, as a key feature of executive power.[52] When the president takes action by issuing an order or an administrative directive, Congress must respond through the cumbersome and time-consuming lawmaking process, overcome internal divisions, and enact legislation that the president may ultimately veto. Moreover, as the political scientist Terry Moe has argued, in such battles Congress faces a significant collective action problem: members are likely to be more sensitive to the substance of a president's actions and its short-term effects on their constituents than to the more general long-term implications of presidential power for the vitality of their institution.[53]

The Limits of Presidential Power

Though the "administrative strategy" has provided presidents with a host of new powers, presidents are not dictators or kings. Their power continues to be limited by Congress and, especially, by the congressional power of the purse. In 2011 and again in 2013, Congress demonstrated that its control over federal spending and borrowing powers could force the president to pay attention to the legislative branch. In the budget battle of 2013, Republicans used their control of the House of Representatives to shut down most government agencies for more than two weeks until a budgetary compromise was reached. So long as Congress controls the purse strings, the president must pay attention to its wishes.

Remember, too, that the president is not omnipotent. Decisions made by leaders in foreign nations who do not answer to the president affect America's economic health, to say nothing of the nation's security. And while the public frequently blames or rewards the president for economic performance, the president's actual impact on the economy is limited. Unemployment and inflation, two important indicators of economic health, are subject to macroeconomic conditions that can never be fully within the president's control, such as consumer demand and the productivity of workers.

The president is also limited in the implementation of his legislative agenda when the opposing party is in control of the House and Senate. As Figure 13.5 shows, presidential success on congressional votes is much higher when his party is in the majority in Congress. In periods of divided government, when one or both houses of Congress are controlled by the opposition party, the president has much more difficulty implementing his agenda. Immigration reform is one example. After his re-election in 2012, President Obama made immigration reform a key policy goal. In June 2013, the Senate, with a Democratic majority, passed a bill that Obama supported. Among other provisions, the bill provided a pathway to citizenship for undocumented immigrants. However, the House, controlled by the Republicans, never allowed the bill to come to a vote, arguing that the president's plan rewarded lawbreakers. And, as we have seen, when Obama issued an executive order on immigration in 2014, the courts questioned the legality of his actions without reaching a definite conclusion.

While presidents are more powerful today than they were 200 years ago, they are still subject to constitutional checks and balances. This process can lead to frustration, such as the 2013 government shutdown.

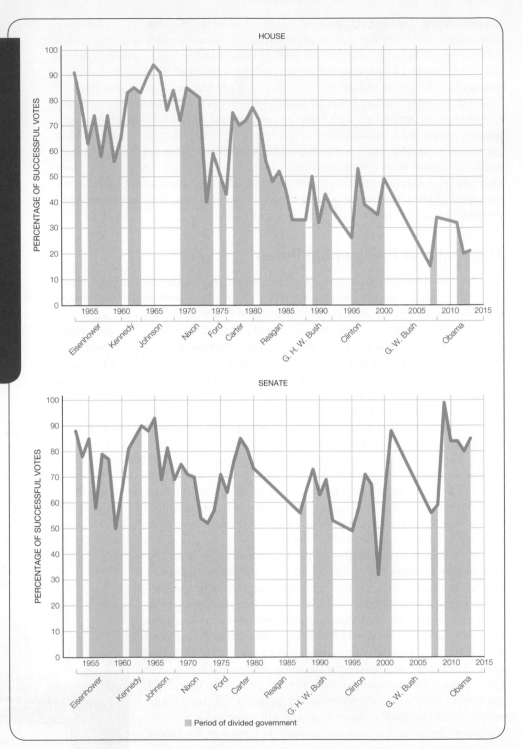

FIGURE 13.5

Presidential Success on Congressional Votes, 1953–2013*

Presidents have more success in Congress when their party is in the majority. Can you identify the periods when presidents had majority support in Congress and when they did not?

*Percentages based on votes on which presidents took a position.
SOURCE: Congressional Quarterly, "CQ's Roll Call's Vote Studies—2013 in Review," http://media.cq.com/votestudies (accessed 3/17/14).

HOUSE

PERCENTAGE OF SUCCESSFUL VOTES

Eisenhower   Kennedy   Johnson   Nixon   Ford   Carter   Reagan   G. H. W. Bush   Clinton   G. W. Bush   Obama

SENATE

PERCENTAGE OF SUCCESSFUL VOTES

Eisenhower   Kennedy   Johnson   Nixon   Ford   Carter   Reagan   G. H. W. Bush   Clinton   G. W. Bush   Obama

■ Period of divided government

Presidential Power
and Your Future

The framers of the Constitution created a system of government in which the Congress and the executive branch were to share power. At least since the New Deal, however, the powers of Congress have waned, whereas those of the presidency have expanded dramatically. There is no doubt that Congress continues to be able to confront presidents and even, on occasion, hand the White House a sharp rebuff. During the 2011 debt crisis, for instance, President Obama was unable to force House Republicans to accept his plan for dealing with the nation's deficits and was compelled to accede to many of the Republican Party's demands in order to prevent a potentially disastrous default on government debt.

In the larger view, however, presidents' occasional defeats, however dramatic, have to be seen as temporary setbacks in a gradual but decisive shift toward increased presidential power. Louis Fisher, a leading authority on the separation of powers, recently observed that in what are arguably the two most important policy arenas, national defense and the federal budget, the powers of Congress have been in decline for at least the past 50 years.[54] The last time Congress exercised its constitutional power to declare war was June 1942, and yet, since that time, American forces have been committed to numerous conflicts around the world by order of the president. The much-hailed 1973 War Powers Resolution, far from limiting presidential power, actually allowed the president considerably more discretionary authority than what was granted by the Constitution, which seems to require congressional authorization before troops can be deployed for even one day. The War Powers Resolution gave the president the authority to deploy forces abroad for 60 days without congressional authority. And presidents have ignored even this stipulation.

As to spending powers, the framers of the Constitution conceived the "power of the purse" to be Congress's most fundamental prerogative. For more than a century this power was jealously guarded by powerful congressional leaders such as Taft-era House speaker "Uncle" Joe Cannon, who saw congressional control of the budget as a fundamental safeguard against "Prussian-style" militarism and autocracy. Since the New Deal, however, successive Congresses have yielded to steadily increasing presidential influence over the budget process. In 1939, Congress allowed FDR to take a giant step toward presidential control of the nation's purse strings when it permitted him to bring the Bureau of the Budget into the newly created EOP. FDR and his successors used the Bureau of the Budget (now called the OMB) effectively to seize the nation's legislative and budgetary agenda. In 1974, Congress attempted to respond to Richard Nixon's efforts to further enhance presidential control of spending when it enacted the Budget and Impoundment Control Act, legislation centralizing Congress's own budgetary process and apparently reinforcing congressional power. Yet, less than 10 years later, Congress watched as President Ronald Reagan essentially seized control of the congressional budget process. Subsequently, Congress has surrendered more and more power to the president.

What might the growth of executive power mean to students reading this book today? It might mean, on the one hand, that policies they favor can more easily become the law of the land. Congress works slowly while the president can work quickly, making law by the stroke of a pen. Presidential strength works both ways, however: for those who oppose a particular policy or have qualms about some aspect of it, the stroke of the presidential pen might seem hasty and autocratic.

Today's students should also consider one of the chief concerns about presidential power expressed by the framers of the Constitution. The framers feared that executives were often too ready to go to war. Legislatures, they thought, were more likely to consider the costs and sacrifices entailed by war. Accordingly, the war power was given to Congress to "leash the dogs of war."[55] The framers possessed a good deal of practical experience, and their views merit consideration. Does presidential unilateralism or congressional deliberation offer better protection from the dogs of war so feared by the framers? In an era of significant international tension and trouble spots, including Iran, North Korea, Iraq, Syria, Libya, and Ukraine, the ease with which the country's leaders enter armed conflict may be a real concern.

A powerful presidency, a weak Congress, and a partially apathetic electorate make for a dangerous mix. Who we vote into the office of the president matters. (The "**Who Participates?**" feature on the facing page shows who voted for Donald Trump in 2016). Presidents have increasingly asserted the right to govern unilaterally and now appear able to overcome most institutional and political constraints. Presidential power, to be sure, can be a force for good. To cite one example from the not-so-distant past, it was President Lyndon Johnson, more than Congress or the judiciary, who faced up to the task of smashing America's racial apartheid system. Yet, as the framers knew, unchecked power—whether executive or legislative—is always dangerous. The framers of the Constitution believed that liberty required checks and balances. However useful presidential power may seem, we should always be mindful of the framers' concern.

Who Voted for Donald Trump in 2016?

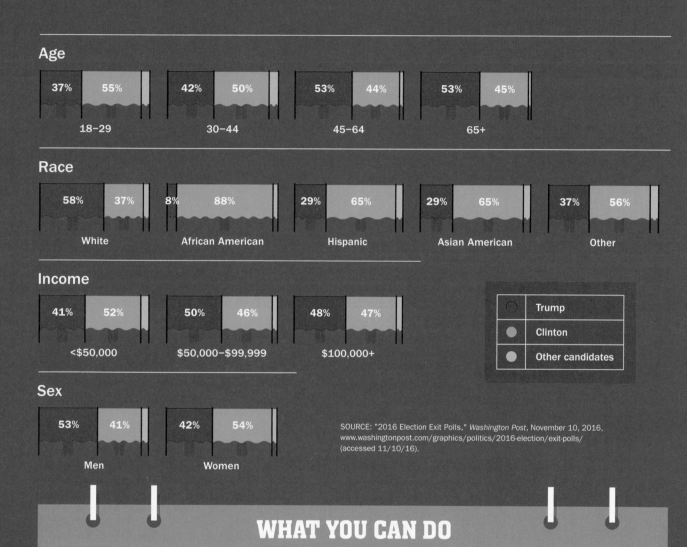

Age

37%	55%	
18–29		

42%	50%	
30–44		

53%	44%	
45–64		

53%	45%	
65+		

Race

58%	37%
White	

8%	88%
African American	

29%	65%
Hispanic	

29%	65%
Asian American	

37%	56%
Other	

Income

41%	52%
<$50,000	

50%	46%
$50,000–$99,999	

48%	47%
$100,000+	

○	Trump
●	Clinton
●	Other candidates

Sex

53%	41%
Men	

42%	54%
Women	

SOURCE: "2016 Election Exit Polls," *Washington Post*, November 10, 2016. www.washingtonpost.com/graphics/politics/2016-election/exit-polls/ (accessed 11/10/16).

WHAT YOU CAN DO

Contact the White House

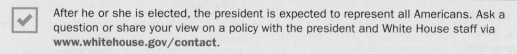

☑ After he or she is elected, the president is expected to represent all Americans. Ask a question or share your view on a policy with the president and White House staff via **www.whitehouse.gov/contact**.

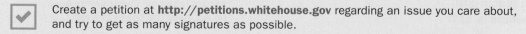

☑ Create a petition at **http://petitions.whitehouse.gov** regarding an issue you care about, and try to get as many signatures as possible.

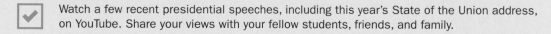

☑ Watch a few recent presidential speeches, including this year's State of the Union address, on YouTube. Share your views with your fellow students, friends, and family.

studyguide

Establishing the Presidency

Explain the role of the president in the American political system and how it has evolved (pp. 507–9)

The framers of the Constitution debated whether executive authority should be concentrated in the hands of one individual and whether this individual should be elected directly by the people. The decision to establish a single president, rather than some form of collectively led executive, was intended to provide for "energy" in the executive. The framers settled on an indirect system of selecting the president (the electoral college) that would make the president responsible to state and national legislators rather than to the public. It was not until the emergence of the national convention system in the 1830s that the presidency obtained the broad popular base needed to increase presidential power.

Practice Quiz

1. Which article of the Constitution describes the basic powers of the presidency and the means of selecting presidents?
   a) Article I
   b) Article II
   c) Article III
   d) Article IV
   e) Article V

2. The Founders chose to select the president through indirect election in order to
   a) increase the strength and influence of political parties.
   b) build an imperial presidency that would overwhelm the power of Congress.
   c) force the president to be responsive to the will of the people.
   d) make the president responsible to state and national legislators.
   e) create a more independent chief executive.

The Constitutional Powers of the Presidency

Understand the expressed, delegated, and inherent powers of the presidency (pp. 509–21)

Presidents have three kinds of powers: expressed, delegated, and inherent. The president's expressed powers, as defined by Article II of the Constitution, include military, judicial, diplomatic, executive, and legislative powers. The expressed powers also entail a set of implied powers, which can be considered necessary in order to carry out the expressed powers. The president's delegated powers are not found in the Constitution but are, instead, the product of congressional statutes and resolutions. The president's inherent powers grow from "the rights, duties and obligations of the presidency" that presidents often assert during times of war and national crisis.

Key Terms

expressed powers (p. 509)
implied powers (p. 509)
delegated powers (p. 509)
commander in chief (p. 510)
executive agreement (p. 512)
executive privilege (p. 512)
veto (p. 513)
pocket veto (p. 513)
legislative initiative (p. 514)
executive order (p. 515)
inherent powers (p. 520)
War Powers Resolution (p. 520)

Practice Quiz

3. Which of the following does *not* require the Senate's approval?
   a) an executive agreement
   b) a treaty
   c) appointment of ambassadors
   d) Supreme Court nominations
   e) All of the above require the advice and consent of the Senate.

4. What did the Supreme Court rule in *United States v. Nixon*?
   a) Nixon had to turn his secret White House tapes over to congressional investigators because presidents do not have the power of executive privilege.

b) Nixon did not have to turn his secret White House tapes over to congressional investigators because, in general, presidents have the power of executive privilege.

c) Nixon had to turn his secret White House tapes over to congressional investigators but, in general, presidents have the power of executive privilege.

d) Nixon did not have to turn his secret White House tapes over to congressional investigators but, in general, presidents do not have the power of executive privilege.

e) All presidents are immune from criminal investigations and cannot, therefore, be tried in any court of law.

5. What are the requirements for overriding a presidential veto?
   a) 50 percent plus one vote in both houses of Congress
   b) two-thirds vote in both houses of Congress
   c) two-thirds vote in the Senate only
   d) three-fourths vote in both houses of Congress
   e) A presidential veto cannot be overridden by Congress.

6. When the president issues a rule or regulation that reorganizes or otherwise directs the affairs of the executive branch, such as the directive that established the Environmental Protection Agency, it is called
   a) an executive agreement.
   b) an executive order.

c) an executive mandate.
d) administrative oversight.
e) legislative initiative.

7. Which of the following military and war powers does the Constitution *not* assign to the president?
   a) command of the army and navy of the United States
   b) the power to declare war
   c) command of the state militias
   d) the power to make treaties
   e) The Constitution assigns all of the powers above to the president.

8. The War Powers Resolution of 1973 was an act passed by Congress that
   a) required the CIA to collect intelligence on all Americans born in a foreign country.
   b) outlawed presidential use of executive agreements.
   c) created the National Security Council.
   d) granted the president the authority to declare war.
   e) stipulated military forces must be withdrawn within 60 days in the absence of a specific congressional authorization for their continued deployment.

The Presidency as an Institution

Identify the institutional resources presidents have to help them exercise their powers (pp. 521–26)

The institutionalized presidency is made up of the Cabinet, the White House staff, the Executive Office of the President, the vice presidency, and the first spouse. Through their advice and assistance, these thousands of individuals give the president a capacity for action that he could never have by himself. When coupled with the president's formal powers, the institutionalized presidency makes the chief executive an important player in the country's policy-making process.

Key Terms

Cabinet (p. 521)

National Security Council (NSC) (p. 522)

White House staff (p. 522)

Kitchen Cabinct (p. 523)

Executive Office of the President (EOP) (p. 523)

Practice Quiz

9. The Office of Management and Budget is part of
   a) the Executive Office of the President.
   b) the White House staff.

c) the Kitchen Cabinet.
d) the Congressional Budget Office.
e) the Bureau of Economic Analysis.

10. Approximately how many people work for agencies within the Executive Office of the President?
    a) 25 to 50
    b) 700 to 1,000
    c) 1,500 to 2,000
    d) 4,500 to 5,000
    e) 25,000 to 30,000

11. Which of the following statements about vice presidents is *not* true?
    a) The vice president succeeds the president in case of death, resignation, or incapacitation.
    b) The vice president casts the tie-breaking vote in the Senate when necessary.
    c) The vice president serves as an honorary member of the Supreme Court.
    d) Eight vice presidents have had to replace American presidents who died in office.
    e) Presidential candidates often select a vice presidential candidate who is likely to bring the support of a state that would not otherwise support the ticket.

The Contemporary Bases of Presidential Power

> **Explain how modern presidents have become even more powerful (pp. 526–36)**

Although Congress was the dominant institution in the American political system throughout the nineteenth century, modern presidents have expanded the policy-making power of their office in a number of ways. While some presidents have relied primarily on the support of party members to advance their legislative goals, contemporary presidents more commonly turn to popular mobilization and executive administration in pursuing policy change.

Key Term

signing statements (p. 533)

Practice Quiz

12. What are two ways that presidents can expand their power?
    a) avoiding popular appeals and loosening their control of executive agencies
    b) using popular appeals and bolstering their control of executive agencies
    c) using popular appeals and loosening their control of executive agencies
    d) avoiding popular appeals and bolstering their control of executive agencies
    e) weakening national partisan institutions and bolstering their control of executive agencies

13. The Supreme Court case *Youngstown Co. v. Sawyer* was significant because
    a) it showed that the courts would never invalidate an executive order.
    b) it showed that the courts would invalidate executive orders that have no statutory or constitutional basis.
    c) it asserted that pocket vetoes were unconstitutional.
    d) it upheld the notion of executive privilege.
    e) it struck down the Budget and Impoundment Control Act.

14. When the president makes an announcement about his interpretation of a congressional enactment that he is signing into law, it is called
    a) a signing statement.
    b) a line item veto.
    c) an executive order.
    d) legislative initiative.
    e) regulatory review.

For Further Reading

Barber, James David. *The Presidential Character*. Englewood Cliffs, NJ: Prentice-Hall, 1992.

Crenson, Matthew, and Benjamin Ginsberg. *Presidential Power: Unchecked and Unbalanced*. New York: W. W. Norton, 2007.

Edwards, George. *Why the Electoral College Is Bad for America*. New Haven, CT: Yale University Press, 2004.

Fisher, Louis. *Constitutional Conflicts between President and Congress*, 6th ed. Lawrence: University Press of Kansas, 2014.

Genovese, Michael, Todd Belt, and William Lammers. *The Presidency and Domestic Policy*. Boulder, CO: Paradigm, 2013.

Gerhardt, Michael J. *The Forgotten Presidents: Their Untold Constitutional Legacy*. New York: Oxford University Press, 2013.

Goldsmith, Jack. *The American Presidency: Power and Constraint*. New York: W. W. Norton, 2012.

Hayes, Stephen F. *Cheney: The Untold Story of America's Most Powerful and Controversial Vice President*. New York: HarperCollins, 2007.

Hendrickson, Ryan. *Obama at War*. Lexington: University Press of Kentucky, 2015.

Maraniss, David. *Barack Obama*. New York: Simon and Schuster, 2013.

Milkis, Sidney. *The American Presidency: Origins and Development*. Washington, DC: CQ Press, 2011.

Nelson, Michael. *The Presidency and the Political System*. Washington, DC: CQ Press, 2013.

Neustadt, Richard E. *Presidential Power: The Politics of Leadership from Roosevelt to Reagan*. Rev. ed. New York: Free Press, 1990.

Pfiffner, James. *Understanding the Presidency*. 6th ed. New York: Longman, 2010.

Skowronek, Stephen. *The Politics Presidents Make: Leadership from John Adams to Bill Clinton*. Cambridge, MA: Belknap Press of Harvard University Press, 1997.

Tatalovich, Raymond, and Steven Schier. *The Presidency and Political Science*. Armonk, NY: M. E. Sharpe, 2014.

Recommended Websites

The American Presidency Project
www.americanpresidency.org

Directed by Gerhard Peters and John T. Woolley at the University of California Santa Barbara, this site contains over 88,000 documents related to the study of the presidency, including party platforms, candidates' remarks, statements of administration policy, documents released by the Office of the Press Secretary, and election debates. This site is also an excellent resource for data related to the study of the presidency.

Dave Leip's Atlas of U.S. Presidential Elections
www.uselectionatlas.org

For information on upcoming and past presidential elections, refer to this website. Experiment with the electoral college calculator to see how your state could affect the electoral outcome.

The National Archives: Executive Branch
www.archives.gov/executive

Research official executive branch documents at the Executive Branch website, provided by the U.S. National Archives and Records Administration.

The White House
www.whitehouse.gov

This is the official website of the White House. Here you can read about current presidential news, the president's Cabinet, executive orders, and presidential appointments.

White House Historical Association
www.whitehousehistory.org

The White House Historical Association is dedicated to the understanding, appreciation, and preservation of the White House. At its website you can find historical facts and take a detailed online tour of the numerous rooms and the property.

The White House: Past First Ladies
www.whitehouse.gov/history/firstladies/

The first lady is an important resource for the president in his role as head of state. Read about the current and past first ladies on this website.

Government bureaucracies affect ordinary Americans in countless ways. For example, the Environmental Protection Agency (EPA) proposes and enforces regulations that protect Americans' health and the environment. Here, an EPA worker vacuums a gasoline-like substance that contains the cancer-causing chemical benzene from the South Platte River, north of Denver, Colorado.

Bureaucracy in a Democracy

WHAT GOVERNMENT DOES AND WHY IT MATTERS Americans depend on government bureaucracies to accomplish the most spectacular achievements as well as the most mundane. Yet they often do not realize that public bureaucracies are essential for providing the services they use every day and rely on in emergencies. On a typical day, a college student might check the weather forecast, drive on an interstate highway, mail the rent check, drink from a public water fountain, check the calories on the side of a yogurt container, attend a class, go online, and meet a relative at the airport. Each of these activities is possible because of the work of a government bureaucracy: the U.S. Weather Service, the U.S. Department of Transportation, the U.S. Postal Service, the Environmental Protection Agency, the Food and Drug Administration, the student loan programs of the U.S. Department of Education, the Advanced Research Projects Agency (which developed the Internet in the 1960s), and the Federal Aviation Administration. Without the ongoing work of these agencies, many of these common activities would be impossible, unreliable, or more expensive. Even though bureaucracies provide essential services that all Americans rely on, they are often disparaged by politicians and the general public alike as "big government" and come into public view only when they are charged with fraud, waste, and abuse.

In emergencies, the national perspective on bureaucracy and, indeed, on "big government" shifts. After the September 11 terrorist attacks, all eyes turned to Washington. The federal government responded by strengthening and reorganizing the bureaucracy to undertake a whole new set of responsibilities designed to keep America safe. In the biggest government reorganization in over half a century, Congress created the Department of Homeland Security in 2002. The massive new department merged 22 existing agencies into a single department employing nearly 170,000 workers.

As we will see in this chapter, Americans have a love–hate relationship with the federal bureaucracy. This ambivalence sometimes prompts politicians to promise that they will slash the federal bureaucracy, yet they rarely follow through on such promises. Americans rely on government in many aspects of their lives—significant reductions in the federal bureaucracy would create more daily disruptions than most realize.

chaptergoals

- Define bureaucracy, and describe the basic features of the executive branch (pp. 547–54)

- Describe the major goals we expect federal agencies to promote (pp. 556–65)

- Evaluate some of the ways politicians have tried to make the bureaucracy more efficient (pp. 566–73)

- Explain why it is often difficult to control the bureaucracy (pp. 573–77)

● Bureaucracy and Bureaucrats

> **Define bureaucracy, and describe the basic features of the executive branch**

Bureaucracy is nothing more nor less than a form of organization, a complex structure of offices, tasks, and rules. *Bureau*, a French word, can mean either "office" or "desk." *Cracy* is from the Greek word for "rule" or "form of rule." Taken together, *bureau* and *cracy* produce an interesting definition: bureaucracy is rule by offices and desks. Each member of an organization has an office, meaning both a place and a set of responsibilities. That is, each "office" comprises a set of tasks that are specialized to the needs of the organization, and the person holding that office (or position) performs those specialized tasks. Specialization and repetition are essential to the efficiency of any organization. Therefore, when an organization is inefficient, it is often because it is not "bureaucratized" enough! But bureaucracies not only perform specialized tasks that require routine action but, as we shall see, also undertake politically controversial tasks that require them to exercise a great deal of discretion and professional judgment. In many areas of policy, Congress writes laws that are very broad, and it is up to the bureaucracy to define what the policy will mean in practice. The decisions that bureaucrats make, often based on professional judgments, can themselves become politically contentious.

At its best, bureaucracy ensures fair, accountable administration overseen by professionals. Bureaucracies are characterized by three features. First, rules are applied to all people in the same way. Second, bureaucracies require that interactions be documented. Documentation allows those who feel they have been treated unfairly to challenge bureaucracies, creating more accountability. Third, administration by professionals ensures that bureaucracies benefit from the skills and professional norms of their workers.

Both routine and exceptional tasks require the organization, specialization, and expertise found in bureaucracies. To provide services, government bureaucracies employ specialists such as meteorologists, doctors, and scientists. To do their jobs effectively, these specialists require resources and tools (ranging from paper to complex computer software), they have to coordinate their work with others (for example, traffic engineers must communicate with construction engineers), and there must be effective outreach to the public (for example, doctors must be made aware of health warnings). Bureaucracy is a means of coordinating the many different parts that must work together for the government to provide useful services.

bureaucracy the complex structure of offices, tasks, rules, and principles of organization that is employed by all large-scale institutions to coordinate the work of their personnel

What Bureaucrats Do

"Government by offices and desks" conveys to most people a picture of hundreds of office workers shuffling millions of pieces of paper. There is a lot of truth in that image, but we have to look more closely at what papers are being shuffled and why. More than 75 years ago, an astute observer defined bureaucracy as "continuous routine business."[1] Almost any organization succeeds by reducing its work to routine tasks performed by different specialists. But with specialization, one worker's output becomes another worker's input, making the timing of such relationships essential and therefore requiring these workers to stay in communication with one another. In fact, bureaucracy was the first information network.

Bureaucrats Implement Laws Congress is responsible for making the laws, but in most cases legislation only sets the broad parameters for government action. Bureaucracies are responsible for filling in the blanks by determining how the laws should be implemented. This requires bureaucracies to draw up detailed rules that guide the process of **implementation** and to play a key role in enforcing the laws. Congress needs the bureaucracy to engage in rule making and implementation for several reasons. One is that bureaucracies employ people who have much more specialized expertise in specific policy areas than do members of Congress. Decisions about how to achieve many policy goals—from managing the national parks to regulating air quality to ensuring a sound economy—rest on the judgment of specialized experts. A second reason that Congress needs bureaucracy is that because updating legislation can take many years, bureaucratic flexibility can ensure that laws are administered in ways that take new conditions into account. Finally, members of Congress often prefer to delegate politically difficult decision making to bureaucrats.

implementation the efforts of departments and agencies to translate laws into specific bureaucratic rules and actions

Bureaucrats Make Rules One of the most important activities that government agencies do is issue rules that provide more detailed and specific indications of what a given congressional policy will actually mean. For example, the Clean Air Act empowers the Environmental Protection Agency (EPA) to assess whether current or projected levels of air pollutants pose a threat to public health, determine whether motor vehicle emissions are contributing to such pollution, and create rules designed to regulate these emissions. Under the George W. Bush administration, the EPA claimed it did not have the authority to regulate a specific group of pollutants commonly referred to as "greenhouse gases" (for example, carbon dioxide). In 2007 the Supreme Court ruled that the EPA did have that authority and had to provide a justification for not regulating such emissions.[2] In the first year of the Obama administration, the agency ruled that greenhouse gases posed a threat to public health and that the emissions from new motor vehicles contributed to greenhouse gas pollution.[3] The agency then imposed new emission standards for automobiles, which would raise the average fuel economy for new vehicles to 35.5 miles per gallon starting in 2016, a standard later boosted to 54.4 miles per gallon by 2025.[4] In 2014, the EPA extended its reach to regulate factories and power plants that emit greenhouse gases. Especially controversial was a set of regulations that requires power plants to reduce greenhouse gas emissions by 32 percent by 2030. Challenges emerged even before the rule—called the Clean Power Plan—was finalized; once it was issued 24 states along with firms in the energy industry filed lawsuits challenging the rule. In 2016 the Supreme Court temporarily blocked implementation of the Clean Power Plan while it is being challenged in court. Litigation was expected to last for years in what one observer predicted would be "the superbowl of climate politics."[5]

The rule-making process is thus a highly political one. Once a new law is passed, the relevant agency studies the legislation and proposes a set of rules to guide implementation. These proposed rules are then open to comment by anyone who wishes to weigh in. Representatives for the regulated industries and advocates of all sorts commonly submit comments. But anyone who wishes to can go to the website www.regulations.gov to read proposed rules, enter comments, and view the comments of others. Once rules are approved, they are published in the *Federal Register* and have the force of law.

During the 1970s and '80s, the length of time required to develop an administrative rule from a proposal to actual publication in the *Federal Register* (when it takes on full legal status) grew from an average of 15 months to an average of 35 to 40 months. Inefficiency? No. Most of the increased time is attributable to

An example of bureaucratic rules that affect Americans both positively and negatively are the regulations set forth by the Environmental Protection Agency (EPA). When President Obama extended the EPA's authority to regulate greenhouse gas emissions in 2014, many people applauded the benefits to the environment, but at the same time, thousands lost jobs because of the new rules.

new procedures requiring more public notice, more public hearings in Washington and elsewhere, more cost-benefit analysis, and stronger legal obligations to prepare "environmental impact statements" demonstrating that the proposed rule or agency action will not have an unacceptably large negative impact on the human or physical environment.[6] Thus, a great deal of what is popularly decried as the lower efficiency of public agencies can be attributed to the political, judicial, legal, and public-opinion restraints and extraordinarily high expectations imposed on public bureaucrats. If a private company such as Apple were required to open up all its decision processes and management practices to full view by the media, its competitors, and all interested citizens, Apple—despite its profit motive and the pressure of competition—would likely appear far less efficient, perhaps no more efficient than public bureaucracies.

Bureaucrats Enforce Laws In addition to rule making, bureaucracies play an essential role in enforcing the laws, thus exercising considerable power over private actors. In 2015, the EPA charged Volkswagen with cheating on emissions tests of its diesel vehicles. For over seven years, the company had installed software that showed emissions at legal levels during testing conditions, but once the cars were on the road emissions were actually 10 to 40 percent higher. After the EPA threatened to bar the company from selling some of its 2016 cars in the United States, Volkswagen admitted that it had cheated. The financial repercussions for the company will be long-lasting. In 2016 the company agreed to a $15.8 billion settlement that required it to buy back the faulty vehicles and compensate owners. As part of the settlement, Volkswagen also agreed to fund several clean air programs. Even with these payments, Volkswagen faced additional lawsuits from states and investors.[7]

Bureaucrats Innovate A good case study of the important role agencies can play is the story of how ordinary federal bureaucrats created the Internet. Yes, it's true: what became the Internet was developed largely by the U.S. Department of Defense, and defense considerations still shape the basic structure of the Internet. In 1957, immediately following the profound American embarrassment over the Soviet Union's launching of *Sputnik*, the first satellite to orbit the earth, Congress authorized the establishment of the Advanced Research Projects Agency (ARPA) to develop, among other things, a means of maintaining communications in the event of a strategic attack on the existing telecommunications network (the telephone system). Since the telephone network was highly centralized and therefore could have been completely disabled by a single attack, ARPA developed a decentralized, highly redundant network with an improved probability of functioning after an attack. The full design, called by the acronym ARPANET, took almost a decade to create. By 1971 around 20 universities were connected to the ARPANET. The forerunner to the Internet was born.[8]

The Merit System: How to Become a Bureaucrat Although they face more inconveniences than their counterparts in the private sector, public bureaucrats are rewarded in part with greater job security than employees of most private organizations. More than a century ago the federal government attempted to imitate business by passing the Civil Service Act of 1883, which was followed by almost universal adoption of equivalent laws in state and local governments. These laws required that appointees to public office be qualified for the job to which they were appointed. This policy came to be called the **merit system**; its goal was not merely to put an end to political appointments under the "spoils system," which awarded jobs based on political connections, but also to create a system of competitive examinations through which the very best candidates were to be hired

merit system a product of civil service reform, in which appointees to positions in public bureaucracies must objectively be deemed qualified for those positions

The State Department's foreign service officer corps represents U.S. interests abroad. To become a foreign service officer, you must take both a written and an oral exam. Approximately 75 percent of the 20,000 or so applicants who take the exam each year do not pass.

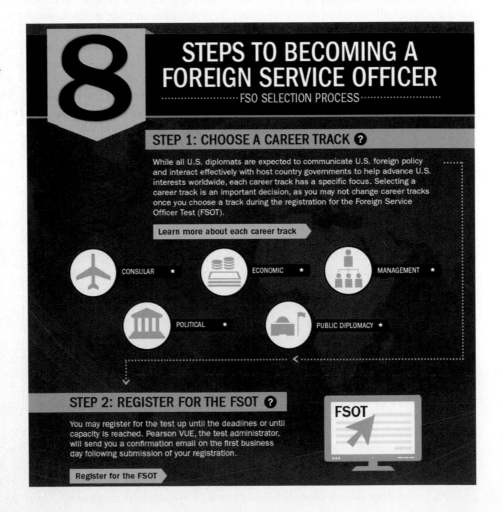

8 STEPS TO BECOMING A FOREIGN SERVICE OFFICER
FSO SELECTION PROCESS

STEP 1: CHOOSE A CAREER TRACK ❓

While all U.S. diplomats are expected to communicate U.S. foreign policy and interact effectively with host country governments to help advance U.S. interests worldwide, each career track has a specific focus. Selecting a career track is an important decision, as you may not change career tracks once you choose a track during the registration for the Foreign Service Officer Test (FSOT).

Learn more about each career track

CONSULAR ★ ECONOMIC ★ MANAGEMENT ★

POLITICAL ★ PUBLIC DIPLOMACY ★

STEP 2: REGISTER FOR THE FSOT ❓

You may register for the test up until the deadlines or until capacity is reached. Pearson VUE, the test administrator, will send you a confirmation email on the first business day following submission of your registration.

FSOT

Register for the FSOT

for every job. At the higher levels of government agencies, including such posts as cabinet secretaries and assistant secretaries, many jobs are filled with political appointees and are not part of the merit system.

As a further safeguard against political interference (and to compensate for the lower-than-average pay given to public employees), merit-system employees (genuine civil servants) were given legal protection against being fired without a show of cause. Reasonable people may disagree about the value of such job security and how far it should extend in the civil service, but the justifiable objective of this job protection, cleansing bureaucracy of political interference while upgrading performance, cannot be disputed.

The Size of the Federal Service

How many people does it take to make rules, implement laws, enforce laws, and innovate in all the areas that the government touches, from aviation safety to national defense to environmental protection to public health? For decades, politicians from both parties have asserted that the federal government is too big. President Ronald Reagan led the way in 1981 with his assertion that government was the problem, not the solution. Fifteen years later President Bill Clinton abandoned the traditional Democratic defense of government, declaring that "the era of big government is over." George W. Bush voiced similar sentiments when he accepted his party's nomination for president in 2000, proclaiming, "Big government is not the answer!" President Barack Obama struck a different tone. Addressing Congress on the topic of health care reform, he noted that while Americans had a "healthy skepticism about government," they also believed that "hard work and responsibility should be rewarded by some measure of security and fair play" and recognized "that sometimes government has to step in to help deliver that promise."[9] Despite fears of bureaucratic growth getting out of hand, however, the federal service has hardly grown at all during the past 35 years; it reached its peak postwar level in 1968, with 3.0 million civilian employees plus an additional 3.6 million military personnel (a figure swollen by the war in Vietnam). The number of civilian federal employees has since fallen to fewer than 2.7 million in 2014; the number of military personnel totals 1.5 million.[10]

The growth of the federal service over the past 50 years is even less imposing when placed in the context of the total workforce and when compared with the size of state and local public employment. Figure 14.1 indicates that since 1950 the ratio of federal employment to the total workforce has in fact *declined* slightly in the past 60 years. Meanwhile, state and local employment has grown: in 1950 there were 4.3 million state and local civil service employees (about 6.5 percent of the country's workforce). In 2015 there were roughly 19.3 million state and local employees (nearly 14 percent of the nation's employed workforce).[11] Federal employment, in contrast, exceeded 6 percent of the workforce only during World War II, and almost all of that temporary growth was military.

Another useful comparison is illustrated in Figure 14.2. Although the dollar increase in federal spending shown by the bars looks impressive, the trend line indicating the relation of federal spending to the gross domestic product remained close to what it had been in 1960. This changed in 2009, when the recession pushed spending up dramatically as the federal government sought to stimulate the economy and spending rose on other recession-related programs, such as unemployment insurance. After 2009 the budget also reflected the costs of the wars in Iraq and Afghanistan, which had not been included in the recent economic Bush administration's budgets.

for critical analysis

How has the size of the federal service changed over the past six decades? How are calls for smaller government related to the size of the federal service?

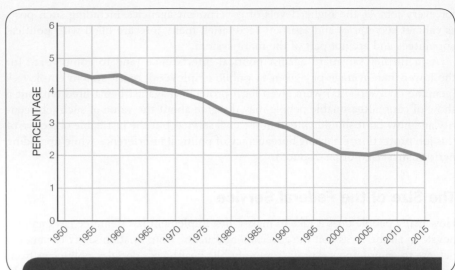

FIGURE 14.1

Employees in the Federal Service as a Percentage of the National Workforce, 1950–2015

Since 1950, the ratio of federal employment to the total workforce has gradually declined. Today, federal employees make up less than 2 percent of the total workforce in the United States. Even at its height, federal employees made up less than 6 percent. What do these numbers suggest about the size of the federal government today?

NOTE: Employment numbers are for December of each year.
SOURCE: Bureau of Labor Statistics, Current Employment Statistics, "Table B-1. Employees on Nonfarm Payrolls by Industry Sector and Selected Industry Detail," www.bls.gov/webapps/legacy/cesbtab1.htm (accessed 7/9/16).

In sum, the national government is indeed "very large," but it has not been growing any faster than the economy or society. Bureaucracy keeps pace with society, despite people's seeming dislike of it, because the control towers, the prisons, the Social Security system, and other essential elements of modern-day society cannot be operated without bureaucracy. Indeed, the recent growth of government spending does not reflect a growth in the federal bureaucracy but rather an increase in payments to individuals for valued social programs such as Social Security and Medicare (which provides health care for people over age 65) and a temporary boost in federal grants to the states to help them weather the recent economic recession.

Although the federal executive branch is large and complex, everything about it is commonplace because its many bureaucracies touch so many aspects of daily life. Government bureaucracies implement the decisions made through the political process. Public bureaucracies are powerful because politicians and the people delegate vast power to them to make sure that society's collective needs are addressed, providing most citizens with the freedom to pursue their private ends.

The Organization of the Executive Branch

department the largest subunit of the executive branch; the secretaries of the 15 departments form the Cabinet

Cabinet **departments**, agencies, and bureaus are the operating parts of the bureaucratic whole. At the top is the head of the department, who in the United States is called the "secretary" of the department.[12] Below the secretary and the deputy

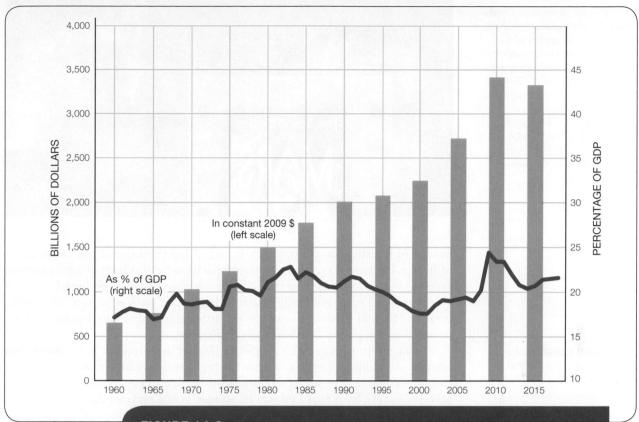

FIGURE 14.2

Annual Federal Outlays, 1950–2018*

As the bars in the figure indicate, when measured in dollars, federal government spending has gone up over time, from $423 billion in 1950 to over $3 trillion in 2015. (The amounts here are measured in constant 2009 dollars, which means the numbers have been adjusted for inflation.) But as the red line shows, federal spending as a percentage of gross domestic product (GDP) has moved up and down just slightly over time. Thus, while government spending has grown, it has basically kept pace with the growing size of the U.S. economy.

*Data for 2016–18 are estimated.
SOURCE: Office of Management and Budget, "Table 1.3—Summary of Receipts, Outlays, and Surpluses or Deficits (–) in Current Dollars, Constant (FY 2009) Dollars, and as Percentages of GDP: 1940–2021," www.whitehouse.gov/omb/budget/historicals (accessed 7/9/16).

secretary is a second tier of "undersecretaries," who have management responsibilities for one or more operating agencies. Those operating agencies are the third tier of the department, yet they are the highest level of responsibility for the actual programs around which the entire department is organized. This third tier is generally called the "bureau level." Each bureau-level agency usually operates under a statute, enacted by Congress, that set up the agency and gave it its authority and jurisdiction. The names of these bureau-level agencies are often quite well known to the public—the Forest Service and the Food Safety and Inspection Service, for example. These are the so-called line agencies, those that deal directly with the public. Sometimes these agencies are officially called "bureaus," such as the Federal

The National Aeronautics and Space Administration (NASA), an independent agency of the federal government, was established by President Eisenhower in 1958. Its mission is "To reach for new heights and reveal the unknown so that what we do and learn will benefit all humankind." Here, NASA public affairs officer Dwayne Brown announces the presence of water on Mars.

independent agency agency that is not part of a Cabinet department

government corporation government agency that performs a market-oriented public service and raises revenues to fund its activities

Bureau of Investigation (FBI), which is part of the third tier of the Department of Justice. But *bureau* is also the conventional term for this level of administrative agency, even though many agencies or their supporters have preferred over the years to adopt a more politically palatable designation, such as "service" or "administration." Each bureau is, of course, even further subdivided into divisions, offices, or units—all are parts of the bureaucratic hierarchy.

Not all government agencies are part of Cabinet departments. Some **independent agencies** are set up by Congress outside the departmental structure altogether, even though the president appoints and directs the heads of these agencies. Independent agencies usually have broad powers to provide public services that are either too expensive or too important to be left to private initiatives. Some examples of independent agencies are the National Aeronautics and Space Administration (NASA), the Central Intelligence Agency (CIA), and the EPA. **Government corporations** are a third type of government agency but are more like private businesses in performing and charging for a market service, such as transporting railroad passengers (Amtrak).

Yet a fourth type of agency is the independent regulatory commission, given broad discretion to make rules. The first regulatory agencies established by Congress, beginning with the Interstate Commerce Commission in 1887, were set up as independent regulatory commissions because Congress recognized that regulatory agencies are "mini-legislatures," whose rules are exactly the same as legislation but require the kind of expertise and full-time attention that is beyond the capacity of Congress. Until the 1960s most of the regulatory agencies set up by Congress, such as the Federal Trade Commission (1914) and the Federal Communications Commission (1934), were independent regulatory commissions. But beginning in the late 1960s and the early 1970s, all new regulatory programs, with two or three exceptions (such as the Federal Election Commission), were placed within existing departments and made directly responsible to the president. After the financial crisis that began in 2008, Congress passed legislation to improve regulation of banks and other nonbank financial institutions. The legislation also created an important new regulatory agency, the Consumer Financial Protection Bureau. The bureau enforces consumer protection laws, for example, regulating bank practices that affect credit cards and mortgages. The agency aims to eliminate deceptive practices and act as the voice of consumers. Its website (www.consumerfinance.gov) also takes complaints from consumers and provides easy-to-understand information on many topics, including student debt repayment.

Bureaucracy in Comparison

As one of the world's largest and most populous countries, the United States has a vast bureaucracy to run government programs and services. However, as a percentage of the labor force, the number of government employees in the United States is not especially high. As the first graph below shows, the size of government bureaucracies, relative to each country's work force, varies widely. For example, the Norwegian government employs almost 35 percent of the labor force, whereas only around 8 percent of Japanese workers work for the government.

We can also see differences in whether most government employees work at the national level or the subnational level in each country. In the United States, most government employees work at the state or local level, rather than the national level. In other countries, such as Turkey, most bureaucrats work for the national government. What do you think accounts for these differences? How does federalism influence American bureaucracy, and what differences do we see in countries like Norway that do not have federalist systems?

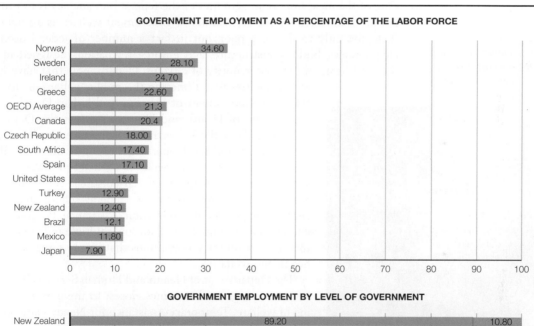

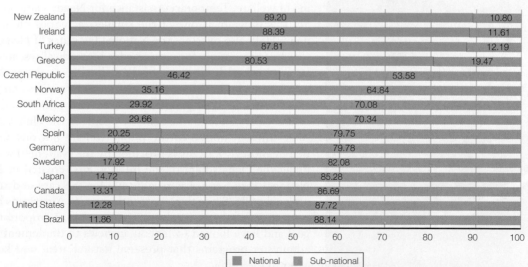

SOURCES: OECD, "Government at a Glance," www.oecd-ilibrary.org/governance/government-at-a-glance-2015_gov_glance-2015-en (accessed 11/18/15), and U.S. data from the U.S. Bureau of Labor Statistics, "Industry Employment and Output Projections to 2022," www.bls.gov/opub/mlr/2013/article/industry-employment-and-output-projections-to-2022-1.htm (accessed 11/18/15).

● Goals of the Federal Bureaucracy

Describe the major goals we expect federal agencies to promote

The different agencies of the executive branch can be classified into three main groups by the services they provide to the American public. The first category of agencies provides services and products that seek to promote the public welfare. The second group of agencies works to promote national security. The third group provides services that help maintain a strong economy. Let us look more closely at what each set of agencies offers to the American public.

Promoting the Public Welfare

One of the most important activities of the federal bureaucracy is to promote the public welfare. Americans often think of government welfare as a single program that goes only to the very poor, but in fact a number of federal agencies provide services, build infrastructure, and enforce regulations designed to enhance the well-being of the vast majority of citizens. Departments that have important responsibilities for promoting the public welfare in this sense include the Department of Housing and Urban Development, the Department of Health and Human Services, the Department of Veterans Affairs, the Department of the Interior, the Department of Education, and the Department of Labor. Ensuring the public welfare is also the main activity of agencies in other departments, such as the Department of Agriculture's Food and Nutrition Service, which administers the federal school lunch program and the Supplemental Nutrition Assistance Program (formerly known as food stamps). In addition, multiple independent regulatory agencies enforce regulations that aim to safeguard the public health and welfare.

The Department of Health and Human Services (HHS) administers the program that comes closest to the popular understanding of welfare: Temporary Assistance for Needy Families (TANF). Yet this program is one of the smallest activities of the department. HHS also oversees the National Institutes of Health (NIH), which is responsible for cutting-edge biomedical research and for two major health programs of the federal government: Medicaid, which provides health care for low-income families and for many elderly and disabled people, and Medicare, which is the health insurance available to most elderly people in the United States.

A different notion of the public welfare but one highly valued by most Americans is provided by the National Park Service, under the Department of the Interior. First created in 1916, the National Park Service is responsible for the care and upkeep of national parks. Since the nineteenth century, Americans have seen protection of the natural environment as an important public goal and have looked to federal agencies to implement laws and administer programs that preserve natural areas and keep them open to the public.

The National Institutes of Health (NIH) is an example of a federal bureaucracy that promotes the public welfare by conducting cutting-edge biomedical research. NIH research has helped doctors to treat diabetes and cardiovascular disease, among many other illnesses. This scientist is studying pancreatic beta cells, which play a role in diabetes

The federal bureaucracy also promotes public welfare through the watchdog activities of many **regulatory agencies**. These include the Food and Drug Administration (FDA), within the HHS; the Occupational Safety and Health Administration (OSHA), in the Department of Labor; as well as numerous independent regulatory commissions, such as the Consumer Product Safety Commission, the Federal Communications Commission, and the EPA. An agency or commission is regulatory if Congress delegates to it relatively broad powers over a sector of the economy or a type of commercial activity and authorizes it to make rules within that jurisdiction. Rules made by regulatory agencies have the force and effect of law.

Often working behind the scenes, regulatory agencies seek to promote the welfare of all Americans. The EPA, for example, works to protect public health by ensuring the provision of clean and safe drinking water. Just as the agency sets standards to limit emissions from automobiles in order to protect the public from air pollutants, as we saw earlier, the EPA also sets national water quality standards to protect against contaminants that may pose health risks. The safety standards apply to the more than 170,000 public water systems around the country that support our access to safe drinking water and are implemented by states, local governments, and water suppliers—all of which are overseen by the EPA to ensure compliance.[13] Unsafe drinking water may seem like a concern of less-developed countries, but in 2016 drinking water in Flint, Michigan, was found to have high levels of lead content, potentially harming children's brain development for life. The state of Michigan and the EPA both failed to act quickly to remedy the problem, although complaints about the water had emerged two years earlier.[14]

Bureaucracies, Clienteles, and the Public Some of the public agencies that provide services are tied to a specific group or segment of American society that is often thought of as the main clientele of that agency. For example, the Department of Agriculture was established in 1862 to promote the interests of farmers. Likewise, the Department of Veterans Affairs has strong links to veterans' organizations such as the American Legion and the Veterans of Foreign Wars. The Department of Education relies on teachers' organizations for support. Figure 14.3 is a representation of this type of politics. This configuration is known as an iron triangle, a pattern of stable relationships among an agency in the executive branch, a congressional committee or subcommittee, and one or more organized groups of agency clientele. (Iron triangles are discussed in detail in Chapter 11.)

These relationships with particular clienteles are often important in preserving agencies from political attack. During his 1980 campaign, Ronald Reagan promised to dismantle the Department of Education as part of his commitment to get government "off people's backs." After his election, Reagan even appointed a secretary of the department who was publicly committed to eliminating it. Yet by the end of his administration, the Department of Education was still standing and barely touched. In 1995 the Republican Congress vowed to eliminate the Department of Education, along with two other departments; but it, too, failed. The educational constituency of the department (its clientele) mobilized to save it each time. Teachers unions and educational administrators formed a powerful alliance to defend the department.

Nevertheless, the ability of clientele groups to get their way is not automatic as agencies have to balance limited resources, competing interests, and political pressures. For example, the Department of Veterans Affairs long resisted the efforts of

regulatory agency department, bureau, or independent agency whose primary mission is to impose limits, restrictions, or other obligations on the conduct of individuals or companies in the private sector

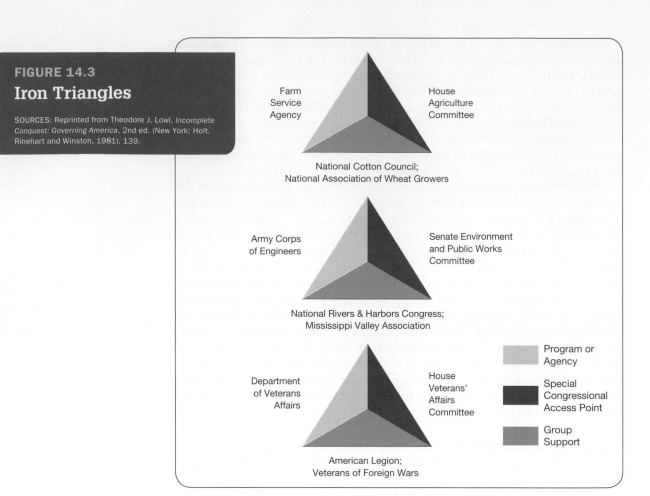

FIGURE 14.3

Iron Triangles

SOURCES: Reprinted from Theodore J. Lowi, *Incomplete Conquest: Governing America*, 2nd ed. (New York: Holt, Rinehart and Winston, 1981), 139.

Farm Service Agency

House Agriculture Committee

National Cotton Council;
National Association of Wheat Growers

Army Corps of Engineers

Senate Environment and Public Works Committee

National Rivers & Harbors Congress;
Mississippi Valley Association

Department of Veterans Affairs

House Veterans' Affairs Committee

Program or Agency

Special Congressional Access Point

Group Support

American Legion;
Veterans of Foreign Wars

Vietnam veterans to be compensated for exposure to Agent Orange, a chemical defoliant used extensively during the Vietnam War. Veterans charged that exposure to Agent Orange had left them with a variety of diseases ranging from cancer to severe birth defects in their children. Only after decades of lobbying, lawsuits, and federally sponsored studies did the Department of Veterans Affairs provide assistance to affected veterans.

Providing National Security

One of the remarkable features of American federalism is that the most vital agencies for providing security for the American people (namely, the police) are located in state and local governments. But some agencies vital to maintaining national security are located in the national government, and they can be grouped into two categories: (1) agencies to confront threats to internal national security and (2) agencies to defend American security from external threats. The departments of greatest influence in these two areas are Homeland Security, Justice, Defense, and State.

Agencies for Internal Security The task of maintaining domestic security changed dramatically after the terrorist attacks of September 11, 2001. The creation of the Department of Homeland Security in late 2002 signaled the high

for critical analysis

What is the impact of iron triangles on government services in the United States? Do the ties among agencies, congressional committees, and organized groups promote the efficient provision of government services?

The Department of Homeland Security (DHS) is tasked with the broad goal of keeping America safe. Its 240,000 employees work in jobs as diverse as aviation security, emergency response, and chemical facility inspection. The DHS also provided security for the 2015 Super Bowl, an event attended by approximately 70,000 people.

priority that domestic security would now have. The orientation of domestic agencies also shifted as agencies geared up to prevent terrorism, a very different task from their former charge of investigating crime. With this shift in responsibility came broad new powers, many of them controversial, including the power to detain terrorist suspects and to engage in extensive domestic intelligence gathering about possible terrorists.

Before September 11, most of the effort put into maintaining internal national security took the form of legal work related to prosecuting federal crimes. The largest and most important unit of the Justice Department is the Criminal Division. Lawyers in the Criminal Division represent the U.S. government when it is the plaintiff enforcing federal criminal laws, except for those cases (about 25 percent) specifically assigned to other divisions or agencies. Criminal litigation is handled by U.S. attorneys, who are appointed by the president. There is one U.S. attorney in each of the 94 federal judicial districts; he or she supervises the work of a number of assistant U.S. attorneys.

The Civil Division of the Justice Department deals with litigation in which the United States is the defendant being sued for injury and damages allegedly inflicted by a government official or agency. The missions of the other divisions of the Justice Department—Antitrust, Civil Rights, Environment and Natural Resources, and Tax—are described by their names.

In 2002 the new Department of Homeland Security joined the Justice Department as the major bureaucracy charged with domestic security. The department took over some of the security-oriented agencies previously controlled by other departments. (See Table 14.1 for a look inside the Department of Homeland Security.) Growing pains were evident in Homeland Security's first years. Different bureaucratic cultures, now part of a single operation, quickly became embroiled in turf battles with one another and with the FBI (which remained in the Justice Department) as the two departments attempted to sort out their

for critical analysis

Why was the Department of Homeland Security created? What problems has the new department faced?

TABLE 14.1

Department of Homeland Security

SELECTED OFFICES	FUNCTION	2016 BUDGET, IN MILLION $	ESTIMATED NUMBER OF EMPLOYEES
Department of Management and Operations	Provides leadership, direction, and management to the Department of Homeland Security	1,069	2,041
Analysis and Operations	Provides intelligence analysis, information sharing, incident management support, and situational awareness	265	791
Office of Inspector General	Conducts and supervises audits, inspections, special reviews, and investigations of the department's programs and operations	161	796
U.S. Customs and Border Protection	Responsible for securing America's borders to protect the United States against terrorist threats and prevent the illegal entry of inadmissible persons and contraband, while facilitating lawful travel, trade, and immigration	13,254	59,808
U.S. Immigration and Customs Enforcement	The principal investigative arm of the Department of Homeland Security	6,154	19,908
Transportation Security Administration	Provides security for the nation's transportation system	7,440	51,309
Coast Guard	Safeguards our nation's maritime interests and natural resources on our rivers, in U.S. ports, on the high seas, and in the maritime domain around the world	10,985	49,366
U.S. Secret Service	Protects national leaders and safeguards the nation's financial infrastructure and payment systems	2,199	6,481
Office of Health Affairs	Advises, promotes, integrates, and enables a safe and secure workforce and nation in pursuit of national health security	125	96
Federal Emergency Management Agency	Manages and coordinates the federal response to and recovery from major domestic disasters and emergencies of all types	16,575	9,515

SOURCE: Susan Dudley and Melinda Warren, "Regulator's Budget from Eisenhower to Obama: An Analysis of the U.S. Budget for Fiscal years 1960 to 2017," Table A-1 Agency Detail of Spending on Federal Regulatory Activity: Current Dollars (Selected Fiscal Years, Billions of Dollars) wc.wustl.edu/files/wc/imce/2017_regulators_budget_05-17-2016.pdf (accessed 7/9/16).

respective responsibilities. These early problems signaled deeper challenges that the Department of Homeland Security has continued to face throughout its existence. The Department of Homeland Security has been unable to establish itself as a strong institutionally coherent presence capable of coordinating government action. Part of the problem is that its portfolio of responsibilities is both large and vague. It is responsible for all kinds of internal security including terrorist attacks, border security, natural disasters, and food safety. At times the agency has emphasized one or the other of these responsibilities so that the overarching goal of "homeland security" has failed to gain traction. In addition, the agency failed to establish strong links with state and local agencies whose activities remain critical to its on-the-ground capabilities.

Agencies for External National Security Two departments occupy center stage in maintaining external national security: the Departments of State and Defense.

The State Department's primary mission is diplomacy. As the most visible public representative of American diplomacy, the secretary of state works to promote American perspectives and interests in the world. For example, in 2015, Secretary of State John Kerry convened a meeting with leaders from Europe and the Middle East—including Iran—to help find a diplomatic solution to the civil war in Syria. Concern about the flow of refugees in Europe, the increased role of Russia in the war, and the growing power of the terrorist group the Islamic State of Iraq and Syria (ISIS) in Syria all led the secretary to step up his efforts to negotiate an end to the war, including the controversial step of including Iran in the talks.[15] Although diplomacy is the primary task of the State Department, diplomatic missions are only one of its organizational dimensions. As of 2016 the State Department comprised 35 bureau-level units, each under the direction of an undersecretary.[16]

These bureaus support the responsibilities of the elite foreign-service officers, who staff U.S. embassies around the world and who hold almost all of the most powerful positions in the department below the rank of ambassador.[17] The ambassadorial positions, especially the plum positions in the major capitals of the world, are filled by presidential appointees, many of whom get their posts by having been important donors to victorious political campaigns.

Despite the importance of the State Department in foreign affairs, fewer than 20 percent of all U.S. government employees working abroad are directly under its authority. By far the largest number of career government professionals working abroad are under the authority of the Defense Department.

In 2002 the Defense Department created the U.S. Northern Command, a regional command charged with ensuring homeland defense, directing military operations inside the nation's borders, and providing emergency backup to state and local governments, which are the first responders to any security disaster. The creation of a regional command within the United States was an unprecedented move, breaching a long-standing line between domestic law enforcement and foreign military operations. As the creation of a military capacity within the United States suggests, addressing the threat of terrorism calls for greater coordination of internal and external security. In 2004 the National Commission on Terrorist Attacks upon the United States (the 9/11 Commission) issued a widely read report that revealed that different departments of the American government had information that, if handled properly, might have prevented the attacks of September 11, 2001.[18] The 9/11 Commission's work prompted a major reorganization of the fragmented intelligence community. In 2005 a new office, the Office of the Director of National Intelligence, took over responsibility for coordinating the efforts of the 16 different agencies that gather intelligence. The Director of National Intelligence reports directly to the president each morning.

National Security and Democracy Of all the agencies in the federal bureaucracy, those charged with providing national security most often come into conflict with the norms and expectations of American democracy. Two issues in particular arise as these agencies work to ensure national security: (1) the trade-offs between respecting the personal rights of individuals versus protecting the general public and (2) the need for secrecy in matters of national security versus the public's right to know what the government is doing. Needless to say, Americans often disagree about what activities the government should be able to pursue to defend U.S. national security.

When national security is at stake, federal agencies have taken actions that are normally considered incompatible with individual rights. For example, during World War II thousands of American citizens of Japanese descent were interned in camps due to national security concerns. Although the Supreme Court approved this action, the federal government has since acknowledged that it constituted unjustified discrimination and has offered reparations to those who were interned.

With the advent of the war on terrorism, the government gained unprecedented powers to detain foreign suspects, carry out wiretaps and searches, conduct secret military tribunals, and build an integrated law-enforcement and intelligence system. Congress hastily enacted many of these sweeping provisions of the USA PATRIOT Act several weeks after the terrorist attacks, with little debate. Since then, extensive doubts about the broad powers of the PATRIOT Act have spread. When Congress debated renewing the PATRIOT Act in 2005–06, these concerns about individual liberties threatened to block renewal. The act that was finally approved in 2006 did include modest revisions. The 2015 renewal of the act, now called the USA Freedom Act, included more significant restrictions on federal surveillance. The restrictions in the new legislations sought to ensure security without jeopardizing privacy.

Protecting national security often requires the government to conduct its activities in secret. Yet, as Americans have come to expect a more open government, many believe that federal agencies charged with national security keep too many secrets from the American public. The effort to make information related to national security more available began in 1966 with the passage of the Freedom of Information Act (FOIA). Strengthened in 1974 after Watergate, the act allows any person to request classified information from any federal agency. The information obtained often reveals unflattering or unsuccessful aspects of national security activities. One private organization, the National Security Archive, makes extensive use of FOIA requests to obtain information about the activities of national security agencies; it has published many of these documents on its website and maintains an archive in Washington, D.C., that is open to the public. The website's "The Torture Archive," for example, is a searchable database of documents related to the authorized use of torture by the American government.

The U.S. media have used Freedom of Information Act requests to obtain important information, such as federal drug safety reports and conditions at local jails. Americans are likely to always debate just how much secrecy their government is entitled to.

The tension between secrecy and democracy sharpened dramatically with the threat of terrorism. Access under the FOIA was curtailed, and the range of information deemed sensitive has greatly expanded. Some analysts worried that secrecy would prevent Congress from carrying out its basic oversight responsibilities. They also claimed that much of the secrecy had nothing to do with national security. The day after President Obama's election, he launched a process that would culminate in an Open Government Directive. He also instructed federal agencies that they should administer the FOIA law liberally: when in doubt, err on the side of openness. In 2011 the Department of Justice created the website www.foia.gov, which presents data about the number of FOIA requests by agency and the size of the backlog in processing those requests (see the "Who Participates?" feature on p. 579). In the most substantive change, at the end of his first year in office, Obama issued an executive order designed to promote more rapid declassification of secret documents.

Obama's campaign to make government more transparent was challenged, however, by national security contract worker Edward Snowden's leak of sensitive national security documents in 2013. The Snowden documents exposed the extent, and potential illegality, of the National Security Agency's (NSA) global surveillance operations. Following the revelation that the NSA was collecting private data on millions of Americans and foreign nationals—tracking not only phone calls but also email messages, web browser histories, and personal contacts—concern mounted among the American public, government watchdog groups, and representatives in Congress, while foreign allies threatened to suspend cooperation on global antiterrorism efforts.[19] President Obama responded to the growing outrage by appointing an independent, five-member panel of intelligence experts to assess the NSA's activities, which determined that its massive data collection "made only a modest contribution to the nation's security." They recommended, among dozens of other reforms, that the government stop the collection program and relinquish the files to a third party.[20] While the Obama administration publicly endorsed many of the panel's findings and outlined changes to the surveillance program—including requiring the agency to obtain prior court approval to access calling records[21]—even after these reforms more Americans disapproved than approved of the government's role in collecting Internet and telephone data.[22] Congress responded to such concerns in 2015 when it barred bulk collection of telephone data and instituted other limits on government surveillance in the USA Freedom Act.

Maintaining a Strong Economy

In our capitalist economic system, the government does not directly run the economy. Yet many federal government activities are critical to maintaining a strong economy. Foremost among these are the agencies responsible for fiscal and monetary policy. Other agencies, such as the Internal Revenue Service (IRS), collect private resources into use for public purposes. Tax policy may also strengthen the economy through decisions about whom to tax, how much, and when. Finally, the federal government, through such agencies as the Department of Transportation, the Commerce Department, and the Energy Department, may directly provide services or goods that bolster the economy.

fiscal policy the government's use of taxing, monetary, and spending powers to manipulate the economy

Fiscal and Monetary Agencies **Fiscal policy** can refer to any government policy having to do with public finance. However, Americans often reserve *fiscal* for taxing and spending policies and use *monetary* for policies having to do with banks, credit, and currency.

While the responsibility for making fiscal policy lies with Congress, the administration of fiscal policy occurs primarily in the Treasury Department. In addition to collecting income, corporate, and other taxes, the Treasury manages the national debt: $19 trillion in 2016.[23] The Treasury Department is also responsible for printing U.S. currency, but currency is only a tiny proportion of the entire money economy. Most of the trillions of dollars used in the transactions of the private and public sectors of the U.S. economy exist virtually—in computerized accounts rather than actual currency.

Federal Reserve System a system of 12 Federal Reserve banks that facilitates exchanges of cash, checks, and credit; regulates member banks; and uses monetary policies to fight inflation and deflation

A key monetary agency is the **Federal Reserve System** (called simply the Fed), which is headed by the Federal Reserve Board. The Fed has authority over the interest rates and lending activities of the nation's most important banks. Congress established the Fed in 1913 as a clearinghouse responsible for adjusting the supply of money and credit to the needs of commerce and industry in different regions of the country. The Fed is also responsible for ensuring that banks do not overextend themselves, a policy that guards against bank failures during a sudden economic scare, such as occurred in 1929. The Treasury and the Federal Reserve took center stage when a string of bank failures threatened economic catastrophe in 2008. These agencies designed a $700 billion bailout package and convinced Congress that a rapid response was needed to avert a worldwide depression. Although the Treasury and the Federal Reserve sprang into action when economic calamity loomed, critics charged that the crisis could have been prevented if these agencies had exercised more regulatory oversight over the financial sector during the previous decade. In 2010, Congress and the president created the Financial Stability Oversight Council to identify systemwide risks to the financial sector. As part of its duties, the council devised a rule to identify "systemically important" nonbank financial companies that would pose a grave threat to U.S.

financial stability in the event that they failed and to prompt stiffer regulatory oversight of those companies.[24]

Revenue Agencies One of the first actions Congress took under President George Washington was to create the Department of the Treasury, and probably its oldest function is the collection of taxes on imports, called tariffs. Now part of the Department of Homeland Security, federal customs agents are located at every U.S. seaport and international airport to oversee the collection of tariffs. But far and away the most important of the **revenue agencies** is the IRS, a bureau within the Treasury Department.

The IRS is the government agency that Americans love to hate. As one expert put it, "probably no organization in the country, public or private, creates as much clientele *dis*favor as the Internal Revenue Service. The very nature of its work brings it into an adversarial relationship with vast numbers of Americans every year [emphasis added]."[25] Taxpayers complain about the IRS's needless complexity, its lack of sensitivity and responsiveness to individual taxpayers, and its overall lack of efficiency. Such complaints led Congress to pass the IRS Restructuring and Reform Act of 1998, which instituted a number of new protections for taxpayers.

The politics of the IRS is interesting because, although thousands upon thousands of corporations and wealthy individuals have a strong and active interest in American tax policy, key taxation decisions are set by agreements among the president, the Treasury Department, and the leading members of the two tax committees in Congress, the House Ways and Means Committee and the Senate Finance Committee. External influence is not spread throughout the 50 states but is much more centralized in the majority political party, a few key figures in Congress, and a handful of professional lobbyists. Suspicions of unfair exemptions and favoritism are widespread, and they do exist; but these exemptions come largely from Congress, *not* from the IRS itself.

Economic Development Agencies Federal agencies also conduct programs designed to strengthen particular segments of the economy or to provide specific services aimed at strengthening the entire economy. Created in 1889, the Department of Agriculture is the fourth-oldest Cabinet department. Its initial mission, to strengthen American agriculture by providing information about effective farming practices, reflected the enormous importance of farming in the American economy. Through its Agricultural Extension Service, the Department of Agriculture established an important presence in rural areas throughout the country. It also built strong support for its activities among the nation's farmers and at the many land-grant colleges, where agricultural research has been conducted for over 100 years.

At first glance, the Department of Transportation, which oversees the nation's highway and air traffic systems, may seem to have little to do with economic development. But effective transportation is the backbone of a strong economy. The interstate highway system, for example, is widely acknowledged as a key factor in promoting economic growth in the decades after World War II. The Small Business Administration, in the Department of Commerce, provides loans and technical assistance to small businesses across the country.

For one picture of how the federal government prioritizes these goals, see the "Who Are Americans?" feature, which shows the number of employees of major executive departments.

revenue agency an agency responsible for collecting taxes. Examples include the Internal Revenue Service for income taxes; the U.S. Customs Service for tariffs and other taxes on imported goods; and the Bureau of Alcohol, Tobacco, Firearms and Explosives for collection of taxes on the sale of those particular products

● Can the Bureaucracy Be Reformed?

Evaluate some of the ways politicians have tried to make the bureaucracy more efficient

When citizens complain that government is too bureaucratic, what they often mean is that government bureaucracies seem inefficient and waste money. The epitome of such bureaucratic inefficiency in the late 1980s was the Department of Defense, which was revealed to have spent $640 apiece for toilet seats and $435 apiece for hammers. In 2015 the government revealed that government databases housed in the Office of Personnel Management had been hacked. Information about more than 22 million federal employees and their friends and families, including sensitive information about security clearances, was now in the hands of hackers, suspected of working for the Chinese government. Critics charged that lax cybersecurity made the agency an easy target.[26] In addition to hearing about poor government performance, many citizens have negative personal experience with the federal government: mountains of forms to fill out, lengthy waits, and unsympathetic service, leading them to wonder why government can't do better.

Do these frustrations mean that bureaucracy needs to be reformed? In a sense, bureaucracy is always in need of reform. Technological change and a dynamic private sector mean that public bureaucracies must always be looking for ways to take advantage of innovations to improve their performance. When bureaucracies fail to implement timely reforms, they can appear out of date and provoke frustration among citizens who rely on them. For example, the application of new technologies and innovative management strategies in the private sector during the 1980s led people to expect faster service and more customer-friendly interactions, which made government agencies look even more lumbering and inefficient by comparison. Yet, reforms may be more difficult to implement in the public sector because it is held to much higher standards of accountability than are private companies. Speedy service delivery can be hindered by the need to act in accordance with the multiple rules and regulations that govern bureaucracies. Moreover, the practices of bureaucracies are much more carefully scrutinized by watchdogs than those of the private sector. The security breaches that attracted negative press have also occurred in many private-sector firms. The tension between accountability and responsiveness, played out in the public eye, makes reform both necessary and challenging for bureaucracies.

The government has sought to find various ways to make the federal bureaucracy more efficient. The key strategies used to promote reform include reinventing bureaucratic procedures, termination, devolution, and privatization. In general, Democratic administrations have aimed to make the existing bureaucracy work more effectively, whereas Republican administrations have sought to sideline the bureaucracy, especially by contracting out government work to private companies.

In 1993, President Bill Clinton launched the National Performance Review—part of his promise to "reinvent government"—to make the federal bureaucracy more efficient, accountable, and effective. The National Performance Review sought to prompt federal agencies to adopt flexible, goal-driven practices. Clinton promised that the result would be a government that would "work better and

Who Are "Bureaucrats"?

Executive Branch Employees, 2015 (in thousands)

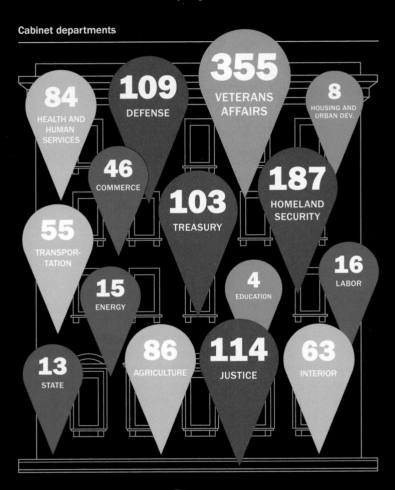

Cabinet departments

84 HEALTH AND HUMAN SERVICES

109 DEFENSE

355 VETERANS AFFAIRS

8 HOUSING AND URBAN DEV.

46 COMMERCE

103 TREASURY

187 HOMELAND SECURITY

55 TRANSPORTATION

15 ENERGY

4 EDUCATION

16 LABOR

13 STATE

86 AGRICULTURE

114 JUSTICE

63 INTERIOR

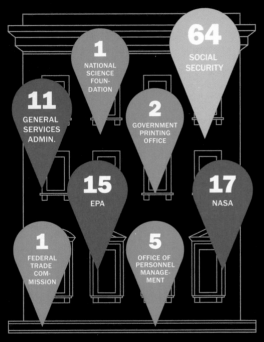

Independent agencies

1 NATIONAL SCIENCE FOUNDATION

64 SOCIAL SECURITY

11 GENERAL SERVICES ADMIN.

2 GOVERNMENT PRINTING OFFICE

15 EPA

17 NASA

1 FEDERAL TRADE COMMISSION

5 OFFICE OF PERSONNEL MANAGEMENT

Number of employees

- ● < 10,000
- ● 10,000–49,999
- ● 50,000–99,999
- ● 100,000–199,999
- ● > 200,000

Location, 2015

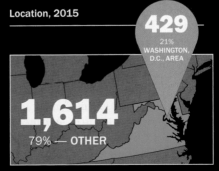

429 21% WASHINGTON, D.C., AREA

1,614 79% — OTHER

SOURCE: U.S. Office of Personnel Management, employment as of March 2015, www.fedscope.opm.gov/ibmcognos/cgi-bin/cognosisapi.dll (accessed 3/6/16).

Contrary to popular notions of "paper pushers," the people who work in the federal bureaucracy perform a range of tasks essential to the functioning of American society. More than 2 million executive branch employees are involved in protecting the nation's security, managing the economy, and promoting public welfare through various means, including environmental protection and health and safety regulations. Most federal employees work outside the Washington, D.C., area.

for critical analysis

1. Which category of departments and agencies—security, economic, or public welfare—employs the most people? Why?

2. With 2 million people working for the executive branch, mostly outside of the Washington, D.C., area, how can Congress and the president be sure that they are serving the public's interests?

In recent decades there have been several attempts to "reinvent government." In 1993, President Bill Clinton and Vice President Al Gore established the National Performance Review for this purpose. Gore promoted this on David Letterman's show, where he railed against the government's procurement requirements, which even specified the number of pieces into which a government ashtray may shatter.

cost less." Virtually all observers agreed that the National Performance Review (later renamed the National Partnership for Reinventing Government) made substantial progress. Its original goal was to save more than $100 billion over five years, in large part by cutting the federal workforce by 12 percent (more than 270,000 jobs) by the end of 1999. In fact, by 2000, $136 billion in savings were already assured through legislative or administrative action, and the federal workforce had been cut by 426,200.[27] The streamlining of government business procedures did help make government work more effectively, but it did not institute the more sweeping approach to reform demanded by some political leaders. These leaders have instead pursued efforts to terminate, devolve, or contract out government functions.

Termination

The only *certain* way to reduce the size of the bureaucracy is to eliminate programs through termination, a rare occurrence. Even in the 12 years of the Reagan and George H. W. Bush administrations, both of which proclaimed a strong commitment to the reduction of the national government, not a single national government agency or program was terminated. In the 1990s, Republicans did succeed in eliminating two small agencies.

The overall difficulty in terminating bureaucracy is a reflection of Americans' love–hate relationship with the national government. As antagonistic as Americans may be toward bureaucracy in general, they benefit from the services being rendered and the protections being offered by particular bureaucratic agencies. They fiercely defend their favorite agencies while perceiving no inconsistency in their hostility toward the bureaucracy in general. A good case in point is the agonizing problem of closing military bases in the wake of the end of the Cold War with the former Soviet Union, when the United States no longer needed so many bases. Since every base was in some congressional member's district, it proved impossible for Congress to decide to close any of them. Consequently, beginning in 1988, Congress established the Defense Base Closure and Realignment Commission (BRAC) to decide on base closings, allowing Congress only an up or down vote on the commission's proposals.[28] Five different BRAC reports, the most recent in 2005, formed the basis for closing bases and modifying the operations in the remaining bases. When the Pentagon proposed another round of base closings in 2014, it met with resistance from members of Congress, few of whom wanted to run the risk that a base in their district could close.[29]

Americans may desire smaller government in the abstract, but they defend the agencies that affect them. Closing military bases in the United States has proved particularly controversial. Citizens mobilized across the country to urge the Base Closure and Realignment Commission not to close military bases in their areas.

Elected leaders have come to rely on a more incremental approach to downsizing the bureaucracy. Much has been done by budgetary means, reducing the budgets of all agencies across the board by small percentages and cutting some less supported agencies by larger amounts. Yet these changes are still incremental, leaving the existence of agencies unaddressed.

Devolution

The next most effective approach to genuinely reducing the size of the federal bureaucracy is **devolution**, downsizing the federal bureaucracy by delegating the implementation of programs to state and local governments. Devolution often alters the pattern of who benefits most from government programs. Opponents of devolution in social policy, for example, charge that it reduces the ability of the government to remedy inequality. They argue that state governments, which cannot run deficits as the federal government does and which have more limited taxing capabilities, will inevitably cut spending on programs that serve low-income residents. They point to the State Children's Health Insurance Program (SCHIP), which was created in 1997 to extend health insurance to low-income children. When the economy was booming, states added children to the rolls and some states even extended benefits to the children's parents. But by 2002, as states faced significant budget crises, many cut back on SCHIP. Although the federal government was initially able to compensate for state funding problems, states have found it difficult to keep pace with the rising number of children without health insurance.

Often the central aim of devolution is to provide more efficient and flexible government services. Yet, by its very nature, devolution entails variation across the states. In some states, government services may improve as a consequence of devolution. In other states, services may deteriorate as the states use devolution as an opportunity to cut spending and reduce services. This has been the pattern in the implementation of the welfare reform passed in 1996, the most significant devolution of federal government social programs in many decades. Some states, such as Wisconsin, have used the flexibility of the reform to design innovative programs that respond to clients' needs; other states, such as Idaho, have virtually dismantled their welfare programs. The recession that began in 2008 provided the first real evidence about what increased state flexibility meant for low-income Americans.

devolution a policy to remove a program from one level of government by delegating it or passing it down to a lower level of government, such as from the national government to the state and local governments

Studies showed that the number of people on public assistance rose by 14 percent even as the unemployment rate increased by 88 percent between 2007 and 2010.[30] Moreover, states varied widely in how they responded: for example, although the unemployment rate rose by 146 percent in Arizona—increasing from 4 percent at the end of 2007 to almost 10 percent in 2010—public-assistance rolls actually fell by 48 percent. In Oregon, by contrast, public-assistance cases rose by 70 percent, although unemployment grew by only 41 percent. The overall lack of growth and state variation in welfare contrast sharply with the rise in food stamp recipients during 2008–09, a program run by the federal government. Recipients of food stamps (now called the Supplemental Nutrition Assistance Program) grew by 45 percent between 2009 and 2010 and pulled an estimated 9 percent of Americans out of poverty in 2009.[31] Critics argued that devolution gave the states too much flexibility in designing their own welfare programs and that the result has been a program unable to assist the poor when they need it most.

This is the dilemma that devolution poses. Up to a point, variation can be considered one of the virtues of federalism. But in a democracy, it is inherently dangerous to have large variations in the provisions of services and benefits.

Privatization

Most of what is called "privatization" is the provision of government goods and services by private contractors under direct government supervision. Except for top-secret strategic materials, virtually all military hardware, from boats to bullets, is produced on a privatized basis by private contractors. Research services worth billions of dollars are bought under contract by governments from universities and from ordinary industrial corporations and private "think tanks." **Privatization** simply means that a formerly public activity is picked up under contract by a private company or companies. But such programs are still very much government programs—paid for by government and supervised by government. Privatization downsizes the government only in that the workers providing the service are no longer counted as part of the government bureaucracy.

The central aim of privatization is to reduce the cost of government. When private contractors can perform a task as well as government can but for less money, taxpayers win. President George W. Bush made privatization a central component of his effort to reform the federal bureaucracy. He introduced new procedures that would subject more than 800,000 federal jobs, nearly half the federal civilian workforce, to competitive outsourcing. If it were determined that a company could do the job more efficiently, the work would be contracted out. Under Bush, government outsourcing grew dramatically as the government sought to staff the new Department of Homeland Security and pursue wars in Afghanistan and Iraq without increasing the numbers of federal employees. Payments for federal contracts grew from $209 billion in 2000 to $537 billion in 2011.[32] Although military contracts account for much of the growth, contracting is common throughout the federal bureaucracy. In fact, contracting has become so widespread that it has been called a "virtual fourth branch of government."[33]

Depending on how it is conducted, competitive outsourcing may not lead to extensive privatization; instead, competition may improve government performance by forcing federal agencies to reexamine how they can do their

for critical analysis

Dissatisfied citizens have supported a range of bureaucratic reforms, including termination of agencies, devolution of responsibility to lower levels of government, and privatization. Are such reforms likely to make the bureaucracy more responsive to public wishes?

privatization a formerly public service that is now provided by a private company but paid for by the government

One strategy to carry out the tasks of government is privatization. The U.S. Military and Department of Defense contract many services to companies such as Booz Allen Hamilton, which provides systems for personnel management, program support, and assessment, among other services.

work more efficiently. But when public bureaucracies are *not* granted a fair chance to bid in the contracting competition and, too, if there is little competition among private firms, private firms have a monopoly on service provision and often end up being less efficient and more costly than government. In 2015 close to 60 percent of all contracts were awarded competitively. But that year was an exception: from 2000 to 2011, less than half of existing contracts were subject to open competition (Figure 14.4). In fact, there is no good evidence that privatization saves the government money.

In most aspects of government activity, contract employees work side by side with government employees in what has been called a "blended workforce."[34] Many agencies that rely on technical expertise, such as the National Oceanographic and Atmospheric Administration, routinely rely on contractors. Although federal regulations forbid the outsourcing of "inherently governmental work," no clear line separates governmental and nongovernmental work. For example, in 2006 the General Services Administration hired a private firm, CACI International, to help it examine cases of fraud by other private contractors. Not only did the private contract workers hired by the General Services Administration in this case cost double what their public counterparts cost, but they were engaged in oversight of other private contractors, a clear conflict of interest.[35]

Concerns about adequate government oversight and accountability of private contractors escalated when the scale of contracting dramatically increased. Consider the use of private contractors in Iraq and Afghanistan. Congressional hearings revealed massive cost overruns by KBR (formerly a subsidiary of Halliburton, the firm that former vice president Dick Cheney headed), which held $9 billion in no-bid contracts to provide services ranging from supplying fuel for the military to preparing cafeteria meals in Iraq. Army auditors challenged $1.9 billion of KBR's bills as improper, citing violations ranging from unserved meals to inflated gas prices.[36]

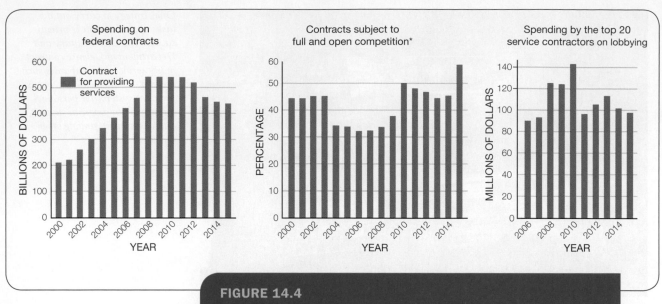

Spending on federal contracts

BILLIONS OF DOLLARS

- Contract for providing services

(Years 2000–2014)

Contracts subject to full and open competition*

PERCENTAGE

(Years 2000–2014)

Spending by the top 20 service contractors on lobbying

MILLIONS OF DOLLARS

(Years 2006–2014)

FIGURE 14.4

Outsourcing the Government

As spending on federal contracts has grown, the number of contracts subject to open competition initially declined but later rose again. The rise in spending by private contractors on lobbying and campaign contributions raises questions about improper political influence on government contracting decisions.

*Includes both new contracts and payments against existing contracts.
SOURCES: "Overview of Awards by FY 2008–2016," USAspending.gov, www.usaspending.gov/Pages /TextView.aspx?data=OverviewOfAwardsByFiscalYearTextView (accessed 7/11/16), and Advanced Data Search, www.usaspending.gov/Pages/AdvancedSearch.aspx (accessed 7/12/16); "Summary of Federal Spending: Financial Assistance and Procurement," www.fedspending.org (accessed 7/11/16); Federal Procurement Data System-Next Generation, "Top 100 Contractors Report," www.fpds.gov/fpdsng_cms /index.php/en/reports/62-top-100-contractors-report3.html (accessed 7/11/16); and Center for Responsive Politics, www.opensecrets.org/lobby/ (accessed 7/11/16).

Along with increased alarm over the activities of contractors have come several efforts to increase accountability. In 2008 Congress responded to the concerns about contractors by creating a "Commission on Wartime Contracting." Its final report sharply criticized the use of private contractors, estimating that the practice had wasted between $31 and $60 billion during the wars in Afghanistan and Iraq. It made numerous recommendations for reform but noted that successful reforms would require congressional action and funding for new oversight capabilities.[37] As part of the 2009 National Defense Authorization Act, Congress called for the creation of a database to keep track of contractors who commit legal or contractual violations,[38] to supplement a database created in 2002 whose aim was to record how well contractors have performed in order to serve as a resource for agencies. However, research by the Government Accountability Office (GAO) found that the earlier database was poorly documented and was seldom used in agency decision making,[39] and government transparency groups have complained that the newer database also suffers from poor documentation.[40]

Some members of Congress have sought far-reaching regulations on contractors, including forbidding contractors from performing sensitive functions in war settings, including interrogations, security, and intelligence functions. Proposals for such major reforms, however, are difficult to enact given the political connections of many federal contractors.

The Obama administration sought to address the concerns about contracting in several ways. In July 2009 the White House Office of Management and Budget (OMB) took steps to reduce the government's reliance on outside contractors. Departments and agencies were told to cut contract spending by 7 percent over the next two years.[41] By 2011 the administration announced that for the first time in 13 years, spending on outside contractors had declined.[42] In 2013 the national security leaks by Edward Snowden and a mass shooting at the Washington Navy Yard, a U.S. military base, both by government contractors, raised fresh concerns about the outsourcing of government and prompted Congress to pass legislation calling for a review of contractors' security clearances.[43] The White House also drafted an executive order requiring government contractors to disclose their political donations, though Congress blocked those efforts by passing a federal spending bill in 2014 that prohibits any funding to require contractors to provide campaign disclosures.[44] In 2015, Obama issued a series of executive orders that responded to a very different set of concerns about federal contractors. Frustrated with his inability to win congressional approval for measures designed to assist workers, he decided to act where he did have authority; one key area included setting requirements for federal contractors. The new provisions compelled contractors to pay a $10.10 minimum wage and to provide paid sick leave for their employees.[45]

for critical analysis

Private firms play a significant role in providing government services, including both internal and external security. What are the advantages and disadvantages of relying on private firms to provide essential services? Can government provide adequate oversight of these private companies?

● Managing the Bureaucracy

Explain why it is often difficult to control the bureaucracy

By their very nature, bureaucracies pose challenges to democratic governance. Although bureaucracies provide the expertise needed to implement the public will, they can also become entrenched organizations that serve their own interests. The public's task is neither to retreat from bureaucracy nor to attack it but to take advantage of its strengths while making it more accountable to the demands of democratic politics and representative government.

We must return to James Madison's observation, "You must first enable the government to control the governed; and in the next place oblige it to control itself."[46] Today, after more than 200 years, millions of employees, and trillions of dollars since the Founding, the problem is the same. Now, though, the process has a name, administrative accountability, which implies that some higher authority will guide and judge the actions of the bureaucracy. The highest authority in a democracy is *demos* ("the people"), and the guidance for bureaucratic action is the popular will. But that ideal of accountability must be translated into practical terms by the president and Congress.

The President as Chief Executive

In 1937, President Franklin Roosevelt's Committee on Administrative Management officially addressed a plea that had been growing increasingly urgent: "The president needs help." The national government had grown rapidly during the preceding 25 years, but the structures and procedures necessary to manage the burgeoning executive branch had not yet been established. The response to the call for "help" for the president initially took the form of three management policies: (1) all communications and decisions that related to executive policy decisions must pass through the White House; (2) in order to cope with such a flow, the White House must have an adequate staff of specialists in research, analysis, legislative and legal writing, and public affairs; and (3) the White House must have additional staff to ensure that presidential decisions are made, communicated to Congress, and carried out by the appropriate agency.

Making the Managerial Presidency The story of the modern presidency can be told largely as a series of responses to the plea for managerial help. Indeed, each expansion of the national government into new policies and programs in the twentieth century was accompanied by a parallel expansion of the president's management authority.[47]

President Jimmy Carter, in particular, was probably more preoccupied with administrative reform and reorganization than any other twentieth-century president. His reorganization of the civil service will long be recognized as one of the most significant contributions of his presidency. The Civil Service Reform Act of 1978 was the first major revamping of the federal civil service since its creation in 1883. The 1978 act created the Merit Systems Protection Board to defend competitive merit recruitment and promotion from political encroachment. The separate Federal Labor Relations Authority was set up to administer collective bargaining and to address individual personnel grievances. The third new agency, the Office of Personnel Management, was created to manage recruiting, testing, training, and the retirement system. The Senior Executive Service, a top management rank for civil servants, was also created to recognize and foster "public management" as a profession and to facilitate the movement of "super-grade" career officials across agencies and departments.[48]

Carter also tried to impose a stringent budgetary process on all executive agencies. Called "zero-based budgeting," it was a method of budgeting from the bottom up whereby each agency was required to rejustify its entire mission rather than merely its next year's increase. Zero-based budgeting did not succeed, but the effort was not lost on President Reagan. From Carter's "bottom-up" approach, Reagan went to a "top-down" approach, whereby the initial budgetary decisions would be made in the White House and the agencies would be required to abide by those decisions. This process converted the OMB into an agency of policy determination and presidential management.[49] President George H. W. Bush took Reagan's centralization strategy even further in using the White House staff instead of Cabinet secretaries for managing the executive branch.[50]

President Bill Clinton was often criticized for the way he managed his administration. His loose approach to administration even included all-night "bull sessions," complete with pizza. Yet, as we have seen, Clinton also inaugurated one of the most systematic efforts "to change the way government does business" in his National Performance Review. Heavily influenced by the theories of management consultants who prized decentralization, customer responsiveness, and employee initiative, Clinton sought to infuse these new practices into government.[51]

George W. Bush was the first president with a degree in business. His management strategy followed a standard business school dictum: select skilled subordinates and delegate responsibility to them. Bush followed this model closely in his appointment of highly experienced officials to Cabinet positions and in his selection of Dick Cheney for vice president. But critics contended that the Bush administration's distrust of the bureaucracy led it to exercise inappropriate political control. Political appointees occupied high agency positions that allowed them to suppress the work of agency experts when they threatened to undercut the administration's political goals.

The Obama administration sought to reinvigorate federal agencies, which reflected the Democrats' greater support for strong government institutions. Obama's approach to the managerial presidency featured a deep belief in the importance of scientific expertise in government service. The president's appointments to head key regulatory agencies, including the EPA, OSHA, and the FDA, reflected this conviction. Some of the new agency leaders were well-known academic experts; others had won recognition for their achievements in state or local administrative settings.

Decades of reform have increased the managerial capacity of the presidency, but such reforms themselves do not ensure democratic accountability—presidents must put their managerial powers to use. Although Ronald Reagan was an enormously popular president, he was faulted for his disengaged management style. During his administration, the National Security Council staff was not prevented from running its own policies toward Iran and Nicaragua for at least two years (1985–86) after Congress had explicitly restricted activities toward Nicaragua and the president had forbidden negotiations with Iran. The Tower Commission, appointed to investigate the Iran-Contra affair, concluded that "at no time did [President Reagan] insist upon accountability and performance review."[52] In 2008, Congress held hearings to investigate the financial crisis. Members grilled banking and insurance executives and the former chair of the Federal Reserve, Alan Greenspan. Greenspan, once hailed as a financial wizard, memorably admitted that inadequate regulation of lending practices had played a role in causing the crisis.[53]

Congressional Oversight

Congress is constitutionally essential to responsible bureaucracy because ultimately the key to bureaucratic responsibility is legislation. When a law is passed and its intent is clear, the accountability for implementation of that law is also clear. Then the president knows what to "faithfully execute," and the responsible agency understands what is expected of it. But when Congress enacts vague legislation, agencies must resort to their own interpretations. The president and the federal courts often step in to tell agencies what the legislation intended. So do the most intensely interested groups. Yet when everybody from president to courts to interest groups gets involved in the actual interpretation of legislative intent, to whom and to what is the agency accountable?

Congress's answer is **oversight**. The more power Congress has delegated to the executive, the more it has sought to re-involve itself in directing the interpretation of laws through committee and subcommittee oversight of each agency. The standing committee system in Congress is well suited to oversight, inasmuch as most of the congressional committees and subcommittees have jurisdictions roughly parallel to one or more departments and agencies, and members of Congress who sit on these committees can develop expertise equal to that of the bureaucrats. The exception is the Department of Homeland Security, whose activities are now overseen by more than 20 committees. One of the central recommendations of the

oversight the effort by Congress, through hearings, investigations, and other techniques, to exercise control over the activities of executive agencies

The most visible aspect of congressional oversight is the use of public hearings. Following the 2012 attack on the U.S. embassy in Benghazi, Libya, Congress held multiple highly publicized—and highly politicized—hearings to investigate the matter, focusing on the activities of former secretary of state Hillary Clinton.

9/11 Commission—as yet unimplemented—was to create a single committee with oversight of the Department of Homeland Security.

The most visible indication of Congress's oversight efforts is the use of public hearings, before which bureaucrats and other witnesses are summoned to discuss and defend agency budgets and past decisions. In 2013 and 2014, for example, Congress held high-profile hearings on topics as diverse as the attack on the American mission in Benghazi, Libya; reform of the Postal Service; and security concerns about the Department of Health and Human Services' new Healthcare.gov website. Oversight hearings can also become highly politicized. In 2015, the House select committee on Benghazi, which was the eighth committee to investigate the matter, called former secretary of state Hillary Clinton to appear for a second time. During the televised hearings Republican members of the committee aggressively questioned the former secretary for more than eight hours. Democrats charged that the hearing was designed to harm Clinton's presidential campaign.[54]

The data drawn from systematic studies of congressional committee and subcommittee hearings and meetings show quite dramatically that Congress has tried through oversight to keep pace with the expansion of the executive branch. The annual number of oversight hearings has grown over time as the bureaucracy has expanded. Oversight hearings in both the Senate and the House increased dramatically in the 1970s in the aftermath of the Watergate scandal. In recent years, oversight has become a topic of substantial political concern. After the Republicans took over Congress in 1995, they concentrated their oversight power on investigating scandal. When George W. Bush became president in 2001, congressional oversight virtually disappeared. After winning back Congress in 2006, the Democrats revived the oversight role, holding hearings on such issues as the use of government contractors in the Iraq and Afghanistan wars and the Troubled Asset Relief Program, which was instituted to help bail out the banks in 2008. When Republicans took control of the House in 2010, oversight hearings focused on the Democratic administration's programs, such as the Consumer Financial Protection Bureau and, in 2013, the troubled rollout of the Affordable Care Act.

Individual members of Congress can also carry out oversight inquiries. Such standard congressional "casework" can address significant questions of public responsibility even when they are motivated only by the demands of an individual constituent. Oversight also encompasses the communications between congressional staff and agency staff. In addition, Congress has created for itself three large agencies whose obligations are to engage in constant research on matters related to the executive branch. These are the GAO, the Congressional Research Service, and the Congressional Budget Office, each designed to give Congress information independent of the information it can get directly from the executive branch through hearings and other communications.[55] Another source of information for oversight is directly from citizens through the FOIA, which, as we have seen, gives ordinary citizens the right to gain access to agency files and agency data. Nevertheless, the information citizens gain through the FOIA can be made effective only through the institutionalized channels of congressional committees and, though rarely, through public interest litigation in the federal courts.

The increasing use of federal contractors raises new questions about democratic accountability. When government work is outsourced, federal monitoring is essential to ensure that funds are spent in accordance with the public will and to confirm that the costs are fair. Yet government contracting is now so extensive that such monitoring has become extremely difficult. Even with monitoring, accountability may be hard to achieve; many of the mechanisms of democratic accountability do not apply to private firms that contract to perform public work. For example, private corporations can resist FOIA requests, and they are not constrained by the same ethics rules as public employees. Moreover, because private firms do not have to disclose information about their operations in the same way that public bureaucracies do, Congress has much more limited oversight. The move to privatization clearly presents major challenges to democratic accountability.

One of the most troubling aspects of outsourcing is that private contractors donate millions of dollars each year to political campaigns and lobbying. As Figure 14.4 shows, the top 20 federal contractors have substantially increased their spending on lobbying in recent years. These expenditures raise troubling questions about how assertive members of Congress are likely to be in scrutinizing the business practices of important political donors or in moving activities from the private to the public sector.

Bureaucracy
and Your Future

Americans' views about the federal government bureaucracy present something of a paradox. On the one hand, the public expresses dislike for "big government," exemplified by bureaucracy. From this perspective, the federal government is too large, inherently wasteful, and at odds with individual freedom. On the other hand, Americans support many government programs and have high expectations for government. Indeed, high expectations lead many Americans to blame bureaucrats when the country faces problems, such as the prolonged economic downturn of recent years. One consequence of these divergent views is that public discussion about bureaucracy is often high on emotion and short on facts.

Arguments contending that the federal government is too large ignore the fact that the number of government employees has not grown disproportionately large when compared with the size of the American workforce. Charges that government wastes the taxpayers' money must also be put into perspective. As we have seen in this chapter, outsourcing government activities to private contractors does not offer a remedy for wasteful spending. In fact, private firms may be more wasteful than the public sector unless there is strong government oversight of private activities. Finally, it is true that bureaucratic rules often limit the freedom of individuals and corporations. But the laws that bureaucracies implement were enacted by our elected representatives in Congress. They are, in fact, the product of our democratic political system. As these considerations suggest, building a bureaucracy that reflects American values is not a simple task. Adequate congressional oversight is one important part of the solution because a bureaucracy that is shielded from the public eye may wind up pursuing its own interests rather than those of the public. Even so, an administration whose every move is subject to intense public scrutiny may be hamstrung in its efforts to carry out the public interest. (The "**Who Participates?**" feature on the facing page shows the public's efforts to get information from the bureaucracy under the Freedom of Information Act.) Finding the right balance between bureaucratic autonomy and public scrutiny is a central task of creating an effective government; it requires both presidential and congressional vigilance to build an effective and responsive bureaucracy.

The emergence of "big data" is likely to change the way bureaucracies operate in the future. The term *big data* refers to very large data sets that compile information on a wide range of topics including climate, traffic, health, and the NSA's huge database of phone calls and use of social media. Big data have the potential to improve government performance by linking sources of information that were previously unconnected. They also will allow the government to analyze information that was stored as text or went uncollected. Advances in government's ability to implement programs in public health, food safety, and transportation are only the beginning of what big data promise. At the same time, however, big data pose a threat to individual privacy, as the revelations about the NSA's data suggest. As bureaucracies tap into the promise of big data to create more effective programs, a close public eye on the implications for the right to privacy will be needed. How might big data improve the government's delivery of services in the future? What additional safeguards might be needed to protect individuals' privacy?

Getting Information from the Bureaucracy

FOIA Requests Received

2009	2010	2011	2012	2013	2014
557,825	597,415	644,165	651,254	704,394	714,231

Backlogged FOIA Requests

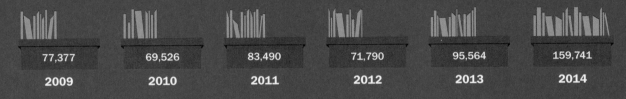

2009	2010	2011	2012	2013	2014
77,377	69,526	83,490	71,790	95,564	159,741

Responses to FOIA Requests, 2014

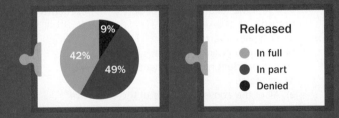

9%
42%
49%

Released
- In full
- In part
- Denied

SOURCE: U.S. Department of Justice, "Summary of Annual FOIA Reports for Fiscal Year 2014," www.justice.gov/sites/default/files/oip/pages/attachments/2015/05/01/fy_2014_annual_report_summary.pdf (accessed 4/12/16), pp. 2, 6, and 9.

WHAT YOU CAN DO

Ask Questions about Federal Agencies

☑ Learn more about the Freedom of Information Act (FOIA), including how to submit your own request, at **www.foia.gov/faq.html**. For a selection of records released under FOIA, go to **www.foia.state.gov/Search/Collections.aspx**.

☑ The Freedom of Information Act only applies to classified information. Federal agencies provide a vast amount of other government information as a standard part of their work. For a list of federal agencies and their websites, go to **www.usa.gov/federal-agencies**.

☑ Ask a question about how federal agencies can help you. Most agencies have FAQ and contact pages on their websites.

studyguide

Bureaucracy and Bureaucrats

Define bureaucracy, and describe the basic features of the executive branch (pp. 547–54)

Bureaucracy is defined as the complex structure of offices, tasks, and rules that private and public organizations use to coordinate the work of their personnel. The federal executive branch is composed of cabinet departments, independent agencies, government corporations, and independent regulatory commissions. Through their rule making and enforcement decisions, the federal service touches on many important aspects of daily life.

Key Terms

bureaucracy (p. 547)

implementation (p. 548)

merit system (p. 550)

department (p. 552)

independent agency (p. 554)

government corporation (p. 554)

Practice Quiz

1. Which of the following statements about Congress and the bureaucracy is *not* true?
   a) Bureaucracies employ people who have much more specialized expertise in specific policy areas than do members of Congress.
   b) Members of Congress often prefer to delegate politically difficult decision making to bureaucrats.
   c) While Congress is responsible for making laws, the bureaucracy is responsible for filling in the blanks by determining how the laws should be implemented.
   d) Congress banned rule making by the federal bureaucracy in 1995.
   e) Congress relies heavily on bureaucratic flexibility in implementing laws because updating legislation can take many years and bureaucrats can ensure that laws are administered in ways that take new conditions into account.

2. State and local laws similar to the Civil Service Act of 1883 require that appointees to public office
   a) pledge an oath of loyalty to the United States.
   b) be qualified for the job to which they are appointed.
   c) not belong to any political party.
   d) cannot be fired for any reason.
   e) cannot serve more than four years.

3. Which of the following best describes the size of the federal service?
   a) The size of the federal service has grown exponentially over the last 35 years.
   b) The size of the federal service has changed very little over the last 35 years.
   c) The size of the federal service reached its peak in 1955 and has been dramatically declining ever since.
   d) The federal service has employed at least 15 percent of the American workforce every year since 1950.
   e) The federal service was eliminated during the 1990s in order to hire more state government employees.

4. Which of the following are *not* part of the executive branch?
   a) Cabinet departments
   b) government corporations
   c) independent regulatory commissions
   d) agencies
   e) All of the above are parts of the executive branch.

5. Which of the following is an example of a government corporation?
   a) National Aeronautics and Space Administration
   b) Amtrak
   c) Federal Bureau of Investigation
   d) Environmental Protection Agency
   e) Department of Justice

Goals of the Federal Bureaucracy

Describe the major goals we expect federal agencies to promote (pp. 556–65)

The federal bureaucracy promotes the public welfare through a diverse set of services, products, and regulations. Some federal agencies, such as the Department of Defense, the Department of Justice, and the Department of Homeland Security, protect the country against internal and external security threats. Other federal agencies, such as the Federal Reserve System and the Internal Revenue Service, promote the public's welfare by helping maintain a strong economy.

Key Terms

regulatory agency (p. 557)

fiscal policy (p. 564)

Federal Reserve System (p. 564)

revenue agency (p. 565)

Practice Quiz

6. A stable relationship between a bureaucratic agency, a clientele group, and a legislative committee is called
   a) a standing committee.
   b) a conference committee.
   c) a cabinet.
   d) an issue network.
   e) an iron triangle.

7. Americans refer to government policy about banks, credit, and currency as
   a) interstate commerce policy.
   b) deficit policy.
   c) fiscal policy.
   d) monetary policy.
   e) regulatory policy.

Can the Bureaucracy Be Reformed?

Evaluate some of the ways politicians have tried to make the bureaucracy more efficient (pp. 566–73)

Many Americans express frustration with the performance of the federal bureaucracy. As a result, politicians have frequently explored various methods of making the federal bureaucracy more efficient. In general, politicians have attempted four strategies to promote bureaucratic reform: "reinventing" government, termination of programs, devolution, and privatization.

Key Terms

devolution (p. 569)

privatization (p. 570)

Practice Quiz

8. Which president instituted the bureaucratic reform of the National Performance Review?
   a) Richard Nixon
   b) Lyndon Johnson
   c) Jimmy Carter
   d) Bill Clinton
   e) George W. Bush

9. *Devolution* refers to
   a) the gradual decline in efficiency that always comes when government begins to implement a new program.

   b) moving all or part of a program from the public sector to the private sector.
   c) a policy of reducing or eliminating regulatory restraints on the conduct of individuals or private institutions.
   d) a policy to remove a program from one level of government by passing it down to a lower level of government.
   e) reducing the overall number of regulatory agencies in the federal bureaucracy.

10. Which of the following statements best describes termination of government programs?
    a) In the 12 years of the Reagan and George H. W. Bush administrations over 50 national government programs were terminated.
    b) In the 12 years of the Reagan and George H. W. Bush administrations over 100 national government programs were terminated.
    c) In the 12 years of the Reagan and George H. W. Bush administrations over 1,000 national government programs were terminated.
    d) Terminating government programs is an easy process that occurs frequently at the federal level.
    e) Terminating government programs is a difficult process that rarely occurs at the federal level.

11. Which of the following best describes the changes in government contracting since 2000?
    a) Spending on government contracts has decreased, while spending by contractors on lobbying and campaign contributions has increased.

b) Spending on government contracts has decreased, while spending by contractors on lobbying and campaign contributions has also decreased.

c) Government contracting ended in 2000 as a result of the Supreme Court's decision in *Immigration and Naturalization Service v. Chadha*.

d) Spending on government contracts has remained constant since 2000 due to a congressional law that limits federal spending on government contracts to $400 billion per year.

e) Spending on government contracts has increased, while spending by contractors on lobbying and campaign contributions also has increased.

Managing the Bureaucracy

Explain why it is often difficult to control the bureaucracy (pp. 573–77)

The federal bureaucracy provides the expertise that is needed to implement the law. However, parts of the bureaucracy can also become entrenched organizations that serve their own interests rather than the public will. While the emergence of the "managerial presidency" during the twentieth century has given the president more authority over the bureaucracy, presidents have sometimes used their managerial capacities to limit rather than promote democratic accountability. Congress can exert control over the federal bureaucracy by enacting specific legislation and engaging in vigorous oversight.

Key Term

oversight (p. 575)

Practice Quiz

12. The executive branch is kept accountable to the public mainly by
    a) the judiciary.
    b) direct, popular election of top bureaucrats.
    c) the president and Congress.
    d) the media.
    e) administrative adjudication.

13. The concept of *oversight* refers to the effort made by
    a) Congress to make executive agencies accountable for their actions.
    b) the president to make executive agencies accountable for their actions.
    c) the president to make Congress accountable for its actions.
    d) the courts to make executive agencies responsible for their actions.
    e) the states to make the executive branch accountable for its actions.

14. Which of the following agencies were created by Congress to engage in research on problems taking place in or confronted by the executive branch?
    a) Government Accountability Office, Congressional Research Service, Congressional Budget Office
    b) Department of Justice, Department of the Interior, Department of the Treasury
    c) Congressional Oversight Organization, Bureau of Government Performance, National Performance Review Association
    d) Office of Management and Budget, Council of Economic Advisers, Oversight and Government Reform
    e) Government Accountability Office, National Performance Review, Troubled Asset Relief Program

For Further Reading

Aberbach, Joel D., and Mark A. Peterson, eds. *Institutions of American Democracy: The Executive Branch*. Institutions of American Democracy Series. New York: Oxford University Press, 2006.

Arnold, Peri E. *Making the Managerial Presidency: Comprehensive Organization Planning*. Princeton, NJ: Princeton University Press, 1986.

Gormley, William, and Stephen Balla. *Bureaucracy and Democracy: Accountability and Performance*. 3rd ed. Washington, DC: CQ Press, 2012.

Kettl, Donald F. *System under Stress: The Challenge to 21st Century Government*. 3rd ed. Los Angeles: Sage/CQ Press, 2014.

Kettl, Donald F., and James W. Fesler. *The Politics of the Administrative Process*. 4th ed. Washington, DC: CQ Press, 2008.

Light, Paul C. *A Government Ill Executed: The Decline of the Federal Service and How to Reverse It*. Cambridge, MA: Harvard University Press, 2008.

Moffitt, Susan. *Making Public Policy: Participatory Bureaucracy in American Democracy*. New York: Cambridge University Press, 2014.

Verkuil, Paul. *Outsourcing Sovereignty: Why Privatization of Government Functions Threatens Democracy and What We Can Do about It*. New York: Cambridge University Press, 2007.

Weiner, Tom. *Legacy of Ashes: The History of the CIA*. New York: Doubleday, 2007.

Wilson, James Q. *Bureaucracy: What Government Agencies Do and Why They Do It*. New York: Basic Books, 1989.

Recommended Websites

Central Intelligence Agency
www.cia.gov

The Central Intelligence Agency (CIA) is one of several bureaucracies responsible for providing national security. A major problem facing this clandestine agency is how to provide security and meet the public's right to know what the government is doing. At the official website for the CIA, see what questions are often asked.

Department of Homeland Security
www.dhs.gov

The Department of Homeland Security was created after 9/11 to promote bureaucratic communication and domestic security. See what the department is doing to protect America from foreign threats.

Federal Emergency Management Agency
www.fema.gov

In the aftermath of Hurricane Katrina, the Federal Emergency Management Agency (FEMA) became infamous for its role in the disaster relief efforts. View the disaster history of your state, and see what FEMA is currently doing to prevent disasters and assist Americans in need.

Official U.S. Executive Branch Websites
www.loc.gov/rr/news/fedgov.html

This resource page at the Library of Congress website provides links to every federal department, independent agency, and regulatory commission in the federal bureaucracy.

Project on Government Oversight
www.pogo.org

The Project on Government Oversight is an independent, nonprofit organization that seeks to make government more accountable by investigating corruption and misconduct. Originally set up to focus on the military, this organization now examines all types of government bureaucracies.

Reason Foundation
reason.org

The Reason Foundation is dedicated to promoting libertarian principles and limited government. Its website includes studies and opinion pieces on a range of policy issues, including many related to the size and effectiveness of the federal bureaucracy.

U.S. Agency for International Development
www.usaid.gov

In 1961 Congress created the U.S. Agency for International Development (USAID) to provide economic and social development assistance to foreign countries. Often criticized for promoting American values and foreign policy objectives, USAID is currently involved in numerous global issues.

Although the Supreme Court is often viewed as the least political of the three branches, its rulings touch on major political issues that affect Americans in many ways. Here, demonstrators call on the other two branches of government to put partisanship aside and fill the Court vacancy left by the death of conservative justice Antonin Scalia.

The Federal Courts

15

WHAT GOVERNMENT DOES AND WHY IT MATTERS The judicial branch of the U.S. government is headed by the Supreme Court. Many Americans view the Supreme Court as aloof and apolitical because, unlike the president and members of Congress, the judges who sit on the Supreme Court are appointed, not elected. Thus, they do not need to campaign the way other politicians do. But the issues the Supreme Court decides are often as political as those voted on in Congress, and the Supreme Court is often asked to hear questions that touch the lives of ordinary Americans, including students, in a very direct and meaningful way.

Since the 1980s, politically conservative justices appointed by Presidents Ronald Reagan, George H. W. Bush, and George W. Bush constituted a conservative majority on the Supreme Court. Though this majority did not prevail in each and every case, many of the most important cases over the past three decades were decided by 5–4 votes in favor of the conservatives.

In February 2016, Justice Antonin Scalia, who spoke for conservative and religious values on the Court, died unexpectedly. Scalia's death gave President Obama an opportunity to create a liberal majority on the Court for the first time in decades, and he quickly nominated Judge Merrick Garland as Scalia's replacement. Garland, a moderate liberal, was supported by most Republican senators when Bill Clinton appointed him to the appeals court in 1997. However, the stakes for the Supreme Court are much higher. In an effort to prevent tipping the ideological balance of the Court toward the liberals, Senate Republicans decided not to act on the Garland nomination, hoping that a Republican president would be elected in 2016 and have the opportunity to nominate another conservative to the Court. While Republicans called on Obama to leave the appointment to his successor, Democrats called on Republicans to fill the vacancy, leaving the matter at a standstill for months. With only eight justices, the Court found itself evenly split on some important matters. For example, on a 4–4 vote the Court let stand a lower-decision striking down President Obama's executive orders blocking the deportation of as many as 5 million undocumented immigrants.[1] During the 2016 presidential campaign, Donald Trump released a list of individuals whom he would consider for the Supreme Court. The list comprised the most respected conservative judges in the United States. With Trump's election it seemed certain that the Court would regain its 5–4 conservative majority.

Every year, nearly 25 million cases are tried in American courts. Cases can arise from disputes between citizens, from efforts by government agencies to punish wrongdoing, from citizens' efforts to prove that their rights have been infringed on as a result of government action—or inaction—and from efforts by interest groups to promote their agendas. Many critics of the U.S. legal system assert that Americans have become too litigious (ready to use the courts for all purposes). But the heavy use that Americans make of the courts is also an indication of the extent of conflict in American society. And given the existence of social conflict, it is far better that Americans seek to settle their differences through the courts than resort to violence or otherwise take matters into their own hands. The framers of the Constitution called the Supreme Court the "least dangerous branch" of American government. Today, though, it is not unusual to hear the Court described as an all-powerful "imperial judiciary." Before we can understand this transformation and its consequences, we must look in some detail at America's judicial process.

chaptergoals

- Identify the general types of cases and types of courts in our legal system (pp. 587–92)
- Describe the different levels of federal courts and their functions (pp. 592–98)
- Explain how the Supreme Court exercises the power of judicial review (pp. 598–606)
- Describe the process the Supreme Court follows in the exercise of its power of judicial review (pp. 606–14)
- Consider the personal and political influences on judges and the courts (pp. 615–20)

● The Legal System

Identify the general types of cases and types of courts in our legal system

Originally, a "court" was the place where a sovereign ruled—where the king or queen governed. Settling disputes between citizens was part of governing. In modern democracies, courts and judges have taken over the power to settle conflicts by hearing the facts on both sides and deciding which side possesses the greater merit. But since judges are not kings and queens, they must have a basis for their authority. That basis in the United States is the Constitution and the law. Courts decide cases by hearing the facts on both sides of a quarrel and applying the relevant law or principle to the facts. This can be a sensitive matter because courts have been given the authority to settle disputes not only between citizens but also between citizens and the government itself, where the courts are obliged to maintain the same neutrality and impartiality as they do in disputes involving two citizens. This is the essence of the "rule of law": that "the state" and its officials must be judged by the same laws as the citizenry.

Cases and the Law

Court cases in the United States proceed under two broad categories of law: criminal law and civil law, each with myriad subdivisions.

Cases of **criminal law** are those in which the government charges an individual with violating a statute that has been enacted to protect public health, safety, morals, or welfare. In criminal cases, the government is always the **plaintiff** (the party that brings charges) and alleges that a criminal violation has been committed by a named **defendant**. Most criminal cases arise in state and municipal courts and involve matters ranging from traffic offenses to robbery and murder. Although the great bulk of criminal law is still a state matter, a large and growing body of federal

criminal law the branch of law that regulates the conduct of individuals, defines crimes, and specifies punishment for proscribed conduct

plaintiff the individual or organization that brings a complaint in court

defendant the one against whom a complaint is brought in a criminal or civil case

In criminal cases, the government charges an individual with violating a statute protecting health, safety, morals, or welfare. Most such cases arise in state and municipal courts. Here, an Illinois county court hears testimony in a murder case.

criminal law deals with matters ranging from tax evasion and mail fraud to acts of terrorism and the sale of narcotics. Defendants found guilty of criminal violations may be fined or sent to jail or prison.

civil law the branch of law that deals with disputes that do not involve criminal penalties

Cases of **civil law** involve disputes among individuals, groups, corporations, and other private entities or between such litigants and the government, in which no criminal violation is charged. Unlike in criminal cases, the losers in civil cases cannot be fined or incarcerated, although they may be required to pay monetary damages for their actions. The two most common types of civil cases involve contracts and torts. In a typical contract case, an individual or corporation charges that it has suffered because of another's violation of a specific agreement between the two. For example, the Smith Manufacturing Corporation may charge that Jones Distributors failed to honor an agreement to deliver raw materials at a specified time, causing Smith to lose business. Smith asks the court to order Jones to compensate it for the damage it allegedly suffered. In a typical tort case, one individual charges that he has been injured by another's negligence or malfeasance. Medical malpractice suits are one example of tort cases. Another important area of civil law is administrative law, which involves disputes over the jurisdiction, procedures, or authority of administrative agencies. A plaintiff may assert, for example, that an agency did not follow proper procedures when issuing new rules and regulations. A court will then examine the agency's conduct in light of the Administrative Procedure Act, the legislation that governs agency rule making.

precedent prior case whose principles are used by judges as the basis for their decision in a present case

In deciding cases, courts apply statutes (laws) and legal **precedents** (prior decisions). State and federal statutes, for example, often govern the conditions under which contracts are and are not legally binding. Jones Distributors might argue that it was not obliged to fulfill its contract with the Smith Manufacturing Corporation because actions by Smith, such as the failure to make promised payments, constituted fraud under state law. Precedents established in previous cases also guide courts' decisions in new cases. Attorneys for a physician being sued for malpractice might search for prior instances in which courts ruled that actions similar to those of their client did not constitute negligence. Such precedents are applied under the doctrine of **stare decisis**, a Latin phrase meaning "let the decision stand."

stare decisis literally, "let the decision stand"; the doctrine that a previous decision by a court applies as a precedent in similar cases until that decision is overruled

If a case involves the actions of the federal government or a state government, a court may also be asked to examine whether the government's conduct was consistent with the Constitution. In a criminal case, for example, defendants might assert that their constitutional rights were violated when the police searched their property. Similarly, in a civil case involving federal or state restrictions on land development, plaintiffs might assert that government actions violated the Fifth Amendment's prohibition against taking private property without just compensation. Thus, both civil and criminal cases may raise questions of constitutional law.

Types of Courts

In the United States, systems of courts have been established both by the federal government and by the governments of the individual states. Both systems have several levels, as shown in Figure 15.1. More than 97 percent of all court cases in the United States are heard in state courts. The overwhelming majority of criminal cases, for example, involve violations of state laws prohibiting such actions as murder, robbery, fraud, theft, and assault. If such a case is brought to trial, it will be heard at a state **trial court**, in front of a judge and sometimes a jury, who will determine whether the defendant violated state law. If the defendant is convicted, she

trial court the first court to hear a criminal or civil case

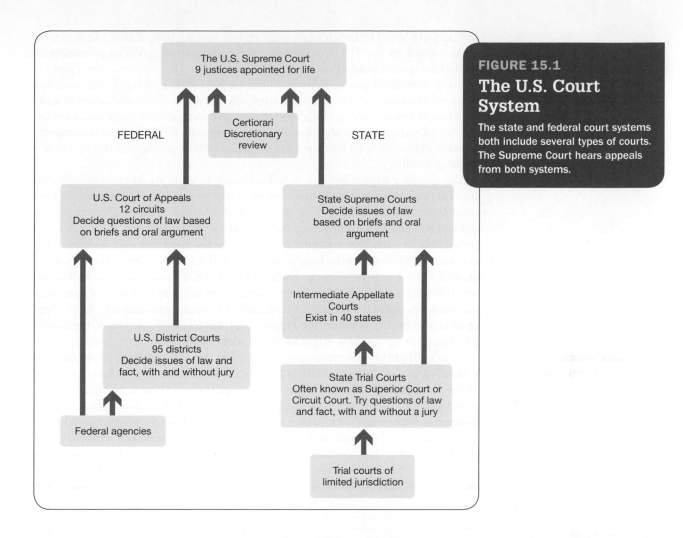

FIGURE 15.1

The U.S. Court System

The state and federal court systems both include several types of courts. The Supreme Court hears appeals from both systems.

The U.S. Supreme Court
9 justices appointed for life

FEDERAL

Certiorari
Discretionary
review

STATE

U.S. Court of Appeals
12 circuits
Decide questions of law based on briefs and oral argument

State Supreme Courts
Decide issues of law based on briefs and oral argument

Intermediate Appellate Courts
Exist in 40 states

U.S. District Courts
95 districts
Decide issues of law and fact, with and without jury

State Trial Courts
Often known as Superior Court or Circuit Court. Try questions of law and fact, with and without a jury

Federal agencies

Trial courts of limited jurisdiction

may appeal the conviction to a higher court, such as a state **court of appeals**, and from there to a court of last resort, usually called the state's **supreme court**. The government is not entitled to appeal if the defendant is found not guilty in a criminal case.

Similarly, in civil cases, most litigation is brought in the courts established by the state in which the activity in question took place. For example, a patient bringing suit against a physician for malpractice would file the suit in the appropriate court in the state where the alleged malpractice occurred. The judge hearing the case would apply state law and state precedent to the matter at hand. (There is some variation in court structure among the 50 states.) In a civil case, such as malpractice, either side may appeal the verdict if it loses.

The party filing an appeal, known as an *appellant*, usually must show that the trial court made a legal error in deciding the case. Appeals courts do not hear witnesses or examine additional evidence and will consider new facts only under unusual circumstances. Thus, for example, a physician who loses a malpractice case might appeal on the basis that the trial court misapplied the relevant law or incorrectly instructed the jury. It should be noted that in both criminal and civil matters most cases are settled before trial through negotiated agreements between the parties. In criminal cases these agreements are called **plea bargains**.

court of appeals a court that hears appeals of trial court decisions

supreme court the highest court in a particular state or in the United States; this court primarily serves an appellate function

plea bargain a negotiated agreement in a criminal case in which a defendant agrees to plead guilty in return for the state's agreement to reduce the severity of the criminal charge or prison sentence the defendant is facing

jurisdiction the sphere of a court's power and authority

Cases are heard in the federal courts if they involve federal laws, treaties with other nations, or the U.S. Constitution; these areas are the official **jurisdiction** of the federal courts. In addition, any case in which the U.S. government is a party is heard in the federal courts. If, for example, an individual is charged with violating a federal criminal statute, such as evading the payment of income taxes, charges are brought before a federal judge by a federal prosecutor. Civil cases involving the citizens of more than one state and in which more than $75,000 is at stake may be heard in either the federal or the state courts, usually depending on the preference of the plaintiff.

But even if a matter belongs in federal court, how do we know which federal court should exercise jurisdiction over the case? The jurisdiction of each federal court is derived from the U.S. Constitution and federal statutes. Over the years, as Congress enacted statutes creating the federal judicial system, it specified the jurisdiction of each type of court it established. For the most part, Congress has assigned jurisdictions on the basis of geography. The nation is currently, by statute, divided into 94 judicial districts. Each of the 94 U.S. district courts, including one court for each of three U.S. territories, exercises jurisdiction over federal cases arising within its district. The judicial districts are, in turn, organized into 11 regional circuits and the D.C. circuit (see Figure 15.2). Each circuit court exercises appellate jurisdiction over cases heard by the district courts within its region.

original jurisdiction the authority to initially consider a case; distinguished from appellate jurisdiction, which is the authority to hear appeals from a lower court's decision

Article III of the Constitution gives the Supreme Court **original jurisdiction** in a limited variety of classes, including (1) cases between the United States and one of the 50 states, (2) cases between two or more states, (3) cases involving foreign ambassadors or other ministers, and (4) cases brought by one state against citizens of another state or against a foreign country. Article III assigns original jurisdiction in all other federal cases to the lower courts that Congress was authorized to establish. Importantly, the Constitution gives the Supreme Court appellate jurisdiction in all federal cases, and almost all cases heard by the Supreme Court today are under its appellate jurisdiction. Courts of original jurisdiction are the courts that

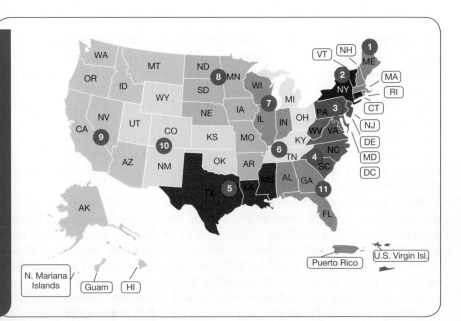

FIGURE 15.2
Federal Appellate Court Circuits

The 94 federal district courts are organized into 12 regional circuits: the 11 shown here, plus the District of Columbia, which has its own circuit. Each circuit court hears appeals from lower federal courts within the circuit. A thirteenth federal circuit court, the U.S. Court of Appeals for the Federal Circuit, hears appeals from a number of specialized courts such as the U.S. Court of Federal Claims.

SOURCE: www.uscourts.gov/court_locator.aspx (accessed 7/27/10).

are responsible for discovering the facts in a controversy and creating the record on which a judgment is based. In courts that have appellate jurisdiction, judges receive cases after the factual record is established by the trial court. Ordinarily, new facts cannot be presented before appellate courts.

Geography, however, is not the only basis for federal court jurisdiction. Congress has also established several specialized courts that have nationwide original jurisdiction in certain types of cases. These include the U.S. Court of International Trade, created to deal with trade and customs issues, and the U.S. Court of Federal Claims, which handles damage suits against the United States. Congress has also established a court with nationwide appellate jurisdiction, the U.S. Court of Appeals for the Federal Circuit, which hears appeals involving patent law and those arising from the decisions of the trade and claims courts. Other federal courts assigned specialized jurisdictions by Congress include the U.S. Court of Appeals for Veterans Claims, which exercises exclusive jurisdiction over cases involving veterans' claims, and the U.S. Court of Military Appeals, which deals with questions of law arising from trials by court-martial.

With the exception of the claims court and the Court of Appeals for the Federal Circuit, these specialized courts were created by Congress on the basis of the powers the legislature exercises under Article I, rather than Article III, of the Constitution. Article III is designed to protect judges from political pressure by granting them life tenure and prohibiting reduction of their salaries while they serve. The judges of Article I courts, by contrast, are appointed by the president for fixed terms of 15 years and are not protected by the Constitution from salary reduction. As a result, these "legislative courts" are generally viewed as less independent than the courts established under Article III of the Constitution. The three territorial courts (for Guam, the U.S. Virgin Islands, and the Northern Mariana Islands) were also established under the provisions in Article I, and their judges are appointed for 10-year terms.

The appellate jurisdiction of the federal courts extends to cases originating in the state courts. In both civil and criminal cases, a decision of the highest state court can be appealed to the U.S. Supreme Court by raising a federal issue. A defendant who appeals a lower-court decision in federal court might assert, for example, that he was denied the right to counsel or was otherwise deprived of the **due process of law** guaranteed by the federal Constitution or that important issues of federal law were at stake in the case. The U.S. Supreme Court is not obligated to accept such appeals and will do so only if it believes that the matter has considerable national significance. In addition, in criminal cases, defendants who have been convicted in a state court may request a **writ of habeas corpus** from a federal district court. Sometimes known as the "Great Writ," habeas corpus is a court order to the authorities to show cause for a prisoner's incarceration. The court will then evaluate the sufficiency of the cause and may order the release of a prisoner deemed to be held in violation of her legal rights. In 1867 its distrust of southern courts led Congress to authorize federal district judges to issue such writs to prisoners who they believed had been deprived of constitutional rights in state court. Generally speaking, state defendants seeking a federal writ of habeas corpus must show that they have exhausted all available state remedies and must raise issues not previously raised in their state appeals. Federal courts of appeals and, ultimately, the U.S. Supreme Court have appellate jurisdiction for federal district court habeas decisions.

Although the federal courts hear only a small fraction of all the civil and criminal cases decided each year in the United States, their decisions are extremely

due process of law the right of every individual against arbitrary action by national or state governments

writ of habeas corpus a court order that the individual in custody be brought into court and shown the cause for detention; habeas corpus is guaranteed by the Constitution and can be suspended only in cases of rebellion or invasion

important. It is in the federal courts that the Constitution and federal laws that govern all Americans are interpreted and their meaning and significance established. Moreover, it is in the federal courts that the powers and limitations of the increasingly powerful national government are tested. Finally, through their power to review the decisions of the state courts, it is ultimately the federal courts that dominate the American judicial system.

● Federal Courts

Describe the different levels of federal courts and their functions

During the year ending in March 2015, federal district courts (the lowest federal level) received 376,905 cases. Though large, this number is approximately 3 percent of the number of cases heard by state courts (see Figure 15.3). The federal courts of appeal listened to 54,244 cases during the same period. Generally, about 15 percent of the verdicts rendered by the lower courts are appealed to the U.S. Supreme Court. Most of the 9,000 or so cases filed with the Supreme Court each year are dismissed without a ruling on their merits. The Court has broad latitude to decide what cases it will hear and generally listens to only those cases it deems raise the most important issues. In recent years, fewer than 80 cases per year have received full-dress Supreme Court reviews.[2]

Federal Trial Courts

Most of the cases of original federal jurisdiction are handled by the federal district courts. Although the Constitution gives the Supreme Court original jurisdiction in several types of cases, such as those affecting ambassadors and those in which a state is one of the parties, most original jurisdiction goes to the lowest courts—the trial courts.

Congress has authorized the appointment of 678 federal district judges to staff the 94 federal district courts. At any given time, some of these positions may be vacant and awaiting the appointment of new judges. District judges are assigned to district courts according to the workload; the busiest of these courts may have as many as 28 judges. Only one judge is assigned to each case, except where statutes provide for three-judge courts to deal with special issues. The routines and procedures of the federal district courts are essentially the same as those of the state trial courts except that federal procedural requirements tend to be stricter. States, for example, do not have to provide a grand jury, a 12-member trial jury, or a unanimous jury verdict. Federal courts must follow all these procedures.

Federal Appellate Courts

Roughly 20 percent of all lower-court cases, along with appeals from some federal agency decisions, are subsequently reviewed by federal appeals courts. As noted, the country is divided geographically into 11 regional circuits and the D.C. circuit, each of which has a U.S. Court of Appeals. A thirteenth appellate court, the U.S. Court of Appeals for the Federal Circuit, has a subject matter, rather than

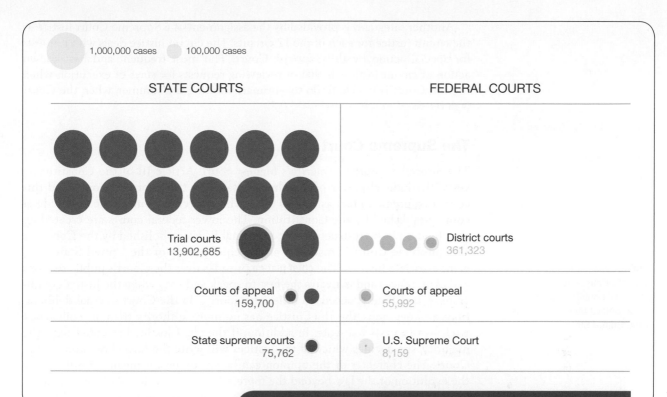

1,000,000 cases · 100,000 cases

STATE COURTS	FEDERAL COURTS
Trial courts 13,902,685	District courts 361,323
Courts of appeal 159,700	Courts of appeal 55,992
State supreme courts 75,762	U.S. Supreme Court 8,159

FIGURE 15.3

Caseloads of American Courts

This figure shows the total incoming caseloads of U.S. courts in 2010 (the most recent year for which complete state court data are available). More than 99 percent of the cases heard in American courts every year are heard in state courts. At both the federal and the state levels, lower-court decisions can be appealed to the appropriate court of appeals. Why do you think a larger percentage of federal district court decisions are appealed compared with state trial court decisions?

SOURCES: Court Statistics Project, National Center for State Courts, www.courtstatistics.org /; Supreme Court, 2010 Year-End Report on the Federal Judiciary, www.supremecourt.gov /publicinfo/year-end/2010year-endreport.pdf (accessed 5/26/14).

a geographical, jurisdiction. Congress has authorized the appointment of 179 court of appeals judges, though, as in the case of the district courts, some spots may be vacant at any given point in time.

Except for cases selected for review by the Supreme Court, decisions made by the appeals courts are final. Because of this finality, certain safeguards have been built into the system. The most important is the provision of more than one judge for every appeals case. Each court of appeals has from 6 to 28 permanent judgeships, depending on the workload of the circuit. Although normally three judges hear appealed cases, in some instances a larger number of judges sit together en banc.

Another safeguard is provided by the assignment of a Supreme Court justice as the circuit justice for each of the 12 circuits. The circuit justice deals with requests for special action by the Supreme Court. The most frequent and best-known action of circuit justices is that of reviewing requests for stays of execution when the full Court is unable to do so—primarily during the summer, when the Court is in recess.

The Supreme Court

The Supreme Court is America's highest court. Article III of the Constitution vests "the judicial power of the United States" in the Supreme Court, and this court is supreme in fact as well as form. The Supreme Court is the only federal court established by the Constitution. The lower federal courts are created by statute and can be restructured or, presumably, even abolished by the Congress. The Supreme Court is made up of the chief justice of the United States and eight associate justices. The **chief justice** presides over the Court's public sessions and conferences and is always the first to speak and vote when the justices deliberate; voting then proceeds in order of seniority. In the Court's actual deliberations and decisions, the chief justice has no more authority than his colleagues. Each justice casts one vote. In addition, if the chief justice has voted with the majority, she decides which of the justices will write the formal opinion for the Court. The character of the opinion can be an important means of influencing the evolution of the law beyond the mere affirmation or denial of the appeal on hand. To some extent, the influence of the chief justice is a function of his own leadership ability. Some chief justices, such as the late Earl Warren, have been able to lead the Court in a new direction. In other instances, forceful associate justices, such as the late Felix Frankfurter or William Brennan, are the dominant figures on the Court.

The Constitution does not specify the number of justices who should sit on the Supreme Court; Congress has the authority to change the Court's size. In the early nineteenth century, there were six Supreme Court justices; later there were seven. Congress set the number of justices at nine in 1869, and the Court has remained that size ever since. In 1937, President Franklin Delano Roosevelt, infuriated by several Supreme Court decisions that struck down New Deal programs, asked Congress to enlarge the Court so that he could add a few sympathetic justices to the bench. Although Congress balked at Roosevelt's "Court packing" plan, the Court gave in to his pressure and began to take a more favorable view of his policy initiatives. The president, in turn, dropped his efforts to enlarge the Court.

How Judges Are Appointed

Federal judges are nominated by the president and confirmed by the Senate. They are generally selected from among the more prominent or politically active members of the legal profession. Many federal judges previously served as state court judges or state or local prosecutors. Before the president makes a formal nomination, however, the senators from the candidate's own state must indicate that they support the nominee. This is an informal but seldom violated practice called **senatorial courtesy**. If one or both senators from a prospective nominee's home state belong to the president's political party, the president will almost invariably consult them and secure their blessing for the nomination. Because the president's

chief justice justice on the Supreme Court who presides over the Court's public sessions and whose official title is "chief justice of the United States"

senatorial courtesy the practice whereby the president, before formally nominating a person for a federal judgeship, seeks the indication that senators from the candidate's own state support the nomination

party in the Senate will rarely support a nominee opposed by a home-state senator from its ranks, this arrangement gives these senators virtual veto power over appointments to the federal bench in their own states. Senators also see nominations to the judiciary as a way to reward important allies and contributors in their states. If the state has no senator from the president's party, the governor or members of the state's House delegation may make suggestions. The practice of "courtesy" generally does not apply to Supreme Court appointments, only to district and circuit court nominations.

Federal appeals court nominations follow much the same pattern. Since appeals court judges preside over jurisdictions that include several states, however, senators do not have so strong a role in proposing potential candidates. Instead, potential appeals court candidates are generally suggested to the president by the Justice Department or by important members of the administration. The senators from the nominee's own state are still consulted before the president will formally act.

There are no formal qualifications for service as a federal judge. In general, presidents endeavor to appoint judges who possess legal experience and good character and whose partisan and ideological views are similar to their own. Once the president has formally nominated an individual, the nominee must be considered by the Senate Judiciary Committee and confirmed by a majority vote in the full Senate. In recent years, a good deal of partisan conflict has surrounded judicial appointments. Senate Democrats have sought to prevent Republican presidents from appointing conservative judges, while Senate Republicans have worked to prevent Democratic presidents from appointing liberal judges. During the early months of the Obama administration, Republicans were able to slow the judicial appointment process through filibusters and other procedural maneuvers so that only three of the president's 23 nominations for federal judgeships were confirmed by the Senate.[3] Some of Obama's allies urged the president to take a more aggressive stance or risk allowing Republicans to block what had been considered a key Democratic priority. In November 2013 the Senate voted 52 to 48 to end the use of the filibuster against all executive branch and judicial nominees except those to the Supreme Court. As of August 2016 the president had secured the appointment of 329 new district court judges, 55 new appeals court judges, and two Supreme Court justices.[4]

Supreme Court Appointments While political factors play an important role in the selection of district and appellate court judges, they are decisive when it comes to Supreme Court appointments. Because the high court has so much influence over American law and politics, virtually all presidents have made an effort to select justices who share their political philosophies.

Four of the eight current justices, as of November 2016, were appointed by Republican presidents (Table 15.1). Before the passing of Antonin Scalia in February 2016, the Court had a conservative majority for 45 years, most recently consisting of Chief Justice Roberts and justices Alito, Kennedy, Scalia, and Thomas. As we saw in this chapter's introduction, this majority propelled the Court in a more conservative direction in a variety of areas. In 2011 and 2012, however, Chief Justice Roberts joined the liberal bloc in two important cases. The first was the Court's decision to invalidate portions of an Arizona law designed to identify

In 2010, President Obama's second nominee to the Supreme Court, Elena Kagan, was sworn in. Although a large Democratic majority in the Senate all but guaranteed that Kagan would be confirmed, Republican senators asked her questions for weeks on her approach to the law.

TABLE 15.1

Supreme Court Justices, 2016 (in Order of Seniority)

NAME	YEAR OF BIRTH	LAW SCHOOL ATTENDED	PRIOR EXPERIENCE	APPOINTED BY	YEAR OF APPOINTMENT
Anthony Kennedy	1936	Harvard	Federal judge	Reagan	1988
Clarence Thomas	1948	Yale	Federal judge	G. H. W. Bush	1991
Ruth Bader Ginsburg	1933	Columbia	Federal judge	Clinton	1993
Stephen Breyer	1938	Harvard	Federal judge	Clinton	1994
John Roberts, Jr. (Chief Justice)	1955	Harvard	Federal judge	G. W. Bush	2005
Samuel Alito	1950	Yale	Federal judge	G. W. Bush	2006
Sonia Sotomayor	1954	Yale	Federal judge	Obama	2009
Elena Kagan	1960	Harvard	Solicitor general	Obama	2010
(vacant seat)*					

*As of November 2016.

and apprehend illegal aliens.[5] The second was the Court's 5–4 decision to uphold the Affordable Care Act, President Obama's major legislative achievement. While Roberts was generally a conservative voice on the Court, he continued to anger Republicans from time to time by supporting the liberal bloc on major issues. Thus, in the 2015 case of *King v. Burwell*, Roberts wrote the majority opinion, once again upholding the constitutionality of Obamacare against a legal challenge.[6]

In recent decades, Supreme Court nominations have come to involve intense partisan struggle. Typically, after the president has named a nominee, interest groups opposed to the nomination mobilize opposition in the media, among the public, and in the Senate. When President George H. W. Bush proposed the conservative judge Clarence Thomas for the Court, for example, liberal groups launched a campaign to discredit Thomas. After extensive research into his background, opponents of the nomination were able to produce evidence suggesting that Thomas had sexually harassed a former subordinate, Anita Hill. Thomas denied the charge. After contentious Senate Judiciary Committee hearings, highlighted by testimony from both Thomas and Hill, Thomas narrowly won confirmation.

Republicans severely criticized Obama's nomination of Sonia Sotomayor in 2009 and Elena Kagan in 2010, though both were ultimately confirmed by the Senate. Because Sotomayor and Kagan replaced liberal justices, they did not affect the balance of power on the Court. In 2016, however, the death of conservative justice Antonin Scalia gave President Obama an opportunity to replace Scalia with a more liberal jurist, and Obama named Judge Merrick Garland. The Senate's Republican leadership responded by refusing to take action on the nomination, preferring to wait and see whether a Republican might be elected to the presidency in 2016 and have the opportunity to nominate another conservative to the Court. With Republican Donald Trump's election in 2016, this strategy seemed to have paid off.

Who Are Federal Judges?

One factor among many that presidents may take into account when selecting judicial nominees is diversity. The number of Supreme Court justices is relatively small, so it is easy to count the number of African Americans who have served as Supreme Court justices (2), female justices (4), and Hispanic justices (1). How diverse is the rest of the federal judiciary? The first section below shows the racial, ethnic, and gender composition of the lower federal courts.

Federal Judges in 2016,* by Race and Gender *As of March 2016

= 10 federal judges

White men 828

African American men 97

Hispanic men 68

Asian American men 18

White women 261

African American women 53

Hispanic women 29

Asian American women 11

Appointments to Federal Courts, by Administration

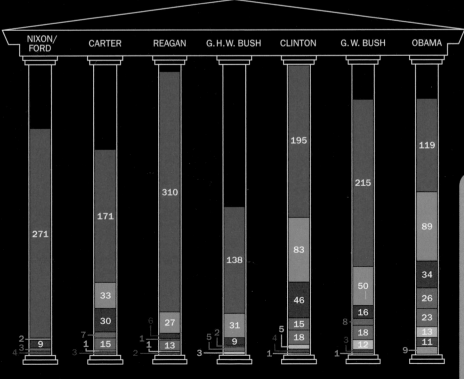

- White men
- White women
- African American men
- African American women
- Hispanic men
- Hispanic women
- Asian American men
- Asian American women

SOURCE: Federal Judicial Center, www.fjc.gov/history/home.nsf/page/judges_diversity.html (accessed 3/6/16).

for critical analysis

1. Would you describe the federal judiciary as diverse? Does racial, ethnic, and gender diversity of federal judges matter? Why or why not?

2. What similarities and differences do you notice among the judicial appointments of the presidents shown? What might account for the differences in terms of the diversity of their appointees?

After the death of conservative justice Antonin Scalia in 2016, Republican senators called on President Obama to leave the nomination of his replacement to the next president. Obama nominated Merrick Garland, a moderate Democrat, hoping to persuade the Senate to hold a hearing and a vote.

In considering Supreme Court nominations, presidents and senators will take account of a variety of factors, including ideology, partisanship, race, gender, and so forth, in addition to legal ability. Presidents seek nominees whose ideas are consistent with their own and whose appointment will please major constituency groups. In deciding whether to support or oppose a nominee, senators will apply a similar calculus.

● The Power of the Supreme Court: Judicial Review

judicial review the power of the courts to review and, if necessary, declare actions of the legislative and executive branches invalid or unconstitutional; the Supreme Court asserted this power in *Marbury v. Madison* (1803)

> **Explain how the Supreme Court exercises the power of judicial review**

The term **judicial review** refers to the power of the judiciary to examine and, if necessary, invalidate actions undertaken by the legislative and executive branches if it finds them unconstitutional. The term is sometimes also used to describe the scrutiny that appellate courts give to the actions of trial courts, but, strictly speaking, this is an improper use. A higher court's examination of a lower court's decisions might be called "appellate review," but it is not judicial review.

Judicial Review of Acts of Congress

Because the Constitution does not give the Supreme Court the power of judicial review over congressional enactments, the Court's exercise of it seems like something of a usurpation. It is not known whether the framers of the Constitution opposed judicial review; but judicial review was debated at the Constitutional Convention. Some delegates expected the courts to exercise this power, while many others were "departmentalists," believing that each branch of the new government would interpret the Constitution as it applied to its own actions, with the judiciary mainly ensuring that individuals did not suffer injustices. Ambiguity over the framers' intentions was settled in 1803 in the case of *Marbury v. Madison*.[7]

This case arose after Thomas Jefferson replaced John Adams in the White House. Jefferson's secretary of state, James Madison, refused to deliver an official commission to William Marbury, who had been appointed to a minor office by Adams and approved by the Senate just before Adams left the presidency. Marbury petitioned the Supreme Court to order Madison to deliver the commission. Jefferson and his followers did not believe that the Court had the power to undertake such an action and might have resisted the order. Chief Justice John Marshall was determined to assert the power of the judiciary but knew he must avoid a direct confrontation with the president. Accordingly, Marshall turned down Marbury's petition but gave as his reason the unconstitutionality of the legislation upon which Marbury had based his claim. Thus, Marshall asserted the power of judicial review but did so in a way that would not provoke a battle with Jefferson. The Supreme Court's decision in this case established the power of judicial review:

> It is emphatically the province and duty of the Judicial Department [the judicial branch] to say what the law is. Those who apply the rule to particular cases must, of necessity, expound and interpret that rule. If two laws conflict with each other, the Courts must decide on the operation of each. . . . So, if a law [e.g., a statute or treaty] be in opposition to the Constitution, if both the law and the Constitution apply to a particular case, so that the Court must either decide that case conformably to the law, disregarding the Constitution, or conformably to the Constitution, disregarding the law, the Court must determine which of these conflicting rules governs the case. This is of the very essence of judicial duty.

The Court's legal power to review acts of Congress has not been seriously questioned since 1803. One reason for that is that the Supreme Court makes a self-conscious effort to give acts of Congress an interpretation that will make them constitutional. For example, in its 2012 decision upholding the constitutionality of the Affordable Care Act, the Court agreed with the many legal scholars who had argued that the Congress had no power under the Constitution's commerce clause to order Americans to purchase health insurance. But, rather than invalidate the act, the Court declared that the law's requirement that all Americans purchase insurance was actually a tax and, thus, represented a constitutionally acceptable use of Congress's power to levy taxes.[8]

In more than two centuries, the Court has concluded that fewer than 160 acts of Congress directly violated the Constitution.[9] These cases are often highly controversial. For example, in 2007 and 2014, the high court struck down key portions of the Bipartisan Campaign Reform Act, through which Congress had sought to regulate spending in political campaigns.[10] The Court found that provisions of the act limiting political advertising violated the First Amendment. These cases are unusual in that the Court rarely overturns acts of Congress.

Judicial Review of State Actions

The power of the Supreme Court to review state legislation or other state action and to determine its constitutionality is neither granted by the Constitution nor inherent in the federal system. But the logic of the **supremacy clause** of Article VI of the Constitution, which declares the Constitution itself and laws made under its authority to be the supreme law of the land, is very strong. Furthermore, in the Judiciary Act of 1789, Congress conferred on the Supreme Court the power to reverse state constitutions

supremacy clause Article VI of the Constitution, which states that laws passed by the national government and all treaties are the supreme law of the land and superior to all laws adopted by any state or any subdivision

Judicial Review across the Globe

A strong, independent judiciary is a major component of most modern democracies today. In 1946 only about a quarter of democracies had a constitutional court that possessed the power of judicial review, whereby the court can review the constitutionality of an act; by 2006 almost 90 percent did.[a]

However, the type of judicial review varies greatly by county. The U.S. Supreme Court has *concrete* judicial review, meaning that the Court can only rule whether or not a law is constitutional if it receives a specific case challenging that law. In contrast, countries with *abstract* judicial review do not require a case to make such a ruling. France's Conseil Constitutionnel, for example, can rule on the constitutionality of a law before the law is even enacted, if it receives a request by an elected official, such as a member of parliament or local government, to review the bill. France was long known for being the only country to use solely abstract review, but in 2010, France's courts gained the power to respond to enacted legislation as well, meaning that the courts now have the power of both abstract and concrete judicial review.

Country	Constitutional Court	Concrete, Abstract, or Both?	What Can Be Reviewed
Brazil	Supreme Federal Court	Both	• National legislation • Lower court decisions • State and local laws
France	Conseil Constitutionnel	Both	• National legislation • Legislation pertaining to cases before other high courts
Germany	Federal Constitutional Court	Both	• National legislation • Actions of other national government institutions • State and local laws • Constitutional amendments • Election law violations
India	Supreme Court	Concrete	• National legislation • Actions of other national government institutions • State and local laws • Lower court decisions and appeals • Past judgments by the Supreme Court
Japan	Supreme Court	Concrete	• National legislation • Local laws • Administrative actions
South Africa	Constitutional Court	Both	• National legislation • Actions of other national government institutions • Local laws • Lower court decisions and appeals
United States	Supreme Court	Concrete	• National legislation • Actions of other national government institutions (e.g., executive orders) • State and local laws • Lower court decisions and appeals

[a]David S. Law and Mila Versteeg, "The Evolution and Ideology of Global Constitutionalism," *California Law Review*, 99, no. 5 (2010): 1163–1257.

In 2011 the Supreme Court struck down a California law that regulated the sale of violent video games to children, saying it violated the First Amendment. California state senator Leland Yee, who proposed the ban, held up some of the games the law would have regulated.

and laws whenever they are clearly in conflict with the U.S. Constitution, federal laws, or treaties.[11] This power gives the Supreme Court appellate jurisdiction over all the millions of cases that American courts handle each year.

The supremacy clause of the Constitution not only established the federal Constitution, statutes, and treaties as the "supreme Law of the Land" but also provided that "the Judges in every State shall be bound thereby, any Thing in the Constitution or Laws of the State to the Contrary notwithstanding." Under this authority, the Supreme Court has frequently overturned state constitutional provisions or statutes, state court decisions, and local ordinances it deems to contravene rights or privileges guaranteed under the federal Constitution or federal statutes.

The civil rights arena abounds with examples of state laws that the Supreme Court has overturned because the statutes violated guarantees of due process and equal protection contained in the Fourteenth Amendment to the Constitution. For example, in the 1954 case of *Brown v. Board of Education*, the Court overturned statutes from Kansas, South Carolina, Virginia, and Delaware that either required or permitted segregated public schools, ruling that such statutes denied black schoolchildren equal protection under the law.[12] In 2003, the Court ruled that Texas's law criminalizing sodomy violated the right to liberty protected by the due process clause.[13]

State statutes in other areas of law are equally subject to challenge. Many of the Supreme Court's recent decisions overturning state law have come in cases concerning election law. In 2015, for example, the Court ruled against an Alabama legislative districting plan that opponents charged was designed to reduce the influence of black voters.[14] During the same year, the Court ruled against an effort by the Arizona legislature to invalidate a districting plan drawn up by an independent commission created by a voter referendum.[15] One realm in which the Court constantly monitors state conduct is that of law enforcement. As we saw in Chapter 4, over the years, the Supreme Court has developed a number of principles regulating police conduct to ensure that the police do not violate constitutional liberties.

These principles, however, must often be updated to keep pace with changes in technology. In a 2012 decision, the Supreme Court found that police use of a GPS tracker—a device invented more than two centuries after the adoption of the Bill of Rights—constituted a "search" as defined by the Fourth Amendment.[16] And in the 2014 case of *Riley v. California*, the Court held that the police could not undertake a warrantless search of the digital contents of a cell phone—another device hardly imagined by the framers.[17]

Judicial Review of Federal Agency Actions

Although Congress makes the law, as we saw in Chapters 12 and 14, it can hardly administer the thousands of programs it has enacted and must therefore delegate power to the president and to a huge bureaucracy to achieve its purposes. For example, if Congress wishes to improve air quality, it cannot possibly anticipate all the conditions and circumstances that may arise with respect to that general goal. Inevitably, Congress must delegate to the executive substantial discretionary power to make judgments about the best ways to bring about improved air quality in the face of changing circumstances. Thus, over the years, almost any congressional program will result in thousands upon thousands of pages of administrative regulations developed by executive agencies nominally seeking to implement the will of the Congress.

Delegation of power to the executive poses a number of problems for Congress and the federal courts. If Congress delegates broad authority to the president, it risks seeing its goals subordinated to and subverted by those of the executive branch.[18] If Congress attempts to limit executive discretion by enacting precise rules and standards to govern the conduct of the president and the executive branch, it risks writing laws that do not conform to real-world conditions and that are too rigid to be adapted to changing circumstances.[19]

Over the past two centuries, the issue of delegation of power has led to a number of court decisions regarding the scope of the delegation. Courts have also been called on to decide whether the regulations adopted by federal agencies are consistent with Congress's express or implied intent.

As presidential power expanded during the New Deal era, one indication of increased congressional subordination to the executive was the enactment of laws that contained few, if any, principles limiting executive discretion. Congress enacted legislation, often at the president's behest, that gave the executive virtually unfettered authority to address a particular concern. For example, the Emergency Price Control Act of 1942 authorized the executive to set "fair and equitable" prices without spelling out what those terms might mean.[20] Although the Court initially challenged these delegations of power to the president during the New Deal, it retreated from its position when faced with a confrontation with President Franklin Delano Roosevelt. Perhaps as a result, no congressional delegation of power to the president since then has been struck down as impermissibly broad. Particularly in recent years, the Supreme Court has found that so long as federal agencies developed rules and regulations "based upon a permissible construction" or "reasonable interpretation" of Congress's statute, the judiciary would accept the views of the executive branch. Generally, the courts give considerable deference to administrative agencies as long as those agencies engage in a formal rule-making process as prescribed by the various statutes governing agency rule making. This principle was recently reaffirmed in the 2014 case of *Chamber of Commerce of the United States v. Environmental Protection Agency*. The Supreme Court was unwilling to overturn a "reasonable" agency interpretation of the Clean Air Act, even though the interpretation did not precisely conform to the language of the statute.[21] Of course, the Court will occasionally rule against a federal agency's interpretation of its powers under the law. In the 2015 case of *Michigan v. Environmental Protection* Agency, for example, the Court ruled that the Environmental Protection Agency had failed to properly interpret its obligations under the Clean Air Act when it did not take into account the likely costs of a set of regulations it developed to implement the Act.[22]

Judicial Review and Presidential Power

The federal courts are also called on to review the actions of the president. On many occasions, members of Congress as well as individuals and groups have challenged presidential orders and actions in the federal courts. In recent years, the federal bench has, more often than not, upheld assertions of presidential power in such realms as foreign policy, war and emergency powers, legislative power, and administrative authority. In June 2004, however, the Supreme Court ruled on three cases involving President George W. Bush's antiterrorism initiatives and claims of executive power and in two of the three cases appeared to place some limits on presidential authority.

One important case was *Hamdi v. Rumsfeld*.[23] Yaser Esam Hamdi, apparently a Taliban soldier, was captured by American forces in Afghanistan and brought to the United States, where he was incarcerated at the Norfolk Naval Station. Hamdi was classified as an enemy combatant and denied civil rights, including the right to counsel, despite the fact that he had been born in Louisiana and held American citizenship. In June 2004, the Supreme Court ruled that Hamdi was entitled to a lawyer and "a fair opportunity to rebut the government's factual assertions." Thus the Supreme Court did assert that presidential actions were subject to judicial scrutiny and that the Court could place some constraints on the president's power.

The courts may be called on to review the actions of the president. When President Obama passed an executive order that would protect millions of immigrants from deportation, opponents of the president's order challenged the legality of his actions. Here, supporters ask the Court to find it constitutional. In 2016 the Court issued a 4–4 tie, calling into question Obama's plan.

But at the same time, the Court affirmed the president's single most important claim: the unilateral power to declare individuals, including U.S. citizens, "enemy combatants," who could be detained by federal authorities under adverse legal circumstances. Several of the justices intimated that once designated an enemy combatant, a U.S. citizen might be tried before a military tribunal, without the normal presumption of innocence.

In the 2006 case of *Hamdan v. Rumsfeld*,[24] Salim Hamdan, a Taliban fighter, was captured in Afghanistan and held at the Guantánamo Bay naval base. The Bush administration planned to try Hamdan before a military commission authorized by a 2002 presidential order. The Supreme Court ruled that the commissions created by the president planned to use procedures that would violate federal law and U.S. treaty obligations. President Bush responded by demanding that Congress rewrite the law. Congress quickly obliged and enacted the Military Commissions Act, which gave the president statutory authority for his actions. In Section 7 of the act, Congress declared that Guantánamo prisoners could not bring habeas corpus petitions to federal courts to seek their release. In the 2008 case of *Boumediene v. Bush*, however, the Supreme Court struck down Section 7 and declared habeas corpus to be a fundamental right.[25] Judicial review of presidential actions is not limited to presidential war powers and the realm of terrorism. In 2013, the Fourth U.S. Circuit Court of Appeals ruled that President Obama violated the Constitution when he made so-called recess appointments to the National Labor Relations Board in order to avoid the need to secure Senate confirmation. Recess appointments are customarily used only when the Senate adjourns at the end of the year, but the president made the appointments in question when the Senate was on a short break. In June 2014, the Supreme Court ruled that a Senate recess of less than 10 days was "presumptively too short" to justify a recess appointment. In this case, the Senate had recessed for only 3 days.[26]

Judicial Review and Lawmaking

Much of the work of the courts involves the application of statutes to the particular case at hand. Over the centuries, judges have also developed a body of rules and principles of interpretation that are not grounded in specific statutes. This body of judge-made law is called **common law**. For example, **tort case**, which determines whether one person is liable for causing harm to another, is based more upon cases and precedents than statute.

The appellate courts, however, are in another realm. Their rulings can be considered laws, but they govern the behavior only of the judiciary. The written opinion of an appellate court is about halfway between common law and statutory law. As in common law, the opinion is judge-made and draws heavily on the precedents of previous cases. But, as in statutory law, it tries to articulate the rule of law controlling the case in question and future cases like it. It differs from a statute in that a statute addresses itself to the future conduct of citizens, whereas a written opinion addresses itself mainly to the future willingness or ability of courts to take cases and render favorable opinions. Decisions by appellate courts affect citizens by opening or closing access to the courts.

A specific case illustrates the distinction. Before the Second World War, one of the most insidious forms of racial discrimination was the "restrictive covenant," a clause in a contract whereby the purchasers of a house agreed that if they later decided to sell the home, they would sell only to a Caucasian. When a case finally

for critical analysis

During his 2005 confirmation hearings, senators asked Chief Justice Roberts why the Supreme Court was more willing to declare acts of Congress unconstitutional than it was to confront the president on the constitutionality of his actions. What reasons might you identify?

common law law made through court precedent rather than legislative enactments

tort case a law suit by one individual (the plaintiff) demanding compensation for harm allegedly caused by the actions of another (the defendant)

reached the Supreme Court in 1948, the Court ruled unanimously that citizens had a right to discriminate with restrictive covenants in their sales contracts but that the courts could not enforce those contracts. Its argument was that enforcement would constitute violation of the Fourteenth Amendment provision that no state shall "deny to any person within its jurisdiction equal protection under the law."[27] The Court was thereby predicting what it would and would not do in future cases of this sort. Restrictive covenants can be found in many old property deeds, but they have no legal validity.

Many areas of civil law have been constructed in the same way: by judicial messages to other judges, some of which are eventually codified into legislative enactments. An example of great concern to employees and employers is that of liability for injuries sustained at work. Courts have sided with employees so often that it has become virtually useless for employers to fight injury cases. It has become "the law" that employers are liable for such injuries, without regard to claims of negligence. But the law in this instance is simply a series of messages to lawyers that they should advise their corporate clients not to appeal injury decisions. In recent years, the Supreme Court has also been developing law in the realm of sexual harassment in the workplace. In a 2006 case, for example, the Court said that a victim of sexual harassment who was transferred from her job could sue her employer even though the company disciplined the perpetrator when the harassment was reported.[28]

The appellate courts cannot decide what types of behavior will henceforth be a crime. They cannot directly prevent the police from forcing confessions from suspects or intimidating witnesses. In other words, they cannot directly change the behavior of citizens or eliminate abuses of government power. What they can do, however, is make it easier for mistreated persons to gain redress.

In redressing wrongs, the appellate courts—and even the Supreme Court itself—often call for a radical change in legal principle. Changes in race relations, for example, would probably have taken a great deal longer if the Supreme Court had not rendered the 1954 decision *Brown v. Board of Education*, which redefined the rights of African Americans.

Similarly, the Supreme Court interpreted the doctrine of the separation of church and state so as to alter significantly the practice of religion in public institutions. For example, in the 1962 case *Engel v. Vitale*, the Court declared that a once widely observed ritual—the recitation of a prayer by students in a public school—was unconstitutional under the establishment clause of the First Amendment.[29] Almost all the dramatic changes in the treatment of criminals and of persons accused of crimes have been made by the appellate courts, especially the Supreme Court. The Supreme Court brought about a veritable revolution in the criminal process with three cases over less than five years: *Gideon v. Wainwright*, in 1963, established the obligation of state courts to provide legal counsel to defendants who could not afford their own attorneys.[30] *Escobedo v. Illinois*, in 1964, gave suspects the right to remain silent and the right to have counsel present during questioning, but the *Escobedo* decision left confusions that allowed differing decisions to be made by lower courts.[31] In *Miranda v. Arizona*, in 1966, the Supreme Court cleared up these confusions by setting forth what is known as the Miranda rule: arrested people have the right to remain silent, the right to be informed that anything they

Due process of law is an area in which federal courts have played a critical role in "making law" since the 1960s. In 2012 the Supreme Court heard the case of Evan Miller, who was tried as an adult on murder charges for a crime he allegedly committed when he was 14 years old and was sentenced to life without parole. The Court ruled that a life-without-parole sentence for a 14-year-old violates the Eighth Amendment's prohibition against cruel and unusual punishment.

say can be held against them, and the right to their own counsel or one provided by the government before and during police interrogation (see Chapter 4).[32] In 2000 the Supreme Court considered overruling *Miranda* in *Dickerson v. United States*, but it decided that the wide acceptance of Miranda rights in the legal culture was "adequate reason not to overrule" it.[33]

One of the most significant changes brought about by the Supreme Court was the revolution in legislative representation unleashed by the 1962 case *Baker v. Carr*.[34] In this landmark case, the Supreme Court held that it could no longer avoid reviewing complaints about the apportionment of seats in state legislatures. Following that decision, the federal courts went on to force reapportionment of all state, county, and local legislatures in the country.

● The Supreme Court in Action

Describe the process the Supreme Court follows in the exercise of its power of judicial review

Given the millions of disputes that arise every year, the job of the Supreme Court would be impossible if it were not able to control the flow of cases and its own caseload. Over the years, the courts have developed specific rules that govern which cases within their jurisdiction they will and will not hear. In order to be heard by the courts, cases must meet certain criteria that are initially applied by the trial court but may be reconsidered by appellate courts. These rules of access can be broken down into three major categories: case or controversy, standing, and mootness.

Article III of the Constitution and Supreme Court decisions define judicial power as extending only to "cases and controversies." This means that the case before a court must be an actual controversy, not a hypothetical one, with two truly adversarial parties. The courts have interpreted this language to mean that they do not have the power to render advisory opinions to legislatures or agencies about the constitutionality of proposed laws or regulations. Furthermore, even after a law is enacted, the courts will generally refuse to consider its constitutionality until it is actually applied.

standing the right of an individual or organization to initiate a court case, on the basis of having a substantial stake in the outcome

Parties to a case must also have **standing**—that is, they must show that they have a substantial stake in the outcome of the case. The traditional requirement for standing has been to show injury to oneself; that injury can be personal, economic, or even aesthetic, such as a neighbor's building a high fence that blocks one's view of the ocean. In order for a group or class of people to have standing (as in class-action suits), each member must show specific injury. This means that a general interest in the environment, for instance, does not provide a group with sufficient basis for standing.

mootness a criterion used by courts to screen cases that no longer require resolution

The Supreme Court also uses a third criterion in determining whether it will hear a case: that of **mootness**. In theory, this requirement disqualifies cases that are brought too late—after the relevant facts have changed or the problem has been resolved by other means. The criterion of mootness, however, is subject to the discretion of the courts, which have begun to relax the rules of mootness, particularly in cases where a situation that has been resolved is likely to come up again. In the abortion case *Roe v. Wade*, for example, the Supreme Court rejected the lower court's argument that because the pregnancy in question had already come to term, the case was moot. The Court agreed to hear the case because no pregnancy was likely to outlast the lengthy appeals process.[35] Related to mootness but less frequently cited is the idea of *ripeness*, which means the readiness of a case for litigation. The courts try to avoid becoming entangled in issues that remain hypothetical or events that may never occur.

Putting aside the formal criteria, the Supreme Court is most likely to accept cases that involve conflicting decisions by the federal circuit courts, cases that present important questions of civil rights or civil liberties, and cases in which the federal government is the appellant. Ultimately, however, the question of which cases to accept can come down to the preferences and priorities of the justices. If a group of justices believes that the Court should intervene in a particular area of policy or politics, they are likely to look for a case or cases that will serve as vehicles for judicial intervention. For many years, the Court was not interested in considering challenges to affirmative action or other programs designed to provide particular benefits to minorities. In recent years, however, several of the Court's more conservative justices have been eager to push back the limits of affirmative action and racial preference and have therefore accepted a number of cases that would allow them to do so. In the 2014 case *Schuette v. Coalition to Defend Affirmative Action*, for example, the Court ruled that a Michigan ballot initiative that resulted in a ban on racial preferences in college admissions was constitutional.[36] The decision paved the way for other states to prohibit the use of race as a factor in college admissions. In the 2016 case of *Fisher v. University of Texas*, however, the Court ruled that race could be one of the factors taken into account in college admissions if the school so desired.[37]

Writs Most cases reach the Supreme Court through a **writ of certiorari**. Certiorari is an order to a lower court to deliver the records of a particular case to be reviewed for legal errors. The term *certiorari* is sometimes shortened to *cert*, and cases deemed to merit certiorari are referred to as "certworthy." An individual who loses in a lower federal court or state court and wants the Supreme Court to review the decision has 90 days to file a petition for a writ of certiorari with the clerk of the U.S. Supreme Court. Petitions for thousands of cases are filed with the Court every year (see Figure 15.4).

writ of certiorari a decision of at least four of the nine Supreme Court justices to review a decision of a lower court; *certiorari* is Latin, meaning "to make more certain"

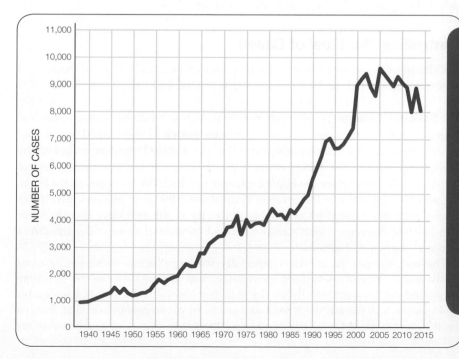

FIGURE 15.4

Cases Filed in the U.S. Supreme Court, 1938–2014 Terms*

*Number of cases filed in term starting in year indicated.
SOURCES: Years 1938–69, 1970–83, 1984–99: reprinted with permission from *The United States Law Week* (Washington, DC: Bureau of National Affairs), vol. 56, no. 3102; vol. 59, no. 3064; vol. 61, no. 3098; vol. 63, no. 3134; vol. 65, no. 3100; vol. 67, no. 3167; vol. 69, no. 3134 (copyright © Bureau of National Affairs Inc.); 2000–05 U.S. Bureau of the Census, *Statistical Abstract of the United States*; 2006–07: Office of the Clerk, Supreme Court of the United States; and Supreme Court of the United States, Cases on Docket, www .uscourts.gov/statistics-reports/caseload -statistics-data-tables (accessed 7/11/16).

Since 1972 most of the justices have participated in a "certiorari pool" in which their law clerks work together to evaluate the petitions. Each petition is reviewed by one clerk, who writes a memo for all the justices participating in the pool, summarizing the facts and issues and making a recommendation. Clerks for the other justices add their comments to the memo. After the justices have reviewed the memos, any one of them may place any case on the "discuss list," which is circulated by the chief justice. If a case is not placed on the discuss list, it is automatically denied certiorari. Cases placed on the discuss list are considered and voted on during the justices' closed-door conference.

For certiorari to be granted, four justices must be convinced that the case satisfies rule 10 of the Rules of the Supreme Court of the United States. Rule 10 states that certiorari is not a matter of right but is to be granted only when there are special and compelling reasons. These include conflicting decisions by two or more circuit courts, conflicts between circuit courts and state courts of last resort, conflicting decisions by two or more state courts of last resort, decisions by circuit courts on matters of federal law that should be settled by the Supreme Court, and a circuit court decision on an important question that conflicts with Supreme Court decisions. It should be clear from this list that the Court will usually take action under only the most compelling circumstances—when there are conflicts among the lower courts about what the law should be, when an important legal question has been raised in the lower courts but not definitively answered, or when a lower court deviates from the principles and precedents established by the high court. Few cases are able to gain the support of four justices needed for certiorari. In recent sessions, although thousands of petitions were filed, the Court has granted certiorari to barely more than 80 petitioners each year—about 1 percent of those seeking a Supreme Court review.

A handful of cases reach the Supreme Court through avenues other than certiorari. One of these is the writ of certification, which can be used when a U.S. court of appeals asks the Supreme Court for instructions on a point of law that has never been decided. A second alternative avenue is the writ of appeal, which is used to appeal the decision of a three-judge district court.

Controlling the Flow of Cases

In addition to the judges, other actors play important roles in shaping the flow of cases through the federal courts: the solicitor general and federal law clerks.

The Solicitor General If any single person has greater influence than individual judges over the federal courts, it is the **solicitor general** of the United States. The solicitor general is the third-ranking official in the Justice Department (below the attorney general and the deputy attorney general) but the top government lawyer in virtually all cases before the Supreme Court in which the government is a party. The solicitor general has the greatest control over the flow of cases; his or her actions are not reviewed by any higher authority in the executive branch. More than half the Supreme Court's total workload consists of cases under the direct charge of the solicitor general.

The solicitor general exercises especially strong influence by screening cases before any agency of the federal government can appeal them to the Supreme Court; indeed, the justices rely on the solicitor general to "screen out undeserving litigation and furnish them with an agenda to government cases that deserve serious consideration."[38] Agency heads may lobby the president or otherwise try

solicitor general the top government lawyer in all cases before the Supreme Court where the government is a party

Solicitor General Donald B. Verrilli, Jr., had experience arguing cases before the Supreme Court as an attorney in private practice before he entered government service. He was confirmed as the forty-sixth solicitor general in 2011. Since then, he has defended the U.S. government's position on the Affordable Care Act and the Voting Rights Act.

to circumvent the solicitor general, and a few of the independent agencies have a statutory right to make direct appeals; but without the solicitor general's support, these requests are seldom reviewed by the Court. Congress has given only a few agencies, including the Federal Communications Commission, the Federal Maritime Commission, and in some cases the Department of Agriculture (even though it is not an independent agency), the right to appeal directly to the Supreme Court without going through the solicitor general.

The solicitor general can enter a case even when the federal government is not a direct litigant by writing an **amicus curiae** ("friend of the court") brief. A friend of the court is not a direct party to a case but has a vital interest in its outcome. Thus, when the government has such an interest, the solicitor general can file an amicus brief or a federal court can invite such a brief because it wants an opinion in writing. Other interested parties may file briefs as well.

In addition to exercising substantial control over the flow of cases, the solicitor general can shape the arguments used before the federal courts. Indeed, the Supreme Court tends to give special attention to the way the solicitor general characterizes the issues. The solicitor general is the person who appears most frequently before the Court and, theoretically at least, is the most disinterested. The credibility of the solicitor general is not hurt when several times each year he comes to the Court to withdraw a case with the admission that the government has made an error.

Law Clerks Every federal judge employs law clerks to research legal issues and assist with the preparation of opinions. Each Supreme Court justice is assigned four clerks, almost always honors graduates of the nation's most prestigious law schools. A clerkship with a Supreme Court justice is a great honor and generally indicates that the fortunate individual is likely to reach the very top of the legal profession. The work of the Supreme Court clerks is a closely guarded secret, but it is likely

amicus curiae literally, "friend of the court"; individuals or groups who are not parties to a lawsuit but who seek to assist the Supreme Court in reaching a decision by presenting additional briefs

Federal judges, including Supreme Court justices, rely on their clerks for research and help in preparing opinions. Serving as a law clerk to a Supreme Court justice is a prestigious position. Three current justices—Roberts, Breyer, and Kagan—clerked for a Supreme Court justice early in their careers.

that some justices rely heavily on their clerks for advice in writing opinions and in deciding whether the Court should hear specific cases. In a recent book, a former law clerk to the late justice Harry Blackmun charged that Supreme Court justices yielded "excessive power to immature, ideologically driven clerks, who in turn use that power to manipulate their bosses."[39]

Lobbying for Access: Interests and the Court

At the same time that the Court exercises discretion over which cases it will review, groups and forces in society often seek to persuade the justices to listen to their problems. Lawyers representing interest groups try to choose the proper client and the proper case so that the issues in question are most dramatically and appropriately portrayed. When possible, they also pick a district or jurisdiction with a sympathetic judge in which to bring the case. Sometimes they even have to wait for an appropriate political climate. They must also attempt to develop a proper record at the trial court level, one that includes some constitutional arguments and even, when possible, errors on the part of the trial court.

One of the most effective strategies that litigants use in getting cases accepted for review by the appellate courts is to bring the same type of suit in more than one circuit (that is, to develop a "pattern of cases"), in the hope that inconsistent treatment by two different courts will improve the chance of a Supreme Court review. The two most notable users of the pattern-of-cases strategy in recent years have been the National Association for the Advancement of Colored People (NAACP) and the American Civil Liberties Union (ACLU). For many years, the NAACP (and its Defense Fund—now a separate group) has worked through local chapters and with many individuals to encourage litigation on issues of racial discrimination and segregation. Sometimes it distributes petitions to be signed by parents and filed with local school boards and courts, deliberately sowing the seeds of future litigation. The NAACP and the ACLU often encourage private parties to bring suit and then join the suit as amici curiae.

In many states, it is considered unethical and illegal for attorneys to engage in "fomenting and soliciting legal business in which they are not parties and have no pecuniary right or liability." The NAACP was sued by the state of Virginia in the late 1950s in an attempt to restrict or eliminate its efforts to influence the pattern of cases. The Supreme Court reviewed the case in 1963, recognized that the strategy was being used, and held that the NAACP strategy was protected by the First and Fourteenth amendments, just as other forms of speech and petition are protected.[40]

Thus, many pathbreaking cases are eventually granted certiorari because repeated refusal to review one or more of them would amount to a rule of law just as much as if the courts had handed down a written opinion. In this sense, the flow of cases, especially the pattern of significant cases, influences the behavior of the appellate judiciary.

The Supreme Court's Procedures

The Supreme Court's decision to accept a case is the beginning of what can be a lengthy and complex process (see Figure 15.5). After a petition is filed and certiorari is granted, the Court considers the reasoning on both sides as presented in briefs and oral argument, the justices discuss the case in conference, and opinions are carefully drafted.

The Preparation First, the attorneys on both sides must prepare **briefs**, written documents in which the attorneys explain why the Court should rule in favor of their client. Briefs are filled with referrals to precedents specifically chosen to show that other courts have frequently ruled in the same way the attorneys are requesting that the Supreme Court rule. The attorneys for both sides muster the most compelling precedents they can in support of their arguments.

briefs written documents in which attorneys explain, using case precedents, why the court should find in favor of their client

As the attorneys prepare their briefs, they often ask sympathetic interest groups for their help. These groups are asked to file amicus curiae briefs that support the claims of one or the other litigant. In a case involving separation of church and state, for example, liberal groups such as the ACLU and People for the American Way are likely to be asked to file amicus briefs in support of strict separation, whereas conservative religious groups are likely to file amicus briefs advocating increased public accommodation of religious ideas. Often, dozens of briefs will be filed on each side of a major case. Amicus filings are one of the primary methods used by interest groups to lobby the Court. By filing these briefs, groups indicate to the Court where they stand and signal to the justices that they believe the case to be an important one.

Oral Argument The next stage of a case is **oral argument**, in which attorneys for both sides appear before the Court to present their positions and answer the justices' questions. Each attorney has only a half hour to present a case, and this time includes interruptions for questions. Certain members of the Court, such as the late Justice Antonin Scalia, are known to interrupt attorneys dozens of times. Others, such as Justice Clarence Thomas, seldom ask questions. For an attorney, the opportunity to argue a case before the Supreme Court is a singular honor and a mark of professional distinction. It can also be a harrowing experience, as when justices interrupt a carefully prepared presentation. Nevertheless, oral argument can be very important to the outcome of a case. It allows justices to understand better the heart of the case and to raise questions that might not have been addressed in the opposing sides' briefs. It is not uncommon for justices to go beyond the strictly legal issues and ask opposing counsel to discuss the implications of the case for the Court and the nation at large.

oral argument the stage in the Supreme Court procedure in which attorneys for both sides appear before the Court to present their positions and answer questions posed by justices

The Conference Following oral argument, the Court discusses the case in its Wednesday or Friday conference, a strictly private meeting that no outsiders are

April 19, 2013

The Chamber of Commerce filed a petition for a writ of certiorari in the case *Chamber of Commerce of the United States of America, et al. v. Environmental Protection Agency, et al.*

May 2013

Filing of briefs and amicus curiae briefs in support of the petitioner, including the Institute for Trade, Standards, and Sustainable Development and Nobel Prize–winning economist Thomas C. Shelling

July 2013

Brief of the solicitor general on behalf of the Environmental Protection Agency (the respondent)

August 7, 2013

The case is distributed for conference.

October 15, 2013

The petition (certiorari) is granted.

November 25, 2013

Date for oral argument is set for February 24, 2014.

December 2013

Briefs and amicus curiae briefs are filed on behalf of petitioner.

January 2014

Briefs and amicus curiae briefs are filed on behalf of respondent.

February 24, 2014

Oral argument of one hour

June 2014

Decision

The Supreme Court allocates just one hour to hear oral arguments, even in difficult and contentious cases. Attorneys for both sides must make their arguments succinctly and respond to questions from the nine justices, which are often very pointed.

permitted to attend. The chief justice presides over the conference and speaks first; the other justices follow in order of seniority. The justices discuss the case and eventually reach a decision on the basis of a majority vote. If the Court is divided, a number of votes may be taken before a final decision is reached. As the case is discussed, justices may try to influence or change one another's opinions. At times, this may result in compromise decisions.

Opinion Writing After a decision has been reached, one of the members of the majority is assigned to write the **opinion**. This assignment is made by the chief justice or by the most senior justice in the majority if the chief justice is on the losing side. The assignment of the opinion can make a significant difference to the interpretation of a decision. Every opinion of the Supreme Court sets a major precedent for future cases throughout the judicial system. Lawyers and judges in the lower courts will examine the opinion carefully to ascertain the Supreme Court's intent. Differences in wording and emphasis can have important implications for future litigation. Thus, in assigning an opinion, the justices must give serious thought to the impression the case will make on lawyers and on the public and to the probability that one justice's opinion will be more widely accepted than another's.

opinion the written explanation of the Supreme Court's decision in a particular case

One of the more dramatic instances of this tactical consideration occurred in 1944, when Chief Justice Harlan F. Stone chose Justice Felix Frankfurter to write the opinion in the "white primary" case *Smith v. Allwright*.[41] The chief justice believed that this sensitive case, which overturned the southern practice of prohibiting black participation in nominating primaries, required the efforts of the most brilliant and scholarly jurist on the Court. But the day after Stone made the assignment, Justice Robert H. Jackson wrote a letter to Stone urging a change of assignment and arguing that Frankfurter, a foreign-born Jew from New England, would not win the South with his opinion, regardless of its brilliance. Stone accepted the advice and substituted Justice Stanley Reed, an American-born Protestant from Kentucky and a southern Democrat in good standing.

Once the majority opinion is drafted, it is circulated to the other justices. Some members of the majority may agree with both the outcome and the rationale but wish to emphasize or highlight a particular point. For that purpose, they draft a concurring opinion, called a *regular concurrence*. In other instances, one or more justices may agree with the majority decision but disagree with the rationale presented in the majority opinion. These justices may draft *special concurrences*, explaining their own rationale for the decision and how it differs from the majority's rationale.

Dissent Justices who disagree with the majority decision of the Court may choose to publicize the character of their disagreement in the form of a **dissenting opinion**. The dissenting opinion is generally assigned by the senior justice among the dissenters. Dissents can be used to express irritation with an outcome or to signal to defeated political forces in the nation that their position is supported by at least some members of the Court. Ironically, the most dependable way an individual justice can exercise a direct and clear influence on the Court is to write a dissent. Because there is no need to please a majority, dissenting opinions can be more eloquent and less guarded than majority opinions. The current Supreme Court often produces 5–4 decisions, with dissenters writing long and detailed opinions that, they hope, will help them persuade a swing justice to join their side on the next round of cases dealing with a similar topic. During the Court's 2006–07 term, Justice Ruth Bader Ginsburg was so unhappy about the majority's decisions in a number of cases that she began to read forceful dissents from the bench, a practice she has continued to underscore her disagreements with several recent decisions and point the way toward other possibilities.

Dissent plays a special role in the work and impact of the Court because it amounts to an appeal to lawyers all over the country to keep bringing similar cases. Therefore, an effective dissent influences the flow of cases through the Court and the arguments that lawyers will use in later cases. Even more important, dissent points out that although the Court speaks with a single opinion, it is the opinion only of the majority—and one day the majority might go the other way.

Often, the division between the majority and the dissenting justices in major cases reflects deep divisions in American society. Take the 2015 same-sex marriage case of *Obergefell v. Hodges* in which the majority opinion, written by Justice Anthony Kennedy, asserted that state same-sex marriage bans violated the Fourteenth Amendment by arbitrarily intruding upon personal choices, "central to individual dignity and autonomy," and thus denying such persons due process and equal protection of the laws.[42] The dissenters, Chief Justice Roberts and Justices Alito, Scalia, and Thomas, declared that the Fourteenth Amendment had never been intended or interpreted as providing a right to same-sex marriage and criticized the majority opinion as little more than an effort by jurists to write their own views into the Constitution. In its split decision, the Court mirrored a division in American society between those who see gay rights as a natural extension of civil rights and those offended, often for religious reasons, by open expressions of same-sex partnership. The dissenting justices hope to encourage further litigation in this realm, but generally speaking, once a right is granted it is seldom subject to revocation.

dissenting opinion a decision written by a justice in the minority in a particular case in which the justice wishes to express his or her reasoning in the case

Supreme Court justices can use a dissenting opinion to express their opposing viewpoint with the hope of influencing future cases on similar questions. Justice Ruth Bader Ginsburg is known for her forceful dissents such as in the 2007 case of Gonzales v. Carhart, *which upheld certain restrictions on abortion.*

Explaining Supreme Court Decisions

> **Consider the personal and political influences on judges and the courts**

The Supreme Court makes its mark on American politics and society through the decisions it hands down. But judicial decision making does not take place in a vacuum, of course. Like other actors in government, justices are influenced by institutional concerns, prior experience, and personal philosophy. In addition, the Court as a whole is affected by the overarching political system in which it plays a role. Over time, that role has shifted as a result of political developments both inside and outside the Court.

Influences on Supreme Court Decision Making

The Supreme Court explains its decisions in terms of law and precedent. But it is the Court itself that decides what the laws actually mean and what importance the precedent will actually have. Throughout its history, the Court has shaped and reshaped the law. In the late nineteenth and early twentieth centuries, for example, the Supreme Court held that the Constitution, law, and precedent permitted racial segregation in the United States. Beginning in the late 1950s, however, the Court found that the Constitution prohibited segregation on the basis of race and indicated that the use of racial categories in legislation was always suspect. By the 1970s and '80s, the Court once again held that the Constitution permitted the use of racial categories—when such categories were needed to help members of minority groups achieve full participation in American society. Since the 1990s, the Court has retreated from this position, too, indicating that governmental efforts to provide extra help to racial minorities could represent an unconstitutional infringement on the rights of the majority.

Institutional Interests The Supreme Court's justices are acutely aware of the Court's place in history, and they care about protecting the Court's power and reputation. This desire to protect the institutional integrity of the Court can sometimes influence judicial thinking. During the 1930s, for example, the Supreme Court became embroiled in a political struggle with President Franklin Roosevelt over his "New Deal" programs. During the 1935–36 term, the Court struck down several of the president's initiatives in a series of 5–4 votes. Furious, the president responded by proposing a Court-reform plan that would have increased the size of the Court to as many as 15 justices. Roosevelt hoped to pack the Court with his own appointees and, thus, win future cases over New Deal programs. Justice Owen Roberts, who had been one of the five justices voting against the president's initiatives, made a sudden reversal, voting in favor of an important New Deal policy he had been expected to oppose. The media dubbed Roberts's shift "The switch in time that saved nine."

Such institutional concerns are not isolated incidents, however. More recently, Chief Justice John Roberts seemed to have institutional concerns in mind when he surprised fellow conservatives by casting the deciding vote in favor of the constitutionality of the Affordable Care Act in 2012. The Court's conservative majority had come under increasing political fire for its positions on such matters as campaign finance and affirmative action. Roberts, according to one commentator, saw himself as "uniquely entrusted with the custodianship of the Court's legitimacy, reputation, and stature" and was determined to show that the Court stood above mere political ideology.[43] As we saw above, Roberts repeated his support of the Affordable Care Act in 2015 in the case of *King v. Burwell*.

Political and Governmental Experience When justices take their places on the Court, they bring to the bench decades of prior career experience as lawyers, public officials, judges on lower courts, and so forth. This prior experience helps to shape their understanding of government and politics and plays a role in their decision making. One area in which prior experience seems to be important is the question of congressional versus presidential power. None of today's justices has ever served in Congress or a state legislature. The last justice to have done so was retired Justice Sandra Day O'Connor, who had previously served as a member of the Arizona state legislature. The past experiences of the current justices have made them more familiar with the operations of the executive branch, so they tend to give the president and the agencies of the executive branch considerable deference, seldom reversing presidential or agency decisions. Congress, on the other hand, is alien territory to the justices. Though they show deference to Congress, they are more inclined to look askance at congressional than executive actions.

Activism and Restraint Judicial philosophy also plays a role in the decisions of all judges, including those on the Supreme Court. One element of judicial philosophy is the issue of activism versus restraint. Over the years, some justices have believed that courts should interpret the Constitution according to the stated intentions of its framers and defer to the views of Congress when interpreting federal statutes. Justice Felix Frankfurter, for example, advocated judicial deference to legislative bodies and avoidance of the "political thicket" in which the Court would entangle itself by deciding questions that were essentially political rather than legal in character. Advocates of **judicial restraint** are sometimes called "strict constructionists" because they look strictly to the words of the Constitution in interpreting its meaning.

The alternative to restraint is **judicial activism**. Activist judges such as Chief Justice Earl Warren believed that the Court should go beyond the words of the Constitution or a statute to consider the broader societal implications of its decisions. Activist judges sometimes strike out in new directions, promulgating new interpretations or inventing new legal and constitutional concepts when they believe these to be socially desirable. For example, Justice Harry Blackmun's opinion in *Roe v. Wade* was based on a constitutional right to privacy that is not found in the words of the Constitution but was, rather, from the Court's prior decision in *Griswold v. Connecticut*.[44] Blackmun and the other members of the majority in the *Roe* case argued that the right to privacy was implied by other constitutional provisions. In this instance of judicial activism, the Court knew the result it wanted to achieve and was not afraid to make the law conform to the desired outcome.

Activism and restraint are sometimes confused with liberalism and conservatism. For example, conservative politicians often castigate "liberal activist" judges and call for the appointment of conservative jurists who will refrain from reinterpreting the law. To be sure, some liberal jurists are activists and some conservatives have been advocates of restraint, but the relationships are by no means synonymous. Indeed, the Rehnquist Court, dominated by conservatives, was among the most activist courts in American history, particularly in such areas as federalism and election law. The Roberts Court is continuing along the same route. For example, in the 2014 case of *McCutcheon v. Federal Election Commission*, the Court struck down one of the major remaining elements of Congress's efforts to regulate campaign finance. The Court's five more conservative justices said that limits on how much individuals could contribute in any given election were a restraint on free speech.[45] This decision could be described as "activist" because it broadens the interpretation of "speech" and overturns congressional legislation that has

judicial restraint judicial philosophy whose adherents refuse to go beyond the clear words of the Constitution in interpreting the document's meaning

judicial activism judicial philosophy that posits that the Court should go beyond the words of the Constitution or a statute to consider the broader societal implications of its decisions

significant public support. As the examples of these conservative courts illustrate, a judge may be philosophically conservative and believe in strict construction of the Constitution but also be jurisprudentially activist and believe that the courts must play an active and energetic role in policy making, if necessary striking down acts of Congress to ensure that the intent of the framers is fulfilled.

Political Ideology and Partisanship The philosophy of activism versus restraint is sometimes a smokescreen for political ideology, and indeed, the liberal or conservative attitudes or partisan leanings of justices play an important role in their decisions.[46] In the past, liberal judges have often been activists, willing to use the law to achieve social and political change, whereas conservatives have been associated with judicial restraint. Interestingly, however, in recent years some conservative justices who have long called for restraint have actually become activists in seeking to undo some of the work of liberal jurists.

From the 1950s to the 1980s, the Supreme Court took an activist role in such areas as civil rights, civil liberties, abortion, voting rights, and police procedures. For example, the Supreme Court was more responsible than any other governmental institution for breaking down America's system of racial segregation. In the following decades, however, the conservative justices appointed by presidents Ronald Reagan, George H. W. Bush, and George W. Bush became the dominant bloc on the Court and, as we saw earlier, moved the Court to the right on a number of issues, including affirmative action and abortion.

The political struggles of recent years amply illustrate the importance of judicial ideology. Is abortion a fundamental right or a criminal activity? How much separation must there be between church and state? Does application of the Voting Rights Act to increase minority representation constitute a violation of the rights of whites? The answers to these and many other questions cannot be found in the words of the Constitution. They must be located, instead, in the hearts and minds of the judges who interpret that text.

Judicial philosophy, ideology, institutional interest, and prior experience all influence the thinking of justices. In the end, however, the Supreme Court is a court of law and must pay heed to statutes and legal precedent. A decision that cannot be justified by law and precedent cannot be issued. To ignore the law would be to undermine the rule of law and to destroy the constitutional structure in which the Supreme Court occupies such a prominent place.

Judicial Power and Politics

One of the most important institutional changes to occur in the United States during the past half-century has been the striking transformation of the role and power of the federal courts, and of the Supreme Court in particular. Understanding how this transformation came about is the key to understanding the contemporary role of the courts in America.

Traditional Limitations on the Federal Courts For much of American history, the power of the federal courts was subject to a number of limitations.[47] First, unlike other governmental institutions, courts cannot exercise power on their own initiative. Judges must wait until a case is brought to them before they can make authoritative decisions. Traditionally, moreover, courts were constrained by judicial rules of standing that limited access to the bench. Claimants who simply disagreed with governmental action or inaction could not obtain access to the courts, which was limited to individuals who could show that they were specifically affected by the government's behavior in some area. This limitation on access diminished the judiciary's capacity to forge links with important political and social forces.

Second, courts were traditionally limited in the character of the relief they could provide. In general, courts acted only to offer relief or assistance to individuals and not to broad social classes, again inhibiting the formation of alliances between the courts and important social forces.

Third, courts lacked enforcement powers of their own and were compelled to rely on executive or state agencies to ensure compliance with their edicts. If the executive or state agencies were unwilling to assist the courts, judicial enactments could go unheeded, as when President Andrew Jackson declined to enforce Chief Justice John Marshall's 1832 order to the state of Georgia to release two missionaries it had arrested on Cherokee lands. Marshall asserted that the state had no right to enter the lands without the Cherokees' assent.[48] Jackson is reputed to have said, "John Marshall has made his decision, now let him enforce it."

Fourth, federal judges are, of course, appointed by the president (with the consent of the Senate). As a result, the president and Congress can shape the composition of the federal courts and ultimately, perhaps, the character of judicial decisions. Finally, Congress has the power to change both the size and jurisdiction of the Supreme Court and other federal courts. In many areas, federal courts obtain their jurisdiction not from the Constitution but from congressional statutes. On a number of occasions, Congress has threatened to take matters out of the courts' hands when it was unhappy with the courts' policies.[49] For example, in 1996, Congress enacted several pieces of legislation designed to curb the jurisdiction of the federal courts. One of these laws was the Prison Litigation Reform Act, which limits the ability of federal judges to issue "consent decrees," under which the judges could take control of state prison systems. As to the size of the Court, on one memorable occasion that we mentioned earlier, presidential and congressional threats to expand the size of the Supreme Court—Franklin Delano Roosevelt's "Court packing" plan—encouraged the justices to drop their opposition to New Deal programs.

As a result of these limitations on judicial power, through much of their history the chief function of the federal courts was to provide judicial support for executive agencies and to legitimize acts of Congress by declaring them to be consistent with constitutional principles. Only on rare occasions have the federal courts dared to challenge Congress or the executive branch.[50]

Two Judicial Revolutions Since the Second World War, however, the role of the federal judiciary has been strengthened and expanded. There have been two judicial revolutions in the United States since then. The first and more visible of these was the substantive revolution in judicial policy. As we saw earlier in this chapter and in Chapters 4 and 5, in many policy areas, including school desegregation, legislative apportionment, and criminal procedure, and in obscenity, abortion, and voting rights, the Supreme Court was at the forefront of a series of sweeping changes in the role of the U.S. government and, ultimately, the character of American society.[51]

At the same time that the courts were introducing important policy innovations, they were also bringing about a second, less visible revolution. During the 1960s and '70s, the Supreme Court and other federal courts instituted a series of changes in judicial procedures that fundamentally expanded the power of the courts in the United States.

First, the federal courts liberalized the concept of standing to permit almost any group that seeks to challenge the actions of an administrative agency to bring its case before the federal bench. In 1971, for example, the Supreme Court ruled that public interest groups could use the National Environmental Policy Act to

for critical analysis

Are the federal courts "imperial," or are they subordinate to the elected branches of government? In what respect does the federal judiciary still play a "checks and balances" role?

challenge the actions of federal agencies by claiming that the agencies' activities might have adverse environmental consequences.[52]

Congress helped to make it even easier for groups dissatisfied with government policies to bring their cases to the courts by adopting Section 1983 of the U.S. Code, which permits the practice of "fee shifting"—that is, allowing citizens who successfully bring a suit against a public official for violating their constitutional rights to collect their attorneys' fees and costs from the government. Thus, Section 1983 encourages individuals and groups to bring their problems to the courts rather than to Congress or the executive branch. These changes have given the courts a far greater role in the administrative process than ever before. Many federal judges are concerned that federal legislation in areas such as health care reform will create new rights and entitlements that give rise to a deluge of court cases. "Any time you create a new right, you create a host of disputes and claims," warned Barbara Rothstein, chief judge of the federal district court in Seattle, Washington.[53]

Second, the federal courts broadened the scope of relief to permit themselves to act on behalf of broad categories or classes of persons in "class-action" cases, rather than just on behalf of individuals.[54] A **class-action suit** is a procedural device that permits large numbers of persons with common interests to join together under a representative party to bring or defend a lawsuit. One example of a class-action suit is the case of *In re Agent Orange Product Liability Litigation*, in which a federal judge in New York certified Vietnam War veterans as a class with standing to sue a manufacturer of herbicides for damages allegedly incurred from exposure to the defendant's product while in Vietnam.[55] The class potentially numbered in the tens of thousands.

Third, the federal courts began to employ so-called structural remedies, in effect retaining jurisdiction of cases until the court's mandate had actually been implemented to its satisfaction.[56] The best known of these instances was the effort

class-action suit a legal action by which a group or class of individuals with common interests can file a suit on behalf of everyone who shares that interest

Today, the Supreme Court is frequently at the center of major political issues. In a historic decision in 2015, the Court declared same-sex marriage a fundamental right protected by the due process and equal protection clauses of the Fourteenth Amendment to the Constitution.

of federal judge W. Arthur Garrity, Jr., to operate the Boston school system from his bench in order to ensure its desegregation. Between 1974 and 1985, Judge Garrity issued 14 decisions relating to different aspects of the Boston school desegregation plan that had been developed under his authority and put into effect under his supervision.[57] In 1985, as a result of a suit brought by the NAACP five years earlier, federal judge Leonard B. Sand imposed fines that would have forced the city of Yonkers, New York, into bankruptcy if it had refused to accept his plan to build public housing in white neighborhoods. Twenty-two years and $1.6 million in fines later, in 2007, the city finally gave in to the judge's ruling.

Through these three judicial mechanisms, the federal courts paved the way for an unprecedented expansion of national judicial power. In essence, liberalization of the rules of standing and expansion of the scope of judicial relief drew the federal courts into linkages with important social interests and classes, while the introduction of structural remedies enhanced the courts' ability to serve these constituencies. Thus, during the 1960s and '70s, the power of the federal courts expanded in the same way the power of the executive expanded during the 1930s: through links with constituencies, such as civil rights, consumer, environmental, and feminist groups, that staunchly defended the Supreme Court in its battles with Congress, the executive, and other interest groups.

for critical analysis

In what ways are courts, judges, and justices shielded from politics and political pressure? In what ways are they vulnerable to political pressure? Are the courts an appropriate place for politics?

The Federal Judiciary
and Your Future

In the original conception of the framers, the judiciary was to be the institution that would protect individual liberty from the government. As we saw in Chapter 2, the framers believed that in a democracy the great danger was what they termed "tyranny of the majority"—the possibility that a popular majority, "united or actuated by some common impulse or passion," would "trample on the rules of justice."[58] The framers hoped that the courts would protect liberty from the potential excesses of democracy. And for most of American history, the federal courts' most important decisions were those that protected the freedoms—to speak, worship, publish, vote, and attend school—of groups and individuals whose political views, religious beliefs, or racial or ethnic backgrounds made them unpopular.

Today, Americans of all political persuasions seem to view the courts as useful instruments through which to pursue their goals rather than protectors of individual rights. Conservatives want to ban abortion and help business maintain its profitability, whereas liberals want to promote school integration and help enhance the power of workers in the workplace. (The "**Who Participates?**" feature on the facing page looks at efforts to influence the Supreme Court through amicus briefs). These may all be noble goals, but they present a basic dilemma for students of American government. If the courts are simply one more set of policy-making institutions, who is left to protect the liberty of individuals?

Students should realize that the decisions made by the Supreme Court today will have important consequences for their lives and futures. The Court's campaign-finance decisions will have consequences for who will govern the nation you inherit. The Court's decisions on health care will influence the type of care you receive and its cost. The Court's decisions in the realm of immigration will affect who will and will not be able to call themselves Americans. The Supreme Court is not an abstract entity in far-off Washington. It reaches directly into your life.

Influencing the Supreme Court?

Average Amicus Briefs per Case

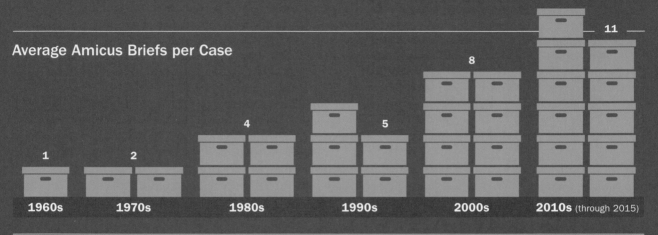

1 — 1960s
2 — 1970s
4 — 1980s
5 — 1990s
8 — 2000s
11 — 2010s (through 2015)

Amicus Briefs for Selected Landmark Cases

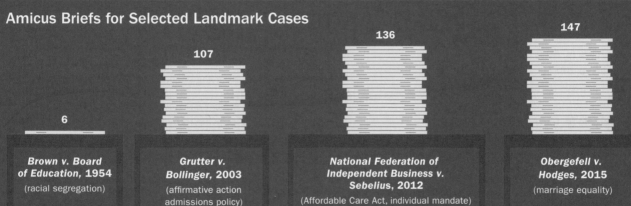

6
Brown v. Board of Education, 1954
(racial segregation)

107
Grutter v. Bollinger, 2003
(affirmative action admissions policy)

136
National Federation of Independent Business v. Sebelius, 2012
(Affordable Care Act, individual mandate)

147
Obergefell v. Hodges, 2015
(marriage equality)

SOURCES: Anthony J. Franze and R. Reeves Anderson, "Record Breaking Term for Amicus Curiae in Supreme Court Reflects New Norm," *The National Law Journal*, August 19, 2015, www.nationallawjournal.com/supremecourtbrief/id=1202735095655/Record-Breaking-Term-for-Amicus-Curiae-in-Supreme-Court-Reflects-New-Norm (accessed 12/8/15); Thomas G. Hansford and Kristen Johnson, "The Supply of Amicus Curiae Briefs in the Market for Information at the U.S. Supreme Court," *Justice System Journal*, 35 no. 4 (2014): 362–82; plus author's updates.

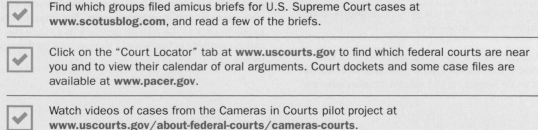

WHAT YOU CAN DO

Look Inside the Federal Courts

☑ Find which groups filed amicus briefs for U.S. Supreme Court cases at **www.scotusblog.com**, and read a few of the briefs.

☑ Click on the "Court Locator" tab at **www.uscourts.gov** to find which federal courts are near you and to view their calendar of oral arguments. Court dockets and some case files are available at **www.pacer.gov**.

☑ Watch videos of cases from the Cameras in Courts pilot project at **www.uscourts.gov/about-federal-courts/cameras-courts**.

studyguide

The Legal System

> **Identify the general types of cases and types of courts in our legal system (pp. 587–92)**

American court cases proceed under two broad categories of law: criminal law and civil law. There are court systems at both the federal and state levels in the United States. While state courts hear only cases involving questions of state law, the federal courts decide cases addressing federal laws, treaties with other nations, and the Constitution.

Key Terms

criminal law (p. 587)

plaintiff (p. 587)

defendant (p. 587)

civil law (p. 588)

precedent (p. 588)

stare decisis (p. 588)

trial court (p. 588)

court of appeals (p. 589)

supreme court (p. 589)

plea bargain (p. 589)

jurisdiction (p. 590)

original jurisdiction (p. 590)

due process of law (p. 591)

writ of habeas corpus (p. 591)

Practice Quiz

1. What is the name for the body of law that involves disputes between private entities such as individuals, groups, and corporations?
   a) civil law
   b) privacy law
   c) plea bargains
   d) household law
   e) common law

2. The doctrine that previous court decisions should apply as precedents in similar cases is known as
   a) habeas corpus.
   b) a writ of certiorari.
   c) stare decisis.
   d) rule of four.
   e) senatorial courtesy.

3. Where do most trials in America take place?
   a) state courts
   b) appellate courts
   c) federal courts
   d) federal circuit courts
   e) the Supreme Court

4. Which of the following is not included in the original jurisdiction of the Supreme Court?
   a) cases between the United States and one of the 50 states
   b) cases brought by one state against citizens of another state or against a foreign country
   c) cases involving challenges to the constitutionality of state laws
   d) cases between two or more states
   e) cases involving foreign ambassadors or other ministers

5. The term *writ of habeas corpus* refers to
   a) a short, unsigned decision by an appellate court, usually rejecting a petition to review the decision of a lower court.
   b) a criterion used by courts to screen cases that no longer require resolution.
   c) a decision of at least four of the nine Supreme Court justices to review a decision of a lower court.
   d) a court order that an individual in custody be brought into court and shown the cause for his or her detention.
   e) a brief filed by the solicitor general when the federal government is not a direct litigant in a Supreme Court case.

Federal Courts

> **Describe the different levels of federal courts and their functions (pp. 592–98)**

The federal courts hear a very small percentage of the cases decided in the United States each year. Presidents typically nominate judges for the federal judiciary who are prominent members of the legal profession and who share their partisan and ideological views. The importance of appointments to the federal judiciary has made the confirmation process in the Senate increasingly contentious in recent years.

Key Terms

chief justice (p. 594)

senatorial courtesy (p. 594)

Practice Quiz

6. The size of the Supreme Court is determined by
   a) the president.
   b) the chief justice.
   c) the Department of Justice.
   d) Congress.
   e) the Constitution.

7. The formal requirements for service as a federal judge include
   a) experience as a state-level judge.
   b) a minimum age of 30.
   c) a minimum of 10 years' legal experience.
   d) a neutral political background.
   e) There are no formal requirements for service as a federal judge.

The Power of the Supreme Court: Judicial Review

Explain how the Supreme Court exercises the power of judicial review (pp. 598–606)

The U.S. Supreme Court has the power to review the constitutionality of acts of Congress and the federal executive branch, as well as state actions. Although this power is not explicitly provided for in the Constitution, the Supreme Court asserted the power of judicial review in its 1803 *Marbury v. Madison* decision; and this power has generally been accepted since then.

Key Terms

judicial review (p. 598)

supremacy clause (p. 599)

common law (p. 604)

tort case (p. 604)

Practice Quiz

8. The Supreme Court's decision in *Marbury v. Madison* was important because
   a) it invalidated state laws prohibiting interracial marriage.
   b) it ruled that the recitation of prayers in public schools is unconstitutional under the establishment clause of the First Amendment.
   c) it established that arrested people have the right to remain silent, the right to be informed that anything they say can be held against them, and the right to counsel before and during police interrogation.
   d) it provided an expansive definition of *commerce* under the interstate commerce clause.
   e) it established the power of judicial review.

9. The U.S. Supreme Court's power to review state actions comes from
   a) tort law.
   b) *Hamdi v. Rumsfeld* and *Hamdan v. Rumsfeld*.
   c) the supremacy clause of the Constitution and the Judiciary Act of 1789.
   d) certiorari and *amicus curiae*.
   e) The Supreme Court does not have the power to review state actions.

The Supreme Court in Action

Describe the process the Supreme Court follows in the exercise of its power of judicial review (pp. 606–14)

Most cases reach the Supreme Court by a writ of certiorari. The Supreme Court is most likely to grant a writ of certiorari to cases that involve conflicting decisions by the federal circuit courts, cases that present important questions of civil rights or civil liberties, and cases in which the federal government is the appellant. Much of the Supreme Court's power in the American political system comes from its power to invalidate actions taken by the legislative and executive branches of government if these actions violate the Constitution.

Key Terms

standing (p. 606)

mootness (p. 606)

writ of certiorari (p. 607)

solicitor general (p. 608)

amicus curiae (p. 609)

briefs (p. 611)

oral argument (p. 611)

opinion (p. 613)

dissenting opinion (p. 614)

10. Which of the following play an important role in shaping the flow of cases heard by the Supreme Court?
    a) the attorney general and the secretary of state
    b) the solicitor general and federal law clerks
    c) the president and Congress
    d) state legislatures
    e) the federal district and circuit courts

11. Which government official is responsible for arguing the federal government's position in cases before the Supreme Court?
    a) the vice president
    b) the attorney general
    c) the chief justice
    d) the U.S. district attorney
    e) the solicitor general

12. Which of the following is a brief submitted to the Supreme Court by someone other than one of the parties in the case?
    a) amicus curiae
    b) habeas corpus
    c) solicitor general
    d) ex post brief
    e) de jure brief

Explaining Supreme Court Decisions

Consider the personal and political influences on judges and the courts (pp. 615–20)

Through most of American history, the federal courts avoided confrontations with the other branches of government and worked primarily to provide support for executive actions and congressional laws by declaring them to be consistent with constitutional principles. During the 1960s and '70s, the federal courts liberalized the concept of standing, broadened the scope of relief courts could provide, and began to employ structural remedies. As a result of these changes, the power of the federal court system expanded dramatically.

Key Terms

judicial restraint (p. 616)
judicial activism (p. 616)
class-action suit (p. 619)

Practice Quiz

13. If a justice favors going beyond the words of the Constitution to consider the broader societal implications of the Supreme Court's decisions, he or she would be considered an advocate of which judicial philosophy?
    a) judicial restraint
    b) judicial activism
    c) stare decisis
    d) judicial liberalism
    e) judicial conservatism

14. Which of the following would *not* be accurately characterized as a traditional limitation on the power of the federal courts?
    a) The president shapes the federal judiciary through the appointment process.
    b) Courts lack enforcement powers of their own and are compelled to rely on executive or state agencies to ensure compliance with their rulings.
    c) Congress has the power to change both the size and jurisdiction of the federal courts.
    d) Courts can act to offer relief or assistance to broad social classes but not to specific individuals.
    e) Courts cannot exercise power on their own initiative and must wait for cases to be brought to them.

For Further Reading

Baum, Lawrence. *The Supreme Court*. 11th ed. Washington, DC: CQ Press, 2012.

Block, Frederick. *Disrobed: An Inside Look at the Life and Work of a Federal Trial Judge*. New York: Westlaw, 2012.

Breyer, Stephen. *The Court and the World: American Law and the New Global Realities*. New York: Knopf, 2015.

Cross, Frank. *Decision Making in the U.S. Courts of Appeals*. Stanford, CA: Stanford University Press, 2007.

Dorsen, David. *Henry Friendly, Greatest Judge of His Era*. Cambridge, MA: Harvard University Press, 2012.

Greenhouse, Linda. *The U.S. Supreme Court: A Very Short Introduction*. New York: Oxford University Press, 2012.

Hall, Kermit L., James W. Ely, Jr., and Joel B. Grossman. *The Oxford Companion to the Supreme Court of the United States*. 2nd ed. New York: Oxford University Press, 2005.

Hirshman, Linda. *Sisters in Law: How Sandra Day O'Conner and Ruth Bader Ginsburg Went to the Supreme Court and Changed the World*. New York: Harper, 2015.

McClosky, Robert, and Sanford Levinson. *The American Supreme Court*. Chicago: University of Chicago Press, 2004.

Peppers, Todd, and Artemus Ward. *In Chambers: Stories of Supreme Court Law Clerks and Their Justices*. Charlottesville: University of Virginia Press, 2012.

Posner, Richard. *Reflections on Judging*. Cambridge, MA: Harvard University Press, 2013.

Raskin, Jamin B. *We the Students: Supreme Court Decisions for and about Students*. Washington, DC: Congressional Quarterly Press, 2003.

Rosenberg, Gerald. *The Hollow Hope: Can Courts Bring about Social Change?* Chicago: University of Chicago Press, 1991.

Rossum, Ralph. *Antonin Scalia's Jurisprudence*. Lawrence: University Press of Kansas, 2006.

Stevens, John Paul. *Five Chiefs: A Supreme Court Memoir*. Boston: Little, Brown, 2011.

Sunstein, Cass. *Are Judges Political?* Washington, DC: Brookings Institution Press, 2006.

Toobin, Jeffrey. *The Nine: Inside the Secret World of the Supreme Court*. New York: Anchor Books, 2008.

Toobin, Jeffrey. *The Oath: The Obama White House and the Supreme Court*. New York: Anchor Books, 2013.

Urofsky, Melvin. *Dissent and the Supreme Court: Its Role in the Court's History and the Nation's Constitutional Dialogue*. New York: Pantheon, 2015.

Whittington, Keith. *Political Foundations of Judicial Supremacy: The President, the Supreme Court, and Constitutional Leadership in U.S. History*. Princeton, NJ: Princeton University Press, 2008.

Recommended Websites

Concourts
www.concourts.net

The U.S. Supreme Court has the responsibility for examining and interpreting the Constitution. The Concourts website assumes a comparative perspective and looks at systems of constitutional review in over 150 countries.

FindLaw
www.findlaw.com

FindLaw's website provides answers to most legal questions and helps individuals find legal counsel.

Justice Talking
www.justicetalking.org

Justice Talking is a public radio program that examines current legal issues and important court cases.

Legal Information Institute
www.law.cornell.edu

The Legal Information Institute at Cornell University is a wonderful website for conducting legal research.

Office of the Solicitor General
www.usdoj.gov/osg

The solicitor general conducts litigation on behalf of the U.S. Supreme Court and has a tremendous amount of control over the cases that it hears. See what cases are currently being considered by this powerful official of the Justice Department.

U.S. Courts
www.uscourts.gov

The U.S. court system consists of trial, appellate, and supreme courts. The U.S. Courts website provides a look at the different types of courts in the federal judiciary.

U.S. Supreme Court
www.supremecourtus.gov

The website for the U.S. Supreme Court provides information on recent decisions. Take a moment to read some oral arguments, briefs, or court opinions.

U.S. Supreme Court Media
www.oyez.com

The website for U.S. Supreme Court Media has a great search engine for finding information on such landmark cases as *Marbury v. Madison*, *Miranda v. Arizona*, and *Roe v. Wade*.

The federal government spent nearly $1 trillion dollars in response to the economic crisis that began in 2008, but unemployment remained a problem in the years that followed. At this hiring fair in New York, long lines of job seekers awaited the opportunity to find work.

16

Government and the Economy

WHAT GOVERNMENT DOES AND WHY IT MATTERS Many Americans are still feeling the impact of the global economic crisis that began in 2008. As a result of the crisis, families lost homes and jobs. Students were financially pressed, with many unable to afford college tuition. Recent graduates were unable to find full-time employment. For many, the American dream of prosperity suddenly seemed beyond reach. Even after the economy recovered, many people continued to suffer from the impact of the "great recession."

Since the 1930s, Americans have counted on the federal government to ensure a prosperous economy. Political leaders have a wide variety of tools they can use to improve economic performance. Among the most widely used are public spending, tax cuts, and interest rate changes, all of which aim to stimulate economic activity or reduce inflation. Policy makers also employ regulations to influence competition among firms. Political leaders' choice of economic tools depends on their perceptions about what the most pressing economic problem is, beliefs about which tools are most likely to be effective, and considerations about who is likely to benefit from a particular economic policy and who is likely to be hurt. Although economic policy is a highly technical field, the choice of policy tools is fundamentally a political one.

In 2008, with the financial sector on the brink of collapse, the federal government launched a series of major interventions designed to prop up failing banks and insurance companies. It was not just financial institutions that faced collapse. As the economic instability spread, Washington bailed out other distressed industries, ending up as a major stakeholder in both the financial sector and the auto industry. The federal government also passed a sweeping package in 2009 to help stimulate the economy, save jobs, and make longer-term investments to help build future prosperity. As the economic crisis began to ebb, however, Congress struggled to implement enduring reforms to the financial regulatory system. Banks argued that the crisis had been resolved and cautioned that too much regulation would impede the economic recovery. On the other hand, some government officials warned that not enough was being done to rein in use of the risky financial instruments that had caused the crisis in the first place. Consumer advocates pressed for more aggressive government regulation of mortgage lenders and credit card issuers to protect borrowers.

These developments raise fundamental questions about the role of the government in the economy. On one side of the spectrum are those who believe that the government should have a minimal role in the economy. Government's main purpose should be to set and enforce rules that ensure economic stability. In this perspective, the government is sometimes called the "night watchman state."[1] At the other end of the spectrum are those who want to see the state actively engaged in shaping economic outcomes. Not only should the government promote economic growth, according to this perspective, but it should also step in to protect individuals from economic harm. The government's role in the economy should be active, to shape the kind of society we want.

American economic policy has historically reflected the belief that individual liberty is the key to a thriving economy. In this view, the government's role is to set the basic rules that govern economic transactions and then stand back and let individuals engage in the market. However, periodically Americans have demanded restrictions on market freedoms to protect the public. An array of laws governing competition and protecting consumers and the environment is the consequence of these democratic demands. Although Americans are often uneasy with the idea of government intervention into the market, they show little support for unraveling existing regulations.

chaptergoals

- Identify the broad reasons government gets involved in the economy (pp. 629–36)
- Explore why economic policy is often controversial (pp. 636–45)
- Describe how the government uses monetary, fiscal, and regulatory policies to influence the economy (pp. 645–59)
- Explain why the government tries to balance economic prosperity with policies that protect the environment (pp. 659–63)

● The Goals of Economic Policy

The job of this and the next chapter is to step beyond the politics and the institutions to look at the goals of government: the public policies. **Public policy** can be defined simply as an officially expressed purpose or goal backed by a sanction (a reward or a punishment). Public policy can be embodied in a law, a rule, a regulation, or an order. This chapter will focus on policies aimed at the economy.

At the most basic level, government makes it possible for the economy to function efficiently by setting the rules for economic exchange and punishing those who violate those rules. Among the most important rules for the economy are those that define property rights, contracts, and standards for goods. This kind of government rule making allows markets to expand by making it easier for people who do not know each other to engage in economic transactions: they no longer have to rely only on personal trust to do business. Likewise, government helps markets expand by creating money and standing behind its value. Money allows diverse goods to be traded and greatly simplifies economic transactions. Without government involvement in providing and standardizing a national currency, it would be very difficult to purchase such basic items as groceries: imagine a world in which different stores used different currencies or in which you needed to trade something you made yourself for your groceries. This would be a major impediment to economic exchange!

Government involvement in the economy now extends far beyond these basic market-creating functions. As we shall see in this section, government has become involved in many aspects of the economy in order to promote the public well-being. Of course, there is often vigorous disagreement about the extent to which government should intervene in the economy. Further, beliefs about which forms of government intervention in the economy are most necessary and most effective have changed over time. Although the policies have changed, government intervention in the economy has, for nearly a century, sought to achieve four fundamental goals: (1) to promote economic stability, (2) to stimulate economic growth, (3) to promote business development, and (4) to protect employees and consumers.

public policy a law, rule, statute, or edict that expresses the government's goals and provides for rewards and punishments to promote those goals' attainment

At the most basic level, government's role in the economy is to make it easier for markets to function. The government sets rules for doing business, creates money, and backs its value— functions that influence even the simplest economic transactions, such as buying groceries at a typical farmer's market.

Promoting Stable Markets

One of the central reasons for government involvement in the economy is to protect the welfare and property of individuals and businesses. Maintaining law and order is one of the most important ways government can protect welfare and property. The federal government has also enacted laws designed to protect individuals and businesses in economic transactions. Federal racketeering laws, for example, aim to end criminal efforts to control businesses through such illegal means as extortion and kickbacks.

Another reason that Congress began to adopt national business regulatory policies was that companies felt burdened by the inconsistent regulations across the various states. Companies often preferred a single, national regulatory authority, no matter how

The interstate highway system is an important public good provided by the government to support the economy. While almost everyone benefits from the highway system, no single participant could afford to provide it alone.

public goods goods or services that are provided by the government because they either are not supplied by the market or are not supplied in sufficient quantities

gross domestic product (GDP) the total value of goods and services produced within a country

burdensome, because it would ensure consistency throughout the United States; the companies could thereby treat the nation as a single market.[2]

The government also promotes economic stability by providing **public goods**. This term refers to facilities the state provides because no single participant can afford to provide those facilities. The provision of public goods may entail supplying the physical marketplace itself—such as the commons in New England towns or an interstate highway system to stimulate the trucking industry. The provision of public goods is essential to market operation, and the manner in which the government provides these goods will affect the market's character.

Promoting Economic Prosperity

In addition to setting the basic conditions that allow markets to function, governments may actively intervene in the economy to promote economic growth. Although the idea that government should stimulate economic growth can be traced back to Alexander Hamilton's views about promoting industry, it was not until the twentieth century that the federal government assumed such a role.

Measuring Economic Growth Since the 1930s the federal government has carefully tracked national economic growth by measuring it in several different ways. The two most important measures are the gross national product, which is the market value of the goods and services produced in the economy, and the **gross domestic product (GDP)**, the same measure but excluding income from foreign investments. In the late 1990s the American economy grew at a rate of over 4 percent a year, considered high by modern standards (see Figure 16.1). Growth was slower during the first decade of the 2000s, averaging 1.9 percent annually. This was largely the result of two recessions: one early after the turn of the century and one that began in 2008. In the middle part of the decade (2003–7), the economy grew at a strong 2.8 percent annually.[3] As Figure 16.1 shows, the recession that began in 2008 led to negative economic growth in 2008 and 2009. Although the economy began to grow again after 2010, it remained below the high levels of growth experienced in the 1990s.

The engine of American economic growth has shifted over the centuries. In the 1800s the nation's rich endowment of natural resources was especially important in propelling growth. Manufacturing industries became the driving force of economic growth during the late nineteenth century as mass production made it possible to manufacture goods at a pace that was once unimaginable. In more recent times, the high-technology boom fostered unanticipated and vigorous economic growth that made the United States the envy of the world. Despite these very different economic engines, the basic prerequisites of growth were similar in each case: strong investment, technological innovation, and a productive workforce. Throughout the nation's history, the federal government has adopted policies to promote each of these conditions needed to sustain economic growth.

The most fundamental way that government affects investment is by promoting business as well as investor and consumer confidence. When businesses fear political instability, unpredictable government action, or widespread disregard of the law, they are unlikely to invest. When consumers are insecure about the future, they are unlikely to spend.

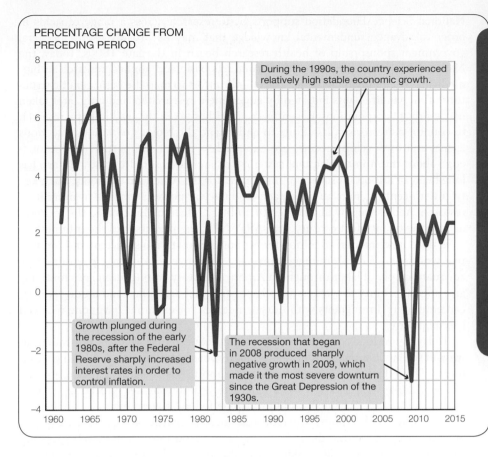

PERCENTAGE CHANGE FROM
PRECEDING PERIOD

During the 1990s, the country experienced relatively high stable economic growth.

Growth plunged during the recession of the early 1980s, after the Federal Reserve sharply increased interest rates in order to control inflation.

The recession that began in 2008 produced sharply negative growth in 2009, which made it the most severe downturn since the Great Depression of the 1930s.

FIGURE 16.1

Changes in Real Gross Domestic Product, 1960–2015

The rates of growth in gross domestic product have varied over time. They were particularly volatile during the 1980s as the economy first plunged into recession and then rapidly recovered with high rates of growth. What was the pattern of growth during the last five presidential election years?

SOURCE: Bureau of Economic Analysis, "Table 1.1.1. Percent Change from Preceding Period in Real Gross Domestic Product [Percent] Seasonally Adjusted at Annual Rates," June 28, 2016, bea.gov /national/pdf/SNTables.pdf (accessed 7/9/16).

The federal government also promotes investment through its regulation of financial markets. The most important federal agency in this regard is the Securities and Exchange Commission (SEC), created after the stock market crash of 1929. The SEC requires companies to disclose information about the stocks and bonds they are selling, inform buyers of the investment risks, and protect investors against fraud. In this way the SEC helps maintain investor confidence and a strong supply of capital for American business. The SEC came in for harsh criticism during the financial crisis in 2008. Analysts pointed to weak SEC oversight and regulation as an important factor in the near collapse of the financial sector. Major financial reforms enacted in 2010 substantially beefed up the SEC's enforcement capabilities and required the agency to take the lead in implementing many of the key regulations.[4]

Public investment is another important source of growth in the American economy. In the 1930s and again in the late 1970s the federal government promoted public investment as a means to spark economic growth. Some kinds of public investment promote growth as a by-product of other, more central objectives. One of the most important of these is spending on the nation's defense. Many analysts credited the rise in military spending associated with the war in Iraq with helping to spur economic growth in 2003.

The second important condition for economic growth is innovation. The federal government has sought to support innovation in a variety of ways. One of the most important is through the National Science Foundation. Created in 1950, the

National Science Foundation supports basic research across a range of fields in order to advance fundamental knowledge that may be broadly useful.[5] Federal government sponsorship of health research began in the late 1800s. Today, the National Institutes of Health (NIH) conducts basic and applied research in biomedicine. The Human Genome Project—the effort to map the basic genetic structure of human life—was initiated by government researchers and only later taken up by private corporations. Recently, the NIH has taken the lead in basic research to counter bioterrorism. Its efforts to understand the biology of various infectious agents and to develop vaccines are expected to produce important new knowledge about the human immune system. Research sponsored by the military has long been an important source of innovation for the American economy. Such key twentieth-century innovations as radar and nuclear power stemmed from military research. And as we saw in Chapter 14, military research also created the technology for the twenty-first century with ARPANET, the precursor to the Internet.

A third fundamental condition for economic growth is a sufficient and productive workforce. Federal immigration policy has played a key role in ensuring an adequate supply of labor throughout American history. Immigration laws routinely give special priority to workers who have skills that are in demand among American employers. Immigrants with nursing degrees, for example, have long received special priority.

Today, a productive workforce is a highly educated workforce. Education, as we will see in Chapter 17, is primarily the responsibility of state and local governments. The federal government, however, supports the development of a productive workforce with a variety of programs to promote higher education, such as educational grants, tax breaks, and loans. The federal government also sponsors a limited array of job-training programs that focus primarily on low-skilled workers. Some analysts argue that the federal government must do much more to support the development of a highly skilled workforce if the United States is to sustain economic growth in the future.

for critical analysis

Why does the unemployment rate matter for the economic health of the country? What policies has the government pursued in the past to help promote employment? What other policies could the government implement?

Full Employment Before the 1930s, neither the federal government nor the state governments sought to promote full employment. Unemployment was widely viewed as an unfortunate occurrence that government could do little to alter. The New Deal response to the prolonged and massive unemployment of the Great Depression changed that view. The federal government put millions of people back to work on public projects sponsored by such programs as the Works Progress Administration. The bridges, parks, and buildings they constructed can still be seen across the United States today. The federal government viewed these programs as temporary measures, however. As the buildup for World War II boosted the economy and unemployment melted away, the employment programs were dismantled.

The New Deal and government wartime spending, however, showed that government could help ensure full employment. Public expectations changed as well: after the war, Americans looked to the federal government to reduce unemployment. Moreover, economic theory now supported their expectations. John Maynard Keynes's theories that government could boost employment by stimulating demand had become very influential.

Federal policy placed the most emphasis on achieving full employment during the 1960s. Keynesian economists—who believe that putting money in the hands of consumers creates a strong economy—in the Council of Economic Advisers persuaded President Kennedy to enact the first tax cut designed to stimulate the economy and promote full employment.[6] The policy was widely seen as a success, and unemployment declined to a low of 3.4 percent in 1968. Favorable economic conditions in the 1990s reduced unemployment to record lows once again.

The worldwide economic recession of 2008 led to the loss of over 8 million American jobs. The Obama administration and Congress responded by passing a sweeping stimulus package called the American Recovery and Reinvestment Act in 2009, to help encourage economic growth, save existing jobs, and make longer-term investments that would encourage job creation, such as in weatherization projects and clean-technology construction. Despite these actions, it was not until 2016 that the unemployment rates dipped below 5 percent.

One reason unemployment rose after 2008 was that numerous companies went out of business. Chrysler laid off thousands of employees before filing for bankruptcy in 2009, when the U.S. government paid $4 billion to bail the company out.

Low Inflation During the 1970s and early 1980s, **inflation**, a consistent increase in the general level of prices, was one of America's most vexing problems. Rising prices harm consumers, especially those on a fixed income such as the elderly. Inflation also undermines the entire economy because it creates uncertainty about future prices, making investors cautious. Inflation was finally reduced from its historic highs of nearly 20 percent down toward 2 and 3 percent a year by the mid-1980s. Since that time, inflation has remained low. Even so, economic policy makers watch prices closely for any sign of inflation.

inflation a consistent increase in the general level of prices

Promoting Business Development

During the nineteenth century, the national government promoted the development of important markets that eventually contributed significantly to the U.S. GDP. National roads and canals were built to tie states and regions together. National tariff policies promoted domestic markets by restricting imported goods; a tax on an import raised its price and weakened its ability to compete with similar domestic products. The national government also heavily subsidized the railroad system. Until the 1840s, railroads were thought to be of limited commercial value. But between 1850 and 1872, Congress granted more than 100 million acres of public-domain land to railroad interests, and state and local governments pitched in an estimated $280 million in cash and credit. Before the end of the century, 35,000 miles of track existed, almost half the world's total at the time.

Railroads were not the only clients of federal support for the private markets. Many sectors of agriculture began receiving federal subsidies during the nineteenth century. Agriculture remains highly subsidized to this day. In 2012, 38 percent of farms in the United States received subsidies; by 2015 the total subsidy was estimated at more than $20 billion.[7] One of the many criticisms of the farm subsidy program is that it disproportionately supports large-scale farmers rather than small family farmers. The list of farm subsidy recipients includes many large corporations.

The national government also promotes business development indirectly through **categorical grants** (see Chapter 3), by which the federal government offers grants to states on condition that the state (or local) government undertake a particular activity. Thus, in order to use motor transportation to improve national markets, a 900,000-mile national highway system was built during the 1930s, based on a formula whereby the national government would pay 50 percent of the cost if the state provided the other 50 percent. Over 20 years, beginning in the late 1950s, the federal government constructed an additional 45,000 miles of interstate

categorical grants congressional grants given to states and localities on the condition that expenditures be limited to a problem or group specified by the law

Since the early nineteenth century, the government has been an important promoter of business development in the United States. Beginning around 1850, federal, state, and local governments gave railroad companies the land on which to lay tracks and financial aid to construct the railroads. Railroads received additional land from the government, which they could sell at low prices to attract settlers to build along their lines.

highways. In this program, the national government agreed to pay 90 percent of the construction costs on the condition that each state provide 10 percent of the costs of any portion of a highway built within its boundaries.[8] The tremendous growth of highways was a major boon to the automobile and trucking industries.

The federal government supports specific business sectors with direct subsidies, loans, and tax breaks. In 1953 the Small Business Administration was created to offer loans, loan guarantees, and disaster assistance to small businesses. Recognizing that such businesses often find it harder to obtain financing and to recover from unexpected events such as fires, the federal government has provided assistance where the market would not. Today, the Small Business Administration provides more than $45 billion in such assistance to small businesses.[9]

Among the many contemporary examples of policies promoting private industry, Sematech may be the most instructive. Sematech is a nonprofit research and development consortium of major U.S. computer microchip manufacturers, set up in 1987 to work with government and academic institutions to reestablish U.S. leadership in semiconductor manufacturing. (The United States appeared to be in danger of losing out to the Japanese in this area during the 1980s.) The results of its research were distributed among the consortium members.[10] For nine years, industry and government together spent $1.7 billion to make the American microchip industry the leader in the world. The government contributed about half of the total expenditures. In 1997 federal funding was phased out. Industry leaders, convinced they no longer needed federal support, themselves initiated the break with government. At a critical moment, the federal government had stepped in to save the chip industry; it stepped out once that goal had been achieved.

Since September 11, 2001, the federal government has taken on a major role in promoting technological innovation related to national security. Even before the September 11 terrorist attacks, the CIA had set up its own venture capital firm, In-Q-Tel (the Q stands for a character in the James Bond movies), to invest in high-tech start-ups whose work could enhance intelligence efforts. More recently, the federal government has aimed to support the alternative energy industry. The Energy Policy Act of 2005 greatly increased the number and cost of tax credits and loan programs for renewable and efficient energy technologies. As the recession hit, Washington stepped up its efforts to support the alternative energy industry, seeing it as a way to expand economic growth in an emerging sector. The Emergency Economic Stabilization Act of 2008 and the American Recovery and Reinvestment Act of 2009 expanded subsidies and created a new program allowing companies to receive a one-time cash grant in lieu of tax credits. Between 2015 and 2019, the federal government is projected to spend $46.5 billion in tax-related support for the production of renewable energy, as well as an additional $3.1 billion to support energy efficiency.[11]

Protecting Employees and Consumers

Stable relations between business and labor are important elements of a productive economy. During the latter half of the nineteenth century, strikes over low wages or working conditions became a standard feature of American economic life. In fact, the United States has one of the most violent histories of labor relations in the world. Yet for most of American history, the federal government did little to regulate relations between business and labor. Local governments and courts often weighed in on the side of business by prohibiting strikes and arresting strikers.

As the economic depression enveloped the United States in the 1930s, plummeting wages and massive strikes for union recognition prompted Congress to pass the 1935 National Labor Relations Act, which set up a new framework for industrial relations. The new law created a permanent agency, the National Labor Relations Board, charged with overseeing union elections and collective bargaining between labor and industry. The federal government weighed in further on the side of organized labor in 1938, when it passed the Fair Labor Standards Act, which created the minimum wage. Because it is not indexed to inflation, the value of the minimum wage declines if it is not raised periodically. Since 1938 conflicts over increasing the minimum wage have been a regular feature of American politics. The federal minimum wage reached its highest value in 1968. It was last raised in 2009 but since then has lost over 8 percent of its value to inflation.[12]

During the 1950s and '60s, the federal government played an active role in industrial relations. The Department of Labor and occasionally even the president directly intervened in labor–management disputes to ensure peaceful industrial relations. Although Democrats were generally seen as more supportive of labor, both parties sought to achieve a balance between business and labor that would promote a strong, stable economy.

President Reagan made a decisive break with this tradition of compromise in 1981, when he fired striking air traffic controllers (who were federal employees) and hired permanent replacements to take their jobs, effectively ceding more power to employers. Politicians are now much less likely to intervene in labor relations.

Economic policies also protect consumers. The idea that the federal government should protect consumers emerged in the first decade of the 1900s. Upton Sinclair's graphic exposé of the meatpacking industry, *The Jungle* (1906), galvanized public concern about unsanitary food processing. These concerns prompted the U.S. Department of Agriculture to inspect packing plants and the meat they produced, stamping approved meats with the now-familiar "USDA" certification. Similar concern about the safety of food, drugs, and cosmetics led to the creation of the Food and Drug Administration in 1927.

The government promotes technological innovation and business growth in specific sectors. For example, businesses that provide renewable energy sources, such as wind power, have benefited from significant federal tax credits and loans in recent years.

The National Highways Traffic Safety Administration (NHTSA) is one government agency that protects consumers, in part by ensuring that vehicles are safe. However, the NHTSA failed to act on complaints about a serious flaw in some GM cars that led to numerous accidents before the cars were recalled in 2014.

for critical analysis

What does the American government do to ensure that the products Americans buy are safe? What challenges does it face in making certain that products are safe?

The movement for consumer protection took off again in the 1960s. The consumer advocate Ralph Nader's 1965 book *Unsafe at Any Speed* helped spark new demands for federal action. Nader's book showed that design flaws in the Corvair, a popular car model, had caused deaths that could have been prevented. Nader's book not only led to the demise of the Corvair but also mobilized calls for more federal action to protect consumers. The first response was the 1966 National Traffic and Motor Vehicle Safety Act, which gave the Department of Transportation responsibility for ensuring vehicle safety. Federal responsibility for consumer safety expanded in 1972, when Congress created the Consumer Product Safety Commission, an independent agency that informs consumers about hazards associated with products and works with industry to set product standards. In cases where safety concerns are severe, the commission will see that such products are recalled. Through the Consumer Product Safety Commission, the Department of Transportation, and the Food and Drug Administration, the federal government continues to play an active role in protecting the public from unsafe products.

In recent years, federal agencies have been very active in ensuring auto safety. Especially serious were charges that General Motors had hidden a problem related to its ignition system, which had caused 13 deaths. Some charged that the flaw may have caused even more fatalities. In response, General Motors recalled 2.6 million cars, but its failure to act earlier triggered a number of government investigations. The Justice Department launched an investigation about whether the company intentionally misled consumers. In addition, the new head of General Motors was called to testify before Senate and House panels about allegations that the company had failed to act even though it knew about the problems with the ignition system. Congressional investigators also probed why a federal agency, the National Highway Traffic Safety Administration, had failed to act when it first learned of the defects.[13] The charges reveal the challenges involved in ensuring consumer safety when the government agencies charged with protecting the public do not take swift action.

The Politics of Economic Policy Making

Explore why economic policy is often controversial

All politicians want a healthy economy, but they often differ in their views about how to attain it. Addressing economic challenges and maintaining a strong economy are extremely important to political leaders. As presidents from Herbert Hoover (who presided over the beginning of the Great Depression of the 1930s) to Jimmy Carter (who faced double-digit inflation) discovered, voters will punish politicians for poor economic performance. In the 50 years that followed the Great Depression and the federal government's first big steps into the economy, politicians from both parties agreed that the government played an important role in ensuring a strong economy, though they often disagreed about what priorities should guide economic policy. Democrats generally expressed more concern about unemployment than did Republicans, who focused more on reducing budget deficits. In the 1980s, however, the differences between the parties on economic policy became much more fundamental. While Democrats and Republicans alike embraced a smaller role for the government in the economy, growing numbers of Republicans began to reject the idea that government should intervene in the economy at all. Instead, they argued that a free market was the best way to ensure economic prosperity. Democrats continued to believe that economic prosperity required government action. Once in power, however, parties acted very differently. Budget deficits have soared under Republican presidents since the 1980s, and Democrats have often taken limited action for fear of upsetting the markets.

How Much Should the Government Intervene in the Economy?

Until 1929 most Americans believed that government had little to do with actively managing the economy. The world was guided by the theory—called laissez-faire economics—that the economy, if left to its own devices, would produce full employment and maximum production. This traditional view of the relationship between government and the economy crumbled in 1929 before the stark reality of the Great Depression of 1929–39. Some misfortune befell nearly everyone. Around 20 percent of the workforce became unemployed, and few of these individuals had any monetary resources or the old family farm to fall back on. Banks failed, wiping out the savings of millions who had been prudent enough or fortunate enough to have any. Thousands of businesses closed, throwing middle-class Americans onto the bread lines alongside unemployed laborers and dispossessed farmers. The Great Depression proved to Americans that the economic system was not, in fact, perfectly self-regulating, as had been generally believed.

Demands grew for the federal government to act. In Congress, some Democrats proposed that the federal government finance public works to aid the economy and put people back to work. Other members introduced legislation to provide federal grants to the states to assist their relief efforts.

When President Franklin Delano Roosevelt took office in 1933, he energetically threw the federal government into the business of fighting the Depression. He proposed a variety of temporary measures to provide federal relief and work programs. Most of the programs he proposed were to be financed by the federal government but administered by the states. In addition to these temporary measures, Roosevelt presided over the creation of several important federal programs designed to provide future economic security for Americans. Since that time, the public has held the government, and the president in particular, responsible for ensuring a healthy economy.

One of the main ways that the federal government sought to keep the economy healthy was through decisions about taxing and spending in accordance with the ideas of the British economist John Maynard Keynes. **Keynesians** argue that by pumping money into the economy, particularly by running deficits during periods of recession, government can stimulate demand and create a cycle of increased production and jobs that will pull the economy out of recession. Governments can do this by increasing public spending through such measures as public works or public employment or by temporary tax cuts. Tax cuts will allow workers to keep more of their earnings; their increased spending power will boost consumption and increase demand.[14]

Keynesians followers of the economic theories of John Maynard Keynes, who argued that the government can stimulate the economy by increasing public spending or by cutting taxes

After World War II, Republicans and Democrats broadly agreed that Keynesian ideas could best guide economic policy. By the 1960s Keynesians believed that economic policy did not need to provoke political controversy because they could ensure ongoing prosperity by "fine-tuning" the economy. Democrats and Republicans often disagreed about how much the government should do to alleviate unemployment or inflation, but they shared a pragmatic view that government intervention could solve economic problems. President Richard Nixon, a Republican, reflected the strong consensus behind Keynesian ideas when he remarked in 1971, "Now I am a Keynesian." The question about whether and how government should intervene in the economy appeared settled.

Partisan Divisions over the Government Role in the Economy By the 1980s the broad consensus about the role of the government in the economy had evaporated. Growing numbers of Republicans began to reject the idea that government could help ensure economic prosperity. Instead, they argued that freeing markets from government intervention would produce the best economic results. As Ronald Reagan put it in his first inaugural address, "Government is not the solution to our problem, government is the problem."[15]

Thus, the ideas of **laissez-faire capitalism** began to make a comeback in American politics. These arguments were first elaborated in the late 1700s by the great Scottish economist Adam Smith. Smith believed that most government involvement in the economy (such as the government-authorized monopolies that dominated trade in his day) suppressed economic growth. Instead, he argued that competition among free enterprises would unleash economic energy, fostering growth and innovation. In his view, the self-seeking behavior of individuals, when subject to the discipline of market competition, would create products that consumers wanted at the best possible price. Smith praised "the invisible hand" of the market, by which he meant that millions of individual economic transactions together create a greater good—far better than the government could create. Smith believed that the government role should be restricted to national defense, establishing law and order (including the protection of private property), and providing basic public goods (such as roads) that facilitate commerce.

Although only a few politicians would entirely remove government from the economy, Republicans draw on the ideas of laissez-faire economics as they argue for significant reductions in nonmilitary spending. Many Democrats, on the other hand, stress the important role of government in promoting a strong economy. This fundamental disagreement between the parties over the appropriate role of government underlies the fierce contemporary political debates over the government role in taxes, spending, and economic regulation.

Taxes Today some of the most intense conflicts between Democrats and Republicans concern taxes. As Republicans embraced the idea that reducing the role of government in the economy would promote investment and spur economic growth, they made tax cuts their highest priority. Rejecting Keynesian ideas, they adopted the idea of **supply-side economics**. This approach maintains that lower tax rates create incentives for more productive and efficient use of resources. When individuals know they can keep more of their earnings, they are more likely to be productive workers and creative investors. In this perspective, low taxes are not

laissez-faire capitalism an economic system in which the means of production and distribution are privately owned and operated for profit with minimal or no government interference

supply-side economics an economic theory that posits that reducing the marginal rate of taxation will create a productive economy by promoting levels of work and investment that would otherwise be discouraged by higher taxes

just a temporary measure to stimulate the economy; taxes should remain low at all times to ensure a growing economy.

Because no one really likes to pay taxes, Republican support for tax cuts creates a political dilemma for Democrats. How can they defend taxes? Polls show that most of the time—although not always—a majority of Americans think that their taxes are too high.[16] Aware of the political damage that might come from opposing tax cuts, many Democratic members of Congress have supported tax cuts. But because most Democrats favor higher levels of public spending than do Republicans, they ultimately need taxes to fund government programs. To resolve this political problem, Democrats have sought to increase taxes on the wealthy. One reliable finding in public opinion polls is that the majority of Americans agree that upper-income people are not paying their fair share of taxes.[17] Raising taxes on the wealthy involves boosting taxes on investment income, which accounts for a much greater share of the income for the wealthy. By making the rich the target for tax increases and highlighting the special tax loopholes they enjoy, Democrats hope to turn the politics of taxes to their advantage.

Spending and Deficits Government spending is another area where the two parties have locked horns. Contending that the federal government has become too big, Republicans argue for reduced government spending. In their view, big government is not only wasteful but also a drag on the economy. Moreover, Republicans argue, excessive spending creates deficits, which can harm the economy. It is not hard to convince Americans that government spending is wasteful or that government is too big or that deficits are bad. When asked, a majority of Americans regularly say they would prefer a smaller government with fewer services.[18]

Yet, polls reveal little support for cutting specific government programs.[19] In fact, the public shows the strongest support for the most expensive government programs. Social Security, which provides pensions to the elderly, and Medicare, which supplies health insurance for the elderly, are both politically popular. Only the most ardent spending foes among Republicans have argued for cutting these programs. Indeed, in 2003 Republicans agreed to a major expansion in Medicare spending by adding a prescription drug benefit to the program. The popularity of these programs reflects the fact that government provides real benefits to real people. President Obama articulated the position that the government should help to provide what individuals cannot provide for themselves. Democrats therefore support government spending on education, infrastructure, health care, and other public programs. Taking away these programs will deny economic opportunities to Americans, they believe, and in so doing hurt the national economy.

Because neither party wishes to cut big, expensive, popular programs and because tax increases have been so difficult to enact, budget deficits have grown periodically over the past three decades. Democratic critics and most economists point to rising deficits as proof that supply-side economics does not work; they argue that the economy would be better off without tax cuts. Some go further, arguing that Republicans deliberately

"Supply-siders" argue that reducing tax rates will spur economic growth as people are able to spend and invest more of their money. In the 1980s, President Ronald Reagan—shown here holding an oversize tax form—sought to simplify the tax laws and reduce taxes.

reduced taxes in order to win support for spending cuts. This strategy, called "starving the beast," suggests that spending cuts would become more popular in the face of rising deficits.[20]

for critical analysis

How does government spending hurt the economy? How does government spending help the economy?

Because it is politically difficult to raise taxes or reduce big-spending programs, most cuts have fallen on smaller programs, often those administered by the states. This is what happened in 2013 after a Republican and Democratic standoff over the deficit led to a set of cuts applied to smaller programs. Unusually, in 2013 these spending reductions also applied to military spending. The 2015 budget deal, a complex compromise between Republicans and Democrats, avoided cutting small programs by raising spending and making targeted cuts in entitlements. Even so, spending for small programs has fallen quite significantly since 2010. Nondefense discretionary spending for 2016, for example, was 12 percent below the 2010 level in inflation-adjusted terms; by 2017, this spending was projected to fall to its lowest level as a share of the economy ever recorded, with data going back to 1962.[21] In general, since 2010, legislation to reduce the deficit has made about $4 in spending cuts for every $1 in new revenue.[22]

Economic Regulation The federal government regulates business to achieve a broad range of objectives, including economic stability, workplace safety, wages and hours, consumer satisfaction, and environmental goals. Economic regulation often attracts intense political conflict as businesses seek to limit the government role and other interests press for stronger government action. Democrats have usually been more favorable toward government regulation than have Republicans. Each party can point to public-opinion polls to support its position. Public views about regulation have shifted over time, but on the whole, Americans agree with the statement that government regulation of business does more harm than good.[23] However, as is the case for spending, Americans tend to express strong support for maintaining or even strengthening current regulations. Only a small percentage of Americans want to roll back existing regulations.

One area of regulation that sharply divides the parties is the minimum wage. As we have seen, the minimum wage was first enacted in 1938 as part of the Fair Labor Standards Act. Because it is not indexed to rise with inflation (see Figure 16.2), it has become a regular target of political conflict as supporters aim to raise it to keep pace with inflation. Most Americans strongly support an increase in the minimum wage, with close to three-quarters of Americans supporting a boost in the minimum wage in 2015.[24] Respondents who identify as Democrats are far more likely to back an increased minimum wage, but about half of Republicans polled also express support.[25]

In the context of growing inequality, upcoming midterm elections in 2014, and a federal minimum wage that had not risen since 2007, Democrats sought to make a minimum wage hike central to their political agenda. President Obama embraced the idea in his 2014 State of the Union address, urging Congress to raise the federal minimum wage from its current value of $7.25 to $10.10 an hour. Twenty-two states and the District of Columbia had already enacted state minimum wages higher than the federal wage. But with business adamantly against raising the minimum wage and the Republican base split, most congressional Republicans opposed the increase. When a Congressional Budget Office (CBO) study showed that raising the minimum wage to $10.10 would reduce jobs by 500,000[26] Republicans faulted Democrats for supporting a policy that would cut jobs when unemployment was still high.[27] Although Democrats challenged the CBO report

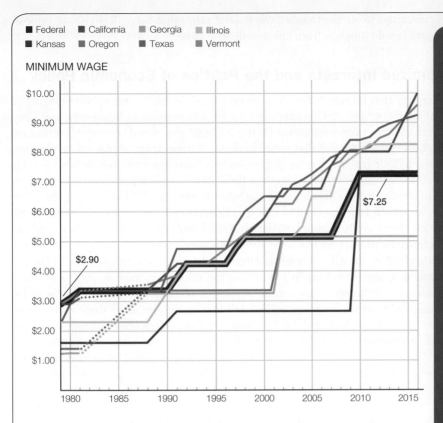

MINIMUM WAGE

Legend:
■ Federal ■ California ■ Georgia ■ Illinois
■ Kansas ■ Oregon ■ Texas ■ Vermont

$2.90

$7.25

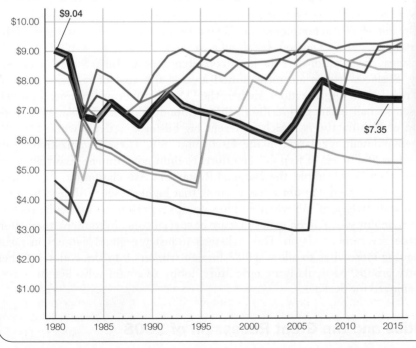

MINIMUM WAGE ADJUSTED FOR INFLATION (2016 DOLLARS)

$9.04

$7.35

FIGURE 16.2

The Minimum Wage, 1979–2016

The federal government and most U.S. states have minimum-wage laws. The minimum wage has increased over time across the United States (see top graph). However, near-constant inflation during this time period has reduced the real value of these wages, so the purchasing power of the minimum wage has declined. California, Oregon, and Vermont have had some of the highest minimum wages in the country. Georgia, Texas, and Kansas have had minimum wages that are among the lowest. How do the data in these graphs relate to arguments for or against a higher federal minimum wage?

NOTE: Department of Labor data are not available for all states for all years. A dotted line indicates a gap of more than two years in the data.
SOURCES: Department of Labor, Wage and Hour Division, "Changes In Basic Minimum Wages In Non-Farm Employment Under State Law: Selected Years 1968 to 2016," www.dol.gov/whd/state/stateMinWageHis.htm (accessed 7/9/16); "Minimum Wage Laws in the States, January 1, 2016," www.dol.gov/whd/minwage/america.htm (accessed 7/9/16); U.S. Department of Labor, Wage and Hour Division, "Changes in Basic Minimum Wages in Non-Farm Employment Under State Law: Selected Years 1968 to 2016," www.dol.gov/whd/state/stateMinWageHis.htm (accessed 7/12/16); and Bureau of Labor Statistics, Consumer Price Index—All Urban Consumers (Current Series), "Databases, Tables & Calculators by Subject: Inflation & Prices, U.S. All Items," http://data.bls.gov/cgi-bin/surveymost?cu (accessed 7/12/16).

and continued to support raising the federal minimum wage, Republican opposition prevented Congress from considering the issue.

Organized Interests and the Politics of Economic Policy

The groups that influence decisions about economic policy are as wide-ranging as the objectives of policy. Consumer groups, environmentalists, businesses, and labor all work to shape economic policy. Of these groups, organized labor and business are the most consistent actors that weigh in across the spectrum of policies. In the past, organized labor was much more important in influencing economic policy than it is today. At the height of their strength in the 1950s, unions represented some 35 percent of the labor force. Today, labor unions, representing 11.1 percent of the labor force, are much less powerful in influencing economic policy.[28] Democratic presidents continue to court labor because unions control resources and votes important to Democratic politicians, but labor's overall power has waned. On particular issues, organized labor can still exercise significant influence. For example, labor played a key role in Congress's decision to increase the minimum wage in 2009 and was a key advocate of boosting the federal minimum wage to $10.10 an hour in 2014. Although most union members make more than minimum wage, some unions have begun to advocate on behalf of low-wage workers, supporting innovative tactics to call attention to the economic problems these workers confront. Among these efforts have been one-day strikes by fast-food workers launched in 100 cities and protests in other cities.[29] In 2012, unions launched a national campaign called "The Fight for Fifteen," to pressure state and local governments to raise the minimum wage to $15 an hour. By 2015, their pressure had led a number of cities and states to increase the minimum wage. Three cities, San Francisco, Los Angeles, and Seattle, voted to raise the minimum wage to $15 or above for all workers. Some states have moved to require the $15 minimum for some categories of workers. Massachusetts and Oregon set $15 an hour for home care workers, while New York state raised the minimum wage to $15 an hour for all state workers.[30]

Business organizations are the most consistently powerful actors in economic policy. Business groups are most united around the goal of reducing government regulation. Organizations, such as the U.S. Chamber of Commerce, which represents small business, and the Business Roundtable and the National Association of Manufacturers, which represent big business, actively worked to roll back government regulation in the 1970s and '80s. These organizations have been vocal supporters of Republican efforts to limit government involvement in the economy. For example, the National Restaurant Association has denounced efforts to raise the minimum wage, warning that higher wages will lead to automation and fewer jobs. Yet when business groups representing particular sectors of the economy weigh in on issues that are of special concern to them, they often embrace government action. The high-tech industry regularly argues in favor of granting more visas to allow skilled foreign workers into the country. Other industry groups, particularly in agriculture, lobby to retain subsidies that they have enjoyed for decades.

Politics and the Great Recession of 2008

The severe economic downturn that began in 2008, often called the "great recession," provoked unprecedented government intervention into the economy. As the

Who Earns the Minimum Wage?

In recent years, many states have passed laws raising the minimum wage, and Congress has debated taking action at the federal level. Most Americans support raising the minimum wage, but there are differences in who earns the minimum wage based on age, gender, and race.

Percentage of Minimum Wage Earners

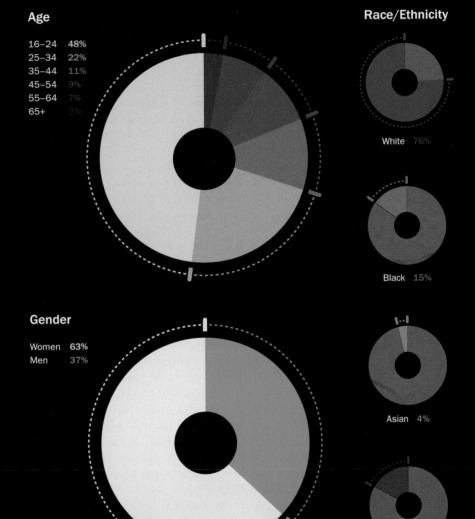

Age

16–24	**48%**
25–34	**22%**
35–44	11%
45–54	9%
55–64	7%
65+	3%

Gender

Women	**63%**
Men	37%

Race/Ethnicity

White   76%

Black   15%

Asian   4%

Hispanic   17%

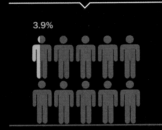

Percentage of all American workers (age 16+) who earn the minimum wage

3.9%

for critical analysis

1. Based on these data, which of these groups are more likely to support raising the minimum wage?

2. Women make up about 47 percent of the workforce. How does this compare to the percentage of minimum wage workers who are women?

SOURCE: U.S. Bureau of Labor Statistics, "Characteristics of Minimum Wage Workers, 2014," April 2015, www.bls.gov/opub/reports/minimum-wage/archive/characteristics-of-minimum-wage-workers-2014.pdf (accessed 4/28/16).

near-collapse of the financial sector in 2008 reverberated throughout the U.S. (and world) economy, thousands of Americans lost their homes, banks refused to lend, and unemployment rose. The federal government, first under George W. Bush and then under Barack Obama, initiated large-scale interventions in the hope of staving off the downward economic spiral. These included emergency measures to bail out failing companies, short-term stimulus to get the economy moving again, and proposals for regulations that would prevent similar financial meltdowns in the future. However, support for these measures wavered as fear of rising deficits, exploding long-term debt, and, more abstractly, "big government" grew.

Propping up the financial sector presented an economic challenge for federal officials. President Bush found he could not count on support from congressional Republicans when he sought to enact a major bailout for the financial sector. A bipartisan group in Congress ultimately approved a $700 billion emergency "bailout" in October 2008 (known as the Troubled Asset Relief Program, or TARP), which the Treasury Department drew on to infuse major financial institutions with capital. It was not just major banking institutions that faced ruin. Auto companies, teetering on the edge of bankruptcy, also received major infusions of cash from the federal government.[31] By late 2010 the economy had stabilized sufficiently that many of the financial institutions that had received funds under TARP were able to pay the federal government back. The CBO estimated that TARP would end up costing taxpayers $34 billion, far less than the initial $700 billion.[32]

Congress also passed a sweeping package in 2009 to help stimulate the economy, save jobs (particularly in the public sector), and make longer-term investments that would help stimulate economic growth. The $789 billion American Recovery and Reinvestment Act (more commonly known as the "stimulus" bill of 2009) contained a number of measures to stimulate growth in the short term and prevent drastic cuts to public services. Among the most important measures in the act were reductions in individual and business taxes by $288 billion in order to generate more spending and job hiring. The measure also spent $195.5 billion on aid, health insurance subsidies, and job training for low-income and unemployed workers and $44.5 billion designed to limit teacher layoffs and cutbacks in local school districts. The rest of the investments aimed not only to create new jobs in the short term but also to be long-term investments in infrastructure and education that would help future growth. The act reflected Keynesian logic that called for public investment during periods of economic downturn.

Although only some Republicans and Democrats had balked at supporting the financial bailout package in 2008, by early 2009 a sharp partisan rift had become evident. No Republicans in the House and only three in the Senate voted to support the 2009 stimulus package. Republicans denounced the House measure as overly tilted toward spending rather than tax cuts. But even when Senate Democrats added significant new tax cuts to the bill, most Republicans still opposed it. While Democrats defended the measure as an infusion of funds needed to prevent a depression, Republicans denounced it as wasteful spending and made their opposition a defining stance toward the Obama administration. Mounting unemployment complicated the political judgments about the stimulus; despite the injection of public funds into the economy, national unemployment rose to a seasonally adjusted rate of 9.6 percent by September 2010, with rates much higher in some states.[33] The nonpartisan CBO estimated that its height in 2010, American Recovery and Reinvestment Act increased the number of full-time jobs by as many as 3.6 million.[34] Yet because unemployment remained high,

The American Recovery and Readjustment Act provided $787 billion to support economic growth following the recession that began in 2008. Among other provisions, the act included funding for projects that would help keep Americans employed during the downturn.

the act did not get much credit from the public for helping the economy, and it attracted considerable criticism for contributing to the budget deficit. When Congress considered a second stimulus bill focused on job creation, it succeeded in enacting a relatively small job-creation package worth $15 billion, most of which consisted of tax credits for businesses that hired new employees.[35]

The Tools of Economic Policy

> **Describe how the government uses monetary, fiscal, and regulatory policies to influence the economy**

The U.S. economy is no accident; it is the result of specific policies that have expanded American markets and sustained massive economic growth. The Constitution provides that Congress shall have the power "To lay and collect Taxes . . . to pay the Debts and provide for the common Defence and general Welfare. . . . To borrow Money. . . . To coin Money [and] regulate the Value thereof." These clauses of Article I, Section 8, are the constitutional sources of the fiscal and monetary policies of the national government. The Constitution says nothing, however, about *how* these powers can be used, although the way they are used shapes the economy. As it works to meet the multiple goals of economic policy, the federal government relies on a broad set of tools that has evolved over time. Let us now turn to the actual tools designed to accomplish the goals of economic policy. As we will see, decisions about which tools to use are not simply technical; they are highly political decisions that reflect political conflicts over whether the government should act at all and, if so, which tools to use and when to use them.

Monetary Policies

Monetary policies manipulate the growth of the entire economy by controlling the availability of money to banks. With very few exceptions, banks in the United States are privately owned and locally operated. Until well into the twentieth century, banks were regulated, if at all, by state legislatures. Each bank was granted a charter, which gave it permission to make loans, hold deposits, and make

monetary policies efforts to regulate the economy through the manipulation of the supply of money and credit; America's most powerful institution in this area of monetary policy is the Federal Reserve Board

investments within that state. Although more than 25,000 banks continue to be chartered by the states, they are less important in the overall financial picture than they used to be as the most important banks now are members of the federal banking system.

Federal Reserve System But banks did not become the core of American capitalism without intense political controversy. The Federalist majority in Congress, led by Alexander Hamilton, did in fact establish a Bank of the United States, in 1791; but it was vigorously opposed by agrarian interests, led by Thomas Jefferson, who feared that the interests of urban, industrial capitalism would dominate such a bank. The Bank of the United States was terminated during the administration of Andrew Jackson, but the fear of a central, public bank lingered eight decades later, when, in 1913, Congress established an institution, the **Federal Reserve System**, to integrate private banks into a single national system. The Federal Reserve System did not become a central bank in the European tradition but rather is composed of 12 Federal Reserve banks, each located in a major commercial city. The Federal Reserve banks are not ordinary banks; they are banker's banks that make loans to other banks, clear checks, and supply the economy with currency and coins. They also play a regulatory role over the member banks. Every national bank must be a member of the Federal Reserve System and must follow national banking rules. State banks and savings and loan associations may also join if they accept national rules. At the top of the system is the Federal Reserve Board—"the Fed"—comprising seven members appointed by the president (with Senate confirmation) for 14-year terms. The chair of the Fed is selected by the president from among the seven members of the board for a four-year term. In all other concerns, however, the Fed is an independent agency (see Chapter 14) inasmuch as its members cannot be removed during their terms except "for cause" and the president's executive power does not extend to them or their policies. Nonetheless, observers charged the longtime Federal Reserve chair, Alan Greenspan, with being attentive to politics, for example, in his endorsement of President George W. Bush's tax cuts. In his 2005 confirmation hearings to head the Fed, the economist Ben Bernanke promised Congress that he would be "strictly independent of all political influences."[36]

The major advantage that a bank gains from being in the Federal Reserve System is that it can borrow from the system. This enables banks to expand their loan operations continually, as long as there is demand for loans in the economy. On the other hand, it is this very access of member banks to the Federal Reserve System that gives the Fed its power: the ability to expand and contract the *amount of credit* available in the United States.

The Fed can affect the total amount of credit through the interest (called the **federal funds rate**) that member banks charge one another for loans. If the Fed significantly decreases the federal funds rate, making it cheaper to borrow money, this can give a boost to a sagging economy. In the steep recession that began in 2008, the Fed acted aggressively. By December 2008 it had cut rates nine times from a high in September 2007 of 4.75 percent to a historically low percentage rate close to zero. Moreover, the Federal Reserve kept interest rates at that same low level well into 2015, in an attempt to encourage lending again and thus economic growth.[37] If the Fed raises the federal funds rate, it can put a brake on the economy because the higher rates make it more expensive to borrow money. This makes it more difficult for new businesses to get loans, for instance.

Federal Reserve System a system of 12 Federal Reserve banks that facilitates exchanges of cash, checks, and credit; regulates member banks; and uses monetary policies to fight inflation and deflation

federal funds rate the interest rate on loans between banks that the Federal Reserve Board influences by affecting the supply of money available

Although the Federal Reserve is responsible for ensuring high employment as well as price stability, it has been particularly important in fighting inflation. During the late 1970s and early 1980s, with inflation at record high levels, Federal Reserve chair Paul Volcker aggressively raised interest rates in order to dampen inflation. Although his actions provoked a sharp recession, they raised the stature of the Fed, demonstrating its ability to manage the economy. Because the Fed is so closely associated with inflation fighting, Senate Democrats pressed Ben Bernanke, President George W. Bush's nominee to head the Fed, to indicate at his nomination hearings that he would view maximum employment as a goal of equal importance to that of fighting inflation. In 2014, Janet Yellen, the new head of the Fed, vowed to continue the focus on employment. But in 2016, as unemployment declined, Yellen signaled that increases in the interest rates would likely occur later in the year.

Another power of the Fed is called **open-market operations**, whereby the Fed buys and sells government securities. When the Fed buys government securities in the open market, it is pumping money into the economy and stimulating economic activity; when it sells securities, it is applying brakes to the economy.

Fostering Investment The federal government also provides insurance to foster credit and encourage private capital investment. The Federal Deposit Insurance Corporation insures bank deposits up to $250,000. Another important promoter of investment is the federal insurance of home mortgages through the Department of Housing and Urban Development. By guaranteeing mortgages, the government can reduce the risks that banks run in making such loans, thus allowing banks to lower their interest rates and making such loans more affordable to middle- and lower-income families. Such programs have enabled millions of families that could not otherwise have afforded it to finance the purchase of a home.

This system began to unravel in the first decade of the 2000s, with the growth of the subprime market for lending. This market made home loans available to people who could not otherwise have afforded to buy a home. At the same time, however, it created new instabilities in the market by offering risky loans that would become more costly due to adjustable interest rates. The slowing housing market in 2007 set off a wave of foreclosures as many homeowners discovered that they could not pay back their loans. After the recession hit in 2008, many more Americans lost their homes to foreclosures: by 2015 over 5 million homes had been lost to foreclosure.[38]

The foreclosure crisis in turn sent shock waves through the financial system as investment banks found themselves holding worthless loans. One casualty of the home loan meltdown was the Wall Street investment bank Bear Stearns, which faced bankruptcy early in March 2008. Seeking to limit the harm to the broader economy that such a bankruptcy would cause, Fed chair Bernanke arranged for Bear Stearns to be bought, at bargain-basement prices, by JPMorgan Chase, another investment bank. In making this move, Bernanke was exercising powers of the Federal Reserve Act that had not been used since the 1930s.[39] After the firm Lehman Brothers collapsed in 2008 and several other investment banks and insurance companies moved closer to insolvency, the Federal Reserve also provided billions of dollars to banks so that they could continue to lend money for student loans, auto loans, and residential mortgages. In all, the Fed gave nearly $1.5 trillion in emergency loans to financial institutions.[40]

Although many were impressed by the swift action undertaken by the Fed, critics charged that its supervision of the banking system prior to the crisis had been too lax. This led to an unusually contentious set of Senate confirmation hearings

At her confirmation hearing in 2013, chair of the Federal Reserve Janet Yellen discussed the role of the Fed in reducing unemployment and in keeping inflation at approximately 2 percent a year.

for critical analysis

Why is the Federal Reserve so important to economic policy?

open-market operations
methods by which the Open Market Committee of the Federal Reserve System buys and sells government securities and other investment instruments to help finance government operations and to reduce or increase the total amount of money circulating in the economy

for Bernanke, whom President Obama had renominated in 2009. Most Democrats prefer that the Federal Reserve take a strong stand in regulating banks and in prioritizing the problem of unemployment. Republicans, on the other hand, fear that excessive regulation will limit economic growth. Republicans are more likely to see unemployment as a problem of workers who lack appropriate job skills, rather than a problem that requires more stimulus of the economy.

Fiscal Policies

fiscal policy the government's use of taxing, monetary, and spending powers to manipulate the economy

Fiscal policy includes the government's taxing and spending powers. Personal and corporate income taxes, which raise most of the U.S. government's revenues, are the most prominent examples. Although the direct purpose of an income tax is to raise revenue, each tax has a different impact on the economy, and government can attempt to plan for that impact.

tariff a tax on imported goods

Taxation During the nineteenth century, the federal government received most of its revenue from a single tax, the **tariff**. It also relied on excise taxes, which are taxes levied on specific products, such as tobacco and alcohol. As federal activities expanded in the 1900s, the federal government added new sources of tax revenue. The most important was the income tax, proposed by Congress in 1909, ratified by the states, and added to the Constitution in 1913 as the Sixteenth Amendment. The income tax is levied on individuals and corporations. With the creation of the Social Security system in 1935, social insurance taxes became an additional source of federal revenue.

Before World War II, individual income taxes accounted for only 14 percent of federal revenues.[41] The need to raise revenue for World War II made the income tax much more important. Congress expanded the base of the income tax so that most Americans paid income taxes after World War II. Figure 16.3 shows several notable shifts that have occurred in taxes since 1966. Social insurance taxes now compose a much greater share of federal revenues, rising from 19.5 percent of revenues in 1966 to an estimated 33 percent in 2016. Receipts from corporate income taxes declined over the same period, dropping from 23 percent of receipts in 1966 to 8.8 percent in 2016. The share of the federal individual income tax has remained fairly stable; it was 42.4 percent in 1966 and estimated at 48.8 percent in 2016.

progressive taxation taxation that hits upper-income brackets more heavily

regressive taxation taxation that hits lower-income brackets more heavily

One of the most important features of the American income tax is that it is a "progressive," or "graduated," tax, with the heaviest burden carried by those most able to pay. A tax is called **progressive** if the rate of taxation goes up with each higher income bracket. A tax is called **regressive** if people in lower-income brackets pay a higher proportion of their income toward the tax than people in higher-income brackets. For example, a sales tax is deemed regressive because everybody pays at the same rate so that people who make less money end up paying a greater share of their income in sales taxes than do people who make more money. The Social Security tax is another example of a regressive tax. In 2016, Social Security law applied a tax of 6.2 percent on the first $118,500 of income for the retirement program and an additional 1.45 percent on all income (without limit) for Medicare benefits, for a total of 7.65 percent in Social Security taxes. This means that a person earning an income of $118,500 pays $9,065 in Social Security taxes, a rate of 7.65 percent. But someone earning twice that income, $237,000, pays a total of $10,783 in Social Security taxes, a rate of 4.55 percent. As one's income continues to rise, the amount of Social Security taxes also rises (until the cap is reached) but

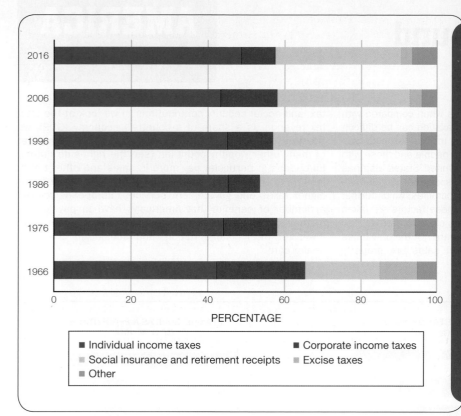

FIGURE 16.3

Federal Revenues by Type of Tax

The federal government collects revenue from a variety of different taxes. Most important is the individual income tax, which has accounted for approximately 45 percent of federal revenue over the past 50 years. Revenues from corporate income tax have fallen considerably over this time period, from 23 percent in 1966 to 8.8 percent in 2016. In the same period, taxes for social insurance and retirement have grown substantially. Does the federal government draw more of its revenue from progressive taxes or regressive taxes?

NOTE: Data for 2016 are estimated.
SOURCE: Office of Management and Budget, "Table 2.2—Percentage Composition of Receipts by Source: 1934-2021." The Budget for Fiscal Year 2017. www.whitehouse.gov/omb/budget /Historicals (accessed 7/13/16).

the rate, or the percentage of one's income that goes to taxes, declines. As part of the Affordable Care Act, high earners (individuals making over $200,000 and couples earning more than $250,000) faced an additional Medicare tax of 0.9 percent on all of their income.

Although the primary purpose of the graduated income tax is, of course, to raise revenue, an important second objective is to collect revenue in such a way as to reduce the disparities of wealth between the lowest and the highest income brackets. We call this a policy of **redistribution**. Another policy objective of the income tax is the encouragement of the capitalist economy by rewarding investment. The tax laws allow individuals or companies to deduct from their taxable income any money they can justify as an investment or a "business expense"; this gives an incentive to individuals and companies to spend money to expand their production, their advertising, or their staff and reduces the income taxes that businesses have to pay. These kinds of deductions are called incentives or "equity" by those who support them; others call them **loopholes**. The tax reforms of the 1980s actually closed a number of important loopholes in U.S. tax laws. But others still exist—on home mortgages and on business expenses, for example—and others will likely return because there is a strong consensus among members of Congress, both Democrats and Republicans, that businesses often need such incentives. The differences between the two parties focus largely on which incentives are justifiable.[42] In addition to benefiting from loopholes, American corporations can limit their taxation by merging with foreign firms. This increasingly common procedure—called "corporate inversion"—allows the merged company to pay the lower foreign tax

redistribution a policy whose objective is to tax or spend in such a way as to reduce the disparities of wealth between the lowest and the highest income brackets

loophole incentive to individuals and businesses to reduce their tax liabilities by investing their money in areas the government designates

Tax Rates around the World

AMERICA
Side *by* Side

Do Americans pay more or less in taxes when compared with people in other wealthy democracies? Taxation can be difficult to compare across countries. Regarding income tax, countries frequently set different rates for married people and those with children (see the left-side graph). The United States also has fewer cash transfer programs (such as social security and un-employment insurance) than other democracies, which further reduces individual tax burdens. When these factors are taken into account, the U.S. income tax rate is close to average.[a]

However, taxes on personal income are not the only taxes governments collect; they also collect sales tax, property tax, and social security contributions. If we look at the total tax revenue as a share of a country's economy (GDP), we see that the U.S. tax burden is significantly less than that of many other wealthy countries (see the right-side graph). Europeans in particular pay more in sales and other taxes, leading to a higher tax burden. There is a tradeoff between higher taxes and government services: Europeans receive a number of benefits that Americans have to pay for out of their personal incomes, including cheaper health care, lower (or free) college tuition, and subsidized child and senior care.[b]

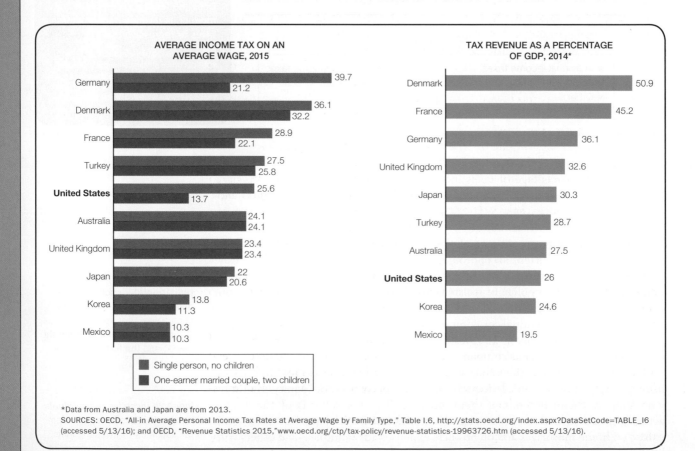

*Data from Australia and Japan are from 2013.
SOURCES: OECD, "All-in Average Personal Income Tax Rates at Average Wage by Family Type," Table I.6, http://stats.oecd.org/index.aspx?DataSetCode=TABLE_I6 (accessed 5/13/16); and OECD, "Revenue Statistics 2015," www.oecd.org/ctp/tax-policy/revenue-statistics-19963726.htm (accessed 5/13/16).

[a]When compared to the average of the members of the Organization for Economic Co-Operation and Development, an international organization of upper- and middle-income democracies.
[b]Steven Hill, "The Myth of Low-Tax America: Why Americans Aren't Getting Their Money's Worth," *The Atlantic*, April 15, 2013, www.theatlantic.com/business/archive /2013/04/the-myth-of-low-tax-america-why-americans-arent-getting-their-moneys-worth/274945/ (accessed 5/13/16).

rate. In 2015, for example, the drug firm Pfizer merged with the Irish company Allergan PLC. The move allowed Pfizer to reduce its income tax from 25 percent to 17 or 18 percent, reflecting the lower corporate taxes in Ireland.[43]

The tax reform laws of 1981 and 1986 significantly reduced the progressiveness of the federal income tax. In the 1960s the highest tax bracket applied a 91 percent tax to income over $200,000 (which is the equivalent of $1.5 million in today's dollars).[44] Drastic rate reductions were instituted in 1986, however. The Tax Reform Act of 1986 established five tax brackets, ranging from a 15 percent tax on those in the lowest income bracket to 39.6 percent on those in the highest income bracket.

Taxes became a controversial issue again during the George W. Bush administration. After passing major cuts in income tax rates in 2001, President Bush proposed, and Congress passed, a sweeping new round of cuts in 2003. Bush's plan was intended to promote investment by reducing taxes on most stock dividends, to spur business activity by offering tax breaks to small businesses, and to stimulate the economy by reducing the tax rates for all taxpayers. In 2006, Congress extended the rate reductions on dividends and capital gains. The tax cuts reduced the federal budget by an estimated $1.3 trillion over 10 years.[45] The argument for the tax cuts was largely a supply-side one: the cuts would make for a prosperous economy. Opponents charge that it made no sense to cut taxes since the benefits of the tax cuts went primarily to the wealthy. Critics also charge that the tax cuts caused the federal budget, which was in surplus when Bush took office, to fall into deficit.[46]

President Obama and the Democratic leadership proposed extending the tax cuts for everyone with annual incomes under $250,000; those making more would have their income taxes revert back to the rates in the 1990s. Republicans preferred to extend the tax cuts for everyone. In late 2010, Congress agreed to a two-year extension of the cuts until December 2012. As the new deadline loomed in 2012, many analysts warned that the pending expiration of the tax cuts, which might amount to as much as $500 billion in additional taxes, coupled with $100 billion in federal spending cuts to which Congress and the president had previously agreed, could push the still-faltering U.S. economy over a "fiscal cliff" if they came to pass. After a series of complex negotiations stretching over three years, Congress struck a deal to raise income taxes on couples making over $450,000 a year from 35 percent to 39.6 percent. Since that time, Congress has not sought to revise the tax code. (See Table 16.1 for the tax brackets in 2016. The brackets go up every year to keep pace with inflation.)

Spending and Budgeting The federal government's power to spend is one of the most important tools of economic policy. Decisions about how much to spend affect the overall health of the economy. They also affect every aspect of American life, from the distribution of income to the availability of different modes of transportation to the level of education in society.

The president and Congress have each created institutions to assert control over the budget process. The Office of Management and Budget (OMB) in the Executive Office of the President is responsible for preparing the president's budget. This budget contains the president's spending priorities and the estimated costs of the president's policy proposals. It is viewed as the starting point for the annual debate over the budget. When different parties control the presidency and Congress, the president's budget may have little influence on the budget that is ultimately adopted. Members of the president's own party also may have different priorities.

for critical analysis

What are the multiple goals of tax policy in America? How else might some of these goals be achieved? In what ways is the tax system in the United States progressive? In what ways is it regressive?

TABLE 16.1

Taxable Income Brackets and Rates, 2016

This table shows the federal tax rates that Americans pay on their income. The United States has a progressive tax system in that the tax rate goes up on Americans with more income.

TAX RATE (%)	INDIVIDUALS	MARRIED COUPLES FILING JOINTLY	HEAD OF HOUSEHOLD FILERS
10	$0 to $9,275	$0 to $18,550	$0 to $13,250
15	$9,275 to $37,650	$18,550 to $75,300	$13,250 to $50,400
25	$37, 650 to $91,150	$75,300 to $151,900	$50,400 to $130,150
28	$91,150 to $190,150	$151,900 to $231,450	$130,150 to $210,800
33	$190,150 to $413,350	$231,450 to $413,350	$210,800 to $413,350
35	$413,350 to $415,050	$413,350 to $466,950	$413,350 to $441,000
39.6	$415,050+	$466,950+	$441,000+

SOURCE: Tax Foundation, http://taxfoundation.org/article/2016-tax-brackets (accessed 12/9/15).

budget deficit amount by which government spending exceeds government revenue in a fiscal year

Congress has its own budget institutions. Congress created the Congressional Budget Office (CBO) in 1974 so that it could have reliable information about the costs and economic impact of the policies it considers. At the same time, it set up a budget process designed to establish spending priorities and to consider individual expenditures in light of the entire budget. A key element of the process is the annual budget resolution, which designates broad targets for spending. By estimating the costs of policy proposals, Congress hoped to control spending and reduce deficits. When the congressional budget process proved unable to hold down deficits in the 1980s, Congress established stricter measures to control spending, including "spending caps" that limit spending on some types of programs.

Not surprisingly, the fight for control over spending is one of the most contentious in Washington as interest groups and politicians strive to determine the priorities and appropriate levels of spending. Decisions about spending are made as part of the annual budget process. During the 1990s, when the federal **budget deficit** first became a major political issue and parties were deeply split on spending, the budget process became the focal point of the entire policy-making process. With the rapid swing from budget surpluses in 2000 to record deficits by 2003, deficits once again emerged as a political issue (Figure 16.4). This time, however, Republican leaders, who had made deficits the focal point of politics in the mid-1990s, largely dismissed their importance. As House majority leader Tom DeLay put it, "The Soviet Union had a balanced budget. Well, you can raise taxes until you balance it, but the economy will go into the toilet."[47]

The deficit once again drove the economic policy agenda between 2010 and 2013, when Republicans in the House of Representatives and Democrats in the Senate and White House engaged in a contentious series of battles over the federal deficit and President Obama's economic policies.[48] The impasse stemmed

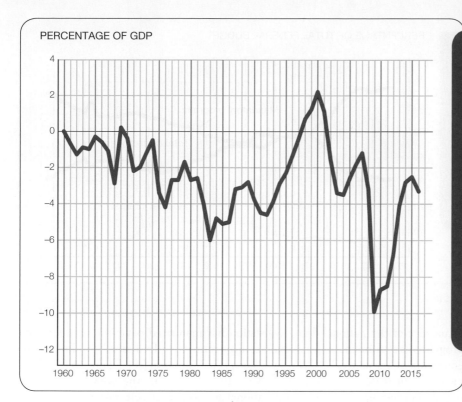

PERCENTAGE OF GDP

FIGURE 16.4

U.S. Budget Deficits and Surpluses, 1960–2016*

The federal deficit grew substantially during the 1980s under President Reagan. During the 1990s, the budget deficit declined significantly but then grew dramatically after 2001. When was the last time that the federal budget showed a surplus? Why did the budget deficit grow so much after 2001?

*Data for 2016 are estimated.
SOURCE: Office of Management and Budget, Fiscal Year 2017, Budget of the U.S. Government, "Historical Tables Table 1.2—Summary of Receipts, Outlays, and Surpluses or Deficits (–) as Percentages of GDP: 1930–2021," www .whitehouse.gov/sites/default/files/omb/budget /fy2017/assets/hist.pdf (accessed 7/9/16).

from Republicans' insistence that the deficit, which had grown substantially in the aftermath of the great recession, be reduced primarily through spending cuts, while Democrats pushed for deficit reduction through a mix of spending cuts and tax increases for the wealthiest Americans. The resolution to the standoff, the Budget Control Act of 2011, achieved $1 trillion in deficit reduction over 10 years, all through spending cuts, but also scheduled additional, automatic across-the-board "sequestration" cuts beginning in 2013 if a bipartisan "super-committee" failed to reach a deal securing an additional $1.2 trillion in deficit reduction. To the frustration of all, the super-committee failed to agree on a new deficit-reduction plan. In March 2013 sequestration cuts finally came into effect after Congress and the White House failed to cancel the cuts. A period of high-stakes back-and-forth negotiation over the debt finally came to an end in October 2013 when another failure to agree on the terms of raising the debt ceiling—with Republicans demanding a one-year delay in the implementation of the Affordable Care Act, further spending cuts on social programs, and negotiations on entitlements reform and Democrats insisting on a clean, no-strings-attached increase in the debt limit—led to a shutdown of the federal government for the first time in almost two decades.[49] The government reopened after 16 days with a resolution cleanly raising the debt limit and funding the government for another two years. In 2015, it appeared that the government once again would shut down as conservative Republicans threatened to withhold their approval. But after the resignation of John Boehner as Speaker and several months of negotiation, Congress was able to enact a budget.

A very large and growing proportion of the annual federal budget is **mandatory spending**, expenditures that are, in the words of the OMB, "relatively uncontrollable." Interest payments on the national debt, for example, are determined by the

mandatory spending federal spending that is made up of "uncontrollables," budget items that cannot be controlled through the regular budget process

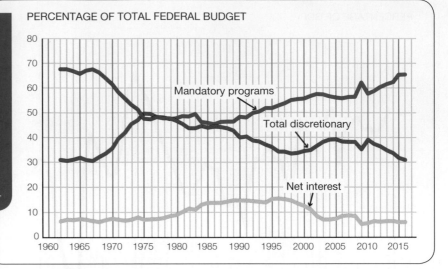

FIGURE 16.5

Mandatory Spending, Discretionary Spending, and Net Interest, 1962–2016*

*Data for 2016 are estimated.
SOURCE: Office of Mangement and Budget, "Table 8.3—Percentage Distribution of Outlays by Budget Enforcement Act Category: 1962–2021," The Budget for Fiscal Year 2017, www.whitehouse.gov/omb/budget/Historicals (accessed 7/13/16).

PERCENTAGE OF TOTAL FEDERAL BUDGET

actual size of the national debt. Legislation has mandated payment rates for such programs as retirement under Social Security, retirement for federal employees, unemployment assistance, Medicare, and farm price supports (see Figure 16.5). These payments increase with the cost of living; they increase as the average age of the population goes up; they increase as national and world agricultural surpluses go up. In 1970, 38.5 percent of the total federal budget was made up of these **uncontrollables**; in 1975, 52.5 percent fell into that category; and by 2016, around 69 percent was in the uncontrollable category. This means that the national government now can do very little **discretionary spending** that will allow it to counteract fluctuations in the business cycle. (Figure 16.6 shows discretionary spending in 2016.)

Government spending as a fiscal policy works fairly well when deliberate deficit spending is used to stop a recession and to speed up the recovery period, but it does not work very well in fighting inflation because elected politicians are often politically unable to make the drastic expenditure cuts and tax hikes necessary to balance the budget, much less to produce a budgetary surplus.

Regulation and Antitrust Policy

Americans have long been suspicious of concentrations of economic power. Federal economic regulation aims to protect the public against potential abuses by concentrated economic power in two ways. First, the federal government can establish conditions that govern the operation of big businesses to ensure fair competition. For example, it can require a business to make information about its activities and account books available to the public. Second, the federal government can force a large business to break up into smaller companies if it finds that the business has established a **monopoly**. This is called **antitrust policy**. In addition to economic regulation, the federal government engages in social regulation. Social regulation establishes conditions on businesses in order to protect workers, the environment, and consumers.

Federal regulatory policy has evolved, in part, as a reaction to public demands. As the American economy prospered throughout the nineteenth century, some

uncontrollables budgetary items that are beyond the control of budgetary committees and can be controlled only by substantive legislative action in Congress; some uncontrollables, such as interest on the debt, are beyond the power of Congress because the terms of payments are set in contracts

discretionary spending federal spending on programs that are controlled through the regular budget process

monopoly a single firm in a market that controls all the goods and services of that market; absence of competition

antitrust policy government regulation of large businesses that have established monopolies

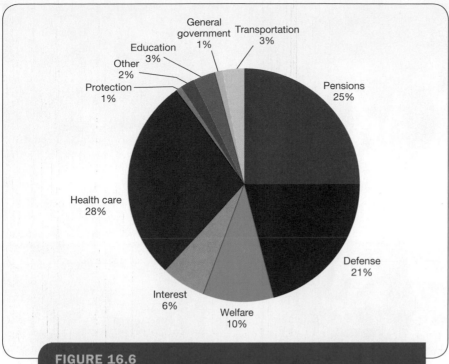

FIGURE 16.6

Discretionary Spending, 2016*

The biggest items in the federal budget are mandatory programs, including Social Security and Medicare. These programs are supported by contributory taxes and enjoy broad support. It is easier to cut discretionary spending because appropriations must be approved each year. With rising budget deficits and congressional unwillingness to raise taxes, discretionary spending—including defense but especially domestic programs—are the easiest programs to cut.

*Estimate

NOTE: Health includes discretionary spending on Medicare. Defense includes discretionary spending on international affairs and assistance for veterans. Protection includes federal law enforcement and correctional activities.

SOURCE: Office of Management and Budget, "Table 3.2—Outlays by Function and Subfunction: 1962–2021," The Budget for Fiscal Year 2017, www.whitehouse.gov/omb/budget/Historicals (accessed 7/14/16).

companies grew so large that they were recognized as possessing "market power." This meant that they were powerful enough to eliminate competitors and to impose conditions on consumers rather than catering to consumer demand. The growth of billion-dollar corporations led to collusion among companies to control prices, much to the dismay of smaller businesses and ordinary consumers. Small businesses, laborers, farmers, and consumers all began to clamor for protective regulation. Although the states had been regulating businesses in one way or another all along, interest groups turned to Washington as economic problems appeared to be beyond the reach of the individual state governments. If markets were national, there would have to be national regulation.[50]

The first national regulatory policy was the Interstate Commerce Act of 1887, which created the first national independent regulatory commission, the

Regulatory policies to protect consumers first emerged in the early twentieth century. The publication of Upton Sinclair's The Jungle *in 1906 exposed the unsanitary practices of the meatpacking industry, spurring concerns about food safety that led to the Federal Meat Inspection Act that same year.*

Interstate Commerce Commission, designed to control the monopolistic practices of the railroads. Three years later, the Sherman Antitrust Act extended regulatory power to cover all monopolistic practices. The Interstate Commerce Commission and the Sherman Antitrust Act were strengthened in 1914 with the enactment of the Federal Trade Commission Act (creating the Federal Trade Commission) and the Clayton Antitrust Act. At the same time, public demands to protect consumers led the federal government to enact a more limited number of social regulations. As we have seen, Upton Sinclair's best-seller about the meatpacking industry, *The Jungle*, led to the Federal Meat Inspection Act of 1906. Two decades later, the Food and Drug Administration was given broad powers to test and regulate products viewed as essential to public health.

The modern era of comprehensive national regulation began in the 1930s. Most of the regulatory programs of the 1930s were established to regulate the conduct of companies within specifically designated sectors of American industry. For example, the jurisdiction of one agency was the securities industry; the jurisdiction of another was the radio (and eventually television) industry. Others included banking, coal mining, and agriculture. At this time, Congress also set the basic framework of American labor regulation, including the rules for collective bargaining and the minimum wage.

When Congress turned once again to regulatory policies in the 1970s, it became still bolder, moving beyond the effort to regulate specific industrial sectors and toward regulating aspects of the entire economy. The scope or jurisdiction of such agencies as the Occupational Safety and Health Administration, the Consumer Product Safety Commission, and the Environmental Protection Agency (EPA) is as broad as the entire economy, indeed the entire society.

Despite occasional high-profile regulatory cases such as the one against Microsoft in the 1990s, the trend since the late 1970s has been against regulation. Over the years, businesses complained about the burden of the new regulations they confronted, and many economists began to argue that excessive regulation was hurting the economy. In the 1980s, Congress and the president responded with a wave of **deregulation**. For example, President Reagan went about the task of changing the direction of regulation by way of "presidential oversight." Shortly after taking office, he gave the OMB authority to review all executive branch proposals for new regulations. By this means, Reagan reduced the total number of regulations issued by federal agencies, dropping the number of pages in the *Federal Register* from 74,000 in 1980 to 49,600 in 1987.[51]

The financial crisis that began in 2008 put regulation on the agenda once again. As the economic emergency subsided, Congress began to consider long-term reform of the financial industry. A central question was how to create regulations that would prevent excessive risk-taking by investors, seen as the principal cause of the recession. The complex reform that Congress enacted in 2010 (the Dodd-Frank Wall Street Reform and Consumer Protection Act) included a range of new regulations on the financial industry. It created the Consumer Financial Protection Bureau, placed under the auspices of the Federal Reserve but independent of it. The new agency has a broad mandate to regulate consumer financial products, such as mortgages and credit cards, to ensure that they are fair and competitive. The reform also created the Financial Stability Oversight Council, headed by the Treasury secretary, with responsibility for identifying risks to the economy before they spread.

deregulation a policy of reducing or eliminating regulatory restraints on the conduct of individuals or private institutions

Subsidies and Contracting

Subsidies and contracting are the carrots of economic policy. Their purpose is to encourage people to do something they might otherwise not do or to get people to do more of what they are already doing. Sometimes the purpose is merely to compensate people for something done in the past.

Subsidies **Subsidies** are simply government grants of cash or other valuable commodities, such as land. Although subsidies are often denounced as "giveaways," they have played a fundamental role in the history of government in the United States. Subsidies were the dominant form of public policy of the national government and the state and local governments throughout the nineteenth century. They continue to be an important category of public policy at all levels of government. The first planning document ever written for the national government, Alexander Hamilton's "*Report on Manufactures,*" was based almost entirely on Hamilton's assumption that American industry could be encouraged by federal subsidies and that these were not only desirable but constitutional.

The thrust of Hamilton's plan was not lost on later policy makers. Subsidies in the form of land grants were given to farmers and to railroad companies to encourage western settlement. Substantial cash subsidies have traditionally been given to shipbuilders to help build the commercial fleet and to guarantee the use of the ships as military personnel carriers in times of war. The effect of any subsidy has to be measured somewhat indirectly in terms of what people *would be doing* if the subsidy were not available. For example, many thousands of people settled in lands west of the Mississippi only because land subsidies were available. Similarly, hundreds

subsidies government grants of cash or other valuable commodities, such as land, to an individual or an organization; used to promote activities desired by the government, reward political support, or buy off political opposition

American farmers have long benefited from government subsidies. Agricultural subsidies are designed to help farmers stay in business even when the markets for their crops are less favorable so that the country can rely on a steady food supply.

of research laboratories exist in universities and corporations only because certain types of research subsidies from the government are available to fund them.

Policies using the subsidy technique continued to be plentiful in the twentieth century and into the twenty-first, even after the 1990s, when there was widespread public and official hostility toward subsidies. For example, in 2007 the annual value of corporate subsidies, not including agriculture, was estimated at more than $92 billion.[52] Politicians have always favored subsidies because subsidies can be treated as "benefits" that can be spread widely in response to many demands that might otherwise produce profound political conflict. Subsidies can, in other words, be used to buy off the opposition.

Contracting Like any corporation, a government agency must purchase goods and services by contract. The law requires open bidding for a substantial proportion of these contracts because government contracts are extremely valuable to businesses in the private sector and because the opportunities and incentives for abuse surrounding contracting are very great. But contracting is more than a method of buying goods and services. It is also an important technique of policy because government agencies are often authorized to use their **contracting power** as a means of encouraging corporations to improve themselves, helping to build up whole sectors of the economy, and encouraging certain desirable goals or behavior, such as equal employment opportunity. For example, the infant airline industry of the 1930s was nurtured by the national government's lucrative contracts to carry airmail. A more recent example is the use of government contracting to encourage industries, universities, and other organizations to engage in research and development on a wide range of issues in basic and applied science.

Military contracting has long been a major element in government spending. So tight was the connection between defense contractors and the federal government during the Cold War that as he was leaving office President Eisenhower warned the nation to beware of the powerful "military–industrial complex." After the Cold

contracting power the power of government to set conditions on companies seeking to sell goods or services to government agencies

War, as military spending and production declined, major defense contractors began to look for alternative business activities to supplement the reduced demand for weapons. For example, Lockheed Martin, the nation's largest defense contractor, began to bid on contracts related to welfare reform. Since the terrorist attacks of 2001, however, the military budget has been awash in new funds, and military contractors are flooded with business. President Bush increased the Pentagon budget by more than 7 percent a year, requesting so many weapons systems that one observer called the budget a "weapons smorgasbord."[53] Military contractors geared up to produce not only weapons for foreign warfare but also surveillance systems to enhance domestic security.

● The Environment and the Economy

> **Explain why the government tries to balance economic prosperity with policies that protect the environment**

One of the most important reasons that the government intervenes in the economy is to protect the environment. Although federal interest in environmental conservation stretches back to the beginning of the twentieth century, federal regulation of industry grew more extensive with the rise of the modern environmental movement in the 1970s. By then the consequences of economic growth that paid little attention to environmental impact were evident all over America. Cleveland's Cuyahoga River, long a dumping ground for industrial waste, caught fire in 1969; and the burning river became an especially vivid symbol of environmental neglect. The first "Earth Day," in 1970, highlighted the new ecological concerns, which became a major feature of American politics in subsequent decades.[54]

for critical analysis

Think about a specific instance of government intervention in the American economy since the New Deal. What economic policy tool was used? What other tools might have been used? In your opinion, when is government action in the economy necessary?

A wave of new laws wrote environmental goals into policy. The 1969 National Environmental Policy Act (NEPA), the Clean Air Act amendments of 1970, the 1972 Clean Water Act, and the 1974 Safe Drinking Water Act together established a new set of goals and procedures for protecting the environment. These acts are properly considered part of economic policy because they affect virtually every aspect of the economy. NEPA, for example, requires federal agencies to prepare an environmental impact statement for every major development project they propose. In this way, environmental impacts routinely become factored into considerations about whether a particular project is feasible or desirable.

Environmental disasters have often drawn attention to new environmental hazards and have prompted greater federal regulation. For example, during the mid-1970s the residents of the Love Canal neighborhood in Buffalo, New York, discovered that their neighborhood had been built on a toxic waste dump. Many of the chemicals in the soil were suspected carcinogens. At federal and state cost, residents were moved to new homes. Partly as a result of this highly publicized incident, Congress passed legislation to facilitate cleanup of hazardous waste sites.

Yet government action and corporate liability are often bitterly contested issues in this area. Protecting the environment presents policy makers with difficult trade-offs. Compliance with environmental regulations can be very costly. Moreover, critics maintain that federal standards are sometimes too high. How clean should the air be? What is the difference between pure drinking water and safe drinking water? Who should bear the costs of protecting the environment? Not only do citizens, consumers, and businesses take different perspectives on these questions but the goals themselves often present a moving target. As new scientific evidence shows (or fails to find evidence for) new or suspected environmental hazards, conflicts emerge over the proper role of government.

The Debate on Climate Change

Nowhere have these conflicts been more acute than in the debate over climate change. A large and growing body of scientific evidence suggests that greenhouse gas emissions from cars, power plants, and other human-made sources are causing temperatures on earth to rise.[55] The projected environmental consequences are dire: melting polar ice caps, extreme weather, droughts, fire, rising sea levels, and disease. All would have profound economic consequences. Yet these projections come with considerable uncertainty. How likely are most catastrophic scenarios? Should we prepare for the most damaging outcomes or only the most likely outcomes of climate change?[56] These questions are important because the costs of transforming the world's carbon-based technologies through lower energy use and newer green technologies are enormous. These questions are especially salient for the United States, which has the world's largest economy and is responsible for 25 percent of the world's greenhouse gas emissions but has only 10 percent of the world's population.[57] And because the United States relies so heavily on fossil fuels for its energy sources, the effort to reduce carbon emission requires a major shift in how we obtain and use energy.

As scientists have learned more about the effects of human activity on the climate, the issue of climate change has risen on the national agenda. But it has become embroiled in partisan politics, with many Republicans challenging the argument that human activity causes global warming. Public opinion has remained split. In 2015, surveys revealed that while 72 percent of respondents believed the

Low-lying coastal areas are particularly vulnerable to the effects of climate change. Rising waters and hurricanes have washed away most of Isle de Jean Charles, Louisiana. In 2016 the federal government provided funding to relocate residents of the island.

world was warming, less than half believed that human activity was the cause.[58] Despite Republican opposition and public ambivalence, the Obama administration made climate change an important focus of attention and encouraged federal agencies to move aggressively on this issue. In 2009 the EPA began to set standards so that it could, for the first time ever, regulate greenhouse gas emissions under the Clean Air Act. In 2014, the EPA moved to regulate factories and power plants that emit greenhouse gases. Especially controversial was a rule that requires coal plants to reduce greenhouse gas emissions by 30 percent by 2030. The largely Republican congressional opposition signaled its disapproval by passing a resolution to block the rules on the eve of the president's appearance at a major international summit on climate change in 2015.[59] The president played a central role in the negotiations that created the Paris climate agreement, an ambitious international agreement to lower the earth's temperature. The United States signed the accord in 2016, but the steps to implement the accord face major political and legal obstacles.

Environmental Policies

Policy makers charged with devising approaches to climate change have identified three basic policy approaches. The first is mitigation, or reduction, of greenhouse gas emissions. The second is large-scale research and development to promote alternative technologies. The third consists of measures that allow us to adapt to a warmer climate. Each of these strategies entails potentially gargantuan costs in the form of higher energy prices, subsidies to industry, infrastructure projects, and relocation decisions. When specific policy proposals are discussed and these costs become apparent, the consensus for addressing climate change breaks down.

Mitigation: Reducing Emissions The mitigation approach, which seeks to reduce greenhouse gas emissions, has garnered the most attention from policy

for critical analysis

What are some of the policies that can be used to address climate change? Which policies have the best chance of being enacted?

One approach to addressing climate change is reducing emissions from factories, power plants, and cars. Capping emissions can be controversial if doing so imposes costs on businesses and ultimately on consumers, but recent cap-and-trade proposals may offer a more efficient way to reduce pollution.

makers. Two proposed policies that aim to achieve this goal, both controversial, are tougher standards for auto fuel mileage and higher taxes on gasoline. Although the public strongly supports higher gas-mileage standards, auto companies resisted such standards for nearly 30 years after they were first put in place in the early 1970s. In 2009 the EPA announced that it would set standards for greenhouse gas emissions for automobiles under the Clean Air Act, raising the fuel economy standards for new vehicles to 35.5 miles per gallon beginning in 2016, a standard later boosted to 54.4 miles per gallon by 2025.[60] As for proposals to increase gasoline taxes, public-opinion polls routinely show that a majority of Americans oppose a tax on gasoline as a way to reduce emissions, and few politicians want to sponsor such an unpopular policy.[61]

Proponents of reducing carbon emissions pinned their hopes on a "cap-and-trade" system as the most politically feasible strategy to achieve their goal. This approach sets a target for carbon emissions for each industry but allows companies to trade "carbon credits" with one another. This market-based system is attractive to political leaders because it achieves its goals by creating incentives for private actors and allows them flexibility as they seek to reduce emissions. More than 23 large firms, including leading automakers, joined environmentalists in a coalition called the U.S. Climate Action Partnership to press for a cap-and-trade system to reduce carbon emissions.[62] In 2009 the House of Representatives passed a landmark cap-and-trade bill aimed at reducing greenhouse gas emissions. However, opposition from some Democrats and most Republicans in the Senate blocked further movement on cap-and-trade legislation.

Promoting Alternative Technologies Many analysts and politicians prefer a second strategy for addressing the problems associated with fossil fuels, one that centers on increased research and development to promote alternative technologies. President Obama came out strongly in favor of a comprehensive energy and climate

change bill that would, among other things, provide funding and large tax incentives for the production and adoption of clean-energy technologies. He also warned that the United States was falling behind other countries, including China, in the production of clean-energy products, arguing that this industry would be a vital source of millions of new jobs over the next few decades.[63] The 2009 Recovery Act allocated nearly $30 billion to support alternative energy technology investment and to improve energy efficiency.

Green technologies may prove to be a boon for the American economy. Because highly skilled labor is required to produce most such technologies, America has a competitive advantage over many other countries. Furthermore, a move toward green technologies could significantly improve American national security. Indeed, some argue that reducing the use of fossil fuels and adopting more fuel-efficient technologies would take money away from regimes that support terrorism against the United States.

One strategy for curtailing the effects of climate change is to reduce the use of fossil fuels in favor of "clean-energy" or "green" technologies. In 2016 the Nellis Air Force Base in Las Vegas opened its array of solar panels, which provides 42 percent of the base's electricity requirements.

Adaptation Policies A final approach to climate change is adaptation to a warmer climate. Adaptation would entail a diverse set of policies, including establishment of green corridors, pest and disease control, water conservation to deal with drought, and new infrastructure such as seawalls to cope with rising sea levels.[64] Many scientists believe that deliberate adaptation has to be part of any approach to climate change because even if we take major steps to mitigate carbon emissions and pour resources into developing new technologies, climate change has already arrived.

Many aspects of a deliberate adaptation strategy would be difficult to implement in the market-oriented, decentralized context of the United States. Although some European countries, such as the low-lying Netherlands, are relocating people as part of their adaptation strategy, American politicians have little stomach for initiating such controversial measures. Moreover, the combination of conservation and new infrastructure requires considerable public resources and broad coordination across multiple public agencies. Both are hard to achieve in the context of American politics. For example, the environmentally sensitive Sacramento delta is extremely vulnerable to rising sea levels. The delta, a swath of land that lies below sea level, is economically important because it supplies much of Northern California, including California agribusiness, with water. Yet decisions about what happens in the delta involve more than 200 government agencies.[65]

Global climate change poses a difficult economic challenge for the United States. It presents the opportunity for American industry to take the lead in developing green technologies, placing the nation's economic prosperity on a fundamentally new base. Yet it also calls for government to enforce the reduction of carbon emissions and adapt current practices to a changing world. Many industries have expressed support for action to address climate change, but such a major economic transformation creates winners and losers. Firms, such as the auto companies, whose profits are jeopardized and workers whose jobs are threatened by change have successfully blocked bold action in the past. The diffuse long-term harms that climate change poses are hard to pit against the specific concentrated costs that industries face today. Nonetheless, growing recognition that climate change is real and poses potentially catastrophic consequences ensures that economic policy and environmental policy will be ever more closely intertwined in the future.

Economic Policy
and Your Future

For three decades, a sharp partisan debate has driven the politics of economic policy. Most Republicans have pressed for freer markets and less government, while most Democrats have defended the need for market regulation and more government intervention in the economy. The partisan divisions have made it difficult for policy makers to come to terms with an economy that has changed radically since the debate over more or less government commenced during the Reagan years. The American economy is now far more open to the rest of the world, and many American firms do most of their production in China and other developing economies, not in the United States. At the same time, the distribution of economic gains in the United States has shifted upward. As the debate about more or less government has led to a series of policy stalemates among politicians, the income of the American middle class has stagnated and the gains going to the top 1 percent have soared.[66] Some Americans think the government should do more to address income inequality through tax policy, for example by taxing the wealthy at higher rates. The **"Who Participates?"** feature on the facing page shows taxes as a percentage of income at both the federal and state and local levels.

Everyone agrees that economic policy should address the needs of the next generation and, indeed, frequently refers to the future to defend their views about economic policy. Yet, the great recession and the divisive politics of economic policy have cut short the debate about how federal economic policy can be reoriented to promote future growth and, at the same time, ensure that all Americans have the opportunity to benefit from that growth. To consider the needs of future generations requires shifting the debate over economic policy from "more or less government" to "what kind of government." Should spending priorities be shifted in the face of an altered global economy and wage stagnation at home? Have the last three decades shown us that less government intervention leads to greater gains for the wealthy? As the federal government has stalled over these issues, the action has shifted to states and localities. We have seen in this chapter that many states and localities have raised their minimum wages well above the federal level. Some states are also moving to make community college free for all students. Three states—Tennessee, Minnesota, and Oregon—have passed laws to make community college free. Ten other states are considering such legislation. These and other state models offer important guideposts that can inform federal policy and perhaps ultimately help to break the stalemate over government's role in the economy.

Who Pays Taxes?

Taxes as a Percentage of Income, 2015

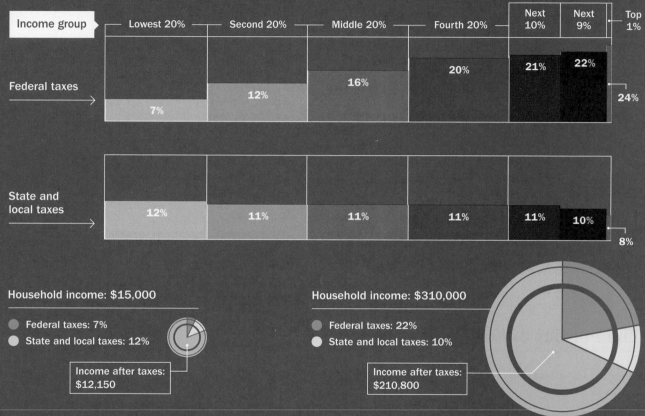

Income group	Lowest 20%	Second 20%	Middle 20%	Fourth 20%	Next 10%	Next 9%	Top 1%
Federal taxes →	7%	12%	16%	20%	21%	22%	24%
State and local taxes →	12%	11%	11%	11%	11%	10%	8%

Household income: $15,000

- Federal taxes: 7%
- State and local taxes: 12%

Income after taxes: $12,150

Household income: $310,000

- Federal taxes: 22%
- State and local taxes: 10%

Income after taxes: $210,800

SOURCE: Citizens for Tax Justice, "Who Pays Taxes in America in 2015?" April 8, 2015, www.ctj.org/pdf/taxday2015.pdf (accessed 1/11/16).

WHAT YOU CAN DO

Compare Tax Rates

 Learn more about how tax rates vary by income, state, and local area at **www.taxfoundation.org**. Contact your representatives at the state or federal level to express your opinion.

 Compare tax rates in the United States to those paid in countries around the world at **www.businessinsider.com/america-taxes-charts-2013-1**.

 Learn more about your rights as a taxpayer, how to get help with your taxes, and how to avoid tax scams from the Internal Revenue Service (**www.irs.gov**).

studyguide

The Goals of Economic Policy

Identify the broad reasons government gets involved in the economy (pp. 629–36)

Public policies, which are officially expressed goals backed by rewards or punishments, can be embodied in laws, rules, regulations, or orders. In contemporary societies, government makes it possible for the economy to function efficiently by setting the rules for economic exchange and punishing those who violate the rules. Through a variety of different policies, the U.S. government has pursued four economic goals over the last century: to promote economic stability, to stimulate economic growth, to promote business development, and to protect employees and consumers.

Key Terms

public policy (p. 629)

public goods (p. 630)

gross domestic product (GDP) (p. 630)

inflation (p. 633)

categorical grants (p. 633)

Practice Quiz

1. Which of the following is *not* one of the goals of government intervention in the economy?
   a) to guarantee economic equality
   b) to promote economic stability
   c) to stimulate economic growth
   d) to promote business development
   e) to protect employees and consumers

2. The total value of goods and services produced within a country is referred to as
   a) the gross national product.
   b) the gross domestic product.
   c) the Dow Jones Industrial Average.
   d) the federal funds rate.
   e) the Gini coefficient.

3. *Inflation* refers to
   a) a lack of change in the general level of prices.
   b) a tax on imported goods.
   c) a consistent increase in the general level of prices.
   d) a consistent decrease in the general level of prices.
   e) an increase in the interest rate on loans between banks.

The Politics of Economic Policy Making

Explore why economic policy is often controversial (pp. 636–45)

Although all politicians want a healthy economy, they often have different views about how to attain it and what the priorities of economic policy should be. The three schools of economic thought that have been most influential with American policy makers, interest groups, and members of the public are Keynesianism, laissez-faire capitalism, and supply-side economics. Government spending is controversial, but there is usually little public support for cutting specific programs. Consumer groups, environmentalists, businesses, and labor all work to shape economic policy.

Key Terms

Keynesians (p. 637)

laissez-faire capitalism (p. 638)

supply-side economics (p. 638)

Practice Quiz

4. The argument for laissez-faire capitalism was first elaborated by
   a) Ben Bernanke.
   b) Milton Friedman.
   c) Alan Greenspan.
   d) James Madison.
   e) Adam Smith.

5. Which of the following economic perspectives argues that government can stimulate economic growth by increasing public spending or by cutting taxes?
   a) Keynesianism
   b) laissez-faire
   c) libertarianism
   d) monetarism
   e) fiscalism

6. Supply-side economics is
   a) an economic theory that argues government regulation of the economy should be limited to environmental protection.
   b) an economic theory that argues for government ownership of the means of production and distribution.
   c) an economic theory that argues tax reductions will spur economic growth because people will be able to spend and invest more of their money.
   d) an economic theory that argues every taxpayer should pay exactly the same tax rate.
   e) an economic theory that argues all taxes should be paid by the consumers of goods and services rather than the suppliers of goods and services.

The Tools of Economic Policy

Describe how the government uses monetary, fiscal, and regulatory policies to influence the economy (pp. 645–59)

The sustained growth of the American economy is the result of specific policies enacted by the U.S. government. The Constitution gives the federal government the power to set monetary and fiscal policies. Monetary policy in the United States is determined primarily by the Federal Reserve Board. Most of the U.S. government's revenues come from personal and corporate income taxes, and most of the federal government's budget is now made up of mandatory, rather than discretionary, spending.

Key Terms

monetary policies (p. 645)
Federal Reserve System (p. 646)
federal funds rate (p. 646)
open-market operations (p. 647)
fiscal policy (p. 648)
tariff (p. 648)
progressive taxation (p. 648)
regressive taxation (p. 648)
redistribution (p. 649)
loophole (p. 649)
budget deficit (p. 652)
mandatory spending (p. 653)
uncontrollables (p. 654)
discretionary spending (p. 654)
monopoly (p. 654)
antitrust policy (p. 654)
deregulation (p. 657)
subsidies (p. 657)
contracting power (p. 658)

Practice Quiz

7. Monetary policy seeks to influence the economy through
   a) taxing and spending.
   b) privatizing and nationalizing selected industries.
   c) controlling the availability of money and credit to banks.
   d) foreign exchange of currency.
   e) administrative regulation.

8. Monetary policy is determined primarily by
   a) state governments.
   b) the Department of the Treasury.
   c) the federal judiciary.
   d) the Federal Reserve Board.
   e) the president.

9. Government attempts to affect the economy by using its taxing and spending powers are called
   a) antitrust policies.
   b) expropriation policies.
   c) monetary policies.
   d) fiscal policies.
   e) redistributive policies.

10. A tax that places a greater burden on those who are better able to afford it is called
    a) regressive.
    b) progressive.
    c) inflationary.
    d) a flat tax.
    e) voodoo economics.

11. A policy whose objective is to tax or spend in such a way as to reduce the disparities of wealth between the highest and lowest income brackets is called
    a) antitrust policy.
    b) deregulation.
    c) discretionary spending.
    d) equalization.
    e) redistribution.

12. Which of the following statements best describes the U.S. budget deficit?
    a) The budget deficit grew substantially in the 1980s and declined substantially in the 1990s before rising sharply again in the 2000s.
    b) The budget deficit declined substantially in the 1980s and grew substantially in the late 1990s into the 2000s.
    c) The budget deficit grew consistently between 1980 and the present.
    d) The budget deficit declined consistently between 1980 and the present.
    e) The budget deficit has remained exactly the same since 1980.

13. Which of the following statements best describes spending in the federal budget?
    a) Mandatory and discretionary spending now make up approximately equal parts of the total budget.
    b) Mandatory spending has been outlawed, and the total budget is now made up of discretionary spending.
    c) Mandatory spending is now a much larger percentage of the total budget than discretionary spending.
    d) Discretionary spending has been outlawed, and the total budget is now made up of mandatory spending.
    e) Discretionary spending is now a much larger percentage of the total budget than mandatory spending.

The Environment and the Economy

Explain why the government tries to balance economic prosperity with policies that protect the environment (pp. 659–63)

The federal government frequently regulates industry in order to protect the environment. One of the most important environmental issues currently facing the U.S. government is climate change. Policy makers charged with devising approaches to the problem of climate change have identified three basic approaches: mitigation of greenhouse emissions, promotion of alternative energy technologies, and adaptation to a warmer climate.

Practice Quiz

14. A cap-and-trade system is an example of which kind of policy approach to global warming?
    a) adaptation to a warmer climate
    b) not in my backyard (NIMBY)
    c) supply-side economics
    d) mitigation of greenhouse gas emissions
    e) promotion of alternative energy technologies

For Further Reading

Baldwin, Robert, Martin Cave, and Martin Lodge. *Understanding Regulation*. New York: Oxford University Press, 2012.

Bernanke, Ben S. *The Federal Reserve and the Financial Crisis*. Princeton, NJ: Princeton University Press, 2013.

Blanchard, Olivier, Paul Romer, Michael Spence, and Joseph Stiglitz. *In the Wake of the Crisis: Leading Economists Reassess Economic Policy*. Cambridge, MA: MIT Press, 2012.

Frank, Robert H. *Falling Behind: How Rising Inequality Harms the Middle Class*. Berkeley: University of California Press, 2007.

Friedman, Milton, and Walter Heller. *Monetary versus Fiscal Policy*. New York: W. W. Norton, 1969.

Hacker, Jacob S., and Paul Pierson. *Winner-Take-All Politics: How Washington Made the Rich Richer—And Turned Its Back on the Middle Class*. New York: Simon and Schuster, 2010.

Harris, Richard A., and Sidney M. Milkis. *The Politics of Regulatory Change*. 2nd ed. New York: Oxford University Press, 1996.

Jacobs, Lawrence, and Theda Skocpol, eds. *Inequality and American Democracy: What We Know and What We Need to Learn*. New York: Russell Sage Foundation, 2005.

McCarty, Nolan, Keith T. Poole, and Howard Rosenthal. *Political Bubbles: Financial Crises and the Failure of American Democracy*. Princeton, NJ: Princeton University Press, 2013.

Page, Benjamin I., and Lawrence R. Jacobs. *Class War: What Americans Really Think about Economic Inequality*. Chicago: University of Chicago Press, 2009.

Schick, Allen. *The Federal Budget: Politics, Policy, Process*. 3rd ed. Washington, DC: Brookings Institution Press, 2007.

Stein, Robert M., and Kenneth N. Bickers. *Perpetuating the Pork Barrel: Policy Subsystems and American Democracy*. New York: Cambridge University Press, 1995.

Stiglitz, Joseph E. *Rewriting the Rules of the American Economy: An Agenda for Growth and Shared Prosperity*. New York: W. W. Norton, 2015.

Waterhouse, Benjamin C. *Lobbying America: The Politics of Business from Nixon to NAFTA*. Princeton, NJ: Princeton University Press, 2014.

Wells, David. *The Federal Reserve System*. Jefferson, NC: McFarland, 2004.

Recommended Websites

Board of Governors of the Federal Reserve System
www.federalreserve.gov

The Federal Reserve System consists of 12 banks that use monetary policy to fight inflation and deflation. Visit the Fed's official website to see how it is working to maintain a strong economy.

Citizens for Tax Justice
www.ctj.org

Review federal, state, and local tax laws at the website of Citizens for Tax Justice. This nonprofit organization is dedicated to educating ordinary citizens about tax laws and reducing the tax burden on low- and middle-income Americans.

National Bureau of Economic Research
www.nber.org

The National Bureau of Economic Research is a nonprofit, nonpartisan organization dedicated to creating a better understanding of the economy. Take a minute to review some of its free research publications.

Tax Foundation
www.taxfoundation.org

The Tax Foundation is a respected organization that has been providing Americans with information about tax policy for more than 50 years. Click on your state to learn about current tax and spending policies.

Treasury Direct
www.treasurydirect.gov/govt/govt.htm

Treasury Direct, part of the U.S. Department of the Treasury, provides a statistical look at federal, state, and public debt.

U.S. Department of Commerce
www.commerce.gov

The U.S. Department of Commerce promotes domestic and international commerce to foster economic progress. Review the initiatives and programs designed to encourage economic development.

U.S. Department of Labor
www.dol.gov

The U.S. Department of Labor seeks to promote the well-being of wage earners, retired workers, and people looking for work. Look under "popular topics" to see some of the ways that the department aims to improve the conditions of workers.

Health care is an area of social policy that has been controversial. Although most Americans support universal access to health care, they disagree about the best way to ensure high-quality health care. Americans were divided over President Obama's 2010 comprehensive health care reform initiative, the Affordable Care Act, which underwent two Supreme Court challenges.

Social Policy

WHAT GOVERNMENT DOES AND WHY IT MATTERS Social policies promote a range of public goals. The first is to protect against the risks and insecurities that most people face over the course of their lives. These include illness, disability, temporary unemployment, and the reduced earning capability that comes with old age. Most spending on social welfare in the United States goes to programs that serve these purposes, such as Social Security and medical insurance for the elderly. These programs are widely regarded as successful and popular. Although large projected deficits in both programs have generated conflict, they are the least controversial areas of social spending.

Comprehensive health care reform is more controversial. Most Americans support universal access to health care, but when it comes to specific proposals, they often express doubts. Democrats experienced the public ambivalence about health care reform after they enacted major changes to the system in 2010. The Affordable Care Act was complex legislation that many people found hard to understand. Some parts of it were clearly popular, such as the provision allowing young people to remain on their parents' insurance until they reached the age of 26 and full coverage of many preventive health services for adults and children. Other features, such as the requirement that everyone purchase insurance, with federal assistance, were unpopular. When the Supreme Court ruled that most of the act, including the individual mandate, was constitutional, the public remained divided. Even after the act was fully implemented in 2014 and survived another challenge in the Supreme Court in 2015, the public was split, with 42 percent of Americans holding unfavorable views of the legislation and 42 percent holding favorable views. Nearly five years after its enactment, Americans could not agree about the role government should play in ensuring health care for all.[1]

Two other goals of social policy have also been controversial: promoting equality of opportunity and assisting the poor. Although Americans admire the ideal of equal opportunity, there is no general agreement about what government should do to address inequalities: groups that have suffered from past inequality generally support much more extensive government action to promote equality of opportunity than do others. Yet most Americans support some government action, especially in the area of education.

The third goal of social policy, to alleviate poverty, has long generated controversy in the United States. Americans take pride in their strong work ethic and prize the value of self-sufficiency. As a result, the majority of Americans express suspicion that the able-bodied poor will not try hard enough to support themselves if they are offered too much assistance or if they receive the wrong kind of assistance. Yet Americans also recognize that poverty may be the product of past inequality of opportunity. Since the 1960s, a variety of educational programs and income-assistance policies have sought to end poverty and promote equal opportunity. Much progress has been made toward these goals. However, the disproportionate rates of poverty among minorities suggest that our policies have not solved the problem of unequal opportunity. Likewise, the high rates of child poverty challenge us to find new ways to assist the poor.

American social policy reflects the nation's views about which risks should be borne by the individual and which should be shared by society as a whole. As such, social policy reflects public wishes, as would be expected in a democracy. However, Americans often have quite different views about how social policy should advance the value of equality. Polls show that two-thirds of Americans believe that the distribution of money and wealth should be more even, and there is broad consensus that equality of opportunity is not only desirable but also an essential part of American culture.[2] There is much less agreement about which social policies are needed to reduce the gulf between the rich and the poor and to promote equality of opportunity.

chapter goals

- Trace the history of government programs designed to promote economic security (pp. 673–84)

- Describe how education, health, and housing policies try to advance equality of opportunity (pp. 685–96)

- Explain how contributory and noncontributory programs benefit different groups of Americans (pp. 696–703)

The Welfare State

Trace the history of government programs designed to promote economic security

For much of American history, local governments and private charities were in charge of caring for the poor. During the 1930s, when this largely private system of charity collapsed in the face of widespread economic destitution, the federal government created the beginnings of an American welfare state. The idea of the welfare state was new; it meant that the national government would oversee programs designed to promote economic security for all Americans—not just for the poor. The American system of social welfare comprises many different policies enacted over the years since the Great Depression. Because each program is governed by distinct rules, the kind and level of assistance available vary widely.

The History of the Social Welfare System

America has always had a welfare system, but until 1935 it was almost entirely private, composed of an extensive system of voluntary donations through churches and other religious groups, ethnic and fraternal societies, communities and neighborhoods, and philanthropically inclined wealthy individuals. Most often it was called "charity," and although it was private and voluntary, it was thought of as a public obligation.

There were great variations in the generosity of charity from town to town, but one thing seems to have been universal—the tradition of distinguishing between two classes of poor: the "deserving poor" and the "undeserving poor." The deserving poor were widows and orphans and others rendered dependent by some misfortune, such as the death or serious injury of the family's breadwinner in the course of war or honest labor. The undeserving poor were able-bodied persons unwilling to work, transients new to the community, and others of whom, for various reasons, the community did not approve. Thus, private charity was a very subjective matter: the givers and their agents spent a great deal of time and resources examining the qualifications, both economic and moral, of the seekers of charity.

Before the Great Depression, much of the private charity was given in cash, called "outdoor relief." But because of fears that outdoor relief spawned poverty rather than relieving or preventing it, many communities set up settlement houses and other "indoor relief" institutions. A still larger institution of indoor relief was the police station, where many of America's poor sought temporary shelter. But even in the severest weather, the homeless could not stay in police stations for many nights without being jailed as vagrants.[3]

The severe limitations on financing faced by private charitable organizations and settlement houses slowly produced a movement by many groups toward public responsibility for some of these charitable or welfare functions. Workers' compensation laws were enacted in a few states, for example; but the effect of such laws was limited because they benefited only workers injured on the job and, of them, only those who worked for certain types of companies. A more important effort, one that led more directly to the modern welfare state, was public aid to mothers with dependent children. Beginning in Illinois in 1911, the movement for mothers' pensions spread to include 40 states by 1926. Initially such aid was viewed as simply an inexpensive alternative to providing "indoor relief" to mothers

During the depression, the government took a more active role in helping poor and struggling Americans. Here, people line up to receive free bread.

and their children. Moreover, applicants not only had to pass a rigorous means test but also had to prove they were deserving because the laws provided that assistance would be given only to individuals who were deemed "physically, mentally, and morally fit." In most states, a mother was deemed unfit if her children were born out of wedlock.[4]

In effect, these criteria proved to be racially discriminatory. Many African Americans in the South and ethnic immigrants in the North were denied benefits on the grounds of "moral unfitness." Furthermore, local governments were allowed to decide whether to establish such pension programs. In the South, many counties with large numbers of African American women refused to implement assistance programs.

Despite the spread of state government programs to assume some of the obligation to relieve the poor, the private sector remained dominant until the 1930s. Even as late as 1928 only 11.6 percent of all relief granted in 15 of the largest cities came from public funds.[5] Nevertheless, the various state and local public experiences provided guidance and precedents for the national government's welfare system.

The traditional approach, dominated by the private sector, with its severe distinction between deserving and undeserving poor, crumbled in the face of the stark reality of the Great Depression in 1929. During the depression, misfortune became so widespread and private wealth shrank so drastically that private charity was out of the question, and the distinction between deserving and undeserving became impossible to draw. Around 20 percent of the workforce immediately became unemployed; this figure grew as the depression stretched into years. Moreover, few of these individuals had any monetary resources or any family farm on which to fall back. Banks failed, wiping out the savings of millions who had been fortunate enough to have any savings at all. Thousands of businesses failed as well, throwing middle-class Americans onto the bread lines along with unemployed laborers, dispossessed farmers, and those who had never worked in any capacity whatsoever. The Great Depression proved to Americans that poverty could be a result of imperfections in the economic system as well as of individual irresponsibility. It also forced Americans to drastically alter their standards regarding who was deserving and who was not.

Once poverty and dependency were accepted as problems inherent in the economic system, a large-scale public policy approach was not far away. By the time the Roosevelt administration took office in 1933 the question was not whether there was to be a public welfare system but how generous or restrictive that system would be.

Foundations of the Welfare State

The founding of the modern welfare state in the United States occurred with the passage of the Social Security Act of 1935. This act created two separate categories of welfare: contributory and noncontributory.

Contributory Programs The category of welfare programs financed by taxation can justifiably be called "forced savings"; these programs force working Americans to contribute a portion of their earnings to provide income and benefits for present-day retirees, with the understanding that younger workers will one day provide for them in the same way. These **contributory programs** are what most people have in mind when they refer to **Social Security** or social insurance. Under the original contributory program, old-age insurance, the employer and the employee were each required to pay equal amounts, which in 1937 were set at 1 percent of the first $3,000 in wages, to be deducted from the paycheck of each employee and matched by the same amount from the employer. This percentage has increased over the years; the contribution in 2016 was 7.65 percent subdivided as follows: 6.2 percent on the first $118,500 of income for Social Security benefits plus 1.45 percent on all earnings for Medicare. Starting in 2014, households earning over $250,000 a year paid an extra 0.9 percent in Medicare taxes due to a provision in the Patient Protection and Affordable Care Act (ACA).[6]

Social Security may seem to be a rather conservative approach to welfare. In effect, the Social Security tax, as a forced saving, sends a message that people cannot be trusted to save voluntarily to take care of their own needs. But in another sense, it is quite radical. Social Security is not real insurance; workers' contributions do not accumulate in a personal account, as they would in an annuity. Consequently, contributors do not receive benefits in proportion to their contributions, and this means that a redistribution of wealth is occurring. The formula by which Social Security benefits are calculated aims to provide lower-income workers with a higher proportion of their contributions than higher-income workers receive. This is because the goal of Social Security is to ensure a basic income to all workers once they retire. Research has shown, however, that due to different mortality rates and other factors, the system does not end up redistributing from well-off to less well-off workers as intended by the formula. The system does redistribute to women, who earn less than men, have fewer years in the workforce (and hence tend to contribute less to Social Security than do men), and live longer than men.[7] In the short term, Social Security redistributes money from the young to the old: the taxes of current workers are paying for the benefits received by retirees. But Social Security also plays a vital role for young people by providing survivor benefits to those whose parents die, retire, or become disabled. Surviving spouses also receive survivor benefits.

Congress increased Social Security benefits every two or three years during the 1950s and '60s. Today the average payment is $1,335 each month.[8] In 1972, Congress decided to end the grind of biennial legislation to increase benefits by establishing **indexing**, whereby benefits paid out under contributory programs would be modified annually by **cost-of-living adjustments (COLAs)** designed to increase benefits to keep up with the rate of inflation. But, of course, Social Security taxes

contributory programs social programs financed in whole or in part by taxation or other mandatory contributions by their present or future recipients

Social Security a contributory welfare program into which working Americans contribute a percentage of their wages and from which they receive cash benefits after retirement or if they become disabled

indexing periodic process of adjusting social benefits or wages to account for increases in the cost of living

cost-of-living adjustments (COLAs) changes made to the level of benefits of a government program based on the rate of inflation

Medicare a form of national health insurance for the elderly and the disabled

noncontributory programs social programs that provide assistance to people on the basis of demonstrated need rather than any contribution they have made

means testing a procedure by which potential beneficiaries of a public-assistance program establish their eligibility by demonstrating a genuine need for the assistance

Medicaid a federally and state-financed, state-operated program providing medical services to low-income people

The Supplemental Nutrition Assistance Program (SNAP), formerly known as "food stamps," helps people in need buy food. Today recipients use a government-provided debit card that is accepted at most grocery stores.

(contributions) also increased after almost every benefit increase. This made Social Security, in the words of one observer, "a politically ideal program. It bridged partisan conflict by providing liberal benefits under conservative financial auspices."[9] In other words, conservatives could more readily yield to the demands of the well-organized and ever-growing constituency of elderly voters if benefit increases were automatic; liberals could cement conservative support by agreeing to finance the increased benefits through increases in the regressive Social Security tax, paid into a special Social Security fund, rather than out of the general revenues coming from the more progressive income tax, which are paid into the Treasury. (See Chapter 16 for a discussion of regressive and progressive taxes.)

The biggest single expansion in contributory programs since 1935 was the establishment in 1965 of **Medicare**, which provides substantial medical services to elderly persons who are already eligible to receive old-age, survivors', and disability insurance under the original Social Security system.

Unemployment insurance is another contributory program that is funded by a combination of federal and state taxes. States set benefit levels and eligibility criteria for receiving unemployment insurance and tax employers to fund the program. In most states, benefits last for a maximum of 26 weeks. In periods of high unemployment, Congress can enact extended benefits that authorize an additional 13 weeks for those who have exhausted their regular benefits. Such benefits are generally funded by federal taxes. Unemployment benefits are meant to help replace lost wages, but they do so at a low level: most workers receive only half of their wages. Moreover, because states impose criteria about how long a person must work or how much she must earn to become eligible for unemployment insurance, only about half of workers who lose their jobs receive unemployment benefits.[10]

Noncontributory Programs Programs to which beneficiaries do not have to contribute—**noncontributory programs**—are also known as "public-assistance programs," or, more commonly, as "welfare." Until 1996 the most important noncontributory program was Aid to Families with Dependent Children (AFDC)—originally called Aid to Dependent Children—which was founded in 1935 by the original Social Security Act. In 1996, Congress abolished AFDC and replaced it with the Temporary Assistance for Needy Families (TANF) block grant. Eligibility for public assistance is determined by **means testing**, a procedure that requires applicants to show a financial need for assistance. Between 1935 and 1965, the government created programs to provide housing assistance, school lunches, and food stamps to other needy Americans.

Like contributory programs, the noncontributory public-assistance programs also made their most significant advances during the 1960s and '70s. The largest single category of expansion was the establishment in 1965 of **Medicaid**, a program that provides extended medical services to low-income Americans. Noncontributory programs underwent another major transformation during the 1970s in the level of benefits they provide. Besides being means-tested, noncontributory programs are state-based; grants-in-aid are provided by the federal government to the states as incentives to establish the programs, but states retain considerable leeway to establish eligibility criteria (see Chapter 3). Thus, from the beginning there were considerable disparities in benefits from state to state. The national government sought to rectify the disparities in levels of old-age benefits in 1974 by creating the Supplemental Security Income (SSI) program to augment benefits for the elderly, the blind, and the disabled. SSI provides uniform minimum benefits across the entire nation and includes mandatory COLAs. States are allowed to be more generous if they wish, but no state is permitted to provide benefits below the minimum level set by the national government. As a result, 25 states increased their SSI benefits to the mandated level.

The TANF program is also administered by the states, and, as with the old-age benefits just discussed, benefit levels vary widely from state to state (see Figure 17.1). For example, in 2015, the states' monthly TANF benefits for a family of three varied from $170 in Mississippi to $923 in Alaska.[11] Even the most generous TANF payments are well below the federal poverty line. In 2016 the poverty level for a family of three included those earning less than $20,160 a year or $1,680 a month.[12]

The number of people receiving AFDC benefits expanded in the 1970s, in part because new welfare programs had been established during the mid-1960s: Medicaid (discussed earlier) and the **Supplemental Nutrition Assistance Program (SNAP)**, which is still sometimes called by its old name, *food stamps*. These programs provide what are called **in-kind benefits**—noncash goods and services that would otherwise have to be paid for in cash by the beneficiary. Because AFDC recipients automatically

Supplemental Nutrition Assistance Program (SNAP) the largest antipoverty program, which provides recipients with a debit card for food at most grocery stores; formerly known as *food stamps*

in-kind benefits noncash goods and services provided to needy individuals and families by the federal government

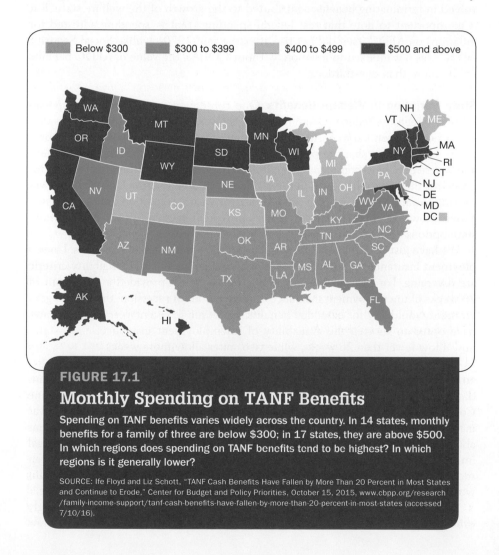

Below $300 $300 to $399 $400 to $499 $500 and above

FIGURE 17.1

Monthly Spending on TANF Benefits

Spending on TANF benefits varies widely across the country. In 14 states, monthly benefits for a family of three are below $300; in 17 states, they are above $500. In which regions does spending on TANF benefits tend to be highest? In which regions is it generally lower?

SOURCE: Ife Floyd and Liz Schott, "TANF Cash Benefits Have Fallen by More Than 20 Percent in Most States and Continue to Erode," Center for Budget and Policy Priorities, October 15, 2015, www.cbpp.org/research /family-income-support/tanf-cash-benefits-have-fallen-by-more-than-20-percent-in-most-states (accessed 7/10/16).

received Medicaid and food stamps, these new programs created an incentive for poor Americans to establish their eligibility for AFDC.

Another, more complex reason for the growth of AFDC in the 1970s was that it became more difficult for the government to terminate people's AFDC benefits for lack of eligibility. In the 1970 case of *Goldberg v. Kelly*, the Supreme Court held that the financial benefits of AFDC could not be revoked without due process— that is, a hearing at which evidence is presented.[13] This ruling inaugurated the concept of **entitlement**, a class of government benefits with a status similar to that of property (which, according to the Fourteenth Amendment, cannot be taken from people "without due process of law"). *Goldberg v. Kelly* did not provide that the beneficiary had a "right" to government benefits; it provided that once a person's eligibility for AFDC was established, and as long as the program was still in effect, that person could not be denied benefits without due process. The decision left open the possibility that Congress could terminate the program and its benefits by way of legislation. If the welfare benefit were truly a property right, Congress would have no authority to deny it.

Thus, the establishment of in-kind benefit programs and the legal obstacles involved in terminating benefits contributed to the growth of the welfare state. But it is important to note that real federal spending (that is, spending adjusted for inflation) on AFDC itself did not rise after the mid-1970s. Unlike Social Security, AFDC was not indexed to inflation; without COLAs, the value of AFDC benefits fell by more than one-third.

State Variation in Welfare Benefits One consequence of the shared responsibility between the federal government and the states for welfare programs is that social benefits can vary considerably by state. State variation is greatest in programs where states share responsibility for funding with the federal government and where they have considerable flexibility to set eligibility criteria, as they do for programs that cover the needy. In the 1970s it appeared that the United States was moving toward a more national set of standards with the creation of SSI, discussed above. However, since that time, changes in federal laws and provisions for more state options have created considerable divergences among the states.

We have just seen the wide variation in TANF benefits across the states. Unemployment insurance is another policy in which state benefits and eligibility criteria are diverging. For most of the program's history, states provided a maximum of 26 weeks of unemployment insurance; but in periods of recession, the federal government would pay for extended benefits. However, in recent years several states have opted to shorten the availability of unemployment insurance: eight states now allow fewer than 26 weeks, while two states allow more weeks.[14]

The provisions for expanding Medicaid under the ACA of 2010, which we examine more closely below, initially aimed to create an expanded Medicaid program that would establish uniformity in eligibility across the states. When the Supreme Court gave states the right to opt out of the expansion, however, the result was increased state variation as 19 states have opted out. States make other decisions about Medicaid eligibility that create state variation. For example, noncitizen legal immigrants are required to reside in the United States for five years before they can receive Medicaid, but states can waive this requirement for children and pregnant women. Twenty-nine states and the District of Columbia waive this requirement.[15]

The political polarization we have seen in national politics is increasingly evident in state choices about social benefits. States governed solely by Democrats

entitlement a legal obligation of the federal government to provide payments to individuals, or groups of individuals, according to eligibility criteria or benefit rules

or solely by Republicans take very different perspectives on social policy. The result is a patchwork that is growing more, not less, diverse.

Welfare Reform

From the 1960s to the 1990s, opinion polls consistently showed that the public viewed welfare beneficiaries as "undeserving."[16] Underlying that judgment was the belief that welfare recipients did not want to work. Common criticisms charged that welfare recipients were taking advantage of the system, that they were irresponsible people who refused to work. These negative assessments were amplified by racial stereotypes. By 1973, 46 percent of welfare recipients were African American. Although the majority of recipients were white, media portrayals helped create the widespread perception that the vast majority of welfare recipients were black. A careful study by Martin Gilens has shown how racial stereotypes of blacks as uncommitted to the work ethic reinforced public opposition to welfare.[17]

Despite negative public sentiment toward welfare and welfare recipients, it proved difficult to reform welfare. While many reformers wanted to require work in exchange for benefits, few wished to be seen as harming children by eliminating benefits. Yet providing services such as child care that would enable single mothers to work would require spending substantially more on welfare, when most reformers wished to spend less on the program. A significant reform in 1988 imposed stricter work requirements but also provided additional support services, such as child care and transportation assistance. This compromise legislation reflected a growing consensus that effective reform entailed a combination of sticks (work requirements) and carrots (extra services to make work possible). The reform also created a new system to identify the absent parent (usually the father) and enforce child-support payments.

These reforms were barely implemented when welfare rolls rose again with the recession of the early 1990s, reaching an all-time high in 1994. Sensing continuing public frustration with welfare, when Bill Clinton was a presidential candidate he vowed "to end welfare as we know it," an unusual promise for a Democrat. Once in office, Clinton found it difficult to design a plan that would provide an adequate safety net for recipients unable to find work. Clinton's major achievement in the welfare field was to increase the Earned Income Tax Credit (EITC). This credit now allows working parents whose annual income falls below $53,300 (for a family of three or more) to file through their income tax return for an income supplement of up to $6,242, depending on their income and family size. The average EITC benefit in 2015 was $2,400.[18]

Congressional Republicans then proposed a much more dramatic reform of welfare, which Clinton, facing a campaign for re-election in 1996, signed. The Personal Responsibility and Work Opportunity Reconciliation Act repealed AFDC. In place of the individual entitlement to assistance, the new law created block grants to the states and allowed states much more discretion in designing their cash-assistance programs to needy families. The new law also established time limits, restricting recipients to two years of assistance at a time and creating a lifetime limit of five years. It imposed new work requirements on those receiving welfare, and it restricted most legal immigrants from receiving benefits. The aim of the new law was to reduce welfare caseloads, promote work, and reduce out-of-wedlock births. Notably, reducing poverty was not one of its stated objectives.

In recent decades, welfare reform has emphasized work requirements and training for unemployed recipients. Here, an instructor provides training in using power tools as part of a Detroit-area welfare-to-work program funded by the federal government.

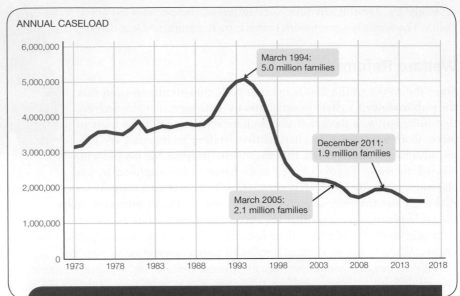

ANNUAL CASELOAD

March 1994:
5.0 million families

December 2011:
1.9 million families

March 2005:
2.1 million families

FIGURE 17.2

Welfare Caseload, 1973–2016

Welfare caseloads began to decline even before the 1996 reform. They have continued to plummet in the years since welfare reform. Welfare caseloads remained low even during the recession that began in 2008. Does the decline in the welfare caseload show that the 1996 reform was successful?

*Average monthly AFDC/TANF and SSP (separate state programs) families caseload.
SOURCE: U.S. Department of Health and Human Services, Administration for Children and Families, "Appendix Table 2:1: Average Monthly AFDC/TANF and SSP Families and Recipients, Fiscal Years 1960–2011," TANF: Tenth Report to Congress, December 12, 2013, www.acf.hhs.gov/sites/default/files /ofa/10th_tanf_report_congress_appendix.pdf; U.S. Department of Health and Human Services, Administration for Children and Families, Data and Reports, Caseload Data, www.acf.hhs.gov/programs/ofa/programs /tanf/data-reports (accessed 4/29/14); U.S. Department of Health and Human Services, Administration for Children and Families, TANF Caseload Data, 2016, 2015, 2014, June 24, 2016, www.acf.hhs.gov /programs/ofa/resource/tanf-caseload-data-2016 (accessed 7/10/16).

for critical analysis

Why was AFDC such an unpopular program? How did the creation of TANF alter welfare, and what has it meant for TANF as an antipoverty program? Should TANF be reformed again?

After this law was enacted, the number of families receiving assistance dropped by 60 percent nationwide (see Figure 17.2). The sharp decline in the number of recipients was widely hailed as a sign that the welfare reform was working. Indeed, former welfare recipients have been more successful at finding and keeping jobs than many critics of the law predicted. One important indicator of how welfare has changed is the proportion of funds it provides in cash assistance. Before the 1996 reform, assistance was provided largely in the form of a cash grant. After the reform, 64 percent of welfare funds were allocated for noncash services and 36 percent for cash assistance.[19] This means that an increasing proportion of welfare funds is spent on such costs as assistance with transportation to work, temporary shelter, or one-time payments for emergencies so that people do not go on the welfare rolls. The orientation of assistance has shifted away from subsidizing people who are not in the labor force and toward addressing temporary problems that low-income people face and providing assistance that facilitates work. But critics point out that most former welfare recipients are not paid enough to pull their families out of poverty. While the 1996 law has helped reduce welfare caseloads, it has done little to reduce the underlying problem of poverty.[20]

As the economy soured in 2009 and 2010, the number of people on welfare rolls began to move upward but at a very slow rate. The American Recovery and Reinvestment Act of 2009 included a TANF Emergency Fund that provided monies for states to create subsidized jobs for low-income parents and young adults. Despite these measures, many advocates for the poor worried that the state TANF programs were not assisting enough poor families. After the Emergency Fund expired in 2011, advocates for the poor charged that, with states making deep cuts to their budgets, TANF was not keeping pace with the growth of poverty caused by the recession.[21] They contrasted it to the growth of the supplemental nutrition program (SNAP, or food stamps), whose growth closely tracked the rise in unemployment and poverty during the recession. In 2007, before the recession took hold, approximately 26.3 million individuals received SNAP benefits. By 2015, that number had risen to approximately 45 million people a month, close to 15 percent of all Americans.[22]

How Do We Pay for the Welfare State?

Since the 1930s, when the main elements of the welfare state were first created, spending on social policy has grown dramatically. Most striking has been the growth of entitlement programs, the largest of which are Social Security and Medicare. The costs of entitlement programs grew from 26 percent of the total federal budget in 1962 to 64.1 percent by 2014. Funds to pay for these social programs have come disproportionately from increases in payroll taxes. In 1970, social insurance taxes accounted for 23 percent of all federal revenues; in 2016, they had grown to 33 percent of all federal revenues.[23] Meanwhile, since 1970, corporate taxes have fallen from 17 to 11.1 percent of all federal revenues. Because the payroll tax is regressive, low- and middle-income families have carried the burden for funding increased social spending.

Although much public attention has centered on welfare and other social spending programs for the poor, such as food stamps, these programs account for only a small proportion of social spending. For example, even at its height, AFDC made up only 1 percent of the federal budget. In recent years, Congress has tightly controlled spending on most means-tested programs, and lawmakers and government officials currently express little concern that spending on such programs is out of control. Spending on SNAP benefits rose substantially during the recession, but even at these historically high rates, spending on programs for the poor is dwarfed by the costs of social insurance programs for the elderly. As Figure 17.3 shows, together the three biggest programs that assist low-income people (SNAP, Medicaid, and unemployment insurance) accounted for 2.6 percent of gross domestic product (GDP) in 2016, while spending on programs targeted at the elderly—Social Security and Medicare—together represented 8.1 percent of GDP.[24]

Spending on Social Security The biggest spending increases to the welfare state have come in social insurance programs that provide benefits to the elderly. Such expenditures are hard to control because these programs are entitlements, and the government has promised to cover all people who fit the category of beneficiary. So, for example, the burgeoning elderly population will require that spending on Social Security automatically increase in the future. Furthermore, because Social Security benefits are indexed to inflation, there is no easy way to reduce benefits. Spending on medical programs (Medicare and Medicaid) has also proved difficult

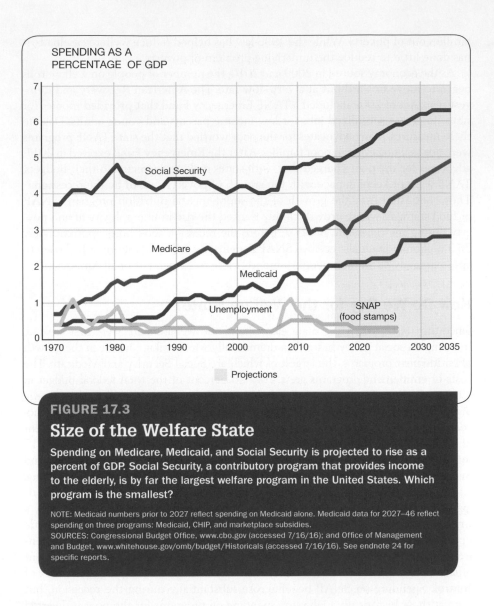

SPENDING AS A
PERCENTAGE OF GDP

Social Security

Medicare

Medicaid

Unemployment

SNAP
(food stamps)

Projections

FIGURE 17.3

Size of the Welfare State

Spending on Medicare, Medicaid, and Social Security is projected to rise as a percent of GDP. Social Security, a contributory program that provides income to the elderly, is by far the largest welfare program in the United States. Which program is the smallest?

NOTE: Medicaid numbers prior to 2027 reflect spending on Medicaid alone. Medicaid data for 2027–46 reflect spending on three programs: Medicaid, CHIP, and marketplace subsidies.
SOURCES: Congressional Budget Office, www.cbo.gov (accessed 7/16/16); and Office of Management and Budget, www.whitehouse.gov/omb/budget/Historicals (accessed 7/16/16). See endnote 24 for specific reports.

to limit, in part because of the growing numbers of people eligible for the programs but also because of rising health care costs. Health care expenditures have risen much more steeply than inflation in recent years.

Concern about social spending has centered on Social Security because the aging of the baby-boom generation will force spending up sharply in the coming decades. In the past, there were always many more young workers than retirees receiving Social Security. That situation is changing as individuals live longer and as the very large generation known as the baby boomers reaches retirement. Indeed, under current law, the Social Security Trust Fund, the special government account from which Social Security payments are made, is projected to experience a shortfall beginning in 2034.[25]

Critics also contend that Americans are not getting their money's worth from Social Security and that workers would be better off if they could take at least part of the payroll tax that currently pays for Social Security and invest it in individual accounts. They highlight unfavorable rates of return in the current system, noting, for example, that a male worker born in 2000 who is single can expect to see a return of only 0.86 percent on his Social Security contributions. This is far below stock market returns over the past decades.[26] These arguments have received less attention since the economic recession which started in 2008 and the stock market volatility that accompanied it.

Because Social Security is such a popular program, proposed changes that might weaken it are generally greeted with suspicion, and politicians often shy away from proposing changes to the system. President George W. Bush was an exception, however; and he came to office supporting Social Security reforms, including the creation of private retirement accounts. Soon after taking office, the president appointed the Social Security Commission, whose final report prominently featured individual accounts as a reform strategy. The commission recommended three reform plans, each of which offered workers the choice of contributing a portion (ranging from 2 to 4 percent) of the payroll tax to an individual account. The worker's traditional benefits would be reduced by the amount diverted to the individual account. According to the commission, individual plans would create a better system because they would allow workers to accumulate assets and build wealth that could be passed on to their children.[27]

Given the politically volatile character of debates about Social Security, Bush backed off from proposing any changes in the program during his first term; but in 2004, immediately after his re-election, Bush announced that he would make Social Security reform a centerpiece of his next administration. Although he did not put forth a precise plan, private accounts were at the heart of his approach to reform. During the first half of 2005, the president toured the country attempting to win support for his ideas. But he immediately faced huge opposition as unions and AARP mobilized to oppose him. AARP launched a national advertising campaign against private accounts. Senate Democrats, displaying unusual unity, closed ranks against the president's ideas. By October 2005 the president had to admit that Social Security reform was dead. When Republicans gained control of the House of Representatives in 2011, they remembered Bush's experience and refrained from proposing changes to Social Security.

Supporters of the current Social Security system contend that the system's financial troubles are exaggerated. They dispute arguments that deficits require cuts in Social Security. They point out that Social Security taxes were raised in 1983 and that the program's trust funds were officially placed "off budget," in a so-called lockbox, so that the program would be prepared to serve the aging baby-boom generation.[28] They argue that instead of saving that money, however, the federal government cut taxes on the wealthy and used Social Security taxes to finance the deficit in the federal operating budget. Advocates of the current system believe that many of Social Security's troubles could be solved by raising income taxes on the wealthy and eliminating the cap on payroll taxes. In 2016 only the first $118,500 in income was subject to the payroll tax. If this cap were lifted, these critics argue, the resulting revenues would cut the expected shortfall in the Social Security Trust Fund in half.

Supporters of the current system are also deeply skeptical about the benefits of individual accounts. They charged that

The Social Security system is one of the most popular government programs, but recent reports have estimated that by 2034 it will be unable to pay full benefits. Both parties have proposed reforms to address the projected shortfall, but the issue remains highly controversial.

When government has tried to re-form Social Security or Medicare, beneficiaries of these programs have rallied together—often successfully—in opposition.

President Bush presented a rosy scenario that overestimated likely gains through the stock market. When more realistic assumptions are adopted and the costs of the private accounts are considered, the critics argue, individual accounts would not provide higher benefits than the current system. Moreover, they note that individual accounts would do nothing to solve the budget crisis that Social Security will face.[29]

Finally, supporters of the present system emphasize that Social Security is not just a retirement account but also a social insurance program that provides "income protection to workers and their families if the wage earner retires, becomes disabled, or dies."[30] Because it provides this social insurance protection, supporters argue, Social Security's returns should not be compared with those of a private retirement account.

In 2010, President Obama appointed a bipartisan commission on reducing the national debt, which recommended reforms to Social Security. The commission recommended increasing Social Security taxes on the wealthy, increasing the age for receiving benefits, and gradually reducing future benefits. But in a charged political context, neither party wanted to take the initiative on reforms that would ensure that Social Security remain solvent.

Spending on Medicare Although much of the public debate has focused on the costs of Social Security, most experts agree that Medicare and Medicaid pose the biggest budget challenge. The rapidly rising cost of health care—often at twice the rate of inflation—makes it much harder to control how much the government spends. Moreover, as more of the large baby-boom generation reaches age 65, the costs of Medicare are expected to skyrocket. While payroll taxes are sufficient to cover Social Security payments fully until 2034 and small changes in benefits and taxes would see the program through the baby-boom retirement years, the cost challenges to Medicare are much more significant. In 2014, payroll taxes accounted for only 38 percent of all Medicare revenues; 41 percent came from general revenues.[31] In 2014, Medicare accounted for 14 percent of the federal budget, and Medicare costs present an ongoing challenge in the effort to reduce the deficit.[32]

A sweeping plan for reforming Medicare and Medicaid came from Paul Ryan (R-Wisc.), who in 2011 proposed replacing the current program with payments—called "premium support"—that could be used to help pay for private insurance. The plan called for converting Medicaid from an entitlement program, where costs are shared between the federal government and the states, to a block grant. The block grant would provide federal funds to the state but would not guarantee eligibility to some groups as does an entitlement.

An analysis of the Ryan plan by the Congressional Budget Office showed that while the plan might reduce the deficit, it would require elderly beneficiaries to pay substantially more for health care and would likely leave current Medicaid beneficiaries without health care coverage.[33] These proposals met with intense opposition from Democrats. Public opposition to the proposed Medicare changes played a significant role in Republican defeat in a 2011 special election for a normally Republican New York state district. After that defeat, Republicans backed off on their proposals to redesign Medicare and Medicaid. Even after Ryan was named Speaker of the House, Republicans did not revive these proposals. However, rising health care expenditures and budget deficits meant that the issue of controlling costs in Medicare and Medicaid will remain on the national agenda.

● Opening Opportunity

> **Describe how education, health, and housing policies try to advance equality of opportunity**

The welfare state not only supplies a measure of economic security but also provides opportunity. The American belief in **equality of opportunity** makes such programs particularly important. Programs that provide opportunity keep people from falling into poverty and offer a hand up to those who are poor. At their best, opportunity policies allow all individuals to rise as high as their talents will take them. Three types of policies are most significant in opening opportunity: education policies, health policies, and housing policies.

equality of opportunity a widely shared American ideal that all people should have the freedom to use whatever talents and wealth they have to reach their fullest potential

Education Policies

Those who understand American federalism (see Chapter 3) already are aware that most of the education of the American people is provided by the public policies of state and local governments. What may be less obvious is that these education policies—especially the policy of universal compulsory public education—are the most important single force in the distribution and redistribution of opportunity in America.

For most of American history, the federal government has played only a minor role in education. In the early years of the nation, the government assisted schools through the Land Ordinance of 1785 and the Northwest Ordinance of 1787, both of which ensured that lands were set aside for public schools and their maintenance. In 1862, Congress established land-grant colleges with the Morrill Act. After World War II the federal government stepped up its role in education policy with the enactment of the GI Bill of Rights of 1944. The GI Bill, however, was aimed almost entirely at postsecondary schooling; the national government did not truly enter the field of elementary education until after 1957.[34]

What finally brought the national government into elementary education was embarrassment that the Soviet Union had beaten the United States into space with the launching of *Sputnik*, the world's first satellite. As a result, in 1958 the federal government adopted the policy under the National Defense Education Act of improving education in science and mathematics. At the same time, the federal government recognized the role of education in promoting equality of opportunity. In 1965 the Elementary and Secondary Education Act offered federal aid for education by allocating funds to school districts with substantial numbers of children from families who were unemployed or earning less than $2,000 a year. By the early 1970s federal expenditures for elementary and secondary education were running over $4 billion per year. Today the federal government spends $79 billion, 10 percent of all spending on K–12 education; states and localities each account for 45 percent of spending. Over time, however, federal education funds have become less targeted on low-income districts as Congress has failed to update the formula for allocating funds.[35]

As we saw in Chapter 5, the federal government also pursued the goal of equal opportunity in education through its support for racial desegregation. This meant dismantling the system of "separate but equal" education in the South and challenging de facto racial segregation in the North. Throughout the 1960s the Justice Department played a major role in pressing for desegregation and in monitoring

U.S. Education Policy: Lagging or Leading?

Much of the push for education reform has been driven by the belief that American students are falling behind students in other countries. Education reform advocates point to recent performance on the Program for International Student Assessment (PISA) surveys, which measure the educational performance of 15-year-old students from around the globe. In recent years, American students have consistently scored lower in mathematics and science than students in many Asian and European countries.[a] For some education advocates, this trend is particularly worrisome as the United States on average spends considerably more per student than many countries whose students scored higher on these tests. Concerns about competitiveness have driven recent education policy decisions in the United States, including the adoption of the Common Core State Standards in most states.

However, some education experts argue that we should not be too quick to label the U.S. education system a failure. They point out that PISA results might not be truly comparable, as the selection of test-takers for the survey may be biased. For example, the U.S. test sample includes students from across the United States who represent many social and economic backgrounds; in contrast, Shanghai's school system (which ranked #1 on the test) excludes most migrant children and poor students whose parents come from China's rural regions.[b] Compared to other developed countries, the United States has greater social inequality and a larger immigrant population, meaning that the education system includes more students from poor and disadvantaged backgrounds—students who traditionally perform poorly on standardized tests. If PISA scores were weighted to take demographics into account, the ranking of the United States would jump significantly.[c]

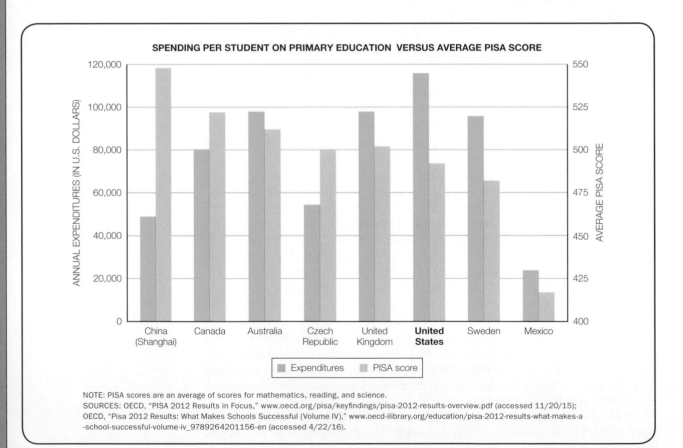

SPENDING PER STUDENT ON PRIMARY EDUCATION VERSUS AVERAGE PISA SCORE

NOTE: PISA scores are an average of scores for mathematics, reading, and science.
SOURCES: OECD, "PISA 2012 Results in Focus," www.oecd.org/pisa/keyfindings/pisa-2012-results-overview.pdf (accessed 11/20/15);
OECD, "Pisa 2012 Results: What Makes Schools Successful (Volume IV)," www.oecd-ilibrary.org/education/pisa-2012-results-what-makes-a-school-successful-volume-iv_9789264201156-en (accessed 4/22/16).

[a]Julian Ryan, "American Schools vs. the World: Expensive, Unequal, Bad at Math," *The Atlantic*, December 3, 2013, www.theatlantic.com/education/archive/2013/12/american-schools-vs-the-world-expensive-unequal-bad-at-math/281983/ (accessed 7/26/16).
[b]Brookings Institute, "Attention OECD-PISA: Your Silence on China Is Wrong," Brookings Institution, December 11, 2013, www.brookings.edu/blogs/brown-center-chalkboard/posts/2013/12/11-shanghai-pisa-scores-wrong-loveless (accessed 7/26/16).
[c]Martin Carnoy and Richard Rothstein, "What Do International Tests Really Show about U.S. Student Performance?" Economic Policy Institute, January 28, 2013, www.epi.org/publication/us-student-performance-testing/ (accessed 7/26/16).

progress of school integration. Yet, 50 years after the Civil Rights Act, this goal has remained elusive. Segregated patterns in housing create segregated schools unless vigorous policy interventions are implemented. However, such policies, including requirements for cross-district busing and provisions for affordable housing in affluent suburbs, have been struck down by the courts.

Ronald Reagan's administration signaled a new focus for federal education policy: the central goal of equal opportunity was replaced by the pursuit of higher standards. In 1983 the Department of Education issued "A Nation at Risk," an influential report that identified low educational standards as the cause of America's declining international economic competitiveness. The report did not suggest any changes in federal policy, but it urged states to make excellence in education their primary goal. This theme was picked up again by President George H. W. Bush. Because Republicans have historically opposed a strong federal role in education, the initiatives of Reagan and Bush remained primarily advisory; but they were very influential in focusing educational reform on standards and testing, now widely practiced across the states.

The federal role was substantially increased by President George W. Bush's signature education act, the No Child Left Behind Act of 2001 (NCLB). Supported by Democrats and Republicans, the law sought to combine the goals of higher standards and equality of opportunity. It aimed to improve standards through stronger federal requirements for testing and school accountability. Every child in grades 3 through 8 had to be tested yearly for proficiency in math and reading. The law aimed to promote equality of opportunity with two provisions: first, for a school to be judged a success, it had to show positive test results for all subcategories of children—minority race and ethnicity, English learners, and disability—not just overall averages; second, parents whose child is in a failing school had the right to transfer the child to a better school. Because of strong congressional opposition to creating a national test, the states were made responsible for setting standards and devising appropriate tests.

As we saw in Chapter 3, although NCLB initially attracted broad bipartisan support, it quickly generated considerable controversy. Many states branded it an unfunded mandate, noting that the law placed expensive new obligations on the schools to improve their performance but provided woefully inadequate resources. Teachers objected that "teaching to the test" undermined critical thinking. In some states, up to half the schools failed to meet the new standards, presenting a costly remedial challenge. Under the federal law, they were required to improve student performance by providing such new services as supplemental tutoring, longer school days, and additional summer school. Moreover, critics charged that NCLB actually undermined equality of opportunity because it ended up punishing underperforming schools—mostly those schools that bear the greatest burden for teaching the neediest students.[36]

Faced with these conflicts, the Obama administration sought a major overhaul of NCLB. But by 2011, with Congress unable to agree on new legislation, the administration initiated its own reform. The president announced that states could apply for waivers that would exempt them from some of the requirements of NCLB. But waivers did not signal a movement away from a standards-based approach to equality of opportunity. In fact, Obama's education initiatives drew many of the same criticisms that surrounded NCLB, especially the emphasis on high-stakes testing. As a condition of receiving waivers, states were required to show that they had adopted a strong set of educational standards and that they linked teacher evaluations to test results. In an effort to show that they had adopted

for critical analysis

Why did the No Child Left Behind Act, initially passed with bipartisan support, become so controversial? Do educational standards promote equality of opportunity? Why or why not?

Education policy is the most important means of providing equal opportunity for all Americans. In 2015, President Obama signed the Every Student Succeeds Act (ESSA) to replace the No Child Left Behind Act. ESSA gives states, rather than the federal government, the authority to evaluate schools and to use broader criteria than test scores to do so.

high educational standards, most states endorsed a set of standards known as the Common Core State Standards. Drawn up by representatives of the National Governors Association and the Council of Chief State School Officers in 2010, the standards set out clear markers for student knowledge. While many educators believe that the standards could serve as a tool for promoting equality of opportunity by improving education in all schools, the testing regime associated with the Common Core drew sharp criticisms as a return to the failed policies of NCLB.[37]

The Obama administration also put its imprint on education with its strong support for charter schools—publicly funded schools that are free from the bureaucratic rules and regulations of the school district in which they are located and free to design specialized curricula and to use resources in ways they think most effective. Since the creation of the first charter schools in Minnesota in 1990, states across the country have passed legislation to authorize them. Many states, however, proceeded slowly, establishing caps on the number of new charter schools that could be created each year. The Obama administration put its weight behind charter schools in one of its first pieces of legislation, the American Reinvestment and Recovery Act, sometimes called the "stimulus bill." The act included a new $4.3 billion program called Race to the Top, which offered competitive grants to state education systems. To be eligible for the grants, states had to agree to lift the caps on the number of charter schools that could be created each year. In the end, the administration awarded sizable grants to 18 states and Washington, D.C., praising the states for proposing bold new programs for assessing teachers and overhauling failing schools.[38] Several years after the program began, it was clear that states had promised more than they could do in the limited time that the funds were provided. While the additional financing helped to shore up school budgets in a period of tremendous financial strain, systemwide improvements proved more elusive.[39]

In 2015 a bipartisan coalition in Congress rejected the strong federal role represented by NCLB and the Race to the Top by enacting a major new education law entitled Every Student Succeeds. The new law returned control to the states for school performance and made them responsible for devising their own methods of ensuring accountability. Controversial federal requirements for teachers' evaluations and mandated standards have been eliminated. Every Student Succeeds continues to mandate testing and disaggregation of testing results by minority race and ethnicity, English learners, and disability. It also requires states to intervene to correct problems in the lowest 5 percent of schools but it leaves the specific remedies up to the states. While many hailed the new law, others charged that it would do little to alter the achievement gap between richer and poorer schools.[40]

Indeed, as policy makers, politicians, and educators have struggled over implementing standards and supporting alternative models for education, such as charter schools, some critics fundamentally question the focus of these efforts.[41] These critics argue that American schools face unprecedented challenges in educating students from impoverished families and growing numbers of English learners in a setting where the goal is to make every student college-ready. From this perspective, the solution does not lie in more testing or in charter schools but rather in providing more assistance to children in poverty, free preschool, and enhanced assistance to the schools that educate low-income students and English learners.

The federal government also plays an important role in helping to fund higher education. As in K–12 education, most funds for public systems of higher education have historically come from the states, not the federal government. However, federal programs have made a big difference in promoting equal access to higher education. Perhaps the most celebrated higher-education program of all is the GI Bill of 1944, which put higher education in reach of a whole generation of World War II veterans who never thought they would attend college. The federal government built on this role in the 1950s and '60s with the National Defense Education Act, which offered low-interest loans to college students, and the Higher Education Act, which supplied assistance directly to colleges and offered additional need-based grants allocated to students by universities. In 1972, Congress created the Pell Grant program, which offered grants directly to lower-income students.

Together these programs opened the doors of higher education much more widely than ever before in American history. Since the mid-1970s, as states have sharply reduced funding for higher education and college tuition has risen dramatically, these financial assistance programs have not kept pace. Whereas Pell Grants had initially provided enough to pay for tuition plus room and board at a four-year public college, by 2015–16, they covered only 61 percent of tuition and fees.[42] The growing costs of higher education have put college out of reach for many lower-income students and have left those who do attend college with a heavy load of debt. In the decade between 2003 and 2013, average student debt grew by nearly 20 percent to $26,900.[43]

Americans have long prided themselves on a system of education—at the primary, secondary, and higher-education levels—that promotes opportunity. A changing world economy that features intense competition from developing economies has put a premium on the importance of a high-skill workforce. Yet, our system of education has fallen short in delivering the benefits of a high-quality education to all children, and higher education is now out of reach for many, even as it grows in importance. These challenges mean that debates about how education can best promote equal opportunity will grow even more intense in the future.

Health Policies

Until recent decades, no government in the United States (national, state, or local) concerned itself directly with individual health. But public responsibility was always accepted for *public* health. After New York City's newly created Board of Health was credited with holding down a cholera epidemic in 1867, most states created statewide public-health agencies.

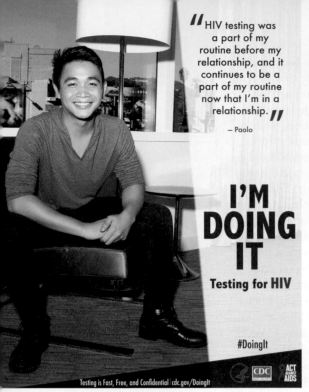

"HIV testing was a part of my routine before my relationship, and it continues to be a part of my routine now that I'm in a relationship."

— Paolo

I'M DOING IT

Testing for HIV

#DoingIt

Testing is Fast, Free, and Confidential | cdc.gov/DoingIt

The Centers for Disease Control has mounted major awareness campaigns about HIV/AIDS to inform the public about preventative measures and treatment options and to encourage people to get tested.

The U.S. Public Health Service has been in existence since 1798 but was a small part of public-health policy until after World War II. Established in 1937 but little noticed for 20 years was the National Institutes of Health (NIH), an agency within the U.S. Public Health Service that was created to do biomedical research. Between 1950 and 2012, NIH expenditures by the national government increased from $160 million to $32.3 billion. NIH research on the link between smoking and disease led to one of the most visible public-health campaigns in American history. The Centers for Disease Control and Prevention, which monitors outbreaks of disease and implements prevention measures, coordinates such public-health campaigns. Subsequently, the NIH's focus turned to cancer and acquired immunodeficiency syndrome (AIDS).

As with smoking, this work on AIDS resulted in massive public-health education as well as new products and regulations. Federal programs for human immunodeficiency virus (HIV)/AIDS research, treatment, prevention, and income support had a budget of $33 billion in 2016, a major increase from the $2.9 billion spent in 1990.[44] President Bill Clinton put greater emphasis on HIV/AIDS by appointing an "AIDS czar" to coordinate federal HIV/AIDS policy and by giving this position Cabinet status. Under Presidents Bush and Obama, the coordinator for national HIV/AIDS policy directed the Office of National AIDS Policy as part of the White House Domestic Council. Although this federal attention to HIV/AIDS has contributed to new treatments that have saved many lives, the rates of infection have remained unchanged for the past decade.[45]

Other recent commitments to the improvement of public health are the numerous laws aimed at cleaning up and defending the environment (including the creation in 1970 of the Environmental Protection Agency) and laws attempting to improve the health and safety of consumer products (regulated by the Consumer Product Safety Commission, created in 1972).

In addition to important public-health campaigns, government now plays a significant role in providing for individual health. Health policies aimed directly at the poor include Medicaid and nutritional programs, particularly SNAP and the school lunch program. In 2016 federal grants to states for Medicaid totaled an estimated $392 billion, up from $41 billion in 1990.[46] Medicaid covers not only the poor but also people who are disabled; it also assists the elderly poor who cannot pay Medicare premiums. Because there is no provision for long-term care in the United States, Medicaid has become the de facto program financing nursing home residents when they have exhausted their savings. In fact, the disabled and elderly account for 65 percent of all Medicaid spending.[47] Medicaid is the single largest medical insurance program in the United States, covering 72.4 million people, a number that rose by 24 percent after the ACA's expansion provisions (discussed below) were put into place.[48]

Health Care Reform Even with the passage of the ACA in March 2010, the United States is the only advanced industrial nation without universal access to health care. Opposition from the American Medical Association, the main lobbying organization of doctors, prevented President Roosevelt from proposing national health insurance during the 1930s, when other elements of the welfare state became law. As a result, the United States developed a patchwork system: in 2014, 55 percent of the nonelderly population received health insurance through their employers, older Americans were covered through Medicare, and the poor and disabled were assisted with Medicaid.[49] However, the growing cost of employer-provided insurance means that increasing numbers of workers cannot afford it. Many small employers cannot even afford to offer benefits because they are so expensive. And both Medicaid and Medicare face severe fiscal strain due to rising costs.

President Bill Clinton made a major effort to reform America's health care system. In 1993, Clinton announced a plan with two key objectives: to limit the rising costs of the American health care system and to provide universal health insurance coverage for all Americans. Clinton's plan, spearheaded by the first lady, Hillary Rodham Clinton, at first garnered enormous public support and seemed likely to win congressional approval in some form. But the plan gradually lost momentum as resistance to it took root among those who feared changes in a system that worked well for them. Following the failure of President Clinton's health care initiative, Congress passed a much smaller program, expanding health insurance coverage for low-income children not already receiving Medicaid, called the State Children's Health Insurance Program (SCHIP).

Medicare Reform In 2003, Congress enacted a major reform of the Medicare program. Most notably, Congress added a prescription drug benefit to the package of health benefits for the elderly as the high cost of prescription drugs had been an issue of growing concern to millions of older Americans. Yet the bill proved very controversial. Critics charged that the bill included a sweetheart deal with drug companies since it prohibited the federal government from using its purchasing power to reduce drug prices. Many Democrats also objected to the legislation because it opened the door for private health plans to play a significant role in health care provision for the elderly, which they feared would significantly weaken Medicare. Fiscal conservatives worried about the costs of the prescription drug package, a concern that escalated when the administration issued new, much higher cost estimates for the prescription drug benefit than the estimates presented when the bill was being debated.

The conflict over Medicare reform highlights the problems surrounding health care more generally. A majority of Americans believe that government should ensure that all people receive adequate health care. Yet how to deliver such benefits and how to pay for them are extremely contentious issues.[50]

Health Care Legislation in 2010 After the 2008 election, the Obama administration and the Democratic Congress pressed forward with comprehensive health reform. Seeking to avoid the conflicts that broke out in Congress over the Clintons' reform proposal, Obama offered Congress broad principles for reform, not a detailed proposal. The administration aimed at covering most Americans who lacked health insurance with a reform strategy that built on the existing system. The plan that ultimately passed had three key features. The first was the creation of new state-based insurance exchanges where individuals could buy health insurance, along with insurance regulation that would prohibit insurers from denying benefits for a variety of reasons such as preexisting conditions. With a few exceptions, the legislation also made insurers cover preventive medicine in full. The second provision of the ACA, known as "the individual mandate," required uninsured individuals to purchase health insurance; those who did not have insurance would be subject to a fine (scheduled to rise over time) of 1 percent of yearly household income or $95, whichever was larger. The third major provision of the ACA was a set of subsidies to help the uninsured and small businesses purchase insurance as well as an expansion of the public programs Medicaid and SCHIP. The Medicaid expansion made more people eligible for the program by opening it to people with incomes up to $27,724 a year.[51] The reform also allowed working-aged adults without dependent children to qualify for the program for the first time. Figure 17.4 shows the projected number of Americans who would have insurance with and without the ACA in 2026.

The politics of health care reform have remained a focus of partisan contention. By 2016 Republican members of the House of Representatives had voted 62 times to repeal the act and the public remained split.[52] In September 2016, 47 percent of those polled expressed an unfavorable opinion compared to 44 percent had favorable views.[53]

The rollout of the state insurance exchanges in fall 2013 reinforced negative public perceptions of the ACA. Massive initial computer problems with the main website, heathcare.gov, meant that some applicants working through the online system were cut off after hours of effort; others could not even get started on their applications. Only after a major reworking of the online system did the federal insurance exchanges begin to work as intended. The administration gradually extended the sign-up deadline, and by April 2014 it announced that more than 8 million people had signed up through the exchanges, a number that exceeded initial expectations.[54] Even so, the disastrous launch of the insurance exchanges represented a missed opportunity for the administration to improve public perceptions of the ACA.

The new health reform law faced challenges from state governments soon after it was enacted. Twenty-one state attorneys general filed lawsuits against the

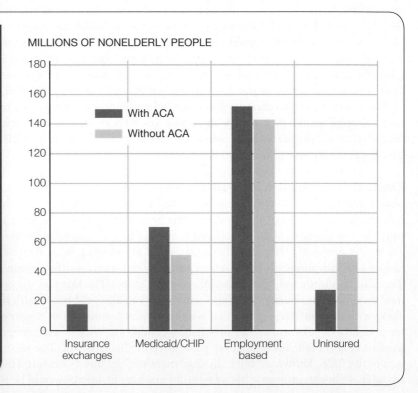

FIGURE 17.4

Projected Insurance Coverage with and without ACA, 2026

These projections by the Congressional Budget Office (CBO) predict that in 2026 over 20 million people would receive health insurance through the exchanges set up by the ACA. The act would also boost the number of people receiving benefits through Medicaid and the Children's Health Insurance Program. The CBO projects that the number of uninsured people will be 30 million lower with the ACA than it would be without the ACA.

SOURCES: Congressional Budget Office, Federal Subsidies for Health Insurance Coverage for People under Age 65: Tables from CBO's March 2016 Baseline, Table 1 Health Insurance Coverage for People under Age 65, Table 4 Effects of the Affordable Care Act on Health Insurance Coverage for People under Age 65, www.cbo.gov/sites/default/files/51298-2016-03-HealthInsurance.pdf (accessed 7/11/16).

MILLIONS OF NONELDERLY PEOPLE

■ With ACA
■ Without ACA

legislation on the grounds that the provision requiring individuals to purchase health insurance expanded the commerce clause beyond its constitutional limits. The states also objected to provisions that required them to expand their Medicaid programs to cover more poor people or lose the Medicaid funds that they received from the federal government. Even though the federal government initially paid for 100 percent of the expansion and starting in 2016 would cover 90 percent of new costs, the states argued that the federal government had overstepped its powers in withdrawing all federal Medicaid funds if states did not comply with new coverage requirements.

The Supreme Court decided these suits in 2012, ruling that most of the act was constitutional.[55] Chief Justice John Roberts, regarded as a conservative, surprised many observers by personally writing the decision that declared the individual mandate constitutional. However, the decision found that the mandate could not be justified as constitutional under the commerce clause, which the administration relied on in its arguments before the Court. Because the mandate regulated economic *inactivity* (i.e., the failure to purchase health insurance), Roberts argued that the commerce clause, which regulates economic *activity*, did not apply. Instead, the Court ruled that the requirement to purchase insurance was legal under Congress's taxing powers (since, under the law, failure to purchase insurance will result in a penalty). The decision on Medicaid, the second contested feature of the act, also came as a surprise. The Court ruled that Congress did not have the power to take existing Medicaid funds away from states if they did not comply with the expansion requirements. The governors of several states, including Florida and South Carolina, immediately announced their intention to opt out of the

Some Americans opposed the 2010 Affordable Care Act because they were concerned that decisions previously left to patients and their doctors would be made by the government.

expansion. Eventually, 19 states decided not to expand their Medicaid programs. In 2015 these state decisions left 3 million people who would have qualified for Medicaid without access to health care.[56]

Another provision that attracted much controversy was the requirement that all employers provide contraceptive services at no cost as part of their insurance plans. Republicans charged that the administration was interfering with religious freedom; Democrats countered that Republicans were trying to take the country back to the 1950s. The president's compromise proposal, which required the insurance companies, not the religious institutions, to provide contraception, did little to quell the controversy. The issue reemerged when Hobby Lobby, an arts and crafts chain store, challenged the federal law because its owners objected to requirements that their insurance cover all forms of contraception, including birth control methods they opposed on religious grounds. In 2014 the Supreme Court ruled, in a 5–4 decision, that "closely held" corporations—where the owners actively manage the companies—were exempt from provisions of law that violated their owners' religious beliefs.[57]

The ACA survived another major challenge in 2015 when the Supreme Court upheld the law in the *King v. Burwell* decision. Conservative opponents of the ACA sued on the grounds that the language of the law prohibited the federal government from providing subsidies to beneficiaries who relied on the federal health insurance exchange. Because only 16 states had set up their own exchanges and the rest relied on the federal exchange, an estimated 6.4 million people would have lost their subsidies to purchase health insurance.[58] The Obama administration defended the law, arguing that the language in question represented nothing more than an error in drafting the legislation. The administration contended that the legislative record clearly indicated Congress's intent to make subsidies available to all who qualified, regardless of the type of health exchange they used to purchase insurance. The Court sided with the administration's interpretation, agreeing that Congress intended to make subsidies available to both types of exchanges. Reacting to the Court's ruling, President Obama proclaimed that "The Affordable Care Act is here to stay."[59]

Even so, the ACA remained a topic of contention in the 2016 presidential race. Democratic nominee Hillary Clinton expressed strong support for the health reform and vowed to expand health coverage. Pushed by her Democratic rival Bernie Sanders, Clinton embraced the idea of allowing people in their 50s to buy into Medicare (under current law, people become eligible for Medicare at age 65). This proposal brought her closer to the single-payer system supported by Sanders.[60] As the Republican nominee, Donald Trump espoused a range of ideas on health care. On the one hand, he strongly denounced the Affordable Care Act and vowed to repeal it. At the same time, however, he proclaimed support for a program that would cover all people. His specific proposals included tax deductions to buy private insurance and to allow insurance companies to operate more easily across state lines. Many health experts and Republican leaders faulted Trump's proposals as overly vague and contended that they would not be sufficient to displace the Affordable Care Act.[61]

Housing Policies

The United States has one of the highest rates of home ownership in the world, and the central thrust of federal housing policy has been to promote home ownership. The federal government has traditionally done much less to provide housing for low-income Americans who cannot afford to buy homes.

Federal housing programs were first created during the Great Depression of the 1930s, when many Americans found themselves unable to afford housing. Through

public housing for low-income families, which originated in 1937 with the Wagner-Steagall National Housing Act, and subsidized private housing after 1950, the percentage of American families living in overcrowded conditions was reduced from 20 percent in 1940 to 9 percent in 1970. Federal policies made an even greater contribution to reducing "substandard" housing, defined by the U.S. Census Bureau as dilapidated houses without hot running water and without some other plumbing. In 1940 almost 50 percent of American households lived in substandard housing. By 1950 this had been reduced to 35 percent and, by 1975, to 8 percent.[62]

Many cities have been replacing high-rise housing projects with new mixed-income units, such as these homes in New Haven, Connecticut.

Despite these improvements in housing standards, federal housing policy until the 1970s was largely seen as a failure. Restricted to the poorest of the poor and marked by racial segregation and inadequate spending, public housing contributed to the problems of the poor by isolating them from shopping, jobs, and urban amenities. Dilapidated high-rise housing projects stood as a symbol of the failed American policy of "warehousing the poor." By the 1980s the orientation of housing policy had changed: most federal housing policy for low-income Americans came in the form of housing vouchers (now called housing choice vouchers) that provided recipients with support to rent in the private market. Although this program did not promote the same kind of isolation of the poor, it was often useless in very active housing markets, where the vouchers provided too little money to cover rental costs. Most cities and suburbs have long waiting lists to receive vouchers, and many housing authorities have closed their lists for 5 to 10 years because they have so few vouchers to hand out. The lack of affordable rental housing in the United States has become an increasingly pressing problem, made much worse by the recession that started in 2008. Neither the federal government nor the states have enacted policies that go far toward addressing this issue.

The Bill Clinton administration at first showed a strong ideological commitment to encouraging housing policies and combating homelessness. But especially after 1994, the Clinton administration began to retreat. Housing and Urban Development (HUD) secretary Henry Cisneros continually had to waive, virtually to the point of abandonment, a long-standing one-for-one HUD rule that provided that for every public housing unit destroyed, another would have to be built. This rule mattered because during the 1990s the main public housing program, called HOPE VI, allowed local public housing authorities to tear down the high-rise public housing that had been such a failure. In its place, city after city dismantled its old public housing projects and replaced them with new mixed-income units. The policy assumed that reducing concentrations of poverty would benefit the poor. Unfortunately, few of the original residents have been able to move into the new units.[63] The Bush administration placed less emphasis on housing policy. It proposed transforming the federal voucher program into a block grant to the states. The initiative, which never came to a vote in Congress, faced opposition from housing proponents who feared that it would greatly reduce assistance to low-income renters.

Beginning in 2007 and 2008, a home loan foreclosure crisis presented the government with a different kind of housing problem. During the housing boom of the early 2000s, many homeowners received loans that they later could not afford to repay. This was due in part to the deregulation of the mortgage industry in 1999. The deregulation allowed many new mortgage companies to form, offering loans that cost little at first but later required large payments from homeowners. This form of "predatory lending" targeted unsophisticated buyers and made it very hard for borrowers to understand the terms of the loans, which contained pages and pages of small print written in legalese. Lending standards were relaxed to the point that rising numbers of borrowers were offered "no-doc" loans, which required no documentation of the borrowers' income. As more and more Americans took out such loans, demand for housing rose, and housing prices skyrocketed. This was the housing bubble—a bubble that was bound to burst because so many borrowers would not be able to pay back their loans. As growing numbers of homeowners began to default on their loans in 2007, banks foreclosed on their houses and the value of housing began to drop. This downward spiral set off the major recession that began in 2007. As borrowers defaulted, banks holding that debt, including the biggest banks in the United States, teetered on the edge of failure and threatened to destabilize the entire economy. Many of the new mortgage companies, which had grown into huge businesses, went bankrupt. As unemployment rose, more families, unable to pay their mortgages, lost their homes. Many homeowners found that their homes were "underwater," meaning the homeowners owed more on their mortgages than the mortgaged properties were now worth.

By 2015 over 5 million homes had been lost to foreclosure.[64] The federal government responded with a plan that would slow the rising interest rates that were the cause of the problem for some homeowners. It also created several additional programs designed to help homeowners facing foreclosure. However, these programs did not experience much success. Many argued that a program that would reduce the amount of principal owed on a mortgage was the only way to stem the foreclosure crisis. But banks objected to such a program, as did a significant segment of the public. Some of the opposition to this kind of homeowner bailout stemmed from different perspectives on who was responsible for the mortgage crisis. While some people blamed predatory lenders, others blamed the borrowers themselves, who had taken out loans they couldn't afford, sometimes misrepresenting their ability to pay.

The federal government and the states continued to look for ways to stem the tide of foreclosures, which remained a major barrier to economic recovery. In 2012 states announced a legal settlement with banks that required the latter to pay $26 billion to homeowners who had received foreclosure notices without proper documentation. In the rush to foreclose on homes, banks had systematically violated the legal requirements, including by employing the practice of "robo-signing," in which documents were forged or never reviewed. However, given the size of the foreclosure crisis, this settlement was unlikely to make a major impact. As the millions of families that have lost their homes struggle to get back on their feet and neighborhoods across the country grapple with vacant homes, the effects of the housing bubble will be felt for many years to come.

● Who Gets What from Social Policy?

Explain how contributory and noncontributory programs benefit different groups of Americans

The two categories of social policy, contributory and noncontributory, generally serve different groups of people. We can understand much about the development of social policy by examining which constituencies benefit from different policies. The "Who Are Americans?" feature shows two of the key areas in which the government provides assistance and presents recent data on the numbers of beneficiaries and the money spent on these programs.

Who Receives Benefits from Social Programs?

Almost all Americans benefit from public welfare programs at some point in their lives. Two important programs in America's safety net are Medicaid, which provides health insurance to the poor, and unemployment insurance, which helps Americans who lose their jobs. Children make up a disproportionate number of the Medicaid enrollees.

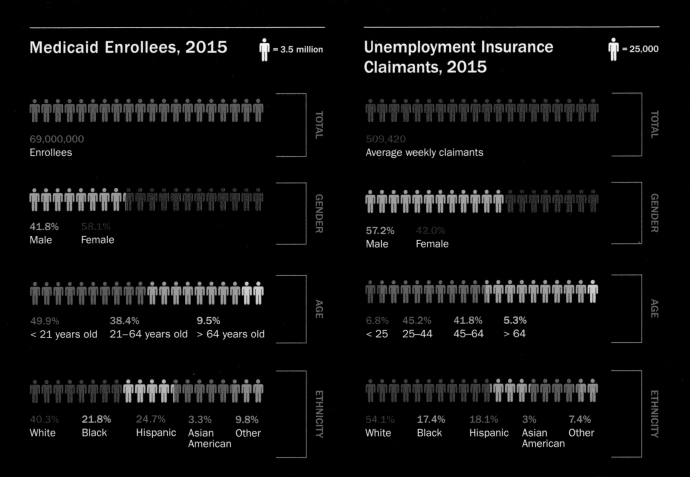

Medicaid Enrollees, 2015
👤 = 3.5 million

TOTAL
69,000,000
Enrollees

GENDER
41.8% Male | 58.1% Female

AGE
49.9% < 21 years old | 38.4% 21–64 years old | 9.5% > 64 years old

ETHNICITY
40.3% White | 21.8% Black | 24.7% Hispanic | 3.3% Asian American | 9.8% Other

Unemployment Insurance Claimants, 2015
👤 = 25,000

TOTAL
509,420
Average weekly claimants

GENDER
57.2% Male | 42.0% Female

AGE
6.8% < 25 | 45.2% 25–44 | 41.8% 45–64 | 5.3% > 64

ETHNICITY
54.1% White | 17.4% Black | 18.1% Hispanic | 3% Asian American | 7.4% Other

for critical analysis

1. What are some of the major differences between the demographics of those on Medicaid and those receiving unemployment compensation?

2. What underlying social patterns relating to poverty and employment do these data suggest?

SOURCE: United States Department of Labor, "Characteristics of the Insured Unemployed."
www.workforcesecurity.doleta.gov/unemploy/csv/ar203.csv (accessed 3/7/16)

The strongest and most generous programs are those in which the beneficiaries are widely perceived as deserving of assistance and politically powerful. Because Americans prize work, constituencies that have "earned" their benefits in some way or those who cannot work because of a disability are usually seen as most deserving of government assistance. Politically powerful constituencies are those who vote as a group, lobby effectively, and mobilize to protect the programs from which they benefit.

When we study social policies from a group perspective, we can see that the elderly and the middle class receive the most benefits from the government's social policies and that children and the working poor receive the fewest. In addition, America's social policies do little to change the fact that minorities and women are more likely than white men to be poor.

The Elderly

The elderly are the beneficiaries of the two strongest and most generous social policies: old-age pensions (what we call Social Security) and Medicare (medical care for the elderly). The aim of these programs is to provide security and prevent poverty. As these programs have grown, they have provided most elderly Americans with economic security and have dramatically reduced the poverty rate among the elderly. In 1959, before very many people over the age of 65 received social insurance, the poverty rate for the elderly was 35 percent; by 2014, it had dropped to 10 percent.[65] Because of this progress, many people call Social Security the most effective antipoverty program in the United States.[66] This does not mean that the elderly are rich, however; in 2014, the median income of elderly households was $36,895, well below the national median income.[67]

Even with the success of these programs at reducing poverty among the elderly, older African Americans and Latinos are much more likely to be poor than are white seniors. In 2014 the poverty rate for African Americans over age 65 and for Latinos over age 65 was 18.1 percent, compared to only 7.8 percent of whites over 65 who were living in poverty. The difference is due in part to the lower wages of these groups during their working years since Social Security benefits are pegged to wages. Social Security may do less to pull immigrants out of poverty depending on the number of years they have worked in the United States.[68]

One reason that Social Security and Medicare are politically strong is that the elderly are widely seen as a deserving population. They are not expected to work because of their age. Moreover, both programs are contributory, and a work history is a requirement for receiving a Social Security pension. But these programs are also strong because they serve a constituency that has become quite powerful. The elderly are a very large group: in 2015, there were 47.8 million Americans over the age of 65.[69] Because Social Security and Medicare are not means-tested, they are available to nearly all people over the age of 65, whether they are poor or not. The size of this group is of great political importance because the rates of voter turnout are greater among the elderly than among the rest of the population.

In addition, the elderly have developed strong and sophisticated lobbying organizations that can influence policy making and mobilize elderly Americans to defend these programs against proposals

AARP has been highly effective at representing the interests of the elderly in social policy. Here, AARP members demonstrate in favor of the right to buy cheaper prescription drugs from Canada under Medicare.

to cut them. One important and influential such organization is AARP. Originally the American Association of Retired Persons, in 1999 the organization changed its name to its initials only because 40 percent of AARP members work full- or part-time. AARP had more than 38 million members in 2015, amounting to one-quarter of all voters. It also has a sophisticated lobbying organization in Washington, which employs 55 lobbyists and a staff of 51 policy analysts.[70] (See Chapter 11 for more discussion of AARP's lobbying efforts.) Although AARP is the largest and the strongest organization of the elderly, other groups, such as the Alliance for Retired Americans, to which many retired union members belong, also lobby Congress on behalf of the elderly. When Congress considers changes in programs that affect the elderly, these lobbying groups pay close attention. They mobilize their supporters and work with legislators to block changes they believe will hurt the elderly.[71]

The Middle and Upper Classes

Americans don't usually think of the middle class or upper class as benefiting from social policies, but government action promotes the social welfare of the middle and upper classes in a variety of ways. First, medical care and pensions for the elderly help the middle class by relieving them of the burden of caring for elderly relatives. Before these programs existed, old people were more likely to live with and depend financially on their adult children. Many middle-class families whose parents and grandparents are in nursing homes rely on Medicaid to pay nursing home bills.

In addition, the middle and upper classes benefit from what some analysts call the shadow welfare state.[72] These are the social benefits that private employers offer to their workers: medical insurance and pensions, for example. The federal government subsidizes such benefits by not taxing the payments that employers and employees make for health insurance and pensions. These **tax expenditures**, as they are called, are an important way the federal government helps ensure the social welfare of the middle and upper classes. (Such programs are called "tax expenditures" because the federal government helps finance them through the tax system rather than by direct spending.) Another key tax expenditure that helps the well-off is the tax exemption on mortgage interest payments: taxpayers can deduct the amount they have paid in interest on a mortgage from the income they report on their tax return. By allowing these payments to be counted as deductions, the government makes home ownership less expensive.

tax expenditures government subsidies provided to employers and employees through tax deductions for amounts spent on health insurance and other benefits

People often don't think of these tax expenditures as part of social policy because they are not as visible as the programs that provide direct payments or services to beneficiaries. But tax expenditures represent a significant federal investment: they cost the national treasury some $1.26 trillion a year and make it easier and less expensive for working Americans to obtain health care, save for retirement, and buy homes.[73] These programs are very popular with the middle and upper classes, and Congress rarely considers reducing them. On the few occasions when public officials have tried to limit these programs—with proposals to limit the amount of mortgage interest that can be deducted, for example—they have quickly retreated.

The Working Poor

People who are working but are poor or just above the poverty line receive only limited assistance from government social programs. This is somewhat surprising, given that Americans value work so highly. But the working poor are typically employed in jobs that do not provide pensions or health care; often, they are renters because they cannot afford to buy homes. This means they cannot benefit from the shadow welfare state that subsidizes the social benefits enjoyed by most middle-class Americans.

Three government programs that assist the working poor include the ACA (described earlier), the EITC, and SNAP (formerly known as food stamps). The EITC was implemented in 1976 to provide poor workers some relief from increases in the taxes that pay for Social Security. As it has expanded, the EITC has provided a modest wage supplement for the working poor, allowing them to catch up on utility bills or pay for children's clothing.

Poor workers can also receive benefits from SNAP. To be eligible, households must earn below 130 percent of the poverty line (about $26,124 a year for a three-person family in 2016). The average monthly benefit for a family of three is $382 a month.[74] Food advocates, such as Feeding America, have encouraged people to take "the SNAP Challenge," in which people who do not need food stamps spend $1.50 a meal (the average for SNAP recipients) for a week. In the words of one high-profile participant, "I was hungry last week—laser-focused on how much food was left in the fridge and how many dollars were left in my wallet. I was scared about eating portions that were too big, and wasn't sure what to do if my food ran out."[75] Because the wages of less educated workers have declined significantly since the 1980s and minimum wages have not kept pace with inflation, the problems of the working poor remain acute.

The working poor are more likely to be in jobs that do not provide health benefits from their employers. By expanding Medicaid to cover workers who earn up to 138 percent of the poverty line ($27,821 for a family of three in 2016), the ACA sought to ensure coverage to this group. However, the decision of 19 states to opt out of Medicaid expansion left a gap in coverage. Latinos and African Americans were especially likely to be harmed by this gap compared to whites: 27 percent of Hispanics and 16 percent of blacks lacked access to health insurance as a result of these state decisions, but only 11 percent of whites were affected in this way.[76]

Even though the working poor may be seen as deserving, they are not politically powerful because they are not organized. There is no equivalent to AARP for the poor. Nonetheless, because work is highly valued in American society, politicians find it difficult to cut the few social programs that help the working poor. In 1995, efforts to cut the EITC were defeated by coalitions of Democrats and moderate Republicans, although Congress did place new restrictions on food stamps and reduced the level of spending on this type of aid.

The Nonworking Poor

The only nonworking, able-bodied poor people who receive federal cash assistance are parents who are caring for children. The primary source of cash assistance for these families was AFDC and now is the state-run TANF program, but they also rely on SNAP and Medicaid. Able-bodied adults who are not caring for children are not eligible for federal assistance other than food stamps. Many states provide small amounts of cash assistance to such individuals through programs called "general assistance," but most states have abolished or greatly reduced their general-assistance programs in an effort to encourage these adults to work. Americans don't like to subsidize adults who are not working, but they do not want to harm children.

AFDC was the most unpopular social spending program ever undertaken by the federal government; as a result, spending on it declined after 1980. Under TANF, states receive a fixed amount of federal funds, whether the welfare rolls rise or fall. Because the number of people on welfare has declined so dramatically since 1994 (by more than 50 percent), states have had generous levels of federal resources for the remaining welfare recipients. Many states, however, have used the windfall of federal dollars to cut taxes and indirectly support programs that benefit the middle class, not the poor.[77] Welfare recipients have little political power to resist cuts to their benefits. During the late 1960s and early 1970s, the short-lived National Welfare Rights Organization sought to represent the interests of welfare recipients. But keeping the organization in operation proved difficult because its members and its constituents had few resources and were difficult to organize.[78] Because welfare recipients are widely viewed as undeserving and are not politically organized, they have played little part in recent debates about welfare.

The deep recession that started in 2008 meant that record numbers of Americans were without work. The numbers of people receiving SNAP benefits during this period soared. At the height in 2013, over 47 million people (15 percent of the population) received SNAP benefits. As the unemployment rate declined, the number of SNAP beneficiaries began to decline as well, although in 2016, 44.7 million people continued to rely on SNAP.[79] These numbers reflect the high levels of need that persisted long after the recession.

Minorities, Women, and Children

Minorities, women, and children are disproportionately poor. Much of this poverty is the result of disadvantages that stem from the position of these groups in the labor market. In 2014 the poverty rate for African Americans was 26.2 percent, and for Latinos it was 23.6 percent. Both rates are more than double the poverty rate for non-Hispanic whites, which was 10.1 percent. The median income for

The poor and working poor (including many single mothers) have little influence on government. Although organized protests representing their interests occasionally do occur, they fail to have the impact of similar protests by other groups, such as senior citizens.

black households in 2014 was $35,398. For Hispanics, it was $42,491, whereas for non-Hispanic white households the median household income was $60,256.[80] Much of this economic inequality occurs because minority workers tend to have low-wage jobs. Minorities are also more likely to become unemployed and to remain unemployed for longer periods of time than are white Americans. African Americans, for example, typically have experienced twice as much unemployment as have other Americans. The combination of low-wage jobs and unemployment often means that minorities are less likely to have jobs that give them access to the shadow welfare state. They are more likely to fall into the precarious categories of the working poor or the nonworking poor.

More than 30 years ago, policy analysts began to talk about the "feminization of poverty," or the fact that women are more likely than men to be poor. This problem is particularly acute for single mothers, who are more than twice as likely to fall below the poverty line as the average American (see Figure 17.5). When the Social Security Act was passed in 1935, the main programs for poor women were Aid to Dependent Children (ADC) and survivors' insurance for widows. The framers of the act believed that ADC would gradually disappear as more women became eligible for survivors' insurance. The social model behind the Social Security Act was that of a male breadwinner with a wife and children. Women were not expected to work, and if a woman's husband died, ADC or survivors' insurance would help her stay at home and raise her children. The framers of Social Security did not envision today's large number of single women heading families. At the same time, they did not envision that so many women with children would also be working. This combination of changes helped make AFDC (the successor program to ADC) more controversial. Many people asked why welfare recipients shouldn't work, if the majority of women who were not on welfare worked. Such questions led to the welfare reform of 1996, which created TANF.

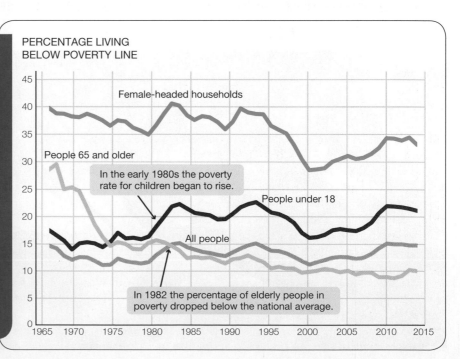

FIGURE 17.5

Poverty Levels in the United States, 1966–2014

Poverty rates in the U.S. population vary considerably. The rate of poverty among female-headed households declined significantly in the 1990s and has been increasing again since 2000. Which group has seen the greatest reduction in its poverty level since 1966?

SOURCES: U.S. Census Bureau, Historical Poverty Tables, "Table 2. Poverty Status of People by Family Relationship, Race, and Hispanic Origin: 1959 to 2014" and "Table 3. Poverty Status of People, by Age, Race, and Hispanic Origin," www.census.gov/data/tables /time-series/demo/income-poverty/historical -poverty-people.html (accessed 7/16/16).

PERCENTAGE LIVING BELOW POVERTY LINE

Female-headed households

People 65 and older

In the early 1980s the poverty rate for children began to rise.

People under 18

All people

In 1982 the percentage of elderly people in poverty dropped below the national average.

The need to combine work and child care was understood as a challenging problem for most single parents. This problem is more acute for single mothers than for single fathers because, on average, women still earn less than men and because working creates new expenses such as child care and transportation costs. Many women working in low-wage jobs do not receive health insurance as a benefit of their jobs; they must pay the cost of such insurance themselves. As a result, many poor women found that once they were working, the expenses of child care, transportation, insurance, and other needs left them with less cash per month than they would have received if they had not worked and had instead collected AFDC and Medicaid benefits. These women concluded that it was not "worth it" for them to leave AFDC and go to work. Some states are now experimenting with programs to encourage women to work by allowing them to keep some of their welfare benefits even when they are working. Although Americans want individuals to be self-sufficient, research suggests that single mothers with low-wage jobs are likely to need continuing assistance to make ends meet.[81]

One of the most troubling issues related to American social policy is the number of American children who live in poverty. The rate of child poverty in 2014 was 21.1 percent—6.3 percentage points higher than that of the population as a whole. African American and Latino children experience much higher rates of poverty than do whites. In 2014 the rate of child poverty for white children was 12.3 percent, while 31.9 percent of Latino children and 37.1 percent of black children lives in poverty.[82] These high rates of poverty stem in part from the design of American social policies. Because these policies do not generously assist able-bodied adults who aren't working and they offer little help to the working poor, the children of these adults are likely to be poor as well.

As child poverty has grown, several lobbying groups have emerged to represent children's interests; the best known of these is the Children's Defense Fund. But even with a sophisticated lobbying operation, and although their numbers are large, poor children do not vote and therefore cannot wield much political power.[83]

Social Policy
and Your Future

The development of social policy in the United States reflects shifts in our views about how government can best help accomplish fundamental national goals. Until the 1930s the federal government did very little in the domain of social policy. The country's major social policy was free public education, which was established by the states and administered locally. Americans placed especially strong emphasis on education because an educated citizenry was seen as an essential component of a strong democracy.[84] Given the strength of these beliefs, it is not surprising that free public education was available in the United States well before European nations established public education systems. To this day the government offers various programs to support education. The "**Who Participates?**" feature on page 705 looks at the growth in student loans and describes some government programs to help students pay off their loans.

Other public social policies, established from the 1930s on, have stirred up much more controversy. Liberals often argue that more generous social policies are needed if the United States is truly to ensure equality of opportunity. Some liberals have argued that the government needs to go beyond simply providing opportunity and should ensure more equal conditions, especially where children are concerned. Conservative critics, on the other hand, often argue that social policies that offer income support take the ideal of equality too far and, in the process, do for individuals what those individuals should be doing for themselves. From this perspective, social policies make the government too big, and big government is seen as a fundamental threat to Americans' liberties.

Where do average Americans fit in these debates? Americans are often said to be philosophical conservatives and operational liberals.[85] When asked about government social policy in the abstract, they say they disapprove of activist government—a decidedly conservative view. But when they must evaluate particular programs, Americans generally express support—a more liberal perspective. Some programs, of course, are preferred over others. Policies in which the recipients are regarded as deserving, such as programs for the elderly, receive more support than those that assist working-age people. Programs that have a reputation for effectiveness and those that require people to help themselves through work are also viewed favorably.[86] In sum, most Americans take a pragmatic approach to social welfare policies: they favor programs that work, and they want to reform those that seem not to work.

Yet reform is often difficult to achieve. The most pressing social policy issue in the coming decades—the rising cost of health care—has been notoriously difficult to address. The United States spends more on health care than any other advanced nation, but many Americans remain without access to care, even after the expansions in the ACA (see Figure 17.4). The share of our economy devoted to health care rose from 7.2 percent in 1970 to 17.5 percent in 2014.[87] The causes of increasing health care costs are many, including new technology, administrative complexity, greater coverage for more people, and an aging population. Can we reap the advantages of our highly advanced health care system and reduce costs at the same time? While most Americans might prefer this outcome, it is very difficult to reach agreement on the reforms needed to attain this goal. The complex system that delivers health care in the United States includes powerful interests that resist changes to current arrangements. Yet the projected increase in the proportion of older Americans in coming decades makes the need to control health care costs especially urgent. What strategies might be used to initiate a national discussion of health care? What are the consequences of inaction for today's young adults? Although discussions of health care costs are often complex and technical, it is vital that more Americans engage in this debate if we are to re-create a health care system that is both affordable and effective.

Government Relief for Student Loans

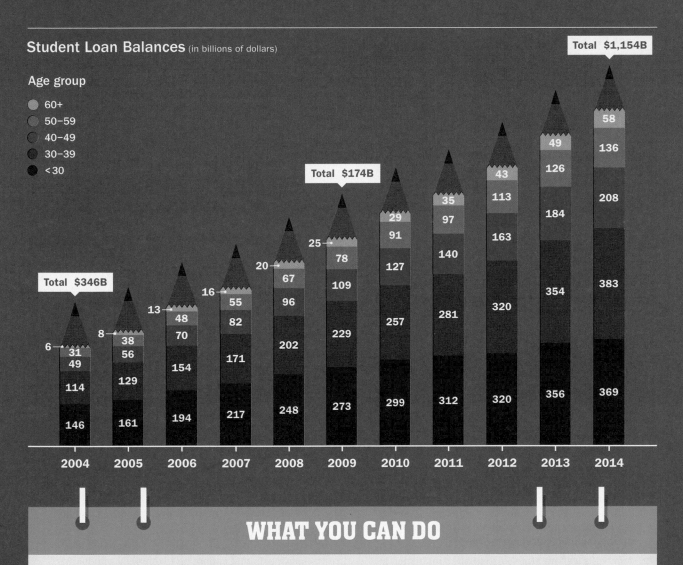

Student Loan Balances (in billions of dollars)

Total $1,154B

Age group
- 60+
- 50–59
- 40–49
- 30–39
- < 30

Total $174B

Total $346B

	2004	2005	2006	2007	2008	2009	2010	2011	2012	2013	2014
60+	6	8	13	16	20	25	29	35	43	49	58
50–59	31	38	48	55	67	78	91	97	113	126	136
40–49	49	56	70	82	96	109	127	140	163	184	208
30–39	114	129	154	171	202	229	257	281	320	354	383
< 30	146	161	194	217	248	273	299	312	320	356	369

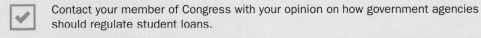

WHAT YOU CAN DO

Contact the Government about Student Loan Issues

☑ Contact your member of Congress with your opinion on how government agencies should regulate student loans.

☑ If your employer is a government organization, a 501(c)(3) nonprofit, or a private company that provides public services, you may qualify to get your federal loans forgiven through the Public Service Loan Forgiveness (PSLF) program: **www.studentaid.ed.gov/sa/repay-loans/ forgiveness-cancellation/public-service**.

☑ If you have Perkins Loans and go to work in public service, including the active duty military, education, health services, and public safety, you might be eligible for Perkins Loans cancellation: **https://studentaid.ed.gov/sa/repay-loans/forgiveness-cancellation**.

studyguide

The Welfare State

Trace the history of government programs designed to promote economic security (pp. 673–84)

Prior to the Great Depression, assistance to the poor was provided mainly by local governments and private charities. The Social Security Act of 1935 gave the federal government a much larger role and created two separate categories of welfare: contributory and noncontributory. Spending on social policy, particularly entitlement programs, has grown dramatically ever since the 1930s; and the costs have been paid primarily through payroll taxes.

Key Terms

contributory programs (p. 675)

Social Security (p. 675)

indexing (p. 675)

cost-of-living adjustments (COLAs) (p. 675)

Medicare (p. 676)

noncontributory programs (p. 676)

means testing (p. 676)

Medicaid (p. 676)

Supplemental Nutrition Assistance Program (SNAP) (p. 677)

in-kind benefits (p. 677)

entitlement (p. 678)

Practice Quiz

1. Prior to 1935, the private welfare system in the United States made a distinction between
   a) contributory and noncontributory programs.
   b) citizens and recent immigrants.
   c) the deserving poor and the undeserving poor.
   d) mandatory and discretionary spending.
   e) religious and secular assistance.

2. America's welfare state was initially constructed in response to
   a) the Civil War.
   b) World War II.
   c) political reforms of the Progressive era.
   d) the Great Depression.
   e) the growth of the military-industrial complex.

3. Which of the following is an example of a contributory program?
   a) Medicaid
   b) Medicare
   c) Temporary Assistance for Needy Families
   d) Supplemental Nutrition Assistance Program
   e) Aid to Families with Dependent Children

4. In 1996, as part of welfare reform, Aid to Families with Dependent Children was abolished and replaced by
   a) the Earned Income Tax Credit.
   b) the DREAM Act.
   c) the Affordable Care Act.
   d) Supplemental Security Income.
   e) Temporary Assistance for Needy Families.

5. Means testing requires that applicants for welfare benefits show
   a) that they are capable of getting to and from their workplace.
   b) that they have the ability to store and prepare food.
   c) a financial need for assistance.
   d) that they have the time and resources to take full advantage of federal educational opportunities.
   e) that they are natural-born citizens who have never been convicted of a felony.

6. Which of the following programs provide in-kind benefits?
   a) Medicaid and the Supplemental Nutrition Assistance Program
   b) Social Security and the Troubled Assets Relief Program
   c) Medicare and unemployment compensation
   d) the GI Bill of Rights and the Equal Rights Amendment
   e) the Earned Income Tax Credit and No Child Left Behind

7. Government programs that provide benefits to individuals that *cannot* be taken away without due process of the law are called
   a) cost-of-living adjustment programs.
   b) noncontributory programs.
   c) entitlement programs.
   d) indexing programs.
   e) tax expenditure programs.

Opening Opportunity

Describe how education, health, and housing policies try to advance equality of opportunity (pp. 685–96)

The federal government enacts three types of policies in order to keep people from falling into poverty and to help those who are already poor: education policies, health policies, and housing policies. Although the federal government played only a minor role in education through most of American history, it has become more active since the late 1950s. Even with the passage of the Patient Protection and Affordable Care Act in 2010, the United States is the only advanced industrial nation without universal access to health care. The federal government has concentrated most of its efforts on housing policy to promote home ownership rather than to provide housing for low-income Americans who cannot afford to buy homes.

Key Term

equality of opportunity (p. 685)

Practice Quiz

8. What event prompted the federal government to enter the field of elementary education?
   a) the Civil War
   b) the Great Depression
   c) World War II
   d) the Soviet Union's launching of Sputnik
   e) the civil rights movement

9. Which of the following was *not* part of the No Child Left Behind Act of 2001?
   a) a provision allowing parents whose child is attending a failing school to transfer the child to a better school
   b) a requirement that all students be proficient in reading and math by 2014
   c) a requirement that schools show positive results for all subcategories of students and not just positive overall averages
   d) a requirement that a national test be used to evaluate every student around the country
   e) a requirement that every child in grades 3 through 8 be tested yearly for proficiency in math and reading

10. A charter school is
    a) a publicly funded school that is free from the rules and regulations of local school districts.
    b) a privately funded school that is subject to the rules and regulations of local school districts.
    c) a privately funded school that is free from the rules and regulations of local school districts.
    d) a school that meets the requirements spelled out in the No Child Left Behind Act of 2001.
    e) a school created by the GI Bill of Rights of 1944.

11. Most nonelderly adults receive health insurance through
    a) Social Security.
    b) Medicare.
    c) Medicaid.
    d) their employers.
    e) local charitable organizations.

Who Gets What from Social Policy?

Explain how contributory and noncontributory programs benefit different groups of Americans (pp. 696–703)

The federal government's social policies tend to provide the largest benefits to those groups that are politically organized and to those groups that the public perceives to be deserving of assistance. As a result, children and the poor receive the fewest benefits from the federal government and the middle class and the elderly receive the most. Government policies do little to change the fact that minorities and women are more likely than white men to be poor.

Key Term

tax expenditures (p. 699)

Practice Quiz

12. In terms of receiving benefits of social policies, what distinguishes the elderly from the working poor?
    a) The elderly are perceived as deserving, whereas the working poor are not.
    b) The elderly receive fewer benefits from the government's social policies.
    c) The elderly are more organized and more politically powerful than are the working poor.
    d) The elderly are less organized and less politically powerful than are the working poor.
    e) There is no significant difference between these two groups.

13. Who are the chief beneficiaries of the "shadow welfare state"?
    a) children
    b) the elderly
    c) the nonworking poor
    d) the working poor
    e) the middle class

14. Which three government programs provide assistance to the working poor?
    a) Temporary Assistance for Needy Families, Medicare, and the Supplemental Nutrition Assistance Program
    b) the Affordable Care Act, the Earned Income Tax Credit, and the Supplemental Nutrition Assistance Program
    c) Temporary Assistance for Needy Families, Social Security, and the Earned Income Tax Credit
    d) Temporary Assistance for Needy Families, Medicare, and the Affordable Care Act
    e) Social Security, Medicaid, and Medicare

15. Which of the following statements about poverty in the United States is most accurate?
    a) African Americans have a lower poverty rate than non-Hispanic whites.
    b) Latinos have a lower poverty rate than non-Hispanic whites.
    c) Latinos have a higher poverty rate than non-Hispanic whites.
    d) The rate of child poverty is less than the rate of adult poverty.
    e) Single mothers are less likely than average Americans to fall below the poverty line.

For Further Reading

Campbell, Andrea Louise. *How Policies Make Citizens: Senior Political Activism and the American Welfare State.* Princeton, NJ: Princeton University Press, 2005.

Cohen, David K., and Susan L. Moffitt. *The Ordeal of Equality: Did Federal Regulation Fix the Schools?* Cambridge, MA: Harvard University Press, 2009.

Edin, Kathryn J., and Luke Shafer. *$2.00 a Day: Living on Almost Nothing in America.* New York: Houghton Mifflin Harcourt, 2015.

Howard, Christopher. *The Welfare State Nobody Knows: Debunking Myths about U.S. Social Policy.* Princeton, NJ: Princeton University Press, 2007.

Katz, Michael. *In the Shadow of the Poorhouse: A Social History of Welfare in America.* New York: Basic Books, 1986.

Katznelson, Ira, and Margaret Weir. *Schooling for All: Race, Class, and the Democratic Ideal.* New York: Basic Books, 1985.

Light, Paul. *Artful Work: The Politics of Social Security Reform.* New York: Random House, 1985.

Marmor, Theodore R., Jerry L. Mashaw, and John Pakutka. *Social Insurance: America's Neglected Heritage and Contested Future.* Washington, DC: CQ Press, 2013.

Mettler, Suzanne. *Degrees of Inequality: How the Politics of Higher Education Sabotaged the American Dream.* New York: Basic Books, 2014.

Mettler, Suzanne. *The Submerged State: How Invisible Government Policies Undermine American Democracy.* Chicago: University of Chicago Press, 2011.

Murray, Charles. *Losing Ground: American Social Policy, 1950–1980.* New York: Basic Books, 1984.

Patterson, James T. *America's Struggle against Poverty in the Twentieth Century.* Cambridge, MA: Harvard University Press, 2000.

Skocpol, Theda. *The Missing Middle: Working Families and the Future of American Social Policy.* New York: W. W. Norton, 2000.

Soss, Joe, Richard C. Fording, and Sanford F. Schramm. *Disciplining the Poor: Neoliberal Paternalism and the Persistent Power of Race.* Chicago: University of Chicago Press, 2011.

Weir, Margaret, Ann Orloff, and Theda Skocpol, eds. *The Politics of Social Policy in the United States.* Princeton, NJ: Princeton University Press, 1988.

Recommended Websites

Center for Retirement Research
http://crr.bc.edu

Americans pay for their retirement with a mix of Social Security, employer-sponsored savings plans, and private savings. This website provides analyses of the challenges that face all aspects of the current arrangements and includes a downloadable "Social Security Fix-It Book."

Center on Budget and Policy Priorities
www.cbpp.org

The Center on Budget and Policy Priorities is a nonpartisan, liberal-leaning nonprofit organization that provides timely data and analysis of social programs that serve low-income Americans. It also studies economic and social changes that affect the well-being of low-income people. Areas of research include the Earned Income Tax Credit, Food Assistance, Social Security, and climate change. The center focuses on state and local policies as well as national programs.

Libertarian Party
www.lp.org

Contrary to many other Americans, libertarians believe that social programs pose a threat to personal freedom and should be eliminated. Go to the Libertarian Party's website to read the organization's opinions and positions on most current social policies.

Medicare
www.medicare.gov

Health care is one of the largest and most controversial social programs in the United States. At the Medicare website, find out what services the Department of Health and Human Services provides.

Modern American Poetry: The Great Depression
www.english.uiuc.edu/maps/depression/depression.htm

The Great Depression changed American opinion about the causes of and responsibility for poverty. This website, by Cary Nelson at the University of Illinois at Urbana-Champaign, provides information, statistics, and photos of this historical period as well as analysis of poems by depression-era writers.

Poverty.com
www.poverty.com

Poverty is a problem that exists in the United States and around the world. Read about how poverty, hunger, and related problems affect people in other areas of the globe.

Public Agenda
www.publicagenda.com

Public Agenda is a nonpartisan organization that tries to bridge the gap between American leaders and public opinion on current social, domestic, and foreign policy issues.

U.S. Department of Education
www.ed.gov

The U.S. Department of Education is dedicated to providing equal access to education and improving academic programs throughout America. At the department's website, you can learn about the No Child Left Behind Act and other policies.

The United States spends hundreds of billions of dollars—far more than any other country—on its military and weapons. However, Americans often disagree on when and how their government should act in international affairs, especially when it comes to deploying the U.S. military.

Foreign Policy and Democracy

WHAT GOVERNMENT DOES AND WHY IT MATTERS Ever since George Washington, in his Farewell Address, warned the American people "to have . . . as little political connection as possible" with foreign nations and to "steer clear of permanent alliances," Americans have been distrustful of foreign policy. But despite their distrust, the United States has had to pursue its national interests in the world through a variety of means, including diplomacy, economic policy, and precisely the sorts of entangling alliances with other nations and involvements with international organizations that would have troubled Washington.

To some college students, foreign policy may seem like a distant or abstract matter, but not too long ago tens of thousands of students were drafted and sent to serve in Korea and Vietnam. Even today, in the era of the all-volunteer military, thousands of recent college graduates (and numerous current college students) have served in America's military forces in Iraq and Afghanistan, and many others know someone who has been wounded or killed on distant battlefields.

It is important to note that war is only one aspect of foreign policy, but the United States has indeed fought a large number of wars. Though Americans like to regard themselves as a peaceful people, since our own Civil War, U.S. forces have been deployed abroad on hundreds of occasions for both major conflicts and minor skirmishes. Writing in 1989, historian Geoffrey Perret commented that no other nation "has had as much experience of war as the United States."[1] Since 1989, U.S. forces have fought two wars in the Persian Gulf and a war in Afghanistan, while engaging in lesser military actions in Panama, Kosovo, Somalia, and elsewhere. Every year, the U.S. military arsenal and defense budget dwarf those of other nations. The United States currently spends nearly $600 billion per year on its military and weapons programs—a figure that represents roughly one-third of the world's total military expenditure and over three times the amount spent by the People's Republic of China, the nation that currently ranks second to the United States in overall military outlays.[2] The debt we incur for these programs is likely to be paid by today's college students for their entire working lives.

Foreign policy, especially military policy, is often a major political issue in the United States. An old American adage asserts that "politics stops at the water's edge." The point of this saying is that unless we put our domestic political disunity aside and work together to protect our nation's political, economic, and security interests in the wider world, all Americans will suffer. In today's world, however, the water's edge does not neatly demarcate the difference in interests between "us" and "them." As the global economic crisis that began in 2008 revealed, "our" economic interests and "their" economic interests are intertwined. Environmental concerns are global, not national. And even in the realm of security interests, some risks and threats are shared and require international rather than national responses. Our national government, created to further our national interests, must find ways of acting internationally and striking the right balance between competition and cooperation in the international arena.

chaptergoals

- Explain how foreign policy is designed to promote security, prosperity, and humanitarian goals (pp. 713–24)
- Identify the major players in foreign-policy making, and describe their roles (pp. 725–32)
- Describe the means the United States uses to carry out foreign policy today (pp. 732–41)

● The Goals of Foreign Policy

Explain how foreign policy is designed to promote security, prosperity, and humanitarian goals

The term *foreign policy* refers to the programs and policies that determine America's relations with other nations and foreign entities. Foreign policy includes diplomacy, military and security policy, international human rights policies, and various forms of economic policy, such as trade policy and international energy policy. Of course, foreign policy and domestic policy are not completely separate categories but are instead closely intertwined: the United States' decisions in its foreign policy impact domestic policies and outcomes. Take security policy, for example. Defending the nation requires the design and manufacture of tens of billions of dollars' worth of military hardware. The manufacture and procurement of this military equipment might provide jobs in American communities where the equipment is built, while paying for it involves raising taxes or choosing not to fund other types of programs.

Many of the basic contours of the foreign policy arena are similar to those of America's other policy domains. The nation's chief foreign-policy makers are the president, Congress, and the bureaucracy. Just as in economic and social policy, battles over foreign policy often erupt among and within these institutions as competing politicians and a variety of organized groups and rival political forces pursue their own versions of the national interest or their own narrower purposes that they seek to present as the national interest. In the foreign policy arena, the institutional powers of the presidency give presidents and their allies an advantage over political forces based in Congress, although Congress is not without resources of its own through which to influence the conduct of foreign policy. Moreover, like domestic policy matters, foreign policy issues often figure prominently in public debate and in national election campaigns as competing forces seek to mobilize popular support for their positions or at least to castigate the opposition for the putative shortcomings of its policies.

In this section we will examine the goals of American foreign policy. Although U.S. foreign policy has a number of purposes, three main goals stand out. These are security, prosperity, and the creation of a better world. These goals overlap with one another, and each can never be pursued fully in isolation. Then, in the following sections, we will discuss the actors and institutions that shape foreign policy. Next, we will analyze the instruments that policy makers have at their disposal to implement foreign policy.

Security

To many Americans, the chief goal of the nation's foreign policy is protection of U.S. security in an often hostile world. Traditionally, the United States has been concerned about threats that might emanate from other countries, such as Nazi Germany during the 1940s and then Soviet Russia until the Soviet Union's collapse in the late 1980s. Today, American security policy is concerned not only with the actions of other nations but also with the activities of terrorist groups and other hostile **non-state actors**.[3] To protect the nation's security from foreign threats, the United States has built an enormous military apparatus and a complex array of intelligence-gathering institutions, such as the Central Intelligence Agency (CIA), charged with evaluating and anticipating challenges from abroad.[4]

non-state actors groups other than nation-states that attempt to play a role in the international system; terrorist groups are one type of non-state actor

Security is, of course, a broad term. Policy makers must be concerned with Americans' physical security. The September 11 terrorist attacks killed and injured thousands of Americans, and the government constantly fears that new attacks could be even more catastrophic. Policy makers must also be concerned with such matters as the security of America's food supplies, transportation infrastructure, and energy supplies. Many of our efforts in the Middle East, for example, are aimed at ensuring continuing American access to vital oil fields. In recent years, cyberspace has become a new security concern. The nation's dependence on computers means that the government must be alert to efforts by hostile governments, groups, or even individual "hackers" to damage computer networks or access sensitive or proprietary information. The U.S. government has often charged Chinese government and military agencies with stealing American secrets through cyber espionage. In 2015 the United States and China signed an agreement to stop cyber attacks against one another, but no one expected the agreement to have much effect; and the Chinese, for their part, did not seem to pause in their efforts to hack American companies.

During the eighteenth and nineteenth centuries, American security was based mainly on the geographic isolation of the United States. Separated by two oceans from European and Asian powers, many Americans thought that the country's security would be best preserved by our remaining aloof from international power struggles. This policy was known as **isolationism**. In his 1796 Farewell Address, President George Washington warned Americans to avoid permanent alliances with foreign powers; and in 1823, President James Monroe warned foreign powers not to meddle in the Western Hemisphere. Washington's warning and what came to be called the Monroe Doctrine were the cornerstones of the U.S. foreign policy of isolationism until the end of the nineteenth century. The United States saw itself as the dominant power in the Western Hemisphere and, indeed, believed that its "manifest destiny" was to expand from sea to sea. The rest of the world, however, should remain at arm's length.

In the twentieth century, technology made oceans less of a barrier to foreign threats, and the world's growing economic interdependence meant that the nation could no longer ignore events abroad. Early in the twentieth century, the United States entered World War I on the side of Great Britain and France when the Wilson administration concluded that a German victory would adversely affect the economic and security interests of the United States. In 1941 the United States was drawn into World War II when Japan, hoping to become the dominant power in the Pacific, attacked the U.S. Pacific fleet anchored at Pearl Harbor, Hawaii. Even before the attack, the Roosevelt administration had concluded that the United States must act to prevent a victory by the German–Japanese–Italian Axis alliance. Until the Japanese attack, however, Roosevelt had been unable to overcome proponents of American isolationism, who declared that our security was best served by leaving foreigners to their own devices. With their attack, the Japanese proved that the Pacific Ocean could not protect the United States from foreign foes and effectively discredited isolationism as a security policy.

Following World War II, the United States developed a new security policy known as **containment** to check or "contain" the growing power of the Soviet Union, which, by the end of the 1940s, had built a huge empire, enormous military forces, and nuclear weapons and intercontinental bombers capable of attacking the United States. The United States was committed to maintaining its own military might as a means of deterrence, to discourage the Soviets from attacking the United States or its allies. Some Americans wanted a more aggressive policy and argued that we

isolationism avoidance of involvement in the affairs of other nations

containment a policy designed to curtail the political and military expansion of a hostile power

should attack the Soviets before it was too late. Others said that we should show our peaceful intentions and attempt to placate the Soviets. This policy is called **appeasement**.

The policies that the United States actually adopted, deterrence and containment, could be seen as midway between preventive war and appeasement. A nation pursuing a policy of deterrence, on the one hand, signals its peaceful intentions but, on the other hand, indicates its willingness and ability to fight if attacked. Thus, during the era of confrontation with the Soviet Union, known as the **Cold War**, the United States frequently asserted that it had no intention of attacking the Soviet Union but also built a huge military force, including a vast arsenal of over 1,500 nuclear warheads, and frequently asserted that, in the event of a Soviet attack, it had the ability and will to respond with overwhelming force. The Soviet Union, which had also built powerful nuclear and conventional military forces, announced that its nuclear weapons were also intended for deterrent purposes. Eventually, the two sides possessed such enormous arsenals of nuclear missiles that each potentially had the ability to destroy the other in the event of war. This heavily armed standoff came to be called a posture of "mutually assured destruction." Eventually, this situation led to a period of "détente," in which a number of arms control agreements were signed and the threat of war was reduced.

A policy of deterrence requires not only the possession of large military forces but also that the nation pursuing such a policy convince potential adversaries that it is willing to fight. Thus, as part of its policy of deterrence, the United States engaged in wars in Korea and Vietnam, where it had no particular interests, because American policy makers believed that if the United States did not fight in these areas, the Soviets would be emboldened to pursue an expansionist policy elsewhere, thinking that the Americans would not respond.

The Soviet Union's dissolution began in 1985, and the final collapse occurred in 1991, partly because the USSR's huge military expenditures undermined its inefficient centrally planned economy. The new Russia, though still a formidable power, seemed to pose less of a threat to the United States. Within a few years, however, new security threats emerged, requiring new policy responses.

A policy of deterrence assumes certainty and rationality. *Certainty* means that a potential adversary must know for sure that the United States will reply with force if attacked. *Rationality* means that, to be deterred, a potential adversary must be capable of rationally assessing the risks and costs of aggression against the United States. These two assumptions may not be valid in the context of contemporary security threats. The September 11 terrorist attacks demonstrated a threat against which some security scholars had long warned: that non-state actors and so-called rogue states might acquire significant military capabilities, including nuclear weapons, and would not be affected by America's deterrent capabilities. Unlike **nation-states**, which are countries with governments and fixed borders, terrorist groups are non-state actors having no fixed geographic location that can be attacked. Terrorists may believe they can attack and melt away, leaving the United States with no one against whom to retaliate. Hence, the threat of massive retaliation does not deter them. Rogue states are nations with unstable and erratic leaders

During the Cold War, the United States and the Soviet Union engaged in an arms race, each acquiring nuclear weapons to deter the other from attacking.

appeasement the effort to forestall war by giving in to the demands of a hostile power

Cold War the period of struggle between the United States and the former Soviet Union lasting from the late 1940s to about 1990

nation-states political entities consisting of a people with some common cultural experience (nation) who also share a common political authority (state), recognized by other sovereignties (nation-states)

who seem to pursue policies driven by ideological or religious fervor rather than careful consideration of economic or human costs. The United States considers North Korea and Iran to be rogue states.

To counter these new security threats, the George W. Bush administration shifted from a policy of deterrence to one of **preventive war**—the willingness to strike first in order to prevent an attack, particularly by enemies that might be armed with weapons of mass destruction. The United States declared that, if necessary, it would take action to disable terrorist groups and rogue states before they could develop the capacity to harm the United States.[5] The Bush administration's "global war on terror" was an expression of prevention, as was the U.S. invasion of Iraq. The United States also refused to rule out the possibility that it would attack North Korea or Iran if it deemed those nations' nuclear programs to be an imminent threat to American security interests. Accompanying this shift in military doctrines was an enormous increase in overall U.S. military spending (see Figure 18.1).

In June 2014 in a commencement address at the U.S. Military Academy at West Point, President Obama signaled a shift in American military policy. The president declared that U.S. policy had led to what he described as too many "military adventures." In the future, said the president, American policy would be based on collective action and restraint. While a military option would remain available if Americans were directly threatened, the president said that nonmilitary options, including diplomacy and economic sanctions, should always be tried first.

This emphasis on diplomacy, sanctions, and collective action seemed to characterize the president's responses to three major foreign policy problems encountered by the administration. These were the Russian annexation of the Crimean area of

preventive war policy of striking first when a nation fears that a foreign foe is contemplating hostile action

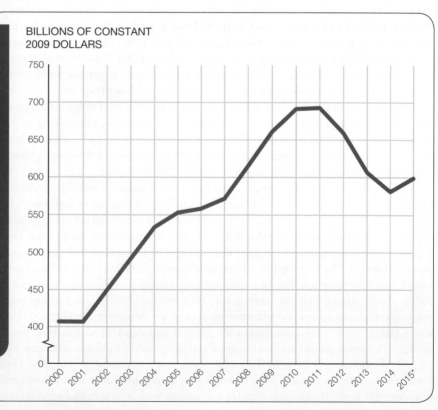

FIGURE 18.1

U.S. Spending on National Defense since 2000

During the 1990s the budget for national defense declined as the country enjoyed a "peace dividend" following the conclusion of the Cold War. After the attacks of September 11 and the commencement of the war on terrorism, however, national defense spending rose steadily; in a decade, spending increased by 70 percent. Since that time, defense spending has fallen, partly as a result of sequestration (see Chapter 16).

*Data for 2015 are estimated.
SOURCE: Office of Management and Budget, "Table 6.1—Composition of Outlays: 1940–2021," www.whitehouse.gov/omb/budget/historicals (accessed 1/7/16).

BILLIONS OF CONSTANT 2009 DOLLARS

Ukraine and Russian actions in Syria, the Iranian nuclear program, and the North Korean effort to build missiles capable of carrying nuclear warheads to American soil.

The crisis in Crimea worsened in March 2014, when Russian forces effectively seized control of the Crimean Peninsula, an area that had been part of the Ukraine. Many of the peninsula's inhabitants were ethnic Russians and apparently preferred Russian rule. Russian prime minister Vladimir Putin said Russia's actions were necessary to prevent disorder and bloodshed and to reassert Russia's historic rights to the region. Russian troops next massed along other portions of the Ukrainian border. The Obama administration urged the Russians to withdraw, announced a program of economic sanctions, and sought through diplomacy to encourage the United States' North Atlantic Treaty Organization (NATO) allies to impose sanctions as well. The result illustrated the difficulties inherent in collective action and the use of sanctions. Many of the United States' European allies depend on Russian energy supplies and engage in a good deal of trade with the Russians. As a result, while all agreed in principle that Russia should withdraw from Crimea, none were prepared to follow the American lead; and it seemed that nothing would be done to dislodge the Russians from Crimea. In 2014, Russia formally annexed Crimea, though the action was not officially recognized by the United States. Subsequently, Russian forces supported separatist groups in several other parts of the Ukraine. After one of these groups shot down a civilian airliner, European governments tightened their economic sanctions, and Russia at least temporarily reduced its level of threatening behavior toward the Ukraine.

In 2015, Russia challenged the United States in another part of the world when Russian forces entered the Syrian civil war in support of the Assad regime, which the United States had sought to oust. Russia claimed that its military actions were aimed at the Islamic State of Iraq and Syria (ISIS) and other terrorist groups, but in reality Russian attacks seemed to be directed at anti-Assad rebels. With American military advisers fighting alongside some of these same rebel groups, there was a danger of a direct clash between Russia and the United States. Obama called for Russian withdrawal and for negotiations to prevent an accidental confrontation between Russian and American military forces. In 2016, Russia claimed to have withdrawn its forces, but it was unclear whether Russia had, in fact, done so.

From the beginning of the Syrian civil war in 2011, the United States has backed rebels against the Bashar al-Assad regime but has increased its involvement in recent years with the aim of targeting ISIS. The United States first deployed Special Operations Forces on the ground in Syria in late 2015.

During the course of the year, the United States and Russia continued to negotiate—and violate—new agreements as the fighting continued.

As to Iran, Iran and the United States have been adversaries since 1979, when Iranians overthrew an unpopular U.S.-backed leader, Shah Reza Pahlavi. For years the United States has worried that Iran is working toward obtaining nuclear weapons with which it could threaten Israel, a close U.S. ally, and possibly the United States itself. To prevent Iran from obtaining nuclear weapons, U.S. presidents have used both carrots and sticks in the form of diplomacy and sanctions. Sanctions made it more difficult for Iran to sell its oil, its major export, hurting its economy. In this case, U.S. allies mostly cooperated with the sanctions regime. In 2015, the United States and Iran signed an agreement in which the Iranians pledged not to build nuclear weapons in exchange for a lifting of the economic sanctions. Critics of the agreement expressed fears that it would not deter the Iranians from continuing with their nuclear program, and during his campaign Donald Trump promised to abrogate the agreement.

In the case of North Korea, however, U.S. diplomacy has been futile because North Korea's major backer and trading partner—China—will not cooperate with any effort by the United States to undermine the North Korean regime. China regards North Korea as a useful pawn on the geopolitical chessboard, preventing the United States and two of its allies, Japan and South Korea, from dominating the Sea of Japan. As a result, the North Koreans have continued to build nuclear warheads and to test missiles capable of carrying them.

The president's speech at West Point also raised concerns among U.S. allies, especially in Asia, that the United States could no longer be counted on to defend them. Japan and South Korea, for example, fear the growth of Chinese economic and military power on their borders and look to the United States as a counterweight to China. Fear that the United States is no longer a reliable protector may well lead the Japanese and South Koreans to build their own nuclear forces—something that each nation certainly possesses the technology to accomplish in short order. Hence, an irony: a more peaceful United States may produce a more dangerous world.

In September 2014, President Obama seemed to shift away from his West Point pronouncements by ordering air strikes against Islamic militants operating in Iraq and Syria. The terrorist group ISIS emerged in the chaos that followed the withdrawal of American troops from Iraq. ISIS was able to overrun large portions of Syria and Iraq and was deemed by the president to pose a threat to American interests. The president seemed to feel that he had shown enough restraint and that it was time to call on the military. Accordingly, in October 2014 the United States launched a series of air attacks designed to blunt the ISIS advance and to provide support for Kurdish forces and others pitted against ISIS troops. In 2015 the president halted the withdrawal of American troops from Afghanistan, one of his major campaign pledges, when it became apparent that Islamic militants seemed likely to increase their influence in that country when the Americans departed. Apparently, diplomacy had reached its limits. Indeed, the limits of diplomacy were underscored in 2015 when ISIS launched terror attacks in Paris to demonstrate its capacity to carry the war directly to its enemies.

Economic Prosperity

A second major goal of U.S. foreign policy is promoting American prosperity. America's international economic policies are intended to expand employment opportunities in the United States, to maintain access to foreign energy supplies at a reasonable cost, to promote foreign investment in the United States, and to lower the prices Americans pay for goods and services.

Among the key elements of U.S. international economic policy is trade policy, which seeks to promote American goods and services abroad. This effort involves a complex arrangement of treaties, tariffs, and other mechanisms of policy formation. Trade policy is always complicated because most Americans benefit from a policy of free trade, which tends to reduce the cost of goods and services. One reason that consumer electronics are so inexpensive is that televisions, smartphones, and other gadgets are imported from all over the world, driving down their prices. However, many American industries and their employees are hurt by free trade if it results in factories and jobs moving abroad. Hence, trade policy always produces huge political battles between those who stand to benefit and those who stand to lose from particular policies. Trade is an area where the line between domestic and foreign policy is blurred. The most important international organization for promoting trade is the **World Trade Organization (WTO)**, established in 1995. The WTO grew out of the **General Agreement on Tariffs and Trade (GATT)**. Since World War II, GATT had brought together a wide range of nations for regular negotiations designed to reduce barriers to trade. Such barriers, many believed, had contributed to the breakdown of the world economy in the 1930s and had helped cause World War II. The WTO has 151 members worldwide, including the United States. Similar policy goals are pursued in regional arrangements, such as the **North American Free Trade Agreement (NAFTA)**, a trade treaty among the United States, Canada, and Mexico.

Working toward freer trade has been an important goal of most presidential administrations since World War II. The Obama administration, for example, reached a free trade agreement with 12 Pacific Rim countries in 2015. Yet as globalization has advanced, concerns about the consequences of free trade, and about the operation of the WTO in particular, have grown. Critics contend that the WTO does not pay sufficient attention to the concerns of developing nations or to such issues as environmental degradation, human rights, and labor practices, including the use of child labor in many countries. Countries in the developing world accuse the United States and Europe of hypocrisy in preaching free trade but then using patents and subsidies to protect their markets. There have been some successes on these issues, notably new WTO guidelines that allow poor countries to override expensive patents. Such patents make desperately needed drugs unavailable to most of the developing world. It has been more difficult to reach agreement on agricultural subsidies. Both the United States and Europe provide massive subsidies to their own agricultural industries. The prospects for resolving this issue are dim. The developed world has been reluctant to confront the economic dislocations and political costs of reducing the subsidies.

Agriculture and Trade One of the most controversial areas of trade liberalization is agriculture. Since 2001 the WTO trade talks—called the Doha Round because they began in Doha, Qatar, in 2001—have focused particularly on reducing trade barriers in agriculture. Since the formation of the WTO, the United States has pressured the developing world to reduce trade barriers. At the same time, however, the United States and Europe have offered heavy subsidies to their own agricultural industries. Such subsidies keep the prices high of commodities like wheat and corn, helping to ensure that farmers make a profit. Developing countries have long imposed tariffs on agricultural products

Word Trade Organization (WTO) international organization promoting free trade that grew out of the General Agreement on Tariffs and Trade

General Agreement on Tariffs and Trade (GATT) international trade organization, in existence from 1947 to 1995, that set many of the rules governing international trade

North American Free Trade Agreement (NAFTA) trade treaty among the United States, Canada, and Mexico to lower and eliminate tariffs among the three countries to limit the entry of these artificially cheap products, which would otherwise destroy their agricultural sector. During the Doha Round, the developing world charged the richer nations with hypocrisy for demanding that poor countries lower tariffs yet refusing to reduce their agricultural subsidies. Of course, both subsidies and tariffs are harmful from the point of view of consumers, who pay higher prices for food products.

Both the United States and Europe have been reluctant to reduce subsidies and tariffs because farmers are important political constituencies. During the mid-1990s, the United States began to cut agricultural subsidies; but in the lead-up to the 2002 elections, President Bush signed a very generous farm bill that reinstated many of these subsidies. By 2006, American farm subsidies neared record highs. U.S. trade officials have sought to persuade American farmers that the costs of reduced subsidies will be far outweighed by the benefits gained from opening new markets for their products.

Jobs and Trade Trade is often a political issue in the United States. In 2008, John McCain accused Barack Obama of promoting protectionist policies, while Obama said Republicans had exported American jobs abroad and allowed an enormous trade deficit to develop. The U.S. trade deficit (a negative trade balance, meaning the country imports more than it exports) was in the triple digits (see Figure 18.2), and job growth in the United States had been low for several years. Analysts predicted that many of the 2.8 million manufacturing jobs lost in the recession of the early 2000s would never return to the United States. Moreover, outsourcing, the practice of moving jobs to other countries, began to hit the white-collar workforce as jobs for workers such as call center operators and computer programmers moved to India and other countries with cheaper labor forces. In 2010 the United States accused China of manipulating trade rules to its own advantage, and China, in return, accused the United States of mismanaging its own economy. In 2012, China announced that it would reduce its purchases

Free-trade agreements can hurt American workers if factories and jobs are outsourced overseas. Many Americans—as well as a majority of members of Congress, including most Democrats—opposed the Obama-backed Trans-Pacific Partnership for just this reason.

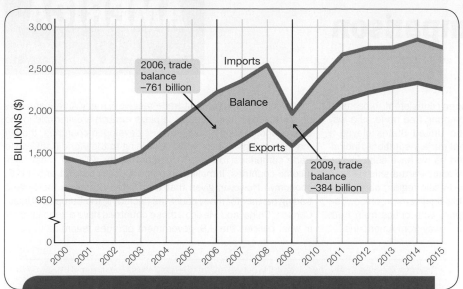

FIGURE 18.2

U.S. International Trade in Goods and Services

The United States has a "trade deficit" with the rest of the world, which means it imports more goods and services from abroad than it exports. Economists argue about whether this is a problem for the U.S. economy. Some assert that a deficit means the United States is a debtor nation, living beyond its means. Others assert that the trade deficit reflects investment in American productive capabilities. Still others argue that imports as well as exports are good for the American economy.

SOURCE: U.S. Census Bureau, Foreign Trade Statistics, www.census.gov/foreign-trade/statistics/historical/index.html (accessed 7/25/16).

of U.S. government securities in order to become less vulnerable to fluctuations in the value of the dollar. The United States pointed out that this might result in a reduction of its imports of Chinese goods.

In 2016, the Trans-Pacific Partnership (TPP)—a free trade agreement negotiated by the Obama administration—was signed by 12 countries along the Pacific Rim. The agreement faced opposition from the public and from both Republican and Democratic members of Congress as another job-killing measure. In the 2016 presidential campaign, Donald Trump accused the Obama administration of having mismanaged trade policy so that foreign countries profited at America's expense. He sharply criticized the TPP and promised to withdraw from the agreement and bring jobs back to the United States.

International Humanitarian Policies

A third goal of American policy is to make the world a better place for all its inhabitants. The main forms of policy that address this goal are international environmental policy, international human rights policy, and international

Trade in Comparison

Since World War II, there has been consistent bipartisan support in the United States for promoting free trade as a way to encourage economic growth.[a] The United States played a key role in creating major international trade institutions, including the World Trade Organization. And as we have seen in this chapter, negotiations over the Trans-Pacific Partnership (TPP), a regional trade agreement in the Asia-Pacific region, were a key priority of President Obama during his final term in office. The TPP did not receive bipartisan support, with critics from both parties arguing that it would take jobs away from Americans.

Given the attention that trade receives, many Americans may be surprised to learn that trade plays a much smaller role in the U.S. economy than it does in most developed countries, though that percentage is increasing. According to the World Bank, while trade comprises roughly 60 percent of the GDP of most high-income countries, it makes up only about 30 percent of the U.S. economy.[b] However, given that the United States is the largest trading partner for many countries (including the European Union, Canada, China, and Mexico), those countries have a keen interest in what policies the U.S. government pursues regarding trade.

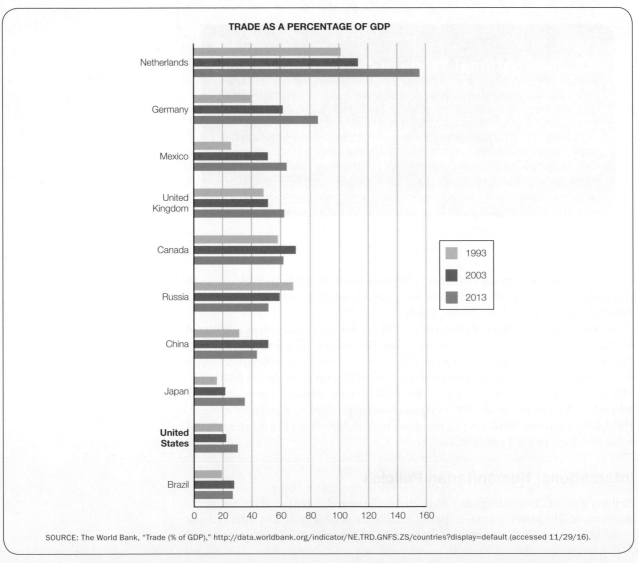

TRADE AS A PERCENTAGE OF GDP

Netherlands, Germany, Mexico, United Kingdom, Canada, Russia, China, Japan, **United States**, Brazil

Legend: 1993, 2003, 2013

0   20   40   60   80   100   120   140   160

SOURCE: The World Bank, "Trade (% of GDP)," http://data.worldbank.org/indicator/NE.TRD.GNFS.ZS/countries?display=default (accessed 11/29/16).

[a]Christopher Alessi and Robert McMahon, "Backgrounder: U.S. Trade Policy," Council on Foreign Relations, www.cfr.org/trade/us-trade-policy/p17859 (accessed 11/23/15).
[b]The World Bank measures trade as the sum of export and imports in goods and services.

peacekeeping. The United States also contributes to international organizations that work for global health and against hunger, such as the World Health Organization. These policies are often seen as secondary to the other goals of U.S. foreign policy and are forced to give way if they interfere with security or foreign economic policy. Moreover, although the United States spends billions annually on security policy and hundreds of millions on trade policy, it spends relatively little on environmental, human rights, and peacekeeping efforts. Some critics charge that the United States has the wrong priorities, spending far more to make war than to protect human rights and the global environment. Nevertheless, a number of important U.S. foreign policy efforts are, at least in part, designed to make the world a better place.

In the realm of international environmental policy, the United States supports various international efforts to protect the environment. These include the United Nations Framework Convention on Climate Change, an international agreement to study and ameliorate harmful changes in the global environment, and the Montreal Protocol, an agreement signed by over 150 countries to limit the production of substances potentially harmful to the world's ozone layer. Other nations have criticized the United States for withdrawing from the 1997 Kyoto Protocol, an agreement setting limits on industrial countries' emissions of greenhouse gases. The United States asserted that the Kyoto Protocol would harm American economic interests. The Kyoto Protocol expired in 2012, but 37 of the original signatories signed the Doha Amendment to renew their commitment to reduce greenhouse gas emissions. The United States refrained from signing this new agreement as well. In 2015, however, the United States did agree to the so-called Paris accords to reduce greenhouse gas emissions. Many Republicans, including Donald Trump, opposed the agreement. Each country agreed to reduce emissions but would set its own contribution to the effort.

The same national priorities seem apparent in the area of human rights policy. The United States has a long-standing commitment to human rights and is a party to most major international human rights agreements. These include the International Covenant on Civil and Political Rights, the UN Convention against Torture, the International Convention on the Elimination of All Forms of Racial Discrimination, and various agreements to protect children. The State Department's Bureau of Democracy, Human Rights, and Labor works cooperatively with international organizations to investigate and focus attention on human rights abuses. In 1998 the United States enacted the International Religious Freedom Act, which calls on all governments to respect religious freedom. The act lists a number of sanctions that the United States and other signatories may employ to punish nations found to be in violation.

Although the United States is committed to promoting human rights, this commitment has a lower priority in American foreign policy than the nation's security concerns and economic interests. Thus, the United States is likely to overlook human rights violations by its major trading partners, such as China, and remain silent in the face of human rights violations by such allies as Saudi Arabia. Nevertheless, human rights concerns do play a role in American foreign policy. For example, beginning in 2007 the United States has annually made available several million dollars in small grants to pay medical and legal expenses incurred by individuals who have been the victims of retaliation in their own countries for working against their governments' repressive practices. In this small way, the United States is backing its often-asserted principles.

U.S. foreign policy also includes support for international peacekeeping efforts. At any time, border wars, civil wars, and guerrilla conflicts flare somewhere in the world—usually in its poorer regions—and can generate humanitarian crises in the form of casualties, disease, and refugees. In cooperation with international agencies and other nations, the United States funds efforts to keep the peace in volatile regions and to address the health care and refugee problems associated with conflict. In 2015 the United States provided nearly $2 billion in humanitarian assistance to help Syrian refugees displaced by the civil war in that nation and by the end of 2016 had donated over $5 billion to the cause.[6] Because the United States was also providing military support to some of the forces battling in Syria, it might be said that it was seeking to solve a humanitarian crisis partially of its own making.

As the world's wealthiest nation, the United States also recognizes an obligation to render assistance to nations facing emergencies. In 2010, for example, the United States sent medical aid, food relief, and rescue teams to Haiti when that impoverished island nation was struck by a devastating earthquake; and in 2011, the United States provided support to Japan when a tsunami devastated a portion of the Japanese coast and damaged a nuclear reactor. In 2014 the United States pledged $300 million in humanitarian aid to the people of South Sudan, a population at grave risk of famine due to military conflict between government and rebel forces.

U.S. humanitarian policies are important, contributing to the success of many international humanitarian programs. In general, though, security and economic interests take precedence over humanitarian concerns. An example of this precedence is American refugee policy. In recent years, fighting in the Middle East has displaced hundreds of thousands of refugees from their homes. Western Europe has been relatively hospitable to these individuals. The United States, however, concerned that ISIS and other terrorist groups might attempt to infiltrate their fighters into the country disguised as refugees, has admitted only a trickle from the vast river of displaced persons.

for critical analysis

Why does the United States pursue international humanitarian policy? Should the United States pay more attention to the human rights records of its trading partners, like China, or allies, like Saudi Arabia?

● Who Makes American Foreign Policy?

Identify the major players in foreign-policy making, and describe their roles

As we have seen, domestic policies are made by governmental institutions and influenced by a variety of interest groups, political movements, and even the mass media. The same is true in the realm of foreign policy. The president and the chief advisers are the principal architects of U.S. foreign policy. However, Congress, the bureaucracy, the courts, political parties, interest groups, and trade associations also play important roles in this realm. Often, the president and Congress are at odds over foreign policy. When the Democrats took control of Congress in 2006, they vowed to force President Bush to end the war in Iraq. The president vowed, in turn, to resist the Democrats' efforts and generally prevailed. Ethnic lobbies such as the pro-Israel lobby and the Armenian lobby also seek to affect foreign policy. In 2007 the Armenian lobby persuaded Congress to condemn Turkey's actions in 1915 that led to the deaths of more than 1 million Armenians. The president, fearing that Turkey, an important U.S. ally, would be offended, blocked the effort. Let us examine the major institutions and forces shaping American foreign policy.

The President

The Constitution assigns the president very clear powers in the realm of foreign and security policy. The president is given the power to make treaties (with the advice and consent of the Senate), appoint ambassadors, and serve as commander in chief of the army and navy of the United States. Presidents have expanded on these powers, claiming that their inherent power to defend the nation serves as the basis for presidential primacy in all matters affecting America's international interests. Since World War II, presidents have declined to ask Congress for a declaration of war as required by the Constitution and have, instead, committed American forces to foreign conflicts under their own authority.

Most American presidents have been domestic politicians who set out to make their place in history through achievements in domestic policy. George W. Bush had virtually no foreign policy preparation prior to taking office. He had traveled very little outside the United States, and he had had virtually no foreign experience as governor of Texas. Nonetheless, Bush was decisive in the initiatives he took to define America's national interest for his administration. Examples include revival of the controversial program to develop a nuclear missile shield ("Star Wars"); his abandonment of the Anti–Ballistic Missile treaty, which alienated Russia; changes in policy priorities away from humanitarian and environmental goals and toward goals more specifically within the realm of national security; and turning America's concerns (by degree or emphasis) away from Europe and toward an "Asia-first" policy.

September 11 and its aftermath immensely accentuated the president's role and his place in foreign policy.[7] By 2002 foreign policy was the centerpiece of the Bush administration's agenda. In a June 1 speech at West Point, the **Bush Doctrine** of preemptive war was announced. Bush argued that "our security will require all Americans . . . to be ready for preemptive action when necessary to defend our liberty and to defend our lives." Bush's statement was clearly intended to justify his administration's plans to invade Iraq, but it had much wider implications for

Bush Doctrine foreign policy based on the idea that the United States should take preemptive action against threats to its national security

Following the events of September 11, 2001, George W. Bush announced the "Bush Doctrine" at a speech at West Point in 2002. The Bush Doctrine marked a shift away from the policy of deterrence, advocating instead for preemptive action against security threats from terrorists and rogue states with unstable leaders.

international relations and for the central role of the American president in guiding foreign policy.

By 2010, President Obama had put his own stamp on American foreign policy, altering the conduct of America's war in Afghanistan and seeking to compel the Israelis and Palestinians to accept a Middle East peace deal. Obama also sought to engage more fully America's allies, who had been miffed by the previous administration's tendency to engage in unilateral action. Thus, the United States worked closely with its NATO allies in 2011 to bring an end to the Libyan dictatorship of Mu'ammar Qaddafi.

During the course of his first year in office, Obama also concluded direct U.S. military involvement in Iraq and began to withdraw American forces from Afghanistan. One of Obama's triumphs was the military raid that resulted in the killing of Osama bin Laden, who had long been sought by the United States for his role in the September 11 terrorist attacks. As we saw, however, President Obama faced a number of challenges as he neared the end of his presidency. Russian prime minister Putin had upset the international order in Europe by seizing the Crimean Peninsula. North Korea continued to test missiles; Iran had not definitively halted its nuclear weapons program; Israel and the Palestinians fought a war in Gaza; ISIS militants sought to win control of Iraq, Syria, and Lebanon, and showed that they could strike in the hearts of European capitals. These and, no doubt, new problems would challenge Obama's successors. Presidents have come to dominate American foreign policy, but U.S. foreign policies are never able to cure the ills of the world.

The Bureaucracy

The major foreign policy actors in the bureaucracy are the secretaries of the Departments of State, Defense, and the Treasury; the Joint Chiefs of Staff, especially the chair; and the director of the CIA. Since 1947 a separate unit in the

White House has overseen the vast foreign policy establishment for the purpose of synthesizing all the messages arising out of the bureaucracy and helping the president make his own foreign policy. This is the National Security Council (NSC). It is a "subcabinet" made up of the president, the vice president, the secretary of defense, and the secretary of state, plus others each president appoints. Since the profound shake-up of September 11, two key players have been added. The first of these was the secretary of the Department of Homeland Security, established in 2002 and composed of 22 existing agencies relocated from all over the executive branch on the theory that their expertise could be better coordinated, more rational, and more efficient in a single organization designed to fight international terrorism and domestic natural disasters. The second key player was imposed at the top as the war in Iraq was becoming a quagmire: a director of national intelligence, to collate and coordinate intelligence coming in from multiple sources and to report a synthesis of all this intelligence to the president on a daily basis.

Since the creation of the CIA in 1947 and the Department of Defense in 1949 (replacing the Department of War), the secretary of defense and the director of the CIA have often been rivals engaged in power struggles for control of the intelligence community.[8] For the most part, secretaries of defense have prevailed in these battles, and the Defense Department today controls more than 80 percent of the nation's intelligence capabilities and funds. The creation of the position of director of national intelligence in 2005 to coordinate all intelligence activities set off new Washington power struggles as the "intelligence czar" faced opposition from both the CIA and the Department of Defense. The Defense Department is generally reluctant to cooperate with civilian intelligence agencies and has moved to expand its own intelligence capabilities at the other agencies' expense.

In addition to these top Cabinet-level officials, key lower-level staff members have policy-making influence as strong as that of the Cabinet secretaries, and occasionally even stronger. These include the two or three specialized national security advisers in the White House, the staff of the NSC (headed by the national security adviser), and a few other career bureaucrats in the Departments of State and Defense. A few civilian intelligence agencies are also involved in foreign policy and national security, the most important of which are the Federal Bureau of Investigation (FBI), the U.S. Citizenship and Immigration Services, and the Internal Revenue Service (IRS).

Since the events of September 11, military and law enforcement agencies have increased their role in America's foreign-policy making.[9] To a significant extent, American foreign policy is driven by military and antiterrorism concerns, and the agencies addressing these concerns play an increased role. Recent American ambassadors have complained about being relegated to secondary status as the White House has looked to military commanders for information, advice, and policy implementation. For every region of the world, the U.S. military has assigned a "combatant commander," usually a senior general or admiral, to oversee operations in that area. In many instances, these combatant commanders, who control troops, equipment, and intelligence capabilities, have become the real eyes, ears, and voices for American foreign policy in their designated regions.

Congress

Although the Constitution gives Congress the power to declare war (see Table 18.1), Congress has exercised this power on only five occasions: the War of 1812, the Mexican War (1846), the Spanish-American War (1898), World War I

TABLE 18.1

Principal Foreign Policy Provisions of the Constitution

	POWERS GRANTED	
	PRESIDENT	CONGRESS
War power	Commander in chief of armed forces	Provide for the common defense; declare war
Treaties	Negotiate treaties	Ratification of treaties by two-thirds majority (Senate)
Appointments	Nominate high-level government officials	Confirm president's appointments (Senate)
Foreign commerce	No explicit powers, but treaty negotiation and appointment powers pertain	Explicit power "to regulate foreign commerce"
General powers	Executive power; veto	Legislative power; power of the purse; oversight and investigation

(1917), and World War II (1941). For the first 150 years of American history, Congress's foreign policy role was limited because the nation's role in world affairs was limited. During this time, the Senate was the only important congressional foreign policy player because of its constitutional role in reviewing and approving treaties. In recent decades, presidents have brought few treaties to the Senate, preferring to rely on executive agreements with other nations. Congress has nevertheless remained influential because most foreign policies require financing, which requires action by both the House of Representatives and the Senate. For example, Congress's first act after September 11, 2001, was to authorize the president to use "all necessary and appropriate force," coupled with a $40 billion emergency appropriations bill for homeland defense. And although President Bush believed he possessed the constitutional authority to invade Iraq, he still sought congressional approval, which he received in October 2002. After the Democrats took control of Congress in 2007, the Democratic leadership proposed a new resolution opposing President Bush's policies in Iraq. The president asserted that he would not be bound by such a vote.

Not only does the president need Congress to provide funding for foreign and military policy initiatives but under the Constitution many presidential agreements with foreign nations also have to be approved by Congress. Article II, Section 2, of the Constitution declares that proposed treaties with other nations must be submitted by the president to the Senate and approved by a two-thirds vote. Because this "supermajority" is usually difficult to achieve, presidents generally prefer a different type of agreement with other nations, called an **executive agreement**. An executive agreement is similar to a treaty and has the force of law but usually requires only a plurality vote in both houses of Congress for approval. There are two types of executive agreements. The first, a *sole executive agreement*, entails only presidential action and does not require congressional approval. While they provide presidents with maximum flexibility, sole executive agreements have limited usefulness since they cannot supersede existing law and Congress is not obligated to provide

executive agreement an agreement, made between the president and another country, that has the force of a treaty but does not require the Senate's "advice and consent"

any funding that might be needed to implement them. The second is called an *executive–congressional agreement*. Such an agreement is negotiated by the president and then submitted to Congress for approval. Approval consists of a majority vote of both houses rather than a supermajority in the Senate. This generally represents a lower hurdle than the constitutional two-thirds vote in the Senate. In some instances, the president and Congress will agree upon a particular procedure for congressional approval of an agreement. In the case of the 2015 Iran agreement, Congress had agreed that it would vote on whether or not to accept the agreement. However, such a vote was subject to a presidential veto. In this way, the constitutional treaty power was turned on its head. Under the Constitution, the president needed two-thirds support in the Senate to carry out his plans. The Iran agreement, however, could have been blocked only if a veto-proof two-thirds of both houses of Congress was prepared to vote against the president's policy.

Another aspect of Congress's role in foreign policy is the Senate's power to confirm the president's nominations of Cabinet members, ambassadors, and other high-ranking officials (such as the director of the CIA, but not the director of the NSC). A final constitutional power of Congress is the regulation of "commerce with foreign nations." This is the power under which Congress enacts tariffs and other foreign trade legislation.

Other congressional players are the foreign policy, military policy, and intelligence committees: in the Senate, these are the Foreign Relations Committee, the Armed Services Committee, and the Homeland Security and Governmental Affairs Committee; in the House, these are the Foreign Affairs and Homeland Security Committees and the Armed Services Committee. Usually a few members of these committees with extensive foreign affairs experience become influential makers of foreign policy. In fact, several members of Congress have left the legislature to become key foreign affairs Cabinet members. After September 11, 2001, congressional committees conducted hearings on the failure of the intelligence agencies; but at the time, most members of Congress were reluctant to take on these agencies or a popular president. In 2007, though, with Congress under Democratic control and the president's popularity fading, a number of congressional committees launched inquiries into the conduct of the war in Iraq and the more general operations of the intelligence and defense communities. Within weeks, congressional testimony revealed flaws in military procurement procedures, military planning, and other aspects of the administration's programs and policies. Congressional investigations and the publicity they generate are weapons Congress frequently uses to blunt presidential power. In 2014 and again in 2015, Republicans held hearings on the 2012 attack on America's consulate in Benghazi, Libya, which resulted in the deaths of the U.S. ambassador and three other Americans. The attack came while Hillary Clinton was secretary of state; Democrats charged that Republicans were hoping to tarnish her image before the 2016 presidential election. The hearings produced little hard evidence of wrongdoing on Clinton's part but did serve to publicize many accusations that the GOP hoped would be damaging to the Democratic candidate.

Interest Groups

Although the president, the executive branch bureaucracy, and Congress are the true makers of foreign policy, the "foreign policy establishment" is a much larger

The American Israel Public Affairs Committee (AIPAC) is a powerful interest group that advocates pro-Israel policies to Congress and the president. Here, Israeli prime minister Benjamin Netanyahu speaks to the group about the emerging White House–backed nuclear deal with Iran, which AIPAC lobbied heavily against, albeit unsuccessfully.

arena, including significant shapers of foreign policy. These unofficial players possess varying degrees of influence depending on their prestige, reputation, socioeconomic standing, and, most important, the party and ideology that are dominant at a given moment.

The most important category of nonofficial player is the interest group—that is, the interest group to which one or more foreign policy issues are of vital relevance. Economic interest groups are reputed to wield the most influence, yet myths about their influence far outweigh the realities. In fact, the influence of organized economic interest groups in foreign policy varies enormously from issue to issue and year to year. Most are "single-issue" groups, most active when their particular issue is on the agenda. On many broader and more sustained policy issues—such as NAFTA, the TPP, and the general question of U.S. involvement in international trade—the larger interest groups, or peak associations, have difficulty getting their many members to speak with a single voice. Some business groups represent export industries, and others represent firms threatened by imports. Hence, "business" has more than one view on trade policy. More successful in influencing foreign policy are the single-issue groups such as the tobacco industry, which has prevented heavy restrictions on international trade in and advertising of tobacco products, and the computer hardware and software industries, which have hardened the United States' attitude toward Chinese piracy of intellectual property rights.

Another type of interest group with significant foreign policy influence comprises people who strongly identify with their country of national origin. Wielding the greatest influence are Jewish Americans with family and emotional ties to Israel. In 2015 many, albeit not all, Jewish groups lobbied heavily but ultimately unsuccessfully against the Obama administration's agreement with Iran, which they argued posed a threat to both the United States and Israel. Similarly, Americans of Irish heritage, despite having lived in the United States for two, three, or four generations, maintain vigilance about U.S. policies toward Ireland and Northern Ireland. Cuban Americans have long been a powerful voice in support of maintaining sanctions against Cuba, which helps explain why relations with Cuba were not normalized until 2015. Many other ethnic and national interest groups wield similar influence over U.S. foreign policy.

These ethnic or national origin interest groups, exhibiting a kind of dual loyalty that Americans generally welcome as a worthy sentiment, are more influential than their counterparts in other democratic countries. But there are limits, especially when national origin is coupled with or tied to countries in which a single religion is dominant. For example, Jews with strong ties to Israel and Catholics with connections to Ireland have on occasion been blocked from group influence on foreign policy because "dual loyalty" can be taken by other groups as "doubtful loyalty."[10] Nevertheless, Irish and Jewish groups, and a variety of other ethnic American interest groups, are vigorously involved in salient aspects of foreign policy; and it is an irrational or nonrational elected politician who disregards their signals. It is quite possible that the "electoral connection"[11] and the politics of representation in Congress (and the White House) are at their most intense when national origin is linked to a foreign policy issue. Many will argue that the rationality principle "need not . . . be equated with such narrowly self-serving actions."[12] However, the nationality interest is often the strongest electoral connection.

A third type of interest group, more prominent in recent decades, is devoted to human rights. Instead of having self-serving economic or ethnic interests in foreign policy, such groups are genuinely concerned about the welfare of people worldwide—particularly those who suffer under harsh political regimes. An example is Amnesty International, whose exposés of human rights abuses have altered the practices of many regimes. In recent years, the Christian right has been a vocal advocate for the human rights of Christians who are persecuted in other parts of the world for their religious beliefs, most notably in China. For example, in the 1990s, the Christian Coalition joined groups such as Amnesty International in lobbying Congress to restrict trade with countries that permitted attacks against religious believers.

A related type of group with rapidly growing influence is the ecological or environmental group, sometimes collectively called "greens." Groups of this nature often depend more on demonstrations than on lobbying and electoral politics. Demonstrations in strategically located areas can have significant influence on American foreign policy. In recent years environmental activists have staged major protests, such as at the 2009 London and 2010 Toronto international economic summits, and at the 2015 Paris environmental summit that led to the signing of the accords discussed above.

A final actor in the realm of foreign policy is public opinion. Americans tend to be concerned mainly with domestic issues, but public opinion does begin to count when the nation is at war. Americans are often impatient with military actions that seem drawn out, producing costs and casualties for reasons that no longer seem clear. Presidents are aware that long wars and casualties are likely to turn public opinion against them and provide ammunition for their political foes. Fear of public opinion is one reason that presidents have favored professional military forces and technologies like drones that would reduce the immediacy of war to America's general public.

Putting It Together

Who actually makes American foreign policy? First, except for the president, the key players vary from case to case. Second, because the one constant is the president's centrality, it is best to evaluate other actors and factors as they interact with the president.[13] Third, influence varies from case to case because each one involves different conditions and time constraints: for issues that arise and are resolved quickly, the opportunity for influence is limited. Fourth, foreign policy experts will usually disagree about the level of influence any player or type of player has on policy making.

But we can make some tentative generalizations to frame the remainder of this chapter. First, when an important foreign policy decision must be made under conditions of crisis, the influence of the presidency is strongest. Second, within these time constraints, access to the decision-making process is limited almost exclusively to the officially and constitutionally designated players of the foreign policy establishment. In other words, in a crisis, the foreign policy establishment works as it is supposed to.[14] As time becomes less restricted, the arena of participation expands to include more government players and more nonofficial, informal players—the most concerned interest groups and the most important journalists. In other words, the arena becomes more pluralistic and, therefore, less distinguishable from the politics of domestic-policy making. Third, because so many other countries have influence and interests on any given issue, there are severe limits on the choices the United States can make. That is, in contrast to domestic politics, U.S. foreign-policy makers are engaged not only in infighting but also in strategically interacting with other nations' policy makers; their choices are made both in reaction to and in anticipation of these strategic interactions. Thus, even though foreign-policy making in noncrisis situations may closely resemble the pluralistic politics of domestic-policy making, foreign-policy making is still a narrower arena with fewer participants.

● The Instruments of Modern American Foreign Policy

> **Describe the means the United States uses to carry out foreign policy today**

Any government has at hand certain instruments, or tools, to use in implementing its foreign policy. An instrument is neutral, capable of serving many goals. There have been many instruments of American foreign policy, and we can deal here only with those instruments we deem most important in the modern epoch: diplomacy, the United Nations, the international monetary structure, economic aid and sanctions, collective security, military force, and arbitration. Each of these instruments will be evaluated in this section for its utility in the conduct of American foreign policy, and each will be assessed in light of the history and development of American values.

Diplomacy

diplomacy the representation of a government to other governments

We begin this treatment of instruments with diplomacy. **Diplomacy** is the representation of a government to other foreign governments. Its purpose is to promote national values or interests by peaceful means.

The first effort to create a modern diplomatic service in the United States was made through the Rogers Act of 1924, which established the initial framework for a professional foreign service staff. But it took World War II and the Foreign Service Act of 1946 to forge the foreign service into a fully professional diplomatic corps.

Diplomacy, by its very nature, is overshadowed by spectacular international events, dramatic initiatives, and meetings among heads of state or their direct personal representatives. The traditional American distrust of diplomacy continues today, albeit in a weaker form. Impatience with or downright distrust of diplomacy has been built into not only all the other instruments of foreign policy but also the modern presidential system itself.[15] So much personal responsibility has been heaped on the presidency that presidents are reluctant to entrust any of their authority or responsibility in foreign policy to professional diplomats in the State Department and other bureaucracies.

In 2008, both parties' presidential candidates criticized the Bush administration for having failed to use diplomacy to secure greater international support for the Iraq War. Both promised to revitalize American diplomacy. President Obama appointed Hillary Clinton as secretary of state in part to underline the importance he attached to diplomacy by choosing such a prominent figure as America's chief diplomat. In 2016, Clinton cited her diplomatic experience as an important credential supporting her presidential bid. Donald Trump dismissed Clinton's claims and asserted that she and President Obama had mismanaged U.S. interests.

The secretary of state is America's chief diplomat. In 2015, Secretary of State John Kerry met with Iranian foreign minister Javad Zarif and other leaders in Switzerland as part of ongoing negotiations regarding the United States' nuclear deal with Iran.

The significance of diplomacy and its vulnerability to politics may be better appreciated as we proceed to the other instruments. While Americans have traditionally distrusted diplomacy, it was an instrument more or less imposed on them as the prevailing means of bargaining among nation-states in the nineteenth century. The other instruments to be identified and assessed here are those that Americans self-consciously crafted for themselves to take care of their own chosen place in the world affairs of the second half of the twentieth century and beyond. The instruments therefore better reflect American culture and values than diplomacy does.

The United Nations

The utility of the **United Nations (UN)** to the United States as an instrument of foreign policy can be too easily underestimated because the UN is a very large and unwieldy institution with few powers and no armed forces to implement its rules and resolutions. Its supreme body is the UN General Assembly, comprising one representative of each of the 192 member states; each member representative has one vote, regardless of the size of the country. Important issues require a two-thirds majority vote, and the annual session of the General Assembly runs only from September to December (although it can call extra sessions). It has little organization that can make it an effective decision-making body, with only six standing committees, few tight rules of procedure, and no political parties to provide priorities and discipline. Its defenders are quick to add that although it lacks armed forces, it relies on the power of world opinion—and this is not to be taken lightly. The powers of the UN devolve mainly to the organization's "executive committee," the UN Security Council, which alone has the real power to make decisions and rulings that member states are obligated by the UN Charter to implement. The Security Council may be called into session at any time, and each member (or a designated alternate) must be present at UN headquarters in New York at all times. The council is composed of 15 members: 5 are permanent (the victors of World War II), and 10 are elected by the General Assembly for unrepeatable two-year terms. The 5 permanent members are China, France, Russia, the United

United Nations (UN) an organization of nations founded in 1945 to be a channel for negotiation and a means of settling international disputes peacefully; the UN has had frequent successes in providing a forum for negotiation and, on some occasions, a means of preventing international conflicts from spreading; on a number of occasions, the UN has been a convenient cover for U.S. foreign policy goals

Kingdom, and the United States. Each of the 15 members has only one vote, and a 9-vote majority of the 15 is required on all substantive matters. But each of the 5 permanent members also has a negative vote, a "veto"; and one veto is sufficient to reject any substantive proposal.

The UN can serve as a useful forum for international discussions and an instrument for multilateral action. Most peacekeeping efforts to which the United States contributes, for example, are undertaken under UN auspices.

The International Monetary Structure

Fear of a repeat of the economic devastation that followed World War I brought the United States together with its allies (except the USSR) to Bretton Woods, New Hampshire, in 1944 to create a new international economic structure for the postwar world. The result was two institutions: the International Bank for Reconstruction and Development (commonly called the World Bank) and the International Monetary Fund. The World Bank's chief mission is development aid to poor countries.

The World Bank was set up to finance long-term capital. Leading nations took on the obligation of contributing funds to enable the World Bank to make loans to capital-hungry countries. (The U.S. quota has been about one-third of the total.)

International Monetary Fund (IMF) an institution established in 1944 that provides loans and facilitates international monetary exchange

The **International Monetary Fund (IMF)** was set up to provide for the short-term flow of money. After the war, the U.S. dollar replaced gold as the chief means by which the currency of one country would be "changed into" the currency of another country for purposes of making international transactions. To permit debtor countries with no international balances to make purchases and investments, the IMF was set up to lend dollars or other appropriate currencies to such needy member countries to help them overcome temporary trade deficits.

During the 1990s the importance of the IMF increased through its efforts to reform some of the largest debtor nations and formerly communist countries, to bring them more fully into the global capitalist economy. For example, in the early

The United States is the most influential member of the World Bank, which provides loans and other assistance to developing countries. Here, workers in Afghanistan work to improve roads. The World Bank has provided hundreds of millions of dollars to help rebuild Afghanistan over the past decade.

1990s, Russia and 13 other former Soviet republics were invited to join the IMF and the World Bank, with the expectation that they would receive $10.5 billion from these two agencies, primarily for a currency stabilization fund. Each republic was to get a permanent IMF representative, and the IMF increased its staff by at least 10 percent to provide the expertise necessary to cope with the problems of these emerging capitalist economies.[16]

The IMF, with tens of billions of dollars contributed by its members, has more money to lend poor countries than does the United States, Europe, or Japan (the three leading IMF shareholders) individually. It makes its policy decisions in ways that are generally consonant with the interests of the leading shareholders.[17] Two weeks after September 11, 2001, the IMF approved a $135 million loan to economically troubled Pakistan, a key player in the war against the Taliban government of Afghanistan because of its strategic location. Turkey, also because of its strategic location in the Middle East, was likewise put back in the IMF pipeline.[18] The future of the IMF, the World Bank, and all other private sources of international investment will depend in part on extension of more credit to developing countries because credit means investment and productivity. But the future may depend even more on reducing the debt that is already there from previous extensions of credit.

Economic Aid and Sanctions

Every year, the United States provides nearly $30 billion in economic assistance to other nations. Some aid has a humanitarian purpose, such as helping to provide health care, shelter for refugees, or famine relief. A good deal of American aid, however, is designed to promote American security interests or economic concerns. For example, the United States provides military assistance to a number of its allies in the form of advanced weapons or loans to help them purchase such weapons. These loans generally stipulate that the recipient must purchase the designated weapons from American firms. In this way, the United States hopes to bolster its security and economic interests with one grant. The two largest recipients of American military assistance are Israel and Egypt, American allies that fought two wars against each other. The United States believes that its military assistance allows both countries to feel sufficiently secure to remain at peace with each other.

Aid is an economic carrot. Sanctions are an economic stick. Economic sanctions that the United States employs against other nations include trade embargoes, bans on investment, and efforts to prevent the World Bank or other international institutions from extending credit to a nation against which the United States has a grievance. Sanctions are most often employed when the United States seeks to weaken what it considers a hostile regime or when it is attempting to compel some particular action by another regime. In 2014, for example, the United States imposed economic sanctions agains Russia in response to the Russian annexation of Crimea, which the United States regards as part of the Ukraine. The United States also uses economic sanctions to advance its international humanitarian policy goals. The United States currently has sanctions in place against a number of governments with records of serious violations of civil and political rights.[19]

Unilateral sanctions by the United States usually have little effect since the target can usually trade elsewhere, sometimes even with foreign affiliates of U.S. firms. If, however, the United States is able to persuade its allies to cooperate, sanctions have a better chance of success. International sanctions against Iran, for example, influenced that regime's decision to enter into negotiations with the United States, culminating in the nuclear weapons deal of 2015.

Collective Security

In 1947 most Americans hoped that the United States could meet its world obligations through the UN and economic structures alone. But when drafting the original UN Charter, most foreign-policy makers anticipated future military entanglements by insisting on language that recognized the right of all nations to provide for their mutual defense independent of the UN. And almost immediately after enactment of the Marshall Plan, designed to promote European economic recovery, the White House and a parade of State and Defense Department officials followed up with an urgent request to the Senate to ratify, and to both houses of Congress to finance, mutual defense alliances.

The Senate, at first quite reluctant to approve treaties providing for national security alliances, ultimately agreed with the executive branch. The first collective security agreement was the Rio Treaty (ratified by the Senate in September 1947), which created the Organization of American States. This was the model treaty, anticipating all succeeding collective security treaties by providing that an armed attack against any of its members "shall be considered as an attack against all the American States," including the United States. A more significant break with U.S. tradition against peacetime entanglements came with the North Atlantic Treaty (signed in April 1949), which created the **North Atlantic Treaty Organization (NATO)**. The Australian, New Zealand, United States Security (ANZUS) Treaty, which tied Australia and New Zealand to the United States, was signed in September 1951. Three years later, the Southeast Asia Treaty created the Southeast Asia Treaty Organization (SEATO).

In addition to these multilateral treaties, the United States entered into a number of **bilateral treaties** (treaties between two countries), such as the treaty with Vietnam

for critical **analysis**

There has been a good deal of debate about whether economic sanctions can convince North Korea to halt its nuclear weapons programs. What factors might help to determine the effectiveness of economic sanctions?

North Atlantic Treaty Organization (NATO) an organization, comprising the United States, Canada, and most of Western Europe, formed in 1949 to counter the perceived threat from the Soviet Union

bilateral treaties treaties made between two nations

The United States joined NATO in 1949 to help counter the threat of the Soviet Union. NATO remains an important institution for multilateral cooperation in international affairs. Here, world leaders from NATO member states discuss the Russian-Crimean crisis at a meeting in Wales in 2014.

that resulted in ultimately unsuccessful American military action to protect that nation's government. As one author has observed, the United States has been a *producer* of security, whereas most of its allies have been *consumers* of security.[20]

This pattern has continued in the post–Cold War era, and its best illustration is in the Persian Gulf War, where the United States provided the initiative, the leadership, and most of the armed forces, even though its allies were obliged to reimburse over 90 percent of the cost.

It is difficult to evaluate collective security and its treaties because the purpose of collective security as an instrument of foreign policy is prevention, and success of this kind has to be measured in terms of what did *not* happen. Critics have argued that U.S. collective security treaties posed a threat of encirclement to the Soviet Union, forcing it to produce its own collective security, particularly the Warsaw Pact.[21] Nevertheless, no one can deny the counterargument that more than 70 years have passed without a world war.

In 1998 the expansion of NATO took its first steps toward including former Warsaw Pact members, extending membership to the Czech Republic, Hungary, and Poland. Most of Washington embraced this expansion as the true and fitting end of the Cold War, and the U.S. Senate echoed this with a resounding 80–19 vote to induct these three former Soviet satellites into NATO. After the collapse of the Soviet Union, the importance of NATO as a military alliance seemed to wane. However, since 2014 the resurgence of Russia as a military power forced NATO members once again to look to one another for support. In 2014, Russia seized the Crimean Peninsula from the Ukraine and appeared to pose a threat to the Baltic states and other portions of the old Soviet empire. Russia also sent military forces to support the Assad regime in Syria. Facing an aggressive new Russia, NATO's period of quiescence seemed to be coming to a close.

The attack on the United States on September 11, 2001, was the first time in its more than 50-year history that Article 5 of the North Atlantic Treaty had to be invoked; it provides that an attack on one country is an attack on all the member countries. In fighting "the war on terror," the Bush administration recognized that no matter how preponderant American power was, some aspects of U.S. foreign policy could not be achieved without multilateral cooperation. On the other hand, the United States did not want to be constrained by its alliances. The global coalition initially forged after September 11, 2001, numbered more than 170 countries. Not all joined the war effort in Afghanistan, but most, if not all, provided some form of support for some aspect of "the war on terror," such as economic sanctions and intelligence.

Two years later, however, the war in Iraq put this coalition to the test. The Bush administration was determined not to make its decision to go to war subject to the UN, NATO, or any other international organization. The breadth of the U.S. coalition was deemed secondary to the coalition's being nonconstraining. As a result, other than the British government, no major power supported the actions of the United States.

Military Force

The most visible instrument of foreign policy is, of course, military force. The United States has built the world's most imposing military, with army, navy, marine, and air force units stationed in virtually every corner of the globe. The United States is responsible for one-third of the world's total military expenditures. The Prussian military strategist Carl von Clausewitz famously called war "politics by other means." By this he meant that nations used force not simply to demonstrate their capacity for violence. Rather, force or the threat of force is a tool nations must sometimes use to achieve their foreign policy goals. Military force may be needed to protect a nation's security interests and

Often, military efforts abroad do not turn out as the government or the public expected. Though most Americans were in favor of U.S. involvement in Afghanistan following September 11, 2001, public opinion on the issue has shifted.

Who Serves in the U.S. Military?

Gender

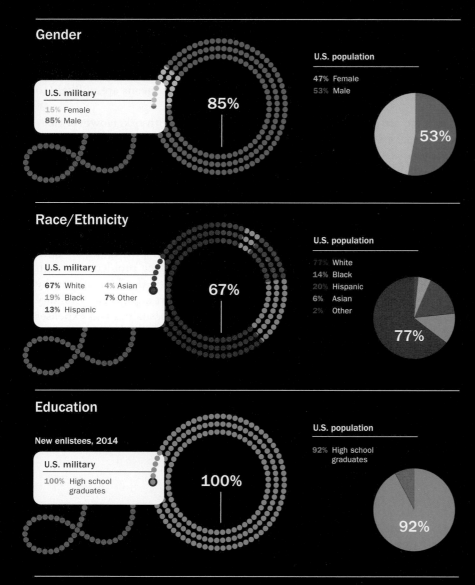

U.S. military
15% Female
85% Male

85%

U.S. population

47% Female
53% Male

53%

Race/Ethnicity

U.S. military

67% White   4% Asian
19% Black   7% Other
13% Hispanic

67%

U.S. population

77% White
14% Black
20% Hispanic
6% Asian
2% Other

77%

Education

New enlistees, 2014

U.S. military

100% High school
graduates

100%

U.S. population

92% High school
graduates

92%

The Department of Defense and the military are often responsible for implementing foreign policy that relates to security. Who are the men and women in the armed forces? The military has a far greater proportion of men to women than the general population, but in terms of race and ethnicity, the military is fairly similar to the United States as a whole. Residents of southern states are significantly more likely to enlist than those from other regions.

NOTE: Civilian comparison groups are 17- to 55-year-olds for gender and race/ethnicity, 18- to 44-year-olds for education, and 18- to 24-year-old noninstitutional civilians for geographic origin. Percentages under race/ethnicity sum to more than 100 because some people identify as more than one race.

SOURCE: Office of the Under Secretary of Defense, Personnel and Readiness, "Population Representation in the Military Services 2014," www.cna.org/pop-rep /2014, appendix B (accessed 3/7/16).

Geographic Origin

U.S. military new enlistees, 2014

13%
24%   19%
44%

Northeast	13%	Midwest	19%
South	44%	West	24%

U.S. population

18%
25%   21%
36%

Northeast	18%	Midwest	21%
South	36%	West	25%

for critical analysis

1. The move to an all-volunteer military in the United States in 1973 resulted in a more educated and professionalized force. However, the United States has used the draft in the past, and some countries require military service of all citizens. Can you think of some arguments for and against each approach?

2. Does it matter if some groups are more heavily represented in the armed forces than others?

economic concerns. Ironically, force may also be needed to achieve humanitarian goals. For example, in 2014 and 2015, international military force was required to protect tens of thousands of Yazidi refugees threatened by ISIS forces in Iraq. Without the use of military force, humanitarian assistance to the Yazidis would have been irrelevent.

Military force is generally considered a last resort and avoided if possible because of a number of problems associated with its use. First, the use of military force is extremely costly in both human and financial terms. In the past 50 years, tens of thousands of Americans have been killed and hundreds of billions of dollars spent in America's military operations. Before they employ military force to achieve national goals, policy makers must be certain that achieving those goals is essential and that other means are unlikely to succeed.

Second, the use of military force is inherently fraught with risk. However carefully policy makers and generals plan for military operations, results can seldom be fully anticipated. Variables ranging from the weather to unexpected weapons and tactics deployed by opponents may turn calculated military operations into costly disasters or convert maneuvers that were expected to be quick and decisive into long, drawn-out, expensive struggles. For example, American policy makers expected to defeat the Iraqi army quickly and easily in 2003—and they did. Policy makers did not anticipate, however, that American forces would still be struggling years later to defeat the insurgency that arose in the war's aftermath. Finally, in a democracy, any government that chooses to address policy problems through military means is almost certain to encounter political difficulties. Generally speaking, the American public will support relatively short and decisive military engagements. If, however, a conflict drags on, producing casualties and expenses with no clear outcome, the public loses patience and opposition politicians point to the government's lies and ineptitude. The wars in Korea, Vietnam, and Iraq are all examples of protracted conflicts whose domestic political repercussions became serious liabilities for the governments that initially decided to make use of military force.

Thus, military force remains a major foreign policy tool, and the United States currently possesses a more powerful and effective set of military forces than any other nation. Nevertheless, even for the United States, the use of military force is fraught with risk and is not to be undertaken lightly.

Arbitration

The final foreign policy tool we shall consider is dispute arbitration. *Arbitration* means referring an international disagreement to a neutral third party for resolution. Arbitration, like diplomacy, is sometimes seen as a form of "soft power" as distinguished from military force, economic sanctions, and other coercive foreign policy instruments. The United States will occasionally turn to international tribunals to resolve disputes with other countries. For example, in February 2008 the U.S. government asked the International Court of Justice to resolve a long-standing dispute with Italy over American property confiscated by the Italian government more than 40 years ago. To take another example, in 1981 the United States and Iran established an arbitral tribunal to deal with claims arising from Iran's seizure of the U.S. embassy in Tehran in 1979; the tribunal resulted in a settlement.

More important, the United States relies heavily on the work of arbitral panels to maintain the flow of international trade on which the U.S. economy depends. U.S. firms would be reluctant to do business abroad if they could not be certain that their property and contractual rights would be honored by other nations. Arbitration helps produce that certainty. Almost every international contract contains an arbitration clause requiring that disputes between the parties will be resolved not by foreign governments but by impartial arbitral panels accepted by both sides. By the terms of the New York Convention, virtually every nation in the world has agreed to accept and enforce arbitral verdicts. The United States has incorporated the terms of the New York Convention into federal law, and U.S. courts vigorously enforce arbitral judgments. The United States may not be happy with the outcome of every arbitral proceeding, but the arbitral system is essential to America's economic interests.

Foreign Policy
and Your Future

The nineteenth-century British statesman Lord Palmerston famously said, "Nations have no permanent friends or allies; they only have permanent interests." Palmerston's comment illustrates what is sometimes known as the "realist" view of foreign policy. The realist school holds that foreign policies should be guided by the national interest (mainly security and economic interest) and that policy makers should steel themselves to the necessity of making decisions that might be viewed from the outside as cold and ruthless if they serve the nation's interests. Although many public officials have denounced such views in public—especially if they were running for office—many became realists once in power. Every one of America's post–World War II presidents, Democrats and Republicans alike, has been willing to order young Americans into battle and to visit death and destruction on the citizens of foreign states if he believed the national interest required it.

The harsh rationality of foreign policy often clashes with America's history and ideals. U.S. democratic and liberal traditions lead Americans to hope for a world in which ideals rather than naked interests govern foreign policy and in which U.S. leaders pay heed to ideals. The ideals that Americans historically have espoused (though not always lived by) assert that U.S. foreign policies should have a higher purpose than the pursuit of self-interest and that the United States is to use force only as a last resort. Since the realities of U.S. foreign policy often clash with these historic ideals, American policy makers often struggle to explain their actions and avoid admitting to motivations that don't embody those ideals.

"Simply stated, there is no doubt that Saddam Hussein now has weapons of mass destruction," said Vice President Dick Cheney in 2002. When it turned out that these weapons did not exist, Assistant Defense Secretary Paul Wolfowitz explained, "For bureaucratic reasons, we settled on one issue, weapons of mass destruction [as justification for invading Iraq], because it was the one reason everyone could agree on."[22] As a candidate for the presidency, Barack Obama was praised for denouncing the Bush administration's treatment of enemy combatants. Obama was especially critical of the Guantánamo detention facility, where some

for critical analysis

In what ways do U.S. ideals affect the nation's foreign policies? Should foreign policies be guided by ideals or determined by national interests?

alleged enemy combatants were incarcerated. Once in office, however, Obama did not rush to close the Guantánamo facility—though he continued to plan for its eventual closure.

Must the United States always choose between its ideals and its interests? The Founders of the Republic believed that America would be different from other nations. They believed that its ideals would be its source of power, that its ideals would allow it to inspire and lead others as a "shining beacon." But international events can make it difficult to always pursue those ideals. The forces of globalization mean that it is easier than ever for small groups of extremists with violent intentions to travel to American shores and carry out their plans. (The "**Who Participates?**" feature on the facing page shows public opinion on security issues and reflects strong concern about international terrorism among all age groups.) On the other hand, those same forces of globalization have been the source of many positive outcomes. Greater trade reduces the price of many products for American consumers as well as those abroad. Furthermore, many scholars believe that the increasing global economic interdependence is a force for peace: it is difficult to go to war with one's major trading partners because the harm domestically would be too great. What can U.S. leaders do in the future to make sure that globalization is a positive force that promotes U.S. security and prosperity? If, in the pursuit of national power and security, our political leaders always choose narrow interests over transcendent ideals, might they be robbing the United States of its true source of international power and global security?

Public Opinion on Security Issues

Percentage Who Think Each Issue Is a Critical Threat

The development of China as a world power

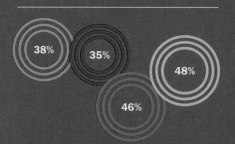

38% 35% 48% 46%

Islamic fundamentalism

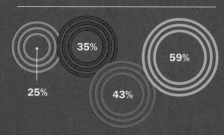

25% 35% 43% 59%

Age group

- <25
- 25–44
- 45–64
- 65+

Immigrants and refugees coming into the United States

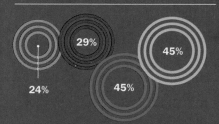

24% 29% 45% 45%

International terrorism

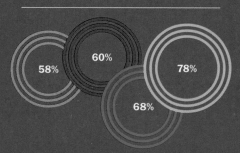

58% 60% 68% 78%

As we learned in this chapter, public opinion can influence foreign policy. However, many Americans are not engaged with or knowledgeable about foreign policy. Moreover, public opinion varies by age. These figures show what percentage of each age group think each issue is a critical threat.

SOURCE: Chicago Council Survey of American Public Opinion and U.S. Foreign Policy, 2014, www.icpsr.umich.edu/icpsrweb/ICPSR/studies/36216 (accessed 11/9/15).

WHAT YOU CAN DO

Stay Informed about International News

 Learn more about the issues above and others through coverage in major U.S. newspapers such as the *New York Times* (**www.nytimes.com**) and the *Wall Street Journal* (**www.wsj.com**).

 Check out foreign news sites for different perspectives on U.S. foreign policies and activities such as Al Jazeera English (**www.aljazeera.com**) and the BBC (**www.bbc.com**).

 For in-depth conversations about world affairs, watch videos at the World Affairs Council (**www.worldaffairs.org**) or the Council on Foreign Relations (**www.cfr.org**).

 Consider working with an interest group on a foreign policy issue you care about, such as Amnesty International (human rights), Move America Forward (supporting American troops), or Just Foreign Policy (equality and justice from a nonpartisan perspective).

studyguide

The Goals of Foreign Policy

Explain how foreign policy is designed to promote security, prosperity, and humanitarian goals (pp. 713–24)

The programs and policies that determine U.S. relations with other nations and foreign entities are referred to as *American foreign policy*. The three main goals of American foreign policy are security, prosperity, and the creation of a better world. Although each of these goals is important in understanding the contours of American foreign policy, most policy makers usually give precedence to security and economic interests over humanitarian concerns.

Key Terms

non-state actors (p. 713)

isolationism (p. 714)

containment (p. 714)

appeasement (p. 715)

Cold War (p. 715)

nation-states (p. 715)

preventive war (p. 716)

World Trade Organization (WTO) (p. 719)

General Agreement on Tariffs and Trade (GATT) (p. 719)

North American Free Trade Agreement (NAFTA) (p. 719)

Practice Quiz

1. Which of the following terms best describes the American posture toward the world prior to the twentieth century?
   a) interventionist
   b) isolationist
   c) appeasement
   d) humanitarian
   e) internationalist

2. *Cold War* refers to the
   a) competition between the United States and Canada over Alaska.
   b) the years between World War I and World War II when the United States and Germany were hostile to one another.
   c) the long-standing conflict over which nation controls Antarctica.
   d) the period of struggle between the United States and the Soviet Union from the late 1940s to the late 1980s.
   e) the economic competition between the United States and Japan today.

3. Which of the following terms describes an effort to forestall war by giving in to the demands of a hostile power?
   a) appeasement
   b) détente
   c) deterrence
   d) containment
   e) "Minuteman" theory of defense

4. In trade policy since World War II, American presidents have generally supported
   a) ending the role of international institutions like the GATT and the WTO.
   b) ending all farm subsidies in the United States.
   c) tight restrictions on U.S. exports.
   d) closing the borders to most imports.
   e) freer trade.

Who Makes American Foreign Policy?

Identify the major players in foreign-policy making, and describe their roles (pp. 725–32)

While the president and the chief advisers are the principal architects of U.S. foreign policy, many other actors in the American political system play an important role in determining how the United States interacts with other nations. Specifically, Congress, the bureaucracy, the courts, political parties, and interest groups all exert some influence over American foreign policy. With the exception of the president, the precise influence of each of these actors varies from case to case.

Key Terms

Bush Doctrine (p. 725)

executive agreement (p. 728)

Practice Quiz

5. *Bush Doctrine* refers to
   a) the idea that the United States should not allow foreign powers to meddle in the Western Hemisphere.
   b) the idea that the United States should avoid future wars by giving in to the demands of hostile foreign powers.
   c) the idea that the United States should take preemptive action against threats to its national security.
   d) the idea that the United States should never take preemptive action against threats to its national security.
   e) the idea that the United States should always secure international approval before taking any military action.

6. The Constitution assigns the power to declare war to
   a) the National Security Council.
   b) the president.
   c) Congress.
   d) the secretary of defense.
   e) the chief justice of the United States.

7. An agreement made between the president and another country that has the force of a treaty but requires only a majority vote (not a supermajority) in both houses of Congress for approval is called
   a) an executive order.
   b) a sole executive agreement.
   c) an executive–congressional agreement.
   d) a diplomatic decree.
   e) arbitration.

8. The making of American foreign policy during noncrisis moments is
   a) dominated entirely by the president.
   b) dominated entirely by Congress.
   c) dominated entirely by interest groups.
   d) dominated entirely by the Department of Defense.
   e) pluralistic, involving a large mix of both official and unofficial players.

The Instruments of Modern American Foreign Policy

Describe the means the United States uses to carry out foreign policy today (pp. 732–41)

The most important tools for the United States in implementing its foreign policy in the modern era have been diplomacy, the United Nations, the international monetary structure, economic aid and sanctions, collective security, military force, and arbitration. Many of the international organizations that influence contemporary American foreign policy, such as the United Nations, the International Monetary Fund, the World Bank, NATO, and the International Court of Justice, were formed in the years immediately following World War II. As a result of the fact that the United States possesses a more powerful and effective military than any other nation, military force is a particularly important tool for American foreign policy.

Key Terms

diplomacy (p. 732)
United Nations (UN) (p. 733)
International Monetary Fund (IMF) (p. 734)
North Atlantic Treaty Organization (NATO) (p. 736)
bilateral treaties (p. 736)

Practice Quiz

9. Which of the following statements about the United Nations is *not* true?
   a) It gives every country one vote in the General Assembly.
   b) It has a powerful army to implement its decisions.
   c) The five permanent members of the UN Security Council are China, France, Russia, the United Kingdom, and the United States.
   d) It was designed to be a channel for negotiation and a means of settling international disputes peaceably.
   e) Important issues require a two-thirds majority vote in the General Assembly.

10. Which of the following were founded during the 1940s in order to create a new international economic structure for the postwar world?
    a) the Federal Reserve System and the Council of Economic Advisers
    b) the North Atlantic Treaty Organization and the Southeast Asia Treaty Organization
    c) the International Monetary Fund and the World Bank
    d) the International Court of Justice and the Warsaw Pact
    e) the Office of Management and Budget and the General Agreement on Tariffs and Trade

11. Which of the following was dedicated specifically to European economic recovery after World War II?
    a) the Marshall Plan
    b) the Lend-Lease Act
    c) the General Agreement on Tariffs and Trade
    d) the North American Free Trade Agreement
    e) the International Monetary Fund

12. The North Atlantic Treaty Organization was formed by the United States,
    a) Canada, and most of Eastern Europe.
    b) Canada, and the Soviet Union.
    c) Canada, and Mexico.
    d) Canada, and most of Western Europe.
    e) Canada, and the United Kingdom.

13. Which statement best describes the military spending of the United States compared to other countries?
    a) The United States spends about the same as most other countries in the world.
    b) The United States spends significantly more than any other country in the world.
    c) The United States spends significantly more than any other country in the world except for China.
    d) The United States spends significantly less than any other country in the world.
    e) The United States spends slightly less than most other countries in the world.

For Further Reading

Art, Robert. *The Use of Force: Military Power and International Politics*. New York: Rowman and Littlefield, 2009.

Bacevich, Andrew. *The Limits of Power: The End of American Exceptionalism*. New York: Metropolitan Books, 2008.

Bacevich, Andrew. *The New American Militarism: How Americans Are Seduced by War*. New York: Oxford University Press, 2006.

Dorman, Andrew, and Joyce Kaufman, eds. *Providing for National Security*. Palo Alto, CA: Stanford University Press, 2014.

Drezner, Daniel. "The Realist Tradition in American Public Opinion." *Perspectives on Politics* (March 2008): 51–70.

Fisk, Robert. *The Great War for Civilization: The Conquest of the Middle East*. New York: Knopf, 2005.

Gaddis, John L. *The Cold War: A New History*. New York: Penguin Press, 2005.

Ginsberg, Benjamin. *The Worth of War*. New York: Prometheus, 2014.

Herring, George C. *From Colony to Superpower: U.S. Foreign Relations since 1776*. New York: Oxford University Press, 2011.

Hook, Steven. *U.S. Foreign Policy: The Paradox of World Power*. Washington, DC: CQ Press, 2010.

Ikenberry, John. *American Foreign Policy*. New York: Wadsworth, 2010.

Jentleson, Bruce W. *American Foreign Policy: The Dynamics of Choice in the 21st Century*. 5th ed. New York: W. W. Norton, 2013.

Kagan, Robert. *Dangerous Nation*. New York: Knopf, 2006.

Kaufman, Joyce. *A Concise History of U.S. Foreign Policy*. New York: Rowman and Littlefield, 2010.

Kennan, George F. *Around the Cragged Hill: A Personal and Political Philosophy*. New York: W. W. Norton, 1993.

Nasr, Vali. *The Dispensable Nation: American Foreign Policy in Retreat*. New York: Anchor, 2014.

Pillar, Paul. *Intelligence and U.S. Foreign Policy*. New York: Columbia University Press, 2011.

Recommended Websites

American Israel Public Affairs Committee
www.aipac.org
Interest groups are some of the main shapers of foreign policy. One of the top lobbies in the nation, the American Israel Public Affairs Committee works to strengthen the U.S.–Israeli relationship.

Foreign Policy Association
www.fpa.org
This nonprofit organization tries to generate interest in and draw attention to global issues and policies.

International Monetary Fund
www.imf.org

World Trade Organization
www.wto.org
The International Monetary Fund (IMF) and the World Trade Organization (WTO) have been considered instruments of modern American foreign policy. Read about how these organizations are trying to promote capitalism, free trade, and economic development.

National Security Council
www.whitehouse.gov/nsc/

The National Security Council was formed in 1947 and consists of senior advisers and Cabinet officials who keep the president informed on all matters of national security and foreign policy.

Peterson Institute for International Economics
www.piie.com

The Peterson Institute for International Economics is dedicated to analyzing international economic policy. Take a minute to review some of the studies that have influenced the policies of such international organizations as NAFTA, the WTO, and the IMF.

United Nations
www.un.org

Founded in 1945, the United Nations (UN) promotes international peace and security. Visit the UN website for information on the General Assembly, the Security Council, economic and social development, and humanitarian issues.

U.S. Department of State
www.state.gov

The U.S. Department of State is the primary bureaucratic department for American diplomacy and national security.

U.S. Senate: Treaties
www.senate.gov/legislative/treaties.htm

The most important foreign policy task of the Senate is reviewing and approving treaties. Learn more about the Senate's treaty-making powers, and find information about treaty action at this U.S. Senate website.

The Declaration of Independence

In Congress, July 4, 1776

The unanimous Declaration of the thirteen united States of America,

When in the Course of human events, it becomes necessary for one people to dissolve the political bands which have connected them with another, and to assume among the powers of the earth, the separate and equal station to which the Laws of Nature and of Nature's God entitle them, a decent respect to the opinions of mankind requires that they should declare the causes which impel them to the separation.

We hold these truths to be self-evident, that all men are created equal, that they are endowed by their Creator with certain unalienable Rights, that among these are Life, Liberty and the pursuit of Happiness.—That to secure these rights, Governments are instituted among Men, deriving their just powers from the consent of the governed.—That whenever any Form of Government becomes destructive of these ends, it is the Right of the People to alter or to abolish it, and to institute new Government, laying its foundation on such principles and organizing its powers in such form, as to them shall seem most likely to effect their Safety and Happiness. Prudence, indeed, will dictate that Governments long established should not be changed for light and transient causes; and accordingly all experience hath shewn, that mankind are more disposed to suffer, while evils are sufferable, than to right themselves by abolishing the forms to which they are accustomed. But when a long train of abuses and usurpations, pursuing invariably the same Object evinces a design to reduce them under absolute Despotism, it is their right, it is their duty, to throw off such Government, and to provide new Guards for their future security.—Such has been the patient sufferance of these Colonies; and such is now the necessity which constrains them to alter their former Systems of Government. The history of the present King of Great Britain is a history of repeated injuries and usurpations, all having in direct object the establishment of an absolute Tyranny over these States. To prove this, let Facts be submitted to a candid world.

He has refused his Assent to Laws, the most wholesome and necessary for the public good.

He has forbidden his Governors to pass Laws of immediate and pressing importance, unless suspended in their operation till his Assent should be obtained; and when so suspended, he has utterly neglected to attend to them.

He has refused to pass other Laws for the accommodation of large districts of people, unless those people would relinquish the right of Representation in the Legislature, a right inestimable to them and formidable to tyrants only.

He has called together legislative bodies at places unusual, uncomfortable, and distant from the depository of their public Records, for the sole purpose of fatiguing them into compliance with his measures.

He has dissolved Representative Houses repeatedly, for opposing with manly firmness his invasions on the rights of the people.

He has refused for a long time, after such dissolutions, to cause others to be elected; whereby the Legislative powers, incapable of Annihilation, have returned to the People at large for their exercise; the State remaining in the mean time exposed to all the dangers of invasion from without, and convulsions within.

He has endeavoured to prevent the population of these States; for that purpose obstructing the Laws for Naturalization of Foreigners; refusing to pass others to encourage their migrations hither, and raising the conditions of new Appropriations of Lands.

He has obstructed the Administration of Justice, by refusing his Assent to Laws for establishing Judiciary powers.

He has made Judges dependent on his Will alone, for the tenure of their offices, and the amount and payment of their salaries.

He has erected a multitude of New Offices, and sent hither swarms of Officers to harrass our people, and eat out their substance.

He has kept among us, in times of peace, Standing Armies without the Consent of our legislatures.

He has affected to render the Military independent of and superior to the Civil power.

He has combined with others to subject us to a jurisdiction foreign to our constitution, and unacknowledged by our laws; giving his Assent to their Acts of pretended Legislation:

For Quartering large bodies of armed troops among us:

For protecting them, by a mock Trial, from punishment for any Murders which they should commit on the Inhabitants of these States:

For cutting off our Trade with all parts of the world:

For imposing Taxes on us without our Consent:

For depriving us in many cases, of the benefits of Trial by Jury:

For transporting us beyond Seas to be tried for pretended offences:

For abolishing the free System of English Laws in a neighboring Province, establishing therein an Arbitrary government, and enlarging its Boundaries so as to render it at once an example and fit instrument for introducing the same absolute rule into these Colonies:

For taking away our Charters, abolishing our most valuable Laws, and altering fundamentally the Forms of our Governments:

For suspending our own Legislatures, and declaring themselves invested with power to legislate for us in all cases whatsoever.

He has abdicated Government here, by declaring us out of his Protection and waging War against us.

He has plundered our seas, ravaged our Coasts, burnt our towns, and destroyed the lives of our people.

He is at this time transporting large Armies of foreign Mercenaries to compleat the works of death, desolation and tyranny, already begun with circumstances of Cruelty & perfidy scarcely paralleled in the most barbarous ages, and totally unworthy the Head of a civilized nation.

He has constrained our fellow Citizens taken Captive on the high Seas to bear Arms against their Country, to become the executioners of their friends and Brethren, or to fall themselves by their Hands.

He has excited domestic insurrections amongst us, and has endeavoured to bring on the inhabitants of our frontiers, the merciless Indian Savages, whose known rule of warfare, is an undistinguished destruction of all ages, sexes and conditions.

In every stage of these Oppressions We have Petitioned for Redress in the most humble terms: Our repeated Petitions have been answered only by repeated injury. A Prince whose character is thus marked by every act which may define a Tyrant, is unfit to be the ruler of a free people.

Nor have We been wanting in attentions to our Brittish brethren. We have warned them from time to time of attempts by their legislature to extend an unwarrantable jurisdiction over us. We have reminded them of the circumstances of our emigration and settlement here. We have appealed to their native justice and magnanimity, and we have conjured them by the ties of our common kindred to disavow these usurpations, which, would inevitably interrupt our connections and correspondence. They too have been deaf to the voice of justice and of consanguinity. We must, therefore, acquiesce in the necessity, which denounces our Separation, and hold them, as we hold the rest of mankind, Enemies in War, in Peace Friends.

We, Therefore, the Representatives of the United States of America, in General Congress, Assembled, appealing to the Supreme Judge of the world for the rectitude of our intentions, do, in the Name, and by Authority of the good People of these Colonies, solemnly publish and declare, That these United Colonies are, and of Right ought to be Free and Independent States; that they are Absolved from all Allegiance to the British Crown, and that all political connection between them and the State of Great Britain, is and ought to be totally dissolved; and that as Free and Independent States, they have full Power to levy War, conclude Peace, contract Alliances, establish Commerce, and to do all other Acts and Things which Independent States may of right do. And for the support of this Declaration, with a firm reliance on the protection of divine Providence, we mutually pledge to each other our Lives, our Fortunes and our sacred Honor.

The foregoing Declaration was, by order of Congress, engrossed, and signed by the following members:

John Hancock

NEW HAMPSHIRE
Josiah Bartlett
William Whipple
Matthew Thornton

MASSACHUSETTS BAY
Samuel Adams
John Adams
Robert Treat Paine
Elbridge Gerry

RHODE ISLAND
Stephen Hopkins
William Ellery

CONNECTICUT
Roger Sherman
Samuel Huntington
William Williams
Oliver Wolcott

NEW YORK
William Floyd
Philip Livingston
Francis Lewis
Lewis Morris

NEW JERSEY
Richard Stockton
John Witherspoon
Francis Hopkinson
John Hart
Abraham Clark

PENNSYLVANIA
Robert Morris
Benjamin Rush
Benjamin Franklin
John Morton
George Clymer
James Smith
George Taylor
James Wilson
George Ross

DELAWARE
Caesar Rodney
George Read
Thomas M'Kean

MARYLAND
Samuel Chase
William Paca
Thomas Stone
Charles Carroll,
 of Carrollton

VIRGINIA
George Wythe
Richard Henry Lee
Thomas Jefferson
Benjamin Harrison
Thomas Nelson, Jr.
Francis Lightfoot Lee
Carter Braxton

NORTH CAROLINA
William Hooper
Joseph Hewes
John Penn

SOUTH CAROLINA
Edward Rutledge
Thomas Heyward, Jr.
Thomas Lynch, Jr.
Arthur Middleton

GEORGIA
Button Gwinnett
Lyman Hall
George Walton

Resolved, That copies of the Declaration be sent to the several assemblies, conventions, and committees, or councils of safety, and to the several commanding officers of the continental troops; that it be proclaimed in each of the United States, at the head of the army.

The Articles of Confederation

Agreed to by Congress November 15, 1777;
ratified and in force March 1, 1781

To all whom these Presents shall come, we the undersigned Delegates of the States affixed to our Names, send greeting. Whereas the Delegates of the United States of America, in Congress assembled, did, on the fifteenth day of November, in the Year of Our Lord One thousand Seven Hundred and Seventy seven, and in the Second Year of the Independence of America, agree to certain articles of Confederation and perpetual Union between the States of Newhampshire, Massachusetts-bay, Rhodeisland and Providence Plantations, Connecticut, New-York, New-Jersey, Pennsylvania, Delaware, Maryland, Virginia, North-Carolina, South-Carolina and Georgia in the words following, viz. "Articles of Confederation and perpetual Union between the states of Newhampshire, Massachusettsbay, Rhodeisland and Providence Plantations, Connecticut, New-York, New-Jersey, Pennsylvania, Delaware, Maryland, Virginia, North-Carolina, South-Carolina and Georgia.

Art. I. The Stile of this confederacy shall be "The United States of America."

Art. II. Each state retains its sovereignty, freedom and independence, and every Power, Jurisdiction and right, which is not by this confederation expressly delegated to the United States, in Congress assembled.

Art. III. The said states hereby severally enter into a firm league of friendship with each other, for their common defence, the security of their Liberties, and their mutual and general welfare, binding themselves to assist each other, against all force offered to, or attacks made upon them, or any of them, on account of religion, sovereignty, trade, or any other pretence whatever.

Art. IV. The better to secure and perpetuate mutual friendship and intercourse among the people of the different states in this union, the free inhabitants of each of these states, paupers, vagabonds and fugitives from Justice excepted, shall be entitled to all privileges and immunities of free citizens in the several states; and the people of each state shall have free ingress and regress to and from any other state, and shall enjoy therein all the privileges of trade and commerce, subject to the same duties, impositions and restrictions as the inhabitants thereof respectively, provided that such restriction shall not extend so far as to prevent the removal of property imported into any state, to any other state, of which the Owner is an inhabitant; provided also that no imposition, duties or restriction shall be laid by any state, on the property of the united states, or either of them.

If any Person guilty of, or charged with treason, felony, or other high misdemeanor in any state, shall flee from Justice, and be found in any of the united states, he shall, upon demand of the Governor or executive power, of the state from which he fled, be delivered up and removed to the state having jurisdiction of his offence.

Full faith and credit shall be given in each of these states to the records, acts and judicial proceedings of the courts and magistrates of every other state.

Art. V. For the more convenient management of the general interests of the united states, delegates shall be annually appointed in such manner as the legislature of each state shall direct, to meet in Congress on the first Monday in November, in every year, with a power reserved to each state, to recall its delegates, or any of them, at any time within the year, and to send others in their stead, for the remainder of the Year.

No state shall be represented in Congress by less than two, nor by more than seven Members; and no person shall be capable of being a delegate for more than three years in any term of six years; nor shall any person, being a delegate, be capable of holding any office under the united states, for which he, or another for his benefit receives any salary, fees or emolument of any kind.

Each state shall maintain its own delegates in a meeting of the states, and while they act as members of the committee of the states.

In determining questions in the united states, in Congress assembled, each state shall have one vote.

Freedom of speech and debate in Congress shall not be impeached or questioned in any Court, or place out of Congress, and the members of congress shall be protected in their persons from arrests and imprisonments, during the time of their going to and from, and attendance on congress, except for treason, felony, or breach of the peace.

Art. VI. No state without the Consent of the united states in congress assembled, shall send any embassy to, or receive any embassy from, or enter into any conference, agreement, or alliance or treaty with any King, prince or state; nor shall any person holding any office or profit or trust under the united states, or any of them, accept of any present, emolument, office or title of any kind whatever from any king, prince or foreign state; nor shall the united states in congress assembled, or any of them, grant any title of nobility.

No two or more states shall enter into any treaty, confederation or alliance whatever between them, without the consent of the united states in congress assembled, specifying accurately the purposes for which the same is to be entered into, and how long it shall continue.

No state shall lay any imposts or duties, which may interfere with any stipulations in treaties, entered into by the united states in congress assembled, with any king, prince or state, in pursuance of any treaties already proposed by congress, to the courts of France and Spain.

No vessels of war shall be kept up in time of peace by any state, except such number only, as shall be deemed necessary by the united states in congress assembled, for the defence of such state, or its trade; nor shall any body of forces be kept up by any state, in time of peace, except such number only, as in the judgment of the united states, in congress assembled, shall be deemed requisite to garrison the forts necessary for the defence of such state; but every state shall always keep up a well regulated and disciplined militia, sufficiently armed and accoutred, and shall provide and constantly have ready for use, in public stores, a due number of field pieces and tents, and a proper quantity of arms, ammunition and camp equipage.

No state shall engage in any war without the consent of the united states in congress assembled, unless such state be actually invaded by enemies, or shall have received certain advice of a resolution being formed by some nation of Indians to invade such state, and the danger is so imminent as not to admit of a delay, till the united states in congress asssembled can be consulted; nor shall any state grant commissions to any ships or vessels of war, nor letters of marque or reprisal, except it be after a declaration of war by the united states in congress assembled, and then only against the kingdom or state and the subjects thereof, against which war has been so declared, and under such regulations as shall be established by the united states in congress assembled, unless such state be infested by pirates; in which case vessels of war may be fitted out for that occasion, and kept so long as the danger shall continue, or until the united states in congress assembled shall determine otherwise.

Art. VII. When land-forces are raised by any state for the common defence, all officers of or under the rank of colonel, shall be appointed by the legislature of each state respectively, by whom such forces shall be raised, or in such manner as such state shall direct, and all vacancies shall be filled up by the state which first made the appointment.

Art. VIII. All charges of war, and all other expences that shall be incurred for the common defence or general welfare, and allowed by the united states in congress assembled, shall be defrayed out of a common treasury, which shall be supplied by the several states in proportion to the value of all land within each state, granted to or surveyed for any Person, as such land and the buildings and improvements thereon shall be estimated according to such mode as the united states in congress assembled, shall from time to time direct and appoint.

The taxes for paying that proportion shall be laid and levied by the authority and direction of the legislatures of the several states within the time agreed upon by the united states in congress assembled.

Art. IX. The united states in congress assembled, shall have the sole and exclusive right and power of determining on peace and war, except in the cases mentioned in the sixth article—of sending and receiving ambassadors—entering into treaties and alliances, provided that no treaty of commerce shall be made whereby the legislative power of the respective states shall be restrained from imposing such imposts and duties on foreigners, as their own people are subjected to, or from prohibiting the exportation of any species of goods or commodities whatsoever—of establishing rules for deciding in all cases, what captures on land or water shall be legal, and in what manner prizes taken by land or naval forces in the service of the united states shall be divided or appropriated—of granting letters of marque and reprisal in times of peace—appointing courts for the trial of piracies and felonies committed on the high seas and establishing courts for receiving and determining finally appeals in all cases of captures, provided that no member of congress shall be appointed a judge of any of the said courts.

The united states in congress assembled shall also be the last resort on appeal in all disputes and differences now subsisting or that hereafter may arise between two or more states concerning boundary, jurisdiction or any other cause whatever; which authority shall always be exercised in the manner following. Whenever the legislative or executive authority or lawful agent of any state in controversy with another shall present a petition to congress stating the matter in question and praying for a hearing, notice thereof shall be given by order of congress to the legislative or executive authority of the other state in controversy, and a day assigned for the appearance of the parties by their lawful agents, who shall then be directed to appoint by joint consent, commissioners or judges to constitute a court for hearing and determining the matter in question: but if they cannot agree, congress shall name three persons out of each of the united states, and from the list of such persons each party shall alternately strike out one, the petitioners beginning, until the number shall be reduced to thirteen; and from that number not less than seven, nor more than nine names as congress shall direct, shall in the presence of congress be drawn out by lot, and the persons whose names shall be so drawn or any five of them, shall be commissioners or judges, to hear and finally determine the controversy, so always as a major part of the judges who shall hear the cause shall agree in the determination: and if either party shall neglect to attend at the day appointed, without shewing reasons, which congress shall judge sufficient, or being present shall refuse to strike, the congress shall proceed to nominate three persons out of each state, and the secretary of congress shall strike in behalf of such party absent or refusing; and the judgment and sentence of the court to be appointed, in the manner before prescribed, shall be final and conclusive; and if any of the parties shall refuse to submit to the authority of such court, or to appear to defend their claim or cause, the court shall nevertheless proceed to pronounce sentence, or judgment, which shall in like manner be final and decisive, the judgment or sentence and other proceedings being in either case transmitted to congress, and lodged among the acts of congress for the security of the parties concerned: provided that every commissioner, before he sits in judgment, shall take an oath to be administered by one of the judges of the supreme or superior court of the state, where the cause shall be tried, "well and truly to hear and determine the matter in question, according to the best of his judgment, without favour, affection or hope of reward:" provided also, that no state shall be deprived of territory for the benefit of the united states.

All controversies concerning the private right of soil claimed under different grants of two or more states, whose jurisdictions as they may respect such lands, and the states which passed such grants are adjusted, the said grants or either of them being at the same time claimed to have originated antecedent to such settlement of jurisdiction, shall on the petition of either party to the congress of the united states, be finally determined as near as may be in the same manner as is before prescribed for deciding disputes respecting territorial jurisdiction between different states.

The united states in congress assembled shall also have the sole and exclusive right and power of regulating the alloy and value of coin struck by their own authority, or by that of the respective states—fixing the standard of weights and measures throughout the united states—regulating the trade and managing all affairs with the Indians, not members of any of the states, provided that the legislative right of any state within its own limits be not infringed or violated—establishing and regulating post-offices from one state to another, throughout all the united states, and exacting such postage on the papers passing thro' the same as may be requisite to defray the expences of the said office—appointing all officers of the land forces, in the service of the united states, excepting regimental officers—appointing all the officers of the naval forces, and commissioning all officers whatever in the service of the united states—making rules for the government and regulation of the said land and naval forces, and directing their operations.

The united states in congress assembled shall have authority to appoint a committee, to sit in the recess of congress, to be denominated "A Committee of the States," and to consist of one delegate from each state; and to appoint such other committees and civil officers as may be necessary for managing the general affairs of the united states under their direction—to appoint one of their number to preside, provided that no person be allowed to serve in the office of president more than one year in any term of three years; to ascertain the necessary sums of Money to be raised for the service of the united states,

and to appropriate and apply the same for defraying the public expenses—to borrow money, or emit bills on the credit of the united states, transmitting every half year to the respective states an account of the sums of money so borrowed or emitted,—to build and equip a navy—to agree upon the number of land forces, and to make requisitions from each state for its quota, in proportion to the number of white inhabitants in such state; which requisition shall be binding, and thereupon the legislature of each state shall appoint the regimental officers, raise the men and cloath, arm and equip them in a soldier like manner, at the expense of the united states; and the officers and men so cloathed, armed and equipped shall march to the place appointed, and within the time agreed on by the united states in congress assembled: But if the united states in congress assembled shall, on consideration of circumstances judge proper that any state should not raise men, or should raise a smaller number than its quota, and that any other state should raise a greater number of men than the quota thereof, such extra number shall be raised, officered, cloathed, armed and equipped in the same manner as the quota of such state, unless the legislature of such state shall judge that such extra number cannot be safely spared out of the same, in which case they shall raise officer, cloath, arm and equip as many of such extra number as they judge can be safely spared. And the officers and men so cloathed, armed and equipped, shall march to the place appointed, and within the time agreed on by the united states in congress assembled.

The united states in congress assembled shall never engage in a war, nor grant letters of marque and reprisal in time of peace, nor enter into any treaties or alliances, nor coin money, nor regulate the value thereof, nor ascertain the sums and expenses necessary for the defence and welfare of the united states, or any of them, nor emit bills, nor borrow money on the credit of the united states, nor appropriate money, nor agree upon the number of vessels of war, to be built or purchased, or the number of land or sea forces to be raised, nor appoint a commander in chief of the army or navy, unless nine states assent to the same: nor shall a question on any other point, except for adjourning from day to day be determined, unless by the votes of a majority of the united states in congress assembled.

The congress of the united states shall have power to adjourn to any time within the year, and to any place within the united states, so that no period of adjournment be for a longer duration than the space of six Months, and shall publish the Journal of their proceedings monthly, except such parts thereof relating to treaties, alliances or military operations, as in their judgment require secrecy; and the yeas and nays of the delegates of each state on any question shall be entered on the Journal, when it is desired by any delegate; and the delegates of a state, or any of them, at his or their request shall be furnished with a transcript of the said Journal, except such parts as are above excepted, to lay before the legislatures of the several states.

Art. X. The committee of the states, or any nine of them, shall be authorised to execute, in the recess of congress, such of the powers of congress as the united states in congress assembled, by the consent of nine states, shall from time to time think expedient to vest them with; provided that no power be delegated to the said committee, for the exercise of which, by the articles of confederation, the voice of nine states in the congress of the united states assembled is requisite.

Art. XI. Canada acceding to this confederation, and joining in the measures of the united states, shall be admitted into, and entitled to all the advantages of this union: but no other colony shall be admitted into the same, unless such admission be agreed to by nine states.

Art. XII. All bills of credit emitted, monies borrowed and debts contracted by, or under the authority of congress, before the assembling of the united states, in pursuance of the present confederation, shall be deemed and considered as a charge against the united states, for payment and satisfaction whereof the said united states and the public faith are hereby solemnly pledged.

Art. XIII. Every state shall abide by the determinations of the united states in congress assembled, on all questions which by this confederation are submitted to them. And the Articles of this confederation shall be inviolably observed by every state, and the union shall be perpetual; nor shall any alteration at any time hereafter be made in any of them; unless such alteration be agreed to in a congress of the united states, and be afterwards confirmed by the legislatures of every state.

And Whereas it hath pleased the Great Governor of the World to incline the hearts of the legislatures we respectively represent in congress, to approve of, and to authorize us to ratify the said articles of confederation and perpetual union. Know Ye that we the undersigned delegates, by virtue of the power and authority to us given for that purpose, do by these presents, in the name and in behalf of our respective constituents, fully and entirely ratify and confirm each and every of the said articles of confederation and perpetual union, and all and singular the matters and things therein contained: And we do further solemnly plight and engage the faith of our respective constituents, that they shall abide by the determinations of the united states in congress assembled, on all questions, which by the said confederation are submitted to them. And that the articles thereof shall be inviolably observed by the states we respectively represent, and that the union shall be perpetual. In Witness whereof we have hereunto set our hands in Congress. Done at Philadelphia in the state of Pennsylvania the ninth day of July, in the Year of our Lord one Thousand seven Hundred and Seventy-eight, and in the third year of the independence of America.

The Constitution of the United States of America

We the People of the United States, in Order to form a more perfect Union, establish Justice, insure domestic Tranquility, provide for the common defence, promote the general Welfare, and secure the Blessings of Liberty to ourselves and our Posterity, do ordain and establish this Constitution for the United States of America.

Article I

SECTION 1

[LEGISLATIVE POWERS]

All legislative Powers herein granted shall be vested in a Congress of the United States, which shall consist of a Senate and House of Representatives.

SECTION 2

[HOUSE OF REPRESENTATIVES, HOW CONSTITUTED, POWER OF IMPEACHMENT]

The House of Representatives shall be composed of Members chosen every second Year by the People of the several States, and the Electors in each State shall have the Qualifications requisite for Electors of the most numerous Branch of the State Legislature.

No Person shall be a Representative who shall not have attained to the Age of twenty five Years, and been seven Years a Citizen of the United States, and who shall not, when elected, be an Inhabitant of that State in which he shall be chosen.

Representatives and *direct Taxes*[1] shall be apportioned among the several States which may be included within this Union, according to their respective Numbers, *which shall be determined by adding to the whole Number of free Persons, including those bound to Service for a Term of Years, and excluding Indians not taxed, three fifths of all other Persons.*[2] The actual Enumeration shall be made within three Years after the first Meeting of the Congress of the United States, and within every subsequent Term of ten Years, in such Manner as they shall by Law direct. The Number of Representatives shall not exceed one for every thirty Thousand, but each State shall have at Least one Representative; *and until such enumeration*

---

[1]Modified by Sixteenth Amendment.

[2]Modified by Fourteenth Amendment.

shall be made, the State of New Hampshire shall be entitled to chuse three, Massachusetts eight, Rhode-Island and Providence Plantations one, Connecticut five, New-York six, New Jersey four, Pennsylvania eight, Delaware one, Maryland six, Virginia ten, North Carolina five, South Carolina five, and Georgia three.[3]

When vacancies happen in the Representation from any State, the Executive Authority thereof shall issue Writs of Election to fill such Vacancies.

The House of Representatives shall chuse their Speaker and other Officers; and shall have the sole Power of Impeachment.

SECTION 3

[THE SENATE, HOW CONSTITUTED, IMPEACHMENT TRIALS]

The Senate of the United States shall be composed of two Senators from each State, *chosen by the Legislature thereof,*[4] for six Years; and each Senator shall have one Vote.

Immediately after they shall be assembled in Consequence of the first Election, they shall be divided as equally as may be into three Classes. The Seats of the Senators of the first Class shall be vacated at the Expiration of the second Year, of the second Class at the Expiration of the fourth Year, and of the third Class at the Expiration of the sixth Year, so that one third may be chosen every second Year; *and if Vacancies happen by Resignation, or otherwise, during the Recess of the Legislature of any State, the Executive thereof may make temporary Appointments until the next Meeting of the Legislature, which shall then fill such Vacancies.*[5]

No Person shall be a Senator who shall not have attained to the Age of thirty Years, and been nine Years a Citizen of the United States, and who shall not, when elected, be an Inhabitant of that State for which he shall be chosen.

The Vice President of the United States shall be President of the Senate, but shall have no Vote, unless they be equally divided.

The Senate shall chuse their other Officers, and also a President pro tempore, in the Absence of the Vice President, or when he shall exercise the Office of President of the United States.

---

[3]Temporary provision.

[4]Modified by Seventeenth Amendment.

[5]Modified by Seventeenth Amendment.

The Senate shall have the sole Power to try all Impeachments. When sitting for that Purpose, they shall be on Oath or Affirmation. When the President of the United States is tried, the Chief Justice shall preside: And no Person shall be convicted without the Concurrence of two thirds of the Members present.

Judgment in Cases of Impeachment shall not extend further than to removal from Office, and disqualification to hold and enjoy any Office of honor, Trust or Profit under the United States: but the Party convicted shall nevertheless be liable and subject to Indictment, Trial, Judgment and Punishment, according to Law.

SECTION 4
[ELECTION OF SENATORS AND REPRESENTATIVES]
The Times, Places and Manner of holding Elections for Senators and Representatives, shall be prescribed in each State by the Legislature thereof; but the Congress may at any time by Law make or alter such Regulations, except as to the Places of chusing Senators.

The Congress shall assemble at least once in every Year, and such Meeting shall be on the first Monday in December, unless they shall by Law appoint a different Day.[6]

SECTION 5
[QUORUM, JOURNALS, MEETINGS, ADJOURNMENTS]
Each House shall be the Judge of the Elections, Returns and Qualifications of its own Members, and a Majority of each shall constitute a Quorum to do Business; but a smaller Number may adjourn from day to day, and may be authorized to compel the Attendance of absent Members, in such Manner, and under such Penalties as each House may provide.

Each House may determine the Rules of its Proceedings, punish its Members for disorderly Behaviour, and, with the Concurrence of two thirds, expel a Member.

Each House shall keep a Journal of its Proceedings, and from time to time publish the same, excepting such Parts as may in their Judgment require Secrecy; and the Yeas and Nays of the Members of either House on any questions shall, at the Desire of one fifth of those Present, be entered on the Journal.

Neither House, during the Session of Congress, shall, without the Consent of the other, adjourn for more than three days, nor to any other Place than that in which the two Houses shall be sitting.

SECTION 6
[COMPENSATION, PRIVILEGES, DISABILITIES]
The Senators and Representatives shall receive a Compensation for their Services, to be ascertained by Law, and paid out of the Treasury of the United States. They shall in all Cases, except Treason, Felony and Breach of the Peace, be privileged from Arrest during their Attendance at the Session of their respective Houses, and in going to and returning from the same; and for any Speech or Debate in either House, they shall not be questioned in any other Place.

No Senator or Representative shall, during the Time for which he was elected, be appointed to any civil Office under the Authority of the United States, which shall have been created, or the Emoluments whereof shall have been encreased during such time; and no Person holding any Office under the United States, shall be a Member of either House during his Continuance in Office.

SECTION 7
[PROCEDURE IN PASSING BILLS AND RESOLUTIONS]
All Bills for raising Revenue shall originate in the House of Representatives; but the Senate may propose or concur with Amendments as on other Bills.

Every Bill which shall have passed the House of Representatives and the Senate, shall, before it become a Law, be presented to the President of the United States: If he approve he shall sign it, but if not he shall return it, with his Objections to that House in which it shall have originated, who shall enter the Objections at large on their Journal, and proceed to reconsider it. If after such Reconsideration two thirds of that House shall agree to pass the Bill, it shall be sent, together with the Objections, to the other House, by which it shall likewise be reconsidered, and if approved by two thirds of that House, it shall become a Law. But in all such Cases the Votes of both Houses shall be determined by yeas and Nays, and the Names of the Persons voting for and against the Bill shall be entered on the Journal of each House respectively. If any Bill shall not be returned by the President within ten Days (Sundays excepted) after it shall have been presented to him, the Same shall be a Law, in like Manner as if he had signed it, unless the Congress by their Adjournment prevent its Return, in which Case it shall not be a Law.

Every Order, Resolution, or Vote to which the Concurrence of the Senate and House of Representatives may be necessary (except on a question of Adjournment) shall be presented to the President of the United States; and before the Same shall take Effect, shall be approved by him, or being disapproved by him, shall be repassed by two thirds of the Senate and House of Representatives, according to the Rules and Limitations prescribed in the Case of a Bill.

SECTION 8
[POWERS OF CONGRESS]
The Congress shall have Power

To lay and collect Taxes, Duties, Imposts and Excises, to pay the Debts and provide for the common Defence and general Welfare of the United States; but all Duties, Imposts and Excises shall be uniform throughout the United States;

To borrow Money on the credit of the United States;

---

[6]Modified by Twentieth Amendment.

To regulate Commerce with foreign Nations, and among the several States, and with the Indian Tribes;

To establish an uniform Rule of Naturalization, and uniform Laws on the subject of Bankruptcies throughout the United States;

To coin Money, regulate the Value thereof, and of foreign Coin, and fix the Standard of Weights and Measures;

To provide for the Punishment of counterfeiting the Securities and current Coin of the United States;

To establish Post Offices and post Roads;

To promote the Progress of Science and useful Arts, by securing for limited Times to Authors and Inventors the exclusive Right to their respective Writings and Discoveries;

To constitute Tribunals inferior to the supreme Court;

To define and punish Piracies and Felonies committed on the high Seas, and Offences against the Law of Nations;

To declare War, grant Letters of Marque and Reprisal, and make Rules concerning Captures on Land and Water;

To raise and support Armies, but no Appropriation of Money to that Use shall be for a longer Term than two Years;

To provide and maintain a Navy;

To make Rules for the Government and Regulation of the land and naval Forces;

To provide for calling forth the Militia to execute the Laws of the Union, suppress Insurrections and repel Invasions;

To provide for organizing, arming, and disciplining, the Militia, and for governing such Part of them as may be employed in the Service of the United States, reserving to the States respectively, the Appointment of the Officers, and the Authority of training the Militia according to the discipline prescribed by Congress;

To exercise exclusive Legislation in all Cases whatsoever, over such District (not exceeding ten Miles square) as may, by Cession of particular States, and the Acceptance of Congress, become the Seat of the Government of the United States, and to exercise like Authority over all Places purchased by the Consent of the Legislature of the State in which the Same shall be, for the Erection of Forts, Magazines, Arsenals, dock-Yards, and other needful Buildings;—And

To make all Laws which shall be necessary and proper for carrying into Execution the foregoing Powers, and all other Powers vested by this Constitution in the Government of the United States, or in any Department or Officer thereof.

SECTION 9

[SOME RESTRICTIONS ON FEDERAL POWER]

The Migration or Importation of such Persons as any of the States now existing shall think proper to admit, shall not be prohibited by the Congress prior to the Year one thousand eight hundred and eight, but a Tax or duty may be imposed on such Importation, not exceeding ten dollars for each Person.[7]

The Privilege of the Writ of Habeas Corpus shall not be suspended, unless when in Cases of Rebellion or Invasion the public Safety may require it.

No Bill of Attainder or ex post facto Law shall be passed.

No Capitation, or other direct, Tax shall be laid, unless in Proportion to the Census or Enumeration herein before directed to be taken.[8]

No Tax or Duty shall be laid on Articles exported from any State.

No Preference shall be given by any Regulation of Commerce or Revenue to the Ports of one State over those of another; nor shall Vessels bound to, or from, one State, be obliged to enter, clear, or pay Duties in another.

No Money shall be drawn from the Treasury, but in Consequence of Appropriations made by Law; and a regular Statement and Account of the Receipts and Expenditures of all public Money shall be published from time to time.

No Title of Nobility shall be granted by the United States: And no Person holding any Office of Profit or Trust under them, shall, without the Consent of the Congress, accept of any present, Emolument, Office, or Title, of any kind whatever, from any King, Prince, or foreign State.

SECTION 10

[RESTRICTIONS UPON POWERS OF STATES]

No State shall enter into any Treaty, Alliance, or Confederation; grant Letters of Marque and Reprisal; coin Money; emit Bills of Credit; make any Thing but gold and silver Coin a Tender in Payment of Debts; pass any Bill of Attainder, ex post facto Law, or Law impairing the Obligation of Contracts, or grant any Title of Nobility.

No State shall, without the Consent of the Congress, lay any Imposts or Duties on Imports or Exports, except what may be absolutely necessary for executing its inspection Laws: and the net Produce of all Duties and Imposts, laid by any State on Imports or Exports, shall be for the Use of the Treasury of the United States; and all such Laws shall be subject to the Revision and Control of the Congress.

No State shall, without the Consent of Congress, lay any Duty of Tonnage, keep Troops, or Ships of War in time of Peace, enter into any Agreement or Compact with another State, or with a foreign Power, or engage in War, unless actually invaded, or in such imminent Danger as will not admit of delay.

Article II

SECTION 1

[EXECUTIVE POWER, ELECTION,
QUALIFICATIONS OF THE PRESIDENT]

The executive Power shall be vested in a President of the United States of America. *He shall hold his Office during the Term of*

---

[7]Temporary provision.

[8]Modified by Sixteenth Amendment.

four Years, and, together with the Vice President, chosen for the same Term, be elected, as follows[9]

Each State shall appoint, in such Manner as the Legislature thereof may direct, a Number of Electors, equal to the whole Number of Senators and Representatives to which the State may be entitled in the Congress: but no Senator or Representative, or Person holding an Office of Trust or Profit under the United States, shall be appointed an Elector.

The electors shall meet in their respective States, and vote by ballot for two Persons, of whom one at least shall not be an Inhabitant of the same State with themselves. And they shall make a List of all the Persons voted for, and of the Number of Votes for each; which List they shall sign and certify, and transmit sealed to the Seat of the Government of the United States, directed to the President of the Senate. The President of the Senate shall, in the Presence of the Senate and House of Representatives, open all the Certificates, and the Votes shall then be counted. The Person having the greatest Number of Votes shall be the President, if such Number be a Majority of the whole Number of Electors appointed; and if there be more than one who have such Majority, and have an equal Number of Votes, then the House of Representatives shall immediately chuse by Ballot one of them for President; and if no Person have a Majority, then from the five highest on the List the said House shall in like Manner chuse the President. But in chusing the President, the Votes shall be taken by States, the Representation from each State having one Vote; A quorum for this Purpose shall consist of a Member or Members from two thirds of the States, and a Majority of all the States shall be necessary to a Choice. In every Case, after the Choice of the President, the person having the greatest Number of Votes of the Electors shall be the Vice President. But if there should remain two or more who have equal Votes, the Senate shall chuse from them by Ballot the Vice President.[10]

The Congress may determine the Time of chusing the Electors, and the Day on which they shall give their Votes; which Day shall be the same throughout the United States.

No Person except a natural born Citizen, or a Citizen of the United States, at the time of the Adoption of this Constitution, shall be eligible to the Office of President; neither shall any Person be eligible to that Office who shall not have attained to the Age of thirty five Years, and been fourteen Years a Resident within the United States.

In Case of the Removal of the President from Office, or his Death, Resignation, or Inability to discharge the Powers and Duties of the said Office, the Same shall devolve on the Vice President, and the Congress may by Law provide for the Case of Removal, Death, Resignation or Inability, both of the President and Vice President, declaring what Officer shall then act as President, and such Officer shall act accordingly, until the Disability be removed, or a President shall be elected.

The President shall, at stated Times, receive for his Services, a Compensation, which shall neither be increased nor diminished during the Period for which he shall have been elected, and he shall not receive within that Period any other Emolument from the United States, or any of them.

Before he enter on the Execution of his Office, he shall take the following Oath or Affirmation:—"I do solemnly swear (or affirm) that I will faithfully execute the Office of President of the United States, and will to the best of my Ability, preserve, protect and defend the Constitution of the United States."

SECTION 2
[POWERS OF THE PRESIDENT]

The President shall be Commander in Chief of the Army and Navy of the United States, and of the Militia of the several States, when called into the actual Service of the United States; he may require the Opinion, in writing, of the principal Officer in each of the executive Departments, upon any Subject relating to the Duties of their respective Offices, and he shall have Power to grant Reprieves and Pardons for Offences against the United States, except in Cases of Impeachment.

He shall have Power, by and with the Advice and Consent of the Senate, to make Treaties, provided two thirds of the Senators present concur; and he shall nominate, and by and with the Advice and Consent of the Senate, shall appoint Ambassadors, other public Ministers and Consuls, Judges of the supreme Court, and all other Officers of the United States, whose Appointments are not herein otherwise provided for, and which shall be established by Law: but the Congress may by Law vest the Appointment of such inferior Officers, as they think proper, in the President alone, in the Courts of Law, or in the Heads of Departments.

The President shall have Power to fill up all Vacancies that may happen during the Recess of the Senate, by granting Commissions which shall expire at the End of their next Session.

SECTION 3
[POWERS AND DUTIES OF THE PRESIDENT]

He shall from time to time give to the Congress Information of the State of the Union, and recommend to their Consideration such Measures as he shall judge necessary and expedient; he may, on extraordinary Occasions, convene both Houses, or either of them, and in Case of Disagreement between them, with Respect to the Time of Adjournment, he may adjourn them to such Time as he shall think proper; he shall receive Ambassadors and other public Ministers; he shall take Care that the Laws be faithfully executed, and shall Commission all the Officers of the United States.

SECTION 4
[IMPEACHMENT]

The President, Vice President and all civil Officers of the United States, shall be removed from Office on Impeachment for,

---

[9]Number of terms limited to two by Twenty-Second Amendment.

[10]Modified by Twelfth and Twentieth Amendments.

and Conviction of, Treason, Bribery, or other high Crimes and Misdemeanors.

Article III

SECTION 1

[JUDICIAL POWER, TENURE OF OFFICE]

The judicial Power of the United States, shall be vested in one supreme Court, and in such inferior Courts as the Congress may from time to time ordain and establish. The Judges, both of the supreme and inferior Courts, shall hold their Offices during good Behaviour, and shall, at stated Times, receive for their Services, a Compensation, which shall not be diminished during their Continuance in Office.

SECTION 2

[JURISDICTION]

The judicial Power shall extend to all Cases, in Law and Equity, arising under this Constitution, the Laws of the United States, and Treaties made, or which shall be made, under their Authority;— to all Cases affecting Ambassadors, other public Ministers and Consuls;—to all Cases of admiralty and maritime Jurisdiction;— to Controversies to which the United States shall be a Party;—to Controversies between two or more States;—*between a State and Citizens of another State;*—between Citizens of different States,— between Citizens of the same State claiming Lands under Grants of different States, *and between a State,* or the Citizens thereof, *and foreign States, Citizens or Subjects.*[11]

In all Cases affecting Ambassadors, other public Ministers and Consuls, and those in which a State shall be Party, the supreme Court shall have original Jurisdiction. In all the other Cases before mentioned, the supreme Court shall have appellate Jurisdiction, both as to Law and Fact, with such Exceptions, and under such Regulations as the Congress shall make.

The Trial of all Crimes, except in Cases of Impeachment, shall be by Jury; and such Trial shall be held in the State where the said Crimes shall have been committed; but when not committed within any State, the Trial shall be at such Place or Places as the Congress may by Law have directed.

SECTION 3

[TREASON, PROOF, AND PUNISHMENT]

Treason against the United States, shall consist only in levying War against them, or in adhering to their Enemies, giving them Aid and Comfort. No Person shall be convicted of Treason unless on the Testimony of two Witnesses to the same overt Act, or on Confession in open Court.

The Congress shall have Power to declare the Punishment of Treason, but no Attainder of Treason shall work Corruption of Blood, or Forfeiture except during the Life of the Person attainted.

Article IV

SECTION 1

[FAITH AND CREDIT AMONG STATES]

Full Faith and Credit shall be given in each State to the public Acts, Records, and judicial Proceedings of every other State. And the Congress may by general Laws prescribe the Manner in which such Acts, Records and Proceedings shall be proved, and the Effect thereof.

SECTION 2

[PRIVILEGES AND IMMUNITIES, FUGITIVES]

The Citizens of each State shall be entitled to all Privileges and Immunities of Citizens in the several States.

A Person charged in any State with Treason, Felony or other Crime, who shall flee from Justice, and be found in another State, shall on Demand of the executive Authority of the State from which he fled, be delivered up, to be removed to the State having Jurisdiction of the Crime.

No person held to Service or Labour in one State, under the Laws thereof, escaping into another, shall, in Consequence of any Law or Regulation therein, be discharged from such Service or Labour, but shall be delivered up on Claim of the Party to whom such Service or Labour may be due.[12]

SECTION 3

[ADMISSION OF NEW STATES]

New States may be admitted by the Congress into this Union; but no new State shall be formed or erected within the Jurisdiction of any other State; nor any State be formed by the Junction of two or more States, or Parts of States, without the Consent of the Legislatures of the States concerned as well as of the Congress.

The Congress shall have Power to dispose of and make all needful Rules and Regulations respecting the Territory or other Property belonging to the United States; and nothing in this Constitution shall be so construed as to Prejudice any Claims of the United States, or of any particular State.

SECTION 4

[GUARANTEE OF REPUBLICAN GOVERNMENT]

The United States shall guarantee to every State in this Union a Republican Form of Government, and shall protect each of them against Invasion; and on Application of the Legislature, or of the Executive (when the Legislature cannot be convened), against domestic Violence.

Article V

[AMENDMENT OF THE CONSTITUTION]

The Congress, whenever two thirds of both Houses shall deem it necessary, shall propose Amendments to this Constitution, or, on the Application of the Legislatures of two thirds of the

---

[11]Modified by Eleventh Amendment.

[12]Repealed by the Thirteenth Amendment.

several States, shall call a Convention for proposing Amendments, which, in either Case, shall be valid to all Intents and Purposes, as Part of this Constitution, when ratified by the Legislatures of three fourths of the several States, or by Conventions in three fourths thereof, as the one or the other Mode of Ratification may be proposed by the Congress; *Provided that no Amendment which may be made prior to the Year One thousand eight hundred and eight shall in any Manner affect the first and fourth Clauses in the Ninth Section of the first Article;*[13] and that no State, without its Consent, shall be deprived of its equal Suffrage in the Senate.

Article VI

[DEBTS, SUPREMACY, OATH]
All Debts contracted and Engagements entered into, before the Adoption of this Constitution, shall be as valid against the United States under this Constitution, as under the Confederation.

This Constitution, and the Laws of the United States which shall be made in Pursuance thereof; and all Treaties made, or which shall be made, under the Authority of the United States, shall be the supreme Law of the Land; and the Judges in every

State shall be bound thereby, any Thing in the Constitution or Laws of any State to the Contrary notwithstanding.

The Senators and Representatives before mentioned, and the Members of the several State Legislatures, and all executive and judicial Officers, both of the United States and of the several States, shall be bound by Oath or Affirmation, to support this Constitution; but no religious Test shall be required as a Qualification to any Office or public Trust under the United States.

Article VII

[RATIFICATION AND ESTABLISHMENT]
The Ratification of the Conventions of nine States, shall be sufficient for the Establishment of this Constitution between the States so ratifying the Same.[14]

Done in Convention by the Unanimous Consent of the States present the Seventeenth Day of September in the Year of our Lord one thousand seven hundred and Eighty seven and of the Independence of the United States of America the Twelfth. *In Witness* whereof We have hereunto subscribed our Names,

---

[13]Temporary provision.

[14]The Constitution was submitted on September 17, 1787, by the Constitutional Convention, was ratified by the conventions of several states at various dates up to May 29, 1790, and became effective on March 4, 1789.

G:⁰ *WASHINGTON—*
Presidt. and deputy from Virginia

NEW HAMPSHIRE
John Langdon
Nicholas Gilman

MASSACHUSETTS
Nathaniel Gorham
Rufus King

CONNECTICUT
Wm. Saml. Johnson
Roger Sherman

NEW YORK
Alexander Hamilton

NEW JERSEY
Wil: Livingston
David Brearley
Wm. Paterson
Jona: Dayton

PENNSYLVANIA
B Franklin
Thomas Mifflin
Robt. Morris
Geo. Clymer
Thos. FitzSimons
Jared Ingersoll
James Wilson
Gouv Morris

DELAWARE
Geo: Read
Gunning Bedford jun
John Dickinson
Richard Bassett
Jaco: Broom

MARYLAND
James McHenry
Dan of St Thos. Jenifer
Danl. Carroll

VIRGINIA
John Blair—
James Madison Jr.

NORTH CAROLINA
Wm. Blount
Richd. Dobbs Spaight
Hu Williamson

SOUTH CAROLINA
J. Rutledge
Charles Cotesworth Pinckney
Charles Pinckney
Pierce Butler

GEORGIA
William Few
Abr Baldwin

Amendments to the Constitution

Proposed by Congress and Ratified by the Legislatures of the Several States, Pursuant to Article V of the Original Constitution.

Amendments I–X, known as the Bill of Rights, were proposed by Congress on September 25, 1789, and ratified on December 15, 1791.

Amendment I

[FREEDOM OF RELIGION, OF SPEECH, AND OF THE PRESS]
Congress shall make no law respecting an establishment of religion, or prohibiting the free exercise thereof; or abridging the freedom of speech, or of the press; or the right of the people peaceably to assemble, and to petition the Government for a redress of grievances.

Amendment II

[RIGHT TO KEEP AND BEAR ARMS]
A well regulated Militia, being necessary to the security of a free State, the right of the people to keep and bear Arms, shall not be infringed.

Amendment III

[QUARTERING OF SOLDIERS]
No Soldier shall, in time of peace be quartered in any house, without the consent of the Owner, nor in time of war, but in a manner to be prescribed by law.

Amendment IV

[SECURITY FROM UNWARRANTABLE SEARCH AND SEIZURE]
The right of the people to be secure in their persons, houses, papers, and effects, against unreasonable searches and seizures, shall not be violated, and no Warrants shall issue, but upon probable cause, supported by Oath or affirmation, and particularly describing the place to be searched, and the persons or things to be seized.

Amendment V

[RIGHTS OF ACCUSED PERSONS IN CRIMINAL PROCEEDINGS]
No person shall be held to answer for a capital, or otherwise infamous crime, unless on a presentment or indictment of a Grand Jury, except in cases arising in the land or naval forces, or in the Militia, when in actual service in time of War or in public danger; nor shall any person be subject for the same offence to be twice put in jeopardy of life or limb; nor shall be compelled in any criminal case to be a witness against himself, nor be deprived of life, liberty, or property, without due process of law; nor shall private property be taken for public use, without just compensation.

Amendment VI

[RIGHT TO SPEEDY TRIAL, WITNESSES, ETC.]
In all criminal prosecutions, the accused shall enjoy the right to a speedy and public trial, by an impartial jury of the State and district wherein the crime shall have been committed, which district shall have been previously ascertained by law, and to be informed of the nature and cause of the accusation; to be confronted with the witnesses against him; to have compulsory process for obtaining witnesses in his favor, and to have the Assistance of Counsel for his defence.

Amendment VII

[TRIAL BY JURY IN CIVIL CASES]
In suits at common law, where the value in controversy shall exceed twenty dollars, the right of trial by jury shall be preserved, and no fact tried by a jury, shall be otherwise reexamined in any Court of the United States, than according to the rules of the common law.

Amendment VIII

[BAILS, FINES, PUNISHMENTS]
Excessive bail shall not be required, nor excessive fines imposed, nor cruel and unusual punishments inflicted.

Amendment IX

[RESERVATION OF RIGHTS OF PEOPLE]
The enumeration in the Constitution, of certain rights, shall not be construed to deny or disparage others retained by the people.

Amendment X

[POWERS RESERVED TO STATES OR PEOPLE]
The powers not delegated to the United States by the Constitution, nor prohibited by it to the States, are reserved to the States respectively, or to the people.

Amendment XI

[*Proposed by Congress on March 4, 1794;*
declared ratified on January 8, 1798.]
[RESTRICTION OF JUDICIAL POWER]
The Judicial power of the United States shall not be construed to extend to any suit in law or equity, commenced or prosecuted against one of the United States by Citizens of another State, or by Citizens or Subjects of any Foreign State.

Amendment XII

[*Proposed by Congress on December 9, 1803;*
declared ratified on September 25, 1804.]
[ELECTION OF PRESIDENT AND VICE PRESIDENT]
The Electors shall meet in their respective states and vote by ballot for President and Vice-President, one of whom, at least, shall not be an inhabitant of the same state with themselves; they shall name in their ballots the person voted for as President, and in distinct ballots the person voted for as Vice-President, and they shall make distinct lists of all persons voted for as President, and of all persons voted for as Vice-President, and of the number of votes for each, which lists they shall sign and certify, and transmit sealed to the seat of the government of the United States, directed to the President of the Senate;—the President of the Senate shall, in presence of the Senate and House of Representatives, open all the certificates and the votes shall then be counted;—The person having the greatest number of votes for President, shall be the President, if such number be a majority of the whole number of Electors appointed; and if no person have such majority, then from the persons having the highest numbers not exceeding three on the list of those voted for as President, the House of Representatives shall choose immediately, by ballot, the President. But in choosing the President, the votes shall be taken by states, the representation from each state having one vote; a quorum for this purpose shall consist of a member or members from two-thirds of the states, and a majority of all the states shall be necessary to a choice. And if the House of Representatives shall not choose a President whenever the right of choice shall devolve upon them, before the fourth day of March next following, then the Vice-President shall act as President, as in the case of the death or other constitutional disability of the President.—The person having the greatest number of votes as Vice-President, shall be the Vice-President, if such number be a majority of the whole number of Electors appointed, and if no person have a majority, then from the two highest numbers on the list, the Senate shall choose the Vice-President; a quorum for the purpose shall consist of two-thirds of the whole number of Senators, and a majority of the whole number shall be necessary to a choice. But no person constitutionally ineligible to the office of President shall be eligible to that of Vice-President of the United States.

Amendment XIII

[*Proposed by Congress on January 31, 1865;*
declared ratified on December 18, 1865.]

SECTION 1
[ABOLITION OF SLAVERY]
Neither slavery nor involuntary servitude, except as a punishment for crime whereof the party shall have been duly convicted, shall exist within the United States, or any place subject to their jurisdiction.

SECTION 2
[POWER TO ENFORCE THIS ARTICLE]
Congress shall have power to enforce this article by appropriate legislation.

Amendment XIV

[*Proposed by Congress on June 13, 1866;*
declared ratified on July 28, 1868.]

SECTION 1
[CITIZENSHIP RIGHTS NOT TO BE ABRIDGED BY STATES]
All persons born or naturalized in the United States, and subject to the jurisdiction thereof, are citizens of the United States and of the State wherein they reside. No State shall make or enforce any law which shall abridge the privileges or immunities of citizens of the United States; nor shall any State deprive any person of life, liberty, or property, without due process of law; nor deny to any person within its jurisdiction the equal protection of the laws.

SECTION 2
[APPORTIONMENT OF REPRESENTATIVES IN CONGRESS]
Representatives shall be apportioned among the several States according to their respective numbers, counting the whole number of persons in each State, excluding Indians not taxed. But when the right to vote at any election for the choice of electors for President and Vice-President of the United States, Representatives in Congress, the Executive and Judicial officers of a State, or the members of the Legislature thereof, is denied to any of the male inhabitants of such State, being twenty-one years of age, and citizens of the United States, or in any way abridged, except for participation in rebellion, or other crime, the basis of representation therein shall be reduced in the proportion which the number of such male citizens shall bear to the whole number of male citizens twenty-one years of age in such State.

SECTION 3
[PERSONS DISQUALIFIED FROM HOLDING OFFICE]
No person shall be a Senator or Representative in Congress, or elector of President and Vice-President, or hold any office, civil or military, under the United States, or under any State, who,

having previously taken an oath, as a member of Congress, or as an officer of the United States, or as a member of any State legislature, or as an executive or judicial officer of any State, to support the Constitution of the United States, shall have engaged in insurrection or rebellion against the same, or given aid or comfort to the enemies thereof. But Congress may by a vote of two-thirds of each House, remove such disability.

SECTION 4
[WHAT PUBLIC DEBTS ARE VALID]
The validity of the public debt of the United States, authorized by law, including debts incurred for payment of pensions and bounties for services in suppressing insurrection or rebellion, shall not be questioned. But neither the United States nor any State shall assume or pay any debt or obligation incurred in aid of insurrection or rebellion against the United States, or any claim for the loss or emancipation of any slave; but all such debts, obligations and claims shall be held illegal and void.

SECTION 5
[POWER TO ENFORCE THIS ARTICLE]
The Congress shall have power to enforce, by appropriate legislation, the provisions of this article.

Amendment XV
[Proposed by Congress on February 26, 1869; declared ratified on March 30, 1870.]

SECTION 1
[NEGRO SUFFRAGE]
The right of citizens of the United States to vote shall not be denied or abridged by the United States or by any State on account of race, color, or previous condition of servitude.

SECTION 2
[POWER TO ENFORCE THIS ARTICLE]
The Congress shall have power to enforce this article by appropriate legislation.

Amendment XVI
[Proposed by Congress on July 2, 1909; declared ratified on February 25, 1913.]
[AUTHORIZING INCOME TAXES]
The Congress shall have power to lay and collect taxes on incomes, from whatever source derived, without apportionment among the several States, and without regard to any census or enumeration.

Amendment XVII
[Proposed by Congress on May 13, 1912; declared ratified on May 31, 1913.]
[POPULAR ELECTION OF SENATORS]
The Senate of the United States shall be composed of two Senators from each State, elected by the people thereof, for six years; and each Senator shall have one vote. The electors in each State shall have the qualifications requisite for electors of the most numerous branch of the State legislatures.

When vacancies happen in the representation of any State in the Senate, the executive authority of such State shall issue writs of election to fill such vacancies: *Provided*, That the legislature of any State may empower the executive thereof to make temporary appointments until the people fill the vacancies by election as the legislature may direct.

This amendment shall not be so construed as to affect the election or term of any Senator chosen before it becomes valid as part of the Constitution.

Amendment XVIII
[Proposed by Congress December 18, 1917; declared ratified on January 29, 1919.]

SECTION 1
[NATIONAL LIQUOR PROHIBITION]
After one year from the ratification of this article the manufacture, sale, or transportation of intoxicating liquors within, the importation thereof into, or the exportation thereof from the United States and all territory subject to the jurisdiction thereof for beverage purposes is hereby prohibited.

SECTION 2
[POWER TO ENFORCE THIS ARTICLE]
The Congress and the several States shall have concurrent power to enforce this article by appropriate legislation.

SECTION 3
[RATIFICATION WITHIN SEVEN YEARS]
This article shall be inoperative unless it shall have been ratified as an amendment to the Constitution by the legislatures of the several States, as provided in the Constitution, within seven years from the date of the submission hereof to the States by the Congress.[1]

Amendment XIX
[Proposed by Congress on June 4, 1919; declared ratified on August 26, 1920.]
[WOMAN SUFFRAGE]
The right of citizens of the United States to vote shall not be denied or abridged by the United States or by any State on account of sex.

Congress shall have power to enforce this article by appropriate legislation.

---

[1]Repealed by the Twenty-First Amendment.

Amendment XX

[*Proposed by Congress on March 2, 1932;
declared ratified on February 6, 1933.*]

SECTION 1
[TERMS OF OFFICE]
The terms of the President and Vice President shall end at noon on the 20th day of January, and the terms of Senators and Representatives at noon on the 3d day of January, of the years in which such terms would have ended if this article had not been ratified; and the terms of their successors shall then begin.

SECTION 2
[TIME OF CONVENING CONGRESS]
The Congress shall assemble at least once in every year, and such meeting shall begin at noon on the 3d day of January, unless they shall by law appoint a different day.

SECTION 3
[DEATH OF PRESIDENT-ELECT]
If, at the time fixed for the beginning of the term of the President, the President elect shall have died, the Vice President elect shall become President. If a President shall not have been chosen before the time fixed for the beginning of his term, or if the President elect shall have failed to qualify, then the Vice President elect shall act as President until a President shall have qualified; and the Congress may by law provide for the case wherein neither a President elect nor a Vice President elect shall have qualified, declaring who shall then act as President, or the manner in which one who is to act shall be selected, and such person shall act accordingly until a President or Vice President shall have qualified.

SECTION 4
[ELECTION OF THE PRESIDENT]
The Congress may by law provide for the case of the death of any of the persons from whom the House of Representatives may choose a President whenever the right of choice shall have devolved upon them, and for the case of the death of any of the persons from whom the Senate may choose a Vice President whenever the right of choice shall have devolved upon them.

SECTION 5
[AMENDMENT TAKES EFFECT]
Sections 1 and 2 shall take effect on the 15th day of October following the ratification of this article.

SECTION 6
[RATIFICATION WITHIN SEVEN YEARS]
This article shall be inoperative unless it shall have been ratified as an amendment to the Constitution by the legislatures of three-fourths of the several States within seven years from the date of its submission.

Amendment XXI

[*Proposed by Congress on February 20, 1933;
declared ratified on December 5, 1933.*]

SECTION 1
[NATIONAL LIQUOR PROHIBITION REPEALED]
The eighteenth article of amendment to the Constitution of the United States is hereby repealed.

SECTION 2
[TRANSPORTATION OF LIQUOR INTO "DRY" STATES]
The transportation or importation into any State, Territory, or Possession of the United States for delivery or use therein of intoxicating liquors, in violation of the laws thereof, is hereby prohibited.

SECTION 3
[RATIFICATION WITHIN SEVEN YEARS]
This article shall be inoperative unless it shall have been ratified as an amendment to the Constitution by conventions in the several States, as provided in the Constitution, within seven years from the date of the submission hereof to the States by the Congress.

Amendment XXII

[*Proposed by Congress on March 21, 1947;
declared ratified on February 27, 1951.*]

SECTION 1
[TENURE OF PRESIDENT LIMITED]
No person shall be elected to the office of President more than twice, and no person who has held the office of President or acted as President, for more than two years of a term to which some other person was elected President shall be elected to the office of the President more than once. But this Article shall not apply to any person holding the office of President when this Article was proposed by the Congress, and shall not prevent any person who may be holding the office of President, or acting as President, during the term within which this Article becomes operative from holding the office of President or acting as President during the remainder of such term.

SECTION 2
[RATIFICATION WITHIN SEVEN YEARS]
This article shall be inoperative unless it shall have been ratified as an amendment to the Constitution by the legislatures of three-fourths of the several States within seven years from the date of its submission to the States by the Congress.

Amendment XXIII

[*Proposed by Congress on June 16, 1960;
declared ratified on March 29, 1961.*]

SECTION 1

[ELECTORAL COLLEGE VOTES FOR THE DISTRICT OF COLUMBIA]
The District constituting the seat of Government of the
United States shall appoint in such manner as the Congress
may direct:

A number of electors of President and Vice President equal
to the whole number of Senators and Representatives in Congress to which the District would be entitled if it were a State,
but in no event more than the least populous State; they shall
be in addition to those appointed by the States, but they shall
be considered, for the purposes of the election of President and
Vice President, to be electors appointed by a State; and they
shall meet in the District and perform such duties as provided
by the twelfth article of amendment.

SECTION 2

[POWER TO ENFORCE THIS ARTICLE]
The Congress shall have power to enforce this article by
appropriate legislation.

Amendment XXIV

[*Proposed by Congress on August 27, 1962;
declared ratified on January 23, 1964.*]

SECTION 1

[ANTI-POLL TAX]
The right of citizens of the United States to vote in any primary or other election for President or Vice President, for electors
for President or Vice President, or for Senator or Representative of Congress, shall not be denied or abridged by the United
States or any State by reason of failure to pay any poll tax or
other tax.

SECTION 2

[POWER TO ENFORCE THIS ARTICLE]
The Congress shall have power to enforce this article by
appropriate legislation.

Amendment XXV

[*Proposed by Congress on July 6, 1965;
declared ratified on February 10, 1967.*]

SECTION 1

[VICE PRESIDENT TO BECOME PRESIDENT]
In case of the removal of the President from office or his death
or resignation, the Vice President shall become President.

SECTION 2

[CHOICE OF A NEW VICE PRESIDENT]
Whenever there is a vacancy in the office of the Vice President,
the President shall nominate a Vice President who shall take
the office upon confirmation by a majority vote of both houses
of Congress.

SECTION 3

[PRESIDENT MAY DECLARE OWN DISABILITY]
Whenever the President transmits to the President pro tempore of the Senate and the Speaker of the House of Representatives his written declaration that he is unable to discharge the
powers and duties of his office, and until he transmits to them
a written declaration to the contrary, such powers and duties
shall be discharged by the Vice President as Acting President.

SECTION 4

[ALTERNATE PROCEDURES TO DECLARE AND
TO END PRESIDENTIAL DISABILITY]
Whenever the Vice President and a majority of either the principal officers of the executive departments, or of such other body
as Congress may by law provide, transmit to the President pro
tempore of the Senate and the Speaker of the House of Representatives their written declaration that the President is unable to discharge the powers and duties of his office, the Vice
President shall immediately assume the powers and duties of
the office as Acting President.

Thereafter, when the President transmits to the President
pro tempore of the Senate and the Speaker of the House of
Representatives his written declaration that no inability exists,
he shall resume the powers and duties of his office unless the
Vice President and a majority of either the principal officers of
the executive department, or of such other body as Congress
may by law provide, transmit within four days to the President
pro tempore of the Senate and the Speaker of the House of
Representatives their written declaration that the President is
unable to discharge the powers and duties of his office. Thereupon Congress shall decide the issue, assembling within forty
eight hours for that purpose if not in session. If the Congress,
within twenty one days after receipt of the latter written declaration, or, if Congress is not in session, within twenty one
days after Congress is required to assemble, determines by
two-thirds vote of both Houses that the President is unable to
discharge the powers and duties of his office, the Vice President shall continue to discharge the same as Acting President;
otherwise, the President shall resume the powers and duties
of his office.

Amendment XXVI

[*Proposed by Congress on March 23, 1971;
declared ratified on July 1, 1971.*]

SECTION 1

[EIGHTEEN-YEAR-OLD VOTE]

The right of citizens of the United States, who are eighteen
years of age or older, to vote shall not be denied or abridged by
the United States or by any State on account of age.

SECTION 2

[POWER TO ENFORCE THIS ARTICLE]

The Congress shall have power to enforce this article by
appropriate legislation.

Amendment XXVII

[*Proposed by Congress on September 25, 1789;
declared ratified on May 8, 1992.*]

[CONGRESS CANNOT RAISE ITS OWN PAY]

No law varying the compensation for the services of the Senators and Representatives, shall take effect, until an election of
representatives shall have intervened.

The Federalist Papers

No. 10: Madison

Among the numerous advantages promised by a well constructed Union, none deserves to be more accurately developed than its tendency to break and control the violence of faction. The friend of popular governments never finds himself so much alarmed for their character and fate, as when he contemplates their propensity to this dangerous vice. He will not fail therefore to set a due value on any plan which, without violating the principles to which he is attached, provides a proper cure for it. The instability, injustice, and confusion introduced into the public councils have, in truth, been the mortal diseases under which popular governments have everywhere perished, as they continue to be the favorite and fruitful topics from which the adversaries to liberty derive their most specious declamations. The valuable improvements made by the American constitutions on the popular models, both ancient and modern, cannot certainly be too much admired; but it would be an unwarrantable partiality to contend that they have as effectually obviated the danger on this side, as was wished and expected. Complaints are everywhere heard from our most considerate and virtuous citizens, equally the friends of public and private faith and of public and personal liberty, that our governments are too unstable, that the public good is disregarded in the conflicts of rival parties, and that measures are too often decided, not according to the rules of justice and the rights of the minor party, but by the superior force of an interested and overbearing majority. However anxiously we may wish that these complaints had no foundation, the evidence of known facts will not permit us to deny that they are in some degree true. It will be found, indeed, on a candid review of our situation, that some of the distresses under which we labor have been erroneously charged on the operation of our governments; but it will be found, at the same time, that other causes will not alone account for many of our heaviest misfortunes; and, particularly, for that prevailing and increasing distrust of public engagements and alarm for private rights which are echoed from one end of the continent to the other. These must be chiefly, if not wholly, effects of the unsteadiness and injustice with which a factious spirit has tainted our public administration.

By a faction I understand a number of citizens, whether amounting to a majority or minority of the whole, who are united and actuated by some common impulse of passion, or of interest, adverse to the rights of other citizens, or to the permanent and aggregate interests of the community.

There are two methods of curing the mischiefs of faction: the one, by removing its causes; the other, by controlling its effects.

There are again two methods of removing the causes of faction: the one, by destroying the liberty which is essential to its existence; the other, by giving to every citizen the same opinions, the same passions, and the same interests.

It could never be more truly said than of the first remedy, that it is worse than the disease. Liberty is to faction what air is to fire, an aliment without which it instantly expires. But it could not be a less folly to abolish liberty, which is essential to political life, because it nourishes faction, than it would be to wish the annihilation of air, which is essential to animal life, because it imparts to fire its destructive agency.

The second expedient is as impracticable, as the first would be unwise. As long as the reason of man continues fallible, and he is at liberty to exercise it, different opinions will be formed. As long as the connection subsists between his reason and his self-love, his opinions and his passions will have a reciprocal influence on each other; and the former will be objects to which the latter will attach themselves. The diversity in the faculties of men, from which the rights of property originate, is not less an insuperable obstacle to a uniformity of interests. The protection of these faculties is the first object of Government. From the protection of different and unequal faculties of acquiring property, the possession of different degrees and kinds of property immediately results; and from the influence of these on the sentiments and views of the respective proprietors, ensues a division of the society into different interests and parties.

The latent causes of faction are thus sown in the nature of man; and we see them everywhere brought into different degrees of activity, according to the different circumstances of civil society. A zeal for different opinions concerning religion, concerning Government, and many other points, as well of speculation as of practice; an attachment to different leaders ambitiously contending for pre-eminence and power; or to persons of other descriptions whose fortunes have been interesting to the human passions, have in turn divided mankind into parties, inflamed them with mutual animosity, and rendered them much more disposed to vex and oppress each other, than to co-operate for their common good. So strong is this propensity of mankind to fall into mutual animosities, that where no substantial occasion presents itself, the most frivolous and fanciful distinctions have been sufficient to kindle their unfriendly passions, and excite their most violent conflicts. But the most common and durable source of factions has been the various and unequal distribution of property. Those who hold and those who are without property have ever formed distinct interests in society. Those who are creditors, and those who are debtors, fall under a like discrimination. A landed interest, a manufacturing interest, a mercantile interest, a moneyed interest, with many lesser interests, grow up of necessity in civilized nations, and divide them into different classes, actuated by different sentiments and views. The regulation of these various and interfering interests forms the principal task of modern Legislation, and involves the spirit of party and faction in the necessary and ordinary operations of Government.

No man is allowed to be judge in his own cause, because his interest would certainly bias his judgment and, not improbably, corrupt his integrity. With equal, nay with greater reason, a body of men are unfit to be both judges and parties at the same time; yet what are many of the most important acts of legislation but so many judicial determinations, not indeed concerning the rights of single persons, but concerning the rights of large bodies of citizens; and what are the different classes of legislators but advocates and parties to the causes which they determine? Is a law proposed concerning private debts? It is a question to which the creditors are parties on one side and the debtors on the other. Justice ought to hold the balance between them. Yet the parties are, and must be, themselves the judges; and the most numerous party, or in other words, the most powerful faction must be expected to prevail. Shall domestic manufacturers be encouraged, and in what degree, by restrictions on foreign manufacturers? are questions which would be differently decided by the landed and the manufacturing classes, and probably by neither with a sole regard to justice and the public good. The apportionment of taxes on the various descriptions of property is an act which seems to require the most exact impartiality; yet there is, perhaps, no legislative act in which greater opportunity and temptation are given to a predominant party to trample on the rules of justice. Every shilling with which they overburden the inferior number is a shilling saved to their own pockets.

It is in vain to say that enlightened statesmen will be able to adjust these clashing interests and render them all subservient to the public good. Enlightened statesmen will not always be at the helm. Nor, in many cases, can such an adjustment be made at all without taking into view indirect and remote considerations, which will rarely prevail over the immediate interest which one party may find in disregarding the rights of another or the good of the whole.

The inference to which we are brought is that the *causes* of faction cannot be removed and that relief is only to be sought in the means of controlling its *effects*.

If a faction consists of less than a majority, relief is supplied by the republican principle, which enables the majority to defeat its sinister views by regular vote. It may clog the administration, it may convulse the society; but it will be unable to execute and mask its violence under the forms of the Constitution. When a majority is included in a faction, the form of popular government, on the other hand, enables it to sacrifice to its ruling passion or interest both the public good and the rights of other citizens. To secure the public good and private rights against the danger of such a faction, and at the same time to preserve the spirit and the form of popular government, is then the great object to which our enquiries are directed. Let me add that it is the great desideratum by which alone this form of government can be rescued from the opprobrium under which it has so long labored and be recommended to the esteem and adoption of mankind.

By what means is this object attainable? Evidently by one of two only. Either the existence of the same passion or interest in a majority at the same time must be prevented, or the majority, having such co-existent passion or interest, must be rendered, by their number and local situation, unable to concert and carry into effect schemes of oppression. If the impulse and the opportunity be suffered to coincide, we well know that neither moral nor religious motives can be relied on as an adequate control. They are not found to be such on the injustice and violence of individuals, and lose their efficacy in proportion to the number combined together, that is, in proportion as their efficacy becomes needful.

From this view of the subject it may be concluded that a pure Democracy, by which I mean a Society consisting of a small number of citizens, who assemble and administer the Government in person, can admit of no cure for the mischiefs of faction. A common passion or interest will, in almost every case, be felt by a majority of the whole; a communication and concert results from the form of Government itself; and there is nothing to check the inducements to sacrifice the weaker party or an obnoxious individual. Hence it is that such Democracies have ever been spectacles of turbulence and contention; have ever been found incompatible with personal security or the rights of property; and have in general been as short in their lives as they have been violent in their deaths. Theoretic politicians, who have patronized this species of Government, have erroneously supposed that by reducing mankind to a perfect equality in their political rights, they would at the same time be perfectly equalized and assimilated in their possessions, their opinions, and their passions.

A Republic, by which I mean a Government in which the scheme of representation takes place, opens a different prospect and promises the cure for which we are seeking. Let us examine the points in which it varies from pure Democracy, and we shall comprehend both the nature of the cure and the efficacy which it must derive from the Union.

The two great points of difference between a Democracy and a Republic are: first, the delegation of the Government, in the latter, to a small number of citizens elected by the rest; secondly, the greater number of citizens and greater sphere of country over which the latter may be extended.

The effect of the first difference is, on the one hand, to refine and enlarge the public views by passing them through the medium of a chosen body of citizens, whose wisdom may best discern the true interest of their country and whose patriotism and love of justice will be least likely to sacrifice it to temporary or partial considerations. Under such a regulation it may well happen that the public voice, pronounced by the representatives of the people, will be more consonant to the public good than if pronounced by the people themselves, convened for the purpose. On the other hand, the effect may be inverted. Men of factious tempers, of local prejudices, or of sinister designs, may, by intrigue, by corruption, or by other means, first obtain the suffrages, and then betray the interests of the people. The question resulting is, whether small or extensive Republics are most favorable to the election of proper guardians of the public weal; and it is clearly decided in favor of the latter by two obvious considerations.

In the first place it is to be remarked that however small the Republic may be, the Representatives must be raised to a certain number in order to guard against the cabals of a few; and that however large it may be they must be limited to a certain number in order to guard against the confusion of a multitude. Hence, the number of Representatives in the two cases not being in proportion to that of the Constituents, and being proportionally greatest in the small Republic, it follows that if the proportion of fit characters be not less in the large than in the small Republic, the former will present a greater option, and consequently a greater probability of a fit choice.

In the next place, as each Representative will be chosen by a greater number of citizens in the large than in the small Republic, it will be more difficult for unworthy candidates to practise with success the vicious arts by which elections are too often carried; and the suffrages of the people being more free, will be more likely to centre on men who possess the most attractive merit and the most diffusive and established characters.

It must be confessed that in this, as in most other cases, there is a mean, on both sides of which inconveniencies will be found to lie. By enlarging too much the number of electors, you render the representative too little acquainted with all their local circumstances and lesser interests; as by reducing it too much, you render him unduly attached to these, and too little fit to comprehend and pursue great and national objects. The Federal Constitution forms a happy combination in this respect; the great and aggregate interests being referred to the national, the local and particular to the State legislatures.

The other point of difference is the greater number of citizens and extent of territory which may be brought within the compass of Republican than of Democratic Government; and it is this circumstance principally which renders factious combinations less to be dreaded in the former than in the latter. The smaller the society, the fewer probably will be the distinct parties and interests composing it; the fewer the distinct parties and interests, the more frequently will a majority be found

of the same party; and the smaller the number of individuals composing a majority, and the smaller the compass within which they are placed, the more easily will they concert and execute their plans of oppression. Extend the sphere and you take in a greater variety of parties and interests; you make it less probable that a majority of the whole will have a common motive to invade the rights of other citizens; or if such a common motive exists, it will be more difficult for all who feel it to discover their own strength and to act in unison with each other. Besides other impediments, it may be remarked, that where there is a consciousness of unjust or dishonorable purposes, communication is always checked by distrust in proportion to the number whose concurrence is necessary.

Hence, it clearly appears that the same advantage which a Republic has over a Democracy in controlling the effects of faction is enjoyed by a large over a small republic—is enjoyed by the Union over the States composing it. Does this advantage consist in the substitution of representatives whose enlightened views and virtuous sentiments render them superior to local prejudices and to schemes of injustice? It will not be denied that the representation of the Union will be most likely to possess these requisite endowments. Does it consist in the greater security afforded by a greater variety of parties, against the event of any one party being able to outnumber and oppress the rest? In an equal degree does the increased variety of parties comprised within the Union increase this security? Does it, in fine, consist in the greater obstacles opposed to the concert and accomplishment of the secret wishes of an unjust and interested majority? Here again the extent of the Union gives it the most palpable advantage.

The influence of factious leaders may kindle a flame within their particular States but will be unable to spread a general conflagration through the other States: a religious sect may degenerate into a political faction in a part of the Confederacy; but the variety of sects dispersed over the entire face of it must secure the national Councils against any danger from that source: a rage for paper money, for an abolition of debts, for an equal division of property, or for any other improper or wicked project, will be less apt to pervade the whole body of the Union than a particular member of it; in the same proportion as such a malady is more likely to taint a particular county or district than an entire State.

In the extent and proper structure of the Union, therefore, we behold a republican remedy for the diseases most incident to Republican Government. And according to the degree of pleasure and pride we feel in being republicans ought to be our zeal in cherishing the spirit and supporting the character of federalist.

PUBLIUS
November 22, 1787

No. 51: Madison

To what expedient, then, shall we finally resort, for maintaining in practice the necessary partition of power among the several departments as laid down in the constitution? The only answer that can be given is that as all these exterior provisions are found to be inadequate the defect must be supplied, by so contriving the interior structure of the government as that its several constituent parts may, by their mutual relations, be the means of keeping each other in their proper places. Without presuming to undertake a full development of this important idea I will hazard a few general observations which may perhaps place it in a clearer light, and enable us to form a more correct judgment of the principles and structure of the government planned by the convention.

In order to lay a due foundation for that separate and distinct exercise of the different powers of government, which to a certain extent is admitted on all hands to be essential to the preservation of liberty, it is evident that each department should have a will of its own; and consequently should be so constituted that the members of each should have as little agency as possible in the appointment of the members of the others. Were this principle rigorously adhered to, it would require that all the appointments for the supreme executive, legislative, and judiciary magistracies should be drawn from the same fountain of authority, the people, through channels having no communication whatever with one another. Perhaps such a plan of constructing the several departments would be less difficult in practice than it may in contemplation appear. Some difficulties, however, and some additional expense would attend the execution of it. Some deviations, therefore, from the principle must be admitted. In the constitution of the judiciary department in particular, it might be inexpedient to insist rigorously on the principle: first, because peculiar qualifications being essential in the members, the primary consideration ought to be to select that mode of choice which best secures these qualifications; second, because the permanent tenure by which the appointments are held in that department must soon destroy all sense of dependence on the authority conferring them.

It is equally evident that the members of each department should be as little dependent as possible on those of the others for the emoluments annexed to their offices. Were the executive magistrate, or the judges, not independent of the legislature in this particular, their independence in every other would be merely nominal.

But the great security against a gradual concentration of the several powers in the same department consists in giving to those who administer each department the necessary constitutional means and personal motives to resist encroachments of the others. The provision for defence must in this, as in all other cases, be made commensurate to the danger of attack. Ambition must be made to counteract ambition. The interest of the man must be connected with the constitutional rights of the place. It may be a reflection on human nature that such devices should be necessary to control the abuses of government. But what is government itself but the greatest of all reflections on human nature? If men were angels, no government would be necessary. If angels were to govern men, neither external

nor internal controls on government would be necessary. In framing a government which is to be administered by men over men, the great difficulty lies in this: You must first enable the government to control the governed; and in the next place oblige it to control itself. A dependence on the people is, no doubt, the primary control on the government; but experience has taught mankind the necessity of auxiliary precautions.

This policy of supplying, by opposite and rival interests, the defect of better motives, might be traced through the whole system of human affairs, private as well as public. We see it particularly displayed in all the subordinate distributions of power, where the constant aim is to divide and arrange the several offices in such a manner as that each may be a check on the other; that the private interest of every individual may be a sentinel over the public rights. These inventions of prudence cannot be less requisite in the distribution of the supreme powers of the State.

But it is not possible to give to each department an equal power of self-defense. In republican government, the legislative authority necessarily predominates. The remedy for this inconveniency is to divide the legislature into different branches; and to render them, by different modes of election and different principles of action, as little connected with each other as the nature of their common functions and their common dependence on the society will admit. It may even be necessary to guard against dangerous encroachments by still further precautions. As the weight of the legislative authority requires that it should be thus divided, the weakness of the executive may require, on the other hand, that it should be fortified. An absolute negative on the legislature appears, at first view, to be the natural defense with which the executive magistrate should be armed. But perhaps it would be neither altogether safe nor alone sufficient. On ordinary occasions it might not be exerted with the requisite firmness, and on extraordinary occasions it might be perfidiously abused. May not this defect of an absolute negative be supplied by some qualified connection between this weaker branch of the stronger department, by which the latter may be led to support the constitutional rights of the former, without being too much detached from the rights of its own department?

If the principles on which these observations are founded be just, as I persuade myself they are, and they be applied as a criterion to the several State constitutions, and to the federal Constitution, it will be found that if the latter does not perfectly correspond with them, the former are infinitely less able to bear such a test.

There are, moreover, two considerations particularly applicable to the federal system of America, which place that system in a very interesting point of view.

First. In a single republic, all the power surrendered by the people is submitted to the administration of a single government; and usurpations are guarded against by a division of the government into distinct and separate departments. In the compound republic of America, the power surrendered by the people is first divided between two distinct governments, and then the portion allotted to each subdivided among distinct and separate departments. Hence a double security arises to the rights of the people. The different governments will control each other, at the same time that each will be controlled by itself.

Second. It is of great importance in a republic not only to guard the society against the oppression of its rulers, but to guard one part of the society against the injustice of the other part. Different interests necessarily exist in different classes of citizens. If a majority be united by a common interest, the rights of the minority will be insecure. There are but two methods of providing against this evil: The one by creating a will in the community independent of the majority—that is, of the society itself; the other, by comprehending in the society so many separate descriptions of citizens as will render an unjust combination of a majority of the whole very improbable, if not impracticable. The first method prevails in all governments possessing an hereditary or self-appointed authority. This, at best, is but a precarious security; because a power independent of the society may as well espouse the unjust views of the major as the rightful interests of the minor party, and may possibly be turned against both parties. The second method will be exemplified in the federal republic of the United States. Whilst all authority in it will be derived from and dependent on the society, the society itself will be broken into so many parts, interests and classes of citizens, that the rights of individuals, or of the minority, will be in little danger from interested combinations of the majority. In a free government the security for civil rights must be the same as that for religious rights. It consists in the one case in the multiplicity of interests, and in the other in the multiplicity of sects. The degree of security in both cases will depend on the number of interests and sects; and this may be presumed to depend on the extent of country and number of people comprehended under the same government. This view of the subject must particularly recommend a proper federal system to all the sincere and considerate friends of republican government: Since it shows that in exact proportion as the territory of the Union may be formed into more circumscribed Confederacies, or States, oppressive combinations of a majority will be facilitated; the best security, under the republican form, for the rights of every class of citizens, will be diminished; and consequently the stability and independence of some member of the government, the only other security, must be proportionally increased. Justice is the end of government. It is the end of civil society. It ever has been and ever will be pursued until it be obtained, or until liberty be lost in the pursuit. In a society under the forms of which the stronger faction can readily unite and oppress the weaker, anarchy may as truly be said to reign as in a state of nature, where the weaker individual is not secured against the violence of the stronger: And as, in the latter state, even the stronger individuals are prompted, by the uncertainty of their condition, to submit to a government which may protect the weak as well as themselves: So, in the former state, will the more powerful factions or parties be gradually induced, by a like motive, to wish for a government which will protect all parties, the weaker as well as the more powerful. It can be little doubted that if the State of Rhode Island was separated from the Confederacy and left to itself, the insecurity of rights under the popular form of government within such narrow limits would be displayed by such reiterated oppressions of factious majorities that some power altogether independent of the people would soon be called for by the voice of the very factions whose misrule had proved the necessity of it. In the extended republic of the United States, and among the great variety of interests, parties, and sects which it embraces, a coalition of a majority of the whole society could seldom take place on any other principles than those of justice and the general good; and there being thus less danger to a minor from the will of the major party, there must be less pretext, also, to provide for the security of the former, by introducing into the government a will not dependent on the latter, or, in other words, a will independent of the society itself. It is no less certain than it is important, notwithstanding the contrary opinions which have been entertained, that the larger the society, provided it lie within a practicable sphere, the more duly capable it will be of self-government. And happily for the *republican cause*, the practicable sphere may be carried to a very great extent by a judicious modification and mixture of the *federal principle*.

PUBLIUS
February 6, 1788

The Anti-Federalist Papers

Essay by Brutus in the *New York Journal*

When the public is called to investigate and decide upon a question in which not only the present members of the community are deeply interested, but upon which the happiness and misery of generations yet unborn is in great measure suspended, the benevolent mind cannot help feeling itself peculiarly interested in the result.

In this situation, I trust the feeble efforts of an individual, to lead the minds of the people to a wise and prudent determination, cannot fail of being acceptable to the candid and dispassionate part of the community. Encouraged by this consideration, I have been induced to offer my thoughts upon the present important crisis of our public affairs.

Perhaps this country never saw so critical a period in their political concerns. We have felt the feebleness of the ties by which these United-States are held together, and the want of sufficient energy in our present confederation, to manage, in some instances, our general concerns. Various expedients have been proposed to remedy these evils, but none have succeeded. At length a Convention of the states has been assembled, they have formed a constitution which will now, probably, be submitted to the people to ratify or reject, who are the fountain of all power, to whom alone it of right belongs to make or unmake constitutions, or forms of government, at their pleasure. The most important question that was ever proposed to your decision, or to the decision of any people under heaven, is before you, and you are to decide upon it by men of your own election, chosen specially for this purpose. If the constitution, offered to your acceptance, be a wise one, calculated to preserve the invaluable blessings of liberty, to secure the inestimable rights of mankind, and promote human happiness, then, if you accept it, you will lay a lasting foundation of happiness for millions yet unborn; generations to come will rise up and call you blessed. You may rejoice in the prospects of this vast extended continent becoming filled with freemen, who will assert the dignity of human nature. You may solace yourselves with the idea, that society, in this favoured land, will fast advance to the highest point of perfection; the human mind will expand in knowledge and virtue, and the golden age be, in some measure, realised. But if, on the other hand, this form of government contains principles that will lead to the subversion of liberty—if it tends to establish a despotism, or, what is worse, a tyrannic aristocracy; then, if you adopt it, this only remaining assylum

for liberty will be shut up, and posterity will execrate your memory.

Momentous then is the question you have to determine, and you are called upon by every motive which should influence a noble and virtuous mind, to examine it well, and to make up a wise judgment. It is insisted, indeed, that this constitution must be received, be it ever so imperfect. If it has its defects, it is said, they can be best amended when they are experienced. But remember, when the people once part with power, they can seldom or never resume it again but by force. Many instances can be produced in which the people have voluntarily increased the powers of their rulers; but few, if any, in which rulers have willingly abridged their authority. This is a sufficient reason to induce you to be careful, in the first instance, how you deposit the powers of government.

With these few introductory remarks, I shall proceed to a consideration of this constitution:

The first question that presents itself on the subject is, whether a confederated government be the best for the United States or not? Or in other words, whether the thirteen United States should be reduced to one great republic, governed by one legislature, and under the direction of one executive and judicial; or whether they should continue thirteen confederated republics, under the direction and controul of a supreme federal head for certain defined national purposes only?

This enquiry is important, because, although the government reported by the convention does not go to a perfect and entire consolidation, yet it approaches so near to it, that it must, if executed, certainly and infallibly terminate in it.

This government is to possess absolute and uncontroulable power, legislative, executive and judicial, with respect to every object to which it extends, for by the last clause of section 8th, article 1st, it is declared "that the Congress shall have power to make all laws which shall be necessary and proper for carrying into execution the foregoing powers, and all other powers vested by this constitution, in the government of the United States; or in any department or office thereof." And by the 6th article, it is declared "that this constitution, and the laws of the United States, which shall be made in pursuance thereof, and the treaties made, or which shall be made, under the authority of the United States, shall be the supreme law of the land; and the judges in every state shall be bound thereby, any thing in the constitution, or law of any state to the contrary notwithstanding." It appears from these articles that there is no need of any intervention of the state governments, between the Congress and the people, to execute any one power vested in the general government, and that the constitution and laws of every state are nullified and declared void, so far as they are or shall be inconsistent with this constitution, or the laws made in pursuance of it, or with treaties made under the authority of the United States.—The government then, so far as it extends, is a complete one, and not a confederation. It is as much one complete government as that of New York or Massachusetts, has as absolute and perfect powers to make and execute all laws, to appoint officers, institute courts, declare offences, and annex penalties, with respect to every object to which it extends, as any other in the world. So far therefore as its powers reach, all ideas of confederation are given up and lost. It is true this government is limited to certain objects, or to speak more properly, some small degree of power is still left to the states, but a little attention to the powers vested in the general government, will convince every candid man, that if it is capable of being executed, all that is reserved for the individual states must very soon be annihilated, except so far as they are barely necessary to the organization of the general government. The powers of the general legislature extend to every case that is of the least importance—there is nothing valuable to human nature, nothing dear to freemen, but what is within its power. It has authority to make laws which will affect the lives, the liberty, and property of every man in the United States; nor can the constitution or laws of any state, in any way prevent or impede the full and complete execution of every power given. The legislative power is competent to lay taxes, duties, imposts, and excises;—there is no limitation to this power, unless it be said that the clause which directs the use to which those taxes, and duties shall be applied, may be said to be a limitation: but this is no restriction of the power at all, for by this clause they are to be applied to pay the debts and provide for the common defence and general welfare of the United States; but the legislature have authority to contract debts at their discretion; they are the sole judges of what is necessary to provide for the common defence, and they only are to determine what is for the general welfare; this power therefore is neither more nor less, than a power to lay and collect taxes, imposts, and excises, at their pleasure; not only [is] the power to lay taxes unlimited, as to the amount they may require, but it is perfect and absolute to raise them in any mode they please. No state legislature, or any power in the state governments, have any more to do in carrying this into effect, than the authority of one state has to do with that of another. In the business therefore of laying and collecting taxes, the idea of confederation is totally lost, and that of one entire republic is embraced. It is proper here to remark, that the authority to lay and collect taxes is the most important of any power that can be granted; it connects with it almost all other powers, or at least will in process of time draw all other after it; it is the great mean of protection, security, and defence, in a good government, and the great engine of oppression and tyranny in a bad one. This cannot fail of being the case, if we consider the contracted limits which are set by this constitution, to the late [state?] governments, on this article of raising money. No state can emit paper money—lay any duties, or imposts, on imports, or exports, but by consent of the Congress; and then the net produce shall be for the benefit of the United States: the only mean therefore left, for any state to support its government and discharge its debts, is by direct taxation; and the United States have also power to lay and collect taxes, in any way they please. Every one who has thought on the subject, must be convinced that but small sums of money can be collected in any country, by direct taxe[s], when the foederal government begins to exercise the right of taxation in all its parts, the legislatures of the several states will find it impossible to raise monies to support their governments. Without money they cannot be supported, and they must dwindle away, and, as before observed, their powers absorbed in that of the general government.

It might be here shewn, that the power in the federal legislative, to raise and support armies at pleasure, as well in peace as in war, and their controul over the militia, tend, not only to a consolidation of the government, but the destruction of liberty.—I shall not, however, dwell upon these, as a few observations upon the judicial power of this government, in addition to the preceding, will fully evince the truth of the position.

The judicial power of the United States is to be vested in a supreme court, and in such inferior courts as Congress may from time to time ordain and establish. The powers of these courts are very extensive; their jurisdiction comprehends all civil causes, except such as arise between citizens of the same state; and it extends to all cases in law and equity arising under the constitution. One inferior court must be established, I presume, in each state, at least, with the necessary executive officers appendant thereto. It is easy to see, that in the common course of things, these courts will eclipse the dignity, and take away from the respectability, of the state courts. These courts will be, in themselves, totally independent of the states, deriving their authority from the United States, and receiving from them fixed salaries; and in the course of human events it is to be expected, that they will swallow up all the powers of the courts in the respective states.

How far the clause in the 8th section of the 1st article may operate to do away all idea of confederated states, and to effect an entire consolidation of the whole into one general government, it is impossible to say. The powers given by this article are very general and comprehensive, and it may receive a construction to justify the passing almost any law. A power to make all laws, which shall be *necessary and proper*, for carrying into execution, all powers vested by the constitution in the government of the United States, or any department or officer thereof, is a power very comprehensive and definite [indefinite?], and may, for ought I know, be exercised in a such manner as entirely to abolish the state legislatures. Suppose the legislature of a state should pass a law to raise money to support their government and pay the state debt, may the Congress repeal this law, because it may prevent the collection of a tax which they may think proper and necessary to lay, to provide for the general welfare of the United States? For all laws made, in pursuance of this constitution, are the supreme law of the land, and the judges in every state shall be bound thereby, any thing in the constitution or laws of the different states to the contrary notwithstanding.—By such a law, the government of a particular state might be overturned at one stroke, and thereby be deprived of every means of its support.

It is not meant, by stating this case, to insinuate that the constitution would warrant a law of this kind; or unnecessarily to alarm the fears of the people, by suggesting, that the federal legislature would be more likely to pass the limits assigned them by the constitution, than that of an individual state, further than they are less responsible to the people. But what is meant is, that the legislature of the United States are vested with the great and uncontroulable powers, of laying and collecting taxes, duties, imposts, and excises; of regulating trade, raising and supporting armies, organizing, arming, and disciplining the militia, instituting courts, and other general powers. And are by this clause invested with the power of making all laws, *proper and necessary*, for carrying all these into execution; and they may so exercise this power as entirely to annihilate all the state governments, and reduce this country to one single government. And if they may do it, it is pretty certain they will; for it will be found that the power retained by individual states, small as it is, will be a clog upon the wheels of the government of the United States; the latter therefore will be naturally inclined to remove it out of the way. Besides, it is a truth confirmed by the unerring experience of ages, that every man, and every body of men, invested with power, are ever disposed to increase it, and to acquire a superiority over every thing that stands in their way. This disposition, which is implanted in human nature, will operate in the federal legislature to lessen and ultimately to subvert the state authority, and having such advantages, will most certainly succeed, if the federal government succeeds at all. It must be very evident then, that what this constitution wants of being a complete consolidation of the several parts of the union into one complete government, possessed of perfect legislative, judicial, and executive powers, to all intents and purposes, it will necessarily acquire in its exercise and operation.

Let us now proceed to enquire, as I at first proposed, whether it be best the thirteen United States should be reduced to one great republic, or not? It is here taken for granted, that all agree in this, that whatever government we adopt, it ought to be a free one; that it should be so framed as to secure the liberty of the citizens of America, and such an one as to admit of a full, fair, and equal representation of the people. The question then will be, whether a government thus constituted, and founded on such principles, is practicable, and can be exercised over the whole United States, reduced into one state?

If respect is to be paid to the opinion of the greatest and wisest men who have ever thought or wrote on the science of government, we shall be constrained to conclude, that a free republic cannot succeed over a country of such immense extent, containing such a number of inhabitants, and these encreasing in such rapid progression as that of the whole United States. Among the many illustrious authorities which might be produced to this point, I shall content myself with quoting only two. The one is the baron de Montesquieu, spirit of laws, chap. xvi. vol. I [book VIII]. "It is natural to a republic to have only a small territory, otherwise it cannot long subsist. In a large republic there are men of large fortunes, and consequently of less moderation; there are trusts too great to be placed in any single subject; he has interest of his own; he soon begins to think that he may be happy, great and glorious, by oppressing his fellow citizens; and that he may raise himself to grandeur on the ruins of his country. In a large republic, the public good is sacrificed to a thousand views; it is subordinate to exceptions, and depends on accidents. In a small one, the interest of the public is easier perceived, better understood, and more within the reach of every citizen; abuses are of less extent, and of course are less protected." Of the same opinion is the marquis Beccarari.

History furnishes no example of a free republic, any thing like the extent of the United States. The Grecian republics were of small extent; so also was that of the Romans. Both of these, it is true, in process of time, extended their conquests over large territories of country; and the consequence was, that their governments were changed from that of free governments to those of the most tyrannical that ever existed in the world.

Not only the opinion of the greatest men, and the experience of mankind, are against the idea of an extensive republic, but a variety of reasons may be drawn from the reason and nature of things, against it. In every government, the will of the sovereign is the law. In despotic governments, the supreme authority being lodged in one, his will is law, and can be as easily expressed to a large extensive territory as to a small one. In a pure democracy the people are the sovereign, and their will is declared by themselves; for this purpose they must all come together to deliberate, and decide. This kind of government cannot be exercised, therefore, over a country of any considerable extent; it must be confined to a single city, or at least limited to such bounds as that the people can conveniently assemble, be able to debate, understand the subject submitted to them, and declare their opinion concerning it.

In a free republic, although all laws are derived from the consent of the people, yet the people do not declare their consent by themselves in person, but by representatives, chosen by them, who are supposed to know the minds of their constituents, and to be possessed of integrity to declare this mind.

In every free government, the people must give their assent to the laws by which they are governed. This is the true criterion between a free government and an arbitrary one.

The former are ruled by the will of the whole, expressed in any manner they may agree upon; the latter by the will of one, or a few. If the people are to give their assent to the laws, by persons chosen and appointed by them, the manner of the choice and the number chosen, must be such, as to possess, be disposed, and consequently qualified to declare the sentiments of the people; for if they do not know, or are not disposed to speak the sentiments of the people, the people do not govern, but the sovereignty is in a few. Now, in a large extended country, it is impossible to have a representation, possessing the sentiments, and of integrity, to declare the minds of the people, without having it so numerous and unwieldly, as to be subject in great measure to the inconveniency of a democratic government.

The territory of the United States is of vast extent; it now contains near three millions of souls, and is capable of containing much more than ten times that number. Is it practicable for a country, so large and so numerous as they will soon become, to elect a representation, that will speak their sentiments, without their becoming so numerous as to be incapable of transacting public business? It certainly is not.

In a republic, the manners, sentiments, and interests of the people should be similar. If this be not the case, there will be a constant clashing of opinions; and the representatives of one part will be continually striving against those of the other. This will retard the operations of government, and prevent such conclusions as will promote the public good. If we apply this remark to the condition of the United States, we shall be convinced that it forbids that we should be one government. The United States includes a variety of climates. The productions of the different parts of the union are very variant, and their interests, of consequence, diverse. Their manners and habits differ as much as their climates and productions; and their sentiments are by no means coincident. The laws and customs of the several states are, in many respects, very diverse, and in some opposite; each would be in favor of its own interests and customs, and, of consequence, a legislature, formed of representatives from the respective parts, would not only be too numerous to act with any care or decision, but would be composed of such heterogenous and discordant principles, as would constantly be contending with each other.

The laws cannot be executed in a republic, of an extent equal to that of the United States, with promptitude.

The magistrates in every government must be supported in the execution of the laws, either by an armed force, maintained at the public expence for that purpose; or by the people turning out to aid the magistrate upon his command, in case of resistance.

In despotic governments, as well as in all the monarchies of Europe, standing armies are kept up to execute the commands of the prince or the magistrate, and are employed for this purpose when occasion requires: But they have always proved the destruction of liberty, and [are] abhorrent to the spirit of a free republic. In England, where they depend upon the parliament for their annual support, they have always been complained of as oppressive and unconstitutional, and are seldom employed in executing of the laws; never except on extraordinary occasions, and then under the direction of a civil magistrate.

A free republic will never keep a standing army to execute its laws. It must depend upon the support of its citizens. But when a government is to receive its support from the aid of the citizens, it must be so constructed as to have the confidence, respect, and affection of the people. Men who, upon the call of the magistrate, offer themselves to execute the laws, are influenced to do it either by affection to the government, or from fear; where a standing army is at hand to punish offenders, every man is actuated by the latter principle, and therefore, when the magistrate calls, will obey: but, where this is not the case, the government must rest for its support upon the confidence and respect which the people have for their government and laws. The body of the people being attached, the government will always be sufficient to support and execute its laws, and to operate upon the fears of any faction which may be opposed to it, not only to prevent an opposition to the execution of the laws themselves, but also to compel the most of them to aid the magistrate; but the people will not be likely to have such confidence in their rulers, in a republic so extensive as the United States, as necessary for these purposes. The confidence which the people have in their rulers, in a free republic, arises from their knowing them, from their being responsible to them for their conduct, and from the power they have of displacing them when they misbehave: but in a republic of the extent of this continent, the people in general would be acquainted with very few of their rulers: the people at large would know little of their proceedings, and it would be extremely difficult to change them. The people in Georgia and New-Hampshire would not know one another's mind, and therefore could not act in concert to enable them to effect a general change of representatives. The different parts of so extensive a country could not possibly be made acquainted with the conduct of their representatives, nor be informed of the reasons upon which measures were founded. The consequence will be, they will have no confidence in their legislature, suspect them of ambitious views, be jealous of every measure they adopt, and will not support the laws they pass. Hence the government will be nerveless and inefficient, and no way will be left to render it otherwise, but by establishing an armed force to execute the laws at the point of the bayonet—a government of all others the most to be dreaded.

In a republic of such vast extent as the United-States, the legislature cannot attend to the various concerns and wants of its different parts. It cannot be sufficiently numerous to be acquainted with the local condition and wants of the different districts, and if it could, it is impossible it should have sufficient time to attend to and provide for all the variety of cases of this nature, that would be continually arising.

In so extensive a republic, the great officers of government would soon become above the controul of the people, and abuse their power to the purpose of aggrandizing themselves, and oppressing them. The trust committed to the executive offices, in a country of the extent of the United-States, must be various and of magnitude. The command of all the troops and navy of the republic, the appointment of officers, the power of pardoning offences, the collecting of all the public revenues, and the power of expending them, with a number of other powers, must be lodged and exercised in every state, in the hands of a few. When these are attended with great honor and emolument, as they always will be in large states, so as greatly to interest men to pursue them, and to be proper objects for ambitious and designing men, such men will be ever restless in their pursuit after them. They will use the power, when they have acquired it, to the purposes of gratifying their own interest and ambition, and it is scarcely possible, in a very large republic, to call them to account for their misconduct, or to prevent their abuse of power.

These are some of the reasons by which it appears, that a free republic cannot long subsist over a country of the great extent of these states. If then this new constitution is calculated to consolidate the thirteen states into one, as it evidently is, it ought not to be adopted.

Though I am of opinion, that it is a sufficient objection to this government, to reject it, that it creates the whole union into one government, under the form of a republic, yet if this objection was obviated, there are exceptions to it, which are so material and fundamental, that they ought to determine every man, who is a friend to the liberty and happiness of mankind, not to adopt it. I beg the candid and dispassionate attention of my countrymen while I state these objections—they are such as have obtruded themselves upon my mind upon a careful attention to the matter, and such as I sincerely believe are well founded. There are many objections, of small moment, of which I shall take no notice—perfection is not to be expected in any thing that is the production of man—and if I did not in my conscience believe that this scheme was defective in the fundamental principles—in the foundation upon which a free and equal government must rest—I would hold my peace.

BRUTUS
October 18, 1787

Presidents and Vice Presidents

	PRESIDENT	VICE PRESIDENT		PRESIDENT	VICE PRESIDENT
1	George Washington *(Federalist 1789)*	John Adams *(Federalist 1789)*	12	Zachary Taylor *(Whig 1849)*	Millard Fillmore *(Whig 1849)*
2	John Adams *(Federalist 1797)*	Thomas Jefferson *(Dem.-Rep. 1797)*	13	Millard Fillmore *(Whig 1850)*	
3	Thomas Jefferson *(Dem.-Rep. 1801)*	Aaron Burr *(Dem.-Rep. 1801)*	14	Franklin Pierce *(Democratic 1853)*	William R. D. King *(Democratic 1853)*
		George Clinton *(Dem.-Rep. 1805)*	15	James Buchanan *(Democratic 1857)*	John C. Breckinridge *(Democratic 1857)*
4	James Madison *(Dem.-Rep. 1809)*	George Clinton *(Dem.-Rep. 1809)*	16	Abraham Lincoln *(Republican 1861)*	Hannibal Hamlin *(Republican 1861)*
		Elbridge Gerry *(Dem.-Rep. 1813)*			Andrew Johnson *(Unionist 1865)*
5	James Monroe *(Dem.-Rep. 1817)*	Daniel D. Tompkins *(Dem.-Rep. 1817)*	17	Andrew Johnson *(Unionist 1865)*	
6	John Quincy Adams *(Dem.-Rep. 1825)*	John C. Calhoun *(Dem.-Rep. 1825)*	18	Ulysses S. Grant *(Republican 1869)*	Schuyler Colfax *(Republican 1869)*
7	Andrew Jackson *(Democratic 1829)*	John C. Calhoun *(Democratic 1829)*			Henry Wilson *(Republican 1873)*
		Martin Van Buren *(Democratic 1833)*	19	Rutherford B. Hayes *(Republican 1877)*	William A. Wheeler *(Republican 1877)*
8	Martin Van Buren *(Democratic 1837)*	Richard M. Johnson *(Democratic 1837)*	20	James A. Garfield *(Republican 1881)*	Chester A. Arthur *(Republican 1881)*
9	William H. Harrison *(Whig 1841)*	John Tyler *(Whig 1841)*	21	Chester A. Arthur *(Republican 1881)*	
10	John Tyler *(Whig and Democratic 1841)*		22	Grover Cleveland *(Democratic 1885)*	Thomas A. Hendricks *(Democratic 1885)*
11	James K. Polk *(Democratic 1845)*	George M. Dallas *(Democratic 1845)*	23	Benjamin Harrison *(Republican 1889)*	Levi P. Morton *(Republican 1889)*

	PRESIDENT	VICE PRESIDENT		PRESIDENT	VICE PRESIDENT
24	Grover Cleveland *(Democratic 1893)*	Adlai E. Stevenson *(Democratic 1893)*	34	Dwight D. Eisenhower *(Republican 1953)*	Richard M. Nixon *(Republican 1953)*
25	William McKinley *(Republican 1897)*	Garret A. Hobart *(Republican 1897)*	35	John F. Kennedy *(Democratic 1961)*	Lyndon B. Johnson *(Democratic 1961)*
		Theodore Roosevelt *(Republican 1901)*	36	Lyndon B. Johnson *(Democratic 1963)*	Hubert H. Humphrey *(Democratic 1965)*
26	Theodore Roosevelt *(Republican 1901)*	Charles W. Fairbanks *(Republican 1905)*	37	Richard M. Nixon *(Republican 1969)*	Spiro T. Agnew *(Republican 1969)*
27	William H. Taft *(Republican 1909)*	James S. Sherman *(Republican 1909)*			Gerald R. Ford *(Republican 1973)*
28	Woodrow Wilson *(Democratic 1913)*	Thomas R. Marshall *(Democratic 1913)*	38	Gerald R. Ford *(Republican 1974)*	Nelson Rockefeller *(Republican 1974)*
29	Warren G. Harding *(Republican 1921)*	Calvin Coolidge *(Republican 1921)*	39	James E. Carter *(Democratic 1977)*	Walter Mondale *(Democratic 1977)*
30	Calvin Coolidge *(Republican 1923)*	Charles G. Dawes *(Republican 1925)*	40	Ronald Reagan *(Republican 1981)*	George H. W. Bush *(Republican 1981)*
31	Herbert Hoover *(Republican 1929)*	Charles Curtis *(Republican 1929)*	41	George H. W. Bush *(Republican 1989)*	J. Danforth Quayle *(Republican 1989)*
32	Franklin D. Roosevelt *(Democratic 1933)*	John Nance Garner *(Democratic 1933)*	42	William J. Clinton *(Democratic 1993)*	Albert Gore, Jr. *(Democratic 1993)*
		Henry A. Wallace *(Democratic 1941)*	43	George W. Bush *(Republican 2001)*	Richard Cheney *(Republican 2001)*
		Harry S. Truman *(Democratic 1945)*	44	Barack H. Obama *(Democratic 2009)*	Joseph R. Biden, Jr. *(Democratic 2009)*
33	Harry S. Truman *(Democratic 1945)*	Alben W. Barkley *(Democratic 1949)*	45	Donald J. Trump *(Republican 2017)*	Michael R. Pence *(Republican 2017)*

glossary

affirmative action government policies or programs that seek to redress past injustices against specified groups by making special efforts to provide members of those groups with access to educational and employment opportunities

agency representation a type of representation in which a representative is held accountable to a constituency if he or she fails to represent that constituency properly; this is incentive for the representative to provide good representation when his or her personal backgrounds, views, and interests differ from those of his or her constituency

agenda setting the power of the media to bring public attention to particular issues and problems

agents of socialization social institutions, including families and schools, that help to shape individuals' basic political beliefs and values

amendment a change added to a bill, law, or constitution

amicus curiae literally, "friend of the court"; individuals or groups who are not parties to a lawsuit but who seek to assist the Supreme Court in reaching a decision by presenting additional briefs

Antifederalists those who favored strong state governments and a weak national government and who were opponents of the Constitution proposed at the American Constitutional Convention of 1787

antitrust policy government regulation of large businesses that have established monopolies

appeasement the effort to forestall war by giving in to the demands of a hostile power

apportionment the process, occurring after every decennial census, that allocates congressional seats among the 50 states

appropriations the amounts of money approved by Congress in statutes (bills) that each unit or agency of government can spend

Articles of Confederation America's first written constitution; served as the basis for America's national government until 1789

attitude (or opinion) a specific preference on a particular issue

authoritarian government a system of rule in which the government recognizes no formal limits but may nevertheless be restrained by the power of other social institutions

autocracy a form of government in which a single individual—a king, queen, or dictator—rules

ballot initiative a proposed law or policy change that is placed on the ballot by citizens or interest groups for a popular vote

bandwagon effect a shift in electoral support to the candidate whom public opinion polls report as the front-runner

bicameral having a legislative assembly composed of two chambers or houses, distinguished from *unicameral*

bilateral treaties treaties made between two nations

bill a proposed law that has been sponsored by a member of Congress and submitted to the clerk of the House or Senate

bill of attainder a law that declares a person guilty of a crime without a trial

Bill of Rights the first 10 amendments to the U.S. Constitution, ratified in 1791; they ensure certain rights and liberties to the people

block grants federal grants-in-aid that allow states considerable discretion in how the funds are spent

briefs written documents in which attorneys explain, using case precedents, why the court should find in favor of their client

broadcast media television, radio, or other media that transmit audio and/or video content to the public

Brown v. Board of Education the 1954 Supreme Court decision that struck down the "separate but equal" doctrine as fundamentally unequal; this case eliminated state power to use race as a criterion of discrimination in law and provided the national government with the power to intervene by exercising strict regulatory policies against discriminatory actions

budget deficit amount by which government spending exceeds government revenue in a fiscal year

bureaucracy the complex structure of offices, tasks, rules, and principles of organization that is employed by all large-scale institutions to coordinate the work of their personnel

Bush Doctrine foreign policy based on the idea that the United States should take preemptive action against threats to its national security

Cabinet the secretaries, or chief administrators, of the major departments of the federal government; Cabinet secretaries are appointed by the president with the consent of the Senate

campaign an effort by political candidates and their supporters to win the backing of donors, political activists, and voters in their quest for political office

categorical grants congressional grants given to states and localities on the condition that expenditures be limited to a problem or group specified by law

caucus (political) a normally closed political party business meeting of citizens or lawmakers to select candidates, elect officers, plan strategy, or make decisions regarding legislative matters

caucuses (congressional) associations of members of Congress based on party, interest, or social group, such as gender or race

checks and balances mechanisms through which each branch of government is able to participate in and influence the activities of the other branches; major examples include the presidential veto power over congressional legislation, the power of the Senate to approve presidential appointments, and judicial review of congressional enactments

chief justice justice on the Supreme Court who presides over the Court's public sessions and whose official title is "chief justice of the United States"

citizen groups groups that claim they serve the general good rather than only their own particular interests

citizen journalism news reported and distributed by citizens, rather than professional journalists and for-profit news organizations

citizenship informed and active membership in a political community

civil law the branch of law that deals with disputes that do not involve criminal penalties

civil liberties areas of personal freedom constitutionally protected from government interference

civil rights obligation imposed on government to take positive action to protect citizens from any illegal action of government agencies and of other private citizens

class-action suit a legal action by which a group or class of individuals with common interests can file a suit on behalf of everyone who shares that interest

"clear and present danger" test used to determine whether speech is protected or unprotected, based on its capacity to present a "clear and present danger" to society

closed primary a primary election in which voters can participate in the nomination of candidates but only of the party in which they are enrolled for a period of time prior to primary day

closed rule a provision by the House Rules Committee limiting or prohibiting the introduction of amendments during debate

cloture a rule or process in a legislative body aimed at ending debate on a given bill; in the U.S. Senate, 60 senators (three-fifths) must agree in order to impose a time limit and end debate

Cold War the period of struggle between the United States and the former Soviet Union lasting from the late 1940s to about 1990

collective goods benefits sought by groups that are broadly available and cannot be denied to nonmembers

commander in chief the role of the president as commander of the national military and the state National Guard units (when called into service)

commerce clause Article I, Section 8, of the Constitution, which delegates to Congress the power "to regulate commerce with foreign nations, and among the several States and with the Indian tribes"; this clause was interpreted by the Supreme Court in favor of national power over the economy

committee markup the session in which a congressional committee rewrites legislation to incorporate changes discussed during hearings on a bill

common law law made through court precedent rather than legislative enactments

concurrent powers authority possessed by *both* state and national governments, such as the power to levy taxes

confederation a system of government in which states retain sovereign authority except for the powers expressly delegated to the national government

conference a gathering of House Republicans every two years to elect their House leaders; Democrats call their gathering the "caucus"

conference committees joint committees created to work out a compromise on House and Senate versions of a piece of legislation

conservative today this term refers to those who generally support the social and economic status quo and are suspicious of efforts to introduce new political formulas and economic arrangements; conservatives believe that a large and powerful government poses a threat to citizens' freedom

constituency the residents in the area from which an official is elected

constitutional government a system of rule in which formal and effective limits are placed on the powers of the government

containment a policy designed to curtail the political and military expansion of a hostile power

contracting power the power of government to set conditions on companies seeking to sell goods or services to government agencies

contributory programs social programs financed in whole or in part by taxation or other mandatory contributions by their present or future recipients

cooperative federalism a type of federalism existing since the New Deal era in which grants-in-aid have been used strategically to encourage states and localities (without commanding them) to pursue nationally defined goals; also known as *intergovernmental cooperation*

cost-of-living adjustments (COLAs) changes made to the level of benefits of a government program based on the rate of inflation

court of appeals a court that hears appeals of trial court decisions

criminal law the branch of law that regulates the conduct of individuals, defines crimes, and specifies punishment for proscribed conduct

de facto literally, "by fact"; refers to practices that occur even when there is no legal enforcement, such as school segregation in much of the United States today

de jure literally, "by law"; refers to legally enforced practices, such as school segregation in the South before the 1960s

dealignment a movement away from the major political parties; a decline in partisan attachment

defendant the one against whom a complaint is brought in a criminal or civil case

delegate a representative who votes according to the preferences of his or her constituency

delegated powers constitutional powers that are assigned to one governmental agency but that are exercised by another agency with the express permission of the first

democracy a system of rule that permits citizens to play a significant part in the governmental process, usually through the election of key public officials

department the largest subunit of the executive branch; the secretaries of the 15 departments form the Cabinet

deregulation a policy of reducing or eliminating regulatory restraints on the conduct of individuals or private institutions

devolution a policy to remove a program from one level of government by delegating it or passing it down to a lower level of government, such as from the national government to the state and local governments

digital citizen a daily Internet user with broadband (high-speed) home Internet access and the technology and literacy skills to go online for employment, news, politics, entertainment, commerce, and other activities

digital divide the gap in access to the Internet among demographic groups based on education, income, age, geographic location, and race/ethnicity

digital political participation activities designed to influence politics using the Internet, including visiting a candidate's website, organizing events online, and signing an online petition

diplomacy the representation of a government to other governments

direct democracy a system of rule that permits citizens to vote directly on laws and policies

discretionary spending federal spending on programs that are controlled through the regular budget process

discrimination the use of any unreasonable and unjust criterion of exclusion

dissenting opinion a decision written by a justice in the minority in a particular case in which the justice wishes to express his or her reasoning in the case

divided government the condition in American government wherein the presidency is controlled by one party while the opposing party controls one or both houses of Congress

double jeopardy the Fifth Amendment right providing that a person cannot be tried twice for the same crime

dual federalism the system of government that prevailed in the United States from 1789 to 1937 in which most fundamental governmental powers were shared between the federal and state governments

due process of law the right of every individual against arbitrary action by national or state governments

early voting the option in some states to cast a vote at a polling place or by mail before the election

elastic clause the concluding paragraph of Article I, Section 8, of the Constitution (also known as the "necessary and proper clause"), which provides Congress with the authority to make all laws "necessary and proper" to carry out its enumerated powers

electoral college the presidential electors from each state who meet after the general election to cast ballots for president and vice president

electoral realignment the point in history when a new party supplants the ruling party, becoming in turn the dominant political force; in the United States, this has tended to occur roughly every 30 years

eminent domain the right of government to take private property for public use

entitlement a legal obligation of the federal government to provide payments to individuals, or groups of individuals, according to eligibility criteria or benefit rules

equal protection clause provision of the Fourteenth Amendment guaranteeing citizens "the equal protection of the laws"; this clause has been the basis for the civil rights of African Americans, women, and other groups

equal time rule the requirement that broadcasters provide candidates for the same political office equal opportunities to communicate their messages to the public

equality of opportunity a widely shared American ideal that all people should have the freedom to use whatever talents and wealth they have to reach their fullest potential

establishment clause the First Amendment clause that says that "Congress shall make no law respecting an establishment of religion"; this law means that a "wall of separation" exists between church and state

ex post facto laws laws that declare an action to be illegal after it has been committed

exclusionary rule the ability of courts to exclude evidence obtained in violation of the Fourth Amendment

executive agreement an agreement, made between the president and another country, that has the force of a treaty but does not require the Senate's "advice and consent"

Executive Office of the President (EOP) the permanent agencies that perform defined management tasks for the president; created in 1939, the EOP includes the OMB, the CEA, the NSC, and other agencies

executive order a rule or regulation issued by the president that has the effect and formal status of legislation

executive privilege the claim that confidential communications between a president and close advisers should not be revealed without the consent of the president

expressed powers specific powers granted by the Constitution to Congress (Article I, Section 8) and to the president (Article II)

federal funds rate the interest rate on loans between banks that the Federal Reserve Board influences by affecting the supply of money available

Federal Reserve System a system of 12 Federal Reserve banks that facilitates exchanges of cash, checks, and credit; regulates member banks; and uses monetary policies to fight inflation and deflation

federalism a system of government in which power is divided, by a constitution, between a central government and regional governments

Federalist Papers a series of essays written by Alexander Hamilton, James Madison, and John Jay supporting ratification of the Constitution

Federalists those who favored a strong national government and supported the Constitution proposed at the American Constitutional Convention of 1787

Fifteenth Amendment one of three Civil War amendments; it guaranteed voting rights for African American men

fighting words speech that directly incites damaging conduct

filibuster a tactic used by members of the Senate to prevent action on legislation they oppose by continuously holding the floor and speaking until the majority backs down; once given the floor, senators have unlimited time to speak, and it requires a vote of three-fifths of the Senate to end a filibuster

fiscal policy the government's use of taxing, monetary, and spending powers to manipulate the economy

501(c)(4)s politically active nonprofits; under federal law, these nonprofits can spend unlimited amounts on political campaigns and not disclose their donors as long as their activities are not coordinated with the candidate campaigns and political activities are not their primary purpose

527 committees nonprofit independent groups established specifically to receive and disburse funds to influence the nomination, election, or defeat of candidates; named after Section 527 of the Internal Revenue Code, which defines and provides tax-exempt status for nonprofit advocacy groups

formula grants grants-in-aid in which a formula is used to determine the amount of federal funds a state or local government will receive

Fourteenth Amendment one of three Civil War amendments; it guaranteed equal protection and due process

framing the power of the media to influence how events and issues are interpreted

free exercise clause the First Amendment clause that protects a citizen's right to believe and practice whatever religion he or she chooses

free riders those who enjoy the benefits of collective goods but did not participate in acquiring or providing them

full faith and credit clause provision from Article IV, Section 1, of the Constitution requiring that the states normally honor the public acts and judicial decisions that take place in another state

gender gap a distinctive pattern of voting behavior reflecting the differences in views between women and men

General Agreement on Tariffs and Trade (GATT) international trade organization, in existence from 1947 to 1995, that set many of the rules governing international trade

general election a regularly scheduled election involving most districts in the nation or state, in which voters select officeholders; in the United States, general elections for national office and most state and local offices are held on the first Tuesday after the first Monday in November in even-numbered years (every four years for presidential elections)

general revenue sharing the process by which one unit of government yields a portion of its tax income to another unit of government, according to an established formula; revenue sharing typically involves the national government providing money to state governments

gerrymandering the apportionment of voters in districts in such a way as to give unfair advantage to one racial or ethnic group or political party

government institutions and procedures through which a territory and its people are ruled

government corporation government agency that performs a market-oriented public service and raises revenues to fund its activities

grand jury jury that determines whether sufficient evidence is available to justify a trial; grand juries do not rule on the accused's guilt or innocence

grants-in-aid programs through which Congress provides money to state and local governments on the condition that the funds be employed for purposes defined by the federal government

grassroots mobilization a lobbying campaign in which a group mobilizes its membership to contact government officials in support of the group's position

grassroots politics political campaigns that operate at the local level, often using face-to-face communication to generate interest and momentum by citizens

Great Compromise the agreement reached at the Constitutional Convention of 1787 that gave each state an equal number of senators regardless of its population but linked representation in the House of Representatives to population

gross domestic product (GDP) the total value of goods and services produced within a country

habeas corpus a court order demanding that an individual in custody be brought into court and shown the cause for detention

home rule power delegated by the state to a local unit of government to manage its own affairs

impeachment the formal charge by the House of Representatives that a government official has committed "Treason, Bribery, or other high Crimes and Misdemeanors"

implementation the efforts of departments and agencies to translate laws into specific bureaucratic rules and actions

implied powers powers derived from the necessary and proper clause of Article I, Section 8, of the Constitution; such powers are not specifically expressed but are implied through the expansive interpretation of delegated powers

in-kind benefits noncash goods and services provided to needy individuals and families by the federal government

incumbency holding the political office for which one is running

incumbent a candidate running for re-election to a position that he or she already holds

independent agency agency that is not part of a Cabinet department

indexing periodic process of adjusting social benefits or wages to account for increases in the cost of living

inflation a consistent increase in the general level of prices

informational benefits special newsletters, periodicals, training programs, conferences, and other information provided to members of groups to entice others to join

inherent powers powers claimed by a president that are not expressed in the Constitution but are inferred from it

institutional advertising advertising designed to create a positive image of an organization

interest group individuals who organize to influence the government's programs and policies

intermediate scrutiny a test used by the Supreme Court in gender discrimination cases that places the burden of proof partially on the government and partially on the challengers to show that the law in question is unconstitutional

International Monetary Fund (IMF) an institution established in 1944 that provides loans and facilitates international monetary exchange

iron triangle the stable, cooperative relationship that often develops among a congressional committee, an administrative agency, and one or more supportive interest groups; not all of these relationships are triangular, but the iron triangle is the most typical

isolationism avoidance of involvement in the affairs of other nations

issue network a loose network of elected leaders, public officials, activists, and interest groups drawn together by a specific policy issue

Jim Crow laws laws enacted by southern states following Reconstruction that discriminated against African Americans

joint committees legislative committees formed of members of both the House and Senate

judicial activism judicial philosophy that posits that the Court should go beyond the words of the Constitution or a statute to consider the broader societal implications of its decisions

judicial restraint judicial philosophy whose adherents refuse to go beyond the clear words of the Constitution in interpreting the document's meaning

judicial review the power of the courts to review and, if necessary, declare actions of the legislative and executive branches invalid or unconstitutional; the Supreme Court asserted this power in *Marbury v. Madison* (1803)

jurisdiction the sphere of a court's power and authority

Keynesians followers of the economic theories of John Maynard Keynes, who argued that the government can stimulate the economy by increasing public spending or by cutting taxes

Kitchen Cabinet an informal group of advisers to whom the president turns for counsel and guidance; members of the official Cabinet may or may not also be members of the Kitchen Cabinet

laissez-faire capitalism an economic system in which the means of production and distribution are privately owned and operated for profit with minimal or no government interference

legislative initiative the president's inherent power to bring a legislative agenda before Congress

Lemon test a rule articulated in *Lemon v. Kurtzman* that government action toward religion is permissible if it is secular in purpose, neither promotes nor inhibits the practice of religion, and does not lead to "excessive entanglement" with religion

libel a written statement made in "reckless disregard of the truth" that is considered damaging to a victim because it is "malicious, scandalous, and defamatory"

liberal today this term refers to those who generally support social and political reform, governmental intervention in the economy, more economic equality, expansion of federal social services, and greater concern for consumers and the environment

libertarian someone who emphasizes freedom and believes in voluntary association with small government

liberty freedom from governmental control

limited government a principle of constitutional government; a government whose powers are defined and limited by a constitution

lobbying a strategy by which organized interests seek to influence the passage of legislation by exerting direct pressure on government officials

logrolling a legislative practice whereby agreements are made between legislators in voting for or against a bill; vote trading

loophole incentive to individuals and businesses to reduce their tax liabilities by investing their money in areas the government designates

majority leader the elected leader of the majority party in the House of Representatives or in the Senate; in the House, the majority leader is subordinate in the party hierarchy to the Speaker of the House

majority party the party that holds the majority of legislative seats in either the House or the Senate

majority rule, minority rights the democratic principle that a government follows the preferences of the majority of voters but protects the interests of the minority

majority system a type of electoral system in which, to win a seat in the parliament or other representative body, a candidate must receive a majority of all the votes cast in the relevant district

majority-minority district an electoral district, such as a congressional district, in which the majority of the constituents belong to racial or ethnic minorities

mandatory spending federal spending that is made up of "uncontrollables," budget items that cannot be controlled through the regular budget process

marketplace of ideas the public forum in which beliefs and ideas are exchanged and compete

material benefits special goods, services, or money provided to members of groups to entice others to join

means testing a procedure by which potential beneficiaries of a public-assistance program establish their eligibility by demonstrating a genuine need for the assistance

media print and digital forms of communication, including television, newspapers, radio, and the Internet, intended to convey information to large audiences

media monopoly the ownership and control of the media by a few large corporations

Medicaid a federally and state-financed, state-operated program providing medical services to low-income people

Medicare a form of national health insurance for the elderly and the disabled

membership association an organized group in which members play a substantial role, sitting on committees and engaging in group projects

merit system a product of civil service reform, in which appointees to positions in public bureaucracies must objectively be deemed qualified for those positions

midterm elections congressional elections that do not coincide with a presidential election; also called *off-year elections*

minority leader the elected leader of the minority party in the House or Senate

minority party the party that holds the minority of legislative seats in either the House or the Senate

Miranda rule the requirement, articulated by the Supreme Court in *Miranda v. Arizona*, that persons under arrest must be informed prior to police interrogation of their rights to remain silent and to have the benefit of legal counsel

mobilization the process by which large numbers of people are organized for a political activity

monetary policies efforts to regulate the economy through the manipulation of the supply of money and credit; America's most powerful institution in this area of monetary policy is the Federal Reserve Board

monopoly a single firm in a market that controls all the goods and services of that market; absence of competition

mootness a criterion used by courts to screen cases that no longer require resolution

nation-states political entities consisting of a people with some common cultural experience (nation) who also share a common political authority (state), recognized by other sovereignties (nation-states)

national convention convened by the Republican National Committee or the Democratic National Committee to nominate official candidates for president and vice president in the upcoming election, establish party rules, and adopt the party's platform

National Security Council (NSC) a presidential foreign policy advisory council composed of the president, the vice president, the secretary of state, the secretary of defense, and other officials invited by the president

necessary and proper clause Article I, Section 8, of the Constitution, which provides Congress with the authority to make all laws "necessary and proper" to carry out its expressed powers

netroots grassroots online activist organizations that have redefined membership and fund-raising practices and streamlined staff structure

New Federalism attempts by presidents Nixon and Reagan to return power to the states through block grants

New Jersey Plan a framework for the Constitution, introduced by William Paterson, that called for equal state representation in the national legislature regardless of population

news aggregator an application or feed that collects web content such as news headlines, blogs, podcasts, online videos, and more in one location for easy viewing

niche journalism news reporting devoted to a targeted portion (subset) of a journalism market sector or for a portion of readers/viewers based on content or ideological presentation

nomination the process by which political parties select their candidates for election to public office

non-state actors groups other than nation-states that attempt to play a role in the international system; terrorist groups are one type of non-state actor

noncontributory programs social programs that provide assistance to people on the basis of demonstrated need rather than any contribution they have made

North American Free Trade Agreement (NAFTA) trade treaty among the United States, Canada, and Mexico to lower and eliminate tariffs among the three countries

North Atlantic Treaty Organization (NATO) an organization, comprising the United States, Canada, and most of Western Europe, formed in 1949 to counter the perceived threat from the Soviet Union

oligarchy a form of government in which a small group—landowners, military officers, or wealthy merchants—controls most of the governing decisions

open primary a primary election in which the voter can wait until the day of the primary to choose which party to enroll in to select candidates for the general election

open rule a provision by the House Rules Committee that permits floor debate and the addition of new amendments to a bill

open-market operations methods by which the Open Market Committee of the Federal Reserve System buys and sells government securities and other investment instruments to help finance government operations and to reduce or increase the total amount of money circulating in the economy

opinion the written explanation of the Supreme Court's decision in a particular case

oral argument the stage in the Supreme Court procedure in which attorneys for both sides appear before the Court to present their positions and answer questions posed by justices

original jurisdiction the authority to initially consider a case; distinguished from appellate jurisdiction, which is the authority to hear appeals from a lower court's decision

oversight the effort by Congress, through hearings, investigations, and other techniques, to exercise control over the activities of executive agencies

partisanship identification with or support of a particular party or cause

party activists partisans who contribute time, energy, and effort to support their party and its candidates

party identification an individual voter's psychological ties to one party or another

party machines strong party organizations in late nineteenth- and early twentieth-century American cities; these machines were led by often corrupt "bosses" who controlled party nominations and patronage

party organization the formal structure of a political party, including its leadership, election committees, active members, and paid staff

party platform a party document, written at a national convention, that contains party philosophy, principles, and policy positions

party polarization the division between the two major parties on most policy issues, with members of each party unified around their party's positions with little crossover

party unity vote a roll-call vote in the House or Senate in which at least 50 percent of the members of one party take a particular position and are opposed by at least 50 percent of the members of the other party

patronage the resources available to higher officials, usually opportunities to make partisan appointments to offices and to confer grants, licenses, or special favors to supporters

penny press cheap, tabloid-style newspaper produced in the nineteenth century, when mass production of inexpensive newspapers first became possible due to the steam-powered printing press; a penny press newspaper cost one cent compared with other papers, which cost more than five cents

permanent absentee ballots the option in some states to have a ballot sent automatically to your home for each election, rather than having to request an absentee ballot each time

plaintiff the individual or organization that brings a complaint in court

platform a party document, written at a national convention, that contains party philosophy, principles, and positions on issues

plea bargain a negotiated agreement in a criminal case in which a defendant agrees to plead guilty in return for the state's agreement to reduce the severity of the criminal charge or prison sentence the defendant is facing

pluralism the theory that all interests are and should be free to compete for influence in the government; the outcome of this competition is compromise and moderation

plurality system a type of electoral system in which, to win a seat in the parliament or other representative body, a candidate need only receive the most votes in the election, not necessarily a majority of the votes cast

pocket veto a presidential veto that is automatically triggered if the president does not act on a given piece of legislation passed during the final 10 days of a legislative session

police power power reserved to the state government to regulate the health, safety, and morals of its citizens

policy entrepreneur an individual who identifies a problem as a political issue and brings a policy proposal into the political agenda

political action committee (PAC) a private group that raises and distributes funds for use in election campaigns

political culture broadly shared values, beliefs, and attitudes about how the government should function; American political culture emphasizes the values of liberty, equality, and democracy

political efficacy the ability to influence government and politics

political equality the right to participate in politics equally, based on the principle of "one person, one vote"

political ideology a cohesive set of beliefs that forms a general philosophy about the role of government

political parties organized groups that attempt to influence the government by electing their members to important government offices

political socialization the induction of individuals into the political culture; learning the underlying beliefs and values on which the political system is based

politics conflict over the leadership, structure, and policies of governments

popular sovereignty a principle of democracy in which political authority rests ultimately in the hands of the people

pork barrel (or pork) appropriations made by legislative bodies for local projects that are often not needed but that are created so that local representatives can win re-election in their home districts

power influence over a government's leadership, organization, or policies

precedent prior case whose principles are used by judges as the basis for their decision in a present case

preemption the principle that allows the national government to override state or local actions in certain policy areas; in foreign policy, the willingness to strike first in order to prevent an enemy attack

preventive war policy of striking first when a nation fears that a foreign foe is contemplating hostile action

primary elections elections held to select a party's candidate for the general election

priming process of preparing the public to bring specific criteria to mind when evaluating a politician or issue

prior restraint an effort by a governmental agency to block the publication of material it deems libelous or harmful in some other way; censorship; in the United States, the courts forbid prior restraint except under the most extraordinary circumstances

private bill a proposal in Congress to provide a specific person with some kind of relief, such as a special exemption from immigration quotas

privatization a formerly public service that is now provided by a private company but paid for by the government

privileges and immunities clause provision, from Article IV, Section 2, of the Constitution, that a state cannot discriminate against someone from another state or give its own residents special privileges

progressive taxation taxation that hits upper-income brackets more heavily

project grants grant programs in which state and local governments submit proposals to federal agencies and for which funding is provided on a competitive basis

proportional representation a multiple-member district system that allows each political party representation in proportion to its percentage of the total vote

prospective voting voting based on the imagined future performance of a candidate or political party

protest participation that involves assembling crowds to confront a government or other official organization

public goods goods or services that are provided by the government because they either are not supplied by the market or are not supplied in sufficient quantities

public opinion citizens' attitudes about political issues, leaders, institutions, and events

public policy a law, rule, statute, or edict that expresses the government's goals and provides for rewards and punishments to promote those goals' attainment

public-opinion polls scientific instruments for measuring public opinion

purposive benefits selective benefits of group membership that emphasize the purpose and accomplishments of the group

push poll a polling technique in which the questions are designed to shape the respondent's opinion

random digit dialing a polling method in which respondents are selected at random from a list of 10-digit telephone numbers, with every effort made to avoid bias in the construction of the sample

recall a procedure to allow voters to remove state officials from office before their terms expire by circulating petitions to call a vote

redistribution a policy whose objective is to tax or spend in such a way as to reduce the disparities of wealth between the lowest and the highest income brackets

redistributive programs economic policies designed to control the economy through taxing and spending, with the goal of benefiting the poor

redistricting the process of redrawing election districts and redistributing legislative representatives; this happens every 10 years, to reflect shifts in population or in response to legal challenges in existing districts

redlining a practice in which banks refuse to make loans to people living in certain geographic locations

referendum the practice of referring a proposed law passed by a legislature to the vote of the electorate for approval or rejection

regressive taxation taxation that hits lower-income brackets more heavily

regulated federalism a form of federalism in which Congress imposes legislation on states and localities, requiring them to meet national standards

regulatory agency department, bureau, or independent agency whose primary mission is to impose limits, restrictions, or other obligations on the conduct of individuals or companies in the private sector

representative democracy (republic) a system of government in which the populace selects representatives, who play a significant role in governmental decision making

reserved powers powers, derived from the Tenth Amendment to the Constitution, that are not specifically delegated to the national government or denied to the states

retrospective voting voting based on the past performance of a candidate or political party

revenue agency an agency responsible for collecting taxes. Examples include the Internal Revenue Service for income taxes; the U.S. Customs Service for tariffs and other taxes on imported goods; and the Bureau of Alcohol, Tobacco, Firearms and Explosives for collection of taxes on the sale of those particular products

right of rebuttal a Federal Communications Commission regulation giving individuals the right to have the opportunity to respond to personal attacks made on a radio or television broadcast

right to privacy the right to be left alone, which has been interpreted by the Supreme Court to entail individual access to birth control and abortions

roll-call vote a vote in which each legislator's yes or no vote is recorded as the clerk calls the names of the members alphabetically

runoff election a "second-round" election in which voters choose between the top two candidates from the first round

same-day registration the option in some states to register on the day of the election, at the polling place, rather than in advance of the election

sample a small group selected by researchers to represent the most important characteristics of an entire population

sampling error (or margin of error) polling error that arises based on the small size of the sample

select committees (usually) temporary legislative committees set up to highlight or investigate a particular issue or address an issue not within the jurisdiction of existing committees

selection bias (news) the tendency to focus news coverage on only one aspect of an event or issue, avoiding coverage of other aspects

selection bias (surveys) polling error that arises when the sample is not representative of the population being studied, which creates errors in overrepresenting or underrepresenting some opinions

selective incorporation the process by which different protections in the Bill of Rights were incorporated into the Fourteenth Amendment, thus guaranteeing citizens protection from state as well as national governments

senatorial courtesy the practice whereby the president, before formally nominating a person for a federal judgeship, seeks the indication that senators from the candidate's own state support the nomination

seniority the ranking given to an individual on the basis of length of continuous service on a committee in Congress

"separate but equal" rule doctrine that public accommodations could be segregated by race but still be considered equal

separation of powers the division of governmental power among several institutions that must cooperate in decision making

signing statements announcements made by the president when signing bills into law, often presenting the president's interpretation of the law

simple random sample (or probability sample) a method used by pollsters to select a representative sample in which every individual in the population has an equal probability of being selected as a respondent

slander an oral statement made in "reckless disregard of the truth" that is considered damaging to the victim because it is "malicious, scandalous, and defamatory"

social desirability effect the effect that results when respondents in a survey report what they expect the interviewer wishes to hear rather than what they believe

social media web- and mobile-based technologies that are used to turn communication into interactive dialogue among organizations, communities, and individuals; social media technologies take on many different forms including text, blogs, podcasts, photographs, streaming video, Facebook, and Twitter

Social Security a contributory welfare program into which working Americans contribute a percentage of their wages and from which they receive cash benefits after retirement or if they become disabled

socialist someone who generally believes in social ownership, strong government, free markets, and reducing economic inequality

socioeconomic status status in society based on level of education, income, and occupational prestige

sociological representation a type of representation in which representatives have the same racial, gender, ethnic, religious, or educational backgrounds as their constituents; it is based on the principle that if two individuals are similar in background, character, interests, and perspectives, then one can correctly represent the other's views

soft money money contributed directly to political parties and other organizations for political activities, such as voter mobilization drives, that is not regulated by federal campaign spending laws

solicitor general the top government lawyer in all cases before the Supreme Court where the government is a party

solidary benefits selective benefits of group membership that emphasize friendship, networking, and consciousness-raising

Speaker of the House the chief presiding officer of the House of Representatives; the Speaker is the most important party and House leader and can influence the legislative agenda, the fate of individual pieces of legislation, and members' positions within the House

"speech plus" speech accompanied by conduct such as sit-ins, picketing, and demonstrations; protection of this form of speech under the First Amendment is conditional, and restrictions imposed by state or local authorities are acceptable if properly balanced by considerations of public order

staff agencies legislative support agencies responsible for policy analysis

staff organization a type of membership group in which a professional staff conducts most of the group's activities

standing the right of an individual or organization to initiate a court case, on the basis of having a substantial stake in the outcome

standing committee a permanent committee with the power to propose and write legislation that covers a particular subject, such as finance or agriculture

stare decisis literally, "let the decision stand"; the doctrine that a previous decision by a court applies as a precedent in similar cases until that decision is overruled

states' rights the principle that the states should oppose the increasing authority of the national government; this principle was most popular in the period before the Civil War

straight-ticket voting selecting candidates from the same political party for all offices on the ballot

strict scrutiny a test used by the Supreme Court in racial discrimination cases and other cases involving civil liberties and civil rights that places the burden of proof on the government rather than on the challengers to show that the law in question is constitutional

subsidies government grants of cash or other valuable commodities, such as land, to an individual or an organization; used to promote activities desired by the government, reward political support, or buy off political opposition

suffrage the right to vote; also called *franchise*

Super PAC an independent political action committee that may raise unlimited sums of money from corporations, unions, and individuals but is not permitted to contribute to or coordinate directly with parties or candidates

Supplemental Nutrition Assistance Program (SNAP) the largest antipoverty program, which provides recipients with a debit card for food at most grocery stores; formerly known as food stamps

supply-side economics an economic theory that posits that reducing the marginal rate of taxation will create a productive economy by promoting levels of work and investment that would otherwise be discouraged by higher taxes

supremacy clause Article VI of the Constitution, which states that laws passed by the national government and all treaties are the supreme law of the land and superior to all laws adopted by any state or any subdivision

supreme court the highest court in a particular state or in the United States; this court primarily serves an appellate function

tariff a tax on imported goods

tax expenditures government subsidies provided to employers and employees through tax deductions for amounts spent on health insurance and other benefits

term limits legally prescribed limits on the number of terms an elected official can serve

third parties parties that organize to compete against the two major American political parties

Thirteenth Amendment one of three Civil War amendments; it abolished slavery

Three-Fifths Compromise the agreement reached at the Constitutional Convention of 1787 that stipulated that for purposes of the apportionment of congressional seats only three-fifths of slaves would be counted

tort case a law suit by one individual (the plaintiff) demanding compensation for harm allegedly caused by the actions of another (the defendant)

totalitarian government a system of rule in which the government recognizes no formal limits on its power and seeks to absorb or eliminate other social institutions that might challenge it

town hall meeting an informal public meeting in which candidates meet with ordinary citizens; allows candidates to deliver messages without the presence of journalists or commentators

traditional political participation activities designed to influence government, including voting and face-to-face activities such as volunteering for a campaign or working on behalf of a candidate or political organization

trial court the first court to hear a criminal or civil case

trustee a representative who votes based on what he or she thinks is best for his or her constituency

turnout the percentage of eligible individuals who actually vote

two-party system a political system in which only two parties have a realistic opportunity to compete effectively for control

tyranny oppressive government that employs cruel and unjust use of power and authority

uncontrollables budgetary items that are beyond the control of budgetary committees and can be controlled only by substantive legislative action in Congress; some uncontrollables, such as interest on the debt, are beyond the power of Congress because the terms of payments are set in contracts

unfunded mandates regulations or conditions for receiving grants that impose costs on state and local governments for which they are not reimbursed by the federal government

unitary system a centralized government system in which lower levels of government have little power independent of the national government

United Nations (UN) an organization of nations founded in 1945 to be a channel for negotiation and a means of settling international disputes peaceably; the UN has had frequent successes in providing a forum for negotiation and, on some occasions, a means of preventing international conflicts from spreading; on a number of occasions, the UN has been a convenient cover for U.S. foreign policy goals

values (or beliefs) basic principles that shape a person's opinions about political issues and events

veto the president's constitutional power to turn down acts of Congress; a presidential veto may be overridden by a two-thirds vote of each house of Congress

Virginia Plan a framework for the Constitution, introduced by Edmund Randolph, that called for representation in the national legislature based on the population of each state

War Powers Resolution a resolution of Congress that the president can send troops into action abroad only by authorization of Congress or if American troops are already under attack or serious threat

whip a party member in the House or Senate responsible for coordinating the party's legislative strategy, building support for key issues, and counting votes

White House staff analysts and advisers to the president, each of whom is often given the title "special assistant"

Word Trade Organization (WTO) international organization promoting free trade that grew out of the General Agreement on Tariffs and Trade

writ of certiorari a decision of at least four of the nine Supreme Court justices to review a decision of a lower court; *certiorari* is Latin, meaning "to make more certain"

writ of habeas corpus a court order that the individual in custody be brought into court and shown the cause for detention; habeas corpus is guaranteed by the Constitution and can be suspended only in cases of rebellion or invasion

endnotes

Chapter 1

1. Pew Research Center, "Beyond Distrust: How Americans View Their Government," November 23, 2015, www.people-press.org/2015/11/23/1-trust-in-government-1958-2015/ (accessed 4/10/16).
2. Pew Research Center, "Beyond Distrust."
3. ANES Guide to Public Opinion and Electoral Behavior, "Trust the Federal Government, 1958–2008," www.electionstudies.org/nesguide/toptable/tab5a_1.htm (accessed 6/8/12).
4. ANES Guide to Public Opinion and Electoral Behavior, "Trust the Federal Government."
5. *New York Times*/CBS News Poll, "Americans' Approval of Congress Drops to Single Digits," October 25, 2011, www.nytimes.com/interactive/2011/10/25/us/politics/approval-of-congress-drops-to-single-digits.html?ref5politics (accessed 6/8/12).
6. Pew Research Center, "Beyond Distrust."
7. Joseph S. Nye, Jr., "Introduction: The Decline of Confidence in Government," in *Why People Don't Trust Government*, ed. Joseph S. Nye, Jr., Philip D. Zelikow, and David C. King (Cambridge, MA: Harvard University Press, 1997), 4.
8. Pew Research Center, "Beyond Distrust."
9. Pew Research Center, "Beyond Distrust."
10. This definition is taken from Norman H. Nie, Jane Junn, and Kenneth Stehlik-Barry, *Education and Democratic Citizenship in America* (Chicago: University of Chicago Press, 1996).
11. Kaiser Family Foundation, "Poll Finds 62% of Americans Approve of the Supreme Court's Decision to Continue Allowing ACA Health Insurance Subsidies in All States, While 32% Disapprove," July 1, 2015, kff.org/health-reform/press-release/poll-finds-62-of-americans-approve-of-the-supreme-courts-decision-to-continue-allowing-aca-health-insurance-subsidies-in-all-states-while-32-disapprove/ (accessed 11/10/15).
12. John B. Horrigan and Lee Rainie, "Americans' Views on Open Government Data," Pew Research Center, April 21, 2015, www.pewinternet.org/2015/04/21/open-government-data/ (accessed 7/22/15).
13. Arch Puddington and Tyler Roylance, *Freedom in the World, 2016*, freedomhouse.org/sites/default/files/FH_FITW_Report_2016.pdf (accessed 4/10/16).
14. Eugen Weber, *Peasants into Frenchmen: The Modernization of Rural France, 1870–1914* (Stanford, CA: Stanford University Press, 1976), chap. 5.
15. V. O. Key, *Politics, Parties, and Pressure Groups* (New York: Crowell, 1964), 201.
16. Harold Lasswell, *Politics: Who Gets What, When, How* (New York: Meridian Books, 1958).
17. Susan B. Carter, Scott Sigmund Gartner, Michael R. Haines, Alan L. Olmstead, Richard Sutch, and Gavin Wright, eds., *Historical Statistics of the United States: Millennial Edition Online* (New York: Cambridge University Press, 2006), Table Aa145-184, Population, by Sex and Race: 1790–1990, 23. Data from 2012 available at U.S. Census Bureau, www.census.gov (accessed 2/25/12).
18. Carter et al., *Historical Statistics of the United States*, Table Aa145-184, Population, by Sex and Race: 1790–1990, 23.
19. Carter et al., *Historical Statistics of the United States*, Table Aa145-184, Population, by Sex and Race: 1790–1990, 23; Table Aa2189-2215, Hispanic Population Estimates,
20. Campbell J. Gibson and Emily Lennon, "Historical Census Statistics on the Foreign-Born Population of the United States: 1850–1990," www.census.gov/population/www/documentation/twps0029/twps0029.html (accessed 4/10/16).
21. Carter et al., *Historical Statistics of the United States*, Table Aa22-35, Selected Population Characteristics.
22. Fischer and Hout, *A Century of Difference*, 24.
23. Michael B. Katz and Mark J. Stern, *One Nation Divisible: What America Was and What It Is Becoming* (New York: Russell Sage Foundation, 2006), 16.

24. Carter et al., *Historical Statistics of the United States*, Table Aa145-184, Population, by Sex and Race: 1790–1990, 23. Karen R. Humes, Nicholas A. Jones, and Roberto R. Ramirez, "Overview of Race and Hispanic Origin: 2010. *2010 Census Briefs*," no. C2010BR-02 (Washington, DC: U.S. Census Bureau, March 2011), 4, www.census.gov/prod/cen2010 /briefs/c2010br-02.pdf (accessed 10/14/2011).

25. U.S. Census Bureau, "Annual Estimates of the Resident Population by Sex, Race, and Hispanic Origin for the United States, States, and Counties: April 1, 2010 to July 1, 2014," www.census.gov/quickfacts/table /PST045215/00#headnote-js-a (accessed 4/11/16).

26. U.S. Census Bureau, "2014 American Community Survey 1-Year Estimates: Selected Social Characteristics in the United States," factfinder.census.gov/bkmk/table/1.0 /en/ACS/14_1YR/DP02/0100000US (accessed 4/11/16).

27. U.S. Census Bureau, "2010–2014 American Community Survey 5-Year Estimates: Selected Characteristics of the Foreign-Born Population by Region of Birth: Latin America," factfinder.census.gov/faces/tableservices /jsf/pages/productview.xhtml?pid=ACS_14_5YR _S0506&prodType=table (accessed 4/11/16).

28. U.S. Census Bureau, "2014 American Community Survey 1-Year Estimate."

29. Michael Hoefer, Nancy Rytina, and Bryan Baker, "Estimates of the Unauthorized Immigrant Population Residing in the United States: January 2011," *Population Estimates*, Office of Immigration Statistics, Department of Homeland Security, March 2012, www.dhs.gov/sites /default/files/publications/ois_ill_pe_2011.pdf (accessed 9/25/13).

30. Anthony Faiola, "States' Immigrant Policies Diverge," *Washington Post*, October 15, 2007, A1.

31. *Plyler v. Doe*, 457 U.S. 202 (1982).

32. Pew Research Center, "2014 Religious Landscape Study," www.pewforum.org/religious-landscape-study /#religions (accessed 4/11/16).

33. Pew Research Center, "2014 Religious Landscape Study."

34. U.S. Census Bureau, "Demographic Trends in the 20th Century, Table 5: Population by Age and Sex for the United States: 1900 to 2000," www.census.gov /prod/2002pubs/censr-4.pdf (accessed 4/11/16); U.S. Census Bureau, "Annual Estimates of the Resident Population for Selected Age Groups by Sex for the United States, States, Counties, and Puerto Rico Commonwealth and Municipios: April 1, 2010 to July 1, 2014," www .census.gov/quickfacts/table/PST045215/00 (accessed 4/11/16).

35. U.S. Census Bureau, "Annual Estimates of the Resident Population for Selected Age Groups by Sex for the United States, States, Counties, and Puerto Rico Commonwealth and Municipios"; Eurostat, Statistics Explained, "Population Structure and Ageing," ec .europa.eu/eurostat/statisticsexplained/index.php /Population_structure_and_ageing (accessed 4/10/16).

36. U.S. Census Bureau, "2010 Census Urban Area Facts," www.census.gov/geo/reference/ua/uafacts.html (accessed 4/11/16).

37. Thomas Piketty and Emmanuel Saez, "Income Inequality in the United States, 1913–1998," *Quarterly Journal of Economics*, 18 no. 1 (2003), (Tables and Figures Updated to 2014), eml.berkeley.edu/~saez/TabFig2014prel.xls (accessed 4/11/16).

38. U.S. Census Bureau, "Income: Historical Income Data. Tables F-2, F-3, and F-6." www.census.gov/hhes/www /income/data/historical/index.html (accessed 4/12/16).

39. U.S. Census Bureau, "Historical Poverty Tables, Table 2: Poverty Status of People by Family Relationship, Race, and Hispanic Origin: 1959 to 2014," www.census.gov /hhes/www/poverty/data/historical/hstpov2.xls (accessed 4/11/16).

40. U.S. Census Bureau, "Table 1. Apportionment Population and Number of Representatives, by State: 2010 Census," www.census.gov/population/apportionment/files /Apportionment%20Population%202010.pdf (accessed 9/25/13).

41. See Judith N. Shklar, *American Citizenship: The Quest for Inclusion* (Cambridge, MA: Harvard University Press, 1991).

42. Herbert McClosky and John Zaller, *The American Ethos: Public Attitudes toward Capitalism and Democracy* (Cambridge, MA: Harvard University Press, 1984), 19.

43. *Burwell v. Hobby Lobby Stores, Inc.*, 573 U.S. __(2014).

44. Kevin McCoy and Kevin Johnson, "U.S. Demands Apple Unlock Phone in Drug Case," April 10, 2016, www .usatoday.com/story/news/2016/04/08/justice-moving -forward-separate-apple-case/82788824 (accessed 4/10/16).

45. J. R. Pole, *The Pursuit of Equality in American History* (Berkeley: University of California Press, 1978), 3.

46. *Plessy v. Ferguson*, 163 U.S. 537 (1896).

47. *Brown v. Board of Education*, 347 U.S. 483 (1954).

48. See Rogers M. Smith, *Liberalism and American Constitutional Law* (Cambridge, MA: Harvard University Press, 1985), chap. 6.

49 The case was *San Antonio Independent School District v. Rodriguez*, 411 U.S. 1 (1973). See the discussion in Smith, *Liberalism and American Constitutional Law*, 163–4.

50. Pew Research Center for the People and the Press and for the Public, "Trends in American Values, 1987–2012, Partisan Polarization Surges in Bush, Obama Years," June 4, 2012, p. 104; Pew Research Center for the People and the Press and for the Public, www.peoplepress.org /2012/03/02/for-the-public-its-not-about-class-warfare -but-fairness (accessed 6/9/12); Pew Research Center, "Global Support for Principle of Free Expression, but Opposition to Some Forms of Speech," November 18, 2015, www.pewglobal.org/files/2015/11/Pew-Research -Center-Democracy-Report-FINAL-November -18-2015.pdf; Public Religion Research Institute poll, June 3–7, 2015, www.pollingreport.com/civil.htm; Pew Research Center, "Changing Attitudes on Gay Marriage,"

July 29, 2015, www.pewforum.org/2015/07/29/graphics
-slideshow-changing-attitudes-on-gay-marriage; Pew Research Center, "Across Racial Lines, More Say Nation
Needs to Make Changes to Achieve Racial Equality,"
August 5, 2015, www.people-press.org/2015/08/05
/across-racial-lines-more-say-nation-needs-to-make
-changes-to-achieve-racial-equality/ (accessed 4/12/16).

51. See the discussion in Eileen McDonagh, "Gender Politi-
cal Change," in *New Perspectives on American Politics*, ed.
Lawrence C. Dodd and Calvin C. Jillson (Washington,
DC: CQ Press, 1994), 58–73. The argument for moving
women's issues into the public sphere is made by Jean
Bethke Elshtain, *Public Man, Private Woman* (Princeton,
NJ: Princeton University Press, 1981).

52. Roger Lowenstein, "The Way We Live Now: The Inequality Conundrum," *New York Times Magazine*, June
10, 2007, 11.

53. Associated Press, "Obama: Tax Cuts Will Be Felt by
April 1," February 21, 2009, www.msnbc.msn.com
/id/29314485/ (accessed 9/28/09).

54. "Americans' Views on Income Inequality and Workers'
Rights," *New York Times*, June 3, 2015, www.nytimes.com
/ineractive/2015/06/03/business/income-inequality-workers
-rights-international-trade-poll.html (accessed 4/10/16).

55. Kevin Phillips, *Arrogant Capital: Washington, Wall Street,
and the Frustration of American Politics* (Boston: Little,
Brown, 1994).

56. FairVote, "Voter Turnout," www.fairvote.org/voter_turnout
#voter_turnout_101 (accessed 4/10/16).

57. Center for the Study of the American Electorate, "2008
Turnout Report: African-Americans, Anger, Fear and
Youth Propel Turnout to Highest Level since 1960,"
news release, December 17, 2008, www.american.edu
/research/news/loader.cfm?csModule=security
/getfile&pageid=23907 (accessed 2/19/16).

Chapter 2

1. Executive Office of the President of the United States,
"Impacts and Costs of the October 2013 Federal Government Shutdown," November 2013, www.whitehouse
.gov/sites/default/files/omb/reports/impacts-and-costs
-of-october-2013-federal-government-shutdown-report
.pdf (accessed 6/13/16).

2. The social makeup of colonial America and some of the
social conflicts that divided colonial society are discussed
in Jackson Turner Main, *The Social Structure of Revolutionary America* (Princeton, NJ: Princeton University
Press, 1965).

3. George B. Tindall and David E. Shi, *America: A Narrative
History*, 8th ed. (New York: W. W. Norton, 2010), 202.

4. For a discussion of events leading up to the Revolution,
see Charles M. Andrews, *The Colonial Background of the
American Revolution* (New Haven, CT: Yale University
Press, 1924).

5. See Carl Becker, *The Declaration of Independence* (New
York: Knopf, 1942).

6. An excellent and readable account of the development
from the Articles of Confederation to the Constitution
will be found in Alfred H. Kelly, Winfred A. Harbison,
and Herman Belz, *The American Constitution: Its Origins and Development*, 7th ed., vol. 1 (New York: W. W.
Norton, 1991), chap. 5.

7. Reported in Samuel E. Morrison, Henry Steele Commager,
and William Leuchtenberg, *The Growth of the American Republic*, vol. 1 (New York: Oxford University Press, 1969), 244.

8. Quoted in Morrison, Commager, and Leuchtenberg,
Growth of the American Republic, 242.

9. Charles A. Beard, *An Economic Interpretation of the Constitution of the United States* (New York: Macmillan, 1913).

10. Max Farrand, ed., *The Records of the Federal Convention of
1787*, Vol. 1 (New Haven, CT: Yale University Press, 1966).

11. Madison's notes, along with the somewhat less complete
records kept by several other participants in the convention, are available in a four-volume set. See Max Farrand,
ed., *The Records of the Federal Convention of 1787*, 4 vols.,
rev. ed. (New Haven, CT: Yale University Press, 1966).

12. Farrand, *Records of the Federal Convention of 1787*, 476.

13. Alexander Hamilton, James Madison, and John Jay, *The
Federalist Papers*, ed. Clinton L. Rossiter (New York:
New American Library, 1961), no. 71.

14. *Federalist Papers*, no. 62.

15. *Federalist Papers*, no. 70.

16. Max Farrand, *The Framing of the Constitution of the United
States* (New Haven, CT: Yale University Press, 1962), 49.

17. Melancton Smith, quoted in Herbert J. Storing, *What the
Anti-Federalists Were For* (Chicago: University of Chicago
Press, 1981), 17.

18. "Essays of Brutus," no. 1, in *The Complete Anti-Federalist*, ed.
Herbert Storing (Chicago: University of Chicago Press, 1981).

19. *Federalist Papers*, no. 57.

20. "Essays of Brutus," no. 15, in Storing, *Complete Anti-
Federalist*.

21. *Federalist Papers*, no. 10.

22. "Essays of Brutus," no. 7, in Storing, *Complete Anti-Federalist*.

23. "Essays of Brutus," no. 6, in Storing, *Complete Anti-
Federalist*.

24. Storing, *What the Anti-Federalists Were For*, p. 28.

25. *Federalist Papers*, no. 51.

26. Quoted in Storing, *What the Anti-Federalists Were For*, 30.

27. *Federalist Papers*, no. 10.

Chapter 3

1. Brady Dennis, "Obama Administration Will Not
Block State Marijuana Laws, If Distribution Is Regulated," *Washington Post*, August 29, 2013, http://articles
.washingtonpost.com/2013-08-29/national
/41566270_1_marijuana-legalization-attorney-general
-bob-ferguson-obama-administration (accessed 11/17/13).

2. The public policy exception stems from developments in case law tracing back to the 1930s. In Section 283 of the Restatement (Second) of Conflict of Laws (1971) a group of judges and academics codified existing case law related to marriage: "A marriage which satisfies the requirements of the state where the marriage was contracted will everywhere be recognized as valid unless it violates the strong public policy of another state which had the most significant relationship to the spouses and the marriage at the time of the marriage." However, in *Baker v. General Motors Corp*, 522 U.S. 222 (1998), the Supreme Court explicitly stated that its decision "creates no general exception to the full faith and credit command."

3. Adam Liptak, "Bans on Interracial Unions Offer Perspective on Gay Ones," *New York Times*, March 17, 2004, A22.

4. *Loving v. Virginia*, 388 U.S. 1 (1967). The Lovings were charged with violating Virginia's miscegenation laws and were sentenced to one year in jail, which would be suspended if they left the state for 25 years. Five years later, with the assistance of the American Civil Liberties Union, the Lovings filed a motion to vacate their conviction. The Supreme Court heard the case and overturned the Lovings' conviction, finding Virginia's miscegenation law unconstitutional under the due process clause and equal protection clause of the Fourteenth Amendment.

5. Ken I. Kersch, "Full Faith and Credit for Same-Sex Marriages?" *Political Science Quarterly* 112 (Spring 1997): 117–36; Joan Biskupic, "Once Unthinkable, Now under Debate," *Washington Post*, September 3, 1996, A1.

6. *United States v. Windsor*, 570 U.S. __ (2013).

7. *Obergefell v. Hodges*, 576 U.S. __ (2015).

8. Elliot C. McLaughlin, "Most States to Abide by Supreme Court's Same-Sex Marriage Ruling, but . . . ," CNN, June 30, 2015, www.cnn.com/2015/06/29/us/same-sex -marriage-state-by-state/ (accessed 8/16/15).

9. *Hicklin v. Orbeck*, 437 U.S. 518 (1978).

10. *Sweeny v. Woodall*, 344 U.S. 86 (1952).

11. Patricia S. Florestano, "Past and Present Utilization of Interstate Compacts in the United States," *Publius* 24 (Fall 1994): 13–26.

12. National Conference of State Legislatures, "National Popular Vote." March 11, 2015. www.ncsl.org/research /elections-and-campaigns/national-popular-vote.aspx (accessed 4/11/16).

13. A good discussion of the constitutional position of local governments is in Richard Briffault, "Our Localism: Part I, the Structure of Local Government Law," *Columbia Law Review* 90, no. 1 (January 1990): 1–115. For more on the structure and theory of federalism, see Larry N. Gerston, *American Federalism: A Concise Introduction* (Armonk, NY: M. E. Sharpe, 2007), and Martha Derthick, "Up-to-Date in Kansas City: Reflections on American Federalism" (1992 John Gaus Lecture), *PS: Political Science and Politics* 25 (December 1992): 671–75.

14. Gary Fields and John R. Emshwiller, "As Criminal Laws Proliferate, More Are Ensnared," *Wall Street Journal*, July 23, 2011, http://online.wsj.com/news/articles/SB10001424052 7487037495045761727141846016 54 (accessed 11/5/13).

15. Rachel Barkow, "Federalism and Criminal Law: What the Feds Can Learn from the States," *Michigan Law Review* 109 (2011): 519–80. http://repository.law.umich .edu/cgi/viewcontent.cgi?article=1165&context=mlr (accessed 11/5/13).

16. For a good treatment of the contrast between national political stability and social instability, see Samuel P. Huntington, *Political Order in Changing Societies* (New Haven, CT: Yale University Press, 1968), chap. 2.

17. *McCulloch v. Maryland*, 4 Wheaton 316 (1819).

18. *Gibbons v. Ogden*, 9 Wheaton 1 (1824).

19. The Sherman Antitrust Act, adopted in 1890, for example, was enacted not to restrict commerce but rather to protect it from monopolies, or trusts, in order to prevent unfair trade practices and to enable the market again to become self-regulating. Moreover, the Supreme Court sought to uphold liberty of contract to protect businesses. For example, in *Lochner v. New York*, 198 U.S. 45 (1905), the Court invalidated a New York law regulating the sanitary conditions and hours of labor of bakers on the grounds that the law interfered with liberty of contract.

20. The key case in this process of expanding the power of the national government is generally considered to be *NLRB v. Jones & Laughlin Steel Corporation*, 301 U.S. 1 (1937), in which the Supreme Court approved federal regulation of the workplace and thereby virtually eliminated interstate commerce as a limit on the national government's power.

21. *United States v. Darby Lumber Co.*, 312 U.S. 100 (1941).

22. W. John Moore, "Pleading the 10th," *National Journal*, July 29, 1996.

23. *United States v. Lopez*, 14 U.S. 549 (1995).

24. *Printz v. United States*, 521 U.S. 98 (1997).

25. See the poll reported in Guy Gugliotta, "Scaling Down the American Dream," *Washington Post*, April 19, 1995, A21. See also John Kincaid and Richard L. Cole, "Citizens' Attitudes toward Issues of Federalism in Canada, Mexico and the United States," *Publius: The Journal of Federalism* 41, no. 1 (2011): 53–75.

26. Kenneth T. Palmer, "The Evolution of Grant Policies," in *The Changing Politics of Federal Grants*, ed. Lawrence D. Brown, James W. Fossett, and Kenneth T. Palmer (Washington, DC: Brookings Institution Press, 1984), 15.

27. Palmer, "Evolution of Grant Policies," 6.

28. Morton Grodzins, *The American System*, ed. Daniel J. Elazar (Chicago: Rand McNally, 1966).

29. See Terry Sanford, *Storm over the States* (New York: McGraw-Hill, 1967).

30. James L. Sundquist, *Making Federalism Work*, with David W. Davis (Washington, DC: Brookings Institution Press, 1969), 271. George Wallace was mistrusted by the

architects of the War on Poverty because he was a strong proponent of racial segregation and "states' rights."

31. See Donald F. Kettl, *The Regulation of American Federalism* (Baton Rouge: Louisiana State University Press, 1983).

32. Cindy Skrzycki, "Trial Lawyers on the Offensive in Fight against Preemptive Rules," *Washington Post*, September 11, 2007, D2.

33. *Gonazales v. Oregon*, 546 U.S. 243 (2006).

34. *Wyeth v. Levine*, 555 U.S. 555 (2009).

35. Philip Rucker, "Obama Curtails Bush's Policy of 'Preemption,'" *Washington Post*, May 22, 2009, A3.

36. See U.S. Advisory Commission on Intergovernmental Relations, *Federal Regulation of State and Local Governments: The Mixed Record of the 1980s* (Washington, DC: Advisory Commission on Intergovernmental Relations, July 1993).

37. Robert Jay Dilger and Richard S. Beth, "Unfunded Mandates Reform Act: History, Impact, and Issues" (Washington, DC: Congressional Research Service, April 19, 2011), 40, http://digital.library.unt.edu/ark:/67531/metadc40084/m1/1/high_res_d/R40957_2011Apr19.pdf (accessed 11/16/13).

38. U.S. Advisory Commission on Intergovernmental Relations, *Federal Regulation of State and Local Governments*, iii. www.cbo.gov/sites/default/files/114th-congress-2015-2016/reports/50051-UMRA2_1.pdf (accessed 5/6/16).

39. Congressional Budget Office, "A Review of CBO's Activities in 2014 under the Unfunded Mandates Reform Act," March 31, 2015. https://www.cbo.gov/sites/default/files/114th-congress-2015-2016/reports/50051-UMRA2_0.pdf (see Appendix B, p. 39) (accessed 8/16/15).

40. Adam Liptak, "Justices to Hear Health Care Case as Race Heats Up," *New York Times*, November 15, 2011, A1.

41. Quoted in Timothy Conlon, *New Federalism: Intergovernmental Reform from Nixon to Reagan* (Washington, DC: Brookings Institution Press, 1988), 25.

42. For the emergence of complaints about federal categorical grants, see Palmer, "Evolution of Grant Policies," 17–18. On the governors' efforts to gain more control over federal grants after the 1994 congressional elections, see Dan Balz, "GOP Governors Eager to Do Things Their Way," *Washington Post*, November 22, 1994, A4.

43. U.S. Advisory Commission on Intergovernmental Relations, *Federal Regulation of State and Local Governments*.

44. For an assessment of the achievements of the 104th and 105th Congresses, see Timothy Conlan, *From New Federalism to Devolution: Twenty-Five Years of Intergovernmental Reform* (Washington, DC: Brookings Institution Press, 1998).

45. Robert Frank, "Proposed Block Grants Seen Unlikely to Cure Management Problems," *Wall Street Journal*, May 1, 1995, 1.

46. Sarah Kershaw, "U.S. Rule Limits Emergency Care for Immigrants," *New York Times*, September 22, 2007, A1.

47. U.S. Committee on Federalism and National Purpose, *To Form a More Perfect Union* (Washington, DC: National Conference on Social Welfare, 1985). See also the discussion in Paul E. Peterson, *The Price of Federalism* (Washington, DC: Brooking Institution Press, 1995), esp. chap. 8.

48. Malcolm Gladwell, "Remaking Welfare: In States' Experiments, a Cutting Contest," *Washington Post*, March 10, 1995, 6.

49. The phrase "laboratories of democracy" was coined by Supreme Court Justice Louis Brandeis in his dissenting opinion in *New State Ice Co. v. Liebman*, 285 U.S. 262 (1932).

50. Insurance Institute for Highway Safety, "Motor Vehicle Fatalities in 1996 Were 12 Percent Higher on Interstates, Freeways in 12 States That Raised Speed Limits," press release, October 10, 1997.

51. *Gonzales v. Raich*, 545 U.S. 1 (2005). For more, see William Yardley, "New Federal Crackdown Confounds States That Allow Medical Marijuana," *New York Times*, May 8, 2011, A13.

52. *Gonzales v. Oregon*, 546 U.S. 243 (2006).

53. Josh Sanburn, "Colorado Approves a 'Right to Die' for Terminally Ill Patients," *Time*, time.com/4563632/colorado-right-to-die-approved/ (accessed 11/10/16).

54. National Conference of State Legislatures, "Collecting E-Commerce Taxes," www.ncsl.org/research/fiscal-policy/collecting-ecommerce-taxes-an-interactive-map.aspx (accessed 11/17/13).

55. Richard Rubin, "States Set Up Fight over Web Sales Tax," *Wall Street Journal*, February 23, 2016, www.wsj.com/articles/states-seek-new-ways-to-tax-online-sales-1456262265 (accessed 4/11/16).

56. National Conference of State Legislatures, "2013 Report on State Immigration Laws (Jan.–June)," www.ncsl.org/research/immigration/immgration-report-august-2013.aspx (accessed 11/3/13).

57. Terry Frieden, "Justice Department Sues Utah over State Immigration Law," CNN, November 22, 2011, www.cnn.com/2011/11/22/us/utah-immigration-law/ (accessed 4/21/16).

58. *Arizona v. United States*, 567 U.S. __ (2012). Adam Liptak, "Blocking Parts of Arizona Law, Justices Allow Its Centerpiece," *New York Times*, June 25, 2012, www.nytimes.com/2012/06/26/us/supreme-court-rejects-part-of-arizona-immigration-law.html (accessed 11/3/13).

59. *United States v. Texas*, 579 U.S. __ (2016).

60. Kate Linthicum, "Obama Ends Secure Communities Program as Part of Immigration Action," *Los Angeles Times*, November 21, 2014, www.latimes.com/local/california/la-me-1121-immigration-justice-20141121-story.html (accessed 8/16/15).

61. White House, Office of the Press Secretary, Memorandum for the Heads of Executive Departments and Agencies, Subject: Preemption, May 20, 2009, www.whitehouse.gov/the-press-office/presidential-memorandum-regarding-preemption (accessed 4/16/16).

62. Adam Liptak, "In Health Law, Asking Where U.S. Power Stops," *New York Times*, November 14, 2011, A1.

63. Robert Barnes, "Affordable Care Act Survives Supreme Court Challenge," *Washington Post*, June 25, 2015, www.washingtonpost.com/politics/courts_law/obamacare-survives-supreme-court-challenge/2015/06/25/af87608e-188a-11e5-93b7-5eddc056ad8a_story.html (accessed 8/16/15).

Chapter 4

1. Alexander Hamilton, James Madison, and John Jay, *The Federalist Papers*, ed. Clinton Rossiter (New York: New American Library, 1961), no. 84, 513.

2. *Federalist Papers*, no. 84, 513.

3. Clinton Rossiter, *1787: The Grand Convention* (New York: W. W. Norton, 1987), 302.

4. Rossiter, *1787*, 303. Rossiter also reports that "in 1941 the States of Connecticut, Massachusetts, and Georgia celebrated the sesquicentennial of the Bill of Rights by giving their hitherto withheld and unneeded assent."

5. *Barron v. Baltimore*, 7 Peters 243, 246 (1833).

6. The Fourteenth Amendment also seems designed to introduce civil rights. The final clause of the all-important Section 1 provides that no state can "deny to any person within its jurisdiction the equal protection of the laws." It is not unreasonable to conclude that the purpose of this provision was to obligate the state governments as well as the national government to take positive actions to protect citizens from arbitrary and discriminatory actions, at least those based on race. Civil rights will be explored in Chapter 5.

7. For example, *The Slaughterhouse Cases*, 16 Wallace 36 (1883).

8. *Chicago, Burlington and Quincy Railroad Company v. Chicago*, 166 U.S. 226 (1897).

9. *Gitlow v. New York*, 268 U.S. 652 (1925).

10. *Near v. Minnesota*, 283 U.S. 697 (1931); *Hague v. C.I.O.*, 307 U.S. 496 (1939).

11. *Palko v. Connecticut*, 302 U.S. 319 (1937).

12. All of these were implicitly included in the *Palko* case as "not incorporated" into the Fourteenth Amendment as limitations on the powers of the states.

13. There is one interesting exception, which involves the Sixth Amendment right to public trial. In the 1948 case *In re Oliver*, 33 U.S. 257, the right to a public trial was, in effect, incorporated as part of the Fourteenth Amendment. However, the issue in that case was put more generally as "due process," and public trial itself was not actually mentioned in so many words. Later opinions, such as *Duncan v. Louisiana*, 391 U.S. 145 (1968), cited the *Oliver* case as the precedent for more explicit incorporation of public trials as part of the Fourteenth Amendment.

14. *Abington School District v. Schempp*, 374 U.S. 203 (1963).

15. *Engel v. Vitale*, 370 U.S. 421 (1962).

16. *Wallace v. Jaffree*, 472 U.S. 38 (1985).

17. *Lemon v. Kurtzman*, 403 U.S. 602 (1971). The *Lemon* test is still good law, but as recently as the 1994 Court term, four justices have urged that the test be abandoned. Here is a settled area of law that may soon become unsettled.

18. *Rosenberger v. Rector and Visitors of the University of Virginia*, 515 U.S. 819 (1995).

19. *Van Orden v. Perry*, 545 U.S. 677 (2005).

20. *McCreary County v. American Civil Liberties Union of Kentucky*, 545 U.S. 844 (2005).

21. *West Virginia State Board of Education v. Barnette*, 319 U.S. 624 (1943). The case it reversed was *Minersville School District v. Gobitus*, 310 U.S. 586 (1940).

22. *Cantwell v. Connecticut*, 310 U.S. 296 (1940).

23. *Holt v. Hobbs*, 574 U.S. __ (2015).

24. *Equal Employment Opportunity Commission v. Abercrombie & Fitch Stores, Inc.*, 575 U.S. __ (2015).

25. *Abrams v. United States*, 250 U.S. 616 (1919).

26. *United States v. Carolene Products Company*, 304 U.S. 144 (1938), n4. This footnote is one of the Court's most important doctrines. See Alfred H. Kelly, Winfred A. Harbison, and Herman Belz, *The American Constitution: Its Origins and Development*, 7th ed., (New York: Norton, 1991), 2:519–23.

27. *Schenk v. United States*, 249 U.S. 47 (1919).

28. *Brandenburg v. Ohio*, 395 U.S. 444 (1969).

29. *Buckley v. Valeo*, 424 U.S. 1 (1976).

30. *McConnell v. Federal Election Commission*, 540 U.S. 93 (2003).

31. *Federal Election Commission v. Wisconsin Right to Life*, 551 U.S. 449 (2007).

32. *Citizens United v. Federal Election Commission*, 558 U.S. 50 (2010).

33. *McCutcheon v. Federal Election Commission*, 572 U.S. __ (2014).

34. Arthur Delaney, "Supreme Court Rolls Back Campaign Finance Restrictions," *Huffington Post*, March 23, 2010, updated May 25, 2011, www.huffingtonpost.com/2010/01/21/supreme-court-rolls-back_n_431227.html (accessed 7/9/12).

35. *Chaplinsky v. State of New Hampshire*, 315 U.S. 568 (1942).

36. *Dennis v. United States*, 341 U.S. 494 (1951), which upheld the infamous Smith Act of 1940 that provided criminal penalties for those who "willfully and knowingly conspire to teach and advocate the forceful and violent overthrow and destruction of the government."

37. *Capital Broadcasting Company v. Acting Attorney General*, 405 U.S. 1000 (1972).

38. *R.A.V. v. City of St. Paul*, 506 U.S. 377 (1992).

39. *Bethel School District No. 403 v. Fraser*, 478 U.S. 675 (1986).

40. *Hazelwood School District v. Kuhlmeier*, 484 U.S. 260 (1988).

41. *Morse v. Frederick*, 551 U.S. 393 (2007).

42. *City Council v. Taxpayers for Vincent*, 466 U.S. 789 (1984).

43. Fisher, *American Constitutional Law*, p. 546.

44. *Bigelow v. Virginia*, 421 U.S. 809 (1975).

45. *Virginia State Board of Pharmacy v. Virginia Citizens Consumer Council*, 425 U.S. 748 (1976). Later cases restored the rights of lawyers to advertise their services.

46. *Lorillard Tobacco v. Reilly*, 533 U.S. 525 (2001).

47. *Hague v. Committee for Industrial Organization*, 307 U.S. 496 (1939).

48. *Texas v. Johnson*, 488 U.S. 884 (1989).

49. Charles Babington, "Senate Rejects Flag Desecration Amendment," *Washington Post*, June 28, 2006, www.washingtonpost.com/wp-dyn/content/article/2006/06/27/AR2006062701056.html (accessed 11/13/13).

50. *Snyder v. Phelps*, 562 U.S. __(2011).

51. For a good general discussion of speech plus, see Louis Fisher, *American Constitutional Law* (New York: McGraw-Hill, 1990), 544–6. The case upholding the buffer zone against the abortion protesters is *Madsen v. Women's Health Center*, 512 U.S. 753 (1994).

52. *Near v. Minnesota*, 283 U.S. 697 (1931).

53. *New York Times Co. v. United States*, 403 U.S. 731 (1971).

54. *Cable News Network, Inc., v. Noriega*, 498 U.S. 976 (1990).

55. *Branzburg v. Hayes*, 408 U.S. 656 (1972).

56. Emily Bazelon, "Obama's War on Journalists: His Administration's Leak Investigations Are Outrageous and Unprecedented," *Slate*, May 14, 2013, www.slate.com/articles/news_and_politics/jurisprudence/2013/05/obama_s_justice_department_holder_s_leak_investigations_are_outrageous_and.html (accessed 11/15/14).

57. *New York Times Co. v. Sullivan*, 376 U.S. 254 (1964).

58. Shannon Hutzler, "Protecting Informed Public Participation," *Valparaiso University Law Review* 41, no. 3 (Spring 2007): 1235–84.

59. See *Zeran v. America Online*, 129 F3d 327 (4th Cir. 1997).

60. *Roth v. United States*, 354 U.S. 476 (1957).

61. Concurring opinion in *Jacobellis v. Ohio*, 378 U.S. 184 (1964).

62. *Miller v. California*, 413 U.S. 15 (1973).

63. *Reno v. American Civil Liberties Union*, 521 U.S. 844 (1997).

64. *United States v. Williams*, 553 U.S. 285 (2008).

65. *United States v. Playboy Entertainment Group*, 529 U.S. 803 (2000).

66. *Brown v. Entertainment Merchants Association*, 564 U.S. __ (2011).

67. *District of Columbia v. Heller*, 554 U.S. 570 (2008).

68. *McDonald v. Chicago*, 561 U.S. 3025 (2010).

69. *In re Winship*, 397 U.S. 361 (1970). An outstanding treatment of due process in issues involving the Fourth through Seventh amendments will be found in Fisher, *American Constitutional Law*, chap. 13.

70. *Horton v. California*, 496 U.S. 128 (1990).

71. *Mapp v. Ohio*, 367 U.S. 643 (1961). Although Mapp went free in this case, she was later convicted in New York on narcotics trafficking charges and served 9 years of a 20-year sentence.

72. For a good discussion of the issue, see Fisher, *American Constitutional Law*, pp. 884–9.

73. *United States v. Grubbs*, 547 U.S. 90 (2006).

74. *National Treasury Employees Union v. Von Raab*, 39 U.S. 656 (1989).

75. *Skinner v. Railroad Labor Executives' Association*, 489 U.S. 602 (1989).

76. *Vernonia School District 47J v. Acton*, 515 U.S. 646 (1995).

77. *Chandler v. Miller*, 520 U.S. 305 (1997).

78. *Florida v. Jardines*, 569 U.S. __ (2013).

79. *United States v. Jones*, 132 S. 565 U.S. __ (2012).

80. *Maryland v. King.* 569 U.S. __ (2013).

81. *Riley v. California*, 572 U.S. __ (2014).

82. *Terry v. Ohio*, 392 U.S. 1 (1968).

83. Marjorie Cohn, "NSA Metadata Collection: Fourth Amendment Violation," JURIST, January, 15, 2014, http://jurist.org/forum/2014/01/marjorie-cohn-nsa-metadata.php (accessed 4/19/16).

84. Edwin S. Corwin and J. W. Peltason, *Understanding the Constitution* (New York: Holt, 1967), 286.

85. *Benton v. Maryland*, 395 U.S. 784 (1969).

86. *Miranda v. Arizona*, 348 U.S. 436 (1966).

87. *Berman v. Parker*, 348 U.S. 26 (1954). For a thorough analysis of the case, see Benjamin Ginsberg, "*Berman v. Parker*: Congress, the Court, and the Public Purpose," *Polity* 4 (1971): 48–75. For a later application of the case that suggests that "just compensation"—defined as something approximating market value—is about all a property owner can hope for protection against a public taking of property, see Theodore Lowi et al., *Poliscide: Big Government, Big Science, Lilliputian Politics*, 2nd ed. (Lanham, MD: University Press of America, 1990), 267–70.

88. *Kelo v. City of New London*, 545 U.S. 469 (2005).

89. *Gideon v. Wainwright*, 372 U.S. 335 (1963).

90. *Wiggins v. Smith*, 539 U.S. 510 (2003).

91. For further discussion of these issues, see Corwin and Peltason, *Understanding the Constitution*, 319–23.

92. *Furman v. Georgia*, 408 U.S. 238 (1972).

93. *Gregg v. Georgia*, 428 U.S. 153 (1976).

94. Death Penalty Information Center, www.deathpenaltyinfo.com (accessed 11/10/16).

95. *Kennedy v. Louisiana*, 554 U.S. 407 (2008).

96. *Snyder v. Louisiana*, 552 U.S. 472 (2008).

97. *Glossip v. Gross*, 576 U.S. (2015).

98. *Hudson v. McMillan*, 503 U.S. 1 (1992).

99. *Miller v. Alabama*, 567 U.S. __ (2012).

100. *Olmstead v. United States*, 227 U.S. 438 (1928). See also David M. O'Brien, *Constitutional Law and Politics*, 6th ed. (New York: W. W. Norton, 2005), 1:76–84.

101. *West Virginia State Board of Education* (1943).

102. *NAACP v. Alabama ex rel. Patterson*, 357 U.S. 447 (1958).

103. *Griswold v. Connecticut*, 381 U.S. 479 (1965).

104. *Griswold*, concurring opinion. In 1972 the Court extended the privacy right to unmarried women: *Eisenstadt v. Baird*, 405 U.S. 438 (1972).

105. *Roe v. Wade*, 410 U.S. 113 (1973).

106. *Webster v. Reproductive Health Services*, 492 U.S. 490 (1989), which upheld a Missouri law that restricted the use of public medical facilities for abortion. The decision opened the way for other states to limit the availability of abortion.

107. *Planned Parenthood of Southeastern Pennsylvania v. Casey*, 505 U.S. 833 (1992).

108. *Ayotte v. Planned Parenthood*, 546 U.S. 320 (2006).

109. *Gonzales v. Carhart*, 550 U.S. 124 (2007).

110. *Bowers v. Hardwick*, 478 U.S. 186 (1986).

111. *Lawrence v. Texas*, 539 U.S. 558 (2003).

112. *Lawrence* (2003).

113. It is worth recalling here the provision of the Ninth Amendment: "The enumeration in the Constitution, of certain rights, shall not be construed to deny or disparage others retained by the people."

114. *Obergefell v. Hodges*, 576 U.S. __ (2015).

115. *Gonzales v. Oregon*, 546 U.S. 243 (2006).

116. Daniel J. Solove, *Nothing to Hide: The False Tradeoff between Privacy and Security* (New Haven, CT: Yale University Press, 2011).

Chapter 5

1. Paula Baker, "The Domestication of Politics: Women and American Political Society, 1780–1920," *American Historical Review* 89 (June 1984): 620–47.

2. *Dred Scott v. Sandford*, 19 Howard 393 (1857).

3. August Meier and Elliott Rudwick, *From Plantation to Ghetto* (New York: Hill and Wang, 1976), 184–8.

4. Jill Dupont, "Susan B. Anthony," New York Notes (Albany: New York State Commission on the Bicentennial of the U.S. Constitution, 1988), 3.

5. *Plessy v. Ferguson*, 163 U.S. 537 (1896).

6. Dupont, "Susan B. Anthony," 4.

7. The prospect of a "fair employment practices" law tied to the commerce power produced the Dixiecrat break with the Democratic Party in 1948. The Democratic Party organization of the States of the Old Confederacy seceded from the national party and nominated its own candidate, the then-Democratic governor of South Carolina, Strom Thurmond, who later became a Republican senator. This almost cost President Truman the election.

8. This was based on the provision in Article VI of the Constitution that "all treaties made . . . under the Authority of the United States" shall be the "supreme Law of the Land." The commission recognized that if the U.S. Senate ratified what became the Universal Declaration of Human Rights (a treaty), then that power could be used as the constitutional umbrella for effective civil rights legislation. The Supreme Court had recognized in *Missouri v. Holland*, 252 U.S. 416 (1920), that a treaty could enlarge federal power at the expense of the states.

9. *Missouri ex rel. Gaines v. Canada*, 305 U.S. 337 (1938).

10. *Sweatt v. Painter*, 339 U.S. 629 (1950).

11. *Smith v. Allwright*, 321 U.S. 649 (1944).

12. *Shelley v. Kraemer*, 334 U.S. 1 (1948).

13. Kermit L. Hall, *The Magic Mirror: Law in American History* (New York: Oxford University Press, 1989), 322–4. See also Richard Kluger, *Simple Justice* (New York: Vintage, 1977), 530–7.

14. The District of Columbia case came up, too; but since the District of Columbia is not a state, this case did not directly involve the Fourteenth Amendment and its equal protection clause. The plaintiffs confronted the Court on the same grounds, however—that segregation is inherently unequal. Their victory in effect was "incorporation in reverse," with equal protection moving from the Fourteenth Amendment to become part of the Bill of Rights. See *Bolling v. Sharpe*, 347 U.S. 497 (1954).

15. *Brown v. Board of Education of Topeka, Kansas*, 347 U.S. 483 (1954).

16. The Supreme Court first declared that race was a suspect classification requiring strict scrutiny in the decision *Korematsu v. United States*, 323 U.S. 214 (1944). In this case, the Court upheld President Roosevelt's executive order of 1941 allowing the military to exclude persons of Japanese ancestry from the West Coast and to place them in internment camps. It is one of the few cases in which classification based on race survived strict scrutiny.

17. The two most important cases were *Cooper v. Aaron*, 358 U.S. 1 (1958), which required Little Rock, Arkansas, to desegregate, and *Griffin v. Prince Edward County School Board*, 377 U.S. 218 (1964), which forced all the schools of that Virginia county to reopen after five years of closing to avoid desegregation.

18. In *Cooper v. Aaron*, the Supreme Court ordered immediate compliance with the lower court's desegregation order and went beyond that with a stern warning that it is "emphatically the province and duty of the judicial department to say what the law is."

19. *Shuttlesworth v. Birmingham Board of Education*, 358 U.S. 101 (1958), upheld a "pupil placement" plan purporting to assign pupils on various bases, with no mention of race. This case interpreted *Brown* to mean that school districts had to stop explicit racial discrimination

but were under no obligation to take positive steps to desegregate. For a while black parents were doomed to a case-by-case approach.

20. For good treatments of this long stretch of the struggle of the federal courts to integrate the schools, see Paul Brest and Sanford Levinson, *Processes of Constitutional Decision-Making: Cases and Materials*, 2nd ed. (Boston: Little, Brown, 1983), 471–80; and Alfred H. Kelly, Winfred A. Harbison, and Herman Belz, *The American Constitution: Its Origins and Development*, 6th ed. (New York: W. W. Norton, 1983), 610–16.

21. Pierre Thomas, "Denny's to Settle Bias Cases," *Washington Post*, May 24, 1994, A1.

22. See Hamil Harris, "For Blacks, Cabs Can Be Hard to Get," *Washington Post*, July 21, 1994, J1.

23. For a thorough analysis of the Office for Civil Rights, see Jeremy Rabkin, "Office for Civil Rights," in *The Politics of Regulation*, ed. James Q. Wilson (New York: Basic Books, 1980).

24. This was an accepted way of using quotas or ratios to determine statistically that blacks or other minorities were being excluded from schools or jobs and then, on the basis of that statistical evidence, to authorize the Justice Department to bring suits in individual cases and class-action suits. In most segregated situations outside the South, it is virtually impossible to identify and document an intent to discriminate.

25. *Swann v. Charlotte-Mecklenberg Board of Education*, 402 U.S. 1 (1971).

26. *Milliken v. Bradley*, 418 U.S. 717 (1974).

27. For a good evaluation of the Boston effort, see Gary Orfield, *Must We Bus? Segregated Schools and National Policy* (Washington, DC: Brookings Institution, 1978), 144–6. See also Bob Woodward and Scott Armstrong, *The Brethren: Inside the Supreme Court* (New York: Simon and Schuster, 1979), 426–7; and J. Anthony Lukas, *Common Ground* (New York: Random House, 1986).

28. *Board of Education v. Dowell*, 498 U.S. 237 (1991).

29. *Parents Involved in Community Schools v. Seattle School District No. 1*, 551 U.S. 701 (2007).

30. John A. Powell, "Segregated Schools Ruling Not All Bad: In Rejecting Seattle's Integration Bid, Top Court Majority Also Held That Avoiding Racial Isolation Is a Legitimate Public Goal," *Newsday*, July 16, 2007, A33.

31. *Griggs v. Duke Power Company*, 401 U.S. 24 (1971). See also Allan Sindler, *Bakke, DeFunis, and Minority Admissions* (New York: Longman, 1978), 180–9.

32. For a good treatment of these issues, see Charles O. Gregory and Harold A. Katz, *Labor and the Law* (New York: W. W. Norton, 1979), chap. 17.

33. In 1970 this act was amended to outlaw for five years literacy tests as a condition for voting in all states.

34. Joint Center for Political Studies, *Black Elected Officials: A National Roster—1988* (Washington, DC: Joint Center for Political Studies Press, 1988), 9–10. For a comprehensive analysis and evaluation of the Voting Rights Act, see Bernard Grofman and Chandler Davidson, eds., *Controversies in Minority Voting: The Voting Rights Act in Perspective* (Washington, DC: Brookings Institution, 1992).

35. Ford Fessenden, "Ballots Cast by Blacks and Older Voters Were Tossed in Far Greater Numbers," *New York Times*, November 12, 2001, A17.

36. Aaron Blake, "Texas Redistricting Case: Five Things You Need to Know," *Washington Post*, December 13, 2011, www.washingtonpost.com/blogs/the-fix/post/texas -redistricting-case-five-things-you-need-to-know/2011 /12/13/gIQAdowHsO_blog.html; Manny Fernandez, "Federal Judges Approve Final Texas Redistricting Maps," *New York Times*, February 28, 2012, www .nytimes.com/2012/02/29/us/final-texas-redistricting -maps-approved.html (accessed 6/22/12).

37. *Shelby County v. Holder*, 570 U.S. __(2013).

38. *Crawford v. Marion County Election Board*, 553 U.S. 181 (2008). See also David Stout, "Supreme Court Upholds Voter Identification Law in Indiana," *New York Times*, April 29, 2008, www.nytimes.com/2008/04/29 /washington/28cnd-scotus.html (accessed 1/13/14).

39. See Douglas S. Massey and Nancy A. Denton, *American Apartheid: Segregation and the Making of the Underclass* (Cambridge, MA: Harvard University Press, 1993), chap. 7.

40. Michael Powell, "Bank Accused of Pushing Mortgage Deals on Blacks," *New York Times*, June 6, 2009, www .nytimes.com/2009/06/07/us/07baltimore.html; Charlie Savage, "Countrywide Will Settle a Bias Suit," *New York Times*, December 22, 2011, B1.

41. *Loving v. Virginia*, 388 U.S. 1 (1967).

42. *FCCV Beach Communications*, 508 U.S. 307 (1993).

43. *Windsor v. United States*, 699 F.3d 169 2nd Cir. (2012).

44. *Adarand Contractors v. Pena*, 515 U.S. 200 (1995).

45. *Fisher v. University of Texas*, 570 U.S. __ (2013).

46. *Fisher v. University of Texas*, 579 U. S. __ (2016).

47. See Jane J. Mansbridge, *Why We Lost the ERA* (Chicago: University of Chicago Press, 1986); and Gilbert Steiner, *Constitutional Inequality* (Washington, DC: Brookings Institution, 1985).

48. See *Frontiero v. Richardson*, 411 U.S. 677 (1973).

49. See *Craig v. Boren*, 423 U.S. 1047 (1976).

50. Claire Zillman, "Barnes & Noble Is Latest Retailer to Face Transgender Discrimination Lawsuit," *Fortune*, May 7, 2015, http://fortune.com/2015/05/07/barnes-noble -transgender-lawsuit/ (accessed 12/23/15).

51. *Franklin v. Gwinnett County Public Schools*, 503 U.S. 60 (1992).

52. Jennifer Halperin, "Women Step Up to Bat," *Illinois Issues* 21 (September 1995): 11–14.

53. Joan Biskupic and David Nakamura, "Court Won't Review Sports Equity Ruling," *Washington Post*, April 22, 1997, A1.

54. Debra DeMeis and Rosanna Hertz, "Sex, Sports, and Title IX on Campus: The Triumphs and Travails," Daily Beast, June 22, 2012, www.dailybeast.com/articles /2012/06/22/sex-sports-and-title-ix-on-campus-the -triumphs-and-travails.html (accessed 6/22/12).

55. *United States v. Virginia*, 518 U.S. 515 (1996).

56. Judith Havemann, "Two Women Quit Citadel over Alleged Harassment," *Washington Post*, January 13, 1997, A1.

57. *Meritor Savings Bank v. Vinson*, 477 U.S. 57 (1986). See also Gwendolyn Mink, *Hostile Environment: The Political Betrayal of Sexually Harassed Women* (Ithaca, NY: Cornell University Press, 2000), 28–32.

58. *Harris v. Forklift Systems, Inc.*, 510 U.S. 17 (1993).

59. *Burlington Industries v. Ellerth*, 524 U.S. 742 (1998); *Faragher v. City of Boca Raton*, 524 U.S. 775 (1998).

60. *Ledbetter v. Goodyear Tire and Rubber Co.*, 550 U.S. 618 (2007).

61. New Mexico had a different history because not many Anglos settled there initially. (*Anglo* is the term for a non-Hispanic white, generally of European background.) Mexican Americans had considerable power in territorial legislatures between 1865 and 1912. See Lawrence H. Fuchs, *The American Kaleidoscope* (Hanover, NH: University Press of New England, 1990), 239–40.

62. *Salvatierra v. Del Rio Independent School District*, 33 S.W.2d 790 (Tex. Civ. App. 1930).

63. *Mendez v. Westminster*, 64 F. Supp. 544 (S.D. Cal. 1946), aff'd, 161 F.2d 774 (9th Cir. 1947) (en banc).

64. On the United Farm Workers and César Chávez, see Marshall Ganz, *Why David Sometimes Wins: Leadership, Organization, and Strategy in the California Farm Worker Movement* (New York: Oxford University Press, 2009); Miriam Pawel, *The Union of Their Dreams: Power, Hope and Struggle in Cesar Chavez's Farm Worker Movement* (New York: Bloomsbury Press, 2010); and Jacques E. Levy, *Cesar Chavez: Autobiography of La Causa* (Minneapolis: University of Minnesota Press, 2007).

65. *United States v. Texas*, 579 U.S. __ (2016).

66. Dick Kirschten, "Not Black and White," *National Journal*, March 2, 1991, 497.

67. Gretchen Gavett, "Controversial 'Secure Communities' Immigration Program Will Be Mandatory by 2013," www .pbs.org/wgbh/pages/frontline/race-multicultural/lost-in -detention/controversial-secure-communities-immigration -program-will-be-mandatory-by-2013 (accessed 12/3/2013).

68. *Arizona v. United States*, 567 U.S. __ (2012); Robert Barnes, "Supreme Court Rejects Much of Arizona Immigration Law," *Washington Post*, June 25, 2012, www .washingtonpost.com/politics/supreme-court-rules-on -arizona-immigration-law/2012/06/25/gJQA0Nrm1V _story.html?hpid5zl (accessed 6/25/12).

69. *United States v. Wong Kim Ark*, 169 U.S. 649 (1898).

70. *Korematsu v. United States*, 323 U.S. 214 (1944).

71. Children of the Camps, "Historical Documents: Civil Liberties Act of 1988," http://pbs.org/childofcamp/history /civilact.html (accessed 2/17/08).

72. *Lau v. Nichols*, 414 U.S. 563 (1974).

73. Not all Native American tribes agreed with this, including the Navajos. See Ronald Takaki, *A Different Mirror: A History of Multicultural America* (Boston: Little, Brown, 1993), 238–45.

74. On the resurgence of Native American political activity, see Stephen Cornell, *The Return of the Native: American Indian Political Resurgence* (New York: Oxford University Press, 1990); and Dee Brown, *Bury My Heart at Wounded Knee* (New York: Holt, Rinehart, 1971).

75. See the discussion in Robert A. Katzmann, *Institutional Disability: The Saga of Transportation Policy for the Disabled* (Washington, DC: Brookings Institution, 1986).

76. For example, after pressure from the Justice Department, one of the nation's largest rental-car companies agreed to make special hand controls available to any customer requesting them. See "Avis Agrees to Equip Cars for Disabled," *Los Angeles Times*, September 2, 1994, D1.

77. For more, see Dale Carpenter, *Flagrant Conduct: The Story of* Lawrence v. Texas (New York: W. W. Norton, 2012).

78. *Bowers v. Hardwick*, 478 U.S. 186 (1986).

79. *Romer v. Evans*, 517 U.S. 620 (1996).

80. *Lawrence v. Texas*, 539 U.S. 558 (2003).

81. *Obergefell v. Hodges*, 576 U.S. __ (2015).

82. Joseph Kane and Adie Tomer, "Income Disparities Holding Back U.S. Internet Adoption," Brookings, *The Avenue* (blog), November 18, 2015, www.brookings.edu/blogs /the-avenue/posts/2015/11/18-income-disparities -internet-adoption-kane-tomer (accessed 12/23/15).

83. The Department of Health, Education, and Welfare (HEW) was the cabinet department charged with administering most federal social programs. In 1980, when education programs were transferred to the newly created Department of Education, HEW was renamed the Department of Health and Human Services.

84. *Regents of the University of California v. Bakke*, 438 U.S. 265 (1978).

85. See, for example, *United Steelworkers v. Weber*, 443 U.S. 193 (1979); and *Fullilove v. Klutznick*, 448 U.S. 448 (1980).

86. *Adarand Constructors v. Peña*, 515 U.S. 200 (1995).

87. *Gratz v. Bollinger*, 539 U.S. 244 (2003).

88. *Grutter v. Bollinger*, 539 U.S. 306 (2003).

89. *Fisher v. University of Texas*.

90. Pew Research Center, "Across Racial Lines, More Say Nation Needs to Make Changes to Achieve Racial Equality," August 5, 2015, www.people-press.org/2015/08/05 /across-racial-lines-more-say-nation-needs-to-make -changes-to-achieve-racial-equality/ (accessed 12/23/15).

91. There are still many genuine racists in America, but with the exception of a lunatic fringe, made up of neo-Nazis

and members of the Ku Klux Klan, most racists are too ashamed or embarrassed to take part in normal political discourse. They are not included in either category here.

92. *Slaughterhouse Cases*, 16 Wallace 36 (1873).

Chapter 6

1. Benjamin Page and Larry Jacobs, *Class War? What Americans Really Think about Economic Inequality* (Chicago: University of Chicago Press, 2009).

2. Bernadette D. Proctor, Jessica L. Semega, and Melissa A. Kollar, "Income and Poverty in the United States: 2015," September 2016, www.census.gov/content/dam/Census/library/publications/2016/demo/p60-256.pdf (accessed 10/8/16).

3. Thomas Piketty and Emmanuel Saez, "Top Incomes and the Great Recession: Recent Evolutions and Policy Implications," *IMF Economic Review* 61 (2013): 456–78.

4. Emmanuel Saez, "Striking It Richer: The Evolution of Top Incomes in the United States," January 25, 2015, https://eml.berkeley.edu/~saez/saez-UStopincomes-2013.pdf (accessed 10/8/16).

5. Bruce Stokes, "The U.S.'s High Income Gap Is Met with Relatively Low Public Concern," Pew Research Center, Fact Tank, December 6, 2013, www.pewresearch.org/fact-tank/2013/12/06/the-u-s-s-high-income-gap-is-met-with-relatively-low-public-concern/ (accessed 1/20/14).

6. Noam Scheiber and Dalia Sussman, "Inequality Troubles Americans across Party Lines, Times/CBS Poll Finds," *New York Times*, June 3, 2015.

7. Milton Lodge and Charles Taber, "Three Steps toward a Theory of Motivated Political Reasoning," in *Elements of Reason: Cognition, Choice, and the Bounds of Rationality*, ed. Arthur Lupia, Mathew D. McCubbins, and Samuel L. Popkin (London: Cambridge University Press, 2000); David Redlawsk, "Hot Cognition or Cool Consideration? Testing the Effects of Motivated Reasoning on Political Decision Making," *Journal of Politics* 64 (2002): 1021–44; David Redlawsk, Andrew Civettini, and Karen Emmerson, "The Affective Tipping Point: Do Motivated Reasoners Ever 'Get It'?" *Political Psychology* 31, no. 4 (2010): 563–93.

8. George E. Marcus, W. Russell Neuman, and Michael MacKuen, *Affective Intelligence and Political Judgment* (Chicago: University of Chicago Press, 2000).

9. "A Year Later, U.S. Campaign against ISIS Garners Support, Raises Concerns," July 22, 2015, Pew Research Center, www.people-press.org/2015/07/22/a-year-later-u-s-campaign-against-isis-garners-support-raises-concerns/ (accessed 3/4/16).

10. Pew Research Center, "A Year Later, U.S. Campaign against ISIS Garners Support, Raises Concerns," July 22, 2015, www.people-press.org/2015/07/22/a-year-later-u-s-campaign-against-isis-garners-support-raises-concerns/ (accessed 5/2/16).

11. George Gao, "What Americans Think about NSA Surveillance, National Security and Privacy," Pew Research Center, Fact Tank, May 29, 2015, www.pewresearch.org/fact-tank/2015/05/29/what-americans-think-about-nsa-surveillance-national-security-and-privacy/ (accessed 11/23/15).

12. Pew Research Center, "Beyond Red vs. Blue: The Political Typology. Section 6: Foreign Affairs, Terrorism and Privacy," June 26, 2014, www.people-press.org/2014/06/26/section-6-foreign-affairs-terrorism-and-privacy/ (accessed 3/11/16).

13. Richard Wike and Katie Simmons, "Global Support for Principle of Free Expression, but Opposition to Some Forms of Speech: Americans Especially Likely to Embrace Individual Liberties," Pew Research Center, November 18, 2015, www.pewglobal.org/2015/11/18/global-support-for-principle-of-free-expression-but-opposition-to-some-forms-of-speech/ (accessed 11/18/15).

14. Milton Lodge and Charles Taber, "Three Steps toward a Theory of Motivated Political Reasoning," in *Elements of Reason: Cognition, Choice, and the Bounds of Rationality*, ed. Arthur Lupia, Mathew D. McCubbins, and Samuel L. Popkin (London: Cambridge University Press, 2000); Marcus, Neuman, and MacKuen, *Affective Intelligence*; David Redlawsk, "Hot Cognition or Cool Consideration? Testing the Effects of Motivated Reasoning on Political Decision Making," *Journal of Politics* 64 (2002): 1021–44; David Redlawsk, Andrew Civettini, and Karen Emmerson, "The Affective Tipping Point: Do Motivated Reasoners Ever 'Get It'?" *Political Psychology* 31, no. 4 (2010): 563–93.

15. Desilver, "5 Facts" (accessed 11/23/15).

16. See Harry Holloway and John George, *Public Opinion* (New York: St. Martin's Press, 1986); Paul R. Abramson, *Political Attitudes in America* (San Francisco: Freeman, 1983).

17. See Paul M. Sniderman and Edward G. Carmines, *Reaching beyond Race* (Cambridge, MA: Harvard University Press, 1997).

18. Lydia Saad, "Conservatives Hang on to Ideology Lead by a Thread," Gallup, January 11, 2016, www.gallup.com/poll/188129/conservatives-hang-ideology-lead-thread.aspx (accessed 10/3/16).

19. Jocelyn Kiley and Michael Dimock, "The GOP's Millennial Problem Runs Deep," September 25, 2014, www.pewresearch.org/fact-tank/2014/09/25/the-gops-millennial-problem-runs-deep/ (accessed 3/4/16).

20. Douglas R. Oxley et al., "Political Attitudes Vary with Physiological Traits," *Science* 321, no. 5896 (September 19, 2008): 1667–70. See also Jeffrey Mondak, *Personality and the Foundation of Political Behavior* (Cambridge: Cambridge University Press, 2010).

21. John Alford, Carolyn Funk, and John Hibbing, "Are Political Orientations Genetically Transmitted?" *American Political Science Review* 99, no. 2 (2005): 153–67;

Rich Morin, "Study on Twins Suggests Our Political Beliefs May Be Hard-Wired," Pew Research Center, Fact Tank, December 9, 2013, www.pewresearch.org/fact-tank/2013/12/09/study-on-twins-suggests-our-political-beliefs-may-be-hard-wired/ (accessed 1/20/14).

22. See Angus Campbell et al., *The American Voter* (New York: Wiley, 1960), 147.

23. Betsy Sinclair, *The Social Citizen: Peer Networks and Political Behavior* (Chicago: University of Chicago Press, 2012).

24. Pew Research Center, "Changing Attitudes on Gay Marriage," July 29, 2015, www.pewforum.org/2015/07/29/graphics-slideshow-changing-attitudes-on-gay-marriage/ (accessed 2/23/16).

25. Jennifer A. Heerwig and Brian J. McCabe, "Education and Social Desirability Bias: The Case of a Black Presidential Candidate," *Social Science Quarterly* 90, no. 3 (2009): 674–86.

26. Raymond E. Wolfinger and Steven J. Rosenstone, *Who Votes?* (New Haven, CT: Yale University Press, 1980). See also Steven J. Rosenstone and John Mark Hansen, *Mobilization, Participation, and Democracy in America* (New York: Macmillan, 1993).

27. Katherine Tate, *Black Faces in the Mirror* (Princeton, NJ: Princeton University Press, 1993).

28. Tate, *Black Faces*.

29. Brakkton Booker, "How Equal Is American Opportunity? Survey Shows Attitudes Vary by Race," National Public Radio, September 21, 2015, www.npr.org/sections/thetwo-way/2015/09/21/442068004/how-equal-is-american-opportunity-survey-shows-attitudes-vary-by-race (accessed 3/11/16).

30. Pew Research Center, "Across Racial Lines, More Say Nation Needs to Make Changes to Achieve Racial Equality," August 5, 2015, www.people-press.org/2015/08/05/across-racial-lines-more-say-nation-needs-to-make-changes-to-achieve-racial-equality/8-4-2015_02a/ (accessed 2/24/16).

31. Michael Tesler and David O. Sears, *Obama's Race: The 2008 Election and the Dream of a Post-Racial America* (Chicago: University of Chicago Press, 2010).

32. Pew Research Center, "Hispanic Population Reaches Record 55 Million but Growth Has Cooled," June 25, 2015, www.pewresearch.org/fact-tank/2015/06/25/u-s-hispanic-population-growth-surge-cools/ (accessed 5/4/16).

33. Anna Brown and Renee Stepler, "Statistical Portrait of the Foreign-Born Population in the United States, 1960–2013," Pew Research Center, September 28, 2015, www.pewhispanic.org/2015/09/28/statistical-portrait-of-the-foreign-born-population-in-the-united-states-1960-2013-key-charts/#2013-fb-origin (accessed 12/22/15).

34. Author analysis of 2014 Cooperative Election Study, Harvard University, released February 2015, http://projects.iq.harvard.edu/cces/home (accessed 3/4/16)

35. Matt Barreto and Gary M. Segura, *Latino America: How America's Most Dynamic Population Is Poised to Transform the Politics of the Nation* (New York: Public Affairs, 2014).

36. Michael X. Delli Carpini and Scott Keeter, "The Gender Gap in Political Knowledge," *The Public Perspective*, July/August 1992, www.ropercenter.cornell.edu/public-perspective/ppscan/35/35023.pdf (accessed 5/4/16).

37. Michael Lipka, Religious "Nones" Are Not Only Growing, They're Becoming More Secular," Pew Research Center, Fact Tank, November 11, 2015, www.pewresearch.org/facttank/2015/11/11/religious-nones-are-not-only-growing-theyre-becoming-more-secular/ (accessed 11/11/15).

38. 2014 Cooperative Comparative Election Study.

39. See Richard Lau and David Redlawsk, *How Voters Decide: Information Processing during an Election Campaign* (New York: Cambridge University Press, 2006).

40. Brian Schaffner and Stephen Ansolabehere, "CCES Common Content, 2014," Havard Dataverse, V2, http://dx.doi.org/10.7910/DVN/XFXJVY (accessed 5/4/16).

41. Morris Fiorina, Samuel Abrams, and Jeremy Pope, *Culture War? The Myth of a Polarized America* (New York: Longman, 2004).

42. 2014 Cooperative Comparative Election Study.

43. Nathan J. Kelly and Peter K. Enns, "Inequality and the Dynamics of Public Opinion: The Self-Reinforcing Link between Economic Inequality and Mass Preferences," *American Journal of Political Science* 54, no. 4 (2010): 855–70; Jacob S. Hacker and Paul Pierson, *Winner-Take-All Politics: How Washington Made the Rich Richer—and Turned Its Back on the Middle Class* (New York: Simon and Schuster, 2010).

44. Larry M. Bartels, "Homer Gets a Tax Cut: Inequality and Public Policy in the American Mind," *Perspectives on Politics* 3, no. 1 (2005): 15–31; Larry Bartels, *Unequal Democracy: The Political Economy of the New Gilded Age* (Princeton, NJ: Princeton University Press, 2008).

45. Thomas E. Mann and Norman J. Ornstein, *It's Even Worse Than It Looks: How the American Constitutional System Collided with the New Politics of Extremism* (New York: Basic Books, 2012).

46. Shaun Bowler, Gary Segura, and Stephen Nicholson, "Earthquakes and Aftershocks: Race, Direct Democracy, and Partisan Change," *American Journal of Political Science* 50 (2006): 146–59. For a more general discussion of the spillover effects of ballot measures on public opinion, see Stephen Nicholson, *Voting the Agenda: Candidates, Elections, and Ballot Propositions* (Princeton, NJ: Princeton University Press, 2005).

47. John R. Zaller, *The Nature and Origins of Mass Opinion* (New York: Cambridge University Press, 1992).

48. Milton Lodge, Kathleen McGraw, and Patrick Stroh, "An Impression-Driven Model of Candidate Evaluation," *American Political Science Review* 83, no. 2 (1989): 399–419.

49. Benjamin I. Page and Robert Y. Shapiro, *The Rational Public: Fifty Years of Trends in Americans' Policy Preferences* (Chicago: University of Chicago Press, 1995); Eugene Wittkopf, *Faces of Internationalism: Public Opinion and Foreign Policy* (Durham, NC: Duke University Press, 1990).

50. Pew Research Center, "In Gay Marriage Debate, Both Supporters and Opponents See Legal Recognition as 'Inevitable,'" June 6, 2013, www.people-press.org/2013/06/06/in-gay-marriage-debate-both-supporters-and-opponents-see-legal-recognition-as-inevitable (accessed 3/19/14).

51. *Varnum v. Brien*, 22 Ill.763 N.W.2d 862 (Iowa 2009) [2009 BL 73739].

52. Rebecca J. Kreitzer, Allison J. Hamilton, and Caroline J. Tolbert, "Does Policy Adoption Change Opinions on Minority Rights? The Effects of Legalizing Same-Sex Marriage," *Political Research Quarterly* (July 10, 2014), http://prq.sagepub.com/content/early/2014/07/07/1065912914540483.abstract.

53. *Obergefell v. Hodges*, 576 U.S. __ (2015)

54. Zaller, *Nature and Origins*.

55. Carroll Glynn et al., *Public Opinion*, 2nd ed. (Boulder, CO: Westview, 2004), 293. See also Michael X. Delli Carpini and Scott Keeter, *What Americans Know about Politics and Why It Matters* (New Haven, CT: Yale University Press, 1996).

56. Adam J. Berinsky, "The Two Faces of Public Opinion," *American Journal of Political Science* 43, no. 4 (1999): 1209–30.

57. Delli Carpini and Keeter, *What Americans Know*.

58. Pilar Marrero, "June Tracking Poll: Immigration Is a Critical Issue for Voters," *Latino Decisions*, June 10, 2011, www.latinodecisions.com/blog/2011/06/10/june-tracking-poll-immigration-is-a-critical-issue-for-voters (accessed 6/6/12).

59. Adam J. Berinsky, "Assuming the Costs of War: Events, Elites and American Support for Military Conflict," *Journal of Politics* 69, no. 4 (2007): 975–97; Zaller, *Nature and Origins*.

60. Richard R. Lau and David P. Redlawsk, "Advantages and Disadvantages of Cognitive Heuristics in Political Decision Making," *American Journal of Political Science* 45 (October 2001): 951–71. Lau and Redlawsk, *How Voters Decide*.

61. For a discussion of the role of information in politics, see Arthur Lupia and Matthew D. McCubbins, *The Democratic Dilemma: Can Citizens Learn What They Need to Know?* (New York: Cambridge University Press, 1998). See also Shaun Bowler and Todd Donovan, *Demanding Choices: Opinion and Voting in Direct Democracy* (Ann Arbor: University of Michigan Press, 1998). See also Samuel Popkin, *The Reasoning Voter: Communication and Persuasion in Presidential Campaigns* (Chicago: University of Chicago Press, 1991); Arthur Lupia, "Shortcuts Versus Encyclopedias: Information and Voting Behavior in California Insurance Reform Elections," *American Political Science Review* 88 (1994): 63–76; and Wendy Rahn, "The Role of Partisan Stereotypes in Information Processing about Political Candidates," *American Journal of Political Science* 37 (1993): 472–96.

62. James Druckman, Erik Petersen, and Rune Slothuus, "How Elite Partisan Polarization Affects Public Opinion Formation," *American Political Science Review* 107, no. 1 (February 2013): 57–79.

63. Lee Rainie et al., "Social Media and Political Engagement," Pew Research Center, October 19, 2012, www.pewinternet.org/2012/10/19/social-media-and-political-engagement (accessed 8/14/14).

64. Tony Dokoupil, "Is the Internet Making Us Crazy? What the New Research Says," *Newsweek*, July 9, 2012, http://mag.newsweek.com/2012/07/08/is-the-internet-making-us-crazy-what-the-new-research-says.html (accessed 3/19/14); Nicholas Carr, *The Shallows: What the Internet Is Doing to Our Brains* (New York: W. W. Norton, 2011).

65. Bartels, *Unequal Democracy*.

66. Benjamin Ginsberg, *The American Lie: Government by the People and Other Political Fables* (Boulder, CO: Paradigm, 2007).

67. Gerald F. Seib and Michael K. Frisby, "Selling Sacrifice," *Wall Street Journal*, February 5, 1993, 1.

68. Peter Marks, "Adept in Politics and Advertising, 4 Women Shape a Campaign," *New York Times*, November 11, 2001, B6.

69. John Zaller and Dennis Chiu, "Government's Little Helper: U.S. Press Coverage of Foreign Policy Crises, 1945–1991," *Political Communications* 13 (1996): 385–405

70. David W. Moore, "Support for Invasion of Iraq Remains Contingent on U.N. Approval," Gallup, November 12, 2002, www.gallup.com/poll/7195/support-invasion-iraq-remains-contingent-un-approval.aspx; Pew Research Center, "Public Attitudes toward the War in Iraq: 2003–2008," March 19, 2008, www.pewresearch.org/2008/03/19/public-attitudes-toward-the-war-in-iraq-20032008 (accessed 2/19/14).

71. *Roe v. Wade*, 410 U.S. 113 (1973).

72. See Gillian Peele, *Revival and Reaction* (Oxford: Clarendon, 1985). See also Connie Paige, *The Right-to-Lifers* (New York: Summit, 1983).

73. See David Vogel, "The Public Interest Movement and the American Reform Tradition," *Political Science Quarterly* 96 (Winter 1980): 607–27.

74. See Shanto Iyengar, *Is Anyone Responsible? How Television Frames Political Issues* (Chicago: University of Chicago Press, 1991); and Shanto Iyengar, *Do the Media Govern?* (Thousand Oaks, CA: Sage, 1997).

75. Campbell et al., *The American Voter*.

76. Benjamin I. Page and Robert Y. Shapiro, "Effects of Public Opinion on Policy," *American Political Science Review* 77, no. 1 (1983): 175–90.

77. Gerald C. Wright, Rober S. Erikson, and John P. McIver, "Public Opinion and Policy Liberalism in the American States," *American Journal of Political Science* 31, no. 4 (November 1987): 980–1001.

78. Pew Research Center, "Mixed Views of Economic Policies and Health Care Reform Persist: Support for Health Care Principles, Opposition to Package," October 8, 2009, www.people-press.org/2009/10/08/mixed-views-of-economic-policies-and-health-care-reform-persist/ (accessed 2/15/14).

79. Christopher Wlezien, "The Public as Thermostat: Dynamics of Preferences for Spending," *American Journal of Political Science*, 39 no. 4 (1995): 981–1000.

80. See Julianna Pacheco, "Attitudinal Policy Feedback and Public Opinion: The Impact of Smoking Bans on Attitudes toward Smokers, Secondhand Smoke, and Anti-Smoking Policies," *Political Research Quarterly* 77, no. 3 (2013): 714–34; Barbara Norrander, "The Multi-Layered Impact of Public Opinion on Capital Punishment Implementation in the American States," *Political Research Quarterly* 53, no. 4 (2000): 771–93; Suzanne Mettler and Joe Soss, "The Consequences of Public Policy for Democratic Citizenship: Bridging Policy Studies and Mass Politics," *Perspectives on Politics* 2, no. 1 (2004): 55–73; Andrea Hetling and Monika L. McDermott, "Judging a Book by Its Cover: Did Perceptions of the 1996 U.S. Welfare Reforms Affect Public Support for Spending on the Poor?" *Journal of Social Policy* 37, no. 3 (2008): 471–87; Joe Soss, "Lessons of Welfare: Policy Design, Political Learning, and Political Action," *American Political Science Review* 93, no. 2 (1999): 363–80; Joe Soss and Sanford F. Schram, "A Public Transformed? Welfare Reform as Policy Feedback," *American Political Science Review* 101, no. 1 (2007): 111.

81. Malcolm E. Jewell, *Representation in State Legislatures* (Lexington: University Press of Kentucky, 1982).

82. Lawrence R. Jacobs and Robert Y. Shapiro, *Politicians Don't Pander: Political Manipulation and the Loss of Democratic Responsiveness* (Chicago: University of Chicago Press, 2000).

83. John Griffin and Brian Newman, "Are Voters Better Represented?" *Journal of Politics* 67 (2005): 1206–27.

84. Bartels, *Unequal Democracy*.

85. Other authors have endorsed Bartels's view that government policy exacerbates income inequality. See, for example, Hacker and Pierson, *Winner-Take-All Politics*.

86. Martin Gilens, "Inequality and Democratic Responsiveness," *Public Opinion Quarterly* 69, no. 5 (2005): 778–96; and Martin Gilens, "Preference Gaps and Inequality in Representation," *PS: Political Science and Politics* 42, no. 2 (2009): 335–41.

87. Robert Dahl, *A Preface to Democratic Theory* (Chicago: University of Chicago Press, 1956).

88. David Redlawsk, Caroline Tolbert, and Todd Donovan, *Why Iowa? How Caucuses and Sequential Elections Improve the Presidential Nominating Process* (Chicago: University of Chicago Press, 2011).

89. Redlawsk, Tolbert, and Donovan, *Why Iowa?*

90. Herbert Asher, *Polling and the Public* (Washington, DC: CQ Press, 2001), 64.

91. Drew DeSilver and Scott Keeter, "The challenges of polling when fewer people are available to be polled," July 21, 2015, www.pewresearch.org/fact-tank/2015/07/21/the-challenges-of-polling-when-fewer-people-are-available-to-be-polled/ (accessed 3/1/16).

92. Michael Kagay and Janet Elder, "Numbers Are No Problem for Pollsters, Words Are," *New York Times*, August 9, 1992, E6.

93. Lynn Vavreck and Douglas Rivers, "The 2006 Cooperative Congressional Election Study," *Journal of Elections, Public Opinion and Parties* 18, no. 4 (2008): 355–66. See also Simon Jackman and Lynn Vavreck, "Primary Politics: Race, Gender, and Age in the 2008 Democratic Primary," *Journal of Elections, Public Opinion and Parties* 20, no. 2 (2010): 153–86.

94. Nate Silver, "FiveThirtyEight's Pollster Ratings," August 5, 2016, FiveThirtyEight, projects.fivethirtyeight.com/pollster-ratings/ (accessed 10/16/16).

95. Dennis Chong and James N. Druckman, "A Theory of Framing and Opinion Formation in Competitive Elite Environments," *Journal of Communication* 57 (2007): 99–118. See also Stephen P. Nicholson and Robert M. Howard, "Framing Support for the Supreme Court in the Aftermath of *Bush v. Gore*," *Journal of Politics* 65, no. 3 (2003): 676–95; and Dennis Chong and James N. Druckman, "Framing Public Opinion in Competitive Democracies," *American Political Science Review* 101, no. 4 (2007): 637–55.

96. Zaller, *Nature and Origins*.

97. Berinsky, "Two Faces of Public Opinion." See also Adam Berinsky, "Political Context and the Survey Response: The Dynamics of Racial Policy Opinion," *Journal of Politics* 64, no. 2 (2002): 567–84.

98. Nate Silver, "Which Polls Fared Best (and Worst) in the 2012 Presidential Race," November 10, 2012, http://fivethirtyeight.blogs.nytimes.com/2012/11/10/which-polls-fared-best-and-worst-in-the-2012-presidential-race/ (accessed 2/24/16).

99. Redlawsk, Tolbert, and Donovan, *Why Iowa?*

100. Sasha Issenberg, *The Victory Lab: The Secret Science of Winning Campaigns* (New York: Broadway Books, 2012); Sasha Issenberg, "A More Perfect Union: How President Obama's Campaign Used Big Data to Rally Individual Voters," *MIT Technology Review*, December 19, 2012, www.technologyreview.com/featuredstory/509026/how-obamas-team-used-big-data-to-rally-voters/ (accessed 11/25/15).

101. Chris Taylor, "Triumph of the Nerds: Nate Silver Wins in 50 States," November 7, 2012, http://mashable.com/2012/11/07/nate-silver-wins/#6aWvyWVGcaqq (accessed 2/24/16).

102. Christopher Wlezien and Stuart Soroka, "The Relationship between Public Opinion and Policy," in *Oxford Handbook of Political Behavior*, ed. Russell Dalton and Hans-Dieter Klingemann (New York: Oxford University Press, 2009), 799–817.

103. Gilens, "Inequality and Democratic Responsiveness"; Bartels, *Unequal Democracy*.

104. Ryan Claassen and Benjamin Highton, "Does Policy Debate Reduce Information Effects in Public Opinion? Analyzing the Evolution of Public Opinion on Health Care," *Journal of Politics* 68, no. 2 (2006): 410–20.

Chapter 7

1. Caroline Tolbert and Ramona McNeal, "Unraveling the Effects of the Internet on Political Participation," *Political Research Quarterly* 56, no. 2 (2003): 175–85. See also Bruce Bimber, "Information and Political Engagement in America: The Search for Effects of Information Technology at the Individual Level," *Political Research Quarterly* 54 (2001): 53–67; Bruce Bimber, *Information and American Democracy: Technology in the Evolution of Political Power* (Cambridge: Cambridge University Press, 2003); and Brian S. Krueger, "Assessing the Potential of Internet Political Participation in the United States," *American Politics Research* 30 (2002): 476–98.

2. Michael Barthel, et al., "The Evolving Role of News on Twitter and Facebook," Pew Research Center, www.journalism.org/2015/07/14/the-evolving-role-of-news-on-twitter-and-facebook/ (accessed 1/14/16).

3. Andrew Chadwick, *The Hybrid Media System: Politics and Power* (New York: Oxford University Press, 2013).

4. Julian P. Boyd et al., ed., *The Papers of Thomas Jefferson* (Princeton, NJ: Princeton University Press), http://press-pubs.uchicago.edu/founders/documents/amendI_speechs8.html (accessed 5/30/14).

5. Pew Research Center, "Amid Criticism, Support for Media's 'Watchdog' Role Stands Out," August 8, 2013, www.people-press.org/2013/08/08/amid-criticism-support-for-medias-watchdog-role-stands-out (accessed 4/27/14).

6. U.S. Census Bureau, Current Population Survey: Computer and Internet Use Supplement, 1998.

7. U.S. Census Bureau, American Community Survey, 2014, www.census.gov/programs-surveys/acs/news/data-releases.html.

8. Robert McChesney and John Nichols, *The Death and Life of American Journalism: The Media Revolution That Will Begin the World Again* (New York: Nation Books, 2010).

9. Ken Doctor, "Newsonomics: 10 Numbers That Define the News Business Today," Nieman Lab, June 25, 2015, www.niemanlab.org/2015/06/newsonomics-10-numbers-that-define-the-news-business-today/ (accessed 1/14/16).

10. Darrell West, *The Next Wave: Using Digital Technology to Further Social and Political Innovation* (Washington, DC: Brookings Institution Press, 2011).

11. Pew Research Center, "Newspapers: Print and Online Ad Revenue," Newspaper Association of America (2003–2013), Pew Research Analysis of BIA/Kelsey Data (2014), www.journalism.org/media-indicators/newspaper-print-and-online-ad-revenue/ (accessed 1/22/16).

12. Amy Mitchell, "State of the News Media 2015," Pew Research Center, Journalism and Media, April 29, 2015, www.journalism.org/2015/04/29/state-of-the-news-media-2015 (accessed 1/22/16).

13. Mitchell, "State of the News Media 2015."

14. Pew Research Center, Project for Excellence in Journalism, "State of the News Media 2013: Overview," 2013, www.stateofthemedia.org/2013/overview-5/ (accessed 3/14/16).

15. Robert O'Harrow, Jr., "Trump's Bad Bet: How Too Much Debt Drove His Biggest Casino Aground," *Washington Post*, January 18, 2016, www.washingtonpost.com/investigations/trumps-bad-bet-how-too-much-debt-drove-his-biggest-casino-aground/2016/01/18/f67cedc2-9ac8-11e5-8917-653b65c809eb_story.html (accessed 3/9/16); Robert O'Harrow, Jr., "Trump Swam in Mob-Infested Waters in Early Years as an NYC Developer," *Washington Post*, October 16, 2015, www.washingtonpost.com/investigations/trump-swam-in-mob-infested-waters-in-early-years-as-an-nyc-developer/2015/10/16/3c75b918-60a3-11e5-b38e-06883aacba64_story.html (accessed 3/9/16).

16. Mitchell, "State of the News Media 2015."

17. Mitchell, "State of the News Media 2015."

18. Pew Research Center, "The Internet's Broader Role in Campaign 2008," January 11, 2008, www.people-press.org/2008/01/11/internets-broader-role-in-campaign-2008/; and "Journalism, Satire or Just Laughs? 'The Daily Show' with Jon Stewart' Examined," May 8, 2008, www.journalism.org/2008/05/08/journalism-satire-or-just-laughs-the-daily-show-with-jon-stewart-examined/ (accessed 9/7/12).

19. Michael Barthel, "In the News Industry, Diversity Is Lowest at Smaller Outlets," Pew Research Center, Fact Tank, www.pewresearch.org/fact-tank/2015/08/04/in-the-news-industry-diversity-is-lowest-at-smaller-outlets/ (accessed 1/14/16).

20. Mitchell, "State of the News Media 2015."

21. For a criticism of the increasing consolidation of the media, see the essays in Patricia Aufderheide et al., *Conglomerates and the Media* (New York: New Press, 1997).

22. Jonathan M. Ladd, *Why Americans Hate the Media and How It Matters* (Princeton, NJ: Princeton University Press, 2012).

23. Andrew Kohut, Carroll Doherty, Michael Dimock, and Scott Keeter, "Views of the News Media 1985–2011: Press Widely Criticized, but Trust More Than Other Information Sources," Pew Research Center, September 22, 2011, www.people-press.org/files/legacy-pdf/9-22-2011%20Media%20Attitudes%20Release.pdf (accessed 6/23/16).

24. West, *The Next Wave*; Edward Glaeser, *Triumph of the City: How Our Greatest Invention Makes Us Richer, Smarter, Greener, Healthier, and Happier* (New York: Penguin Press, 2011).

25. Pew Research Center, "Internet Use over Time," 2014, www.pewinternet.org/datatrend/internet-use/internet-use-over-time (accessed 4/29/2014).

26. Amy Mitchell, Jeffrey Gottfried, and Katerina Eva Matsa, "Millennials and Political News: Social Media—The Local TV for the Next Generation?" June 1, 2015, Pew Research Center, www.journalism.org/2015/06/01/millennials-political-news/ (accessed 1/14/16).

27. Aaron Smith and Maeve Duggan, "Online Political Videos and Campaign 2012," Pew Research Center, November 2, 2012, www.pewinternet.org/2012/11/02/online-political-videos-and-campaign-2012 (accessed 4/29/2014).

28. Jeffrey Gottfriend and Elisa Shearer, "News Use across Social Media Platforms 2016," Pew Research Center, May 26, 2016, www.journalism.org/2016/05/26/news-use-across-social-media-platforms-2016/ (accessed 6/17/16).

29. Antony Wilhelm, *Digital Nation: Toward an Inclusive Information Society* (Cambridge, MA: MIT Press, 2006); Paul DiMaggio, et al., "Social Implications of the Internet," *Annual Review of Sociology* 27, no. 1 (2001): 307–36.

30. Karen Mossberger, Caroline Tolbert, and Allison Hamilton, "Measuring Digital Citizenship: Mobile Access and Broadband," *International Journal of Communication* 6 (2012): 2492–528; Brian A. Krueger, "A Comparison of Conventional and Internet Political Mobilization," *American Politics Research* 34, no. 6 (2006): 759–76.

31. Karen Mossberger, Caroline Tolbert, and Mary Stansbury, *Virtual Inequality: Beyond the Digital Divide* (Washington, DC: Georgetown University Press, 2003); Pippa Norris, *Digital Divide: Civic Engagement, Information Poverty, and the Internet Worldwide* (New York: Cambridge University Press, 2001).

32. John B. Morris, "Language and Citizenship May Contribute to Low Internet Use among Hispanics," National Telecommunications & Information Administration, November 17, 2015, https://www.ntia.doc.gov/blog/2015/language-and-citizenship-may-contribute-low-internet-use-among-hispanics (accessed 1/14/16).

33. U.S. Census Bureau, "Nearly 8 in 10 Americans Have Access to High-Speed Internet," American Community Survey, November 13, 2014, www.census.gov/newsroom/press-releases/2014/cb14-202.html (accessed 3/2/16). Section 1.02 31. U.S. Census Bureau, "Nearly 8 in 10 Americans."

34. National Telecommunications & Information Administration, *Digital Nation: 21st Century America's Progress towards Universal Broadband Access* (Washington, DC: U.S. Department of Commerce, 2011).

35. Kenneth Olmstead and Elisa Shearer, "Digital News—Audience: Fact Sheet," Pew Research Center, April 29, 2015, www.journalism.org/2015/04/29/digital-news-audience-fact-sheet/ (accessed 1/14/16).

36. Olmstead and Shearer, "Digital News."

37. Jesse Holcomb, "5 Key Takeaways about Today's Washington Press Corps," Pew Research Center, December 3, 2015, www.pewresearch.org/fact-tank/2015/12/03/key-takeaways-washington-press-corps/ (accessed 1/14/16).

38. "Number of Monthly Active Facebook Users Worldwide as of 2nd Quarter 2016 (in Millions)," Statistica, www.statista.com/statistics/264810/number-of-monthly-active-facebook-users-worldwide/ and "Number of Facebook Users in the United States from 2014 to 2021 (in Millions)," Statistica, www.statista.com/statistics/408971/number-of-us-facebook-users/ (accessed 10/4/16).

39. Gottfriend and Shearer, "News Use across Social Media Platforms 2016."

40. Amy Mitchell, Jeffrey Gottfried, and Katerina Eva Matsa, "Political Interest and Awareness Lower among Millennials," Pew Research Center, June 1, 2015, www.journalism.org/2015/06/01/political-interest-and-awareness-lower-among-millennials/ (accessed 12/7/15).

41. Michael Barthel et al., "The Evolving Role of News on Twitter and Facebook," Pew Research Center, July 14, 2015, www.journalism.org/2015/07/14/the-evolving-role-of-news-on-twitter-and-facebook/ (accessed 1/14/16).

42. Richard Davis, "Interplay: Political Blogging and Journalism," in *iPolitics: Citizens, Elections, and Governing in the New Media Era*, ed. Richard L. Fox and Jennifer M. Ramos (Cambridge: Cambridge University Press, 2012), 76–99.

43. Pew Research Center Publications, "State of the News Media 2010," March 15, 2010, http://pewresearch.org/pubs/1523/state-of-the-news-media-2010 (accessed 9/11/12); West, *The Next Wave*.

44. Karen Mossberger and Caroline J. Tolbert, "Digital Democracy: How Politics Online Is Changing Electoral Participation," in *Oxford Handbook of American Elections and Political Behavior*, ed. Jan E. Leighley (New York: Oxford University Press, 2010), 200–18.

45. Tolbert and McNeal, "Unraveling the Effects of the Internet."

46. Karen Mossberger, Caroline Tolbert, and Ramona McNeal, *Digital Citizenship: The Internet, Society, and Participation* (Cambridge, MA: MIT Press, 2008). See Richard L. Fox and Jennifer M. Ramos, eds., *iPolitics: Citizens, Elections, and Governing in the New Media Era* (Cambridge: Cambridge University Press, 2011).

47. W. R. Neuman, M. R. Just, and A. N. Crigler, *Common Knowledge: News and the Construction of Political Meaning* (Chicago: University of Chicago Press, 1992).

48. A. Healy and D. McNamara, "Verbal Learning and Memory: Does the Modal Model Still Work?" in *Annual Review of Psychology*, Vol. 47, ed. J. Spense, J. Darley, and D. Foss (Palo Alto, CA: Annual Reviews, 1996), 143–72.

49. Cass Sunstein, *Republic.com* (Princeton, NJ: Princeton University Press, 2001). See also Mossberger and Tolbert, "Digital Democracy."

50. Michael Margolis and David Resnick, *Politics as Usual: The Cyberspace "Revolution"* (Thousand Oaks, CA: Sage, 2000).

51. West, *The Next Wave*; McChesney and Nichols, *Death and Life of American Journalism*.

52. Dianne Bystrom, "Advertising, Web Sites, and Media Coverage: Gender and Communication along the Campaign Trail," in *Gender and Elections: Shaping the Future of American Politics*, 2nd ed., ed. Susan J. Carroll and Richard L. Fox (Cambridge: Cambridge University Press, 2010), 239–62.

53. Matthew A. Baum, "Preaching to the Choir or Converting the Flock: Presidential Communication Strategies in the Age of Three Medias," in *iPolitics: Citizens, Elections, and Governing in the New Media Era*, ed. Richard L. Fox and Jennifer M. Ramos (Cambridge: Cambridge University Press, 2012), 183–205.

54. Eli Pariser, *The Filter Bubble: What the Internet Is Hiding from You* (New York: Penguin Press, 2011).

55. Mossberger, Tolbert, and Stansbury, *Virtual Inequality.*

56. Jill Carle, "Climate Change Seen as Top Global Threat: Americans, Europeans, Middle Easterners Focus on ISIS as Greatest Danger," Pew Research Center, July 14, 2015, www.pewglobal.org/2015/07/14/climate-change-seen -as-top-global-threat/ (accessed 12/8/15).

57. David J. Garrow, *Protest at Selma: Martin Luther King, Jr., and the Voting Rights Act of 1965* (New Haven, CT: Yale University Press, 2001).

58. See Todd Gitlin, *The Whole World Is Watching* (Berkeley: University of California Press, 1980).

59. Tim Groseclose, *Left Turn: How Liberal Media Bias Distorts the American Mind* (New York: St. Martin's Press, 2011).

60. Pew Research Center, "How Journalists See Journalists in 2004: Views on Profits, Performance and Politics," May 2004, http://people-press.org/files/legacy-pdf/214 .pdf (accessed 9/7/2012).

61. Doris Graber, ed., *Media Power in American Politics*, 5th ed. (Washington, DC: Congressional Quarterly Press, 2006).

62. Amber E. Boydstun, Stefaan Walgrave, and Anne Hardy, "Two Faces of Media Attention: Media Storms vs. General Coverage," *Political Communication* 31, no. 4 (2014): 509–31.

63. George Robert Boynton et al., "The Political Domain Goes to Twitter: Hashtags, Retweets and URLs," *Open Journal of Political Science* 4, no 1 (2014): 8–15.

64. Larry M. Bartels, *Presidential Primaries and the Dynamics of Public Choice* (Princeton, NJ: Princeton University Press, 1988).

65. David Redlawsk, Caroline Tolbert, and Todd Donovan, *Why Iowa? How Caucuses and Sequential Elections Improve the Presidential Nominating Process* (Chicago: University of Chicago Press, 2011).

66. Larry Bartels, *Unequal Democracy: The Political Economy of the New Gilded Age* (Princeton, NJ: Princeton University Press, 2008).

67. Robert Entman, "Framing: Toward Clarification of a Fractured Paradigm," *Journal of Communication* 43, no. 4 (1993): 51–8.

68. Shanto Iyengar and Donald R. Kinder, *News That Matters: Television and American Opinion* (Chicago: University of Chicago Press, 1987), 63.

69. Larry M. Bartels and Wendy M. Rahn, "Political Attitudes in the Post-Network Era" (presented at the Annual Meeting of the American Political Science Association, Washington, DC, August 31–September 3, 2000); Michael X. Delli Carpini and Scott Keeter, *What Americans Know about Politics and Why It Matters* (New Haven, CT: Yale University Press, 1996); Thomas R. Palfrey and Keith T. Poole, "The Relationship between Information, Ideology, and Voting Behavior," *American Journal of Political Science* 31, no. 3 (1987): 511–30; Sidney Verba, Kay Lehman Schlozman, and Henry E. Brady, *Voice and Equality: Civic Voluntarism in American Politics* (Cambridge, MA: Harvard University Press, 1995).

70. Markus Prior, "News vs. Entertainment: How Increasing Media Choice Widens Gaps in Political Knowledge and Turnout," *American Journal of Political Science* 49, no. 3 (2005): 577–92.

71. Delli Carpini and Keeter, *What Americans Know about Politics.*

72. Sunstein, *Republic.com.*

73. *New York Times v. United States*, 403 U.S. 713 (1971).

74. Michael Massing, "The Press: The Enemy Within," *New York Review of Books*, December 15, 2005, 6.

75. Chris Cillizza, "This E-Mail Story Just Keeps Getting Worse for Hillary Clinton," *Washington Post*, August 12, 2015, www.washingtonpost.com/news/the-fix/wp/2015 /08/12/this-e-mail-story-keeps-getting-worse-for -hillary-clinton/ (accessed 12/7/15).

76. Mark Lander and Eric Lichtblau, "F.B.I. Director James Comey Recommended No Charges for Clinton on Email," July 5, 2016, *New York Times*, www.nytimes .com/2016/07/06/us/politics/hillary-clinton-fbi-email -comey.html (accessed 10/16/16).

77. *Red Lion Broadcasting Company v. FCC*, 395 U.S. 367 (1969).

78. United Nations General Assembly, "Report of the Special Rapporteur on the Promotion and Protection of the Right to Freedom of Opinion and Expression," 2011, www.ohchr.org/EN/Issues/FreedomOpinion/Pages /OpinionIndex.aspx (accessed 3/14/16).

79. Andrew Chadwick, *Internet Politics: States, Citizens, and New Communication Technologies* (Oxford: Oxford University Press, 2006).

80. See Martin Linsky, *Impact: How the Press Affects Federal Policymaking* (New York: W. W. Norton, 1986).

Chapter 8

1. U.S. Census Bureau, "Voter Turnout Increases by 5 Million in 2008 Presidential Election, U.S. Census Bureau Reports," Newsroom Archive, www.census.gov /newsroom/releases/archives/voting/cb09-110.html (accessed 2/29/16).

2. Michael McDonald, "2016 November General Election Turnout Rates," United States Elections Project, www .electproject.org/2016g (accessed 11/11/16).

3. U.S. Census Bureau, "Table 10. Reasons for Not Voting, by Selected Characteristics: November 2012," Voting and Registration, www.census.gov/hhes/www /socdemo/voting/publications/p20/2012/tables.html.

4. National Conference of State Legislatures, "Same Day Voter Registration," June 2, 2015, www.ncsl.org/research /elections-and-campaigns/same-day-registration.aspx (accessed 2/29/16).

5. Domenico Montanaro, "Would Automatic Voter Registration Increase Turnout?" NPR, March 18, 2015, www.npr .org/sections/itsallpolitics/2015/03/18/393645667 /would-automatic-voter-registration-increase-turnout (accessed 11/14/16).

6. Shoichet, Catherine E., "Is Racism on the Rise? More in U.S. Say It's a 'Big Problem,' CNN/KFF Poll Finds," CNN, Race & Reality in America, November 25, 2015, www.cnn.com/2015/11/24/us/racism-problem-cnn-kff -poll/ (accessed 2/29/16).

7. Pew Research Center, "No Consensus about Whether Nation Is Divided into 'Haves' and 'Have-Nots,'" U.S. Politics & Policy, September 29, 2011, http:// pewresearch.org/pubs/2109/haves-have-nots-economic -divisions (accessed 9/14/12).

8. Sidney Verba, Kay Lehman Schlozman, and Henry E. Brady, *Voice and Equality: Civic Voluntarism in American Politics* (Cambridge, MA: Harvard University Press, 2005), chap. 3, for kinds of participation; 66–67 for prevalence of local activity.

9. Michael P. McDonald, "American Voter Turnout in Historical Perspective," in *The Oxford Handbook of American Elections and Political Behavior*, ed. Jan Leighley (New York: Oxford University Press, 2010), 125–43.

10. Todd Donovan and Shaun Bowler, *Reforming the Republic: Democratic Institutions for the New America* (Upper Saddle River, NJ: Pearson Education, 2004).

11. For a discussion of the decline in voter turnout over time, see Ruy A. Teixeira, *The Disappearing American Voter* (Washington, DC: Brookings Institution Press, 1992). See also Michael McDonald and Samuel Popkin, "The Myth of the Vanishing Voter," *American Political Science Review*, 95 (2001): 963–74; and Michael McDonald, "2012 November General Election Turnout Rates," *United States Election Project*, www.electproject .org/2012g (accessed 9/14/12).

12. McDonald, "2016 November General Election Turnout Rates."

13. Jeffrey Gottfried and Elisa Shearer, "News Use Across Social Media Platforms, 2016," Pew Research Center, May 26, 2016, www.journalism.org/2016/05/26 /news-use-across-social-media-platforms-2016/ (accessed 6/6/16).

14. Lee Rainie, et al., "Social Media and Political Engagement," Pew Research Center, Internet, Science & Tech, www.pewinternet.org/2012/10/19/social-media-and -political-engagement/ (accessed 6/24/14).

15. Katerina Eva Matsa and Amy Mitchell, "8 Key Takeaways about Social Media and News," March 26, 2014, Pew Research Center, Journalism & Media, www.journalism .org/2014/03/26/8-key-takeaways-about-social-media -and-news/ (accessed 1/12/16).

16. Michael Barthel, et al., "News Habits on Facebook and Twitter," Pew Research Center, Journalism & Media, July 14, 2015, www.journalism.org/2015/07/14/news -habits-on-facebook-and-twitter/ (accessed 2/9/16).

17. Amy Mitchell and Emily Guskin, "Twitter News Consumers: Young, Mobile and Educated," Pew Research Center, Journalism & Media, November 4, 2013, www .journalism.org/2013/11/04/twitter-news-consumers -young-mobile-and-educated/ (accessed 2/9/16).

18. David Karpf, *The MoveOn Effect: The Unexpected Transformation of American Political Advocacy* (New York: Oxford University Press, 2012).

19. Pew Research Center, "The Internet News Audience Goes Ordinary," U.S. Politics & Policy, January 14, 1999, www.people-press.org/1999/01/14/the-internet -news-audience-goes-ordinary/; Pew Research Center, "Internet Use over Time," Internet, Science & Tech, http://www.pewinternet.org/data-trend/internet-use /internet-use-over-time/ (accessed 4/11/16).

20. Monica Anderson, "More Americans Are Using Social Media to Connect with Politicians," Pew Research Center, Fact Tank, May 19, 2015, www.pewresearch .org/fact-tank/2015/05/19/more-americans-are -using-social-media-to-connect-with-politicians/ (accessed 2/12/16).

21. Andrew Chadwick, *The Hybrid Media System: Politics and Power* (New York: Oxford University Press, 2013).

22. Karen Mossberger, Caroline Tolbert, and Ramona McNeal, *Digital Citizenship: The Internet, Society and Participation* (Cambridge, MA: MIT Press, 2008); B. S. Krueger, "Assessing the Potential of Internet Political Participation in the United States," *American Politics Research* 30 (2002): 476–98; B. S. Krueger, "A Comparison of Conventional and Internet Political Mobilization," *American Politics Research* 34, no. 6 (2006): 759–76; Andrew Chadwick, *Internet Politics: States, Citizens, and New Communication Technologies* (New York: Oxford University Press, 2006); Bruce Bimber, *Information*

and *American Democracy: Technology in the Evolution of Political Power* (Cambridge: Cambridge University Press, 2003); and Rachel Gibson, Wainer Lusoli, and Steven Ward, "Online Participation in the UK: Testing a 'Contextualized' Model of Internet Effects," *British Journal of Politics and International Relations* 7, no. 4 (2006): 561–83.

23. Pew Research Center, "Politics Fact Sheet," Internet, Science & Tech, http://www.pewinternet.org/fact-sheets /politics-fact-sheet/ (accessed 4/11/16).

24. Verba, Schlozman, and Brady, *Voice and Equality*.

25. Caroline Tolbert and Ramona McNeal, "Unraveling the Effects of the Internet on Political Participation," *Political Research Quarterly* 56, no. 2 (2003): 175–85; see also Bruce Bimber, "Information and Political Engagement in America: The Search for Effects of Information Technology at the Individual Level," *Political Research Quarterly* 54 (2001): 53–67; Bimber, *Information and American Democracy*; and Krueger, "Assessing the Potential"; J. Thomas and G. Streib, "The New Face of Government: Citizen-Initiated Contacts in the Era of E-Government," *Journal of Public Administration Theory and Research* 13, no. 1 (2003): 83–102; D. V. Shah, et al., "Information and Expression in a Digital Age: Modeling Internet Effects on Civic Participation," *Communication Research* 32, no. 5 (2005): 531–65; K. Kenski and N. J. Stroud, "Connections between Internet Use and Political Efficacy, Knowledge, and Participation," *Journal of Broadcasting and Electronic Media* 50, no. 2 (2006): 173–92; Arthur Lupia and G. Sin, "Which Public Goods Are Endangered? How Evolving Communication Technologies Affect the Logic of Collective Action," *Public Choice* 117 (2003): 315–31.

26. Karen Mossberger and Caroline J. Tolbert, "Digital Democracy: How Politics Online Is Changing Electoral Participation," in *Oxford Handbook of American Elections and Political Behavior*, ed. Jan E. Leighley (New York: Oxford University Press, 2010), 200–18.

27. W. R. Neuman, M. R. Just, and A. N. Crigler, *Common Knowledge: News and the Construction of Political Meaning* (Chicago: University of Chicago Press, 1992).

28. David P. Redlawsk, "Hot Cognition or Cool Consideration: Testing the Effects of Motivated Reasoning," *Journal of Politics* 64 (2002): 1021–44.

29. Manuel Castells, *The Rise of the Network Society: The Information Age: Economy, Society, and Culture* (Oxford: Blackwell, 1997).

30. Bimber, *Information and American Democracy*; Bruce Bimber and Richard Davis, *Campaigning Online: The Internet in U.S. Elections* (Cambridge: Cambridge University Press, 2003).

31. Russell Dalton, *The Good Citizen: How a Younger Generation Is Reshaping American Politics* (Washington, DC: CQ Press, 2008).

32. Robert Putnam, *Bowling Alone: The Collapse and Revival of American Community* (New York: Simon and Schuster, 2000).

33. Karen Mossberger, Allison Hamilton, and Caroline Tolbert, "Measuring Digital Citizenship: Mobile Access and Broadband," *International Journal of Communication* 6 (2012): 2492–528; Pippa Norris, *Digital Divide: Civic Engagement, Information Poverty, and the Internet Worldwide* (New York: Cambridge University Press, 2001); Benjamin Barber, "The New Telecommunications Technology: Endless Frontier or the End of Democracy?" *Constellations* 4, no. 2 (2011): 208–28; Tolbert and McNeal, "Unraveling the Effects of the Internet"; H. Rheingold, *The Virtual Community: Homesteading on the Electronic Frontier* (Reading, MA: Addison-Wesley, 1993).

34. "Same-Sex Marriage Tweets Takeover the Internet," *USA Today*, June 27, 2015, www.usatoday.com/story /news/nation-now/2015/06/27/same-sex-marriage -scotus-gay-marriage-twitter-love-wins-trending /29389167/ (accessed 1/7/16).

35. Russell Dalton, "Citizenship Norms and the Expansion of Political Participation," *Public Choice* 56 (2008): 76–98.

36. Mossberger, Tolbert, and McNeal, *Digital Citizenship*.

37. U.S. Census Bureau, "Nearly 8 in 10 Americans Have Access to High-Speed Internet," Newsroom, November 13, 2014, www.census.gov/newsroom/press-releases/2014/cb14 -202.html (accessed 2/29/16).

38. Norris, *Digital Divide*. See also Karen Mossberger, Caroline Tolbert, and May Stansbury, *Virtual Inequality: Beyond the Digital Divide* (Washington, DC: Georgetown University Press, 2003).

39. See, e.g., *Citizens United v. Federal Election Commission*, 558 U.S. __ (2010), and *McCutcheon v. Federal Election Commission*, 572 U.S. __ (2014).

40. *Citizens United v. Federal Election Commission*.

41. Anthony Downs, *An Economic Theory of Democracy* (New York: Harper and Row, 1957); William H. Riker and Peter C. Ordeshook, "A Theory of the Calculus of Voting," *American Political Science Review* 62, no. 1 (1968): 25–42.

42. Julianna Pacheco and Jason Fletcher, "Incorporating Health into Studies of Political Behavior: Evidence for Turnout and Partisanship," *Political Research Quarterly* (December 23, 2014): doi: 10.1177/1065912914563548.

43. U.S. Census Bureau, "Voting and Registration in the Election of November 2012—Detailed Tables," 2012 Current Population Survey, www.census.gov/hhes/www /socdemo/voting/publications/p20/2012/tables.html (accessed 1/17/16).

44. Angus Campbell, et al., *The American Voter* (New York: Wiley, 1960); Steven Rosenstone and John Mark Hansen, *Mobilization, Participation, and Democracy in America* (New York: Macmillan, 1993); Kay Lehman Scholzman, Sidney Verba, and Henry E. Brady, *The Unheavenly Chorus: Unequal Political Voice and the Broken Promise of*

American Democracy (Princeton, NJ: Princeton University Press, 2012).

45. U.S. Census Bureau, "Table 7. Reported Voting and Registration of Family Members, by Age and Family Income: November 2012," Voting and Registration, https://www.census.gov/hhes/www/socdemo/voting/publications/p20/2012/tables.html.

46. Sidney Verba and Norman H. Nie, *Participation in America: Political Democracy and Social Equality* (New York: Harper and Row, 1972).

47. U.S. Census Bureau, "Reported Voting by Region, Educational Attainment, and Labor Force: November 2012," May 2013, www.census.gov/data/tables/2012/demo/voting-and-registration/p20-568.html (accessed 11/14/16).

48. Pew Research Center, "Fewer Voters Report Getting Robo-Calls, Campaign Ads Still Pervasive," U.S. Politics & Policy, October 28, 2014, www.people-press.org/2014/10/28/fewer-voters-report-getting-robo-calls-campaign-ads-still-pervasive/ (accessed 1/7/16).

49. Emily Hoban Kirby and Kei Kawashima-Ginsberg, "The Youth Vote in 2008," Center for Information and Research on Civic Learning and Engagement, August 17, 2009, http://www.civicyouth.org/PopUps/FactSheets/FS_youth_Voting_2008_updated_6.22.pdf (accessed 11/25/09).

50. Julia Glum, "Youth Turnout for 2014 Midterm Election Lowest in 40 Years: Report," *International Business Times*, July 22, 2015, www.ibtimes.com/youth-voter-turnout-2014-midterm-election-lowest-40-years-report-2019813 (accessed 11/14/16).

51. Julianna Pacheco, "Political Socialization in Context: The Effect of Political Competition on Youth Voter Turnout," *Political Behavior* 30, no. 4 (2008): 415–36.

52. Michael DeCourcy Hinds, "Youth Vote 2000: They'd Rather Volunteer," *Carnegie Reporter* 1, no. 2 (Spring 2001): 2.

53. Tyler Kingkade, "Youth Vote 2012 Turnout: Exit Polls Show Greater Share of Electorate than in 2008," Huffington Post, www.huffingtonpost.com/2012/11/07/youth-vote-2012-turnout-exit-polls_n_2086092.html (accessed 5/24/14).

54. Jennifer Lawless and Richard Fox, 2015. *Running from Office: Why Young Americans Are Turned Off to Politics* (New York: Oxford University Press, 2015).

55. Emily Hoban Kirby, Karlo Barrios Marcelo, and Kei Kawashima-Ginsberg, "Volunteering and the College Experience," Center for Information and Research on Civic Learning and Engagement, August 2009, www.civicyouth.org (accessed 11/25/09).

56. Connie Cass, "'Motor Voters' Impact Slight," *Chattanooga News-Free Press*, June 20, 1997, A5. On the need to motivate voters, see Marshall Ganz, "Motor Voter or Motivated Voter?" *American Prospect*, no. 28 (September–October 1996): 41–9. On the hopes for Motor Voter, see Frances Fox Piven and Richard A. Cloward, "Northern Bourbons: A Preliminary Report on the National Voter Registration Act," *PS: Political Science and Politics* 29, no. 1 (March 1996): 39–42. On turnout in the 1996 election, see Barbara Vobejda, "Just under Half of Possible Voters Went to the Polls," *Washington Post*, November 7, 1996, A3.

57. Lawrence Bobo and Franklin D. Gilliam, "Race, Sociopolitical Participation, and Black Empowerment," *American Political Science Review* 24, no. 2 (June 1990): 377–93.

58. Rene Rocha, et al., "Race and Turnout: Does Descriptive Representation in State Legislatures Increase Minority Voting?" *Political Research Quarterly* 63, no. 3 (2010): 890–907.

59. Susan Banducci, Todd Donovan, and Jeffrey Karp, "Minority Representation, Empowerment and Participation," *Journal of Politics* 66, no. 2 (2004): 534–56.

60. Mark Hugo Lopez and Paul Taylor, "Dissecting the 2008 Electorate: Most Diverse in U.S. History," Pew Research Center, Hispanic Trends, April 30, 2009, www.pewhispanic.org/2009/04/30/dissecting-the-2008-electorate-most-diverse-in-us-history/ (accessed 9/14/12).

61. Thom File, "The Diversifying Electorate—Voting Rates by Race and Hispanic Origin in 2012 (and Other Recent Elections)," U.S. Census Bureau, Current Population Survey, May 2013, www.census.gov/prod/2013pubs/p20-568.pdf (accessed 4/11/16).

62. See William Julius Wilson, *The Truly Disadvantaged: The Inner City, the Underclass, and Public Policy* (Chicago: University of Chicago Press, 1987); and Douglas Massey and Nancy Denton, *American Apartheid: Segregation and the Making of the American Underclass* (Cambridge, MA: Harvard University Press, 1993).

63. Michael Dawson, *Black Visions: The Roots of Contemporary African-American Political Ideologies* (Chicago: University of Chicago Press, 2003).

64. File, "The Diversifying Electorate."

65. Matt Barreto and Gary Segura, *Latino America: How America's Most Dynamic Population Is Poised to Transform the Politics of the Nation* (New York: Public Affairs, 2014).

66. Matt Barreto, Gary Segura, and Nathan Woods, "The Mobilizing Effect of Majority–Minority Districts on Latino Turnout," *American Political Science Review* 98 (2004): 65–75, and authors' update.

67. Pew Research Center, "Looking Forward to 2016: The Changing Latino Electorate," January 19, 2016, www.pewhispanic.org/2016/01/19/looking-forward-to-2016-the-changing-latino-electorate/ (accessed 11/11/16).

68. Barreto and Segura, *Latino America*.

69. Loren Collingwood, Matt Barreto, and Sergio García-Rios, "Revisiting Latino Voting: Cross-Racial Mobilization in the 2012 Election," *Political Research Quarterly*, 67 (2014): 4.

70. John Griffin and Brian Newman, *Minority Report: Evaluating Political Equality in America* (New York: Cambridge University Press, 2008); Rodney R. Hero, *Latinos and the U.S. Political System: Two-Tiered Pluralism* (Philadelphia: Temple University Press, 1992); Daniel Bowen and

Christopher Clark, "Revisiting Descriptive Representation in Congress: Assessing the Effect of Race on the Constituent–Legislator Relationship," *Political Research Quarterly* 67, no. 3 (2014): 695–707.

71. Adrian Pantoja and Gary Segura, "Does Ethnicity Matter? Descriptive Representation in the Statehouse and Political Alienation Among Latinos," *Social Science Quarterly* 84 (2003): 441–60.

72. File, "The Diversifying Electorate."

73. U.S. Census Bureau, "Voting and Registration in the Election of November 2012," May 2013, www.census .gov/data/tables/2012/demo/voting-and-registration /p20-568.html (accessed 11/14/16).

74. "Election 2016: Exit Polls," *New York Times*, November 8, 2016, www.nytimes.com/interactive/2016/11/08/us /politics/election-exit-polls.html (accessed 11/11/16).

75. 2014 Cooperative Comparative Election Study (CCES).

76. "Election 2016: Exit Polls."

77. Kira Sanbonmatsu, "Political Parties and the Recruitment of Women to State Legislatures," *Journal of Politics* 64, no. 3 (August 2002): 791–809; Jennifer L. Lawless and Richard L. Fox, *Why Are Women Still Not Running for Public Office?* (Washington, DC: Brookings Institution Press, 2008).

78. Center for American Women and Politics, *The Impact of Women in Public Office: Findings at a Glance* (New Brunswick, NJ: Rutgers University Press, 1991).

79. *Engel v. Vitale*, 370 U.S. 421 (1962); *Abington School District v. Schempp*, 374 U.S. 203 (1963).

80. Laurie Goodstein, "Bush's Charity Plan Is Raising Concerns for Religious Right," *New York Times*, March 3, 2001, A1.

81. David E. Campbell, "Religious 'Threat' in Contemporary Presidential Elections," *Journal of Politics* 68, no. 1 (2006): 104–15.

82. See Richard A. Brody, "The Puzzle of Political Participation in America," in *The New American Political System*, ed. Anthony King (Washington, DC: American Enterprise Institute, 1978), chap. 8.

83. Rosenstone and Hansen, *Mobilization, Participation, and Democracy*, 59.

84. Alan S. Gerber and Donald P. Green, "The Effects of Canvassing, Telephone Calls, and Direct Mail on Voter Turnout: A Field Experiment," *American Political Science Review* 94, no. 3 (September 2000): 660.

85. Donald P. Green and Alan S. Gerber, "Getting Out the Youth Vote: Results from Randomized Field Experiments," December 29, 2001, pp. 26–27, http://s3 .amazonaws.com/fieldexperiments-papers/papers /00260.pdf (accessed 3/8/08).

86. Robert M. Bond et al., "A 61-Million-Person Experiment in Social Influence and Political Mobilization," *Nature* 489 (2012): 295–8.

87. Bond et al., "A 61-Million-Person Experiment."

88. Katerina Eva Matsa and Kristine Lu, "10 Facts about the Changing Digital News Landscape," Pew Research Center, September 14, 2016, www.pewresearch.org/ fact-tank/2016/09/14/facts-about-the-changing-digital-news-landscape/ (accessed 10/16/16).

89. Theda Skocpol, *The Tea Party and the Remaking of Republican Conservatism* (New York: Oxford University Press, 2013).

90. Michael P. McDonald and John Samples, eds., *The Marketplace of Democracy: Electoral Competition and American Politics* (Washington, DC: Brookings Institution Press, 2006).

91. Mark N. Franklin, "Electoral Participation," in *Comparing Democracies: Elections and Voting in Global Perspective*, ed. Lawrence LeDuc, Richard G. Niemi, and Pippa Norris (Thousand Oaks, CA: Sage, 1996), 216–35; G. Bingham Powell, "American Voter Turnout in Comparative Perspective," *American Political Science Review* 80, no. 1 (1986): 17–43.

92. Todd Donovan, "A Goal for Reform: Make Elections Worth Stealing," *PS: Political Science and Politics* 40, no. 4 (2007): 681–6.

93. Donovan, "A Goal for Reform"; Gary W. Cox and Michael C. Munger, "Closeness, Expenditures, and Turnout in the 1982 U.S. House Elections," *American Political Science Review* 83, no. 1 (1989): 217–31; James G. Gimpel, Karen M. Kaufmann, and Shanna Pearson-Merkowitz, "Battleground States versus Blackout States: The Behavioral Implications of Modern Presidential Campaigns," *Journal of Politics* 69, no. 3 (2007): 786–97.

94. Donovan and Bowler, *Reforming the Republic*; McDonald and Samples, *Marketplace of Democracy*; Gary Jacobson, *The Politics of Congressional Elections*, 7th ed. (New York: Longman, 2008).

95. Samuel C. Patterson and Gregory A. Caldeira, "Getting Out the Vote: Participation in Gubernatorial Elections," *American Political Science Review* 77, no. 3 (1983): 675–89; Gregory A. Caldeira and Samuel C. Patterson, "Contextual Influences on Participation in U.S. State Legislative Elections," *Legislative Studies Quarterly* 7, no. 3 (1982): 359–81; Cox and Munger, "Closeness, Expenditures, and Turnout"; Gary W. Copeland, "Activating Voters in Congressional Elections," *Political Behavior* 5, no. 4 (1983): 391–401; Robert A. Jackson, "The Mobilization of U.S. State Electorates in the 1988 and 1990 Elections," *Journal of Politics* 59, no. 2 (1997): 520–37; Thomas M. Holbrook and Scott D. McClurg, "The Mobilization of Core Supporters: Campaigns, Turnout, and Electoral Composition in United States Presidential Elections," *American Journal of Political Science* 49, no. 4 (2005): 689–703; Andre Blais, "What Affects Voter Turnout?" *Annual Review of Political Science* 9 (2006): 111–25; Andre Blais and Agnieszka Dobrzynska, "Turnout in Electoral Democracies," *European Journal of Political Research* 33, no. 2 (2003): 239–61.

96. Gimpel, Kaufmann, and Pearson-Merkowitz, "Battleground States versus Blackout States"; Julianna Sandell Pacheco, "Political Socialization in Context: The Effect of Political Competition on Youth Voter Turnout," *Political Behavior* 30, no. 4 (2008): 415–36; Keena Lipsitz, "The Consequences of Battleground and 'Spectator' State Residency for Political Participation," *Political Behavior* 31, no. 2 (2009): 187–209.

97. David Redlawsk, Caroline Tolbert, and Todd Donovan, *Why Iowa? How Caucuses and Sequential Elections Improve the Presidential Nominating Process* (Chicago: University of Chicago Press, 2011).

98. Caroline Tolbert, Daniel C. Bowen, and Todd Donovan, "Initiative Campaigns: Direct Democracy and Voter Mobilization," *American Politics Research* 37, no. 1 (2009): 155–92.

99. Caroline Tolbert, John A. Grummel, and Daniel A. Smith, "The Effects of Ballot Initiatives on Voter Turnout in the American States," *American Politics Research* 29, no. 6 (2001): 625–48; Mark A. Smith, "The Contingent Effects of Ballot Initiatives and Candidate Races on Turnout," *American Journal of Political Science* 45, no. 3 (2001): 700–6; Caroline J. Tolbert and Daniel A. Smith, "The Educative Effects of Ballot Initiatives on Voter Turnout," *American Politics Research* 33, no. 2 (2005): 283–309; Daniel A. Smith and Caroline J. Tolbert, *Educated by Initiative: The Effects of Direct Democracy on Citizens and Political Organizations in the American States* (Ann Arbor: University of Michigan Press, 2004).

100. Stephen Nicholson, *Voting the Agenda: Candidates, Elections, and Ballot Propositions* (Princeton, NJ: Princeton University Press, 2005).

101. John Myers, "That Blockbuster California Ballot Will Be a $452-Million Battle," *Los Angeles Times*, February 18, 2016, www.latimes.com/local/california /la-pol-sac-november-ballot-500-million -20160215-story.html (accessed 10/18/16).

102. Daniel Smith and Caroline Tolbert, *Educated by Initiative: The Effects of Direct Democracy on Citizens and Political Organizations in the American States* (Ann Arbor: University of Michigan Press, 2004); Frederick Boehmke and Daniel Bowen, "Direct Democracy and Individual Interest Group Membership," *Journal of Politics* 72, no. 3 (2010): 659–71.

103. Bruce E. Cain, Todd Donovan, and Caroline J. Tolbert, *Democracy in the States: Experiments in Election Reform* (Washington, DC: Brookings Institution Press, 2008).

104. National Conference of State Legislatures, "Voter Identification Requirements," www.ncsl.org/research/elections -and-campaigns/voter-id.aspx (accessed 10/12/16).

105. National Conference of State Legislatures, (accessed 1/7/16).

106. Rene R. Rocha and Tetsuya Matsubayashi, "The Politics of Race and Voter ID Laws in the States: The Return of Jim Crow?" *Political Research Quarterly* 67, no. 3 (2014): 666–79.

107. National Conference of State Legislatures, "Felon Voting Rights," January 4, 2016, www.ncsl.org/research /elections-and-campaigns/felon-voting-rights.aspx (accessed 1/7/16).

108. E. Ann Carson, "Prisoners in 2013," U.S. Department of Justice, Bureau of Justice Statistics, September 30, 2014, www.bjs.gov/content/pub/pdf/p13.pdf (accessed 4/11/16).

109. Justin Wolfers, David Leonhardt and Kevin Quealy, "1.5 Million Missing Black Men," The Upshot, *New York Times*, April 20, 2015, www.nytimes.com /interactive/2015/04/20/upshot/missing-black-men. html?_r=0&abt=0002&abg=1 (accessed 1/6/16).

110. Jean Chung, *Felong Disenfranchisement: A Primer* (Washington, DC: The Sentencing Project, 2016), www.sentencingproject.org/wp-content/uploads /2015/08/Felony-Disenfranchisement-Primer.pdf (accessed 10/12/16).

111. National Conference of State Legislatures, "Same Day Voter Registration," June 2, 2015, www.ncsl .org/research/elections-and-campaigns/same-day -registration.aspx (accessed 2/29/16).

112. Robert A. Jackson, Robert D. Brown, and Gerald C. Wright, "Registration, Turnout and the Electoral Representativeness of U.S. State Electorates," *American Politics Quarterly* 26, no. 3 (July 1998): 259–87. See also Benjamin Highton, "Easy Registration and Voter Turnout," *Journal of Politics* 59, no. 2 (April 1997): 565–87.

113. Highton "Easy Registration and Voter Turnout"; Stephen Knack and James White, "Election-Day Registration and Turnout Inequality," *Political Behavior* 22, no. 1 (2000): 29–44; Craig Leonard Brians and Bernard Grofman, "When Registration Barriers Fall, Who Votes? An Empirical Test of a Rational Choice Model," *Public Choice* 99 (1999): 161–76; Michael J. Hanmer, *Discount Voting: Voter Registration Reforms and Their Effects* (New York: Cambridge University Press, 2009); Mary Fitzgerald, "Greater Convenience but Not Greater Turnout: The Impact of Alternative Voting Methods on Electoral Participation in the United States," *American Politics Research* 33, no. 6 (2005): 842–67; Caroline J. Tolbert, et al., "Election Day Registration, Competition, and Voter Turnout," in *Democracy in the States: Experiments in Election Reform*, ed. Bruce E. Cain, Todd Donovan, and Caroline J. Tolbert (Washington, DC: Brookings Institution Press, 2008), 83–98.

114. Cain, Donovan, and Tolbert, eds., *Democracy in the States*.

115. McDonald, "2012 November General Election" (accessed 4/23/14).

116. National Conference of State Legislatures, "Absentee and Early Voting," January 5, 2016, www.ncsl.org /research/elections-and-campaigns/absentee-and -early-voting.aspx (accessed 2/12/16).

117. Paul Gronke, Eva Galanes-Rosenbaum, and Peter Miller, "Early Voting and Turnout," *PS: Political Science and Politics* 40, no. 4 (October 2007): 639–45; Fitzgerald "Greater Convenience but Not Greater Turnout"; Adam J. Berinsky, "The Perverse Consequences of Electoral Reform in the United States," *American Politics Research* 33, no. 4 (2005): 471–91.

118. Jeffrey Karp and Susan Banducci, "Going Postal: How All-Mail Elections Influence Turnout," *Political Behavior* 22, no. 3 (2000): 223–39.

119. McDonald, "2012 November General Election" (accessed 5/25/14).

120. Michael C. Herron and Daniel A. Smith, "Race, Party, and the Consequences of Restricting Early Voting in Florida in the 2012 General Election," *Political Research Quarterly* 67, no. 3 (July 2014): 646–65.

121. Michael J. Hamner, *Discount Voting: Voter Registration Reforms and Their Effects* (New York: Cambridge University Press, 2009).

122. John Griffin, and Michael Keane, "Are Voters Better Represented?" *Journal of Politics* 67, no. 4 (2005): 1206–27.

123. Larry Bartels, *Unequal Democracy: The Political Economy of the New Gilded Age* (Princeton, NJ: Princeton University Press, 2008).

Chapter 9

1. Center for Responsive Politics, "2016 Presidential Race," www.opensecrets.org/pres16/ (accessed 6/21/16).

2. Jeff Stein, "The 7 Trumpiest Things Donald Trump Said during His 'Counter-Debate,'" Vox.com, January 29, 2016, www.vox.com/2016/1/29/10868360/trump -quotes-counter-debate (accessed 3/10/16).

3. Walter Dean Burnham, *Critical Elections and the Mainsprings of American Politics* (New York: W. W. Norton, 1970).

4. E. E. Schattschneider, *The Semisovereign People: A Realist's View of Democracy in America* (New York: Holt, Rinehart & Winston, 1960).

5. Larry Bartels, *Unequal Democracy: The Political Economy of the New Gilded Age* (Princeton, NJ: Princeton University Press, 2008).

6. Kathleen Bawn et al., "A Theory of Political Parties: Groups, Policy Demands and Nominations in American Politics." *Perspectives on Politics* 10, no. 3 (2012): 571–97.

7. Morris Fiorina, Samuel Abrams, and Jeremy Pope, *Culture War? The Myth of a Polarized America* (New York: Pearson Longman, 2004).

8. Todd Donovan and Shaun Bowler, *Reforming the Republic: Democratic Institutions for the New America* (Upper Saddle River, NJ: Prentice Hall, 2003).

9. James Madison, *The Federalist Papers*, no. 10, http://thomas .loc.gov/home/histdox/fed_10.html (accessed 11/11/12).

10. John H. Aldrich, *Why Parties? A Second Look* (Chicago: University of Chicago Press, 2011).

11. Raymond J. La Raja, "Political Parties in the Era of Soft Money," in *The Parties Respond: Changes in American Parties and Campaigns*, 4th ed., ed. Sandy L. Maisel (Boulder, CO: Westview Press, 2002), 163–88.

12. For an excellent analysis of the parties' role in recruitment, see Paul Herrnson, *Congressional Elections: Campaigning at Home and in Washington* (Washington, DC: CQ Press, 1995).

13. Marty Cohen et al., *The Party Decides: Presidential Nominations before and after Reform* (Chicago: University of Chicago Press, 2008).

14. Seth E. Masket, *No Middle Ground: How Informal Party Organizations Control Nominations and Polarize Legislatures* (Ann Arbor: University of Michigan Press, 2011).

15. Sasha Issenberg, *Victory Lab: The Secret Science of Winning Campaigns* (New York: Crown, 2012).

16. Glen Justice, "F.E.C. Declines to Curb Independent Fund Raisers," *New York Times*, May 14, 2004, A16.

17. See Harold Gosnell, *Machine Politics: Chicago Model*, rev. ed. (Chicago: University of Chicago Press, 1968).

18. For a useful discussion, see John Bibby and Thomas Holbrook, "Parties and Elections," in *Politics in the American States*, ed. Virginia Gray and Herbert Jacob (Washington, DC: CQ Press, 1996), 78–121.

19. Daniel Galvin, *Presidential Party Building: Dwight D. Eisenhower to George W. Bush* (Princeton, NJ: Princeton, University Press, 2009).

20. "Election 2016: Exit Polls," *New York Times*, November 8, 2016, www.nytimes.com/interactive/2016/11/08/us /politics/election-exit-polls.html (accessed 11/11/16).

21. Alex Leary, "Hispanics Voting in Record Numbers In Florida, Other States, Boosting Hillary Clinton," *Miami Herald*, November 6, 2016, www.miamiherald.com /news/politics-government/election/article112958953 .html (accessed 11/11/16).

22. "Election 2016: Exit Polls."

23. "Election 2016: Exit Polls."

24. Pew Research Center, Religious Landscape Study, www .pewforum.org/religious-landscape-study/ (accessed 12/16/15).

25. Christopher Shea, "Who Are You Calling Working Class?" *Boston Globe*, February 12, 2006, www.boston .com/news/globe/ideas/articles/2006/02/12/who_are _you_calling_working_class/ (accessed 2/24/08).

26. Pew Research Center, "Beyond Red vs. Blue: The Political Typology," U.S. Politics & Policy, June 26, 2014, www.people-press.org/2014/06/26/the-political -typology-beyond-red-vs-blue (accessed 2/28/16).

27. Shaun Bowler, Gary Segura, and Stephen Nicholson, "Earthquakes and Aftershocks: Race, Direct Democracy, and Partisan Change," *American Journal of Political Science* 50 (January 2006): 146–59.

28. "Election 2016: Exit Polls."

29. Jeffrey A. Karp and Caroline J. Tolbert, "Support for Nationalizing Presidential Elections," *Presidential Studies Quarterly* 40, no. 4 (2010): 771–93.

30. Jeffrey M. Jones, "Democratic, Republican Identification Near Historical Lows," Gallup, January 11, 2016, www .gallup.com/poll/188096/democratic-republican -identification-near-historical-lows.aspx (accessed 8/3/16).

31. Renata Sago, Ben Markus, and Jude Joffe-Block, "Sick of Political Parties, Unafilliated Voters Are Chaning Politics," NPR Politics, February 28, 2016, www .npr.org/2016/02/28/467961962/sick-of-political -parties-unaffiliated-voters-are-changing-politics (accessed 10/18/16); Secretary of State of Colorado, "September 2016 Total Registered Voters by Party Affiliation and Status," September 6, 2016, www.sos.state.co.us/pubs /elections/VoterRegNumbers/2016/September/Voters- ByPartyStatus.pdf (accessed 10/18/16).

32. See Morris Fiorina, "Parties and Partisanship: A Forty Year Retrospective," *Political Behavior* 24, no. 2 (2002): 93–115.

33. On the limited polarization among ordinary voters, see Fiorina, Abrams, and Pope, *Culture War?*; on growing partisan attachment among a subset of voters, see Alan Abramowitz and Kyle Saunders, "Why Can't We Just Get Along? The Reality of a Polarized America," *The Forum* 3, no. 2 (2005): 1–22.

34. See Matthew Crenson and Benjamin Ginsberg, *Downsizing Democracy* (Baltimore: Johns Hopkins University Press, 2002).

35. Benjamin Ginsberg, *The Consequences of Consent* (New York: Random House, 1982), chap. 4.

36. "CQ Roll Call's Vote Studies—2013 in Review," Feburary 3, 2014, http://media.cq.com/votestudies/ (accessed 7/25/16).

37. "Statistics and Historical Comparison," GovTrack.us, www .govtrack.us/congress/bills/statistics (accessed 3/16/16).

38. Donovan and Bowler, *Reforming the Republic.*

39. Fiorina, Abrams, and Pope, *Culture War?*

40. For a discussion of third parties in the United States, see Daniel Mazmanian, *Third Parties in Presidential Elections* (Washington, DC: Brookings Institution Press, 1974).

41. See Maurice Duverger, *Political Parties* (New York: Wiley, 1954).

42. Donovan and Bowler, *Reforming the Republic.*

43. Andri Blais, *To Keep or to Change First Past the Post? The Politics of Election Reform* (New York: Oxford University Press, 2008).

44. Stanley Kelley, Jr., Richard E. Ayres, and William Bowen, "Registration and Voting: Putting First Things First," *American Political Science Review* 61 (June 1967): 359–70.

45. David H. Fischer, *The Revolution of American Conservatism* (New York: Harper & Row, 1965), 93.

Chapter 10

1. *Baker v. Carr* 369 U.S. 186 (1962); *Gray v. Sanders*, 372 U.S. 368 (1963); *Wesberry v. Sanders*, 376 U.S. 1 (1964); *Reynolds v. Sims*, 377 U.S. 533 (1964).

2. *Thornburg v. Gingles*, 478 U.S. 613 (1986).

3. Louis Jacobson, "Congress Has 11% Approval Rating but 96% Incumbent Reelection Rate, Meme Says," Politifact, November 11, 2014, www.poltifact.com/truth-0-meter /statements/2014/nov/11/facebook-posts/congress-has -11-approval-ratings-96-incumbent-re-e/ (accessed 8/8/16).

4. *Shaw v. Reno*, 509 U.S. 113 (1993).

5. David Redlawsk, Caroline J. Tolbert, and Todd Donovan, *Why Iowa? How Caucuses and Sequential Elections Improve the Presidential Nomination Process* (Chicago: University of Chicago Press, 2011).

6. Redlawsk, Tolbert, and Donovan, *Why Iowa?*

7. State legislatures determine the system by which electors are selected. Almost all states use this "winner-take-all" system. Maine and Nebraska, however, provide that one electoral vote goes to the winner in each congressional district and two electoral votes go to the winner statewide.

8. *Bush v. Gore*, 531 U.S. 98 (2000).

9. Jeffrey Karp and Caroline J. Tolbert, "Polls and Elections: Support for Nationalizing Presidential Elections." *Presidential Studies Quarterly*, 40, no. 4 (2010): 771–93

10. See National Popular Vote, www.nationalpopularvote .com, for details (accessed 5/27/14).

11. Karp and Tolbert, *"Explaining Support"*; Daron Shaw, *The Race to 270: The Electoral College and the Campaign Strategies of 2000 and 2004* (Chicago: University of Chicago Press, 2006).

12. Todd Donovan and Shaun Bowler, *Reforming the Republic: Democratic Institutions for the New America* (Upper Saddle River, NJ: Pearson Press, 2003).

13. André Blais, *To Keep or to Change First Past the Post? The Politics of Electoral Reform* (Oxford: Oxford University Press, 2008).

14. Adam Nagourney, "Court Strikes Down Ban on Gay Marriage in California," *New York Times*, February 7, 2012, www.nytimes.com/2012/02/08/us/marriage-ban -violates-constitution-court-rules.html (accessed 8/21/12).

15. Daniel Smith and Caroline J. Tolbert, *Educated by Initiative: The Effects of Direct Democracy on Citizens and Political Organizations in the American States* (Ann Arbor: University of Michigan Press, 2004).

16. Shaun Bowler, Todd Donovan, and Caroline J. Tolbert. *Citizens as Legislators: Direct Democracy in the United States* (Columbus: Ohio State University Press, 1998).

17. BallotPedia, "2016 Ballot Measures," www.ballotpedia .org/2016_ballot_measures (accessed 10/16/16).

18. Stephen Nicholson, *Voting the Agenda: Candidates, Elections, and Ballot Propositions* (Princeton, NJ: Princeton University Press, 2005).

19. Ryan Grim and Sabrina Siddiqui, "Call Time for Congress Shows Dominates Bleak Work Life," *Huffington Post*, January 9, 2013, www.huffingtonpost.com/2013/01/08/call-time-congressional-fundraising_n_2427291.html (accessed 8/8/16).

20. OpenSecrets.org, "Outside Spending," www.opensecrets.org/outsidespending/summ.php?cycle=2014&disp=R&pty=A&type=A (accessed 6/23/16)

21. Stephen Ansolabehere and James Snyder, "Campaign War Chests and Congressional Elections," *Business and Politics* 2 (2000): 9–34.

22. Gary W. Cox and Eric Magar, "How Much Is Majority Status in the U.S. Congress Worth?" *American Political Science Review* 93 (1999): 299–309.

23. John Greer, *In Defense of Negativity: Attack Ads in Presidential Campaigns* (Chicago: University of Chicago Press, 2006).

24. David Horsey, "Donald Trump Makes an Art of Commandeering Free Media," *Los Angeles Times*, March 10, 2016, www.latimes.com/opinion/topoftheticket/la-na-tt-trump-media-20160309-story.html (accessed 6/23/16).

25. Aaron Smith and Maeve Duggan, "Online Political Videos and Campaign 2012," Pew Research Center, Internet, Science & Tech, November 2, 2012, www.pewinternet.org/2012/11/02/online-political-videos-and-campaign-2012/ (accessed 10/13/14).

26. Brian Stelter, "Debate Breaks Record as Most-Watched in U.S. History," CNN Money, September 27, 2016, www.money.cnn.com/2016/09/27/media/debate-ratings-record-viewership/ (accessed 10/17/16).

27. D. Sunshine Hillygus and Todd G. Shields, *The Persuadable Voter: Wedge Issues in Political Campaigns* (Princeton, NJ: Princeton University Press, 2009).

28. Sasha Issenberg, *The Victory Lab: The Secret Science of Winning Campaigns* (New York: Crown, 2012).

29. Alan S. Gerber and Donald P. Green, "The Effects of Canvassing, Telephone Calls, and Direct Mail on Voter Turnout: A Field Experiment," *American Political Science Review* 94, no. 3 (2000): 660.

30. Timothy Clark, "The RNC Prospers, the DNC Struggles as They Face the 1980 Election," *National Journal*, October 27, 1980, 1619.

31. M. Ostrogorski, *Democracy and the Organization of Political Parties* (New York: Macmillan, 1902).

32. For discussions of the consequences of this, see Thomas Edsall, *The New Politics of Inequality* (New York: W. W. Norton, 1984). See also Thomas Edsall, "Both Parties Get the Company's Money—but the Boss Backs the GOP," *Washington Post*, National Weekly Edition, September 16, 1986, 14; and Benjamin Ginsberg, "Money and Power: The New Political Economy of American Elections," in *The Political Economy*, ed. Thomas Ferguson and Joel Rogers (Armonk, NY: M. E. Sharpe, 1984).

33. Center for Responsive Politics, "Cost of Election," www.opensecrets.org/overview/cost.php (accessed 11/9/16).

34. *Buckley v. Valeo*, 424 U.S. 1 (1976).

35. *Citizens United v. Federal Election Commission*, 558 U.S. 50 (2010).

36. *Citizens United*.

37. *McCutcheon et al. v. Federal Election Commission*, 572 U.S. __ (2014).

38. Martin Gilens, *Affluence and Influence: Economic Inequality and Political Power in America* (New York: Princeton University Press, 2012).

39. *McCutcheon et al.*

40. OpenSecrets.org, Sen. Bernie Sanders, www.opensecrets.org/politicians/summary.php?cid=N00000528 (accessed 6/23/16).

41. *Buckley*.

42. Aaron Blake, "More Young People Voted for Bernie Sanders than Trump and Clinton Combined," *Washington Post*, June 20, 2016, www.washingtonpost.com/news/the-fix/wp/2016/06/20/more-young-people-voted-for-bernie-sanders-than-trump-and-clinton-combined-by-a-lot/ (accessed 11/14/16).

43. Linda Qui, "No, Donald Trump, Bernie Sanders Wouldn't Have Won Even If super Delegates Were Nixed," *Politifact*, July 25, 2016, www.politifact.com/truth-o-meter/statements/2016/jul/25/donald-trump/no-donald-trump-bernie-sanders-wouldnt-have-won-ev/ (accessed 11/14/16).

44. Steve Phillips, "What About White Voters?" *Center for American Progress*, February 5, 2016, www.americanprogress.org/issues/race/news/2016/02/05/130647/what-about-white-voters/ (accessed 11/14/16).

45. Martin, Sussman, and Thee-Brenan, "Voters Express Disgust."

46. GDELT Project, "Presidential Campaign 2016: Candidate Television Tracker," television.gdeltproject.org/cgi-bin/iatv_campaign2016/iatv_campaign2016 (accessed 11/11/16).

47. David Barstow, et al., "Donald Trump Tax Records Show He Could Have Avoided Taxes for Nearly Two Decades, The Times Found," *New York Times*, October 1, 2016, www.nytimes.com/2016/10/02/us/politics/donald-trump-taxes.html (accessed 11/11/16).

48. Michael McDonald, "2016 November General Election Turnout Rates," United States Election Proejct, www.electproject.org/2016g (accessed 11/11/16).

49. Chris Cillizza, "The 13 Most Amazing Findings in the 2016 Exit Poll," *Washington Post*, November 10, 2016, www.washingtonpost.com/news/the-fix/wp/2016/11/10/the-13-most-amazing-things-in-the-2016-exit-poll/ (accessed 11/14/16).

50. "Election 2016: Exit Polls," *New York Times*, November 8, 2016, www.nytimes.com/interactive/2016/11/08/us/politics/election-exit-polls.html (accessed 11/11/16).

51. Rebecca Harrington and Skye Gould, "Americans Neared a Voter-Turnout Record—Here's How 2016 Compares to Past Elections," *Business Insider*, November 10, 2016, www.businessinsider.com/trump-voter-turnout

-records-history-obama-clinton-2016-11 (accessed 11/11/16).

52. Henry Grabar, "Maine Just Voted for a Better Way to Vote," *Slate*, November 9, 2016, www.slate.com/articles /business/moneybox/2016/11/maine_just_passed _ranked_choice_voting_bravo.html (accessed 11/10/16).

53. Rebecca Shabad, "What Are the Major Ballot Measures That Voters Approved at the Polls?" CBS News, November 9, 2016, www.cbsnews.com/news/what-are-the-major -ballot-measures-that-voters-approved-at-the-polls/ (accessed 11/10/16).

54. Craig Silverman, "Viral Fake Election News Outper-formed Real News On Facebook In Final Months of the US Election," November 16, 2016, www.buzzfeed.com /craigsilverman/viral-fake-election-news-outperformed -real-news-on-facebook?utm_term=.bvR73wjQd# .ic6olvY6V (accessed 11/18/16).

Chapter 11

1. Alexis de Tocqueville, *Democracy in America*, ed. J. P. Mayer and trans. George Lawrence (New York: Harper Collins, [1835–40] 1988), 513.

2. Alexander Hamilton, James Madison, and John Jay, *The Federalist Papers*, ed. Clinton L. Rossiter (New York: New American Library, 1961), no. 10, 83.

3. *The Federalist Papers*, no. 10.

4. The best statement of the pluralist view is in David Truman, *The Governmental Process* (New York: Knopf, 1951), chap. 2.

5. Martin Gilens and Benjamin Page, "Testing Theories of American Politics: Elites, Interest Groups, and Average Citizens," *Perspectives on Politics* 12, no. 3 (Sept. 2014): 564–81.

6. Beth L. Leech, National Survey of Governmental Relations, 2012; Center for Responsive Politics, "Political Action Committees," www.opensecrets.org/pacs/.

7. Frank Baumgartner et al., *Lobbying and Policy Change: Who Wins, Who Loses, and Why* (Chicago: University of Chicago Press, 2009).

8. Baumgartner et al., *Lobbying and Policy Change*.

9. Erika Falk, Erin Grizard, and Gordon McDonald, "Legislative Issue Advertising in the 108th Congress: Pluralism or Peril?" *Harvard International Journal of Press/Politics* 11, no. 4 (Fall 2006): 148–64.

10. Betsy Wagner and David Bowermaster, "B.S. Economics," *Washington Monthly* (November 1992): 19–21.

11. Truman, *Governmental Process*.

12. For an exploration of lower-class interest groups and social movements, see Frances Piven and Richard Cloward, *Poor People's Movements* (New York: Vintage, 1978).

13. E. E. Schattschneider, *The Semisovereign People: A Realist's View of Democracy in America* (New York: Holt, Rinehart and Winston, 1960).

14. Kay Lehman Schlozman and John T. Tierney, *Organized Interests and American Democracy* (New York: Harper and Row, 1986), 60.

15. Clay Shirky, *Here Comes Everybody: The Power of Organizing without Organizations* (New York: Penguin Press, 2008).

16. Mancur Olson, *The Logic of Collective Action* (Cambridge, MA: Harvard University Press, 1965).

17. David Karpf, *The MoveOn Effect: The Unexpected Transformation of American Political Advocacy* (New York: Oxford University Press, 2012).

18. John Herbers, "Special Interests Gaining Power as Voter Disillusionment Grows," *New York Times*, November 14, 1978.

19. L. Brooke Conaway, "Explaining Interest Group Activity across US States" (working paper, John E. Walker Department of Economics, Clemson University, Clemson, SC, 2008), http://myweb.clemson.edu/~maloney/download /SpringFellowships-09/Conaway/Explaining%20 Interest%20Group%20Activity%20Across%20US%20 States.doc (accessed 2/10/14).

20. Amber van der Graaf, Simon Otjes, and Anne Rasmussen, "Weapon of the Weak: The Social Media Landscape of Interest Groups," *European Journal of Communication* (October 2015), http://ejc.sagepub.com/content /early/2015/10/28/0267323115612210.abstract (accessed 12/11/15).

21. Center for Responsive Politics, "Lobbying Database," www.opensecrets.org/lobby/ (accessed 12/17/13).

22. For discussions of lobbying, see Allan J. Cigler and Burdett A. Loomis, eds., *Interest Group Politics* (Washington, DC: CQ Press, 1983). See also Jeffrey M. Berry, *Lobbying for the People* (Princeton, NJ: Princeton University Press, 1977).

23. Marie Jojnacki, "Interest Groups' Decisions to Join Alliances or Work Alone," *American Journal of Political Science* 41 (1997): 61–87; Kevin W. Hula, *Lobbying Together: Interest Groups Coalitions in Legislative Politics* (Washington, DC: Georgetown University Press, 1999).

24. Andrew Chin, "A Case of Insecure Browsing," Newsobserver.com, September 30, 2004, www.unclaw .com/chin/scholarship/nando.pdf (accessed 3/30/16).

25. Common Cause, "The Microsoft Playbook: A Report from Common Cause," September 25, 2000.

26. Michael Barbaro, "A New Weapon for Wal-Mart: A War Room," *New York Times*, November 1, 2005, 1.

27. Center for Responsive Politics, "Organization Profiles," www.opensecrets.org/orgs (accessed 10/13/14).

28. "Editorial: Obama's Lobbyists," *Washington Times*, May 7, 2009, www.washingtontimes.com/news/2009 /may/07/obamas-lobbyists (accessed 9/6/12).

29. For an excellent discussion of the political origins of the Administrative Procedure Act, see Martin Shapiro, "APA: Past, Present, Future," *Virginia Law Review* 72, no. 477 (March 1986): 447–92.

30. David Kirkpatrick, "Congress Finds Ways of Avoiding Lobbyist Limits," *Washington Post*, February 11, 2007, 1.

31. *Brown v. Board of Education of Topeka, Kansas*, 347 U.S. 483 (1954).

32. *Obergefell v. Hodges*, 576 U.S. __(2015).

33. *Roe v. Wade*, 410 U.S. 113 (1973).

34. *Webster v. Reproductive Health Services*, 492 U.S. 490 (1989).

35. E. Pendleton Herring, *Group Representation before Congress* (New York: McGraw-Hill, 1936).

36. "How the NRA Relies More on Grassroots Mobilization Rather Than Lobbying," *U.S. News and World Report*, December 18, 2012, http://usnews.tumblr.com/post/38229308383/how-the-nra-relies-more-on-grassroots-mobilization (accessed 12/11/15).

37. Julia Preston, "Grass Roots Roared and Immigration Bill Collapsed," *New York Times*, June 10, 2007, A1.

38. Center for Responsive Politics, "Behind the Candidates: Campaign Committees and Outside Groups," www.opensecrets.org/pres16/raised-summ (accessed 11/10/16).

39. *Citizens United v. Federal Election Commission*, 558 U.S. 50 (2010).

40. Center for Responsive Politics, "2016 Outside Spending, by Super PAC," www.opensecrets.org/outsidespending/summ.php?chrt=V&type=S (accessed 11/10/16).

41. Richard L. Burke, "Religious-Right Candidates Gain as GOP Turnout Rises," *New York Times*, November 12, 1994, 10.

42. Elisabeth R. Gerber, *The Populist Paradox* (Princeton, NJ: Princeton University Press, 1999).

43. Gerber, *Populist Paradox*.

44. *The Federalist Papers*, no. 10.

45. Olson, *Logic of Collective Action*.

Chapter 12

1. Clinton T. Brass, *Shutdown of the Federal Government: Causes, Processes, and Effects*: Congressional Research Service, Sept. 8, 2014, www.fas.org/sgp/crs/misc/RL34680.pdf (accessed 6/11/16).

2. Spenser S. Hsu, "Waiting for Next President, Confirmations of Federal Trial Judges Stall," *Washington Post*, June 5, 2016, www.washingtonpost.com/local/public-safety/waiting-for-next-president-confirmations-of-federal-trial-judges-stall/2016/06/05/9b626aa4-222f-11e6-9e7f-57890b612299_story.html (accessed 6/11/16).

3. Jennifer E. Manning, *Membership of the 113th Congress: A Profile* (Washington, DC: Congressional Research Service, October 31, 2013), www.senate.gov/CRSReports/crs-publish.cfm?pid=%260BL%2BR%5CC%3F%0A (accessed 12/1/13).

4. Jennifer E. Manning, "Membership of the 114th Congress," Congressional Research Service, September 7, 2016 www.senate.gov/CRSpubs/c527ba93-dd4a-4ad6-b79d-b1c9865ca076.pdf (accessed 11/10/16); Ballotpedia, "U.S. Senate" and "U.S. House," www.ballotpedia.org (accessed 11/10/16); and U.S. Census Quick Facts, www.census.gov/quickfacts/table/PST045215/00 (accessed 11/10/16).

5. Manning, *Membership of the 113th Congress*.

6. Jennifer E. Manning, *Membership of the 114th Congress: A Profile* (Washington, DC: Congressional Research Service, June 11, 2015), www.fas.org/sgp/crs/misc/R43869.pdf (accessed 9/14/15).

7. Manning, *Membership of the 113th Congress*.

8. For a discussion, see Benjamin Ginsberg, *The Consequences of Consent* (New York: Random House, 1982), chap. 1.

9. See Kristen D. Burnett, *Congressional Apportionment*, U.S. Census Bureau, November 2011, www.census.gov/prod/cen2010/briefs/c2010br-08.pdf (accessed 1/23/12). For some interesting empirical evidence, see Angus Campbell et al., *Elections and the Political Order* (New York: Wiley, 1966), chap. 11; for more recent considerations about the relationship between members of Congress and their constituents, see Lawrence Jacobs and Robert Y. Shapiro, *Politicians Don't Pander: Political Manipulation and the Loss of Democratic Responsiveness* (Chicago: University of Chicago Press, 2000); and Larry M. Bartels, *Unequal Democracy: The Political Economy of the New Gilded Age* (Princeton, NJ: Princeton University Press, 2008).

10. Norman J. Ornstein et al., *Vital Statistics on Congress* (Washington, DC: Brookings Institution, 2014), Tables 5–3 and 5–4, www.brookings.edu/~/media/Research/Files/Reports/2013/07/vital-statistics-congress-mann-ornstein/Vital-Statistics-Full-Data-Set.pdf?la=en (accessed 9/14/15). Norman J. Ornstein, Thomas E. Mann, and Michael J. Malbin, *Vital Statistics on Congress 2008* (Washington, DC: Brookings Institution, 2009), 111–12.

11. Ashley Parker, "Spotlighting Constituents to Buoy Congressional Candidates," *New York Times* (October 8, 2014), www.nytimes.com/2014/10/09/us/politics/out-of-the-mouths-of-constituents-candidates-find-a-message.html (accessed 9/14/15); Juana Summers, "Constituent Services Give Voters Something to Remember," National Public Radio, www.npr.org/2014/10/28/359615965/constituent-services-give-voters-something-to-remember (accessed 9/14/15).

12. Linda Fowler and Robert McClure, *Political Ambition: Who Decides to Run for Congress* (New Haven, CT: Yale University Press, 1989); and Alan Ehrenhalt, *The United States of Ambition: Politicians, Power, and the Pursuit of Office* (New York: Three Rivers Press, 1992).

13. Center for Responsive Politics, "Reelection Rates over the Years," www.opensecrets.org/bigpicture/reelect.php (accessed 9/14/15) and author's calculations from Ballotpedia, www.ballotpedia.org.

14. Ballotpedia, "Margin of Victory Analysis for the 2014 Congressional Elections," ballotpedia.org/Margin_of_victory_analysis_for_the_2014_congressional_elections (accessed 9/14/15).

15. Michael Leahy, "House Rules," *Washington Post*, June 10, 2007, W12.

16. Barbara C. Burrell, *A Woman's Place Is in the House: Campaigning for Congress in the Feminist Era* (Ann Arbor: University of Michigan Press, 1994); and David Broder, "Key to Women's Political Parity: Running," *Washington Post*, September 8, 1994, A17.

17. Dan Balz, "Dodd, Dorgan, and Ritter to Retire as Democrats Face a Difficult Mid-Term Year," *Washington Post*, January 7, 2010.

18. U.S. Census Bureau, "Map: Apportionment of the U.S. House of Representatives Based on the 2010 Census," www.census.gov/population/apportionment/files/2010map.pdf (accessed 2/6/12).

19. Mark Hugo Lopez and Paul Taylor, "The 2010 Congressional Reapportionment and Latinos," Pew Research Center, www.pewhispanic.org/2011/01/05/the-2010-congressional-reapportionment-and-latinos/ (accessed 2/24/14).

20. Greg Giroux, "Republicans Win Congress as Democrats Get Most Votes," Bloomberg, March 18, 2013, www.bloomberg.com/news/2013-03-19/republicans-win-congress-as-democrats-get-most-votes.html (accessed 12/2/13).

21. Eric McGhee, "Are the Democrats Still at a Disadvantage in Redistricting?" *The Monkey Cage* (blog), July 9, 2013, themonkeycage.org/2013/07/09/are-the-democrats-still-at-a-disadvantage-in-redistricting/ (accessed 12/2/13).

22. Royce Crocker, *Congressional Redistricting: An Overview* (Washington, DC: Congressional Research Service, November 21, 2012), www.fas.org/sgp/crs/misc/R42831.pdf (accessed 12/2/13).

23. Adam Liptak, "Supreme Court Rebuffs Lawmakers over Independent Redistricting Plan," *New York Times*, June 29, 2015, www.nytimes.com/2015/06/30/us/supreme-court-upholds-creation-of-arizona-redistricting-commission.html?_r=0 (accessed 9/14/15).

24. "Did Redistricting Sink the Democrats?" *National Journal*, December 17, 1994, 2984.

25. *Miller v. Johnson*, 515 U.S. 900 (1995).

26. Bernie Becker, "Reapportionment Roundup," *New York Times*, December 24, 2009, http://thecaucus.blogs.nytimes.com/2009/12/24/reapportionment-roundup/ (accessed 1/31/10).

27. *Shelby County v. Holder*, 570 U.S. __ (2013); L. Paige Whitaker, *Congressional Redistricting and the Voting Rights Act: A Legal Overview* (Washington, DC: Congressional Research Service, August 30, 2013), www.fas.org/sgp/crs/misc/R42482.pdf (accessed 12/2/13).

28. Chris Cillizza, "What the Supreme Court's Voting Rights Act Decision Means for Politics," *Washington Post*, June 25, 2013, www.washingtonpost.com/blogs/the-fix/wp/2013/06/25/what-the-voting-rights-act-decision-means-for-politics/ (accessed 12/2/13).

29. Tarini Parti, "High Court Reasserts Voting Rights Act in Alabama Decision," *Politico*, March 25, 2015, www.politico.com/story/2015/03/supreme-court-alabama-redistricting-ruling-116384 (accessed 9/14/15).

30. Tom Hamburger and Richard Simon, "Everybody Will Know if It's Pork," *Los Angeles Times*, January 6, 2007, A1.

31. Don Seymour, "House Republicans Renew Earmark Ban for 113th Congress," website of the Speaker of the House, November 16, 2012, www.speaker.gov/general/house-republicans-renew-earmark-ban-113th-congress (accessed 12/1/13).

32. Martin Frost and Tom Davis, "How to Fix What Ails Congress: Bring Back Earmarks," *Los Angeles Times*, February 8, 2015, www.latimes.com/opinion/op-ed/la-oe-frost-earmark-spending-20150209-story.html (accessed 9/14/15).

33. Paul Ryan, "Constituent Services," paulryan.house.gov/constituentservices/ (accessed 6/11/16).

34. Richard Fenno, Jr., *Home Style: House Members in Their Districts* (Boston: Little, Brown, 1978).

35. Edward Epstein, "Dusting Off Deliberation," CQ *Weekly*, June 14, 2010, 1436–42. Sarah Binder, "Where Have All the Conference Committees Gone?" *The Monkey Cage* (blog), December 21, 2011, themonkeycage.org/blog/2011/12/21/where-have-all-the-conference-committees-gone/ (accessed 2/7/12).

36. Derek Willis, "Republicans Mix It Up When Assigning House Chairmen for the 108th," *Congressional Quarterly Weekly*, January 11, 2003, 89.

37. Rebecca Kimitch, "CQ Guide to the Committees: Democrats Opt to Spread the Power," *Congressional Quarterly Weekly*, April 16, 2007, 1080.

38. Richard E. Cohen, "Crackup of the Committees," *National Journal*, July 31, 1999, 2210–16.

39. See, for example, the announcement of an agreement on the Agricultural Act of 2014, House Committee on Agriculture, "House–Senate Negotiators Announce Bipartisan Agreement on Final Farm Bill," press release, http://agriculture.house.gov/news/documentsingle.aspx?DocumentID=1220 (accessed 9/21/15).

40. Norman J. Ornstein, et al., *Vital Statistics on Congress* (Washington, DC: Brookings Institution and American Enterprise Institute, July 2013), chap. 5, www.brookings.edu/research/reports/2013/07/vital-statistics-congress-mann-ornstein (accessed 6/13/16).

41. Susan Crabtree, "After Four-Month Impasse, House Ethics Taps Staff Director," *Talking Points Memo*, May 2, 2011, talkingpointsmemo.com/muckraker/after-four-month-impasse-house-ethics-taps-staff-director (accessed 11/30/13).

42. H.R. 1111: Department of Peacebuilding Act of 2015, govtrack.us, www.govtrack.us/congress/bills/114/hr1111 (accessed 9/21/15).

43. "Statistics and Historical Comparisons: Bills by Final Status," govtrack.us, www.govtrack.us/congress/bills/statistics (accessed 9/21/15).

44. U.S. Senate, "Senate Actions on Cloture Motions," www.senate.gov/pagelayout/reference/cloture_motions/clotureCounts.htm (accessed 11/29/13).

45. Jeremy W. Peters, "Senate Vote Curbs Filibuster Power to Stall Nominees," *New York Times*, November 22, 2013, A1.

46. Burgess Everett and Daniel Strauss, "Filibuster Divides GOP 2016 Contenders," *Politico*, July 6, 2015, www

.politico.com/story/2015/07/filibuster-divides-gop
-2016-contenders-119750 (accessed 9/21/15).

47. Jonathan Weisman, "House Votes 411–18 to Pass Ethics
    Overhaul," *Washington Post*, August 1, 2007, A1.

48. Leigh Munsil, "Graham Won't Lift Nominee-Hold
    Threat over Benghazi," *Politico*, November 11, 2013,
    www.politico.com/blogs/politico-live/2013/11/graham
    -wont-lift-nomineehold-threat-over-benghazi-177154
    .html (accessed 11/30/13).

49. Sean Sullivan and Mike DeBonis, "Congress Averts
    Homeland Security Shutdown with One-Week Ex-
    tension," *Washington Post*, February 28, 2015, www
    .washingtonpost.com/politics/house-gop-hopes-to-pass
    -stopgap-dhs-funding-before-midnight-shutdown
    /2015/02/27/22021530-be88-11e4-b274-e5209a3bc9a9
    _story.html (accessed 9/21/15).

50. John W. Kingdon, *Congressmen's Voting Decisions* (New
    York: Harper and Row, 1973), chap. 3; and R. Douglas
    Arnold, *The Logic of Congressional Action* (New Haven,
    CT: Yale University Press, 1990).

51. Lauren French, Jake Sherman, and John Bresnahan,
    "Democrats Deal Obama Huge Defeat on Trade," *Po-
    litico*, June 12, 2015, www.politico.com/story/2015/06
    /barack-obama-capitol-hill-trade-deal-118927 (accessed
    9/21/15).

52. Jane Fritsch, "The Grass Roots, Just a Free Phone Call
    Away," *New York Times*, June 23, 1995, A1.

53. Eric Lipton and Ben Protess, "Banks' Lobbyists Help in
    Drafting Financial Bills," *New York Times*, May 23, 2013,
    dealbook.nytimes.com/2013/05/23/banks-lobbyists
    -help-in-drafting-financial-bills/ (accessed 9/21/15);
    Michael Corkery, "Citigroup Becomes the Fall Guy in the
    Spending Bill Battle" *New York Times*, December 12, 2014,
    dealbook.nytimes.com/2014/12/12/citigroup-becomes
    -the-fall-guy-in-the-spending-bill-battle/ (accessed
    9/21/15).

54. Eliza Newlin Carney, "For Ethics Hawks, Congress
    Could Be Next," *National Journal Online*, February 17,
    2009, http://freerepublic.com/focus/f-new/2187821/posts
    (accessed 2/5/10).

55. Holly Idelson, "Signs Point to Greater Loyalty on Both
    Sides of the Aisle," *Congressional Quarterly Weekly
    Report*, December 19, 1992, 3849.

56. "2015 Vote Studies: Party Unity Remained Strong,"
    CQ Weekly, February 8, 2016, https://library.cqpress
    .com/cqweekly/document.php?id=weeklyreport114
    -000004830472&type=hitlist&num=9 (accessed 6/13/16).

57. Center for Responsive Politics, "Contributions to Federal
    Candidates, 2016," www.opensecrets.org/pacs/pacgot
    .php?cmte=C00525600&cycle=2016 (accessed 10/13/16).

58. Kimitch, "CQ Guide to the Committees," p. 1080.

59. Leahy, "House Rules," W12; Marin Cogan, "Freshmen
    Jump Line for Floor Speeches," *Politico*, January 18, 2011,
    www.politico.com/news/stories/0111/47791.html
    (accessed 2/9/12).

60. Daniel Newhauser, "Three Booted from GOP Whip
    Team as Leaders Crack Down," *National Journal*, June 16,
    2015, www.nationaljournal.com/congress/2015/06/16/
    Three-Booted-From-GOP-Whip-Team-Leaders-Crack
    -Down (accessed 9/21/15).

61. James J. Kilpatrick, "Don't Overlook Corn for Porn Plot,"
    Chicago Sun-Times, January 3, 1992, 23.

62. Dennis McDougal, "Cattle Are Bargaining Chip of the
    NEA," *Los Angeles Times*, November 2, 1991, F1.

63. Drew DeSilver, "In a Late Spurt of Activity Con-
    gress Avoids 'Least Productive' Title," Pew Research
    Center, December 19, 2014, www.pewresearch.org
    /fact-tank/2014/12/29/in-late-spurt-of-activity
    -congress-avoids-least-productive-title/4 (accessed
    9/21/15); "Statistics and Historical Comparison: Bills by
    Final Status," govtrak.us, www.govtrack.us/congress/bills
    /statistics (accessed 9/21/15).

64. Jonathan Weisman and Jeremy W. Peters, "Government
    Shuts Down in Budget Impasse," *New York Times*, Septem-
    ber 30, 2013, www.nytimes.com/2013/10/01/us/politics
    /congress-shutdown-debate.html (accessed 12/1/13).

65. Caren Bohan and Rachelle Younglai, "Boehner Warns
    against Shutting U.S. Government over 'Obamacare,'"
    Reuters, August 23, 2013, www.reuters.com/article
    /2013/08/23/us-usa-healthcare-republicans-idUS-
    BRE97L15120130823; Ashley Parker, "Conservatives with a
    Cause: 'We're Right,'" *New York Times*, September 30, 2013,
    www.nytimes.com/2013/10/01/us/politics/conservatives
    -with-a-cause-were-right.html (accessed 12/1/13).

66. Jonathan Weisman and Ashley Parker, "Republicans
    Back Down, Ending Crisis over Shutdown and Debt
    Limit," *New York Times*, October 16, 2013, www
    .nytimes.com/2013/10/17/us/congress-budget-debate
    .html (accessed 12/1/13).

67. Mike Zapler, "Boehner Unloads on GOP's 'false proph-
    ets,'" *Politico*, September 27, 2015, www.politico.com
    /story/2015/09/john-boehner-gop-false-prophets
    -214120 (accessed 9/27/15).

68. Nick Gass, "GOP Congress Earns Low Marks from
    Public," *Politico*, August 12, 2015, www.politico.com
    /story/2015/08/poll-congress-approval-rating-gop
    -leadership-121285 (accessed 9/28/15).

69. Pew Research Center, U.S. Politics and Policy, "Negative
    Views of New Congress Cross Party Lines," May 21, 2015,
    www.people-press.org/2015/05/21/negative-views-of
    -new-congress-cross-party-lines/ (accessed 9/28/15).

70. Molly E. Reynolds, "Speaker Ryan Meets the Realities
    of Governing," Brookings Institution, June 10, 2016,
    www.brookings.edu/blogs/fixgov/posts/2016/06
    /10-paul-ryan-amendments-appropriations-reynolds
    (accessed 6/13/16).

71. Geoffrey C. Layman, Thomas M. Carsey, and Juliana
    Menasce Horowitz, "Party Polarization in American Pol-
    itics: Characteristics, Causes, and Consequences," *Annual
    Reivew of Political Science*, no. 9 (2006): 83–110.

72. For example, Fredreka Schouten, "Club for Growth Plans New Push in House Races," *USA Today*, August 17, 2015, http://onpolitics.usatoday.com/2015/08/17/club-for-growth-plans-new-push-in-house-races/ (accessed 9/21/15).

73. Elizabeth Williamson, "Revival of Oversight Role Sought; Congress Hires More Investigators, Plans Subpoenas," *Washington Post*, April 25, 2007, A1.

74. Susan Milligan, "Congress Reduces Its Oversight Role; Since Clinton, a Change in Focus," *Boston Globe*, November 20, 2005, A1; Bill Shaikin, "Clemens Is Star Attraction at Hearing," *Los Angeles Times*, February 12, 2008, D1.

75. Eric Lipton and Sheryl Gay Stolberg, "Health Law Rollout Provides Rich Target for Oversight Chief," *New York Times*, November 12, 2013, www.nytimes.com/2013/11/13/us/politics/health-law-rollout-provides-rich-target-for-oversight-chief.html?_r50 (accessed 12/12/13).

76. Michael S. Schmidt and Maggie Haberman, "Aides for Hillary Clinton and Benghazi Committee Dispute Testimony Plan," *New York Times*, July 25, 2015, www.nytimes.com/2015/07/26/us/clinton-to-testify-publicly-before-house-committee-investigating-benghazi-attacks.html (accessed 9/21/15).

77. Gregory Krieg, "FBI Boss Comey's 7 Most Damning Lines on Clinton," CNN, July 5, 2016, www.cnn.com/2016/07/05/politics/fbi-clinton-email-server-comey-damning-lines/ (accessed 9/21/16).

78. *United States v. Pink*, 315 U.S. 203 (1942). For a good discussion of the problem, see James W. Davis, *The American Presidency* (New York: Harper and Row, 1987), chap. 8.

79. U.S. House, "Impeachment," http://history.house.gov/Institution/Origins-Development/Impeachment/ (accessed 4/18/14).

80. Carroll J. Doherty, "Impeachment: How It Would Work," *Congressional Quarterly Weekly Report*, January 31, 1998, 222.

81. Kenneth A. Shepsle, "Representation and Governance: The Great Legislative Trade-Off," *Political Science Quarterly* 103, no. 3 (1988): 461–84.

Chapter 13

1. *Myers v. United States*, 272 U.S. 52 (1926).

2. These statutes are contained mainly in Title 10 of the U.S. Code, Sections 331, 332, and 333.

3. The best study covering all aspects of the domestic use of the military is that of Adam Yarmolinsky, *The Military Establishment* (New York: Harper and Row, 1971). Probably the most famous instance of a president's unilateral use of the power to protect a state "against domestic violence" was President Grover Cleveland's dealing with the Pullman strike of 1894. The famous Supreme Court case that ensued was *In re Debs*, 158 U.S. 564 (1895).

4. In *United States v. Pink*, 315 U.S. 203 (1942), the Supreme Court confirmed that an executive agreement is the legal equivalent of a treaty, despite the absence of Senate approval. This case approved the executive agreement that was used to establish diplomatic relations with the Soviet Union in 1933. An executive agreement, not a treaty, was used in 1940 to exchange "fifty over-age destroyers" for 99-year leases on some important military bases.

5. *United States v. Nixon*, 418 U.S. 683 (1974).

6. For a different perspective, see William F. Grover, *The President as Prisoner: A Structural Critique of the Carter and Reagan Years* (Albany: State University of New York Press, 1988).

7. A third source of presidential power is implied from the provision for "faithful execution of the laws." This is the president's power to impound funds—that is, to refuse to spend money Congress has appropriated for certain purposes. One author referred to this as a "retroactive veto power" (Robert E. Goostree, "The Power of the President to Impound Appropriated Funds," *American University Law Review* 11 [January 1962]: 32–47). This impoundment power has been used freely and to considerable effect by many modern presidents, and Congress has occasionally delegated such power to the president by statute. But in reaction to the Watergate scandal, Congress adopted the Congressional Budget and Impoundment Control Act of 1974, which was designed to circumscribe the president's ability to impound funds by requiring that the president must spend all appropriated funds unless both houses of Congress consented to an impoundment within 45 days of a presidential request. Therefore, since 1974, the use of impoundment has declined significantly. Presidents have had either to bite their tongues and accept unwanted appropriations or to revert to the older and more dependable but politically limited method of vetoing the entire bill.

8. For more on the veto, see Robert J. Spitzer, *The Presidential Veto: Touchstone of the American Presidency* (Albany: State University of New York Press, 1989).

9. Dan Eggen, "Bush Announces Veto of Waterboarding Ban," WashingtonPost.com, March 8, 2008, www.washingtonpost.com/wp-dyn/content/article/2008/03/08AR2008030800304.html (accessed 6/10/10).

10. For a good review of President Clinton's legislative leadership in the first session of his last Congress, see *Congressional Quarterly Weekly*, November 13, 1999, especially the cover story by Andrew Taylor, "Clinton Gives Republicans a Gentler Year-End Beating," 2698–700.

11. Kenneth F. Warren, *Administrative Law*, 3rd ed. (Upper Saddle River, NJ: Prentice-Hall, 1996), 250.

12. *J. W. Hampton & Co. v. United States*, 276 U.S. 394 (1928).

13. National Industrial Recovery Act, 48 Stat. 200 (1933).

14. Theodore J. Lowi, *The End of Liberalism*, 2nd ed. (New York: W. W. Norton, 1979), 117.

15. Jerry L. Nashaw, *Greed, Chaos, and Governance: Using Public Choice to Improve Public Law* (New Haven, CT: Yale University Press, 1997), 106.

16. *Henry C. Black, Black's Law Dictionary*, 6th ed. (St. Paul, MN: West Publishing, 1991), 539.

17. James G. Randall, *Constitutional Problems under Lincoln* (New York: Appleton, 1926), chap. 1.

18. Edward S. Corwin, *The President: Office and Powers*, 4th rev. ed. (New York: New York University Press, 1957), 229.

19. Congress has made 11 declarations of war in its history. In June 1942, Congress declared war against Bulgaria, Hungary, and Romania, which were allies of Germany in World War II. See www.senate.gov/pagelayout/history/h _multi_sections_and_teasers/WarDeclarationsbyCongress .htm (accessed 4/21/14).

20. Adam Clymer, "The Transition: Push for Diversity May Cause Reversal on Interior Secretary," *New York Times*, December 23, 1992, 1.

21. A substantial portion of this section is taken from Theodore J. Lowi, *The Personal President* (Ithaca, NY: Cornell University Press, 1985), 141–50.

22. All the figures since 1967, and probably 1957, are understated because additional White House staff members were on "detail" service from the military and other departments (some secretly assigned) and are not counted here because they were not on the White House payroll.

23. "2012 Annual Report to Congress on White House Staff," www.whitehouse.gov/briefing-room/disclosures /annual-records/2012 (accessed 12/7/13).

24. The actual number is difficult to estimate because, as with White House staff, some EOP personnel, especially in national security work, are detailed to the EOP from outside agencies.

25. Article I, Section 3, provides that "The Vice-President . . . shall be President of the Senate, but shall have no Vote, unless they be equally divided." This is the only vote the vice president is allowed.

26. David Ignatius, "A Skeptical Biden's Role," RealClear-Politics.com, November 26, 2009, www.realclearpolitics .com/articles/2009/11/26/a_skeptical_bidens_role _99320.html (accessed 5/12/09).

27. Samuel Kernell, *Going Public: New Strategies of Presidential Leadership*, 3rd ed. (Washington, DC: CQ Press, 1997); also Jeffrey K. Tulis, *The Rhetorical Presidency* (Princeton, NJ: Princeton University Press, 1987).

28. Tulis, *Rhetorical Presidency*, 91.

29. Sidney M. Milkis, *The President and the Parties* (New York: Oxford University Press, 1993), 97.

30. James MacGregor Burns, *Roosevelt: The Lion and the Fox* (New York: Harcourt, Brace, 1956), 317.

31. Burns, *Roosevelt*, 317.

32. Kernell, *Going Public*, 79.

33. Claire Cain Miller, "How Obama's Internet Campaign Changed Politics," *New York Times*, November 7, 2008, bits.blogs.nytimes.com/2008/11/07/how-obamas -internet-campaign-changed-politics/?_php=true& _type=blogs&_r=o (accessed 4/7/14); David Plouffe, *The Audacity to Win: The Inside Story and Lessons of Barack Obama's Historic Victory* (New York: Viking, 2009).

34. Gallup, www.gallup.com/poll/124922/presidential-approval -center.aspx (accessed 3/14/14).

35. Lowi, *Personal President*.

36. Lowi, *Personal President*, 11.

37. Milkis, *President and the Parties*, 128.

38. Milkis, *President and the Parties*, 160.

39. The classic critique of this process is Lowi, *End of Liberalism*.

40. Kenneth Culp Davis, *Administrative Law Treatise* (St. Paul, MN: West Publishing, 1958), 9.

41. John M. Broder, "Powerful Shaper of U.S. Rules Quits, Leaving Critics in Wake," *New York Times*, August 4, 2012, A1.

42. A complete inventory is provided in Harold C. Relyea, "Presidential Directives: Background and Review," Congressional Research Service Report 98–611 (Washington, DC: Library of Congress, November 9, 2001).

43. Terry M. Moe and William G. Howell, "The Presidential Power of Unilateral Action," *Journal of Law, Economics and Organization* 15, no. 1 (January 1999): 133–4.

44. Moe and Howell, "Presidential Power of Unilateral Action," 164.

45. *United States v. Texas*, 579 U.S. __ (2016)

46. *Youngstown Sheet & Tube Co. v. Sawyer*, 346 U.S. 579 (1952).

47. Philip Cooper, *By Order of the President* (Lawrence: University Press of Kansas, 2002), 201.

48. Corwin, *The President*, 283.

49. Cooper, *By Order of the President*, 203.

50. Cooper, *By Order of the President*, 216.

51. The American Presidency Project, "Presidential Signing Statements," www.presidency.ucsb.edu/signingstatements .php?year=2016&Submit=DISPLAY (accessed 11/10/16).

52. Alexander Hamilton, James Madison, and John Jay, *The Federalist Papers*, ed. Clinton Rossiter (New York: New American Library, 1961), no. 70, 423–30.

53. Terry Moe, "The Presidency and the Bureaucracy: The Presidential Advantage," in *The Presidency and the Political System*, ed. Michael Nelson (Washington, DC: Congressional Quarterly Press, 2002), 416–20.

54. Louis Fisher, *Congressional Abdication on War and Spending* (College Station: Texas A&M Press, 2000).

55. Letter from Thomas Jefferson to James Madison (Sept. 6, 1789), in *The Papers of Thomas Jefferson*, 392, 397 (Julian P. Boyd ed., 1958).

Chapter 14

1. Arnold Brecht and Comstock Glaser, *The Art and Techniques of Administration in German Ministries* (Cambridge, MA: Harvard University Press, 1940), 6.

2. Linda Greenhouse, "Justices Say E.P.A. Has Power to Act on Harmful Gases," *New York Times*, April 3, 2007, www.nytimes.com/2007/04/03/washington/03scotus.html?ex51333339200&en5e0d0a1497263d879&ei55124&partner5permalink&exprod5permalink (accessed 2/15/10).

3. Environmental Protection Agency, "Endangerment and Cause or Contribute Findings for Greenhouse Gases under Section 202(a) of the Clean Air Act," www.epa.gov/climatechange/endangerment/ (accessed 5/19/16).

4. Environmental Protection Agency, "Regulations and Standards: Light Duty," www3.epa.gov/otaq/climate/regs-light-duty.htm#new1 (accessed 7/9/16).

5. Juliet Eilperin and Steve Mufson, "Everything You Need to Know about the EPA's Proposed Rule on Coal Plants," *Washington Post*, June 2, 2014, www.washingtonpost.com/national/health-science/epa-will-propose-a-rule-to-cut-emissions-from-existing-coal-plants-by-up-to-30-percent/2014/06/02/f37f0a10-e81d-11e3-afc6-a1dd9407abcf_story.html; Coral Davenport, "Court Gives Obama a Climate Change Win," *New York Times*, June 9, 2015, www.nytimes.com/2015/06/10/us/coal-epa-clean-power-plan.html (accessed 9/30/15); Amy Harder Brent Kendall, "Obama Carbon Rules to Face Lawsuits, Congressional Tests," *Wall Street Journal*, October 23, 2015, www.wsj.com/articles/obama-carbon-rules-to-face-lawsuits-congressional-tests-1445611059 (accessed 10/29/15).

6. Juliet Eilperin, "EPA Needed More Data before Ruling on Greenhouse Gas Emissions, Report Says," *Washington Post*, September 28, 2011, www.washingtonpost.com/national/health-science/epa-needed-more-data-before-ruling-on-greenhouse-gas-emissions-report-says/2011/09/28/gIQABs2X5K_story.html (accessed 1/2/12).

7. Margaret Cronin Fisk, Kartikay Mehrotra, Alan Katz, and Jeff Plungis, "Volkswagen Agrees to $15 Billion Diesel-Cheating Settlement," Bloomberg News, June 28, 2016, www.bloomberg.com/news/articles/2016-06-28/volkswagen-to-pay-14-7-billion-to-settle-u-s-emissions-claims (accessed 7/8/16).

8. Gary Bryner, *Bureaucratic Discretion* (New York: Pergamon Press, 1987).

9. "Obama's Health Care Speech to Congress," *New York Times*, September 9, 2009, www.nytimes.com/2009/09/10/us/politics/10obama.text.html (accessed 2/10/10).

10. Office of Personnel and Management, Data, Analysis & Documentation Federal Employment Reports, "Historical Federal Workforce Tables, Total Government Employment since 1962," www.opm.gov/policy-data-oversight/data-analysis-documentation/federal-employment-reports/historical-tables/total-government-employment-since-1962/ (accessed 7/15/16).

11. Bureau of Labor Statistics, Current Employment Statistics, "Table B-1. Employees on Nonfarm Payrolls by Industry Sector and Selected Industry Detail." www.bls.gov/webapps/legacy/cesbtab1.htm (accessed 7/15/16).

12. There are historical reasons that American Cabinet-level administrators are called "secretaries." During the Second Continental Congress and the subsequent confederal government, standing committees were formed to deal with executive functions related to foreign affairs, military and maritime issues, and public financing. The heads of those committees were called "secretaries" because their primary task was to handle all correspondence and documentation related to their areas of responsibility.

13. Environmental Protection Agency, "Drinking Water Contaminants—Standards and Regulation," May 9, 2016, www.epa.gov/dwstandardsregulations (accessed 5/20/16).

14. Merrit Kennedy, "Lead-Laced Water in Flint: A Step-by-Step Look at the Makings of a Crisis," National Public Radio, April 20, 2016, www.npr.org/sections/thetwo-way/2016/04/20/465545378/lead-laced-water-in-flint-a-step-by-step-look-at-the-makings-of-a-crisis (accessed 7/9/16).

15. Thomas Erdbrink, Sewell Chan, and David E. Sanger, "After a U.S. Shift, Iran Has a Seat at Talks on War in Syria," *New York Times*, October 28, 2015, www.nytimes.com/2015/10/29/world/middleeast/syria-talks-vienna-iran.html (accessed 10/19/15).

16. U.S. Department of State, "Department Organization Chart: (image map) March 2014," www.state.gov/r/pa/ei/rls/dos/99494.htm (accessed 7/9/16).

17. For more details, consult John E. Harr, *The Professional Diplomat* (Princeton, NJ: Princeton University Press, 1972), 11; and Nicholas Horrock, "The CIA Has Neighbors in the 'Intelligence Community,'" *New York Times*, June 29, 1975, sec. 4, 2. See also Morton H. Halperin and Priscilla Clapp, *Bureaucratic Politics and Foreign Policy*, 2nd ed., with Arnold Kanter (Washington, DC: Brookings Institution Press, 2007).

18. National Commission on Terrorist Attacks upon the United States, *The 9/11 Commission Report: Final Report of the National Commission on Terrorist Attacks upon the United States* (New York: W. W. Norton, 2004).

19. Louise Osborne, "Europeans Outraged over NSA Spying, Threaten Action," *USA Today*, October 29, 2013, www.usatoday.com/story/news/world/2013/10/28/report-nsa-spain/3284609/ (accessed 1/24/14).

20. Warren Strobel and Mark Hosenball, "White House Review Panel Proposes Curbs on Some NSA Programs," Reuters, December 18, 2013, www.reuters.com/article/2013/12/18/us-usa-surveillance-obama-idUSBRE9BG1AQ20131218 (accessed 1/24/14).

21. Strobel and Hosenball, "White House Review Panel."

22. Mary Madden and Lee Rainie, "Americans' Views about Data Collection and Security," Pew Research Center, Internet, Science, and Tech, May 20, 2015 www.pewinternet.org/2015/05/20/americans-views-about-data-collection-and-security/ (accessed 9/30/15).

23. U.S. Department of the Treasury, "The Debt to the Penny and Who Holds It," www.treasurydirect.gov/NP/debt/current (accessed 7/716).

24. Financial Stability Oversight Council, "Designations," www.treasury.gov/initiatives/fsoc/designations/Pages/default.aspx (accessed 1/23/14).

25. Lisa Rein, "IRS Conference in Anaheim Featured Gifts, Other Excesses Approved by Top Officials, Report Says," *Washington Post*, June, 6, 2013, www.washingtonpost.com/blogs/federal-eye/wp/2013/06/04/irs-conference-in-anaheim-featured-gifts-other-excesses-approved-by-top-officials-report-says/ (accessed 1/31/14).

26. Ellen Nakashima, "Hacks of OPM Databases Compromised 22.1 Million People, Federal Authorities Say," *Washington Post*, July 5, 2015, www.washingtonpost.com/blogs/federal-eye/wp/2015/07/09/hack-of-security-clearance-system-affected-21-5-million-people-federal-authorities-say/ (accessed 9/30/15).

27. Vice President Gore's National Partnership for Reinventing Government, "Appendix F, History of the National Partnership for Reinventing Government: Accomplishments, 1993–2000, A Summary," http://govinfo.library.unt.edu/npr/whoweare/appendixf.html (accessed 3/28/08).

28. Public Law 101-510, Title XXIX, Sections 2,901 and 2,902 of Part A (Defense Base Closure and Realignment Commission); see the 2005 commission's website, Defense Base Closure and Realignment Commission, www.brac.gov (accessed 1/3/12).

29. Walter Pincus, "For Pentagon, It's Always a Tough Battle to Get Congress to Close Military Bases, Facilities," *Washington Post*, March 17, 2014, www.washingtonpost.com/world/national-security/for-pentagon-its-always-a-tough-battle-to-get-congress-to-close-military-bases-facilities/2014/03/17/a7eda064-a887-11e3-8599-ce7295b6851c_story.html (accessed 9/30/15).

30. Sheila R. Zedlewski, Pamela J. Loprest, and Erika Huber, "What Role Is Welfare Playing in This Period of High Unemployment?" Urban Institute, Fact Sheet 3, August 17, 2011, www.urban.org/UploadedPDF/412378-Role-of-Welfare-in-this-Period-of-High-Unemployment.pdf (accessed 7/4/12).

31. Sabrina Tavernise, "Food Stamps Helped Reduced Poverty Rate, Study Says," *New York Times*, April 10, 2012, A16.

32. Paul C. Light, "The New True Size of Government," Organizational Performance Initiative, Research Brief no. 2, Wagner School of Public Service, New York University, 8, https://wagner.nyu.edu/files/performance/True%20Size%20Research%20Brief.pdf (accessed 3/11/08). OMB Watch, "Total Spending by Year," FedSpending.org, www.fedspending.org/fpds/chart_total.php (accessed 1/2/12).

33. Scott Shane and Ron Nixon, "In Washington, Contractors Take On Biggest Role Ever," *New York Times*, February 4, 2007, A1.

34. Daniel Patrick Moynihan, "The Culture of Secrecy," *Public Interest* (Summer 1997): 55–71.

35. Thomas E. Mann and Norman J. Ornstein, *The Broken Branch: How Congress Is Failing America and How to Get It Back on Track* (New York: Oxford University Press, 2006), 155.

36. Matt Kelley, "GAO Challenges $150B Contract Awarded by Army," *USA Today*, October 31, 2007, 5A.

37. For the estimates on waste, see Commission on Wartime Contracting in Iraq and Afghanistan, *Transforming Wartime Contracting: Controlling Costs, Reducing Risks: Final Report to Congress*, 18, August 2011, www.wartimecontracting.gov (accessed 1/4/12).

38. Neil Gordon, "Move over FCMD, Make Way for FAPIIS," Project on Government Oversight, September 11, 2009, http://pogoblog.typepad.com/pogo/2009/09/move-over-fcmd-make-way-for-fapiis.html (accessed 2/26/10).

39. Government Accountability Office, *Federal Contractors: Better Performance Information Needed to Support Agency Contract Award Decisions*, April 2009, GAO-09-374, www.gao.gov/new.items/d09374.pdf (accessed 2/26/10).

40. Tom Lee, "FAPIIS May Be the Worst Government Website We've Ever Seen," Sunlight Foundation, April 19, 2011, sunlightfoundation.com/blog/2011/04/19/fapiis-may-be-the-worst-government-website-weve-ever-seen/ (accessed 1/23/14).

41. Joe Davidson, "OMB Moves to Cut Outside Contractors," Federal Diary, *Washington Post*, July 29, 2009, www.washingtonpost.com/wp-dyn/content/article/2009/07/28/AR2009072802812.html (accessed 2/18/10).

42. Joe Davidson, "Deficit-Cutters Must Also Weigh the Cost of Contractors," Federal Diary, *Washington Post*, February 4, 2011, www.washingtonpost.com/wp-dyn/content/article/2011/02/03/AR2011020306809.html?nav5emailpage (accessed 1/2/12).

43. Marjorie Censer, "Five Provisions in the New Defense Policy Legislation for Contractors to Watch," *Washington Post*, January 5, 2014, www.washingtonpost.com/business/capitalbusiness/five-provisions-in-the-new-defense-policy-legislation-for-contractors-to-watch/2014/01/0/f6dd00ec-6c10-11e3-a523-fe73f0ff6b8d_story.html (accessed 1/24/14).

44. Dan Egan, "Democrats Proposing New Limits on Corporate Campaign Donations," *Boston Globe*, February 12, 2010, www.boston.com/news/nation/washington/articles/2010/02/12/democrats_proposing_new_limits_on_corporate_campaign_donations/ (accessed 2/27/10).

45. Peter Baker, "Obama Orders Federal Contractors to Provide Workers Paid Sick Leave," *New York Times*, September 7, 2015, www.nytimes.com/2015/09/08/us /politics/obama-to-require-federal-contractors-to -provide-paid-sick-leave.html?_r=0 (accessed 9/30/15).

46. Alexander Hamilton, James Madison, and John Jay, *The Federalist Papers*, ed. Clinton Rossiter (New York: New American Library, 1961), no. 51, 322.

47. The title of this section was inspired by Peri Arnold, *Making the Managerial Presidency* (Princeton, NJ: Princeton University Press, 1986).

48. For more details and evaluations, see David Rosenbloom, *Public Administration* (New York: Random House, 1986), 186–221; Charles H. Levine, *The Quiet Crisis of the Civil Service: The Federal Personnel System at the Crossroads*, with the assistance of Rosslyn S. Kleeman (Washington, DC: National Academy of Public Administration, 1986).

49. Lester Salamon and Alan Abramson, "Governance: The Politics of Retrenchment," in *The Reagan Record*, ed. John Palmer and Isabel Sawhill (Cambridge, MA: Ballinger, 1984), 40.

50. Colin Campbell, "The White House and the Presidency under the 'Let's Deal' President," in *The Bush Presidency: First Appraisals*, ed. Colin Campbell and Bert A. Rockman (Chatham, NJ: Chatham House, 1991), 185–222.

51. John Micklethwait, "Managing to Look Attractive," *New Statesman* 125, November 8, 1996, 24.

52. Quoted in I. M. Destler, "Reagan and the World: An 'Awesome Stubborness,'" in *The Reagan Legacy: Promise and Performance*, ed. Charles O. Jones (Chatham, NJ: Chatham House, 1988), 244–57. The source of the quote is *Report of the President's Special Review Board* (Washington, DC: Government Printing Office, 1987).

53. Edmund L. Andrews, "Greenspan Concedes Error on Regulation," *New York Times*, October 23, 2008, www .nytimes.com/2008/10/24/business/economy/24panel .html (accessed 7/6/16).

54. Michael D. Shear and Michael S. Schmidt, "Benghazi Panel Engages Clinton in Tense Session," *New York Times*, October 22, 2015, www.nytimes.com/2015/10/23/us /politics/hillary-clinton-benghazi-committee.html? _r=0 (accessed 10/29/15).

55. The Office of Technology Assessment was a fourth research agency serving Congress until 1995. It was one of the first agencies scheduled for elimination by the 104th Congress. Until 1983, Congress had still another tool of legislative oversight: the legislative veto. Each agency operating under such provisions was obliged to submit to Congress every proposed decision or rule, which would then lie before both chambers for 30 to 60 days. If Congress took no action by one-house or two-house resolution explicitly to veto the proposed measure during the prescribed period, the measure became law. The legislative veto was declared unconstitutional by the Supreme Court in 1983 on the grounds that it violated the separation of powers—the resolutions Congress passed to exercise its veto were not subject to presidential veto, as required by the Constitution. See *Immigration and Naturalization Service v. Chadha*, 462 U.S. 919 (1983).

Chapter 15

1. *United States v. Texas*, 579 U.S. __ (2016).

2. U.S. Courts Statistical Tables, www.uscourts.gov /statistics-reports/analysis-reports/statistical-tables -federal-judiciary (accessed 9/19/2015).

3. Michael A. Fletcher, "Obama Criticized as Too Cautious, Slow on Judicial Posts," *Washington Post*, October 16, 2009, www.washingtonpost.com/wp-dyn/content/article /2009/10/15/AR2009101504083.html (accessed 3/1/10).

4. Russell Wheeler, "Judicial Nominations and Confirmations after Three Years—Where Do Things Stand?" Brookings, January 13, 2012, www.brookings.edu /research/papers/2012/01/13-nominations-wheeler (accessed 8/27/14).

5. *Arizona v. United States*, 567 U.S. __ (2012).

6. *King v. Burwell*, 576 U.S. __ (2015).

7. *Marbury v. Madison*, 5 U.S. 137 (1803).

8. *National Federation of Independent Business v. Sebelius*, 567 U.S. __ (2012).

9. Acts of Congress held unconstitutional in whole or in part by the Supreme Court of the United States, General Printing Office, www.gpo.gov/fdsys/pkg/GPO-CONAN-2013 /pdf/GPO-CONAN-2013-11.pdf (accessed 4/20/14).

10. *Federal Election Commission v. Wisconsin Right to Life*, 551 U.S. 449 (2007); *McCutcheon v. Federal Election Commission*, 572 U.S. __ (2014).

11. This review power was affirmed by the Supreme Court in *Martin v. Hunter's Lessee*, 1 Wheat. 304 (1816).

12. *Brown v. Board of Education*, 347 U.S. 483 (1954).

13. *Lawrence v. Texas*, 539 U.S. 558 (2003).

14. *Alabama Legislative Black Caucus v. Alabama*, 575 U.S. __ (2015).

15. *Arizona State Legislature v. Arizona Independent Redistricting Commission*, 576 U.S. __ (2015).

16. *United States v. Jones*, 565 U.S. __ (2012).

17. *Riley v. California*, 573 U.S. __ (2014).

18. Theodore J. Lowi, *The End of Liberalism*, 2nd ed. (New York: W. W. Norton, 1979); also David Schoenbrod, *Power without Responsibility: How Congress Abuses the People through Delegation* (New Haven, CT: Yale University Press, 1993).

19. Kenneth Culp Davis, *Discretionary Justice* (Baton Rouge: Louisiana State University Press, 1969), 15–21.

20. Emergency Price Control Act, 56 Stat. 23 (1942).

21. *Chamber of Commerce of the United States v. Environmental Protection*, No. 12-1272 (2014).

22. *Michigan v. Environmental Protection Agency*, 576 U.S. __ (2015).

23. *Hamdi v. Rumsfeld,* 542 U.S. 507 (2004).

24. *Hamdan v. Rumsfeld,* 548 U.S. 557 (2006).

25. *Boumediene v. Bush,* 553 U.S. 723 (2008).

26. *National Labor Relations Board v. Noel Canning,* 572 U.S. __ (2014).

27. *Shelley v. Kraemer,* 334 U.S. 1 (1948).

28. *Burlington Northern v. White,* 548 U.S. 53 (2006).

29. *Engel v. Vitale,* 370 U.S. 421 (1962).

30. *Gideon v. Wainwright,* 372 U.S. 335 (1963).

31. *Escobedo v. Illinois,* 378 U.S. 478 (1964).

32. *Miranda v. Arizona,* 384 U.S. 436 (1966).

33. *Dickerson v. United States,* 530 U.S. 428 (2000).

34. *Baker v. Carr,* 369 U.S. 186 (1962).

35. *Roe v. Wade,* 410 U.S. 113 (1973).

36. *Schuette v. Coalition to Defend Affirmative Action,* 572 U.S. __ (2014).

37. *Fisher v. University of Texas,* 579 U.S. __ (2016).

38. Robert Scigliano, *The Supreme Court and the Presidency* (New York: Free Press, 1971), 162. For an interesting critique of the solicitor general's role during the Reagan administration, see Lincoln Caplan, "Annals of the Law," *New Yorker,* August 17, 1987, 30–62.

39. Edward Lazarus, *Closed Chambers* (New York: Times Books, 1998), 6.

40. *NAACP v. Button,* 371 U.S. 415 (1963). The quotation is from the opinion in this case.

41. *Smith v. Allwright,* 321 U.S. 649 (1944).

42. *Obergefell v. Hodges,* 576 U.S. __ (2015).

43. Charles Krauthammer, "Why Roberts Did It," *Washington Post,* June 29, 2012, www.washingtonpost.com/opinions/charles-krauthammer-why-roberts-did-it/2012/06/28/gJQA4X0g9V_story.html (accessed 4/22/14).

44. *Griswold v. Connecticut,* 381 U.S. 479 (1965).

45. *McCutcheon v. Federal Election Commission,* 572 U.S. __ (2014).

46. R. W. Apple, Jr., "A Divided Government Remains, and with It the Prospect of Further Combat," *New York Times,* November 7, 1996, B6.

47. For limits on judicial power, see Alexander Bickel, *The Least Dangerous Branch* (Indianapolis, IN: Bobbs-Merrill, 1962).

48. *Worcester v. Georgia,* 6 Pet. 515 (1832).

49. Walter Murphy, *Congress and the Court* (Chicago: University of Chicago Press, 1962).

50. Robert Dahl, "The Supreme Court and National Policy Making," *Journal of Public Law* 6 (1958): 279.

51. Martin Shapiro, "The Supreme Court: From Warren to Burger," in *The New American Political System,* ed. Anthony King (Washington, DC: American Enterprise Institute, 1978).

52. *Citizens to Preserve Overton Park v. Volpe,* 401 U.S. 402 (1971).

53. Toni Locy, "Bracing for Health Care's Caseload," *Washington Post,* August 22, 1994, A15.

54. See "Developments in the Law—Class Actions," *Harvard Law Review* 89 (1976): 1318.

55. *In re Agent Orange Product Liability Litigation,* 100 F.R.D. 718 (D.C.N.Y. 1983).

56. Donald Horowitz, *The Courts and Social Policy* (Washington, DC: Brookings Institution Press, 1977).

57. *Morgan v. McDonough,* 540 F2d 527 (1 Cir., 1976; *cert. denied,* 429 U.S. 1042 [1977]).

58. Alexander Hamilton, James Madison, and John Jay, *The Federalist Papers,* ed. Clinton Rossiter (New York: New American Library, 1961), no. 10, 78.

Chapter 16

1. Robert Nozick, *Anarchy, State and Utopia* (New York: Basic Books, 1974; repr., Oxford: Blackwell, 2003).

2. Compare with Gabriel Kolko, *The Triumph of Conservatism* (New York: Free Press, 1963), chap. 6.

3. Bureau of Economic Analysis, National Economic Accounts, Gross Domestic Product (GDP), Percent Change from Preceeding Period, www.bea.gov/national/index.htm#gdp (accessed 7/10/16).

4. U.S. Securities and Exchange Commission, Implementing the Dodd- Frank Wall Street Reform and the Consumer Protection Act, www.sec.gov/spotlight/dodd-frank.shtml (accessed 7/10/16).

5. See David M. Hart, *Forged Consensus: Science, Technology and Economic Policy in the United States, 1921–1953* (Princeton, NJ: Princeton University Press, 1998).

6. See Margaret Weir, *Politics and Jobs: The Boundaries of Employment Policy in the United States* (Princeton, NJ: Princeton University Press, 1992).

7. U.S. Department of Agriculture, 2012 Census of Agriculture, issued May 2014, www.agcensus.usda.gov/Publications/2012/Full_Report/Volume_1,_Chapter_1_US/usv1.pdf; The $20 billion figure includes forecasted "direct government payments" ($11 billion) and crop insurance program cost for 2015 ($9 billion). The forecasted direct government payments: USDA Economic Research Service, Farm Income and Wealth Statistics, (November 2015), www.ers.usda.gov/data-products/farm-income-and-wealth-statistics/government-payments-by-program.aspx; the crop insurance program cost: Government Accountability Office, GAO Highlights, Crop Insurance, GAO-15-215, Feb. 2015, www.gao.gov/assets/670/668358.pdf (accessed 7/10/16). Crop Insurance (accessed 12/16/15).

8. The act of 1955 officially designated the interstate highways as the National System of Interstate and Defense Highways. It was indirectly a major part of President Dwight Eisenhower's defense program. But it was just as obviously a "pork-barrel" policy as any rivers and harbors legislation.

9. Small Business Administration, Agency Financial Report: Fiscal Year—2015, p. 9, www.sba.gov/sites/default/files/aboutsbaarticle/Agency_Financial_Report_FY_2015.pdf (accessed 12/16/15).

10. The members included AMD, Digital, Hewlett-Packard, IBM, Intel, Lucent, Motorola, National Semiconductor, Rockwell, and Texas Instruments.

11. Molly Sherlock and Jeffrey M. Stupak, "Energy Tax Policy: Issues in the 114th Congress," Congressional Research Service, June 15, 2016, www.fas.org/sgp/crs/misc/R43206.pdf (accessed 7/9/16).

12. Drew Desilver, "5 Facts about the Minimum Wage," Pew Research Center, Fact Tank, July 23, 2015, www.pewresearch.org/fact-tank/2015/07/23/5-facts-about-the-minimum-wage/ (accessed 12/9/15).

13. Matthew L. Wald, "U.S. Agency Knew about G.M. Flaw but Did Not Act," *New York Times*, March 30, 2014, www.nytimes.com/2014/03/31/business/us-regulators-declined-full-inquiry-into-gm-ignition-flaws-memo-shows.html (accessed 4/27/14).

14. For a good summary of Keynes's ideas, see Robert Lekachman, *The Age of Keynes* (New York: McGraw-Hill, 1966).

15. Ronald Reagan, Inaugural Address, January 20, 1981, http://www.presidency.ucsb.edu/ws/?pid543130. (accessed 4/27/14).

16. Gallup, Taxes, www.gallup.com/poll/1714/taxes.aspx (accessed 4/27/14).

17. Gallup, Taxes.

18. Pew Research Center, "Beyond Distrust: How Americans View Their Government," U.S. Politics & Policy, November 23, 2015, www.people-press.org/2015/11/23/2-general-opinions-about-the-federal-government/ (accessed 6/1/16).

19. Pew Research Center, "As Sequester Deadline Looms, Little Support for Cutting Most Programs," U.S. Politics & Policy, February 22, 2013, www.people-press.org/2013/02/22/as-sequester-deadline-looms-little-support-for-cutting-most-programs/ (accessed 4/27/14).

20. See, for example, Paul Krugman, "The Bankruptcy Boys," *New York Times*, February 21, 2010, www.nytimes.com/2010/02/22/opinion/22krugman.html?_r50 (accessed 4/27/14).

21. Robert Greenstein, "Budget Deal, Though Imperfect, Represents Significant Accomplishment and Merits Support," Center on Budget and Policy Priorities, October 27, 2015, www.cbpp.org/press/statements/greenstein-budget-deal-though-imperfect-represents-significant-accomplishment-and (accessed 12/16/15).

22. Harry Stein, "Congress Passed a Budget Deal. Now What?" Center for American Progress, November 2, 2015, www.americanprogress.org/issues/budget/news/2015/11/02/124733/congress-passed-a-budget-deal-now-what/ (accessed 12/16/15).

23. Pew Research Center, "Section 2: Views of Government Regulation," U.S. Politics & Policy, February 23, 2012, www.people-press.org/2012/02/23/section-2-views-of-government-regulation/ (accessed 4/27/14).

24. Pew Research Center, "As Election Year Nears, Public Sees Mixed Economic Picture," www.people-press.org/2015/12/22/as-election-year-nears-public-sees-mixed-economic-picture/ (accessed 7/13/16).

25. Desilver, "5 Facts about the Minimum Wage."

26. Congressional Budget Office, "The Effects of a Minimum-Wage Increase on Employment and Family Income," February 18, 2014, www.cbo.gov/publication/44995 (accessed 4/27/14).

27. Josh Boak, "CBO: Stimulus Added up to 3.3M Jobs," *Politico*, November 22, 2011, www.politico.com/story/2011/11/cbo-stimulus-added-up-to-33m-jobs-068965 (accessed 12/7/15).

28. Bureau of Labor Statistics, "Union Members Summary," January 8, 2016, www.bls.gov/news.release/union2.nr0.htm (accessed 7/9/16).

29. Steven Greenhouse, "Wage Strikes Planned at Fast-Food Outlets," *New York Times*, December 1, 2013, www.nytimes.com/2013/12/02/business/economy/wage-strikes-planned-at-fast-food-outlets-in-100-cities.html?_r50 (accessed 4/27/14).

30. Sophie Quinton, "States Battle Cities over Minimum Wage," Pew Charitable Trusts, Stateline, July 13, 2015, www.pewtrusts.org/en/research-and-analysis/blogs/stateline/2015/07/13/states-battle-cities-over-minimum-wage; Jesse McKinley, "Cuomo to Raise Minimum Wage to $15 for All New York State Employees," *New York Times*, November 10, 2015 www.nytimes.com/2015/11/11/nyregion/andrew-cuomo-and-15-minimum-wage-new-york-state-workers.html (accessed 12/7/15).

31. David E. Sanger, David M. Herszenhorn, and Bill Vlasic, "Bush Aids Detroit, but Hard Choices Await Obama," *New York Times*, December 19, 2008, www.nytimes.com/2008/12/20/business/20auto.html?r53&hp (accessed 3/7/10).

32. Reuters, "CBO Raises TARP Cost Estimate to $34 Billion," December 16, 2011, www.reuters.com/article/2011/12/16/us-usa-tarp-cost-idUSTRE7BF1W920111216 (accessed 7/3/12).

33. Bureau of Labor Statistics, "United States Unemployment Rate," www.tradingeconomics.com/united-states/unemployment-rate (accessed 7/3/12).

34. Congressional Budget Office, "Estimated Impact of the American Recovery and Reinvestment Act on Employment and Economic Output from January 2012 through March 2012," Table 1, May 2012, www.cbo.gov/sites/default/files/cbofiles/attachments/05-25-Impact_of_ARRA.pdf (accessed 7/10/16).

35. Ben Pershing, "House Passes $15 Billion Jobs Bill," *Washington Post*, March 5, 2010, www.washingtonpost.com/wp-dyn/content/article/2010/03/04/AR2010030402757.html (accessed 3/5/10).

36. Kevin G. Hall, "Bernanke to Stay on Greenspan Path, but Not All the Way," *Seattle Times*, November 16, 2005, C1.

37. Federal Reserve Board, *Intended Federal Funds Rate, 1990 to Present*, www.federalreserve.gov/monetarypolicy/openmarket.htm (accessed 3/8/10).

38. Annamaria Andriotis, Laura Kusisto, and Joe Light, "After Foreclosures Home Buyers Are Back," *Wall Street Journal*, April 8, 2015, www.wsj.com/articles/after-foreclosures-home-buyers-are-back-1428538655 (accessed 11/6/15).

39. Steven R. Weisman, "Bernanke Faces Bear Stearns Queries," *New York Times*, April 2, 2008, C1.

40. Federal Reserve, "Why Did the Federal Reserve Lend to Banks and Other Financial Institutions during the Financial Crisis?" www.federalreserve.gov/faqs/why-did-the-Federal-Reserve-lend-to-banks-and-other-financial-institutions-during-the-financial-crisis.htm (acccessed 12/7/15).

41. Executive Office of the President of the United States, GPO Access, "Budget of the United States Government: Historical Tables Fiscal Year 2009," Table 2.2—Percentage Composition of Receipts by Source: 1934–2013, www.gpo.gov/fdsys/pkg/BUDGET-2009-TAB/pdf/BUDGET-2009-TAB-4-2.pdf. (accessed 5/9/08).

42. For a systematic account of the role of government in providing incentives and inducements to business, see C. E. Lindblom, *Politics and Markets* (New York: Basic Books, 1977), chap. 13. For a detailed account of the dramatic Reagan tax cuts and reforms, see Jeffrey Birnbaum and Alan Murray, *Showdown at Gucci Gulch: Lawmakers, Lobbyists, and the Unlikely Triumph of Tax Reform* (New York: Random House, 1987).

43. Jonathan D. Rockoff, "Pfizer Weighs Splitting Up New Drug Behemoth," *Wall Street Journal*, November 23, 2015, www.wsj.com/articles/pfizer-and-allergan-to-merge-in-huge-inversion-deal-1448280652 (accessed 12/9/15).

44. See Tax Foundation, "U.S. Federal Individual Income Tax Rates History, 1862–2013 (Nominal and Inflation-Adjusted Brackets)," http://taxfoundation.org/article/us-federal-individual-income-tax-rates-history-1913-2013-nominal-and-inflation-adjusted-brackets (accessed 3/30/14).

45. Glen Kessler, "Revisiting the Costs of the Bush Tax Cuts," *Washington Post*, May 10, 2011, www.washington-post.com/blogs/fact-checker/post/revisiting-the-cost-of-the-bush-tax-cuts/2011/05/09/AFxTFtbG_blog.html (accessed 12/7/15).

46. Center on Budget and Policy Priorities, "Tax Cuts: Myths and Realities," November 16, 2007, www.cbpp.org/9-27-06tax.htm (accessed 6/1/16).

47. Jay Heflin, "House Dems Want Bush Tax Cuts to Expire, but Say It's Tough Sell," *The Hill*, February 8, 2010, http://thehill.com/homenews/house/80133-democrats-supporting-ending-tax-cut-but-see-it-as-tough-sell (accessed 3/8/10).

48. Jackie Calmes, "Demystifying the Fiscal Impasse that Is Vexing Washington," *New York Times*, November 15, 2012, www.nytimes.com/2012/11/16/us/politics/the-fiscal-cliff-explained.html; Jonathan Weisman, "Answers to Questions on Capital's Top Topic," *New York Times*, February 21, 2013, www.nytimes.com/2013/02/22/us/politics/questions-and-answers-about-the-sequester.html (accessed 4/26/14).

49. David Espo, "Shutdown Orders Issued as Congress Misses Deadline," Associated Press, October 1, 2013, bigstory.ap.org/article/health-law-challenge-threatens-government-shutdown (accessed 4/26/14).

50. For an account of the relationship between mechanization and law, see Lawrence Friedman, *A History of American Law* (New York: Simon and Schuster, 1973), 409–29.

51. The *Federal Register* is the daily publication of all official acts of Congress, the president, and the administrative agencies. A law or executive order is not legally binding until it is published in the *Federal Register*.

52. Veronique de Rugy, "Hold on to Your Wallet: The Cost of Corporate Welfare and Rent-Seeking," *National Review Online*, July 25, 2012, www.nationalreview.com/corner/312251/hold-your-wallet-cost-corporate-welfare-and-rent-seeking-veronique-de-rugy# (accessed 9/26/12).

53. James Dao, "The Nation; Big Bucks Trip up the Lean New Army," *New York Times*, February 10, 2002, www.nytimes.com/2002/02/10/weekinreview/the-nation-big-bucks-trip-up-the-lean-new-army.html?pagewanted5all (accessed 9/26/12).

54. See Samuel P. Hays, *Beauty, Health, and Permanence: Environmental Politics in the United States, 1955–1985* (Cambridge: Cambridge University Press, 1987).

55. Pew Center on Global Climate Change, "Climate Change 101: The Science and Impacts," www.pewclimate.org/docUploads/101_Science_Impacts.pdf (accessed 3/21/08).

56. See the discussion in Peter R. Orszag, director Congressional Budget Office, "Issues in Climate Change" (presentation for the CBO Director's Conference on Climate Change, November 16, 2007), http://www.cbo.gov/sites/default/files/cbofiles/ftpdocs/88xx/doc8819/11-16-climatechangeconf.pdf (accessed 3/21/08).

57. Energy Information Administration, "Greenhouse Gases, Climate Change, and Energy," www.eia.doe.gov/oiaf/1605/ggccebro/chapter1.html (accessed 3/21/08).

58. Care Funk and Lee Raine, "Chapter 2: Climate Change and Energy Issues," Pew Research Center, Internet, Science & Tech, www.pewinternet.org/2015/07/01/chapter-2-climate-change-and-energy-issues/ (accessed 12/9/15).

59. Coral Davenport, "Senate Votes to Block Obama's Climate Change Rules," *New York Times*, November 17, 2015, www.nytimes.com/2015/11/18/us/politics/senate-blocks-obamas-climate-change-rules.html?_r=0 (accessed 12/9/15).

60. Michael Austin, "Breaking Down the New 2016 Fuel Economy Standards," *Car and Driver*, April 2, 2010, http://blog.caranddriver.com/breaking-down-the-new-2016-fuel-economy-standards/ (accessed 9/26/12).

61. Some research has shown that when taxes are linked to specific projects, public opinion is more favorable. See Department of Transportation, Office of Research and Technology, *UTC Spotlight*, "Will Americans Support Fuel Tax Increases? The Answer Could Be Surprising," March 2014, www.rita.dot.gov/utc/sites/rita.dot.gov.utc/files/utc_spotlights/pdf/spotlight_0314.pdf (accessed 7/10/16.)

62. Steve Mufson, "Coalition Agrees on Emissions Cuts," *Washington Post*, January 15, 2009, www.washingtonpost.com/wp-dyn/content/article/2009/01/14/AR2009011403850.html, (accessed 7/10/16).

63. Hendrik Hertzberg, "Cooling on Warming," *New Yorker*, February 7, 2011, 21.

64. Orszag, "Issues in Climate Change," 6–7.

65. Joe Palca, "California Turns to Holland for Flood Expertise," National Public Radio, January 14, 2008, www.npr.org/templates/story/story.php?storyId=18080442 (accessed 3/21/08).

66. Steven Greenhouse, "Our Economic Pickle," *New York Times*, January 12, 2013, www.nytimes.com/2013/01/13/sunday-review/americas-productivity-climbs-but-wages-stagnate.html?_r50 (accessed 5/2/14).

Chapter 17

1. Henry J. Kaiser Family Foundation, "Kaiser Health Tracking Poll: The Public's Views on the ACA," kff.org/interactive/kaiser-health-tracking-poll-the-publics-views-on-the-aca/#?response=Favorable—Unfavorable&aRange=twoYear (accessed 10/31/15).

2. "Americans' Views on Income Inequality and Workers' Rights," *New York Times*, June 3, 2015, www.nytimes.com/interactive/2015/06/03/business/income-inequality-workers-rights-international-trade-poll.html (accessed 10/31/15).

3. A good source of pre-1930s welfare history is James T. Patterson, *America's Struggle against Poverty, 1900–1994* (Cambridge, MA: Harvard University Press, 1994), chap. 2.

4. Patterson, *America's Struggle against Poverty*, 27.

5. This figure is based on a Works Progress Administration study by Ann E. Geddes, reported in Merle Fainsod et al., *Government and the American Economy*, 3rd ed. (New York: W. W. Norton, 1959), 769.

6. Social Security Administration, "2016 Social Security Changes," www.ssa.gov/news/press/factsheets/colafacts2016.html (accessed 11/19/15).

7. C. Eugene Steuerle, Adam Carasso, and Lee Cohen, *How Progressive Is Social Security and Why?* (Washington, DC: Urban Institute, 2004), www.urban.org/research/publication/how-progressive-social-security-and-why (accessed 5/3/14).

8. Social Security Administration, "Social Security Basic Facts," www.ssa.gov/news/press/basicfact.html (accessed 10/31/15).

9. Edward J. Harpham, "Fiscal Crisis and the Politics of Social Security Reform," in *The Attack on the Welfare State*, ed. Anthony Champagne and Edward Harpham (Prospect Heights, IL: Waveland, 1984), 13.

10. Workers must have lost their job through no fault of their own. For a full description of the program, see Chad Stone and William Chen, "Introduction to Unemployment Insurance," Center on Budget and Policy Priorities, July 30, 2014, www.cbpp.org/research/introduction-to-unemployment-insurance (accessed 11/18/15).

11. Ife Floyd and Liz Schott, "TANF Cash Benefits Have Fallen by More Than 20 Percent in Most States and Continue to Erode," Center on Budget and Policy Priorities, October 15, 2015, www.cbpp.org/research/family-income-support/tanf-cash-benefits-have-fallen-by-more-than-20-percent-in-most-states (accessed 10/31/15).

12. This poverty threshold is for a household of three persons that includes two children. Department of Health and Human Services, Office of the Assistant Secretary for Planning and Evaluation, Poverty Guidelines, January 25, 2016, http://aspe.hhs.gov/poverty-guidelines (accessed 7/10/16).

13. *Goldberg v. Kelly*, 397 U.S. 254 (1970).

14. Center on Budget and Policy Priorities, "Policy Basics: How Many Weeks of Unemployment Compensation Are Available?" May 23, 2016, www.cbpp.org/research/economy/policy-basics-how-many-weeks-of-unemployment-compensation-are-available (accessed 6/1/16).

15. Centers for Medicare and Medicaid Services, "Eligibility for Non-Citizens in Medicaid and CHIP," www.medicaid.gov/medicaid-chip-program-information/by-topics/outreach-and-enrollment/downloads/overview-of-eligibility-for-non-citizens-in-medicaid-and-chip.pdf (accessed 10/31/15).

16. See Martin Gilens, *Why Americans Hate Welfare* (Chicago: University of Chicago Press, 1999), chaps. 3, 4.

17. Gilens, *Why Americans Hate Welfare*.

18. EITC and Other Refundable Credits, "Statistics for Tax Returns with EITC," www.eitc.irs.gov/EITC-Central/eitcstats (accessed 7/10/16).

19. U.S. Government Accountability Office, "Temporary Assistance for Needy Families," December 2012, www.gao.gov/assets/660/650635.pdf (accessed 10/31/15).

20. Center on Budget and Policy Priorities, Chart Book TANF at 19, March 29, 2016, www.cbpp.org/research/family-income-support/chart-book-tanf-at-19 (accessed 7/10/16).

21. LaDonna Pavetti and Liz Schott, "TANF's Inadequate Response to Recession Highlights Weakness of Block-Grant Structure," Center on Budget and Policy Priorities, July 14, 2011, www.cbpp.org/research/family-income-support/tanfs-inadequate-response-to-recession-highlights-weakness-of-block (accessed 6/1/16).

22. Center for Budget and Policy Priorities, "Chartbook: SNAP Helps Struggling Families Put Food on the Table," April 18, 2012, www.cbpp.org/research/food -assistance/chart-book-snap-helps-struggling-families -put-food-on-the-table (accessed 6/1/16); U.S. Department of Agriculture, Food and Nutrition Service, "Supplemental Nutrition Assistance Program (SNAP)," www .fns.usda.gov/pd/34SNAPmonthly.htm (accessed 5/3/14).

23. Office of Management and Budget, "Table 2.2— Percentage Composition of Receipts by Source: 1934–2012," The Budget for Fiscal Year 2017, www.whitehouse.gov /omb/budget/Historicals (accessed 7/13/16).

24. Congressional Budget Office, Long-Term Budget Projections (July 2016), "Table 1. Summary Data for the Extended Baseline," www.cbo.gov/about/products /budget_economic_data (accessed 7/16/16); Congressional Budget Office, "Updated Budget Projections: 2016 to 2026," "Table 4. Mandatory Outlays Projected in CBO's Baseline," www.cbo.gov/sites/default/files/114th -congress-2015-2016/reports/51384-MarchBaseline _OneCol.pdf (accessed 7/16/16); Congressional Budget Office, Historical Budget Data (March 2016), "Table 5. Mandatory Outlays," www.cbo.gov/about/products /budget_economic_data (accessed 7/16/16); Congressional Budget Office, Baseline Projections for Selected Programs, Medicaid (Mar 2016), "Detail of Spending and Enrollment for Medicaid for CBO's March 2016 Baseline," www.cbo.gov/sites/default/files/51301-2016 -03-Medicaid.pdf (accessed 7/16/16); Office of Management and Budget, Historical Tables, "Table 11.3—Outlays for Payments for Individuals by Category and Major Program: 1940–2021," www.whitehouse.gov/omb/budget /Historicals (accessed 7/16/16).

25. Social Security Administration, "A Summary of the 2015 Annual Reports: Social Security and Medicare Boards of Trustees," www.ssa.gov/oact/trsum/ (accessed 11/14/15).

26. President's Commission to Strengthen Social Security, "Strengthening Social Security and Creating Personal Wealth for All Americans," December 21, 2001, www .ssa.gov/history/reports/pcsss/Final_report.pdf (accessed 3/26/08).

27. President's Commission, "Strengthening Social Security."

28. Alicia H. Munnell, "Are the Social Security Trust Funds Meaningful?" Center for Retirement Research at Boston College, May 2005, http://crr.bc.edu/briefs /are-the-social-security-trust-funds-meaningful/ (accessed 3/25/08); see also Social Security Administration, "Summary of P.L. 98-21, (H.R. 1900) Social Security Amendments of 1983—Signed on April 20, 1983," www.ssa .gov/history/1983amend.html (accessed 3/25/08).

29. Christian E. Weller, "Undermining Social Security with Private Accounts," Economic Policy Institute Issue Brief, December 11, 2001, www.epi.org/content.cfm /issuebriefs_ib172; Robert Greenstein, "Social Security Commission Proposals Contain Serious Weaknesses but May Improve the Debate in an Important Respect," Center on Budget and Policy Priorities, December 26, 2001, www.cbpp.org/archives/12-11-01socsec.htm (accessed 3/26/08).

30. Quoted in Jill Quadragno, "Social Security Policy and the Entitlement Debate," in Social Policy and the Conservative Agenda, ed. Clarence Y. H. Lo and Michael Schwartz (Malden, MA: Blackwell, 1998), 111.

31. Henry J. Kaiser Family Foundation, "The Facts on Medicare Spending and Financing," July 24, 2015, http://kff.org/medicare/fact-sheet/medicare-spending -and-financing-fact-sheet/ (accessed 7/10/16).

32. Henry J. Kaiser Family Foundation, "Facts on Medicare Spending and Financing."

33. Congressional Budget Office, "Long Term Analysis of a Budget Proposal by Chairman Ryan," April 5, 2011, www.cbo.gov/publication/22085 (accessed 7/6/12); see also the discussion in Kaiser Family Foundation Program on Medicare Policy, "Proposed Changes to Medicare in the 'Path to Prosperity': Overview and Key Questions," April 14, 2011, www.kff.org/medicare/upload/8179.pdf (accessed 3/1/12).

34. There were a couple of minor precedents. First was the Smith-Hughes Act of 1917, which made federal funds available to the states for vocational education at the elementary and secondary levels. Second, the Lanham Act of 1940 made federal funds available to schools in "federally impacted areas," that is, areas with an unusually large number of government employees and/or where the local tax base was reduced by large amounts of government-owned property.

35. New America Foundation, "Federal, State and Local K–12 School Finance Overview," June 29, 2015, http://atlas .newamerica.org/school-finance (accessed 7/10/16).

36. David K. Cohen and Susan L. Moffitt, The Ordeal of Equality: Did Federal Regulation Fix the Schools? (Cambridge, MA: Harvard University Press, 2009).

37. For a positive view of the standards, see Sonja Brookins Santelises, "Abandoning the Common Core Is Taking the Easy Way Out," The Equity Line, March 31, 2014, https:// edtrust.org/the-equity-line/abandoning-the-common -core-is-taking-the-easy-way-out/; for a critique see Valerie Strauss, "The Coming Common Core Melt-down," Washington Post, January 23, 2014, www.washingtonpost .com/blogs/answer-sheet/wp/2014/01/23/the-coming -common-core-meltdown (accessed 5/11/14).

38. Department of Education, Fundamental Change: Innovation in America's Schools under Race to the Top, 2015, www2 .ed.gov/programs/racetothetop/rttfinalrptexecsumm .pdf (accessed 7/11/16).

39. Elaine Weiss, "Mismatches in Race to the Top Limit Educational Improvement: Lack of Time, Resources, and Tools to Address Opportunity Gaps Puts Lofty State Goals Out of Reach," Economic Policy Institute, September 12, 2013, www.epi.org/publication/race-to-the-top-goals/ (accessed 5/11/14).

40. Valerie Strauss, "The Successor to No Child Left Behind Has, It Turns Out, Big Problems of Its Own," *Washington Post*, December 7, 2015, www.washingtonpost.com /news/answer-sheet/wp/2015/12/07/the-successor-to -no-child-left-behind-has-it-turns-out-big-problems-of -its-own/ (accessed 7/11/16).

41. One of the most vocal proponents of this viewpoint is former assistant secretary of education Diane Ravitch, *The Life and Death of the Great American School System* (New York: Basic Books, 2011).

42. The College Board, "Trends in Student Aid 2015," 2015, 34, trends.collegeboard.org/sites/default/files/trends -student-aid-web-final-508-2.pdf (accessed 11/6/15).

43. The College Board, "Trends in Student Aid 2015," (accessed 7/10/16).

44. Henry J. Kaiser Family Foundation, "U.S. Federal Funding for HIV/AIDS: Trends over Time," June 10, 2016, http://kff.org/global-health-policy/fact-sheet /u-s-federal-funding-for-hivaids-trends-over-time/ (accessed 7/11/16).

45. Noam N. Levey, "Obama's HIV/AIDS Policy Hailed for Targeting Spread of Disease," *Los Angeles Times*, July 14, 2010, http://articles.latimes.com/2010/jul/14/nation/la-na-obama -aids-20100714 (accessed 3/1/12); Henry J. Kaiser Family Foundation, "The HIV/AIDS Epidemic in the United States," April 7, 2014, http://kff.org/hivaidsfact-sheet/the -hivaids-epidemic-in-the-united-states/ (accessed 5/10/14).

46. Office of Management and Budget, Fiscal Year 2017, Historical Tables, "Table 12.3, Total Outlays for Grants to State and Local Governments, by Function, Agency, and Program: 1940–2017," www.whitehouse.gov/sites /default/files/omb/budget/fy2017/assets/hist.pdf (accessed 7/11/16).

47. Henry J. Kaiser Family Foundation, "*Medicaid: A Primer —Key Information on the Nation's Health Coverage Program for Low-Income People*," March 1, 2013, https: //kaiserfamilyfoundation.files.wordpress.com /2010/06/7334-05.pdf (accessed 6/2/16) (see p. 26).

48. Henry J. Kaiser Family Foundation, "Total Monthly Medicaid and CHIP Enrollment," http://kff.org/health -reform/state-indicator/total-monthly-medicaid-and -chip-enrollment/ (accessed 11/4/15).

49. Henry J. Kaiser Family Foundation, "Health Insurance Coverage of Non-Elderly, 0–64," http://kff.org/other /state-indicator/nonelderly-0-64 (accessed 7/10/16).

50. For a comparison of opinion in 1993 when the Clinton plan was considered and opinion in 2009 as reform was just beginning again, see Pew Research Center, "Obama's Ratings Remain High Despite Some Policy Concerns," U.S. Politics & Policy, June 18, 2009, www.people-press. org/2009/06/18/obamas-ratings-remain-high-despite -some-policy-concerns/ (accessed 7/6/12).

51. Henry J. Kaiser Family Foundation, "The Coverage Gap: Uninsured Poor Adults in States that Do Not Expand Medicaid—An Update," January 21, 2016, kff.org /health-reform/issue-brief/the-coverage-gap-uninsured -poor-adults-in-states-that-do-not-expand-medicaid-an -update/ (accessed 6/2/16).

52. Jennifer Steinhauer, "House Votes to Send Bill to Repeal Health Law to Obama's Desk," *New York Times*, January 6, 2016, www.nytimes.com/2016/01/07/us /politics/house-votes-to-send-bill-to-repeal-health-law -to-obamas-desk.html (accessed 7/11/16).

53. Henry J. Kaiser Family Foundation, "Kaiser Health Tracking Poll: The Public's Views on the ACA," http://kff.org/interactive/kaiser-health-tracking-poll -the-publics-views-on-the-aca/#?response=Favorable- -Unfavorable&aRange=twoYear (accessed 10/19/16).

54. White House, "Fact Sheet: Affordable Care Act by the Numbers," www.whitehouse.gov/the-press-office/2014/ 04/17/fact-sheet-affordable-care-act-numbers (accessed 5/12/14).

55. *National Federation of Independent Businesses v. Sebelius*, 567 U.S. __ (2012).

56. Henry J. Kaiser Family Foundation, "The Coverage Gap."

57. *Burwell v. Hobby Lobby Stores*, Inc., 573 U.S. __ (2014).

58. *King v. Burwell*, 576 U.S. __ (2015); Lena H. Sun, "6.4 million Americans Could Lose Obamacare Subsidies, Federal Data Show," *Washington Post*, June 2, 2015, www.washingtonpost.com/national/health-science /64-million-americans-could-lose-obamacare-subsidies -federal-data-show/2015/06/02/fe0c87be-095a-11e5 -95fd-d580f1c5d44e_story.html (accessed 11/4/15).

59. Robert Barnes, "Affordable Care Act Survives Supreme Court Challenge," *Washington Post*, June 25, 2015, www.washingtonpost.com/politics/courts_law/obam- acare-survives-supreme-court-challenge/2015/06/25 /af87608e-188a-11e5-93b7-5eddc056ad8a_story.html (accessed 11/4/15).

60. Alan Rappeport and Margot Sanger-Katz, "Hillary Clinton Takes a Step to the Left on Health Care," *New York Times*, May 10, 2016, www.nytimes.com/2016/05/11 /us/politics/hillary-clinton-health-care-public-option .html (accessed 7/11/16).

61. Robert Pear and Maggie Haberman, "Donald Trump's Health Care Ideas Bewilder Republican Experts," *New York Times*, April 8, 2016, www.nytimes.com /2016/04/09/us/politics/donald-trump-health-care .html?_r=0 (accessed 7/11/16).

62. John E. Schwarz, *America's Hidden Success*, 2nd ed. (New York: W. W. Norton, 1988), 41–2.

63. See, for example, Lawrence Vale, "Housing Chicago: Cabrini-Green to Parkside of Old Town," https:// placesjournal.org/article/housing-chicago-cabrini-green-to -parkside-of-old-town/ (accessed 3/1/12).

64. Annamaria Andriotis, Laura Kusisto, and Joe Light, "After Foreclosures, Home Buyers Are Back," *Wall Street Journal*, April 8, 2015, www.wsj.com/articles /after-foreclosures-home-buyers-are-back-1428538655 (accessed 11/6/15).

65. U.S. Census Bureau, "Table 3. Poverty Status of People, by Age, Race, and Hispanic Origin," www.census.gov /data/tables/time-series/demo/income-poverty/historical -poverty-people.html (accessed 7/17/16).

66. See, for example, Theodore R. Marmor, Jerry L. Mashaw, and Philip L. Harvey, *America's Misunderstood Welfare State* (New York: Basic Books, 1990), 156.

67. U.S. Census Bureau, "Income and Poverty in the United States: 2014," www.census.gov/content/dam/Census /library/publications/2015/demo/p60-252.pdf (accessed 7/16/16).

68. U.S. Census Bureau, "Table 3. Poverty Status of People, by Age, Race, and Hispanic Origin."

69. U.S. Census Bureau, "Annual Estimates of the Resident Population for Selected Age Groups by Sex: April 1, 2010 to July 1, 2015," www.census.gov/popest/data /national/asrh/2015/index.html (accessed 7/17/16).

70. AARP, "AARP Member Opinion Survey, Issue Spotlight: Work," December 2012, http://www.aarp. org/content/dam/aarp/research/surveys_statistics /general/2012/2012-AARP-Member-Opinion-Survey -Issue-Spotlight-Work-AARP.pdf (accessed 11/11/15); Thom File, "Who Votes? Congressional Elections and the American Electorate: 1978–2014," U.S. Census Bureau, July 2015, www.census.gov/content/dam/Census /library/publications/2015/demo/p20-577.pdf; AARP, "AARP Survey: 76% of People 50-Plus Pleased with Pope," September 22, 2015, www.aarp.org/about-aarp /press-center/info-09-2015/aarp-survey-76-percent -50-plus-pleased-with-pope.html; Center for Responsive Politics, "Profile for 2014 Election Cycle," www.opensecrets .org/orgs/summary.php?id=D000023726&cycle=; AARP, "About the AARP Public Policy Institute," www .aarp.org/ppi/about-ppi/#experts (accessed 11/11/15).

71. See Andrea Louise Campbell, *How Policies Make Citizens: Senior Political Activism and the American Welfare State* (Princeton, NJ: Princeton University Press, 2005).

72. Christopher Howard, *The Hidden Welfare State: Tax Expenditures and Social Policy in the United States* (Princeton, NJ: Princeton University Press, 1999); Jacob S. Hacker, *The Divided Welfare State: The Battle over Public and Private Benefits in the United States* (New York: Cambridge University Press, 2002).

73. Center on Budget and Policy Priorities, "Policy Basics: Federal Tax Expenditures," updated February 23, 2016, www.cbpp.org/research/federal-tax/policy-basics -federal-tax-expenditures (accessed 7/11/16).

74. U.S. Department of Agriculture, Food and Nutrition Service, "Supplemental Nutrition Assistance Program (SNAP)," www.fns.usda.gov/snap/eligibility#Income (accessed 7/11/16); Center on Budget and Policy Priorities, "Policy Basics: Introduction to the Supplemental Nutrition Assistance Program (SNAP)," updated March 24, 2016, www.cbpp.org/research/policy-basics -introduction-to-the-supplemental-nutrition-assistance -program-snap (accessed 7/11/16)

75. "Panera CEO: On Food Stamps, I Can't Eat in My Own Restaurant," September 25, 2013, http://eatocracy.cnn .com/2013/09/25/panera-ceo-on-food-stamps-i-cant -eat-in-my-own-restaurant (accessed 5/12/14).

76. Samantha Artiga, Anthony Damico, and Rachel Garfield, "The Impact of the Coverage Gap for Adults in States not Expanding Medicaid by Race and Ethnicity," October 26, 2015, kff.org/disparities-policy/issue-brief /the-impact-of-the-coverage-gap-in-states-not -expanding-medicaid-by-race-and-ethnicity/ (accessed 11/11/15).

77. Raymond Hernandez, "Federal Welfare Overhaul Allows Albany to Shift Money Elsewhere," *New York Times*, April 23, 2000, 1.

78. Frances Fox Piven and Richard Cloward, *Poor People's Movements* (New York: Pantheon, 1977), chap. 5.

79. U.S. Department of Agriculture, Food and Nutrition Service, "National and/or State Level Monthly and/or Annual Data," April 2016; www.fns.usda.gov/pd /supplemental-nutrition-assistance-program-snap (accessed 7/11/16).

80. U.S. Census Bureau, "Table 2. Poverty Status of People by Family Relationship, Race, and Hispanic Origin: 1959 to 2014," www.census.gov/data/tables/time-series /demo/income-poverty/historical-poverty-people.html (accessed 7/16/16); U.S. Census Bureau, "Income and Poverty in the United States: 2014."

81. See, for example, Sharon Hayes, *Flat Broke with Children: Women in the Age of Welfare Reform* (New York: Oxford University Press, 2004).

82. U.S. Census Bureau, "Table 2. Poverty Status of People by Family Relationship, Race, and Hispanic Origin: 1959 to 2014" and "Table 3. Poverty Status of People, by Age, Race, and Hispanic Origin."

83. U.S. Census Bureau, "Poverty: Historical Poverty Tables—People," "Table 2. Poverty Status, of People by Family Relationship, Race, and Hispanic Origin: 1959–2014" www.census.gov/hhes/www/poverty/data /historical/people.html (accessed 2/20/12). For an argument that children should be given the vote, see Paul E. Peterson, "An Immodest Proposal," *Daedalus* 121, no. 4 (Fall 1992): 151–74.

84. On the relationship between education and democracy in the United States, see Ira Katznelson and Margaret Weir, *Schooling for All: Race, Class, and the Democratic Ideal* (New York: Basic Books, 1985).

85. See L. Free and Hadley Cantril, *The Political Beliefs of Americans* (New York: Simon and Schuster, 1968).

86. See Fay Lomax Cook and Edith Barrett, *Support for the American Welfare State* (New York: Columbia University Press, 1992); and Hugh Heclo, "The Political Foundations of Antipoverty Policy," in *Fighting Poverty: What Works and What Doesn't*, ed. Sheldon H. Danziger

and Daniel H. Weinberg (Cambridge, MA: Harvard University Press, 1986), 312–40.

87. Henry J. Kaiser Family Foundation, Peterson Kaiser Health System Tracker, Health Spending Explorer, December 7, 2015, www.healthsystemtracker.org/interactive/health-spending-explorer/?display=As%2520a%2520%2525%2520of%2520GDP&service=&range Type=single&years=2014 (accessed 7/11/16).

Chapter 18

1. Geoffrey Perret, *A Country Made by War* (New York: Random House, 1989), 558.

2. Sam Perlo-Freeman and Carina Solmirano, "Trends in World Military Expenditure, 2013," Stockholm International Peace Research Institute, April 2014, http://books.sipri.org/files/FS/SIPRIFS1404.pdf (accessed 6/12/14).

3. Rupert Smith, *The Utility of Force: The Art of War in the Modern World* (New York: Vintage, 2008).

4. D. Robert Worley, *Shaping U.S. Military Forces: Revolution or Relevance in a Post–Cold War World* (Westport, CT: Praeger Security International, 2006).

5. Colin S. Gray, "The Implications of Preemptive and Preventive War Doctrines," Strategic Studies Institute, July 2007, www.strategicstudiesinstitute.army.mil/pdffiles/pub789.pdf (accessed 8/1/14).

6. Better World Campaign, "How the U.S. Funds the UN," https://betterworldcampaign.org/us-un-partnership/how-the-us-funds-the-un/ (accessed 9/19/14).

7. Matthew Crenson and Benjamin Ginsberg, *Presidential Power: Unchecked and Unbalanced* (New York: W. W. Norton, 2007).

8. Benjamin Ginsberg, *The American Lie: Government by the People and Other Political Fables* (Boulder, CO: Paradigm, 2007).

9. Paul R. Pillar, *Terrorism and American Foreign Policy* (Washington, DC: Brookings Institution Press, 2003).

10. For a good treatment of this in regard to Irish Catholics and Catholics in general, see Timothy Byrnes, *Catholic Bishops and American Politics* (Princeton, NJ: Princeton University Press, 1991). For a (controversial) discussion of the role of Jewish groups, see John J. Mearsheimer and Stephen M. Walt, *The Israel Lobby and U.S. Foreign Policy* (New York: Farrar, Straus and Giroux, 2007).

11. This felicitous term is from David R. Mayhew, *Congress: The Electoral Connection* (New Haven, CT: Yale University Press, 1974).

12. John H. Aldrich, *Why Parties? The Origin and Transformation of Political Parties in America* (Chicago: University of Chicago Press, 1995), 278.

13. A very good brief outline of the centrality of the president in foreign policy is found in Paul E. Peterson, "The President's Dominance in Foreign Policy Making," *Political Science Quarterly* 109 (Summer 1994): 215–34.

14. One confirmation of this is found in Theodore Lowi, *The End of Liberalism: The Second Republic of the United States*, 2nd ed. (New York: W. W. Norton, 1979), 127–30; another is found in Stephen Krasner, "Are Bureaucracies Important?" *Foreign Policy* 7 (Summer 1972): 159–79. However, it should be noted that Krasner was writing his article in disagreement with Graham T. Allison, "Conceptual Models and the Cuban Missile Crisis," *American Political Science Review* 63, no. 3 (September 1969): 689–718.

15. See Theodore Lowi, *The Personal President: Power Invested, Promise Unfulfilled* (Ithaca, NY: Cornell University Press, 1985), 167–9.

16. "Sleeve-Rolling Time: IMF," *The Economist*, May 2, 1992, 98–9.

17. James Dao and Patrick E. Tyler, "U.S. Says Military Strikes Are Just a Part of Big Plan," *The Alliance*, September 27, 2001; and Joseph Kahn, "A Nation Challenged: Global Dollars," *New York Times*, September 20, 2001, B1.

18. Turkey was desperate for help extricating its economy from its worst recession since 1945. The Afghanistan crisis was going to hurt Turkey all the more; Turkey's strategic location helped its case with the IMF. "Official Says Turkey Is Advancing in Drive for I.M.F. Financing," *New York Times*, October 6, 2001, A7.

19. For information on current U.S. sanctions programs, visit U.S. Department of the Treasury, "Sanctions Programs and Country Information," www.treasury.gov/resource-center/sanctions/Programs/Pages/Programs.aspx (accessed 6/1/14).

20. George Quester, *The Continuing Problem of International Politics* (Hinsdale, IL: Dryden Press, 1974), 229.

21. The Warsaw Pact was signed in 1955 by Albania, Bulgaria, Czechoslovakia, Hungary, the German Democratic Republic (East Germany), Poland, Romania, and the Soviet Union. Albania later dropped out. The Warsaw Pact was terminated in 1991.

22. Ginsberg, *The American Lie*, 3.

answer key

Chapter 1
1. e
2. b
3. a
4. d
5. c
6. c
7. c
8. b
9. a
10. d
11. e
12. b
13. e
14. a
15. a

Chapter 2
1. b
2. a
3. b
4. c
5. e
6. c
7. c
8. d
9. b
10. e
11. e
12. b
13. e
14. a

Chapter 3
1. c
2. c
3. b
4. e

5. a
6. c
7. d
8. b
9. c
10. b
11. b
12. a
13. d
14. d

Chapter 4
1. a
2. e
3. b
4. e
5. b
6. e
7. e
8. b
9. d
10. b
11. a
12. c
13. a
14. d

Chapter 5
1. b
2. e
3. a
4. c
5. b
6. d
7. a
8. a
9. d
10. a

11. d
12. c
13. a
14. b

Chapter 6
1. c
2. b
3. b
4. d
5. e
6. d
7. c
8. a
9. c
10. b
11. a
12. b

Chapter 7
1. b
2. a
3. b
4. c
5. e
6. c
7. b
8. c
9. b
10. e
11. b
12. c
13. c

Chapter 8
1. e
2. a
3. d

4. e
5. e
6. c
7. d
8. d
9. b
10. d
11. d
12. c

Chapter 9
1. a
2. c
3. b
4. d
5. d
6. a
7. d
8. e
9. e
10. c
11. d
12. e
13. d

Chapter 10
1. b
2. e
3. d
4. c
5. c
6. c
7. c
8. b
9. d
10. b
11. d
12. b

13. c
14. a

Chapter 11
1. a
2. b
3. c
4. c
5. d
6. b
7. e
8. d
9. a
10. e
11. c
12. a
13. e

Chapter 12
1. b
2. a
3. d
4. c
5. d
6. c
7. a
8. a
9. b
10. d
11. e
12. c
13. a
14. a

Chapter 13
1. b
2. d
3. a

4. c
5. b
6. b
7. b
8. e
9. a
10. c
11. c
12. b
13. b
14. a

Chapter 14
1. d
2. b
3. b
4. e
5. b
6. e

7. d
8. d
9. d
10. e
11. e
12. c
13. a
14. a

Chapter 15
1. a
2. c
3. a
4. c
5. d
6. d
7. e
8. e

9. c
10. b
11. e
12. a
13. b
14. d

Chapter 16
1. a
2. b
3. c
4. e
5. a
6. c
7. c
8. d
9. d
10. b

11. e
12. a
13. c
14. d

Chapter 17
1. c
2. d
3. b
4. e
5. c
6. a
7. c
8. d
9. d
10. a
11. d
12. c

13. e
14. b
15. c

Chapter 18
1. b
2. d
3. a
4. e
5. c
6. c
7. c
8. e
9. b
10. c
11. a
12. d
13. b

credits

TEXT

Figure 4.1: Map: "Gun Ownership, State by State" from "This Map Shows Where America's Gun Owners Are," by Julia Lurie. MotherJones.com, July 8, 2015. Reprinted courtesy of Mother Jones Magazine.

Figure 8.3: Figure from "More Americans Are Using Social Media to Connect with Politicians," by Monica Anderson, Pew Research Center, Washington, DC (May, 2015) http://www.pewresearch.org/fact-tank/2015/05/19/more-americans-are-using-social-media-to-connect-with-politicians/. Reprinted with permission.

Figure 9.4: Figure from "Millennials Increasingly Identify as Political Independents," Pew Research Center, Washington, DC (March, 2014) http://www.pewsocialtrends.org/2014/03/07/millennials-in-adulthood/sdt-next-america-03-07-2014-1-01/. Reprinted with permission.

Figure 9.6: Figure from "More Democrats Take Liberal Positions, More Republicans Take Conservative Positions," Pew Research Center, Washington, DC (June, 2014) http://www.people-press.org/2014/06/12/section-1-growing-ideological-consistency/pp-2014-06-12-polarization-1-03/. Reprinted with permission.

Table 11.1: Table: "Top Spending on Lobbying Activities by Industry, 1998-2015" from OpenSecrets.org. Reprinted by permission of Center for Responsive Politics.

Figure 14.3: "Iron Triangles" republished with permission of Wadsworth, a division of Cengage Learning from *Incomplete Conquest: Governing America*, 2nd ed. by Theodore J. Lowi (New York: Holt, Rinehart and Winston, 1981), p. 139. © 1981 by CBS College Publishing; permission conveyed through Copyright Clearance Center, Inc.

PHOTOS

Chapter 1: p. 2: JG Photography/Alamy; p. 5: Screenshot 2016 U.S. Department of Education Office of Federal Student Aid; p. 8: Daniel Acker/Bloomberg via Getty Images; p. 11: Richard B. Levine/Alamy Live News; p. 14 (top): Bettmann/Corbis via Getty Images; p. 14 (bottom): Bettmann/Corbis via Getty Images; p. 17: Library of Congress; p. 18: Rue des Archives/Granger, NYC—All rights reserved; p. 21: Jim West/Alamy Stock Photo; p. 23: Ed Zurga/Getty Images; p. 26: Bettmann/Corbis via Getty Images; p. 28: Blend Images/Alamy Stock Photo; p. 30: Mike Nelson/EPA/Newscom; p. 31: Don Emmert/AFP/Getty Images

index

Page numbers in *italic* refer to figures or photos.

incorporation into Fourteenth
Amendment, 116–18, *118–19*
liberties contained in, 113
nationalization of, 116–20
personal liberties and rights in, 26
rights and liberties in, 153
and right to die, 144
and right to privacy, 140, 142–43, 145
bills, 480–85. *See also* lawmaking
Bimber, Bruce, 298
bin Laden, Osama, 264, 505, 726
Bipartisan Campaign Reform Act of 2002
(BCRA; McCain-Feingold Act),
124–25, *338*, 396, 446, 599
birth control, 140, 142
"birther" controversy, 266, *266*
BISC (Ballot Initiative Strategy Center),
448
Bismarck, Otto von, 15
Black Chamber, 145–46
Black Lives Matter movement, *152*, 154,
165, 211, 289–90, *344*, *444*
Blackmun, Harry, 610, 616
Blankfein, Lloyd, *230*
block grants, 96, 98
blogs, 263
Bloomberg News, 260
blue states, 345
Boehner, John, 358, *490*, 491–93, 498, 653
Boston, Massachusetts, 168, *168*
Boston Massacre, 42
Boston Tea Party, 42–43, *43*
Boumediene v. Bush, 604
bourgeoisie, 14
Bowers v. Hardwick, 143, 186
Boydstun, Amber, 271
BRAC (Defense Base Closure and
Realignment Commission),
569
Brady Handgun Violence Prevention
Act, 88
Brandeis, Louis, 140
Brandenburg, Charles, 124
Brandenburg v. Ohio, 124
BRCA. *See* Bipartisan Campaign Reform
Act of 2002
Brennan, William J., Jr., 130
Breyer, Stephen, 122
briefs, 611
broadcast media, 251, 254–57
Brown, Linda, 162
Brown, Michael, 211, 289, 528
Brown, Oliver, 162
Brown University, 177
Brown v. Board of Education, 28, 162–64,
180, 442, 601, 605
*Brown v. Entertainment Merchants
Association*, 131
Bryan, William Jennings, 352, 355
Buchanan, James, 526

Buckley v. Valeo, 124, 396
budget, federal, 651–54, *655*
Budget and Impoundment Control Act, 537
Budget Control Act of 2011, 653
budget deficit, 652–53, *653*
budget surplus, *236*, 653
burden of proof, 189–91
bureaucracy, 544–79
agencies of executive branch, 556
defined, 547
in a democracy, 577–78
employment figures (2015), *567*
FOIA requests, *579*
and foreign policy, 726–27
goals of, 556–65
for maintaining a strong economy,
564–65
managing, 573–77
organization of the executive branch,
552–54
for promotion of the public welfare,
556–58
for providing national security, 558–64,
560
reformation of, 566, 568–73
size in various countries, 555, *555*
size of federal service, 551–52, *552*
Burger, Warren, 176
Burnham, Walter Dean, 329
Bush, George H.W., and administration, *726*
attempts to shrink bureaucracy`, 568
centralization strategy, 574
education policies, 687
election of 1988, 388
judicial appointments, 585, 596, 617
momentum in election of 1980, 376
signing statements of, 534
Bush, George W., and administration
administrative directives, 530
antiterrorism initiatives, 603–4
approval ratings, 528–29
on big government, 551
Dick Cheney and, 525
communications strategies, 534
as "compassionate conservative," 207
congressional scrutiny of, 495
courting of religious groups, 345
economic policies, 644
education policies, 687
election of 2000, 240, 354, 359,
374, 380
election of 2004, 382
and farm subsidies, 720
and financial crisis of 2008, 644
foreign policy, 725–26
foreign policy after 9/11 attacks, 226–29
and gender gap, 345
and greenhouse gas emissions, 548
growth of government under, 101
and HIV/AIDS policy, 690

housing policies, 695
and Hurricane Katrina, 511
immigration law enforcement, 182
and Iraq War, 226, 227, 725–26, 728,
738
judicial appointments, 585, 617
lack of congressional oversight under,
576
management strategy, 574–75
and media priming, 273
and micro-targeting, 390
military spending, 635
Pentagon budget under, 659
and popular vote, 82
presidential initiatives, 515
preventive war policy, 716
privatization under, 570
public opinion of tax cuts, 217, 224
public relations by, 528
and religious conservatives, 309
SCHIP regulation under, 98
signing statements, 534
and Social Security reform, 683
tax cuts, 272, 646, 651
and United Nations, *734*
veto power used by, 513
voter mobilization in 2004 election, 311
war on terror, 271
and war on terror, 520
Bush, Jeb, 272, 346
Bush Doctrine, 725–26, *726*
Bush v. Gore, 380
business conservatives, 346
business development, promoting, 633–35
business interest groups, 423
business organizations, 642
Business Roundtable, 642
busing, school desegregation via,
168–69
butterfly ballots, *373*
Bystrom, Dianne, 266

C

cabinet, 521–22
Cable News Network (CNN), 128, 254
cable television, 255
CACI International, 571
Calhoun, John C., *87*, 87–88
California
Asian Americans, 183–84, 306
automatic voter registration in, 287–88,
318
gun laws, 131
immigration and voter demographics,
345
initiative campaigns in, 382
marijuana laws, 75
migrant workers in, 180
Proposition 30, 313
Proposition 187, 181

Clinton, Bill, and administration
administrative directives of, 530
administrative strategies, 534
approval rating of, 529
on big government, 551
block grant vetos, 96
congressional investigation of, 495
diverse cabinet of, 521–22
election of 1992, 380
election of 1996, 354
Merrick Garland and, 585
and gays in the military, 186
health care reform initiative of, 526, 691
on Hillary's role in administration, 526
and HIV/AIDS policy, 690
housing policy, 695
impeachment inquiry, 486, *496*, 497
Monica Lewinsky scandal, 254, 272
management strategy of, 574
National Performance Review, 566, 568, *568*
as "new Democrat," 341
polls on use for budget surplus under, 236
public relations by, 226, 528
on welfare reform, 679
White House staff of, 523
Clinton, Hillary, *23, 230, 344, 383*
ACA support in 2016 campaign, 694
African American support for, 344
Asian American support for, 307
Benghazi hearings, 476, 495–96, 576, 729
and *Citizens United* case, *125*
in debates, 390
election of 2008, 303
election of 2016, 303, 369–70, *379*, 380
email server as campaign issue, 277
as first lady, 526
and gender gap, 307, 345
health care reform, 691
Latino support for, 213, 222, 306
media agenda-setting in 2008 election, 272
momentum in 2016 primaries, 376
as Secretary of State, 733
superdelegates and, 379
trustworthiness issue, 400
Twitter use in 2016 election, 528
voter race/ethnicity, 345
youth vote, 348
closed primaries, 372
closed rule, 482
cloture, 483
CNN (Cable News Network), 128, 254
coercion, power of, 79
COLAs (cost-of-living adjustments), 675–76
Colbert, Stephen, 256
Cold War, 715, 737

collective goods, 429
collective security, 736–38
colleges, 689
Collingwood, Loren, 306
colonists, political strife among, 42–43
Colorado, 15, 102, 159, 348
comedy talk shows, 256
Comey, James, 496
comity, 55–56
comity clause, 81
commander in chief, 510
commerce clause, 85, 87, 105
Commerce Department, 565, 719
commercial speech, 126–27
Commission on Wartime Contracting, 572
committee markup sessions, 482
committee system (Congress), 341, 473–78, 489–90, 495–96
Common Cause, 228, 420
Common Core, 101, 688
common law, 604
Communications Decency Act (CDA), 130, 278
community, online, 297–98
Community Reinvestment Act of 1977, 173
compacts, 81–82
computer security, 714
computer security breaches, 566
concurrent powers, 79
confederation, 44
conference, 473, 611, 613
conference committees, 476–77, 484–85
Congress, *456, 456–99. See also* House of Representatives; Senate
advice and consent by, 496
and Affordable Care Act, 105
and budget process, 652–54
caucuses, 480
committee system of, 473–78, *475*
conference committees, 484–85
constitutional powers of, 645
Constitutional provision for, 52–54
decision making by, 485–94
and democracy, 497–98
differences between House and Senate, *459*, 459–60
direct patronage by, 470–72
election of, 465–70
federal courts and, 618
and foreign policy, 713, 727–29
and impeachment, 496–97
implied powers of, 77
influence of interest groups on, *437*, 437–41
iron triangles, 440
and limits of presidential power, 535
lobbying, 437–41
majority party structure, *474*
member demographics, *463*
organization of, 472–80

oversight by, 495–96, 575–77
parties in, 341–42
party leadership in, 473, 487–91
party polarization in, 340, 357–58, *494*
and population shift, 23, 24
powers delegated by, 516, 518
power under Articles of Confederation, 44–45, 47
and presidency, 509
and presidential policy-making, 534–35, *536*
profile of, *463*
and recession of 2008, 644–45
representation by, *472*
rules of lawmaking in, 480–85, *481*
and separation of powers, 58, *58*
sociological vs. agency representation, 461–62, 464–65
staff system of, *478*, 478–79
and Supreme Court, 616
tax committees in, 565
and tax cuts, 651
and TPP, 721
and Twenty-Seventh Amendment, 65, 67
unemployment insurance extension authorization, 676
unfunded mandates of, 94–95
and voter demographics, *499*
war power of, 520
Congressional Black Caucus, *464*
Congressional Budget Office (CBO), 644, 652
congressional campaign committees, 339
Congressional investigations, 729
Connecticut, 140, 142
Connecticut Compromise, 50. *See also* Great Compromise
conservatism, 206, *207*, 357, 358, 616–17, 704
constituency, 459, 464–65, 485–86, *486*
constituent services, 471
Constitution, U.S., 39–40, 52–59
amending, 56. *See also* amendments to the Constitution
Annapolis Convention, 46
Articles of Confederation vs., *53*
Bill of Rights, 59
on congressional powers, 645
continuing value of, 39, 40
executive branch, 54–55
on federal courts, 590
federalism in, 77–82
foreign policy provisions of, 727, 728, *728*
judicial branch, 55
legislative branch, 52–54
liberty in, 24
limits on power of national government, 56, 58–59

and labor groups, 642
and laissez-faire economics, 638
Latino voters, 305–6, 344–45
and lower-income voters, 346
members' characteristics, 215–16
and minimum wage, 640, 642
origins of, 351–53
party identification, 342–44
and polarization, 357, 358
and primary delegates, 378
and Progressive Party reforms,
    360–61
and proportional representation
    voting, 337, 378
and public works financing, 89–90
recruitment of candidates by, 466
and redistricting, 469–70
and regulation, 640, 642
religious affiliations of members, 215
responsiveness of, 330
tax and social spending views of, 346,
    639–40
and tax debate, 30
and TPP, 721
and voter ID laws, 314, 316
voter mobilization, 311
voter registration reform and, 288
and white southerners, 218
and young Americans, 348, *348*
and youth vote, 348
democratic socialism, 207
demonstrations, 443
Dennis v. United States, 125
department, defined, 552
deportation policies, 104–5, 118
deregulation, 657
descriptive representation, 306
desegregation, 510–11
deterrence, 715–16
devolution, 96, 98–100, 569–70
DHS. *See* Homeland Security,
    Department of
Dickerson v. United States, 606
digital advertising, 258–59
digital citizens/citizenship, 11–12, 259. *See
    also* Internet
defined, 11, 259
offline political participation of, 297–98
digital divide, 12, 260, 299
digital journalism, 260–61
digital literacy, 12
digital media. *See also* Internet
as news source, 249
and presidential campaigns, 389
digital political participation, 295–99
digital revolution, 249
diplomacy, 732–33
diplomatic power (president), 511–12
direct-action politics, 16
direct democracy, 15, 381–82

direct elections, 507
direct lobbying, 436–41
direct mail campaigns, 390, 391
direct patronage, 470–72
Disability Rights Education and Defense
    Fund, 185
disabled Americans, civil rights for, 185
discretionary spending, 654, *654*, *655*
discrimination. *See also* segregation
against Asian Americans, 183–84
based on sexual orientation, 185–87
against citizens of other states, 81
defined, 155
against disabled Americans, 185
employment, 166, 167, 169, 189
gender, 175–79
in housing, 172–73
against Latinos/Hispanics, 180–83, *181*
in lending, 172–73
against Native Americans, 185
positive, 192
racial, 155–74, 604–5, 674
against women, 166
dissenting opinion, 614
district courts, federal, *590*, 591, 592
district judges, appointment of, 592
District of Columbia, 75, 80, 138, 162, 316,
    318
District of Columbia v. Heller, 131–32
diversity, news media and, 255–56
divided government, 355
DNA testing, 135
DNC. *See* Democratic National
    Committee
Dodd–Frank Act, 487
Dodd–Frank Wall Street Reform and
    Consumer Protection Act of
    2010, 505, 657
Doha Amendment to the Kyoto
    Protocol, 723
Doha Round, 719–20
Dole, Bob, 88
donations (political campaigns).
    See fund-raising
Donovan, Todd, 240, 312
"Don't Ask, Don't Tell," 186
double jeopardy, 117, 136
Douglas, Stephen, 231
Douglas, William O., 142
Douglass, Frederick, 157
Drake, Thomas, 129
DREAM Act, 181–82, *182*, 222
Dred Scott v. Sandford, 156
Druckman, James, 223
Druckman, Jamie, 237
Drudge Report, 254
Drug Enforcement Agency, U.S.
    (DEA), 75
drug testing, 134–35
dual federalism, 83–85, *92*

Du Bois, W.E.B., 159
due process clause, 117
due process of law, 133–40, 153
cruel and unusual punishment, 139–40
defined, 591
double jeopardy, 136
eminent domain, 137–38
grand juries, 136
right to counsel, 138–39
and same-sex marriage ruling, 187
searches and seizures, 133–36
self-incrimination, 137
Dukakis, Michael, 388
Duke Power Company, 169

E
Early, Stephen, 527
early voting, 319
earmarks, 470–71
Earned Income Tax Credit (EITC), 679,
    700
East India Company, 42, 43, *43*
e-commerce, 102
economic aid and sanctions, 735–36
economic class, public opinion and, 217
economic crisis of 2008. *See* financial crisis
    and recession of 2008
economic development agencies, 565
economic equality/inequality, 23–24,
    25, 28
economic freedom, 26–27
economic growth
environmental policy vs., 232
measuring, 630–32
economic inequality. *See* income
    equality/inequality
Economic Opportunity Act, 92
economic policy, 627–65
for business development, 633–35
for economic prosperity, 630–34
and the environment, 659–63
fiscal policies, 648–54
and foreign policy, 713
goals of, 629–36
government spending, 639–40
monetary policies, 645–48
politics of, 636–45
to protect employees and consumers,
    635–36
public opinion on, 199–200
regulation, 640, 642
regulation and antitrust policy,
    654–57
and special interest groups, 642
for stable markets, 629–30
subsidies and contracting, 657–58
taxation, 638–39
economic populism, 345–46
economic power, political power
    and, 31

equal protection clause, 155, 174–75
"equal rights," 153–54
Equal Rights Amendment (ERA), 67, 176
equal time rule, 278
Erikson, Robert, 230
Ernst, Joni, 489
Escobedo v. Illinois, 605
ESEA (Elementary and Secondary Education Act of 1965), 685
Espionage Act of 1917, 124
establishment clause, 120–22
ethics, congressional, 471, 478, 487
ethnic diversity
    in congressional representation, 461–62, *462*, *463*, 464
    global changes in, 22, *22*
    and immigration, 17–18
    and political culture, 17–21, *19*
ethnicity
    party affiliation and, 344–45
    public opinion and, 213
Europe. *See also individual countries*
    and free trade, 719
    as market for American goods, 720
    proportional representation in, 373
European immigrants, 21
Evangelical Christians
    and conservatism, 215
    and political participation, 309, *309*
    and right-to-life movement, 228
Every Student Succeeds, 688–89
exclusionary rule, 133–34
executive agreement, 496, 512, 728–29
executive branch. *See also* presidency
    agencies of, 556
    Constitutional provisions for, 54–55
    lobbying of, 439–40
    organization of, 552–54
    separation of powers, 58, *58*
executive-congressional agreement, 729
Executive Office of the President (EOP), 516, 523, 530
executive orders, 104, 515–16, 531–33, *532*, 573
executive power (president), 512–13
executive privilege, 512
exit polls, 300
ex post facto laws, 115
expressed powers, 54, 77, 509–16
expressive politics, 298–99
external mobilization, 331

F

Facebook
    and election of 2016, 295–96
    as news source, 249, 259, 261, 262
    Obama's page on, 226, 528
    political uses of, 261, 262

prevalence of, 261
    as shaper of public opinion, 210
    and Supreme Court same-sex marriage decision, *298*, 298–99
    as tool in 2016 election, 295–96
    and voter mobilization, 310–11
    and voter participation, *297*
face-to-face surveys, 237, *237*
FactCheck.org, 265, *265*
Fair Housing Act, 172–73
Fair Housing Amendments Act, 173
Fair Labor Standards Act of 1938, 635, 640
fairness doctrine, 278
Fallon, Brian, *383*
Falwell, Jerry, 129
family, political socialization by, 209–10
Family and Medical Leave Act, 101–2
farm subsidy program, 633
Farook, Syed, 113, 135
Faubus, Orval, 163, 510
Faulkner, Shannon, 177
FBI. *See* Federal Bureau of Investigation
FCC (Federal Communications Commission), 277–78
FCC v. Beach Communications, 175
FDA. *See* Food and Drug Administration
FDIC (Federal Deposit Insurance Corporation), 647
FEC (Federal Election Commission), 395
Fed, the. *See* Federal Reserve Board
federal agencies, judicial review of, 602–3
federal aid, *93*
Federal Bureau of Investigation (FBI), 27, 113–14, 135, 496, 559, 727
Federal Communications Commission (FCC), 277–78
federal courts, *589*, 598–621. *See also individual courts, e.g.:* Supreme Court
    appellate courts, 592–94
    caseloads, *593*
    court cases, 587–88
    and judicial revolutions, 618–20
    and the legal system, 587–92
    Supreme Court, 598–620
    traditional limitations on, 617–18
    transformation of role and power of, 617–20
    trial courts, 592
    types of courts, 588–92
Federal Deposit Insurance Corporation (FDIC), 647
Federal Election Campaign Act of 1971, 395, 445
Federal Election Commission (FEC), 395
Federal Election Commission v. Wisconsin Right to Life, 124–25
Federal Emergency Management Agency (FEMA), 511

federal funds rate, 646
federal government. *See also* bureaucracy; government(s)
    Constitutional limits on power of, 56, 58–59
    Constitutional provisions on power of, 55–56, 58–59
    and dual federalism, 83–85
    effect on daily life at state universities, *78*
    growth in power of, 85–87
    relationship of state governments and, 76, 82–89. *See also* federalism
    role as defined in Articles of Confederation, 44
    spending by, *553*
federal grants, 90, *91*, *93*, 96
federalism, 74–107
    and changing role of states, 87–89
    in the Constitution, 52, 58–59, 77–82
    cooperative, 91–92, *92*
    defined, 52, 77
    and devolution, 98–100
    dual, 83–85
    dual vs. cooperative, *92*
    federal grants, 90, *91*
    and growth of national government's power, 85–87
    New Deal, 89–90
    New Federalism, 96–105
    public spending, *103*
    public spending and, 89–95
    regulated, 92–95, *98*, *99*
    relationship of federal and state governments, 82–89
    since 2000, 100–105
Federalist Papers, 60–61
Federalists
    and bill of rights, 115
    defined, 60
    and electoral realignment, 355
    and Jeffersonian Republicans, 362
    origin of, 331
    and ratification of the Constitution, *60*, 60–63
    and states' powers amendment, 79
    and two-party system, 332, 350–51
federal judges, 594–95, *597*
Federal Labor Relations Authority (FLRA), 574
Federal Meat Inspection Act of 1906, 656, *656*
Federal Register, 657
Federal Regulation of Lobbying Act of 1946, 436
Federal Reserve Act, 647
Federal Reserve banks, 646
Federal Reserve Board (the Fed), 564, 646–47
Federal Reserve System, 564, 646–47, 656

federal service, 551–52, *552. See also* bureaucracy
federal system, 77, *83*, 97, *97*, 371. *See also* federalism
Federal Trade Commission (FTC), 656
Federal Trade Commission Act of 1914, 656
Feeding America, 700
fee shifting, 619
Feingold, Russell, 396
Feinstein, Diane, *220*
felons, voting rights of, 316
FEMA (Federal Emergency Management Agency), 511
Ferguson, Missouri, 165, 211, 289, 528
Fifteenth Amendment, 31, 157, 291
Fifth Amendment, 136–38
    double jeopardy, 136
    eminent domain, 137–38
    grand juries, 136
    incorporated in Fourteenth Amendment, 118
    provisions of, 117
    rights of the accused, 67
    right to privacy, 140, 142
    self-incrimination, 137
fighting words, 125
filibuster, 358, 483, 498
financial crisis and recession of 2008, *626, 633*
    and federal deficit, 653
    Federal Reserve's response to, 646
    and financial industry regulation reform, 657
    foreclosure crisis, 647, 696
    and global economy, 712
    government response, 627–28, 644
    and public opinion, 220
    and SNAP benefits, 701
    stimulus package, 633
financial industry reform, 657
Financial Stability Oversight Council, 564–65, 657
Fiorina, Morris, 216–17
firearms. *See* gun control
First Amendment, 116, 120–31, *121*
    and campaign contribution limits, 392, 393, 599
    and freedom of religion, 120–23. *See also* freedom of religion
    and freedom of speech, 123–28. *See also* freedom of speech
    and freedom of the press, 128–31
    incorporated in Fourteenth Amendment, 118
    and lobbying, 437
    and press freedom around the world, 279
First Continental Congress, 43
First Founding, 41–45

"first past the post," 332, 333
first spouse, 525–26
fiscal agencies, 564–65
fiscal policies, 564, 648–54
Fisher, Abigail, *191*
Fisher, Louis, 537
Fisher v. University of Texas, 191, *191*, 607
501(c)(4) politically active nonprofits, 338–39, 395
527 committees, 338, 395, 446. *See also* Super PACs
flag burning, 127
Flint, Michigan water crisis (2014–), *271*
Florida
    congressional seats of, 468
    election of 2000, 171, *373*, 374, 380
    election of 2012, 319, 380
FLRA (Federal Labor Relations Authority), 574
FOIA. *See* Freedom of Information Act
Food and Drug Administration (FDA), 94, 635, 656
Ford, Gerald, 511, 524–25
foreclosure crisis, 696
foreclosures, 647
foreign aid, 724, 735–36
foreign policy, 227, 710–43
    after 9/11 attacks, 228–29
    and America's role in the world, 742
    arbitration, 740–41
    for collective security, 736–38
    diplomacy, 732–33
    for economic aid and sanctions, 735–36
    for economic prosperity, 718–21
    goals of, 713–24
    instruments of, 732–41
    international humanitarian policies, 721, *723*, 723–24
    and international monetary structure, 734–35
    makers of, 725–32
    and military force, *712*, 738–40
    for security, 713–18
    and the United Nations, 733–34
Foreign Service Act of 1946, 732
formula grants, 90
foundations, as media revenue source, 264
Founding, 39–51, 63–64
    American demographics at time of, 16
    Articles of Confederation, 44–45
    and British taxes, 41–42
    and colonists' political strife, 42–43
    Declaration of Independence, 44
    First, 41–45
    Second, 45–51
Fourteenth Amendment, 81, 614
    citizenship for freed slaves, 18
    civil rights, 155
    and double jeopardy, 136

due process clause, 117
equal protection, 153, 157, 159, 187
first definitive interpretation of, 192
incorporation of Bill of Rights into, 116–18, *118–19*
levels of scrutiny under equal protection clause, 174–75
Obergefell v. Hodges, 187
and voting rights, 165–66
Fourth Amendment, 113–14, 133–36, 140, 142
Fourth of July (Independence Day) celebration, *44*
Fox News, 254, 257
fracking, *418*, 419
framing, 272–73
    of events, by mass media, 228–29
    of survey questions, 237–38
France, 22, 41, 77, 97, 733
Frankfurter, Felix, 594, 613, 616
Franklin, Benjamin, 44
Franklin v. Gwinnett County Public Schools, 177
Frederick, Joseph, 126
Freedom Caucus, 493
Freedom of Information Act (FOIA), 562–63, *563*, 577, 579
freedom of religion, 120–23
    free exercise clause, 122–23
    separation of church and state, 120–22
freedom of speech, 123–28
    and campaign contribution limits, 392, 393, 599, 616
    and political parties, 362
freedom of the press, 250, 279, *279*
free exercise clause, 122–23
free markets, 26
free media, 390
free riders, 429–30
Free Soil Party, 156
French and Indian War, 41
FTC (Federal Trade Commission), 656
full faith and credit clause, 79–80
Fulton, Robert, 86
fund-raising (election campaigns), 328, 362, 384–86, *385*, 391–96, *394*, 411–12, *413. See also* Bipartisan Campaign Reform Act of 2002

G

Gadsden, Christopher, 43
Gallup polls, 227, 239
GAO (Government Accountability Office), 572
García-Rios, Sergio, 306
Gardner, Cory, 489
Garland, Merrick, 493, 585–86, 596, *598*
Garner, Eric, 211
Garrity, W. Arthur, Jr., 168, 619–20

minimum wage, *30, 198,* 200, 204, 217, 231, 635, 640, *641,* 642, *643*

Minnesota, 99, 314, 664

minorities, 701–3. *See also specific minority groups*

minority leader, 473

minority party, 341

minority rights, 31

Miranda, Ernesto, 137

Miranda rule, 137, 605

Miranda v. Arizona, 606

Mississippi, 98, 157, 171, 314

Missouri, 160, 165

Missouri Compromise, 156

mixed regime, 58

mobile devices, as news source, 260, 296–97

mobilization
defined, 310
in early days of American elections, 362
in formation of parties, 331
for political participation, 310–11
of public opinion by interest groups, 442–45
of voters, 335–36

Moe, Terry, 535

momentum, 273, 376

monetary agencies, 564–65

monetary policies, 645–48

monetary structure, international, 734–35

money, politics and, 31, *385,* 391–96, 411–12. *See also* fund-raising

"money bills," 480

monopolies, 654

Monroe, James, 714

Monroe Doctrine, 714

Montana, 469

Montesquieu, Baron de la Brède et du, 56, 58

Montgomery bus boycott, 164–65, *165*

Montreal Protocol, 723

mootness, 606

Moral Majority, 309

Morrill Act of 1862, 685

Morse v. Frederick, 126

mortgage lending crisis, 647, 695–96

Mott, Lucretia, 156, 157

MoveOn.org, 228, 311, 431–33, *432*

MSPB (Merit Systems Protection Board), 574

multiculturalism, news media and, 255–56

multi-party systems, *333*

Murdoch, Rupert, 257, 270

Murguia, Janet, *23*

Muslims, 21

Myers v. United States, 509

N

NAACP. *See* National Association for the Advancement of Colored People

NAACP Legal Defense and Educational Fund, 161

Nader, Ralph, 359, *359,* 428, *429,* 636

NAFTA (North American Free Trade Agreement), 719

Nashaw, Jerry L., 518

National Aeronautics and Space Administration (NASA), 554, *554*

National American Woman Suffrage Association (NAWSA), 159–60

National Association for the Advancement of Colored People (NAACP), 140, 159, *161,* 442, 610–11

National Association of Evangelicals, *341*

National Association of Manufacturers, 642

national bank, 85–86

National Commission on Terrorist Attacks upon the United States (9/11 Commission), 561–62, 576

national committees, 338–39

national conventions, 337–38, *338,* 378–79, 508

national debt, 653–54

National Defense Authorization Act of 2009 (NDAA), 572

National Defense Education Act of 1958 (NDEA), 685, 689

National Endowment for the Arts (NEA), 491

National Environmental Policy Act of 1969 (NEPA), 618–19, 660

national government. *See* federal government

National Highway Traffic Safety Administration, 636

National Hurricane Center, 4

National Industrial Recovery Act of 1933, 518

National Institutes of Health (NIH), 556, *556,* 632, 690

National Labor Relations Act of 1935, 635

National Labor Relations Board (NLRB), 604, 635

National Opinion Research Center, 235

National Organization for Women (NOW), 175–76, *227,* 228

National Origins quota system, 18

National Park Service, 556

National Performance Review (NPR), 566, 568, *568*

National Popular Vote compact, 82

National Public Radio (NPR), 256

National Restaurant Association, 642

National Rifle Association (NRA), 420, 422, 443–44, 448

National Science Foundation, 631–32

national security
bureaucracy for providing, 558–64, *560*
and green technologies, 663

liberty vs., 113
technological innovation for, 635

National Security Agency (NSA), 27, 129, 136, 145, 275, 563

national security alliances, 736

National Security Archive, 562

National Security Council (NSC), 522, 523, 575, 727

national standards
regulated federalism and, 92–95
and unfunded mandates, 94–95

National Traffic and Motor Vehicle Safety Act of 1966, 636

national unity
Constitutional provisions for, 55–56
and obligations among states, 79, 81

National Weather Service, 4

National Welfare Rights Organization, 701

National Woman's Party, 160

National Women's Political Caucus, 307

nation-states, 715

Native Americans, 16, *17,* 18, 185

NATO. *See* North Atlantic Treaty Organization

NAWSA (National American Woman Suffrage Association), 159–60

NDAA (National Defense Authorization Act of 2009), 572

NDEA (National Defense Education Act of 1958), 685, 689

NEA (National Endowment for the Arts), 491

Near v. Minnesota, 128

necessary and proper clause, 77, 85–86

negative campaign advertising, 388

Negotiated Rulemaking Act of 1990, 439–40

NEPA (National Environmental Policy Act of 1969), 618–19, 660

Netanyahu, Benjamin, *730*

Netflix, 260

Netherlands, 333

netroots, 429, 431–32, 443

Nevada, 468

New Deal, *89,* 89–90, 353, 360–61
and African American voters, 344
and Democratic Party, 218
and employment, 632
and government expansion, 85, 89–90
and income-based voting, 346
and Jewish voters, 345
and judicial review of federal agency actions, 602
and middle class, 23
and party affiliation, 346
and Supreme Court, 594, 615, 618

Newdow, Michael A., 121–22

New Federalism, 96–105, *98*

New Hampshire primaries, 313, 376, 378

New Jersey, 469

New Jersey Plan, 48
Newman, Brian, 231
new media, 258–67, 362
New Politics movement, 435
news, 249–50. *See also* media
    Americans' main sources for, 249, 251, *252*, 259
    in broadcast media, 254–57
    content and character of, 267
    followers by age, income, and education, 269
    from new media, 258–67
    online, 258–60, 264–65, 297
    in print media, 251–54
    types of coverage, 274–77
news aggregators, 258
News Corporation, 257
newspapers, *251*, 251–54, *253*, 257, 272, 276
New York, 156–57
New York City
    Eric Garner incident, 211
    stop and frisk, 135–36
New York Convention, 741
New York Times, 175–76
    circulation, 252–53
    diversity and, 255
    Pentagon Papers, 128, 228, 275
    revenue for, 252–53
    Vietnam coverage, 276–77
    Watergate coverage, 268
New York Times v. Sullivan, 129
New York Times v. United States, 128.
    See also Pentagon Papers
New Zealand, 97, 736
niche journalism, 260
NIH. *See* National Institutes of Health
9/11 attacks. *See* September 11, 2001 attacks
9/11 Commission, 561–62, 576
Nineteenth Amendment, 31, 160, 292
Nixon, Richard, and administration, *390*
    and block grants, 96
    and budget process, 537
    and election of 1968, 353
    and employment discrimination, 169
    on Keynesians, 638
    and media coverage, 268
    pardon of, 511
    and party polarization, 257
    in presidential debates, 389, *390*
    resignation of, 525
    and school segregation, 168
    "southern strategy" of, 354, *354*
    and War Powers Resolution, 520
    Watergate, 268, 272, 277, 445, 476, 512–13, *513*
    White House staff of, 523
NLRB (National Labor Relations Board), 604, 635

No Child Left Behind Act of 2001, 101, 687, 688
"no excuse" absentee voting, 318–19
nominating conventions. *See* national conventions
nominations, 335, 372, 375–80, 508
noncontributory welfare programs, 676–77, 696
nonenforcement of laws, 534
nonprofit journalism, 263–64
nonprofit organizations, 338
non-state actors, 713
nonworking poor, social policy for, 700–701, *701*
Noriega, Manuel, 128
North
    Republican Party in, 352
    slavery in, 156
    and Three-Fifths Compromise, 50–51
North American Free Trade Agreement (NAFTA), 719
North Atlantic Treaty, 736
North Atlantic Treaty Organization (NATO), 717, 726, 736–38, *737*
North Carolina, 176–77
North Dakota, voter registration in, 314
North Korea, 715–18
Northwest Ordinance of 1787, 685
NOW. *See* National Organization for Women
NPR (National Performance Review), 524, 566, 568, *568*
NPR (National Public Radio), 256
NRA. *See* National Rifle Association
NSA. *See* National Security Agency
NSC. *See* National Security Council
"nuclear option," 483
nullification, 87–88

O

OAS (Organization of American States), 736
oaths of office, 56
Obama, Barack, and administration, *512*
    and 2009 economic stimulus package, 644–45
    administrative directives of, 530
    Affordable Care Act, 8, 95
    and African American voters, 304
    background checks for gun owners, 132
    Biden chosen by, 524
    "big data" use in election campaigns, 240
    "birther" controversy, 266
    campaign funding of, 396
    campaign strategies, 386
    on *Citizens United*, 125
    classified information leak cases, 129
    climate change focus of, 661–63
    Hillary Clinton and, 369–70

    and Clinton's appointment as Secretary of State, 733
    continuation of George W. Bush's policies, 207–8
    diplomatic power, 511–12
    "Don't Ask, Don't Tell" repeal, 186
    DREAM act, 222
    on earmarks, 471
    economic policies of, 644, 652–53
    and economic recession of 2008, 633
    education policies, 687–88, *688*
    election campaign of 2008, 212, 272, 304, 336, 354, 378, 390
    election campaign of 2012, 239, 306, 319, 392, 448
    on energy and climate change, 662–63
    executive orders of, 531, 533, *533*
    Facebook page, 528
    false beliefs about, 266
    on federal contractors, 573
    and federal deficit, 652–53
    and federal regulation of state laws, 94
    and financial crisis of 2008, 644
    as first black president, 154, *192*
    foreign policy of, 716–17, 726
    on function of government, 551
    on government programs, 639
    on government secrecy, 563–64
    and greenhouse gas emissions, 548
    and Guantánamo Bay prison camp, 741–42
    health care, *439*, 505, 690–94
    HIV/AIDS policy, 690
    holds on nominees of, 484
    immigration law, 104–5, *533*, 535
    international initiatives, 521
    Internet used by, 528
    Iran nuclear deal, 718
    and Israel, 730
    issues focus in campaigns of, 398
    judicial appointments, 585–86, 596
    and judicial appointments, 595
    and Latino voters, 222, 306, 344–45
    and LBGT rights, 176–77
    liberalism under, 205
    Lily Ledbetter Fair Pay Act, 178
    and limits of presidential power, 535, 537
    on lobbyists, 439
    managerial presidency of, 575
    and media agenda-setting, 272
    media agenda-setting in 2008 election, 272
    and military powers, 520–21
    and minimum wage, 640, 642
    natural gas issue, 419
    and No Child Left Behind Act, 101, 687
    and nonenforcement of laws, 534
    NSA investigation, 563–64
    policy failures, 505–6

United Nations (UN), 724, 733–34, 736
United Nations, declaration of Internet access as human right, 278, 280
United Nations Framework Convention on Climate Change (UNFCCC), 723
UN Security Council, 733–34
United States v. Grubbs, 134
United States v. Jones, 135
United States v. Lopez, 88
United States v. Nixon, 513, *513*
United States v. Playboy Entertainment Group, 130–31
United States v. Williams, 130
United States v. Wong Kim Ark, 183
University of California, 189–90
University of Michigan, 190–91
University of Texas, 191
unreasonable searches. *See* searches and seizures
Unsafe at Any Speed (Nader), 636
upper class, social policy for, 699
urban areas, American population in, 23
U.S. Chamber of Commerce. *See* Chamber of Commerce, U.S.
U.S. Citizenship and Immigration Services, 727
U.S. Climate Action Partnership (USCAP), 662
U.S. Commission on Civil Rights, 165, 171
U.S. Court of Appeals, 592
U.S. Court of Appeals for the Federal Circuit, 591–93
U.S. Court of Appeals for Veterans Claims, 591
U.S. Court of Federal Claims, 591
U.S. Court of International Trade, 591
U.S. Court of Military Appeals, 591
U.S. Northern Command, 561
U.S. Public Health Service (USPHS), 690
USA Freedom Act, 564
USA PATRIOT Act, 101, 521, 562
USCAP (U.S. Climate Action Partnership), 662
USPHS (U.S. Public Health Service), 690
Utah, 159, 182, 468

V

values
    consensus on, 204, *204*
    in the Constitution, 68
    defined, 201
    democracy, 30–31
    equality, 27–30
    immigration and, 24
    liberty, 26–27
    political, 203–5
Van Ordern v. Perry, 122
Varnum v. Brien, 221
Vermont, voting rights of felons in, 316

Verrilli, Donald B., Jr., *609*
Veterans Affairs, Department of, 557–58
veto, 485, 513–14, *514*, *515*
vice presidency, 523–25
video, streaming, 260
Vietnam War, *276*
    deterrence policy, 715
    domestic repercussions, 740
    draft card burning, 127
    draft evader amnesty, 511
    media and, 268
    media coverage, 276–77
    and New Deal coalition, 353
    Pentagon Papers case, 128, 275
    and presidential power, 520
    and public interest groups, 435
    secret presidential agreements, 496
    shaping of political environment by, 218, 347
    and Twenty-Sixth Amendment, *68*, 292
    veterans with Agent Orange exposure, 558, 619
Virginia, 80, 162, 316
Virginia Military Institute (VMI), 177
Virginia Plan, 48
VMI (Virginia Military Institute), 177
Volcker, Paul, 647
Volkswagen diesel emissions scandal, 549
voter fraud, ID laws and, 314, 316
voter ID laws, *171*, 171–72, 314, 316
voter mobilization, 336
voter registration
    automatic, 287–88
    same-day, 287
    by social group, *315*
    state requirements, 314, 316
voters
    demographics in 2016, *539*
    election decision making by, 397–400
voter turnout, 31, *107*, 292–94, *293*, 300–310
    battleground vs. non-battleground states, 312–13
    election campaign of 2008, 330
    international variations in, 294, *294*
    percentages (1976-2012), *302*
    primaries and caucuses, *363*
    and voter ID laws, 316
    voter registration reform and, 287–88
voting, 14, *286*, 287–88, 290–94, 300–319
    in Congress, 484
    for congressional representatives, *499*
    in election of 2008, *31*
    in election of 2016, *31*
    formal barriers to, 316
    importance of, 371
    by mail, 319

and political knowledge, 220
political participation through, 290–92
split-ticket, 348, 374
state electoral laws, 314–19, *317*
straight-ticket, 373
turnout. *See* voter turnout
voting rights, 31, *170*, 170–72, 286, 290–92
    for African Americans, *155*, 157, 291, 304
    Amendments regarding, 69
    Twenty-Sixth Amendment, *68*
    and voter turnout, 292
    for women, 31, 155, *157*, 158–60, *160*, 292, *292*
Voting Rights Act of 1965 (VRA), 31, *170*, 170–72, 184, 185, 291, 354, 469, 470
Vox Media, 260
VRA. *See* Voting Rights Act of 1965

W

wage(s). *See* minimum wage
wage inequality, 178, *179*
Wagner-Steagall National Housing Act of 1937, 695
Wales, Jimmy, 280
Walker, Scott, *207*, 382
Wallace, George, 92, 354
Wal-Mart, 438
War on Poverty, 92
war on terror/terrorism, 226, 271, 520–21, 562–64, 715–16, 737–38
war power (president), 520–21, 538
War Powers Resolution, 520–21, 537
Warren, Earl, 137, 180, 594, 616
Warren, Elizabeth, 9, *206*
Warsaw Pact, 737
Washington, George, 332, 512, 711, 714
Washington Post
    as nonprofit, 263–64
    Trump business history investigation, 254
    Vietnam coverage, 276–77
    Watergate coverage, 268
Washington State, 75, 102, 468, 469
Watergate, 268, 272, 277, 445, 476, 512–13, *513*
Waters, Maxine, 478
Watson, Gregory, 67
WEAL (Women's Equity Action League), 176
wealth, political influence and, 230–31
wealth inequality. *See* income equality/ inequality
Webster v. Reproductive Health Services, 143, 442
wedge issues, 390
welfare programs
    beneficiaries of, *697*

Voter Registration Information

State	Registration Deadline before Election*	Early Voting Permitted?**	Identification Required to Vote?**	More Information
Alabama	14 days	No	Photo ID requested	alabamavotes.gov
Alaska	30 days	Yes	ID requested; photo not required	elections.alaska.gov
Arizona	29 days	Yes	ID required; photo not required	azsos.gov/election
Arkansas	30 days	Yes	ID requested; photo not required	sos.arkansas.gov
California	15 days	Yes	No	sos.ca.gov
Colorado	8 days by mail or online; no in-person deadline	Yes (all voting by mail)	ID requested; photo not required	sos.state.co.us
Connecticut	14 days by mail; 7 days in person; election-day registration permitted	No	ID requested; photo not required	ct.gov/sots
Delaware	24 days	No	ID requested; photo not required	elections.delaware.gov
District of Columbia	30 days by mail or online; no in-person deadline	Yes	No	dcboee.org
Florida	29 days	Yes	Photo ID requested	dos.myflorida.com/elections
Georgia	28 days	Yes	Photo ID required	sos.ga.gov
Hawaii	30 days	Yes	Photo ID requested	hawaii.gov/elections
Idaho	25 days	Yes	Photo ID requested	idahovotes.gov
Illinois	27 days	Yes	No	elections.il.gov
Indiana	29 days	Yes	Photo ID required	in.gov/sos/elections
Iowa	10 days	Yes	No	sos.iowa.gov
Kansas	21 days	Yes	Photo ID required	kssos.org
Kentucky	29 days	No	ID requested; photo not required	elect.ky.gov
Louisiana	30 days	Yes	Photo ID requested	sos.la.gov
Maine	21 days by mail; no in-person deadline	Yes	No	maine.gov/sos
Maryland	21 days	Yes	No	elections.state.md.us
Massachusetts	20 days	No	No	www.sec.state.ma.us
Michigan	30 days	No	Photo ID requested	michigan.gov/sos
Minnesota	21 days	Yes	No	mnvotes.org
Mississippi	30 days	No	Photo ID required	sos.ms.gov
Missouri	Fourth Wednesday prior to election	No	ID requested; photo not required	sos.mo.gov
Montana	30 days by mail; no in-person deadline	Yes	ID requested; photo not required	sos.mt.gov

with tarpaulins in wet weather; and in fair uncovered, to let in the more air. Some also have made small ports, or lights along the sides at proper distances, well secured with thick iron bars, which they open from time to time for the air; and that very much contributes to the preservation of those poor wretches, who are so thick crowded together.

The Portuguese of Angola, a people in many respects not to be compared to the English, Dutch or French, in point of neatness aboard their ships, though indeed some French and English ships in those voyages for slaves are slovenly, foul, and stinking, according to the temper and the want of skill of the commanders; the Portuguese, I say, are commendable in that they bring along with them to the coast, a sufficient quantity of coarse thick mats, to serve as bedding under the slaves aboard, and shift them every fortnight or three weeks with such fresh mats: which, besides that it is softer for the poor wretches to lie upon than the bare deals or decks, must also be much healthier for them, because the planks, or deals, contract some dampness more or less, either from the deck being so often washed to keep it clean and sweet, or from the rain that gets in now and then through the scuttles or other openings, and even from the very sweat of the slaves; which being so crowded in a low place, is perpetual, and occasions many distempers, or at best great inconveniencies dangerous to their health: whereas, lying on mats, and shifting them from time to time, must be much more convenient; and it would be prudent to imitate the Portuguese in this point, the charge of such mats being inconsiderable.

We are very nice in keeping the places where the slaves lie clean and neat, appointing some of the ship's crew to do that office constantly, and several of the slaves themselves to be assistant to them in that employment; and thrice a week we perfume betwixt decks with a quantity of vinegar in pails, and red-hot iron bullets in them, to expel the bad air, after the place has been well washed and scrubbed with brooms: after which, the deck is cleaned with cold vinegar, and in the daytime, in good weather, we leave all the scuttles open, and shut them again at night.

It has been observed before, that some slaves fancy they are carried to be eaten, which makes them desperate; and others are so on account of their captivity: so that if care be not taken, they will mutiny and destroy the ship's crew in hopes to get away.

To prevent such misfortunes, we use [sic] to visit them daily, narrowly searching every corner between decks, to see whether they have not found means, to gather any pieces of iron, or wood, or knives, about the ship, notwithstanding the great care we take not to leave any tools or nails, or other things in the way: which, however, cannot be always so exactly observed, where so many people are in the narrow compass of a ship.

We cause as many of our men as is convenient to lie in the quarter-deck and gunroom, and our principal officers in the great cabin, where we keep all our small arms in a readiness, with sentinels constantly at the door and avenues to it; being thus ready to disappoint any attempts our slaves might make on a sudden.

These precautions contribute very much to keep them in awe; and if all those who carry slaves duly observed them, we should not hear of so many revolts as have happened. Where I was concerned, we always kept our slaves in such order, that we

Gabler, Neal, **6**:524
Gabriel, Islamic belief in, **6**:594
Gagarin, Yuri, **6**:187
Gaius Cestius, **1**:522
Galbraith, John Kenneth, **6**:19, 40, 111, 120
Galen: Byzantine medicine (Middle Ages) based on, **2**:188; on castration, **2**:74; on evolution, **1**:297; life of, **1**:300; medical writings of, **1**:295; medicine, role in, **1**:301; **2**:182; **3**:193; Mongolian medicine (Middle Ages) based on, **2**:192; Muslim study of, **2**:178; scientific theory of, **4**:227
Galicia as part of Spanish Empire, **3**:288
Galician language, **3**:161
Galileo, **3**:191
Galleons, **4**:326
Galleys, sentence to: Italy (15th & 16th Centuries), **3**:309; Spain (15th & 16th Centuries), **3**:305
Gambling: England (15th & 16th Centuries), **3**:319; England (17th & 18th Centuries), **4**:421; England (Victorian era), **5**:403; Europe (Middle Ages), **2**:372–73; India (ancient), **1**:449; Italy (15th & 16th Centuries), **3**:315, 323–24; Japan (17th & 18th Centuries), **4**:422–23; Madrid, **3**:321; Middle Ages, **2**:368, 369; New England, colonial, **4**:426; Rome (ancient), **1**:415–16, 441; seamen, **4**:428; 17th & 18th Centuries, **4**:419; Seville, **3**:321; Spain (15th & 16th Centuries), **3**:315; United States (Civil War era), **5**:428; United States (Western Frontier), **5**:59–60, 434, 436–37
Games: ancient world, **1**:404–19; Australia, colonial, **4**:432–33; Australian Aboriginals, **1**:418–19; Aztec, **3**:326–28; China (Tang Dynasty), **2**:375–77; England (15th & 16th Centuries), **3**:58, 316–20; England (17th & 18th Centuries), **4**:418, 419–22; Europe (Middle Ages), **2**:369, 370–73, 371; France (17th & 18th Centuries), **4**:422; Greece (ancient), **1**:410–14; Inca, **3**:328; India (19th Century), **5**:78; Islamic World (Middle Ages), **2**:401; Italy (15th & 16th Centuries), **3**:63, 321–24; Japan (17th & 18th Centuries), **4**:422–25; life at sea (17th & 18th Centuries), **4**:427–28; Maya, **3**:324–26; Mesopotamia, **1**:405–8; Middle Ages, **2**:368–77; Native Americans (colonial frontier of North America), **4**:68; New England, colonial, **4**:425–27; Nubia, **1**:416–18; Puritans, **4**:419, 426–27; Rome (ancient), **1**:414–16; 17th & 18th Centuries, **4**:417–28; Spain (15th & 16th Centuries), **3**:320–21; Vikings, **2**:373–75. *See also* Gambling; Sports; *specific types of games*
Gamming (17th & 18th Centuries), **4**:442–43
Gandhi, Indira, **6**:10, 47, 79, 389
Gandhi, Mohandas K. (Mahatma), **5**:291, 303; **6**:9, 105; on caste system, **6**:126, 136; on health and medicine, **6**:286; rise of, **6**:388; on women, **6**:611–12
Gandhi, Rajiv, **6**:10, 47, 79
Gandhi, Sanjay, **6**:47, 79
Gandía, Duke of, **3**:210
Gangs: Latin America (20th Century), **6**:420; Soviet Union, **6**:554
Gangster movies, **6**:520
Gannett Co., **6**:227

Gans, Herbert J., **6**:168, 169
Gaozong, **2**:10, 58
Gaozu (emperor of China), **2**:7, 153
Garbage disposal. *See* Waste disposal
Garbo, Greta, **6**:518
García, José Mauricio Nunes, **5**:426
Gardening: England (15th & 16th Centuries), **3**:239; India (20th Century), **6**:344; Italy (15th & 16th Centuries), **3**:337; Japan (17th & 18th Centuries), **4**:278; Maya, **3**:101; North American colonial frontier, **4**:244–45; Rome (ancient), **3**:336; United States (Western Frontier), **5**:62
Gardens of Babylon, **1**:3
Garibaldi shirts, **5**:274
Garland, Hamlin, **5**:63, 73, 103, 278–79
Garnet, Henry H., **5**:345
Garrick, David, **4**:450
Garrison, William L., **5**:343, 344, 345–46, 380, 382
Garrison houses, **4**:332–33
Garum, **1**:256
Gas as weapon in World War I, **6**:266, 349
"Gas gangrene," **6**:264, 265
Gaskell, Elizabeth, **5**:181, 191, 192, 283
Gas masks, **6**:267
Gas prices and shortage: United States (1973), **6**:363–64; United States (1990), **6**:478
Gaston de Blondeville (Radcliffe), **5**:183
Gastric fever, **5**:208
Gas utilities, **6**:336
Gates, Bill, **6**:252
Gates of Eden: American Culture in the Sixties (Dickstein), **6**:222
Gauchos, **5**:19, 289
Gaul. *See* France
Gauntlets, **4**:435
Gauze, **2**:253
Gay, John, **4**:208, 450
Gay, Sidney H., **5**:382
Gazeta Medica Da Bahia, **5**:214
Gazpacho, **3**:241
Geb, **1**:475, 476
Gebel Barkal, **1**:467
Geese, **5**:228
Geisel, Theodore, **6**:228
Geisha, **4**:153, 160–61, 311–12
Gelb, Ernest, **6**:91–95
Gender roles. *See* Men; Women
Genê, **1**:25, 348
Genealogy: Africa (17th & 18th Centuries), **4**:366, 368; Aztec, **3**:217; Italy (15th & 16th Centuries), **3**:179, 276
General Electric, **6**:244, 335
General Foods, **6**:308
General Historie (Smith), **4**:205–6
General Motors, **6**:115, 276, 358
General Post Office (England), **5**:139
Genesis, Book of, **3**:395
Geneva and Calvinism, **3**:366
Genghis Khan (Chinggis Khan): creating of kinship out of multiple tribes, **2**:31, 37; on drunkenness, **2**:221; on garments and decorations, **2**:266; history of, **2**:20, 22; hunting viewed as preparation for warfare, **2**:377, 384; laws of, **2**:342, 343; shaman, dealings with, **2**:428; symbolic gestures involving clothing, **2**:246; warfare waged by, **2**:362, 363
Genius loci, **1**:483
Genoa: economy in 15th & 16th Centuries, **3**:8. *See also* Italy (15th & 16th Centuries)
Gentildonnas, **3**:277
Gentilhuomos, **3**:269
Gentleman's Agreement (film), **6**:445

Gentleman's Magazine, **4**:505–6
Gentleman status (England): 15th and 16th Century, **3**:270–71; Victorian era, **5**:50–52
Gentry: China (19th Century), **5**:114; England (17th & 18th Centuries), **4**:374–75
Geography: United States (Western Frontier), **5**:4, 6; Vikings, **2**:162
Geology, **4**:176
Geomancy, **5**:144, 157
Geometry: Europe (Middle Ages), **2**:149, 160; Islamic World (Middle Ages), **2**:166; Mesopotamia, **1**:219; Vikings, **2**:152
Geoponika, **2**:130, 131, 209, 284
Georgiana, duchess of Devonshire, **4**:56
Germanic languages, **2**:146, 167, 168
German settlers in North American colonial frontier, **4**:373, 470
Germany (18th Century) and treatment of Jews, **6**:142
Germany (Middle Ages): expulsion of Jews, **6**:143; historical overview, **2**:2, 135; Holy Roman Empire, part of, **3**:18, 276, 283, 287; law codes, **2**:327–28; printing press, **3**:205; Protestant reformation, **3**:365
Germany (1910–20): diet, **6**:303; women and the military, **6**:64; workers' strikes, **6**:113. *See also* World War I
Germany (20th Century): authors post-World War II, **6**:218; film, **6**:513, 514–15; invasion of Russia, **6**:487–89; trench warfare (1914–19), **6**:459, 460; weapons, **6**:350; World War II, death toll statistics, **6**:489. *See also* Europe (20th Century); Holocaust; Nazis; World War II
Germ theory, **5**:150, 209–10
Gerusalemme liberata (Tasso), **3**:214
Gettysburg, Battle of, **5**:43–44, 100, 185, 315
Ghazan, **2**:192
Ghettos, Jewish, **6**:142
Ghosts: Mesopotamia, **1**:509–10, 529. *See also* Magic and superstition
Giant (film), **6**:445
Giants in the Earth (Rolvaag), **5**:207
Gibbs, Mary, **4**:83
GI Bill: education subsidies, **6**:17, 119, 201, 202, 205; excerpts from, **6**:625–27; housing subsidies, **6**:162, 166, 169, 338
Gift exchanging: India (ancient), **1**:449; Rome (ancient), **1**:441
Gilding, use in ancient Rome, **1**:499, 506
Gilgamesh, Epic of: Akkadians, **1**:196; on death, burial, and the afterlife, **1**:473, 507, 508–9, 510; Mesopotamian traditions and, **1**:194; sports and games stories, **1**:405–6; "The Great Flood," **1**:541–45
Gillies, Harold, **6**:266
Gin, **4**:261
Ginsberg, Allen, **6**:225–26, 542
Giovedi Grasso, **3**:135
Girl Guides, **6**:90
Giza pyramids, **1**:4, 160
Gladiators: Byzantium, **2**:402; India (ancient), **1**:449; Rome (ancient), **1**:442–45
Gladius, **1**:386, 399
Glagolitic alphabet, **3**:166
Glasgow East India (19th Century) Company, **5**:303
Glass: Byzantium, **2**:107; Europe (Middle Ages), **2**:277; Islamic World (Middle Ages), **2**:283; Mesopotamia, **1**:121; Vikings, **2**:101
Glasse, Hannah, **4**:246
Glavlit, **6**:235, 256
Glavrepertkom, **6**:235–36
Glazunov, Ilya, **6**:138